Individuals as Organizational Members

- Individuals in Organizations: Perception, Personality, and Cultural Differences
- Attitudes in Organizations
- Work Motivation
- Behavior in Organizations

The management of organizational behavior is a complex and challenging task. Managers must understand their philosophies regarding management, as well as society's expectations for organizational behavior. This in turn affects managers' decisions, which result in the creation of the organizational behavior context, groups in organizations, and the use of contemporary management practices. All of this affects employee perceptions, attitudes, motivation, and behavior. Successful managers use their knowledge of organizational behavior to maximize employee and organizational effectiveness through the strategic management of the decisions they make and their management practices.*

*J. Child. 1972. Organization structure, environment, and performance: The role of strategic choice. *Sociology* 6: 369–393.

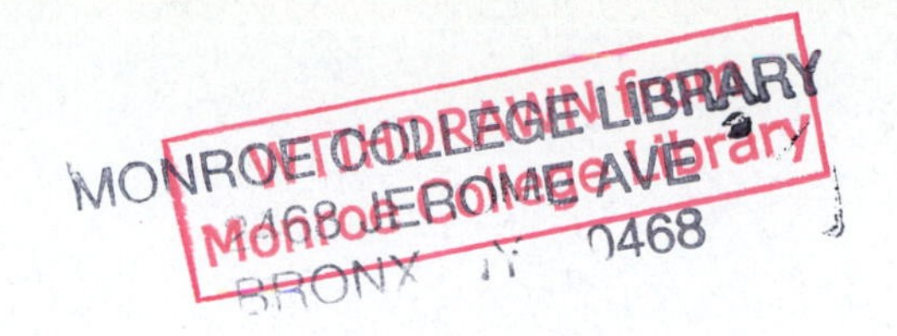

MANAGEMENT AND ORGANIZATIONAL BEHAVIOR

AN INTEGRATED PERSPECTIVE

JON L. PIERCE
University of Minnesota Duluth

DONALD G. GARDNER
James Cook University, Australia
University of Colorado at Colorado Springs

with

RANDALL B. DUNHAM
University of Wisconsin—Madison

SOUTH-WESTERN
THOMSON LEARNING™

Australia · Canada · Mexico · Singapore · Spain · United Kingdom · United States

Management and Organizational Behavior: An Integrated Perspective
by Jon L. Pierce and Donald G. Gardner

Vice President/Publisher: Jack Calhoun
Executive Editor: John Szilagyi
Developmental Editor: Theresa Curtis, Ohlinger Publishing Services
Marketing Manager: Rob Bloom
Production Editor: Barbara Fuller-Jacobsen
Media Technology Editor: Vicky True
Media Developmental Editor: Kristen Meere
Media Production Editor: Mark Sears
Manufacturing Coordinator: Sandee Milewski
Photo Manager: Deanna Ettinger
Photo Research: Susan van Etten
Internal Design: Joe Devine
Cover Design: Christy Carr
Cover Photograph: PhotoDisc
Production House: Lachina Publishing Services
Compositor: Lachina Publishing Services
Printer: Quebecor World—Versailles, KY

Printed in the United States of America
1 2 3 4 5 04 03 02 01

Library of Congress Cataloging-in-Publication Data

Pierce, Jon L. (Jon Lepley)
Management and organizational behavior: an integrated perspective / Jon L. Pierce, Donald G. Gardner.
p. cm.
Includes bibliographical references and index.
ISBN 0-324-04958-7
1. Management. 2. Organizational behavior. I. Gardner, Donald G. II. Title.

HD31 .P488 2001
658—dc21

2001031098

For more information contact South-Western, 5101 Madison Road, Cincinnati, Ohio 45227 or find us on the Internet at http://www.swcollege.com

For permission to use material from this text or product, contact us by
- Telephone: 1-800-730-2214
- Fax: 1-800-730-2215
- Web: http://www.thomsonrights.com

To a small group of scholars who have had a profound impact upon me and my academic career—Professors Larry L. Cummings, Randall B. Dunham, Andre L. Delbecq, Bruce Pannier, and Donald G. Gardner. Thank you for caring and for your mentoring. Thank you for your friendship and our working relationships. Finally, to my wife Janet, whose love and social-emotional support was very important during the creation of this book.

—Jon L. Pierce

To Professors Eugene F. Stone-Romero and Chris J. Berger, who started me on my academic journey. To Professors Jon L. Pierce, Larry L. Cummings, and Randall B. Dunham, who helped me sustain my journey. Finally and most importantly, to my wife Karen, whose substantial opportunity costs made this book possible. Thanks to all of you for your friendship and support.

—Donald G. Gardner

Brief Contents

Contents

PART II

Individuals as Organizational Members 148

PART V
Managing in the 21st Century 572

Preface

A long-standing tradition in collegiate schools of business has been the offering of a survey course in management, often called principles, or fundamentals, of management. Historically, the principles course has covered the mechanics of management—planning, organizing, directing, and controlling. Yet, ever since the Ford Foundation's call (in the 1950s) to recognize organizations as human communities, the behavioral sciences rightly have had a markedly enhanced presence in the business school curriculum. Courses in organizational behavior, with their emphasis on individuals and groups as organizational members, have become a part of the education of tomorrow's managers. Successful managers not only must have a command of the practice of management and an understanding of organizations, they must concern themselves with the human side of organizations.

This book represents a blending of the traditional management and organizational behavior topics, highlighting the essence of the management process, presented in such a fashion that it simultaneously illuminates organizational behavior. By weaving together the management process and organizational behavior literature, we have created a text appropriate for an integrated course in management and organizational behavior and also viable for introduction to management or organizational behavior. Our approach presents a coverage of material that emphasizes the technical aspects of management and management practice, as well as its social-psychological and behavior consequences.

In constructing this management/organizational behavior text, we believe we have produced a whole that is greater than the sum of its specialized parts and, we don't mind saying, one that is better than any standalone management or organizational behavior text now available. We discuss the essence of the management process, emphasizing its technical aspects, while simultaneously illuminating the behavior of organizations and of the individuals who inhabit them. We take a comparative view, revealing the social-psychological consequences of behavior within a management context. We believe that an understanding of the management of organizations that recognizes the organization as a social system forms a powerful analytical construct and a framework for decisive action. Similarly, we believe that a mature understanding of the essential nature of organizational behavior enriches one's understanding of the management process and of organization design. As noted above, we believe that the fusion of the traditional principles of management course with the course in organizational behavior is, in many ways, quite instinctive. With this text we believe that we have—without sacrificing performance—combined these two courses and achieved a new point of view, a new buoyancy, a distinctive personality. *Management and Organizational Behavior: An Integrated Perspective* delivers to your students both a cohesive way of thinking and a platform for learning more.

From the Ground Up

The bedrock of *Management and Organizational Behavior: An Integrated Perspective* is a composite of three interrelated concepts: management, the organization, and the individual as an organizational member. We will unearth the causal relationships among these concepts. We will draw on a diverse blend of noted scholars and successful business professionals. We will mine the sources of information on management and organizational behavior and discuss their possible limits. We will address how management philosophies, decisions, and practices give rise to particular organization designs and how both management practice and organization design affect employee attitudes, motivation, and behaviors.

The model that guides our thinking about organizational behavior is depicted below. It construes management philosophy as a force that shapes both the practice of management and the design of organizations. The combination of these activities provides the very rich contexts out of which organizational behavior arises. Our objective is to drill deeply into these topics and thereby shed light on the effects that management and organization have on employees.

The Organization Behavior Model

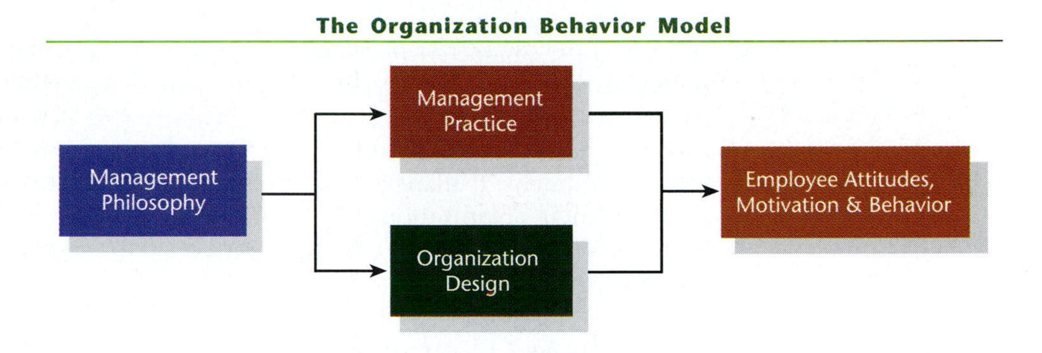

As a manager, you will be called upon to "manage" the management process and "design" the organization so as to have a significant impact on the employee attitudes, motivation, and behaviors that serve the particular needs of the organization and those of its employees. Good strategic choices and your ability to act intelligently will rest on your sturdy understanding of management, organization, the individual as an organizational member, and the interrelationships that play out among these three building blocks.

From the Outside In: The Organization of this Book

Out of our collaboration on this integrative model came not only the energy and ideas for this book but its full design as well. *Management and Organizational Behavior* has a macro-to-micro tilt. We focus on macro issues (management practice and organizational design) and then on micro issues (effects on the individual), but all the while weighing one against the other.

First, in Part I, the student will be introduced to the concepts of management and organizations. Management practices and the design of organizations are two of the major causes of organizational behavior. In Part I, we explore the nature and purpose of organizations, and we peer into management as a process universal to all organizations. Two major approaches to management and organizational design are discussed, along with issues pertaining to ethical and socially responsible behavior.

In Part II we add a layer of complexity to our discussions. This part focuses on the individual as an organizational member. We sift through traditional organizational behavior topics, examining the fine-grained details of individual differences, perception, work-related attitudes, motivation, and behaviors. Our treatments of the individual as an organizational member and of behavior in organizations (Chapters 5 and 8) are particularly distinctive.

Part III delves into the functions of management and into the organizational behavior context more deeply and more systematically than does Part I. Aspects of this discussion will lead the student to inquire into the nature of the management process and into the nature of organizations—to reach the lower strata, so to speak. The student will explore the impact that different approaches to the process of management have on organizational members and on their work-related attitudes, motivation, and behaviors. We will examine planning, decision making, and controlling as a part of the management process. In addition, the student will confront employee responses, where and how they interact with the design of organizations.

Part IV highlights the need for and utilization of work groups and teams in organizations. Characteristics of the processes that occur within work groups are closely covered and documented. Finally, Part V deciphers management issues critical to organizational success in the twenty-first century: job/work design, work scheduling, employee ownership, productivity, and organizational change and development. If managers fail to manage these issues effectively, eruptions all along their organizational fault lines are inevitable. They, along with their organizations, are likely to fall prey to more adaptive and agile competitors in the worldwide marketplace.

From Theory to Practice: A Model Approach

To bolster the reader's understanding of the multilayered topics presented in this book and of the texture of their interrelationships, we position the integrative model at crucial junctures throughout the book. We've taken on many influences over the years, but the model represents our fundamental approach to linking together the wide range of topical choices. It emphasizes the fact that managers make decisions that affect how organizations are structured, how groups are utilized, and how they affect individuals in the organization. Follow its progression at the beginning of each of the text's five parts. It is our hope that by repeatedly connecting back to this model, the reader will develop a deeper, more integrated understanding of management and organizational behavior and see clearly the relevance of the real-life examples we employ.

One final aspect of this book is worth highlighting. You will find that much of the book is written in an engaging, conversational tone. We have not done this, however, at the expense of rigor. By relying on organizational behavior research that is based on sound scientific methods we have created an amalgam of leading-edge theories firmly grounded in the real world and mindful of accepted wisdom. We sought to avoid the trap of focusing only on a series of trendy topics (such as easily forgotten time-management principles of the 1970s). Instead, we set our target on what would have lasting value for the student, what would create a useful experience. Anything less would be a disservice to students as well as to our academic colleagues. Management may be partly skill and partly art, but our growing knowledge of organizational behavior is based on science.

From the Opaque to the Transparent: An Environment That Puts Learning within Reach

Coming to understand management and organizational behavior can be stimulating, challenging, and rewarding, not to mention occasionally fun. To facilitate this process, we have developed a broad system that incorporates a variety of learning devices into this book. These unique features were designed to raise interest, unlock aspects of the managerial profession, encourage the internalization of a significant body of knowledge, and give future managers lots to look forward to.

Overall, our learning system is a migration toward the useful. It follows this progression:

Integrated Approach Our integration of the management process literature with the organization behavior literature takes a macro-to-micro focus, exploring what management is, what organizations are, and how the two affect the attitudes, motivation, and behaviors of organizational members.

Integrated Model The integrated model presented at the outset of each of the book's five major sections highlights that portion of the book about which the student will be learning next.

Part Openers The book is divided into five parts, each of which begins with a brief part opener. The openers provide an overview to this section of the book, highlighting the major themes and their relationship to the integrative model.

Integrative Video Case Each of the five parts of the book ends with a comprehensive case on Horizons, a media technology company located in Columbus, Ohio. The case is accompanied by a 7 to 12 minute video that highlights Horizons' executives, managers, and team members utilizing many of the theories and techniques described in the text.

Each of the text's 18 chapters contain these complementary features.

Chapter Outlines list the main topics that will be covered in each chapter.

Learning Objectives guide students as they read the text.

A First Look opening vignettes present a hypothetical situation that touches on a theme from the chapter. Questions are posed for the student to keep in mind as they study the chapter material.

Key Terms are highlighted in the text, defined in the margin, listed at the end of the chapter with page numbers, and are listed in alphabetical order in the Glossary at the end of the book.

BusinessLink Video Case Margin Notes direct students to video cases that highlight and expand on topics in the chapter. Use of these cases is optional and at the instructor's discretion.

Inside Look boxes provide in-depth coverage of chapter topics and apply the theories to real world situations.

Self-Assessments allow students to gauge their own strengths and weaknesses as they learn new management and organizational behavior theories.

A Final Look closing vignettes connect with the opening vignettes by providing students with a possible solution to the situation set up at the beginning of the chapter.

Chapter Reviews can be used in conjunction with the learning objectives to guide students in their review of the chapter content.

Issues for Review and Discussion are provided as a means to generate classroom discussion.

Exercises, individual and group, allow students to apply the knowledge and theories they have learned in each chapter. Internet and InfoTrac activities provide a base for further research.

End-of-Chapter Cases provide opportunities for students to analyze situations and sharpen their problem-solving skills.

In addition, we have prepared or overseen the development of several supplements to accompany our book, including:

Instructor's Manual (ISBN 0-324-04959-5). Prepared by Shannon Studden at the University of Minnesota Duluth, the Instructor's Manual includes lecture notes; key points; answers to end of chapter material including Questions for Review and Discussion, Exercises, and Cases. Video cases with questions and answers are provided for 10 of the 18 chapters. Additional questions and activities are provided that are not in the text.

Test Bank (ISBN 0-324-04961-7). Prepared by Jon Kalinowski of Minnesota State University, Mankato, the Test Bank contains over 1800 questions with a combination of true/false, multiple choice, short answer, and scenario type questions.

PowerPoint® Slides (ISBN 0-324-04960-9). Prepared by Charlie Cook of the University of West Alabama, the PowerPoint presentation enhances the lecture materials and presents the key topics in each chapter in an electronic format. Available for download at http://pierce.swcollege.com and also on the Instructor's Resource CD-ROM.

Instructor's Resource CD-ROM (ISBN 0-324-12879-7). The Instructor's CD is available to instructors and contains all the above-named instructional supplements in electronic format plus ExamView testing software. ExamView is a computerized testing program that contains all of the questions in the printed test bank and is an easy-to-use test-creation software, compatible with Microsoft Windows. Instructors can add or edit questions, instructions, and answers; and select questions by previewing them on the screen, selecting them randomly, or selecting them by number. Instructors can also create and administer quizzes online, whether over the Internet, a local area network, or a wide area network.

Management POWER

Management Power! PowerPoint Slides (ISBN 0-324-13380-4). *Management Power!* is a CD-ROM of PowerPoint slides covering 14 major management and organizational behavior topics: communication, control, decision making, designing organizations, ethics and social responsibility, foundations of management, global management, human resources, innovation and change, leadership, motivation, planning, strategy, and teams. These easy-to-use, multimedia-enriched slides can be easily modified and customized to suit individual preferences.

Student CD-ROM. A student CD comes free with every new copy of the text. It includes the Glossary from the text; a General Business Glossary, in both English and Spanish; the Horizons Integrative Video Case (actual video segments and their textual counterparts), and pertinent Web site links.

InfoTrac College Edition. Free with each new text, InfoTrac provides access to an online library of articles from hundreds of journals. It offers a database that is updated daily with full-length articles. Keyword searches allow you to scan the database quickly and efficiently.

CNN Video: Management and Organizations (ISBN 0-324-13495-9). Forty-five minutes of short segments from CNN's Headline News, CNNfn (the financial network), CNN Today, Movers with Jan Hopkins, and other programs to use as lecture launchers, discussion starters, topical introductions, or directed inquiries.

BusinessLink Video (VHS ISBNs 0-324-04963-3, 0-324-14957-3, 0-324-14958-1) A library of 15 video case studes is available free to instructors on VHS cassettes. Videos provide an excellent platform for classroom analysis of the experiences and challenges facing a range of businesses, including Valassis Communications, Archway Cookie, and the Vermont Teddy Bear Company.

WebTutor™. WebTutor harnesses the power of the Internet to deliver innovative learning aids that actively engage students. Instructors can incorporate WebTutor as an integral part of the course, or students can use it on their own as a study guide. Benefits to students include automatic and immediate feedback from quizzes and exams; interactive, multimedia-rich explanation of concepts; online exercises that reinforce what they've learned; flashcards that include audio support; and greater interaction and involvement through online discussion forums. South-Western/Thomson Learning has partnered with two of the leading course management systems available today—Blackboard and WebCT—to deliver WebTutor content cartridges to instructors around the world. Visit http://webtutor.swcollege.com for more information.

Web Site. http://pierce.swcollege.com is the address of the web site that supports *Management and Organizational Behavior: An Integrated Perspective*. The site provides teaching resources, learning resources, and an Interactive Study Center with key concepts and terms, online quizzes, Internet applications, links to relevant management and organizational behavior web sites, and many more features.

ACKNOWLEDGMENTS

We would like to take this opportunity to thank all of those individuals whose time, efforts, insight, and hard work has contributed to the development of our book. Without your assistance this project would have never been realized.

First and foremost, we want to thank and acknowledge Dr. Randall B. Dunham. The three of us have been friends and colleagues for more than two decades. Much of our understanding of management and organizations emerged as a result of our collaborative relationship with Randy. It is difficult for either of us to write about the majority of topics covered in this book without being reminded of the important role that he has played in forming our thinking about management and organizational behavior and without recognizing that he was a research partner in much of our own work that is cited in this book. For these reasons we acknowledge Randy as a virtual co-author of our book.

The manuscript was reviewed by a number of Management and Organizational Behavior professors. We appreciate the time and effort that the following individuals put into the reading of the manuscript as well as their many suggestions for improvement:

Clarence Anderson, Walla Walla College
Sara Barbor, Winona State University
Shawn Carraher, Texas A&M University-Commerce
Marios Katsioloudes, West Chester University of Pennsylvania
Douglas McCabe, Georgetown University
Michael McCuddy, Valparaiso University
Robert J. Paul, Kansas State University
Peter P. Poole, Lehigh University
William L. Smith, Emporia State University

Many individuals At South-Western Publishing played an important role in the creation of this text. We would like to thank the following: John Szilagyi, Executive Editor; Judy O'Neill, Developmental Editor; Barb Fuller Jacobsen, Production Editor; Rob Bloom, Marketing Manager; and the many individuals who work behind the scenes.

We also want to thank the supplement preparers including Jon Kalinowski of Minnesota State University, Mankato (Test Bank), Charlie Cook of the University of West Alabama (Power Point), and Shannon Studden of the University of Minnesota Duluth (Instructor's Manual). In addition, we'd like to thank Carolyn Lawrence, who contributed end-of-chapter cases, Bruce Barringer for the Horizons Video Case, Ross Stapeton-Gray for his work on chapter video cases, and Mrs. Carmel Store of James Cook University for her excellent administrative and listening skills.

Finally, we want to thank Barbara Neiberg from the University of Colorado at Colorado Springs and Theresa Curtis from Ohlinger Publishing Services. Barbara prepared the opening and closing vignettes, as well as most of the Inside Look features. For two years, Theresa watched over our every word and move, never letting us stray far from the original plan. Thanks, Barbara and Theresa, for all of your commitment and hard work—now we *are* going fishing!

Jon L. Pierce
Donald G. Gardner

ABOUT THE AUTHORS

Jon L. Pierce is Professor of Management and Organization in the School of Business and Economics at the University of Minnesota Duluth. He received his Ph.D. in management and the organizational sciences at the University of Wisconsin—Madison. Professor Pierce is a charter member of the Academy of Management Journal's Hall of Fame. He has authored and published over 50 articles, and has co-authored and edited six other books. He was a visiting scholar in the Department of Psychology at the University of Waikato in New Zealand. Professor Pierce is the recipient of the Yoder-Heneman Research Award, and he has served on the editorial review board for several American and British management and organization journals. He teaches courses in management, leadership, and organizational studies. His research interests focus on the individual-organization relationship. He has published research focused on job design, work scheduling, employee ownership, work environment structure, psychological focus of attention, organization-based self-esteem, and psychological ownership within the organizational context.

Donald G. Gardner is currently Establishment Professor of Management at James Cook University in Queensland, Australia. Prior to that, he was a Professor of Management and Organization at the University of Colorado at Colorado Springs for 18 years. He received his Ph.D. in administrative sciences from the Krannert Graduate School of Management at Purdue University. He teaches courses in management, organizational behavior, human resources management, and labor relations. He has been a visiting scholar at the University of Wisconsin—Madison, the Helsinki School of Economics, and at the Australian Graduate School of Management. His research focuses on employee attitudes and behavior, with specific interests in the causes and consequences of employee self-esteem, and management of organizational change. His research has been published in such prestigious journals as the *Academy of Management Journal, Organizational Behavior and Human Decision Processes,* and *the Journal of Applied Psychology.*

Randall B. Dunham is the Procter & Gamble Bascom Professor of Management, in the Granger School of Business, at the University of Wisconsin—Madison. He received his Ph.D. in industrial and organizational psychology at the University of Illinois. At the University of Wisconsin he has served as Chair of the Management Department, Associate Dean of Graduate Programs, and Senior Associate Dean. A former Cargill faculty fellow, Dunham has been actively involved in the academic, professional, and business communities. He has taught management, organizational behavior, compensation, research methods, data analysis, and doctoral seminars and has received multiple teaching awards and research grants. Dunham's current research focuses on the management of organizational change, organizational commitment, the design of work in organization, distance education effectiveness, and global/cross-cultural issues in management. His publications include over 40 journal articles and six books, and he has designed computer software to enhance the learning experience. He has served as a management consultant and trainer for many private and public organizations, including IBM, Rockwell, GE, and Arthur Andersen. He has consulted with over 50 schools of business from 15 countries on the effectiveness of instructional technology. He is a fellow of the American Psychological Association and the American Psychological Society and is a charter member of the Academy of Management Journal's Hall of Fame.

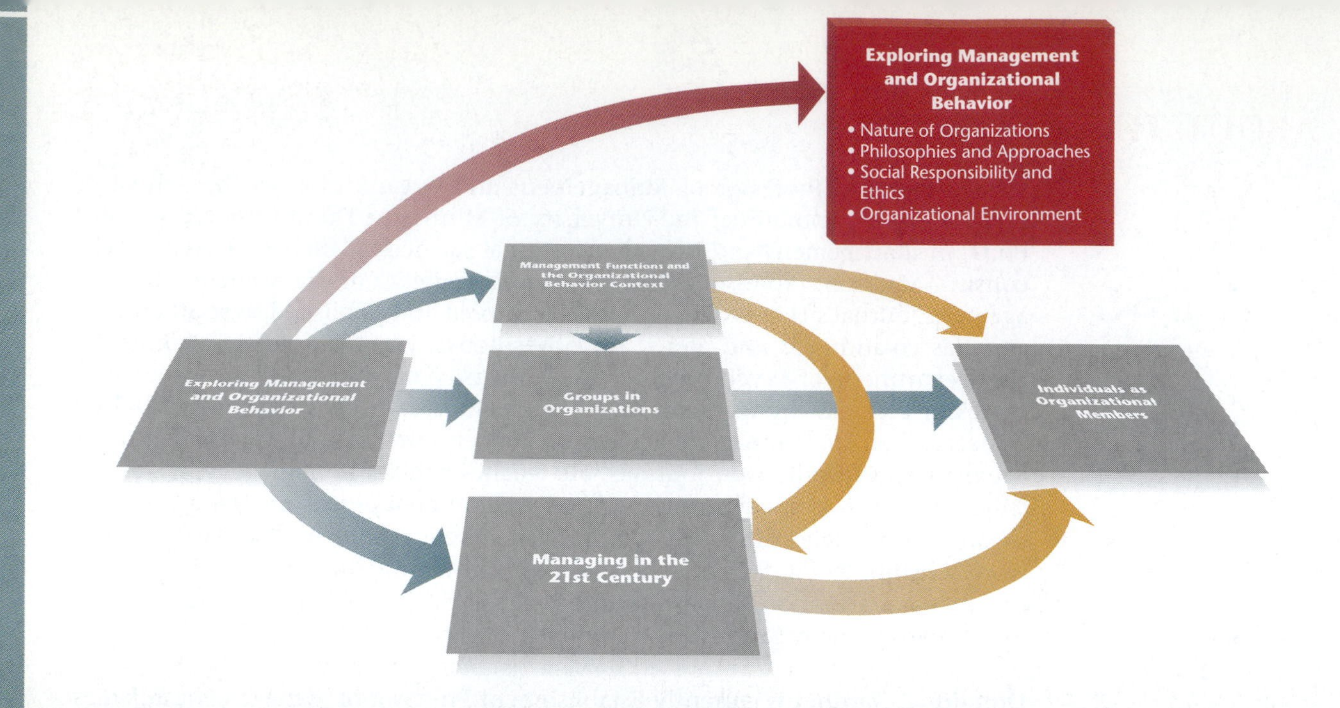

PART I
Exploring Management and Organizational Behavior

1. The Nature of Organizations and Management
2. Philosophies and Approaches to Management Practice
3. Social Responsibility and Ethics
4. The Organizational Environment

The management of organizational behavior is a complex and challenging task. Managers must understand their philosophies toward work, people, and organization, as well as the process of managing. Managers must also be aware of the environment within which their organization operates and society's expectations. These forces affect managerial decisions leading up to the creation of the organizational behavior context, groups in organizations, and the use of contemporary management practices. This in turn affects employee perceptions, attitudes, motivation, and behavior. Successful managers use their knowledge of organizational behavior to maximize employee and organizational effectiveness through the strategic management of the decisions that they make and their managerial practices.* The **integrative model** presented above summarizes this process. The highlighted portion reveals our focus in Part I.

In order to come to an understanding of organizational behavior, there are three basic building blocks and a causal relationship that we need to address. The three building blocks are "management," "organization," and the "individual employee as an organizational member." The causal relationship addresses how management and organization influence the employee's work-related attitudes, motivation, and behavior. These three building blocks and the critical relationship among them are

* J. Child. 1972. Organization structure, environment and performance: The role of strategic choice. *Sociology* 6:369–393.

FIGURE I-1

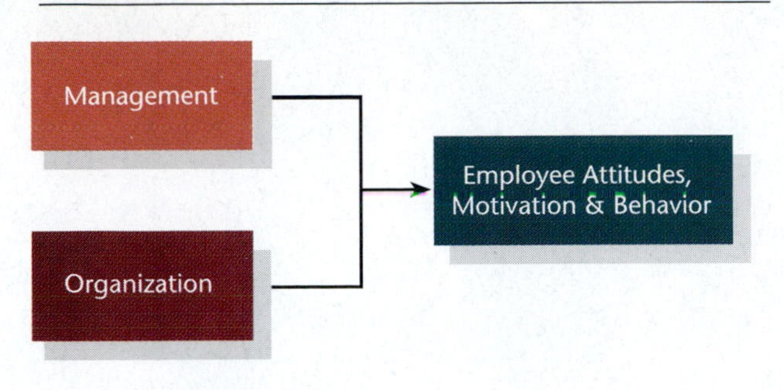

shown in Figure I-1. This model illustrates the "macro-to-micro" focus of our book. We'll explore management and organization and their impact upon employee responses (attitudes, motivation, and behavior).

In Chapter 1, you will be introduced to two important concepts—*"organization"* and *"management."* In Chapters 2 and 3, we continue to explore the concept of management. In Chapter 2, we suggest that the way organizations are managed is shaped by the attitudes, beliefs, opinions, and assumptions that managers have about people, work, action, and organization. In this chapter we introduce you to two major schools of thought (theories) that address how organizations in our society are managed. Specifically, you will learn about control-oriented management and its mechanistic (bureaucratic) organization, and involvement-oriented management and its organic organization.

As a continuation of our discussion of management philosophy, two extremely important sets of managerial values—ethics and social responsibility—are discussed in Chapter 3. Both "mindsets" translate into managerial behavior that has an impact upon those with whom the organization interacts and the community in which the organization resides. We believe that any time managers and organizations have to deal with people—inside and outside of the organization—an important question needs to be asked: What is the right and socially responsible thing to do? As a part of this discussion we call your attention to ethics as they pertain to the individual-organization relationship.

The final chapter continues our examination of the concepts of management and organization. In this chapter we discuss management and the organization's external and internal environment. The external environment represents the entire milieu (for example, societal needs and values, customer wants, and competitor's strategies) that is external to and impacting the organization. The organization's internal environment is presented as the primary setting in which the employee operates, and it is the characteristics of this environment that have a large impact on the employee's responses (as reflected in Figure I-1). Understanding the internal environment will help you understand the nature and anatomy of the organization.

Upon completion of Part I, you will realize that organizational goals (that is, the organization's "reason for being"), management philosophy (assumptions about people, work, ethics, social responsibility, and organization), and the external environment influence the strategic choices that managers make about their management practices and the design of the organization (see Figure I-2). We'll explore management practices and organization design in greater depth later in the text, along with the impact that each has upon the attitudes, motivation, and behavior of the organizational member.

Before we turn our attention to an exploration of the impact that management practices and organizational designs have upon the attitudes, motivation, and behavior of the organizational member, we will introduce you to the third building block of organizational behavior. In Part II (Chapters 5–8), we consider the "individual as an organizational member."

FIGURE I-2

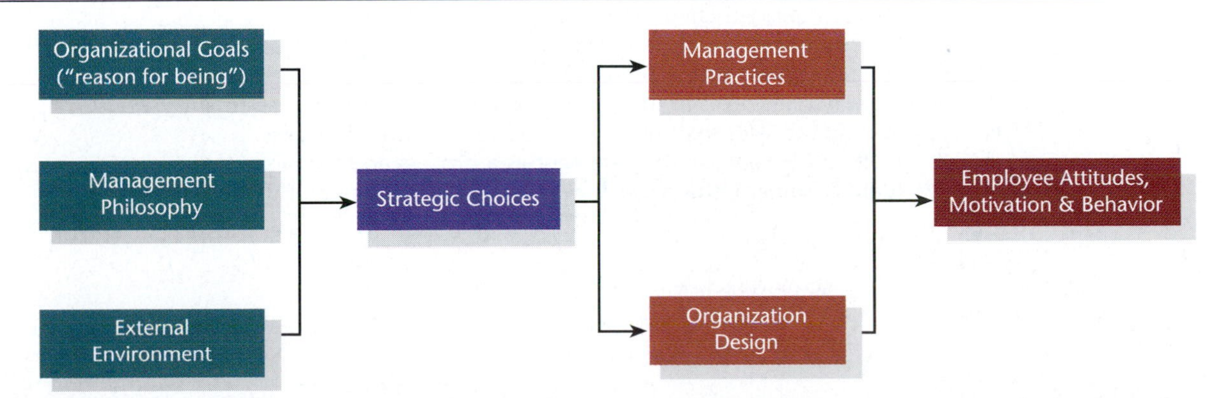

Outline

PHOTO: © CRAIG LOVELL/CORBIS

CHAPTER 1

The Nature of Organizations and Management

Learning Objectives

After reading this chapter, you should be able to

1. Discuss what organizations are and why they exist.
2. Define management and understand what managers do.
3. Distinguish between the sociological and process perspectives on management.
4. Discuss some of the different types of managers.
5. Identify differences in the way managers execute the management process.
6. Specify the skills that managers need to perform effectively.
7. Distinguish between management as a process and management as a set of roles.
8. Identify some of the forces that are redefining the role of the manager.

A FIRST LOOK

The buzz around small, privately owned Vinton Enterprises is that the international telecommunications company, Global TC, is negotiating a takeover. Global TC is a company that everyone in the industry knows and emulates. Vinton management seems to know something that no one else knows, and the tension is palpable. Speculation is rampant. If the takeover occurs, what happens to Vinton Enterprises? Do current employees keep their jobs? If so, how will their responsibilities and lives change as a result?

One day, the president meets with the upper-level and middle managers and announces that the takeover is official. Middle managers in particular fear for their jobs. Innovative organizations like Global TC advocate a "flat" management style, and many middle managers in other organizations have seen their positions change drastically or be eliminated altogether.

Fast forward to several weeks later. The CEO of Global TC has come to town. After discussing the Global TC mission statement, vision, and core values with Vinton managers, the CEO makes the expected but still disturbing statement that Vinton employees should prepare for radical change and restructuring.

Vinton employees at lower levels of the company feel left in the dark. They had little firsthand information about the restructuring and have relied on their immediate supervisors, the middle managers, for news. Not surprisingly, office morale and productivity plummet.

Questions: How could Global TC alleviate the fears of the Vinton Enterprises employees? If you were a mid-level manager at Vinton, would you fear or embrace the takeover? Do you think that Vinton employees will have difficulty adjusting to an entirely different system of management?

Many organizational members routinely go home at the end of the day feeling good about their work accomplishments and looking forward to another good day tomorrow. They find their relationship with the organization meaningful and full of responsibility. Their behavior contributes to the success of the organization. Unfortunately this is not the case for others. For many organizational members, the expressions "Blue Monday," "Hump Day," and "TGIF" take on a great deal of meaning. These expressions signal that something is wrong with their world of work. The employees who have internalized these expressions don't feel a strong sense of ownership for the work they do, and work is neither a central life interest nor a major contributor to their self-worth. The casual observer of both groups is quick to learn that management practices and forces stemming from characteristics of the organization (for example, organizational size) are major contributors to the work-related attitudes, motivation, and behaviors of organizational members.

Our objective in this text is to understand organizational behavior by gaining insight into the individual-organization relationship. We are interested in the management and organizational forces that contribute, for example, to employee job satisfaction, work motivation, performance, and acts of good organizational citizenship. We are also interested in the forces that contribute to employee absenteeism and turnover as well as the forces that produce a strong commitment to the organization.

This journey necessitates our understanding organization, management, and the nature of the individual as an organizational member. In this the opening chapter, we will start to explore two concepts: "organization" and "management." We look first at the concept of organization, as this defines the setting within which management is performed. Second, we define management. While our overall objective is to understand organizational behavior, management and organizations serve as the context within which this behavior unfolds. As the following model shows, management practices and organization design represent two major causes of the attitudes, motivation, and behaviors of our organizational members.

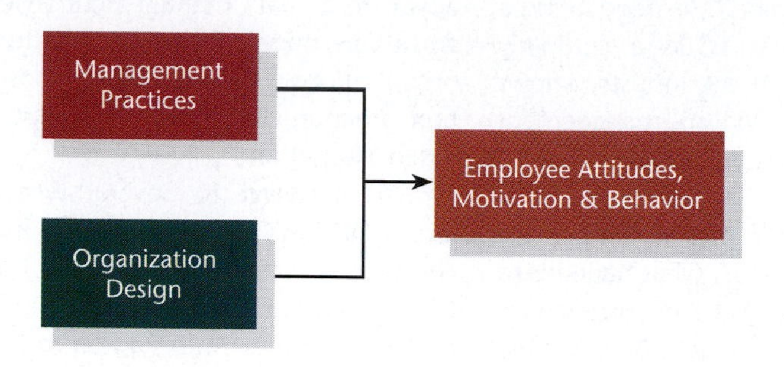

THE NATURE OF ORGANIZATIONS

Their Reason for Being

If we were to look across the landscape of society, we would quickly notice that there are a large number of organizations and many different types of organizations. A natural question to ask is "why": Why do organizations exist? Why are there so many organizations? And why are there so many different types of organizations spread out across society?

Sociologist Talcott Parsons provides us with insight into these questions. He suggests that, like you and me, society has needs. If our individual needs are not fulfilled, our physical health and mental well-being will be severely challenged. Similarly, unless society's needs are satisfied, that society as we know it will fail to prosper and survive.[1] Organizations, Parsons observes, come into existence to help society satisfy its needs.

Society has at least four fundamental needs. All societies have, for example, a need to adapt to their environments. We can call this the *adaptation need* of society. The adaptation need gives rise to *production organizations*. These organizations come into existence to make goods that are consumed by society and that help society adapt to its environment. Como Oil and Gas and Helly Hansen Clothing play a significant role in one of your authors' adaptation to the cold winter weather in northern Minnesota. In addition to the adaptation need, all societies have goals and values (that is, the ideals that it stands for). These values need to be articulated, and resources need to be mobilized in order to help society attain its valued goals. This *goal achievement need* of society gives rise to *political organizations*. Political organizations seek to ensure that society attains its goals and values.

http://www.hellyhansen.com

Not only do societies have adaptation and goal achievement needs, societies also have a need to maintain and continue themselves across time. Parsons calls this the *pattern maintenance need*. Out of this need emerges *socializing organizations*. Among the most visible socializing organizations are our religious, cultural, and educational institutions. Each of these organizations works to pass along the values, traditions, language, customs, and beliefs of a society. Inevi-

FIGURE 1-1

The Origin of Organizations

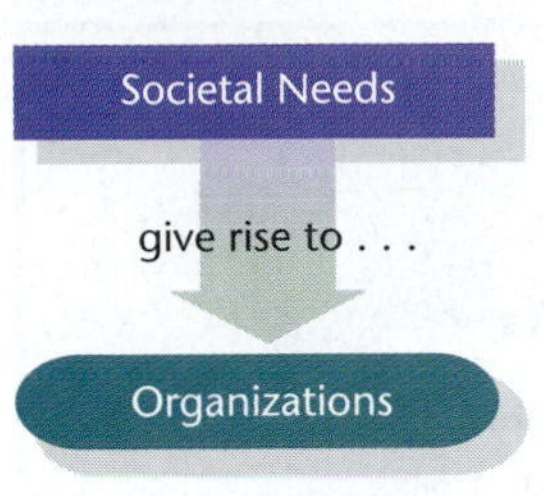

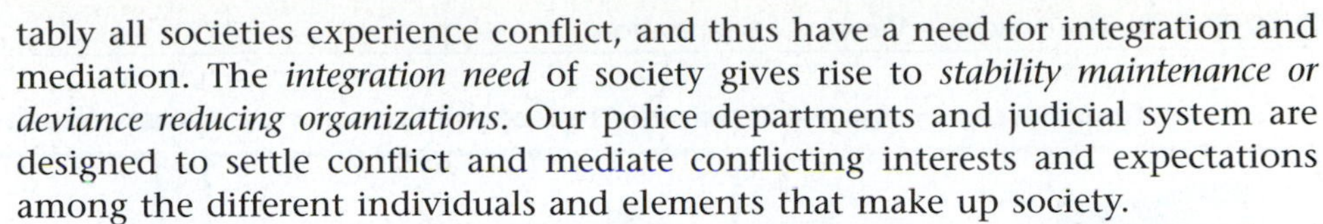

tably all societies experience conflict, and thus have a need for integration and mediation. The *integration need* of society gives rise to *stability maintenance or deviance reducing organizations*. Our police departments and judicial system are designed to settle conflict and mediate conflicting interests and expectations among the different individuals and elements that make up society.

In summary, an organization's reason for being is to satisfy the needs of society. Society has at least four major needs (adaptation, goal achievement, pattern maintenance, and integration) that give rise to four types of organizations (production, political, socializing, and stability maintenance). These relationships are depicted in Figures 1-1 and 1-2. The origin of organizations and their differentiation is in the needs of society—that is, societal needs give rise to organizations, and different societal needs give rise to different types of organizations. That society is large and geographically dispersed contributes to the rise of many organizations that serve the same societal need. For obvious reasons, there are numerous grocery stores in most towns and fire and police departments within all states and counties.

FIGURE 1-2

The Origin of Different Types of Organizations

Organization Defined

There are two major perspectives on the definition of organization. Building on the view of organizations as a response to societal needs, organizations can be defined as social instruments. An organization can be seen as a system that transforms inputs (for example, raw materials, capital, human ideas and effort) into the goods and services required to serve a societal need.

This perspective provides us with a "machine" approach to the definition of organizations. That is, organizations are viewed as machines that import raw materials from the external environment (for example, barley, sick patients, uneducated people), transform these inputs, and export a product or service (beer, healthy and educated people) back into the organization's external environment (see Figure 1-3).

Picture Steinlagger Brewery in New Zealand, Frog's Leap Winery in the Napa Valley of California, the Vancouver Canucks hockey team from Vancouver, British Columbia, and the 3M Corporation of St. Paul, Minnesota, and you will see four very different looking organizations, at least as different as a hammer, saw, screwdriver, and pliers. These tools differ in their parts, shape, and design because they serve different purposes. The same is true for these four companies. Each of these organizations has a different anatomy. The parts of an organization needed to brew beer are different from the parts of an organization needed to play hockey.

The vineyard is only one part of a winery's organization. Many other parts need to function effectively for a winery to be successful.

If someone sounded the fire alarm in your local hospital and in the process removed all of the doctors, nurses, technicians, assistants, patients, plant services, and administrative personnel to the other side of the street, can we still say that the vacant building is a hospital? We can certainly conclude that it is no

FIGURE 1-3 The Machine View of Organization

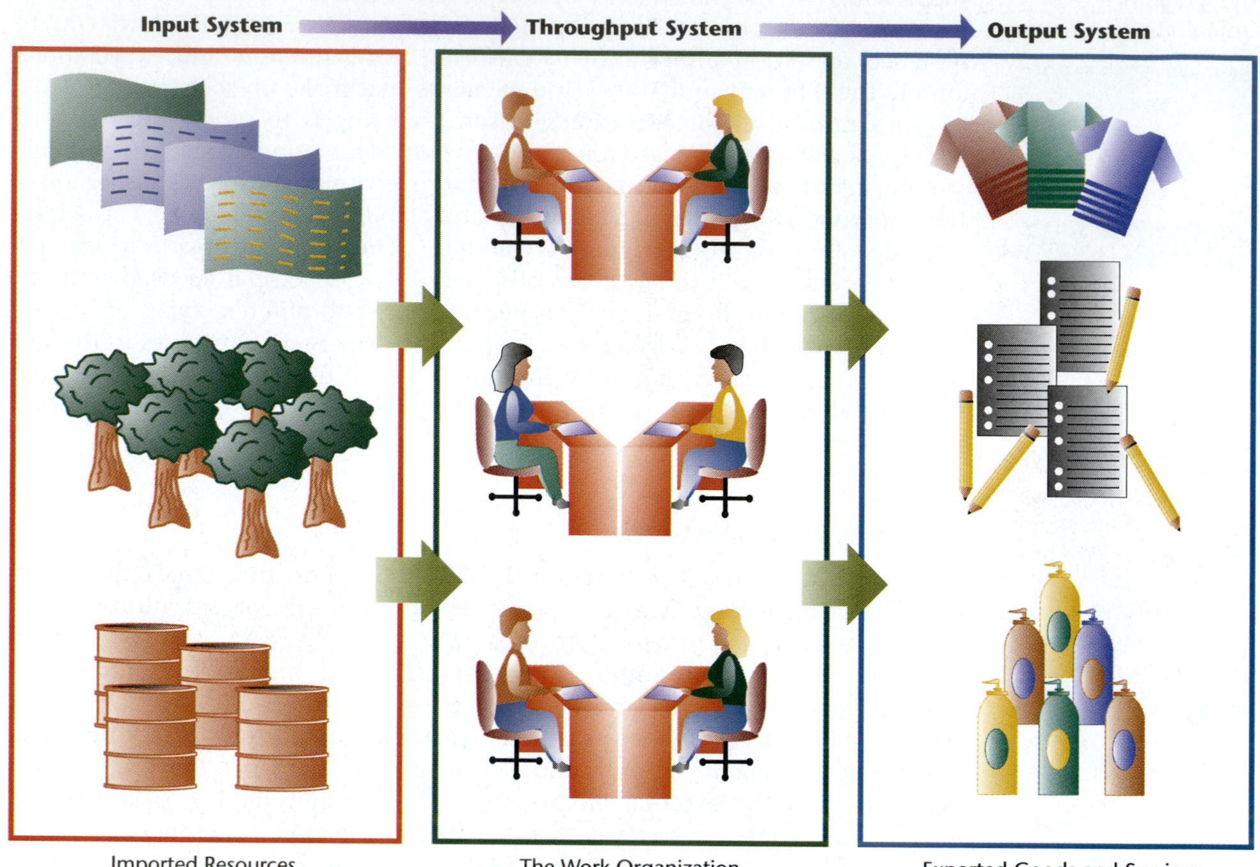

longer an effective health care delivery system. Now, if you walk in with a broken arm what happens? Nothing! Why? Because the doctors and nurses have left—the essence of what this organization is has been disrupted.

This example reveals a second and different perspective on the definition of organizations. Organizations are social systems: two or more people with a conscious, common purpose linked by a communication and command system, possessing both the ability and willingness to contribute to the attainment of the organization's goals.[2] While organizations may own buildings and equipment, these do not define the nature or essence of the organization. Organizations are social systems characterized by relatively enduring interaction patterns that link people to people and people to work as they pursue organizational goals.[3] Take away the interaction patterns in a hospital, for example, that link nurses with doctors, doctors with technicians, the medical staff with administrators, and all of these people with the patients that they care for, and the essence of the hospital as a health care delivery system vanishes. The buildings and equipment remain, but the organization is gone.

http://www.nhl.com

As we envision the interaction patterns that link people to people and people to work that reflect the work of St. Mary's Hospital, we see different interaction patterns than those needed to win the Stanley Cup. No nurses, doctors, pregnant mothers, or interaction patterns needed for successfully delivering a baby are part of the Vancouver Hockey team, and for obvious reasons.

organization a tool or technical system, as well as a social system

In summary, note that there are two dominant views of and definitions for **organization.** The first suggests that organizations are technical or mechanical systems—that is, tools, machines, or vehicles designed to achieve a particular goal. The second definition defines organizations as social systems. Both approaches suggest that organizations are designed differently (have a different anatomy) from one another as a function of the purpose (goals) for which they were created (see Figure 1-4).

FIGURE 1-4

Causes of Organizational Differentiation

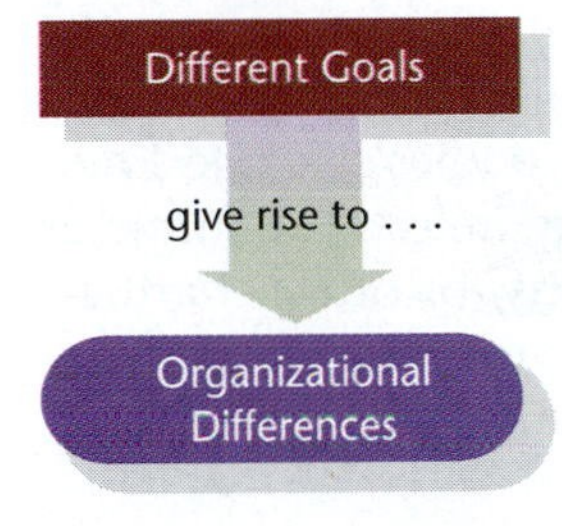

Organizations as Socio-Technical Systems

At this juncture, it is appropriate to ask if there is a correct view of organization. Is it better to define organization as a technical system, a tool, machine, or mechanical device designed to transform inputs into outputs? Or is it more appropriate to define organizations as social systems?

We believe that the definition managers use for their organization influences how they manage the organization. An organization seen as a machine leads to a management approach that emphasizes different aspects of the organization than one seen as a social system. The latter naturally attends carefully to developing cohesion and teamwork, and to satisfying individual member needs. The former attends to the design of efficient input, throughput, and output systems.

socio-technical system an organization is both a social and technical system

Viewing organizations as **socio-technical systems** is an important integrating perspective. Organizations are both social and technical systems. Both systems should be seen as having different needs that must be managed and met simultaneously. If any one system is not carefully managed, the organization will inevitably be less efficient than would be the case if both systems function appropriately.

http://www.indy500.com

Consider Menard's Racing. John Menard recently attempted to win the Indianapolis 500. In order to win this prestigious race, he needed to develop an extremely powerful, fast, and efficient racing machine. Yet with the best and fastest car on the track, where would he be if his car arrived in the pit only to find those who were to service it were late to work, hung-over, unmotivated, not committed to winning, and functioning without coordination? Similarly, with the most motivated, committed, cohesive, and coordinated pit crew, he can't win the Indianapolis 500 without a good racing machine. The same is true for any organization.

Organizations—what are they? They are clearly both a social and technical system, thus referred to as socio-technical system. Organizations are machines and mechanical devices, and simultaneously they are social systems—a relatively enduring network of people-to-people and people-to-work interaction patterns. As a social system, organizations are two or more people with a conscious, common purpose, a willingness and ability to contribute to goal attainment, and with a command and communication system that harmonizes their collective action. Both systems (that is, the technical and social systems) have needs that must be carefully attended to—managed in concert and harmony with one another. IBM's design for the world's fastest computer that is user *un*friendly will result in lower levels of efficiency than a fast computer that is simultaneously responsive to the needs of its user.*

http://www.ibm.com

* *Efficiency* can be seen as a ratio that reflects a comparison of some aspect of unit performance to the cost incurred for that performance. Organizational *effectiveness* should be defined in terms of the degree to which an organization has met such goals as productivity, profit, growth, morale, and manager and human resource development.

Some Additional Perspectives on Organizations

Organizations differ in both degree of permanence and complexity.[4] Each organization has a distinct structure and a set of goals, norms, boundaries, and internal systems. Each also has a relatively enduring pattern of interaction among those within the organization, an external environment and relationships to it, and a social order. Communities, societies, social movements, families, friendship groups, governmental bodies, charitable foundations, and businesses are all organizations. *Work organizations* are systems that import resources from outside the organization, convert them into products and/or services, and export the results to their consumers.

Most of us use the term *organization* to refer to a legal or registered entity. The term *organization* thus brings to mind corporations like Hallmark, Microsoft, Ford, Molson, and General Electric or governmental bodies like the Environmental Protection Agency, Congress, or city hall. You may also think of organizations like the American Cancer Society, United Way, or other charities, or of police and fire departments, or school systems. All of these are organizations. These readily identifiable and legally registered organizations usually contain other organizations embedded within them.

organizational nesting organizations embedded within organizations

Organizations are commonly *nested* within organizations. Sometimes it is easy to spot an **organizational nesting.** Citigroup has Travelers Insurance, Smith Barney, and CitiBank nested within it. The University of Minnesota has the Minneapolis, St. Paul, Duluth, Morris, and Crookston campuses embedded within it. The Duluth campus is divided into several collegiate units (for example, School of Business and Economics, College of Science and Engineering, School of Medicine), each consisting of several departments (faculty). Each unit has distinct interaction patterns that link people to people and people to work, members who share goals and transform resources into goods and services. Therefore, the University of Minnesota is an organization, as is the Duluth campus of the University of Minnesota (University of Minnesota Duluth), its School of Business and Economics, and its Department of Management Studies, and that department's curriculum committee.

This text examines the management and organizational behavior of all organizations, obvious or subtle, large or small. Whether a manufacturing organization or a governmental agency, a free-standing corporation or a tiny organization embedded in another, every organization must be managed. Every organization is a socio-technical system, and the way that it is managed will affect the attitudes, motivation, and behavior of all of its members.

The Work of Organizations

There are several ways for us to think about the work of organizations. We will address the issue of organizational work from three perspectives.

Societal Need The work that organizations do is, in part, defined in terms of the societal need that the organization chooses to address. The St. Louis County Historical Society, like your college, has chosen to respond to society's pattern maintenance need, while Cub Foods has chosen to respond to the adaptation need. Similarly, the Maricopa Sheriff Department is responding to society's integration need, while Minnesota Governor Jesse Ventura and his Independence Party are attempting to respond to society's goal achievement needs.

http://www.sdm-cub.com

http://www.eindependence.org

Organizational Functions At the turn of the century, French businessman Henri Fayol wrote about the general principles of management.[5] He addressed the work of organizations by suggesting that all organizations perform six functions. Fayol referred to this work as **organizational functions.** They consist of production, marketing, finance, accounting, human resources, and management.

organizational functions the work of organizations, which consists of production, marketing, finance, accounting, human resources, and management

According to Fayol, all organizations perform a *production* function. That is, there is some good or service that each organization "produces" and delivers to its external environment. All organizations perform a *marketing* function. Marketing consists of the discovery of customer needs, advertising, and the sale and delivery of the organization's goods and services to the marketplace. All organizations perform a *financial* function. Organizations in our society need capital (money) in order, for example, to purchase buildings, production machines, and raw materials and to hire and staff the organization. All organizations perform an *accounting* function as well. Organizations need to maintain a record of their current state (accounts payable, receivable, land value), which is generally done in financial terms. In addition, all organizations have a *human resource* function. Quite simply, organizations are social systems, and they need to locate, hire, train, and retain people in order to carry out their production, marketing, accounting, and financial functions. Finally, Fayol notes that all organizations have a *management* function. In addition to executing each of the other organizational functions (Ford's production of automobiles; Procter & Gamble's marketing of Tide), each organizational function must be managed. Thus, management is the sixth and final organizational function. (In the next section we explore in greater detail the nature of the management activity.)

Organizational Need Finally, organizations have several needs, three of which provide us with another perspective on the nature of the work of the organization. The organization's **institutional-level needs** reflect the fact that if the organization is going to survive, it must integrate with its external environment and deliver to that environment something that the environment values. This is the price that the organization pays because it takes valued resources from the external (outside) environment in order to support its very existence. To fulfill the institutional need, two activities get performed. First, it is important for the organization to identify needs of the external environment and to find ways in which the organization can satisfy those needs. Second, the organization needs to devote some resources to establish its importance to the external community by informing people outside the organization of its usefulness to that environment.

institutional-level need the organizational need to become integrated with the external environment

Technical core needs are those directly concerned with producing and delivering the organization's goods and services to the external environment. Regardless of which societal need the organization is working to fulfill, certain day-to-day activities need to be performed. In the university, these activities consist of teaching classes, advising students, and conducting research, while at the local hospital the technical core activities are those directly concerned with the delivery of health care.

technical core need the organizational need to accomplish the day-to-day activities associated with producing a product or delivering a service

The organization's **administrative-level needs** focus on the fulfillment of two internal integrative activities. First, the administrative activities focus on the integration of institutional and technical core activities. Vision formulation for the organization unfolds as an institutional-level activity, while vision implementation represents a technical core activity. The road between vision formulation and vision implementation is a long one. Visions formulated at the

administrative-level need the organizational need to integrate the institutional level with the technical core and the diverse work systems within the technical core institutional level need to be interpreted, a meaningful set of short- and medium-range goals need to be created, action plans have to be formulated so that the vision is appropriately represented and those responsible for the performance of the technical core activities have purposeful directions for their day-to-day work activities. In addition to integrating institutional-level and technical core activities, administrative activities are also concerned with integrating the diverse activities that make up the organization's technical core activities. Earlier it was noted that there are several organizational functions—for example, production, marketing, accounting, finance, and human resources. These diverse activities need to be integrated with one another. Production needs to build a product that marketing can successfully sell, which needs to be a product that the human resources are sufficiently trained to produce, and at the same time all of this needs to be done within the organization's financial means and budget. Administrative activities are directed toward this often complex, integrative task.

These three organizational needs and the application of a division of labor result in the traditional organization, which can be envisioned as a three-layer cake. *Institutional-level* responsibilities are commonly positioned at the top, the *technical core* responsibilities at the bottom, with the *administrative level* sandwiched in between the two. Recall, however, that there are organizations nested within organizations and that all organizations have to be managed. Thus, the School of Management Studies at the University of Waikato in Hamilton, New Zealand, has institutional, technical core, and administrative-level needs, as does the University of Waikato.

In summary, the work of organizations can be thought about in terms of three important categories. The societal need served by the organization contributes to our understanding of what it is that organizations do. The work of organizations has also been categorized in terms of six organizational functions—all organizations have a production, marketing, finance, accounting, human resource, and management set of activities. Finally, the work of organizations has been reflected in terms of three organizational needs—all organizations need to integrate themselves with their external environment, fulfill day-to-day activities in terms of the goods and services delivered to the external environment, and integrate and harmonize the internal operations of the organization.

THE NATURE OF MANAGEMENT

The study of organizational management is relatively young. Consequently, there is no universally accepted language, set of symbols, or theoretical underpinning that managers can use to analyze, understand, explain, or make predictions about the management of organizations. This lack of consensus becomes apparent as soon as one tries to define management. Nearly every manager and writer about management has a favorite way to define management. Perhaps the best reaction to this diversity is to take it as grist for the mill, to treat the many definitions as a useful variety that add to your stock of knowledge. Most often, management has been seen simply in terms of "getting things accomplished through other people."

Before turning to the dominant definitions of management, we believe that, first and foremost, management is a philosophy, a set of attitudes and beliefs about people, work, action, and organization. Some managers have a well-developed and conscious theory of management, while many others operate from implicit assumptions about task performance and goal attainment. We'll address the two most dominant theories of management (assumptions and beliefs about organizations and their management) in Chapter 2. As a part of this discussion, we highlight the two most dominant approaches to managing (management practices) that characterize contemporary organizations.

While many definitions exist, there appear to be two major approaches to the definition of management. They are known as the sociological and the process perspectives. The former defines management according to the *social position* that one occupies within the organization, while the latter focuses on *activities* performed within organizations.

The Sociological Perspective

For many, the word "management" calls up an image of a certain group of individuals in an organization. Talk to any unionized employee and mention the word "management," and you will quickly be reminded that what comes to their mind is *a certain group of organizational members,* individuals who sit on the "other side of the fence."

Sociologists study groups of people. As the organizational sociologists view the organization, they see two major social positions, much like the union employee. These two social positions give rise to two kinds of organizational members: managers and "others." The **sociological perspective** thus defines *management* as that group of organizational members who occupy the social positions responsible for making sure that the organization achieves its mission (that is, the organization's reason for being). As you would expect, people who do the managing are called *managers.* The second group of organizational members—the "others" or "everyone else"—are the workers, employees, associates, laborers, troops, rank-and-file, support staff, technical analysts—the *nonmanagers.*

sociological perspective the belief that management consists of a certain group of people in the organization

organizational chart a schematic drawing that depicts the hierarchical relationship among all positions within the organization

The **organizational chart,** such as the one depicted in Figure 1-5, diagrams the formal positions within an organization and their static superior-subordinate and departmental interrelationships. It can be used to distinguish among these social positions. Notice that, in Figure 1-5, the management group spans several different levels and units (departments, sections, divisions) in the organizational hierarchy (that is, its managerial levels of authority and responsibility). The organizational chart has been criticized for its failure to depict the dynamics of true relationships and organizational processes.[6] That is, organizational charts don't show how the work actually gets done. The organizational chart is useful in that it depicts, for example, reporting relationships and the organization's authority structure (the chain of command or authority/influence relationships among organizational members).

Other factors distinguish managers from nonmanagers. Managers generally have more power, influence, rewards, status, and responsibility than do nonmanagers. The two groups also have different organizational roles to fulfill. Managers are often hired, fired, promoted, and demoted according to whether their organization achieves its objectives: selling enough airline tickets, earning enough profits, serving enough hamburgers, and so on. Managers' primary responsibility is to design, pursue, and achieve organizational objectives by working with and through the nonmanagers. Nonmanagers are usually hired to perform specific technical tasks such as operating machinery, maintaining clerical records,

FIGURE 1-5 Organizational Chart

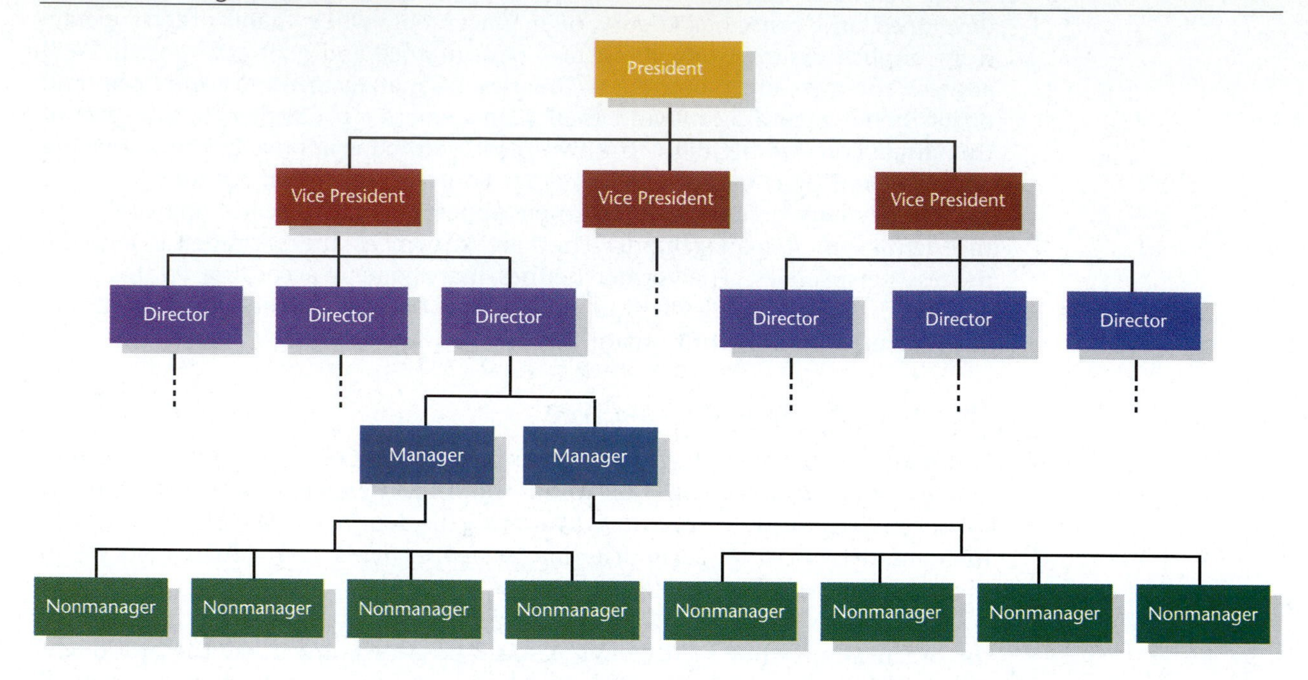

flipping hamburgers, teaching courses, mending broken arms, or maintaining accounts receivable. Their rewards usually are closely tied to how well they apply their technical skills. As organizations move toward high-involvement systems and skill-based pay systems, nonmanagerial people will increasingly be selected based on their commitment to continuous learning and a willingness to perform a variety of tasks as time and organizational need dictate. Increasingly, this group of organizational members may even be called on to devote time and energy to managing—managing their work, their work group, and related activities. It is to the notion of management as a process that we now turn our attention.

The Process Perspective

One of the oldest and most widely adopted definitions of management is the "art of getting things done through people." Mary Parker Follett, a pioneer in the study of management, described management as an activity concerned with the orchestration of people, work, and systems in the pursuit of organizational goals.[7] These two definitions suggest that management is a process (activity). The way in which managers accomplish this is the basis for the **process perspective.** We adopt the process perspective and, in this book, we explore the roles, activities, and processes that organizational members engage in as they plan, organize, direct, and control their organization. We'll treat the process of management as a major organizational force that shapes the attitudes, motivation, and behavior of its organizational members.

process perspective an activity concerned with the orchestration of people, work, and systems in the pursuit of organizational goals

In 1916, French industrialist Henri Fayol described a "functional approach to management" (a process perspective) and suggested that *all* managers perform similar activities, hence, his reference to the *universalism of management* (see Figure 1-6). Whether they are top-level or low-level managers, whether their organization is as small as a sub sandwich shop or as large as the U.S. government, whether they manage a manufacturing organization or a health care institution, all managers must execute a universal set of management processes.[8] Fayol's universal set of management functions included planning, organizing, commanding, coordinating, and controlling.[9]

Following Fayol, theorists such as Chester Barnard, Ralph C. Davis, and Lyndall Urwick revised the idea of universal management functions (see Table 1-1).[10] The result is a process definition that is popular and useful today. It modifies Fayol's categories into four universal management functions: planning, organizing (which includes Fayol's coordinating activities), directing (which includes Fayol's commanding activities), and controlling. **Management**, therefore, can be defined as the process of planning, organizing, directing, and controlling organizational resources (human, financial, physical, and informational) in the pursuit of organizational goals. **Managers** are the members of the organization assigned primary responsibility for carrying out the management process. As you will discover, there can be many levels of management in organizations and many activities that managers must plan for, organize, direct, and control. Among these are the functions of the organization, products (services), processes, special projects, and geographical areas. The concept of high-involvement organization demands that all members, even those with technical responsibilities, share responsibility for the management processes; thus, all members do some managing.

management the process of planning, organizing, directing, and controlling organizational resources in the pursuit of organizational goals

managers those members of the organization assigned the primary responsibility for carrying out the management process

FIGURE 1-6 The Universalism of Management

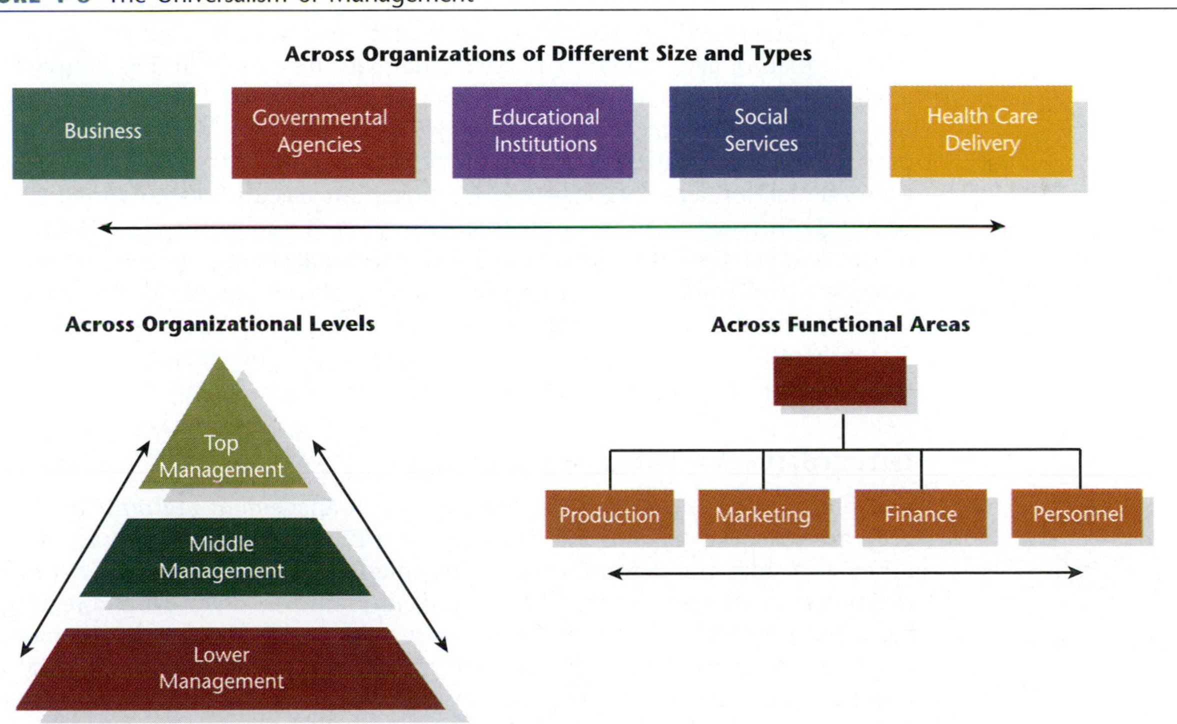

TABLE 1-1 The Range of Management Activities

Planning	Representing	Staffing
Organizing	Activating	Motivating
Commanding	Administering	Innovating
Coordinating	Investigating	Decision making
Controlling	Communicating	Evaluating
Directing	Securing efforts	
Leading	Formulating purposes	

planning defining goals and the methods by which these goals are to be attained

organizing designing, structuring, and coordinating the components of an organization to meet organizational goals

directing orchestrating interpersonal activities, leading, and motivating employees to work effectively and efficiently in the pursuit of organizational goals

controlling monitoring the behavior of organizational members and the effectiveness of the organization itself to determine whether organizational goals are being achieved, and taking corrective action if necessary

The **planning** function involves establishing organizational goals and defining the methods by which these goals are to be attained. The **organizing** functions involve designing, structuring, and coordinating the components (such as reporting relationships) of an organization to meet organizational goals. Organizing is that activity directed toward structuring (restructuring) the socio-technical system (for example, creating the people-to-people networks). The **directing** function involves managing interpersonal activities, leading, and motivating employees so that they will effectively and efficiently accomplish the task necessary to realize organizational goals. The **controlling** function involves monitoring both the behavior of organizational members and the effectiveness of the organization itself, determining whether plans are achieving organizational goals, and taking corrective action as needed. These functions will be explored in Part III. As shown in Figure 1-7, managers use all four functions when applying the organization's resources to achieve the organization's goals. These functions are explored in greater detail in Chapters 9–12.

Fayol's view of management as a process is very much in keeping with the "machine view" of organizations in that management is defined in terms of a series of integrated and mechanical tasks that need to be performed—set a goal, create a plan of action, design a system that can implement and accomplish the goal, orchestrate people in the performance of their tasks, and monitor (control) on-going activities in accordance with the planned course of action. As a process, management might be seen through a set of lenses similar to viewing the organization as a social system. Management has also been defined as a set of human interactions,[11] supposedly in the pursuit and satisfaction of the goals of an organization (to satisfy the need of management, its employees, customers, and members of the community in which the organization resides) as a human community. Great managers communicate their vision to others, interact with others with integrity, and show respect for their employees as well as the organization's larger external community.[12]

Integrative View on Management

The process and sociological perspectives on management are both useful. Yet they are perspectives and not an everyday reality, as theory and practice often differ. Consider the definition of management as a set of activities. Does that make you a manager any time you engage in planning, organizing, directing, or controlling? Possibly, yet most of us sense a basic difference between managerial and nonmanagerial organizational members and between managerial and nonmanagerial work. This is particularly true in traditional (low-involvement) organizations. This is due primarily to a *division of labor* (breaking up work into

FIGURE 1-7 The Management Process

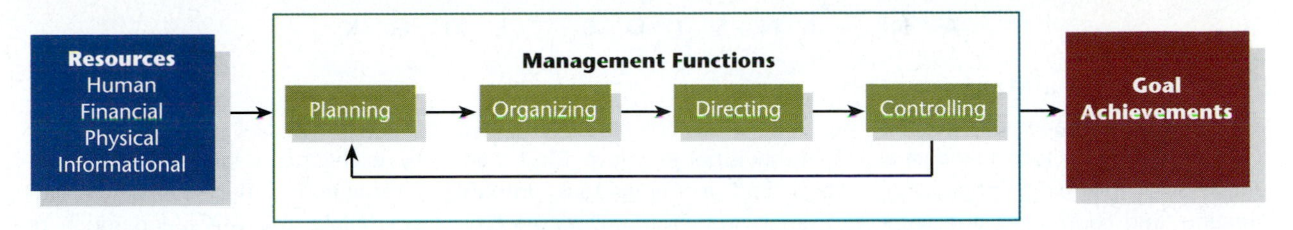

Source: Adapted from G. Terry. 1972. *Principles of management*. Homewood, IL: Irwin, 4.

relatively narrow, standardized, and repetitive jobs) that managers create by assigning activities to individuals and groups in organizations. Managers traditionally assign different kinds of tasks to holders in each of the two social positions. Nonmanagers typically are assigned technical tasks, such as operating machines, sweeping floors, removing tonsils, teaching classes, selling, and calculating the firm's taxes. Managers are assigned broader tasks of planning, organizing, directing, and controlling the individuals, resources, and tasks of the nonmanagerial group. The high-involvement model assigns at least some level of the management process to all members while leaving major decisions to management.

Most managers are involved in all four sets of management functions, though rarely in a controlled and systematic fashion.[13] Managers navigate through their days by following a sequence of planning (identifying goals), organizing (designing the systems needed to meet goals), directing (energizing people), and controlling (measuring results against the plan.)[14] But this sequence doesn't mean that managers plan on Monday, organize on Tuesday, direct on Wednesday, control on Thursday, and golf on Friday. Rather, their day is a sea of scheduled and unscheduled events, opportunities, and crises through which they navigate by using the four functions. (See *An Inside Look* at the daily life of a manager.) Even for the highest-level managers, half of their activities last less than nine minutes. As recently observed by Harvard University Business School Professor John P. Kotter, "GMs [general managers] spend most of their time with others in short, disjointed conversations."[15] Only 10 percent of managerial activities exceed one hour.[16] As portrayed in Figure 1-8, the job of a manager often resembles a day in the swamp.

THE MOVE TOWARD THE HIGH-INVOLVEMENT ORGANIZATION AND MANAGEMENT SYSTEM

The distinction between managers and nonmanagers and the responsibility differences that accompany these two social positions (managers being responsible for planning, organizing, directing, and controlling) are becoming increasingly blurred. Many organizations are moving in the direction of highly participative systems. Information is being decentralized (dispersed throughout and pushed to lower organizational levels), people are becoming empowered, responsibility for performance and quality is being transferred to all organizational members, and decisions are being made by those who carry out the decisions. In essence, organizations are evolving into systems characterized by high involvement

AN INSIDE LOOK

The Daily Life of a Manager

Much of the management process is centered on the four managerial functions of planning, organizing, directing, and controlling, and techniques that managers can use to carry out those functions. Real life for the manager, however, is seldom as organized and systematic. Managers don't plan on Monday, organize on Tuesday, direct on Wednesday, control on Thursday, and golf and drink martinis on Friday!

We encourage you to shadow a manager or two for a day and examine their daily routines. You might be interested in what the future holds in store if you become a manager.

For one thing, you can expect to work long hours. Most managers work at least fifty hours a week; some put in as many as ninety. If you are like most managers, you will spend most of this time working inside your own organization. Despite the importance of outside factors—such as customers, competitors, and suppliers—most managers spend little time interacting directly with these groups. They spend over 90 percent of their time inside the walls of their own workplace.

Expect not to be bored, especially if you become a first-level manager. There will be plenty to keep you busy. First-level managers perform from 200 to 400 separate activities in a single eight-hour day. The work is not repetitive. Most managers find a tremendous amount of variety in their job. During a typical workday, a manager completes paperwork, makes and takes phone calls, attends scheduled and unscheduled meetings, conducts inspection tours and visits at the workplace, has personal contact with many people, and addresses a wide range of work-related issues.

This level of activity will not allow you much time for contemplation. First-level managers encounter a new demand on their time almost every minute of the workday; therefore, most of their activities tend to be of very short duration. Trivial and important matters are often interspersed, and you will be expected to isolate and handle problems in rapid-fire order. Although this pace gives most managers little time to reflect or plan systematically, you should try to reserve some time for these activities. As you will see later in this book, one of the factors that distinguishes effective from ineffective managers is how well they reflect on their work and systematically plan their actions.

Most managers do most of their work orally, not in writing. Managers need to be able to communicate well with their superiors, subordinates, and peers. You can expect to exchange a lot of information. Information is the soul of a manager's job. You will spend much of your day getting and giving information. If you do not get the information you need, you will not make good decisions or plans. If you do not give information to the people who need it, your activities will be in vain.

The reality of what a manager's life is actually like is not necessarily what it should be like. The reality, from a manager's perspective, also is not necessarily what others see. If you were to ask managers how many hours they spend at work, how often they are interrupted, how much time they spend working inside their organization, or other aspects about how they spend their time, their answers would not match one another. Managers usually do not know how much time they devote to specific activities, and that is a problem. If managers do not know how they spend their day, how can they modify it to become more effective?

These *de*scriptions of a typical managerial day are, therefore, not *pre*scriptions. The reality is that a manager's day is hectic; however, managers must attack the management process more systematically in order to improve effectiveness.

FIGURE 1-8 The Management Process under Pressure

When you are up to your elbows in alligators, it's hard to remember that your objective was to drain the swamp.

(see *An Inside Look* at the high-involvement perspective). These efforts are being undertaken in an effort to positively impact employee attitudes, motivation, and behavior, and the organization's competitive position and profitability.

With this movement toward high involvement, we see more extreme and more widely integrated planning, organizing, directing, and controlling activities. At Harley-Davidson, for example, a team of workers might decide on the supplies to be ordered, on the number of units they can produce, and on the particular team members who will do the work. In addition, they may reengineer a portion of the production line. All of these are tasks traditionally performed by managers. Participative management and the delegation of authority (both of which are discussed more fully in later chapters) blur the traditional distinction between the two social positions.

http://www.harley-davidson.com

WHY ORGANIZATIONS NEED MANAGERS

http://www.sunhealth.org/hospitals/boswell.com

http://www.lakesuperiorbrewing.com

Organizations have been defined as tools created to achieve a set of objectives. Boswell Hospital in Sun City, Arizona, was created to deliver quality health care. Carroll College in Waukesha, Wisconsin, was created to provide a sound liberal arts education for college students. The Lake Superior Brewing Company, in Duluth, Minnesota, was created to make a profit by manufacturing and selling beer. Every organization has a set of technical tasks that must be performed to

AN INSIDE LOOK

The High-Involvement Perspective

Extensions of the *human-resource model* created by the behavioral scientists have slowly become the driving ideology for an increasing number of managers. When fully integrated into managerial thinking and practice, the high-involvement organization replaces the top-down hierarchical-driven organization designed and managed by those managers who subscribe to "Taylorism" and Fayol and Weber's approach to organizational management and design.

Those managing in accord with the principles of the classical school of management sincerely believe that those who guide organizations have the genius to create vision and be the architects of the necessary means to achieve organizational goals in a competitive, efficient, and effective manner. The challenge or "the essence of management is getting the ideas out of the heads of the bosses and into the hands of labor."*

The classical school casts the typical employee as someone who is basically lazy and incapable of making a commitment to the organization and its goals. Adherents believe that the employee is economically motivated. Why else would anyone work eight, twelve, or fourteen hours a day, five or six days per week, year in and year out, other than for money, more and more money?

It quite simply never occurred to the hard-core proponents of control-oriented management and the mechanistic organization that employees are capable of self-direction and self-control; that they are intrinsically motivated to do meaningful work and find satisfaction in doing so; that commitment, responsibility, and good organizational citizenship find their roots in people coming to feel a sense of attachment toward, involvement with, belonging to, and ownership of the organization. Throughout much of the 20th century, there were "managers" and "laborers."

The philosophical gurus, the organizational architects, and the managers who have implemented the high-involvement organization employ an entirely different vocabulary that is coupled with a different set of beliefs. They don't think and talk in terms of laborers, but rather in terms of partners, associates, owners, and organizational members. Managers are teachers, facilitators, cheerleaders, and leaders. While these labels can be viewed as mere semantics, those who use them feel they represent an entirely different philosophical orientation than that promoted by those who practice classical management techniques.

This approach to management implies that management (that is, the process of planning, organizing, directing, and controlling) will be carried out extensively by people at *all* levels and in *all* positions throughout the organization and especially by those who make the products and deliver the organization's services. It makes extensive use of job enrichment, self-directed and cross-functional teams, quality circles, and other participative strategies. Through and as a part of each of these participative processes, the emphasis is on providing organizational members with the skills/training needed to perform and continuously improve, the information needed to make sound organizational decisions, the power to make things happen, and a sharing in the rewards that are associated with increases in organizational efficiency and effectiveness.

The high-involvement approach to organizational management will be discussed in more detail in Chapter 3. In addition, we will link the high-involvement theme to our discussion of each phase of the management process.

* M. J. Kiernan. 1993. The new strategic architecture: Learning to compete in the twenty-first century. *Academy of Management Executive* 7(1): 14.

convert its mission into reality. It is through management that specific goals are set, plans of action are formulated, the necessary work systems to carry out plans are organized, people are encouraged, and behavior is regulated. According to management guru Peter Drucker, the task of management is to make people capable of joint performance by giving them common goals and values, the right environment within which to operate, and the ongoing training so that they can perform and respond to change.[17] It is managers who achieve this very important work by attending to the needs of social systems—the need for plans, organization, direction, and control.

http://www.pfdf.org

TYPES OF MANAGERS

Now that you have an idea of what the management process is, let's consider the roles of managers themselves. A number of classification schemes are commonly employed to identify different types of managers, particularly in traditional organizations. It is possible, for example, to classify managers by organizational responsibility; hierarchical level; functional area; line versus staff positions; product, process, and geographical area; projects and tasks; and self and team responsibilities. We describe these differences in this section.

Organizational Responsibility Served

As a part of our discussion of the work of organizations, you were introduced to the institutional, administrative, and technical core needs of the organization. In many organizations, managers can be classified by the nature of the organizational responsibility that they carry out. Managers who carry out institutional-level responsibilities focus their energies on vision formulation and integrating the organization with its external environment. Jack Welch's vision to have General Electric be either number one or two in every one of its businesses reflects institutional-level management. Managers of the organization's technical core manage the day-to-day production, marketing, accounting, finance, and human resource activities of the organization. Managers with responsibility for administrative needs find themselves integrating the diverse activities within the organization's technical core (for example, integrating the production and marketing activities) and bringing vision formed at the institutional level into an operational plan that is executed in the organization's technical core.

In large organizations, such as GE, the job of managing is sufficiently large and complex that certain organizational members are exclusively assigned to one area of organizational responsibility. At Dun-Rovin resort on the Big Chippewa in northern Wisconsin, this family-owned and controlled business sees the owners—a husband-and-wife team—wearing multiple organizational responsibility hats all within the same day. At certain times, one or both of them address institutional-level responsibilities as they deal with the Department of Natural Resources' proposed fishing regulations for the upcoming season, only to change hats to wrestle with problems in the kitchen as the kitchen staff prepares for this evening's menu. They go from institutional-level to technical core responsibilities in a matter of minutes. The small organization's division of management labor rarely parallels that of large organizations like GE.

http://www.dnr.state.wi.us

http://www.ge.com

Hierarchy Distinctions

Managers can also be classified by their position in the organization's hierarchy. The lowest level at which the management process is executed, especially in the high-involvement organization, is through self-management and self-managing work teams in the organization's technical core. Within the ranks of formal and traditionally defined managers, the lowest level of managers are **first-level managers.** They are involved primarily with managing the organization's technical core and are the only managers who direct nonmanagerial organizational members. First-level managers often have titles such as "unit manager" or "department manager." Those who manage first-level managers are referred to as **second-level managers.** Next come third-level managers, and so on, up to top-level management. People often describe managers' general positions in a hierarchy as lower, middle, and upper level.

first-level managers those managers at the lowest level in the organization

second-level managers those managers who direct first-level managers

Functional Area

Managers are also classified according to their area of specialized activity (also known as the organizational function served). They are the organization's **functional managers.** "I'm in accounting," says one manager. "I've been transferred from production to marketing," says another. Functional areas should not be confused with the general management functions of planning, organizing, directing, and controlling. Instead, specialized functional areas describe the specific set of activities that the manager oversees. While these vary somewhat depending on the industry, it is common for organizations to have operations (production), marketing, finance, accounting, and human resource functions. In some contemporary organizations, functional separation is reduced in favor of cross-functionally integrated teams.

functional managers those managers responsible for the organization's functions of production, marketing, finance, accounting, and human resources

Virtually any manager may be classified by the several schemes discussed in this section. For example, there are likely to be top, middle, and lower-level managers, a hierarchical-level classification of managers, within each functional area. Thus, a senior vice president for production at Cisco is also a top-level manager, while several lower-level production managers may be assigned to a single Cisco product.

http://www.cisco.com

Line and Staff Distinctions

Another helpful way to classify managers is according to whether they are directly involved in producing the organization's goods or services. **Line managers** have a *direct* responsibility for producing the service or product line of the organization. At Goodyear, for example, the department supervisor in charge of a tire molding department is a line manager. Each manager, from the technical core to the institutional level, who links the tire molding department supervisor with the president of Firestone is a line manager. Thus, there are upper-level, middle-level, and lower-level line managers. Line managers are usually given considerable command authority; that is, they can tell subordinates "what to do," "how to do it," and "when it should be done."

line managers those managers who have "direct" responsibility for producing the organization's products and/or services

It is the job of **staff managers** to *support* line managers, but staff managers are not directly involved in the production of goods or services. Staff managers, who are found in all zones of responsibility, usually are not given command authority, but instead wield influence based on their personal skill and knowledge. For example, staff managers in the legal department at Dairycraft, Inc., a manufacturer of stainless steel products for the dairy industry, don't manage

staff managers managers whose responsibility it is to "support" line managers the production or sales of stainless steel containers. Rather, they supervise the lawyers who advise the line managers who establish contractual relationships with suppliers, customers, and employees. Legal department staff managers cannot *order* line managers to sign or reject a purchasing contract. They can only use personal legal knowledge to help line managers decide whether the contract is a good one and one that should be signed. Line managers are responsible for the decisions made and actions taken; staff managers are responsible for the quality of the advice that they give to line managers.

Product, Process, and Geographical Area Managers

It is not uncommon to find organizations dividing the work of the organization and responsibilities around factors other than organizational functions (production, marketing, human resources). It is common, for example, to witness the following divisions within organizations: product divisions (GM Truck and Automobile Divisions), geographical territories (Western Europe, Africa, North America, South Pacific), or processes employed (welding, assembly, cutting, stamping). Those individuals who manage these organizational divisions are commonly referred to as **product**, **territory**, and **process managers**, respectively.

product, territory, and **process managers** those who manage an organization's product, territorial, and process divisions

Task and Project Managers

Often organizations identify special projects (tasks) that need to be completed. Individuals responsible for a particular task or project are commonly called **task (project) managers.** Task managers work to develop the plan that will guide the completion of the project. They frequently build the project team, manage its day-to-day activities, and close down the project once it has been completed. John Szilagyi, at South-Western College Publishing, served as the project manager for the creation of this book. He identified the market, signed the authors, developed the table of contents, and assembled both the production team needed for the development of the book and the marketing team needed for the marketing of the final product.

task (project) managers individuals who have been assigned responsibility for a particular organizational task or project

Self and Team Managers

Two major changes reflect the movement toward the high-involvement organization: the **empowerment** of individual organizational members who are given considerable autonomy to exercise discretion in the performance of their jobs and the increased utilization of self-managed work teams (also commonly referred to as autonomous work groups). These teams are given the autonomy and opportunity to exercise discretion in the performance of team jobs.

empowerment state that exists when an organizational member experiences power to exercise discretion in the performance of their job

These two trends create self managers and team managers. **Self managers** not only perform the technical side of their organizational roles, but also devote substantial time to problem solving, decision making, planning, and controlling. In similar fashion, **team managers** assume responsibility for facilitating (orchestrating) group activity as it pertains to the performance of both the team's technical and managerial activities.

self managers individuals who manage themselves and the performance of their own work; thus, they plan, problem-solve, make decisions, and control their own work activities

team managers those who assume responsibility for the orchestration of group performance activities

Organizational Type Distinctions

As you might expect, the societal need or the sector of the economy (for example, government, education, health care, finance, entertainment, manufacturing) in which an organization operates also influences the nature of the manager's job and, often, the titles used to designate the manager's position. While chancellors and provosts are common to universities, neither title or role is likely to be found in a manufacturing organization.

http://www.amfam.com

The vice president of claims at American Family Insurance may have an editorial vice president counterpart at South-Western College Publishing and an under-secretary of state in the federal government. A head nurse in a hospital can be the counterpart of a supervisor in a manufacturing shop. The dean of a medical school may be doing work on a level comparable to that of a manufacturing organization's division head. Confusion is often created when there is a lack of specificity and common meaning associated with these titles across organizations and industries. Unfortunately, this is a fact of organizational life with which we have to live.

VARIATIONS IN THE MANAGER'S JOB

"A rose is a rose is a rose" and "Management is management is management." There is a universal aspect to management—*all* managing involves performance of the same functions—planning, organizing, directing, and controlling. Yet this statement flies in the face of both common sense and empirical evidence.[18] Managers at Hermantown High School and managers at Northern States Power, for example, plan, organize, direct, and control their organizations' operations. But in one case, the focus is on the education of children. In the other, the focus is on the manufacture and delivery of electricity. In addition to differences in content of issues or problems dealt with, management jobs differ in several ways: the time frame managers must consider, the allocation of time across functions, the scope of the organization for which they are accountable, and the specific skills performed. Wide variations exist in the jobs of managers, both between organizations and within.

Time Perspective

In the traditional organization, those managing the organization's technical core commonly deal with matters that involve the here and now. As we move from lower to higher management levels, a manager's time frame shifts toward the distant future. Lower-level managers are usually concerned with delivering current services and meeting current production schedules. Upper-level managers focus more on issues that will have impact 5–15 years in the future. As John W. Teets, former Chairman of the Board for Greyhound Corporation, put it, "Management's job is to see the company not as it is . . . but as it can become."[19] In many of Japan's leading organizations, it is not uncommon for the CEO to believe that it is their responsibility to see several decades into the future. Thus, institutional-level managers plan, organize, direct, and control an organization's future while managers in the technical core carry out the same activities, but focus on delivering today's services and meeting current production schedules.

http://www.greyhound.com

Time Allocation Differences

One of the biggest variations among managers is in how much time they devote to each of the four management functions. It has been observed that lower-level managers spend about half as much time planning as upper-level managers. In addition, lower-level managers appear to devote almost twice as much time to directing compared to their upper-level managerial counterparts.[20]

Figure 1-9 shows how managers at different hierarchical levels distribute their time. It should be noted that, in high-involvement organizations, these patterns can change substantially. In those organizations, for example, it is not unusual for low-level managers and nonmanagers to spend substantial time involved in planning and controlling activities.

Time allocation also differs for managers from various functional areas.[21] Figure 1-10 shows this allocation for middle-level managers. As you can see, production, marketing, and financial managers spend the largest percentage of their time controlling. Human resource managers, on the other hand, spend the least amount of their time controlling. Instead, they devote more of their time to the planning function.

Organizational Scope

The manner in which managers plan, organize, direct, and control varies according to the scope of the organization. Top-level managers devise strategic plans that encompass the entire organization. Managers in the technical core usually concentrate their planning on only the organizational work unit (for example, department, project, team) for which they are responsible. Thus, the organizational scope toward which their planning, organizing, directing, and controlling activities are directed is much more narrow (limited) than that of the organization's chief executive officer (CEO).

Skills Needed

Because the jobs of managers vary, the specific skill needed for success also varies. The manager responsible for planning the strategies that make an aerospace company competitive in the world arena needs a different mixture of skills than does the manager who trains astronauts or who assembles rocket booster engines. Daniel Katz, a psychology professor at the University of Michigan, examined the skills managers use and placed them into three categories: conceptual, human, and technical.[22]

technical skills the ability to use and understand the use of tools, procedures, and techniques needed to perform a task

Technical skills enable managers to understand and use the tools, procedures, and techniques needed to perform a task. Managers at the lowest levels, particularly in the technical core, usually need considerable technical skills to understand the various components of their work unit and the work of those whom they supervise. The relative importance of the technical skills to managerial performance decreases for managers at higher levels in an organization.

FIGURE 1-9 Hierarchical-Level Differences among Managers

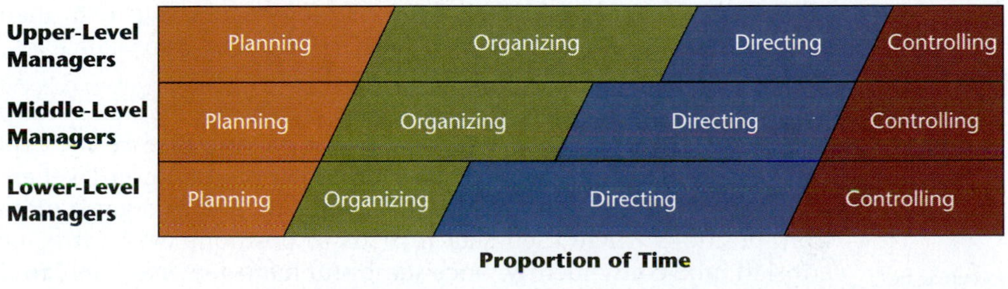

Upper-Level Managers: Planning | Organizing | Directing | Controlling
Middle-Level Managers: Planning | Organizing | Directing | Controlling
Lower-Level Managers: Planning | Organizing | Directing | Controlling

Proportion of Time

FIGURE 1-10 Functional-Area Managerial Differences

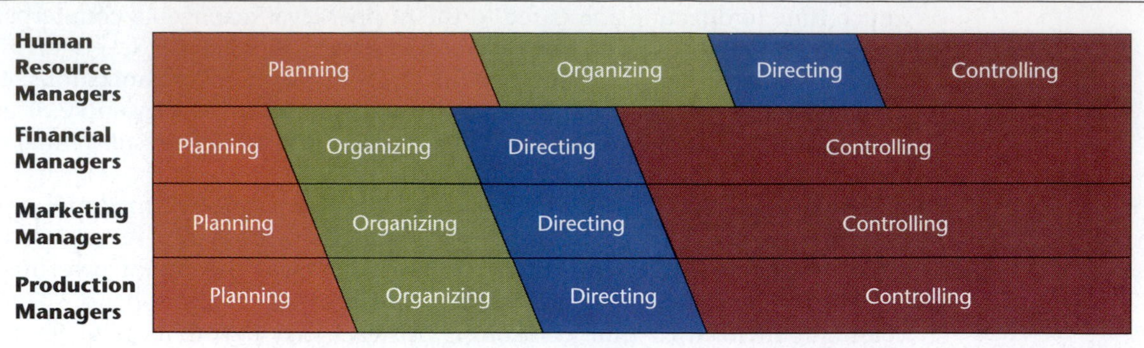

Source: Based on data from J. Horne and T. Lupton. 1965. The work activities of middle managers: An exploratory study. *Journal of Management Studies* 2:14–33.

human (interpersonal) skills the ability to work with and understand others, to lead, motivate, resolve conflict, and build group effort

Human (interpersonal) skills enable managers to work with and understand others, to lead, to motivate, to manage conflict, and to build group effort. Human skills are equally important to all managers in the social system. Mary Parker Follett observed that management is the orchestration of people, and that management has traditionally been defined as "getting work done through others"—hence the importance of human skills. Some have suggested that management is an art and that a competitive advantage can be achieved by "tapping employee's most essential humanity, their ability to create, judge, imagine, and build relationships."[23]

conceptual skills the ability to examine, diagnose, understand, and evaluate complex concepts at an abstract level of analysis; to reason, store, and retrieve information

Conceptual skills refer to an individual's intellectual functioning. These enable managers to examine, diagnose, understand, and evaluate concepts at an abstract level of analysis. Not only do conceptual skills enable managers to think abstractly; they contribute to the ability to reason, to engage in inductive and deductive thought. The conceptual skills contribute to the ability to process, store, retrieve, and understand large amounts of complex information. Individuals with good conceptual skills have the capacity to envision and think long-term. Although everyone needs conceptual skills, they are most important to managers who deal with institutional-level responsibilities, who must devise plans based on probabilities, patterns, and abstract connections. Conceptual skills provide upper-level managers with the ability to visualize the future, to strategize, and to anticipate changes or to estimate the value of corporate strategies.

According to Katz, all managers must have all of these three skills to be effective. He also notes that the skill levels required for successful managerial performance vary from level to level and from organization to organization.

Human skills are important to managerial success among first-level, middle-level, and upper-level managers. The picture for the conceptual and technical skills is different. Successful managerial performance among upper-level managers is somewhat more dependent on the conceptual skills than is the case at lower levels in the organizational hierarchy. Just the reverse is true for the technical skills. The technical skills have a strong relationship with managerial success among first-level managers, and the relative importance of these skills decreases as one rises to upper-level management.

The fact that a different mix of skills is required for successful performance at different levels in the organization might provide at least one explanation for why promotions based on successful performance at a lower level are not always met with success. Often, upward advancement moves organizational members from positions where their skill mix fits to positions where they need a different skill mix; consequently, once-successful managers may need to develop new skills in order to continue to succeed. The *Peter Principle* was coined to refer to

http://pespmcl.vub.ac.be/PETERPR.htm

this phenomenon. The Peter Principle refers to the tendency of organizational members to rise through promotions to their level of incompetence.[24] Once individuals reach their level of incompetence, they are no longer promoted, and seldom do organizations move organizational members back down to those jobs where their configuration of skills fits the job. We might anticipate that those organizations in which the Peter Principle is operative may well be organizations in which morale, motivation, and performance are lower than would be the case where people's skills and abilities match their job demands.

The importance of human resource development shows as the nature of organizations and the roles of their members change. As lower-level organizational members become empowered through high involvement, human and conceptual skills become ever more important for members of the organization's technical core. In addition, the skills successful CEOs of the 21st century need are changing as well. Visionary leadership will likely become the most valued standard for tomorrow's CEO. Also increasing dramatically in importance for Manager 2000 will be the ability to communicate their vision for the organization so that other organizational members embrace it and to manage a broad range of human resource practices.[25]

MANAGERIAL ROLES

interpersonal role the organizational role that involves serving as figurehead, leader, and liaison for an organization

informational role the organizational role that involves monitoring, disseminating, and serving as a spokesperson for an organization

Managers wear many hats as they carry out the four management functions. Henry Mintzberg, management professor from Canada's McGill University, identifies three major roles that managers perform as they carry out the work of management: interpersonal, informational, and decisional.

Interpersonal Roles

Managers actually perform several **interpersonal roles.** As a *figurehead,* managers symbolize the organization, signing legal documents and participating in such events as ground-breaking ceremonies or the opening of new branch offices. As a *leader,* managers use power, coordination techniques, and motivational tools to integrate the needs of individual subordinate organizational members with the needs of the organization as it pursues its objectives. As a *liaison,* managers develop and cultivate relationships with individuals and groups outside their area of direct responsibility. A supervisor, for example, may develop a network with other supervisors, and the chief executive officer with other CEOs.

Henry Mintzberg identified interpersonal, informational, and decisional as the three major roles that managers perform.

Informational Roles

As a result of their interpersonal role, managers collect and disperse information, thereby giving rise to their **informational role.** The informational role is actually made up of three subroles. As a *monitor,* managers collect information about the organization and its environment from all available sources. As a *disseminator,* managers transmit information to others in the organization. This can involve factual information

("We must fill an order for 1000 widgets by Thursday") and value information ("The director of marketing wants us to be more aware of and responsive to our customers' actual needs"). As a *spokesperson,* managers transmit information about the organization (such as its policies or plans) to individuals and groups outside the organization.

Decisional Roles

decisional (strategy-making) role the organizational role that involves serving as entrepreneur, disturbance handler, resource allocator, and negotiator for an organization

The third major role that managers play is the **decisional** or **strategy-making role.** As an *entrepreneur,* managers identify opportunities for, and threats to, the organization and initiate changes to capitalize on these. As a *disturbance handler,* managers react to and attempt to resolve crises, such as conflicts between individuals or problems with other organizations. As a *resource allocator,* managers schedule their time, program the work of subordinates, and control decisions involving the allocation of other resources, such as money, supplies, and equipment. As a *negotiator,* managers attempt to obtain beneficial solutions for the organization in nonroutine situations, such as arranging a contract with a supplier or negotiating a tax break from a state government in exchange for building a new plant in that state.

Although neither the functional (process) nor the role approach provides complete insight into all aspects of a manager's daily routine, they do comprise a comprehensive and useful way of looking at the nature of management. Managers can, and should, integrate the role-oriented approach with the traditional four-function process perspective because it is, in part, through the interpersonal, informational, and decisional roles that managers execute the planning, organizing, directing, and controlling functions.

According to Mintzberg, these three managerial roles are interrelated. As managers carry out their interpersonal roles, they come into contact with others. Through these interactions, they gain access to information that will be important to the organization's future functioning. Possession of important information, when coupled with the manager's position of power and responsibility, makes the manager a central figure in organizational decision making. Thus, the interpersonal role leads to their informational role, which, in turn, when coupled with the power and responsibility of their organizational position, gives rise to their key decisional role. (See Figure 1-11.)

Emerging Roles

For nearly a century, we have seen management as a process (activity) where managers in virtually all organizations assumed the primary responsibility for planning, organizing, directing, and controlling the affairs of the organization. As a part of the process, managers assumed interpersonal, informational, and decisional roles.

During the past few decades, new forms of organization have been emerging, accompanied by new approaches to managing. In many organizations, like Johnsonville Foods of Sheyboygan, Wisconsin, the "be-all" manager (commander, gang-boss, top honcho, big dog) is being replaced with a manager whose roles include mentor, coach, facilitator, enabler, teacher, and cheerleader. Increasingly, traditional nonmanagers devote a meaningful portion of their time to problem solving, planning, organizing, directing, and controlling. Production employees at Johnsonville Foods are not only involved in producing bratwurst, but in performing many activities that were once the exclusive domain of their lower- and middle-level line and staff managers.

http://johnsonville.com

FIGURE 1-11 Mintzberg's Three Managerial Roles: The Interrelationship

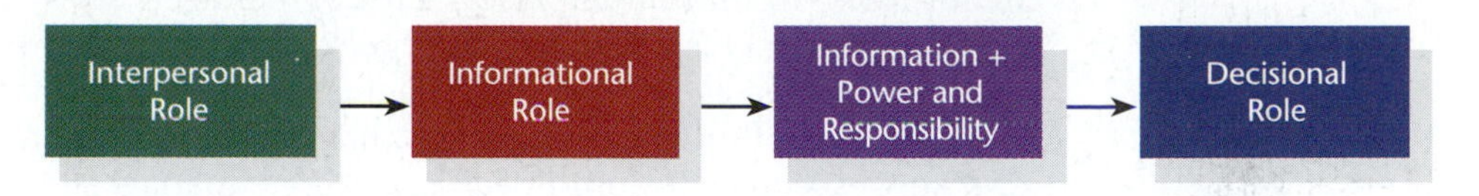

Johnsonville's owner-CEO, Ralph Stayer, describes his role as one of establishing the philosophy for the organization. People working for Stayer describe him as their mentor and in turn define their own roles as that of teachers. Apple's Steve Jobs has talked about the role of the manager as coach and cheerleader. A keen observer of the business and management community, Peter Drucker believes that the new role of the manager will be more like a minister bringing together different units into a community.[26] While these are new roles for today's manager, they reinforce Mintzberg's observation of the interpersonal role of the manager.

http://www.apple.com

THE NATURE OF ORGANIZATIONS AND MANAGEMENT IN REVIEW

In this text we assume that organizations are socio-technical systems—social systems whose technical system is driven by its people. It is the nature of the employee-organization relationship—that is, the level of employee commitment, identification, and psychological ownership for the organization (its mission and work to be done)—that defines whether the organization as a "machine" is driven at 50, 100, or 120 percent of its technical capacity. It is the organization that is managed as a high-involvement system that will lead the way into this, the 21st century. The high-involvement organization is characterized as a participative system that places a premium on human resource development, the decentralization of information, the empowerment of people, and rewarding people for their own growth and development and the organization's successful performance.

There are at least two perspectives on, and many, many definitions of, management. This book uses a definition based on the process perspective of management. We view management as the processes of planning, organizing, directing, and controlling an organization's resources in pursuit of organizational goals. These four processes are put into effect by people called managers. All managers plan, organize, direct, and control, so this set of functions can be considered universal. Yet the specific ways in which managers apply the four functions vary with the specific type of management position held.

Management positions vary according to organizational need; line or staff; hierarchical level; functional area; product, process, and geographical territory; tasks (projects); self and team; and organizational type. Differences among types of managers produce differences in time perspectives, in the allocation of time among the four functions, and in the profile of skills needed for effective management. For example, upper-level managers deal with the long term as they plan the organization's future; they allocate a great deal of their time to planning; and they rely on conceptual skills to develop an organization's strategy. Lower-level managers, on the other hand, deal with daily time frames and production schedules, allocating much of their time to directing and controlling functions, and thus need good technical skills.

In carrying out the four major management functions, managers play three major roles. To fulfill interpersonal roles, managers serve as figureheads, leaders, and liaisons. Increasingly, the interpersonal role is also being defined in terms of the manager as philosopher, teacher, coach, facilitator, mentor, and cheerleader. To fulfill informational roles, managers become monitors, disseminators, and spokespeople. To fulfill decisional roles, managers act as entrepreneurs, disturbance handlers, resource allocators, and negotiators. As organizations become increasingly high-involvement systems, the informational and decisional roles are increasingly shared with lower and nonmanagerial organizational members.

The planning, organizing, directing, and controlling functions and the activities that managers perform as they apply these functions to their organization are discussed in detail throughout the remainder of this book. As these are addressed, distinctions will frequently be made between traditional organizations and high-involvement organizations. In addition, we address how differences in organization design, structure, and process and differences in approaches to management and managing impact organizational members—influencing their satisfaction and commitment to the organization, levels of work motivation, and the behaviors (for example, performance) that they engage in as organizational members.

A FINAL LOOK

Global TC brings in a team of takeover consultants to Vinton Enterprises to assist in organizing the transition from small private company to large international conglomerate. They begin by meeting with individuals from each level of the company to explain how the restructuring will occur. They describe how they will move to a "project teams" format in which many middle managers would no longer be "in charge" of a group of people and responsible for communicating projects and the company's vision to these employees. They intend to spend less time controlling employee activities and time. Project managers will be assigned, and employees in general will have more input. Global TC 's philosophy is that empowered employees are satisfied and therefore productive employees.

This may not alleviate all the anxiety of the Vinton employees, but most of them now feel confident that they will be valued in the new organization. Many are even excited about the possibilities that they see for professional growth in the Global TC organization and feel more motivated than they have in quite some time.

KEY TERMS

ISSUES FOR REVIEW AND DISCUSSION

1. What are organizations?
2. What is meant by the work of organizations and how might we describe this work?
3. Describe the management process.
4. List and define the four managerial functions, and explain how they are interrelated.
5. Explain the concept of universalism of management.
6. Identify three types of skills needed by effective managers, and relate their importance to the managers' position in the hierarchy.
7. What is the high-involvement organization?
8. Name three managerial roles and the duties managers perform.
9. Discuss how the role of manager is changing.

EXERCISES

WHAT DO MANAGERS DO?

INTRODUCTION

Students of management have attempted to develop a comprehensive description of the managerial job for many years. Fayol (1916) was one of the first to propose looking at managerial work in terms of the functions performed by a manager. Other approaches have been suggested as well, but the result has been a "jungle" of theoretical frameworks and empirical findings (Koontz, 1961), rather than a convergence toward a shared view of the managerial job.

More recently, the work of Henry Mintzberg has attracted considerable attention and acclaim. Based on his observations of managers at work, Mintzberg has developed a role model of the managerial job. Ten roles, falling into three broad categories or "families" of roles, were identified by Mintzberg. These ten roles form the basis of the interview you will conduct in this exercise.

PROCEDURE

After you read the assignment, interview a manager, using the interviewing questionnaire that follows. Follow the instructions for the questionnaire carefully; be sure that you have read them over and understand them before you begin the interview.

For purposes of this assignment, a manager is any person whose job primarily involves *supervising the work of other people.* The manager may work in a business, public or private agency, or school. The nature of the duties, not the type of organization, is the important criterion.

The Mintzberg roles are given—though not labeled—on the questionnaire in the following order:

Interpersonal roles	*Informational roles*	*Decisional roles*
1. Figurehead	4. Monitor ("Nerve Center" in Mintzberg)	7. Entrepreneur
2. Leader	5. Disseminator	8. Disturbance handler
3. Liaison	6. Spokesman	9. Resource allocator
		10. Negotiator

The role titles are left unlabeled on the questionnaire because managers tend to respond to the title rather than the content of the role. Bring the completed interview to the session specified by your group leader. The data will be summarized and discussed by the entire group.

INSTRUCTIONS

On the following pages, you will find a list of ten "roles"—functions described in studies of managerial work. Not every manager performs every role; not every role is equally important in each manager's job. And there may be functions managers do that are not on the list. Note that there is an "Other" category for listing important roles not already on the form.

The objective of this assignment is to collect information on what contributions managers make to achieving the organization's goals. Remember, for purposes of this study, a *manager is anyone whose job consists primarily of supervising other people.*

1. Find a manager and conduct the interview, using the attached questionnaire as a guide. Obtain numerical answers, using the scale provided, for *all* of the questions in the first two columns:
   a. Which are the most *important* roles—those that contribute to effective performance on the job?
   b. Which are the most *time-consuming*?
   For the third column, ask the manager for an example of this role.
2. Discuss the interview results with the manager. Ask: Were there any roles that you had expected to be more (or less) important before the interview? Were there any roles where the time consumed seemed disproportionate to the importance of the role? Which are the most difficult roles? You may think of other questions you wish to ask, as well.
3. Take notes on the interview and bring them with you to refer to in the group discussion.
4. *You do not need to supply the name of the manager interviewed.* We are interested only in developing a sample of managerial job views. The responses will be *anonymous*, and you should treat the interview as a *confidential* communication.

Ten roles and the typical activities involved in them are listed below, together with a space for you to list items that may be important but not provided for. For each role, enter the appropriate numbers based on the scale shown. In column I, enter a number reflecting *how important the role is to effective* job performance for the manager. Next, in column II, enter a number from the scale to describe *how time-consuming the role is for the manager*.

Scale values

Column I	*Column II*
1 = Of no importance	1 = No time consumed
2 = Of minimal importance	2 = Minimal time consumed
3 = Of some importance	3 = Some time consumed
4 = Of considerable importance	4 = Considerable time consumed
5 = Of very high importance	5 = A very high amount of time consumed

Finally, in column III, briefly note an example of the job duties performed in fulfilling this role. Fill in columns I and II for every job role, even if you have difficulty identifying an example for column III.

INTERVIEWING QUESTIONNAIRE

Role Activities and Examples	I. Importance to effective performance on the job	II. Time-consuming parts of the job	III. A typical example
1. Acts as legal and symbolic head; performs obligatory social, ceremonial, or legal duties (retirement dinner, luncheon for employees, plant dedication, annual dinner dance, civic affairs, signs contract on behalf of firm)			
2. Motivates, develops, and guides subordinates; staffing, training, and associated duties (management by objectives, provides challenging assignments, develops people, selects personnel, encourages subordinates, trains new employees)			
3. Maintains a network of contacts and information sources outside own group to obtain information and assistance (attends staff meetings, takes customer to lunch, attends professional meetings, meets with manager of department X, keeps abreast of upcoming design changes)			

4. Seeks and obtains information to understand organization and environment. Acts as nerve center for organization (chart work flow, work place meetings, audits expense control statements, reviews exception reports, reviews quotations, meets with production control)			
5. Transmits information to subordinates within own organizational area of responsibility (work place meetings, disseminates results of meetings, transmits policy letters, briefs subordinates, sends out copies of information, posts schedules and forecasts)			
6. Transmits information to persons outside of organizational area of responsibility (works with product committee, prepares weekly status reports, participates in meetings, deals with customer's coordinator, field sales)			
7. Searches organization and its environment for "improvement projects" to change products, processes, procedures, and organization, supervises design and implementation of change projects as well (cost reduction program, plans trip to X Division, changes forecasting system, brings in subcontract work to level work load, reorganizes department).			
8. Takes corrective action in time of disturbance or crisis (handles union grievances, negotiates sales problems, redistributes work during "crash programs," handles customer complaints, resolves personal conflicts, assigns engineers to problem jobs)			
9. Allocates organizational resources by making or approving decisions. Scheduling, budgeting, planning, programming of subordinate's work, etc. (budgeting, program scheduling, assigns personnel, strategic planning, plans manpower load, sets objectives)			
10. Represents organization in negotiating of sales, labor, or other agreements. Represents department or group negotiating with other functions within the organization (negotiates with suppliers, assists in quoting on new work, negotiates with union, hires, resolves jurisdictional dispute with department X, negotiates sales contract)			
Other:			

Source: D. T. Hall, D. D. Bowen, R. J. Lewicki, and F. S. Hall. 1982. *Experiences in management and organizational behavior* (2nd ed.). New York: Wiley. Reprinted by permission of John Wiley & Sons, Inc. Originally developed by D. D. Bowen. Based on the theoretical framework proposed by Mintzberg.

SUGGESTED READINGS

Fayol, H. (1916). *Administration industrielle et generale* (Paris: Dunod). Available in English as *General and Industrial Management* (London: Pitman, 1949).

Koontz, H. (1961). The management theory jungle. *Academy of Management* 4:174–88.

Koontz, H. (1980). Retrospective comment. In L. E. Boone and D. D. Bowen (eds.), *The great writings in management and organizational behavior.* Tulsa: PPC Books, 271–276. Koontz's "The management theory jungle" is also reprinted in this volume.

Mintzberg, H. (1973a). *The nature of managerial work.* New York: Harper & Row.

Mintzberg, H. (1973b). A new look at the chief executive's job. *Organizational Dynamics* 1:20–41.

INFOTRAC 

The articles listed below are a sampling of those available through Infotrac College Edition. You can search for them either by title or by the author's name.

Articles

1. Are you a coach, a cop, or Clark Kent? (sales managers) (Brief Article) (Statistical Data included) Don Beveridge. *Industrial Distribution* Dec 1999 v88 i12 p84 Bus.Coll.: 121P1915
2. Women, men and management styles. Marie-Therese Claes. *International Labour Review* Winter 1999 v138 i4 p431
3. The X Styles. (communication styles of Generation Xers) (includes related articles on communicating with young employees) (Cover Story) Cheryl O'Donovan. *Communication World* Dec 1997 v15 n1 p17(4)
4. Customized Management. (Theory X, Y, Z management styles) Stephen Van Winkle. *Public Management* August 1997 v79 n8 p26(1)
5. Good Leadership: What's its gender? (masculine and feminine management styles; includes bibliography) Jon Entine, Martha Nichols. *Executive Female* Jan-Feb 1997 v20 n1 p50(3)

Questions

For Article 2:

Chapter 1 explains the roles that managers must assume. Marie-Therese Claes' article describes the differences in management styles of women and men and pays particular attention to the topic of communication. Go to a local coffee house, restaurant, or other public gathering spot. Listen to and record the conversation styles and communication strategies of men and women. Form small groups and share your observations with members of your group. Discuss how these observations reflect the research in Claes' article. As a group, also discuss how a man and woman might effectively co-manage a production assembly line of widgit makers. How would their communication and behavior be different and yet be effectively combined?

For Other Articles:

Have members of your group choose different articles from this list. After reading them, discuss the additional insight they provide you about the necessary skills for an effective manager.

WEB EXERCISE

Fortune, Business Week, Forbes, Time, Newsweek, and *The Wall Street Journal* are just a few of the many sources of information about organizations. Articles commonly appear in them that inform us about management, organizations, and their ongoing activities. The World Wide Web is yet another important source. Most large organizations also have detailed websites. You can find many of these websites through search engines such as Yahoo (**http://www.yahoo.com**), Alta Vista (**http://www.altavista.digital.com**), or HotBot (**http://www.hotbot.com**).

Identify and visit the website for a large corporation that you're familiar with. Scan the website to get an overview of the company, then read about the organization's CEO (or any other top level manager who is profiled on the website). Using Chapter 2's discussion of management practices as a guide, how would you characterize this person's approach to managing?

CASE
Larry Ross: A Manager in His Own Words

The corporation is a jungle. It's exciting. You're thrown in on your own and you're constantly battling to survive. When you learn to survive, the game is to become the conqueror, the leader.

"I've been called a business consultant. Some say I'm a business psychiatrist. You can describe me as an advisor to top management in a corporation." He's been at it since 1983.

I started in the corporate world, oh gosh—'57. After kicking around in the Depression, having all kinds of jobs and no formal education, I wasn't equipped to become an engineer, a lawyer, or a doctor. I gravitated to selling. Now they call it marketing. I grew up in various corporations. I became the executive vice president of a large corporation and then of an even larger one. Before I quit I became president and chief executive officer of another. All nationally known companies.

Eighty-three, we sold out our corporation. There was enough money in the transaction where I didn't have to go back in business. I decided that I wasn't going to get involved in the corporate battle any more. It lost its excitement, its appeal. People often ask me, "Why weren't you in your own business? You'd probably have made a lot of money." I often ask it myself, I can't explain it, except . . .

Most corporations I've been in, they were on the New York Stock Exchange with thousands and thousands of stockholders. The last one—whereas, I was the president and chief executive—I was always subject to the board of directors, who had pressure from the stockholders. I owned a portion of the business, but I wasn't in control. I don't know of any situation in the corporate world where an executive is completely free and sure of his job from moment to moment.

Corporations always have to be right. That's their face to the public. When things go bad, they have to protect themselves and fire somebody. "We had nothing to do with it. We had an executive that just screwed everything up." He's never really ever been his own boss.

The danger starts as soon as you become a district manager. You have men working for you and you have a boss above. You're caught in a squeeze. The squeeze progresses from station to station. I'll tell you what a squeeze is. You have the guys working for you that are shooting for your job. The guy you're working for is scared stiff you're gonna shove him out of his job. Everybody goes around and says, "The test of the true executive is that you have men working for you that can replace you, so you can move up." That's a lot of baloney. The manager is afraid of the bright young guy coming up.

Fear is always prevalent in the corporate structure. Even if you're a top man, even if you're hard, even if you do your job—by a slight flick of a finger, your boss can fire you. There's always the insecurity. You bungle a job. You're fearful of losing a big customer. You're fearful so many things will appear on your record, stand against you. You're always fearful of the big mistake. You've got to be careful when you go to corporation parties. Your wife, your children have to behave properly. You've got to fit in the mold. You've got to be on guard.

When I was president of this big corporation, we lived in a small Ohio town, where the main plant was located. The corporation specified who you could socialize with, and on what level. (His wife interjects: "Who were the wives you could play bridge with.") The president's wife could do what she wants, as long as it's with dignity and grace. In a small town they didn't have to keep check on you. Everybody knew. There are certain sets of rules.

Not every corporation has that. The older the corporation, the longer it's been in a powerful position, the more rigid, the more conservative they are in their approach. Your swinging corporations are generally the new ones, the upstarts, the *nouveau riche*. But as they get older, like duPont, General Motors, General Electric, they became more rigid. I'd compare them to the old, old rich—the Rockefellers and the Mellons—that train their children how to handle money, how to conserve their money, and how to grow with their money. That's what happened to the older corporations. It's only when they get in trouble that they'll have a young upstart of a president come in and try to shake things up.

The executive is a lonely animal in the jungle who doesn't have a friend. Business is related to life. I think in our everyday living we're lonely. I have only a wife to talk to, but beyond that . . . When I talked business to her, I don't know whether she understood me. But that was unimportant. What's important is that I was able to talk out loud and hear myself—which is the function I serve as a consultant.

The executive who calls me usually knows the answer to his problem. He just has to have somebody to talk to and hear his decision out loud. If it sounds good when he speaks it out loud, then it's pretty good. As he's talking, he may suddenly realize his errors and he corrects them out loud. That's a great benefit wives provide for executives. She's listening and you know she's on your side. She's not gonna hurt you.

Gossip and rumor are always prevalent in a corporation. There's absolutely no secrets. I have always felt every office was wired. You come out of the board meeting and people in the office already know what's happened. I've tried many times to track down a rumor, but never could. I think people have been there so many years and have developed an ability to read reactions. From these reactions they make a good, educated guess. Gossip actually develops into fact.

It used to be a ploy for many minor executives to gain some information. "I heard that the district manager of California is being transferred to Seattle." He knows there's been talk going on about changing district managers. By using this ploy—"I know something"—he's making it clear to the person he's talking to that he's been in on it all along. So it's all right to tell him. Gossip is another way of building up importance within a person who starts the rumor. He's in, he's part of the inner circle. Again, we're back in the jungle. Every ploy, every trick is used to survive.

When you're gonna merge with a company or acquire another company, it's supposed to be top secret. You have to do something to stem the rumors because it might screw up the deal. Talk of the merger, the whole place is in a turmoil. It's like somebody saying there's a bomb in the building and we don't know where it is and when it's going to go off. There've been so many mergers where top executives are laid off, the accounting department is cut by sixty percent, the manufacturing is cut by twenty percent. I have yet to find anybody in a corporation who was so secure to honestly believe it couldn't happen to him.

They put on a front: "Oh, it can't happen to me. I'm too important." But deep down, they're scared stiff. The fear is there. You can smell it. You can see it on their faces. I'm not so sure you couldn't see it on my face many, many times during my climb up.

I always used to say—"rough, tough Larry"—I always said, "If you do a good job, I'll give you a great reward. You'll keep your job." I'll have a sales contest and the men who make their quota will win a prize—they'll keep their jobs. I'm not saying there aren't executives who instill fear in their people. He's no different than anybody walking down the street. We're all subject to the same damn insecurities and neuroses—at every level. Competitiveness, that's the basis of it.

Why didn't I stay in the corporate structure? As a kid, living through the Depression, you always heard about the tycoons, the men of power, the men of industry. And you kind of dream that. Gee, these are supermen. These are the guys that have no feeling, aren't subject to human emotions, the insecurities that everybody else has. You get in the corporate structure, you find they all button their pants the same way everybody else does. They all get the same fears.

The corporation is made up of many, many people. I call 'em the gray people and the black—or white—people. Blacks and whites are definite colors, solid. Gray isn't. The gray people come there from nine to five, do their job, aren't particularly ambitious. There's no fear there, sure. But they're not subject to great demands. They're only subject to dismissal when business goes bad and they cut off people. They go from corporation to corporation and get jobs. Then you have the black—or white—people. The ambitious people, the leaders, the ones who want to get ahead.

When the individual reaches the vice presidency or he's general manager, you know he's an ambitious, dedicated guy who wants to get to the top. He isn't one of the gray people. He's one of the black-and-white vicious people—the leaders, the ones who stick out in the crowd.

As he struggles in this jungle, every position he's in, he's terribly lonely. He can't confide and talk with the guy working under him. He can't confide and talk to the man he's working for. To give vent to his feeling, his fears, and his insecurities, he'd expose himself. This goes all the way up the line until he gets to be president. The president really doesn't have anybody to talk to, because the vice presidents are waiting for him to die or make a mistake and get knocked off so they can get his job.

He can't talk to the board of directors, because to them he has to appear as a tower of strength, knowledge, and wisdom, and have the ability to walk on water. The board of directors, they're cold, they're hard. They don't have any direct-line responsibilities. They sit in a staff capacity and they really play God. They're interested in profits. They're interested in progress. They're interested in keeping a good face in the community if it's profitable. You have the tremendous infighting of man against man for survival and clawing to the top. Progress.

We always saw signs of physical afflictions because of the stress and strain. Ulcers, violent headaches. I remember one of the giant corporations I was in, the chief executive officer ate Gelusil by the minute. That's for ulcers. Had a private dining room with his private chef. All he ever ate was well-done steak and well-done hamburgers.

There's one corporation chief I had who worked, conservatively, nineteen, twenty hours a day. His whole life was his business. And he demanded the same of his executives. There was nothing sacred in life except the business. Meetings might be called on Christmas Eve or New Year's Eve, Saturdays, Sundays. He was lonesome when he wasn't involved with his business. He was always creating situations where he could be surrounded by his flunkies, regardless of what level they were, presidential, vice presidential. . . . It was his life.

In the corporate structure, the buck keeps passing up until it comes to the chief executive. Then there ain't nobody to pass the buck to. You sit there in your lonely office and finally you have to make a decision. It could involve a million dollars or hundreds of jobs or moving people from Los Angeles, which they love, to Detroit or Winnipeg. So you're sitting at the desk, playing God.

You say, "Money isn't important. You can make some bad decisions about money, that's not important. What is important is the decisions you make about people working for you, their livelihood, their lives." It isn't true.

To the board of directors, the dollars are as important as human lives. There's only yourself sitting there making the decision, and you hope it's right. You're always on guard. Did you ever see a jungle animal that wasn't on guard? You're always looking over your shoulder. You don't know who's following you.

The most stupid phrase anybody can use in business is loyalty. If a person is working for a corporation, he's supposed to be loyal. This corporation is paying him less than he could get somewhere else at a comparable job. It's stupid of him to hang around and say he's loyal. The only loyal people are the people who can't get a job anyplace else. Working in a corporation, in a business, isn't a game. It isn't a collegiate event. It's a question of living or dying. It's a question of eating or not eating. Who is he loyal to? It isn't his country. It isn't his religion. It isn't his political party. He's working for some company that's paying him a salary for what he's doing. The corporation is out to make money. The ambitious guy will say, "I'm doing my job, I'm not embarrassed taking my money. I've got to progress and when I won't progress, I won't be here." The schnook is the loyal guy, because he can't get a job any place else.

Many corporations will hang on to a guy or promote him to a place where he doesn't belong. Suddenly, after the man's been there twenty-five years, he's outlived his usefulness. And he's too old to start all over again. That's part of the cruelty, you can't only condemn the corporation for that. The man himself should be smart enough and intuitive enough to know he isn't getting any place, to get the hell out and start all over. It was much more difficult at first to lay off a guy. But if you live in a jungle, you become hard, unfortunately.

When a top executive is let go, the king is dead, long live the king. Suddenly he's a *persona non grata*. When it happens, the shock is tremendous. Overnight.

He doesn't know what hit him. Suddenly everybody in the organization walks away and shuns him because they don't want to be associated with him. In corporations, if you back the wrong guy, you're in his corner, and he's fired, you're guilty by association. So what a lot of corporations have done is when they call a guy in sometimes they'll call him in on a Friday night and say, "Go home now and come in tomorrow morning and clean out your desk and leave. We don't want any farewells or anything. Just get up and get the hell out." It's done in nice language. We say, "Look, why cause any trouble? Why cause any unrest in the organization? It's best that you just fade away." Immediately his Cadillac is taken away from him. His phone extension on the WATS* line is taken away from him. All these things are done quietly and—bingo! he's dead. His phone at home stops ringing because the fear of association continues after the severance. The smell of death is there.

We hired a vice president. He came highly recommended. He was with us about six months and he was completely inadequate. A complete misfit. Called him in the office, told him he was gonna go, gave him a nice severance pay. He broke down and cried. "What did I do wrong? I've done a marvelous job. Please don't do this to me. My daughter's getting married next month. How am I going to face the people?" He cried and cried and cried. But we couldn't keep him around. We just had to let him go.

I was just involved with a gigantic corporation. They had a shake-up two Thursdays ago. It's now known as Black Thursday. Fifteen of twenty guys were let go overnight. The intelligent corporations say, "Clear leave tonight, even if it's midweek. Come in Saturday morning and clean your desk. That's all. No good-byes or anything." They could be guys that have been there anywhere from a year to thirty years. If it's a successful operation, they're very generous. But then again, the human element creeps in. The boss might be vindictive and cut him off without anything. It may depend on what the corporation wants to maintain as its image.

And what it does to the ego! A guy in a key position, everybody wants to talk to him. All his subordinates are trying to get an audience with him to build up their own positions. Customers are calling him, everybody is calling him. Now his phone's dead, he's sitting at home and nobody calls him. He goes out and starts visiting his friends, who are busy with their own business, who haven't got time for him. Suddenly he's a failure. Regardless what the reason was—regardless of the press release that said he resigned—he was fired.

The only time the guy isn't considered a failure is when he resigns and announces his new job. That's the tipoff. "John Smith resigned, future plans unknown" means he was fired. "John Smith resigned to accept the position of president of X Company"—then you know he resigned. This little nuance you recognize immediately when you're in corporate life.

*Wide-area telecommunications service. A prerogative granted important executives by some corporations: unlimited use of the telephone to make a call anywhere in the world.

Discussion Questions

1. Larry Ross (not his real name) was interviewed by writer Studs Terkel over 30 years ago. Do you think most managers in the 21st century would describe their jobs in the same way?
2. Does Larry Ross provide an accurate and realistic picture of how organizations operate? If you think so, is it true of all, most, some, or only a few organizations? Why did you answer as you did?
3. Is the organization better (or worse) off if managers behave like Larry Ross? Why? Do you think Larry Ross would be successful in most 21st-century organizations?
4. Assuming that you would like to become an executive in a large organization, would you be willing to do the things Ross does to achieve your goal? Why?
5. Do you see Larry Ross as a person who has largely contributed to his own problems, or as a person who simply goes along with a world he did not create? Why?

Source: "Larry Ross" is from S. Terkel, Working: People talk about what they do all day and how they feel about what they do. *Copyright 1972, 1974 by Studs Terkel. Adapted by D. D. Bowen. Originally used as a case in A. R. Cohen, S. L. Fink, H. Gadon, and R. D. Willits. 1976.* Effective behavior in organizations. *Homewood, IL: Irwin. From D. T. Hall, D. D. Bowen, R. J. Lewicki, and F. S. Hall. 1982.* Experiences in management and organizational behavior (2nd ed.). *New York: Wiley. Reprinted by permission of John Wiley & Sons, Inc.*

Outline

PHOTO: © PREMIUM STOCK/CORBIS

CHAPTER 2

Philosophies and Approaches to Management Practice

Learning Objectives

After reading this chapter, you should be able to

1. Identify early pioneers in management and organizational behavior and their contributions to the classical theory of management.
2. Discuss the major elements of Taylor's approach to scientific management.
3. Explain the significance of the Hawthorne studies.
4. Identify the major contributors to the behavioral theory of management, their view of organizations, and their contributions to the management literature.
5. Discuss the meaning of the human resources model and its relationship to the high-involvement approach to organizational management.
6. Identify and discuss several contemporary perspectives on the nature of organization and management practice.

A FIRST LOOK

Union Pottery is a company of approximately 150 employees located in King's Falls, an area with low unemployment. King's Falls has not always been so prosperous. During the 1980s, Union Pottery turned away many applicants. Now, however, the company is struggling to retain employees. Three new high-tech companies are luring many residents of King's Falls with strong employment prospects and innovative benefits packages.

During exit interviews, the director of human resources for Union Pottery has been listening to employees' reasons for leaving the company. She is surprised to learn of the attractive benefits packages offered by the new companies. In particular, people are excited about generous tuition reimbursement plans and the opportunity to pursue their education and learn new skills that could assist them professionally. Union Pottery does not provide tuition reimbursement for employees seeking to continue their education.

The director of human resources reports to the president of Union Pottery that the primary cause of employee attrition seems to be the opportunity to take advantage of education benefits. The president scoffs, "How can we afford such an investment? The employees will probably leave us anyway if they earn a degree, so where is our payoff?"

Questions: Is the concern of the Union Pottery president valid? What are some other ways that the company could accommodate the professional development needs of its employees? What would you do next if you were the director of human resources?

http://www.usx.com

http://www.michelinas.com

http://www.hallmark.com

If you could visit USX, Michelina's Frozen Foods, Hallmark Cards, and Lake Superior Paper Industries, you would quickly conclude that not all organizations are managed the same. The differences in the "climates" of these organizations are readily noticeable. You would soon learn that the culture of each organization is different, as are their approaches to decision making, human resource management, organization and work design, and other organizational processes. Employee behavior would tell you that not everyone displays the same levels of job satisfaction and organizational commitment, nor do they all engage in acts of good organizational citizenship.

Why do these differences exist? What assumptions about people, work, and organizations have been made that lead to these differences in managing as well as in employee reactions to those differences? We will explore the issue of differences in management and organizational practices in this chapter.

As indicated in Chapter 1, we believe that, first and foremost, management is a philosophy: a set of attitudes, beliefs, opinions, and assumptions that those who manage hold with regard to work, people, and organization. These philosophical differences result in different management practices. While some managers have a well developed theory of management, we do not assume that this is true for all managers. Yet the managerial behaviors of even this latter group of managers are driven by implicit assumptions that they have made about the nature of people, work, and organizations. In fact, there may be as many theories of management as there are managers. We'll use this chapter to identify and discuss the origin and content of two of the most dominant theories of management. Most management practices, whether it is the managerial behavior at USX, Michelina's Frozen Foods, Hallmark Cards, Lake Superior Paper Industries, or any other organization, appear to be an offshoot of one of these two theoretical perspectives.

THE CLASSICAL SCHOOL OF MANAGEMENT THOUGHT AND PRACTICE

For a very long time, people responsible for the management of organizations have recognized the need for efficient planning, organizing, staffing, directing, and control systems. In early Greek and Roman times, however, there were no books or journals about management, no professional management societies, and no schools of business to which a manager could turn. People accumulated knowledge about organizations and management through trial and error while managing families, tribes, armies, commercial organizations, and political entities. Although history provides some insight into managerial practice, it was the organizational complexities brought on by the Industrial Revolution that stimulated sustained and systematic efforts to understand organizations and their management.

classical school management thought and practice that emerged during the late 1800s and early 1900s

The **classical school** of management thought and practice emerged during the late 1800s and early 1900s as managers struggled with the "running" of larger organizations that were becoming increasingly complex. These new organizations, with their relatively sophisticated technologies, required inventory and production control. They demanded that managers schedule and coordinate work, integrate diverse work systems, and manage human resources. A group of industrial managers, most of whom had engineering backgrounds, embarked on a systematic search for practical solutions to these problems.

The early contributors to classical management theory and its traditional approach to organizational management believed that a basic set of laws and principles govern the correct ways of performing work, the design of the organizational machine, and management practices. Thus, they believed that there was a "one best way" to manage a complex industrial organization. Their theories and prescriptions attempted to identify these important principles. In addition, their theories focused primarily on the idea that *economic rationality* controlled the behavior of and decisions made by managers and individual employees. In other words, this new breed of managers assumed that people were driven by an economic motive and that they made logical and rational decisions when trying to maximize personal returns from a work experience.

The classical school of management thought reflects the thinking about organizations and management that stems from the almost simultaneous occurrence of the scientific management movement that unfolded in the United States, Henri Fayol's work in France on administrative management, and the work of German sociologist Max Weber on the development of the bureaucratic organization.

The Scientific Management Movement

scientific management that kind of management which conducts a business or affairs by standards established by facts or truths gained through systematic observation, experiment, or reasoning

Scientific management refers to "that kind of management which conducts a business or affairs by standards established by facts or truths gained through systematic observation, experiment, or reasoning."[1] Promoters of the scientific management movement tried to increase labor efficiency primarily by managing the work of employees in the organization's technical core (on the shop floor). This approach produced several pioneers who used experiments and systematic observation to develop effective management techniques. Each of these pioneers was essentially concerned with the design of work and the day-to-day management of the production floor as a way to increase organizational efficiency and productivity.

Charles Babbage contributed to the early scientific management movement and advocated division of labor, training employees to perform small tasks quickly and effectively, and conducting time studies to determine how long it should take to perform each "small" task. This thinking came to characterize the control-oriented classical school of management.

Charles Babbage. Charles Babbage (1792–1871) was one early contributor to the scientific management movement. He argued that organizations could realize greater profit if employees *specialized* in performing a specific set of job activities. Along with classical economist Adam Smith, Babbage advocated a division of labor and the design of jobs so that each employee performed only a small set of simple tasks. Managers, he argued, should train workers to perform each of these small tasks as efficiently as possible and offer incentives for executing them quickly and effectively. Babbage believed that managers should conduct "time studies" to determine how long it should take to perform each task and noted that "if the observer stands with his watch in his hand before a person heading a pin, the workman will almost certainly increase his speed."[2] (This thinking led to "close" forms of supervision that came to characterize the classical school and its "control-oriented" management practices.) Managers could then use such time-study information to establish standards for performance levels and to reward employees with bonuses for exceeding those standards.

Frederick W. Taylor. The best known of the scientific management theorists was Frederick W. Taylor (1856–1915). He is frequently referred to as the "father of scientific management." Taylor's contributions build on the work of Babbage and others to propel the scientific management movement forward during the late 1800s and early 1900s. Taylor, an engineer and consultant, observed firsthand what he considered to be inexcusable work methods at such organizations as Midvale Steel, Simonds Rolling Machine, and Bethlehem Steel. At that time, industries were plagued by an inadequate supply of skilled labor, and Taylor maintained that organizations were using available employees ineffectively and that managers needed to act decisively to increase labor efficiency.

http://attila.stevens-tech.edu/~rdowns

In the steel industry, Taylor observed and documented many factors that contributed to low production rates and inefficiency.[3] Workers often brought their own tools to the workplace, and these were often poorly designed for the work to be done. Job training was typically haphazard, and workers themselves often determined machine speed and work pace. Hiring frequently was on a "first-come, first-hired" basis rather than on one based on the individual's skills and abilities. Managers commonly worked side by side with laborers, often ignoring such management responsibilities as planning and organizing work. As a result, inadequately trained employees were repeatedly left in charge of planning, decision making, scheduling, and controlling shop-floor activities.

Taylor severely criticized managers for failing to manage effectively and for allowing workers to determine their own methods and pace. He believed that managers should develop and implement the "science of work"—the underlying laws, or principles, that govern various work activities. Laborers could function effectively by following these scientific principles and, in the process, organizational productivity, efficiency, and profitability would rise.

Taylor applied his belief in the scientific approach to management to the task of handling pig iron, a basic task in the steel industry. He observed inefficiencies and wasted energy in the methods used to carry 92-pound pieces of iron from the fabrication site to railroad cars. He was convinced that, using scientific principles, he could identify the "one best way" to pick up a 92-pound piece of pig iron, hold it, walk with it, and lay it down. Through time-and-motion studies and fatigue studies, Taylor identified a "science" of pig iron handling, which enabled an average laborer to increase the amount of pig iron handled from 12½ tons to 48 tons a day.

By using the same approach, Taylor created "sciences" of shoveling coal, iron ore, and ash. He developed shovels with scoops tailored to the particular substance being shoveled and capable of handling the load that, through systematic study, he determined as "ideal." Taylor called for managers to develop a science of all jobs in an organization's technical core. An example of the level of detail that Taylor expected is found in the science he identified for handling the shovel:

> Press the forearm hard against the upper part of the right leg just below the thigh, . . . take the end of the shovel in your right hand, . . . and when you push the shovel into the pile, instead of using the muscular effort of your arms which is tiresome . . . throw the weight of your body on the shovel. . . .[4]

Taylor believed that an organizational revolution could take place—a major transformation in the way organizations were managed and in the way work was performed, which would ultimately impact organizational productivity and profitability. He also believed in "mutuality of interest" that bonded management and the industrial employee together, thereby making this revolution possible. This mutuality of interest was rooted in the classical economic model of the individual. According to this perspective, both managers and employees are economically motivated. Managers want to increase profits, and employees want to increase their personal economic gains. Through this mutual interest, Taylor believed that management and labor would cooperate to satisfy their respective needs. If both parties want a larger and larger portion of the economic pie, a rational and logical solution to the problem would be to increase the size of the pie—a solution without conflict, simultaneously satisfying the needs of labor and management. Taylor believed that this could be achieved by raising organizational productivity and efficiency through application of the principles of scientific management and by asking the rational and economically motivated employee to *listen and comply* with prescriptions on the scientifically defined ways of work performance.

As a way of bringing "order to the workplace," Taylor's scientific management consisted of these prescriptions:

- *Develop the science of work* by using time, motion, and fatigue studies to identify the "one best way" to perform a job and the level at which it can be performed.
- *Emphasize an absolute adherence to work standards* and do not allow the daily production rate that was scientifically identified to be changed by anyone's arbitrary whim.
- *Scientifically select, place, and train workers* and assign them to the most interesting and profitable tasks for which they are suited.
- *Apply a financial incentive system* that encourages workers to perform efficiently and effectively by tying pay to output: Low production leads to low pay, high production to high pay.

FIGURE 2-1 Functional Supervision and Unity of Command

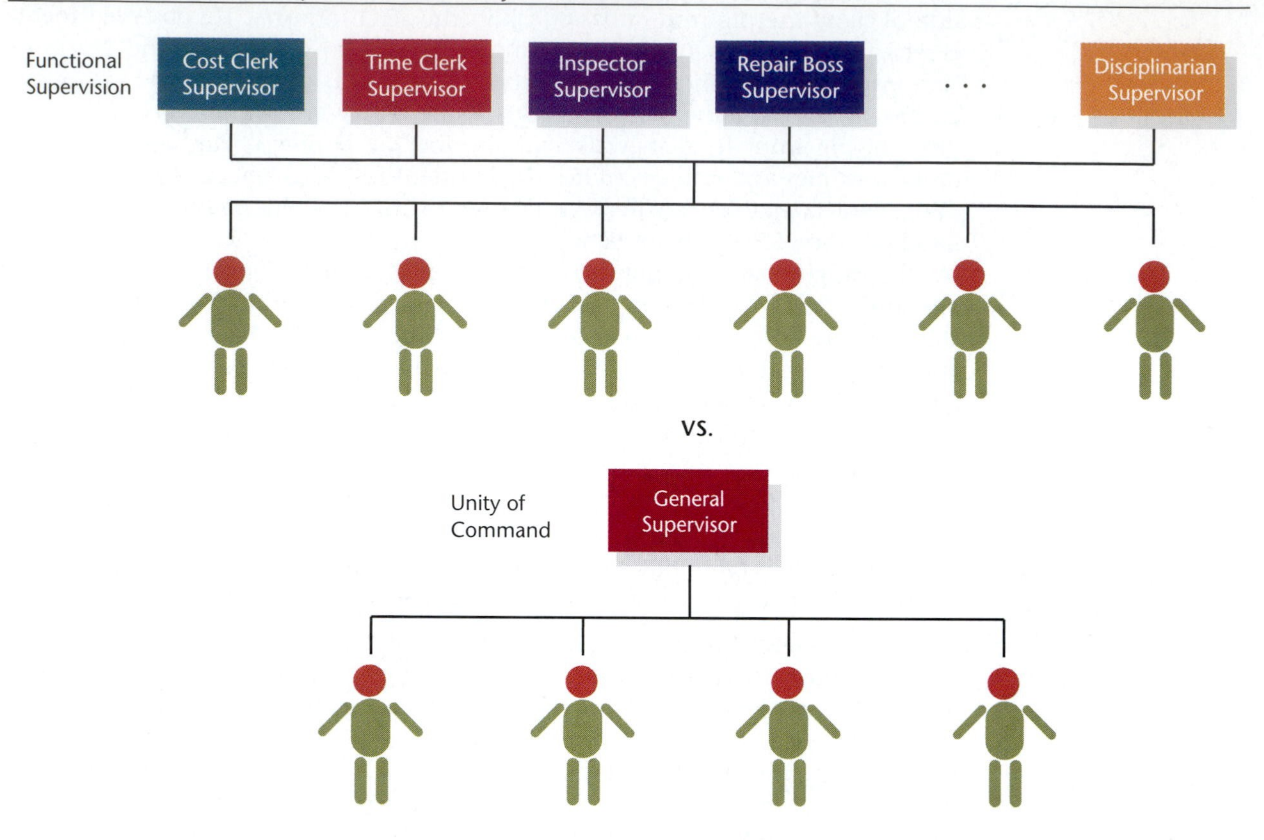

- *Utilize specialized functional supervision* so that, instead of one general manager, a number of expert managers (see Figure 2-1) would supervise a department's employees on the different aspects of their work. (Taylor referred to this as "functional foremanship." We will refer to it as *functional supervision.*)
- *Develop and maintain friendly labor-management relations,* because a cooperative alliance between employee and employer helps ensure the willing application of the scientific principles of work.[5]

Although Taylor's scientific management presented many technical mechanisms, one of the far-reaching aspects of his work was its new philosophical approach to managing work and people. To be successful, Taylor stated, the scientific management approach would require a mental revolution on the part of both labor and management. Employees and managers would have to understand the scientific management principles and work together in harmony, accepting new work roles and new methods. Only through this mental revolution would labor and management achieve both higher wages and increased output.

The Gilbreths. Frank and Lillian Gilbreth, a husband and wife team, also were pioneers in the scientific management movement. Frank Bunker Gilbreth (1868–1924) focused on improving work methods to enhance productivity and efficiency. With her background in psychology and management, Lillian Moller Gilbreth (1878–1972) viewed scientific management as a technique to help workers reach their full potential.

The Gilbreths developed a scheme to classify the motions used in the performance of a job. A motion was referred to as a *therblig,* their name spelled backwards. Their classifications included such motions as grasping, holding, and moving. The motion scheme documented the relationship between types and frequencies of motion and worker fatigue, demonstrating that unnecessary motions wasted energy. By separating appropriate from inappropriate motions, the Gilbreths helped make more of a worker's energy available for job performance.

Frank Gilbreth carefully studied and improved methods used for bricklaying. He observed that different bricklayers used different procedures and was amazed that one of the oldest crafts in the world had never been standardized. Even on relatively casual inspection, bricklaying seemed full of inefficiency. Convinced that bricklayers' efficiency could be improved substantially, Gilbreth analyzed motion pictures of bricklaying and discovered that the process typically used 18 distinct movements. He timed the various activities, explored fatigue factors, and proposed an alternative procedure that reduced the number of movements from 18 to 5. He designed a special scaffold that positioned bricks, mud, and the bricklayer at appropriate levels and created a formula for making a consistent, uniform mixture of mud. He also divided the bricklaying job into parts. One worker delivered bricks and mud while the person who had developed the craft of laying brick would devote full time to that activity. Gilbreth's prescriptions increased the average output of individual bricklayers from 120 to 250 bricks an hour.

Lillian Gilbreth's Ph.D. thesis at Brown University was entitled "The Psychology of Management" and was published in 1914. She pioneered modern human resource management, especially the scientific selection, placement, and training of employees. She served on the faculty of Purdue University, where she became the first female professor of management. In addition to serving Presidents Hoover, Roosevelt, Eisenhower, Kennedy, and Johnson in the areas of aging and rehabilitation of the physically disabled, Lillian Gilbreth held faculty appointments at the University of Wisconsin, Rutgers University, New Jersey University, and Newark College of Engineering; received 20 honorary degrees; and was named an honorary member of the American Society of Mechanical Engineers.

Together, the Gilbreths were interested in developing individual workers through training programs; they were also interested in improved work environments and a healthy psychological outlook among workers. They were so convinced of the benefits of such efforts that they even applied their management principles to raising their 12 children, as described in the book and movie *Cheaper by the Dozen.*

http://www.bethsteel.com

Henry Gantt. Henry Gantt (1861–1919), an associate of Taylor's at Midvale, Simonds, and Bethlehem Steel, added two techniques to scientific management: the Gantt chart and a minimum-wage-based incentive system.

In an attempt to increase managers' control over planning, designing, and monitoring work activities, Gantt developed the *Gantt chart,* which is still in use today. Managers use the Gantt chart to summarize work activities and identify those that should be performed simultaneously or sequentially. As shown in Figure 2-2, for a home builder's remodeling job, plans must be drawn before any other activity can commence, but rough electrical work and ordering cabinets can occur concurrently. Wallboard installation can overlap a bit with final electrical work, but cabinets cannot be installed before wallboard installation

FIGURE 2-2 Gantt Chart for Classic Home Contractors

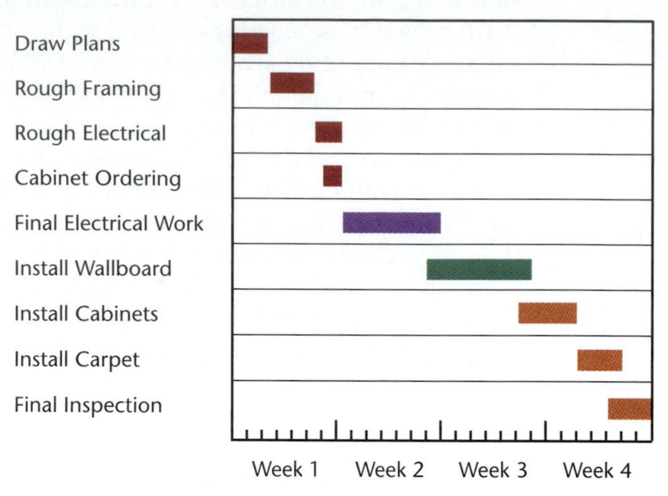

Source: Adapted from J. G. Monks. 1982. *Operations management: Theory and problems.* New York: McGraw-Hill, 549.

has been completed. In addition to assisting with work scheduling, the Gantt chart can be used as a work-monitoring tool. Managers can record on the chart the amount of time it actually took to complete a task and can compare it to the amount of time originally planned for completion.

Gantt promoted the idea that employees should receive a minimum daily wage whether or not they achieved their specified daily work objectives. Acknowledging the economically motivated model of the employee, he also recommended that employees receive monetary incentives in the form of bonuses for work above and beyond the expected standard. Furthermore, Gantt proposed bonuses for supervisors whose subordinates reached their daily standard and additional bonuses if all workers reached their goals, because he felt that this would encourage supervisors to manage subordinates effectively.

Administrative Management and the Bureaucratic Organization

Whereas scientific management focuses on an organization's technical core, contributors to administrative management and organizational bureaucratization concentrated on the management of an entire organization. The contributors were concerned with the structure of an organization and with designing processes that would make its operations rational, ordered, predictable, efficient, and effective. This group of organizational theorists viewed organizations as giant machines created to achieve goals, and they believed in a basic set of universal laws, or principles, that should govern the design and run those "machines" effectively. Henri Fayol was a major contributor to administrative management, and the work of Max Weber gave rise to the contemporary bureaucratic organization.

Administrative Management and Henri Fayol. Henri Fayol (1841–1925) worked for 58 years with Commentry-Fourchambault, a French coal and iron processing organization. His perspectives on management grew out of this experience and his formal training as a mining engineer. Fayol attributed his success as a manager to the methods he used rather than to personal talent. He felt that other managers could be as successful as he was if they had appropriate guidelines for managing complex organizations.

Fayol paid particular attention to managerial activities. He believed that all managers, regardless of their organizational function (for example, production, marketing, human resources), perform all five managerial functions (planning, organizing, commanding, coordinating, and controlling). Yet he also recognized that the nature of managerial work differs from manager to manager according to such factors as the size of an organization and a manager's location in its hierarchy.

A central part of Fayol's views on organizations and the management of organizations can be captured by a set of 14 principles that he believed should guide the management of organizations and that he himself followed:

1. *Division of labor*—improve levels of efficiency through specialization, resulting in reduced learning time, fewer activity changes, and increased skill development.
2. *Authority*—the right to give orders should always carry responsibility fitting to its privilege.
3. *Discipline*—relies on respect for the rules, policies, and agreements that govern an organization; should be achieved by the clear and fair presentation of all agreements between an organization and its employees.
4. *Unity of command*—each employee reports to only one superior, thus avoiding confusion and conflict.
5. *Unity of direction*—one manager for each organizational plan and a single plan for operations within the organization that deal with the same objective.
6. *Subordination of individual interest to the common good*—the needs of individuals and groups within an organization should not take precedence over the needs of the organization as a whole.
7. *Remuneration*—wages should be equitable and satisfactory to employees and superiors.
8. *Centralization*—levels at which decisions are made should depend on the specific situation; no level of centralization or decentralization is ideal for all situations.
9. *Scalar chain*—the relationship among all levels in the organizational hierarchy and exact lines of authority should be unmistakably clear and followed at all times.
10. *Order*—there should be a place for everything (and everyone), and everything (and everyone) should be in its place.
11. *Equity*—employees should be treated with kindness and justice.
12. *Stability of tenure*—the employee population should be stable so that people can learn the nature of their jobs and the larger context within which their jobs are performed.
13. *Initiative*—subordinates should be encouraged to conceive and carry out their ideas.
14. *Esprit de corps*—teamwork, a sense of unity and togetherness, should be fostered and maintained.

Fayol felt that the application of these principles should be flexible enough to match each specific organizational situation. He wrote:

> For preference I shall adopt the term principles whilst dissociating it from any suggestion of rigidity, for there is nothing rigid or absolute in management affairs, it is all a question of proportion. Seldom do we have to apply the same

principle twice in identical conditions; allowance must be made for different changing circumstances, ...[6]

Despite Fayol's call for flexibility, many of the managers who adopted his 14 principles applied them rigidly. It is the strict application of Fayol's principles that characterizes the control-oriented approach to management that grows out of the classical school of management thought. As a result, the principles of esprit de corps and initiative failed to become an integral part of the classical approach to the practice of management. For Fayol, however, the flexible application of these 14 principles helped him guide the nearly bankrupt Commentry-Fourchambault back to prosperity.

The Bureaucratic Organization and Max Weber. Concerned about the inefficiencies and lack of commitment common in many European organizations that permitted hiring practices based on personal relationships rather than skills, Max Weber (1864–1920) envisioned an organization managed on an impersonal and rational basis. Weber, a German lawyer and sociologist, is often considered the architect of the bureaucratic organization. In Weber's "rational organization" (see Table 2-1),[7] labor should be divided according to specialization. Each employee's authority and responsibility should be clearly defined as the official duties of the position and not as the duties of the particular individual who holds that position. Weber also proposed that a well defined hierarchy be set up to eliminate ambiguity and to specify the nature of relationships among jobs within the organization.

TABLE 2-1 The Anatomy of Weber's Bureaucracy

Goals of a Bureaucratic Model

- Speed
- Precision
- Order
- Unambiguity
- Continuity
- Predictability

Structure of the Bureaucratic Model

- The division of labor is based on functional specialization.
- A well-defined hierarchy of authority exists.
- A system of rules specifies the rights and duties of employees.
- A system of rules and work procedures specifies the methods for dealing with work situations.
- An interpersonal network is characterized by the impersonality of interpersonal relations.
- Selection into the organization is based on technical competence and organizational need.
- Promotion inside the organization is based on technical competence and comprehensive knowledge of the organization, which comes through seniority.
- Employment is intended to reflect a lifetime commitment to a career.
- A clearly specified career path to the top of the organization is provided for those who qualify.
- Office management consists of the creation and maintenance of extensive written records of organizational transactions.

Weber's vision of an ideal organization included an elaborate set of rules specifying the rights and duties of employees and a second set of rules containing the procedures involved in each work situation. These rules were to be applied uniformly throughout the organization. As a result, Weber's bureaucratic organization would be impersonal, and employees would be managed without personal affection or enthusiasm for individual or personal accomplishments. Managers were to conform to this atmosphere of impersonality and were to avoid giving special individual considerations. According to Weber, the bureaucratic organization would provide a clear career path for competent individuals. Written rules would govern all major activities, and all management activities and decisions would be documented. A bureaucratic organization would be impersonal, rigid, and routine in meeting its goals of speed, precision, order, unambiguity, continuity, and predictability.

http://www.usps.com

The bureaucratic organization, much like that envisioned by Weber, is alive today. Michelina's Frozen Foods, the U.S. Postal Service, and many of the organizations that are "yesterday's smoke stack industries" (for example, the iron mines of northern Minnesota) find themselves managed in accord with control-oriented management practices. A more detailed discussion of control-oriented management practices as well as the bureaucratic organization is presented in Part III—Management Functions and the Organizational Behavior Context.

Contributions and Limitations of the Classical School

Although the classical school of management did not provide a totally unified approach to management, there were many similarities among the views expressed by Babbage, Taylor, the Gilbreths, Gantt, Fayol, and Weber. Classical management was, to a very large extent, prescriptive in nature—it describes how people *should* manage organizations. Just as engineers specify the appropriate way to build bridges, managers were to follow a rational approach and a set of principles to build and operate organizations. Through their efforts to identify the "one best way," systems were developed that led to greater organizational productivity. In some ways, these systems still characterize contemporary bureaucratic organizations.

Another contribution of these early management pioneers is that their efforts to create an ideal organization spurred additional scientific inquiry into management and organizational systems. Although the various contributors to the classical school of management agreed on many issues (such as the importance of a division of labor, order, the development of standard operating procedures, and centralization of authority), they also had a few areas of disagreement. For example, they had radical differences in thinking about supervision in the technical core. Fayol talked about "unity of command" while Taylor called for "functional supervision." Fayol argued that each employee should report to and be directed by only one superior to avoid confusion and conflict. However, Taylor believed that employees should have multiple supervisors so that they could benefit from various types of specialized knowledge.

Another area of disagreement became evident when managers put the prescriptions from the classical contributors into practice. Fayol instructed managers to apply his 14 principles flexibly, making adjustments to fit each situation. In practice, however, classical management tended to be closed and rigid. Similarly, Taylor called for friendly labor-management relations, but the typical classical approach was often cool, impersonal, and adversarial. Unfortunately, many contemporary organizations have become slaves to a set of inflexible bureaucratic principles and have grown large and sluggish as a result.

TABLE 2-2 Dominant Features of the Classical Model

- Control-oriented management practices
- Mechanistic (bureaucratic) organization design
  - a controlling organization
  - a machine view of the organization
    - rigid and highly structured
    - well-defined hierarchy of authority with power concentrated at the top of the organization
    - division of labor based on functional specialization
    - routine jobs with a short time cycle
    - rules defining the rights and duties of employees
    - well-defined work procedures
    - impersonality of interpersonal relationships
    - pre-programmed system
    - closed system
- Model of the employee—rational and economically motivated

The classical school of management thought has a number of critics. Many argue that its description of organizational members as rational and economically motivated is incomplete. These critics claim that when managers ignore the social needs of workers, organizations do not provide adequate motivation and reinforcement programs. If managers think of organizations as machines rather than social systems, they treat employees as resources to be manipulated for organizational ends. The result has been confrontation between labor and management as managers direct and control employees, work methods, and the pursuit of organizational goals.

A second area of criticism of the classicists revolves around their attempts to identify universal principles for efficient management. Although many of the classical principles of management may be appropriate for organizations operating in simple, nonturbulent environments, they are less well suited to conducting business in shifting and heterogeneous environments (see Chapter 4).

In summary, the classical school gives us the "control-oriented" approach to organizational management and a bureaucratic (mechanistic) organizational design (see Table 2-2 for some of the distinguishing features). It results in a rigid and rational system that emphasizes a well-defined hierarchy of authority controlled from the top-down, one that operates with an elaborate system of written rules and standard operating procedures that are employed to control employee behavior. Standardized and narrowly defined tasks coupled with close supervision are employed in an effort to achieve compliance and order.

THE HAWTHORNE STUDIES: A TRANSITION IN THOUGHT AND PRACTICE

Hawthorne studies worker productivity studies carried out at Western Electric

Between 1924 and 1933, a series of worker productivity studies was conducted at the Hawthorne Plant of the Western Electric Company in Chicago. These studies, widely known as the **Hawthorne studies**, have strongly influenced the course of the second school of management—behavioral management theory[8]—and opened the door to a very different approach to the practice of management and organizational design. As we have seen thus far, managers worked to increase organizational efficiency, productivity, and profitability primarily through developing better tools and work methods. Managers at the Hawthorne plant, very much in keeping with the scientific management tradition, were also interested in increasing productivity, efficiency, and profitability. Managers at the Hawthorne facility, like Taylor, conducted a careful set of systematic studies focused on improving performance. Unlike Taylor, they emphasized the context (work environment) within which employees performed their work while Taylor emphasized work and work methods.

The Hawthorne studies focused on the relationship between worker productivity and such factors as the illumination of the workplace, the length of coffee breaks, the length of the workday, provisions for free lunches, and the nature of pay plans. The researchers expected that improvements in the work environment would yield improvements in productivity. (See the description of the Hawthorne studies in *An Inside Look*.*)

Surprisingly, the results of these studies were often inconsistent with expectations. In fact, at times, productivity actually increased when decreases were expected. For example, in the first set of studies, starting in 1924 and continuing to 1927, the quality of lighting for an experimental group of workers decreased over successive periods while lighting conditions were held constant for a control group (comparison group) of workers. At times, performance in both groups rose even though lighting conditions for the experimental group became so dim that the workers complained that they could hardly see. When lighting conditions reached the approximate candle power of a full moon, performance did decline as predicted.

While the researchers concluded that factors other than lighting were at play, they were extremely perplexed by their observations. After all, they still believed that the quality of the work environment *should* have an impact on performance. Starting in 1927, successive studies were implemented. Each represented a continuation of the original study, which was directed toward investigating the effects of the work environment on employee productivity.

The second and third wave of studies produced both interesting and perplexing observations, and simply put, the researchers failed to find a simple and straightforward relationship between the quality of the work environment and employee productivity. In an attempt to understand the confusing results, the Hawthorne researchers interviewed a large number of workers. The interviews suggested that a human/social element operated in the workplace and that productivity increases were as much an outgrowth of group dynamics as of managerial demands and physical factors. The idea that the employee was something other than a "rational and economic being" emerged. Thus, the Hawthorne studies were catalytic in the emergence of the social model of the employee.

The Hawthorne studies also leave us with the idea that social factors might be as powerful a determinant of worker productivity as financial motives. Classical management theorists expected that each employee in a group would work to maximize his/her pay by producing as many units as possible. Instead,

* The Hawthorne studies have been much discussed and often misrepresented. The discussion here is consistent with the review of the Hawthorne studies published by the Academy of Management as part of its celebration of 100 years of modern management: R. G. Greenwood and C. D. Wrege. 1986. The Hawthorne studies. In D. A. Wren and J. A. Pearce II (eds.), *Papers dedicated to the development of modern management.* Chicago: Academy of Management, 24–35.

AN INSIDE LOOK

The Hawthorne Studies

A series of studies conducted at the Hawthorne Works of the Western Electric Company near Chicago, usually referred to as the Hawthorne studies, has had a significant impact on the management of work.* A set of studies involving illumination levels was conducted at the Hawthorne plant between November 1924 and April 1927 by D. C. Jackson and G. A. Pennock. These studies were intended to identify lighting levels that would produce optimal productivity. In the first illumination experiment, however, productivity increased when illumination was increased and when it was decreased. Overall, productivity bounced up and down without an apparent direct relationship to illumination level.

A second illumination study had an experimental group which experienced illumination changes and a control group for which illumination was held constant. In this experiment, production increased in both groups to an almost equal extent. In yet a third illumination experiment, lighting levels were decreased over time. As a result, productivity levels increased for both experimental and control groups (at least until an extremely low level of illumination was reached).

The first major study of the Hawthorne studies themselves was conducted over 24 experimental sessions between April 25, 1927, and February 8, 1933. These relay assembly test room ("RATR") experiments explored the degree to which variations in length of rest periods, of the working day, and of the working week influenced productivity. As was the case for the illumination study, productivity fluctuated during the various stages of the RATR experiments. Again, these variations in productivity could not be explained by the expected factors.

Many reports of the Hawthorne studies suggest that any change conducted during the studies increased productivity. This is not exactly true, and it is not the primary reason that these studies are so important. The importance of the RATR and Hawthorne experiments is a function of how researchers and scholars explained the unexpected findings. As early as September 1928, an extensive interviewing program elicited comments from workers that helped identify the causes of fluctuations in productivity. Conclusions as to why the Hawthorne effects occurred vary. According to Elton Mayo, for example,

> What actually happened was that six individuals became a team and the team gave itself wholeheartedly and spontaneously to cooperation in the experiment. The consequence was that they felt themselves to be participating freely and without afterthought, and were happy in the knowledge that they were working without coercion from above or limitations from below.†

Mayo seemed to feel that the experiments satisfied workers' needs and shifted their attention from personal problems to productivity.

George Pennock, who conducted the RATR experiments, stated that

> Emotional status was reflected in performance; and the major component of this emotional condition was attitude toward supervisor. The inference from these studies was inescapable that the dominant factor in the performance of these employees was their mental attitude.‡

Another perspective on the Hawthorne effects comes from the independent writings of Whitehead and Chase, who both suggested that a major reason the "Hawthorne effect" produced increases in productivity was that being a part of the experiments made the workers feel important.§ Even members of control groups felt important; thus, their productivity was said to increase as a result.

* R. G. Greenwood and C. D. Wrege. 1986. The Hawthorne studies. In D. A. Wren and J. A. Pearce II (eds.), *Papers dedicated to the development of modern management.* Chicago: Academy of Management, 24–35.

† E. Mayo. 1945. *The social problems of an industrial civilization.* Boston: Division of Research, Graduate School of Business Administration, Harvard University, 72–73.

‡ G. A. Pennock. 1930. Industrial research at Hawthorne: An experimental investigation of rest periods, working conditions and other influences. *Personnel Journal* 8:297.

§ T. N. Whitehead. 1938. *The industrial worker* (2 vols.). Cambridge: Harvard University Press; S. Chase. 1941. What makes workers like to work? *Reader's Digest,* 15–20.

Harvard professor Elton Mayo observed that *informal work groups* emerged with their own leaders, influence systems, norms for appropriate behavior, and pressures for conformity to acceptable levels of performance. Any individual who produced above the group's norm was considered a "rate-buster" and was pressured by co-workers to slow down. Anyone who produced under the acceptable norm was labeled a "chiseler" and urged to speed up. The social pressures within the group powerfully affected workers' productivity, even in the presence of an individual-based wage incentive system designed to encourage higher levels of performance.

The Hawthorne studies failed to uncover a simple relationship between improvements in physical working conditions and increases in worker productivity, but they did discover the importance of human considerations for worker effectiveness. For the first time, the tremendous impact of an informal work group and the social environment on workers' attitudes and behaviors was documented. The studies provided a transition between the classical and behavioral management schools of thought. The classicists were task oriented and believed that managers should enhance productivity through technical systems. The emerging human relations (behavioral) approach to management focused on employees and directed managers to guide individuals' needs for recognition and peer interaction. A social model of employees was beginning to compete with the rational-economic model of the classical management school.

THE BEHAVIORAL SCHOOL OF MANAGEMENT THOUGHT AND PRACTICE

behavioral school management thought and practice that views the organization from a social and psychological perspective

The classicists' preoccupation with the organization as a mechanical system left a void. This space was filled by those people who hold a very different set of assumptions and beliefs about organizations and about the nature of the individual as an organizational member. We'll refer to them and their management philosophy as the behavioral school. Members of the **behavioral school** of thought viewed organizations from a social and psychological perspective. Increasingly, the organization was seen as a social system. The employee, instead of being a mere cog in the industrial wheel, was initially seen as possessing a social need (giving rise to the human relations model of the employee) and eventually came to be seen as needing to make a meaningful contribution (giving rise to the human resource model of the employee). This view should be contrasted with the classicists' view of the employee as a rational and economically motivated being.

Early Contributors and Contributions

Instead of viewing organizations as machines with perfectly designed mechanical systems, behavioral thinkers envisioned the organization as a social system. This social system ought to contain people-to-people and people-to-work networks so smoothly linked and efficient that they would accomplish organizational goals. Effective management of this social system would require managers to understand the nature of individuals, groups, and their patterns of interaction.

Robert Owen. British industrialist Robert Owen (1771–1858) was one of the first managers to recognize the need for good overall management of an organization's human resources. Owen called for managers who treat workers with respect and dignity, provide better working conditions, reduce hours of work, offer meals for the work force, and restrict the use of children as a source of labor.

Hugo Munsterberg. Considered the father of industrial psychology, Hugo Munsterberg (1863–1916) concentrated on applying psychological concepts to organizational settings. While on the faculty at Harvard University he documented the psychological conditions associated with different levels of productivity[9] and taught managers to use empirically based psychological findings to match workers with jobs and to motivate these workers after placing them in jobs.[10] In his groundbreaking book *Psychology and Industrial Efficiency,* published in 1913, Munsterberg popularized the notion that managers can use psychology to enhance organizational effectiveness.

Walter Dill Scott. While on the faculty at Northwestern University, Walter Dill Scott (1869–1955) argued that managers were not effectively using the human factor in organizations. Although Scott agreed that employees are economically motivated, he emphasized that they are also social creatures with needs for recognition and membership in social groups. Scott argued that if managers did not consider employees' social needs, organizational effectiveness would be hindered. He believed that managers placed too much emphasis on developing the technology for getting work done and not enough on developing good employee selection and supervision. Scott asserted that management should work at improving employee attitudes and motivation as a means to increase worker productivity.

Mary Parker Follett. Management philosopher, consultant, and educator, Mary Parker Follett (1868–1933) called management "the art of getting things done through others" and wrote about the issues of power, authority, leadership, and coordination.[11] She believed that a natural order between management and employees could be achieved through leadership. This leadership was not, however, to be accomplished through the traditional use of formal authority by superiors over subordinates. Rather, Follett asserted that managers' influence and power should flow naturally from their knowledge and skill. She also encouraged managers to coordinate work activities through personal contact rather than through impersonally structured work systems or written rules, as advocated in Weber's bureaucratic model.[12]

Chester Barnard. Chester Barnard (1886–1961), past president of New Jersey Bell, provided an important insight into the concept of organization and its social dimensions. Barnard discussed the concept of formal and informal organizations. A formal organization is an entity managers consciously create to achieve organizational goals. An informal organization arises spontaneously as employees interact and form bonds. (Recall the observation of the informal organization in the Hawthorne studies; work groups had their own leaders, influence systems, norms for appropriate behavior, social pressures, and standards for acceptable and unacceptable levels of performance.) Whereas classical management thinking asked managers to focus on the design and management of the formal organization, Barnard's work sensitized managers to the informal organization's ability to aid communication, provide leadership, maintain cohesiveness, and strengthen individual feelings of integrity and self-respect.

The Human Relations Model

FIGURE 2-3
The Human Relations Model

Worker Satisfaction

leads to . . .

Enhanced Worker Performance

Rising negative reactions to the impersonality of scientific management and bureaucratic theory, combined with evidence from the Hawthorne studies, helped ignite the *human relations movement.* As noted earlier, findings from the Hawthorne studies, when coupled with the writings of some of the earlier behavioral scientists (for example, Munsterberg, Scott, Barnard), gave rise to a different model of the employee than the rational-economic one advocated by the classical school of management. This new model portrayed the *employee as a social being* motivated by the need for recognition, acceptance, and inclusion.

Turning from task-oriented styles of management, human relations advocates focused on the social needs of organizational members (see Figure 2-3). Thus, the **human relations model** sees the employee as socially motivated and operates from the assumption that a satisfied worker is a productive worker. This model suggests that increases in worker productivity depend on the degree to which organizations meet workers' needs for recognition, acceptance, and group membership. A manager following the guidelines of the human relations movement would, therefore, be supportive and paternalistic, creating and nurturing cohesive work groups and a psychologically supportive environment for workers.

human relations model a management model that views the employee as socially motivated and operates from the assumption that a social need–satisfied worker is a productive worker

In keeping with the human relations perspective, many of today's successful organizations, such as DuPont, GTE, Johnson & Johnson, Merck, and Motorola, have implemented work- and family-oriented programs. These programs

In the human relations model, employees are socially motivated and are also motivated by the need for recognition, acceptance, and inclusion. Work-family programs (such as parental leave and flextime) fall within the human relations model.

are designed to give the employee more flexible work schedules (in Chapter 17, we discuss flexible work schedules in greater detail) so that they can meet family-related needs while still maintaining their work and organizational obligations. On the other side of the coin, there are many organizations who are insensitive to the lives their employees have away from work and the work/ nonwork life interface.[13]

The Behavioral Science Influence

behavioral science movement a movement that stressed the need to conduct systematic and controlled field and laboratory studies of workers and their motivation, attitudes, and behavior

Those contributing to the **behavioral science movement** stressed the need to conduct systematic and controlled field and laboratory studies of workers and their motivation, attitudes, and behavior. These ideas contributed significantly to the rise of organizational behavior as a discipline. Behavioral scientists consider both the rational-economic model and the social model of the employee to be incomplete representations of the individual as an organizational member. They present a model that suggests that employees have a strong need to explore, to know and to understand, to grow, to develop, to feel competent and efficacious relative to their environment, and to maintain a high level of self-regard.

Among the major contributors to contemporary behavioral management philosophy and practice are Abraham Maslow, Douglas McGregor, Chris Argyris, Rensis Likert, Raymond Miles, and Edward E. Lawler, III. We'll briefly introduce you to these organizational scholars and their contributions to the behavioral school and to the organizational sciences.

Abraham Maslow. In 1943, psychologist Abraham Maslow (1908–1970) advanced a theory of human motivation that has had tremendous impact on current views of the organization, the practice of management, and the organization's relationship with its employees. Specifically, Maslow identified sets of basic human needs and suggested that they are arranged in a hierarchy based on their motivational importance to the individual.[14]

Maslow's need hierarchy theory had important implications for managers. To motivate people, an organization must offer its members the opportunity to satisfy their active personal needs. Maslow helped managers identify the types of needs that employees have, the order in which employees are likely to satisfy these needs, and the specific actions that organizations can take to try to satisfy these needs. Among his major contributions was the identification of the importance of *growth needs*—the need for self-regard, and the individual's need to know and understand—as a major cause of motivation and behavior. Recognition of the growth needs calls for a different style of management from that proposed by classical or human relations advocates.

Abraham Maslow and his theories are discussed at length in Chapter 7.

Douglas McGregor. Douglas McGregor (1906–1964) first presented his ideas on Theory X and Theory Y management in a classic article, "The Human Side of Enterprise."[15] Before proceeding with McGregor's theories, we encourage you to profile your Theory X and Theory Y beliefs by completing the self-assessment.

SELF-ASSESSMENT Theory X and Theory Y Beliefs

Instructions: In the section below, you will see a series of statements. Please indicate your agreement or disagreement with an "X." There is no right or wrong answer. Only your opinion matters here.

	Strongly Agree	Agree	Undecided	Disagree	Strongly Disagree
1. The average human being prefers to be directed, wishes to avoid responsibility, and has relatively little ambition.	______	______	______	______	______
2. The use of rewards (pay, promotion, etc.) and punishment (failure to promote, etc.) is the best way to get subordinates to do their work.	______	______	______	______	______
3. A good leader should give detailed and complete instructions to his or her subordinates rather than merely giving them general directions and relying on their initiative to work out the details.	______	______	______	______	______
4. Group goal setting offers advantages that cannot be obtained by individual goal setting.	______	______	______	______	______
5. A superior should give his or her subordinates only the information they need to do their immediate tasks.	______	______	______	______	______
6. The average human being inherently dislikes work and inherently prefers leisure.	______	______	______	______	______
7. People, while working for others, are capable of exercising self-direction and self-control.	______	______	______	______	______
8. People by nature are passive and resistant to organizational change.	______	______	______	______	______

Scoring:

First, for each question, assign:

5 points for "strongly agree"
4 points for "agree"
3 points for "undecided"
2 points for "disagree"
1 point for "strongly disagree"

Second, subtract your numerical score for question 7 from 6. This is your new score for question 7. Next, sum your answer to questions 1, 2, 3, 4, 5, 6, 7, and 8, and then divide by 8. This is your Theory X/Theory Y belief score.

Interpretation: A high score (4 and higher) reflects a Theory X belief structure. A low score (2 or less) reflects a Theory Y belief structure.

Source: Patterned after M. Haire, E. E. Ghiselli, and L. W. Porter. 1966. *Managerial thinking: An international study.* New York: Wiley.

SELF-ASSESSMENT

Theory X a management view of the worker as inherently disliking work, lacking work-related motivation, resistant to change, gullible and dull, and indifferent to the needs of the organization

McGregor called the traditional approach to management Theory X. **Theory X** describes the worker as inherently disliking work, lacking work-related ambition, resistant to change, gullible and dull, and essentially indifferent to organizational needs and goals. As a consequence, Theory X assumes that the average worker will avoid work if possible; needs to be coerced, controlled, directed, and threatened with punishment in order to put forth adequate effort; and prefers to be directed and wishes to avoid responsibility. Theory X includes the following propositions:

1. Management is responsible for organizing the elements of productive enterprise—money, materials, equipment, people—in the interest of economic goals.
2. With respect to people, this is a process of directing their efforts, motivating them, controlling their actions, and modifying their behavior to fit the needs of the organization.
3. Without this active intervention by management, people would be passive—even resistant—to organizational needs. They must therefore be persuaded, rewarded, punished, and controlled—their activities must be directed.[16]

Theory Y a management view of the worker as liking work, motivated to achieve objectives, capable of self-direction and self-control, and for whom the expenditure of effort at work is as natural as play

In contrast, the **Theory Y** view of management paints a very different picture of the employee. Theory Y describes the worker as liking work; motivated to achieve objectives to which they are committed; capable of self-direction and self-control; neither passive nor resistant to change by nature, although organizational and work-related experiences can make employees passive and resistant to change. As a consequence, Theory Y makes several assumptions, among them: The expenditure of effort (physical and mental) in work is as natural as play or rest. People are motivated to achieve objectives to which they are committed. When people are committed to a set of goals, self-direction and self-control replace the need for the threat of punishment and external control. Commitment to objectives is a function of the rewards associated with their achievement. Under proper conditions, people will seek responsibility. The capacity for the exercise of imagination, ingenuity, and creativity in the solution of organizational problems is widely, not narrowly, distributed in the work population. People are not considered passive or resistant to organizational needs by nature, although they may have become so as a result of their experiences in organizations.

According to the Theory Y approach to management:

1. Organizations should create work conditions that permit employees to exercise imagination, ingenuity, and creativity in the solution of organizational problems.
2. Organizations should create working conditions that promote the acceptance of responsibility.
3. Management needs to create the opportunity to satisfy the ego and self-actualization needs through work-related effort.
4. The essential task of management is to arrange organizational conditions and methods of operation so that people can achieve their own goals best by directing their own efforts toward organizational objectives.[17]

These managers strive to design structures and processes that actively involve employees in executing their organizational roles. Decentralization and delegation of authority, job enlargement, participative and consultative management, and goal setting are some of the management practices Theory Y managers use to encourage and facilitate desirable behavior from organizational members. (Each of these management practices is discussed in greater detail in Chapters 9–13.)

McGregor's Theory Y, like the work of Maslow, focuses managers' attention on a model of the employee as an organizational member who is more complex than either the rational-economic employee or the social model employee. Theory Y depicts employees as having complex motivational patterns with behavior strongly influenced by their *need to exercise self-direction and self-control* in pursuit of their full human potential.

Chris Argyris. While on the faculty at Harvard University, Chris Argyris concentrated on how organizational and management systems affect employees' attitudes and behaviors. He argued that the demands placed on people by bureaucratic organizations are essentially incompatible with the needs of a mature personality. As people mature, for example, they move from being highly dependent to independent. The bureaucratic organization, with its strong emphasis on control, denies people the occasion to engage in independent thought and action. As a result of this incongruence, the individual and organization inevitably clash. To avoid these dysfunctional consequences, Argyris advocated the development of open and flexible organizations that permit employees the occasion to exercise (as McGregor called for in his Theory Y) self-direction and self-control.[18]

Rensis Likert. Rensis Likert was a professor of psychology and sociology at the University of Michigan. His observations led him to conclude that the classical approach to management fails to motivate organizational members to the same levels of organizational efficiency and effectiveness as achieved by managers who make their subordinates feel personal importance and self-worth. He further observed that organizational members attain higher standards of achievement and self-respect with extensive group participation in decision making and supervision. Likert advocated the development of open and flexible organizations. He stressed teamwork and a group approach to organizational design and management, which he called System 4.[19] (Likert also identified several alternative approaches to organizational design and management, which he labeled Systems 1–3.)

Organizational Humanism. A variety of forces (for example, the emergence of industrial psychology; the Army's use of psychologists and the development of the Army's Alpha test to aid in selection and placement during World War I; the Hawthorne studies) contributed to the emergence of organizational humanism. **Organizational humanism** placed a primary concern on employee satisfaction and well-being. To these ends, it called for management practices that permit employee participation in organizational decision making. In 1932, the first major study of employee job satisfaction was published.[20] Subsequent investigations into job satisfaction and the human relations assumption that promotion of job satisfaction was the key to increases in productivity led Brayfield and Crockett,[21] in the mid-1950s, to conclude that the relationship between satisfaction and performance is a complex one. They opened the door to the possibility that the relationship might run in the opposite direction—a productive worker is a satisfied worker—than that proposed in the human relations model. Organizational humanism was catalytic in promoting an interest in

organizational humanism a system that promoted an interest in understanding the psychological forces that tie individuals to organizations, and promoted management practices that lead to employee satisfaction and well-being employee behavior in organizations and understanding the psychological forces that tie individuals to organizations.

At this stage, sociologists interested in organizations and psychologists interested in the individual within the organizational context give rise to the emergence of the organizational sciences as a discipline, an interest in understanding the organization as a social system, and an interest in the impact of organizations on their members' motivation, attitudes, and behavior.

human resource model the belief that through employee involvement in organizational decision making performance would be enhanced, leading to employee satisfaction, commitment and motivation for further involvement

The Human Resource Model. Professor Raymond Miles from the University of California at Berkeley, in his call for expanded employee involvement in organizational affairs, provided us with the **human resource model.** Believing that the organization's employees represented a major and essentially untapped resource, Miles suggested that managers involve workers more in the affairs of the department. Employee involvement in organizational decision making should increase organizational performance because of the ideas and perspectives that they bring to the decision-making (problem-solving) process. According to Miles, when performance improves, employees derive satisfaction that heightens their willingness to become even more involved in organizational activities.[22] These ideas gave rise to the human resources model portrayed in Figure 2-4—a set of beliefs on how to manage for increased organizational performance, employee satisfaction, commitment, and motivation for organizational involvement.

high-involvement management and organization a participative process that uses the entire capacity of workers, designed to encourage employee commitment to organizational success

Several years later, Edward E. Lawler, III, professor of management at the University of Southern California, introduced us to **high-involvement management and organization.**[23] As previously noted, high involvement refers to "a participative process [that uses] the entire capacity of workers, designed to encourage employee commitment to organizational success."[24] The concept of high involvement suggests that the management functions are carried out by people at *all* levels and in *all* positions throughout the organization, and especially those who make the products and deliver the organization's services. The concept implies an organization where management has achieved a fit among its people, tasks/technology, information processes, rewards, and organization structure. It is an approach to management that builds its participative system around providing its organizational members with information, the skills (knowledge and ability) to perform, the power to control and influence organization events, and a reward system that shares organizational gains with those who

FIGURE 2-4 The Human Resources Model

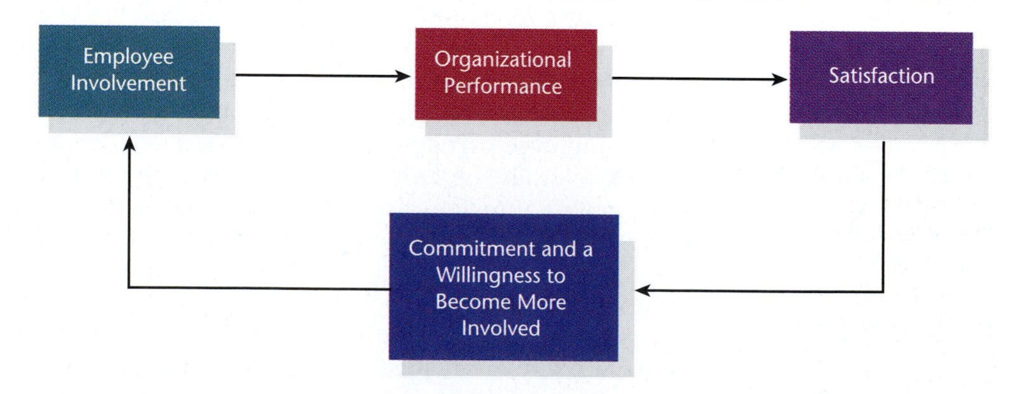

make it all possible. Each organizational member assumes responsibility for their work and for the mission of the organization because they feel a sense of ownership for their work and for the organization.

Contributions and Limitations of the Behavioral School

The behavioral scientists' focus on the importance of personal and social considerations got managers thinking about employees and the need to design organizations that are more open and flexible than those modeled after Weber's bureaucratic model. This influence is evident today as many of the concepts introduced by the behavioral school of thought are operative in contemporary organizations, especially in the high-involvement organization (see *An Inside Look*). American companies with a reputation for excellence, such as Herman Miller and Johnsonville Foods, treat employees as central to their success and growth.[25] It is frequently claimed that the success of Japanese organizations like Honda and Sony lies in their integration of employees into the organizations' technical systems.[26]

http://www.hermanmiller.com

http://www.honda.com

http://www.sony.com

AN INSIDE LOOK

Partners in Beans

Starbucks Coffee (http://www.starbucks.com) has revolutionized the way in which we Americans drink our coffee. One secret of their success lies in their management philosophy: to fully involve all Starbucks employees in the company by offering them incentives such as stock options and utilizing cross-functional project teams to make decisions. Starbucks employees, from the coffee roasters to the cappuccino servers, are known as partners. This terminology demonstrates to even new employees that the success of the company is based on their level of dedication and commitment to excellence.

At the beginning of their Starbucks careers, partners attend classes that include topics such as customer service, brewing techniques, and retail skills. Managers attend even more detailed training sessions on project management, hiring, and evaluating employees.

After working at Starbucks for at least 20 hours per week for six months, partners are eligible for stock options in the "Bean Stock" plan. This innovative demonstration of employee ownership made Starbucks the first private company to offer stock options to employees, both full and part-time, and fulfilled the vision of Starbucks' CEO to provide a work environment that values and involves employees at all levels of the organization.

Partners who own Starbucks' stock have a vested interest in the success of their company. The company therefore sends annual reports on the Bean Stock plan to all partners. Starbucks also encourages employee participation in open forums that provide partners and other stockholders with information on plans for expansion, environmental issues, and other strategic topics.

At its coffee bean roasting plants, Starbucks uses self-managed work teams in which partners have responsibility for decision-making and the daily operations of the team. New partners are hired by a cross-functional team of employees who represent the many facets of the organization.

Besides being a leader in the stylish coffee industry, Starbucks has also demonstrated that they are a trendsetter in the movement toward high-involvement organizations. With the knowledge that Starbucks respects their employees and provides a quality work environment as well as a quality product, your next mocha latte from Starbucks might taste better than ever!

Source: Adapted from B. Nelson, How Starbucks is offering not just jobs but careers. *Workforce Online* (**http://www.workforceonline.com/archive/article/000/16/83.xci**).

A primary contribution from the behavioral science movement was its introduction of the growth model of the employee. The powerful motivating forces associated with intrinsic rewards and the drive for self-esteem and self-efficacy were emphasized. From the perspective of organizational design and management processes, this model called for less bureaucratization, more open and flexible organizations, and higher levels of employee involvement. The organization and employee philosophy espoused by the behavioral science movement laid the foundation for today's high-involvement organization.

Behavioral management thinking does have several limitations, however. First, it lacks a good language for communicating the importance of its ideas to managers. Behavioral scientists often use jargon that is not easily understood, and many of their theories can be highly abstract. Second, behavioral scientists have not done well at getting the attention and respect of key managers in top positions. As a consequence, many managers still see organizations as mechanical systems or purely in terms of the financial bottom line. The third limitation is that, in many ways, behavioral management theorists still assume that there is "one best way" to manage, even though some managerial situations demand varied approaches. This dilemma is addressed by contemporary management theorists.

In summary, the behavioral school of management (see Table 2-3) brings to us a different approach to organizational management than that presented by the classical school of management thought. The hierarchy of authority is less rigid and more fluid and flexible. Fewer rules and standard operating procedures prescribe the way work is to be accomplished. Employees are more empowered; their ideas and opinions tend to be solicited as a part of the problem-solving process. Out of this school in general and the human resource model in particular emerges the "high-involvement organization." Finally, the behavioral school is launched with the human relations movement and its social model of the employee. During this era, paternalistic management practices attempt to satisfy the social needs of employees. Emergent contributions from the behavioral sciences (Maslow, McGregor) give us a model of the employee as "growth-oriented." Subsequently, the human resource model and its employee involvement management practices have been incorporated into many organizations.

TABLE 2-3 Dominant Features of the Behavioral Model

- Involvement-oriented management practices
- Organic organization design
  - organization is a social system (human community)
  - involvement-oriented organization
    - flexible structure
    - dynamic tasks, loosely defined
    - consultative communications
    - authority flows from knowledge and expertise vs. position
    - low levels of standardization
    - extensive use of groups/teams
    - open system
- Model of the employee
  - human relations movement—social being
  - human resource movement—growth being

OTHER MANAGEMENT PERSPECTIVES

The past few decades have been marked by the refinement, extension, and synthesis of both classical and behavioral management thinking. The socio-technical perspective on organizations (see Chapter 1), for example, tries to counteract the one-sided approach taken by the classical and behavioral schools by balancing the technical and social-psychological sides of an organization.[27] The perspectives of both classical and behavioral management have been incorporated into various contingency theories (for example, Fiedler's contingency theory of leadership, which we discuss in Chapter 11).

In addition to the classical and behavioral schools of management thought, there have been other lenses through which organizations and management practice have been viewed. These other perspectives include contingency theory, total quality management, systems theory, Theory Z, and the McKinsey 7-S framework.

Contingency Perspectives

You will recall that both classical and behavioral management theorists searched for the "one best way" to manage. Contemporary theorists, however, see such an approach as too simplistic. They believe that, although a particular managerial strategy may succeed in some situations, it may fail in others; therefore, strict adherence to one approach can have disastrous results.

contingency perspective the belief that the techniques appropriate for a manager to use depend on the specific situation

According to various **contingency perspectives,** the techniques appropriate for a manager to use depend (are *contingent*) on the situation. Although managers always need to plan, organize, direct, and control, they need to do so situation by situation. A contingency theory of decision making, for example, might suggest that the centralized authority and highly directive leadership style found in the classical approach is effective when a manager has a well-developed body of knowledge that defines the most effective way of proceeding. For example, if workers and managers have a body of knowledge that defines an effective way to convert iron ore into pig iron, there is very little need for them to collaborate in deciding which techniques should be used to perform this task.

When there is a high level of environmental uncertainty and little or no developed knowledge to guide work methods, however, a different decision-making strategy is needed. A manager who faces high levels of environment-based and task-based uncertainty needs to use more consultative and participative decision strategies.

Contingency perspectives thus suggest that, as situations vary, the consequences of a particular approach to planning, organizing, directing, and controlling events also vary. The resulting challenge facing management scientists is to identify, understand, and explain these critical contingencies. For managers, this challenge has three aspects (see Figure 2-5). First, managers must develop diagnostic skills that enable them to identify situational demands and characteristics. Second, they must identify a management style appropriate for the demands of the situation. Finally, they must develop the flexibility to move from one managerial style to another as demands change.

Throughout the remainder of this book, contingency perspectives guide our discussion of the management process from planning through controlling. These perspectives show the usefulness as well as the limitations of the earlier classical and behavioral approaches. Given the complexity of modern organizations,

FIGURE 2-5 Demands on Effective Management: Contingency Perspectives

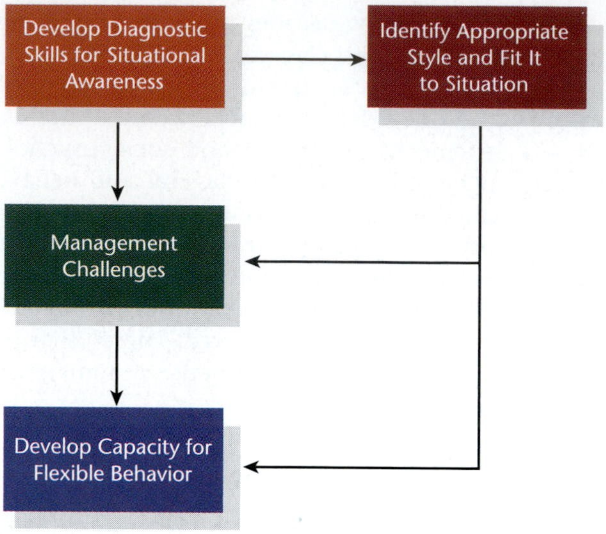

Develop Diagnostic Skills for Situational Awareness

Identify Appropriate Style and Fit It to Situation

Management Challenges

Develop Capacity for Flexible Behavior

effective managers must rely on contingency theories to go beyond the simplistic strategies of the past.

The Total Quality Management Perspective

For decades, the dominant management paradigm centered on mass production. An organization's ability to manufacture large volumes of a product in a cost-effective manner made goods and services available to large numbers of people at relatively low costs. Post–World War II reconstruction of Japan and Japan's desire to become a major player on the world's economic stage led to an attempt to change the rules by which organizations compete in the marketplace. Under the influence of an American scholar, the late W. Edwards Deming (1900–1994), the Japanese started a quality revolution. Eventually the dominant business paradigm shifted from one of quantity to one of quality.

quality management perspective an approach to management that has as its goal the achievement of customer satisfaction by providing high-quality goods and services

total quality management (TQM) a management philosophy and way of managing with the goal of getting everyone committed to quality, continuous improvement, and the attainment of customer satisfaction by meeting or exceeding customer expectations

During the latter two decades of the 20th century, a large number of organizations began to look for ways to become quality producers. This has led to an emerging management perspective that we refer to here as the **quality management perspective.** The quality perspective has as its goal the achievement of customer satisfaction by providing high quality goods and services.

This movement toward quality has resulted in the emergence of **total quality management**, commonly referred to as **TQM.** TQM is a philosophy and way of managing with the goal of getting everyone committed (that is, an organizationwide commitment) to quality, continuous improvement, and the attainment of customer satisfaction by meeting or exceeding customer expectations.

W. Edwards Deming, Joseph Juran, and Karoru Ishikawa, the pioneers of TQM, envisioned that the organization's primary purpose was to stay in business—preservation of the health of the organization is of central importance so that the organization can promote the stability of the community in which it lives, provide products and services that are useful to its customers, and provide a setting for the satisfaction and growth of its members.

The systems perspective sees the organization as part of, and dependent upon, a larger system; therefore, communication between members of the organization is crucial.

© R. W. JONES

TQM management practices are rooted in several assumptions, among them: (1) Quality—it is assumed to be less costly for an organization to turn out quality than poorly produced products and services. (2) People—organizational members are seen as naturally caring about the quality of the work that they do and they are willing to make the effort to improve upon the quality of their work. (3) Organizations—these are systems made up of many highly interdependent parts, and therefore problems faced by organizations cut across functional lines. (4) Senior management—quality and continuous improvement is the ultimate responsibility of top management. (5) Continuous learning and improvement—the long-term health of an organization is dependent on treating quality improvement as a never-ending process, achieved through the development of organizational members and the continuous study of work processes in an effort to find ways to reduce costs, increase productivity, and enhance quality.[28]

http://caes.mit.edu/deming

Organizations that have a quality focus woven into the fabric of their management practices are driven by many principles initially laid out by Dr. Deming. Deming's prescriptions have implications for a number of different management activities; among them, his quality management addresses: goal setting, training, work incentives, the use of quality control departments and quality inspection, the locus of the authority and responsibility for quality, employee involvement, performance appraisals, employee communications, intra-organizational competition, and teams.[29]

The Systems Perspective

An examination of systems theory or a close look at the functioning of human or other biological systems quickly highlights a number of attributes that are of particular importance to organizational functioning. While we need to be careful in our comparisons, in many respects, organizations are living systems. Systems

systems theory a view of an organization as made up of a number of interrelated elements, each functioning to contribute to the purpose of the whole

theory provides us with an important set of lenses to look at and understand organizations and ways to manage. While **systems theory** is not limited to management, it is presented here as a way of viewing organizations.[30]

From the perspective of systems theory, an organization is a system composed of a number of interrelated elements, each functioning to contribute to the purpose of the whole. All systems are a part of a larger whole, and, if we wish to understand the whole, we must understand the context within which the system is embedded as well as the parts of the system and the interrelationships that connect the parts to define the whole. Thus, organizational systems theorists see organizations as complex networks of interrelated and interdependent parts that exist in an interdependent relationship with the external environment.

Among some of the valuable perspectives that we can gain from systems theory that should shape our thinking about the management of organizations are the following:

- The organization is a part of and dependent on a larger system (the external environment) from which it imports critical resources and to which it exports a valued product or service.
- The organization is an input-throughput-output system. It derives its inputs (land, labor, capital, materials, information) from the external environment, and plans, organizes, directs, and controls the flow of these inputs such that there is a transformation of inputs into outputs (goods and services) that are exported back to the external environment.
- The organization is a unified whole, yet it consists of a number of interrelated subsystems (divisions, teams).
- In order to understand the organization, we need to understand its context, its subsystems, and the way these subsystems are interconnected with one another.
- The activity of any one part of the organization affects, to varying degrees, the entire system.
- While all organizations are embedded in a larger environment, some organizations are more open (or closed) than others. Open organizations attempt to interact with and build into their operations the external environment, while closed systems attempt to seal themselves off from the external environment.
- A feedback system communicates to each part of the organization information that is germane to subsequent input and transformation processes.
- Left unattended, there is a natural tendency for a system to run down (entropy), degenerate, and eventually die.

As a result of the organization-environment dependency and the interdependency of different parts of the organization, managers and all organizational members need to communicate with one another. They also need to understand the degree to which the activities of their own work unit affect and are affected by the activities of other organizational units. Internal boundaries need to be more open. Departments within the organization will find it useful to envision their relationships with others within the organization from the perspective of supplier, customer, and partner. From the same perspective, the relationship between organizational members and their internal units and the external environment also needs to be an open relationship.[31] Managers are expected to be sensitive to the needs of the environment as they take resources from, and interact with, it while pursuing organizational goals. The current emphasis placed on heeding customer demands for nonsmoking areas at work and in public places reflects an awareness of the importance of this relationship.

The McKinsey 7-S Framework

McKinsey 7-S framework a perspective on management that calls for the harmonious management of strategy, structure, systems, staff, style, skills, and superordinate goals (shared goals)

The **McKinsey 7-S framework** provides yet another perspective on organizational management; it is a perspective which is grounded in systems theory. This theory stems from the work of contemporary management gurus Tom Peters, Robert Waterman, Richard Pascale, and Anthony Athos while they were employed by McKinsey and Company, a large management consulting organization.[32] Their research into America's effective organizations revealed that seven interdependent factors in organizations must be managed harmoniously.

The critical components in the McKinsey 7-S framework—S factors—include the following:

http://www.coca-cola.com

1. *Strategy*—the plans or courses of action that allocate an organization's scarce resources and commit it to a specified action, over time, to reach identified goals. Example: Coca-Cola's decision to increase its control over its distribution system by purchasing JTL, the nation's largest Coca-Cola bottler.
2. *Structure*—an organization's design, such as the number of its hierarchical levels, its divisions, and the location of authority within them.
3. *Systems*—proceduralized reports and routinized processes, such as those governing the standard operating procedures for handling depreciation of an organization's assets and absenteeism.
4. *Staff*—important personnel groups within an organization, described demographically. Example: the ages of engineers, the functional background of MBAs.
5. *Style*—the way key managers behave when pursuing an organization's goals; also refers to an organization's cultural style. Example: consultative or dictatorial.
6. *Skills*—the distinctive capabilities of an organization's key personnel.
7. *Superordinate goals* (shared values)—the significant meanings or guiding concepts that an organization instills in its members. Example: when organization members are encouraged to experiment with new methods even if they risk failure.[33]

Because of their interdependent relationship, a change in one S factor alerts managers to the need to adjust others. A change in an organization's strategy, for example, may call for a change in its structure. According to the McKinsey model, effective managers achieve a good fit among these seven variables.

The Theory Z Perspective

During the 1970s and 1980s, many U.S. companies were seriously affected by Japanese competitors and American productivity problems. The Japanese played a significant role in changing the business paradigm from one of quantity to quality. This paradigm shift enabled them to make serious inroads to many markets that had been primarily American.

American scholars identified a number of management practices common to effective Japanese organizations that appeared to account for much of their success. Whether these practices could be transplanted successfully to U.S. organizations was hotly debated. Some argued that unique cultural differences would prevent U.S. organizations from adapting Japanese management practices. Others felt that the Japanese practices could be successful in the United States, often noting that they were basically American in origin anyway.

Theory Z a theory of management based upon an integration of the best Japanese and American practices

In 1981, UCLA management professor William Ouchi offered **Theory Z** to integrate the merits of the Japanese (Theory J) and American (Theory A) management styles (see Figure 2-6).[34] Theory Z is less a major theory of management than it is a set of organizational and management style characteristics. As summarized in Figure 2-6, Theory Z emphasizes terms of employment, decision making, responsibility, evaluation and promotion, control, career paths, and concern for employees. Some successful American organizations that experienced success using methods consistent with Theory Z management included Eastman Kodak, Hewlett-Packard, IBM, and Procter & Gamble. For years, IBM prided itself on finding ways to relocate, rather than laying off, its workforce in times of decline—a practice they no longer attend to nor address as a part of their organizational culture.

http://www.kodak.com

http://www.hp.com

http://www.pg.com

FIGURE 2-6 A Comparison of American, Japanese, and Theory Z Organizations

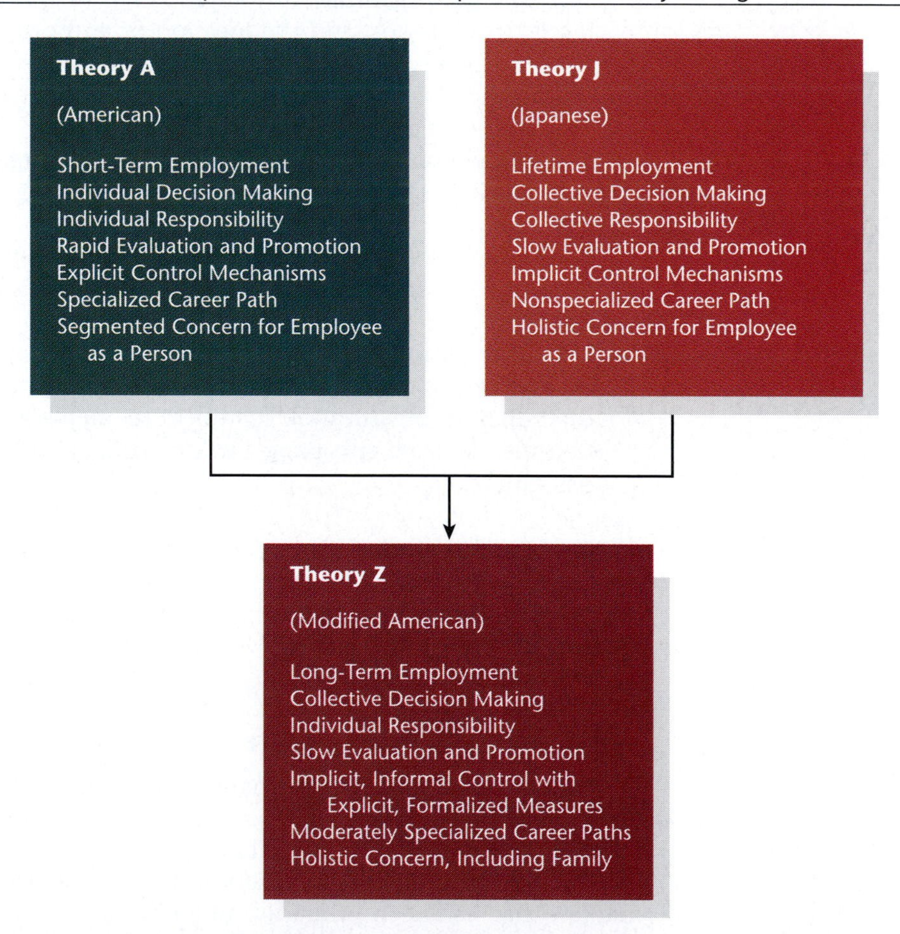

Source: Adapted from W. Ouchi. 1981. *Theory Z.* Reading, MA: Addison-Wesley, 58.

Theory Z is not a contingency theory of management. Ouchi suggested that this style of management is universally better than the traditional American approach and prescribes Theory Z as appropriate for almost any management situation. In fact, in many ways, Theory Z reflects a return to the outdated "one best way" thinking of behavioral management theory. In the tradition of behavioral management, Theory Z identifies employees as a key component of organizational productivity and effectiveness. It prescribes how employees "should be" managed so that organizational efficiency and effectiveness improve. Ouchi's universal management prescriptions call for long-term employment and a concern for employees' total life.

Theory Z is not a complete theory. It does not, for example, fully explain processes through which the prescribed management practices are expected to create an effective organization. Nevertheless, Ouchi's work has again heightened U.S. managers' awareness of the variety of management techniques that can be effective under particular circumstances.

Contributions and Limitations of the Contemporary Schools

Two major contributions have come from the contemporary schools of management thought. First, they have had a unifying effect, combining the technical side of organizations that the classicists examined and the social elements that were the focus of the behavioralists. This strong emphasis on multidimensionality has alerted managers to the interdependence of organizational subsystems and the importance of integrating them to achieve efficiency and effectiveness. Second, many of these contemporary perspectives sensitize managers to the fact that no one set of management principles is appropriate in all situations. Under some circumstances, the classical approach is effective. Under other circumstances, the behavioral model is effective. Under still others, managers should integrate and apply ideas from both the classical and behavioral models while simultaneously working to enhance quality and worker integration.

There are two primary limitations of contemporary management approaches. The first is that each perspective is more complex than either classical or behavioral theory. This complexity can make their use more difficult and their adoption less likely. The second limitation is that no contemporary management perspective has been thoroughly researched. It is likely that, in their current state, these theories are incomplete. Despite these limitations, the contemporary perspectives appear superior to the behavioral and classical approaches because they build on the strengths of the older schools of thought but avoid many of their limitations.

PHILOSOPHIES AND APPROACHES TO MANAGEMENT PRACTICE IN REVIEW

Our understanding of the practice of management comes to us from three primary sources. First, we have the writings of management practitioners and consultants. They offer insights based on their day-to-day organizational experiences. It is apparent that a great deal can be learned from the stories and experiences of the great business people of the past century (like Henry Ford, Alfred P. Sloan, Carly Fiorina, Tom Watson, Jr., Mary Kay Ash, and Bill Gates).[35] Second, we learn much by listening to the voices of management philosophers.

Every discipline has its gurus, those men and women who spend their time thinking about organizations and management and sharing their insights. Peter Drucker, Abraham Maslow, and Mary Parker Follett are among the greater contributors to our understanding of management practices. Finally, we have the management and organization scientists. These individuals have applied the scientific method to develop an objective understanding of organizational behavior.

Management practitioners, philosophers, and scientists help managers understand and anticipate organizational events and, thus, allow them to manage more effectively and efficiently. There are several schools of management thought and, therefore, various approaches to the practice of management. Although no one grand theory has emerged from these schools to guide a manager's every step, each offers a distinctly useful perspective.

The classical school of management thought included work from the scientific-management movement, administrative management, and the development of the bureaucratic organization. It emphasized the economic rationality of decisions made by organizations and their members and the role of economic incentives as primary motivators. Classical management theorists, although occasionally paying lip service to the importance of a friendly labor-management climate, tended to focus on the mechanical side of an organization. Workers were treated as nonthinking, nonfeeling robots and were reduced to the role of cogs on the organizational wheel. The classicists felt that their prescriptions for designing and running the organizational machine defined the one best way to manage.

The Hawthorne studies provided a transition from classical to behavioral management theories, which focused on the human side of organizations and the importance of personal and social factors as motivators. The human relations movement saw organizations as social systems and proposed that the way to increase productivity was to keep workers satisfied. The behavioral scientists saw employee involvement as the key to greater organizational efficiency and effectiveness. Like the classicists, behavioralists believed that their theories provided the one best way to manage organizations.

Companies may opt for different approaches to management, depending on what factors they can control. See how a cleaning company, software engineering firm, and a cookie manufacturer choose to address this issue in the Evolution of Management: Sunshine Cleaning, Jian, Archway Cookies video.

The contemporary school of management thought draws from the best of earlier theories. Although some contemporary theories, such as Theory Z, provide "new" management ideas, the most important recent advances develop contingency perspectives. Recognizing that organizations are not merely machines or social systems, contingency theories arising from this systems-theory perspective deal with both the technical and the human side of organizations. Managers must recognize the interdependence of these two systems when making decisions and performing other managerial duties.

Contemporary management theories propose that there is no one best way to practice management. Instead, managers must develop diagnostic skills to assess each situation, identify the appropriate managerial style for that situation, and be flexible enough to match their behavior to that demanded by the situation. The information they draw on to perform this balancing act is considered the fruit of the science of management. The manner with which they apply this knowledge is an art.

A FINAL LOOK

The director of human resources for Union Pottery distributes a climate survey to the employees to learn more about employee morale and motivation. She is surprised by the high rate of response.

Amongst themselves, the employees discuss how pleased they are to be asked about their work environment. They are still pessimistic about the likelihood of change in such a traditional hierarchical organization, but many believe that the upper-level management is trying to understand their needs.

Results from the survey show that employees would consider leaving Union Pottery for another organization if the opportunities for advancement appear to be better. The survey also shows that employees want more opportunities for professional and personal development. Tuition benefits are also a big draw, as is the ability to work flexible hours and to have greater input into the company operations. The human resources director is surprised to learn that overall, employees are loyal to the company and prefer to stay if development opportunities improve. Employees display a great deal of personal investment in the company and want to see it succeed.

In her report to the president, the director of human resources recommends instituting a revised benefits plan and a professional development plan for each employee. She knows it will be difficult to persuade her boss; however, the benefits in terms of employee retention are obvious and well worth the difficulties in changing old policies and ways of thinking.

KEY TERMS

behavioral school, 51
behavioral science movement, 54
classical school, 39
contingency perspective, 61
Hawthorne studies, 48
high-involvement management and organization, 58
human relations model, 53
human resource model, 58
McKinsey 7-S framework, 65
organizational humanism, 57
quality management perspective, 62
scientific management, 39
systems theory, 64
Theory X, 56
Theory Y, 56
Theory Z, 66
total quality management (TQM), 62

ISSUES FOR REVIEW AND DISCUSSION

1. Who were the major contributors to the scientific management movement and what were their respective contributions?
2. What were Taylor's prescriptions for scientific management?
3. Discuss the major differences between Taylor's contributions to the classical school of management, and those stemming from his European counterparts (that is, Henri Fayol and Max Weber).
4. What were the Hawthorne studies? What effect did they have on the practice of management?
5. Discuss the behavioral science movement and in the process identify its major contributors and the nature of their contributions.
6. Compare and contrast the human relations model of the employee and the human resource model.
7. Why do you think that contingency management emerged? How do these theories differ from the classical and behavioral schools of management?
8. Briefly identify the central perspectives offered by quality management, the McKinsey 7-S framework, and Theory Z.

EXERCISES

ORGANIZATION–PERSON FIT QUESTIONNAIRE

In addition to technology, size, and the external environment, organizational structure must also fit employee personalities. This exercise is designed to help you better understand the type of organization that best fits you and your needs. Read each statement below and respond to each statement by scoring it according to the following scale.

5 = Very descriptive of the type of organization I like to work in.
4 = Somewhat descriptive of the type of organization I like to work in.
3 = Slightly descriptive of the type of organization I like to work in.
2 = Unlike the type of organization I like to work in.
1 = Very much unlike the type of organization I like to work in.

____ 1. Work should be routine and stable with few interruptions.
____ 2. People who are in higher-level positions should have authority over those in lower-level positions.
____ 3. The way work is done should be stable and not subject to much change.
____ 4. Rules and regulations should be applied equally and impersonally.
____ 5. Decisions I would have to make should deal with routine issues.
____ 6. Efficiency and predictability should be two of the most important values.
____ 7. Bottom-line performance should be the main emphasis.
____ 8. People should specialize in the performance of tasks.
____ 9. The organization should be structured in a hierarchy so that everyone knows where he or she fits.
____10. Goals should be established by top-level managers and communicated downward.
____11. Reward for performance should be tangible, such as pay increases, larger offices, and reserved parking.
____12. Work should be performed according to one's job description with little, if any, deviation.
____13. Plans should be made by top-level managers and communicated downward.
____14. The organization should be in an industry that is relatively stable.
____15. Rules and procedures should be followed without question.

Scoring:

Total your points for each statement to arrive at a grand total. Write that score here: ________

Interpretation

If your score is:

61–75 You would most likely enjoy working in an organization that is highly mechanistic.
46–60 You would probably enjoy working in a moderately mechanistic organization.
31–45 You would enjoy working in an organization that has a mixture of mechanistic and organic attributes.
16–30 You would probably enjoy working in a moderately organic organization.
0–15 You would most likely enjoy working in an organization that is highly organic.

Source: Excerpt from *Organizational behavior: Learning guide/experiential exercises* by Bruce Kemelgor, copyright © 1988 by The Dryden Press, reprinted by permission of the publisher.

INFOTRAC

INFOTRAC COLLEGE EDITION

The articles listed below are a sampling of those available through InfoTrac College Edition. You can search for them either by title or by the author's name.

Articles

1. Insanely Great Customer Service. (Sara Lee Bakery standard quality) Debbie Selinsky. *Success* Sept 2000 v47 i4 p59
2. Trends that never died: TQM and re-engineering. (Industry trend or event) (Column) Allan E. Alter. *Computerworld* May 29, 2000 p33
3. The New Public Service: Servicing Rather than Steering. Robert B. Denhardt, Janet Vinzant Denhardt. *Public Administration Review* Nov 2000 v60 i6 p549
4. Where silenced voices speak out: the hidden power of informal communication networks. Stacy L. Young. *Women and Language* Fall 1998 v21 i2 p21(1)
5. The Very Superior Boss. (Brief Article) Abraham H. Maslow. *Across the Board* Feb 2000 v37 i2 p7

Questions

Chapter 2 introduces the Total Quality Management perspective. The article entitled "Trends that never died: TQM and re-engineering," describes the process that new management practices go through. Break into small groups and discuss the evolution of a "Big New Idea" that you are familiar with. What conclusions can you draw about management practices from this discussion?

The article also makes the point that e-commerce companies must adopt TQM practices to survive. Explain why and how this might be done. Describe the re-engineering processes (or lack thereof) in specific e-commerce companies and their resultant success (or failure).

For Other Articles:

Have members of the group read the other articles on this list. Discuss the philosophies and management approaches these writers think are important. What new information have you acquired about these ideas and practices from your reading of the articles?

WEB EXERCISE

Look at Hewlett-Packard's website (**http://www.hp.com**) and its company information page. What are the main elements of the "HP way"—its approach to management?

CASE
A Job Interview with Sterling Manufacturing

Clayton Odland sat in disbelief as the manager explained to him, "You see, our experience with young men such as yourself is that you will stay with us only long enough to gain some experience and then leave to go to work for a smaller company."

"How can she say that?" Clayton thought. "I want to work for Sterling. Where did I go wrong?" Shaken by the realization that he was not going to get a job offer, Clayton thought back over the events of the day to try to understand what he had said or done to make the manager decide not to offer him a job.

Clayton's first interview with Sterling Manufacturing had been on the campus of State University, where Clayton was nearing the end of his senior year. Majoring in human resource management and scheduled to graduate with honors, Clayton had been sure that he would have many job opportunities, but the offer to visit a Sterling plant was especially exciting for him. Sterling was one of the largest manufacturers in the world, with plants located throughout the United States, Canada, and Europe. Former Sterling executives served on the Cabinet of the President of the United States. A career with Sterling seemed to offer unlimited possibilities.

Despite Sterling's size and enormous prestige, at the on-campus interview Clayton had felt relaxed and confident. Donald Vodicka, the Sterling manager conducting the interview, was a State University graduate himself and had advanced to a position of considerable responsibility in the twelve years he had been with Sterling. An accounting graduate whose position was in the financial area at Sterling headquarters, he assured Clayton that he could arrange for him to visit one of Sterling's divisions to interview for a position in human resource management.

About two weeks after the interview, Clayton received a letter inviting him to visit a Sterling facility in Michigan. Now, as he sat in a red leather chair in the manager's impressive paneled office, Clayton's mind raced back over the events of the day.

He had arrived at the Sterling building on schedule, traveling by cab from the hotel at which the company had made a reservation for him. The first person he met was Jim Pflanz, who was not much older than Clayton and had been working for Sterling for only a year. He talked about his work for Sterling, which mainly consisted of interviewing applicants for jobs and occasionally traveling to a college campus to interview seniors for management trainee positions. He also outlined Clayton's schedule for the day, which was to consist of a series of interviews with managers within the human resources department; lunch in the executive dining room; and a final interview with Ms. Merrigan, the head of the division's human resource department.

The second person Clayton saw that day was Louise Portillo. Ms. Portillo described the manner in which Sterling prepared its young management trainees for positions of responsibility. Clayton could expect to spend his first four to six years with Sterling in a series of appointments of six months' to two years' duration. He would probably spend some months interviewing job applicants, as had Jim Pflanz. He would probably have an assignment working in industrial relations as the first level of appeal in grievances filed by the union. He would no doubt spend some time learning the details of administering Sterling's pension and health benefits. The details of the company's training program varied somewhat for different people, but it was the company's policy to ensure that its managers were well prepared through both experience and training before investing them with substantial authority.

Clayton asked Ms. Portillo about her responsibilities at Sterling. Ms. Portillo replied that she was responsible for reviewing the way departments were organized in the division. Clayton had enjoyed his college course in organization theory and asked about the possibility of a training assignment with Ms. Portillo. Ms. Portillo replied that she often did have a management trainee assigned to her, but as the work was rather complex and required some knowledge of the way in which the company worked, trainees were assigned there only after three or four years of experience.

At the close of Clayton's interview with Ms. Portillo, Jim Pflanz appeared and escorted Clayton to his next stop, which was with Stuart Davis. Mr. Davis worked in the industrial relations section, which was responsible for administering the labor contract that covered the employees of this division of Sterling. Mr. Davis described the functions of his department and the types of assignments typically filled by management trainees. Although apparently less intellectually challenging than the work of Ms. Portillo's department, the thought of having the opportunity to resolve real conflict gave the industrial relations department a lot of appeal to Clayton.

After Mr. Davis finished describing the industrial relations function, he asked Clayton if he had any questions. Clayton then asked what Sterling did to motivate its employees. At this, Mr. Davis seemed a little annoyed. As if he were explaining something to a child, he leaned forward and said, "Listen it's very simple. Every job has a standard. If people meet that standard, we leave them alone. When they don't meet the standard, we take disciplinary action." This was not the approach favored by Clayton's professors at State University, but he did not comment.

At the close of their session, Mr. Davis escorted Clayton to the executive dining room, which was on the top floor of the building. He ushered Clayton into a richly appointed small restaurant, where they were joined by Ms. Portillo and three other executives, including Elizabeth Merrigan, the head of the human resource function for the division. Ms. Merrigan led the way to a table for six, where she took a seat at one end and invited Clayton to sit at her right hand. Clayton noted that Jim Pflanz had not joined them but supposed that he had other obligations.

The lunch was a heady experience for Clayton. The surroundings were sumptuous, befitting a corporation of Sterling's reputation, and the lunch was delicious. Two waiters hovered at their table, filling water glasses and coffee cups and attending to every word or gesture from Ms. Merrigan and the others. The conversation centered on labor problems in the divisions's plant in Great Britain and on Sterling's difficulty in dealing with British labor unions. The Sterling executives included Clayton in the discussion, explaining the differences in labor law between Great Britain and the United States. Clayton commented that it was too bad that relations between the company and its workers were so rigid.

At the close of the meal, Mr. Davis asked Clayton what he thought of the dining room. Clayton expressed his delight at so magnificent a place and Mr. Davis laughed. "Well if you come to work here, it will be many years before you see the inside of it again." Clayton then understood why Jim Pflanz had not joined them.

After lunch, Clayton had one more interview before meeting with Ms. Merrigan. It was with one of the executives who had joined them for lunch, and who, as it turned out, was responsible for administering the division's benefits. The work he described seemed terribly dull, more clerical than managerial, but Clayton could recognize the necessity to become familiar with it.

The final stop before checking out with Jim Pflanz was his interview with Ms. Merrigan. Despite the prospect of a long and probably often boring training period,

Clayton was enthusiastic about the opportunity to someday be a member of the inner circle at this large, powerful company. He expressed that enthusiasm to Ms. Merrigan but immediately saw that the decision had already been made, and there would be no job at Sterling Manufacturing for Clayton Odland.

Questions

1. What school of management thought appears to underlie the management practices at Sterling Manufacturing?
2. How are these assumptions reflected in Sterling practices?
3. What school of management thought does Clayton Odland appear to ascribe to?
4. How did he express these assumptions?
5. What do you think would have happened if Clayton had gone to work for Sterling?

Source: This case was prepared by and is used with the permission of Phil Fisher of the University of Southern Indiana. It describes actual events, but the names of persons and the company have been disguised.

Outline

CHAPTER 3

Social Responsibility and Ethics

Learning Objectives

After reading this chapter, you should be able to

1. Define social responsibility and trace its historical development.
2. Name and discuss three levels of commitment to social responsibility.
3. Compare and contrast two divergent views on corporate social responsibility.
4. Define and distinguish ethics from social responsibility.
5. Discuss the individuals' and organizations' responsibility for ethical behavior and list sources of unethical behavior.
6. Identify the three ethical standards and discuss how they affect decision making.
7. Discuss steps managers can take to encourage ethical behavior in organizations.
8. Discuss the ethical challenge associated with efforts to "manage" employee work-related attitudes, motivation, and behavior.
9. Discuss the ethical issues associated with workplace diversity.

A FIRST LOOK

After meeting with representatives from Birmingham Industries, Tom Grey, the CEO of Jamison Hospital, returns to his office both elated and doubtful. Birmingham Industries is offering to fund the new cardiac wing that Jamison Hospital so badly needs in exchange for naming it the Birmingham Cardiac Wing.

Birmingham Industries has endured a lot of negative publicity in the past year due to the fact that tobacco products are responsible for 75 percent of their profits. By doing something this visible for the hospital, the company hopes to improve their image.

When Tom heard that a corporation was considering funding the wing, he was thrilled because this could be the answer to the hospital's seemingly unsolvable funding problems. But when he discovered that the prospective donor manufactures tobacco products, his heart sank. How can his organization, whose mission is to be a leader in preventative health care, accept a donation from a company whose product jeopardizes the health of thousands of local people?

Questions: Should Jamison Hospital be concerned with the source of the funding, or should it focus more on the potential for improved facilities? If it were your decision, would you accept the donation or turn it down and seek a less controversial donor?

As a manager you affect the lives and well-being of many individuals, those with and for whom you work, those who work for you, and those in the broader community. It is incumbent upon you that your moral and ethical compass point "true north," and that you let your guide be that which is the "right and socially responsible thing to do." Standards for ethical and socially responsible behavior should guide *all* of your human interactions. While the actions of some managers raise serious questions as to their ethics and social responsiveness, most managers behave honorably as they pursue their organization's goals. Several years ago, for example, Johnson & Johnson took action that cost them more than 150 million dollars. Seven people in the Chicago area died after taking Tylenol capsules laced with cyanide. While the FBI told company executives that the probability of contaminated capsules showing up outside the Chicago area was extremely low, Johnson & Johnson ordered that supplies of all Tylenol be removed from store shelves and warehouses and sent back to the company.

http://www.johnsonandjohnson.com

http://www.microsoft.com

Bill Gates ("Mr. Microsoft") and his wife Melinda recently set aside one billion dollars to fully fund college education for academically qualified, but economically disadvantaged minority students in the fields of engineering, mathematics, science, and education. At the time of the award, their gift represented the largest academic donation ever, and the Gates Foundation had already pledged four billion dollars to various causes.[1] In addition to individual philanthropists making significant contributions to important causes, many organizations routinely demonstrate a keen social consciousness as well. Eli Lilly and several other Indianapolis firms, for example, made a 2.5 million dollar commitment of equity capital to form an investment company for minority entrepreneurs.[2] An increasing number of universities are taking steps to ensure that their university logo-bearing clothing lines are not produced in foreign sweatshops employing child labor.[3] Exxon, Coca-Cola, RJR Nabisco, Citicorp,

http://www.elililly.com

http://www.exxon.com

http://www.nabisco.com

and IBM have undertaken a major role in attempting to improve public school education.[4]

http://www.texaco.com

Other organizations and their members do not do as well. In 1996, Texaco paid out 175 million dollars to settle a racial discrimination lawsuit filed by some of its African-American employees.[5] Almost daily, the media tells us about organizations that illegally dump toxic wastes and trucking companies and manufacturers that cut corners on their air pollution emissions. Shell Oil discharged over 6600 tons of oil into surface water during 1997. They discharged approximately 20,000 tons the year before. An impressive improvement, perhaps, yet it is difficult to argue that discharging 6000 tons of pollutants is socially responsible.[6]

The Attorney General of the State of Minnesota recently charged US Bancorp with selling privileged information about its banking customers to telemarketers. While not pleading guilty to these charges, US Bancorp recently paid a three million dollar fine.[7] Many of their customers were outraged to learn that "their bank" sold, for financial gain, personal, private, and privileged information. During 1999, State Farm Insurance was charged with repairing policyholder automobiles with aftermarket parts without informing them of their practices, and Humana Hospital was charged with paying doctors cost-saving incentive bonuses to disencourage them from ordering costly tests and making expensive referrals. On September 30, 1999, a significant nuclear accident occurred in Japan, and countries continue to struggle with the problem of nuclear waste—what to do with it, where to store it. Such incidents raise the question, Was the creation and use of nuclear energy the socially responsible thing to do, before problems associated with its waste had been solved?

http://www.statefarm.com

Each of these examples reveals something about the ethics and socially responsible—or irresponsible—behavior of managers and organizations. They also reveal something about the relationships between organizations and various groups in their environments who have an interest in the decisions and actions made by organizational members. Contemporary managers must continually examine how they respond to their communities: Managers today must ask, What is our responsibility here?

The issues of ethics and social responsibility are of special importance to us as we consider the management of organizational behavior. As managers of your organization's social systems, you will be called upon to deal with the organization's members. You will actively manage employee behavior as you strive to cement the employee's relationship with the organization. You will therefore actively seek to manage employee work-related attitudes, work-related motivation, and work-related behavior. Thus, the importance of the question, What is the right and socially responsible thing to do? will stand before you.

THE NATURE OF SOCIAL RESPONSIBILITY

Many members of society argue strongly that managers must consider the impact of their decisions and actions on society as a whole and that they must assume responsibility for their activities. It is argued that managers should take steps to protect and improve the welfare of society. Some have suggested (see Chapter 1 and our discussion of the organization's "reason for being") that organizations exist for the purpose of serving the needs of society. Therefore, being a steward of the needs of society is a socially responsible, appropriate, and natural act.[8] In short, managers must evaluate their decisions and actions, not merely from the perspective of organizational effectiveness, but also from the perspective of the greater good.[9]

social responsibility an organization's obligation to engage in activities that protect and contribute to the welfare of society

Managers must, of course, obey the law, but social responsibility goes beyond the letter of the law. **Social responsibility** is an organization's obligation to engage in activities that protect and contribute to the welfare of society.[10] An organization's social responsibilities are always shaped by the culture and the historical period in which the organization operates.[11] Just as a society's values, norms, and mores change over time, so does the definition of what is socially responsible behavior. Differences in societal values and the shift of public attitude can be seen in the tobacco industry, and in the public's response to the genetic alteration of seeds and dairy products. In the tobacco industry, the "old thinking" was that "if you smoke cigarettes, whatever happens to your heart and lungs is your own fault. Cigarettes are legal and are voluntarily purchased and consumed. Don't come whining to the courts when you see a shadow on the X ray. Caveat fumor." During the latter part of the 20th century, the old thinking shifted to the "new thinking" that "Big Tobacco knowingly sells a defective product that when used exactly as intended (that is, you smoke the thing), addicts the consumer to nicotine and eventually sickens and kills him. Big Tobacco should pay billions. . . . "[12] What was once considered socially acceptable and legal is now considered socially irresponsible, and it has been punished to the tune of billions of dollars! Passions in many Western European countries ran extremely high during the 1990s with regard to importing U.S. dairy products, which use growth hormones to stimulate milk production. Similar feelings do not exist throughout much of the United States—this activity is not judged the same here as it is in Western Europe.

So, just exactly what *is* an organization's social responsibility? It is, for one thing, a matter of intense debate! At one extreme, there are those who strongly believe that organizations are in business solely to produce goods and services that societies want—be they atomic weapons, legal advice, or life-saving drugs—and that they are entitled to make a profit in return. For these people, social responsibility is, simply, not an issue. At the other extreme, there are those who believe that organizations should be allowed to do business only if they do no harm, help solve social problems, and put some of the profits they earn back to work for society. This disagreement does not lend itself to quick and easy resolution.

The Law and Social Responsibility

As we suggested above, the two concepts "legality" and "social responsibility" are not one and the same. Social responsibility is often seen as acts that "go beyond" what is prescribed by the law. In fact, many individuals believe that certain existing laws do not encourage socially responsible behavior. For example, oceangoing ships are currently (and legally) allowed to dump their ballast water into the Great Lakes. This water brings many nonnative species to the Great Lakes, such as lamprey, which nearly destroyed the trout population in Lake Superior, and zebra muscles, which have damaged the water intake systems of communities and businesses located along the lakes. The dumping of ballast water may be legal but it is not socially responsible.

Thinking about legality and responsibility identifies four distinct organizational approaches to social responsibility: illegal and irresponsible, illegal and responsible, irresponsible and legal, and legal and responsible.

Illegal and Irresponsible Some organizations behave illegally and irresponsibly. For example, an investigation was launched to examine claims that some companies took advantage of the catastrophic Pennsylvania Ashland Petroleum tank collapse by dumping their own toxic wastes into the already polluted Monongahela River. Dumping this type of material into the river is prohibited by law, and it was clearly irresponsible to further contaminate the water. In recent years there have been numerous reports of contractors illegally dumping asbestos removed from schools as a way of avoiding the costs associated with proper disposal. Today, an illegal and irresponsible strategy is a high-risk strategy and may be fatal to an organization, because a broad spectrum of society will no longer tolerate such behavior.

http://www.ashland.com

Illegal and Responsible Some organizations follow strategies that are socially conscious and responsible, but that violate the letter of the law. Greenpeace has on many occasions engaged in illegal acts in an effort to protect the environment. For example, during the mid-1990s they attempted to block French nuclear tests in the South Pacific by illegally occupying French territory and harassing French military operations.

http://www.greenpeace.org

Irresponsible and Legal Some organizations operate without violating a single law, but still do not act in a socially responsible manner. For example, beer companies produce commercials that appeal to underage drinkers, and casinos sometimes make special offers that encourage people to trade their Social Security checks for gambling chips. These organizations are acting within the letter of the law but not the spirit of the law.

Although this advertisement was completely legal, many people believed that the cartoon character Joe Camel directly appealed to young people and sent the message that smoking is "cool." RJR Reynolds eventually discontinued the ad amid the criticism.

http://www.patagonia.com

http://www.audubon.com

http://www.tnc.org

http://www.benandjerrys.com

Legal and Responsible Finally, some organizations obey the law and at the same time engage in socially responsible behavior. For example, since 1984 Patagonia has given 10 percent of its pre-tax profits to such groups as Audubon Society, Nature Conservancy, and the Wolf Fund. Ben & Jerry's gives 7.5 percent of their pre-tax profits, while Hallmark Corporation for the past 80 years has donated more than 5 percent of its corporate pre-tax profits to charitable causes.[13] These charitable acts on the part of Patagonia, Ben & Jerry's, and Hallmark are both legal and highly socially responsible.

An Historical Perspective

At the start of the 20th century, there were few corporate acts of charity. Instead, wealthy business people gave as individuals from their personal wealth to charitable causes. How, then, did corporate commitment to social responsibility evolve? Two principles provided the foundation for contemporary views on social responsibility.[14] The first of these, the **principle of charity**, is rooted in religious tradition and suggests that those who have plenty should give to those who do not. Under the influence of this principle, individuals in the business community increasingly decided to use some of their corporate power and wealth for the social good. For example, steel magnate Andrew Carnegie put much of his great wealth to work for education. Henry Ford adopted a paternalistic style of management and made recreational and health programs available to Ford employees. Over time, an increasing number of business leaders adopted and spread the idea that business has a responsibility to society beyond simply providing necessary goods and services.[15]

principle of charity suggests that those who have plenty should give to those who do not

A second principle that shaped corporate social responsibility is the **principle of stewardship.** This principle asserts that organizations have an obligation to see that the public's interests are served by corporate actions and the way in which profits are spent. Because corporations control vast resources, because they are powerful, and because this power and wealth come from their operations within society, they have an obligation to serve society's needs. In this way, managers and corporations become the stewards, or trustees, for society.[16] Under the influence of this principle, the popular press, Congress, and other factions started to attack many large and powerful organizations whose attitudes they perceived to be both anticompetitive and antisocial. Antitrust laws and other legislation began to place constraints on the actions of organizations.[17] In general, there was a shift in the public perception of a corporation's place within and obligations to society.

principle of stewardship suggests that organizations have an obligation to see that the public's interests are served by corporate action and the ways in which profits are spent

Attitudes about what is and is not considered socially responsible behavior also have changed substantially over time.[18,19] This change is reflected by the following three phases:

Phase One: Profit-Maximizing Management During the period of economic scarcity in the 19th and early part of the 20th century, most American business managers felt they had one primary responsibility to society. They were to underwrite the country's economic growth and oversee the accumulation of wealth. Business managers could pursue, almost single-mindedly, the objective of maximizing profits. Managers essentially felt that what was good for business was good for the country. This strong business ethos was shattered, however, by the Great Depression of the 1930s.

profit-maximizing management the belief that business's primary responsibility to society is to underwrite the country's economic growth and to oversee the accumulation of wealth

trusteeship management the belief that corporate managers need to maintain an equitable balance among the competing interests of all groups with a stake in the organization

Phase Two: Trusteeship Management After the Great Depression, the number of privately held American corporations began to decline. Organizations found themselves having to respond to the demands of both internal and external groups, such as stockholders, customers, suppliers, and creditors. As a consequence, organizations had to shift their orientation to social responsibility, and the result was the emergence of trusteeship management. Corporate managers needed to maintain an equitable balance among the competing interests of all groups with a stake in the organization. Pressure from these groups led to the use of some of the corporate wealth to meet social needs.

quality-of-life management the belief that managers have to do more than achieve narrow economic goals, but that they should manage the quality-of-life by helping develop solutions for society's ills

Phase Three: Quality-of-Life Management In the 1960s, a new set of national priorities began to develop, and the pressure on managers to behave in socially responsible ways intensified. Such issues as poverty, environmental pollution, and deteriorating inner cities raised widespread concern about the quality of life in the United States. The consensus was that managers had to do more than achieve narrow economic goals. They are to enhance our quality of life by helping solve society's ills.[20] The principles of charity and stewardship were firmly in place (see Figure 3-1 and Table 3-1).

http://www.cdc.com

An illustration of this approach to social responsibility can be seen in the community involvement of the Control Data Corporation (CDC). CDC built plants in Minneapolis, St. Paul, and Washington, D.C., to provide jobs and develop an economic base for inner-city residents of poor urban areas. They have also undertaken numerous other projects to assist the disabled with vocational training programs, and have created Rural Ventures and City Venture Corporation to encourage rural and urban revitalization projects.

Social Responsibility and Organizational Stakeholders

The internal and external groups that emerged during the trusteeship period have grown in strength and size. Today, every manager must be aware of the needs of the stockholders; customers; suppliers; creditors; and all the men and women, managers and nonmanagers, who work full- or part-time for the organization. This philosophy is reflected in Johnson & Johnson's credo: "We believe

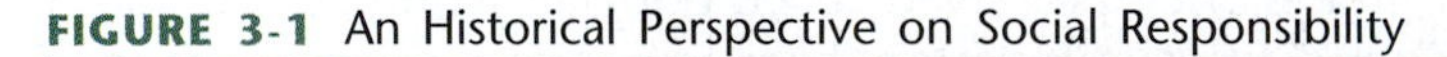

FIGURE 3-1 An Historical Perspective on Social Responsibility

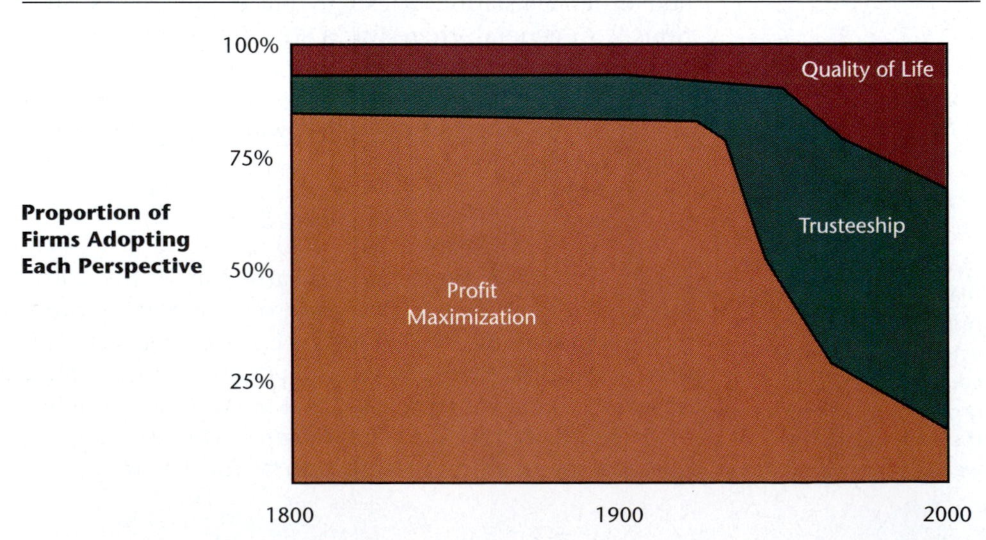

TABLE 3-1 Comparison of Managerial Values

Profit Maximization Management	Trusteeship Management	Quality-of-Life Management
Economic Values		
1. Raw self-interest	1. Self-interest 2. Contributor's interest	1. Enlightened self-interest 2. Contributors' interests 3. Society's interests
What's good for me is good for my country.	What's good for GM is good for our country.	What is good for society is good for our company.
Profit maximizer	Profit satisfier*	Profit is necessary, but . . .
Money and wealth are most important.	Money is important, but so are people.	People are more important than money.
Let the buyer beware. (*caveat emptor*)	Let us not cheat the customer.	Let the seller beware. (*caveat venditor*)
Labor is a commodity to be bought and sold.	Labor has certain rights, which must be recognized.	Employee dignity has to be satisfied.
Accountability of management is to the owners.	Accountability of management is to the owners, customers, employees, suppliers, and other contributors.	Accountability of management is to the owners, contributors, and society.
Technology Values		
Technology is very important.	Technology is important but so are people.	People are more important than technology.
Social Values		
Employee personal problems must be left at home.	We recognize that employees have needs beyond their economic needs.	We hire the whole person.
I am a rugged individualist, and I will manage my business as I please.	I am an individualist, but I recognize the value of group participation.	Group participation is fundamental to our success.
Political Values		
That government is best which governs least.	Government is a necessary evil.	Business and government must cooperate to solve society's problems.
Environmental Values		
The natural environment controls the destiny of humankind.	Human beings can control and manipulate the environment.	We must preserve the environment in order to lead a quality life.
Esthetic Values		
Esthetic values? What are they?	Esthetic values are okay, but not for us.	We must preserve our esthetic values, and we will do our part.

* *Profit satisfier* means generating a satisfactory return.

Source: Adapted from R. Hay and E. Gray. 1974. Social responsibilities of business managers. *Academy of Management Journal* 17:142.

our first responsibility is to the doctors, nurses and patients, to mothers and fathers and all others who use our products and services. . . . We are responsible to our employees, the men and women who work with us throughout the world. . . . We are responsible to the communities in which we live and work and to the world community as well. . . . Our final responsibility is to our stockholders. . . . "[21]

Johnson & Johnson's credo reflects a relatively new concept—that there are a variety of individuals and groups who are organizational stakeholders. These individuals, both inside and outside the organization, have a direct interest in the organization (see Figure 3-2). The large number of stakeholders complicates management's social responsibility. An organization should be responsive to everyone; but there are many groups, each with its own particular set of needs, and these needs can, and often do, conflict. How, for example, can an organization meet the needs and interests of its investors, while simultaneously meeting its community's needs for money to build a new library?

social audit a detailed examination and evaluation of an organization's social performance

One way in which organizations can identify and communicate issues of public interest to both internal and external stakeholders is through a social audit. A **social audit** is a detailed examination and evaluation of an organization's social performance.[22] A thorough social audit involves sophisticated strategic planning and evaluation. Figure 3-3 shows the audit process followed by some organizations.

FIGURE 3-2 Organizational Stakeholders

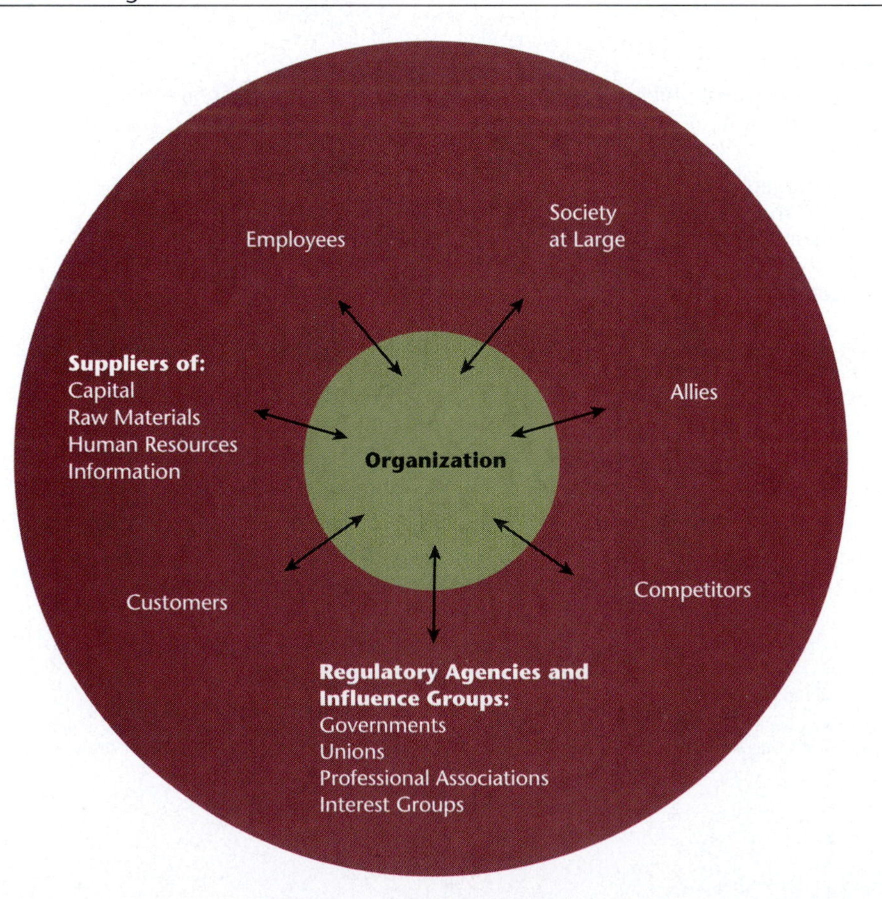

FIGURE 3-3 The Social Audit

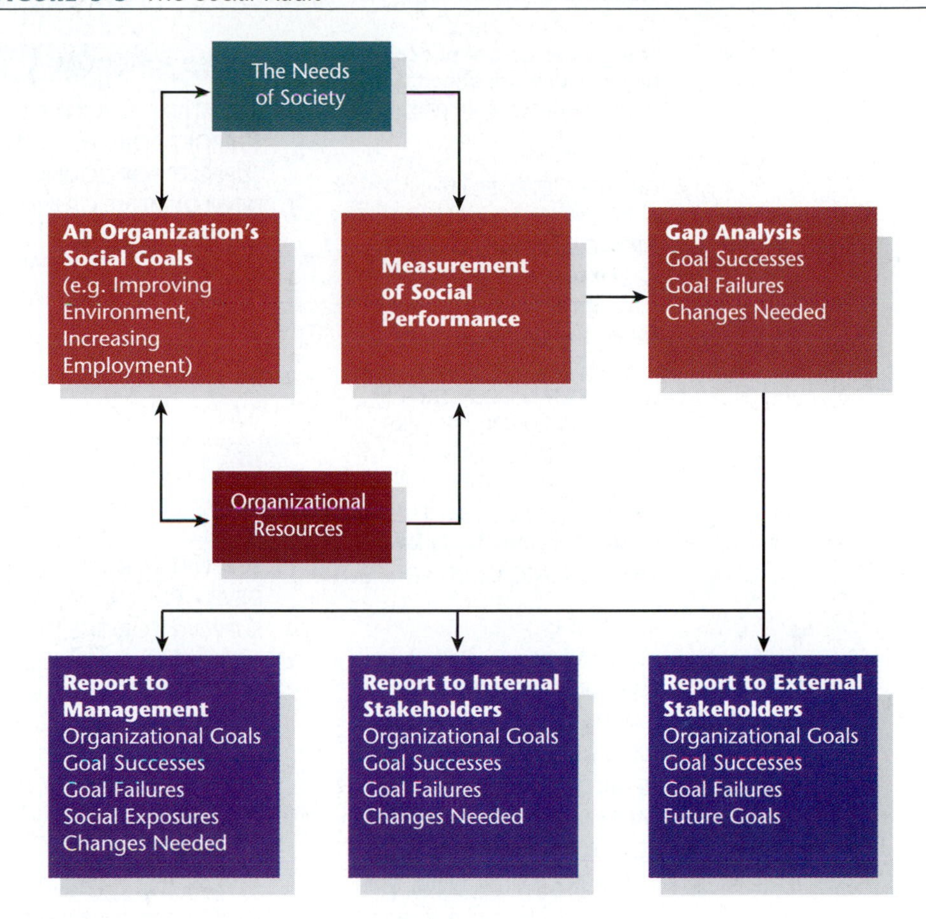

The majority of the top 500 corporations in the United States include information about their social performance in their annual reports. *Triple-bottom-line reporting* is an attempt to make public information on the organization's financial, social, and ethical performance. As early as the mid-1970s, the National Aeronautics and Space Administration (NASA) issued "spinoff" reports that detail the many ways in which technology developed by NASA has been applied to nonaerospace uses. Inspection of Grand Metropolitan's annual report (see Table 3-2) shows the scope of their community involvement in such areas as inner-city regeneration, support for the disabled and young, education, and arts and culture.[23] Today, public accounting firms are getting into the business of preparing social and ethical audits. The Environmental Services Group for Ernst & Young, a large public accounting firm, has conducted a detailed inspection of BP Amoco's operations on the Alaskan oil fields at Prudhoe Bay. The results of this inspection went into BP Amoco's annual report describing the company's environmental behavior for the public.[24]

http://www.nasa.gov

http://www.ey.com

http://www.bpamoco.com

Levels and Types of Social Commitment

What makes managers in some organizations respond so vigorously to social issues, while others seem to do only what the law forces them to do? The intensity with which managers involve their organization in social issues varies

TABLE 3-2 Community Activities for Grand Metropolitan Corporation

The greater part of our community activities are undertaken by the following companies:	
In the UK:	**UNITED KINGDOM**
GRAND METROPOLITAN BREWING (London)	INITIATIVES FOR INNER CITY REGENERATION
GRAND METROPOLITAN COMMUNITY SERVICES (Brighton)	SUPPORT FOR THE DISABLED
GRAND METROPOLITAN ESTATES (Uxbridge)	SUPPORT FOR YOUNG PEOPLE
GRAND METROPOLITAN FOODS EUROPE (Ruislip)	DEVELOPMENT OF INDUSTRY AND EDUCATION LINKS
GRAND METROPOLITAN RETAILING (Uxbridge)	GRAND METROPOLITAN CHARITABLE TRUST
INTERNATIONAL DISTILLERS AND VINTNERS (Harlow)	GRAND METROPOLITAN COMMUNITY SERVICES TRUST
THE DOMINIC GROUP (Harlow)	OTHER INITIATIVES
In the USA:	**USA**
ALPO (Allentown, Pa.)	INITIATIVES FOR YOUTH AND CHILDREN IN NEED
BURGER KING (Miami, Fl.)	SUPPORT FOR THE DISABLED
CARILLON (Teaneck, NJ.)	DEVELOPMENT OF EDUCATION PROGRAMMES
HÄAGEN-DAZS (Teaneck, NJ.)	SUPPORT FOR THE DISADVANTAGED
HEUBLEIN (Farmington, Ct.)	EMPLOYMENT VOLUNTEERISM, ARTS & CULTURE
PADDINGTON (Fort Lee, NJ.)	
PEARLE (Dallas, Tx.)	
PILLSBURY (Minneapolis, Mn.)	

Source: Grand Metropolitan Annual Report—Partnership with the Community. 1999, p. 2.

according to the principles that motivate them (see Table 3.3).[25] At the lowest level of social commitment are the organizations whose managers adhere to the principle of *social obligation.* These managers confine their responses to social issues to those mandated by prevailing laws and the operation of the economic system. They engage in philanthropic acts only when they believe their organization will benefit directly from them. Social contributions are viewed as the responsibility of individuals and not of an organization. Such organizations might adhere to the letter of federal and local environmental protection laws, yet willingly allow pollution when no legal punishment is likely.

At an intermediate level of commitment are organizations who are *socially responsible;* their managers go beyond merely fulfilling their social obligations. Their approach to social responsibility acknowledges the importance of ethical and socially responsible behaviors. Thus, these managers voluntarily pursue their social responsibilities. They recognize that laws often change more slowly than society's expectations, and they try to make their actions keep pace with social norms, values, and expectations of performance.[26] Frequently seen as "good corporate citizens," socially responsible organizations are willing to assume a

TABLE 3-3 Levels of Social Commitment

Social Obligation	Social Responsibility	Social Responsiveness
Low →		*High*
Reactive	Prescriptive	Proactive
Proscriptive*	Does more than required by law	Anticipates and prevents problems
Adheres to legal requirements	Does more than required by economic considerations	Searches for socially responsible acts
Adheres to economic considerations	Avoids public stands on issues	Takes public stands on issues

*Proscriptive means the firm reacts when its action is called (or threatened to be called) to the public's attention.

broader responsibility than that prescribed by law and economic requirements. For example, these organizations are likely to take steps to reduce pollution if they consider certain levels to be dangerous, even if these levels are acceptable by legal standards.

At the highest level of social commitment are organizations whose managers are *socially responsive*. Managers in socially responsive organizations are proactive (leaders) in their dealing with social issues. They attempt to anticipate social issues. Organizations in this category, for example, take the lead in adopting new processes to protect the environment. 3M, for example, formalized their commitment to environmental issues in a strategic policy statement to (a) prevent pollution at the source, whenever possible; (b) solve its own pollution and conservation problems beyond compliance requirements; (c) assist regulatory and government agencies concerned with environmental activities; and (d) develop products that have a minimal negative effect on the environment.[27] Minnesota Power, a major electrical utility company located in northern Minnesota, like many other "environmentally conscious" organizations, has articulated its commitment to the natural environment. Its Environmental Ethics statement is shown in Figure 3-4.

http://www.mmm.com

http://www.minnesotapower.com

How do organizations in the United States measure up when they are rated on these criteria? Although organizations are still driven by the principle of social obligation, since the 1950s many have demonstrated a growing social consciousness. More and more are adopting attitudes of social responsibility and social responsiveness.[28] Some of the most visible initiatives in recent years relate to environmental issues and the conduct of *green business*. Johnson & Johnson has one of the longest-standing commitments to social responsibility in environmentalism. During the 1940s, its Credo stated, "We must maintain in good order the property we are privileged to use," which was revised in 1979 to also read "protecting the environment and natural resources." Part of this commitment is reflected by their creation of the position of Vice President for Worldwide Environmental Affairs.[29]

Discussions of social responsibility must also acknowledge the fact that some firms take an *obstructionist* approach to social responsibility. Obstructionist

FIGURE 3-4 Minnesota Power's Environmental Ethic

Recognizing that all human activities affect the natural environment, the people of Minnesota Power are sensitive to the environmental effects of our conduct as individuals and collectively as a company.

We will be leaders in environmental stewardship. And, consistent with public policy, we will:

- Meet or surpass all environmental compliance criteria.
- Seek and adopt safeguards to prevent injury to the environment, and be prepared to respond quickly should an accident occur.
- Promote land, air, water and energy conservation by encouraging customers and employees to use our products and services efficiently.
- Solicit public and regulatory agency views about environmental concerns and company activities.

In addition, we seek ways to:

- Reduce adverse environmental impacts of our activities.
- Prevent waste by stressing efficiency, recycling and reduced consumption.
- Enhance the environment as we carry out our responsibilities.
- Demonstrate conservation of land, air, water and energy.

ENVIRONMENTAL ETHICS

Source: Minnesota Power—Environmental Ethic, 1998.

managers choose to push the socially irresponsible envelope as far as they can.[30] They consciously engage in questionable and at times illegal acts, in the hope that they won't get caught, and in the hope that if they do get caught, the fine imposed will be less than the benefits incurred. These firms often work to prevent knowledge of their behavior becoming visible. Evidence revealed during the late 1990s suggests that many individuals in the tobacco industry supposedly concealed evidence as to the harmful health risks associated with tobacco.[31] Their "sleight of hand" was revealed during a congressional hearing, when several of the presidents and CEOs from the industry appeared to blatantly lie to Congress when asked if nicotine was addictive—each of them said that they did not believe that it was!

DIVERGING VIEWS ON SOCIAL RESPONSIBILITY

Not everyone agrees that contemporary organizations should be driven by the principles of charity and stewardship. This should not, however, be seen as an argument for obstructionism. Proponents of corporate social responsibility have suggested that firms that take a major role in tackling social issues are good investment risks and will eventually be more profitable than less socially responsive firms.[32] Current research, however, does not show a simple or a consistent relationship between social responsibility and profitability.[33] TIAA/CREF, a teacher retirement organization, reports that the rate of return among their list of "Social Choice" stocks was 10.8 percent for 1999 compared to 21, 36, and 33 percent for their Stock, Global Equity, and Growth accounts, respectively. A look at the research focusing on the relationship between corporate social performance and financial performance reveals a very mixed picture: Some studies report a positive relationship, while others report a negative one.

http://www.tiaacref.com

These mixed findings should not be interpreted as a contradiction, nor are they intended to confuse you. What they tell us is that although socially responsible behavior can favorably impact an organization's bottom line, unfortunately, this is not always the case. At times the financial costs of being socially responsible force firms into an unfavorable financial position versus firms that are not socially responsive.[34] What is not clear from the research at this point is *when* it will be financially profitable to be socially responsible and when it will not. A profitability claim cannot legitimately be used to argue either for or against corporate social responsibility. Other arguments, however, need to be considered.

Arguments for and against Social Responsibility

Those who argue in favor of organizations acting in socially responsible ways offer many reasons. Among them:

- The assumption of social responsibility balances corporate power with corporate responsibilities.
- The voluntary assumption of social responsibility discourages the creation and imposition of government regulations.
- Acts of social responsibility by organizations help correct the social problems (such as air and water pollution) that organizations create.
- Organizations, as members of society, have a moral obligation to help society deal with its problems and to contribute to its welfare.[35]

Sociologists have suggested that, because society has many needs, an organization can be categorized according to (1) the needs it fulfills and (2) the benefits that society derives from the organization's existence.[36] Critics of corporate social responsibility have, in essence, used the sociologists' analysis to propose that each type of organization in society should specialize. In their view, corporations exist solely to provide goods and services and to earn profits. Thus, curing society's social ills becomes the responsibility of other organizations, including governmental and charitable organizations. Among the major arguments against corporate social responsibility are

- The costs of socially responsible behavior lower a corporation's operating efficiency and thus weaken its ability to offer goods and services at the lowest possible competitive cost.
- The costs of socially responsible behavior are often passed along in the form of lower dividends to stockholders, lower wages for employees, or higher prices for consumers.
- Accepting social responsibility sends mixed signals about an organization's goals to both organization and community members. Organization members may have difficulty meeting goals if they do not know whether their primary mission is to make a profit or to act responsibly. Community members may develop unrealistic expectations that the organization is unable to fulfill. For example, expecting an organization to keep a plant open to protect jobs in the community, even when the plant becomes unprofitable, may be asking too much of the organization.
- By assuming social responsibilities, corporations would become even more powerful, and many already exercise too much power over society.
- Business people are trained in such areas as marketing, finance, and manufacturing, not in how to deal with social problems.[37]

These arguments for and against corporate social responsibility have led to the emergence of two distinct sides in the social responsibility debate.

An Argument Against Economist Milton Friedman, while at the University of Chicago, argued that managers should not be required to earn profits for business owners while simultaneously trying to enhance societal welfare.[38] In his view, these two goals are incompatible and will lead to the demise of business as we know it. Friedman has also suggested that forcing organizations to engage in socially responsible behavior may be unethical, because it requires managers to spend money that belongs to other individuals—money that otherwise would be returned to stakeholders in the form of higher dividends, wages, and the like.

An Argument in Favor Keith Davis, professor emeritus of management at Arizona State University, provides another perspective on corporate social responsibility.[39] To him, organizations are members of society. Because they take resources from society for their own use, they have a responsibility to return to society a value for those resources. Society should be able to determine the nature of the value to be returned and to expect organizations to assist in solving social problems. After all, organizations are social instruments that exist and operate at the discretion of society.

Corporate America's Recent Past

Given the many arguments both for and against corporate involvement in addressing the needs of society, it seems appropriate to ask, "How socially responsible is corporate America?" While this is both an important and interesting question, it is not an easy one to answer, as no single and simple barometer is used to measure the social responsiveness of the business community. On a yearly basis, *Fortune* magazine publishes its "the world's most admired companies" list. The results of a survey of executives and analysts for 1999 saw

http://www.fortune.com

http://www.intel.com
http://www.homedepot.com

General Electric, for the second year in a row, rated as the world's most admired organization, followed by Microsoft, Coca-Cola, Intel, Berkshire Hathaway, and IBM. IBM, Procter & Gamble, and Home Depot were judged to be the most socially and environmentally responsible enterprises in the world.[40]

Surveys report that during the 1970s organizations did begin to become socially responsive (Figure 3.5 represents data gathered from a management survey measuring the growth in attention to social issues),[41] and that by the end of the 20th century "Many of the changes that were anticipated in the Sixties and Seventies have in fact taken place. . . ."[42]

A survey of CEOs and college business school deans during the mid-1980s provides us with another glimpse into this question. Responses suggest that many consider it important that today's corporations take an active role in solving social problems.[43] The study also shows that both CEOs and business school deans believe that business support of corporate involvement in addressing social problems has increased (see Tables 3.4 and 3.5).

The Role of Corporate Boards

The role of the corporate board of directors is also a potentially important one when it comes to organizations meeting their legal and social responsibilities. Yet there are questions about the role that should be played by the board and issues surrounding its composition. It has been argued that most corporate boards of directors have done an inadequate job of monitoring the social responsibility of managerial decisions and behaviors. As Harold Geneene, past

FIGURE 3-5 The Growth of Attention to Social Issues

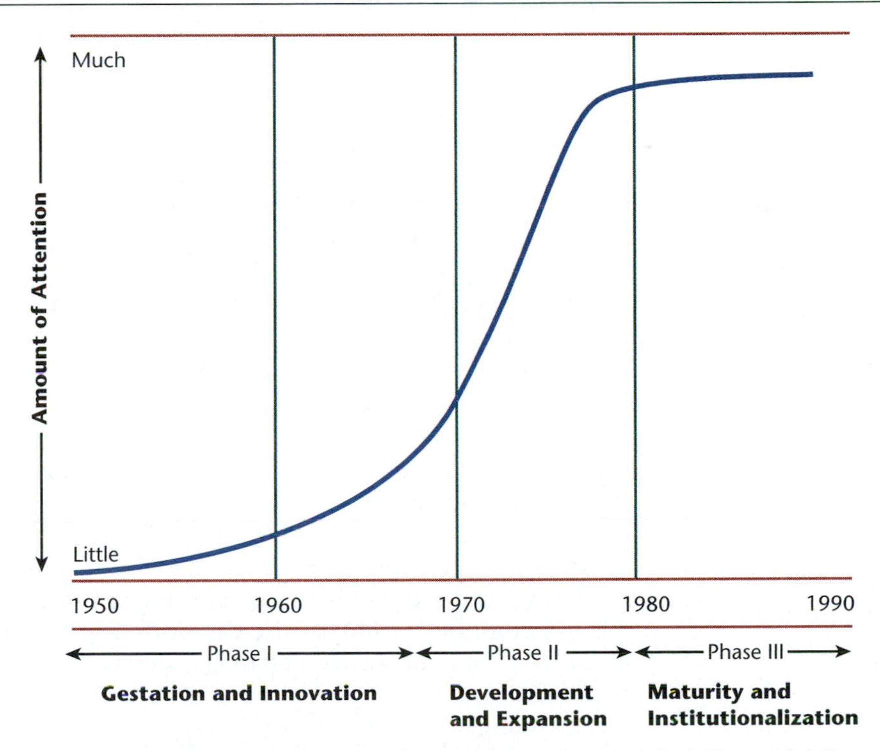

Source: L. E. Preston. 1986. Social issues in management: An evolutionary perspective. In D. A. Wren and J. A. Pearce (eds.), *Papers dedicated to the development of modern management.* Chicago: Academy of Management, 52. Copyright 1986 by Academy of Management. Reproduced with permission of Academy of Management in the format Textbook via Copyright Clearance Center.

TABLE 3-4 Agreement with Statements for Corporate Acceptance of Social Responsibility

Statements	Total % of Respondents Who Agree Strongly and Mildly Agree	
	CEOs	Deans
Reponsible corporate behavior can be in the best economic interest of the stockholders.	92.2%	90.1%
Efficient production of goods and services is no longer the only thing society expects from business.	88.8	92.1
Long-run success of business depends on its ability to understand that it is part of a larger society and to behave accordingly.	87.0	86.1
Involvement by business in improving its community's quality of life will also improve long run profitability.	78.4	75.7
A business that wishes to capture a favorable public image will have to show that it is socially responsible.	77.6	76.2
Social problems, such as pollution control, sometimes can be solved in ways that produce profits from the problem solution.	71.9	75.6
If business is more socially responsible, it will discourage additional regulation of the economic system by government.	70.7	68.3
If business delays dealing with social problems now, it may find itself increasingly occupied with bigger social issues later such that it will be unable to perform its primary business tasks.	55.2	57.4
The idea of social responsibility is needed to balance corporate power and discourage irresponsible behavior.	36.5	55.0
Other social institutions have failed in solving social problems so business should try.	27.8	32.3
Since businesses have such a substantial amount of society's managerial and financial resources, they should be expected to solve social problems.	16.6	31.8

Source: R. Ford and F. McLaughlin. 1984. Perceptions of socially responsible activities and attitudes: A comparison of business school deans and corporate chief executives. *Academy of Management Journal* 27:670. Copyright 1984 by Academy of Management. Reproduced with permission of Academy of Management in the format Textbook via Copyright Clearance Center.

president of International Telephone and Telegraph, commented, "The boards of directors of U.S. industry include numerous first-rate people doing what amounts to a second-rate job."[44] Others have argued that the design of a board restricts the independence of its members and basically renders them ineffective in their monitoring role.[45]

One solution might lie in inviting people outside an organization to become board members.[46] Outsiders give a board a broader base of power and knowledge and enable it to become more independent and, therefore, better able to monitor objectively the decisions and actions taken by management.[47] In spite of these potential advantages, today a large number of U.S. firms allow their CEO to chair their board of directors as well.[48] This situation presents certain dangers.[49] On the one hand, a CEO makes strategic decisions for an organization. On the other hand, a board of directors sits in judgment of management. For one person to assume both roles raises serious questions about conflicts of interest. In an effort to reduce the number of illegal and irrespon-

TABLE 3-5 Disagreement with Statements Against Corporate Acceptance of Social Responsibility

Statements	Total % of Respondents Who Mildly Disagree and Disagree Strongly	
	CEOs	Deans
Business already has too much social power and should not engage in social activities that might give it more.	77.0%	73.1%
If business does become socially involved, it will create so much friction among dissident parties that it will be unable to perform its economic mission.	69.3	77.2
A firm that ignores social responsibility can obtain a competitive advantage over a firm that does not.	69.3	44.1
Involvement in socially responsible activities threatens business by diverting time and money away from its primary business purpose.	68.1	60.9
It is unwise to allow business to participate in social activities where there is no direct way to hold it accountable for its actions.	67.6	67.0
Business is most socially responsive when it attends strictly to its economic interests and leaves social activities to social institutions.	64.7	57.4
Business leaders are trained to manage economic institutions and not to work effectively on social issues.	60.5	49.5
Business will become uncompetitive if it commits many economic resources to social responsibility.	49.1	47.3
If social programs add to business costs it will make business uncompetitive in international trade.	44.7	33.8
Business will participate more actively in social responsibility in prosperous economic times than in recession.	24.6	9.0
Consumers and the general public will bear the costs of business social involvement because businesses will pass these costs along through their pricing structure.	15.8	5.0

Source: R. Ford and F. McLaughlin. 1984. Perceptions of socially responsible activities and attitudes: A comparison of business school deans and corporate chief executives. *Academy of Management Journal* 27:671. Copyright 1984 by Academy of Management. Reproduced with permission of Academy of Management in the format Textbook via Copyright Clearance Center.

sible acts committed by corporations, critics have argued that boards should be made up of men and women who are not members of management.

Although the arguments for outsiders sitting on boards are strong, the existing (although limited) evidence shows no significant relationship between the number of insiders on boards and corporate involvement in illegal acts.[50] Perhaps insiders are simply more effective at concealing illegal activities. At any rate, it still appears likely that responsible behavior is encouraged by outside members who feel free to ask hard questions without worrying whether it will affect their jobs or working relationships.

In sum, to act in a socially responsible way requires managers to consider the effect of their decisions on the well-being of society; thus, managers must ask themselves what their actions do *to* society and what their actions do *for* society. When similar considerations are made at a personal level, managers must rely on their ethics to help them choose an appropriate course of action.

THE NATURE OF MANAGERIAL ETHICS

ethics the set of standards and code of conduct that defines what is right, wrong, and just in human actions

Ethics is the set of standards and code of conduct that defines what is right, wrong, and just in human actions. Ethics, therefore, serve to help us answer the question, What is "the right thing to do"? Managers' decisions and actions affect the health, safety, morale, motivation, and behavior of all organization members, as well as many stakeholders outside of the organization. Plant closings following large pay increases for high-level executives at General Motors and withholding of important information about the O-rings on the space shuttle *Challenger* (which resulted in the death of the entire crew)—these both raise the ethics question—What is the right thing to do, and how do we decide?

Unfortunately, ethical issues don't often fall into tidy categories of right and wrong (see *An Inside Look*). Attempts to do what is ethical can be complex, revealing that there are varying degrees of rightness and wrongness: What standards are to be applied? Whose standards are to be applied? Which ethical theory should guide this judgment?[51] Suppose, for example, that two students miss passing their organizational behavior course by only five points. The first student wants the professor to adjust his grade in exchange for sexual favors. The second student wants the professor to adjust her grade because her grandmother died during the semester and she received passing grades on all exams except the one that she took the day after the funeral. Most people would agree that the professor who agrees to adjust the first student's grade is acting unethically. The second student's case is not so clear-cut. Behaving ethically often involves more than just helping others and behaving honestly.

Ethical considerations, like considerations of social responsibility, are influenced by existing social values, norms, and mores. The two are also similar in that both revolve around concerns for the well-being of others; however, ethical considerations differ from those of social responsibility in certain ways. Ethical judgments are based on personal values that have been learned over a number of years. They usually are involved in situations that do not influence society as a whole. Frequently, in fact, ethical judgments affect only one person, the people in a manager's organization, or an organization's stakeholders, rather than society as a whole. Ethics usually involve one person's judgment and behavior; social responsibility usually involves those of entire organizations. In short, ethics are primarily a personal issue; social responsibility is more an organizational issue.

Sources of Ethics

People in all societies create standards and codes of conduct to govern their dealings with one another, but not all societies define right, wrong, and just in terms of the same behaviors. In the United States, for example, kickbacks to purchasing agents generally are considered unethical. In some countries, however, kickbacks are an accepted business custom. According to sociologist Talcott Parsons, all societies need to maintain patterns of stability and continuity to pass on their culture from one generation to the next.[52] This need is fulfilled by religious, educational, and cultural organizations, as well as by the family unit. Organizations and families teach social values and norms through the process of **socialization.** Societies have beliefs about what is right, wrong, and just. Through the socialization process, new members of the society adopt at

socialization the process through which people develop beliefs about what is right, wrong, and just

AN INSIDE LOOK

Integrity in the Workplace

- Is it wrong to use the office computer for Internet shopping?
- Is it wrong to use an office envelope to mail a personal bill?
- Is it wrong to read a confidential memo addressed to someone else?
- Is it wrong to accept a monetary gift from your boss?
- Is it wrong to accept a monetary gift from a client?

Are there black-and-white answers to these questions? Most companies would agree that while there are no "right" or "wrong" answers, there are preferred office ethics to which employees are expected to adhere. Modern organizations are discovering that employees do not instinctively know the preferred answers. As a result, companies are becoming more proactive in training employees in workplace ethics.

Lockheed Martin, for example, has a virtual ethics training session called "Ethics Challenge" to help their employees develop a sense of right and wrong in the workplace. Employees take a series of online quizzes that cover topics such as insider trading, kickbacks, and sexual harassment. The Ethics Challenge must be taken by each employee at least once a year to ensure continuous ethical development. Lockheed Martin uses "Ethics Challenge" as a preventive measure: Not only does it train employees on important issues before they arise, but it also protects the company in case of lawsuits filed by employees dismissed on ethics violations.

In recent years, many companies have instituted ethics hot lines or ethics officers. These resources help employees facing difficult situations understand the potential consequences of their actions and develop an appropriate response. However companies address the issue of ethics, many see the wisdom of educating employees to prevent problems before they arise.

Source: Adapted from M. J. McCarthy. October 21, 1999. How one firm tracks ethics electronically. *The Wall Street Journal,* B, 1–5.

least some of the values, norms, and mores of that society and develop a definition of ethical conduct.

Moral Development

While people develop their ethical values from societal values, there are stages in an individual's *moral development*. Different theories of ethics, and two models in particular, address the moral development of the individual; these are the *ethic of care* and the *ethic of justice* model.[53] The ethic of care model judges an act as ethical depending on whether the act derives from feelings, emotions, and empathy for others. The ethic of justice model, on the other hand, uses abstract rules to define which actions are fair and which actions are not.

Both models highlight the stages that the individual passes through in moral development. The ethic of care model starts with a focus on the self (a stage commonly seen in young children), which is followed by a move away from the self focus and toward a focus on others and personal relationships. If an individual reaches the mature stage of development, they are characterized by a reflective understanding and caring for others.

The ethic of justice model also commences with self-centeredness, while at the mature stage the person has developed a set of principles that guide behavior. At this stage of moral development, the individual is assumed to be free and their behaviors guided by personally chosen moral principles, also referred to as ethical standards.

Several sets of moral principles have evolved in the Western society. For example, utilitarian theory, rights theory, and theory of justice, which we discuss later in this chapter, set out guidelines (standards) that define or promote ethical behavior.

Managerial Ethics

Managerial ethics are not fundamentally different from other ethics; usually they are only a matter of applying personal ethics within the context of the management of organizations. What are a manager's ethical responsibilities? Managers are responsible for the decisions and actions they take on their own initiative. They also are ethically responsible for actions that they take at the direction of another. In other words, managers are not relieved of ethical responsibility just because their boss "ordered" them to behave unethically. Managers who must choose whether to behave unethically or lose their job face painful decisions, but the ethical choice is to lose the job. (If you are placed in a situation in which you must either cheat on an exam or fail a course, you are behaving unethically if you cheat, regardless of the consequences.)

Managers also are ethically responsible for the behavior of subordinates who are following their instructions. If managers tell subordinates to behave in a manner that the managers consider unethical, the managers are responsible for the subordinates' unethical behavior. Managers are equally responsible if they instruct subordinates to behave in a manner that the subordinates consider unethical. Managers are even ethically responsible when they fail to act, if their inaction allows unethical behavior to occur. They are also responsible if the organizational policies, practices, and structures they create lead to unethical behavior.

An Organization's Responsibility

The preceding discussion makes it sound as if managers are ethically responsible for everything that happens inside organizations. In fact, some people argue that the "real role of the chief executive is to manage the values of the organization."[54] Top managers, with their key organizational roles and formal authority, can and should infuse a sense of moral reasoning and ethically guided decisions and behavior into their organization's culture. By being good role models, by reinforcing ethical behavior and punishing unethical behavior, and by making explicit what ethical conduct is, top managers help ensure that the expectation of ethical behavior, as well as ethical behavior itself, permeates the organizational culture.[55] In fact, research has shown that unethical behavior can be reduced through steps as simple as issuing organizational statements that support ethical behavior, establishing an ethical code of conduct, and making ethical behavior a part of the organization's "way of doing business." Minnesota Power distributes a booklet to all of its employees that details "Ethical Standards—The Minnesota Power Way." Noting that ethics is everyone's responsibility, the firm sets forth its beliefs and expectations in relation to several areas of business activity (for example, fairness and relations with individuals and groups both inside and outside of the organization, gifts and favors, expense accounts, use of company property, drug and alcohol use, political processes).

Of course, top management is not exclusively responsible for instilling and enacting ethical behavior. Every organizational member carries the values, norms, and mores of society into the organization. With this comes responsibility for personal conduct. The responsibility for moral reasoning and ethical conduct falls on each member. With this in mind, some organizations encourage their members to report unethical behavior. The term **whistleblowing** refers to a member's disclosure that someone within the organization has engaged in an illegal, immoral, unethical, or illegitimate act.[56] Traditionally, whistleblowing has been discouraged both by group norms and by company practice, but today more and more organizations are actively encouraging such action, because it is the responsible thing to do.

whistleblowing
a member's disclosure that someone within the organization has engaged in an illegal, immoral, unethical, or illegitimate act

In order to persuade employees to blow the whistle inside an organization rather than to the press or to regulatory agencies, many organizations have set up systems to handle internal complaints.[57] When surveyed about corporate ethics, over 70 percent of the U.S. corporations responding said that they had written codes of conduct, and over 35 percent had formal training programs encouraging ethical behavior.[58] Some companies, such as General Dynamics, have an ombudsperson, whose job includes soliciting and dealing with whistleblowing in-house. Control Data Corporation's Finance Committee has assigned a member the role of "ethics advocate," with the responsibility to push the group with the question, Is this the right thing to do? Unfortunately, whistleblowing can be a risky act in some organizations. Recently, individuals working for the Alaskan pipeline have warned of serious problems and the potential for a major environmental disaster at the Port of Prince William Sound, only to experience threats of personal violence from company officials.

http://www.gd.com

ETHICAL AND UNETHICAL MANAGERIAL BEHAVIOR

> It has always been the policy and practice of the Company [Johnson & Johnson] to conduct its affairs ethically and in a socially responsible manner. This responsibility is characterized and reflected in the Company's Credo and Policy on Business Conduct which are distributed throughout the Company. Management maintains a systematic program to ensure compliance with these policies.[59]

http://www.dupont.com

> The company's [DuPont] business ethics policy is the cornerstone of our internal control system. This policy sets forth management's commitment to conduct business worldwide with the highest ethical standards and in conformity with applicable laws.[60]

http://www.pepsico.com

> We're [Pepsico] committed to being environmentally responsible and to minimizing the impact of our businesses on the Earth. We encourage conservation, recycling and energy use programs that promote clean air and water and reduce landfill.[61]

These excerpts from corporate annual reports illustrate that some organizations attempt to make ethics an integral part of the organization's culture and control systems. It is also quite easy to confirm that ethical behavior does not characterize the actions of all managers and their organizations.

Surveys reveal that the public does not view business executives as among society's ethical leaders. It has been said that business ethics is an oxymoron, to which many managers counter—good ethics is good business. In the public's eye, business executives don't stack up all that well. A recent survey ranked executives in the middle of the pack, with only a 20 percent endorsement, when compared with other professional groups.[62] Observations of widespread illegality, unethical behavior, and cynicism have led two professors of managerial values to conclude that it is important to keep a "continual vigilance . . . focusing attention on values and ethical behavior."[63] It is concerns of this nature that have led to the emergence of organizations like London's Institute of Social and Ethical AccountAbility and their efforts to establish standards for ethical and social behavior and the public accounting of behavior along both of these lines.[64]

http://www.accountability.org.uk

Influences on Unethical Behavior

Why do managers choose to behave unethically? Sometimes they behave unethically simply because they don't take the time to think about the implications of their behavior. Managers are commonly overworked and highly stressed. Under these conditions, people sometimes do things they later regret. Managers sometimes behave unethically for other reasons. The behavior of one's supervisors is one of the strongest influences on employees and the ethical or unethical decisions that they make.[65]

Personality characteristics also appear to influence unethical behavior.[66] Persons most likely to behave unethically are those who believe that the ends justify the means; things that happen are due to luck or chance, not to their actions; and economic and political values are of great importance. In a later chapter on personality, we discuss several traits that appear to make some people less ethical than others. For example, people who rate low on conscientiousness are more likely to steal from their employers than people who rate high on this personality dimension. It has also been shown that people placed in competitive situations are more likely to behave unethically.

As shown in Figure 3-6, rewards and punishments are among the most powerful determinants of ethical and unethical behavior. People who are rewarded for unethical behavior (such as receiving a pay increase for providing a kickback to a customer) are much more likely to behave unethically than those who are punished for unethical behavior—people, after all, generally do that for which they are rewarded. Punishing unethical behavior frequently leads to

FIGURE 3-6 The Impact of Rewards and Punishment on Unethical Behavior

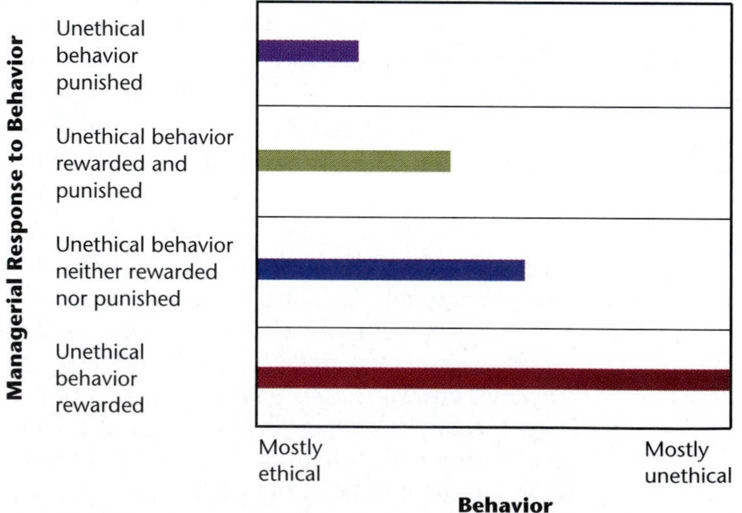

Source: W. H. Hegarty and H. P. Sims, Jr. 1979. Organizational philosophy, policies, and objectives related to unethical decision behavior: A laboratory experiment. *Journal of Applied Psychology* 64:331–338.

higher levels of ethical behavior. Rewards and punishment probably influence the ethics of behavior both because rewards increase the likelihood that behavior will be repeated and punishment decreases the likelihood of repetition, and because they call attention to the potentially unethical behavior.

Ethical Standards and a Manager's Dilemma

An independent set of standards does not exist for ethical behavior in organizations. Ethics for organizations derive from the ethics of the society within which they exist. Thus, societal standards are the ultimate guides for managers. When managers confront an ethically difficult decision, they should consider how societal standards apply to their situation and should try to incorporate the most relevant ones within their moral reasoning.[67]

utilitarian theory concentrates on social consequences; an action is considered morally right if its consequences for everyone affected by the action are greater than those which would be realized by a different action

rights theory concentrates on respecting the rights to which people are entitled (e.g., the right to privacy)

theory of justice emphasizes engaging in acts that are fair and impartial

procedural justice while the outcomes to all may not be equal, the procedures employed to make outcome allocations are experienced (perceived) as fair

Managers can look to several theories to guide their decision making. **Utilitarian theory** concentrates on the social consequences that an action is likely to produce.[68] An action is considered morally right if its consequences for everyone affected by the action are greater than those which would be realized by a different action. Labor unions often negotiate across-the-board pay raises for the employees that they represent. Everyone gets the same pay increases in such situations. This is despite the fact that some employees perform at higher levels than others, and perhaps deserve a larger pay increase. Unions resist this notion, because they believe they can maximize the total return to all members by focusing on the size of the increase for everyone, not just a few. In **rights theory**, decision makers are concerned with respecting the rights to which people are entitled—these may be legal rights or moral rights. In the United States, these rights include the right of free consent, the right to privacy, the right to freedom of conscience, the right to free speech, and the right to due process. Managers operating under a rights theory would not prohibit organizational members from speaking in favor of a gay rights bill, endorsing gay partner benefits, or participating in a same-sex marriage. Managers who subscribe to the **theory of justice** emphasize engaging in acts that are fair and impartial. They would not consider a managerial action as just if it benefited some, while resulting in an injustice to others. Managers operating under a theory of justice try to prevent their subordinates from feeling as if they have been cheated. For example, they make their expectations for performance clear to everyone, and then reward most those employees who have met or exceeded those expectations. Everyone may not get a large pay increase, but they understand how the pay increases were determined. This is what researchers in organizational behavior call **procedural justice**.[69] See Table 3.6 for an analysis of several ethical standards.

The suggestion that managers should consider the social consequences, the rights of others, and other ethical standards when making decisions sounds reasonable; however, doing so will not prevent managers from encountering *ethical dilemmas* from time to time. Consider, for example, the dilemma posed by new scientific developments. In one recent case, the Environmental Protection Agency caused public controversy by announcing that it would allow BioTechnica International, Inc., to test genetically altered organisms on a Wisconsin farm.[70] Many European countries prohibit the importation of genetically altered foods into their markets. The dilemma is whether the potential benefit to the human race is greater than the cost and risks associated with releasing genetically altered organisms into the environment. Should the decision favor a new technology or favor minimizing health and safety risks?

TABLE 3-6 Five Major Ethical Systems

	Nature of the Ethical Belief	Problems in the Ethical System
Eternal Law	Moral standards are given in an Eternal Law, which is revealed in Scripture or apparent in nature and then interpreted by religious leaders or humanist philosophers; the belief is that everyone should act in accordance with the interpretation.	There are multiple interpretations of the Law, but no method to choose among them beyond human rationality, and human rationality needs an absolute principle or value as the basis for choice.
Utilitarian Theory	Moral standards are applied to the outcome of an action or decision; the principle is that everyone should act to generate the greatest benefits for the largest number of people.	Immoral acts can be justified if they provide substantial benefits for the majority, even at an unbearable cost or harm to the minority; an additional principle or value is needed to balance the benefit-cost equation.
Universalist Theory	Moral standards are applied to the intent of an action or decision; the principle is that everyone should act to ensure that similar decisions would be reached by others, given similar circumstances.	Immoral acts can be justified by persons who are prone to self-deception or self-importance, and there is no scale to judge between "wills"; an additional principle or value is needed to refine the Categorical Imperative concept.
Distributive Justice	Moral standards are based on the primacy of a single value, which is justice. Everyone should act to ensure a more equitable distribution of benefits, for this promotes individual self-respect, which is essential for social cooperation.	The primacy of the value of justice is dependent on acceptance of the proposition that an equitable distribution of benefits ensures social cooperation.
Personal Liberty	Moral standards are based on the primacy of a single value, which is liberty. Everyone should act to ensure greater freedom of choice, for this promotes market exchange, which is essential for social productivity.	The primacy of the value of liberty is dependent on acceptance of the proposition that a market system of exchange ensures social productivity.

Source: L. Hosmer. 1987. *The ethics of management*. Homewood, IL: Irwin, 106.

Many ethical dilemmas arise when we balance utilitarian and formalistic needs. Managerial decision making in the utilitarian ethic is future oriented. It seeks innovations, encourages new practices, improves techniques, and promotes organizational change as ways to meet organizational goals and the changing needs of the external environment. Decision making in the formalistic ethic is concerned with preserving current definitions of right and just, maintaining tradition, and perpetuating the heritage of an organization and of society. The two-headed Roman god Janus illustrates the dilemma.[71] Janus, the god of gates and entryways, has two heads—one faces forward and one faces backward. The forward-looking face represents the utilitarian ethic, which is future oriented, anticipating opportunities and results. According to this ethic, today's decisions should respond to future social needs and conditions. The god's backward-looking face represents the formalistic ethic concerned with maintaining the cultural heritage established by tradition, language, and law. According to this ethic, today's decisions should conform to and preserve our cultural heritage.

© ARALDO DE LUCA/CORBIS

Janus, the two-headed Roman god, represents the dilemma of balancing a future-oriented (or utilitarian) ethic and a status quo (or formalistic) ethic.

Encouraging Ethical Behavior

What guides managers as they cope with ethical decisions and the dilemmas they pose? It is clear that the individual's standards of right and wrong are not the sole determinant of their decisions.[72] Personal beliefs about right and wrong interact with other individual characteristics (such as locus of control—I shape my own destiny versus my destiny is shaped by forces outside of me) and situational forces (an organization's rewards and punishments and its culture) that shape the ethics of decisions and the resulting behavior. This interactive process is illustrated in Figure 3-7. People sometimes engage in acts they consider unethical when the culture of their organization and its prevailing reward structure overwhelm personal belief systems.

How can organizations guide managers as they cope with ethical decisions and the dilemmas they pose? Organizations can encourage ethical behavior by considering both long- and short-term factors.[73] For the long term, managers should develop their organization's culture so that it supports the learning—and, if necessary, relearning—of personal values that promote ethical behavior. For example, when decisions are made, managers should explicitly and publicly explain the ethical factors that accompany each alternative considered. Managers also should nurture an organizational culture that supports and values ethical behavior—for example, by encouraging organization members to display signs of ethical values through whistleblowing.

To encourage ethical standards in the short term, managers can

- Consider the personality characteristics of people applying to join the organization. Either avoid personalities that are prone to unethical behavior or make sure that policies block unethical tendencies.
- Make public statements that ethical behavior is important and expected.
- Identify and articulate the organization's values and ethical standards by creating a formal **code of ethics**.
- Develop policies that specify ethical objectives.
- Reward ethical behavior and avoid inadvertently rewarding unethical behavior.
- Punish unethical behavior and avoid inadvertently punishing ethical behavior.
- When placing members into competitive situations, be sensitive to the potential for unethical behavior and take appropriate steps to avoid it.[74]
- Remember that when decisions require moral judgment, group decision making generally results in higher levels of moral reasoning than does individual decision making.[75]

code of ethics an organizationally created code used to encourage ethical behavior by all organizational members

FIGURE 3-7 The Interactionist Model of Ethical Decision Making in Organizations

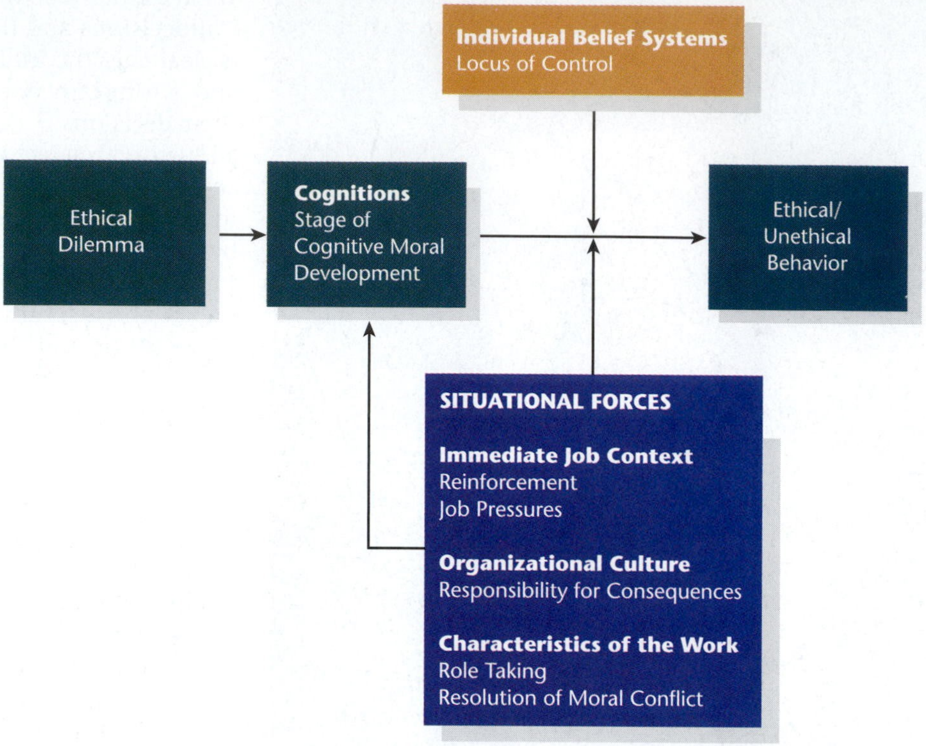

Source: Modified from L. K. Trevino. 1986. Ethical decision making in organizations: A person-situation interactionist model. *Academy of Management Review* 11:603.

Many organizations encourage ethical behavior by creating an *ethical code of conduct.*[76] This naturally raises the question as to their effectiveness at promoting ethical behavior. Popular belief suggests that a "well-written code" can promote ethical behavior. Vague codes are ineffectual. Unfortunately, we don't have a large number of studies that give us answers to the effectiveness question. Some studies indicate that a clear ethics policy deters unethical behavior.[77] However, recent study in the banking industry suggests that while firms with ethical codes of conduct fared better than those without, the differences are not significant.[78] The strongest single influence on employees' behavior is what the "top dogs" do. Do they "walk their talk"? If senior level managers and their staff personnel are seen as valuing and engaging in ethical (unethical) behavior, these actions set the tone for the entire organization.[79] Unfortunately, many organizations who have ventured down the "ethical policy statement and ethical code of conduct road" have "committed to the low-cost, possibly symbolic side of ethics management."[80] In the process they are likely to promote a very weak commitment and compliance to ethical behavior.

moral audit an internal assessment of a firm's moral and ethical conduct

In recognition that an organization's culture is influenced by what flows from the top down, an increasing number of American businesses are investing in ethics programs. Many organizations have *ethics officers,* who are charged with improving the level of ethical decision making by employees. These officers are conducting **moral audits**—an internal assessment of the firm's moral and ethical conduct.[81] One survey found that 78 percent of the participating firms indicated that they had a code of ethics, 51 percent employed the telephone system for reporting ethical concerns, and 30 percent had special offices designated for dealing with ethical complaints.[82] During the 1990s, a professional association, the Ethics Officer Association, emerged with the mission of encouraging dialogue and increasing ethical practices in business organizations. In addition, the *Journal of Business Ethics* is devoted to creating a body of knowledge focused on business ethics.

Does Ethical Behavior Make a Financial Difference?

It is relatively easy to develop the argument that individuals, managers, and organizations should be guided by the "right thing to do" code. It can even be reasoned that the question of "what is the right thing to do" should not be answered from a financial perspective. There have, however, been efforts to look at the relationship between a firm's financial performance and its emphasis on ethics as an aspect of corporate governance.

Recent evidence demonstrates that ethics and financial performance are linked. In a recent study of the 500 largest U.S. public corporations, those that claim a commitment to ethical behavior toward their stakeholders have a better financial performance than those firms that do not.[83] While these results do not demonstrate a causal relationship between ethics and performance, the findings hint at the presence of a relationship between the two.

ETHICS AND THE EMPLOYEE-ORGANIZATION RELATIONSHIP

The human resource model and high-involvement management argues that the individual as an organizational member is a valuable organizational resource, in fact more valuable than the organization's buildings, equipment, and inventories. High-involvement management and the human resource model see the organization's human resource as one of the few resources that grows, develops, and increases in value with the "right use." For example, as people become better informed about the affairs of the organization, they increase in their value to the firm as future decision makers. Thus, effective organizational management calls for the careful, strategic, efficient, and effective utilization of all the organization's resources. If, for example, it makes sense for Bison Transport, a Calgary-based trucking company, to engage in regular maintenance of its fleet of trucks so that they perform well, does it not make sense for the company to invest time and resources in motivating employees to perform well?

http://www.bisontransport.com

As we saw in the last chapter, contributors to the behavioral school of management have endeavored to understand the individual-organization relationship. Managers who use knowledge about human attitudes and motivation to influence behavior that contributes to the organization's functioning need to be sensitive to the ethical nature of their actions.

Classical economics and classical management theory tell us that employees are economically motivated. Knowing that employees have economic needs, should a manager offer economic incentives to encourage employees to come to work and to come to work on time? The Hawthorne studies and the human relations model sensitized us to the idea that social needs motivate behavior in the workplace. Knowing that employees have social needs, should a manager engage in paternalistic management practices to shape employee attitudes and promote job satisfaction so that they will be less likely to seek employment elsewhere? From Maslow we learned that individuals have the need to know and the need to understand. Knowing that employees have these growth needs, should a manager provide employees with opportunities to grow and develop with the belief that this will motivate the employee to higher levels of performance? Knowing that salespeople with a strong need for achievement generally have more job satisfaction and are higher performers, should managers profile job applicants on the strength of their need for achievement to improve the selection process?

In each of these instances, managers consciously use knowledge about personality, employee attitudes, and motivation to influence behavior that serves the organization's needs. Is this ethical? Are they ethical in some instances and not in others? What ethical standards guide the management of the individual-organization relationship? If managers intend no harm to the employee, if their actions produce positive effects for the employee *and* positive effects for the organization—is this ethical behavior?

These are important questions. Throughout this book we offer comments on this delicate balancing act—for example, on management practices and how they influence employee job satisfaction, organizational commitment, and psychological ownership. We will return again and again to the inevitable question: What is the "right" thing to do? Is it ethical for a manager to consciously engage in management practices, design social systems (organizations), and structure the work that people do with an "eye toward" impacting employee motivation, job satisfaction, organizational commitment and identification, work as a central life interest, psychological ownership, work attendance, and performance?

While this is a question that you must ultimately answer for yourselves, we encourage you to develop the habit and to create organizational systems that ask the question—What is the socially responsible and ethical thing to do?—each and every time a decision is made.

With regard to job satisfaction, many different arguments are given as to why job satisfaction is important. Among them, some argue from: (1) A motivational perspective—job satisfaction is important because it impacts employee motivation. (2) A utilitarian perspective—job satisfaction is important because it impacts the organization's bottom line through tardiness, absenteeism, turnover, union activity, and performance. (3) A societal welfare perspective—job satisfaction is important because prolonged job dissatisfaction contributes to poor mental health that carries with it costs to society. (4) An altruistic perspective—job satisfaction is a valued outcome in the lives of people as an end in and of itself. (5) A rights perspective—employees have a right to job satisfaction. Building on the "rights" argument, it is our position that as managers we have no right to make the work lives of those who work for us "miserable"—thus, job dissatisfying. While we are not arguing that it is management's responsibility to create job satisfaction for everyone, we do believe that organizational decision making should, in part, be guided by a concern for the welfare of all organizational members. The managerial compass points "true north" (a metaphor employed here for that which is socially responsible and the right thing to do) when management effectively strives to prevent the onset of job dissatisfaction.

The idea that management should consciously engage in strategies that strengthen employee commitment and loyalty also has ethical implications. We are of the opinion that commitment has a beneficial symmetry relationship. Therefore, ethical management actively commits to employees in the hope that employees will actively commit to the organization. We question the ethicality of consciously attempting to build employee commitment to management and the organization that is greater than the strength of the commitment that the organization is willing to extend to the organizational member.

Thus far, we have addressed only the issues pertaining to job satisfaction/dissatisfaction and commitment. There are many more employee attitudes, motives, and behaviors that managers affect for which a question of ethics arises. What prescriptions can management employ to encourage ethical and socially responsible behavior? In general we encourage the use of what we refer to as a *quality-of-work life barometer.* The quality-of-work life barometer measures whether a managerial/organizational act creates an upward or downward pressure on the organizational member's current quality-of-work life. If an act is anticipated and intended to be neutral or to have a positive impact on the quality-of-work life, it can usually be judged as socially responsible and ethical. If, however, the act is intended or anticipated to lower the quality-of-work life, the act can be judged as socially irresponsible and unethical.

Recognize that virtually every managerial act impacts the attitudes, motivation, and behavior of the members of the organization. It is, in our opinion, better (that is, more ethical and socially responsible) to consciously direct managerial actions toward enhancing of the quality of the organizational member's work life than not. Thus, we believe that so long as the manager's intention is to "do no harm to the employee" and to "try to increase the quality-of-work life," the conscious management of employee work-related attitudes, motivation, and behavior is not an unethical act *per se*.

Implications for Managers

The guidelines for promoting ethical behavior discussed in this chapter are just that—suggestions that may be used to encourage ethical behavior. No one can tell you which one or how many of these guidelines you should adopt. Any decision you make that involves ethics is likely to be based on values you have already embraced and experiences you have already had. Rest assured, as a manager you *will* be asked to make decisions that involve ethics. Some of these decisions will affect only you. Others will affect subordinates, superiors, or even the organization. What, for example, will you do when you encounter organizational policies and practices that you consider inappropriate? Are you willing to blow the whistle on those policies and practices? Are you willing to take a personal stand and perhaps put your own career at risk?

A bank can encounter many ethical issues in the course of safeguarding both money and customer information, as shown in the video *Ethics in Business: Bank of Alma.*

Ethics are rarely clear-cut. Although many behaviors are clearly ethical or unethical, the vast majority of decisions managers make concern "gray" areas. When others cannot agree on whether a particular behavior is ethical, your personal values and the cultural values of an organization come into play. Think about the nature of ethics and the various guidelines discussed in this chapter. Then let your behavior reflect your values.

DIVERSITY—A CONTEMPORARY ISSUE OF ETHICS AND SOCIAL RESPONSIBILITY

A myriad of contemporary ethical and social responsibility issues confront organizations and their members today. Among them are ethics and use of the Internet in general and e-commerce in particular, stewardship of financial resources, environmental stewardship, sweatshops, the exploitation of labor in general and child labor in particular, genetic engineering, the emergence of mega-organizations and the potential reduction of competition in a variety of industries, the "businessization" of health care and education, and issues revolving around diversity in the workplace.

organizational diversity the goal of having a hetereogeneous work group where no one group occupies a majority position, and all members are expected to work effectively with people different from themselves

In the remainder of this chapter, we address issues pertaining to managerial attitudes toward **organizational diversity.** This issue is an extremely important philosophical issue intimately linked to ethics and socially responsive behavior.

One of the most important challenges facing businesses in America today is the changing nature of the workforce.[84] In the last 10 years, the gender and ethnicity of the American workforce has changed. For 300 years, the white male was the "typical" member in our workforce; he now accounts for less than half (approximately 47%) of all workers. It is estimated that by the year 2005, the workforce will be 73 percent white, 12 percent African-American, 11 percent Hispanic, and 4 percent Asian and other minorities.[85] By the middle of the 21st century, whites (males and females) will make up less than half the workforce. In other words, whites will be a minority, along with African-Americans, Hispanics/Latinos, Native Americans, and Asian-Americans. No one group will occupy a majority position.

Compounding this workforce challenge is the fact that many companies are having a difficult time finding, hiring, and keeping skilled workers.[86] Many companies, in their efforts to remain competitive, are keeping workers whom they may have ignored or discarded just 10 years ago. These workers include not only people who have historically been victims of discrimination in the United States, such as African-Americans, Native Americans, and women, but also older workers, people with disabilities, people with a wider variety of educational and socio-economic backgrounds, and people who are gay or lesbian. In short, the workforce will be ever more diverse. What this means—for everyone—is that henceforth we will all be expected to work effectively with people who are different from ourselves (see *An Inside Look*).

For more than 30 years, American businesses have been aware that they may not intentionally or unintentionally discriminate in employment on the basis of race, color, creed (religion), sex, national origin, or age. Title VII of the 1964 Civil Rights Act and the 1967 Age Discrimination in Employment Act guarantee all eligible workers in the United States those rights. Even though few laws *require* businesses to diversify their workforces, many organizations are actively pursuing diversification. Why? One major reason is that they really don't have much choice. In most large cities in the United States, where most large companies conduct their business, the influx of immigrants combined with the decreasing workforce participation rates of whites means that the new applicant pools are increasingly diverse. For example, in Miami over 60 percent of the population is either foreign-born or second-generation Americans. In New York the figure is 42.2 percent,

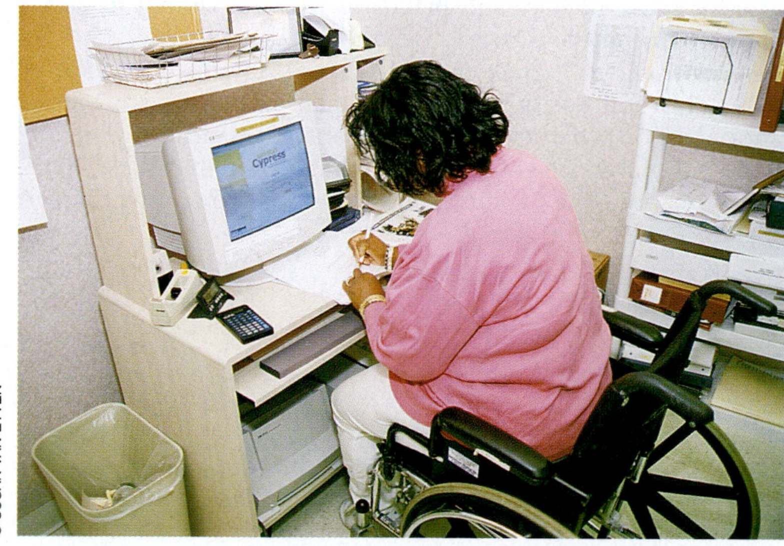

Companies can stay competitive in employee recruiting and retention by creating a workplace that is accessible to all people.

TABLE 3-7 How Companies Define and Value Diversity

Microsoft Corporation: "At Microsoft, we believe that diversity enriches our performance and products, the communities in which we live and work, and the lives of our employees. As our workforce evolves to reflect the growing diversity of our communities and global marketplace, our efforts to understand, value, and incorporate difference become increasingly important. At Microsoft, we have established a number of initiatives to promote diversity within our own organization, and to demonstrate this commitment nationwide."

http://www.ti.com

Texas Instruments: "Our effectiveness at using the talents of people of different backgrounds, experiences and perspectives is key to our competitive edge. . . . Diversity is a core TI value; valuing diversity in our workforce is at the core of the TI values statement. . . . " (See http://www.ti.com/corp/docs/diversity/worldwd.htm for the complete TI definition of diversity.)

http://www.csc.com

Computer Sciences Corporation: "We value the diversity of our employees and the unique perspectives they bring to CSC. Diversity at CSC includes functional roles within the company, the markets and industries we serve, our length of service, geographic location, educational background, age, race, gender, ethnicity, and whether we joined CSC independently or through an acquisition. By valuing differences, we demonstrate our commitment to treating everyone with fairness and respect."

Source: Society for Human Resource Management. 1999. *Workplace diversity: A product of the SHRM diversity initiative.* Alexandria, VA: The Society for Human Resource Management.

and in San Diego it is 42.6 percent.[87] In addition, most large companies have come to understand that they have an ethical and social responsibility to create and value diversity among their employees (see Table 3-7).

Why Value Diversity?

Valuing diversity is ethical—doing what is right and just in human actions. Our commonsense definitions of justice and fairness are usually in line with the principle that individuals should not encounter discrimination because of some unchangeable characteristic they possess, like their age. We agree that discriminating against people who are short, have brown eyes, or were born in Milwaukee is not ethical, because it is not fair. Similarly, it isn't ethical to treat Hindus, older, obese, and/or unathletic people with any less dignity or respect than people who are Christian, young, slim, or athletic.

Valuing diversity is socially responsible. Earlier we defined social responsibility as an organization's expectation to "protect and contribute to the welfare of society." Widespread disdain for "the other" eventually leads to hatred and societal destructiveness, as brutally demonstrated in Nazi Germany, and more recently in Rwanda, Bosnia, and Serbia. When companies promote diversity, and train and require all workers to treat each other with respect, irrespective of their backgrounds, they advance the organizational community. Every person's unique talents and perspectives can be better used to the benefit of all.

Valuing Diversity Is Good Business

As noted above, some managers are not convinced that they or their organizations have a responsibility to respond to societal needs. They focus only on maximizing shareholder wealth. However, a recent survey suggests that such

AN INSIDE LOOK

Challenges of Leading a Diverse Work Group

Ultimately it is the employees of the organization who must learn to recognize and appreciate the qualities that everyone brings to the organization. Managers can help their subordinates in this transition from a homogeneous workplace to a heterogeneous one. Like any other major change in an organization, managers must provide the leadership to make the change an effective one. Managers provide the direction and the confidence to make the change work.

However, the progression to a diverse work group will not be without its challenges for a manager. There are many potential issues managers will need to overcome to build an effective, diverse work team. Some of these* are:

1. *Changes in Power:* As work teams become more diverse, the traditional constituents of the work team (white males) may feel that their influence on the work team has been eroded. They must now consider and respect the opinions of people who are different from them. As influence (power) becomes more widely distributed in the work group, those who perceive that they lost standing within the team may become less committed to the team and the organization. For example, one study showed that as traditionally male work groups became more diverse (with the influx of women), the men became less committed and psychologically attached to the organization.† It is not an easy transition for the newly hired diverse employees either. Any new member of a work team feels the need to earn acceptance by the team. It is even more difficult for someone who brings a different background and perspective to the team.

Managers in such situations walk a fine line. They must show respect for the newcomers while still valuing the opinions of the more tenured employees. They must avoid the appearance of showing favoritism to any one or any group. To ease the transition, managers should pair diverse workers (male-female, white-black) together to work on various team projects. In time, both parties may become comfortable enough to ask questions and learn about the other person at a personal level. Team-building exercises may also be effective. A constant focus on the qualities that each member brings to the group and the importance of the role that each member fulfills helps to erode the perception that any one type of person has more power than another. Everyone should be seen as a contributor.

2. *Diversity of Opinions:* As the work group becomes more diverse, so too will opinions on objectives and procedures. By definition, diverse employees will bring different frames of reference to decisions. It is highly probable that diverse employees will perceive the same situation in different ways. Managers in such situations must keep all of the members focused on the decision at hand and the need to make a quality decision. The manager must reinforce, repeatedly, that all members' opinions are valued and respected by everyone on the team. The manager must be willing to act on and implement the opinion of a minority on the team if that opinion represents the best alternative.

When conflict arises, the manager must maintain the peace. One way to do this is by constantly reiterating

---

managers are in the minority. Of executives at Fortune 500 companies, 84 percent think diversity management is important, as do 67 percent of human resource management professionals in companies outside the Fortune 500.[88] Union Bank of California, Fannie Mae, Public Service Company of New Mexico, Sempra Energy, Toyota Motor Sales, Advantica, SBE Communications, Lucent Technologies, Darden Restaurants, and Wal-Mart Store were listed as the top ten of *Fortune*'s "50 Best Companies for Asians, Blacks, and Hispanics" at the close of the 20th century.[89]

http://www.fanniemae.gov
http://www.toyota.com
http://www.lucent.com

Fortunately, it turns out that valuing diversity is compatible with maximizing profits. Organizations (like Ortho Pharmaceuticals, Avon, Inland Steel) often

http://www.ortho-mcneil.com

what needs to be done and what each member of the team has contributed. Zero tolerance for name calling and personal attacks should be standard operating procedures for any effective, professional work group.

3. *Tokenism:* Tokenism occurs in organizations when employees are hired primarily because of their race or gender. Because a job applicant is a woman or a racial minority, she or he might be hired instead of a more qualified white male. In the extreme, a woman or person of color might be hired who is not qualified for the position. This sort of situation is not good for the organization, the manager, the work team, or the person who was hired. Organizations sometimes do this because they have imposed quotas on themselves. They may do it because of pressure from governmental agencies that enforce equal employment opportunity regulations. Or, they may do it because officers of the organization believe that it is the only way they may overcome prejudice on the part of hiring managers.

Fortunately, this is a very rare occurrence. No company can stay in business for long if it knowingly hires less qualified applicants over more qualified applicants. Even though real tokenism is rare, the perception that it exists is common. Many employees think that a women or minority person is present amongst them because the organization had to hire them, not because they are qualified. This is sometimes called the stigma of affirmative action. It is an extremely difficult situation. The new hires are not accorded respect because group members believe they should not have been hired in the first place. Their opinions are ignored, they are given the worst tasks in the group, and they are generally ostracized. This, in turn, can lower the new hires' self-esteem and their motivation to contribute to the team. Lower performance may result, reinforcing the misbeliefs of the dominant group. As the dominant group becomes distracted by the presence of the new team members, their performance too can suffer. In all, it can be a very costly situation for a company.

Quotas or hiring by the numbers should be avoided. Applicants should be hired for jobs based on their qualifications, not their gender or race. Rather than hiring based on physical characteristics, organizations need to "cast a wide net" in their recruiting efforts so as to find women and minorities who are the most qualified applicants for vacant positions. Managers should communicate to work group members what qualifications (including nontraditional ones like personal experiences) the new person brings to the group and why he or she was more qualified than the other applicants. Managers must ascertain the unique skills that the new member brings to the group. Then the manager must capitalize on those skills by giving the new member meaningful, visible tasks and projects. The manager must ensure their success by mentoring and/or providing the necessary resources. And, the manager should make sure the dominant group members know when the new member has achieved success in the team, celebrate their successes, and ensure that everyone knows that the new member is in fact capable and qualified.

* J. R. W. Joplin and C. S. Daus. 1997. Challenges of leading a diverse workforce. *Academy of Management Executive* 11(3):32–47.

† A. Tsui, T. Egan, and C. O'Reilly. 1992. Being different: Relational demography and organizational attachment. *Administrative Science Quarterly* 37:549–579.

improve their bottom-line when they put diversity management strategies in place.[90] *Fortune* observes that many of the "best companies for minorities" matched the Standard and Poor's 500 over the past year and their performance surpassed them over the past three and five years.[91] Lucent Technology's CEO Rich McGinn states, "The company adopted its diversity stance because it made good business sense, . . . in addition, it was the right thing to do." He goes on to state that "Diversity is a competitive advantage. Different people approach similar problems in different ways."[92] In fact, there are several reasons why diversity programs can add to a company's bottom-line, as Table 3-8 shows. Valuing diversity is, simply put, good business.

TABLE 3-8 Reasons Why Valuing Diversity Is Good Business

1. *Diversity improves the workforce.* When employees treat one another with respect, less time is wasted on interpersonal conflicts and politicking. More time is devoted to working together to maximize organization effectiveness.

2. *Diversity facilitates hiring the best and brightest employees.* As noted above, many companies are finding it difficult to find qualified workers, especially well-educated professionals. When companies develop a reputation for supporting people of all backgrounds with respect, people from diverse backgrounds are more likely to seek employment there. The employer gets to choose from the "cream of the crop."

3. *Diversity increases creativity.* How we view the world is not a random process. Our attitudes, values, and beliefs vary with such demographic variables as age, race, religion, and gender. When a company has a diverse workforce, it brings together different world views; this enhances creativity.

4. *Diversity enhances organizational flexibility.* If employees from diverse backgrounds can learn to adapt to each other, they can learn to adapt to other changes in the organization and the larger environment.

5. *Diversity reduces turnover and absenteeism.* When people feel that they are not valued, or worse, feel discriminated against, they have little emotional investment in the organization's success. They grow dissatisfied with their job and eventually seek employment elsewhere.

6. *Diversity helps to prevent discrimination lawsuits.* If employees value and treat one another with respect, they will be less likely to sue for employment discrimination. Discrimination lawsuits can be costly, as Texaco found out when it lost a $176 million judgment in 1996.[93] The prevention of just one discrimination lawsuit may far outweigh the potential costs of any diversity initiatives.

7. *Diversity improves marketplace understanding.* Just as diversity promotes creativity in decision making, so too do diverse perspectives bring a broader understanding of the marketplace. The spending power of ethnic minorities in the United States will be $650 billion in the early 21st century.[94] Tapping into this lucrative market requires understanding their needs and values.

8. *Diversity capitalizes on new markets.* Consumers eventually know which companies value people from all backgrounds. Diverse consumers are more likely to make purchases from companies who value employees like themselves. Conversely, they are less likely to make purchases from companies they perceive as discriminatory.

9. *Diversity produces higher quality decisions.* Heterogeneous groups (members have different skills and experiences) generally make better decisions than homogenous groups (members have similar backgrounds). Groups that take advantage of their diversity make better decisions. This seems to be especially true at the executive level.[95]

10. *Diversity facilitates the building of global relationships.* Companies who are comfortable with diversity do better in the global marketplace. Becoming truly at ease with diversity is no longer an option; it is a necessity. Managers who are leaders in diversity will be seen as essential members of their organization.

Sources: Adapted from G. Robinson and K. Dechant. 1997. Building a business case for diversity. *Academy of Management Executive* 11(3):21–31; and Society for Human Resource Management. 1999. *Workplace diversity: A product of the SHRM diversity initiative.* Alexandria, VA: The Society for Human Resource Management.

A Final Word on Diversity

It has been your authors' experience in teaching that young people often think that discrimination and prejudice are things of the past. Perhaps you were taught to value diversity in the public school system you attended. Perhaps your high school had a diverse and harmonious student body. Nevertheless, that racially motivated crimes still occur in the United States stands in the face of this belief. Indeed, in a poll conducted right before the year 2000, Americans mentioned racism and prejudice as the number one problem facing the United States in the 21st century.[96] We would caution you to realize that sometimes stereotyping and prejudice are subconscious. The fact that whites still socialize almost exclusively with whites, and blacks likewise with blacks, and so on, shows that we still have a long way to go before we become a truly harmonious multicultural society.

SOCIAL RESPONSIBILITY AND ETHICS IN REVIEW

Organizations at the start of the 20th century were concerned mostly with making profits and leaving the well-being of others up to individual acts of charity. After the Great Depression, however, people began to demand that organizations use some of their profits to improve society. Today, all managers must be aware of what society expects from their organizations and whether their actions will meet expectations.

This is not an easy task. There are many external and internal stakeholders, and one group's needs may conflict with another's. Also complicating the situation is the fact that the social issues that are considered important change as society changes. Many organizations try to specify current social issues and their response to them through a social audit. The level of commitment found in an organization's response is determined largely by the principles it follows and ranges from performing only those socially responsible acts that are imposed by laws and regulations to initiating policies and programs that try to anticipate and react to social issues before they become problems.

There are many arguments for and against corporate social responsibility. These arguments have been encapsulated into two points of view. Those who believe that organizations should not be concerned about social responsibility base their argument on the costs involved and on the idea that organizations are not obligated to shoulder those costs on behalf of society. Those who favor corporate social responsibility feel that organizations benefit from society and, therefore, have an obligation to improve it. Although there is no universal agreement, surveys and other reports indicate that many organizations are, in fact, becoming increasingly active in addressing social concerns.

An organization's response to social issues can be classified according to its relationship with the law. Organizations who behave illegally and irresponsibly flout the law and public opinion. Some organizations obey the letter of the law but not the spirit. Other organizations break the law even as they attempt to act responsibly. A fourth category of organizations manages to adhere to laws and regulations and still respond to society's needs. One way to promote an organization's adherence to the law and attention to social issues is to put its board of directors in charge of monitoring decisions and behaviors. This charge is best met if the board includes members from outside as well as inside the organization.

The societal values, norms, and mores that shape an organization's social responsibilities also influence the ethics of individuals. Every society has a set of values that shape the behavior of its citizens, although acceptable codes of conduct for one society may not be acceptable for another. Like social responsibilities, ethical considerations address the well-being of others, but on a smaller scale. These personal values are learned through our family, religious, educational, and cultural experiences.

A manager's personal ethics become managerial ethics when applied to situations in organizations. Managers bear a tremendous ethical responsibility for the actions they take, for the actions others take at their behest, and even for the results of their failure to act. They are also responsible for encouraging others to act ethically. Although many people might behave unethically under certain conditions, there are steps managers can take to promote ethical behavior, including developing an organizational culture and organizational policies and practices that reflect a high ethical standard for both managers and nonmanagers.

The work of organizations gets done through its people. Managers are therefore called upon continually to make decisions and engage in activities that influence the attitudes, motivation, and behavior of organizational members. We noted that much of this book will provide you with insights into the impact that management practices and organizational design have on employees. You will learn about ways to improve employee job satisfaction, organizational commitment, motivation, work attendance and turnover, and performance. In this chapter we suggested that any attempt to manage employee attitudes, motivation, and behavior should be accompanied by the question, What is the right and socially responsible thing to do? As a part of our discussion of the "ethical employee-organization relationship" we provided insights into when the management of employee attitudes, motivation, and behavior is an ethical or unethical act.

Finally, we discussed the issue of diversity. Diversity has both ethical and socially responsible underpinnings. Changes in the demographic characteristics of the United States, the emergence of a free trade agreement in North America, and the globalization of business make diversity an ever-increasing reality of organizational life. It therefore becomes critical for managers to develop a mindset that values diversity and sees diversity as an organizational resource, while also seeing the integration of diversity into the organization's culture as the right and socially responsible thing to do.

A FINAL LOOK

Tom Grey calls an emergency meeting of the Jamison Hospital Board. When he tells the board that a donor has offered to fund the new cardiac wing, the board members are visibly relieved and excited. With a new cardiac facility, the hospital can now compete with the cutting-edge facilities at their competitor, Memorial Hospital. Then Tom reveals the identity of the donor. Two board members from the community don't feel that this is a problem; as far as they are concerned, the amount of the donation is large enough to justify the conflict of interest. However, the others, some of whom are employed by Jamison Hospital, are concerned that the hospital would be sending mixed messages to the community. "Stop smoking to save lives" is not exactly consistent with "Trust your future to the new cardiac wing donated by Birmingham Industries!"

After much soul-searching, the board votes to decline Birmingham's generous donation offer. They feel it would not be socially responsible for a health-oriented organization to appear to condone the activities of a company that produces tobacco products. The search for a donor will continue.

KEY TERMS

code of ethics, 99
ethics, 92
moral audit, 100
organizational diversity, 104
principle of charity, 79
principle of stewardship, 79
procedural justice, 97
profit-maximizing management, 79
quality-of-life management, 80
rights theory, 97
social audit, 82
social responsibility, 77
socialization, 92
theory of justice, 97
trusteeship management, 80
utilitarian theory, 97
whistleblowing, 95

ISSUES FOR REVIEW AND DISCUSSION

1. Define both ethics and social responsibility. How are they alike? How do they differ?
2. Discuss the managerial values associated with profit-maximizing management, trusteeship management, and quality-of-life management.
3. Identify and discuss the two principles guiding contemporary acts of social responsibility.
4. What are the major points of disagreement between Milton Friedman and Keith Davis on corporate social responsibility?
5. Distinguish between social obligation, social responsibility, and social responsiveness.
6. List several sources of unethical managerial behaviors.
7. Discuss the steps that managers can take to encourage ethical behavior by all employees.
8. Describe the ethical dilemma symbolized by the two heads of the Roman god Janus.
9. What ethical issues confront managers as they deal with managing organizational members?
10. Discuss the meaning of diversity and why diversity is "good business" and ethical and socially responsible.

EXERCISES

ETHICAL WORK CLIMATE QUESTIONNAIRE

Answer the questions by circling the number that best describes an organization you have worked for.

	Disagree				**Agree**
1. What is best for everyone in the company is the major consideration here.	1	2	3	4	5
2. Our major concern is always what is best for the other person.	1	2	3	4	5
3. People are expected to comply with the law and professional standards over and above other considerations.	1	2	3	4	5
4. In this company, the first consideration is whether a decision violates any law.	1	2	3	4	5
5. It is very important to follow the company's rules and procedures here.	1	2	3	4	5
6. People in this company strictly obey the company policies.	1	2	3	4	5
7. In this company, people are mostly out for themselves.	1	2	3	4	5
8. People are expected to do anything to further the company's interests, regardless of the consequences.	1	2	3	4	5
9. In this company, people are guided by their own personal ethics.	1	2	3	4	5
10. Each person in this company decides for him- or herself what is right and wrong.	1	2	3	4	5

Total Score _______

Scoring:

Add up your score. These questions measure the dimensions of an organization's ethical climate. Questions 1 and 2 measure caring for people, questions 3 and 4 measure lawfulness, questions 5 and 6 rules adherence, questions 7 and 8 emphasis on financial and company performance, and questions 9 and 10 individual independence. Questions 7 and 8 are to be reverse scored—thus, subtract your answer to each of these questions from 6. Now a score of 1 becomes 5, a score of 2 becomes 4, and so on. A total score above 40 indicates a very positive ethical climate. A score from 30 to 40 indicates above-average ethical climate. A score from 20 to 30 indicates a below-average ethical climate, and a score below 20 indicates a very poor ethical climate.

Go back over the questions and think about changes that you could have made to improve the ethical climate in the organization. Discuss with other students what you could do as a manager to improve ethics in future companies you work for.

Sources: Excerpt from *Management* (3rd ed.) by R. L. Daft, copyright © 1994 by The Dryden Press, reprinted by permission of the publisher. Ethical work climate on pages 174–175 is based on B. Victor and J. B. Cullen. March 1988. The organizational bases of ethical work climate. *Administrative Science Quarterly* 33(1):101–125.

INFOTRAC

INFOTRAC® COLLEGE EDITION

The articles listed below are a sampling of those available through InfoTrac College Edition. You can search for them either by title or by the author's name.

Articles

1. Indulging Our Differences; Whether successful diversity is the goal of a great work environment or merely a by-product, the action plan is the same—recognize each employee as a valuable asset with unique needs. (Industry Trend or Event) Kathleen Melymuka. *Computerworld* June 19, 2000 p56(1)
2. White Males See Diversity's Other Side. (Workplace diversity) Gillian Flynn. *Workforce* Feb 1999 v78 i2 p52(4) Bus.Coll.: 114X2330
3. Fraudbusting Ethics. Basil Orsini, Diane McDougall. *CMA Management* June 1999 v73 i5 p18(4) Bus.Coll.: 117P1077
4. WHAT WOULD YOU DO? (Tackling the ethics question in business). (Brief Article) Frank C. Bucaro. *Manage* Feb 2000 v51 i3 p14
5. Why it pays to be good (eventually). Charles Leadbeater. *New Statesmen* (1996) March 6, 2000 v129 i4476 p26 Mag.Coll.: 102M2717

Questions

For Articles 1 and 2:

Using "Indulging our differences" and "White males see diversity's other side" as a springboard, form into small groups and discuss how you would go about designing a one-day diversity training program for a service organization. For this situation, you have a limited budget, and your manager has said that you must draw upon in-house personnel and resources as much as possible. Who would you choose as speakers? What would the content cover? What factors would you consider in designing a specific program? What location would you choose? How would you evaluate the success of your program?

For Other Articles:

Again, form into small groups. From your individual readings of this chapter and the ethics articles on this list, as well as your personal experience as a consumer and an employee, explain how you feel about whistle-blowing and why you have the opinions you do.

WEB EXERCISES

1. Identify and visit the website for a major news source (for example, *Chicago Tribune*, *New York Times*, *Washington Post*, *L.A. Times*, *Business Week*, *Newsweek*). Locate and summarize a story that reflects either an ethical or unethical, or socially responsible or irresponsible act, and explain how and why you judge the act as you do.
2. Explore Ben & Jerry's website (**http://benandjerrys.com**) and examine its mission statement. Describe their stance on ethics and social responsibility.
3. In late summer 2000, problems with more than seven million Firestone tires, especially those installed on Ford's Explorer, caused the most massive recall in U.S. history. At the time of this writing, more than 60 deaths and millions of dollars of damage have been attributed to this tire. Review, from a social responsibility perspective, the history of the Firestone/Ford case. Did Firestone and Ford act in a socially responsible manner? Why? Why not? If you prefer to choose another organizational incident, identify the case, summarize the incidents, then discuss what you think is the ethical and/or social responsibility question. What conclusions do you draw? Why?

CASE
Frank Pearson and the Allied Research Corporation

Dr. Frank Pearson was an associate director of medical research for the Allied Research Corporation, where he supervised a research team assigned to develop therapeutic drugs. The team's duties included establishing procedures to test drugs for effectiveness, safety, and marketability. Dr. Pearson was the only physician on the research team and had been employed by Allied since 1990.

In the spring of 1995, the team was engaged in the development of loperamide, a liquid drug for treatment of diarrhea in infants, children, and the elderly. The proposed formula contained 44 times the concentration of saccharin permitted by the Federal Drug Administration (FDA) in 12 ounces of a soft drink. Accordingly, the team agreed that the formula was unsuitable for use and suspended work on the project.

In March of 1996, Allied's marketing division issued a directive to resume the research and development of loperamide. The company intended to file an investigational new drug application with the FDA, to continue laboratory studies on loperamide, and to complete the formula. In Dr. Pearson's professional judgment, however, there was no justification for seeking permission from the FDA to continue to develop the drug because of the heated controversy over the safety of saccharin. He made his position clear to the other team members. The team, however, decided to continue the research despite Dr. Pearson's objections.

Dr. Pearson met with his supervisor, Dr. Antonucci. During the meeting, Dr. Pearson stated that, in his professional opinion, the decision to pursue the development of loperamide was medically unsound. He also told Dr. Antonucci that he believed continuing his work on the loperamide research would violate his Hippocratic oath, a generally accepted standard of medical ethics. The risk, he said, that saccharin might be harmful should prevent testing the formula on children or the elderly, especially when an alternative formula might soon be available.

Dr. Antonucci responded that the company had no intention of testing the formula on any human subjects unless and until the FDA gave its approval. He assured Dr. Pearson that all proper procedures would be scrupulously observed in the development and testing of the drug. He emphasized the differences between the development and testing phases of research projects in general and suggested that continuing to do research would, in his opinion, violate no law or professional code of ethics. He also stressed the need to work constructively with the marketing division.

At the end of the meeting, Dr. Pearson remained unpersuaded, and Dr. Antonucci asked him to choose another research project. He assured Dr. Pearson that the request would be honored and that no salary adjustment would be made. Dr. Pearson responded that even so, he interpreted this offer as a demotion.

Later in the day, Dr. Pearson submitted his letter of resignation to Dr. Antonucci. It said, in part, "Upon learning that you believe that I have not 'acted as a Director' and have displayed inadequacies as to my inability to relate to the marketing division and that I am now—or soon will be—demoted, I find it impossible to continue my employment at Allied." Dr. Antonucci accepted the resignation without comment.

Questions

1. What are the ethical issues in this case?
2. If the FDA had given permission to test the drug, would that permission make the testing ethical? Explain.
3. What alternatives were open to Dr. Antonucci? Which should he have taken?
4. Was Dr. Antonucci correct in dealing with Dr. Pearson as he did?

Source: This case was prepared by David B. Thompson (deceased) and Michael J. DiNoto of the University of Idaho. Used with the permission of Michael J. DiNoto.

Outline

CHAPTER 4

The Organizational Environment

PHOTO: © ROGER RESSMEYER/CORBIS

Learning Objectives

After reading this chapter, you should be able to

1. Identify and discuss key aspects of the organization's general environment and task environments.
2. Identify the major problems that confront managers as a result of the relationship between their organization and its external environment.
3. Identify tactics that managers can use to increase their power over the task environment.
4. Explain how differences in environmental stability and segmentation influence the approach to managing and organizational design.
5. Explain the concepts of mechanistic and organic organizations, and open and closed management systems.
6. Understand the importance of the boundary-spanning process.
7. Differentiate between the organizations' external and internal environments.

A FIRST LOOK

The Ivy College of Business enjoys a reputation as one of the oldest and most respected management programs in the nation. So it comes as a surprise to Dean Atwood that enrollments are steadily decreasing. After considering the latest enrollment statistics, he calls an emergency faculty meeting.

At the meeting, several professors propose that the college is losing students because of changing demographics. While the school traditionally attracted students straight out of high school, these students are not attending Ivy in the numbers they once had. The faculty debates whether the reason is the format and scheduling of classes or their hesitation to use technology in the classroom. Perhaps they need to transform their thinking and make themselves more accessible to nontraditional working students.

One of the younger faculty members suggests teaching some business classes online in a distance format. He has just come from a university that offers online degree programs, and this institution's enrollments have skyrocketed. Distance education is particularly effective in attracting highly qualified working students from around the world.

While some favor this proposal, the Dean and many other faculty members initially oppose it. Distance education is fine for institutions with lesser reputations, but not for Ivy!

Questions: How is the organizational environment of the Ivy College of Business affecting its ability to attract new students? Should Ivy continue to uphold its traditional methods, or look outside of the organization for new inspiration?

In Chapter 1, we noted that organizations come into existence to help serve the needs of society. We also suggested that society has many different needs that give rise to many different types of organizations. The idea of an organization operating within and surrounded by society suggests that all organizations have an external environment.

external environment a set of conditions, circumstances, and influences that surround and affect the functioning of an organization

The organization's **external environment** represents a set of conditions, circumstances, and influences that surround and affect the functioning of an organization. As those who manage the activities of the organization carry out their roles, they are affected by the forces that operate within the external environment. In order to understand management and ultimately organizational behavior, you must understand the nature of this environment. Effective organizations develop management systems that integrate management practice and organizational design with characteristics of their external environment.

Forces outside the organization can have a tremendous impact on the organization. During November of 1999, the court ruled that Microsoft was a monopoly and that they had engaged in unfair competition. Coca-Cola quickly reintroduced its original-formula soft drink—Classic Cola—after a disappointing attempt to introduce "new" Coke. Rumor of, and the eventual acquisition of, Norwest Bank by Wells Fargo produced high levels of anxiety, feelings of job insecurity, and stress among many of the personnel at Norwest. Examples such as these suggest that forces in the organization's external environment reach inside and affect the organization and its internal operations.

internal environment all that is the organization—such as its space, climate, machines/equipment, work and work processes, management and management practices, and organizational members

The notion that the external environment extends beyond the formal boundaries of the organization suggests a second environment. This environment is internal to the boundaries of the organization and is referred to as the internal environment. The **internal environment** represents all that is the organization—for example, its space, climate, machines/equipment, work and work processes, management and management practices, and organizational members. The internal environment will be discussed in detail in Part III, Management Functions and the Organizational Behavior Context. We will, however, briefly introduce the internal environment at the end of this chapter to begin to familiarize you with the nature and anatomy of the organization.

THE EXTERNAL ENVIRONMENT

The external environment, by definition, lies outside the formal boundaries of an organization. Every organization has a boundary that separates the organization from its external environment.

While all organizations have a boundary, like each of us has a layer of skin that separates "us" from "not us," not all organizational boundaries look the same nor appear in the same place. A prison, for example, places its boundary around its clients (prisoners) and keeps them inside the organization (housing, clothing, feeding, and providing medical care), while the Pine Cone Truck Stop at the intersection of Highway 51 and Interstate 94 places its boundary around those who are formally employed by the truck stop. The prison's boundary is closed and difficult to penetrate, while Pine Cone's boundary is quite open to the customer's "comings and goings" for breakfast, lunch, dinner, and late-night coffee and snacks.

The organization's external environment is made up of many different individuals (customers, members of other organizations, local citizens); organizations (suppliers, civic groups, labor unions); and government bodies (regulatory agencies, legislators, local officials). It includes people who are capable of influencing an organization and its management system, as well as those who might be affected by the organization's actions. For most organizations, the external environment is large, diverse, and complex. As a result, scholars partition it into two sections—the general and task environments, both of which we discuss below. The *general environment* refers to the general milieu (environment, setting, surroundings) in which an organization operates. The *task environment* is the more specific and immediate environment in which the organization conducts its business. Many organizations operate within the same general environment, while each organization has its own task environment. Organizations must cope with both facets of the external environment.

http://www.embassysuites.com

http://www.ohare.com

Consider for a moment the general and task environments of Embassy Suites, a hotel chain specializing in "all-suite" accommodations. It built a hotel in Schaumburg, Illinois, to capitalize on the potential market offered by O'Hare Airport and a number of nearby national corporate headquarters. Current economic conditions of the entire country—its external environment—are relevant to the managers of Embassy Suites. The economic prosperity of the late 1990s, for example, increased optional overnight business travel and the willingness of many corporations to pay for suites.

The task environment for Embassy Suites includes not only the local hotel, restaurant, and bar market, but also weekend hotel business in the Chicago area. Managers at the Schaumburg hotel must be concerned about the continued robustness of the economy, as it strongly influences the nature of their business and business success. Continued long-term success of this hotel therefore depends on management being aware of, and coping effectively with, both their general and task environments.

The General Environment

general environment that part of the external environment that represents the organization's sociocultural, economic, technological, legal/political, and international domains

The **general environment** of an organization includes its social and cultural context, the economic system surrounding the organization, the legal and political atmosphere, the technology from which knowledge and tools for reaching goals are derived, and international climate. The major components of an organization's general environment consist of sociocultural, economic, technological, legal/political, and international domains. Managers in different general environments often adopt different management systems.[1]

The organization is affected by pressure from the general environment. The legal/political system, for example, creates a political climate within which organizations must function, while the economic system creates parameters that define how businesses compete with one another. Organizations are not totally passive players in the environment-organization relationship. To a limited extent, organizations can engage in various strategies that impact the external environment. For example, many organizations lobby the U.S. Congress hoping to affect the political climate. The recent acquisition of Honeywell by Allied Signal, and Honeywell's release of 2000 plus employees, impacted the economy of the state of Minnesota. The ability of the general environment to influence and shape organizational activity, however, is seen as much greater than the organization's capacity to influence its external environment.

http://lcweb.loc.gov/global/legislative/congress.html

http://www.honeywell.com

sociocultural domain the values, customs, mores, and demographic characteristics of the people within a society

The Sociocultural Domain

The **sociocultural domain**[2] consists of the values, customs, mores, and demographic characteristics (ages, education levels, mobility patterns, and the like) of the people within a society. As we noted in Chapter 1, organizations have a special place within cultures, as they are that culture's "answers to the problems encountered by human beings in achieving their collective ends."[3] Because most organizations are created to serve the needs of certain members of a society, it's easy to see how society's values, customs, and mores influence organizations and their management systems. Organizations are manifestations of social and cultural forces.

The environmental movement in the United States, for example, has increasingly pressured organizations to act as stewards for the environment. The protests of children, during the early 1990s, prompted McDonalds to dramatically reduce its use of packaging that pollutes the environment. Managers, as leaders and organizational decision makers, must be alert to social and cultural forces, because society will drive, affect, and evaluate their actions.

http://www.mcdonalds.com

The Economic Domain

Although organizations may be strongly influenced by the sociocultural domain, fulfilling their mission requires resources (for example, land, labor, and capital). Whenever people enter relationships that involve the transfer of land, labor, capital, goods, and services, rules emerge to govern these transactions. As societies evolve, these rules take the form of increasingly formalized economic systems and represent an organization's **economic domain.**

economic domain the rules and economic institutions that regulate business activity and govern the transfers of land, labor, capital, goods, and services that an organization needs to fulfill its goals

All organizations operate in an economic system—socialist, communist, or capitalist, or some combination thereof. Each system has its own standards and institutions governing economic activity. Not only does the dominant economic system affect organizational activity, so does the economic health of the external environment. Managers in both for-profit and not-for-profit organizations are influenced by such economic conditions as inflation, recession, depression, and interest rates.

technological domain the knowledge, processes, means, systems, hardware, and software available to an organization to convert its inputs (raw materials, unfinished goods, energy) into outputs (products or services)

The Technological Domain Technology is the means by which an organization converts its inputs (such as raw materials, unfinished goods, energy) into outputs (products or services). The **technological domain** includes the knowledge, processes, means, systems, hardware, and software available to an organization for this transformation process. In the past few decades, for example, optic fibers have facilitated communications, robots have revolutionized manufacturing, computers have facilitated the processing of enormous amounts of information, digitalization has enhanced sound and image delivery, and lasers have replaced scalpels in some surgical procedures.

Technology changes continually, and so managers must keep abreast of emerging trends.

Computers have revolutionized many organizations and management practices, giving rise to widespread downsizing. The work of numerous former middle managers, hired to help organizations process large amounts of information with computers, is now done by workers at lower levels in the organization. For example, computers provide the men and women who assemble Harley-Davidson motorcycles with information that they need to manage this phase of the production process by themselves. Clearly, technological advances can have a profound effect on the management of organizations. Managers must, therefore, constantly monitor the technological domain for emerging developments and their possible impact on organizational activities. In the control-oriented organization, this activity is often assigned to specialists, while in the involvement-oriented organization, part of this boundary-spanning activity becomes everybody's responsibility. The men and women who operate printing machines at Quad/Graphics, in Pewaukee, Wisconsin, routinely deal with suppliers as a way of bringing into the organization critical technological information.

legal/political domain those systems that allocate power among various groups in society and settle disputes as they arise, and that develop, administer, and enforce the law

The Legal/Political Domain The sociocultural system establishes the spirit and sets the tone for acceptable and unacceptable organizational behavior. Social values are then translated into laws designed to control and influence members of the society. The laws, made by legislators and interpreted by courts, are expected to apply "the will of the people"; thus, legal and political systems are inextricably linked. This domain allocates power among various groups in the society and settles disputes as they arise. It also develops, administers, and enforces the law. Societies use their legal and political systems to ensure compliance with the values of the society and to thereby maintain the existence of the society.[4] To achieve these ends, the **legal/political domain** controls members of society and social institutions. If necessary, physical force can be used to achieve this control.[5]

Within any society, certain political ideologies prevail at particular times. Sometimes the ideology leans toward the liberal end of the spectrum, sometimes toward the conservative end. Organizations and managers must operate within this ideological climate. Political ideology affects organizations in many ways, including a governing body's enforcement or nonenforcement of selected laws, its tendency to add or subtract regulations that affect business, and its support for particular levels of taxes and interest rates. The "pro–Big Business" attitude brought to Washington by the Reagan administration, for example, resulted in the deregulation of a number of industries and stimulated a wide range of mergers. This attitude—at the conservative end of the ideological spectrum—caused yet another wave of mergers and acquisitions during the 1990s (for example, Travelers Insurance and Citibank; British Airways and Delta Airlines; Chrysler and Mercedes Benz; World Com and MCI; Tribune and *L.A. Times*), leading once again to the mega-organization. Such an attitude would not have gotten very far during earlier and less "pro–Big Business" eras.

http://www.travelers.com

http://www.citibank.com

http://www.britishairways.com

http://www.delta.com

http://www.chrysler.com

http://www.mercedes.com

http://www.mci.worldcom.com

http://www.latimes.com

http://www.tribune.com

In sum, the legal and political components of the environment strongly affect organizational behavior and, therefore, must continually garner managers' attention. Managers must monitor not only the laws that govern organizational activity, but also the shifts in ideology as different groups gain the upper hand in the legal/political domain.

The International Domain For a variety of reasons, an increasing number of organizations are interacting with organizations and cultures of other countries. Limited domestic resources, the availability of international currency, the search for new markets, and increasingly more vigorous competition cause companies to think globally. The American automobile industry faces stiff competition from Japanese and German automobile producers. Even local wine stores are influenced by international factors, such as the weather conditions in the Bordeaux region of France.

international domain organizations and the economic, legal/political, technological, and sociocultural domains of other countries with which they have contact

There are a variety of ways in which organizations become engaged by the **international domain**. At the simplest level, foreign companies start operating in your domestic market. Competition on what was once "home turf" has become virtually impossible to avoid—foreign manufactured automobiles, appliances, clothing, liquors, cosmetics and pharmaceuticals, tools—the list goes on. A number of vehicles enable organizations to "go international," including importing, exporting, joint ventures, licensing agreements, franchises, wholly owned subsidiaries, and countertrade. As business in foreign markets expands, as firms form wholly owned subsidiaries across different countries, when a significant proportion of the organization's work force is outside the home country, a firm becomes known as a *multinational corporation*. The *global enterprise* represents an extreme involvement in the international domain. Global enterprises respond to world markets through a unified strategy. Michael Porter from the Harvard Business School defines a global enterprise as one in which "a firm's competitive position in one country is significantly influenced by its position in other countries."[6] Television, semiconductor, automobile, and pharmaceutical manufacturers are but a few of the industries that exhibit a global pattern.

Firms that find themselves operating in the international domain will see this sector of the organization's external environment as impacting not only its management process and organizational design, but also each of its functions. Accepted accounting practices in the United States are not the norm worldwide, and these differences need to be addressed. In the area of finance issues pertaining to foreign exchange risk, import and export financing become important. Marketing has to contend with promotion, product, pricing, and physical distribution cross-cultural issues. Human resources will find itself impacted, for example, by new recruitment, selection, placement, training, and cultural diversity issues.

In "going international," an organization's external environment becomes more complicated. Its general environment contains a greater number and variety of actors. If your organization, for example, is operating out of Christchurch, New Zealand, it is going to contend with sociocultural, economic, technological, legal/political, and international domains that differ somewhat from those which its North American operations confront. In addition, the organization's task environment grows larger and more complex (for example, an increase in the number and variety of customers, as well as regulatory agencies standing at your door).

Going international not only enlarges and complicates the organization's general and task environments, the management process also becomes more complex. Environmental scans needed to aid in the decision-making and planning processes, for example, become more complicated, new kinds of organizational structures may be needed, directing strategies have to cope with a variety of cultural differences, and organizational control systems need to be larger, more elaborate, and capable of integrating a greater variety of information.

In terms of understanding attitudes, motivation, and behavior of organizational members, the sociocultural side of the international domain provides management with its greatest challenge. As organizations increasingly find themselves operating across cultural frontiers, they inevitably confront employees with different social values and mores. It has been observed that the French have often found "freedom" in bureaucratic organizations, while many North Americans find bureaucracies as alienating—"overly controlling, limiting, and stifling."[7]

Geert Hofstede, professor of organizational anthropology and international management at the University of Limburg in The Netherlands, gives a useful framework for understanding cultural forces that managers must confront as the international domain impacts their organizations.[8] His framework employs societal values, the preferences that different cultures express for a certain state of affairs.[9] According to Hofstede, five dominant value patterns enable us to compare and contrast different societies in which our organizations operate. These value patterns also give rise to differences in effective management practices. Hofstede's value patterns—individualism-collectivism (values related to the closeness of relationships); power distance (values related to inequality among people); uncertainty avoidance (values related to coping with the uncertainty of the future); masculinity-femininity (values related to the division of roles between the sexes); and time orientation (values with regard to the future)—are discussed in greater detail in Chapter 5.

The Task Environment

Every organization has its own task environment, which is embedded in, and influenced by, the general environment. It is the organization's task environment that exercises the most immediate influence on the organization and its operations. While the U.S. legal system defines basic legal parameters, David Lavold, owner and operator of Lavold's Car Company, must comply with the laws of the community of Monona and the state laws of Wisconsin.[10] In particular, the state's "lemon" law is important to him. This law gives car buyers certain rights if a car purchased from Lavold's plagues them with repeated problems. Lavold is bound by these regulations even if he sells a car in good faith that turns out to be a "lemon." The laws of Wisconsin and the city of Monona are part of the legal/political domain, but they are also part of this automobile dealer's task environment.

As depicted in Figure 4-1, the task environment has the most direct and immediate organizational consequences. The general environment's influence on the organization is generally the result of the general environment's influence over the task environment. Inspection of Figure 4-1 suggests that managers and organizations can take steps to influence the task environment. For example, lobbying city hall and signing contracts with suppliers represent two ways that organizations can exercise some influence over their task environment. Organizations are also more likely to be able to influence their task environment than their general environment.

task environment that part of the external environment that consists of the organization's suppliers, customers/markets, regulatory and influence groups, competitors, and allies

Sociologists William R. Dill and James D. Thompson used the term **task environment** to identify four important components of the organization's external environment.[11] These critical four components are the organization's:

1. *Suppliers*—all organizations have their suppliers, the providers of materials, labor, capital, equipment, and work space.
2. *Customers/markets*—all organizations have customers and/or markets, those who are the distributors and users of the organization's goods and services.
3. *Regulatory and influence groups*—all organizations have a group of regulatory agencies and influence groups that they have to respond to, such as government agencies, unions, and professional associations. (Originally Dill and Thompson dealt only with regulatory groups. We have included unions, professional associations, and outside influence groups—such as the environmental movement—to this category.)
4. *Competitors*—all those organizations that the organization competes with for both markets and resources.

A fifth component of the task environment includes *allies*. Allies might be those with whom one forms a partnership for a joint venture.[12] Minnesota Power and Pentair formed a partnership to establish a new paper manufacturing firm, Lake Superior Paper Industries, which since its inception has been owned by Consolidated Paper and now Stora Enso Oyj, a Finnish corporation.

FIGURE 4-1 Relationship between the Task and General Environments and the Organization

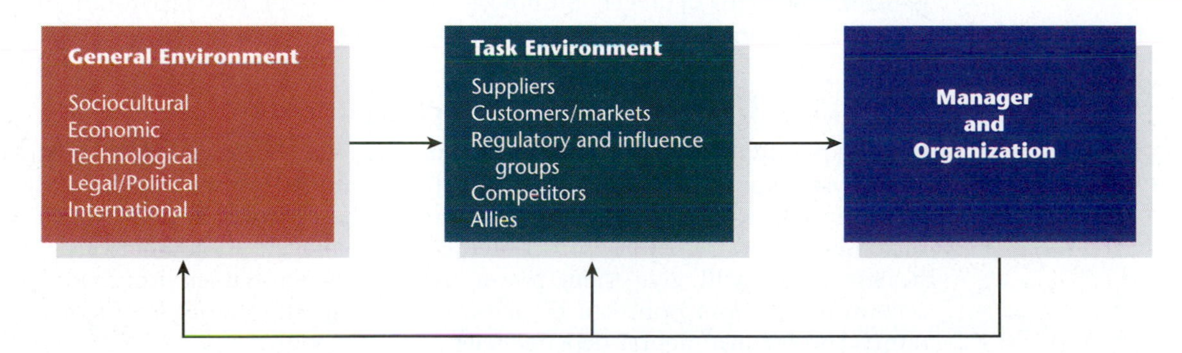

The relationships between organizations and their task environments are dynamic. Much as the task environment influences an organization, managers can engage in strategies aimed at controlling and influencing the task environment. Most managers would agree that it is better to study and manage the external environment than to allow it to control their organization. The environment will attempt to exercise control over the organization to the degree that managers surrender their ability to manage the organization-environment relationship.

THE ORGANIZATION-ENVIRONMENT RELATIONSHIP

In order to fulfill its mission and satisfy its customers, a company must have managers who understand and can successfully navigate the organization through the external environment. The external environment will attempt to exercise power over the organization, as it is an instrument of societal need, in an effort to get the organization to do that which serves the needs of society. As an organization interacts with its external task environment, managers confront two kinds of problems—the problem of uncertainty and the problem of interdependence. A major challenge for those managing organizations will be to deal with these two organizational problems.

The Problems of Uncertainty and Interdependence

Inevitably, managers and their organizations interact with the external environment (that is, with its customers, competitors, suppliers, regulatory agencies, and allies). Under most circumstances, managers can neither control nor predict everything that will happen in this interaction. As a consequence, organizational members are faced with varying amounts of *environmental uncertainty*. This is the source of one kind of problem that those managing organizations must deal with.

A second kind of problem arises as a natural part of doing business. Organizations develop a variety of exchange relationships with, for example, suppliers, customers, and allies. Through purchases, sales, and joint projects, *interdependencies* between organizations doing business begin to develop. For example, Northwest Outlet, a retailer in northwestern Wisconsin, depends on the Hudson Bay Company, a manufacturer of wool blankets and clothing, to supply them with their much-sought-after Hudson Bay wool blankets and jackets.

http://www.hbc.com

Uncertainty and organizational interdependence represent two forces that often constrain managers' activities. Unless managed effectively, these forces can interfere with the attainment of organizational goals. A number of strategies that can help managers minimize the power of the task environment over the organization have been identified and will be discussed next.

Managing Uncertainty and Interdependence

It is frequently argued that those who manage the organization-environment relationship should attempt to control the amount of power that the external environment exercises over the operations of the organization. Organizational sociologist James D. Thompson contends that managers should actively pursue strategies that will give them power over their external environment. This, according to Thompson, can be achieved through the management of uncertainty and environmental dependencies.

Thompson offers two sets of strategies for managers to deal with the problems of uncertainty and interdependence,[13] and Jack Welch's management style at GE reveals a third strategy. The first represents attempts to manage the boundary that separates an organization from its environment. This approach aims to minimize the degree to which environmental forces penetrate an organization and affect its daily operations. Managers frequently engage in strategies aimed at "sealing off" their organization from the environment's control and influence. Sealing off the organization from the forces in the external environment resembles the efforts of those who live in the northern climate to seal off their homes from the cold winter weather, and the efforts of prisons to close their boundary with the external environment to minimize the interface between prisoners and members of society at large.

Organizations that engage in strategies to seal themselves off from forces in the external environment are attempting to protect their technical core from environmental disruptions. After all, it is in the technical core that the day-to-day affairs of the organization are conducted. It is here that Detroit Edison generates electricity for its customers, it is here that St. Mary's hospital delivers babies and mends broken arms, and it is here that your university offers the classes that you take on a daily/weekly basis. Organizations want to protect their technical core so that the day-to-day activities can transpire smoothly, without disruptions from the external environment.

http://www.detroitedison.com

While it is unrealistic to believe that an organization can completely isolate itself from environmental influences, managers can engage in strategies that insulate it from erratic and potentially damaging environmental demands. Among some of the strategies employed by organizations for minimizing these environmentally induced disruptions are

http://www.goodyear.com

- **Buffering.** Organizations can buffer themselves by stockpiling resources or warehousing outputs. For example, Goodyear may stockpile lampblack (an ingredient used in the manufacture of tires) and then warehouse finished tires to avoid potential shortages and to be ready for unexpected demands. These buffering techniques enable organizations to maintain operations in the event of shortages in raw resources, and during peaks and valleys in product demand. Through buffering, organizations absorb environmental fluctuations much as shock absorbers stabilize a car's ride over bumps and potholes. The just-in-time (JIT) inventory system (that is, contracting for the arrival of raw materials just as the organization needs them in order to avoid stockpiling costs) leaves organizations vulnerable to unanticipated strikes, for example, by a major supplier's employees.
- **Smoothing.** Through smoothing, or leveling, managers attempt to influence the behavior of the environment. During low-demand periods, organizations may offer inducements, such as price reductions, to encourage consumers to buy their products and services. During peak periods, they may charge a premium rate, thereby discouraging excessive demand. Smoothing explains why snow tires are cheaper during the summer and air conditioners are less expensive during the winter.
- **Anticipating and adapting.** Under some circumstances, managers can anticipate changes in environmental conditions and adapt appropriately. With forecasting data, managers can help their organizations adapt internally to anticipated environmental demands. Bars and restaurants in popular summer vacation areas, for example, anticipate the tourist season and increase their supplies of liquor, food, and employees.

- **Rationing.** "When buffering, leveling, and forecasting do not protect their technical core from environmental fluctuations, organizations . . . [may] resort to rationing."[14] Rationing establishes priorities for using an organization's resources. Many organizations, under conditions of economic decline, ration existing work across the current work force instead of laying off some people and keeping the remaining employees working full time. In this way, they reduce the total number of hours worked by each employee but retain their human capital.[15]

These four strategies can go a long way toward protecting organizations from environmental stresses. A second set of strategies also affects an organization's relationship with its external environment. These strategies allow managers and their organizations to reduce the level of uncertainty and dependency on the environment through their efforts to increase its control over that environment.

- **Prestige.** If an organization can develop a favorable image in its task environment, and if it can make forming relationships with it "the thing to do," the organization gains power over members of its task environment.
- **Contracting.** An organization often enters into an agreement with a member of its task environment. When an organization enters into a contract with another organization, for example, to purchase needed raw material, the contract serves to reduce uncertainty about the availability of raw materials by giving the organization some control over a member of its task environment.
- **Co-opting.** Co-opting is the process of absorbing part of the task environment into an organization. For example, an organization may place someone from a major lending institution on its board of directors. As a result of co-opting organizations can gain support for their actions.[16]
- **Coalescing.** Coalescing refers to merging or joining into a venture with a member of the task environment. A coalition is formed, and those involved in the coalition become allies. A merger combines the resources of both organizations. In a joint venture, however, only those resources relevant to the common activity are combined.

Although he retired in 2001, Jack Welch's boundaryless organizational model at GE is one of the innovative management strategies that made him one of the most admired CEOs in the United States.

Jack Welch and GE's management team worked to create a "boundaryless" (seamless) organization. Boundaries, according to Welch, are an impediment to movement, costing organizations time and money as they work to get around, over, under, or through boundaries. (To understand Jack Welch's concept, envision a house in the northern climate and one in the tropics. In tropical homes, very few walls separate the inside and outside of houses—simple curtains can be easily raised, lowered, or pushed aside; entry and exit are easy, quick, and without a great deal of inconvenience. In northern Minnesota, on the other hand, walls are solid and filled with insulation, not easy to move, and the only simple way in and out of the house is through the door, which, of course, always seems to be on the other side of the house!) Welch believed that, to the extent that GE becomes a boundaryless organization, organizational flexibility, speed, efficiency, and productivity will ultimately increase, helping GE become Number One or Two in each of its businesses.

http://www.boeing.com

Welch's strategy, in part, can be seen as one of integrating the organization with its external environment—becoming "one with that environment." Boeing, too, has worked to eliminate boundaries that traditionally separated the organization from elements within its task environment. As Boeing designs the next generation of airplanes, their aeronautical engineers will be assisted by their customers and suppliers—working as one integrated team, as opposed to separate and distinct groups.

Stanford University management professor Jeffrey Pfeffer identifies several tactics that managers can use to reduce uncertainty and interdependence:[17]

http://www.compaq.com

- **Selective recruitment** of key employees. By hiring knowledgeable individuals from key organizations in the external environment, managers bring into their fold people with information and knowledge about the operations and policies of competitors. In this way, they reduce interdependence and uncertainty. This is exactly what Compac does each time it hires a former IBM employee.
- **Regulation.** Organizations can encourage and support various forms of control by regulatory agencies. Regulations often affect the interdependence of organizations and the level of uncertainty. In the 1980s, for example, U.S. car makers encouraged the government to restrict the number of cars imported from Japan. The immediate result of this regulation was to reduce competition for U.S. companies, allowing them to charge higher prices than they could otherwise command.
- **Political activity.** Managers participate in the political process not only to influence regulations, but also to exercise political power in ways that favorably affect the organization. For example, many university administrators secure funds for projects through government officials. Columbia University built a new chemistry laboratory with funds from the Department of Energy, Rochester Institute of Technology received money from the Defense Nuclear Agency for its Center for Microelectronic Engineering, and Northeastern University funded a library through the Air Force's electronics research fund.[18]

Thus, managers have a wide variety of tactics by which they can reduce the uncertainty and power of the external environment.

Environmental Change and Segmentation

environmental change reflects the degree to which the organization's task environment is stable/shifting

While the organization's external environment is multidimensional in nature, James Thompson observes that two aspects of an organization's task environment significantly influence the behavior of effective managers and, subsequently, of organizational design. These two environmental dimensions are the degree of environmental change and of environmental segmentation.[19] **Environmental change** reflects the degree to which an organization's task environment is *stable* (undergoing few and slow changes) or *shifting* (dynamic—undergoing frequent and rapid changes). During the 1970s, for example, domestic airlines operated in a fairly stable environment. During the 1980s, however, the U.S. government deregulated the airlines, which caused numerous and frequent changes in flight schedules, airfares, and even airline ownership. Competition for new routes intensified, as did competition for new passengers, whom the airlines tried to attract with low fares. The 1990s marked the second decade during which rapid change, high levels of turbulence, and uncertainty continued to characterize this industry. Clearly, this previously stable environment changed rapidly, as has come to typify an increasing number of industries. Management guru Tom Peters suggests that the 21st century will continue to be characterized as a time during which organizations will need to learn how to "thrive on chaos."[20]

The degree of environmental change influences the level of environmentally induced uncertainty experienced by the organization. Stable environments provide management with time to study and learn the environment, thereby helping them lower the level of uncertainty. The more dynamic the market, the more challenging and difficult this learning process becomes. Environmental stability plays a significant role in determining the degree to which managers can develop rules, regulations, and standard operating procedures to guide internal operation and interactions with the external environment. These are hallmarks of control-oriented management practices and the mechanistically designed organization.

environmental segmentation reflects the degree of homogeneity (similarities) and heterogeneity (differences) among components of the organization's task environment

Environmental segmentation describes the similarities and differences among components of the task environment and the demands that they place on an organization. In other words, it describes whether an organization's suppliers, customers, competitors, and regulatory agencies differ in their demands on the organization. A *homogeneous task environment* is characterized by very little segmentation. That is, components of the task environment place similar demands on an organization. For example, nearly all of the customers at Jingle's, a student bar near Camp Randall Stadium at the University of Wisconsin, place essentially the same demands on Jingle's. Most of the bar's suppliers and its competitors also place similar demands. Because of the similarity in the demands, these segments of the Jingle's task environment can be regarded as homogeneous. Conversely, a *heterogeneous task environment* is highly segmented or differentiated. For example, IBM developed its personal computer line to target part of a highly segmented market. Computer customers have very different demands. Some want word processors, some graphics capabilities, some spreadsheets, and still others want scholarly capabilities. The computer needs of the Pentagon, the college student, and the business executive differ greatly.

The degree of environmental segmentation, like the degree of environmental change, influences the level of environmentally caused uncertainty confronting the organization. Once again, simple environments are easier to study and learn, thereby reducing the level of uncertainty presented to the organization by its external environment. As the environment becomes more complex (that is, segmented into highly heterogeneous units), the level of uncertainty increases, as there are simply more parts of the environment that need to be understood. Environmental segmentation plays a significant role in determining the number of specialized subsystems (jobs, departments, divisions) within the organization, each of which deals with a different segment of the external environment. As these specialized roles are created, the internal structure of the organization becomes increasing complex.

The stability and segmentation of the task environment combine to define the four environmental conditions that managers encounter: (1) stable and homoge-

FIGURE 4-2 Environmental Conditions

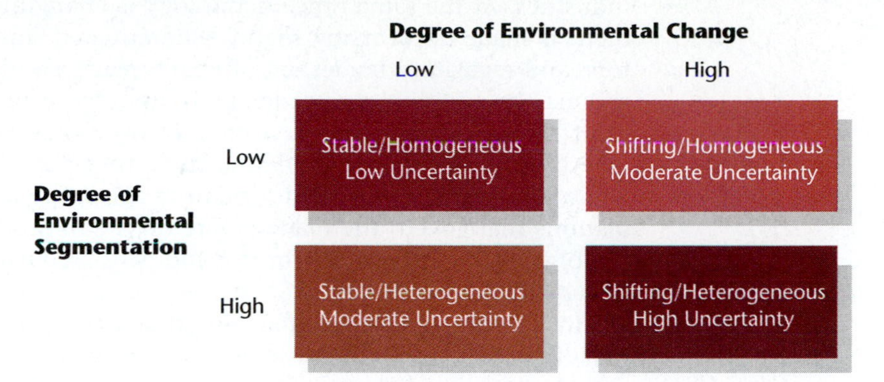

Source: J. D. Thompson. 1967. *Organizations in action.* New York: McGraw-Hill, 72. Reproduced with permission of The McGraw-Hill Companies.

neous, (2) stable and heterogeneous, (3) shifting and homogeneous, or (4) shifting and heterogeneous (see Figure 4-2). Management's challenge is to design an organization and management system that can handle the conditions presented by its task environment.

Organizational Responses to Environmental Conditions

How do effective organizations deal with the uncertainties presented by environmental change and segmentation? To give you a sense for how organizations respond to these environmental conditions, we highlight the two environments that differ most from one another, as most organizations face variations on one of these two environments.

Stable and Homogeneous Environments When the environment is stable and homogeneous, managers face a relatively low level of uncertainty. Under these conditions, management can develop rules, regulations, and standard operating procedures that guide internal operations and interactions with the external environment. The structure of an organization operates efficiently with clearly defined areas of responsibility, authority, information systems, and division of labor. In addition, the structure of the organization can be relatively simple. Without a highly segmented external environment, the organization doesn't need to create a large number of highly specialized roles (jobs, department, divisions) that concentrate their efforts on one segment of the organization's large and complex environment.

For decades, the control-oriented management of the U.S. car industry fit their relatively stable and homogeneous environment very well—until the invasion of foreign car manufacturers. This organization-environmental match, while it lasted, produced high levels of corporate profits.

Shifting and Heterogeneous Environments At the other end of the spectrum, we have firms operating in shifting (dynamic) and segmented (heterogeneous) environments. When the environment is shifting and filled with heterogeneous segments, managers face high degrees of uncertainty. This is currently the case in the cable television industry, where market demands are changing rapidly, and a variety of distinct viewing groups exist. City, state, and federal regulations are relevant. Competition is increasing between cable companies and traditional broadcast stations, as well as with the videotape and satellite TV industries. At the same time, technology is changing rapidly. The task environment is made up of many highly differentiated suppliers, customers, competitors, and regulatory bodies, all of which place a variety of demands on organizations. In addition, these demands undergo rapid change. Customers may want modifications made to a product or service; at the same time, suppliers may change the nature of the materials they are capable of delivering. Meanwhile, legislators, courts, and regulatory agencies may rewrite the laws and regulations that govern the manufacture or sale of products and services. Many of the organizations operating in this industry are facing a shifting and heterogeneous task environment.

In a shifting and heterogeneous environment, each boundary-spanning system (that is, organizational members who work to integrate the organization with individuals, groups, and organizations that fall outside of the organization's boundaries) must be attuned to its special segment of the external environment. In addition, managers must create internal communication and authority systems for processing incoming information so that their organization effectively responds to environmental conditions.

When an organization's environment changes rapidly, creating standard routines for handling activities becomes increasingly difficult. Critical environment clues let managers know when and how to act. Thus, the organization's boundaries must be open so that information flows quickly from the environment into the organization and to the appropriate point for action. Such openness is a hallmark of the high-involvement organization, and is a part of its commitment to decentralizing the flow of information.

Specialized roles (jobs, departments, divisions) are created, each responsible for dealing with a component of the external market. The internal structure of the organization thus becomes more complex—making organizational planning, coordinating, and controlling more difficult.

Organizations that operate in rapidly shifting environments hire people with high levels of specialization, education, and professionalism. These people are placed in key positions and given substantial authority for making decisions. The changeability of the environment requires a more professional work force, fewer operating procedures, and shared decision making.

http://www.bcbs.com

In recent years, an increasing number of insurance companies have recognized that this is the new face of their environment. Many, like Blue Cross/Blue Shield, have responded by creating small teams that handle all phases of the insurance process for a specific group of clients. Team members have a great deal of latitude and flexibility in their dealings with clients. To meet this challenge Blue Cross/Blue Shield employs more involvement-oriented management practices and is creating a flexible organization with a highly decentralized authority structure. The company is therefore more organic and open in its design and operations.

In sum, the challenge facing managers is to design an organization/management system that can handle the conditions presented by the task environment. Task environments vary according to the degree of environmental change, segmentation, and uncertainty. A manager's approach to organizing should differ with each combination of environmental conditions. As the external environment becomes increasingly complex and turbulent, designing fluid, open, flexible, and fast organizations becomes critical to competitive success. This challenge has led an increasing number of organizations like Motorola and Herman Miller to move to the high-involvement organization.

Two Classic Studies of the Organization-Environmental Relationship

An organization's external task environment strongly affects its organization design and management practice (this relationship is shown in Figure 4-3). Results from two major studies provide us with insight into the environment-organization relationship.

FIGURE 4-3

Causes of Differentiation in Organization Design and Management Practice

One of the first major studies to concentrate on the relationship between organizations and their environments was conducted by British researchers Tom Burns and George Stalker.[21] They examined the relationships among environmental conditions, management practice, and organizational design in 20 manufacturing firms in England and Scotland. The study, which has had tremendous impact on the management and organizational sciences, focused on the rate of environmental change in the firms' scientific technology and product markets. Their results identified two types of organizations: *organic* and *mechanistic* (see Table 4-1).

The **organic organization** is characterized, for example, by

organic organization an organization whose structure is fluid and flexible

- A flexible structure that changes when confronted with different kinds of task demands
- Loosely defined tasks to be performed by employees
- Consultative-type communications (as opposed to commands)
- Authority that flows more from knowledge centers (individuals, groups, or specialized departments) and the nature of relationships rather than from strict hierarchical positions
- Receptive to change
- Relies on self and peer control processes

Hallmark, Lake Superior Paper Industries, Johnsonville Foods, and Herman Miller have moved toward the organic organization. Many research and development departments adopt an organic structure in the belief that its openness and lack of structure are more conducive to innovation and creativity.

TABLE 4-1 Mechanistic and Organic Organizations

	Mechanistic	**Organic**
Structure	Rigid	Flexible
Tasks	Well defined, stable, standardized	Dynamic, loosely defined
Change	Resistant	Receptive
Authority source	From hierarchy and position	From knowledge and expertise
Control	Hierarchy	From self and peers
Communication direction	Command-type and downward	Consultative-type, up, down, horizontal, and diagonal
Communication content	Instructions and decisions issued by superiors	Information and advice

Source: T. Burns and G. Stalker. 1961. *The management of innovation.* London: Tavistock.

mechanistic organization an organization whose structure is fixed and rigid (also referred to as a bureaucracy)

In contrast, a **mechanistic organization** is characterized by

- Clear definition and relative stability of tasks and responsibility
- Vesting of authority in position and its arrangement according to hierarchical level
- Communications in the form of a downward flow of instructions issued as commands
- A rigid hierarchy of authority with control embedded in the hierarchy
- Resistant to change

http://www.army.mil

http://www.clorox.com

Many organizations in contemporary society still model themselves on the mechanistic organization. Among the most visible ones are the Catholic Church, the U.S. Army and Postal Service, USX, Goodyear, and many firms associated with the "smoke-stack industries" of the early 1900s. Clorox plant manager Cindy Ransom moved her organization from a mechanistic one to an involvement-oriented organic arrangement.[22] Ransom asked her 100 plant members to redesign the plant's operations. A team of hourly workers reorganized the traditional assembly-line oriented, top-down controlled organization into five customer-focused business units. Ransom viewed her job as that of coach, sponsor, and empowerer as her organization shifted from a mechanistic to a more organic system.

Burns and Stalker argued that organic and mechanistic organizations are appropriate for different environmental conditions. In similar fashion and more than three decades later, Edward Lawler, III, noted that control-oriented management and the mechanistic organization, and involvement-oriented management and the organic organization are appropriate approaches under entirely different environmental conditions.[23] Environments in which uncertainty is high and unique problems and events often arise require an organic and involvement-oriented system. The mechanistic or control-oriented system is more compatible with low levels of environmentally induced uncertainty. Rather than proposing that one management system is superior to the other, these organization scholars suggested that an organization's task environment plays a major role in determining the system that works best. The organization's external environment is seen as another major determinant of organizational design and management practice.

Police forces are generally highly mechanistic organizations.

A second study of the relationship between organizations and their environments was conducted by Harvard University researchers Paul Lawrence and Jay Lorsch.[24] They found that effective organizations operating in highly uncertain environments had management systems different from effective organizations operating in relatively stable environments. Specifically, firms that operate in highly uncertain environments had more differentiated or segmented management systems than did those that operated in highly certain environments. Firms in stable environments had internal divisions, such as departments, that operated with similar goals, time frames, interpersonal coordination, and structures. Firms in highly uncertain environments had internal divisions that differ from one another in all of these respects.

When structures, goals, and temporal and interpersonal orientations were dissimilar, managers in the studies found it more difficult to coordinate and control organizational activities. Lawrence and Lorsch found that managers of effective organizations in highly uncertain environments achieved successful integration of their organizational units by using personal and informal integrating mechanisms. Managers operating in more certain environments achieved integration through rules, policies, and standard operating procedures. Lawrence and Lorsch concluded their reports by noting that effective organizations develop designs and management systems to fit the environment in which they operate.

The work of Thompson, Burns and Stalker, and Lawrence and Lorsch leads to a number of observations. First, there appears to be a relationship between characteristics of the task environment and the type of management systems that develop. To be effective, an organization must find the best possible fit between its environment and its management system(s). Second, organizations create different management systems to deal with the different amounts of uncertainty that managers face in performing their jobs. Organic systems appear appropriate for high levels of environmental change and segmentation, mechanistic systems for more stable environments and lower levels of uncertainty.

Closed and Open Organizational Systems

One way to characterize the different ways managers approach their external environments is by the degree to which management opens the organization to its external environment. Thus, organizations come to be characterized as "closed" or "open" systems.

Closed Systems Years ago, classical management theorists proposed that organizations are rational systems that can be designed according to a specific set of laws. They asserted that organizations will be efficient if managers properly define the nature of the work, standardize work procedures, assign an appropriate division of labor, group tasks into departments, and specify appropriate authority and responsibility relationships. These primary forces, they said, are internal to the system and arise from the nature of the work itself. Thus, according to this perspective, an organization could be designed appropriately if managers paid attention to the relationships among the system parts. Much as an engineer designs a bridge according to the principles of physics, followers of classical management theories believed managers can design an organization by adhering to the principles of organization.

In contrast, behavioral management theorists believe that the forces defining an effective management system are to be found in the nature of individuals and groups. They reason that management systems must accommodate workers' social and self-fulfillment needs. Both the classical and behavioral management theories concentrate on the inner workings of organizations in an effort to achieve order, consistency, efficiency, and predictability. They consider that managers working in such systems don't have to pay particular attention to the external environment. In fact, neither classical nor behavioral management theories include the environment in their models.

From both the classical and behavioral perspectives, managers look only within an organization to improve productivity and efficiency. The organization is considered a **closed system** that operates as though it were in a world by itself. As Figure 4-4 shows, the "walls" of a closed system are thick. They block out ideas, information, and external forces. Whatever environmental uncertainty penetrates the walls of an organization is absorbed at the institutional and administrative levels. Operations in the organization's technical core are not disrupted. The American automobile industry's refusal to believe in the shift to quality and to small and fuel-efficient cars in the 1970s and 1980s is a classic example of a closed system at work. In a similar vein, IBM's refusal to see that their future lay in PCs as opposed to mainframe computers can also be viewed as a closed system. The goal of those in a closed system is to eliminate or control the uncertainty that originates in the external environment so that the management process is as easy and predictable as possible.

closed system an organization that is "shut-off" to its external environment and one in which managers look internally for ideas on productivity and efficiency improvements

As noted earlier, while no organization can close itself off absolutely from external forces, managers can and do design systems that minimize the uncertainty, pressures, information, and ideas of outside influences. For example, if managers assign all boundary-spanning activities to people at the institutional level of their organization, such as to a president or CEO, the effects of external forces on the technical core and the administrative zone are minimized. In addition, if managers at the institutional level adopt a closed-system perspective, they further reduce the intrusion of the external environment into their organization's internal affairs.

Open Systems A second perspective of an organization in relation to its external environment is the **open system** (review Figure 4-4). According to this perspective, an organization is a system that interacts with and depends on other systems. Consider the situation faced by banks in the United States. Banks cannot survive unless people and companies make deposits, take out loans, and purchase other banking services. They are also dependent on the federal government, which sets the cost of loaning money, as well as on state and federal regulations governing their bank charters.

open system an organization that attempts to integrate itself with its external environment and looks to the outside for ideas on productivity and efficiency improvements

". . . [O]rganizations are not autonomous entities; instead, the best laid plans of managers have unintended consequences and are conditioned or upset by other social units—other complex organizations or publics—on whom the organization is dependent."[25] An organization's survival depends on its ability to mesh with the larger environment. Open-systems advocates believe that this meshing allows organizational members to deal effectively with the external environment. To cope with the external environment's inevitable intrusion and uncertainty, organizations must create open management systems. Rather than designing systems that ignore the external environment, they must design systems sensitive and responsive to the environment.

Managers who view their organization as an open system, therefore, face a major challenge. They must play an active role as organizational boundary spanners. They must carry information outward to influence the external environment and simultaneously serve as conduits through which external environ-

FIGURE 4-4 Open and Closed Systems of Management

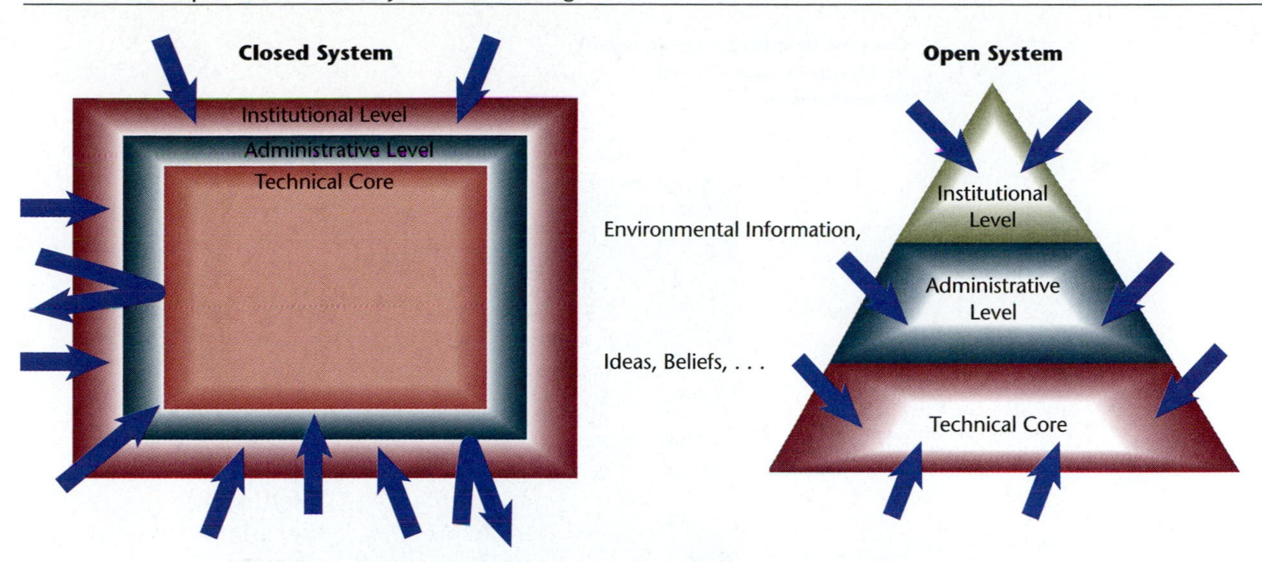

Note: The arrows represent forces in the environment that attempt to penetrate the system.

mental factors can influence internal operations. Such managers meet the public, talk to the press, and actively lobby regulatory and legislative bodies. Henry Mintzberg has noted that in all three critical managerial roles—interpersonal, informational, and decisional—effective managers deal well with environments external to their organization.[26] Open management systems facilitate this.

The open systems model suggests that an organization should create a number of open windows to let ideas, beliefs, information, and pressures from the environment influence the organization at each of its three levels—institutional, administrative, and technical core. As was noted in Chapter 1, rapidly changing conditions mean that first-level managers increasingly will become externally oriented.[27] The institutional zone of management becomes more and more important as organizations come to depend on coalitions with other organizations, as business regulation expands and society expects more social responsibility from organizations. Effective organizations will have to become more open to environmental information, allowing it to flow in at each hierarchical level and permitting organizations to influence the environment at each level as well.

Figure 4-5 summarizes the organization-environment relationship. Control-oriented management and mechanistic and closed organizations tend to be congruent with low levels of environmental uncertainty. Involvement-oriented management practices and open and organic organizations are most compatible with high levels of environmental uncertainty. Based on evidence from environmental studies, it is unlikely that the former approach to management and organizational design can be successful operating under complex and highly turbulent environmental conditions.

FIGURE 4-5 The Influence of Environmental Uncertainty

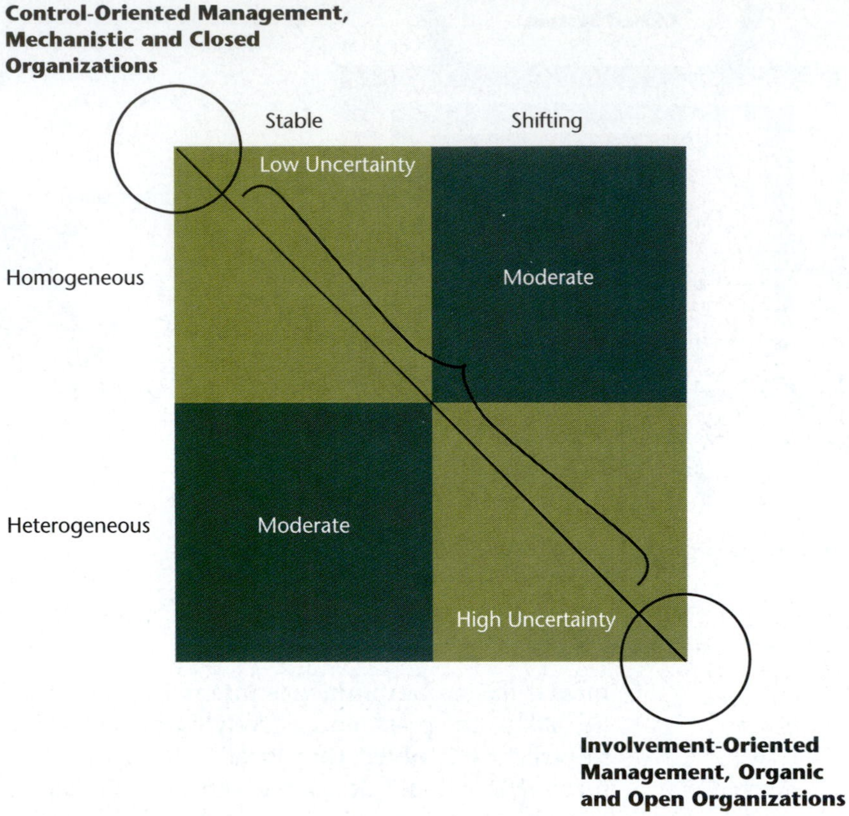

LINKING ENVIRONMENTS AND ORGANIZATIONS

It is often difficult to determine where an organization ends and its environment begins. If someone asked you how large your college is, you would probably refer to the number of students enrolled, but are the students part of the organization or part of the external environment? If asked to describe the size of your hairstylist's shop, would you refer to the number of stylists who work there or to the number of customers? Although the external environment is defined as separate and distinct from an organization, it is seldom easy to locate the exact boundary between the two. In fact, many organizations (such as hospitals and universities) attempt to encompass various aspects of the environment within their boundaries. Many of the tactics described in the previous section help them accomplish this goal. When an organization buys its key suppliers, co-opts a board member, hires an important employee away from a competitor, shapes the laws and regulations that govern its business, or builds partnerships with members of its task environment, it assimilates part of its external environment. In such cases, although an organization and its environment are separate, they have an interdependent relationship.

As we'll see in this section, the relationship between an organization and its environment is one of critical importance. The degree of fit that an organization achieves between its internal and external environments is strongly related to its effectiveness. Consequently, it is important to carefully manage the organization's boundaries and its linking processes.

The Boundary-Spanning Process

boundary-spanning process the means by which managers link the organization with its external environment.

boundary roles those positions in organizations that link the organization with its external environment

boundary spanners individuals whose job it is to span the organization's boundaries and integrate the organization with external environment

Many tactics described earlier for reducing uncertainty and managing interdependence help organizations span their boundaries. Because organizations exist within and depend on their external environments, managers need to link carefully with the external environment. The **boundary-spanning process** is one means through which organizations conduct transactions with their external environment. At General Mills, for example, when the market research department brings information into the organization about customer preferences, it performs a boundary-spanning activity, and when Patrick Miner brings customers into the weekly management meetings at his grocery store, another type of boundary-spanning activity is being performed. **Boundary roles** are the positions that link an organization to its external environment. Sales representatives, market researchers, and organizational lobbyists occupy boundary roles. **Boundary spanners** are the individuals who fill these roles. A boundary spanner operates both within and outside an organization, as when a manager acts as a liaison between the organization and the external environment. The various roles played by managers—figureheads and spokespeople—enable them to span the boundaries between the organization and the environment.[28]

As you have learned, individuals other than managers also perform the role of organizational boundary spanners. Purchasing agents, salespeople, lawyers, technological specialists, and lobbyists often link organizations to their suppliers, customers, regulatory bodies, and informational resources. Although some positions are created specifically as boundary-spanning functions, many individuals are informal carriers of information across organizational boundaries. A waiter, for example, might learn about an especially good wine from customers and suggest to the wine steward that it be considered for inclusion in the restaurant's wine selection.

In the high-involvement organization, a considerable amount of boundary-spanning activity between organization, customer, and supplier gets carried out by production teams. At Harley-Davidson, major product changes were made by production employees who dealt directly with the company's vendors. Today production employees routinely collect information pertaining to capacities of new machinery, costs, and so on, then draft proposals and present them to the company president. Weyerhaeuser has exchanged some employees with their suppliers so that the Weyerhaeuser employee "stays in touch" with suppliers and improves the company's operations. These examples show how production employees facilitate organizational learning by performing the boundary-spanning function.

http://www.weyerhaeuser.com

THE INTERNAL ENVIRONMENT

The second environment that needs to be managed is the organization's internal environment. The internal environment of an organization consists of a wide range of factors within its formal boundaries. Essentially, it represents all that is the organization. The internal environment includes the jobs that people perform; the work units, departments, teams, divisions, and other structures in which they perform those jobs; the technologies employed to develop services and/or products; the processes used to guide workers; and, of course, the people who do the work—both managers and nonmanagers—together with their values and beliefs. In addition, the internal environment is strongly influenced by management style (control-oriented or involvement-oriented).

While Part III, Management Functions and the Organizational Behavior Context, provides a detailed and in-depth look at the organization's internal environment, we briefly introduce internal environment here so that you gain more insight into what we mean by organization. We'll explore management functions and the organizational behavior context and their impact on the employee attitudes, motivation, and behavior in greater detail in Part III.

In Chapter 1, we indicated that if we could show you a picture of Steinlagger Brewery in New Zealand, Frog's Leap Winery in Napa Valley, the Vancouver Canucks in Vancouver, British Columbia, and the 3M Corporation in St. Paul, Minnesota, each picture would look very different. Each organization has a different anatomy, each serves a different purpose.

An organization's internal environment can be thought of as its anatomy. Important features of that anatomy consist of structures and processes, people and their beliefs, management practices and organizational functions, and overall climate of the organization.

Structures and Processes

Several structures define the internal environment. Three salient sources of structure that researchers have identified are the design of the jobs/work that employees do, the structural arrangement of the organization and its work units (such as departments and divisions), and the technology used to produce products and/or services (see *An Inside Look*).[29]

Several important processes unfold in organizations that are also a part of the internal environment. Each affects the character of the organization and impacts the attitudes, motivation, and behavior of its members. Three of these processes are coordination (how people, jobs, departments, levels, and other components are linked), decision making (how decisions are made), and communications (how information is disseminated).

People and Their Beliefs

Of course, the most carefully structured organization and smoothly applied managerial processes would be worthless without people in place to use them. A critical component of the internal environment is thus its social system, which includes organizational members (management, formal leaders, and nonmanagerial employees) and the values and beliefs they share.

organizational culture
a pattern of basic assumptions invented, discovered, or developed by a given group as it learns to cope with problems of external adaptation and internal integration

In addition to the beliefs and opinions held by organizational members, organizations develop beliefs as well. These beliefs represent the **organizational culture**, which is defined as ". . . a pattern of basic assumptions invented, discovered, or developed by a given group as it learns to cope with its problem of external adaptation and internal integration. . . ."[30] Understanding an organization's culture is crucial for managers because, once established, culture is relatively stable and highly resistant to change. New suggestions may be countered with such remarks as "We don't do things that way." When asked why not, employees often have no logical explanation. Instead, they seem to rely on tradition or a mystical embodiment of organizational values.[31]

AN INSIDE LOOK

Jobs versus Work

One of the most intriguing concepts in the field of management today often makes people stop and scratch their heads. What is the difference between a *job* and *work*?

Before the age of industrialization, most people did not have positions defined by job descriptions. Instead, different tasks that needed to be done comprised their work for the day. These tasks would change depending on the time, weather and other variables. Then, during Industrialization, specific jobs were created to improve the efficiency of factory workers. Jobs were conceptualized as a set of repetitive tasks, and employees were recruited who could adequately perform these tasks.

In those days, change was slow in occurring, and employees were not viewed as holistic beings who had complex needs beyond survival. In today's world, managers widely recognize that employees are motivated not only by financial needs but also by their desire to make a contribution to the organization and realize goals for personal as well as professional growth. So why is it that the notion of jobs as unchanging sets of responsibilities has not evolved as well?

Leading-edge management thinkers are attempting to change the paradigm used by most managers to organize employee responsibilities. The concept of *having a job* is becoming obsolete; instead, individuals *have work that needs to be accomplished*. This work includes different tasks that will constantly evolve. Now that many organizations are using the project management concept to organize work teams, an individual may shift from one project team to another depending on his or her areas of expertise and interest. Innovative companies like Amazon.com no longer seek individuals with a specific set of qualifications to fill job openings. Instead, they hire employees with certain key characteristics that they feel will benefit the organization in a multitude of ways.

In order for this new system of accomplishing work to be successful, organizations must be flexible. Traditionally rigid organization structures will not adapt well to this new way of thinking, and managers must be non-territorial and willing to allow employees to move to different project teams as the need arises. A significant benefit to the organization is that employees may use more innovative and creative approaches to solving problems as they continually gain new perspectives and experience different projects.

Organizations who learn to think "outside the box" and use this new paradigm will have an advantage in the ever-changing workplace of the 21st century. Making the shift to thinking how to accomplish work and projects instead of how to fill static job descriptions may help organizations suffering from a labor shortage be better prepared to take advantage of the strengths of current as well as prospective employees. Flexibility is the key to survival in the unpredictable and fast-moving modern world, and organizations should be ready to change their ways of thinking.

Source: Adapted from S. Caudron. 2000. Jobs disappear: When work becomes more important. *Workforce* 79(1):30–32.

An organization's culture influences how its employees address challenges and contributes to the company's mission, as shown in the video *Culture in an Organization: W. B. Donor.*

This combination of shared beliefs, values, perceptions, language, and reactions to situations is a critical part of the internal environment. In fact, an organization's very survival may depend on its culture. The Hay Group, a major consulting firm, notes that corporate cultures of high-performing companies differ dramatically from those of the average company. These firms have strong cultures and are among *Fortune*'s Most Admired Companies. Firms like 3M, Toyota, Bristol-Myers Squibb, and Intel have cultures that revolve around teamwork, customer focus, fair treatment of employees, initiative, and innovation.[32] In addition to the strong internal focus, researchers have observed that corporate culture influences the strategies that organizations pursue and their effectiveness in doing so.[33]

Management Practices and Organizational Functions

To address the components of their organization's internal environment, managers oversee the performance of many different types of activities. To orchestrate such activities, managers frequently group them according to the organizational functions served, such as operations, marketing, accounting, finance, and human resource management (see Chapter 1). These activities and the organization as a whole are managed through the execution of several activities—planning, organizing, directing, and controlling—and the carrying out of several roles—interpersonal, informational, and decisional. These managerial practices and organizational functions reflect part of the organization's internal environment (see Figure 4-6).

As noted in Chapters 1 and 2, the two dominant models of management practice are control-oriented and involvement-oriented management. Both models have a profound impact on the attitudes, motivation, and behavior of organizational members.

Organizational Climate

Much as the physical climate of an area is composed of such factors as temperature, humidity, and precipitation, an organizational climate is composed of such factors as structure, processes, and people and their beliefs (see Figure 4-7). Thus **organizational climate** is the prevailing organizational condition and reflects an organization's overall character or tone.[34] Prior to the court-ordered breakup of AT&T, comedienne Lily Tomlin played a telephone operator who answered customers' complaints with "We don't care. We don't have to. We're the telephone company."—a succinct characterization of a company's climate or "personality."

organizational climate the prevailing organizational condition that reflects the overall organizational tone or character

The climate within an organization is a function of both its internal environment and its reactions to the external environment. You have seen that variations in culture, job design, organizational and work unit structures, technologies, managerial processes, and employees create a wide range of environments. The organizational climate affects, and is affected by, employees' attitudes, motivation, and work-related behaviors. For example, the extent to which employees are willing to perform above and beyond the call of duty is likely to result from the type of climate within the organization.

FIGURE 4-6 Managerial and Organizational Functions

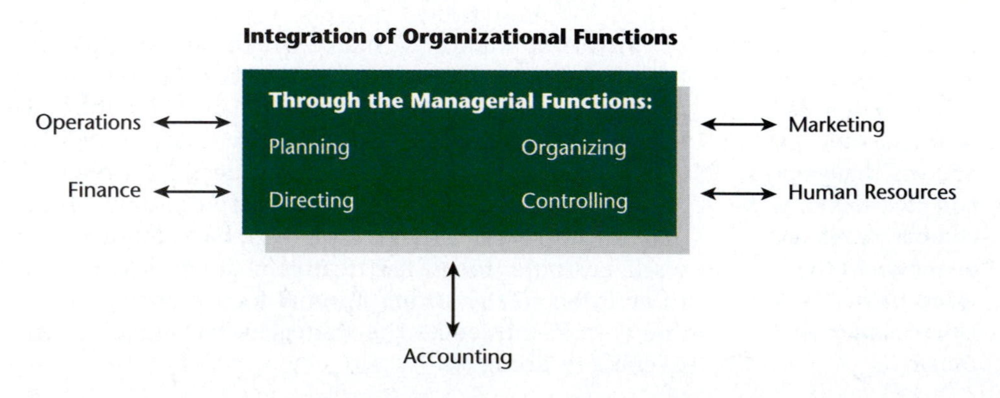

FIGURE 4-7 The Internal Environment and Organizational Climate

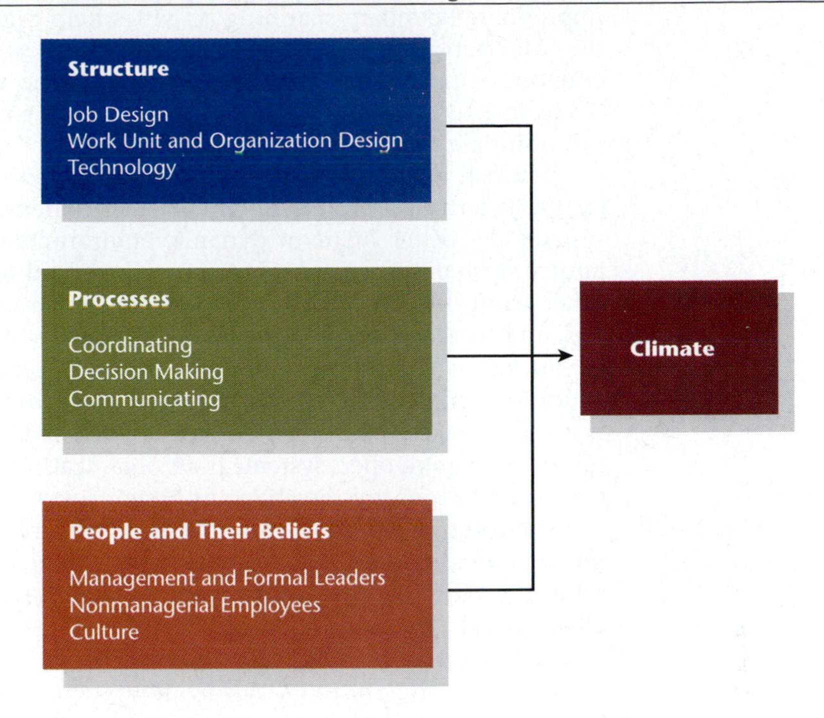

The challenge for managers is to be aware of the climate that they produce with their managerial style. They cannot forget that an organization is a social system. An organization's level of innovation, the quality of its performance, and the way that its workers react to management are largely the result of its employees' attitudes. These attitudes are influenced to a certain degree by an organization's climate, and the climate is shaped largely by management.

THE ORGANIZATIONAL ENVIRONMENT IN REVIEW

Managers must contend with environments both inside and outside their organization. In the ordinary course of events, organizations interact dynamically with their external environments. Managers strive to control forces in the external environment, and the external environment concurrently exerts pressures on the organization. The external environment is large and complex, and contains both general and task components. The general components include the sociocultural domain in which the organization operates, the economic climate, the technological domain, the legal/political atmosphere, and global forces. The task component includes an organization's suppliers, customers, competitors, a number of regulatory and influence groups, and allies.

Through interaction with the external environment, managers face varying degrees of uncertainty and change, as well as various degrees of dependency on members of the task environment. Managers adopt a variety of tactics as they attempt to increase their power over the external environment and manage this uncertainty and interdependence. Ways to deal effectively with the external environment are discussed in more detail in later chapters.

Organizations exist, not in isolation, but within a broader external reality. Appropriate boundary-spanning activities help organization members exchange the information and knowledge necessary to deal effectively with the external environment. Boundary spanning identifies the techniques for dealing effectively and appropriately with the nature of the environment in which an organization operates.

Research has shown that management systems are, and should be, influenced by the external environment. Involvement-oriented management and organic systems are better fitted to dynamic environments with high levels of uncertainty. Mechanistic systems and control-oriented management practices, on the other hand, fit better with stable external environments. Although rules, policies, and standardized procedures can be effective in the absence of environmental uncertainty, more personal and informal procedures are preferable under conditions of high uncertainty. Classical management theorists suggested closed systems to isolate organizations from their environments. Contemporary environments require open systems if an organization is to survive. The most effective organizations are sensitive and responsive to their external environment.

The internal environment consists of a number of different factors, including structure, organizational processes, and people and their beliefs, that determine the climate of the organization. These environmental factors affect an organization's decisions and actions and must be managed to achieve efficiency and effectiveness.

Managers attempt to do this by grouping organizational activities according to the function they serve: operations, marketing, accounting, finance, and human resource management. Each of these functions must be managed effectively, as must their interrelationships.

In sum, managers do not operate in isolation. They practice inside organizations, and organizations conduct business under pressure from both the external and internal environments. As we'll see later in this book, each component of the organization's internal environment impacts the attitudes, motivation, and behaviors of employees. It therefore becomes crucial that each environmental factor is consciously and carefully managed so that intended and beneficial effects are realized, in an ethical and socially responsible manner.

A FINAL LOOK

Despite his skepticism, Dean Atwood decides to hold focus groups made up of students and business leaders to gauge their reaction to the proposal to offer Ivy business courses online. After noting the positive reactions from many of the focus group participants, the college decides that distance education can meet the needs of many prospective students.

Ivy College of Business is energized by this new approach to delivering education. An interdepartmental team made up of faculty from each discipline area, students, and business and university leaders spearheads the distance education effort. The input of this diverse group leads to more innovative ideas, and the College decides to develop an entire online degree in e-commerce.

Distance education not only helps Ivy increase its enrollment but also sparks other changes in the College of Business. Because of the innovations suggested by the focus groups, Dean Atwood concentrates more on the external environment than on the college's internal environment and begins to broadly and positively engage the local business community. Ivy College gains a reputation for being responsive to student and business needs alike. No longer seen as a dusty, stodgy ivory tower, Ivy College's new image as an innovator has students lining up in droves.

KEY TERMS

boundary roles, 135
boundary spanners, 135
boundary-spanning process, 135
closed system, 132
economic domain, 117
environmental change, 125
environmental segmentation, 126
external environment, 115
general environment, 117
internal environment, 115
international domain, 119
legal/political domain, 118
mechanistic organization, 130
open system, 132
organic organization, 129
organizational climate, 138
organizational culture, 136
sociocultural domain, 117
task environment, 121
technological domain, 118

ISSUES FOR REVIEW AND DISCUSSION

1. Identify and briefly discuss each component of the general external environment.
2. What is an organization's task environment? Name the five components of the task environment.
3. What is the relationship between the general and task environments? What is their relationship with an organization?
4. What four strategies help managers seal off an organization from environmental forces?
5. Pfeffer identified a set of tactics that managers use to control the level of environmentally induced uncertainty and interdependence. Identify and briefly discuss each strategy.
6. Who acts as an organizational boundary spanner?
7. Explain why organizations need boundary spanners.
8. Discuss why management planning and decision making should be different under conditions of low stability and high segmentation than under conditions of high stability and low segmentation.
9. How do closed and open management systems differ?
10. Discuss the components of organizational climate and its challenges for managers.

EXERCISES

EXPERIENCING ORGANIZATIONAL CULTURES

DIRECTIONS
Consider an organization that you're all familiar with, such as the institution that sponsors this class. (Another possibility would be to consider the company you work for.)

Step 1: Completing and Scoring the Questionnaire
Complete the following questionnaire, describing first the ideal and then the actual state of the organization, as you see it. (The "organization" can be this class, a work group, your employer, or any other organization.) Then compute your ideal and actual scores on the six dimensions of culture given at the end of the questionnaire. Compute the gap between ideal and actual states on each dimension.

Step 2: Computing Group Averages and Discrepancies
If other members of your organization or group have also completed the questionnaire, meet with them and compute group means for the ideal and actual organizational climate. Also compute the gap between ideal and actual scores on each group mean.

Where do the greatest gaps occur? Discuss the reasons for this state of affairs. What could be done to reduce this gap?

Where do the smallest gaps occur? What accounts for this state of affairs?

ORGANIZATION CULTURE QUESTIONNAIRE

Using the spaces in the left-hand column, first characterize the ideal practices and procedures you would like to see in this organization. Next, using the spaces in the right-hand column, describe what you believe *actually* happens in this organization. Put a number in the space beside each statement according to the following key.

1 = almost never; 2 = infrequently; 3 = sometimes; 4 = frequently; 5 = very frequently.

Ideal		Actual
_____	1. This organization takes care of the people who work for it.	_____
_____	2. Members enjoy keeping up with national and international current events.	_____
_____	3. People in this organization ask each other how they are doing in reaching their goals.	_____
_____	4. Management effectively balances people problems and production problems.	_____
_____	5. There are definite "in" and "out" groups in the organization.	_____
_____	6. This organization encourages employees to exercise their own initiative.	_____
_____	7. This organization takes an active interest in the progress of its members.	_____
_____	8. Members of this organization have a wide range of interests.	_____
_____	9. More experienced members of this organization take the time to help newer members.	_____
_____	10. The management runs a people-oriented organization.	_____
_____	11. Members of this organization always have grievances no matter what is done to correct them.	_____
_____	12. This organization willingly accepts the ideas of its members for change.	_____
_____	13. This organization recognizes that its success depends on its members.	_____
_____	14. Members stay informed on many topics besides their immediate job-related activities.	_____
_____	15. People in this organization speak openly about each others' shortcomings.	_____
_____	16. There is a sense of purpose and direction in this organization.	_____
_____	17. Members are prone to overstate and exaggerate their accomplishments.	_____
_____	18. Management does not exercise authoritarian control over members' activities.	_____

Scoring:

Scale	*Add Items*	*Ideal Total*	*Actual Total*	*Gap (Ideal – Actual)*
Organizational support	1,7,13	_____	_____	_____
Member quality	2,8,14	_____	_____	_____
Openness	3,9,15	_____	_____	_____
Supervisory style	4,10,16	_____	_____	_____
Member conflict	5,11,17	_____	_____	_____
Member autonomy	6,12,18	_____	_____	_____

Source: D. T. Hall, D. D. Bowen, R. J. Lewicki, and F. S. Hall. 1982. *Experiences in management and organizational behavior* (2nd ed.). New York: Wiley. Reprinted by permission of John Wiley & Sons, Inc. Originally developed by B. Schneider and C. J. Bartlett. This version of the questionnaire is not presented for research purposes. Those interested in the total set of items should contact Benjamin Schneider, Department of Psychology, University of Maryland.

INFOTRAC

INFOTRAC COLLEGE EDITION

The articles listed below are a sampling of those available through InfoTrac College Edition. You can search for them either by title or by the author's name.

Articles

1. Why is corporate culture important? William G. Bliss. *Workforce* Feb 1999 v78 i2 pW8(2) Bus.Coll.: 114X2390
2. Business segmentation and location revisited: innovation and the terra incognito of large firms. Roger Hayter, Jerry Patchell, Kevin Rees. *Regional Studies* July 1999 v33 i5 p425(8)
3. From text to context: an open systems approach to research in written business communication. (Discipline Formation in Business Communication) Jim Suchan, Ron Dulek. *The Journal of Business Communication* Jan 1998 v35 n1 p87(24)
4. Disciplined imagination: from scenarios to strategic options. (preparing for the Future: Developing Strategic Flexibility from a Competence-Based Perspective) Paul J. H. Schoemaker. *International Studies of Management & Organization* Summer 1997 v27 n2 p43(28)
5. Flexible organizations: using organizational design as a competitive advantage. Miles H. Overholt. *Human Resource Planning* March 1997 v20 n1 p22(10)

Questions

For Article 1:

The article entitled "Why is corporate culture important?" makes the point that an organization-wide acceptance of its perceived culture is important for all employees from senior executives down through the ranks. It describes how costly it is to hire a new employee who does not know and does not learn and accept the organization's culture. Divide into small groups and read this article. Then discuss the process and methods you would use if you were senior managers in a corporation to ensure new employees' integration into the organization's culture.

For Other Articles:

Have members of your small group read the other articles on this list. What new information do they offer about the organizational environment?

WEB EXERCISE

Visit the *Fortune Global 500* listing of the largest firms in the world. You can use the following web address (**http://pathfinder.com/fortune/global 500/**) in this search. What home country (or countries) represent the largest number of firms? Identify one or two firms that are of interest and visit their home page to learn more about their business, organization, and management practices. How does their environment differ from that of their competitors in other countries?

CASE

Scient Rises and Falls with the Dot-com Boom

Scient (**http://www.scient.com**), an Internet consulting firm, was riding high. Demand for the firm's Internet design and strategy services was skyrocketing as businesses rushed to jump on the e-commerce bandwagon. In a little over a year, Scient grew from a start-up to a business with over 1100 employees in offices around the world. Scient went public in 1999, and by early 2000, its stock price had shot up to $133 a share on news that the firm had earned $156 million in annual revenues.

Scient's clients demanded speed. They wanted to get on the Internet before their competitors beat them to the Web. They were willing to pay handsomely if Scient could help them meet that goal. "These days clients have more money than time," said Steve Ariana, a Scient executive. "You don't have to be right when you get it done. Early is better than accurate." In this fast-paced environment, Scient quickly earned a reputation for developing Internet sites at warp speed. Although Scient handled website development projects for major corporations, about half the firm's revenues came from Internet start-ups.

Robert Howe, Scient's CEO, joined the company after heading IBM's consulting division. "I was running a pretty big part of IBM," Howe said in 1999. "But I came here because I became convinced that electronic commerce and electronic business are going to change the world. I really think this is going to be the greatest service firm in the history of business."

One of Howe's main challenges was to build a corporate culture that could keep up with rapid change. Many of Scient's employees were young, lured from top engineering colleges. While technically savvy, most lacked real business experience. To build a cohesive team, Scient's executives identified six core values for the company: innovation, growth, excellence, community, spirit, and urgency.

Because Scient's hectic pace required long hours and high employee commitment, Howe named Joe Galuszka to the position of "chief morale officer." He was charged with keeping employees motivated and excited about the work they were doing. Rallies, parties, and other special events helped keep morale pumped up. Employees working off-site at client offices were sent regular care packages containing CDs, T-shirts, and other gifts. "That's to let them know that we are concerned and love them," explained Galuszka.

Then, just as quickly as it had soared, the demand for Internet consulting services slowed. Dot-com firms began running out of money and investors were hesitant to provide new funding. Some of Scient's dot-com clients, like Living.com, a furniture e-tailer, and Miadora .com, an online jeweler, went out of business. Other clients seemed ready to follow.

As the dot-com boom slowed, Scient's large corporate clients also started to feel less urgency about getting their Internet initiatives up and running. Many cut back on technology spending. Others were no longer willing to pay just to get on the Internet; now they wanted proof that an Internet investment would be worth the cost. At the same time, traditional management consulting firms like Accenture began offering Internet consulting services in addition to their human resources, accounting, and management consulting services. Competition for large corporate clients became even more intense for Internet-only consulting firms like Scient, especially when it became clear that these established consulting firms were willing to reduce their prices in order to gain new clients.

In December 2000, Scient executives announced that the firm's revenues had dropped by 28 percent. The company's stock price plunged to less than $10 a share. To cut costs, Scient closed its Silicon Valley and Austin, Texas, offices and laid off 460 employees. "This is the worst day in our history," said a Scient executive when the layoffs were announced.

Howe and his executive team have decided that to survive, Scient must broaden its focus. While the company will continue to offer Web design services, Scient plans to also offer more traditional consulting services to help clients integrate technology, including the Internet, throughout their operations. "We're looking at a choppy, rocky, stormy market," admits Christopher Lochhead, Scient's marketing director. "And we don't know when that's going to end."

Questions

1. How has Scient's environmental uncertainty changed? Identify at least three external forces affecting the firm.
2. Do you agree or disagree with Scient's decision to broaden its services? Will this strategy change Scient's external environment? How?
3. Will Scient need to change its internal environment? How?
4. Suggest other strategies to help Scient deal with new environmental conditions.

Sources: B. Barrow, July 27, 2000. Bringing happy days to the office. The Daily Telegraph, *31; E. Brown. April 12, 1999. The E-Consultants.* Fortune, *116; M. A. Farmer. October 26, 2000. Scient gives itself a new lease on life.* CNET News.com, *downloaded from* **http://www.cnet.com**; *K. H. Hammonds. February 1, 2001. Scient's near-death experience.* Fast Company, *99; C. Tatum. August 31, 2000. IBM apostle makes Scient his blue heaven.* The Chicago Tribune, *downloaded from* **http://www.chicagotribune.com**.

VIDEO COHESION CASE FOR PART I

Horizons: A Values-Based Company with a Bright, Yet Challenging, Future

Horizons' Home Page: **http://www.horizonsmedia.com**

Introduction

In 1983 Don Lee, a recent graduate of Ohio State University, stood in a small office just off Lane Avenue in Columbus. All of 22 years old, he turned to his friend Jim Haring and told him, "These four walls define the size of our company." What Don Lee didn't envision at the time was that success facilitates growth. The small video production company soon moved from its original location to a larger one, and it has moved several more times to its present location. Today, the company employs 70 people, has annual revenues of ten million dollars, and is one of the Midwest's largest and most comprehensive media production companies.

As a full-service media production company, Horizons now has offices in Columbus, San Diego, and Nashville. The company offers a rich array of media services, including film, video, music, sound design, computer graphics, animation, and website design. The atmosphere of the company is light and has the type of "high-tech" feel one would expect from a media company. There is no dress code, and employees come and go based on the demands of their schedules. CEO Don Lee has shoulder-length hair and a pleasant demeanor. The organizational structure is flat, and employees are grouped into project teams to complete specific assignments for clients. Although the pace is often hectic, the company operates on two basic principles. First, provide the client with an exceptionally good product, and second, have fun doing it.

So far, the company's formula has worked. It is profitable, is growing, and has been able to attract and retain talented and motivated employees. Its client list includes some of the best-known names in the United States, including ESPN, The Limited, Motorola, Red Roof Inns, and Wendy's International. It has also been recognized for excellence in its work. In 1999, for example, the company won the coveted Dove Award for Enhanced CD of the Year. The Dove Award is the gospel music equivalent of the Grammy. The CD was custom designed for Point of Grace, a contemporary Christian music group. In recent years, Horizons has also garnered an Addy Award, a Golden Link Award, an Emmy nomination, and several Citations for Excellence from the Advertising Federation.

Like any other company, however, Horizons faces challenges. The media industry is a tough industry, particularly for smaller firms. In addition, the company's unique culture and family-style atmosphere, which have been instrumental to its success, are under threat. In the next five years, the company plans to bid on larger projects, build new facilities, and add more employees. Will it be able to maintain its culture and family-style atmosphere as it continues to grow? Also, the flat organizational structure that has served it so well may need to be reevaluated. Will a more formal structure need to be implemented as the company expands? These questions, along with an "insider's" look at what has made Horizons successful, will form the basis of this case.

The Company

Horizons is a multiskilled company that provides custom-designed media products for its clients. The majority of the company's employees are in Columbus, with a small production group in San Diego and a sales office in Nashville. The company's clients are spread all across the country. The bulk of the company's work is in video and film. In addition to doing work for corporate clients, the company is often called upon to do special assignments for television networks. For example, Horizons produced stories about children recovering in hospitals following the Oklahoma City bombing in 1995. Other examples include Ohio segments for "America's Most Wanted" and ESPN sports interviews.

Structure

Although the company is not highly structured, it does include nine distinct divisions or (as CEO Don Lee likes to say) teams. The divisions include Video and Film, Web Development, Media F/X, Interactive, Animation, Audio, Music, Education, and Entertainment. A description of the nature of the work performed by each division is included in Table 1. The multifaceted nature of these divisions helps Horizons meet a range of its clients' needs. In addition, because many media projects require overlapping technologies (for example, CDs for some recording artists now include a combination of sound, video, and animation), Horizons is able to draw quickly from its various divisions to assemble a project team to meet a specific need.

TABLE 1 Horizons' Operating Divisions

Division	Nature of Work Performed
Video and Film	• Feature films • Television commercials • Marketing videos • Special assignments for television networks
Web Development	• Multimedia website design and development • Website enhancement
Media F/X	• Integration of traditional media and new media • Using technology to manage information • Synchronizing audio and video media products
Interactive	• Compact disc development and production • Making CDs, websites, and other forms of media interactive • Video, audio, and graphic support for traditional media
Animation	• Creating digital characters for all forms of media • Animating corporate videos • Developing 2D and 3D animation for CDs, websites, and film
Audio	• Full-service sound production, mixing, and mastering • Voice-overs in multiple languages
Music	• Producing music for various artists under the company's own music label, "Grandma Katherine's Music"
Entertainment	• Original films, videos, CDs, and other media products • Original scripts for film and television
Education	• Interactive CDs • Educational game shows produced on video • Classroom-oriented videos (end-of-chapter reviews and textbook supplements)

Operations and the "Art of the Deal"

Unlike a small retail store or a service provider with an established clientele, Horizons is more a series of deals than a traditional business. The company is typically retained on a work-for-hire basis to complete a specific project. For example, a corporation may need a promotional video for a new product. Horizons will make a pitch for the project and, if hired, will pull together the resources necessary to produce the video. This process typically involves assembling a project team that may involve freelance artists from outside the firm. Part of the company's success hinges on its ability to transform one-time deals into more lasting relationships. For example, after it produces the promotional video for the corporation described above, Horizons might suggest that it place a short video stream about the new product on its website. If the corporation agrees and hires Horizons to do it, then Horizons has another deal, additional revenue, and a more lasting relationship with the client. In the media industry this process is often referred to as the "art of the deal." The "art" is the ability to conceive additional projects for existing clients and to sell the clients on the merits of these ideas.

Values

Ethics

A distinctive attribute of Horizons is that the company's behavior is guided by a strong set of ethical and religious values. CEO Don Lee talks openly about his own personal faith and how his faith helped him build and shape the company. Lee is also fond of talking about the importance of treating people right and maintaining a healthy balance between work and family. Lee has publicly stated that "if each business made it their goal to build each person up—instead of the bank account—I think they'd probably get both."

Horizons employees at all levels also talk openly about the importance of integrity, honesty, and fairness in business and personal relationships. The company's strong sense of values has resulted in at least two positive outcomes. First, in selecting clients, Horizons strives to build relationships and repeat business rather than constantly trying to find new clients. Reflecting on this topic and the importance of strong ethical values, one employee remarked, "One thing that goes a long way toward bringing clients into the fold and keeping them there is honesty and maintaining integrity in the marketplace." The second positive outcome of strong values for Horizons has been internal rather than external. The company's employees work primarily in teams. There is a general belief in the company that honest, fair-minded employees make the best co-workers and teammates.

Social Responsibility

In addition to strong ethical values, Horizons has a strong bent toward social responsibility. Don Lee is involved in a number of civic and charitable organizations. The company is committed to recycling and other environmentally sound practices, and it has used its resources to create video programs for organizations such as Franklin County (Ohio) Children's Services and the Humane Society. The company's values can also be seen in the projects it does and does not select. Horizons deliberately steers away from the clients that would threaten to compromise its ethics, integrity, or professional standards. In contrast, it embraces projects that espouse educational and moral values. For example, Horizons is currently producing the first educational CD-ROM to star Garfield in collaboration with a company called Brighter Child Interactive. The Garfield CD will be the fourth collaboration between Horizons and Brighter Child Interactive. Previous titles have included "The Beginner's Bible" and "Adventures with Kanga Roddy."

Future Challenges

Based on outward appearances, everything is moving in the right direction for Horizons. The company is successful, has strong leadership, is growing, and has been able to attract and retain high-quality clients and employees. But, as briefly mentioned above, Horizons has challenges ahead. Its laid-back, family-like organizational culture has served it well as a small company, but will it be able to sustain that culture as it continues to grow? Don Lee, the company's CEO, is the hands-on manager who has hired everyone who works for Horizons and is clearly the inspirational leader for the firm's 70 employees. But what will happen when the company gets too large for Lee to be personally involved in every hiring decision and to know the first name of every employee? In addition, the firm is rather "loose" in terms of its structure and operating processes. For example, there are no formal titles, no formal organizational structure, no standard track for promotion, and no formal vacation and sick leave policies. Will this informal organizational environment, which has been an asset up to this point, become a liability as the company grows? And if it does become a liability, will Don Lee recognize it soon enough and be willing to make the necessary changes? All of these issues represent future challenges for Horizons and its leadership team.

Related Websites

Grandma Katherine's Music: **http://www.gkmusic.com**
Brighter Child Interactive:
http://www.brighterchild.com
DiscCity: **http://www.disccity.com**

For Discussion

1. Characterize the "management" of Horizons. In what sense is Horizons a technical system, and in what sense is it appropriately seen as a social system?
2. How would you characterize the management philosophy that is operating at Horizons? Does Don Lee's approach to organization and management suggest that he follows the human resource model? What evidence do you see in support of, or as a contradiction to, this model?
3. Is Don Lee a Theory X or Theory Y manager? Explain your answer.
4. Describe Horizons' management style and organization design in terms of the school of management thought that it most closely resembles. What leads you to this conclusion?
5. What do you think the ethical climate of Horizons is like? Similarly, how do you think that Don Lee and his colleagues address issues pertaining to social responsibility? What is the basis for your thoughts?
6. Discuss Horizons' external environment. What can you say about its general environment, task environment, and level of environmental complexity and change?
7. Do you see Horizons as an open or closed management system? Why?
8. If you were involved in steering the direction taken by Horizons, what would you be doing today to help this organization address the challenges it will confront in the future?

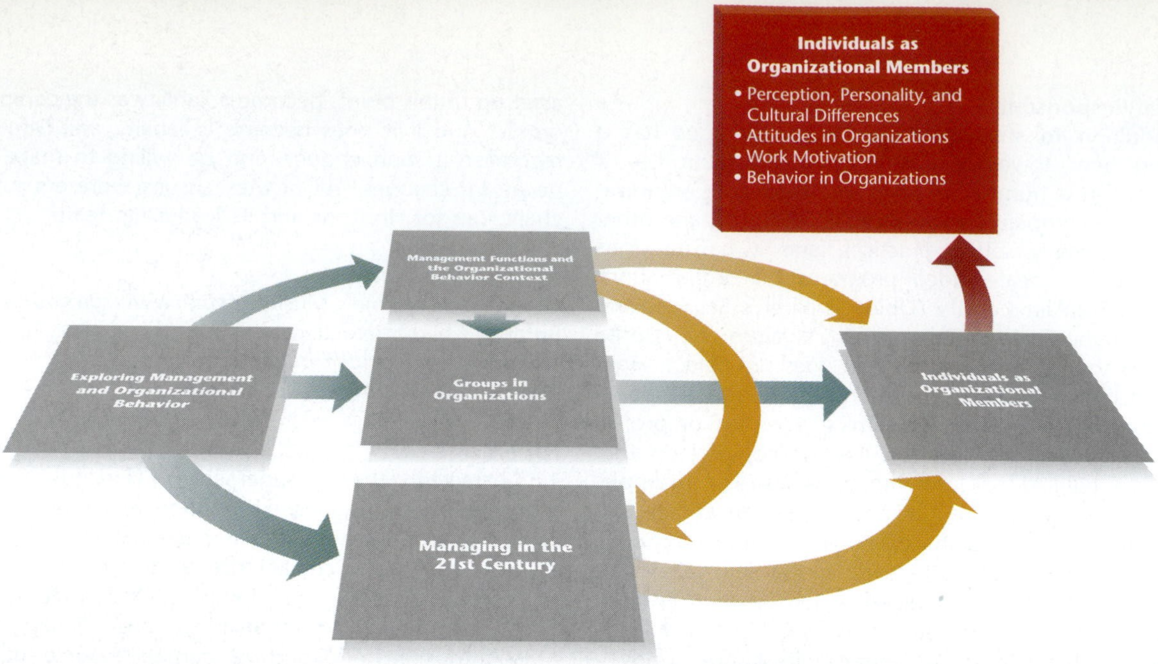

Individuals as Organizational Members

- Perception, Personality, and Cultural Differences
- Attitudes in Organizations
- Work Motivation
- Behavior in Organizations

Management Functions and the Organizational Behavior Context

Exploring Management and Organizational Behavior

Groups in Organizations

Individuals as Organizational Members

Managing in the 21st Century

PART II Individuals as Organizational Members

5. Individuals in Organizations: Perception, Personality, and Cultural Differences
6. Attitudes in Organizations
7. Work Motivation
8. Behavior in Organizations

The **integrative model** presented above highlights the material we will be covering in Part II. In Part I, we introduced two of the three building blocks in organizational behavior. We examined in detail the concepts "organization" and "management."

As we explored the ideas that comprise management, we noted that not all organizations are managed in the same way. This is pretty obvious, but *why* this occurs is an important question, one that has engaged organizational behavior researchers for many years. Managers possess radically different philosophies about work, people, systems, and processes. Many approaches have been tried, and many have failed. Today, as we have noted, approaches to management fall into two camps—control-oriented management with its mechanistic organization, and involvement-oriented management with its organic organization.

Now we turn our attention to the third building block in organizational behavior—*the individual as an organizational member.* Note that the "Individuals as Organizational Members" box is placed on the right side of the integrative model. This is because *everything* discussed in this text (see Figure II-1) ultimately has to do with people, the individuals who make up an organization. Because the individual is key to organizational success, finding practices that promote positive employee attitudes, motivation, and behaviors and discouraging practices that do not is also a key to success. To achieve this, we must understand several aspects of the individual as organizational member. In Chapter 5, we

FIGURE II-1 Management Practices and Organizational Design Affect Employees

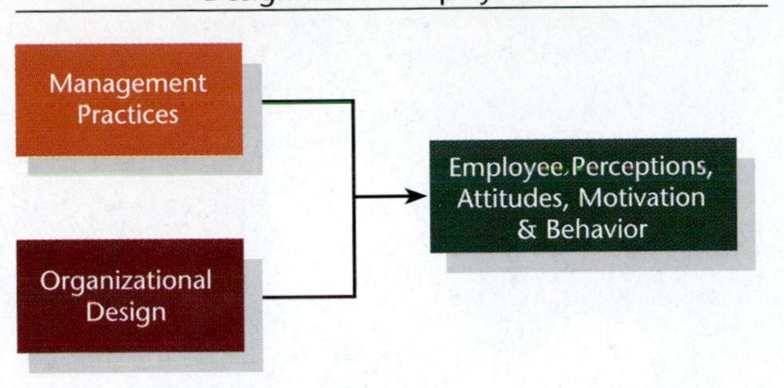

introduce perception and the individual differences that arise from our personalities and the cultural values that shape our perception, thoughts, and behaviors. Because no two people are alike, and because the perceptual process is prone to errors, employees react to managerial decisions about organization policies, procedures, and design in different ways. Chapter 5 examines how these individual differences affect organizational behavior.

In Chapter 6, we explore attitudes. Employees form many work and organization-related attitudes. And work attitudes both influence motivation and shape employee behaviors. Managers must continually be sensitive to employee morale, because negative consequences ensue if they are not.

Chapter 7 explores motivation. Several theories help us understand, explain, and predict the behavior of organizational members. In this chapter, we introduce you to the most popular motivation theories. Together, these theories will help you understand why people react to workplace events with particular attitudes and behaviors. These insights will assist you in predicting how individuals will likely react to future events. This is important because this is one of the contexts that surrounds every organizational decision. The theories cannot tell you which decision is best, but they do provide guidance and suggest new ways to view organizational behavior.

In Chapter 8, the final chapter in Part II, we examine several important organizational behaviors. Managers are keenly interested in the behaviors of their group members, especially when those behaviors influence the efficiency, effectiveness, and reputation of the organization. Therefore, we spend some time exploring the relationships between work attitudes and behaviors. We focus on the common assumption that "a happy worker is a productive worker" and reveal the fallacy behind it. Contrary to commonly held notions, unhappy workers *can* be very productive workers—this relationship is a complex one. We examine the organizational causes of withdrawal behavior (that is, absenteeism and turnover), citizenship behavior, and management strategies for preventing and managing the devastating behaviors of workplace violence and substance abuse, and we look at how profoundly incivility affects the workplace.

Outline

CHAPTER 5

Individuals in Organizations: Perception, Personality, and Cultural Differences

Learning Objectives

After reading this chapter, you should be able to

1. Define perception, describe the perceptual process, and explain how perception affects organizational behavior.
2. Explain what a self-fulfilling prophecy is and its importance to managers.
3. Describe the Johari window and how it is used to improve employee interactions.
4. Describe attribution theory and how it is used to circumvent perceptual problems in organizations.
5. Define personality and how knowledge of employees' personalities may be used by managers to promote organizational effectiveness.
6. Describe the relevance of the following personality traits to organizational behavior: organization-based self-esteem, locus of control, Machiavellianism, and the "Big Five."
7. Define culture and explain its importance to the management of organizations.
8. Describe Hofstede's five cultural dimensions.

PHOTO: © WOLFGANG KAEHLER/CORBIS

A FIRST LOOK

Jong Kim is eating lunch with his Korean co-workers at the Alabama car assembly plant. The mood at the table is somber. Their parent company in Korea has posted Kim's team to Alabama so they can learn more about American production methods. In a year, the company hopes to manufacture these American models in Korea.

As head of the Korean team, Jong listens with concern to his co-workers' complaints. After a month at the U.S. site, the Koreans are uncomfortable with their American colleagues. In particular, they are shocked by the American focus on individual performance. The American manager offers individual employees pay incentives for reaching certain levels of production. The Koreans are accustomed to teamwork that stresses cooperation over competition, and they are uneasy with rewarding individual performance. The lack of explicit written rules presents another difficulty for the Korean team. In Korea, strict, clear-cut policies regulate many facets of employee behavior.

Kim's team also has ideas for improving the U.S. production process. However, even Jong is apprehensive about bringing them to the attention of the Americans. He has been taught to respect authority and doesn't like to challenge those with more experience. However, Jong knows that something has to be done to make his group feel like part of the American team, or it is going to be a very long year.

Questions: How might the Korean team's cultural assumptions be affecting their perception of the American plant? Do you think the American managers will be receptive to their ideas for change? Why or why not?

In this chapter we embark on our exploration of the individual as an organizational member and individual differences by looking at perception—the process by which we come to experience the organization and management practices. We also look at personality—those relatively enduring characteristics that define who we are and affect how we react to the world of work. Lastly, we examine culture and its effects. Understanding a person's culture and background provides useful insights into the individual differences that characterize organizational members. These three phenomena affect how people in organizations react to managerial actions (that is, control- and involvement-oriented management) and organizational design (mechanistic and organic). In subsequent chapters we'll continue to look at the individual as an organizational member and consider their work-related attitudes, motivation, and behaviors.

http://www.perceptionweb.com

Effective organizations have effective employees due largely to the fact that such organizations promote a work environment in which organizational members can and do cooperate with and trust one another. They accept each other, they have common goals, and in a phrase, "they just get along." In ineffective organizations the opposite occurs. Managers engage in "turf battles." Employees dislike each other. To extend the phrase, "they just *don't* get along."

These very different outcomes occur because none of us perceive the work environment in exactly the same way. **Perception** is the process by which people organize and obtain meaning from the sensory stimuli they receive from the environment. It is the process by which we make sense of our world. It is not foolproof. No two people in the same situation will perceive it in exactly the same way. Have you ever been in a class where you thought the instructor was excellent, while some of your classmates thought otherwise? And whose (if either) perception was correct?

perception the process by which people organize and obtain meaning from the sensory stimuli they receive from the environment

personality the collection of psychological characteristics or traits that determines a person's preferences and individual style of behavior

culture the way in which a society as a whole perceives the world and how it should operate

Personality also plays an important role in influencing organizational behavior. Personality is a major way in which people differ from one another, and a failure to understand that there is no one "best" personality can cause poor working relationships. **Personality** is the collection of characteristics or traits that determines a person's preferences and individual style of behavior. It is these enduring characteristics that make you, you.

Lastly, we consider perception and personality from an international perspective. We explore the concept of **culture**, which can be defined as how a society as a whole perceives the world and how it should operate. Different cultures have different values and assumptions about how the world should function. This affects in fundamental ways how people in those cultures react to the world about them. In this chapter we examine the role that culture plays in creating the individual differences that can enhance or sabotage an organization.

PERCEPTION

The Importance of Perception: Objective and Perceived Reality

objective reality what exists in the physical world

perceived reality what individuals experience through one or more of the human senses, and the meaning they ascribe to those experiences

As noted earlier, perception is the process by which we become aware of, and give meaning to, events around us. It is through our perceptions that we come to define "reality." There are, however, two realities. **Objective reality** is what truly exists in the physical world to the best abilities of science to measure it. **Perceived reality** is what individuals experience through one or more of the human senses, and the meaning they ascribe to those experiences. At times, these two realities converge. At other times, they are significantly at odds. Many organizational members perceive their compensation strictly in terms of their paycheck, when objective reality also includes the organization's contributions to the employee's medical, dental, and life insurance, as well as to their retirement account. An individual's perceived reality doesn't always mesh well with objective reality, and when this occurs, behavioral problems can arise in the workplace.

Our perceived reality is important because we base our responses to cues in our environment on these very perceptions. If a person perceives that a coworker is receiving greater rewards for similar contributions, even if untrue, that person may come to feel that things are not fair (we call this inequity). Concerns about being treated unfairly can have negative consequences in terms of job satisfaction, motivation, and performance (see the discussion of equity theory in Chapter 7).

Those of you who will be called upon to lead others must be keenly attuned to both the objective and perceived realities of yourself and of your team, to the fact that the two realities don't always mesh, and to the idea that people respond primarily to their perceived reality.

The Perceptual Process

Perception is the process by which we detect events in our environment, organize them, and then attach meaning to them. Because psychologists have been studying human perception for over 100 years, much is now known about the perceptual process. The process involves four major stages: sensation, selection, organization, and translation. Each stage acts, in sequence, as both filter and

FIGURE 5-1 The Perceptual Process

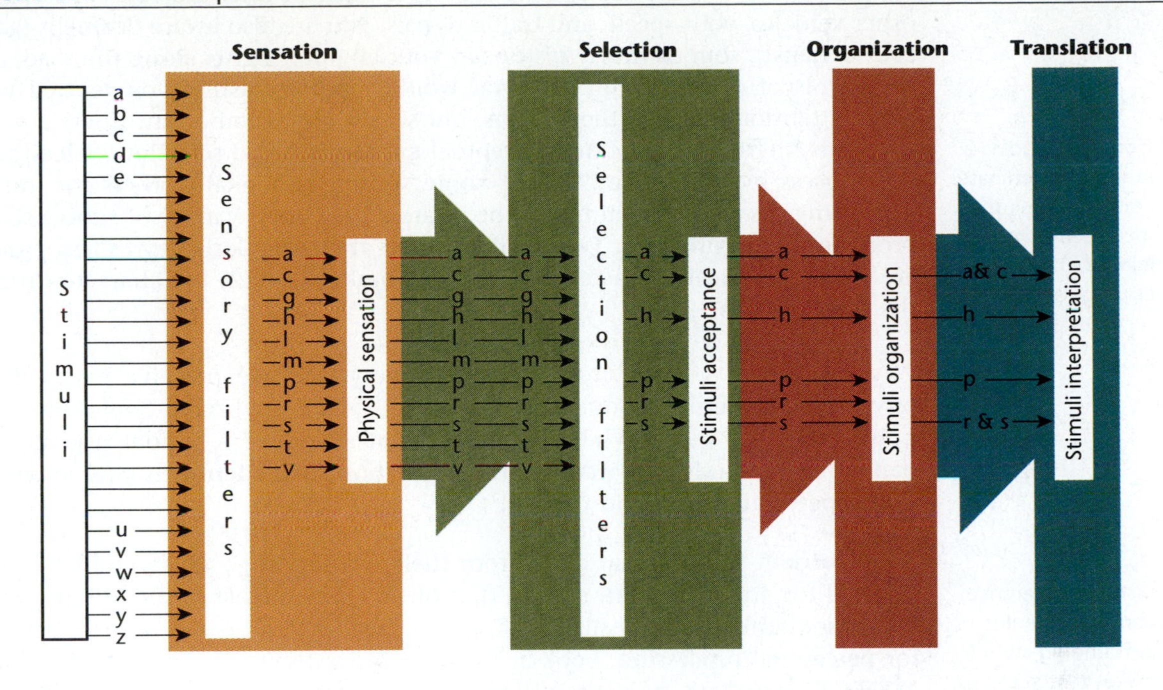

organizer of the world around us (see Figure 5-1). Together, they determine how we make sense of the world, and what that sense is.

Sensation

sensation our ability to detect stimuli in our immediate environment

Sensation is our ability to detect something—a stimulus—in our immediate environment. A flash of light, our supervisor, and warm rays from the sun are all stimuli that we sense. Each of us has multiple sensory systems, yet there are millions of stimuli that we do not perceive. Can you sense the parts per million oxygen that you are breathing at this moment? Do you feel the invisible radio and television signals that bombard every human on earth? Can you sense your heart rate? Can you sense the thoughts (not words) of others? The answer, of course, is no. The human body does not detect these stimuli without the aid of physical measuring instruments.

We humans recognize and react to only a very small number of the stimuli that impinge on us. For much of the stimuli that we do sense, we try to control the degree to which we experience them. Wearing sunglasses to decrease glare is one example. Turning down the volume on your roommate's stereo is another. Of course, people differ in terms of the amount of stimulation they find tolerable or enjoyable. (Why else would you be turning down your roommate's stereo?) The ability to sense things varies widely from person to person, because of heredity, injury, and aging.

Selection

The fact that we sense only certain stimuli is fortunate. Our bodies filter out vast amounts of stimulation. What if you reacted to every possible stimulus? Your nervous system would immediately overload, rendering you incapable of coherent behavior. Let's say you're driving a car. Not only are you conscious of other vehicles, your speed, and traffic signals, you are also aware of smells (gasoline, exhaust), sounds (noisy pistons in your engine), sights along the road, and thousands of other stimuli. But you would rapidly crash if you reacted with equal attention to all of them. Thus, our senses act as important filters.

selection the process a person uses to eliminate some of the stimuli that have been sensed and to retain others for further processing

This filtering stage of our perceptual process is called selection. **Selection** is the process by which we "ignore" some stimuli and retain others for further processing. As we select stimuli to be aware of, we use a variety of subconscious processes (see Figure 5-1). Two attributes that are particularly key in this process are (1) the physical characteristics of the stimulus, and (2) the characteristics of the perceiver (us).

Physical Characteristics of Stimuli Everything we perceive varies in its physical characteristics. Some things are dark, others are bright. Some things are noisy, others are quiet. What determines what we sense? A famous psychologist named Daniel Berlyne researched these questions and identified criteria we use in the perceptual selection process.[1]

contrast the difference between one stimulus and surrounding stimuli that makes that stimulus more likely to be selected for perceptual processing

Contrast. Stimuli that differ from their surroundings are more likely to be selected for attention than stimuli that blend in. **Contrast** is the difference between something and its surroundings that makes it more likely to be selected for perceptual processing. Look at Figure 5-2. See how the words "FROM" and "EFFECT" stand out from the others? The reason is contrast—contrast in terms of color, and contrast in terms of size. That's why key words in textbooks (including this one) are printed in **boldface** to help you remember them. For the same reason, some people are more "noticeable" than others; that is, they contrast with others in the group. People who dress casually in a formal work environment, who are more talkative than those around them, or who are of a different nationality than their co-workers are all likely to receive attention. Of course, these people become less noticeable after awhile, because of another process termed habituation. We get "used to" these "different" people.

novelty when the stimulus we are sensing differs from stimuli we have experienced in the past

Novelty. Remember the commercial a few years ago that featured a cow dribbling a soccer ball? It was wildly successful, but why? One major reason is **novelty.** Not many commercials have cows dribbling soccer balls. Something is novel when it differs from what we have experienced in the past. All else constant, we will select for attention that which is novel. We tend to be more

FIGURE 5-2 Contrast Effect

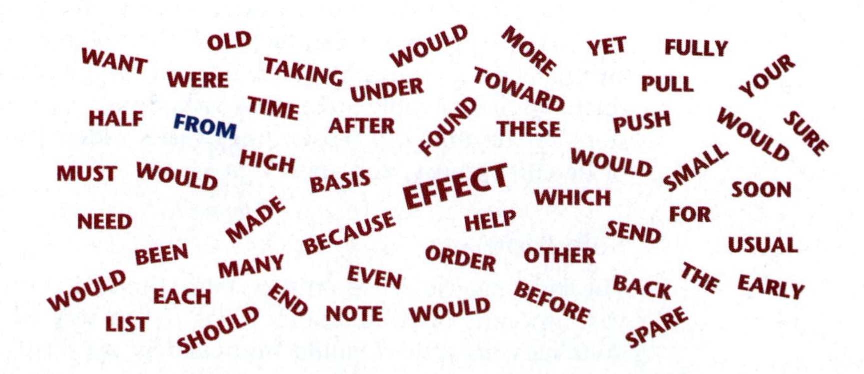

Roller coaster rides demonstrate how different people react to intense stimuli: Some people can't wait for the newest taller, faster roller coasters; other people are content to ride the merry-go-round.

attentive in novel situations. Of course, such situations can be good or bad. Sky diving for the first time can be just as novel as having your car break down at midnight in the middle of nowhere!

Intensity. Why do we like to ride roller coasters? Because it is an intense experience. **Intensity** is the forcefulness of an experience; it enhances the likelihood that a stimulus will be selected for perceptual processing. That is, intense experiences are stronger or more concentrated experiences—like thrills—than we usually find ourselves in. Intensity can be evaluated for a number of different dimensions (brightness, loudness, smell). Overall, we select for perception more intense stimuli than less, although there are limits to what we find tolerable (this is true for all of the physical characteristics discussed here).

Change. Earlier we noted that people get used to, or habituate to, stimuli in time. For example, someone who wears jeans to work at a place where the usual attire is formal is quite noticeable at first. After awhile, they becomes less and less noticeable because of their dress. But, what if that person comes to work one day dressed in a formal business suit? They again become noticeable, even though they have eliminated the contrast that made them noticeable in the first place. This is because they have made a change in the stimuli that we sense. **Change** can cause a stimulus to be selected for perceptual processing. When we sense something that is different than we expect, we are more likely to select it for attention.

intensity the forcefulness that enhances the likelihood that a stimulus will be selected for perceptual processing

change the variety that causes a stimulus to be selected for perceptual processing

Other Dimensions. There are numerous ways in which the physical characteristics of stimuli affect the degree to which they are selected for attention (frequency, number of senses stimulated, number of stimuli, and so on). Generally speaking, the more a stimulus stands out, the more likely it will be selected for further conscious processing.

Characteristics of the Perceiver Human motives and personality factors make you more (or less) sensitive to certain types of stimuli. The probability of noticing stimuli such as food odors or pictures of food, for example, is influenced by your hunger level (a motive). If you are sexually deprived, you probably will notice many stimuli with sexual connotations. You are more likely to respond to job-threatening comments if you feel insecure about your job. Power seekers (a personality dimension) are more likely to notice power-related stimuli (such as the size of co-workers' desks in relation to their own). Extroverts pay attention to interpersonal stimuli (like the degree to which co-workers socialize after work). In short, people are likely to notice stimuli relevant to their current active motives and compatible with their major personality characteristics.

Organization

The stimuli that pass through our selection filters (see Figure 5-1) do not enter our consciousness randomly. Were that the case, everything that we perceive would seem chaotic and without order. Instead, we automatically organize stimuli into recognizable images. In the **organization** stage of the perceptual process, we place selected perceptual stimuli in a framework for "storage." Like the sensation and selection stages, we don't consciously organize stimuli that we have attended to. However, research has shown that our brains organize (sort) stimuli by similarity, proximity in space and time, figure-ground differentiation, and closure.

organization the process of placing selected perceptual stimuli into a framework for "storage"

Similarity The physical resemblance of some stimuli, their **similarity**, causes them to be associated during perceptual organization. We tend to group similar stimuli when we begin to think about them and assign meaning to them. We group objects and events that are similar in color or size or pattern; for example, labels for floppy discs often come color-coded so that the contents are easily organized (all memos are saved on red-labeled floppies, for example). Organizations and society take advantage of our capacity to organize things by similarity. What does a flashing red light mean? In virtually every country in the world it means stop and look around, whether you are driving or on foot. Flashing red lights are universally associated with caution. (Imagine what the world would be like if this were not true, and flashing red meant stop in some situations and go in others.)

similarity the physical resemblance of some stimuli that causes them to be associated during perceptual organization

proximity in space occurs when the physical nearness of stimuli to one another affects their perceptual organization

proximity in time occurs when one stimulus is observed at about the same point in time as another stimulus

Proximity in Space and Time Humans tend to group people, objects, and events that are close to one another, either physically or in time. We may avoid a grocery store in a high-crime area because we perceive it as risky. Yet, it may have no more incidence of crime than a store in a low-crime area. We are grouping the store by **proximity in space**, when the physical nearness of stimuli to one another affects their perceptual organization. We group by **proximity in time** when we observe one stimulus at about the same point in time as another stimulus. An example would be a situation in which a neutral stimulus is followed by a pleasant or aversive one. If you've ever gotten a speeding ticket, you may perceive police officers as people to avoid. On the other hand, if a police officer saved your life once, you will no doubt have quite different feelings. The important thing to remember here is that because we organize information this way, and use it to organize future information, we must take care to do it correctly.

figure-ground differentiation the tendency to distinguish and focus on a stimulus that is classified as figure as opposed to background (ground)

FIGURE 5-3

Figure-Ground Illustration

Figure-Ground Differentiation Our minds classify everything we look at as either *figure* or *ground,* and this affects how we organize stimuli. This is **figure-ground differentiation**, the tendency to distinguish and focus on a stimulus that is classified as figure as opposed to background (ground). Usually, what is perceived as figure receives more attention than its ground. Figure 5-3 is a classic example. Focus on the dark part of the illustration, making it the figure and the light part the ground, and you will see two faces looking at each other. Focus on the light part of the illustration, making it the figure, and you will see a table or a vase. How you perceive the illustration depends on which part you classify as figure.

field dependence a characteristic of people that reflects the degree to which they differ in their ability to differentiate figure from ground

It is worth noting here that people vary widely in the extent to which they differentiate figure from ground. This characteristic is called **field dependence,** and much research indicates that people who are high on the characteristic (called field dependents) differ in many ways from people who are low on the characteristic (called field independents). For example, field dependents are more likely to rate a professor lower if he or she has a reputation for giving low grades.[2] The same sort of thing can happen in the workplace when field-dependent supervisors rate their subordinates low because of things that have nothing to do with job performance (their race or sex, for example).

closure the tendency to organize perceptual stimuli so that, together, they form a complete message

Closure As we sense stimuli, we tend to "fill in the gaps" (see Figure 5-4). Many stimuli we perceive are incomplete, yet we are able to organize our sensations into images and thoughts. This is **closure,** the ability to organize stimuli so that together they form a complete message. Because of prior experiences and associations, we can mentally "piece together" the missing and selected parts into a recognizable whole. Figure 5-4 demonstrates the closure process. But closure also operates in areas that are not visual—when, for example, we talk to people ("you make me so mad I could just ________!"). Because we are able to mentally complete other people's sentences so quickly, we often end up finishing their sentences for them. If this has ever happened to you, you know it can be quite irritating. Thus, the closure process can cause problems in interpersonal communication.

FIGURE 5-4

Closure

Source: Reprinted with permission from *Introduction to psychology: Explorations and applications* by Dennis Coon, Copyright © 1977 by West Publishing Company. All rights reserved.

The organization stage in the perceptual process is the first point at which you begin to manipulate perceptual information. At this point you have subconsciously organized stimuli into forms that can be interpreted, or from which meanings can be derived. The moment you begin to ascribe meanings to something that you have perceived, you have started what is called the **translation** stage. Note that the way in which you organize your perceptions will affect how you interpret them and store them into memory. Also, people organize stimuli differently; thus, two people in the same situation may perceive and interpret the situation in contradictory ways. An effective way to reduce interpersonal conflict in organizations is to have the conflicting parties describe their perceptions of what has happened to cause the conflict. Sometimes simply identifying and clarifying differences in perceptions resolve the conflict.

Translation

translation the stage of the perceptual process at which stimuli are interpreted and given meaning

At this point in the perceptual process, stimuli from your environment have been sensed, selected for further attention, and organized into images and ideas that can be interpreted. Of course, the perceptual process varies considerably in terms of the complexity of the stimuli sensed. When most people smell smoke, it takes very little time for them to translate that sensation into the thought that fire is nearby. On the other hand, study Figure 5-5. What is going on in this picture? It could be one of several things. Many of the situations we encounter in organizations are similarly ambiguous, so it behooves us to be cautious in ascribing meaning to them.

The entire perceptual process thus far is influenced by characteristics of the stimulus (for example, novelty), the surroundings (contrast effects), and the perceiver (personality). These factors also affect the translation stage of the perceptual process. Of particular interest to organizations are several phenomena

FIGURE 5-5 Illustration of Translation Process

What do you think these people are doing?

that influence the translation: primacy/recency effects, stereotyping, halo effects, projection, selective perception, attributions, and expectancy effects. More times than not, these phenomena distort our perceptions (subjective reality) of objective reality. That is, they cause errors in perception. But, since people can react only to how they perceive the world, it is critical that organizations pay significant attention to the entire perceptual process.

http://www.siop.org

Primacy/Recency Effects "You never have a second chance to make a good first impression." This oft-stated axiom has much basis in the perceptual process. Our first encounter with a stimulus, whether it is test-driving an automobile or working with a new supervisor, biases what we think of the stimulus in later encounters. Humans tend to weight first impressions of a stimulus more heavily than later experiences. This is the **primacy effect,** which is quite pervasive in the workplace. Research has shown, for example, that when people interview applicants for jobs, they often make their overall evaluation of that individual in the first few minutes. A bad start in an interview often causes otherwise qualified job applicants to be rejected. Even when inconsistent information is perceived later, it is disregarded in favor of the initial judgment. The moral, of course, is that we should all be cautious in our initial judgments.

primacy effect the disproportionately high weight given to the first information obtained about a stimulus

A related type of translation error occurs in the opposite time direction. Humans remember more recent events better than less recent ones. This **recency effect** occurs most often in interactions between people. When a person we've disliked over a period of time suddenly becomes friendly, we tend to forget all prior unpleasant encounters. Many students are aware of the recency effect. They try to make a favorable impression on their teachers right before final grades are assigned. Similarly, supervisors experience more criticism, hard feel-

recency effect the disproportionately high weight given to the last information obtained about a stimulus

We evaluate others in a few minutes, so it is important to make that good first impression.

ings, and compliments from their employees after performance appraisals than they do at other times.

In organizations, recency effects often distort performance evaluations. Because supervisors are often asked to provide a summary judgment about performance over 6- and 12-month periods, there is a tendency to remember recent performance best. If this isn't representative of the entire review period, unduly lenient or harsh ratings can result. For this reason, many organizations ask supervisors to keep weekly diaries about employee performance throughout the review period. This is good advice.

stereotyping occurs when a person has certain beliefs about a class of stimulus objects, and then generalizes those beliefs to encounters with members of that class of objects

Stereotyping Stereotyping is a particularly insidious type of translation error because more often than not it results in unfairly negative judgments. **Stereotyping** occurs when a person has certain beliefs about a class of stimuli, and then generalizes those beliefs to encounters with individual members of that class. An innocuous example of this would be the case where someone believes that Japanese-made cars are superior in quality to American-made cars. Through the stereotyping process, you could expect this person to criticize your Chevrolet no matter how well it has performed for you.

A more common, and damaging, example of stereotyping occurs when people mistakenly and unfairly associate a wide range of negative characteristics (lazy, stupid, unreliable, emotional) with an identifiable group of persons (such as obese, Latino, female, foreign). Such stereotyping often leads to employment discrimination. This is of course illegal in most circumstances, but it nevertheless continues to occur. Students often like to think that they are above racial and sexual stereotyping, but what percentage of your friends are of a different race than yours? Or, how many people actually prefer female heart surgeons to male when they have cardiac problems?

Sexual and racial stereotyping may not be as blatant today, but it is more pervasive than we care to admit.[3] And, even when people are relatively free of racial and sexual stereotypes, they stereotype other categories of people (union members, blue-collar workers, students from wealthy families, and so on). This is human nature; it allows us to simplify our world—we don't have to, nor do we want to, diagnose from scratch every situation we encounter. In our ever more diverse world, however, we must continually examine and reexamine perceptions that cause us to distort objective reality. Remember, stereotyping is not only an efficient way to perceive others, it also distorts characteristics we see in others (for example, unusual people are perceived as radical).[4] Thus, stereotyping is not only unfair to the people you meet, it is oftentimes illegal.

Halo Effects At the university where one of the authors works, students complete a course-evaluation questionnaire at the end of the semester that rates professors on such things as accessibility, fairness of grading, motivation of students, and so on. Students spend on average about three minutes completing the twelve-item survey. It never fails to amaze faculty that most students rate them at the same point on a 5-point scale for all these different dimensions of performance. That is, one student rates a professor as a 4 on all items, another as all 5's. How likely is it that a professor would perform equally well (or poorly) on all of these different facets of performance? Moreover, how can students complete the questionnaires so quickly if they are thinking back over the entire semester to render a judgment about twelve different aspects of teaching effectiveness?

The answer is, most students base their ratings on their overall impression (good, average, or poor) of the professor. And this impression may use only a single distinguishing characteristic ("She is really good because I am never bored in class"). This general impression then affects more specific impressions ("She's really good so she must use a good textbook"). This process of generalizing from an overall evaluation to specific characteristics is called the **halo effect.** Halo effects, which can be positive or negative (a reverse halo), are not always inaccurate (a professor might actually be high on all twelve dimensions). But they probably are wrong more often than they are right.

halo effect the process of generalizing from an overall evaluation of an individual to specific characteristics of the person

Halo effects pervade organizational life. A supervisor might rate an employee's performance unduly high because she is always on time, and well-dressed to boot. Or an interviewer might rate a job applicant's previous work experience low because he graduated from the "wrong" school. Just like stereotyping, it is in our nature to commit halo errors. In organizational life, where our judgments affect the welfare of those we work with, it becomes paramount to block halo effects (that is, not rely on global impressions) and to consider all the different contributions that people make.

Projection Have you ever noticed that some of the worst drivers you know complain continually about everyone else's driving? Or, when you are angry, you see anger in those around you? These are examples of **projection,** a process by which people attribute their own feelings and characteristics to other people. Cheaters perceive others to be bigger cheaters than themselves; shoplifters justify their behaviors by believing that everyone steals; and so on. Usually, these attributions are negative, because projection is by and large a psychological defense mechanism. If a person felt that only he or she possessed such negative traits, it would be depressing and anxiety-producing. By believing that others also have these traits (or worse ones), people are better able to accept themselves and their own flaws.

projection the process by which people attribute their own feelings and characteristics to other people

How does this affect organizational behavior? One way is in terms of performance. Oftentimes the worst performers in a work group do not believe they are so. In their perception, there are always others who perform worse. This makes it difficult for supervisors to give constructive feedback to such employees. Another way in which projection impairs work relationships is when hostile employees project their hostility onto others. Such people are difficult to work with because they are uncooperative and often make trouble for the entire group. We can't prevent projection, so it is best to acknowledge that it exists and try to recognize it in ourselves and others. As we discuss below, perceptual checking reduces the negative effects of projection.

selective perception occurs when people select for perception those things that are consistent with their views of themselves and the world, and reject or argue against those that are inconsistent

Selective Perception Another old saying is that "we hear what we want to hear and see what we want to see." The technical term for this is **selective perception,** which occurs when people select for perception those things that are consistent with their views of themselves and the world, and reject or argue against those views that are inconsistent. In organizations, for example, people with high self-esteem (discussed later in this chapter) believe that they are highly competent and tend to reject criticisms of their performance. They are said to have set up a perceptual defense, to protect their high level of self-esteem. A **perceptual defense** is the way a person retains existing perceptions in the face of new information that conflicts with the existing perceptions. In other cases, selective perception may preserve a stereotype. A manager might continue to believe that obese people are lazy, despite personally supervising an obese person who is a top performer ("Well, Herb is an exception").

perceptual defense the way a person retains existing perceptions in the face of new information that conflicts with those perceptions

Expectancy Effects Often, prior to meeting a person for the first time, we have expectations about what they will be like (friendly, motivated, shy, intelligent). When we actually meet the person, we tend to confirm our expectations, whether they are accurate or not. In the **expectancy effect**, we perceive stimuli in ways that will confirm our expectations. For example, if you perceive that someone you are about to meet is going to be boring (a friend told you so), then you tend to perceive only those behaviors and statements that confirm your expectations, and ignore those that don't. A classic study on the expectancy effect was conducted by Robert Rosenthal and his associates at Harvard University.[5] In that study, grade school teachers were told that some of their students were more intelligent than others. In fact, those students were randomly selected, meaning that on average they were neither more nor less intelligent than the rest of the class. The teachers nevertheless confirmed their expectations. They later reported that the designated students were indeed brighter and performed better in the classroom than students who were not singled out. In follow-up research, the supposedly "bright" students actually showed signs of increased intellectual capacity, while the other students remained unchanged. The researchers attributed this to a **self-fulfilling prophecy effect** (also called a **Pygmalion effect**), which occurs when people unconsciously adjust their behaviors to either reflect or justify expectations. The teachers, believing that the randomly selected students were highly intelligent, behaved differently toward them. They engaged these students in classroom activities that sparked intellectual development, but not the other students, who would not benefit from the "special attention."

expectancy effect occurs when people perceive stimuli in ways that will confirm their expectations

self-fulfilling prophecy (Pygmalion) effect occurs when people unconsciously adjust their behaviors to reflect their expectations in a situation

Expectancy effects and self-fulfilling prophecies occur in organizations quite frequently. If interviewers believe that an applicant is well qualified prior to an interview, that is what they will end up finding. In other cases, if new employees, as a result of their orientation program, believe they are going to like their new employer, they will tend to notice those things that confirm their expectations, and ignore those that don't (at least for awhile). Managers should try to use the expectancy effects to their advantage, as well as for the benefit of their employees. How? By constantly affirming that people have the ability and means to perform their jobs at a high level, people will attempt to make the "prophecy" come true!

http://www.accel-team.com/pygmalion

Perceiving Ourselves

Thus far we have talked about the perceptual process in general terms, how we come to perceive "stimuli" in our environments. But what if the stimulus is us? Do the same sorts of processes occur? The answer is a qualified yes. The same processes that lead to both accurate and inaccurate perceptions apply to how we perceive ourselves. Some things about ourselves we perceive accurately, some things we perceive inaccurately, and still other things we simply do not perceive at all. In addition, we have a special vantage point: We know things about ourselves that no one else knows. Only you would know that you harbor socially undesirable attitudes (for example, neo-Nazi) if you don't express them in the presence of others.

But as we know, the perceptual process does err. This means you hold perceptions of yourself that are not true. You may think of yourself as having average skills when you may in fact be above average. Yet you hold onto this misconception in spite of positive feedback from teachers, supervisors, co-workers, and friends. There are also no doubt aspects of yourself that you either don't perceive, or perceive but ignore. Our self-estimations are never completely accurate, and others may give us important feedback that we should pay attention to.

Johari window one way to conceptualize the possible combinations of what you know about yourself and what others know about you

Self-Perceptions: The Johari Window One way to conceptualize the possible combinations of what you know about yourself and what others know about you is shown in Figure 5-6. This figure (called a **Johari window**, after its authors, Joe Luft and Harry Ingraham[6]) suggests four possible combinations. The first is called the open area, because it contains perceptions that you have of yourself, and that others also have of you. The open area represents self-knowledge that you openly share with others ("I am dedicated to my job"). The second frame is called the hidden area, and contains those things you know about yourself, but which you hide from others ("I am afraid to confront my boss"). The third frame is the blind area, which represents those characteristics that you possess but that you don't perceive. We often call this a blind spot; we are "blind" to this aspect of ourselves ("J.R. *thinks* he cares about his employees, but nothing could be further from the truth"). The fourth and final frame is the unknown area, and represents those things that are true about you, but which neither you nor others perceive (you have deep-seated hostilities toward authority figures).

FIGURE 5-6 The Johari Window

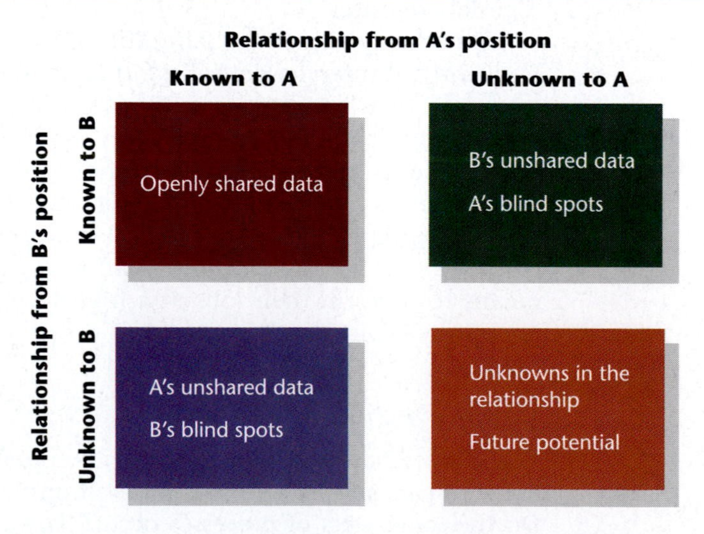

Source: This model is a modification of the "Johari Window," a concept presented in J. Luft. 1970. *Group Processes.* Palo Alto, CA: National Press Books.

http://www.theselfimprovementsite.com/johariwindow.html

In healthy organizations, employees' Johari windows contain large open areas, and smaller hidden, blind, and unknown areas. Why? Because such windows signify that people trust one another enough that they are not afraid to share perceptions of themselves that could lead to ridicule or disdain (things usually reserved for the hidden area). Also, in a healthy work environment, people feel free to share perceptions with one another. They encourage the giving and receiving of feedback about behavior, so that everyone can be the best employee that they can be, as well as grow and develop as individuals through greater self-insight.

The fewer blind spots you have as an organizational member, the more you will understand how your behaviors affect those around you.[7] In addition, the more you know about yourself, the more options you will have in dealing with others in the organization. This means that you need to be confident enough in yourself to solicit feedback from others, and not be defensive when they give it to you. This can be a painful thing to do. But, the alternative is to be misjudged or misunderstood because of characteristics about you that you are unaware of. You can't change ineffective behaviors you don't know about. In reciprocation, you should be willing to offer feedback to others whom you feel have blindspots that hamper their effectiveness. This, of course, should be done only when you are quite certain the person will trust the constructive feedback you are giving him or her. If they then choose to ignore it, at least you know that you have tried to help them grow as an employee and as a person.

Perceiving Others

Just as perceptions about ourselves represent a special case of the perceptual process, so too does the way in which we perceive others. As is true with self-perceptions, some of the traits and attitudes we perceive in others are accurate, some are not, and still others we don't perceive at all. Some of the ways in which our perceptions of others become distorted are discussed above. In addition, three others sets of factors exist in organizations that affect how we perceive others: characteristics of the person perceived, the organization, and the perceiver.

Characteristics of the Person Perceived What springs to mind when you think of a college football player? High athletic ability? Probably. What about high intelligence? Or, mature behavior? Eating habits? Study habits? Behavior around female students? Many times we think we know a lot about someone on the basis of their belonging to one group or another. In fact, we tend to be quite confident in our predictions about how they will behave.[8] When we do this, we are constructing an **implicit personality theory** about them; that is, we are ascribing personality traits solely on the basis of their sharing certain characteristics with others. Prior experiences with members of a certain group (football players, professors), combined with what we read in newspapers and magazines, what television would have us believe about these groups, and what our friends tell us is true, cause us to have images of what certain types of people are like. Implicit personality theories have almost no basis in fact. *Very* few individuals may actually reflect the personality profile widely assumed for this group's members. Yet, what happens when we meet someone for the first time for whom we hold such a theory? We expect them to reflect our image "of people like them." Self-fulfilling prophecies may then prevent us from correcting

implicit personality theory the tendency to ascribe personality traits to people because they share certain characteristics with others the distortion when we observe their actual behaviors. Joe Linebacker is dumb because he's a football player, not because of anything he's said or done. This of course is not fair to the person perceived, and leads to some unfortunate circumstances (Joe Linebacker could find out that you've told others that he's dumb!). We should be careful about how we perceive others when we first meet them. Group membership is at best only a rough indication of what you can expect to learn about a new acquaintance.

The status of the person perceived also affects our perceptions. What esteem (or lack thereof) that others hold them in, or their position in the organization, or the power (or lack thereof) they have over others—all contribute to biases in perception. If you meet someone for the first time, and he tells you he's a custodian, what would you assume about his education level? Yet he could very well be a college student like yourself who is working as a custodian to pay his tuition. Your preconceptions may be wrong, and they might later adversely affect your relationships with that person. Of course the opposite occurs, too. A new acquaintance might tell you she's a "captain of industry," yet have the motivation level of the George Costanza character on *Seinfeld*!

Characteristics of the Organization Research suggests that the context in which people are perceived affects the traits we ascribe to them.[9] The workplace is a powerful context. Some organizations are very desirable to work for. Others are miserable. *Organizational culture* (discussed in more detail in Chapter 4) is the pattern of basic assumptions invented, discovered, or developed by a given group as it learns to cope with its problems of external adaptation and internal integration.[10,11] Despite the difficulty in identifying an organization's culture, it does exist and can bias what its members perceive. Let's imagine a manufacturing firm in an idyllic town that was the model for the New England village romanticized in Thornton Wilder's "Our Town."[12] We would expect this firm to have a warm, perhaps paternalistic, culture where employees feel like one big happy family. Indeed, this was the culture of our hypothetical firm for many years. The only problem was that with the advent of international competition for its product, it began to lose money. When the company was sold to a Japanese firm, the new owners implemented radical changes to make it profitable. They laid off workers, timed each worker's production efficiency, and even took away stools and chairs to reduce the temptation to sit down! Needless to say, workers now perceive this firm's culture as one where employees are "just numbers on a budget sheet." How do you think workers will perceive the new company-appointed managers? Their skepticism might cause them to propagate unfair rumors about the new managers, despite the fact that the managers have ideas that will make workers' jobs easier and that will enhance profitability, making their jobs more secure. Contrast this scenario with what might have happened to new managers 40 years ago and you can see how organizational culture affects employee perceptions.

http://www.ford.com

Industry competition can affect perception. For example, "At Ford, Quality Is Job 1." That wasn't always the case, as Ford Motor Company will openly admit. Only with the advent of global competition in automobile quality and price, most notably from the Japanese, did quality become a major issue for Ford (as well as for hundreds of other companies). The net result is that companies not only routinely train workers in quality control procedures, they encourage a questioning culture such that the first thing asked when presented with something new is "what will it do to product quality?" Similar changes have occurred in service organizations, where customer service is a focal point. In these examples, organizations' responses to competition in the marketplace have led them to train employees to consciously manipulate that which they perceive in the organization. This was unheard of in the history of American management, but it helped to restore the competitiveness of American business in the global marketplace.

Characteristics of the Perceiver Think of someone whom you really dislike. It might be somebody you work with, a fellow student, or a friend of a friend. Now, can you think of many behaviors of that person that you consider effective? Chances are you cannot. An active like or dislike for someone biases how we perceive them in later encounters. That is because previous experiences influence our future expectations. We all tend to ignore the flaws of those we like, and focus on the irritating behaviors of those we dislike. If we believe that our supervisor plays favorites, we will perceive many of their actions as self-serving. If we like our co-workers, we may ignore the fact that they're usually late for work (and leave early to make up for it!). Why does this phenomenon occur? Like the expectancy effect discussed above, once we have an "image" of what other people (and things) are like, we tend to perceive them in ways that are consistent with our expectations. Only when the actual behavior that makes it through the perceptual process differs significantly from what we expect (the co-worker doesn't come to work at all) do we perceive events as they really are.

Imagine you are rushing to get a report done for your boss. It's due tomorrow and you turn it in to your assistant, Mark, with strict instructions that it be finished by the end of the day. How will you perceive Mark if he tells you he's taking the rest of the day off and can't do it? This is where *attributions* can affect the perceptual process. If you believe Mark's behavior is due to *external causes,* something out of his direct control (like a sick child), you will probably try to understand and cope with the situation. On the other hand, if you believe that his behavior is due to *internal causes,* those that are characteristic of him (low motivation) or that he can control (wants to go bird-watching), you may develop a negative perception of Mark.

attribution theory explains how people assign responsibility and the cognitive processes by which they interpret the causes of their own behavior and the behavior of other people

locus of causality occurs when people observe the behavior of others and attribute the behavior to internal causes (ability, effort) or external causes (luck, easy or difficult task)

fundamental attribution error our tendency to overestimate the effects of internal causes and underestimate the effects of external causes when we judge other peoples' actions

This phenomenon of trying to attribute the causes of behavior of other people, and of ourselves, has been a major area of research for social psychologists, called attribution theory.[13] **Attribution theory** examines how we assign responsibility and the cognitive processes by which we interpret the causes of our own behavior and the behavior of others. Usually, when we observe the behavior of others, we attribute the behavior to internal causes (ability, effort) or external causes (luck, easy or difficult task). This is termed the **locus of causality** in attribution theory. What we do in response to our perceptions can be biased by whether we attribute people's behaviors to internal or external causes. For example, when a co-worker is performing exceptionally well, we might believe it is due to high ability or motivation (internal causes). We would conclude that the co-worker is a good employee. On the other hand, if we believe that she's performing well because she has an easy job (an external cause), we may not conclude that she's a good employee so quickly. Research has shown that we tend to overestimate the effects of internal causes and underestimate the effects of external causes when we judge other people's actions. This is called the **fundamental attribution error.**[14] We tend to blame people for their own problems and inadequacies instead of considering the circumstances that led up to them.

Although women are breaking into traditionally male jobs in ever-increasing numbers, they must still overcome perceptions about their qualifications and job performance.

Another aspect of attributions is the stability of the cause. Whether an attribution is internal or external, we still may think of it as being stable (enduring) or unstable (unreliable). Continuing the previous example, if we attribute a co-worker's good performance to high motivation, we could also make the attribution that it is unstable, because she has been less motivated on past occasions. On the other hand, we could also perceive high motivation as being stable if the co-worker has always been highly motivated.

This perceptual phenomenon has major implications for managing organizational behavior. When we attribute the behavior of others to internal or stable causes, we tend to develop a stereotype about that person based on our perceptions of the causes of their behavior (smart, lazy, and so on). On the other hand, if we perceive the causes of the behavior to be external or unstable, we are less likely to form an overall impression of the person. Luck runs out, and task difficulty changes. Next week their behavior may be due to something else. The problem occurs when we generate false attributions for failure. Continuing the example above, you might give a low performance review to your assistant Mark if you thought he chose birdwatching over getting the report done. But what if he really went home to attend to his sick child? You would no doubt have an entirely different perception of the incident.

Problems with attribution are accentuated when women perform jobs that are traditionally considered "male." Madeline Heilman, a leading researcher on effects of sexual stereotypes in organizations, found that when women perform well in "male jobs" (for example, as engineers or managers), their success tends to be attributed to external causes (good luck). On the other hand, if females perform poorly in "male jobs," their failure tends to be attributed to internal factors (lack of ability). The opposite occurs with men in "male jobs." The net result of these mistaken attributions is predictable: Women tend to receive lower performance reviews than men who perform at the same level.[15] This unfortunate error in the perceptual process is less pervasive today as increasing numbers of women perform traditionally male jobs. Nevertheless, it serves as a warning that we need to carefully evaluate what causes the behaviors of people around us.

An Inside Look examines recent research that focuses on another characteristic affecting the perceptual process—emotional IQ.

AN INSIDE LOOK

Emotional Intelligence in the Workplace

For years, many organizations valued "hard skills" such as financial and technical expertise much more than "soft skills" such as communication, trust, and adaptability. Soft skills were taught in training courses, but in lean financial times these courses were frequently cut in favor of courses in more tangible areas such as computer skills. Thanks to the ideas of a revolutionary management thinker, however, corporate leaders are recognizing that employees' interpersonal skills and ability to manage their emotions can have twice the impact as technical ability or IQ on success in the workplace.

Daniel Goleman's books *Emotional Intelligence: Why It Can Matter More than IQ* and *Working with Emotional Intelligence* have opened many managers' eyes to the importance of character and personality on the job. Even more substantially, these books prove that emotional intelligence, unlike IQ, can be taught and improved with training.

While there is no one definitive model of emotional intelligence, many will agree that the individual emotional skills valuable to organizations include empathy, leadership, communication, conflict management, collaboration, self-confidence, initiative, and trustworthiness. Studies have shown that employees who demonstrate these emotional competencies are more likely to be top achievers in their organization and to be considered candidates for promotion to upper management. In some organizations, emotional intelligence was also found to be a better predictor of success than education level, gender, and age.

Goleman's pioneering works may take much of the credit for bringing emotional intelligence back into the limelight. However, the changing face of the modern corporate environment also helps to explain why these qualities are valued. As corporate culture becomes more horizontal and collaborative and middle management disappears, organizational leaders and followers must work closely and effectively as teams. Maintaining positive relationships with team members in this type of environment is essential and allows organizations to respond more quickly and effectively than ever before.

Emotional intelligence also plays an important role in the retention of employees. If employees feel respected and valued by their colleagues, they are more likely to remain with the organization. Emotional intelligence at work leads to a work environment that is conducive to encouraging employees to invest in the success of their organization, which in turns leads to greater employee retention.

Emotional intelligence cannot be developed overnight, or even over a few days. Emotions are behavioral patterns that have been learned over the course of a lifetime, and they are not modified with a quick fix. Organizations must provide ongoing training and support for employees if they truly hope to see results. With commitment to focusing on their employees' emotional intelligence, organizations benefit by having more productive and satisfied employees, which in turn affects the bottom line.

Source: Adapted from S. Caudron. 1999. The hard case for soft skills. *Workforce* 78(7):60–64, 66; and D. Goleman. 1998. What makes a leader? *Harvard Business Review* 76(6):92–102.

Reducing Perceptual Errors

Much of the preceding discussion implies that we are poor judges of what goes on around us. This is not true. If our perceptual processes were so fraught with error, the world would be chaotic indeed—as if everyone was on hallucinogenic drugs! Nevertheless, errors in perception are subtle and certainly do exist. Misperceptions create major problems for organizations, so it is important that organizational members endeavor to ensure that their perceptions are accurate before taking action. There is no surefire way to validate perceptions, or problems of misperception would be less prevalent. Some ways in which perceptual errors can be reduced include self-understanding, conscious information processing, and reality testing.

self-understanding acknowledgment that you and people who interact with you are susceptible to perceptual errors

Self-Understanding **Self-understanding** means you acknowledge that you and people who interact with you are susceptible to perceptual errors. In most cases, misperceptions are not borne out of malice or affection, but are unconscious influences in how we perceive the world. Because these perceptual shortcuts tend to function subconsciously, simply being aware of their pitfalls is the first major step toward defeating them. Careful attention to the perceptual process and a conscious awareness of the role of such factors as stereotypes increase the synchronicity between objective and subjective reality.

Conscious Information Processing You must carefully and consciously examine the "facts" during the perceptual process. Thus, at the selection stage, you document and systematically select the specific pieces of information you need. At the organization stage, you examine the selected information and arrange it for future recall according to its meaning (rather than on the basis of physical similarity, temporal proximity, and so on). At the translation stage, you focus on information directly relevant to the issue at hand, as opposed to irrelevant factors such as the sex or race of a person involved. In short, **conscious information processing** involves consciously questioning the accuracy of what you perceive, especially in those instances where there are multiple possible interpretations of what is being perceived (the United Nations' reaction to Serbia's invasion of Kosovo, for example).

conscious information processing involves consciously questioning the accuracy of what you perceive

reality testing occurs when you compare your perceptions about a stimulus object to some other measure of that object

http://www.un.org

Reality Testing **Reality testing**—comparing your perceptions about a stimulus to some other measure of it—can be a very effective technique for determining whether your perceptions are accurate. One of the most common methods is to compare your perceptions to those formed by someone else who has observed the same situation. You could, however, compare your perceptions to those of another person, find they match, conclude that your perceptions are accurate, and still be wrong. The obvious limitation is that the other person may share some of your perceptual errors (such as stereotypes). Imagine two Green Bay Packer fans discussing the merits of the Chicago Bears! So, comparing your perceptions with another's is useful, but still susceptible to error. Reality testing also can be performed by comparing your perceptions to one or more objective measures of the person being perceived. For example, instead of perpetuating the perception of a salesperson as a "superstar," you might look up their monthly sales figures.

Reality testing is most useful for determining whether your perceptions are in error or are accurate. Unless the object under consideration has measurable physical characteristics (such as weight, color, or size), a reality test can neither prove nor disprove accuracy. Reality testing does, however, make you more aware of your perceptual processes and helps to focus your attention on potential perceptual problems.

PERSONALITY

Importance in Organizational Behavior

The theories and practices described in this text work most of the time. Were that not the case, we wouldn't be discussing them. Yet, why don't they work all of the time? Managers often feel like "no good deed shall go unpunished" in dealing with their employees. They give a high-performing employee additional responsibilities to develop her job skills, and she complains. They give another high-performing employee the highest pay raise in the work group, and he still threatens to quit (while the lowest performer seems content with no increase in pay!). The first law of behavior is, People are different![16] What one person considers a golden opportunity, another considers a threat.

http://www.od-online.com/webpage/Intro.htm

There are thousands of ways in which people differ from one another. Some are tall, some are short. Some are highly intelligent, others are less so. Some are African-American, others are Hispanic. But one way in which people differ that is particularly useful in the study of organizational behavior is personality (sometimes called individual differences). As noted earlier, personality describes the consistent preferences and behaviors of people. When we describe a person's personality, we are summarizing that person's behaviors and attitudes in relation to a wide range of events. For example, if we say someone is shy, we predict that they are quiet and unassuming in social situations (behaviors). We might further predict that a shy person does not like loud, boisterous parties.

Personality, then, consists of characteristics or traits that describe how people are likely to behave in a given situation. One of the most important areas of research in organizational behavior, personality is useful in predicting and understanding the general feelings, thoughts, and behaviors of individuals at work. We know that personality has a direct effect on employee responses (such as satisfaction and performance). We also know that an individual's personality can determine how they will react to a managerial practice. For example, people with low self-esteem (see below) react much more strongly to negative feedback than do people with high self-esteem. This means that effective managers must adjust their leadership styles and practices to the personalities of their different employees.

Even with a knowledge of personality, we can never predict with 100 percent accuracy how someone will behave in a particular situation. Knowledge of personality is simply one of many tools in the managerial toolkit that, if used properly, makes us more effective managers. Considering the personalities of each team member as job assignments are made makes everyone more effective.

That said, managers need to avoid certain pitfalls as they assess personalities in the work group. Managers are often too quick to make judgments about personalities. On the basis of a few observations of a subordinate's behavior, they think that they know what the person "is like." Then, because of the self-fulfilling prophecy effect, they tend to see only behaviors that reaffirm their judgment. Indeed, research suggests that people are quite tolerant of behaviors that are inconsistent with their perceptions of the individual's personality.[17] Perhaps you find yourself in a situation where you have to decline to work some overtime. You certainly wouldn't want your boss to base her assessment of your motivation on this one instance.

The fact that we are often poor judges of personality does not imply that managers should ignore personality altogether. Neither does it imply that managers should administer personality inventories, like a behavioral scientist might do. Use personality insights to guide your actions, but always be cautious in your judgments.

The study of personality has produced a wide range of theories. The famous personality psychologist Henry Murray once counted several hundred different personality traits that were being researched.[18] Each personality theory presents a distinctive formulation of the factors that appear to determine personality and their impact on attitudes and behaviors. We make no attempt to explore the full range of personality theories or the complete set of personality characteristics.

Instead, in this section we focus on personality traits that interest researchers of organizational behavior. Other personality traits will be introduced as we explore the relationship of the individual and organization in subsequent chapters.

Determinants of Personality

There are two fundamental determinants of personality, our heredity and our past interactions with our environment. Psychologists have termed these causes "nature" and "nurture." **Nature** advocates assume that personality is shaped largely by heredity, that is, much of what we are is "hard-wired." While there is no "personality gene" per se (it's much more complex than this), research at the University of Minnesota suggests that as much as 50 percent of our personalities is genetically determined.[19] **Nurture** advocates argue that personality is shaped primarily by life experiences, especially those from early childhood. There is no definitive answer to the issue of how much nature and nurture affect personality. We do know that our genetic makeup sets upper and lower limits for our personality traits, and our life experiences determine where within that range we will end up.

nature advocates assume that part of personality finds its origins in biology—our heredity

nurture advocates argue that personality finds its basis in life experiences, especially those experienced early in life

Self-esteem Self-esteem is probably the most-researched personality trait in organizational settings.[20] It is thus appropriate that we elaborate on its role. **Self-esteem**, sometimes referred to as self-concept, is how individuals perceive themselves in terms of their abilities, competencies, effectiveness, and the like. People with high self-esteem perceive themselves to be capable, significant, and worthy.[21] These individuals believe they are competent, have strong abilities, and are therefore confident in their ability to succeed in a wide range of endeavors. People with low self-esteem, on the other hand, tend to perceive themselves as neither competent nor capable. They see themselves as possessing low ability levels, and thus are less likely to predict success for themselves.

self-esteem how we perceive ourselves in terms of our abilities, competencies, and effectiveness

Self-esteem is what researchers call a "multi-level" personality variable. What this means is that there are different dimensions in which people develop self-esteem. The most general dimension is global self-esteem, which is more or less the overall impression we have of ourselves. In a sense, global self-esteem is a summary, or average, of our self-perceived competencies across a wide range of situations and tasks. High global self-esteem individuals strongly agree with statements like "I am a person of worth, on an equal plane with others."[22] Low self-esteem individuals are reluctant to agree with such statements. Another dimension of self-esteem is role-specific self-esteem, a self-evaluation of our competencies in the various roles we perform in life (parent, student, spouse, sumo wrestler). It is possible to have high self-esteem in one role (parent), and low self-esteem in others (student, spouse). We tend to assign less importance to roles for which we have low self-esteem, or don't perform very often, so they don't have as much impact on our global self-esteem. Probably 99.9 percent of the world's population would fare poorly as sumo wrestlers, but that fact hasn't bruised many egos.

Another widely researched dimension of self-esteem in organizational behavior is job-based self-esteem.[23] This is our self-evaluation of our competence on the job. Employees with high job-based self-esteem are usually better performers and are more satisfied with their jobs than individuals with low job-based self-esteem. Of course, this only makes sense; if our job-based self-esteem is low, it's highly probable we aren't performing very well. Still, people do err in their assessments that comprise their job-based self-esteem. Managers encounter this when they offer constructive feedback to employees who see no reason why they need to improve.

organization-based self-esteem (OBSE) our evaluation of our personal adequacy (worthiness) as an organizational member

Jon L. Pierce, Donald G. Gardner, and their colleagues have been researching a dimension of self-esteem they call organization-based self-esteem.[24] **Organization-based self-esteem (OBSE)** reflects our evaluation of our personal adequacy and worthiness as an organizational member. People want to view themselves as important, meaningful, and worthwhile employees in their organization. People high in organization-based self-esteem agree strongly with job-related statements like "I count around here" and "I make a difference around here" (see the self-assessment below for the complete scale). For the high OBSE individual, these are strongly held beliefs. Pierce and his colleagues tested the hypothesis that employees will generally behave in ways, and have attitudes, consistent with their level of organization-based self-esteem, and found extensive support for their hypothesis.[25] High OBSE employees perform better, have more favorable attitudes about their employer, and are less likely to think about quitting their jobs than are low OBSE employees. That is, high organization-based self-esteem employees are, on average, more effective employees.

SELF-ASSESSMENT Organization-Based Self-Esteem

Think about your influence in the company where you currently work, or in your most recent job. Using the following scale, indicate the degree to which you agree or disagree with the 10 items below:

1	2	3	4	5
Strongly Disagree	**Disagree**	**Neither Agree nor Disagree**	**Agree**	**Strongly Agree**

_____ 1. I COUNT around here.
_____ 2. I am TAKEN SERIOUSLY around here.
_____ 3. There is FAITH IN ME around here.
_____ 4. I am TRUSTED around here.
_____ 5. I am HELPFUL around here.
_____ 6. I am a VALUABLE PART OF THIS PLACE.
_____ 7. I am EFFICIENT around here.
_____ 8. I am an IMPORTANT PART OF THIS PLACE.
_____ 9. I MAKE A DIFFERENCE around here.
_____ 10. I am COOPERATIVE around here.

Scoring:

Add up your scores for the 10 items. The following key indicates how high or low you are on the scale, based on extensive research by your authors.

High = 45 to 50
Medium = 35 to 44
Low = 5 to 34

Discussion:

1. Do you agree with the interpretation of your scores? Why or why not?
2. What could your manager do to increase your organization-based self-esteem? Should he or she ever try to decrease it?

SELF-ASSESSMENT

Causes and Consequences of Self-Esteem. Why has self-esteem been studied so extensively in organizational behavior? Because it is clear that high self-esteem people make better employees. They perform better, persist longer in the face of adversity, are more satisfied with their work, are loyal and committed to the organization, are less likely to quit or be absent, and generally try to add as much value to the organization as they can. And effective employees make for effective organizations. In other words, high self-esteem has good consequences for the individual and the organization.

Given these findings, organizational behavior researchers have attempted to identify the organizational and managerial policies and practices that contribute most to the development of employee self-esteem. Generally what they have found is that the jobs and managerial practices that lead employees to believe they are successful, competent, valued, trusted, and "liked" result in high levels of self-esteem. Employees exposed to involvement-oriented management practices and organically designed organizations tend to have stronger organization-based self-esteem than employees exposed to control-oriented management and mechanistically designed organizations.[26]

Implications. Obviously, managers and co-workers need to be sensitive to self-esteem issues. So, what can managers (and team members to a lesser extent) do to foster high self-esteem? Reaffirm employees' worth to the organization. Tell them when they do something well, and give constructive (not destructive) criticism when they don't. Trust them to perform a job well without monitoring their progress every minute, and without constantly suggesting how they should have done it. Give them enriched work that challenges their knowledge, skills, and abilities (see the job enrichment discussion in Chapter 16). Don't bombard them with so many rules and procedures that they have no discretion in performing their jobs. Send them to training programs where they can develop new skills, which reaffirms that the organization considers them valuable investments. Treat them as you would like to be treated. Everyone wins in such a work environment.

Other Dimensions of Personality

locus of control the degree to which people believe their actions determine what happens to them in life

internal locus of control occurs when people believe that internal factors like their skills and ability are the primary determinants of their destiny

external locus of control occurs when people believe that external factors such as luck, other people, or organizations are the primary determinants of their destiny

Locus of Control What controls our fate? The **locus of control** dimension is the degree to which we believe our own actions determine what happens to us. Even though most of us score about average on this dimension, psychologists do characterize people as having primarily an internal or external locus of control. Locus of control represents our beliefs about "what causes what."

A person with an **internal locus of control** believes they control their own fate. A person with an **external locus of control**, on the other hand, believes that other factors (such as luck, other people, or the organization) are the primary determinants of their destiny. Locus of control beliefs range from totally external ("My behavior has absolutely no impact on what happens to me") to totally internal ("I and I alone am responsible for my life"). Table 5-1 presents questions frequently used to measure locus of control. This scale was developed by Julian B. Rotter, who has made major contributions to the identification and measurement of locus of control and has helped to determine its impact on behavior.[27]

Note that if your locus of control is internal, you don't necessarily experience more or less successful outcomes than does a person whose locus is external; you simply believe that the outcomes occurred because of factors within http://www.psychtests.com/lc.html

TABLE 5-1 Measuring Locus of Control

I more strongly believe that

Internal Control	External Control
Promotions are earned through hard work and persistence.	Making a lot of money is largely a matter of getting the right breaks.
In my experience I have noticed that there is usually a direct connection between how hard I study and the grades I get.	Many times the reactions of teachers seem haphazard to me.
The number of divorces indicates that more and more people are not trying to make their marriages work.	Marriage is a legal gamble.
When I am right I can convince others.	It is silly to think that one can really change another person's basic attitudes.

Source: Derived from Rotter's I-E test. J. B. Rotter. 1971. External control and internal control. *Psychology Today* 5(1):37–42, 58–59.

your control. The external locus individual being promoted may conclude "I got lucky." The internal locus individual is more likely to conclude "I earned this."

The locus of control dimension has a number of significant implications for organizations.[28] Management techniques such as Organizational Behavior Modification and Management by Objectives (discussed in Chapters 10 and 16) are more likely to work for internal locus individuals. External locus people, because they don't believe their behavior influences outcomes, are less motivated by such programs. There is no research to support the hypothesis that externals are worse performers than internals. But, from an organizational behavior perspective, it is important that managers be sensitive to the fact that externals may require "extra convincing" that their actions do have effects on the organization and on themselves.

Machiavellian personalities believe that it is appropriate to behave in any manner that will meet their needs

Machiavellianism If you have a **Machiavellian personality,** you believe that it is appropriate to behave in any manner that will meet your needs. Your primary focus is on obtaining and using power to further your own ends, regardless of the impact on others. In short, you are not a team player. You contribute to the needs of organizations or individuals only to the extent that "there is something in it for me." This personality dimension can be present to any degree, although moderate levels of Machiavellianism are more common than extreme levels.

Machiavellianism is named after Niccolo Machiavelli, who wrote *The Prince* over 450 years ago.[29] The concept has not died, however, as is witnessed by recent research.[30] High Machiavellian personalities tend to behave with psychological detachment and little emotion. They are not easily influenced by others, but effectively manipulate others through convincing lying and the use of false praise, and by using any other tools available to meet their personal objectives.

Table 5-2 presents some of the questions developed by Christie and Geis for measuring the Machiavellian dimension. Surprisingly, research has shown that

TABLE 5-2 Measuring Machiavellianism

	Strongly Disagree	Disagree	Neutral	Agree	Strongly Agree
1. The best way to handle people is to tell them what they want to hear.	1	2	3	4	5
2. One should take action only when sure it is morally right.*	1	2	3	4	5
3. There is no excuse for lying to someone else.*	1	2	3	4	5
4. It is safe to assume that all people have a vicious streak that will come out when given a chance.	1	2	3	4	5

* Reverse scored.

Source: Excerpt from Christie & Geis's Scale. R. Christie and F. L. Geis (eds.). 1970. *Studies in Machiavellianism.* New York: Academic Press. Copyright 1970 by Academic Press, reproduced by permission of the publisher.

a significant number of people score relatively high on this scale. Managers and co-workers need to be sensitive to this fact. Some people will make the achievement of their personal goals such a high priority that it does not bother them if they prevent others from achieving their goals. This makes it especially incumbent on organizations and managers to define what they want out of employees and to reinforce it. Machiavellians are not necessarily poor performers. Organizations that reward good performance and cooperation both help Machiavellians achieve their personal, materialistic goals, and make the organization more effective.

"Big Five" personality theory the view that all personality traits can be distilled into five big ones: extroversion, adjustment, agreeableness, conscientiousness, and inquisitiveness

The "Big Five" One of the more interesting developments to occur in the study of personality is what is known as the **"Big Five" personality theory.**[31] For many years, psychologists developed and studied thousands of different personality dimensions (especially need-based ones like the needs for achievement, power, affiliation, and many more). Such research was largely unproductive for the study of organizational behavior because the tremendous number of potential personality traits made it difficult to validate which dimensions organizations should focus on. However, in the early 1990s, it became and is still widely accepted that all of these personality dimensions can be "distilled" into five "big" ones:

- **Extroversion:** The degree to which a person is sociable, outgoing, assertive, talkative, and expressive.
- **Adjustment:** The degree to which a person is emotionally stable, secure, content, and free from depression.
- **Agreeableness:** The degree to which a person is polite, trusting, good-natured, accepting, co-operative, and forgiving.

© R. W. JONES/CORBIS

Extroverts perform best at jobs such as sales and managerial, that require a lot of interaction with clients and co-workers.

- **Conscientiousness:** The degree to which a person is dependable, organized, thorough, perseverant, and honest.
- **Inquisitiveness:** The degree to which a person is curious, imaginative, artistic, playful, and creative.

Research in the 1990s demonstrated that these broad personality dimensions predict how well employees will adjust to the workplace. For example, conscientious people perform better at virtually all jobs than less conscientious people. Extroverts perform better at jobs that require extensive interactions with people, such as management and sales. Extroverts and people who score high on inquisitiveness do better in job training programs than their counterparts.[32] What this means for managers who understand personality is that employees should be placed in the types of jobs that play to their strengths.

Earlier cautions to the contrary, it doesn't take a lot of time to determine whether an individual is introverted or extroverted (of course, most of us fall somewhere between these two extremes). Extroverts have readily identifiable behaviors (they talk a lot) as do introverts (they talk very little). But, what implications does such an assessment have for maximizing performance? The possibilities are numerous. Obviously, extroverts will do better in jobs that require significant amounts of interaction with clients and/or co-workers. On the other hand, introverts do better in jobs that are repetitive and/or require a lot of concentration. In fact, research indicates that extroverts become more physiologically stressed than introverts (showing, among other factors, higher blood pressure) while performing tedious tasks.[33] This doesn't mean that introverts *like* to perform repetitive work. They simply tolerate it better than extroverts. Redesigning jobs so that they minimize monotony and fatigue is a better solution for everyone (discussed in Chapter 16).

CULTURAL DIFFERENCES AMONG ORGANIZATIONAL MEMBERS

As is often said, our world is getting smaller. Air travel, telephones, satellite communications, e-mail, and the Internet make business interactions with people in different countries routine today. Combined with the fact that most businesses have at least thought about marketing and/or creating their products in countries outside their home country (see Chapter 4), it is imperative that employees learn to recognize, value, and respond appropriately to people from other parts of the world. When we talk about the different values and assumptions that different people hold and make about how the world is and what the world should be, we are talking about culture. Earlier we examined cultural diversity within the borders of the United States (see Chapter 3). Here we discuss culture more broadly, from a global perspective. Differences in the world's cultures result in organizational members who differ from one another in key ways in terms of values, perceptions, attitudes, motivation, and work-related behaviors, and in such subtle ways as personal space.

Culture Defined

http://www.expatriates.com

Culture may be defined as how a society perceives the world and how it should operate. Culture includes the beliefs, values, attitudes, and expectations for behavior that the society believes to be good, effective, desirable, and beneficial. Because culture is seen as a good thing, it is passed from generation to generation. The knowledge, beliefs, laws, morals, art, assumptions, customs, and habits that comprise a culture are conveyed to children through parenting, education, religious activities, law enforcement, and entertainment. Cultures serve an extremely important purpose for humankind. In innumerable ways, culture prevents chaos. Common beliefs and expectations for behavior are the threads that weave a people together, and cultural beliefs are strongly held.

This is not to say that all people (everyone) in a particular society subscribe to the precepts of the dominant culture (as we discussed in Chapter 3 for the United States). Were this the case, we would not need prisons for individuals who do not comply with society's expectations for behavior. Nevertheless, the vast majority of people in a particular society do in fact share the same values and beliefs, or are at least aware of them. As a result, and very importantly, the majority of people in a particular society will react similarly (not exactly) to a given situation.

The Importance of Cultural Awareness to Managers

expatriates employees who are sent on assignments in foreign countries

People on assignments in foreign countries are called **expatriate** employees. It is extremely important that expatriates receive training on the cultural differences they are likely to experience. Research is pretty clear that expatriates ill-prepared for their foreign assignments often become dissatisfied and think about quitting.[34] Many expatriates return home early (estimates range from 16% to 50%[35]), or are fired altogether. This comes at great expense to their employers (estimated at up to $1 million per failure[36]). It also comes at great personal and emotional cost to expatriates and their families.

http://www.expat.or.id

Managers also need to understand cultural differences from a leadership perspective. Practices and decisions that are effective in the United States may not be at all effective in other countries. Culture directs belief systems in subtle and complex ways. As a result, people from different cultures will differ radically in their responses to such American practices as high-participation decision making. Understanding culture is a key strategy in the global workplace, and without such understanding, success is problematic.

Entire books have been written about how different cultures affect organizational behavior and the practice of management.[37] Here we summarize some of the most important ways in which societies differ. Noting these differences is a good start to becoming an effective and satisfied expatriate. These cultural dimensions were identified and researched by Geert Hofstede, a former IBM employee.[38] Most people (and most societies) fall closer to the middle on each dimension than at either extreme. And in all societies, as in ours, certain individuals will "buck the trend" and not value aspects of their culture as highly as the majority does. Nevertheless, researchers like Hofstede have been able to differentiate predominant cultures using these dimensions.

According to Hofstede, five dimensions characterize and differentiate the value systems of most countries and their people: individualism-collectivism, power distance, uncertainty avoidance, masculinity-femininity, and time orientation.

Individualism-Collectivism

individualism-collectivism the degree to which individuals in a society prefer to act as individuals, as opposed to a group

Individualism-collectivism is the degree to which individuals in a society prefer to act as individuals, as opposed to a group. Cultures high on the individualism dimension believe that individuals are responsible for their own actions. In these cultures, people prefer to work alone, and to depend on others only to the extent that it is necessary. They feel good about themselves when they have successfully completed a task or achieved a goal mostly through their own efforts and thus base their self-esteem on their value as an individual. Cultures high on the collectivism dimension emphasize the group over the individual. In these cultures, people feel good about themselves to the extent that they contribute to the success of their group, and they prefer to work in groups rather than on their own. They experience success when the group successfully completes a task or achieves a goal. They base their self-esteem to a large extent on how well their group succeeds.

Table 5-3 shows how different countries score on the individualism-collectivism dimension. Most countries fall near the middle on the dimension; extremes are rare. It probably doesn't surprise you that the United States scores very high on individualism, and that Asian countries score very high on collectivism.

TABLE 5-3 Cultural Differences for 10 Countries

	Individualism	High Power Distance	High Uncertainty Avoidance	Masculinity	Long-Term Time Orientation
High	USA Netherlands Germany France	Russia China France Hong Kong Indonesia West Africa	Japan France Russia	Japan U.S. Germany Hong Kong	China Japan Hong Kong
Medium	Russia Japan	Japan	West Africa China Germany Netherlands	China West Africa Indonesia France	Netherlands Germany
Low	China West Africa Indonesia Hong Kong	Netherlands Germany USA	Indonesia USA Hong Kong	Russia Netherlands	West Africa Indonesia France USA Russia
	Collectivism	**Low Power Distance**	**Low Uncertainty Avoidance**	**Femininity**	**Short-Term Time Orientation**

Source: G. Hofstede. 1993. Cultural constraints in management theories. *Academy of Management Executive* 7(1):81–94. Copyright 1993 by Academy of Management. Reproduced with permission of Academy of Management in the format Textbook via Copyright Clearance Center.

These differences have profound implications for organizational behavior and management. Common practices in companies in the United States will probably not work well in collectivist cultures. For example, U.S. employees assume, accept, and expect their individual performance to be rated by their supervisors. Companies base rewards and compensation packages on how much the individual contributes. Few U.S. employers rate contributions to work group success (although this is changing). In collectivist cultures, this focus on the individual is perceived as odd, if not threatening: Too much focus on the individual may be disruptive to the group's success (survival). Indeed, people in collectivist cultures often perceive employees from individualist countries as self-serving and disloyal. Clearly, as American managers interact with employees from collectivist cultures, they must be sensitive to such nuances.

Power Distance

In no country on earth is power shared equally. Some people have less money, status, influence, and political power than others in the same country. In some countries the government is structured to minimize the differences in power between the most and least powerful people. Through taxation and social entitlement programs, differences in living standards for the wealthy and the poor are not as great as in other countries. This acceptance of large differences in power between the most and least powerful in a society is termed **power distance.** In some cultures, like The Netherlands, there is low acceptance of large differences in power between the "haves" and "have nots." The Netherlands, as a society, has low power distance. In other cultures, such as China, there is greater acceptance that some people will have much greater power (and especially wealth) than others. China is high on the power distance dimension.

power distance the acceptance of large differences in power between the most and least powerful in a society

What sorts of implications does this have for American managers? The United States is low on the power distance dimension. American workers are comfortable challenging a manager's directives if they believe the manager is wrong. In high power distance cultures, this is unacceptable: The boss is the boss for a reason, and workers comply (or else!) with his orders. Unless they've actively studied the culture and its implications for management behavior, American managers who work in high power distance cultures are often surprised to find that the employees do not embrace such practices as participation in decision making. Employees in such cultures expect their bosses to make the decisions—employees are simply there to implement them. It will be more difficult to involve workers from high power distance cultures in the decision-making process.

Uncertainty Avoidance

Cultures differ in the extent to which they tolerate uncertainty. In some countries (such as Japan), **uncertainty avoidance** is very high. People in these countries are, as a rule, uncomfortable in situations where alternatives and outcomes are not well defined, and thus develop rules that address nearly every facet of their behavior. People don't worry about what to do in many situations because numerous and explicit rules govern their choices. In other countries (such as Denmark and Sweden), ambiguity is tolerated, even embraced. People are content with a level of ambiguity in their lives, and may even resent situations that have too many rules ("red tape"). Uncertainty avoidance is low.

uncertainty avoidance the degree to which cultures differ in the extent to which they tolerate uncertainty

Expatriate managers in countries with high levels of uncertainty avoidance need to attend carefully to employees when major changes are planned. Typically, companies in high avoidance countries have developed many rules and highly stable ways of doing things. Employees asked to change how they perform their jobs may resist. Change reduces certainty, yet, as the global marketplace becomes more and more competitive, change will be the only constant for these workers. On the other hand, high uncertainty avoidance has its strengths as well. By its very nature, operations are consistent. Highly structured organizations, often found in cultures with high uncertainty avoidance, can run like well-oiled machines. Once effective procedures have been identified, they are used repeatedly ("by the rules") until they are no longer effective. But, just like machines that perform the same function over and over, highly structured organizations tend not to be flexible in dealing with their environments (see Chapter 4).

Masculinity-Femininity

masculinity-femininity the degree to which a society displays mostly traditionally male or traditionally female traits

Societies that emphasize values like competition, assertiveness, and acquisition of material possessions are said to be high on the masculinity scale. High masculinity countries value those traits often associated with men (though women can exhibit these traits, too). Japan is high on the masculinity scale. Societies that focus on the well-being of their members, the quality of relationships, and the standard of living are said to be high on the femininity scale. High femininity countries value those traits often associated with women (though men exhibit them too). The countries in Scandinavia are high on the femininity scale. **Masculinity-femininity** is the degree to which a society displays mostly traditionally male or traditionally female traits. The masculinity-femininity dimension should not be confused with our common meanings for "masculine" and "feminine." As used in everyday language, these terms describe individuals who are "macho," or who display strong maternal instincts. To clarify this difference, imagine going up to a Finnish hockey player and telling him he is feminine because Finland is high on the femininity scale! If you survive, you will understand that a society's embracing of values that show concern for people is quite different than describing an individual in that society as being feminine.

Organizations and their managers need to adjust to cultural differences in masculinity-femininity. Employees in feminine cultures will expect to be nurtured by the organization. They will expect a high level of concern to be shown for employees and their families (as may also be required by law). This might be reflected in generous paid parental-leave policies, or greater understanding when employees leave work for family emergencies. American managers, for example, shouldn't belittle Scandinavian managers who take extended leave from work to be with their children during their formative years. Similarly, Scandinavian managers shouldn't assume that American managers are cold-hearted when they work on weekends at the expense of their family lives. These are simply manifestations of different cultural values. Changing the cultural values of people from outside our culture isn't an option, but understanding these differences and managing around them is.

Time Orientation

time orientation the degree to which cultures possess a short or long perspective on time

Societies and countries also differ in the degree to which they possess a short or long **time orientation.** Some countries, especially China and Japan, have very long planning horizons. China was famous for its 5- and 10-year economic plans. Contrast that with the United States, where short time frames are the norm. If a newly elected President developed a 10-year economic plan instead of reacting to the latest voter polls, eyebrows would raise, and he or she might not get reelected. Americans are famous for their short-term perspectives (some might legitimately say short-sighted). They sometimes sacrifice long-term success for short-term advantages. On the other hand, societies must also be able to adapt to short-term changes in their environment. China's 10-year plans were not great successes, because (in part) they didn't account for unforeseen changes in the world economy.

There are many implications for the two time orientations. Long-term cultures place much greater value on their history and their traditions. They are more tolerant when the economy seems not to be going well. They emphasize thrift and persistence, as payoffs come in the future. Short-term cultures, like the United States, tend to support behaviors that often have negative connotations—instant gratification, failure to plan for retirement, low savings rates, and so on. However, the United States is also recognized as one of the most creative countries in the world, in no small part because it is not bound by its past. For managers everywhere, these differences in time orientation become most obvious when planning for the organization (see Chapters 9 and 10). If a long-term Japanese manager is engaging in strategic planning with a short-term American, it can be a trying experience for both. Japanese managers invest corporate resources for long-term profitability. American managers strive for profits as quickly and consistently as possible. These are not always compatible goals, but understanding each other's time perspective is a step in the right direction.

PERCEPTION, PERSONALITY, AND CULTURAL DIFFERENCES IN REVIEW

Our purpose in Part II of this text is to familiarize you with the individual as an organizational member. To this end we have examined in this chapter the notion of individual differences. We explored perception, personality, and culture—the differences in values that characterize organizational members.

Perception is the process by which we become aware of, and give meaning to, the organizational events that surround and impact us. The attitudes, motivation, and behavior that organizational members display derive from their perceptions of their work experiences. The perceptual process has four distinct stages: sensation, selection, organization, and translation. Each stage is influenced by the characteristics of the stimulus, the environment in which the stimulus exists, and the characteristics of the perceiver. It is unlikely your perceptions will be exactly "correct," but you can take steps to increase the accuracy of your perceptions and the perceptions of others in your organization. Because of the pervasive impact of perception on attitudes and behaviors, it is imperative that both individuals and organizations recognize and deal with perception issues.

From your personal experiences, you know that people vary widely in personality. And, of course, people often (but not always) behave differently when faced with the same situation. Although the brief and incomplete discussion of personality characteristics presented here cannot do justice to the tremendous amount of research on personality, you are now aware of some of the personality factors important in organizational behavior. Knowing how these factors shape people's reactions to events can prove very useful in choosing and utilizing management strategies.

Cultures differ in significant and documented ways. As noted, they differ in terms of individualism-collectivism, power distance, uncertainty avoidance, masculinity-femininity, and time orientation. Like perception and personality, differences can dramatically affect, in unforeseen ways, the outcome of the most well-meaning management strategy.

A FINAL LOOK

Jong requests a meeting with Ken Arnold, the Korean team's American liaison, to discuss the Koreans' unease with individual competition as well as their desire for more clear-cut rules. He wants to gauge Ken's reaction to these issues before he makes suggestions for improving production procedures.

Ken is interested in the Korean team's impression of the American system. The plant manager has used the individual incentive concept for years; however, he feels that the team concept he's been reading about might increase productivity and employee satisfaction. Ken and a pleasantly surprised Jong agree to write a proposal to the plant manager about moving toward team incentives.

Ken is also puzzled by the Korean need for clearer rules. He tells Jong that Americans generally don't like specific behavioral rules, and he doubts that requiring the American workers to conform to additional rules will go over well. However, they decide that a question-and-answer session to clarify plant policies will ease the Koreans' transition and be a good opportunity to build rapport.

Jong is encouraged by Ken's willingness to listen and respect his requests, and so he ventures a suggestion about making the production line more efficient. To his surprise, Ken welcomes the advice and isn't at all insulted. They agree to meet regularly to discuss ways they can ease the Korean team's discomfort and improve the overall effectiveness of the production area.

KEY TERMS

attribution theory, 165
"Big Five" personality theory, 174
change (of stimuli), 155
closure, 157
conscious information processing, 168
contrast (of stimuli), 154
culture, 152
expatriates, 176
external locus of control, 172
expectancy effect, 161
field dependence, 157
figure-ground differentiation, 156
fundamental attribution error, 165
halo effect, 160
implicit personality theory, 163
individualism-collectivism, 177
intensity (of stimuli), 155
internal locus of control, 172
Johari window, 162
locus of causality, 165
locus of control, 172
Machiavellian personality, 173
masculinity-femininity, 179
nature, 170
nurture, 170
novelty (of stimuli), 154
objective reality, 152
organization, 156
organization-based self-esteem (OBSE), 171
perceived reality, 152
perception, 151
perceptual defense, 161
personality, 152
power distance, 178
primacy effect, 158
projection, 160
proximity in space, 156
proximity in time, 156
reality testing, 168
recency effect, 158
selection, 154
selective perception, 160
self-esteem, 170
self-fulfilling prophecy (Pygmalion) effect, 161
self-understanding, 168
sensation, 153
similarity, 156
stereotyping, 159
time orientation, 179
translation, 157
uncertainty avoidance, 178

ISSUES FOR REVIEW AND DISCUSSION

1. Describe a situation in which you had a conflict with another person (or group). Did perceptual errors play a role in the conflict? How?
2. Using the terms of perceptual selection discussed in the text, explain why (1) amusement parks are fun for most people; (2) TV ads are louder than the regular programs; (3) people usually don't like to see the same movie more than once in the same month; and (4) extroverted people often choose bright-colored clothes.
3. "Can't see the forest for the trees" is an old saying. What perceptual process does this colloquialism reflect?
4. Describe the Johari window. Has anyone ever pointed out one of your "blind spots"? What was your initial reaction?
5. Describe attribution theory. Provide an example from work where you or someone else committed the fundamental attribution error.
6. Describe a situation that you did not perceive accurately. What could you have done differently, using the techniques described in this chapter, to prevent your misperception from occurring?
7. Do you think you have high or low self-esteem? Why? What can managers do to enhance the organization-based self-esteem of employees?
8. Give an example where a manager effectively utilized knowledge of an employee's personality.
9. Is everyone in the United States high on the individualism and masculinity dimensions? Why or why not?

EXERCISES

THE T-TEST: AN EXPERIMENTAL PERSONALITY TEST

This exercise is quite simple. Take out a blank sheet of paper and a pen or pencil. Your instructor will tell you what to do next. Afterwards your instructor will lead a discussion about how we infer the personality traits of other people.

INFOTRAC

The articles listed below are a sampling of those available through InfoTrac College Edition. You can search for them either by title or by the author's name.

Articles

1. A five-year study of upward feedback: what managers do with their results matters. Alan G. Walker, James W. Smither. *Personnel Psychology* Summer 1999 v52 i2 p393(3)
2. Mutual Intercultural Perception: How Does it Affect Technical Communication? Jan M Ulijn, Kirk St. Aman. *Technical Communication* May 2000 v47 i2 p220
3. THE BIG FIVE PERSONALITY CHARACTERISTICS AS PREDICTORS OF EXPATRIATE'S DESIRE TO DETERMINE THE ASSIGNMENT AND SUPERVISOR RATED PERFORMANCE. (Statistical Data Included) Paula M. Caligiuri. *Personnel Psychology* Spring 2000 v53 i1 p67
4. Moderating Effects of Organization-Based Self-esteem on Organizational Uncertainty: Employee Response Relationships. Chun Hui, Cynthia Lee. *Journal of Management* March 2000 v26 i2 p215 Bus.Coll.: 116S2357
5. Sex Differences in Business Ethics: The Importance of Perceptions. Maureen L. Ambrose, Marshall Schminke *Journal of Managerial Issues* Winter 1999 v11 i4 p454 Bus.Coll.: 122X0079

Questions

For Article 2:

"Mutual Intercultural Perception: How Does it Affect Technical Communication?" investigates how individuals from different cultures perceive questioning and pausing/interrupting behavior. In today's diverse workplace, we encounter individuals from many cultures. After reading the article, break into groups and discuss the different responses to the negotiation tape presented in the article. Have you ever encountered circumstances where you misinterpreted or were misinterpreted because of cultural differences? Think of practical ways you could combat miscommunication in the workplace.

For Other Articles:

Have members of your group read the other articles on this list. Discuss any new information you gather about perceptions, self-esteem, the Big Five, locus of control, and cultural differences among organizational members.

WEB EXERCISE

Several journals (*Journal of Personality and Social Psychology, Journal of Applied Psychology, Journal of Personality*) publish articles that focus on personality and individual differences. Employing a search engine (for example, ABI Inform, PsyLit, Firstsearch) available through your university (college) library, access one of these journals and choose a recently published article that focuses on some aspect of perception, personality, and individual differences. Read and summarize the author's findings about this topic. In addition, speculate on how this individual difference factor might impact individuals within the work and organizational context.

CASE

Virtual Teamwork

Sendad Hadzic is an IT project manager for Englehard Corporation, a specialty chemical manufacturer. Hadzic supervises several teams of employees and suppliers located in different offices who are working on new software applications for Englehard. Making sure team members communicated with one another and kept on top of deadlines used to be a never-ending struggle for Hadzic. "There was always a bottleneck," he says. "Every time someone on a team wanted to add a task or have somebody else do a task, it had to be centralized and go through a central approval process, and that would be me."

Recently, Englehard installed Inovie Software's TeamCenter software on the company's computers. Now, team members sign on to a centralized, interactive website to share up-to-date information, ideas, and documents; they also participate in real-time planning and problem solving. "TeamCenter has provided a way for our team members to see one another's work and to leave their knowledge in detail with their task," says Hadzic. "There is no longer a need for me to be directly involved and give assignments."

Like Hadzic, Carolyn Sechler, owner of a successful accounting firm in Phoenix, Arizona, must also manage a far-flung team of workers. All of her employees, and Sechler herself, work from home—some from as far away as Nebraska, Missouri, and Michigan. When it comes time to develop ideas or work on projects as a team, Sechler and her employees log on to the Internet for a virtual meeting using an Internet chat service. If employees need to check a file, or get information on a project's progress, they also sign on to the Internet. All of the company's files, including spreadsheets, correspondence, and accounting ledgers, are stored on a company server at an Internet service provider.

Matt Light, an analyst with the research firm GartnerGroup, says Sechler and Hadzic are part of a growing trend using Internet technology to tie together workers and team members located in different places. "The knowledge base for today's fast-growing companies resides in virtual teams," he says. "Successful team collaboration and a new style of virtual management will be essential for these companies to compete."

Questions

1. How would personality affect an individual's ability to work within a virtual team? What personality characteristics do you believe would contribute to success in this environment? What characteristics do you believe would impede success?
2. Recall the section of the text on perceptual errors. Can you think of situations where operating completely within a virtual team would increase the risk of perceptual error? Explain your answer.
3. Review the "Big Five" personality dimensions identified in the chapter (extroversion, adjustment, agreeableness, conscientiousness, inquisitiveness). Within a virtual team, do you believe that each of these dimensions becomes more or less important as a determinant of employee adjustment and organizational effectiveness?
4. Identify Hofstede's five cultural dimensions. Which type of culture in each of these dimensions do you believe would be most responsive to working in a virtual team? For example, would members of a high uncertainty avoidance or low uncertainty avoidance culture be more likely to value and enjoy working within a virtual team?

Sources: C. Sandlund. March 27, 2000. Remote control. Business Week, *downloaded from* **http://www.businessweek.com**; *C. Sandlund. March 27, 2000. Tools of the remote trade.* Business Week, *downloaded from* **http://www.businessweek.com**; *L. Vaas. May 15, 2000. Taming rush-hour projects.* eWeek, *downloaded from* **http://www.zdnet.com**; *March 29, 2000. Teaming is fundamental to ensuring e-business success.* PR Newswire, *downloaded from* **http://www.prnewswire.com**.

Outline

CHAPTER 6

Attitudes in Organizations

Learning Objectives

After reading this chapter, you should be able to

1. Understand how employee attitudes affect organizations.
2. Describe the three major components of employee attitudes: cognitive, affective, and behavioral tendency.
3. Understand the attitude formation process.
4. Describe some ways in which managers might try to change employee attitudes.
5. Define job satisfaction, organizational commitment, work and job involvement, and psychological ownership, and understand their central role and importance to organizations.
6. Explain why it is important for organizations and managers to try to influence employee attitudes.
7. Understand that employee attitudes have a financial impact on an organization's profitability.

PHOTO: © R. W. JONES/CORBIS

A FIRST LOOK

Absenteeism at Gunnison Semiconductors is at an all-time high, and Human Resource Director Claire Nylund has been asked to discover the cause. After studying absenteeism records from the past two months, Claire discovers a pattern: The workers who call in sick are very often the technical employees newly arrived from India.

Claire invites some Indian employees whom she knows well to lunch and begins to listen. "Management does not appreciate us," one employee says. "I heard a group of managers complaining about the smell of the 'ethnic' food in the cafeteria and employee lounge. They think this place has really gone downhill since we came!" Another employee states quietly that she requested a day off during a religious festival and was turned down because it was right before a project deadline. Claire is sorry to hear how isolated these employees feel and has a hunch that it has a lot to do with their absenteeism. She decides to investigate further.

Questions: Are the attitudes of these employees emotional or cognitive? How are they affecting their involvement with Gunnison Semiconductors? How might Claire work to improve the attitudes of managers toward these employees?

attitude an individual's predisposition to think, feel, perceive, and behave in certain ways toward a particular tangible or intangible phenomenon

http://www.attitudefactor.com

Much is written about attitudes and organizational behavior. This is because employee attitudes can heavily impact organizational effectiveness. An **attitude** is an individual's predisposition to think, feel, perceive, and behave toward a particular tangible or intangible phenomenon.[1] We call the phenomenon associated with an attitude an "attitude object." Our attitudes reflect what we think, how we feel, and how we intend to act toward an attitude object. Organizational attitude objects run the gamut from ease of parking, to supervisors and co-workers, to an organization's trust of employees and its reward policies. Employees develop attitudes about many different facets of organizations. It would be a formidable task to review all of the work attitudes that researchers have examined over the years in their studies of people at work. In this chapter we discuss only a sample of work attitudes, and how they impact employee behavior. We also discuss how attitudes form, and once formed, how they can be changed.

Although attitudes are related to perception, personality, culture, values, and beliefs, they are not the same. As we've discussed, perception is what we sense in our environment. Personality is the consistent behavior patterns that we exhibit in a wide variety of situations. Our values are about how we think the world and everyone in it should behave. Our beliefs are what we hold to be true about the world. Perceptions, personality, values, and beliefs affect the attitudes we develop. But, attitudes are conceptually different from those other characteristics.

Like the previous chapter on perception and personality, the study of attitudes in organizational behavior cannot be overemphasized. There are several reasons why attitudes are important to the study of organizational behavior. First, many of the theories and managerial techniques discussed in this text have at their core the development of healthy work attitudes. These techniques are based on an assumption that under certain conditions attitudes will cause behaviors. Some of these attitude-behavior relations are discussed in this chapter. Second, organizations have an interest in developing good work attitudes as an end in itself. That is, they want their employees to be happy working for the organization, independent of the effects that attitudes have on work behaviors. They want their employees to experience what is called a high "quality of work life." Lastly, favorable work attitudes do contribute to the financial health of organizations. In recent years, researchers have demonstrated that good work attitudes mean bigger profits. Profits get attention. Managers can no longer "afford" (pun intended!) to be nonchalant about employee attitudes.

ATTITUDES AND THEIR COMPONENTS

Attitudes are much more than whether we like something, or how we act around someone. Earlier we noted that attitudes reflect what we think, how we feel, and how we intend to behave toward an attitude object. Our attitudes by themselves are complex in nature. We have many of them—some would say too many! Many of our attitudes conflict, and each one has several components, which we discuss next. Figure 6-1 shows how the components combine to create an attitude.

Cognitive Component

cognitive component of an attitude is what we know, or think we know, about the attitude object

The **cognitive component** of an attitude is what we know, or think we know, about the attitude object. It consists of information, facts, statistics, data, and so on, that we believe to be true about the attitude object. We may in fact be incorrect, but we *think* it is true. The cognitive component of the attitude "Bill Gates is a very successful businessman" is "successful"; the attitude object is Bill Gates. The cognitive component (is successful) is associated with the attitude object (Bill Gates).

Affective Component

affective component of an attitude consists of the feelings a person has toward an attitude object

The **affective component** of an attitude consists of the feelings we have toward an attitude object. This involves evaluation and emotion and is often expressed as like or dislike. Affective components can range from disgust, to indifference, to adoration, and differ from cognitive components in that they involve intensity of feeling, and often a wide range of it. Cognitive components are neutral

FIGURE 6-1 Illustration of the Attitude → Behavior Relationship

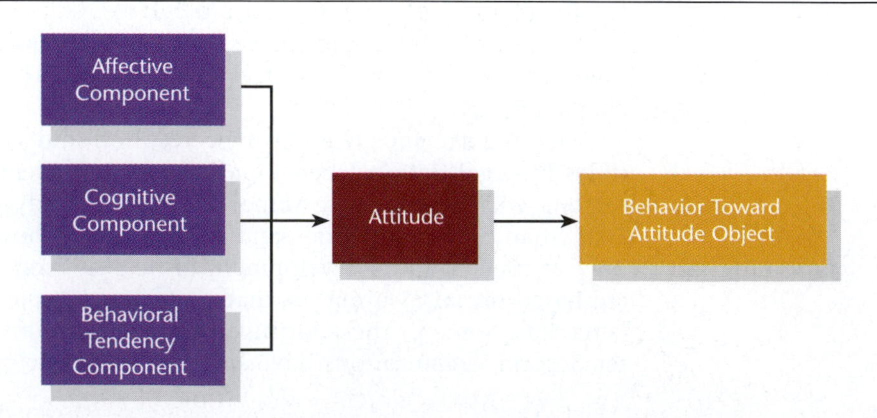

statements of the facts. One way to distinguish between the two is to remember the old saying "Just tell me the facts."

The affective component of an attitude is really our reaction to the cognitive component. As such, the particular pattern of beliefs we hold about a person or thing (the cognitive component) exerts a major influence on our feelings toward that object. However, we use different evaluative processes as we react to our beliefs, because of different values, motivations, perceptions, and so on. Thus, people can have very different affective attitude components even though they possess similar cognitive components. Two students agree that their professor is knowledgeable. Yet, one likes the professor (eager to share her knowledge) while the other student dislikes the professor (hates "know-it-alls").

Behavioral Tendency Component

behavioral tendency component of an attitude is the way an individual is inclined to behave toward an attitude object

The final component of attitudes is the **behavioral tendency component.** This is the way we're inclined to behave toward an attitude object, that is, how the object "makes" us want to behave. Behavioral intentions are strong predictors of future behavior. It is this component that draws researchers to the study of attitudes. If attitudes didn't eventually translate into behavior, they would be of much less consequence to organizations. Researchers assess employee attitudes, and then attempt to predict how the employees will behave on the basis of that assessment.

http://www.attitudesmagazine.com

Both cognitive and affective components of attitudes influence the way people behave toward an attitude object. However, many different behavioral tendencies are possible depending on the particular pattern of cognitive and affective attitude components. Recall the previously mentioned example of two students who similarly believe that a professor is knowledgeable. One may ultimately attend all regularly scheduled classes, while the other student shows up only on examination dates.

As we all know, the attitudes people hold are complex, contradictory, and often counterintuitive, to name a few reasons why they are not always easy to sort out. If we try to sort out an attitude by its components, we must remember that attitudes have three components, each of which affects the others. Let's take a person's attitude toward the company they work for. The cognitive components might include information about the size of the organization, the age of his or her manager, and the amount of money the worker believes a co-worker earns. The affective component could include the worker's dislike of the organization's small size, concern that the manager is too young to exercise authority, and unhappiness that a co-worker is paid more. The behavioral tendency component could range from an intention to leave a small company for a larger one, to ask to be reassigned to an older manager, or to request a pay raise. These are quite a few items to ponder.

ATTITUDE FORMATION

http://www.psych.wisc.edu/emotivelab

We are not born with our attitudes.* Instead, our attitudes develop through the experiences that we have with attitude objects (for example, pay, supervision, work). There are four major sources of such experiences and thus of our attitudes: personal experience, association, social learning, and heredity.

* We'll discuss hereditary tendencies to acquire certain types of attitudes later in this chapter.

Feeling overworked can often lead us to develop attitudes about our companies and those around us. For instance, we may think that we are working harder than others are or that the company is not concerned about our workload. Or, we may think that the workload is challenging and that we are working hard as part of a team.

Personal Experience

Personal experience means that we have come in direct contact with the attitude object. Through this encounter, we perceive certain characteristics or traits of the attitude object. Some of these perceptions are transformed into our attitude about the object. Personal experiences usually have their first impact on the cognitive component. From their first experiences on the job, new employees might form these cognitive components of their attitude toward the company:

1. There are many employees at this company.
2. My job is very difficult.
3. My supervisor isn't as busy as I am.
4. My co-workers complain a lot.

Remember that given the same situation, two people may or may not form the same cognitive component. One may ignore certain factors that the other finds important. Even given the same cognitive components (the ones just listed, for example), two people may use them to form entirely different affective components. Thus, one new hire may conclude "I like having lots of people around; I like the challenge of my duties; I'm grateful my supervisor has time to check my work; I don't understand why my co-workers aren't satisfied." Another new hire, *given the same cognitive components,* might conclude "I feel paranoid around so many people; I didn't expect to work so hard at my first job; I think it's disgusting that I've got more to do than my supervisor; I'm going to take another job the moment something better turns up."

personal experience in forming attitudes occurs by coming in direct contact with an attitude object

association occurs when a person transfers parts or all of an attitude about an old object to a new attitude object

Association

When we "transfer" parts or all of our attitude about an old attitude object to a new one, **association** is forming the new attitude. Two attitude objects can be associated in a variety of ways. Perhaps you notice that a new employee, Raul, is spending a lot of time with Jon, a co-worker who is competent and whom you like personally. To the degree that you associate Raul and Jon, your attitude toward Raul will include competence and liking. Two attitude objects can be associated for a variety of reasons (similarity of appearance, location, and so on). Anything that causes you to associate two attitude objects creates the possibility that you will transfer your attitude from the first to the second. These transfers may be accurate; frequently, they are not. If your attitude toward one supervisor is favorable, you may generalize that attitude to a future supervisor because of association. Personal experience, however, may cause you to revise your attitude if you find that the new supervisor behaves quite differently from your previous supervisor.

Social Learning

social learning of attitudes occurs when people with whom a person works affect the attitudes one develops

A very common and powerful source of attitude formation comes from social learning. **Social learning** of attitudes occurs when people we work with influence our attitudes. We often form attitudes toward objects we haven't personally experienced; instead, we take up the attitude of someone we trust who has experience with the object. The attitude of others can override our predisposition to form attitudes by association. In short, our beliefs are frequently molded by others. All too often, however, the cognitive components shared by others are not accurate. Since we have no direct experience with the attitude object, we can't always evaluate the accuracy of the information.

Social learning affects not only beliefs but affective reactions and behavioral tendencies as well. Many people believe that Harvard students are rich, spoiled, pompous, self-centered individuals who are not as smart as they think they are, who take advantage of their employers, and who exploit co-workers. But how many of us have ever met a Harvard student? Analogously, how many racial, sexist, and ethnic prejudices are learned—that is, have no basis in personal experience? Finally, although people we know (family, friends, co-workers) are our most common sources for social learning, there are many others, including formal education and reading material.

Social learning of work attitudes is especially powerful for new employees. If new employees are placed in a group populated with disgruntled workers, they'll likely develop negative attitudes toward the organization. In contrast, if new employees are placed in groups populated with satisfied co-workers, they'll probably develop positive work attitudes.

Heredity

heredity the transmission from parents to offspring of certain defining characteristics; a genetic predisposition to behave or think in certain ways

One line of research has suggested that people have genetic predispositions to develop certain types of attitudes.[2] **Heredity** is the transmission from parents to offspring of certain defining characteristics (life events may modify these characteristics). A genetic predisposition is an inherited propensity to behave or think in certain ways. Our intelligence is due in large part to the genes we inherit. The environment we're raised in also affects our intelligence, although researchers disagree on the extent of its influence. (This is the old "nature versus nurture" controversy that we discussed in Chapter 5.) Heredity plays a part in our tendencies to develop certain types of attitudes. Some people are genetically programmed to have positive (or negative) attitudes toward certain classes of objects (like jobs; see below). Recent research suggests that up to 30 percent of the attitudes we possess, especially the affective component, may have a genetic component.[3] Still, the other determinants of attitudes combine to have a far stronger influence.

ATTITUDE CHANGE

Just as attitudes are formed through personal experience, association, and social learning, so are attitudes changed through personal experience, association, and social learning. Attitude change requires the addition, removal, or modification of one or more parts of any of the three components. One or two components of an attitude can change while the others remain the same. Once an attitude is formed, it becomes an integral part of us. Simply put, changing our attitudes changes us. It comes as no surprise then that we strongly resist attempts by others to change our attitudes.

There are, however, a number of strategies for endeavoring to change the attitudes of others. First, try to directly change one component. To change the cognitive component, present new information about the attitude object ("Our pay is actually higher than that offered by comparable employers"). Or, try to modify existing beliefs ("The professor is knowledgeable and also receives a lot of respect from other professors"). If the cognitive component can be changed, it may cause a change in the affective component as well. For that reason, most attitude-change interventions in organizations focus on the cognitive component.

Another strategy attempts to change the affective component directly by presenting a different emotional reaction to some attitude object ("Well, I think management's new initiative is good for the employees") or by modeling a different (and desired) behavior ("I plan on participating fully in the new quality improvement program"). Changing the cognitive and/or affective components may lead to changes in the behavioral tendency component.

cognitive dissonance an unpleasant psychological state that occurs when a person possesses conflicting thoughts about an attitude object

If new information about an attitude object conflicts with existing information, it has the potential to change attitudes. But it usually doesn't. Often this contrary information is filtered out of a person's consciousness as unnecessary (see the discussion of perceptual filtering in Chapter 5). Or, the contrary information is treated as suspect. People will actively resist changing the "right" attitude (theirs) for the "wrong" attitude (someone else's). No one likes to admit they are wrong. People also experience what is called **cognitive dissonance** when they are being encouraged to develop a different belief about an attitude object.[4] Cognitive dissonance, when a person possesses conflicting thoughts about an attitude object, is an unpleasant psychological state. For example, Sally wouldn't be "caught dead" in an American car. Yet, she has a secret liking for Cadillacs, one that she's rather embarrassed about "because they're for old people." People will often perceptually distort the cognition (Sally will find a way to make liking Cadillacs acceptable—"they've got that new NavStar thing; it's really cool, I'll never get lost again"). All of these processes reduce the likelihood of attitude change occurring. For these reasons, in trying to effect attitude change with new information, it's best to do it incrementally. Don't expect to turn a Yankees fan into a Mets fan all at once. Instead, first try convincing the Yankees fan that it's good for New York City to support both teams, at least to outsiders.

Providing a new experience with the attitude object that conflicts with the person's prior attitude is yet another strategy. For example, personal computer instructors need to overcome their students' negative attitudes toward computers. They often do this by playing computer games the first day, or by starting with relatively simple but productive tasks like word processing.[5]

Or you can create new associations with the attitude object. For example, Jamie doesn't like Donna, her supervisor. To change that attitude, find opportunities to admire Donna's abilities—"Donna is only doing her job, which makes all of our jobs even more secure." Or better yet, take Jamie and Donna out to lunch!

Relying on the effects of social learning can sometimes change attitudes. People are more likely to change an attitude if someone who is more knowledgeable about, or has had greater experience with, an attitude object has a different attitude toward the object. Advertisers use this strategy all the time when they have experts peddle their products. Think of star athletes peddling shoes and sports equipment or actor physicians and nurses recommending painkillers.

This idea works on the job as well. Try citing the CEO's attitude toward teamwork, for instance. An especially effective way to change attitudes is to cite someone with a favorable image (attractive, funny, wealthy, prestigious). That's why celebrities (like Bill Cosby) get paid millions to endorse products.

What types of attitude are more difficult to change? Those based on an expert's opinion (cognitive basis)? Or those developed because of the endorser's image (affective basis)? Research indicates that both are equally amenable to change. But attitude change will be more successful if the change strategy matches the origin of the attitude.[6] So, to change an expert-based attitude, you would be well-advised to counter with another expert's opinion (preferably one with greater weight). That is, use a physician's opinion to override a nurse's on the value of some painkiller. The same is true with an image-based attitude—for example, using Jennifer Lopez to overcome a Madonna endorsement.

One final strategy: Start with the behavior. That is, changing behavior can sometimes change attitudes. This theory underlies the many attempts to integrate public schools in the United States. Children often adopt the negative racial prejudices of their parents, even though they have no personal experiences that corroborate these attitudes. Giving children opportunities to have positive personal experiences (schools expect certain levels of civility—a behavior) that directly refute myths and biases of social learning can and does change attitudes. The same thing can happen in the workplace.[7]

It is important for organizations and managers to actively foster positive employee attitudes toward the organization. Just as our attitudes affect our behaviors in all manner of contexts, so do our work attitudes affect our work behaviors. The relationship between attitudes and behaviors is not a simple one, though. There are a wide variety of causes of human behavior, many of which we discuss in this text. One major driver of behavior is intention—our desire to behave in a certain way toward an attitude object, consistent with our cognitive and affective reactions to the object. These are, of course, the three components of attitude. When the cognitive and affective components are positive, it is likely that the behavioral intentions will be too.[8] In organizations, desirable work attitudes are often positively related to outcomes the organization values, like higher productivity and less turnover.

Many managers dismiss the importance of *attitude* and conscious attempts to monitor, interpret, and manage them; however, they consider *behavior*—job performance, absenteeism, tardiness, turnover, and various forms of union activity—to be quite important. It may seem *easier* to monitor and regulate behavior, but it may be more *effective* to change attitude. Remember, positive attitudes make for desirable behaviors.

WORK-RELATED ATTITUDES

People form a wide range of attitudes about their work environment. Of the three components, the cognitive component (what employees think about their jobs) is the one that organizations can influence most directly, although as noted below, it doesn't always receive the most attention. Organizations accomplish this by attempting to influence "objective reality" in the hope that workers will base their beliefs on that reality. For example, an organization might increase everyone's pay an equal percentage in the hope that employees will develop a favorable attitude about their pay.

On the other hand, the attitude component that most directly impacts organizations is behavioral tendency. Remember, intention drives behavior. Surveys of employee attitudes often include a question about intentions to quit the organization because intention to quit is the single best predictor of whether an employee will actually quit.[9]

Job Satisfaction

The affective component of attitudes receives the most attention from organizations. In fact, many organizations focus almost entirely on this component when measuring worker attitudes because they view it as the most crucial reaction a worker has. After all, this component directly affects important aspects of the workplace—job satisfaction, loyalty, and so on. Job satisfaction is the most widely researched of the job attitudes; thus we spend the most time discussing it.

job satisfaction the attitude that results from the appraisal of one's job as attaining or enabling the attainment of one's important job values

http://www.meaningatwork.com

What *is* job satisfaction? The most widely accepted definition was proposed by Edwin Locke.[10] "**Job satisfaction** results from the appraisal of one's job as attaining or allowing the attainment of one's important job values, providing these values are congruent with or help to fulfill one's basic needs."[11] What this means is that most people engage in paid work to satisfy multiple needs. To satisfy our safety and security needs (see Maslow's hierarchy of needs in Chapter 7), we need a home; to pay the mortgage or rent on our home, we need to earn money, and organizations pay us money for our work. Similarly, to satisfy our needs for growth, we can learn new skills and thereby gain the respect of our co-workers. Our basic needs give rise to our values, the things we seek to gain and/or keep. People who have very strong security needs value (seek) jobs that pay well. People who have strong growth needs value jobs that are meaningful and challenging (see Chapter 16).

When people believe their jobs enable them to attain their values, either directly (from performing the job) or indirectly (from the pay they receive), they develop a positive attitude toward the job and the organization (the attitude objects). Rare is the case, however, where a job completely allows us to achieve all of our values. Nevertheless, the more that our jobs allow for value attainment, actually acquiring what it is that we value (such as pay), the more satisfied we will be. Conversely, the greater the discrepancy between what we value and our actual experience of attaining it on the job, the more likely we will become dissatisfied with our job and the organization. To summarize, job satisfaction is a reflection of the gap between what we want from a job (values), and what we experience. The greater the gap, the greater the dissatisfaction.

Facets of Job Satisfaction As is the case with most affective attitude components, job satisfaction is complex. Job satisfaction consists of a variety of satisfaction facets ("parts") involving workers' feelings toward various aspects of the work environment. Thus, our job satisfaction includes our feelings about the work itself, about pay, about co-workers, and so on. The most common and most important facets of job satisfaction are the characteristics of the work itself, the amount of work, the physical working conditions, co-workers, supervision, compensation, promotional opportunities, and organizational policies and practices. The work itself, what we do day to day on the job, is often referred to as the *job content* facet. The other facets are generally referred to as *job context* facets, because they provide the context, or environment, in which the job is performed.

Each facet is involved to one degree or another in the job satisfaction of almost all workers, in virtually all organizations. Each facet is associated with a corresponding dimension of the work environment, and each one has a corresponding cognitive attitude component. For example, the organization's pay scale primarily impacts the beliefs you hold about pay. This, in turn, exerts its primary influence on your satisfaction or dissatisfaction with your pay. Keep in mind that two employees can be paid exactly the same and have entirely different reactions to it; both their affective and behavioral tendency components may be different, even though their cognitive component is the same. Thus, one person making $50,000 a year might be very satisfied with this pay, while another making the same amount could be very dissatisfied.

Our feelings about one facet often spill over and influence our feelings about other facets. Although this "spillover" may be moderate in degree, it is very common. Our satisfaction with promotion opportunities, for example, will likely impact our satisfaction with pay. That is, if we're unhappy with our prospects for advancement, we're probably unhappy with our pay. In spite of the spillover effect, each facet does involve a distinct feeling. For example, it's possible to be very satisfied with pay but rather unhappy with co-workers. Under these circumstances, satisfaction with pay may spill over and keep co-worker satisfaction from being as low as it would be otherwise. Similarly, low satisfaction with co-workers might spill over and prevent pay satisfaction from being as high as it could be. The point here is, you cannot fully understand a worker's affective reactions unless you consider each facet.

overall job satisfaction
a combination of facet satisfactions that describes a person's overall affective reaction to a set of work and work-related factors

Overall Job Satisfaction **Overall job satisfaction** (sometimes called "general job satisfaction") describes a person's overall affective reaction to the set of work and work-related factors. Our job satisfaction includes our overall job satisfaction as well as our facet satisfactions. Overall job satisfaction is a combination of our facet satisfactions. This doesn't mean, however, that each facet is equally important to us. Certain facets might be more important than others and, therefore, have a larger impact on overall job satisfaction. Figure 6-2 shows overall satisfaction and facet satisfactions for Carole and Marni. Their overall satisfaction is moderate. They both have relatively low satisfaction with the work itself, supervision, and promotional opportunities, and moderate levels of satisfaction with the amount of work and organizational policies. They both have high satisfaction with the physical conditions. But their satisfaction with their co-workers and compensation differ substantially. Marni's satisfaction with co-workers is very high; Carole's is low. Conversely, Carole's satisfaction with her compensation is high, while Marni's is low. If we considered only their overall satisfaction, we wouldn't get a complete picture of the job satisfaction of either worker. The behavioral tendency components of Carole's and Marni's attitudes toward work could be very different due to the differences in their facet satisfactions. Therefore, despite the fact that they share similar overall satisfaction levels, their subsequent work behavior could also be very different. Furthermore, any actions the organization could take to improve the satisfaction of these two workers would be heavily influenced by this pattern of facet satisfactions. Understanding and applying techniques for improving worker satisfaction involves differentiating between the various facets.

FIGURE 6-2 Satisfaction Levels for Two Co-Workers

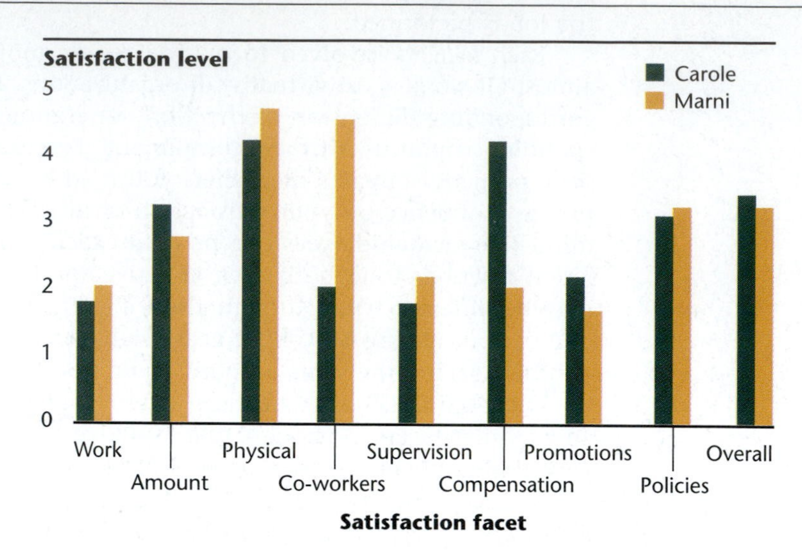

Source: Based on data collected by the authors.

Causes of Job Satisfaction What creates job satisfaction? Experience, association, social learning, and heredity all affect it, just like any other type of attitude. Experience with various elements of the work environment certainly affects our attitudes toward them. If a job is tedious and not challenging, chances are that we won't be satisfied with it (even if we're satisfied with our supervisor). In fact, organizations expend a tremendous amount of effort on making jobs more interesting. This is called job enrichment and is discussed further in Chapter 16. Research (also discussed in Chapter 16) indicates that job content factors (the work we do day after day) play a powerful role in employee job satisfaction/dissatisfaction. Employees whose jobs actively engage them experience more job satisfaction than those whose jobs involve routine, repetitive, short-time-cycle, and low-skill-level work.

Association also plays a role in job satisfaction. If an employee believes her job is similar to one she had in the past, she may generalize the prior satisfaction levels to the present job. Research has demonstrated that people are quite consistent in the levels of job satisfaction they develop throughout their work lives, even in widely different jobs in different organizations.[12] Association accounts for at least some of this consistency.

Social learning also plays an important role in developing job satisfaction. Have you noticed that groups of people develop similar attitudes? The same thing tends to happen in work groups, at least ones where the members interact frequently and perform the same job. They all tend to feel the same way about their supervisors, the work they perform, their pay, and so on. This is because they reinforce each other's comments and reactions. One person says something like "This job really bores me," and the rest of the group nod their heads in agreement. In time, they develop similar job satisfaction levels. Some organizational behavior researchers contend that these social influence effects can be quite substantial.[13]

Research in the past few years has identified other causes of job satisfaction. One line of research suggests that people have genetic predispositions to develop certain levels of job satisfaction. A controversial study conducted on identical twins who grew up in different families suggests that up to 30 percent of job satisfaction is due to genetic factors.[14] This is quite a large effect on an attitude once thought to be caused primarily by on-the-job experiences. Of course, that still leaves job experiences as the major cause of the other 70 percent of job satisfaction.

Yet another study suggests that some people have personalities that predispose them to develop high or low levels of job satisfaction.[15] We've all met people who are constantly cynical and irritable as well as people who are so happy-go-lucky they seem unaware of the problems in their lives, so this idea is not counterintuitive. These researchers found that people high on a personality dimension called negative affectivity are consistently less satisfied with their jobs than people low on the dimension. Such people tend to dwell on the negative aspects of their jobs, which eventually leads to job dissatisfaction. It should be noted, however, that the degree to which their jobs were interesting had a much larger impact on job satisfaction than did the negative affectivity dimension.

Relating the preceding discussion to Part I of this book, which discussed such issues as management philosophies and ethics, it seems safe to say that management's goals and beliefs are translated into actions and policies that lead to employees' satisfaction with the various aspects of work. If management emphasizes profit-maximization, this can be reflected in below-market pay levels. The latter in turn can cause high dissatisfaction with pay. Similarly, if management believes strongly in the organization's social responsibilities, this often filters down to employees feeling like their jobs contribute to society as well as to the organization's profits. This can in itself create high job satisfaction. Thus, managers need to carefully consider their philosophies toward employees and the organization as it ultimately affects employee job satisfaction. Managers also need to consider new ways to promote favorable attitudes. *An Inside Look* at sabbaticals describes one new approach to building employee morale.

Company policies that provide opportunities for employees to further their education are one way to increase morale.

In Part III of this book, we'll discuss specific management practices, such as how managers make decisions, how they engage in strategic planning, how they lead, how they organize work tasks, and how they structure the organization. This is what is termed the organizational behavior context, and it too has direct effects on job satisfaction. For example, when managers use an autocratic decision-making style, simply handing employees decisions without their participation, employees may become dissatisfied with their management. The bottom line is that the decisions managers make and how they manage eventually affect employee job satisfaction.

AN INSIDE LOOK

Sabbaticals: Not Just for Academics Anymore

In the past decade, the corporate world has seen a shift in employee desires and motivations. No longer satisfied with financial perks and extensive retirement packages, employees whose lives are stretched by the hectic pace of work responsibilities and busy family lives are requesting more time off. In an effort to increase employee loyalty and motivation and decrease turnover, some corporations are reviving the sabbatical concept.

Historically, sabbaticals have been available to university professors to allow them to take time off from teaching responsibilities to develop research interests, prepare for publication, and serve as an overall rejuvenator. After World War II, the first companies began to consider the concept of offering employee sabbaticals, and in the 1960s mill workers negotiated a 13-week sabbatical as part of a contract negotiation for the purposes of retraining.

These days, every organization differs in their approach to employee sabbatical policies. Some companies offer employees five days off per year in addition to their annual vacation time, which can be accrued or taken at the end of every year. Other companies offer employees the opportunity to take as much as two years of unpaid leave. Xerox specifies that applicants applying for a sabbatical must use the time for community-service projects, while Ralston Purina Co. allows employees to choose how to spend their time away from work. Some might spend it traveling around the world, while others might return to school to further their education or spend time at home with children or aging parents.

Sabbatical policies do have their opponents, however. Some employers fear that employees will use their sabbatical time to search for a better position. Other employers note the difficulty in having employees who remain at work cover both their own responsibilities and the responsibilities of their co-worker who is on sabbatical. Some companies who are hesitant to implement a full-blown sabbatical policy are instead implementing vacation bonuses and other flex-time options for employees. Some organizations take a very proactive approach and use an employee's time away from his or her position to allow a person with less responsibility to take over the absent employee's responsibilities. In this way, talent is developed internally and the organization finds itself in a win-win situation.

Regardless of specific policies, companies with a sabbatical policy recognize that their employees have lives and goals outside of their immediate professional responsibilities. Whether those goals be family-oriented, community-oriented, or even career-oriented, most employers agree that employees who return from sabbatical are more well-rounded, focused, and productive.

Source: Adapted from S. Greengard. February 7, 2000. It's about time. *Industry Week* 47, 49–50.

Measuring Job Satisfaction Job satisfaction, like all attitudes, exists only inside a person's head. It cannot be measured directly, the way we measure physical factors such as height, weight, or distance. However, because satisfaction is so important to organizations, researchers have developed procedures for measuring it indirectly. These include observing worker behavior, interviewing workers about satisfaction levels, and distributing questionnaires to obtain this information systematically. Most measures of satisfaction in use today have poor reliability (consistency) and validity (accuracy). The people who developed them typically are not trained in the field of psychometrics (the science of test development). The quality of their satisfaction measures suffers as a result. However, a tremendous amount of energy has been expended by organizational behavior researchers to demonstrate that a few good measures do indeed provide high-quality indirect measures of satisfaction. These measures have been used by managers and researchers alike to obtain reliable, valid measures of satisfaction facets and overall satisfaction.[16]

http://www.managingemployees.com

One of the simplest approaches to measuring job satisfaction is shown in Figure 6-3, which presents the "Faces" technique.[17] The Faces scale measures overall satisfaction. It can also measure any facet of satisfaction simply by reworking the directions to focus on the facet of interest (such as pay). This measure of satisfaction is straightforward, requires very simple language skills, and very little employee time. It has been shown to possess good reliability and validity.

The self-assessment on the following page shows sample items from another questionnaire called the Minnesota Satisfaction Questionnaire (MSQ).[18] To get a feel for its effectiveness, complete the questionnaire and score it for a job you've had or currently have. The MSQ is also relatively straightforward. It asks workers to report how satisfied they are with issues relating to a variety of satisfaction facets. The MSQ provides reliable and valid information about satisfaction; it's more precise than the Faces approach, but also takes longer, as there are 100 items listed (we present the short version of the questionnaire here). Also, as is true for the Faces technique, some respondents may distort their answers to demonstrate their satisfaction or dissatisfaction in a stronger manner.

Table 6-1 presents sample items from the Job Descriptive Index (JDI), which is one of the most widely used job satisfaction questionnaires.[19] This measure takes an interesting approach. A series of adjectives is presented to workers, and they are asked to indicate whether or not each adjective describes their work situation. Thus, the JDI doesn't measure the affective component of the work attitude but, rather, addresses the cognitive component. Normally, this is not an acceptable approach, because people can have different affective reactions to the same information. However, developers of the JDI took very careful steps to identify adjectives that consistently lead to positive or negative affective reactions. In fact, over 85 percent of all workers agreed that an adjective was associated with a satisfying or unsatisfying job. In using this "descriptive" approach to measuring job satisfaction, the JDI avoids many of the problems associated with asking a person to "tell me how satisfied you are." In exchange, however, the JDI measures satisfaction somewhat less directly than do many other measures.

FIGURE 6-3 Faces Technique for Measuring Job Satisfaction

Consider all aspects of your job. Circle the face which best describes your feelings about your job in general.

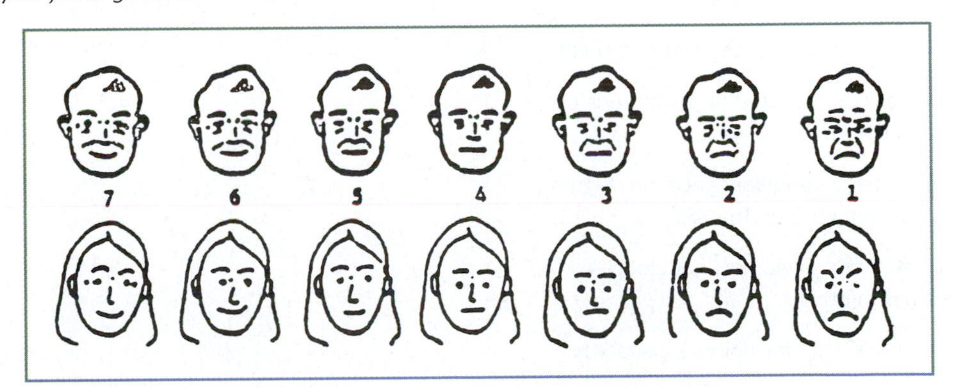

The male faces were originally developed by T. Kunin (1955) as reported in *Personnel Psychology* 8:65–78. The matching female faces were created by R. B. Dunham and J. B. Herman and published in the *Journal of Applied Psychology* 60: 629–631. Copyright 1975 by the American Psychological Association. Reprinted with permission of the publisher and authors.

SELF-ASSESSMENT Minnesota Satisfaction Questionnaire Items for Measuring Job Satisfaction

Think of your current job, or a job that you have had in the past. Then mark your answers to the following 20 items on the scale provided.

On my present (past) job, this is how I feel (felt) about . . .	**Not Satisfied**	**Slightly Satisfied**	**Satisfied**	**Very Satisfied**	**Extremely Satisfied**
Being able to keep busy all the time	1	2	3	4	5
The chance to work alone on the job	1	2	3	4	5
The chance to do different things from time to time	1	2	3	4	5
The chance to be "somebody" in the community	1	2	3	4	5
The way my boss handles his employees	1	2	3	4	5
The competence of my supervisor in making decisions	1	2	3	4	5
Being able to do things that don't go against my conscience	1	2	3	4	5
The way my job provides for steady employment	1	2	3	4	5
The chance to do things for other people	1	2	3	4	5
The chance to tell people what to do	1	2	3	4	5
The chance to do something that makes use of my abilities	1	2	3	4	5
The way company policies are put into practice	1	2	3	4	5
My pay and the amount of work I do	1	2	3	4	5
The chances for advancement on this job	1	2	3	4	5
The freedom to use my own judgment	1	2	3	4	5
The chance to try my own methods of doing the job	1	2	3	4	5
The working conditions (heating, lighting, ventilation, etc.) on this job	1	2	3	4	5
The way my co-workers get along with each other	1	2	3	4	5
The praise I get for doing a good job	1	2	3	4	5
The feeling of accomplishment I get from the job	1	2	3	4	5

Scoring:

1. Add up the values of each number that you circled. Your total should be between 20 and 100.
2. Interpreting your score: 1–72 = very low (bottom 25%); 73–79 = below average (25–50%); 80–85 = above average (51–75%); and 86–100 = very satisfied (top 25%).

Source: Adapted from Minnesota Satisfaction Questionnaire by D. J. Weiss, R. V. Davis, G. W. England, and L. H. Lofquist, *Manual for the Minnesota Satisfaction Questionnaire* (University of Minnesota Vocational Psychology Research, 1967).

http://www.jobsatisfactionsurveys.com

The methods for measuring job satisfaction described here provide adequately reliable, valid, and efficient information. A group of 50–100 workers can complete one of these questionnaires in less than 20 minutes. Each of these approaches can be used with a wide range of employees and organizations. The standardized format of the questionnaires allows comparison of results across jobs, departments, and companies. Nevertheless, realize that none of them is perfect.[20]

Satisfaction measures are used to assess worker reactions to the job and work environment. An investigation by the American Society for Personnel Administration (now called the Society for Human Resource Management) found that over 40 percent of employers conduct attitude surveys of their employees.[21] This is true across all types of industries, large and small alike. Most of these organizations measure overall satisfaction and one or more facets of satisfaction. The study also revealed that over 70 percent of organizations conducting surveys use questionnaires constructed by members of the organization. Unfortunately, only a small percentage of these questionnaires are reliable and valid. This is not surprising, since it took years of work to develop good measures such as the MSQ and JDI. More organizations should take advantage of these reliable, valid measures of satisfaction.

TABLE 6-1 Job Descriptive Index Item for Measuring Job Satisfaction

Directions: Think of the work you do at present. How well does each of the following words or phrases describe your job?

Circle YES if it describes your work.
Circle NO if it does NOT describe your work.
Circle ? If you cannot decide.

Work on present job			
Fascinating	YES	NO	?
Pleasant	YES	NO	?
Job in general			
Pleasant	YES	NO	?
Worse than most	YES	NO	?
Worthwhile	YES	NO	?

Source: JDI and JIG copyright 1997 by Bowling Green State University. Reproduced with permission. Licensing for this and related scales (e.g., Abridged JDI, Stress in General Scale, Retirement Descriptive Index, and Survey of Work Values) can be obtained from the Department of Psychology at Bowling Green State University, Bowling Green, Ohio 43403.

Consequences of Job Satisfaction Job satisfaction is associated with a number of behaviors that are helpful to organizations. Employees who are satisfied with their jobs are less likely than dissatisfied employees to think about or actually quit, be absent or tardy, or refuse to be good citizens. In fact, job satisfaction is one of the strongest determinants of citizenship behaviors.[22] These behaviors are discussed further in Chapter 8.

But what about job performance? Are happy workers more productive than unhappy workers? Research over 50 years in organizational behavior suggests that the short answer is no. In most studies there is no significant relationship between satisfaction and performance. Yet this seems to be counterintuitive. While many theories have been offered to explain this apparent lack of relationship, none have been universally accepted.[23]

OK, you say, but are productive workers happy workers? Frequently the answer to this question is yes. Most people feel good when they perform well. They reward themselves. Also, managers treat their good performers differently than their poor performers. They often take steps to administer rewards (praise, wage increases) to their productive employees. Receipt of this recognition also feels good. Thus, there is some evidence to support the idea that the performance-causes-satisfaction relationship may be stronger than the satisfaction-causes-performance relationship. For "the happy worker is a productive worker" thesis to be correct, we need to know more about the employee's work-related motives (needs, goals, values) and behavioral intentions, since intention is such a significant driver of employee behavior.

The observation of a weak causal relationship between satisfaction and performance may stem from the fact that in many organizations, performance is not measured very well. Poor performance measures, even when coupled with good measures of job satisfaction, are likely to result in a weak correlation between the two, leading to the erroneous conclusion that satisfaction and performance are at best weakly related. Thus, our inability to create good measures of performance may prevent organizational behavior researchers from proving the relationship. The relationship between satisfaction and performance is explored further in Chapter 8.

Organizational Commitment

Some people sincerely care about the organizations they work for. They value the company and their roles in it, care about its future, and wish to remain associated with it. This is the essence of the attitude termed organizational commitment. Lyman Porter, Richard Mowday, and Richard Steers have been researching the organizational commitment concept for over 20 years.[24] They define **organizational commitment** as

organizational commitment the relative strength of an individual's identification with and involvement in a particular organization

> . . . the relative strength of an individual's identification with and involvement in a particular organization. Conceptually, it can be characterized by at least three factors: (a) a strong belief in and acceptance of the organization's goals and values; (b) a willingness to exert considerable effort on behalf of the organization; and (c) a strong desire to maintain membership in the organization (Mowday et al., 1982, p. 27).

Unlike job satisfaction and work/job involvement (discussed later in this chapter), organizational commitment has a strong behavioral tendency component to it. People high in organizational commitment engage in behaviors that are beneficial to the organization. Good organizational citizenship, absenteeism, and turnover behavior—these are all affected by organizational commitment.

affective commitment an emotional attachment to the organization and its mission; an employee's emotional attachment to, identification with, and involvement in the organization

normative commitment is based on the belief that commitment is the "right" thing to do and is based on an employee's moral and personal value system

continuance commitment is based on the costs an employee associates with leaving the organization

Components of Organizational Commitment Three distinct components of organizational commitment have been documented.[25] **Affective commitment** results from an emotional attachment to the organization and its mission. It is an employee's emotional attachment to, identification with, and involvement in the organization. **Normative commitment** is the belief that commitment is the "right" thing to do. It is based on employees' morals and personal values, and their belief in their obligation to continue to support the organization. **Continuance commitment** derives from the costs an employee associates with leaving the organization. It is calculative and rational, and reflects employees' judgments that the costs of leaving the organization are too high; thus they will continue to maintain their affiliation with the organization.

While all three components of commitment can strengthen the link between the employee and the organization, some important distinctions have recently been identified. Employees committed primarily for affective reasons are likely to continue their commitment as long as the organization "earns" it by treating the employee well. These employees stay with the organization because they "want to." Employees committed primarily for normative reasons may continue commitment for some period of time even in the face of poor treatment. These employees stay with the organization because they feel that they "ought to." Employees committed mostly for continuance reasons will continue commitment as long as they see no better opportunity in some other organization. In the meantime, however, they may work only hard enough to be retained by the organization. These employees stay with the organization because they "need to."[26]

Causes of Organizational Commitment Some evidence suggests that people who commit to organizations do so for a number of reasons. They may have a propensity to such commitment, may possess certain personal characteristics, and may have worked in jobs that promoted a sense of meaningfulness and responsibility.[27] By knowing about these factors, managers can choose employees who are likely to become and remain committed. Managers can also use this knowledge to identify the types of work experiences that foster employee commitment. The potential importance of organizational commitment is shown in Figure 6-4, which specifies a number of the determinants and consequences of organizational commitment. It is important to note that one primary determinant of organizational commitment is the nature of the work that people perform. People performing involvement-oriented work tend to have stronger commitment than employees who perform routine, repetitive, short-time-cycle, and low-skill-level work. This figure also makes clear that both the determinants and consequences of organizational commitment involve a complex process.

Although employee commitment is usually emphasized, commitment can flow from the organization to the employee as well. An organization's commitment to employees can be a key component for developing trust and for generating and maintaining employee commitment to the organization. Commitment demonstrated to the employee is believed to be of particular importance for the development and sustainment of high-involvement organizations. Companies such as Ford Motor and Dow of Europe follow this belief and have made attempts to reengineer their company structures, policies, and objectives to foster an environment in which employee commitment provides an edge over the competition.[28] Many firms in Japan also secure intense levels of employee loyalty (commitment).

http://www.dow.com

FIGURE 6-4 Causes and Consequences of Organizational Commitment

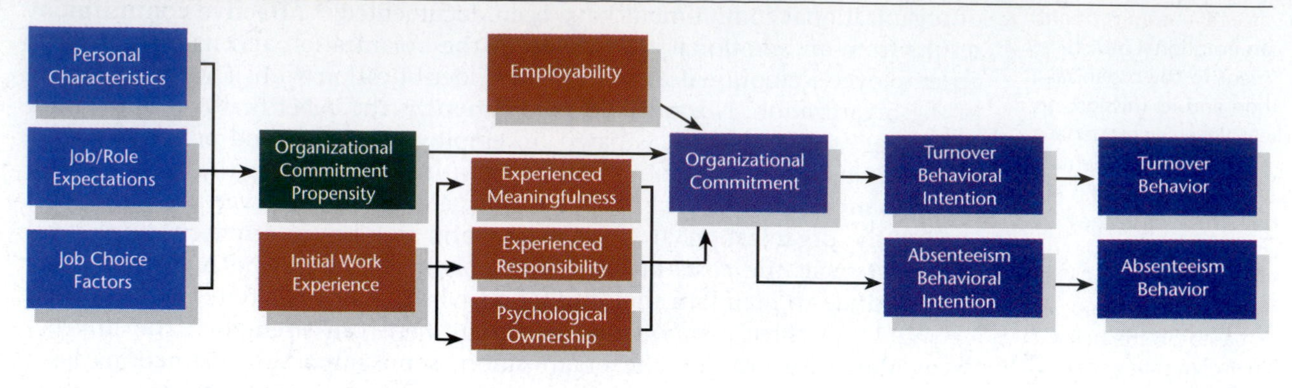

http://www.ibm.com

IBM takes organizational commitment very seriously. CEO Louis V. Gerstner, Jr., worried about the "brain drain" at IBM, has taken steps to strengthen employee commitment by demonstrating IBM's commitment. Gerstner opened up access to the company's stock-option program to a wider group of employees. An additional 1.3 billion dollars was made a part of the company's performance-related bonus system.[29]

Recent Research on Job Satisfaction and Commitment

In the preceding discussion, we examined the general causes of job satisfaction (experience, association, and social learning). However, we also know much about the specific causes of job satisfaction and organizational commitment. Most of the attitude determinants are discussed in subsequent chapters, especially those describing the organizational behavior context (Part III). As noted above, a majority of studies in organizational behavior include at least one of these attitude measures. In the most recent study completed on the causes of job satisfaction and commitment, Lease reviewed the research from 1993 to 1997.[30] Her results are summarized in Figure 6-5. The most consistent predictors of satisfaction and commitment include tenure/career stage, work-family conflict, supervisor and co-worker support, and promotional opportunities. As can be seen from the figure, many of the satisfaction and commitment determinants can be proactively managed by organizations, to the great benefit of the organization and its members.

Job and Work Involvement

Job and work involvement are attitudes relating to specific jobs and work in general. These attitudes deserve special attention because of their importance to both workers and organizations. The term *involvement* has been treated many different ways by both researchers and practitioners. Some refer to involvement as actual behaviors people engage in (such as attendance, timeliness, and performance). Such a behavioral perspective is inappropriate. Involvement is an attitude, and, as such, a variety of behaviors might be associated with a particular level of this attitude. Therefore, involvement is treated here as a psychological aspect of organizational members—an attitude.[31] We define it as the degree to which an employee's job and work are central parts of their lives.

job involvement an employee's psychological involvement with a particular job

Job involvement concerns an employee's psychological involvement with a particular job. It is learned primarily from a person's experiences on a specific

FIGURE 6-5 Major Causes of Job Satisfaction and Organizational Commitment

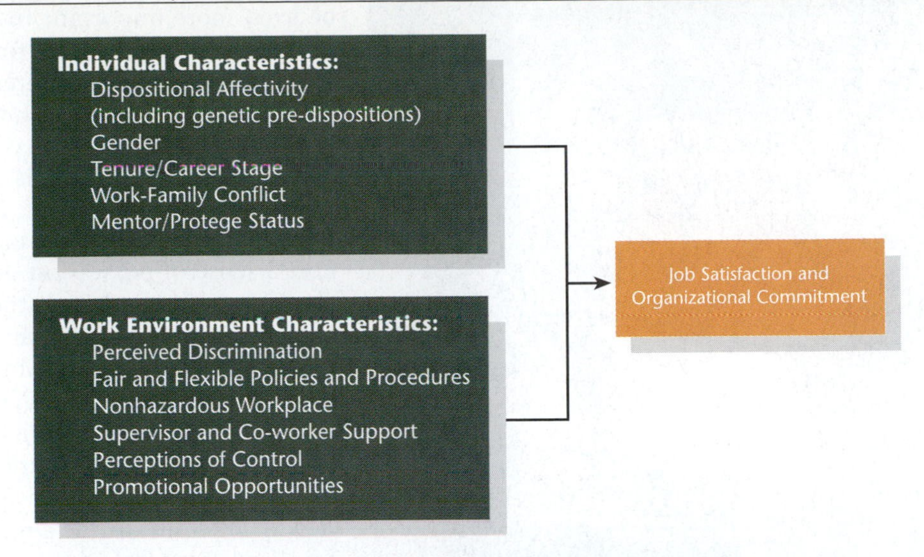

Source: S. Lease. 1998. Annual review, 1993–1997: Work attitudes and outcomes. *Journal of Vocational Behavior* 53:154–183. Copyright 1998 by Academic Press, reproduced by permission of the publisher.

work involvement an employee's devotion to or alienation from work in general

job. Employees with a high level of job involvement are strongly psychologically attached to their jobs. **Work involvement** refers to an employee's devotion to or alienation from work in general. In contrast to job involvement, work involvement develops out of people's experiences with work at school and in all of their jobs. Although job and work involvement are often similar—a person with strong involvement in one is likely to have strong involvement in the other—they can also differ substantially. This happens when, for example, a person who has been highly involved in work over the years is placed in a job for which he or she is overqualified. It also happens when a person with relatively low work involvement is "turned on" by a particular job and becomes highly job-involved.

http://www.eia.com

Both job and work involvement include three aspects. First, they include a person's conscious desire and choice to participate actively in or to avoid a job, or work in general. Second, they include the extent to which a person considers job and work central or marginal to their life. Third, they include how important the work or job is to a person's self-concept (people evaluate who they are at least in part through reference to their work and job).

Psychological Ownership

The concept of ownership as an important work-related attitude is on the rise. Management consultant T. L. Brown noted that "the key to effectively managing in the 1990s and the 21st century will be knowing how to instill psychological ownership. It's psychological ownership that makes the competitive difference," and knowing how to instill ownership will be key to effectively managing in highly uncertain and turbulent environments.[32] For a plant manager at a General Motors components plant, creating a work environment in which people have a sense of ownership has led to dramatic improvements in productivity. Management consultant Tom Peters claims that a sense of ownership resulted in Harley-Davidson's spectacular turnaround in the 1980s.

© STEVE CHENN/CORBIS

Psychological ownership develops through empowerment, self-management opportunities, expanded roles in managing the production process, and participation in problem solving.

We can predict that psychological ownership will be even more important in the 21st century as organizations continue to confront environmental turbulence, uncertainty, and intense competition, and the need for change, continuous improvement, and innovation. **Psychological ownership** is the state in which an individual feels as though the target of ownership (or a piece of that target) is theirs (It's MINE!).[33] The feelings associated with this state reflect a sense of possession. In the work environment, this sense of ownership attaches to work and to the organization. The importance of psychological ownership is underscored by the findings of a study conducted by the Strategic Planning Institute in Cambridge, Massachusetts. Their results indicate that a company's sustainable market share is directly related to the product or service quality the customer perceives, which in turn is a reflection of the employees' degree of commitment and psychological ownership.[34]

An employee's psychological ownership develops through empowerment, self-management opportunities, expanded roles in managing the production process, and participation in organizational problem solving. More specifically, it is through control of their work that individuals come to experience a sense of ownership for their company. In addition, as individuals come to know the company intimately, and through the investment of their time, ideas, skills, decisions, and energies in their work, this sense of possession (ownership) for the job and organization increases.

psychological ownership the state in which an individual feels as though the target of ownership (or a piece of that target) is theirs

The consequences of psychological ownership in organizations are numerous and very powerful. As shown in Figure 6-6, those who experience it tend to assume more personal risk, engage in more constructive helping behaviors, assume greater personal responsibility for their work and organizational outcomes, and experience higher levels of job satisfaction and organizational commitment.[35] Take Lake Superior Paper Industries (LSPI), for example. On Hallo-

FIGURE 6-6 Causes and Consequences of Employee Psychological Ownership

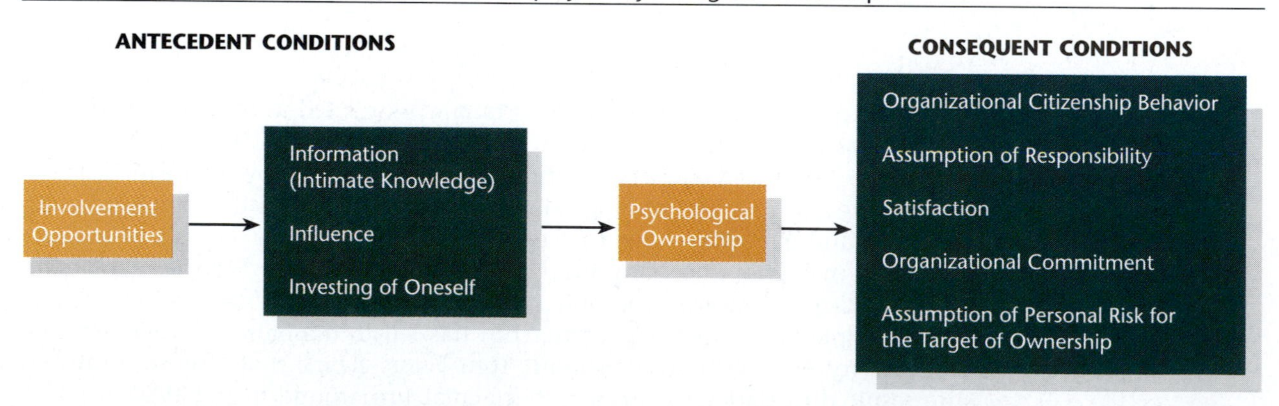

ween 1991, an early and massive amount (40 inches!) of snow fell on Duluth, Minnesota, LPSI's home office. The city was at a standstill—businesses, schools, and city and county government were all closed. The grip of winter did not, however, stop dozens of LPSI employees, who took to cross-country skies, snowshoes, and snowmobiles to find their way to work. Why take such risks? In a word, ownership. LPSI is an involvement-oriented organization. When one worker was asked why he and so many other LPSI employees went to such lengths to get to work, he simply said, "OUR company needed to stay open."

THE IMPORTANCE OF WORK-RELATED ATTITUDES

The relationship between employee attitudes and work-related behaviors is neither simple nor straightforward.[36] For example, increases in job satisfaction don't always cause immediate increases in an employee's performance. In spite of the fact that the relationship is not immediate and direct, attitudes do direct work-related behaviors, and this relationship is thus very significant for the organization.

Unionization and union activity, tardiness and absenteeism, and turnover are costly to organizations. The level of employee job satisfaction is significantly related to each of these behaviors. The more dissatisfied the work force, the more frequent and widespread these behaviors.

As job dissatisfaction grows and organizational commitment weakens, people begin to consider quitting their jobs. With stronger dissatisfaction and a further erosion in commitment, thoughts of quitting come more often and with greater intensity. After a while, "quitting thoughts" trigger a search for a new job and, ultimately, the decision to stay or quit.[37] This relationship between the commitment attitude (as well as job satisfaction), and absenteeism and turnover is shown in Figure 6-4.

Employees who experience a sense of ownership of both their job and the organization tend to be among their organization's high performers.[38] While the relationship between job and work involvement and job satisfaction and performance is complex, it is also often positive in nature. Under the right conditions, employees who experience or anticipate experiencing satisfaction from performing well tend to work hard. Under these conditions, where increases in effort translate into improved performance, we often see a favorable relationship between satisfaction and performance.

http://www.ge.com

Jack Welch, the legendary CEO at General Electric, noted that the level of job satisfaction among GE's employees is one of the most important targets for his management activities. His and other executives' experiences, combined with the knowledge accumulated through organizational research, make clear that employees' attitudes significantly affect the success of organizations and should thus be a key target of management activity.[39]

THE MANAGEMENT OF EMPLOYEE ATTITUDES

Many *attributes* of an organization—job design, technology, organization structure, climate, culture, co-workers, supervisors—describe the organization (see Chapters 4, 12, and 13). As shown in Figure 6-7, all these attributes impact employees, and thereby shape their attitudes.

FIGURE 6-7 Organizational Influences on Employee Attitudes

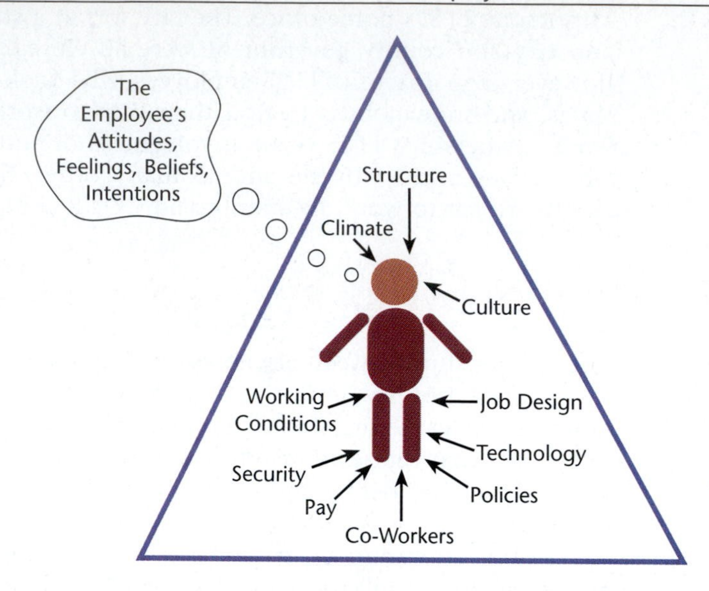

Because each organizational attribute influences employee attitudes, managing attitudes is challenging. It is, however, possible. Managers should recognize that certain organizational attributes are experienced by employees more directly, frequently, and regularly than others. As a consequence, they play a large role in shaping such attitudes as job satisfaction, organizational commitment, and ownership. It is these organizational attributes that should be the primary focus of managers' attention as they endeavor to manage work-related attitudes.

Of all of the organizational features that influence employee attitudes, the nature of the work and the design of the jobs figure as among the most important.[40] After all, people are hired by organizations to perform jobs. They get up in the morning and go to work. Throughout each workday, employees continually respond to the demands of their jobs. At the end of the day, they go home and think about what they should have done and what they need to do tomorrow. It is, therefore, the *nature* of the work that consumes an employee's time and energy on a day-to-day basis.

http://www.amfam.com
http://www.harley-davidson.com

Numerous organizations, such as American Family Insurance, Harley-Davidson, Ford, and General Mills, have discovered that routine, repetitive, short-time-cycle, and low-skill-level jobs produce lower levels of motivation and satisfaction than enriched jobs, characterized by variety, autonomy, significance, and the opportunity to perform whole and identifiable pieces of work. They have also discovered that the nature of work is frequently more important than company policy, the nature of supervision, and the structure of the organization in its impact on member attitudes.

Thus, a significant part of attitude management should be directed toward the nature of the work and the design of the jobs. Complex jobs, demanding and challenging work that involves the employee—these jobs (as opposed to routine and repetitive jobs) produce high levels of job satisfaction, organizational commitment, and ownership, and ultimately strengthen work involvement.

In general, organizations prefer employees who are satisfied and involved with their job and the workplace, who are committed to the organization, and who experience a sense of ownership for both their work and the organization. These favorable attitudes are not, however, without risk. Employees who are marginal performers and who simultaneously have extreme job satisfaction are unlikely to seek employment elsewhere, even though it may be to the organization's advantage for them to leave. The strong sense of partnership that accompanies ownership can increase conformity behavior and groupthink at times when challenging the status quo may be more beneficial to the organization. Finally, unhealthy possessiveness may prevent overly committed employees from being effective team members.

While we have suggested that the most significant determinants of attitudes are the design of jobs and work experiences, other organizational features also affect employee attitudes. The discussion in Chapter 7 on motivating organizational members provides an extensive look at ways to influence attitudes.

THE FINANCIAL IMPACT OF ATTITUDES

> A favorite cliche for the president's letter in corporate annual reports is "Our employees are our most important—our most valuable—asset." Turning from the president's letter and looking to the remainder of the report, one might ask, "where is this human asset on these statements which serve as reports on the firm's resources and earnings?" What is the value of this "most important" or "most valuable" asset? Is it increasing, decreasing, or remaining unchanged? What return, if any, is the firm earning on its human assets? Is the firm allocating its human assets in the most profitable way? No answers are to be found.[41]

human resource accounting the application of accounting principles and practices to the evaluation and management of human assets

behavioral accounting treats attitudinal measures as indicators of subsequent employee behavior, which in turn have economic implications for organizations that can be assessed using cost-accounting procedures

The article in which this quote appeared introduced for the first time the concept of human resource accounting. **Human resource accounting** is the application of accounting principles and practices to the evaluation and management of human assets. Since the appearance of this article, a number of accounting models have been developed for the purpose of attaching monetary values to the behaviors of organizational members.[42] A methodology developed by Philip Mirvis and Edward Lawler greatly facilitates measurement of the financial impact of employee attitudes. This procedure, known as **behavioral accounting,** " . . . treats attitudinal measures as indicators of subsequent employee behavior, which in turn have economic implications for the organizations that can be assessed using cost-accounting procedures."[43] Despite its promise, however, this approach has not yet caught on. In fact, it is quite controversial.

As a manager, it would be extremely useful to be able to estimate the potential benefits as well as costs of actions designed to change employee attitudes. The behavioral accounting approach enables you to estimate both the current financial impact of attitudes on organizations and the probable financial effects of changes in attitudes. Combining cost estimates with predicted financial benefits of subsequent attitude changes allows you to evaluate the potential cost-effectiveness of contemplated programs aimed at enhancing worker attitudes.

In this section we briefly outline the procedures for measuring the financial impact of employee attitudes (this presentation is based primarily on the Mirvis and Lawler behavioral accounting approach).[44] This will give you an overview of the process and is not intended to be a detailed guide. Remember, however, that behavioral accounting has not yet reached the level of precision usually associated with traditional cost-accounting procedures. It is not possible, for example, to identify all of the cost factors associated with behaviors such as absenteeism and turnover. Secondly, current behavioral accounting practices are based primarily on sources of knowledge (cross-sectional and longitudinal studies) that are not capable of proving cause-and-effect-relationships. Therefore, exercise appropriate caution when using behavioral accounting information. Estimates of the financial impact of attitudes should be treated as exactly that—estimates. Refrain from generalizing findings over time and across locations until you have documentation that generalization is appropriate.

It goes without saying that other factors besides attitudes also impact employee behaviors. The intangible impact of employee attitudes (for example, quality of life) has great (albeit not direct financial) value. Despite these qualifications, behavioral accounting promises to be a valuable management tool. When lower-level managers initiate human resource development programs (like employee involvement programs), they attempt to gain approval from upper management by projecting their positive effects on employee attitudes. Upper managers sometimes resist such programs because they believe the organization is not in the "happy people" business. Showing how these programs impact the "bottom line" enhances their chances for being approved. When they are effective, employees, managers, and the organization all benefit.

A Procedure for Measuring the Financial Impact of Attitudes

Step 1: Identifying and Measuring Relevant Attitudes In this first step in the behavioral accounting process, you identify attitudes you have reason to believe may be related to valued employee behaviors. The research literature can help in this process. Consider the issue of generalizing as you evaluate the experiences of other organizations. Evaluate the research on organizations similar to yours, with employees and jobs similar to yours. Remember that the attitudes of greatest importance may vary from organization to organization. A good place to begin as you identify relevant attitudes is the wide range of job satisfaction facets, but other attitudes may also be important. Mirvis and Lawler, for example, found that organizational involvement and intrinsic motivation are important determinants of behavior. At this stage of the process, you are playing an educated guessing game. Later you will refine the set of attitudes of interest.

Once you identify the relevant attitudes, you must measure them (usually through an attitude survey). This is not particularly difficult or unusual, since most large organizations measure employee attitudes. The critical consideration here is to be sure that your measures of worker attitudes are reliable and valid. There are a number of well-established surveys for measuring employee attitudes (see pages 196–199).[45] The behavioral accounting process will not function effectively unless attitudes are measured properly!

Step 2: Identifying and Measuring Relevant "Cost Items" Now you are ready to identify and measure employee behaviors that you expect will relate to the attitudes measured in step 1 and that can impact your organization financially. In practice, these first two steps are usually conducted concurrently. Again, the literature can be helpful. Look for behaviors that have been shown to be related to attitudes in similar organizational settings. Since particular behaviors are heavily influenced by attitudes (absenteeism, turnover, union activity, discussed in more detail in Chapter 8), determine whether these exist in your situation and to what extent. But be sure to look at other behaviors as well. Research has identified cases in which attitude influenced learning speed, on-the-job accident rates, and industrial sabotage.

Once you have identified the relevant behaviors, you must measure them. Sometimes this is relatively easy, especially if your organization systematically collects good measures of absenteeism on a regular basis. Often, unfortunately, measurement is more difficult, as in differentiating avoidable from unavoidable absenteeism. Behavioral measures should not be used unless there is evidence that they are both reliable and valid.[46]

Step 3: Pricing Behavioral "Cost Items" The next step in this process involves pricing each behavioral cost item. If, for example, absenteeism is selected as a relevant behavior, you must determine the cost of a lost day of work. William Macy and Philip Mirvis provide extensive suggestions for pricing behaviors, as does the Bureau of National Affairs Policies and Practices Guide.[47] Remember that pricing must be accurate both for your organization and for the types of jobs being studied.

http://www.bna.com

Step 4: Identifying the Relationship Between Attitudes and Behavioral "Cost Items" Our earlier examination of typical relationships between attitudes and several relevant behaviors should give you some idea of the types of relationships you can expect to find in your organization (step 1). However, you must also estimate the relationship of the actual attitude to behavior in your organization. The nature of these relationships can be determined using a variety of techniques, from straightforward visual inspection of data to very sophisticated statistical analyses. Regardless of the technique used, the questions remain the same: Is there a relationship between this attitude and this behavior? And, if so, how strong is the relationship?

Step 5: Estimating the Financial Impact of Attitude Changes Once you have established the relationship between an attitude and a behavior, you can estimate the impact that an increase or decrease in attitude levels may have. If you estimate, for example, that an overall increase of "one unit" in satisfaction would lead to an annual decrease of two days of sick leave per employee, and previous cost estimates indicate that the average cost of a day of work is $180, then an overall increase of "one unit" in satisfaction may lead to an annual savings of $360 per employee.

For comparative (and conjectural) purposes, some interesting numbers for the United States are given in the box on the following page entitled "An Estimate of the National Financial Impact of Attitudes." In both cases, don't focus too much on the exact numbers and calculations. Instead, realize from these estimates just how much attitudes affect the bottom line.

Some Qualifying Remarks

The behavioral accounting technique is a good one, but it is not perfect and a number of cautions are in order. Mirvis and Lawler point out that the time lag selected for examining the impact of attitudes on behaviors is critical, and no rule of thumb currently exists for identifying appropriate time lags. They used

AN INSIDE LOOK

An Estimate of the National Financial Impact of Attitudes

The following analysis was conducted to obtain a rough estimate of the direct financial impact that would occur if job satisfaction increased an average of .1 SD (a relatively modest increase) across all members of the American work force.

Data Used

1. The typical correlation between satisfaction and turnover was estimated at –.25 by Porter and Steers.[a]
2. The typical correlation between satisfaction → absenteeism would also be –.25.[b]
3. National turnover rates were estimated at about 15.6% on an annual basis, with a standard deviation of about 8.5%.[c]
4. Absenteeism rates are about 5 days per year per employee, with a standard deviation of about 2.67.[d]
5. The national work force was estimated at approximately 120 million.[e]
6. Average compensation (wages plus benefits) was estimated at $158.08/day and $41,100/year.[f]

Analysis

Impact of increase of .1 SD in satisfaction on turnover using Mirvis and Lawler equation [(.1) (SD) (correlation)]:

(.1) (8.5) (.25) = .213% turnover reduction
(120,000,000 employees) (.213) = 255,000 fewer turnovers
If cost of turnover were only 10% of compensation . . .
(255,000) (.10) ($41,100) = $1,048,100,000 savings

Impact of increase of .1 SD in satisfaction on absenteeism:

(.1) (2.67) (.25) = .067 days/year less absenteeism/worker
(120,000,000 employees) (.067) = 8,040,000 fewer absences
If cost of absenteeism is only average daily compensation . . .
(8,040,000) ($158.08) = $1,271,000,000 savings

$1,048,100,000 + $1,271,000,000 = $2,319,100,000 Total financial impact

THAT'S TWO BILLION, THREE HUNDRED NINETEEN MILLION, ONE HUNDRED THOUSAND DOLLARS!!

[a] L. W. Porter and R. M. Steers. 1973. Organizational, work, and personal factors in employee turnover and absenteeism. *Psychological Bulletin* 80:151–176.

[b] V. H. Vroom. 1964. *Work and motivation.* New York: Wiley.

[c] Information obtained from Bureau of National Affairs (BNA) reports on national turnover rates. Standard Deviation is from Dunham 1984.

[d] BNA reports. Standard deviation is from Dunham 1984.

[e] *Occupational Employment and Wage 1997.* Washington, D.C.: Bureau of Labor Statistics.

[f] *Employer Costs for Employee Compensation, 1986–98.* Washington, D.C.: Bureau of Labor Statistics.

Source: R. B. Dunham. 1984. *Organizational Behavior: People and processes in management.* Homewood, IL: Irwin.

a three-month lag, which they felt was consistent with the literature, but an organization would be well advised to consider a variety of intervals. It is also important for an organization to continue to study the relationship between attitudes and behaviors over time, since both the magnitude and nature of the relationships can change (particularly when you consider that variables other than attitudes also influence behaviors).

Nevertheless the procedure and concept of behavioral accounting has promise:

> There are a number of obvious advantages to the method. . . . It provides a practical approach to the problem of relating attitudes to costs . . . and it has the potential to increase significantly the impact and usefulness of attitudinal data. An attitude report to managers containing this information could serve to focus attention on the whole concept of employee satisfaction and motivation; and it could also stimulate them to introduce changes that would improve satisfaction and motivation. One useful feature of the model used in this paper is that it relates attitudes to future costs. Thus, organizations could use it as a way of diagnosing future costs and could initiate programs designed to reduce those costs. . . . Ultimately, the method could be used for undertaking a cost-benefit analysis of programs designed to improve employee satisfaction, motivation, group functioning, or supervision.[48]

ATTITUDES IN ORGANIZATIONS IN REVIEW

Job and work attitudes are some of the most studied topics in organizational behavior because employee attitudes affect organizational effectiveness. Organizational members who have positive job, work, and organizational attitudes are more likely to be key contributors to the organization's success than members who have negative attitudes. It is important for managers to understand this, and to actively manage those aspects of the organization that lead to positive work attitudes.

All attitudes, whether work-related or not, share three components. The affective component addresses how much a person likes the attitude object. The cognitive component consists of the thoughts and beliefs the person has regarding the attitude object. The behavioral intention component is how the person plans to behave around or toward the attitude object.

People develop attitudes toward the phenomenon they perceive (the attitude object) in three primary ways: (1) by personally experiencing the attitude object; (2) through association, whereby we generalize an attitude from the past to a new and similar attitude object; and (3) by letting other people influence our own attitudes, which is called social learning.

At least four strategies exist for changing employee attitudes: (1) Directly change the affective or cognitive component, by challenging the person's beliefs or evaluation of the attitude object. (2) Provide new experiences with the attitude object that differ from prior experiences. (3) Create new associations with the attitude object, such as by associating a negative attitude with something positive. And, (4) use social learning, in which a respected or well-liked individual tries to change the member's attitude.

Numerous job, work, and organizational attitudes have been studied by organizational behavior researchers. Job satisfaction, organizational commitment, job and work involvement, and psychological ownership are some of the more important ones. Job satisfaction, and its facets, measure how satisfied or dissatisfied employees are with their jobs, including specific aspects of the job. Organizational commitment measures how committed an employee is to helping the organization succeed. Three distinct dimensions of organizational commitment have been documented.[49] Affective commitment results from an emotional attachment to the organization and its mission. Normative commitment is based on the belief that commitment is the "right" thing to do. Continuance commitment is based on the belief that the costs of leaving an organization are too high. Job and work involvement reflect the degree to which organizational members are psychologically identified or involved with their jobs, or work in general. Psychological ownership is the degree to which employees sense or perceive that they "own" their jobs or their organizations. Employees high on the ownership dimension are motivated to contribute to and enhance those things that they own.

Tremendous financial implications accrue from successful management of employee attitudes. We now have methods for determining the financial consequences of these attitudes. Research has demonstrated that slight increases in such attitudes as job satisfaction and organization commitment can result in thousands, if not millions, of dollars of increased profitability. Simply put, organizations improve their profitability if they manage employee attitudes well.

A FINAL LOOK

Claire conducts a climate survey to gather feedback from Gunnison employees about their attitudes toward the workplace. Claire's hunch is correct: Many of the new Indian employees feel isolated from their American colleagues and misunderstood by them. On the other hand, some American workers state that there are so many foreigners in the company that they're beginning to feel like a minority.

Claire forms an ad hoc task force of a diverse group of employees and requests candid input on ways to improve the organization's climate. The international employees express their desire for greater integration and respect. The American employees respond that the international employees often stay together at social functions and don't try to get better acquainted. After much discussion, the task force recommends that Gunnison diversify work teams and sponsor functions to educate employees about other cultures—specifically, Indian culture. They hope that by exposing all members of the organization to diverse viewpoints, employees will feel free to express themselves rather than silently protest through absenteeism. Claire knows the organization has a long way to go, but is encouraged by the employees' avowed willingness to change their attitudes.

KEY TERMS

affective commitment, 201
affective component, 186
attitude, 185
association, 188
behavioral accounting, 207
behavioral tendency component, 187
cognitive component, 186
cognitive dissonance, 190
continuance commitment, 201
heredity, 189
human resource accounting, 207
job involvement, 202
job satisfaction, 192
normative commitment, 201
organizational commitment, 200
overall job satisfaction, 193
personal experience, 188
psychological ownership, 204
social learning, 189
work involvement, 203

ISSUES FOR REVIEW AND DISCUSSION

1. Occasionally we say that another person "has a bad attitude." What exactly does that mean in the contexts of the three attitude components—cognitive, affective, and behavioral tendency? Give an example of each.
2. Why is it so difficult to change people's attitudes? Think of a co-worker who has a negative attitude toward his or her supervisor. What can the supervisor do to change that attitude to a positive one?
3. When people have conflicting thoughts, we say they are experiencing "cognitive dissonance." How can a manager use cognitive dissonance to change a subordinate's attitude?
4. Why is job satisfaction considered to be the most important job attitude? Give five examples of managerial actions that might affect employee job satisfaction.
5. Have you ever felt committed to an organization, either an employer or some other organization in which you were a member? Describe your commitment. Can you identify any of the organizational commitment components (affective, continuance, or normative) in your attitude?
6. Differentiate the following attitudes: job involvement, work involvement, and psychological ownership. Which seems the most important to you? Why?
7. You are a manager at a large firm, and you want the firm to invest five million dollars in a program to improve employee morale. How would you justify the expenditure to top management?

EXERCISES

ATTITUDES AND BEHAVIORS

Purpose

In this exercise you will examine the relationships between attitudes and behaviors. Use the questionnaire below to measure your attitude toward movies, and then answer the questions following it.

Read each statement and decide the extent to which you agree or disagree with it. Circle the number that most closely represents your true feelings.

SD = strongly disagree, D = disagree, N = neutral, A = agree, SA = strongly agree

	SD	D	N	A	SA
1. I really enjoy going to the movies.	1	2	3	4	5
2. Movies are an expensive waste of time.	1	2	3	4	5
3. Going to a movie is a great fantasy experience for me because I escape from reality and identify with the characters in the movie.	1	2	3	4	5
4. Excessive sex and violence in movies is damaging to our society.	1	2	3	4	5
5. Going to movies together is great family entertainment.	1	2	3	4	5
6. I get really irritated at the greasy armrests, sticky floors, and litter scattered in movie theaters.	1	2	3	4	5
7. The motion picture producers have made hundreds of outstanding movies over the years.	1	2	3	4	5
8. Most movie stars don't deserve the wealth and social status they have gained. It is basically unfair.	1	2	3	4	5

Scoring:

Compute your score by adding the numbers you circled for the odd items, and subtracting the numbers you circled for the even items. Your score will be somewhere between –16 and +16.

1. Within the past month, how many movies have you seen at the theater?
2. Within the past month, how many movies have you seen on a VCR?
3. Within the past month, how many movies have you seen on television?

Questions

1. Does there appear to be any relationship between your attitudes toward movies and the number of movies you have seen?
2. If you correlated movie attitudes and movie attendance for your entire class, what do you think the correlation coefficient would be?
3. If you computed the correlations for your class, you would probably find that movie attitudes are more highly correlated with movies seen on TV than in theaters. How do you explain this relationship?

Source: D. J. Cherrington. Copyright © 1989. *Organizational behavior: The management of individual and organizational performance.* Boston: Allyn & Bacon, 332–333. Reprinted by permission of Pearson Education, Inc., Upper Saddle River, NJ 07458.

INFOTRAC

INFOTRAC® COLLEGE EDITION

The articles listed below are a sampling of those available through InfoTrac College Edition. You can search for them either by title or by the author's name.

Articles

1. Training Motivation in Organizations: An Analysis of Individual-Level Antecedents [*]. Dawn S. Carlson, Dennis P. Bozeman, K. Michele Kacmar, Patrick M. Wright, Gary C. McMahan. *Journal of Managerial Issues* Fall 2000 v12 i3 p271
2. Down and Out: An Investigation of the Relationship Between Mood and Employee Withdrawal Behavior. (Statistical Data Included) Lisa Hope Pelled, Katherine R. Xin. *Journal of Management* Nov 1999 v25 i6 p875 Bus.Coll.: 121T0382

3. Multidimensional constructs in structural equation analysis: an illustration using the job perception and job satisfaction constructs. Kenneth S. Law, Chi Sum Wong. *Journal of Management* March–April 1999 v25 i2 p143(1)
4. The influence of job satisfaction, organizational commitment, and fairness perceptions on organizational citizenship behavior. Stephen P. Schappe. *The Journal of Psychology* May 1998 v132 n3 p277(14)
5. LOYALTY IN BUSINESS IS A TWO-WAY STREET. (Brief Article) *USA Today* (Magazine) May 1999 v127 i2648 p6(1)

Questions

For Article 1:

"Training Motivation in Organizations: An Analysis of Individual-Level Antecedents" presents a model and a case study that examine individuals' attitudes and motivation toward training. What implications do this model and case study have for managers who want to identify and select the most appropriate employees for various training programs?

For Other Articles:

Assign the other articles to members of your group. After reading these articles, discuss what new information you have acquired about job satisfaction.

WEB EXERCISES

1. Many organizations undertake initiatives to increase employee job satisfaction and strengthen organizational commitment. Find the website of an organization that has done this with attitudes. What initiatives has this organization undertaken? Do you believe that they will be successful? Why or why not?
2. Several journals (*Academy of Management Journal, Academy of Management Review, Human Relations, Journal of Applied Psychology, Journal of Organizational and Occupational Psychology, Organizational Behavior and Human Decision Processes*) routinely publish articles that focus on topics in organizational behavior. Select an attitude (for example, job satisfaction, organizational commitment, job or work involvement) that you want to learn more about. Employing a search engine (ABI Inform, PsyLit, Firstsearch) available through your university (college) library, access one of these journals and search for a recently published article that focuses on the attitude that you've selected. Read and summarize the authors' findings.
3. Use a search engine available through your university (college) library to access an organization and/or management journal that focuses on an organizational effort to enhance employee attitudes. What actions did this organization take? What were their results?

CASE
Teamwork at GE Medical Systems

In late 1986, GE Medical Systems began forming work teams (called GEMS teams) at its Florence, South Carolina, factory. Initially, some of the employees were skeptical. Teamwork meant a shift in responsibility from traditional management to employee-directed work teams. The skepticism resulted from disbelief on the part of many rank-and-file employees that managers would give up any of their power. However, from the beginning, the teams were successful, and the employees could see that management had a genuine interest in seeing the teams succeed. By 1988, all of the employees at the plant were involved at some level in a work team. This was not accomplished at a small cost. To provide employees with the skills that complement teamwork, a high level of training was required, particularly in the areas of communication and feedback skills. The move from traditional management to employee-directed work teams also demanded a change in the factory's culture.

Today, there are 26 employee-directed work teams in the factory. The teams are involved in a wide variety of activities, ranging from routine production to problem solving and special projects. Most employees say they see teamwork as a positive development that has increased their output and the pride they have in their work. They also feel that the shift from traditional management to employee-directed work teams has had a positive effect on the culture of the factory. Because the plant managers often work closely with the teams, the traditional walls that separate managers and rank-and-file employees are coming down. One employee remarked that she is no longer nervous when a manager walks through the factory. She said that she is now more nervous about disappointing a team member than a manager. Another employee remarked that for the first time she believes that everyone in the plant is working toward the same goals.

The movement toward employee-directed work teams at the Florence plant has placed the managers in a coaching, rather than a traditional, management role. One manager indicated that when he had a problem to solve prior to the implementation of employee-directed work teams, he would have simply found a solution and told the workers what to do. Now, he indicated that he would take the problem to the team that would most likely be affected and act as a coach in helping the team arrive at a solution. Once a solution was agreed upon, the team would then implement their solution, rather than his idea, in making the change.

Clearly, the implementation of employee-directed work teams at GE Medical in Florence has been a success. The experience of this organization can serve as a model for other firms interested in improving organizational effectiveness through employee-directed work teams.

Questions

1. Review the first paragraph of the case above. Identify employee attitudes that may have affected the success of the work teams. As a manager, how would you deal with the negative attitudes expressed by employees regarding the work teams?
2. Aside from those mentioned in the case, identify three ways in which managers might have changed the initial reaction to work teams.
3. In what ways has the implementation of work teams at GE Medical Systems increased job satisfaction, organizational commitment, and job involvement?
4. Do you believe that the shift from a negative attitude to a positive attitude regarding work teams had a financial impact on GE Medical Systems? Why or why not?

Source: Management: Challenges in the 21st century (3rd ed.), *by P. S. Lewis, S. H. Goodman, and P. M. Fandt, copyright 2001. Reprinted with the permission of South-Western, a division of Thomson Learning. Fax 800-730-2215.*

Outline

Motivation: direction and intensity

Content theories of motivation

Process theories of motivation

Recent research on motivation theories

Motivation in review

PHOTO: © BETTMAN/CORBIS

CHAPTER 7

Work Motivation

Learning Objectives

After reading this chapter, you should be able to

1. Define motivation and distinguish direction and intensity of motivation.
2. Describe a content theory of motivation.
3. Compare and contrast the main content theories of motivation: manifest needs theory, learned needs theory, Maslow's hierarchy of needs, Alderfer's ERG theory, Herzberg's motivator-hygiene theory, and self-determination theory.
4. Distinguish extrinsic and intrinsic motivation and describe their relationship.
5. Distinguish content and process theories of motivation.
6. Compare and contrast the main process theories of motivation: operant conditioning theory, equity theory, goal theory, and expectancy theory.
7. Describe and distinguish the concepts of reinforcement, punishment, negative reinforcement, and extinction.
8. Describe how to use the equity and goal-setting motivation theories.
9. Discuss the main concepts and managerial implications of expectancy theory.

A FIRST LOOK

Bridget Anderson thought life would be perfect out in the "real world." After earning her degree in computer science, she landed a well-paying job as a programmer for a large non-profit organization whose mission she strongly believed in. And—initially—she was happy with her job.

Lately however, Bridget gets a sick feeling in her stomach every morning when her alarm goes off. Why this feeling of misery? After all, she's working in her chosen field in an environment that matches her values. What else could she want? She's more puzzled than anyone.

It's the end of her second year with the organization, and Bridget apprehensively schedules her annual performance evaluation. She knows she's a competent programmer, but she also knows that lately, she's been motivated to do only the minimum required to get by. Her heart is just not in her work with this organization. Not exactly how she thought things would turn out, that's for sure.

Bridget's manager Kyle Jacobs surprises her when he begins the evaluation by inquiring about her professional goals. She admits that she hasn't thought much about her future. Kyle asks if she's content in her current position and if she feels that anything is missing. Suddenly, Bridget realizes that she *does* want more professionally.

Question: Are Bridget's motivational problems intrinsic or extrinsic? Which of her needs are currently not being met? What steps should she and her manager take to improve her motivation and ultimately her performance?

"New Incentive Plan: Work or Be Fired"

(Sign posted by an anonymous employee on a company bulletin board)

http://www.appliedmotivation.com

If you've ever worked with a group of people, and we all have, you have no doubt noticed differences in their performance. Researchers have pondered these differences for many years. Indeed, John B. Watson first studied this issue in the early 1900s. Performance is, of course, an extremely important issue to employers because organizations with high-performing employees will almost always be more effective.

To better understand why people perform at different levels, researchers consider the major determinants of performance: ability, effort (motivation), accurate role perceptions, and environmental factors (see Figure 7-1). Each performance determinant is important, and a deficit in one can seriously affect the others. People who don't understand what is expected of them will be constrained by their own inaccurate role perceptions, even if they have strong abilities and motivation and the necessary resources to perform their job. None of the performance determinants can compensate for a deficiency in any of the other determinants. Thus, a manager cannot compensate for an employee's lack of skills and ability by strengthening their motivation.

ability the knowledge, skills, and receptiveness to learning that an individual brings to a task or job

Ability refers to the knowledge, skills, and receptiveness to learning that a person brings to a task or job. Knowledge is what a person knows. Skill is their capacity to perform some particular activity (like welding or accounting), including knowing what is expected of them (called accurate role perceptions). Receptiveness to learning is a function of how quickly a person acquires new knowledge. Some people have more ability than others, and high-ability people

FIGURE 7-1 Determinants of Performance

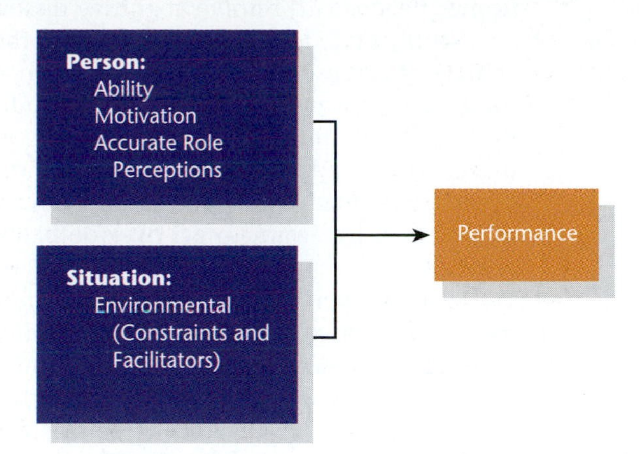

generally perform better than low-ability people (although we shall see that this is not always the case).[1]

role perceptions the set of behaviors employees think they are expected to perform as members of an organization

Accurate **role perceptions** refer to how well an individual understands their organizational role. This includes the goals (outcomes) the person is expected to achieve and the process by which the goals will be achieved. An employee who has accurate role perceptions knows both their expected outcomes *and* how to go about making those outcomes a reality. Incomplete or inaccurate role perceptions limit employees' capacity to meet expectations, regardless of their abilities and motivation.

performance environment refers to those factors that impact employees' performance but are essentially out of their control

The **performance environment** refers to those factors that impact employees' performance but are essentially out of their control. Many environmental factors influence performance. Some factors facilitate performance, while others constrain it. A word processor who has to work with a defective personal computer is certainly not going to perform at peak levels, regardless of ability or desire. Students who are working full time and carrying a full load of classes may not do as well on an exam as they would if they could cut back on their work hours, despite the fact that they have high ability and high motivation.

motivation an internal state that energizes, directs, and sustains behavior

Motivation is the fourth major factor that determines whether a person will perform a task well. **Motivation** is a state of mind that energizes, directs, and sustains behavior. Generally speaking, motivation arises as a consequence of a person's desire to (1) fulfill unmet needs, or (2) resolve conflicting thoughts that produce anxiety (an unpleasant experience). There are many ways in which we describe and categorize human needs, as we shall see later in this chapter. Certain needs are fundamental to our existence, like the need for food and water. When we are hungry, we are energized to satisfy that need by securing and ingesting food. Our other needs operate in a similar manner. When a need is unfulfilled, we are motivated to engage in behaviors that will satisfy it. The same is true for situations in which we experience conflicting thoughts (called cognitive dissonance; see Chapter 6). When we find ourselves in situations inconsistent with our beliefs, values, or expectations, we endeavor to eliminate the inconsistency. We either change the situation, or we change our perception of it. In both cases, motivation arises out of our interaction with, and perception of, a particular situation. We perceive the situation as satisfying our needs, or not. Motivation is thus a result of our interacting with situations to satisfy unmet needs or to resolve cognitive dissonance.

work motivation the amount of effort a person exerts to achieve a level of job performance

Simply stated, **work motivation** is the amount of effort a person exerts to achieve a certain level of job performance. Some people try very hard to perform their jobs well. They work long hours, even if it interferes with their family life. Highly motivated people go the "extra mile." High scorers on an exam make sure they know the examination material to the best of their ability, no matter how much midnight oil they have to burn. Other students who don't do as well may just want to get by—football games and parties are a lot more fun, after all.

Motivation is of great interest to employers: *All* employers want their people to perform to the best of their abilities. They take great pains to screen applicants to make sure they have the necessary abilities and motivation to perform well. They endeavor to supply all the necessary resources and a good work environment. Yet motivation remains a difficult factor to manage. As a result, it receives the most attention—from organizations and researchers alike, who ask the perennial question, What motivates people to perform well?

In this chapter we look at current answers to this question. What work conditions foster motivation? How can theories of motivation help us understand the general principles that guide organizational behavior? Rather than analyze why a particular student studies hard for a test, we'll look at the underlying principles of our general behavior in a variety of situations (including test-taking). We also discuss the major theories of motivation, along with their implications for management and organizational behavior. By the end of this chapter you should have a better understanding of why some people are more motivated than others.

MOTIVATION: DIRECTION AND INTENSITY

direction what a person is motivated to achieve

intensity the degree to which people try to achieve their targets

Our discussion thus far implies that motivation is a matter of effort. This is only partially true. Motivation has two major components: direction and intensity. **Direction** is *what* a person wants to achieve, what they intend to do. It implies a target that motivated people try to "hit." That target may be to do well on a test. Or it may be to perform better than anyone else in a work group. **Intensity** is *how hard* people try to achieve their targets. Intensity is what we think of as effort. It represents the energy we expend to accomplish something. If our efforts are getting nowhere, will we try different strategies to succeed? (High intensity-motivated people are persistent!)

It is important to distinguish the direction and intensity aspects of motivation. If *either* is lacking, performance will suffer. A person who knows what they want to accomplish (direction) but doesn't exert much effort (intensity) will not succeed. (Scoring 100% on an exam—your target—won't happen unless you study!) Conversely, people who haven't got a direction (what they want to accomplish) probably won't succeed either. (At some point you have to decide on a major if you want to graduate, even if you do have straight A's.)

http://www.motivation.com

Employees' targets don't always match with what their employers want. Absenteeism (some employees call this "calling in well") is a major example.[2] Pursuing your favorite hobby (your target) on a workday (your employer's target) is a conflict in direction; below, we'll examine some theories about why this conflict occurs.

© VINCE STREANO/CORBIS

Successful employees know what they want to achieve (direction), and they persist until they achieve their goals (intensity).

There is another reason why employees' targets are sometimes contrary to their employers'—when employers do not ensure that employees understand what the employer wants. Employees can have great intensity, but poor direction. It is management's job to provide direction: Should we stress quality as well as quantity? Work independently or as a team? Meet deadlines at the expense of costs? Employees flounder without direction. Clarifying direction results in accurate *role perceptions,* the behaviors employees think they are expected to perform as members of an organization. Employees with accurate role perceptions understand their purpose in the organization and how the performance of their job duties contributes to organizational objectives. Some motivation theorists assume that employees know the correct direction for their jobs. Others do not. These differences are highlighted in the discussion of motivation theories below.

At this point, as we begin our discussion of the various motivation theories, it is reasonable to ask, why isn't there just one motivation theory? The answer is that the different theories are driven by different philosophies of motivation. Some theorists assume that humans are propelled more by needs and instincts than by reasoned actions. Their **content motivation theories** focus on *the content of what* motivates people. Other theorists focus on the process by which people are motivated. **Process motivation theories** address *how* people become motivated—that is, how people perceive and think about a situation. Content and process theories endeavor to predict motivation in a variety of situations. However, none of these theories can predict what will motivate an individual in a given situation 100 percent of the time. Given the complexity of human behavior, a "Grand Theory" of motivation will probably never be developed.

content motivation theories focus on what motivates people

process motivation theories focus on the how and why of motivation

A second reasonable question at this point is, which theory is best? If that question could be easily answered, this chapter would be quite short. The simple answer is, there is no "one best theory." All have been supported by organizational behavior research. All have strengths and weaknesses. However, understanding something about each theory is a major step toward effective management practice.

CONTENT THEORIES OF MOTIVATION

need a human condition that becomes energized when people feel deficient in some respect

The theories presented in this section focus on the importance of human needs. A common thread through all of them is that people have a variety of needs. A **need** is a human condition that becomes "energized" when people feel deficient in some respect. When we are hungry, for example, our need for food has been energized. Two features of needs are key to understanding motivation. First, when a need has been energized, we are motivated to satisfy it. We strive

hedonism assumes that people are motivated to satisfy mainly their own needs (seek pleasure, avoid pain)

manifest needs are needs motivating a person at a given time

instincts our natural, fundamental needs, basic to our survival

to make the need disappear. **Hedonism**, one of the first motivation theories, assumes that people are motivated to satisfy mainly their own needs (seek pleasure, avoid pain). Long since displaced by more refined theories, hedonism clarifies the idea that needs provide direction for motivation. Second, once we have satisfied a need, it ceases to motivate us. When we've eaten to satiation, we are no longer motivated to eat. Other needs take over and we endeavor to satisfy them. A **manifest need** is whatever need is motivating us at a given time. Manifest needs dominate our other needs.

Instincts are our natural, fundamental needs, basic to our survival. Our needs for food and water are instinctive. Many needs are learned. We are not born with a high (or low) need for achievement—we learn to need success (or failure). The distinction between instinctual and learned needs sometimes blurs; for example, is our need to socialize with other people instinctive or learned?

Manifest Needs Theory

One major problem with the need approach to motivation is that we can make up a need for every human behavior. Do we "need" to talk or be silent? The possibilities are endless. In fact, around the 1920s, some 6000 human needs had been identified by behavioral scientists!

primary needs are instinctual in nature and include physiological needs for food, water, and sex (procreation)

secondary needs are learned throughout one's life span and are psychological in nature

manifest needs theory assumes that human behavior is driven by the desire to satisfy needs

latent needs cannot be inferred from a person's behavior at a given time, yet the person may still possess those needs

Henry A. Murray recognized this problem and condensed the list into a few instinctive and learned needs.[3] Instincts, which Murray called **primary needs**, include physiological needs for food, water, sex (procreation), urination, and so on. Learned needs, which Murray called **secondary needs**, are learned throughout one's life and are basically psychological in nature. They include such needs as the need for achievement, for love, and for affiliation (see Table 7-1).[4]

Murray's main premise was that people have a variety of needs, but only a few are expressed at a given time. When a person is behaving in a way that satisfies some need, Murray called the need manifest. **Manifest needs theory** assumes that human behavior is driven by the desire to satisfy needs. Lucretia's chattiness probably indicates her need for affiliation. This is a manifest need. But what if Lucretia also has a need to dominate others? Could we detect that need from her current behavior? If not, Murray calls this a latent need. A **latent need** cannot be inferred from a person's behavior at a given time, yet the person may still possess that need. The person may not have had the opportunity to express the need. Or he or she may not be in the proper environment to solicit behaviors to satisfy the need. Lucretia's need to dominate may not be motivating her current behavior because she is with friends instead of co-workers.

Manifest needs theory laid the groundwork for later theories, most notably McClelland's learned needs theory, that have greatly influenced the study of organizational behavior. The major implication for management is that some employee needs are latent. Managers often assume that employees do not have certain needs because the employees never try to satisfy them at work. Such needs may exist (latent needs); the work environment is simply not conducive to their manifestation (manifest needs). A reclusive accountant may not have been given the opportunity to demonstrate his need for achievement because he never received challenging assignments.

Learned Needs Theory

David C. McClelland and his associates (especially John W. Atkinson) built on the work of Murray for over 50 years. Murray studied many different needs, but very few in any detail. McClelland's research differs from Murray's in that

TABLE 7-1 Sample Items from Murray's List of Needs

Social Motive	Brief Definition
Abasement	To submit passively to external force. To accept injury, blame, criticism, punishment. To surrender. To become resigned to fate. To admit inferiority, error, wrongdoing, or defeat. To confess and atone. To blame, belittle, or mutilate the self. To seek and enjoy pain, punishment, illness, and misfortune.
Achievement	To accomplish something difficult. To master, manipulate, or organize physical objects, human beings, or ideas. To do this as rapidly and as independently as possible. To overcome obstacles and attain a high standard. To excel oneself. To rival and surpass others. To increase self-regard by the successful exercise of talent.
Affiliation	To draw near and enjoyably cooperate or reciprocate with an allied other (an other who resembles the subject or who likes the subject). To please and win affection of a coveted object. To adhere and remain loyal to a friend.
Aggression	To overcome opposition forcefully. To fight. To revenge an injury. To attack, injure, or kill another. To oppose forcefully or punish another.
Autonomy	To get free, shake off restraint, break out of confinement. To resist coercion and restriction. To avoid or quit activities prescribed by domineering authorities. To be independent and free to act according to impulse. To be unattached, irresponsible. To defy convention.
Counteraction	To master or make up for a failure by restriving. To obliterate a humiliation by resumed action. To overcome weaknesses, to repress fear. To efface a dishonor by action. To search for obstacles and difficulties to overcome. To maintain self-respect and pride on a high level.
Defendance	To defend the self against assault, criticism, and blame. To conceal or justify a misdeed, failure, or humiliation. To vindicate the ego.
Deference	To admire and support a superior. To praise, honor, or eulogize. To yield eagerly to the influence of an allied other. To emulate an exemplar. To conform to custom.
Dominance	To control one's human environment. To influence or direct the behavior of others by suggestion, seduction, persuasion, or command. To dissuade, restrain, or prohibit.
Exhibition	To make an impression. To be seen and heard. To excite, amaze, fascinate, entertain, shock, intrigue, amuse, or entice others.
Harmavoidance	To avoid pain, physical injury, illness, and death. To escape from a dangerous situation. To take precautionary measures.
Infavoidance	To avoid humiliation. To quit embarrassing situations or to avoid conditions which may lead to belittlement, the scorn, derision, or indifference of others. To refrain from action because of the fear of failure.
Nurturance	To give sympathy and gratify the needs of a helpless object: an infant or any object that is weak, disabled, tired, inexperienced, infirm, defeated, humiliated, lonely, dejected, sick, mentally confused. To assist an object in danger. To feed, help, support, console, protect, comfort, nurse, heal.
Order	To put things in order. To achieve cleanliness, arrangement, organization, balance, neatness, tidiness, and precision.
Play	To act for "fun" without further purpose. To like to laugh and make jokes. To seek enjoyable relaxation from stress. To participate in games, sports, dancing, drinking parties, cards.
Rejection	To separate oneself from a negatively valued object. To exclude, abandon, expel, or remain indifferent to an inferior object. To snub or jilt an object.
Sentience	To seek and enjoy sensuous impressions.
Sex	To form and further an erotic relationship. To have sexual intercourse.
Succorance	To have one's needs gratified by the sympathetic aid of an allied object. To be nursed, supported, sustained, surrounded, protected, loved, advised, guided, indulged, forgiven, consoled. To remain close to a devoted protector. To always have a supporter.
Understanding	To ask or answer general questions. To be interested in theory. To speculate, formulate, analyze, and generalize.

Source: C. S. Hall and G. Lindzey, *Theories of Personality.* Sample items from Murray's List of Needs. Copyright 1957 by John Wiley & Sons, New York. Reprinted by permission of John Wiley & Sons, Inc.

McClelland studied three needs in depth: the need for achievement, the need for affiliation, and the need for power (often abbreviated, in turn, as nAch, nAff, and nPow).[5] McClelland believes that these three needs are learned, primarily in childhood. But he also believes that each need can be taught, especially nAch. McClelland's research is important because much of current thinking about organizational behavior is based on it.

need for achievement (nAch) the need to excel at tasks, especially tasks that are difficult

Need for Achievement The **need for achievement (nAch)** is how much people are motivated to excel at the tasks they are performing, especially tasks that are difficult. Of the three needs studied by McClelland, nAch has the greatest impact. The need for achievement varies in intensity across individuals. This makes nAch a personality trait as well as a statement about motivation. When nAch is being expressed, making it a manifest need, people try hard to succeed at whatever task they're doing. We say these people have a high achievement motive. A **motive** is a source of motivation; it is the need that a person is attempting to satisfy. Achievement needs become manifest when individuals experience certain types of situations.

motive a source of motivation; the need that a person is attempting to satisfy

To better understand the nAch motive, it's helpful to describe high-nAch people. You probably know a few of them. They're constantly trying to accomplish something. One of your authors has a father-in-law who would much rather spend his weekends digging holes (for various home projects) than going fishing. Why? Because when he digs a hole, he gets results. In contrast, he can exert a lot of effort and still not catch a fish. A lot of fishing, no fish, no results equal failure!

McClelland describes three major characteristics of high-nAch people:

1. They feel personally responsible for completing whatever tasks they are assigned. They accept credit for success, and blame for failure.
2. They like situations where the probability of success is moderate. High-nAch people are not motivated by tasks that are too easy, or extremely difficult. Instead, they prefer situations where the outcome is uncertain, but in which they believe they can succeed if they exert enough effort. They avoid both simple and impossible situations.
3. They have very strong desires for feedback about how well they are doing. They actively seek out performance feedback. It doesn't matter whether the information implies success or failure. They want to know whether they have achieved or not. They constantly ask how they are doing, sometimes to the point of being a nuisance.

http://www.usmotivation.com

Why is nAch important to organizational behavior? The answer is, the success of many organizations is dependent on the nAch levels of their employees.[6] This is especially true for jobs that require self-motivation and managing others. Employees who continuously have to be told how to do their jobs require an overly large management team, and too many layers of management spell trouble in the current marketplace. Today's flexible, cost-conscious organizations have no room for top-heavy structures; their high-nAch employees perform their jobs well with minimal supervision.

Many organizations manage the achievement needs of their employees poorly. A common perception about people who perform unskilled jobs is that they are unmotivated and content doing what they are doing. But, if they have achievement needs, the job itself creates little motivation to perform. It is too easy. There are not enough workers who feel personal satisfaction for having the cleanest floors in a building. Designing jobs that are neither too challenging nor too boring is key to managing motivation. Job enrichment (discussed in Chapter 16) is one effective strategy; this frequently entails training and rotating employees through different jobs, or adding new challenges.

need for affiliation (nAff) the need to establish and maintain warm and friendly relationships with other people

Need for Affiliation This need is the second of McClelland's learned needs. The **need for affiliation (nAff)** reflects a desire to establish and maintain warm and friendly relationships with other people. As with nAch, nAff varies in intensity across individuals. As you would expect, high-nAff people are very sociable. They're more likely to go bowling with friends after work than to go home and watch television. Other people have lower affiliation needs. This doesn't mean that they avoid other people, or that they dislike others. They simply don't exert as much effort in this area as high-nAff people do.

The nAff has important implications for organizational behavior. High-nAff's like to be around other people, including other people at work. As a result, they perform better in jobs that require teamwork. Maintaining good relationships with their co-workers is important to them, so they go to great lengths to make the work group succeed because they fear rejection. So, high-nAff employees will be especially motivated to perform well if others depend on them. In contrast, if high-nAff people perform jobs in isolation from other people, they will be less motivated to perform well. Performing well on this job won't satisfy their need to be around other people.

http://www.peoplemanagement.com

Effective managers carefully assess the degree to which people have high or low nAff. Employees high in nAff should be placed in jobs that require or allow interactions with other employees. Jobs that are best performed alone are more appropriate for low-nAff employees, who are less likely to be frustrated.

need for power (nPow) the need to control things, especially other people; reflects a motivation to influence and be responsible for other people

Need for Power The third of McClelland's learned needs, the **need for power (nPow)**, is the need to control things, especially other people. It reflects a motivation to influence and be responsible for other people. An employee who is often talkative, gives orders, and argues a lot is motivated by the need for power over others.

Employees with high nPow can be beneficial to organizations. High-nPow's do have effective employee behaviors, but at times they're disruptive. A high-nPow person may try to convince others to do things that are detrimental to the organization. So, when is this need good, and when is it bad? Again, there are no easy answers. McClelland calls this the "two faces of power."[7] A *personal power seeker* endeavors to control others mostly for the sake of dominating them. They want others to respond to their wishes whether or not it is good for the organization. They "build empires" and they protect them.

McClelland's other power seeker is the *social power seeker.* A high social power seeker satisfies needs for power by influencing others, like the personal power seeker. They differ in that they feel best when they have influenced a work group to achieve the group's goals, and not some personal agenda. High social power seekers are concerned with goals that a work group has set for itself, and are motivated to influence others to achieve the goal. This need is oriented toward fulfilling responsibilities to the employer, not to the self.

McClelland has argued that the high need for social power is the most important motivator for successful managers. Successful managers tend to be high in this type of nPow. High need for achievement can also be important, but it sometimes results in too much concern for personal success and not enough for the employer's success. The need for affiliation contributes to managerial success only in those situations where the maintenance of warm group relations is as important as getting others to work toward group goals.

The implication of McClelland's research is that organizations should try to place people with high needs for social power in managerial jobs. It is critical, however, that those managerial jobs allow the employee to satisfy the nPow through social power acquisition. Otherwise, a manager high in nPow may satisfy this need through acquisition of personal power, to the detriment of the organization.

Maslow's Hierarchy of Needs

http://www.maslow.com

Any discussion of needs that motivate performance would be incomplete without considering Abraham Maslow.[8] Thousands of managers in the 1960s were exposed to Maslow's theory through the popular writings of Douglas McGregor.[9] Many of them today still talk about employee motivation in terms of Maslow's theory.

Maslow was a psychologist who, based on his early research with primates (monkeys), observations of patients, and discussions with employees in organizations, theorized that human needs are arranged hierarchically. That is, before one type of need can manifest itself, other needs must be satisfied first. For example, our need for water takes precedence over our need for social interaction (this is also called *prepotency*). We will always satisfy our need for water before we satisfy our social needs; water needs have prepotency over social needs. Maslow's theory differs from others that preceded it because of this hierarchical, prepotency concept.

Maslow went on to propose five basic types of human needs. This is in contrast to the thousands of needs that earlier researchers had identified, and also fewer than Murray identified in his theory. Maslow condensed human needs into a manageable set. Those five human needs, in the order of prepotency in which they direct human behavior, are

1. *Physiological and survival needs.* These are the most basic of human needs, and include the needs for water, food, sex, sleep, activity, stimulation, and oxygen.
2. *Safety and security needs.* These needs invoke behaviors that assure freedom from danger. This set of needs involves meeting threats to our existence, including extremes in environmental conditions (heat, dust, and so on), assault from other humans, tyranny, and murder. In other words, satisfaction of these needs prevents fear and anxiety while adding stability and predictability to life.
3. *Social needs.* These needs reflect human desires to be the target of affection and love from others. They are especially satisfied by the presence of spouses, children, parents, friends, relatives, and others to whom we feel close. Feelings of loneliness and rejection are symptoms that this need has not been satisfied.
4. *Ego and esteem.* Esteem needs go beyond social needs. They reflect our need to be respected by others, and to have esteem for ourself (self-esteem; see Chapter 5). It is one thing to be liked by others. It is another thing to be respected for our talents and abilities. Ego and esteem needs have internal (self) and external (others) focuses. An internal focus includes desires for achievement, strength, competence, confidence, and independence. An exter-

nal focus includes desires to have prestige, recognition, appreciation, attention, and respect from others. Satisfaction of external esteem needs can lead to satisfaction of internal esteem needs.

5. *Self-actualization.* Self-actualization needs are the most difficult to describe. Unlike the other needs, the need for self-actualization is never completely satisfied. Self-actualization involves a desire for self-fulfillment, "to become more and more what one is, to become everything that one is capable of becoming."[10] Because people are so different in their strengths and weaknesses, in capacities and limitations, the meaning of self-actualization varies greatly. Satisfying self-actualization needs means developing all of our special abilities to their fullest degree.

http://www.accel-team.com/human_relations/hrels_02_maslow.html

Figure 7-2 illustrates Maslow's proposed hierarchy of needs. According to his theory, people first direct their attention to satisfying their lower-order needs. Those are the needs at the bottom of the pyramid (physiological, safety, and security). Once those needs have been satisfied, the next level, social needs, become energized. Once satisfied, we focus on our ego and esteem needs. Maslow believed that most people become fixated at this level. That is, most people spend much of their lives developing self-esteem and the esteem of others. But, once those esteem needs are satisfied, Maslow predicted that self-actualization needs would dominate. There are no higher levels in the pyramid, because self-actualization needs can never be fully satisfied. They represent a continuing process of self-development and self-improvement that, once satisfied on one dimension (painting), create motivation to continue on other dimensions (sculpting). One wonders if athletes like Deion Sanders are self-actualizing when they participate in multiple sporting endeavors at the professional level.

FIGURE 7-2 Maslow's Hierarchy of Needs

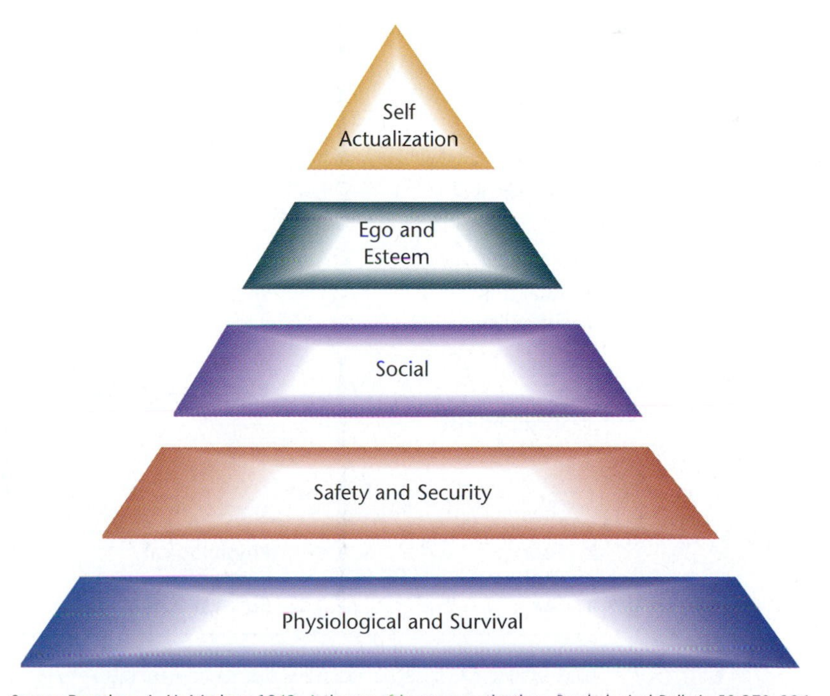

Source: Based on A. H. Maslow. 1943. A theory of human motivation. *Psychological Bulletin* 50:370–396.

An overriding principle in this theory is that a person's attention (direction) and energy (intensity) will focus on satisfying the lowest-level need that is not currently satisfied. Needs can also be satisfied at some point but become active (dissatisfied) again. Needs must be "maintained" (we must continue to eat occasionally). According to Maslow, when lower-level needs are reactivated, we once again concentrate on that need. That is, we lose interest in the higher-level needs when lower-order needs are energized.

The implications of Maslow's theory for organizational behavior are as much conceptual as they are practical. The theory posits that to maximize employee motivation, employers must try to guide workers to the upper parts of the hierarchy. That means that the employer should help employees satisfy lower-order needs like safety and security, and social needs. Once satisfied, employees will be motivated to build esteem and respect through their work achievements. Table 7-2 shows how Maslow's theory relates to factors that organizations can influence. For example, by providing adequate pay, safe working conditions, and cohesive work groups, employers help employees satisfy their lower-order needs. Once satisfied, challenging jobs, additional responsibilities, and prestigious job titles can help employees satisfy higher-order esteem needs.

Maslow's theory is still popular among practicing managers. Organizational behavior researchers, however, are not as enamored with it because research

TABLE 7-2 Maslow's Hierarchy of Needs

General Factors	Ascending order	Need Levels	Basic → Mature	Organizational Specific Factors
1. Growth 2. Achievement 3. Advancement	↑	Self-actualization	Mature	1. Challenging job 2. Creativity 3. Advancement in organization 4. Achievement in work
1. Recognition 2. Status 3. Self-esteem 4. Self-respect		Ego and Esteem	↑	1. Job title 2. Merit pay increase 3. Peer/supervisory recognition 4. Work itself 5. Responsibility
1. Companionship 2. Affection 3. Friendship		Social		1. Quality of supervision 2. Compatible work group 3. Professional friendships
1. Safety 2. Security 3. Competence 4. Stability		Safety and Security		1. Safe working conditions 2. Fringe benefits 3. General salary increases 4. Job security
1. Air 2. Food 3. Shelter 4. Sex		Physiological and Survival	Basic	1. Heat and air conditioning 2. Base salary 3. Cafeteria 4. Working conditions

Source: Adapted from A. D. Szilagyi, Jr. and M. J. Wallace, Jr. 1980. *Organizational behavior and performance* (2nd ed.). Santa Monica, CA: Goodyear Publishing. Data for "General Factors" and "Need Levels" columns drawn from A. H. Maslow. 1970. A theory of human motivation. In *Motivation and personality* (2nd ed.). Copyright © 1970 by Abraham H. Maslow. New York: Harper & Row, Inc.

results don't support Maslow's hierarchical notion. Apparently, people don't go through the five levels in a fixed fashion. On the other hand, there is some evidence that people satisfy the lower-order needs before they attempt to satisfy higher-order needs. Refinements of Maslow's theory in recent years reflect this more limited hierarchy.[11] The self-assessment below will allow you to evaluate the strength of your five needs.

SELF-ASSESSMENT Applying Maslow's Hierarchy of Needs

Below are several characteristics or qualities that could be associated with a job. For each characteristic, rate *how important* the characteristic is to you personally to have in your job. This exercise is self-scored, so no one will see your answers. You should be as honest with yourself as possible in answering each item.

1. The feeling of self-esteem I get from my work.
   Very Unimportant 1 2 3 4 5 6 7 Very Important
2. The opportunity for personal growth and development I get from my work.
   Very Unimportant 1 2 3 4 5 6 7 Very Important
3. The prestige of my job inside the company where I work.
   Very Unimportant 1 2 3 4 5 6 7 Very Important
4. The opportunity for independent thought and action in my work.
   Very Unimportant 1 2 3 4 5 6 7 Very Important
5. The feeling of security in my work.
   Very Unimportant 1 2 3 4 5 6 7 Very Important
6. The feeling of self-fulfillment I get from being in my job, that is, the feeling of being able to use my own capabilities, realizing my potential.
   Very Unimportant 1 2 3 4 5 6 7 Very Important
7. The prestige of my job position outside the company in which I work (the regard received from others not in the company).
   Very Unimportant 1 2 3 4 5 6 7 Very Important
8. The feeling of worthwhile accomplishment in my job.
   Very Unimportant 1 2 3 4 5 6 7 Very Important
9. The opportunity, in my job, to give help to other people.
   Very Unimportant 1 2 3 4 5 6 7 Very Important
10. The opportunity, in my job, for participation in the setting of goals.
    Very Unimportant 1 2 3 4 5 6 7 Very Important
11. The opportunity, in my job, for participation in the determination of methods and procedures.
    Very Unimportant 1 2 3 4 5 6 7 Very Important
12. The authority connected with my job.
    Very Unimportant 1 2 3 4 5 6 7 Very Important
13. The opportunity to develop close friendships in my job.
    Very Unimportant 1 2 3 4 5 6 7 Very Important

Scoring:

Compute your need scores using the form below. For each item indicated, write down the number you circled for the indicated item. The need categories do not correspond exactly to Maslow's hierarchy of needs because it is assumed that all jobs will satisfy basic physiological needs. The autonomy need scale was developed by Porter in his research on need theories.

	Security	Social	Esteem	Autonomy	Self-Actualization
	5 = ____	9 = ____	1 = ____	4 = ____	2 = ____
		13 = ____	3 = ____	10 = ____	6 = ____
			7 = ____	11 = ____	8 = ____
				12 = ____	
Total Score for Need:	____	____	____	____	____
Divide by:	1	2	3	4	3
Final Score:	____	____	____	____	____
National Average for 1,916 U.S. Managers (Porter 1964)	5.33	5.36	5.28	5.92	6.35

Interpretation: How did the importance of job characteristics to you compare to the national sample? Arrange your scores from highest to lowest. Where in Maslow's hierarchy do you think your needs are most prepotent? Given that, what type of job do you think you would enjoy?

Source: Based loosely on L. W. Porter. 1964. *Organizational patterns of job attitudes.* New York: American Foundation for Management Research.

Alderfer's ERG Theory

ERG theory compresses Maslow's five need categories into three: existence, relatedness, and growth

Clayton Alderfer observed that very few attempts had been made to test Maslow's full theory. Further, the evidence accumulated provided only partial support. During the process of refining and extending Maslow's theory, Alderfer provided another need-based theory and a somewhat more useful perspective on motivation.[12] Alderfer's **ERG theory** compresses Maslow's five need categories into three: existence, relatedness, and growth.[13] In addition, ERG theory details the dynamics of an individual's movement between the need categories in a somewhat more detailed fashion than typically characterizes interpretations of Maslow's work.

As shown in Figure 7-3, the ERG model addresses the same needs as those identified in Maslow's work:

- *Existence needs* include physiological and material safety needs. These needs are satisfied by material conditions and not through interpersonal relations or personal involvement in the work setting.
- *Relatedness needs* include all of Maslow's social needs, plus social safety and social esteem needs. These needs are satisfied through the exchange of thoughts and feelings with other people.

FIGURE 7-3 Alderfer's ERG Theory

- *Growth needs* include self-esteem and self-actualization needs. These needs tend to be satisfied through one's full involvement in work and the work setting.

Figure 7-4 identifies a number of ways in which organizations can help their members satisfy these three needs.

Four components—satisfaction progression, frustration, frustration regression, and aspiration—are key to understanding Alderfer's ERG theory. The first of these, *satisfaction progression,* is in basic agreement with Maslow's process of moving through the needs. As we increasingly satisfy our existence needs, we direct energy toward relatedness needs. As these needs are satisfied, our growth needs become more active. The second component, *frustration,* occurs when we attempt but fail to satisfy a particular need. The resulting frustration may make satisfying the unmet need even more important to us—unless we repeatedly fail to satisfy that need. In this case, Alderfer's third component, *frustration regression,* can cause us to shift our attention to a previously satisfied, more concrete, and verifiable need. Lastly, the *aspiration* component of the ERG model notes that, by its very nature, growth is intrinsically satisfying. The more we grow, the more we want to grow. Therefore, the more we satisfy our growth need, the more important it becomes, and the more strongly we are motivated to satisfy it.

Alderfer's model is potentially more useful than Maslow's in that it doesn't create false motivational categories. For example, it is difficult for researchers to ascertain when interaction with others satisfies our need for acceptance and when it satisfies our need for recognition. ERG also focuses attention explicitly on movement through the set of needs in both directions. Further, evidence in support of the three need categories and their order tends to be stronger than evidence for Maslow's five need categories and their relative order.

FIGURE 7-4 Satisfying Existence, Relatedness, and Growth Needs

Herzberg's Motivator-Hygiene Theory

Clearly one of the most influential motivation theories throughout the 1950s and 1960s was Frederick Herzberg's motivator-hygiene theory.[14] This theory is a further refinement of Maslow's theory. Herzberg argued that there are two sets of needs, instead of the five sets theorized by Maslow. He called the first set "motivators" (or growth needs). **Motivators,** which relate to the jobs we perform, and our ability to feel a sense of achievement as a result of performing them, are rooted in our need to experience growth and self-actualization. The second set of needs he termed "hygienes." **Hygienes** relate to the work environment and are based in the basic human need to "avoid pain." According to Herzberg, growth needs motivate us to perform well and, when these needs are met, lead to the experience of satisfaction. Hygiene needs, on the other hand, must be met to avoid dissatisfaction (but do not necessarily provide satisfaction or motivation).[15]

motivators relate to the jobs that people perform, and people's ability to feel a sense of achievement as a result of performing them

hygienes relate to the work environment and are based on the basic human need to "avoid pain"

Hygiene factors are not directly related to the work itself (job content). Rather, hygienes refer to job context factors (pay, working conditions, supervision, and security). Herzberg also refers to these factors as "dissatisfiers" because they are frequently associated with dissatisfied employees. These factors are so frequently associated with dissatisfaction that Herzberg claims they never really provide satisfaction. When they're present in sufficient quantities, we avoid dissatisfaction, but they do not contribute to satisfaction. Furthermore, since meeting these needs does not provide satisfaction, Herzberg concludes that they do not motivate workers.

http://www.iavalley.cc.ia.us

http://www.ed.gov/motivationtheory

Motivator factors involve our long-term need to pursue psychological growth (much like Maslow's esteem and self-actualization needs). Motivators relate to *job content.* Job content is what we actually *do* when we perform our job duties. Herzberg considered job duties that lead to feelings of achievement and recognition to be motivators. He refers to these factors as "satisfiers" to reflect their ability to provide satisfying experiences. When these needs are met, we experience satisfaction. Because meeting these needs provides satisfaction, they motivate workers. More specifically, Herzberg believes these motivators lead to high performance (achievement), and the high performance itself leads to satisfaction.

The unique feature of Herzberg's theory is that job conditions that prevent dissatisfaction do not cause satisfaction. Satisfaction and dissatisfaction are on different "scales" in his view. Hygienes can cause dissatisfaction if they are not present in sufficient levels. Thus, an employee can be dissatisfied with low pay. But paying him more will not cause long-term satisfaction *unless* motivators are present. Good pay *by itself* will only make the employee neutral toward work; to attain satisfaction, employees need challenging job duties that result in a sense of achievement. Figure 7-5 illustrates this unusual aspect of Herzberg's theory. Employees can be dissatisfied, neutral, or satisfied with their jobs, depending on their levels of hygienes and motivators. Herzberg's theory even allows for the possibility that an employee can be satisfied and dissatisfied at the same time—the "I love my job but I hate the pay" situation!

Herzberg's theory has made lasting contributions to organizational research and managerial practice. Researchers have used it to identify the wide range of factors that influence worker reactions. Previously, most organizations attended primarily to hygiene factors. Because of Herzberg's work, organizations today realize the potential of motivators. Job enrichment programs are among the many direct results of his research (see Chapter 16).

FIGURE 7-5 Herzberg's versus Traditional View of Satisfaction and Dissatisfaction

(a) Herzberg's view of satisfaction and dissatisfaction

Dissatisfaction

High
D
B
Low
C
A
Low
High

Satisfaction

(b) Traditional view of satisfaction and dissatisfaction

Great dissatisfaction
Great satisfaction

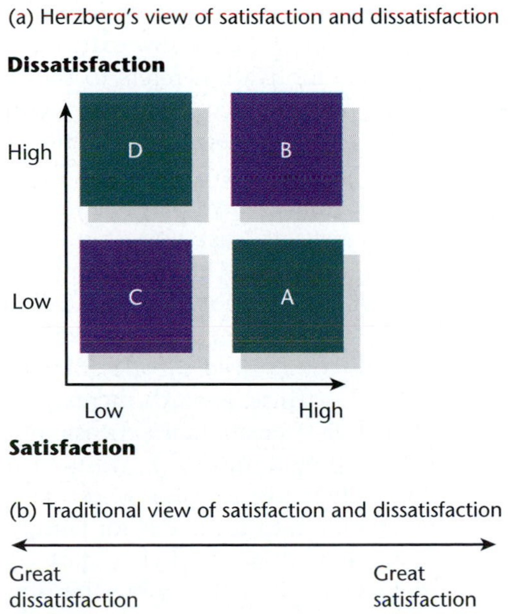

Herzberg's work suggests a two-stage process for managing employee motivation and satisfaction. First, managers should address the hygiene factors. Intense forms of dissatisfaction distract employees from important work-related activities and tend to be demotivating.[16] Thus, managers should make sure that such basic needs as adequate pay, safe and clean working conditions, and opportunities for social interaction are met. They should then address the much more powerful motivator needs, in which workers experience recognition, responsibility, achievement, and growth. If motivator needs are ignored, neither long-term satisfaction nor high motivation is likely. When motivator needs are met, however, employees feel satisfied and are motivated to perform well.

Self-Determination Theory

One major implication of Herzberg's motivator-hygiene theory is the somewhat counterintuitive idea that managers should focus more on motivators than on hygienes. (After all, doesn't everyone want to be paid well? Organizations have held this out as a chief motivator for decades!) Why might concentrating on motivators give better results? To answer this question, we must examine *types* of motivation. Organizational behavior researchers often classify motivation in terms of what stimulates it. In the case of **extrinsic motivation,** we endeavor to acquire something that satisfies a lower-order need. Jobs that pay well and that are performed in safe, clean working conditions, with adequate supervision and resources, satisfy directly or indirectly these lower-order needs. These "outside the person" factors are *extrinsic rewards.*

extrinsic motivation occurs when a person performs a given behavior to acquire something that will satisfy a lower-order need

Factors that cause people to perform tasks that are "inside" the person, **intrinsic motivation,** arise out of performing a task in and of itself, because it is interesting or "fun" to do. The task is enjoyable, so we continue to do it *even in the absence* of extrinsic rewards. That is, we are motivated by *intrinsic rewards,* rewards that we more or less give ourselves. Intrinsic rewards satisfy higher-order needs like relatedness and growth in ERG theory. When we sense that we are valuable contributors, are achieving something important, or are getting better at some skill, we like this feeling and strive to maintain it.

intrinsic motivation arises out of performing a behavior in and of itself, because it is interesting or "fun" to do

Self-determination theory (SDT) seeks to explain not only what causes motivation, but also how extrinsic rewards affect intrinsic motivation.[17] In SDT, extrinsic motivation refers to the performance of an activity in order to attain some valued outcome, while intrinsic motivation refers to performing an activity for the inherent satisfaction of the activity itself. SDT specifies when an activity will be intrinsically motivating and when it will not. Considerable numbers of studies have demonstrated that tasks are intrinsically motivating when they satisfy at least one of three higher-order needs: competence, autonomy, and relatedness. These precepts from SDT are entirely consistent with earlier discussions of theories by McClelland, Maslow, Alderfer, and Herzberg.

self-determination theory (SDT) seeks to explain not only what causes motivation, but also the effects of extrinsic rewards on intrinsic motivation

SDT takes the concepts of extrinsic rewards and intrinsic motivation further than the other need theories. SDT researchers have consistently found that as the level of extrinsic rewards increases, the amount of intrinsic motivation *decreases.* That is, SDT posits that extrinsic rewards not only do not provide intrinsic motivation, they diminish it. Think of this in terms of hobbies. Some people like to knit, others like to carve wood. They do it because it is intrinsically motivating; the hobby satisfies needs for competence, autonomy, and relatedness. But what happens if these hobbyists start getting paid well for their sweaters and carvings? Over time the hobby becomes less fun and is done in order to receive

© JAMES L. AMOS/CORBIS

According to self-determination theory, skilled workers who are given a chance to hone their skills and the freedom to practice their craft will be intrinsically motivated.

extrinsic rewards (money). Extrinsic motivation increases as intrinsic motivation decreases! When extrinsic rewards are present, people do not feel like what they do builds competence, is self-determined, or enhances relationships with others.

SDT theory has interesting implications for the management of organizational behavior. Some jobs are by their very nature uninteresting and unlikely to be made interesting. Automation has eliminated many such jobs, but they are still numerous. SDT would suggest that the primary way to motivate high performance for such jobs is to make performance contingent on extrinsic rewards. Relatively high pay is necessary to sustain performance on certain low-skill jobs. On the other hand, SDT would suggest that to enhance intrinsic motivation on jobs that are interesting, don't focus only on increasing extrinsic rewards (like large pay bonuses). Instead, create even more opportunities for employees to satisfy their needs for competence, autonomy, and relatedness. That means giving them opportunities to learn new skills, to perform their jobs without interference, and to develop meaningful relationships with other customers and employees in other departments. Such actions enhance intrinsic rewards.

You may have noticed that content theories are somewhat quiet about what determines the intensity of motivation. For example, some people steal to satisfy their lower-order needs (they have high intensity). But most of us don't steal. Why is this? Process theories of motivation attempt to explain this aspect of motivation by focusing on the intensity of motivation as well as its direction.

PROCESS THEORIES OF MOTIVATION

Process theories of motivation try to explain *why* behaviors are initiated. These theories focus on the mechanism by which we choose a target, and the effort that we exert to "hit" the target. There are four major process theories: (1) operant conditioning, (2) equity, (3) goal, and (4) expectancy.

Operant Conditioning Theory

Operant conditioning theory is the simplest of the motivation theories. It basically states that people will do those things for which they are rewarded, and will avoid doing things for which they are punished. This premise is sometimes called the "law of effect." However, if this were the sum total of conditioning theory, we would not be discussing it here. Operant conditioning theory does offer greater insights than "reward what you want and punish what you don't," and knowledge of its principles can lead to effective management practices.

operant conditioning a learning process based on the results produced by a person "operating on" the environment

Operant conditioning focuses on the learning of voluntary behaviors.[18] The term **operant conditioning** indicates that learning results from our "operating on" the environment. After we "operate on the environment" (that is, behave in a certain fashion), consequences result. These consequences determine the likelihood of similar behavior in the future. Learning occurs because we do something to the environment. The environment then reacts to our action, and our subsequent behavior is influenced by this reaction.

operant conditioning theory posits that people learn to behave in a particular fashion as a result of the consequences that followed their past behaviors

The Basic Operant Model According to **operant conditioning theory**, we learn to behave in a particular fashion because of consequences that resulted from our past behaviors.[19] The learning process involves three distinct steps (see Table 7-3). The first step involves a *stimulus* (S). The stimulus is any situation or event we perceive that we then respond to. A homework assignment is a stimulus. The second step involves a *response* (R), that is, any behavior or action we take in reaction to the stimulus. Staying up late to get your homework assignment in on time is a response. (We use the words response and behavior interchangeably here.) Finally, a *consequence* (C) is any event that follows our response and that makes the response more or less likely to occur in the future. If Colleen Sullivan receives praise from her superior for working hard, and if getting that praise is a pleasurable event, then it is likely that Colleen will work hard again in the future. If, on the other hand, the superior ignores or criticizes Colleen's response (working hard), this consequence is likely to make Colleen avoid working hard in the future. It is the experienced consequence (positive or negative) that influences whether a response will be repeated the next time the stimulus is presented.

reinforcement occurs when a consequence makes it more likely a behavior will be repeated in the future

extinction occurs when a consequence or lack of a consequence makes it less likely that a behavior will be repeated in the future

Reinforcement occurs when a consequence makes it more likely the response/behavior will be repeated in the future. In the previous example, praise from Colleen's superior is a reinforcer. **Extinction** occurs when a consequence makes it less likely the response/behavior will be repeated in the future. Criticism from Colleen's supervisor could cause her to stop working hard on any assignment.

There are three ways to make a response more likely to recur: positive reinforcement, negative reinforcement, and avoidance learning. In addition, there are two ways to make the response less likely to recur: nonreinforcement and punishment.

TABLE 7-3 General Operant Model: $S \rightarrow R \rightarrow C$

Ways to Strengthen $S \rightarrow R$ Link	
1. $S \rightarrow R \rightarrow C+$	(Positive Reinforcement)
2. $S \rightarrow R \nrightarrow C-$	(Negative Reinforcement)
3. $S \rightarrow R \rightarrow$ (no C–)	(Avoidance Learning)
Ways to Weaken $S \rightarrow R$ Link	
1. $S \rightarrow R \rightarrow$ (no C)	(Nonreinforcement)
2. $S \rightarrow R \rightarrow C-$	(Punishment)

Making a Response More Likely According to reinforcement theorists, managers can encourage employees to repeat a behavior if they provide a desirable consequence, or reward, after the behavior is performed. A **positive reinforcement** is a desirable consequence that satisfies an active need or that removes a barrier to need satisfaction. It can be as simple as a kind word or as major as a promotion. Companies that provide "Dinners for Two" as awards to those employees who go the extra mile are utilizing positive reinforcement. It is important to note that there are wide variations in what people consider to be a positive reinforcer. Praise from a supervisor may be a powerful reinforcer for some workers (like high-nAch individuals), but not others.

positive reinforcement occurs when a desirable consequence that satisfies an active need, or that removes a barrier to need satisfaction, increases the likelihood of a behavior reoccurring

negative reinforcement occurs when a behavior causes something undesirable to be removed, increasing the likelihood of the behavior reoccurring

Another technique for making a desired response more likely to be repeated is known as **negative reinforcement.** When a behavior causes something undesirable to be taken away, the behavior is more likely to be repeated in the future. Managers use negative reinforcement when they remove something unpleasant from an employee's work environment in the hope that this will encourage the desired behavior. Ted doesn't like being continually reminded by Philip to work faster (Ted thinks Philip is nagging him), so he works faster at stocking shelves to avoid being criticized. Philip's reminders are a negative reinforcement for Ted.

Approach using negative reinforcement with extreme caution. Negative reinforcement is often confused with punishment. Punishment, unlike reinforcement (negative or positive), is intended to make a particular behavior go away (not be repeated). Negative reinforcement, like positive reinforcement, is intended to make a behavior more likely to be repeated in the future. In the previous example, Philip's reminders simultaneously punished one behavior (slow stocking) and reinforced another (faster stocking). The difference is often a fine one, but it becomes clearer when we identify the behaviors we are trying to encourage (reinforcement) or discourage (punishment).

avoidance learning occurs when people learn to behave in a certain way to avoid encountering an undesired or unpleasant consequence

A third method of making a response more likely to occur involves a process known as avoidance learning. **Avoidance learning** occurs when we learn to behave in a certain way to avoid encountering an undesired or unpleasant consequence. We may learn to wake up a minute or so before our alarm clock rings so we can turn it off and not hear the irritating buzzer. Some workers learn to get to work on time to avoid the harsh words or punitive actions of their supervisors. Many organizational discipline systems rely heavily on avoidance learning by using the threat of negative consequences to encourage desired behavior. When managers warn an employee not to be late again, when they threaten to fire a careless worker, or when they transfer someone to an undesirable position, they are relying on the power of avoidance learning.

Making a Response Less Likely At times it is necessary to discourage a worker from repeating an undesirable behavior. The techniques managers use to make a behavior less likely to occur involve doing something that frustrates the individual's need satisfaction or that removes a currently satisfying circumstance. **Punishment** is an aversive consequence that follows a behavior and makes it less likely to reoccur.

punishment an aversive consequence that follows a behavior and makes it less likely to reoccur

nonreinforcement occurs when no consequence follows a worker's behavior

Note that managers have another alternative, known as **nonreinforcement,** in which they provide no consequence at all following a worker's response. Nonreinforcement eventually reduces the likelihood of that response reoccurring, which means that managers who fail to reinforce a worker's desirable behavior are also likely to see that desirable behavior less often. If Philip never rewards Ted when he finishes stocking on time, for instance, Ted will probably stop trying to beat the clock. Nonreinforcement can also reduce the likelihood that employees will repeat undesirable behaviors, although it doesn't produce results as quickly as punishment does. Furthermore, if other reinforcing consequences are present, nonreinforcement is unlikely to be effective.

While punishment clearly works more quickly than does nonreinforcement, it has some potentially undesirable side effects. Although punishment effectively tells a person what *not* to do and stops the undesired behavior, it does not tell them what they *should* do. In addition, even when punishment works as intended, the worker being punished often develops negative feelings toward the person who does the punishing. Although sometimes it is very difficult for managers to avoid using punishment, it works best when reinforcement is also used. An experiment conducted by two researchers at the University of Kansas found that using nonmonetary reinforcement in addition to punitive disciplinary measures was an effective way to decrease absenteeism in an industrial setting.[20]

Schedules of Reinforcement When a person is learning a new behavior, like how to perform a new job, it is desirable to reinforce effective behaviors every time they are demonstrated (this is called *shaping*). But in organizations it is not usually possible to reinforce desired behaviors every time they are performed, for obvious reasons. Moreover, research indicates that constantly reinforcing desired behaviors, termed *continuous reinforcement,* can be detrimental in the long run. Behaviors that are learned under continuous reinforcement are quickly extinguished (cease to be demonstrated). This is because people will expect a reward (the reinforcement) every time they display the behavior. When they don't receive it after just a few times, they quickly presume that the behavior will no longer be rewarded, and they quit doing it. Any employer can change employees' behavior by simply not paying them!

schedules of reinforcement the frequency at which effective employee behaviors are reinforced

If behaviors cannot (and should not) be reinforced every time they are exhibited, how often should they be reinforced? This is a question about **schedules of reinforcement**, or the frequency at which effective employee behaviors should be reinforced. Much of the early research on operant conditioning focused on the best way to maintain the performance of desired behaviors. That is, it attempted to determine how frequently behaviors need to be rewarded so that they are not extinguished. Research zeroed in on four types of reinforcement schedules:

Fixed Ratio. With this schedule, a fixed number of responses (let's say five) must be exhibited before any of the responses are reinforced. If the desired response is coming to work on time, then giving employees a $25 bonus for being punctual every day from Monday through Friday would be a fixed ratio of reinforcement.

Variable Ratio. A variable-ratio schedule reinforces behaviors, *on average,* a fixed number of times (again let's say five). Sometimes the tenth behavior is reinforced, other times the first, but on average every fifth response is reinforced. People who perform under such variable-ratio schedules like this don't know *when* they will be rewarded, but they do know that they *will* be rewarded.

Fixed Interval. In a fixed-interval schedule, a certain amount of time must pass before a behavior is reinforced. With a one-hour fixed-interval schedule, for example, a supervisor visits a employee's work station and reinforces the first desired behavior she sees. She returns one hour later and reinforces the next desirable behavior. This schedule doesn't imply that reinforcement will be received automatically after the passage of the time period. The time must pass *and* an appropriate response must be made.

Variable Interval. The variable interval differs from fixed-interval schedules in that the specified time interval passes *on average* before another appropriate response is reinforced. Sometimes the time period is shorter than the average; sometimes it is longer.

Which type of reinforcement schedule is best? In general, continuous reinforcement is best while employees are learning their jobs or new duties. After that, variable-ratio reinforcement schedules are superior. In most situations the fixed-interval schedule produces the least effective results, with fixed ratio and variable interval falling in between the two extremes. But remember that effective behaviors must be reinforced with some type of schedule, or they may become extinguished.

Equity Theory

Suppose you have worked for a company for several years. Your performance has been excellent, you have received regular pay increases, and you get along with your boss and co-workers. One day you come to work to find that a new person has been hired to work at the same job that you do. You are pleased to have the extra help. Then, you find out the new person is making $100 more per week than you, despite your longer service and greater experience. How do you feel? If you're like most of us, you're quite unhappy. Your satisfaction has just evaporated. Nothing about your job has changed—you receive the same pay, do the same job, and work for the same supervisor. Yet, the addition of one new employee has transformed you from a happy to an unhappy employee. This feeling of unfairness is the basis for equity theory.

equity theory states that human motivation is affected by the outcomes people receive for their inputs, compared to the outcomes and inputs of other people

Equity theory states that motivation is affected by the outcomes we receive for our inputs, compared to the outcomes and inputs of other people.[21] This theory is concerned with the reactions people have to outcomes they receive as part of a "social exchange." According to equity theory, our reactions to the outcomes we receive from others (an employer) depend both on how we value those outcomes in an absolute sense *and* on the circumstances surrounding their receipt. Equity theory suggests that our reactions will be influenced by our perceptions of the "inputs" provided in order to receive these outcomes ("Did I get as much out of this as I put into it?"). Even more important is our comparison of our inputs to what we believe others received for their inputs ("Did I get as much for my inputs as my co-workers got for theirs?").

The Basic Equity Model The fundamental premise of equity theory is that we continuously monitor the degree to which our work environment is "fair." In determining the degree of fairness, we consider two sets of factors, inputs and outcomes (see Figure 7-6). **Inputs** are any factors we contribute to the organization that we feel have value and are relevant to the organization. Note that the value attached to an input is based on *our* perception of its relevance and value. Whether or not anyone else agrees that the input is relevant or valuable is unimportant to us. Common inputs in organizations include time, effort, performance level, education level, skill levels, and bypassed opportunities.

inputs any factors that a person views as having value and that are relevant to the organization

FIGURE 7-6 The Equity Theory Comparison

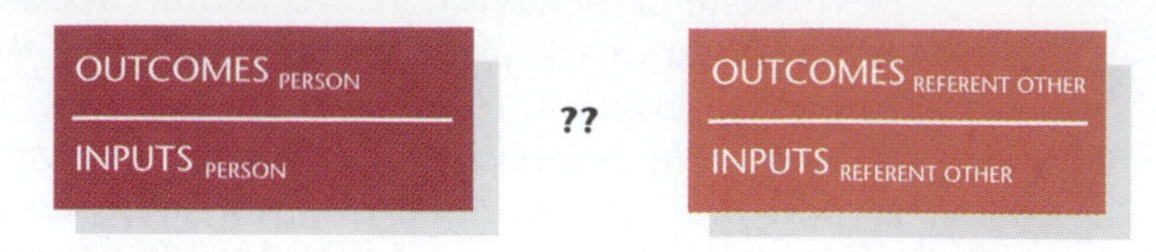

Since any factor we consider relevant is included in our evaluation of equity, it is not uncommon for factors to be included that the organization (or even the law) might argue are inappropriate (such as age, sex, ethnic background, social status).

outcomes anything a person perceives as getting back from an organization in exchange for the person's inputs

Outcomes are anything we perceive as getting back from the organization in exchange for our inputs. Again, the value attached to an outcome is based on our perceptions and not necessarily on "objective reality." Common outcomes from organizations include pay, working conditions, job status, feelings of achievement, and friendship opportunities. Both positive and negative outcomes influence their evaluation of equity. Stress, headaches, and fatigue are also potential outcomes. Since any outcome we consider relevant to the exchange influences our equity perception, we frequently include unintended factors (peer disapproval, family reactions).

Equity theory predicts that we will compare our outcomes to our inputs in the form of a ratio. On the basis of this ratio we make an initial determination of whether or not the situation is equitable. If we perceive that the outcomes we receive are commensurate with our inputs, we are satisfied. If we believe that the outcomes are not commensurate with our inputs, we are dissatisfied. This dissatisfaction can lead to ineffective behaviors for the organization if they continue. The key feature of equity theory is that it predicts that we will compare our ratios to the ratios of other people. It is this comparison of the two ratios that has the strongest effect on our equity perceptions. These other people are called referent others because we "refer to" them when we judge equity. Usually, referent others are people we work with who perform work of a similar nature. That is, **referent others** perform jobs that are similar in difficulty and complexity to the employee making the equity determination (see Figure 7-6).

referent others workers that a person uses to compare inputs and outcomes, and who perform jobs similar in difficulty and complexity to the employee making an equity determination

state of equity occurs when people perceive their input/outcome ratios to be equal to that of their referent other

overreward inequity occurs when people perceive their input/outcome ratios to be greater than that of their referent other

underreward inequity occurs when people perceive their input/outcome ratios to be less than that of their referent other

Three conditions can result from this comparison. Our outcome to input ratio could equal the referent other's. This is a **state of equity.** A second result could be that our ratio is greater than the referent other's. This is a state of **overreward inequity.** The third result could be that we perceive our ratio to be less than that of the referent other. This is a state of **underreward inequity**.

Equity theory has a lot to say about basic human tendencies. The motivation to compare our situation to that of others is strong. For example, what is the first thing you do when you get an exam back in class? Probably look at your score and make an initial judgment as to its fairness. For a lot of people, the very next thing they do is look at the scores received by fellow students who sit close to them. A 75 percent score doesn't look so bad if everyone else scored lower! This is equity theory in action.

Most workers in the United States are at least partially dissatisfied with their pay.[22] Equity theory helps explain this. Two human tendencies create feelings of inequity that are not based in reality. One is that we tend to overrate our performance levels. For example, one study conducted by your authors asked more than 600 employees to anonymously rate their performance on a 7-point scale (1 = poor, 7 = excellent). The average was 6.2, meaning the *average* employee rated his or her performance as *very good to excellent.* This implies that the average employee also expects excellent pay increases, a policy most employers cannot afford if they are to remain competitive. Another study found that the average employee (one whose performance is better than half of the other employees, and worse than the other half) rated his or her performance at the 80th percentile (better than 80 percent of the other employees, worse than 20 percent).[23] Again it would be impossible for most organizations to reward the average employee at the 80th percentile. In other words, most employees inaccurately overrate the inputs they provide to an organization. This leads to perceptions of inequity that are not justified.

The second human tendency that leads to unwarranted perceptions of inequity is our tendency to *overrate* the outcomes of others.[24] Many employers keep the pay levels of employees a "secret." Still other employers actually forbid employees to talk about their pay. This means that many employees don't know for certain how much their colleagues are paid. And, because most of us overestimate the pay of others, we tend to think that they're paid more than they actually are, and the unjustified perceptions of inequity are perpetuated.

The bottom line for employers is that they need to be sensitive to employees' need for equity. Employers need to do everything they can to prevent feelings of inequity because employees engage in effective behaviors when they perceive equity, and ineffective behaviors when they perceive inequity.

Perceived Overreward Inequity When we perceive that overreward inequity exists (that is, we unfairly make more than others), it is rare that we are so dissatisfied, guilty, or sufficiently motivated that we make changes to produce a state of perceived equity (or we leave the situation). Indeed, feelings of overreward, when they occur, are quite transient. Very few of us go to our employers and complain that we're overpaid! Most people are less sensitive to overreward inequities than they are to underreward inequities.[25] However infrequently they are used for overreward, the same types of actions are available for dealing with both types of inequity.

Perceived Underreward Inequity When we perceive that underreward inequity exists (that is, others unfairly make more than we do), we will likely be dissatisfied, angered, and motivated to change the situation (or escape the situation) in order to produce a state of perceived equity. As we discuss shortly, people can take many actions to deal with underreward inequity.

Reducing Underreward Inequity. A simple situation helps explain the consequences of inequity. Two automobile workers in Detroit, John and Mary, fasten lug nuts to wheels on cars as they come down the assembly line, John on the left side and Mary on the right. Their inputs are equal (both fasten the same number of lug nuts at the same pace), but John makes \$500 per week and Mary makes \$600. Their equity ratios are thus

$$\text{John: } \frac{\$500}{\text{10 lug nuts/car}} < \text{Mary: } \frac{\$600}{\text{10 lug nuts/car}}$$

As you can see, their ratios are not equal; that is, Mary receives greater outcome for equal input. Who is experiencing inequity? According to equity theory, both John *and* Mary—underreward inequity for John, and overreward inequity for Mary. Mary's inequity won't last long (in real organizations), but in our hypothetical example, what might John do to resolve this?

Adams identified a number of things people do to reduce the tension produced by a perceived state of inequity. They change their own outcomes or inputs, *or* they change those of the referent other. They distort their own perceptions of the outcomes or inputs of either party by using a different referent other, or they leave the situation in which the inequity is occurring.

1. Alter inputs of the person. The perceived state of equity can be altered by changing our own inputs, that is, by decreasing the quantity or quality of our performance. John can effect his own mini slowdown and install only nine lug nuts on each car as it comes down the production line. This, of course, might cause him to lose his job, so he probably won't choose this alternative.
2. Alter outcomes of the person. We could attempt to increase outcomes to achieve a state of equity, like ask for a raise, a nicer office, a promotion, or other positively valued outcomes. So John will likely ask for a raise. Unfortunately, many people enhance their outcomes by stealing from their employers.
3. Alter inputs of the referent other. When underrewarded, we may try to achieve a state of perceived equity by encouraging the referent other to increase their inputs. We may demand, for example, that the referent other "start pulling their weight," or perhaps help the referent other to become a better performer. It doesn't matter that the referent other is already pulling their weight—remember, this is all about perception. In our example, John could ask Mary to put on two of his ten lug nuts as each car comes down the assembly line. This would not likely happen, however, so John would be motivated to try another alternative to reduce his inequity.
4. Alter outcomes of the referent other. We can "correct" a state of underreward by directly or indirectly reducing the value of the other's outcomes. In our example, John could try to get Mary's pay lowered to reduce his inequity. This too would probably not occur in the situation described.
5. Distort perceptions of inputs or outcomes. It *is* possible to reduce a perceived state of inequity without changing input or outcome. We simply distort our own perceptions of our inputs or outcomes, *or* we distort our perception of those of the referent other. Thus, John may tell himself that "Mary does better work than I thought," or "she enjoys her work much less than I do," or "she gets paid less than I realized."
6. Choose a different referent other. We can also deal with both over- and underreward inequities by changing the referent other ("my situation is really more like Ahmed's"). This is the simplest and most powerful way to deal with perceived inequity: It requires neither actual nor perceptual changes in anybody's input or outcome, and it causes us to look around and assess our situation more carefully. For example, John might choose as a referent other Bill, who installs dashboards but makes less money than John.
7. Leave the situation. A final technique for dealing with a perceived state of inequity involves removing ourselves from the situation. We can choose to accomplish this through absenteeism, transfer, or termination. This approach is usually not selected unless the perceived inequity is quite high or other attempts at achieving equity are not readily available. Most automobile workers are paid quite well for their work. John is unlikely to find an equivalent job, so it is also unlikely that he will choose this option.

Implications of Equity Theory Equity theory is widely used, and its implications are clear. In the vast majority of cases, employees experience (or perceive) underreward inequity rather than overreward. As discussed above, few of the behaviors that result from underreward inequity are good for employers. Thus, employers try to prevent unnecessary perceptions of inequity. They do this in a number of ways. They try to be as fair as possible in allocating pay. That is, they measure performance levels as accurately as possible, then give the highest performers the highest pay increases. Second, most employers are no longer secretive about their pay schedules. People are, naturally, curious about how much they are paid relative to others in the organization. This doesn't mean that employers don't practice discretion—they usually don't reveal specific employees' exact pay. But they do tell employees the minimum and maximum pay levels for their jobs, and the pay scales for the jobs of others in the organization. Such practices give employees a factual basis for judging equity.

http://www.topachievement.com

Supervisors play a key role in creating perceptions of equity. "Playing favorites" ensures perceptions of inequity. Employees want to be rewarded on their merits, not the whims of their supervisors. In addition, supervisors need to recognize differences in employees in their reactions to inequity. Some employees are highly sensitive to inequity, and a supervisor needs to be especially cautious around them.[26] Everyone is sensitive to reward allocation.[27] But "equity sensitives" are even more sensitive. A major principle for supervisors then is, simply, implement fairness. Never base punishment or reward on whether or not you like an employee. Reward behaviors that contribute to the organization, discipline those that do not. Make sure employees understand what is expected of them and praise them when they do it. These practices make everyone happier and your job easier.

Goal Theory

No theory is perfect. If it was, it wouldn't be a theory. It would be a set of facts. Theories are sets of propositions that are right more often than they are wrong, but they are not infallible. However, the basic propositions of goal theory* come close to being infallible. Indeed, it is one of the strongest theories in organizational behavior.

goal theory states that people will perform better if they have difficult, specific accepted performance goals or objectives

The Basic Goal Setting Model **Goal theory** states that people will perform better if they have difficult, specific accepted performance goals or objectives.[28, 29] The first and most basic premise of goal theory is that people will attempt to achieve those goals that they *intend* to achieve. Thus, if we intend to do something (like get an A on an exam), we will exert effort to accomplish it. Without such goals, our effort at the task (studying) required to achieve the goal is less. Students whose goals are to get A's study harder than students who don't have this goal—we all know this. This doesn't mean that people without goals are unmotivated. It simply means that people with goals are more motivated. The intensity of their motivation is greater, and they are more directed.

The second basic premise is that *difficult* goals result in better performance than easy goals. This does not mean that difficult goals are always achieved, but our performance will usually be better when we intend to achieve harder goals.

* Sometimes goal theory is referred to as goal setting theory.

Goal theory holds that people will exert effort to accomplish goals if those goals are difficult to achieve, accepted by the individual, and specific in nature.

Your goal of an A in Classical Mechanics at Cal Tech may not get you your A, but it may earn you a B+, which you wouldn't have gotten otherwise. Difficult goals cause us to exert more effort, and this almost always results in better performance.

Another premise of goal theory is that *specific* goals are better than vague goals. We often wonder what we need to do to be successful. Have you ever asked a professor "What do I need to do to get an A in this course?" If he responded "Do well on the exams," you weren't much better off for having asked. This is a vague response. Goal theory says that we perform better when we have specific goals. Had your professor told you the key thrust of the course, to turn in *all* the problem sets, to pay close attention to the essay questions on exams, and to aim for scores in the 90s, you would have something concrete on which to build a strategy.

A key premise of goal theory is that people must *accept* the goal. Usually we set our own goals. But sometimes others set goals for us. Your professor telling you your goal is to "score at least a 90 percent on your exams" doesn't mean that you'll accept this goal. Maybe you don't feel you can achieve scores in the 90s. Or, you've heard that 90 isn't good enough for an A in this class. This happens in work organizations quite often. Supervisors give orders that something must be done by a certain time. The employees may fully understand what is wanted, yet if they feel the order is unreasonable or impossible, they may not exert much effort to accomplish it. Thus, it is important for people to accept the goal. They need to feel that it is also their goal. If they do not, goal theory predicts that they won't try as hard to achieve it.

goal commitment the degree to which people dedicate themselves to achieving a goal

Goal theory also states that people need to *commit* to a goal in addition to accepting it. **Goal commitment** is the degree to which we dedicate ourselves to achieving a goal. Goal commitment is about setting priorities. We can accept many goals (go to all classes, stay awake during classes, take lecture notes), but we often end up doing only some of them. In other words, some goals are more important than others. And we exert more effort for certain goals. This also happens frequently at work. A software analyst's major goal may be to write a new program. Her minor goal may be to maintain previously written programs. It is minor because maintaining old programs is boring, while writing new ones is fun. Goal theory predicts that her commitment, and thus her intensity, to the major goal will be greater.

Allowing people to participate in the goal setting process often results in higher goal commitment. This has to do with ownership, discussed in Chapter 6. And when people participate in the process, they tend to incorporate factors they think will make the goal more interesting, challenging, and attainable. Thus, it is advisable to allow people some input into the goal setting process.

Imposing goals on them from the outside usually results in less commitment (and acceptance).

The basic goal setting model is shown in Table 7-4. The process starts with our values. Values are our beliefs about how the world should be or act, and often include words like "should" or "ought." We compare our present conditions against these values. For example, Randi holds the value that everyone should be a hard worker. After measuring her current work against this value, Randi concludes that she doesn't measure up to her own value. Following this, her goal setting process begins. Randi will set a goal that affirms her status as a hard worker. Table 7-4 lists the four types of goals. Some goals are self-set. (Randi decides to word process at least 70 pages per day.) Participative goals are jointly set. (Randi goes to her supervisor, and together they set some appropriate goals for her.) In still other cases, goals are assigned. (Her boss tells her that she must word process at least 60 pages per day.) The fourth type of goal, which can be self-set, jointly determined, or assigned, is a "do your best" goal. But note this goal is vague, so it usually doesn't result in the best performance.

Depending on the characteristics of Randi's goals, she may or may not exert a lot of effort. For maximum effort to result, her goals should be difficult, specific, accepted, and committed to. Then, if she has sufficient ability and lack of constraints, maximum performance should occur. Examples of constraints could be that her old computer frequently breaks down or her supervisor constantly interferes.

The consequence of endeavoring to reach her goal will be that Randi will be satisfied with herself. Her behavior is consistent with her values. She'll be even more satisfied if her supervisor praises her performance and gives her a pay increase!

In Randi's case, her goal achievement resulted in several benefits. However, this doesn't always happen. If goals are not achieved, people may be unhappy with themselves, and their employer may be dissatisfied as well. Such an experience can make a person reluctant to accept goals in the future. Thus, setting difficult yet attainable goals cannot be stressed enough.

Goal theory can be a tremendous motivational tool. In fact, many organizations practice effective management by using a technique called "Management-by-Objectives" (MBO). MBO is based on goal theory and is quite effective when implemented consistent with goal theory's basic premises. Because MBO is such an important and prevalent tool, we discuss it in detail in Chapter 10.

TABLE 7-4 The Goal Setting Process

Personal Values →	**Present Situation** →	**Goal Setting** →	**Goal Characteristics** →	**Consequences**
How the world should be.	Am I consistent with my values?	1. Self-set	1. Difficulty	1. Performance
		2. Participative	2. Specificity	2. Satisfaction
		3. Assigned	3. Acceptance	3. Rewards
		4. Do your best	4. Commitment	

Despite its many strengths, several cautions about goal theory are appropriate. Locke has identified most of them.[30] First, setting goals in one area can lead people to neglect other areas. (Randi may word process 70 pages per day, but neglect her proofreading responsibilities.) It is important that goals be set for most major duties. Second, goal setting sometimes has unintended consequences. For example, employees set easy goals so that they look good when they achieve them. Or it causes unhealthy competition between employees. Or an employee sabotages the work of others so that only he has goal achievement.

http://mbs.umd.edu/mao/elocke

Some managers use goal setting in unethical ways. They may manipulate employees by setting impossible goals. This enables them to criticize employees even when the employees are doing superior work and, of course, causes much stress. Goal setting should never be abused. Perhaps the key caution about goal setting is that it often results in too much focus on quantified measures of performance. Qualitative aspects of a job or task may be neglected because they aren't easily measured. Managers must keep employees focused on the qualitative aspects of their jobs as well as the quantitative ones. Finally, setting individual goals in a teamwork environment can be counterproductive.[31] Where possible, it is preferable to have group goals in situations where employees depend on one another in the performance of their jobs.

The cautions noted here are not intended to deter you from using goal theory. We note them so that you can avoid the pitfalls. Remember, employees have a right to reasonable performance expectations and the rewards that result from performance, and organizations have a right to expect high performance levels from employees. Goal theory should be used to optimize the employment relationship.

Expectancy Theory

expectancy theory posits that people will exert high effort levels to perform at high levels so that they can obtain valued outcomes

Expectancy theory posits that we will exert much effort to perform at high levels so that we can obtain valued outcomes. It is the motivation theory that many organizational behavior researchers find most intriguing, in no small part because it is currently also the most comprehensive theory. Expectancy theory ties together many of the concepts and hypotheses from the theories discussed earlier in this chapter. In addition, it points to factors that other theories miss. Expectancy theory has much to offer the student of management and organizational behavior.

Expectancy theory is sufficiently general that it is useful in a wide variety of situations. Choices between job offers, between working hard or not so hard, between going to work or not—virtually any set of possibilities can be addressed by expectancy theory. Basically, the theory focuses on two related issues:

1. When faced with two or more alternatives, which will we select?
2. Once an alternative is chosen, how motivated will we be to pursue that choice?

Expectancy theory thus focuses on the two major aspects of motivation, *direction* (which alternative?) and *intensity* (how much effort to implement the alternative?). The attractiveness of an alternative is determined by our "expectations" of what is likely to happen if we choose it. The more we believe that the alternative chosen will lead to positively valued outcomes, the greater its attractiveness to us.

Expectancy theory states that, when faced with two or more alternatives, we will select the most attractive one. And, the greater the attractiveness of the chosen alternative, the more motivated we will be to pursue it. Our natural hedonism, discussed earlier in this chapter, plays a role in this process. We are motivated to maximize desirable outcomes (a pay raise) and minimize undesirable ones (discipline). Expectancy theory goes on to state that we are also logical in our decisions about alternatives. It considers people to be *rational.* People evaluate alternatives in terms of their "pros and cons," and then choose the one with the most "pros" and fewest "cons."

The Basic Expectancy Model The three major components of expectancy theory reflect its assumptions of hedonism and rationality: effort-performance expectancy, performance-outcome expectancy, and valences.

effort-performance expectancy E1, the perceived probability that effort will lead to performance (or E → P)

The **effort-performance expectancy**, abbreviated E1, is the perceived probability that effort will lead to performance (or E → P). Performance here means anything from doing well on an exam to assembling 100 toasters a day at work. Sometimes people believe that no matter how much effort they exert, they won't perform at a high level. They have weak E1s. Other people have strong E1s and believe the opposite—that is, that they can perform at a high level if they exert high effort. You all know students with different E1s—those who believe that if they study hard they'll do well, and those who believe that no matter how much they study they'll do poorly. People develop these perceptions from prior experiences with the task at hand, and from self-perceptions of their abilities. The core of the E1 concept is that people don't always perceive a direct relationship between effort level and performance level.

performance-outcome expectancy E2, the perceived relationship between performance and outcomes (or P → O)

http://www.nasa.gov

The **performance-outcome expectancy**, E2, is the perceived relationship between performance and outcomes (or P → O).* Many things in life happen as a function of how well we perform various tasks. E2 addresses the question "What will happen if I perform well?" Let's say you get an A in your Classical Mechanics course at Cal Tech. You'll be elated, your classmates may envy you, and you are now assured of that plum job at NASA. But let's say you got a D. Whoops, that was the last straw for the dean. Now you've flunked out, and you're reduced to going home to live with your parents (perish the thought!). Likewise, E2 perceptions develop in organizations, although hopefully not as drastically as your beleaguered career at Cal Tech. People with strong E2s believe that if they perform their jobs well, they'll receive desirable outcomes—good pay increases, praise from their supervisor, and a feeling that they're really contributing. In the same situation, people with weak E2s will have the opposite perceptions—that high performance levels don't result in desirable outcomes, that it doesn't really matter how well they perform their jobs as long as they don't get fired.

valences the degree to which a person perceives an outcome as being desirable, neutral, or undesirable

Valences are the easiest of the expectancy theory concepts to describe. Valences are simply the degree to which we perceive an outcome as desirable, neutral, or undesirable. Highly desirable outcomes (a 25 percent pay increase) are positively valent. Undesirable outcomes (being disciplined) are negatively valent. Outcomes that we're indifferent to (where you must park your car) have neutral valences. Positively and negatively valent outcomes abound in the

* Sometimes E2s are called *instrumentalities,* because they are the perception that performance is instrumental in getting some desired outcome.

workplace—pay increases and freezes, praise and criticism, recognition and rejection, promotions and demotions. And as you would expect, people differ dramatically in how they value these outcomes. Our needs, values, goals, and life situations affect what valence we give an outcome. Equity is another consideration we use in assigning valences. We may consider a 10 percent pay increase desirable until we find out that it was the lowest raise given in our work group.

Figure 7-7 summarizes the three core concepts of expectancy theory. The theory states that our perceptions about our surroundings are essentially predictions about "what leads to what." We perceive that certain effort levels result in certain performance levels. We perceive that certain performance levels result in certain outcomes. Outcomes can be **extrinsic**, in that others (our supervisor) determine whether we receive them, or **intrinsic**, in that we determine if they are received (our sense of achievement). Each outcome has an associated valence (outcome A's valence is V_a). Expectancy theory predicts that we will exert effort that results in the maximum amount of positive-valence outcomes.* If our E1 or E2 is weak, or if the outcomes are not sufficiently desirable, our motivation to exert effort will be low. Stated differently, an individual will be motivated to try to achieve the level of performance that results in the most rewards.

extrinsic outcomes are awarded or given by other people (like a supervisor)

intrinsic outcomes are awarded or given by people to themselves (such as a sense of achievement)

Implications of Expectancy Theory Expectancy theory has major implications for the workplace. Basically, expectancy theory predicts that employees will be motivated to perform well on their jobs under two conditions. The first is when employees believe that a reasonable amount of effort will result in good performance. The second is when good performance is associated with positive outcomes, and low performance is associated with negative outcomes. If neither of these conditions exists in the perceptions of employees, their motivation to perform will be low.

Why might an employee perceive that positive outcomes are not associated with high performance? Or that negative outcomes are not associated with low performance? That is, why would employees develop weak E2s? This happens for a number of reasons. The main one is that many organizations subscribe too strongly to a principle of equality (not to be confused with equity). They give all of their employees equal salaries for equal work, equal pay increases every year (these are known as across-the-board pay raises), and equal treatment wherever possible. Equality-focused organizations reason that some employees "getting more" than others leads to disruptive competition and feelings of inequity.

In time employees in equality-focused organizations develop weak E2s because no distinctions are made for differential outcomes. If the best and the worst salespeople are paid the same, in time they will both decide that it isn't worth the extra effort to be a high performer. Needless to say, this is not the goal of competitive organizations and can cause the demise of the organization as it competes with other firms in today's global marketplace.

* It can also be expressed as an equation:

$$\text{Force to Choose a Level of Effort} = E1 \times \Sigma(E2_o \times V_o)$$

V_o is the valence of the outcome. The effort level with the greatest force associated with it will be chosen by the individual.

FIGURE 7-7 The Expectancy Theory of Motivation

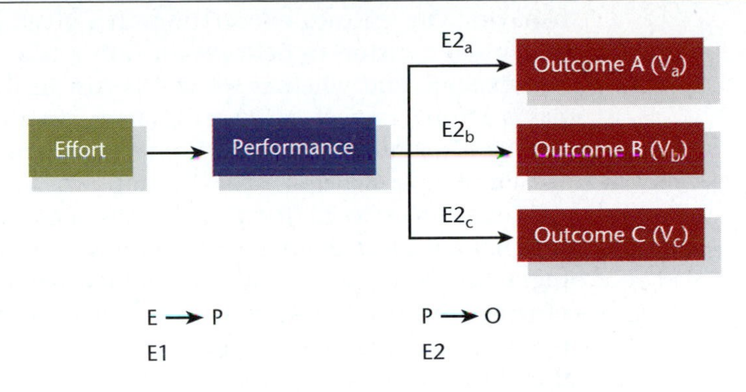

1. Effort ⟶ Performance Expectancy (E → P; E1)
2. Performance ⟶ Outcome Expectancy (P → O; E2)
3. Valences (V) of Outcomes (V_o)

Expectancy theory states that to maximize motivation, organizations must make outcomes contingent on performance. This is the main contribution of expectancy theory: It makes us think about *how* organizations should distribute outcomes. If an organization, or a supervisor, believes that treating everyone "the same" will result in satisfied and motivated employees, they will be wrong more times than not. From equity theory we know that some employees, usually the better-performing ones, will experience underreward inequity. From expectancy theory we know that employees will see no difference in outcomes for good and poor performance, so they will not have as much incentive to be good performers. Effective organizations actively need to encourage the perception that good performance leads to positive outcomes (bonuses, promotions) and that poor performance leads to negative ones (discipline, termination). Remember, there is a big difference between treating employees equally and treating them equitably.

What if an organization ties positive outcomes to high performance, and negative outcomes to low performance? Employees will develop strong E2s. But will this result in highly motivated employees? The answer is, maybe. We have yet to address employees' E1s. If employees have weak E1s, they will perceive that high (or low) effort does *not* result in high performance and thus will not exert much effort. It is important for managers to understand that this can happen despite rewards for high performance.

self-efficacy a belief about the probability that one can successfully execute some future action or task, or achieve some result

Task-related abilities are probably the single biggest reason why some employees have weak E1s. **Self-efficacy** is our belief about whether we can successfully execute some future action or task, or achieve some result. High self-efficacy employees believe that they are likely to succeed at most or all of their job duties and responsibilities. And as you would expect, low self-efficacy employees believe the opposite. Specific self-efficacy reflects our belief in our capability to perform a specific task, at a specific level of performance. If we believe that the probability of our selling $30,000 of jackrabbit slippers in one month is .90, our self-efficacy for this task is high. Specific self-efficacy is our judgment about the likelihood of successful task performance measured immediately before we expend effort on the task. As a result, specific self-efficacy is much more variable than more enduring notions of personality. Still, there is little doubt that our state-based beliefs are some of the most powerful motivators of behavior. Our efficacy expectations at a given point in time determine not only our initial decision to perform (or not) a task, but also the amount of effort we will expend, and whether we will persist in the face of adversity.[32] Self-efficacy has a strong impact on the E1 factor. As a result, self-efficacy is one of the strongest determinants of performance in any particular task situation.[33]

Employees develop weak E1s for two reasons. First, they don't have sufficient resources to perform their jobs. Resources can be internal or external. Internal resources include what employees bring to the job (such as prior training, work experience, education, ability, and aptitude) and their understanding of what they need to do to be considered good performers. The second resource is called role perceptions—how employees believe their jobs are done and how they fit into the broader organization. If employees don't know *how* to become good performers, they will have weak E1s. External resources include the tools, equipment, and labor necessary to perform a job. The lack of good external resources can also cause E1s to be weak.

The second reason for weak E1s is an organization's failure to measure performance accurately. That is, performance *ratings* don't correlate well with actual performance *levels*. How does this happen? Have you ever gotten a grade that you felt didn't reflect how much you learned? This also happens in organizations. Why are ratings sometimes inaccurate? Supervisors, who typically give out ratings, well, they're human. Perhaps they're operating under the mistaken notion that similar ratings for everyone will keep the team happy. Perhaps they're unconsciously playing favorites. Perhaps they don't know what good and poor performance levels are. Perhaps the measurements they're expected to use don't fit their product/team/people. Choose one or all of these. Rating people is rarely easy.

Whatever the cause of rating errors, some employees may come to believe that no matter what they do they will never receive a high performance rating. They may in fact believe that they are excellent performers but that the performance rating system is flawed. Expectancy theory differs from most motivation theories because it highlights the need for accurate performance measurement. Organizations cannot motivate employees to perform at a high level if they cannot identify high performers.

Organizations exert tremendous influence over employee choices in their performance levels and how much effort to exert on their jobs. That is, organizations can have a major impact on the direction and intensity of employees' motivation levels. Practical applications of expectancy theory include

1. Strengthening the effort → performance expectancy by selecting employees who have the necessary abilities, providing proper training, providing experiences of success, clarifying job responsibilities, etc.
2. Strengthening the performance → outcome expectancy with policies that specify that desirable behavior leads to desirable outcomes, and undesirable behavior leads to neutral or undesirable outcomes. Consistent enforcement of these policies is key—workers must believe in the contingencies.
3. Systematically evaluating which outcomes employees value. The greater the valence of outcomes offered for a behavior, the more likely employees will commit to that alternative. By recognizing that different employees have different values and that values change over time, organizations can provide the most highly valued outcomes.

4. Ensuring that effort actually translates into performance by clarifying what actions lead to performance and by appropriate training.
5. Ensuring appropriate worker outcomes for performance through reward schedules (extrinsic outcomes) and appropriate job design (so the work experience itself provides intrinsic outcomes).
6. Examining the level of outcomes provided to workers. Are they equitable, given the worker's inputs? Are they equitable in comparison to the way other workers are treated?
7. Measuring performance levels as accurately as possible, making sure that workers are capable of being high performers.

Expectancy Theory: An Integrative Theory of Motivation

More so than any other motivation theory, expectancy theory can be tied into most concepts of what and how people become motivated. Consider the following examples.

1. *Need theories* state that we are motivated to satisfy our needs. We positively value outcomes that satisfy unmet needs, negatively value outcomes that thwart the satisfaction of unmet needs, and assign neutral values to outcomes that do neither. In effect, the need theories explain how valences are formed.
2. *Operant conditioning theories* state that we will probably repeat a response (behavior) in the future that was reinforced in the past (that is, followed by a positively valued consequence or the removal of a negatively valued consequence). This is the basic process involved in forming performance → outcome expectancies. Both operant theories and expectancy theory argue that our interactions with our environment influence our future behavior. The primary difference is that expectancy theory explains this process in cognitive (rational) terms.
3. *Equity theories* state that our satisfaction with a set of outcomes depends not only on how we value them but also on the circumstances surrounding their receipt. Equity theory, therefore, explains part of the process shown in Figure 7-7. If we don't feel that the outcomes we receive are equitable compared to a referent other, we will associate a lower or even negative valence with those outcomes.
4. *Goal theory* can be integrated with the expanded expectancy model in several ways. Locke has noted that expectancy theory explains how we go about choosing a particular goal.[34] A reexamination of Table 7-4 reveals other similarities between goal theory and expectancy theory. Locke's use of the term "goal acceptance" to identify the personal adoption of a goal is similar to the "choice of an alternative" in the expectancy model. Locke's "goal commitment," the degree to which we commit to reaching our accepted (chosen) goal, is very much like the expectancy description of choice of effort level. Locke argues that the difficulty and specificity of a goal are major determinants of the level of performance attempted (goal-directed effort), and expectancy theory appears to be consistent with this argument (even though expectancy theory is not as explicit on this point). We can reasonably conclude that the major underlying processes explored by the two models are very similar and will seldom lead to inconsistent recommendations.

RECENT RESEARCH ON MOTIVATION THEORIES

Employee motivation continues to be a major focus in organizational behavior.[35] We briefly summarize current motivation research here.

Content Theories There is some interest in testing content theories (including Herzberg's two-factor theory), especially in international research. Need theories are still generally supported, with most people identifying such workplace factors as recognition, advancement, and opportunities to learn as the chief motivators for them. This is consistent with need satisfaction theories. However, most of this research does not include actual measures of employee performance. Thus, questions remain about whether the factors that employees *say* motivate them to perform actually do.

Operant Conditioning Theory There is considerable interest in operant conditioning theory, especially within the context of what has been called organizational behavior modification. Oddly enough, there has not been much research using operant conditioning theory in designing reward systems, even though there are obvious applications. Instead, much of the recent research on operant conditioning focuses on punishment and extinction. These studies seek to determine how to use punishment appropriately. Recent results still confirm that punishment should be used sparingly, only after extinction does not work, and should not be excessive or destructive.

Equity Theory Equity theory continues to receive strong research support. The major criticism of equity theory, that the inputs and outcomes people use to evaluate equity are ill-defined, still holds. Because each person defines inputs and outcomes, researchers are not in a position to know them all. Nevertheless, for the major inputs (performance) and outcomes (pay), the theory is a strong one. Major applications of equity theory in recent years incorporate and extend the theory into the area called *organizational justice.* When employees receive rewards (or punishments), they evaluate them in terms of their fairness (as discussed earlier). This is *distributive justice.* Employees also assess rewards in terms of how fair the processes used to distribute them are. This is *procedural justice.* Thus during organizational downsizing, when employees lose their jobs, people ask whether the loss of work is fair (distributive justice). But they also assess the fairness of the process used to decide *who* is laid off (procedural justice). For example, layoffs based on seniority may be perceived as more fair than layoffs based on supervisors' opinions.

Goal Theory It remains true that difficult, specific goals result in better performance than easy and vague goals, assuming they are accepted. Recent research highlights the positive effects of performance feedback and goal commitment in the goal setting process. Monetary incentives enhance motivation when they are tied to goal achievement, by increasing the level of goal commitment. There are negative sides to goal theory as well. If goals conflict, employees may sacrifice performance on important job duties. For example, if both quantitative and qualitative goals are set for performance, employees may emphasize quantity because this goal achievement is more visible.

Expectancy Theory The original formulation of expectancy theory specifies that the motivational force for choosing a level of effort is a function of the multiplication of expectancies and valences. Recent research demonstrates that the individual components predict performance just as well, without being multiplied. This does not diminish the value of expectancy theory. Recent research also suggests that high performance results not only when the valence is high, but also when employees set difficult goals for themselves.

One last comment on motivation: As the world of work changes, so will the methods organizations use to motivate employees. New rewards—time off instead of bonuses; stock options; on-site gyms, cleaners, and dental services; opportunities to telecommute, and others will need to be created in order to motivate employees in the future. *An Inside Look* at corporate spirituality examines one unusual motivational strategy.

AN INSIDE LOOK

Corporate Spirituality

In the 1990s, corporations began to sense a change in what motivated employees to be successful and productive. Surprisingly, it wasn't 401(k) plans, health or dental benefits that inspired employees most. Instead, studies found that people sought greater personal connection to the pursuits on which they worked. Employees longed to introduce personal concerns and values to their workplace to help them to feel more a part of the organization rather than just a cog in the machine.

Enter corporate spirituality. Spirituality in the workplace is not intended to give employees free reign to attempt to convert those who believe differently than they do. Rather, corporate spirituality implies acknowledging that all employees are spiritual beings who live by a set of core values. If employee values are recognized and incorporated into daily work, then employees should have greater motivation to succeed and to see the organization prosper.

Organizations have not always been comfortable with expression of spirituality in the workplace. Now, however, many companies have instituted a wellness model for the health and development of their employees that encourages not only personal and professional development but also spiritual growth. Participating organizations feel that employees who are better able to balance their work and personal life will be more satisfied, productive, and creative employees.

In some organizations, spirituality is expressed through meditation time at the beginning or end of the day to ease the transition from the workday to home, or vice versa. In other organizations, employees are encouraged to incorporate spiritual values into workgroups and teams. This integration tends to make the teams more cohesive and sensitive to other members' individual approaches and perspectives.

Vancouver City Savings Credit Union (VanCity) focuses on ethics and community as a way of addressing the spiritual needs of both its employees and the community it serves. VanCity stresses its connection to the community in addition to making a profit, demonstrating another key aspect of spirituality—connection. While it can be difficult for large organizations to recognize spirituality, connection to the community at large helps organizations understand how their decisions affect the external environment. Viewing the organization as part of the world as a whole emphasizes the interrelatedness of business and society.

Besides motivating employees to live their values at work and be more invested in their organizations, spirituality in the workplace has other related benefits. One benefit is the accompanying shift from a competitive environment motivated by fear to a more collaborative team-oriented workplace. A collaborative, open workplace is one that promotes creativity and intuition. Another advantage to corporate spirituality is its positive effect on reducing employee turnover due to greater satisfaction. In addition, spiritual thinking can help employees to communicate better with others, a key to success in the fast-paced modern business world. All of these factors combined help organizations reach their peak performance, which benefits not only the organization and its employees, but the community as a whole.

Source: Adapted from J. J. Laabs. 1995. Spirituality at work. *Personnel Journal* 74(9):60–62, 64; and M. Conlin. November 1999. Religion in the workplace: The growing presence of spirituality in corporate America. *Business Week,* 150–158.

WORK MOTIVATION IN REVIEW

This chapter has covered the major motivation theories in organizational behavior. Motivation theories endeavor to explain how people become motivated. Motivation has two major components: direction and intensity. Direction is what a person is trying to achieve. Intensity is the degree of effort a person expends to achieve the target. All motivation theories address the ways in which people develop direction and intensity.

Motivation theories are classified as either content or process theories. Content theories focus on what motivates behavior. The basic premise of content theories is that humans have needs. When these needs are not satisfied, humans are motivated to satisfy the need. The need provides direction for motivation. Murray's manifest needs theory, McClelland's learned needs theory, Maslow's hierarchy of needs, and Herzberg's motivator-hygiene theory are all content theories. Each has something to say about the needs that motivate humans in the workplace.

Process theories focus on how people become motivated. Operant conditioning theory states that people will be motivated to engage in behaviors for which they have been reinforced (rewarded). It also states that people will avoid behaviors that are punished. The rate at which behaviors are rewarded also affects how often they will be displayed. Equity theory's main premise is that people compare their situations to those of other people. If a person feels that they are being treated unfairly relative to a referent other, the person may engage in behaviors that are counterproductive for the organization. Employers should try to develop feelings of fairness in employees. Goal theory is a strong theory. It states that difficult, specific goals will result in high performance if employees accept the goals and are committed to achieving them.

Expectancy theory is a process theory. It also is the broadest of the motivation theories. Expectancy theory predicts that employees will be motivated to be high performers if they perceive that high performance leads to valued outcomes. Employees will be motivated to avoid being low performers if they perceive that it leads to negative outcomes. Employees must perceive that they are capable of achieving high performance, and they must have the appropriate abilities and high self-efficacy. Organizations need to provide adequate resources and to measure performance accurately. Inaccurate performance ratings discourage high performance. Overall, expectancy theory draws attention to how organizations structure the work environment and distribute rewards.

A FINAL LOOK

Once Bridget admits that she's unhappy with her position as a computer programmer, she's ready to explore other possibilities. She and Kyle brainstorm for tasks that will motivate her and bring her greater job satisfaction. Bridget tells Kyle that while she enjoys programming, she feels isolated and misses interacting with other groups in the organization. She also realizes that once she had mastered the initial learning curve, she felt bored. Bridget is ready for a challenge.

Kyle recommends that Bridget move to an information systems team as their technical representative. The team can use Bridget's knowledge of programming, and Bridget will be able to collaborate more frequently with others in the organization.

Bridget and Kyle set specific goals to satisfy her needs to achieve and to work collaboratively. One of Bridget's goals is to take graduate classes in management and information systems. She hopes that this will lead to an MBA and, eventually, to a position as a team leader. Suddenly the prospect of going to work doesn't seem so grim—and lately, Bridget's been beating her alarm!

KEY TERMS

ability, 218
avoidance learning, 237
content motivation theories, 221
direction, 220
effort-performance expectancy, 247
equity theory, 239
ERG theory, 230
expectancy theory, 246
extinction, 236
extrinsic motivation, 234
extrinsic outcomes, 248
goal commitment, 244
goal theory, 243
hedonism, 222
hygienes, 232
input, 239
instincts, 222
intensity, 220
intrinsic motivation, 234
intrinsic outcomes, 248
latent needs, 222
manifest needs, 222
manifest needs theory, 222
motivation, 219
motivators, 232
motive, 224
need for achievement (nAch), 224
need for affiliation (nAff), 225
need for power (nPow), 225
need, 221
negative reinforcement, 237
nonreinforcement, 237
operant conditioning, 236
operant conditioning theory, 236
outcome, 240
overreward inequity, 240
performance environment, 219
performance-outcome expectancy, 247
positive reinforcement, 237
primary needs, 222
process motivation theories, 221
punishment, 237
referent others, 240
reinforcement, 236
role perceptions, 219
schedules of reinforcement, 238
secondary needs, 222
self-determination theory (SDT), 234
self-efficacy, 249
state of equity, 240
underreward inequity, 240
valences, 247
work motivation, 220

ISSUES FOR REVIEW AND DISCUSSION

1. Discuss the benefits that accrue when an organization has a good understanding of employee needs.
2. How might Maslow explain why organizational rewards that motivate workers today may not motivate the same workers in 5 or 10 years?
3. Describe the process by which needs motivate workers.
4. Discuss the importance of Herzberg's motivators and hygienes.
5. Describe a work situation in which it would be appropriate to use a continuous reinforcement schedule.
6. Discuss the potential effectiveness and limitations of punishment in organizations.

7. How can equity theory explain why a person who receives a high salary might be dissatisfied with their pay?
8. Equity theory specifies a number of possible alternatives for reducing perceived inequity. How could an organization influence which of these alternatives a person will pursue?
9. What goals would be most likely to improve your learning and performance in an organizational behavior class?
10. Identify two reasons why a formal goal setting program might be dysfunctional for an organization.
11. What steps can an organization take to increase the motivational force for high levels of performance?
12. Discuss how supervisors sometimes unintentionally weaken employees E → P and P → O expectancies.
13. How can an employee attach high valence to high levels of performance, yet not be motivated to be a high performer?
14. Is there a "one best" motivation theory? Explain your answer.

EXERCISES

DECIDING PAY INCREASES

In the College of Business, all salary changes, including merit increases and cost-of-living adjustments, are decided by the department heads. This year, the dean's office has decided to award a total of $16,000 for salary increases to the six members of the Business Communications department. The names of the six faculty members and some information about them are shown below.

In the past, pay raises have largely been tied to the rate of inflation, and everyone has received about the same percentage increase. The rate of inflation this year has been about 6 percent, and everyone would normally receive a cost-of-living adjustment of at least that amount. However, during its fall retreat, the college's executive committee decided that pay increases should be based primarily on performance rather than on changes in the cost of living. The committee concluded that greater efforts should be made to reward outstanding faculty members for teaching, research, and professional service to the university or to society. When this decision was announced, some of the faculty members objected, and the dean responded that everyone would probably receive some increase, but that weak faculty members might not get enough to keep up with inflation.

Directions. You are the department head who must justify these decisions to faculty members. Decide how you would allocate the $16,000, using the following information. After you have made your decisions, discuss your recommendations with four or five other classmates and try to reach a group consensus based on similar arguments.

Professor	Present Salary	Years of Teaching	Performance Information
Brooks	$44,800	15	Students say he's a horrible teacher. Never keeps his office hours, spends most of his time doing outside consulting, and hasn't written anything but consulting project reports for nine years.
Falco	$32,100	3	Excellent researcher; good teacher of graduate classes; receives mixed evaluations from undergraduate students because most class activities are used to collect research data. Published six articles last year in leading journals.
Aboud	$45,100	12	Students say she's a very good teacher and is also very helpful to students; a member of the College Advisory Council; published three articles last year in practitioner journals and one article in an academic journal

Petlansky	$30,200	2	New to the job; students say she is entertaining in class, but her lectures are weak because she lacks experience; spent first year finishing dissertation and has been working on other research projects since then, but nothing is finished.
O'Neil	$55,600	28	Former associate dean and department head; influential in college politics, but not on any committees; author of three books, including a textbook that he revised eight years ago. Has written nothing in the last four years. Students complain that his lectures are boring and obsolete. He spends much of his time training dogs.
Walker	$52,200	26	Considered an outstanding teacher at graduate and undergraduate levels. Served on several thesis committees last year; involved in two major research projects; has solo-authored two articles and co-authored six; wrote about 40 percent of a textbook last year; serves on the review board for a research journal.

Source: D. J. Cherrington. Copyright © 1989. *Organizational behavior: The management of individual and organizational performance.* Boston: Allyn & Bacon, 243–244. Reprinted by permission of Pearson Education, Inc., Upper Saddle River, NJ 07458.

INFOTRAC

INFOTRAC® COLLEGE EDITION

The articles listed below are a sampling of those available through InfoTrac College Edition. You can search for them either by title or by the author's name.

Articles

1. 6 Degrees of Motivation. Barbara Moses. *Black Enterprise* Nov 2000 v31 i4 p155
2. Motivation by the Book. (Management theory and techniques for employee) (Brief Article) Deanne Bryce. *Training and Development* Nov 2000 v54 i11 p66
3. Jumping the Motivation Hurdle. (Brief Article) Bob Rosner. Workforce Nov 2000 v79 i11 p104
4. On Motivation. Michael R. Maude. *Direct Marketing* Oct 1997 v60 i6 p18
5. Accountability, impression management, and goal setting in the performance evaluation process. Dwight D. Frink, Ferris, Gerald R. *Human Relations* Oct 1998 v51 n10 p1259(25)

Questions

For Article 3:

The article "Jumping the Motivation Hurdle" reports on employees who were asked to look at their motivation and factors that may diminish it. Form a small group and discuss the questions that Bob Rosner, the author, asks. How do these factors apply to your motivation to complete your college education? If you are also employed, how do these factors affect your roles as student and employee?

For Other Articles:

Many of the other articles on this list identify specific, hands-on ways that employers and managers can motivate workers. Have members of your group read them, then discuss the connection between the practical examples offered in the articles and the content and process theories of motivation discussed in this chapter.

WEB EXERCISE

Visit the web site for The Foundation for Enterprise Development (**http://www.fed.org/library/index.html**) to identify the motivational techniques and programs that different organizations employ. The Foundation is a nonprofit organization whose mission is to help managers implement performance enhancement programs. Within its website, look at their "case studies of private (or public) companies." Select one or two companies that interest you. Describe the approach to employee motivation adopted by each organization.

CASE
Delights Restaurant

Jeremiah accepted the job as manager for a restaurant called Delights, located in Washington. It was one of 36 restaurants in a chain with a reputation for having excellent food and loyal employees.

He didn't realize the problems he'd encounter with the employees in his restaurant. Often employees complained to one another about other staff members. For example, the cooks treated the wait staff with little respect, and they made it clear that they didn't like to redo a customer's order. Employees often were impolite to customers and kept them waiting while they talked in the back. Incorrect orders were supposed to go back to the kitchen, but the wait staff often told customers that the cooks complained if orders came back. Turnover was high among the wait staff, and dishwashers normally lasted only a few weeks. Tardiness and absenteeism were common. This caused some employees to put in extra hours to prevent the restaurant from being shorthanded, thus reducing customer service.

Jeremiah's wages were based on salary and a quarterly bonus. His bonus was reflected by the performance of his restaurant. The more money the restaurant made, the more money he made. The flow of customers was fair when he became the new manager, but it slowly began slipping. Jeremiah believed that if his employees would change their behavior, business would pick up again and revenue would increase.

For Discussion

1. Identify and describe the central motivational problems at Delights.
2. Imagine that you are Jeremiah and you have scheduled a meeting with the entire staff. Using the information in Chapter 7, what would you say to the employees at the meeting? What would your plan be to increase motivation among the employees?
3. Which of the major process theories do you think would be most effective in this situation? For example, do you believe Jeremiah needs to make pay more equitable, set goals, or expect more of his employees? Do you believe Jeremiah could use a combination of several of these theories?
4. If you apply the operant conditioning theory, which of the four techniques (positive reinforcement, extinction, punishment, negative reinforcement) is Jeremiah currently using? Do you believe another technique would be more effective in this situation?

Source: Management: Challenges in the 21st century (3rd ed.), *by P. S. Lewis, S. H. Goodman, and P. M. Fandt, copyright 2001. Reprinted with the permission of South-Western, a division of Thomson Learning. Fax 800-730-2215.*

Outline

Individual performance

Withdrawal

Organizational citizenship

Aggression, violence, and civility

Drug and alcohol abuse

Employee behaviors in review

CHAPTER 8

Behavior in Organizations

Learning Objectives

After reading this chapter, you should be able to

1. Define and describe the importance of individual employee performance.
2. Distinguish objective and subjective performance appraisal techniques.
3. Describe a performance improvement plan and identify when it is appropriate to use.
4. Discuss when and how to terminate an employee.
5. Evaluate the belief that satisfaction causes performance.
6. Distinguish physical and psychological withdrawal.
7. Identify major costs associated with absenteeism and turnover, and how to prevent them.
8. Define organizational citizenship behaviors, and describe why organizations depend on them.
9. Describe four types of employee deviance behaviors.
10. Relate deviance behavior categories to workplace violence and aggression, and substance abuse.
11. Describe the manager's role in preventing workplace violence and substance abuse.

A FIRST LOOK

Paul Mercer dreads June, when his annual performance evaluation comes up. In his three years at the bank, Paul has yet to receive anything more than an average evaluation. He knows that co-workers in his group regularly earn above-average and outstanding performance appraisals from Andrea Hartley, their manager, so he can't blame his unimpressive ratings on any tendency of hers to give conservative ratings. He suspects that workplace politics are playing a part in his lackluster ratings, and that bothers him for two reasons: his pride—and he wants to be paid better!

Paul has been unhappy at the bank for a while now and frequently toys with leaving. However, his daughter has acute asthma, and the bank's health insurance covers nearly all of her extensive medical expenses.

Paul is right to dread the performance evaluation. Only this time his dread quickly turns to anger when his manager, Andrea Hartley, accuses him of drug use! Paul does *not* do drugs! He vehemently denies the charge, but Andrea is unmoved and urges him to seek help from the Employee Assistance Program. "If you don't do something about this, we'll have no choice but to take more serious action." Paul leaves, numb with fury. Now there's no doubt, his career *is* being sabotaged.

Questions: Do you think Paul's poor performance evaluations are partially or completely inaccurate? What would you do next if you were Paul? What do you think is going on here?

In this chapter we explore the major behaviors of employees in the workplace. Many managerial practices affect employee behaviors directly and also indirectly through such processes as perception, attitudes, and motivation. The decisions managers make about how the organization is to be run ultimately affect every person in the organization.

http://www.workforce.com

Generally speaking, employees behave in accordance with the motivation theories discussed in Chapter 7. If employees believe that acting in a certain way will lead to desirable outcomes, and also that they can actually perform the behavior, they will attempt to do so (expectancy theory). If employees feel they are underpaid, they will attempt to increase outcomes; these attempts range from asking for a raise to stealing company property (equity theory). If employees have a goal to perform at 125 percent of base performance, they are more likely to do so (goal theory). So, while we talked about behaviors in general terms in the last chapter, now we will focus on specific behaviors that are of particular importance to organizations. These behaviors are performance, withdrawal, organizational citizenship, aggression, and drug abuse. They are important because they directly affect the organization's profitability (see Chapter 6). The more an organization affects these behaviors positively, the stronger its effectiveness and the greater its profitability. If an organization doesn't motivate positive behaviors in its employees, the organization may not survive.

INDIVIDUAL PERFORMANCE

performance the behaviors of organizational members that help meet organizational objectives

Performance Defined

No employee behavior has been researched more than performance. In this text we treat **performance** as the behaviors of organizational members that help the organization meet its objectives. It is the degree to which employees meet the expectations of the organization as they execute the required duties of their jobs. **Effort** is the energy we direct toward achieving an organizational objective. Our performance is the degree to which we meet that objective. As you can see, performance and effort are not the same. High-performing employees behave in ways that produce the results identified as important objectives by the organization. In contrast, low-performing employees do little to help the organization achieve its objectives.

effort the human energy directed toward achieving an organizational objective

Objectives vary as much as organizations. They address quantity, quality, efficiency, waste reduction, customer service, and many other things. Eventually these organizational objectives are reflected in employees' jobs. At the job level we call these objectives job duties. **Job duties** are the activities, tasks, and behaviors expected of anyone performing a particular job. Often these duties are codified in great detail for each job in an organization, in documents called **job descriptions.** Employees are expected to perform their job duties at acceptable levels (in exchange for rewards given to them). These job duties are designed to help the organization achieve its objectives. **Job performance** is how well (or poorly) employees perform their job duties. A job duty can be assembling car parts, or disassembling them (in a recycling organization). Job duties can involve concrete activities (building a product) or abstract activities (supervision, planning, decision making). Performance is how well the line worker assembles or disassembles the car parts and how well the supervisor plans and makes decisions.

job duties the activities, tasks, and behaviors expected of anyone performing a particular job

job description a written document that identifies the job duties for a particular job in an organization

job performance how well (or poorly) employees perform their job duties compared to expectations for the job

As we look to what determines performance, it is important to understand that the determinants of virtually any behavior (performance, withdrawal, aggression) originate in both the person (unmet needs, attitudes, values) and in the situation (time limits, tools, social pressures). Essentially, behavior is the person interacting with the situation:

$$\text{Behavior} = f\,[(\text{Person})(\text{Situation})].$$

Effort is a necessary component of performance: No effort, no performance. Effort alone, however, is not enough; many other factors affect performance. Foremost among them is how skilled individuals are in their job duties. "A hard worker who just doesn't get the job done" is putting in plenty of effort. Effort must be supported by clearly defined job duties (accurate role perceptions) and proper tools (supplies, materials, support systems). If any one of these factors is deficient, performance will be impaired.

The first job of a manager who observes an employee not performing up to expectations is to diagnose the situation. What is causing the performance deficiency? Is it lack of ability, lack of skills, motivation, role perception, resource factors, or something else? Then and only then should the manager take corrective action. Training often solves ability and skill problems, while changing the reward system can improve motivation. Clearly delineating job duties addresses role perception problems. Deficient resources are often oversights and are easily redressed.

Don't always assume that lack of motivation is the only factor in a performance problem (recall the fundamental attribution error from Chapter 5). Figure 8-1 illustrates how different factors come into play in performance. Note that given better resources, Tom's performance improves, but not as much as Cindy's. Their supervisor should consider training or coaching to improve Tom's job-related ability, and new incentives to increase his motivation.

FIGURE 8-1 Sample Performance Improvement Comparison

Tom and Cindy work on identical punch press machines at ACME Tool and Die Works. They both know how to operate their presses, but their skill levels differ. Tom puts a reasonable amount of effort into his work, but his performance is low compared to the other workers (100 punches per hour). Cindy exerts considerably more effort than Tom; she is also more skilled—her punch rate is 150 per hour. On June 27, new punch press machines are installed. Tom's rate on the new machines is 170 punches per hour and Cindy's is 300.

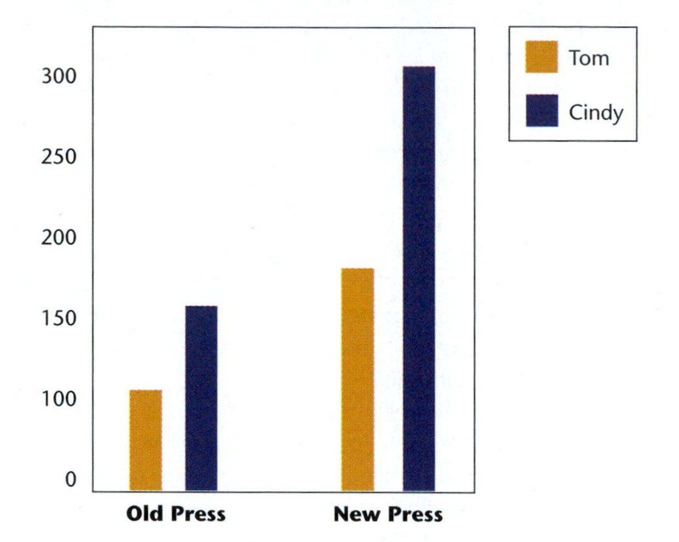

Performance Appraisal

How well is an employee doing? What exactly are they doing well? What needs improvement? Does anyone need to be promoted, warned, or trained? Answering these questions is one of the most important—and most difficult—tasks that managers face. **Performance appraisal** is the process of evaluating how effectively members are fulfilling their job responsibilities and accomplishing organizational goals. It is no surprise that performance appraisal is difficult. To appraise performance accurately and fairly, managers must know the organization's expectations for a job, must monitor the employee's behaviors and results, and must compare and measure these observed behaviors and results against expectations. A crucial part of the appraisal process is feedback, a process that can raise strong (and oftentimes negative) feelings.

performance appraisal the process of evaluating how effectively members are fulfilling their job responsibilities and contributing to organizational goals

Although difficult to conduct, it goes without saying that performance appraisals, in whatever form they take, are extremely important to organizations. They tell organizations whether their hiring standards are effective. They show where training, development, and motivational programs are needed and later gauge whether these have been effective. In fact, many organizational policies and practices are evaluated, in large part, through their impact on performance. Performance appraisals, after all, are the basis for decisions about compensation, promotion, and dismissal. Organizations also use the appraisal interview to recognize jobs done well and to motivate employees. In short, without performance appraisals, it would be very difficult to identify and encourage organizational

© R. W. JONES/CORBIS

The essay method of performance appraisal gives the employee a personalized description of what they do well and what they need to do to improve.

effectiveness. Because formal appraisals are so important, the vast majority of organizations conduct them.[1]

In traditional organizations managers alone assess a worker's behavior. In high-involvement organizations, appraisals are conducted by team members, peers, suppliers, customers, employees from other departments, and upper-level managers. This empowers the work force, increasing both their sense of ownership and the effectiveness of the organization. Management's role in such situations is to see that the appraisals are conducted in a valid and responsible manner. Receiving feedback from a number of sources (peers, subordinates, and so on) is called multi-rater, or **360° feedback.**[2] Many successful companies, like Merck, have implemented 360° programs.

360° feedback occurs when employees (especially managers) receive feedback from a number of sources

http://www.three-sixty.com

Appraisal Techniques Managers compare actual to expected performance in two ways. They assess an employee's output through *objective methods* using verifiable physical objects or events. Objective appraisal methods require "counting things." One objective measure used by the Producers Color Lab in Detroit, for example, counts the number of frames of film processed. Sales performance is measured by units or dollars of product or service sold. Banking institutions such as First Chicago and Wells Fargo have found that cost management assessments provide good, objective measures of performance.[3] Objective methods are useful because numbers are readily understood and easy to explain.

subjective performance appraisal methods include all of those performance appraisal methods that require one employee (usually a manager) to rate another employee

graphic rating scale a method of performance appraisal that requires the rater to judge the performance of the ratee on dimensions (criteria) using scaled standards (poor, excellent, etc.)

For many jobs, however, objective measures are neither possible nor adequate. In some jobs, performance is the combined effort of many workers. How is a manager to determine who made the car at a General Motors plant? Hundreds of workers assemble any given car, and thousands more are responsible for the design, delivery, and sale of the vehicle. In other cases, an objective count does little to inform the manager and employee on the quality of performance. An artist's performance, for example, is not judged on the number of paintings completed in a year. For these reasons, managers also use subjective methods to judge performance. **Subjective performance appraisal methods** include all of those methods that require one person rating another. Total Quality Management, for example, defines performance as meeting customers' expectations; this is a subjective measure.

There are many types of subjective appraisal methods. The most frequently used method is the graphic rating scale (also called a traditional rating method). **Graphic rating scales** require the rater to rate performance on criteria using descriptive standards (poor, excellent). Figure 8-2 shows a completed graphic rating scale.[4] Graphic rating scales often use broad criteria (like quality) that apply

FIGURE 8-2 Graphic Rating Scale

Sloan Tool & Die, Inc.
Duluth, Minnesota

Employee Rating Scale

Employee: Javier Alva
Department: Accounting
Rated by: Irene Muharsky
Date: 3/17/01

Behavior:	Unsatisfactory	Questionable	Satisfactory	Outstanding
A. Quantity of work	1	2	3	(4)
B. Quality of work	1	2	(3)	4
C. Work initiative	1	(2)	3	4
D. Efficiency	1	2	(3)	4
E. Overall	1	2	(3)	4

to a wide variety of jobs. Organizations can thus compare performance across different jobs (a welder versus a word processor). However, such flexibility comes at a cost, as it makes graphic rating scales susceptible to a wide variety of errors. Therefore, they should rarely be used by themselves. Also, graphic rating scales are not especially effective at describing items for specific feedback. For example, what exactly does the "3" in quality of performance mean in Figure 8-2? The scale doesn't identify what the employee can do differently to become a "4."

Another widely used subjective appraisal method is the essay. Essays require the evaluator to write a narrative about employee strengths and weaknesses, as well as ways they can improve their job performance. The **essay method** gives employees a detailed description of what they do well on their job, what they don't do well, and what they need to do in the future to improve. Essays are an excellent way to provide feedback. On the other hand, no two essays are the same. This makes comparing different employees difficult. In addition, managers often resist writing essays. They are time-consuming, intellectually demanding, and require careful, ongoing record-keeping on the part of the manager. Many managers procrastinate when it comes to writing performance essays, so evaluations don't always happen in a timely manner.

essay method of performance appraisal requires the rater to write a narrative about the employee's performance strengths and weaknesses, as well as ways the employee can improve job performance

Using the graphic rating scale and essay together plays to the strengths of both methods and rounds out the appraisal process. Rating every employee on a scale like the one in Figure 8-2 also focuses the manager's thoughts, making it easier to write the paragraphs that both explain and justify the ratings and also tell employees what they need to do differently to earn a higher rating.

Behaviorally anchored rating scales (BARS) are intended to improve the accuracy and usefulness of graphic rating scales.[5] BARS use a scale for each relevant dimension of performance, but each scale has explicit behavioral anchors, which describe specific and observable behaviors that reflect varying degrees of performance effectiveness. The evaluator chooses the description most characteristic of an employee's actual performance (see Figure 8-3). However, the BARS approach is a complex and expensive performance appraisal method relative to graphic rating scales and essays.

behaviorally anchored rating scales (BARS) use a scale for each relevant dimension of performance, but each scale has explicit behavioral anchors

FIGURE 8-3 Sample of a Behaviorally Anchored Rating Scale

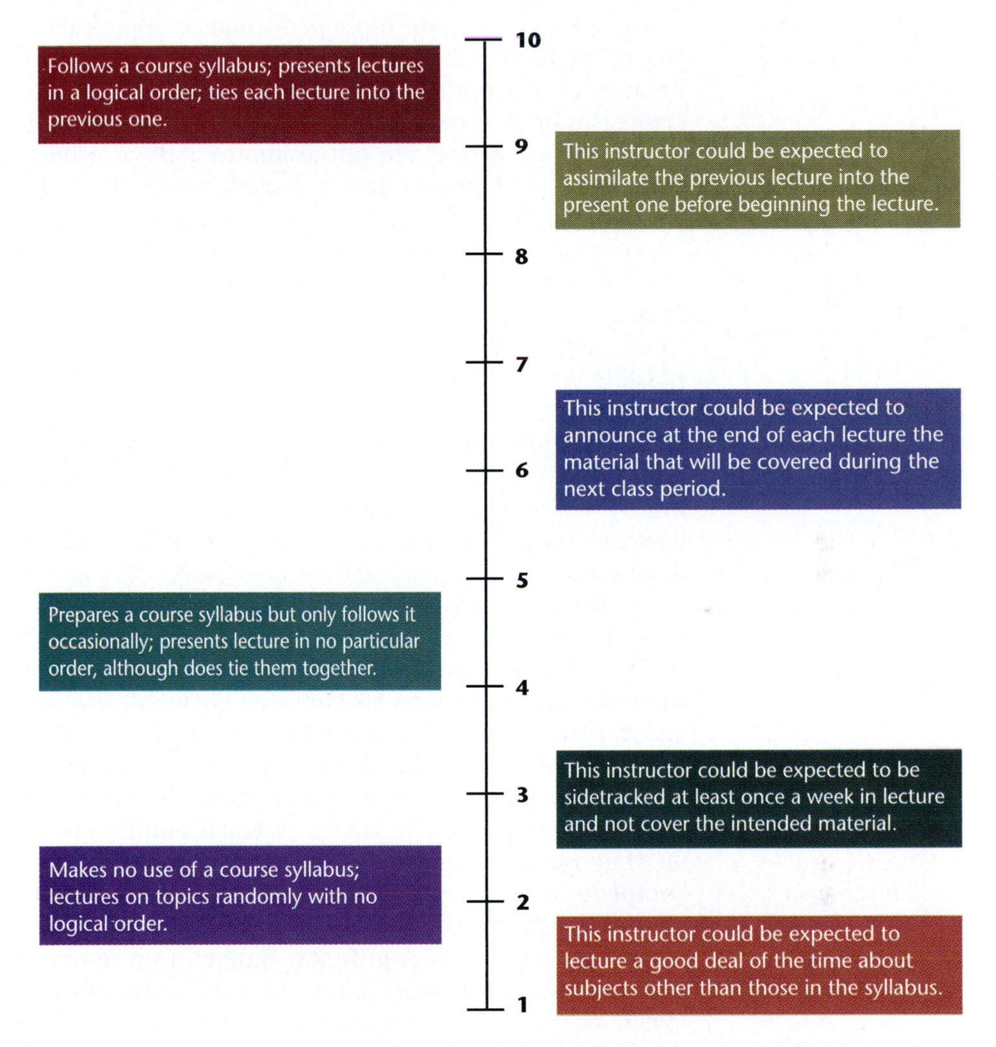

Source: Adapted from H. J. Bernardin. 1977. Behavioral expectation scales versus summated scales: A fairer comparison. *Journal of Applied Psychology* 62:422–477.

comparative method of performance appraisal requires supervisors to compare the performance of each worker to the performance of all co-workers

Other subjective approaches include the **comparative method**, in which supervisors compare each worker's performance to those of co-workers. Employees' performance is ranked in one of two ways. *Straight ranking* simply lists the employees from best to worst. Thus, ten employees would be ranked from "1" (best) to "10" (worst). With *forced distribution,* supervisors create categories (such as average, above average, and superior) and then place a certain number of employees into each category. There are major problems with comparative approaches. They are poor for feedback by themselves (what does it mean to be ranked 5 out of 10?). They assume there is a best (excellent) and worst (poor) employee in each work group when this may not be true. The lowest ranked employee in a work group might be quite satisfactory, just not as good as the others.

Plus, comparative methods assume that all work groups are equally effective. Comparative methods assume that the best employee in group A is equal in performance to the best employee in group B. This may not be true, and probably is only rarely true.

rater error occurs when an employee's performance rating does not reflect their true or actual performance level

Rater Errors Because most performance appraisals rely in large part on subjective methods, they are influenced by the perceptions of the raters, and because of perceptual problems (discussed in Chapter 5), subsequent rating errors can arise. One of the biggest problems with performance appraisal is the fact that most people are not accurate raters of others' performance. When an employee's performance rating doesn't reflect their true or actual performance, we say a **rater error** has occurred. Thousands of studies have been conducted on rater errors and ways to prevent them. When performance appraisal systems don't measure performance well, employees will ignore or reject the ratings, making the whole process irrelevant. Organizational behavior researchers have thus endeavored over the years to make the process as foolproof and valid as possible, and in doing so have identified the most common rater errors.[6]

Halo/Horn. This error occurs when the rater gives the person similar scores on each scale. For example, the rater might give the employee all 5s (outstanding) when he or she is actually outstanding on some dimensions, but only satisfactory on others. This is a halo error. When the ratings are all low, it is a horn error.

Central Tendency, Leniency, and Severity. These errors occur when the rater is required to rate a number of employees using the same set of scales (like those in Figure 8-2). However, the rater may give everyone in the group about the same scores—that is, all high (leniency), all low (severity), or all about average (central tendency)—despite the fact that they did not perform at the same level. This is often unintentional. The rater is unaware that they are clustering the performance ratings. In other cases, managers commit rater errors intentionally. Perhaps they're trying to teach employees a "lesson" (severity error). Or, they want to avoid conflict ("everyone gets the same ratings, so nobody can complain"). Or they don't want to justify their ratings ("it makes me uncomfortable"). If everyone gets a high rating (leniency error), who is likely to complain? These cluster errors in time end up motivating no one. The highest performers are discouraged because their extra effort means nothing, and the lowest performers have no incentive to improve.

Politics and Prejudice. Managers sometimes intentionally bias ratings to achieve political objectives. Perhaps they want to help a valued employee get promoted. Perhaps they want to get rid of someone they don't like. Intentionally biasing ratings in this manner is not always a bad situation for organizations. When performance appraisals communicate a message about behaviors and attitudes that aren't necessarily impacting performance but that are undesirable (like complaining too much), they can still be effective.[7] On the other hand, when managers give employees low ratings for reasons unrelated to work (be it personal dislike or because of their sex, age, or race) it reduces work unit effectiveness—and it is usually illegal.

Problems with performance ratings can arise for reasons other than rater error. One of the most severe problems occurs when the ratings are unreliable. This can happen when more than one rater is evaluating the same person, particularly if they are using different techniques. Some raters are more lenient than the others. Some do not like to differentiate among employees. When multiple ratings diverge significantly, problems arise. Whose rating is correct?

http://www.goodperformance.com

Managing Appraisal Problems. How can managers and employees do a better job of appraising performance? Improvements require an integrated set of actions. First, raters should be taught to recognize and avoid the pitfalls just discussed. Rating instruments must also be improved and raters trained in how to use them properly. Then, dimensions of performance and the scales for rating them must be described in unambiguous terms. The rating procedures should be standardized, and the raters expected to follow them. Finally, top-level managers must recognize that rating performance is an important part of every manager's job, and they must assess managers in part on how effectively they perform this task. Pay and promotions for managers should also be based, in part, on the effectiveness of their performance appraisals.

Improving Performance

It's easy to overstate problems in the performance appraisal process. But the reality is that in most organizations, performance appraisal systems achieve their goals reasonably well; otherwise, the practice would not be nearly as widespread as it is. If performance appraisals were consistently and substantially inaccurate, they would have been dropped long ago like numerous management fads of the last 100 years (remember sensitivity training groups?). Most performance ratings are more accurate than inaccurate, or human resources departments would be inundated with grievances about them.

http://opm.gov/perform/overview.htm

When consistently high performers are identified, we know from motivation theories (see Chapter 7) how to work with them. Organizations strive to reward them (in any number of ways) so that they continue to be high performers. Good managers realize that high performers usually have long-term plans; they intend to rise up through the organization by way of promotions and strategic transfers. Good managers will not only reinforce past superior performance, but will also help such employees develop a plan to acquire the knowledge and skills they will need in future, higher-level positions in the organization. Career plans may actually be written down and put in employees' personnel files.

When consistently poor performers are identified, the manager's job is much more difficult. From motivation theories we know that deficient performance should not be rewarded, especially when the poor performance is caused by lack of effort. Reinforcing undesirable work behaviors does not extinguish them. However, sometimes the withholding of rewards by itself does not motivate poor performers to become better performers. In some situations poor performance might be caused by lack of training or inadequate resources. If such employees don't have the skills they need to perform at a satisfactory level, training programs may be in order. In other cases, transferring them to jobs that better utilize their existing skills may be the answer. Making sure they have adequate physical, financial, and time resources may also solve the problem.

performance improvement plan
a formal agreement between a manager and an employee that covers (1) the employee's performance problem, (2) why performance is deficient, and (3) what the employee must do and by when to eliminate the performance problem

Confronting employees with their motivation problems and trying to help them improve is always challenging. When poor performance is caused by a lack of motivation (or effort), as opposed to lack of skills or resources, performance improvement plans can help. A **performance improvement plan** is a formal agreement between a manager and an employee that covers (1) the employee's performance problem, (2) why performance is deficient, and (3) what the employee must do and by when to eliminate the problem. In practice, the manager must meet with the employee first to discuss the problem. After the employee and the manager agree that a performance problem exists, they then try to identify the cause. Once that is agreed on, together they develop plans for the employee to implement that should eliminate the problem. In some cases the employee simply agrees to try harder not to engage in counterproductive work behaviors. In other cases the employee might be given a goal, such as no unexcused absences for the next six months. Once all of this is decided, including the deadline by which the employee must improve performance, the plan is put into writing and both the manager and employee sign the plan. If the employee does not improve by the deadline, in accordance with the plan, then the employee will be subject to discipline, up to and including termination. If the employee refuses to discuss the problem with the manager, or refuses to sign the plan, then the employee can be subjected to immediate discipline.

The performance improvement plan has come to be an invaluable management tool, especially in American companies. It is a rational approach to what can be an emotionally charged situation. It is also helpful in responding to employee litigation, which we discuss below under termination.

Performance improvement plans also help managers implement the major guidelines from expectancy theory (see Chapter 7). They identify what behaviors are required for different performance levels. They address the effort → performance expectancies. They cover actions that can affect the effort → performance contingencies. And they increase the positive valence of satisfactory performance, and make the valence of poor performance quite negative. Performance improvement plans demonstrate the practical uses of expectancy theory and underscore why it is such a useful tool for managers.

Termination

On rare occasions a manager is not able to improve the performance of a problem employee. Such employees may require termination ("firing") for at least two reasons. First, they are costing the organization money. Second, problem employees are "bad examples"; even if their work behavior is not copied, they can still cause morale problems.

termination the unilateral canceling of an employment contract by an organization, whether the contract is written or not

Termination is the unilateral canceling of an employment contract by an organization, whether the contract is written or not. When an employee is terminated, the employee no longer works for the organization, and of course no longer receives a paycheck. Indeed, the former employee is usually not welcome in company facilities after termination. Termination is considered the "capital punishment of the workplace" because of its severity and finality within the work context. As such, it should always be considered as an option of last resort in dealing with poor performers.

Managers should follow certain guidelines before terminating any employee:[8]

1. Never summarily discharge. That is, never terminate "on the spot" (immediate discharge). Even if an employee is caught in the act of stealing, it is prudent to send the employee home for the day to allow you time to investigate the situation and to consider alternatives (such as progressive discipline). One instance of inadequate performance (such as being late for work) is not grounds for termination. Poor performance should be documented over time, and the discipline should be commensurate with the infraction.

Employees should almost never be terminated while you are emotionally charged, which clouds judgment.

2. Get all the facts and document them. Before confronting a poor performer, you should have a written record, including dates if possible, of the occasions the employee engaged in unsatisfactory work behaviors. Be prepared to prove to the employee (and potentially others) that the employee's performance is deficient.
3. Conduct discussions with the employee with care and deliberation. A good manager will focus on the performance problem and less so on the employee. Endeavor to work with the employee to identify the cause of the performance problems. If the discussion deteriorates into a name-calling, emotionally charged yelling contest, you have failed both the organization and the employee. The problem will remain and nothing will have been resolved.
4. Don't delay. Ignoring a performance problem only increases the potential for unproductive confrontations. And document, document, document. It is imperative to do so as the situation unfolds; waiting until later does not build solid and effective documentation.
5. Use a "final filter." It is always wise to have an impartial third party assess the situation to ensure that justice is being served for the employee and for the employer. Usually this is someone in the human resources department, who reviews your notes and the performance improvement plan(s). It may also be an attorney used by the employer in discrimination lawsuits.
6. Make clear the cause of the discharge. If a performance improvement plan has failed to improve employee performance, then refer to the plan as the basis for the termination. Be specific when identifying the cause of a termination.
7. Inform the employee personally that you are terminating them. There should be no surprises at this point if you have followed the recommendations above. This is never a pleasant task, but it is your task and not someone else's. You can reiterate the reasons for the termination and allay any doubts that the employee has indeed been terminated.

   Endeavor to preserve the dignity of the employee. Employees who feel humiliated by the termination meeting are more likely to seek revenge by filing a wrongful termination or discrimination lawsuit against the employer, or by destroying company property. Managers must be alert to the possibility of *wrongful termination* or *wrongful discharge* lawsuits, which can be expensive even if the organization wins, and cost millions of dollars if the organization loses. For this reason, organizations handle terminations very carefully. Managers must provide documentation that demonstrates beyond any reasonable doubt that the employee's performance was in fact deficient, caused by a lack of effort, and that the employee refused to improve. Performance improvement plans help managers prevent wrongful termination lawsuits.

The Satisfaction-Performance Relationship

Happy workers are more productive than unhappy workers, right? This statement appeals to our common sense. If employees are happy with their jobs, they should be motivated to perform them to the best of their abilities (and resources). Similarly, if employees approach work each day with a sense of despair and gloom, we might predict that they aren't all that eager to perform their job duties at a high level of excellence. This is sometimes called the "happy worker thesis" and was the basis for the Human Relations Movement (see Chapter 2). Because the Human Relations Movement is not widely practiced anymore, one might infer that the happy worker thesis is wrong. By and large, that inference would be correct. Hundreds of studies in organizational behavior have measured workers' job satisfaction levels (see Chapter 6) and then compared them with supervisory ratings or objective measures of performance for those workers. In the majority of situations, the correlation is weak or nonexistent.[9] When researchers test the happy worker thesis with scientific methods, it is usually disproved.

Why would such a commonsense notion be consistently proven false? There are a number of reasons:

1. For reasons detailed above, performance of employees is not always measured with a high degree of accuracy. Performance appraisals are often inaccurate. If researchers correlate job satisfaction with inaccurate ratings, they are not testing the happy worker thesis. They are correlating employee satisfaction with managers' ratings, and the latter don't always reflect employee performance.
2. Employees don't always have the resources they need to perform their jobs. A happy worker might be highly motivated to perform well. But if he or she doesn't have the tools necessary to perform, then high performance will not be possible.
3. Some jobs aren't amenable to high performance. Imagine employees working along a Ford Motor Company assembly line in Dearborn, Michigan. No matter how happy or motivated they may be, they can only work as fast as the assembly line moves.
4. A worker may derive satisfaction on the job from facets that are unrelated to performance levels. For example, a worker might enjoy her colleagues and supervisor, yet be the worst performer in the work group. The highest performer, in contrast, may dislike the working conditions and the fact that he often has to work on weekends. Situations like this, if common, tend to disprove a relationship between satisfaction and performance.
5. The Total Quality Management (TQM) approach to organization management also argues that individual employee performance levels are due to what are called system factors.[10] **System factors** are impediments to job performance over which employees have no direct control. Equipment breakdowns and seasonal demand for a company's products are examples of system factors. Many TQM advocates state that 80 percent of the differences in performance across workers is not under worker control. Factoring out first system factors and then differences in ability leaves little in performance that is accounted for by employee motivation. Therefore, TQM advocates assert that if motivation doesn't account for much of employee performance, it doesn't matter how happy the employees are. This assertion has not been thoroughly tested in organizational behavior research, and has been challenged.[11] In fact, were it to prove true, it would not make much sense for organizations to put time or effort into screening applicants for jobs! Nevertheless, TQM reminds us how important system factors are in job performance. Managers need to acknowledge this when appraising performance.

system factors
impediments to job performance over which the employee has no direct control

Despite the foregoing, the happy worker thesis has not been laid entirely to rest:

1. While a great number of studies establish the validity of job satisfaction measures (see Chapter 6), those measures may not measure happiness. Instead, they measure employees' affective (like/dislike) reactions to various facets of the work environment. The latter may not get at the core of what it means to be happy. Recent research suggests that when pure trait measures of happiness ("dispositional positive affect") are used, there are correlations between happiness and performance.[12] On the other hand, people who consistently have positive moods are also viewed by others as being energetic, enthusiastic, and task focused. Perhaps we falsely assume that they are also better job performers, when in fact they are not.
2. Correlations between job satisfaction and performance have been obtained in situations where employers measure performance accurately and give larger rewards to high performers. As a result, high performers are happier with their jobs. This turns around the happy worker thesis: High performance leads to happy workers!

Whether or not satisfaction leads to performance is still debated; that is, the research is not conclusive. However, because job satisfaction is consistently related to such employee behaviors as absenteeism and turnover, it behooves managers to create agreeable work environments. Moreover, happy employees are just more pleasant to work with than disgruntled employees.[13]

WITHDRAWAL

Individual performance continues to be a major focus of research in organizational behavior. That is because organizational behavior researchers have an implicit goal to improve the work lives of employees as well as to help organizations become more effective. All else constant, high performing employees are better adjusted to work life. Organizational behavior researchers thus continue to endeavor to understand the hows and whys of performance because the global marketplace allows no one to rest on the laurels of excellent *past* performance. Continual improvement in performance is a must.

withdrawal the physical and/or psychological avoidance by employees of their workplace

Another set of employee behaviors and attitudes—*withdrawal*—contributes to (or detracts from) organizational effectiveness. **Withdrawal** is the physical and/or psychological avoidance by employees of their workplace. Generally speaking, employees will avoid their workplace when they are dissatisfied with one or more aspects of the organization. At first they might try to change the work feature that is causing dissatisfaction (recall equity theory from Chapter 7). They might, for example, ask for a pay raise. If attempts to change the work environment fail, then they begin to withdraw from it.

physical withdrawal the act of physically removing oneself from the work environment through such behaviors as tardiness, absence, and turnover

Employees withdraw from the workplace in two major ways. The first is through **physical withdrawal**, the act of physically removing oneself from the work environment through such behaviors as tardiness, absenteeism, and turnover. Employees engage in physical withdrawal to prevent themselves from experiencing the negative aspects of their work environments. If they are not at work, they don't experience the offensive situation and thus reduce or postpone their feelings of distress. When employees cannot find acceptable alternative employment (turnover), they may become habitually tardy and absent, within the limits of company policy.

psychological withdrawal a mental state in which an employee is disengaged from the work environment

Employees also withdraw psychologically from the workplace. **Psychological withdrawal** is a mental state in which an employee is disengaged from the work environment. Psychologically withdrawn employees are physically present, but their "minds are elsewhere." They do just enough work to get by. Psychologically withdrawn employees are not interested in improving themselves or their job performance, or in helping the organization achieve its goals, nor do they care to socialize with their co-workers. They have neither job nor work involvement (see Chapter 6). Research has shown that employees who don't think very much about their jobs (they think about other things) are less likely to react to either good or bad features of the workplace (like supervision).[14] Psychologically withdrawn workers would prefer to be absent, but cannot for fear of losing their jobs. As you might expect, psychologically withdrawn employees often terminate their employment (physically withdraw) as soon as they find acceptable alternative employment.

absenteeism occurs when an employee does not report to work when scheduled

excused absences are those in which employees notify their employer in advance that they will not be at work on a given day, and the employer approves of the absence

unexcused absences occur when an employee, with no advance approval, simply fails to show up for work when scheduled

voluntary absenteeism occurs when an employee chooses not to go to work when they could have (they are not ill) and should have (they were expected)

involuntary absenteeism occurs when an employee is absent because of illness or factors out of the employee's direct control

Physical Withdrawal

The two major manifestations of physical withdrawal are absence and turnover. Because absenteeism and turnover are very costly to employers, and reflect a dissatisfied state on the part of employees, we explore them in some detail.

Absence **Absenteeism** occurs when employees habitually do not report to work when scheduled.[15] Tardiness may be considered a form of absenteeism in that the employee reports to work late. Less is known about the causes and consequences of tardiness than absenteeism. Because many jobs are paid a salary instead of an hourly wage, employers typically don't keep records of when salaried employees start and stop work. Workers paid by the hour do keep such records (they "punch a clock"), but they can make up for being late by working longer than scheduled at the end of the day. As a result, data on tardiness tends to be variable in quality and availability.

Much more is known about absenteeism. Most organizations differentiate between "excused" and "unexcused" absences. **Excused absences** are those in which employees notify their employer in advance that they won't be at work on a given day, and the employer approves of the absence (such as when the employee is scheduled for surgery). **Unexcused absences** are more problematic and are of greater concern to organizations. They occur when employees, with no advance approval, simply fail to show up for work when scheduled. Of course, many unscheduled absences have legitimate reasons—illness, for example. When the reasons given cannot be verified or are untrue, the absence is considered unexcused. Around 25 percent of American workers admit to "calling in sick" at least once per year when in fact they are not ill and simply want to do something else instead of attending work.[16] **Voluntary absenteeism** occurs when employees choose not to go to work when they could have (they are not ill) and should have (they were expected). It may be excused or unexcused, but reflects discretion on the part of the employee. **Involuntary absenteeism** occurs when employees are absent because of illness or factors out of their direct control (such as a car accident on the way to work). These employees would prefer to attend work but are unable to do so.

Absenteeism Costs. Unexcused absences are a major problem. In the United States, on any given day, approximately 1.8 percent of employees are not at work when they are scheduled to be.[17] Absenteeism is thus an expensive employee behavior. Table 8-1 highlights just how expensive absenteeism is. It is not unusual to see estimates of $500 per day for each instance of absence in the United States. Using the 1.8 percent figure means that, for the typical 500-employee company, absenteeism costs about $4,500 per day, or $1,170,000 annually!

What are the most consistent causes of absenteeism? A recent review of research on absenteeism is unequivocal.[18] Long-term causes include depression, smoking, alcohol abuse, drug abuse, and lack of exercise. Intermediate-term causes include job dissatisfaction, low job involvement and low organizational commitment, monotonous work, work group norms that encourage absence, and inflexible work hours. Short-term causes include lack of attendance incentives, unhealthy employees, and lack of work group pressure to attend. Organizations can address many of these causes by simultaneously encouraging attendance and discouraging absence. Methods include:

1. periodically surveying employee job and work attitudes and striving to resolve known sources of dissatisfaction (see Chapters 6 and 18)
2. implementing flexible work schedules for employees such that they can be absent (with permission) on some days but make up the time on other days
3. creating incentives for attendance; offering individual and/or groups of employees rewards (bonuses, gift certificates, merchandise) for good attendance records
4. initiating employee involvement programs that give workers greater levels of autonomy, responsibility, and participation in the organization
5. promoting and subsidizing employee wellness programs, which help employees lose weight, quit smoking, resolve drug addictions, and so on
6. keeping accurate attendance records and using progressive discipline for employees who are absent excessively
7. ensuring that the workplace is clean and safe so that employees don't fear for their health when they come to work

TABLE 8-1 Costs Associated with Employee Absenteeism

- Pay for time not worked (when the absence is paid through sick leave policies)
- Benefits payments
- Premium pay for temporary workers who substitute for the absent worker
- Premium pay for overtime as co-workers make up for the lost productivity of the absent worker
- Salaries and benefits for supervisors who have added administrative tasks associated with the absence
- Underutilized facilities (overhead is paid even when employees are absent)
- Substandard quantity and quality of production (substitute workers are rarely as productive as an experienced but absent worker)
- Increased inspection and supervision costs

Many of these recommendations are, of course, just good management practices that we offer as examples throughout this textbook. Managing absenteeism is one more example of effective management practices and policies.

turnover occurs when an employee or employer cancels the employment relationship

involuntary turnover occurs when the organization, against an employee's preferences, discontinues their employment

Turnover **Turnover** occurs when an employee or employer cancels the employment relationship. The rate of turnover is very important because a stable work force is key to high productivity. Hiring and training new employees and going through their learning curve is expensive. If a company has a high rate of turnover, something is wrong. Like absenteeism, there are two types of turnover. **Involuntary turnover** occurs when the organization, against employee preferences, discontinues the employment of an individual. With the exception of the death of an employee, involuntary turnover is initiated by an organization. There are a number of reasons why an organization might terminate an employee. As discussed above, one major reason is that the employee has failed to perform their job up to expectations. After being given a chance to improve (perhaps guided by a performance improvement plan), the employee continues to perform at an unacceptable level. Poor performance cannot be tolerated by an organization, and as a result the employee is terminated to eliminate the problem. Another major reason for involuntary turnover is financial duress. Downsizing and layoffs occur because an industry may be experiencing a long- or short-term decline, technology may be eliminating jobs—any number of reasons can precipitate large-scale terminations. In such cases, employees are usually chosen for termination in one of two ways: (1) through seniority, with the most recent hires being terminated first, and (2) through special monetary incentives for voluntary resignations. The "golden parachute" retirement incentive plans are examples of the latter method.

voluntary turnover occurs when the employee chooses to leave an organization

The second type of turnover—**voluntary turnover**—occurs when employees choose to leave the organization for other jobs. Here it is the employee, not the organization, who initiates the termination. This occurs for three reasons: (1) changes in circumstance (serious illness, planned retirement, spousal relocation, and so on—employers can usually do little to prevent this type of attrition), (2) employees secure jobs with different employers, or (3) employees quit because they are unhappy with their present work situation. The second and third reasons are areas of concern for the organization. Employees are telegraphing that jobs with other employers and unemployment are more attractive than staying with their current company. Employers compete for good employees, and keeping them is a major goal. Thus, it is crucial for organizations to ferret out the reasons behind high rates of voluntary turnover.

avoidable voluntary turnover occurs when a valuable employee elects to leave the organization and the employer could have prevented it by improving the employee's work conditions

Sometimes, what appears to be voluntary turnover really is not. Employees whose performance has been inadequate may elect to resign rather than suffer the embarrassment of termination, and they may thereby also get severance pay. Avoidable voluntary turnover, however, is a different situation altogether. **Avoidable voluntary turnover** occurs when employers can reduce the turnover rate by improving work conditions. This is the worst kind of turnover. Organizations lose substantial amounts of money when valuable employees leave (discussed later in this chapter). Organizations must incur both cost and uncertainty as they endeavor to replace capable employees. New employees are unknown commodities—there is no guarantee that they will perform as well as those they're replacing. Perhaps they will, but in the meantime, the organization faces uncertainty, something they try to avoid (see Chapter 9). As a result,

TABLE 8-2 Correlates and Causes of Turnover

Personal Characteristics	Effect on Turnover
Family responsibilities	Negative
Age	Negative
Tenure	Negative
Job-Related Factors	
Job satisfaction	Negative
Organizational commitment	Negative
Job involvement	Negative
Met expectations	Negative
Quality of supervision	Negative
Work group cohesion	Negative
Satisfaction with co-workers	Negative
Accurate role perceptions	Negative
Role overload	Positive
Role conflict	Positive
Job stress	Positive
Satisfaction with promotions	Negative
Actual number of promotions	Negative
Challenging work	Negative
Withdrawal Behavior	
Attractive alternative employment	Positive
Intent to search for other work	Positive
Intent to quit	Positive
Previous absenteeism	Positive
Quality of performance	Negative

Source: P. W. Hom and R. W. Griffeth. 1995. *Employee turnover.* Cincinnati: South-Western.

a great deal of research focuses on the causes and prevention of avoidable voluntary turnover.

A review of the existing research on turnover identifies several consistent and strong predictors, which are shown in Table 8-2.[19] Note that some of the following predictors are under an organization's control (job satisfaction) while others are not (family responsibilities).

- *Personal Characteristics.* Employees with more children and who are married, for example, are less likely to quit. Older and more tenured employees are also less likely to resign. In general, personal characteristics that tend to bind employees to organizations—that is, needs for financial stability or lack of attractive job alternatives—decrease the probability of turnover.
- *Job-Related Factors.* Consistent with much of the previous discussion, job satisfaction is by far the strongest predictor of turnover in this group. Less satisfied employees, especially those dissatisfied with promotion opportunities, are most likely to quit. To a lesser extent, whether jobs meet expectations also predicts turnover. This is followed in strength by lack of job

involvement (see Chapter 6) and lack of job challenge (see Chapter 16). These are factors that organizations have some control over.

- *Withdrawal Behaviors.* Whether employees perceive that desirable jobs are available elsewhere is a strong predictor of their quitting. Thus, good job markets bring higher rates of turnover as the marketplace competes for a too-small supply of employees. When employees perceive few or no alternatives to their current jobs, they are less likely to quit.

  Another strong predictor of turnover is intent to quit, along with thoughts about quitting and intent to search for other jobs. These results are consistent with our discussion in Chapter 6 on attitudes. Intent to engage in some behavior is one of the best predictors of that behavior.

  Employees who are frequently absent are also more likely to quit, for two reasons. One, they usually have to be absent from work as they look for other jobs. Second, as noted earlier, frequently absent employees find their work environments distressing, and the ultimate way to avoid it is to quit. Hom and Griffeth also include job performance in this category. As expected, better job performers are less likely to quit than poor job performers.

In sum the research confirms that employees who are dissatisfied with one or more aspects of their work environment, or are poor performers, are more likely to quit their jobs.

It is worth noting that a recent line of research challenges the idea that most avoidable turnover is precipitated by job dissatisfaction.[20] T. W. Lee and colleagues have found that most turnover is caused by a "shock"—a life event that can be positive, negative, or neutral, and expected or unexpected. Getting married or pregnant, having a child, receiving an unsolicited job offer, and company mergers are all examples of shocks. In some cases, employees may have made employment decisions in advance of the "shock," such as when a woman plans to leave the work force after getting pregnant. The key feature of shocks is that they stimulate employees to evaluate their current job situation, and may motivate them to seek alternative jobs. According to Lee et al., only about 28 percent of their sample (accountants) left their jobs because of ongoing job dissatisfaction. However, only two studies have examined this model, so it remains to be seen whether this view of turnover becomes widely accepted. It nevertheless has provoked new ways of thinking about the turnover process.

Turnover Costs. Turnover is expensive. Consider the actual and/or potential costs of turnover (see Table 8-3).[21] It is not unusual to find total replacement costs for a professional employee to be in the $75,000 to $150,000 range. Coupled with the fact that, in the United States, turnover is averaging 1.3 percent per month, or 15.6 percent per year, the annual costs of turnover can easily reach into the millions for larger organizations.[22]

http://www.employee-satisfaction-surveys.com

How can employers prevent costly turnover? As you might suspect, strategies that prevent absence (a physical withdrawal behavior) also prevent turnover (another physical withdrawal behavior). Regular use of employee attitude surveys can pinpoint factors in the organization that are causing widespread dissatisfaction, and subsequent turnover. Surveys that focus on which facets of the organization are failing to meet employee expectations also show promise.[23] Likewise, flexible work schedules, special compensation programs, and job enrichment can reduce both employee turnover and absenteeism. Other suggestions for reducing turnover include the following:[24]

© WALTER HODGES/CORBIS

Exit interviews identify the employee's reasons for leaving and are critical for evaluating employee turnover.

• *Use Exit Interviews.* Once an employee notifies the organization of their resignation, an interview with a manager or someone in human resources should be scheduled. This is the exit interview, used to identify the major causes of employee decisions to leave. The interviewer asks employees why they are leaving, and targets such key factors as pay and benefits, supervisor and co-worker relationships, working conditions, and (especially) career opportunities within the organization. The employee may also be asked for suggestions that would improve working conditions in the organization. Exit interviews are critical tools for analyzing employee turnover. Attitude surveys identify general trends that are useful predictors of turnover, but determining actual causes is always helpful.

• *Create Career Planning Programs.* In many studies, lack of career opportunities has been the strongest predictor of intent to quit. That being the case, it is cost-effective to have career planning programs in place. Such programs identify employees' strengths and weaknesses, career objectives, and development efforts they need to undertake to achieve career objectives. Often, career planning is done in conjunction with performance appraisals.

TABLE 8-3 Costs Associated with Employee Turnover

- Lost productivity while the job is vacant
- Preparing for recruiting (writing new job descriptions and position requirements)
- Recruiting costs (such as advertising fees)
- Screening costs (such as reviewing resumes and responding to applicant inquiries)
- Interviewing costs (time spent contacting applicants, preparing for and conducting interviews)
- Evaluation costs (time spent meeting to evaluate multiple job candidates)
- Cost of making a job offer (time spent negotiating with a candidate)
- Training costs (cost of training a new employee, including orientation training)
- Cost of reduced efficiency and quality of performance as new employee learns a new job
- Other costs (such as lost productivity of new employee's co-workers as they learn to work with the new employee)

- *Practice Open Communication.* Around 65 percent of employees consider open communication to be very important in evaluating jobs. Yet, only 36 percent say that their employer actively seeks their opinions on how to run the organization.[25] Ways to promote two-way communications between managers and employees include (1) 50/50 meetings, where managers talk half the time and employees the other half; (2) management by walking around, where managers make a concerted effort "to stay out of their offices"—that is, they interact frequently with employees in the work areas; and (3) employee task forces whose objectives are to research and communicate to management solutions to problems, or opportunities to become more effective.
- *Balance Work and Nonwork.* People born after 1960 are fast becoming the largest segment of the work force, as baby boomers retire and are replaced by so-called Generation X. It is widely believed that Gen Xers are not as motivated by money as their parents' generation. Indeed, one survey of American workers found that Gen Xers would reduce their compensation by an average of 21 percent in exchange for more personal and family time.[26] Besides flexible work schedules, organizations can create a climate that acknowledges that people have other priorities in life besides work, encourage employees to use flexible work hour options, and create new ways to accommodate employee needs for time away from work (such as telecommuting, job sharing, or part-time options).
- *Create a Compelling Organizational Culture.* Employees are less likely to leave organizations that reflect values that they embrace. Employees feel most comfortable working for companies whose values mirror their own. If employers convey the message that all they care about is profit, then employees begin to feel like they exist only to service that profit motive. If employers affirm the value of their employees to the organization, encourage volunteer work in the community, and show genuine concern for employee welfare, turnover rates often drop dramatically.
- *Implement High-Involvement Work Processes.* There are many ways to make employees feel like important, contributing members of the organization.[27] Giving employees both the information and the authority to make decisions on their jobs benefits the organization.[28] In successful high-involvement programs, employees are "empowered," psychologically involved, and committed to the organization (see Chapter 6). Examples of such programs include participation in decision making, quality circles, and profit-sharing.

Table 8-4 summarizes the strategies that organizations use to combat employee withdrawal behaviors. Most of these operate directly on psychological with-

TABLE 8-4 Strategies for Preventing Absenteeism and Turnover

- Employee attitude surveys
- Incentives and special compensation programs
- Wellness programs
- Accurate record keeping
- Job enrichment
- Safe and clean work environment
- Exit interviews
- Career planning
- Open communication
- Work and nonwork balance options
- Flexible work schedules
- Compelling organizational culture
- High-involvement work processes

drawal, which in turn prevents physical withdrawal. It cannot be emphasized enough that the organizational and managerial practices discussed throughout this book dramatically affect work attitudes. And these attitudes in turn affect absenteeism and turnover. The choices managers make day in and day out can mean the difference between keeping and losing valuable employees.

ORGANIZATIONAL CITIZENSHIP

Imagine an organization whose members perform only the tasks and duties listed in their formal job descriptions, at barely acceptable levels, and only during scheduled work hours. Assemblers only assemble, sales people only sell, human resource people only grudgingly listen to complaints, managers only manage when they have to. Who will work the extra hours to complete major projects on time? Who will cooperate with employees in other departments who make special requests? Who will talk favorably about the organization in social contexts after work, and support the organization's favorable reputation? Who will put their "heart and soul" into their work? In our "work-to-the-rule" organization, no one will. And the organization will no doubt cease to exist. Organizations cannot specify every single behavior needed to make them successful. Employees must recognize and undertake such behaviors themselves.

As organizational environments become increasingly turbulent and uncertain, organizations count on employees to perform activities that are not in their job descriptions, that are not formalized expectations, and that cannot be foreseen as even being needed. Long ago Katz and Kahn called these "innovative and spontaneous behaviors."[29] They are what employees do to benefit the organization that they are not explicitly required to do. These behaviors are neither rewarded when displayed nor punished when they are not. Some researchers call these behaviors "extra-role behaviors."[30] The term most often used to describe them in recent years has been organizational citizenship behaviors. **Organizational citizenship behaviors (OCBs)** are behaviors that employees exhibit on and off their jobs that reflect sacrifices for, and commitment to, the prosperity of the organization. Employees who exhibit these behaviors are the "good soldiers," those who act selflessly on behalf of the organization. OCBs have these key features in common:

organizational citizenship behaviors (OCBs) behaviors that employees exhibit on and off their jobs that reflect sacrifices for, and commitment to, the prosperity of the organization

- They are voluntary on the part of the employee.
- They are intentional; the employee consciously decides to perform them.
- They are intended to be positively valued by the employee and the organization.
- The behavior primarily benefits the organization (or co-workers) and not the employees themselves.

It is important to distinguish organizational citizenship behaviors from excellent job performance. Employees can perform their jobs at a high level (sell a lot of products) without exhibiting OCBs (refusing to stay late to help a customer). Employees demonstrate OCBs when they act to benefit the employer in ways not formally expected of them.

Types of Organizational Citizenship Behaviors

A substantial amount of research has focused on OCBs in the last 20 years. Researchers classify OCBs in five different ways:[31]

- *Altruism.* These behaviors are intended to help another person at work (such as a co-worker or supervisor). An employee who works unpaid overtime to help an employee in another department is displaying altruism.
- *Compliance.* These behaviors benefit the organization but surpass enforceable work standards. An employee who demonstrates exemplary attendance and respect for company property is displaying compliance behaviors.
- *Sportsmanship.* These behaviors reflect a high tolerance for annoyances on the job. An employee who is frequently interrupted but who doesn't complain displays good sportsmanship.
- *Courtesy.* These behaviors reflect consideration of how work decisions might affect other employees. An employee who asks how a new computer application will affect other people's work is displaying courtesy.
- *Civic Virtue.* These behaviors reflect active involvement in organizational activities not required by their jobs. Employees who attend company-sponsored events (such as awards dinners), attend nonmandatory meetings (such as information sessions about new policies), and keep up with organization activities by reading the company newsletter and their e-mails are demonstrating civic virtue.

Recently Van Dyne and her colleagues have expanded earlier research in this area.[32] Building on political science research, they posited that people who engage in OCBs will demonstrate organizational obedience, loyalty, and participation:

- *Organizational Obedience.* These behaviors reflect the need for rational rules and regulations, demonstrated by acceptance of, and compliance with, organizational rules and policies.
- *Organizational Loyalty.* These behaviors reflect identification with, and allegiance to, organizational leaders and the organization as a whole, going beyond employees' own self-interests. Defending the organization against threats, speaking favorably about it, and cooperating with co-workers exemplify loyalty.
- *Organizational Participation.* These behaviors reflect an interest in organizational affairs by full and responsible involvement in organizational management. This dimension was subsequently refined to include *social participation* (noncontroversial interactions with others), *advocacy participation* (publicly challenging existing policies, suggesting improvements), and *functional participation* (personal development that enhances organization performance).

The self-assessment lists samples of these behaviors from Van Dyne's research, and gives you an opportunity to measure your own level of OCB.

SELF-ASSESSMENT Measuring Organizational Citizenship Behaviors

Think of the organization you work for now or one that you worked for in the past. If you have never worked for an organization, even on a voluntary basis, think of how you might normally behave on the job. Then answer each item using this scale:

1	2	3	4	5	6	7
Strongly Disagree	**Mildly Disagree**	**Disagree**	**Neither Agree nor Disagree**	**Agree**	**Mildly Agree**	**Strongly Agree**

_____ 1. I represent my organization favorably to outsiders.
_____ 2. I go out of my way to defend my organization against outside threats.
_____ 3. I tell outsiders this is a good place to work.
_____ 4. I defend my organization when other employees criticize it.
_____ 5. I actively promote my organization's products and services.
_____ 6. I rarely waste time while at work.
_____ 7. I produce as much as I am capable of at all times.
_____ 8. I always come to work on time.
_____ 9. Regardless of circumstances, I produce high-quality work.
_____ 10. I meet all deadlines set by the organization.
_____ 11. I attend work-related meetings only if required by job.
_____ 12. I share ideas for new projects or improvements.
_____ 13. I frequently make creative suggestions to co-workers.
_____ 14. I use professional judgment to assess right/wrong for my organization.
_____ 15. I pursue additional training to improve my job performance.

Scoring:

1. Add up your answers to items 1–5. This is your LOYALTY score: _____
2. Add up your answers to items 6–10. This is your OBEDIENCE score: _____
3. Add up your answers to items 11–15. This is your PARTICIPATION score: _____

Interpreting your scores:

	1. LOYALTY	2. OBEDIENCE	3. PARTICIPATION
HIGH	32–35	29–35	29–35
AVERAGE	23–31	20–28	20–28
LOW	5–22	5–19	5–19

For group discussion:

1. Do you agree with your scores? Why or why not?
2. Do you think the behaviors described in these items represent the meaning of organizational citizenship? Why or why not?
3. What are some other behaviors you perform that you think represent good organizational citizenship?

Source: L. Van Dyne, J. W. Graham, and R. M. Dienesch. 1994. Organizational citizenship behavior: Construct redefinition, measurement, and validation. *Academy of Management Journal* 37:765–802.

covenantal relationships exist between employees and employers when there is a state of mutual commitment and trust, and shared values

Van Dyne and her colleagues explored the OCB concept further by identifying its primary antecedent, the covenantal relationship. A **covenantal relationship** exists between an employee and employer when there is a state of mutual commitment and trust, and shared values. Both employees and employers find this to be a desirable, mutually beneficial state. The employer is expected to act in ways that show commitment and trust in the employee, and vice versa. These behaviors and actions cannot be specified in advance, but support the covenantal relationship as situations arise. Employees demonstrate support for the covenantal relationship through their OCBs. Organizations demonstrate their support of the covenantal relationship by providing job security, investing heavily in employee training, and providing above-average wages and benefits, and so on. The key aspect of the covenantal relationship is that both employee and employer will do what they have to to continue the relationship. VanDyne's research, involving almost 1000 employees in a variety of companies, provides general support for the idea that the covenantal relationship leads to employee OCBs.

Determinants of Organizational Citizenship Behaviors

Organ and Ryan, in their review of research on the causes of OCB, examined 55 different studies of the OCB concept.[33] Factors that lead to employees displaying OCBs were categorized as being either attitudinal (like job satisfaction) or dispositional (a characteristic of the employee). The researchers concluded that the following attitudinal factors have reliable relationships with employee OCBs:

- *Job satisfaction*—how well employees are satisfied with different facets of their jobs, and the job and work as a whole (see Chapter 6).
- *Fairness*—how happy employees are with the way rewards (like pay) are allocated (Chapter 7).
- *Commitment*—whether employees identify with and wish to continue working for an organization (termed affective and continuance commitment in Chapter 6).
- *Leader supportiveness*—whether employees perceive their supervisor as providing the direction and resources needed for employees to perform their jobs.

In addition, the following dispositional (employee) factors have reliable relationships with OCBs:[34]

- *Conscientiousness*—whether a person is dependable, organized, thorough, perseverant, and honest.
- *Agreeableness*—whether a person is polite, trusting, good-natured, accepting, cooperative, and forgiving.
- *Positive and negative affectivity*—the general tendency to exhibit a positive, pleasant disposition or a negative, disagreeable one. (This may be inherited; see Chapter 6.)

Organ and Ryan also came to an interesting conclusion about OCBs. Analogous to the fact that ability is usually the single strongest predictor of performance, they offer the hypothesis that employee morale (as reflected in job attitudes) is the single best predictor of whether employees will display OCBs. Van Dyne and her colleagues show that morale (positive job attitudes) affects OCBs through its effect on the covenantal relationship. That is, consistent with the discussion above, employees will perceive a positive covenantal relationship and help their employer with OCBs only when they perceive most aspects of the work environment as satisfying. Management practices described throughout this book have direct and indirect effects on employee attitudes. Once again we find that organizations and managers need to be aware of and promote positive attitudes in their employees.

AGGRESSION, VIOLENCE, AND INCIVILITY

In the early morning of November 2, 1999, what should have been yet another quiet day in Honolulu, a city with one of the lowest violent crime rates in the United States, quickly turned into tragedy. Bryan Uyesugi, a Xerox copy machine repairman for five years, calmly walked to a conference room where he, his supervisor, and his co-workers were to discuss Bryan's "light workload."[35] Moments later, Uyesugi killed his supervisor and six co-workers. He then waved goodbye to another co-worker as he drove off in a Xerox van.

Intense media attention to such incidents—indeed, "going postal" is now a part of our language—gives the impression that workplaces are dangerous places. In reality, at work we are safer from violence than in most other places.[36] We are twice as likely to be struck by lightning as murdered by a co-worker. In fact, because organizations have implemented many safety devices and procedures in the last 10 years, murders in the workplace actually declined from 1,074 in 1993 to 709 in 1998, out of more than 100 million workers. The Occupational Safety and Health Administration (OSHA) continues to develop new standards that will bring that number down even further, especially in high-risk businesses like convenience stores.

http://www.osha.gov

Despite the relatively few cases of workplace homicide, we cannot conclude, unfortunately, that violence in the workplace is not a problem. Other statistics tell a different story.[37] According to the American Society for Industrial Safety, the number of incidents of workplace violence *other than* homicides has tripled since the 1970s.[38] The Department of Justice estimates that more than two million workers are victims of workplace violence each year. Another estimate suggests that workplace violence causes over 500,000 employees to miss some 1.8 million workdays annually.[39] Physical assaults, robberies, and rapes are included in such statistics, but less severe forms of violence like verbal assaults and threats are not. Many, if not most, fistfights between co-workers are not reported to the police (or to OSHA). Yet, human resource professionals in a survey on conditions in their organizations reported incidents of verbal threats (41 percent), pushing and shoving (19 percent), fistfights (9 percent), and stalking (9 percent) in their workplaces between 1996 and 1999. Still another survey found that executives rate workplace violence as the top security threat to their firms, ahead of Internet security, disaster recovery, and white-collar crime.[40] From these surveys we must reluctantly conclude that violence in the workplace is in fact not only common but growing.

This violence comes with great costs. It goes without saying that the suffering of the victims and their families is enormous. There are other costs as well. Lost work time due to workplace violence is estimated to cost over $55 million each year. Employers must pay workers who are unable to work because of injuries sustained in the violence. Add in litigation costs, diminished productivity, and medical, disability, and workers compensation costs, and the estimate balloons to $36 billion.[41] Other costs include insurance losses, property damage, tarnished reputations, public relations expenses, lost business, low morale, and higher turnover.[42] Clearly, of the many obligations that organizations have to their employees, prevention of workplace violence is a fundamental one. Implementing violence prevention measures cannot only preclude employee suffering, it can also result in major cost savings.

deviant behavior voluntary behavior that violates significant organizational norms and in doing so threatens the well-being of an organization, its members, or both

production deviance deviant behavior that is minor and directed at the organization

property deviance deviant behavior that is serious and directed at an organization

political deviance deviant behavior that is minor and directed at a specific individual

personal aggression deviant behavior that is serious and directed at a specific individual(s)

Workplace violence is just one type of deviant behavior in organizations. **Deviant behavior** is voluntary behavior that violates significant organizational norms and in so doing threatens the well-being of an organization, its members, or both.[43] Deviant behavior is classified along two dimensions. The first dimension is minor versus serious infractions. A minor infraction might be when an employee is consistently half an hour late for work. A serious infraction might be when an employee steals a computer. The second dimension is interpersonal versus organizational. Deviant behavior can be directed at the employer or at a specific person (or persons) in the organization. Table 8-5 classifies deviant behaviors four ways using these two dimensions. Employee behavior that is minor and directed at the organization is called **production deviance.** Leaving work early without permission is an example. Behaviors that are serious and directed at an organization are called **property deviance.** Willfully destroying equipment is a typical example. *An Inside Look* discusses the problem of workplace sabotage. Behaviors that are minor and directed at a specific person are called **political deviance.** An employee who spreads false rumors is engaging in political deviance. Behaviors that are serious and directed at an individual (or individuals), such as physically attacking a co-worker, are called **personal aggression.** Workplace violence is the epitome of personal aggression and is the topic we focus on here.

Workplace violence is not going to fade away quietly. It is epidemic in the United States for numerous reasons, including[44]

- Firearms are readily available.
- Violence depicted in the media and entertainment ("Rambo") implies that violence is a viable way to resolve conflicts.

TABLE 8-5 Classification of Employee Deviant Behaviors

Severity		Target of Behavior: Organization	Target of Behavior: Individual
Severity	Minor	Production Deviance	Political Deviance
Severity	Serious	Property Deviance	Personal Aggression

Source: S. L. Robinson and R. J. Bennett. 1995. A typology of deviant behaviors: A multidimensional scaling study. *Academy of Management Journal* 38:555–572.

AN INSIDE LOOK

Sabotage in the Workplace

Physical violence in the workplace is an unfortunate phenomenon that deservedly receives a great deal of attention. However, there is another more subtle form of workplace violence that is rarely publicized—employee sabotage. Employee sabotage takes many forms. In some cases, acts of sabotage are directed against co-workers or managers, and in other cases the focus of the sabotage is the organization. Both forms can be extremely harmful to the organization's reputation as well as finances.

Deliberately damaging a co-worker's standing is one way that employees may try to advance their own agendas or careers. Personality conflicts, competition for promotions, and perceptions of favoritism or unfair treatment can all contribute to an individual's motivation to undermine a colleague's position or professional status.

A newer kind of workplace sabotage involves computer-oriented crimes. Disgruntled or dishonest employees have been known to destroy company databases storing valuable information or to use computer access to cheat their employer out of profits. In fact, the threat to databases from current or former employees is said to be much greater than threats from hackers outside of the organization.

Modern management trends have inadvertently contributed to the growing frequency of employee sabotage. For example, the phenomenon of downsizing is always disruptive to employees' lives, and employees who take layoffs or terminations personally may lash out at the organization. Flat management styles can also provide employees with more opportunities for sabotage. With fewer controls in organizational structures, employees looking to cause harm have greater opportunities to do so. Reducing productivity on purpose to harm an organization is easier in an organization where control is decentralized.

Trends in workplace violence demonstrate that employees who are most likely to commit sabotage are those who feel that they have been wronged by their employer. In particular, employees who have been terminated are more likely than any other group to attempt harm to the organizations or individuals within the organization. Labor disputes and strikes are other instances of environments where sabotage may be likely to occur. Since downsizing, termination, and labor disputes are facts of life in today's world, how do organizations go about preventing workplace sabotage?

Experts agree that the key to avoiding this particular kind of workplace violence is proper treatment of employees. Organizations who let employees go either temporarily or permanently should work with these individuals in a sensitive manner to avoid feelings of powerlessness and anger and ultimately to prevent any desire for revenge. Employees who are treated fairly and with respect are less likely to attempt sabotage against the organization or co-workers. Creating an open organizational culture in which employees' input is solicited and valued is an essential part of a safe workplace. Employees who are in tune with the organization's mission and values are more likely to work for rather than against its success.

Source: Adapted from J. Labbs. 1999. Employee sabotage: Don't be a target! *Workforce* 78(7): 32–42.

- Corporate downsizings and increased workloads have eroded the covenantal relationship between the organization and employees.
- Employees don't feel they have choices when they are unhappy and dissatisfied.
- In today's tight labor markets, employers are often lax in screening applicants and checking references.
- Increased workplace diversity without appropriate training can result in interpersonal conflicts.
- Alcohol and drug abuse can cause otherwise healthy workers to commit workplace violence.

Traffic jams are good examples of an environment that fosters aggressive behavior. One person honks the horn, others often follow suit (modeling). Aggressive drivers are often rewarded by getting ahead in the line (incentive inducements). And the physical environment of the highway (noisy, smelly, hot, crowded) can stimulate aggressive behavior.

Certain organizational characteristics tend to foster workplace aggression. O'Leary and her colleagues suggest that organizations can inadvertently instigate aggression in the following ways:[45]

http://aggressionmanagement.com

- *Modeling Aggressive Behavior.* Employees learn to be aggressive if the organization tolerates aggressive behaviors, or fails to punish them. Employees become less inhibited about their own aggressive intentions when they see aggressive behaviors go unpunished (or even rewarded). In the extreme, a group of employees can take on mob-like characteristics. Women who have been sexually harassed or even assaulted by groups of male co-workers probably worked in environments where sexual harassment was tolerated.
- *Aversive Treatment.* Organizations control many rewards that employees desire (pay raises, promotions, time off from work). If employees perceive that rewards are allocated capriciously or in a discriminatory manner, they may interpret this as aversive treatment and react by engaging in aggressive behaviors.
- *Incentive Inducements.* Organizations implicitly and/or unconsciously reward some aggressive behaviors. For example, an organization that promotes an employee who has succeeded by manipulating and harming colleagues is providing incentives for aggression. In some cases, aggressive behaviors are rewarded by co-workers ("You sure showed her").
- *Factors in the Physical Environment.* Research shows that physical conditions like overcrowding, uncomfortable temperatures, poor air quality, and noise play a role in stimulating aggressive behavior. Given that organizations provide the physical context for work, employees may take out their frustrations over poor physical conditions through violence.

It is incumbent upon organizations and managers to implement workplace violence prevention programs and to learn the symptoms of workplace violence.

Experts have concluded that incidents of workplace violence are rarely unpredictable. Employees usually display certain characteristic behaviors that precede the violence and serve as warning signs.

Warning Signs

Behaviors that warn of workplace violence are well documented. The problem is that we cannot always predict when these behaviors will escalate to violence. Most employees who display the warning signs do not commit workplace violence. Nevertheless, it is worthwhile for employees and managers to know the signs. Even if an employee who appears to be prone to violence never actually commits a violent act, requiring people to report pre-violent behavior to management is the only way interventions can happen. That is, preventive action at the onset of warning signals is the only way to proactively prevent workplace violence, even at the risk of "false positives." (False positives are employees who are falsely identified as violence-prone.) The potential consequences of *not* taking action are dire.

Employees (and managers) should be expected to report warning signs whenever they occur. Over 90 percent of individuals who commit workplace violence are males, and over 80 percent of victims are male. However, gender is only part of the picture (obviously there are millions and millions of male workers who never commit workplace violence). Other risk factors to look for are presented in Table 8-6.[46] Table 8-7 is a sample checklist managers might use to assess a person's potential for violence. While a single indicator may not be enough to identify the violence-prone, usually the more descriptors checked, the more likely an employee will commit violence.

TABLE 8-6 Warning Signs of Workplace Violence

The employee

- has a past history of violence (such as in a criminal record or arrests for domestic violence)
- is in an acute phase of mental illness
- abuses drugs and/or alcohol
- has poor social behaviors (quick temper, uncontrolled anger, throws or kicks inanimate objects, binge drinker)
- uses profanity extensively
- is in a stressful life circumstance (divorce, job demotion, death of a loved one)
- is preoccupied with violence (talks about revenge fantasies, watches violent movies, reads violent books)
- verbally threatens violence (direct or veiled threats to harm others)
- perceives a history of injustice (that others have treated him unfairly)
- is unable to let go of the past and deal with the present (can't forgive others who have "betrayed" him)
- feels he has nothing to lose
- perceives loss of personal security or control (sense of helplessness)
- has low self-esteem (perceives himself as ineffectual in the organization)
- is intimidating, belligerent, harassing, bullying, or exhibits other inappropriate and aggressive behaviors
- has numerous conflicts with supervisors and other employees
- owns several firearms and is fascinated with weapons
- brings a weapon to the workplace
- frequently makes statements that reflect a fascination (or respect) for incidents of workplace violence; identifies with others who have committed workplace violence
- approves of violence as a way to resolve problems
- makes statements that indicate despair to the point of suicide
- exhibits extreme changes in behavior (attire, hygiene, appearance, spending habits)
- constantly denigrates the workplace and/or colleagues
- makes co-workers feel as if they have to be extra careful in what they say around him (they have to "walk on eggshells")
- has few if any friends at work (or off work)

TABLE 8-7 Workplace Violence—Behavior and Performance Checklist

Tardiness and Absenteeism	Interpersonal Relationships
■ Taking frequent breaks	■ Inappropriate emotional outbursts
■ Taking long lunches	■ Mood swings early and late in day
■ Repeated tardiness	■ Overreacts to criticism
■ Arriving late and leaving early	■ Constantly blaming others
■ Absence from area or office	■ Making inappropriate statements
■ Frequent visits to restroom	■ Rambling, incoherent speech
■ Unexplained absences	■ Isolation from co-workers and others
■ Absences due to unusual accidents	■ Physically volatile
■ Absence before and after paydays	■ Exaggerated self-importance
■ Absence before and after holidays	■ Unbending and unreasonable
■ Absent Mondays and Fridays	■ Excessive time on the telephone
■ Immediate use of earned vacation	■ Failure to keep commitments
■ Sick after denial of vacation extensions	■ Failure to keep appointments
■ Requests for sick leave extensions	
Performance	**Appearance and Mood**
■ Repeated procrastination	■ Inappropriate clothing or dress
■ Repeatedly late in completing work	■ Personal hygiene ignored
■ Irresponsibility in completing work	■ Body odor, unkempt appearance
■ Faulty decision making	■ Glazed or red eyes
■ Unnecessary wasted materials	■ Slurred speech
■ Unnecessary damage to equipment	■ Staggered gait
■ Assigned tasks take too long	■ Outbreaks of heavy perspiration
■ Difficulty recalling instructions	■ Inappropriate wearing of sun glasses
■ General disinterest in work	■ Withdrawn
■ Difficulty recalling mistakes	■ Unusual deep sadness
■ Inconsistent productivity	■ Inappropriate laughter
■ Missed deadlines	■ Suspiciousness
■ Mistakes due to poor judgment	■ Paranoia
■ Customer or client complaints	■ Extreme sensitivity
■ Inappropriate behaviors	■ Unusual irritability
■ General carelessness	

Source: Based on E. F. Ferraro. 1995. *What every employer should know about workplace violence.* Golden, CO. ASET.

So, what do we do when employees display these warning signs? This is an extremely delicate issue. On the one hand, reporting such employees to the appropriate authority in the organization might prevent harm. On the other hand, profiling can falsely stereotype completely innocent employees (such as loners or shy people). The indicators are not hard science; they are merely indicators. Judgment and common sense are crucial, as is training people to respond appropriately to such information. Sometimes the response is simply to watch an employee more carefully; other times it may be appropriate to counsel the employee or refer them to counseling. In extreme cases, managers should not hesitate to call security guards or police.

Managers must also be sensitive to issues of privacy. An employee who reports a fellow employee's inappropriate behaviors should not be identified to anyone who does not need to know. Identifying such employees might jeopardize their safety or result in their ostracism. Similarly, an employee who has been reported for acting inappropriately should be counseled privately. "Praise in public, criticize in private" is always good advice.

Actions That Prevent Workplace Violence

In the majority of situations where employees have been observed displaying one or more of the warning signs of workplace violence, their manager's first response should be to observe the employee more carefully than usual and take progressive steps to remedy the situation. Violence-prone employees frequently go through a progression of behaviors before they commit a violent act.[47] They test the reactions of the organization to see how much aggression they can "get away with." A manager who carefully observes employees may be able to detect the progression and intervene before destructive behaviors occur.

In the first phase of the progression, the employee is passively aggressive, refuses to cooperate with co-workers (who are viewed as enemies), frequently argues, is belligerent to customers, and generally relishes their disruptive influence. It is appropriate at this stage for the manager to advise the employee that such behaviors are unprofessional and unproductive, and can result in discipline (including termination). In many situations, the progression toward workplace violence ends at this phase.

In the second phase, the aggression becomes more overt. The employee blatantly violates organizational policies (such as absence rules), articulates desires to harm co-workers, and obsessively complains about mistreatment by the organization. At this point, discipline is usually required as long as the employee has first been counseled that such behaviors will not be tolerated. Alternatively, the manager might ask the employee to seek counseling, either for personal problems (drug addictions) or for anger management.

In phase three, the employee acts out his (or her) aggression. They might vandalize equipment, sabotage work in progress, begin to push or shove other workers, and threaten violence to specific co-workers. At this point, the employee should either be terminated, given an administrative leave without pay, or be taken into custody by police (depending on the severity of the behavior). At all phases, it is potentially dangerous for managers to ignore the behaviors or to engage in denial ("Joe is just going through a bad time").

There are a number of other preventative actions organizations should implement to deal with workplace violence. These are discussed next.

Develop a Workplace Violence Policy The first step is to develop a comprehensive, written policy on what the organization will do to prevent violence, including formal expectations for the behavior of employees. This should include such provisions as

- a zero tolerance for employee violence (including threats of violence)
- a description of the prohibited behaviors
- a description of the procedure employees should use to report potentially violent co-workers
- a policy of no reprisals against employees who report (in good faith) other employees' inappropriate behaviors

- methods for ensuring confidentiality and privacy
- disciplinary procedures for employees who violate the policy
- methods by which the policy will be communicated to employees
- methods that will be used to monitor workplace safety
- who is responsible for ensuring that actions are taken to respond to potentially violent employees

http://www.crnha.org

Training and Education All employees should know how to identify and report incidents of violent, intimidating, threatening, and other disruptive behavior. Employees should be well versed in the workplace violence policy. Other forms of training might include

- encouragement to report incidents
- ways to diffuse volatile situations
- when to recognize that the employee is in danger and should physically withdraw from a situation
- conflict resolution skills
- location of security devices, such as alarms
- personal security measures
- emergency evacuation procedures
- how to use a company employee assistance program (called an EAP) whereby all employees may seek counseling for personal problems (like family problems or addictions)

Supervisors should be given additional training on how to confront and counsel a potentially violent employee, basic emergency procedures, and how to screen applicants for aggressive tendencies.

Create a Threat Assessment Team This is a group of professionals, which may include consultants or contractors, whose purpose it is to prevent and resolve incidents of workplace violence. The team normally includes managers, human resource employees, security experts, employment attorneys, public law enforcement officials, private investigators, and clinical psychologists/psychiatrists. Smaller firms may not be able to afford an extensive team but should nevertheless designate a group or person who performs this role for the organization. The team should perform a work site audit to identify potential problem areas that would facilitate an act of violence (such as unlit passageways); evaluate security and safety measures (bulletproof windows, alarms) and policies; develop emergency procedures; and articulate procedures to be used when potentially violent employees are identified.

http://jobcandidateprofile.com

Screen Job Applicants for Aggressive Behaviors A major way to keep employees from committing violence is to screen applicants who are violence-prone. This is not easily done, but at a minimum employers can legally check an applicant's references and former employers, require applicants to pass a preemployment drug test, inquire about criminal records, and hire agencies to conduct background checks on applicants. The focus of this thorough screening is to determine whether an applicant has an aggressive and/or hostile personal or work history.

Stress Management Training In many cases, a disturbed employee commits violence at work because on-the-job stress is more than the employee can handle, given problems in their personal life, or the job stress itself triggers the violence. Managers should be aware of common stressors in the work environment (like work overload) and eliminate them. Employees should be trained in ways to manage stress, such as talking to trusted co-workers or supervisors, maintaining proper rest and diet, asking for help when needed, and managing time.

Incidents of workplace violence may seem random and unpredictable. However, thoughtful preparation can go a long way toward handling it effectively if not preventing it altogether.

Incivility in the Workplace

A final comment on workplace violence is appropriate here. The preceding discussion focuses on deviant behavior at its worst, at the end of the behavior spiral into violence and aggression. Perhaps we are starting at the wrong place—a simple, very basic idea may do more to prevent workplace violence than all the complex procedures and manuals combined. It is well known that civility in the workplace (and indeed in modern life) is on the decline. In one major survey of Americans, 90 percent of the respondents considered incivility to be a major problem.[48] Other research suggests that incivility permeates the workplace.[49] Uncivil behaviors at work range from neglecting to say please and thank you, answering the telephone with a "yeah," throwing trash on the floor for others to pick up, to making obscene gestures to co-workers.

Research on criminal behavior suggests that incivility can and does lead to physical aggression. It doesn't take too great of a leap to propose that such incivility at work can also lead to workplace violence.[50] This is the spiraling effect—once the cycle begins, it feeds back and exacerbates itself in a way that escalates the intensity over time. A rude comment attracts an obscene gesture, which leads to a push, then a punch, and so on. This suggests that managers might achieve a number of objectives by demonstrating zero tolerance for incivility, rudeness, and discourtesies among their employees. A culture of civility creates a professional and comfortable place to work and, by discouraging deviant behaviors, may thereby prevent the tragic spiral into workplace violence. There are no reasons to tolerate incivility in the workplace.

DRUG AND ALCOHOL ABUSE

Costs and Prevalence of Substance Abuse

http://www.regionaldruginitiative.org/workplace.html

In our final discussion in this chapter we address drug and substance abuse. Like workplace violence, there is no shortage of statistics that confirm that substance abuse is a major problem in the United States.[51] Approximately 11 percent of all employees use illegal drugs (controlled substances, which is our focus here). Of the millions of drug users in the United States, 71 percent are employed, and some 60 percent of them work in small firms who can ill afford employees' addictions. Employees under the influence of drugs and alcohol function at only 50 to 67 percent of their capacity. The National Institutes for Health estimates that each drug abuser costs the employer $7000 per year in lost productivity, theft, and overuse of benefits (such as medical insurance and sick leave). For a 1000-employee company, that's about $770,000 per year! All told, drug use is estimated to cost U.S. employers about $120 billion per year.

The statistics for alcohol fare no better.[52] Around 6 to 10 percent of the U.S. work force are alcoholics. Another 14 percent of Americans admit to consuming at least five alcoholic drinks on five different occasions in a 30-day span. It is estimated that this results in around 500 million lost workdays per year due to intoxication or its aftereffects ("hangovers"). This estimate does not include lost productivity of employees who perform at barely acceptable levels because they are hung over. Alcoholism is estimated to cost employers $47 billion per year.

Substance abuse (drug and alcohol) causes many major problems for employers. Employees are much more likely to engage in deviant behaviors when they are under the influence of drugs than when they are sober. The model of deviant behavior in Table 8-5 confirms this. Impaired employees are more likely to damage company property, either intentionally or unintentionally (property deviance). They are more likely to avoid work (productivity deviance). They are more likely to waste time at work belittling the work and reputation of other employees, especially those who do not also abuse drugs (political deviance). And certainly the vast majority of physical assaults in the world are stimulated by abuse of drugs and/or alcohol, including those that lead to workplace violence (personal aggression). It can be argued that employers have no right to regulate the activities of employees when they are away from work, including such activities as ingesting alcohol and drugs. However, because substance abuse does lead to all manner and intensity of deviant behaviors on the job, ethicists argue that employers not only have the right but perhaps a moral obligation to prevent substance abuse among their employees.[53]

It is well beyond the scope of this book to examine why people turn to substance abuse as a way of life. Substance abuse is a withdrawal behavior, and most experts agree that it is one way to deal with the stresses of life. The effects of impairment (being "high") are a form of psychological withdrawal, while the lethargy and work avoidance associated with impaired states are a physical withdrawal. Because work is a central life activity for most of us, it represents a major potential stressor in life that some people may endeavor to mitigate through the abuse of drugs.

Preventing Substance Abuse

In an ideal world we could prevent substance abuse by providing everyone with a sufficiently fulfilling life (including work life) so that they would never feel the need to escape from it through substance abuse. Indeed, there is probably a genetic predisposition to abuse drugs, in which case the provision of fulfilling lives might not help many substance abusers. As a result, society (including employers) must usually deal with people who have abuse problems (including addictions) after they already exist.

Organizations must first identify those who abuse drugs, and then try to rectify the situation. For employers, this has meant testing job applicants and current employees for the presence of illegal drugs in their bodies.* It is imperative that organizations have a formal, written drug testing policy before testing

* The controlled substances that most employers test for are amphetamines, methamphetamines, marijuana, cocaine, opiates (heroin), and phencyclidine ("Angel Dust").

employees, and that they train employees in its provisions and requirements.[54] Estimates vary, but around 74 percent of large firms (more than 500 employees) test job applicants and/or current employees for the presence of drugs.[55] Job applicants are typically told that they will be tested, when and where they will be tested, and informed that an employment offer is contingent on their passing (not failing) the drug test. Applicants then provide a sample (urine, blood, saliva, and/or hair) that is analyzed for the presence of drugs (specifically, their remnants, or metabolites, after being processed by the human body). Applicants who fail may be told that they failed and be given another chance to produce a clean sample. Others may be given a chance to have the sample evaluated by a laboratory of their own choosing for independent verification. Still others may not be told anything other than the employer hired someone else who is "more qualified" for the position. The objective for employers is to screen out substance abusers before they become a member of the organization and can engage in the deviant behaviors discussed above. Failed applicants thus become society's problem to "fix."

http://dol.gov/elaws/drugfree.htm

Employers may also test their current employees for impairment. Employees must provide a sample to be tested for the presence of drugs, just like a job applicant. Employers most often test for the presence of illegal drugs, but increasingly they also test for the presence of alcohol (around 28 percent of employers test employees for alcohol).[56] If the employee fails, he or she may be advised or required to seek counseling for the abuse problem, perhaps through a company-sponsored Employee Assistance program (EAP). Alternatively, if the employer has a zero-tolerance approach to substance abuse, the employee might be summarily terminated. There is no legal requirement for an employer to continue employing a person who comes to work under the influence of drugs, and who is job-impaired. However, because employees do have other legal rights, most employers choose to allow the employee to attempt to rehabilitate themselves (on their own or through an EAP). In addition, given the high costs of avoidable turnover (see above), it makes good business sense for most employers to try to help an effective employee overcome their substance abuse problems. There is also evidence that drug testing programs are effective and benefit employers, employees, and society overall. The failure rates for applicants and employees for the presence of drugs dropped from 18.1 percent in 1987 to 5 percent in 1997.[57]

There are usually three conditions under which an employer might ask an employee to undergo a drug test. The first is when the employer has a random drug testing program. A certain percentage of employees, from the lowest to highest levels of the organization, are randomly chosen to provide samples for drug testing. Employers with a strict, perhaps zero-tolerance, approach to drug use are most likely to adopt this approach, despite its huge cost (up to $250 per test). However, most employers test "for cause" rather than by random selection. Cause may be defined as any accident or mishap that occurs in the workplace (including such actions as horseplay and vandalism). Everyone involved in a situation that causes harm to property or other employees is immediately sent to a laboratory where the appropriate tests are done. Still other employers may include managers' observations in their definitions of "cause." If a manager suspects that an employee is under the influence of drugs (including alcohol), the manager can require the employee to undergo drug testing. This is a powerful right of authority for managers, and they must be trained not to misuse it by harassing employees they don't like or are trying to induce to resign.

It is also very important that managers be trained to recognize the physical and behavioral signs of drug influence.[58] The signs for chronic drug impairment are the same as those that lead to workplace violence, because drug impairments and psychological impairments tend to manifest themselves in the same ways (see Table 8-7). In addition, people under the influence of drugs may display tremors, have dilated pupils, complain of chronic fatigue or be hyperactive, and refuse to perform work orders (are insubordinate). Managers must be able to document a pattern of these symptoms over time before requiring an employee to undergo drug testing. We all occasionally have "off days" when our performance is suboptimal.

When managers suspect that an employee's work performance is deteriorating because of substance abuse, it is important that the manager not criticize, become a counselor, or even accuse the employee of being a drug abuser. Instead managers should be trained to[59]

- Carefully observe and identify the employee's unacceptable behavior.
- Document specific work performance thoroughly, accurately, and objectively.
- Learn the common symptoms of drug abuse, not for diagnosis, but to improve the accuracy of their perceptions.
- Consult with higher levels of management, share documentation with other managers, and discuss possible action.
- Confront the employee, discussing specific performance problems and inviting explanations.
- Implement a performance improvement plan, as discussed above.
- Follow company procedures if performance does not improve.
- Suggest sources of help if an employee seems ready to make changes or asks for assistance.
- Know what the organization or community can offer by way of an Employee Assistance Program (EAP).

Managers must be careful not to act as a professional in an area where they have no training, or become an enabler by ignoring an employee's symptoms of drug abuse. Table 8-8 lists behaviors managers should avoid in dealing with employees who have drug problems. Like workplace violence, managers can make a real difference to the organization by effectively managing substance abuse. In addition, helping employees with drug abuse problems within the parameters of the company's policy is good citizenship.

TABLE 8-8 Actions to Avoid with Drug Abusers

Managers should ***not:***

- Diagnose the employee's drug problems; that is to be left to the testing laboratories and the company's policy.
- Moralize, preach, or make value judgments; most people react negatively to statements that make them feel like they are immoral, sinners, or villains.
- Get involved with the employee's problems; not only are most managers ill-trained as clinical psychologists, this can expose them to personal liability lawsuits when the situation worsens.
- Discuss suspicions about drug abuse with anyone but the employee's supervisors.
- Act alone if he or she discovers drugs at a workstation; the information should be passed on to higher management or law enforcement authorities.
- Show favoritism; it can precipitate a discrimination lawsuit.

BEHAVIOR IN ORGANIZATIONS IN REVIEW

Managers play a key role in motivating employees to behave in ways that benefit both the employee and employer. One important behavior that virtually all managers must be focused on is individual performance. Managers must ensure that their employees are performing at least at satisfactory levels and contributing to the attainment of organizational goals. When employees are not performing at acceptable levels, managers must initiate corrective action. This may be in the form of counseling or coaching, and a performance improvement plan. When performance improvement efforts fail, managers must consider involuntary termination of the employee.

There are two major types of employee withdrawal, psychological and physical. Psychological withdrawal occurs when employees mentally disengage from the workplace. Physical withdrawal occurs when the employees voluntarily terminate their employment, or are absent from work when they are scheduled to be there. Absenteeism and turnover are very costly to organizations. Job attitudes are reliable predictors of absenteeism and turnover. Managers should periodically measure employee work attitudes to ensure that policies and practices are not causing unnecessary work dissatisfaction.

Organizations could not continue to exist without employees engaging in behaviors that directly benefit the organization but that are not specified as formal expectations for employees. These spontaneous actions are called organizational citizenship behaviors (OCBs). Employees who have favorable work attitudes are more likely to display OCBs.

Workplace violence and drug abuse by employees are epidemic in the United States. Deviant workplace behaviors are costly and can affect morale. It is important that managers learn the warning signs for both, and that they intervene before employees harm themselves or others.

A FINAL LOOK

After spending a dark weekend fuming over his terrible evaluation, Paul decides to confront Andrea about the allegations of drug use. Paul and Andrea don't have a particularly good working relationship, and he's unsure if this confrontation will make things worse. However, his job is obviously on the line, and Paul feels he has no choice.

In the meeting, Paul asks Andrea for proof of the suspected drug use, and she sheepishly admits she has nothing more than office gossip, which began several months ago. Paul was depressed and withdrawn back then, which made the rumors all the more believable. Paul admits that he is depressed about his daughter's illness and about being trapped in a job he can't leave, even though he's consistently underappreciated. Andrea was unaware of Paul's personal problems and agrees to destroy the previous evaluation and reevaluate him using a different method. They also agree to communicate better in the future.

This incident prompts the bank to revise its evaluation system. The new system will use multiple reviewers and include co-workers and customers as well as bank managers. Serious allegations of inappropriate behavior will require complete documentation. This system of 360° feedback takes more time but has already led to more satisfied employees and more effective evaluations.

KEY TERMS

360° feedback, 263
absenteeism, 272
avoidable voluntary turnover, 274
behaviorally anchored rating scales (BARS), 264
comparative method, 265
covenantal relationship, 282
deviant behavior, 284
effort, 261
essay method, 264
excused absences, 272
graphic rating scale, 263
involuntary absenteeism, 272
involuntary turnover, 274
job duties, 261
job description, 261
job performance, 261
organizational citizenship behaviors (OCBs), 279
performance, 260
performance appraisal, 262
performance improvement plan, 267
personal aggression, 284
physical withdrawal, 271
political deviance, 284
production deviance, 284
property deviance, 284
psychological withdrawal, 272
rater error, 266
subjective performance appraisal methods, 263
system factors, 270
termination, 268
turnover, 274
unexcused absences, 272
voluntary absenteeism, 272
voluntary turnover, 274
withdrawal, 271

ISSUES FOR REVIEW AND DISCUSSION

1. How does a manager know when an employee is not performing up to expectations? What must the manager communicate to this employee? To one who is performing well above expectations?
2. How would you approach an employee you are about to terminate? What would you do in advance? What would you say to the employee?
3. What is the difference between excused and unexcused employee absences? What are some actions a manager can take to prevent unexcused absences?
4. Do voluntary and involuntary turnover have similar causes? How can managers prevent avoidable turnover? Is all turnover bad?
5. Give five examples of organizational citizenship behaviors. Why are organizations so dependent on organizational citizenship behaviors?
6. Give specific examples of the following: productivity deviance, property deviance, political deviance, and personal aggression. Which is worst for an organization?
7. Workplace violence and substance abuse are widespread. What can managers do to help resolve these problems?

EXERCISES

CONSTRUCTIVE DISCIPLINE

Daniel Salazar, age 23, is the son of an immigrant family of seven children. Despite the family's poverty, Dan stayed in school and graduated from technical school in drafting. His father has been dead for seven years. His mother receives welfare and is raising the four youngest members of the family. It is well known at the company that part of Dan's earnings help to support the brood.

During his schooling, Dan denied himself ordinary social activities because he was required to work part-time to help his family. Within the past year, however, he has made several remarks suggesting that he has felt a little resentful at having to spend so many hours working, and would now like to have more social contacts.

Dan's performance at work has been outstanding. Both his supervisors and his co-workers were impressed with how rapidly he learned his job. Recently, however, his supervisor has become concerned about an attendance problem. On one occasion, Dan called his supervisor and requested a substitute because of illness. A substitute was not available, so the other members of his department decided to complete Dan's work. That evening the supervisor called to see how Dan was feeling and found that he was on a date. The supervisor noted the incident on Dan's record and warned him that a similar occurrence would lead to disciplinary action. In the past Dan has maintained a good relationship with the other members of the department, although some of them felt irritated when they learned that Dan was not actually ill and they had had to cover for him.

Two months later it was again learned that in a period of claimed illness, Dan was not at home. He was reprimanded by the supervisor, but he claimed he was helping an older sister take care of a family emergency. In the past week it has come to the attention of the supervisor that a similar breach of conduct has occurred. The supervisor consulted with the area supervisor, who contacted the plant manager. The plant manager decided that the other area supervisors should be involved in the development of a general policy.

The plant manager has accordingly called a meeting involving all the area supervisors plus Dan's supervisor. The purpose of the meeting is to determine what course of action should be taken regarding Dan's problem.

Alternatives:

In your group, discuss the arguments for and against each of these alternatives:

1. Be supportive of Dan and try for the time being to overlook his misbehavior.
2. Counsel with Dan regarding both his personal and family problems and help him to manage them more effectively so that they do not interfere with his work.
3. Make it very clear to Dan that he has violated the standards of the plant, and help him see the difficulty that his absence creates for others. Make arrangements for him to make up the time.
4. Tell Dan that he is now on probation and that another incident of this nature will lead to his dismissal.
5. Tell Dan that since he has been warned about missing work, he is now terminated, but give him a favorable recommendation to help him find another job.
6. Since Dan has ignored two previous warnings and continued in the same pattern, he should be terminated from the plant, and this termination should appear on any recommendation for future employment.

Your instructor will ask each group to present its conclusions to the rest of the class.

Source: D. J. Cherrington. Copyright © 1989. *Organizational behavior: The management of individual and organizational performance.* Boston: Allyn & Bacon, 241–242. Reprinted by permission of Pearson Education, Inc., Upper Saddle River, NJ 07458.

INFOTRAC

INFOTRAC® COLLEGE EDITION

The articles listed below are a sampling of those available through InfoTrac College Edition. You can search for them either by title or by the author's name.

Articles

1. Click for health. (video games) Herb Brody. *Technology Review (Cambridge, Mass.)* Jan 1, 1999 v102 i1 p24(1)
2. Zero tolerance: making it work. (Cover Story) Samuel Greengard. *Workforce* May 1999 v78 i5 p28(6) Bus.Coll.: 117N1459
3. Mandatory binding arbitration-ensure your plan is usable. (interview with lawyer David Tyra) (Interview) Gillian Flynn. *Workforce* June 1997 v76 n6 p121(4)
4. Confronting discrimination in your workplace. (includes related article on employment practices liability insurance) (Special Report on Diversity) Helen Hemphill, Ray Haines. *HR Focus* July 1998 v75 n7 pS5(2)
5. The relationship between drinking and hangovers to workplace problems: an empirical study. Genevieve M. Ames, Joel W. Grube, Roland S. Moore. *Journal of Studies on Alcohol* Jan 1997 v58 n1 p37(11)

Questions

For Article 2:

Read the article entitled "Zero tolerance: making it work." In a small group, write a zero tolerance policy for a corporation that employs approximately 500 people at two different sites. What behaviors should you identify in the policy? For each behavior that you identify, define specifically what will not be tolerated. What will be the consequences for those who perform these behaviors the first time? Subsequent times? Who will be responsible for informing and educating employees about this policy? And specifically, how will employees be educated about the policy?

For Other Articles:

Some of the other articles in this list analyze various organizational behaviors. Assign members of your group to read them and then summarize each in group discussion.

WEB EXERCISE

Several journals *(Academy of Management Journal, Academy of Management Review, Human Relations, Journal of Applied Psychology, Journal of Management, Journal of Organizational Behavior, Journal of Organizational and Occupational Psychology, Organizational Behavior and Human Decision Processes)* routinely publish articles that focus on topics in organizational behavior. Select a behavior (for example, absenteeism, aggression, citizenship, cooperation, performance, turnover, violence) that unfolds within the organizational context that you're interested in learning more about. Employing an Internet search engine (ABI Inform, PsyLit) available through your university (college) library, access one of these journals and search for a recently published article that focuses on this behavior. Read and summarize the author's findings.

CASE
Critical Absence Crisis

It is Monday morning. Alan Haynes, Chief Executive of Hampton Health Trust, a large acute treatment hospital, received a disturbing phone call last night. David Smith, one of his senior managers, has been arrested and charged with manslaughter following a fatal car accident. He had been drinking and was well over the legal limit.

David is responsible for strategic planning and major service developments. Three operational managers report directly to him, one of whom, Alice Jones, joined the Trust only the week before. John Peters has worked with David for several years and is a close friend. The third manager, Michelle Wright, has a more difficult working relationship with him and has recently complained about aspects of his management style to the Human Resources Director, Jane Patterson. She spoke of his irritability and aggressive attitude, of how easily he loses his temper. Although she hasn't reported it to anyone, Michelle has noticed David drinking at lunchtime on several occasions. He's late to work a lot, often muttering about a "heavy night" and looking seriously hung over.

Alan had cause to raise concerns with him earlier last week. Although he claims to put in long hours at work, David's performance is not satisfactory. He's been missing key deadlines and makes careless errors in his presentations. Morale in his area seems to be poor, and Jane has been concerned about his impact on the company. However, both she and Alan also know that David has had family problems. They were hoping that, once he resolved them, his performance and attitude at work would improve. Nevertheless, Alan laid it on the line recently—while he wanted to support David, given his level of seniority, he could not allow standards to fall and expected to see some progress, and soon. David was contrite and assured Alan that pressures at home were diminishing and he would soon be back to par.

Today, in David's office, his secretary, Mary Francis, is in floods of tears, and people are suggesting that she go home. His office is a mess with piles of papers everywhere. Mary says he was never an organized person and wouldn't let her file things regularly. "He liked to hold on to current papers himself." The telephone is ringing off the hook. People want to know whether the buzz is true. The press has deluged the front office, wanting confirmation and a statement from the Trust: "Aren't you the organization that's been promoting healthy living and responsible drinking?"

David's diary for this week is full. It includes among other things:

Today

10 A.M. A very important meeting as lead person for the Trust with the health authority social services and other local Trusts to negotiate an agreement involving a potential joint development worth $91 million to the Trust.

This meeting has been difficult to set up because of the schedules of all these senior people. National development monies are involved, and the negotiations are constrained by tight, externally set deadlines. No one else in the Trust has been involved in the preparation for this meeting, apart from David having consulted one or two clinicians.

2:30 P.M. A disciplinary meeting with staff member; Jane (HR) said she'd be there.

Tomorrow

9 A.M. Job planning with Alice Jones, the new hire.

11 A.M. Meeting with the senior doctors to hear their grievances about nurse staffing levels on the wards. Mary Francis says that this meeting was hard to arrange around doctors' clinics, and they have been pressing for it for several weeks.

Questions

1. What could the Trust have done differently to prevent such a crisis from occurring?
2. What policies or procedures might have prevented this?
3. What does the Trust do now?

Source: C. Clegg, K. Legge, and S. Walsh. 1999. The experiencing of managing: A skills guide. *Hampshire, England: Macmillan, 73–75.*

VIDEO COHESION CASE FOR PART II

Horizons: The Importance of People, Human Resource Management, and a Strong Corporate Culture

The Importance of People

A pervasive theme at Horizons is the importance of people. This notion comes from the top, because CEO Don Lee rarely talks about Horizons without talking about the critical importance of the company's personnel. This sentiment was typified in a recent interview Don Lee gave to a company that was conducting a survey titled "What Keeps Managers Up At Night." Of all the things he could have talked about (for example, raising capital, keeping customers happy, learning new technologies), Lee said that he spends the majority of his time "keeping people engaged and working on the quality of life for everybody at the company."

Top-Level Management Team

At the top of Horizons, Lee has hand-picked a group of managers who lead the company's nine divisions and manage its finances and operations. The names of six of the top-level managers, along with a brief description of their primary responsibilities, time with Horizons, and professional backgrounds, is included in Table I. Attributes shared by the top-level managers are that they are all loyal to Lee, believe in the company's mission, and are passionate about the future of Horizons. To complement his longtime employees, Lee periodically brings new blood into his management team. Jim Haring, the chief financial officer, came to Horizons after spending 12 years with a "Big Five" accounting firm and 5 years with an investment and venture capital fund. Similarly, Dave Fullen, the head of the Interactive Division, is a seasoned producer, writer, and musician who joined Horizons within the past couple of years.

To a person, the strength of Lee's management team is its technical savvy, industry experience, and ability to function effectively within the Horizons culture. It is unlikely that a manager who didn't reflect Lee's values and embrace Horizons' team-oriented culture would last long. According to Cherie Hatton, Lee's longtime second in command, most people who join Horizons and find that they do not fit the Horizons culture self-select themselves out of the organization. These occasions, however, are rare, according to Hatton, because of careful selection procedures.

There is an appealing sense of playfulness among Horizons' top-level management team. Don Lee occasionally allows himself to be called the "Big Kahuna," which in turn prompts him to call Cherie Hatton the "Little Kahuna." Mark Rigsby, a longtime Horizons employee, is often called the "Protocol Man" or "Number 2 Guy." The company also has certain terms that it uses to describe operational activities. For example, when Don Lee tells an employee that he or she will be getting a "new toy," that means that he is purchasing the employee a new software package or industrial gadget.

Rank-and-File Employees

Because Horizons has a rather flat organizational structure—meaning that there are very few layers of management between CEO Don Lee and entry-level employees—most of the firm's employees are either experts in their media-related craft or are young new hires.

Managing Human Resources

Selection

The selection process at Horizons is not well structured, which is something that may need to change as the company continues to grow and needs more employees. Many of the new employees begin as college interns, which gives Horizons a chance to "try them out" before a permanent employment relationship is established. The company is clearly looking for people who fit the Horizons culture and will make a meaningful contribution. This notion is exemplified in the employment notice the company has posted on its website. The notice reads:

Horizons Companies is looking for qualified individuals to fill a variety of available positions. We're not just looking for a particular skill-set, we're looking for creative individuals who can work hard to produce compelling digital experiences and can have a good time.

Supervision

Most of Horizons' employees set their own hours and come and go based on the demands of their job. The employees work in teams and are primarily accountable to their team leader and other teammates. Because the company's structure is flat, it is not unusual for employees to communicate directly with a top-level manager or Don Lee when they have a problem or concern. The focus is on getting the job done, rather than on filling out paperwork or adhering to the protocol of a rigid corporate hierarchy.

Although the rather loose structure may cause some people to be skeptical of the rigor of Horizons' work environment, the structure is not likely to change—at least anytime soon. Commenting on his company's work ethic, Lee has said, "There is a ton of high morals

TABLE 1 Horizon's Top Management Team

Name	Primary Responsibility	Time with Horizons and Professional Background
Don Lee	Founder and CEO	Founder and longtime CEO of Horizons
Cherie Hatton	Vice-President of Operations and Head of Education Division	Longtime Horizons employee; 16 years of additional management experience
Mark Rigsby	Vice-President and Head of Video and Film Division	Longtime Horizons employee; previous experience in radio and television
Jim Haring	Chief Financial Officer	Fairly new Horizons employee; lengthy career in accounting (including six years with Coopers & Lybrand)
Dave Fullen	Head of Interactive Division	Fairly new Horizons employee; 30 years of electronic media experience in a variety of capacities
Randy Taggert	Head of Web Development Division	Fairly new Horizons employee; previous experience in graphic design and multimedia production

and ethics here. The group controls itself. Most of them aren't here at 9:00 A.M., but they're still here at 7:00 P.M. when I leave. I don't track time, but I bet if I did, I'd be the guy winning."

Rewards

The company provides its employees both financial and nonfinancial rewards. The financial rewards include competitive pay, benefits, and a 401K plan. Because Horizons is a private company, it also has the discretion to provide its employees additional financial rewards as occasions arise. For example, at the end of 1999, Don Lee announced to his employees that he was matching their 401K contributions 100 percent. There has also been at least one occasion when all the employees in the firm were given one extra week's pay for their efforts on completing an important project on time.

The employees also receive nonfinancial rewards in the form of a flexible work environment, supportive leadership, and a healthy work-family balance. As evidence of the salience of these issues, the company recently surveyed its employees and asked them to name the five things that they liked the most about working at Horizons. The number one response was that Horizons allows its employees to maintain a healthy work-family balance in their lives. Other quality-of-life responses in the top five included "Horizons is a fun, friendly place to work" and "employees are given a lot of creative freedom." There is also a certain amount of excitement and vitality involved with working on creative projects, which is the essence of what Horizons does. Although this "reward" is difficult to quantify, it nonetheless exists.

Employee Concerns

Although Horizons' approach to managing human resources has strengths, it also has limitations, which are becoming more pronounced as the company gets larger. For example, the company has no formal vacation or sick leave policy. Instead, the company has operated on an honor system and has worked things out with employees on a case-by-case basis. The firm also allows its employees to use their own discretion in terms of taking "comp days" following periods of extraordinarily long hours. Although this unusual amount of flexibility appears attractive, employees have started asking for more structure, particularly in terms of better-defined vacation and sick leave policies. Although it may be an overstatement to characterize this as an employee concern, more structure in human resource management is a topic the company will need to address in the near future.

Culture

As described throughout the case, Horizons has a strong organizational culture. Everything the company does, from hiring decisions, to selecting projects, to planning new facilities, is done with the maintenance of the organizational culture in mind. It is clear that the culture us a direct reflection of the company's founder, Don Lee. Lee himself is a laid-back, introspective, people-type person, and those traits are reflected in the organization he has built. Even when talking about growth, the company's employees talk about the risks that growth poses to their organizational culture. The people at Horizons clearly believe that their company is something special, and they worry that growth and change will threaten their way of life.

At the same time, the company does not seem to fear change. To his credit, Lee has been willing to hire people from outside the Horizons culture to assume major leadership roles, as shown in Table I. In addition, statements like "if you're not moving forward, you're moving backward" seem to resonate with the company's employees. The company is also very forward looking when it comes to technology, as evidenced by its major new initiatives into DVD. Although the company seems fixated on maintaining its current culture, it has not done that to a fault when it comes to hiring new people and embracing new technologies.

For Discussion

1. How would you characterize the personalities of the people employed by Horizons?
2. What is meant by the concept of organizational culture (from Chapter 4)? Describe Horizons' culture.
3. Now that you have been introduced to several of Horizons' employees, comment on job satisfaction, organizational commitment, and psychological ownership as it exists within Horizons.
4. Drawing on our discussion of "management attitudes and approaches to managing" in Chapter 2, discuss Don Lee's management philosophy.
5. What observations do you have that address the work-related motivation (that is, the motivation to come to work, to remain attached to Horizons, and to perform well) among Horizons' employees?
6. What type of work-related behaviors would you expect to see among Horizons' employees? Why?

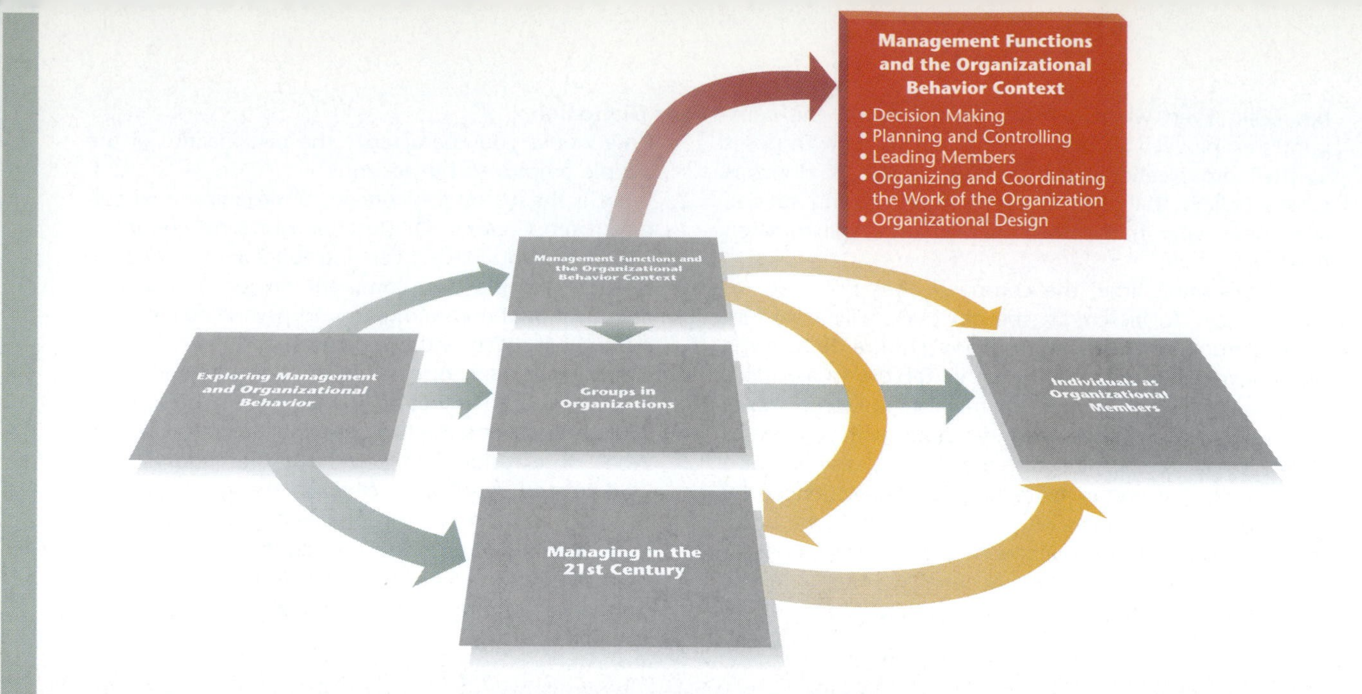

PART III Management Functions and the Organizational Behavior Context

The **integrative model** presented above highlights this portion of your text. At the outset of this book we indicated that three concepts and their interrelationship are at the center of a solid understanding of organizational behavior. In Part I, we briefly introduced two of the building blocks, management and organization. In Part II, we examined the individual as an organizational member, the third building block.

Here in Part III, we endeavor to provide you with a deeper and richer understanding of management and organization. Specifically, we'll explore organizational decision making, planning, controlling, leading, organizing, and organization design. In so doing, we define the *context of organizational behavior* (the OB *context*)—that setting in which the organizational member carries out their organizational role.

The two major features of this context are management practices (decision making, planning and controlling, leading, and organizing, and the way each practice is implemented) and the different features of the organization itself (for example, its size, structure, technology, and processes). The OB context is shaped (see Figure III-1) by the actions of managers in accord with the attitudes, beliefs, opinions, and assumptions that they hold with regard to people, work, and the organization. Rounding this out is the manner in which managers fulfill their social and ethical responsibilities. In Chapter 2, we introduced you to two dominant management philosophies and two approaches to man-

FIGURE III-1

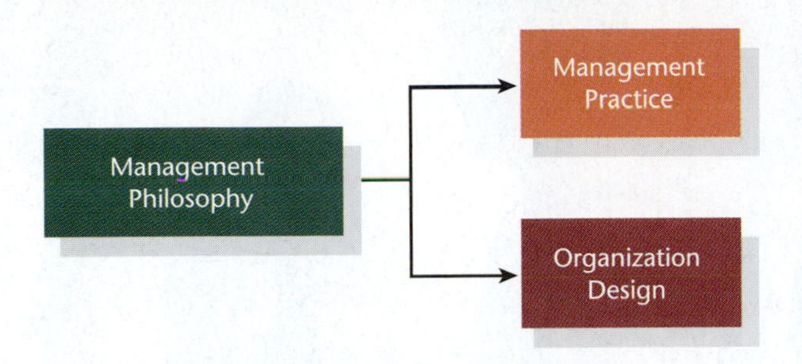

FIGURE III-2

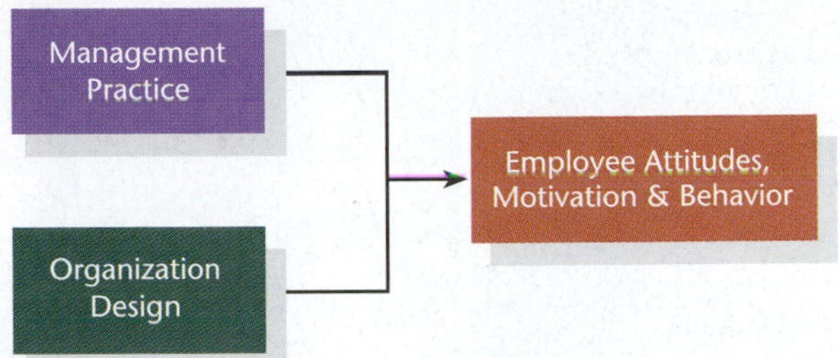

aging. In Chapter 3, we addressed ethics and social responsibility.

The OB context consists of that environment which most immediately surrounds organizational members while they work. As such, this context is the organization's internal environment. To a very large extent, this environment is built on the management practices chosen and implemented and the design of the organization. Each of these dimensions (Figure III-2) has a large impact on the attitudes, motivation, and behaviors of organizational members.

As you may recall from Chapter 2, two dominant and opposing approaches to the practice of management and organization design are control-oriented management as practiced by the mechanistic (bureaucratic) organization, and involvement-oriented management as practiced by the organic organization. In Chapters 9–12, we look at activities that managers engage in, namely decision making, planning, controlling, leading, and organizing. As we explore each activity, differences in the two management approaches will emerge. We will also discuss how these differences in approach impact employee attitudes, motivation, and behavior.

In addition, the design of the organization and the different systems in the organization profoundly influence the attitudes, motivation, and behavior of its members. In the final chapter of Part III we explore this relationship.

Outline

CHAPTER 9

Organizational Decision Making

Learning Objectives

After reading this chapter, you should be able to

1. Describe the nature of decision making. What is decision making, what types of conditions surround the decision-making process, and what types of decisions confront organizational members?
2. Describe and distinguish between the different approaches to decision making.
3. Compare and contrast the rational/economic (classical) and administrative (behavioral) models of decision making.
4. Explain how individual attributes, such as cognitive style, personality, and motivation, affect decision making.
5. Identify and discuss the most common problems that managers face when making decisions.
6. Discuss participative decision making and its relationship with job satisfaction and performance.
7. Explain the role individual differences play in the decision-making process.
8. Compare and contrast approaches to decision making under control-oriented and involvement-oriented management practices.

PHOTO: © R. W. JONES/CORBIS

A FIRST LOOK

Deborah Janus's heart sinks as she turns in the marketing portion of the annual report for Voyagers Travel. As marketing director, she encouraged the travel agency to move to a primarily online inquiry and booking system. Given the boom in Internet travel services, she was sure that Voyagers' customers would like the convenience of booking travel online. Deborah used the idea that Voyager could reduce personnel to convince the president and board of directors to move into the online travel business. Since clients wouldn't be making personal calls to the office itself, Voyagers could scale down and put its resources into state-of-the-art technology.

But Deborah's annual report for the marketing division shows that their marketing plan has not been as successful as they had hoped. In fact, customers are irritated and frustrated with the online system, and business is slowing down. Deborah knows that the board of directors will hold her accountable and wonders how she can prepare for that encounter.

Questions: Why do you think Voyagers' online travel services are failing? Was this a group decision or an individual one? What could Deborah and the board of directors have done differently to avoid this situation?

http://www.cdc.gov

http://www.faa.gov

The summer of 1999 saw the outbreak of an unknown mosquito-borne virus in New York. The Centers for Disease Control and Prevention was slow in identifying the cause because their search focused on rodents and mammals as the source of the virus, and failed to respond to an ornithologist who thought she recognized the symptoms. The animal researchers did not initially share blood samples with her because they were convinced that, like many other mosquito-carried diseases, its origin had to be with rodents or mammals—not birds. During the late 1980s, the nation's air traffic controllers were on the verge of unionizing. One of their major grievances was that the powers within the Federal Aviation Administration (FAA) were making policy decisions about air safety without consulting them—the ones on the front lines. Many claimed that the number of near collisions was rising dramatically and could be traced directly to these policy decisions. In 1986, the space shuttle *Challenger* exploded, killing the seven people aboard and significantly setting back the U.S. space program. Those responsible for the final decision to launch the *Challenger* claimed that they were not fully aware of lower-level engineers' long-expressed concerns over the booster's "O-rings" and concerns that the temperature on the morning of the launch was too low for a safe launch.

What do these incidents have in common? Each characterizes a closed-system perspective of managerial decision making (closed and open systems were discussed in Chapter 4—The Organizational Environment). In each incident, the decision makers were insulated from critical information sources. This highlights a significant challenge for management: developing effective organizational decision-making and problem-solving systems.

Some people equate managing with decision making, because it permeates every aspect of the management of organizations. Decisions need to be made about which goals to pursue and the means to make these goals a reality. Decisions need to be made about how to structure the organization, how to motivate organizational members, and what to do when organizational performance does not measure up to expectation. Thus, decision making is key to the four management functions—planning, organizing, directing, and controlling.

In this chapter we explore the nature of decision making. We introduce a systematic process that facilitates effective decision making. You will discover that not all managers approach the decision-making process systematically; some muddle through, and others simply rely on their gut and intuition. Common problems confronting decision makers are identified, accompanied by observations on how to improve organizational decision making. Finally, we examine the impact that participative decision making has on organizational members.

THE NATURE OF DECISION MAKING

Decision making is the lifeblood of organizations and the very essence of management.[1] It is not unusual for managers to face decisions about hiring and firing, product specifications, return on investment, and the problem employee all in the same business day. Some managers confront decisions rationally and coolly; others decide impulsively or use only part of the information available. Some people avoid making decisions consciously; however, even passive people have a philosophy about how they will confront problems. This passive, problem avoidance approach to decision making is a decision itself—to run away from problems rather than rationally select alternatives.

Managers and others called on to make decisions on behalf of the organization often find themselves confronting decisions about hiring and firing, marketing strategies, plant location, and new technologies. Each of these decisions is usually embedded in a sea of uncertainty, risk, conflict, organizational politics, and lack of clear definition.

What Is Decision Making?

Managers and all organizational members are confronted with occasions to make decisions as a normal part of organizational life. **Decision making** is the process of identifying a set of feasible alternatives and, from these, choosing a course of action. **Decisions** are judgments that directly affect a course of action.[2] While still in high school, for example, Jodi Prohaska had to decide what to do after graduation—look for a job or seek further education. After deciding on college, Jodi collected information about various schools, reviewed the material, narrowed her list to a few alternatives, evaluated each alternative, applied to several schools, and then chose to attend the University of Wisconsin, in Madison. In other words, Jodi did not merely "go to college." She made a decision to go to a particular university.

decision making the process of identifying a set of feasible alternatives and from these, choosing a course of action

decision judgment that directly affects a course of action

Although many use the terms choice making, decision making, and problem solving interchangeably, these three activities are different.[3] *Choice making* refers to the narrow set of activities associated with choosing one option from a set of already identified alternatives. Jodi chose from several possible colleges and universities. Choice making occurs when a manager hires one of five applicants for a quality control job opening. *Decision making* is an intermediate-sized set of activities. It begins with problem identification, proceeds to identifying and evaluating of a set of alternatives, and ends with choice making. *Problem solving* refers to the broad set of activities needed to find and implement a course of action to correct an unsatisfactory situation. It includes not only decision making, but also implementing, monitoring, and maintaining the decision. Problem solving occurs when all of the choice-making and decision-making steps are followed, and when employees implement the chosen course of action and follow up to make certain that the course of action appropriately responds to the occasion that prompted the decision in the first place. Thus, as depicted in Figure 9-1, the problem-solving process includes both decision-making and choice-making processes, and the decision-making process includes choice making.

Many occasions give rise to the need for decisions.[4] First, a current state of affairs may fall short of a goal or an ideal.[5] A publisher, for example, may find that its book sales are not reaching target projections for the current fiscal year. Second, a problem or crisis may arise like what confronted managers of PepsiCo when they were accused of negligence after a number of hypodermic needles were found in their soft drink cans. Third, managers may want to take advantage of an opportunity. For example, several years ago DuPont was one of four companies developing a sucrose polyester in the hope that it would become the food industry's next aspartame (NutraSweet™). Accidentally discovered during research to help premature babies gain weight, this sucrose polyester is now being substituted for fat in cooking. It helps foods retain their traditional taste—but not their calories, because the artificial substance cannot be digested by the human body. A fourth occasion for making decisions is, of course, to maintain the status quo—to preserve a high sales volume, to maintain suppliers' contentment, to keep a consultant, and so on. The fifth reason why managers make decisions is proactive in nature. Carrying out an entrepreneurial role, managers create new opportunities and ventures for their organizations. The decision by Daig Corporation and St. Jude Medical to purchase Kendall Healthcare Products, manufacturer of angio-seal, was characterized by a search for a new venture that would contribute to Daig's objective of becoming a dominant player in the health care products industry. Similarly, during the early 1960s Ford Motor Company's marketing research group identified a major market for a small, sporty, economically priced car that at that time was not being produced by any of their competitors. Ford responded to this opportunity, and their success with the Mustang is legendary. Decision situations need not be limited to one purpose. A hijacking presents a government with a crisis, but, simultaneously, offers the opportunity to forge a closer alliance with another government or to strengthen certain areas of its foreign policy.

http://www.pepsico.com

http://www.dupont.com

FIGURE 9-1 Decision Making, Choice Making, and Problem Solving

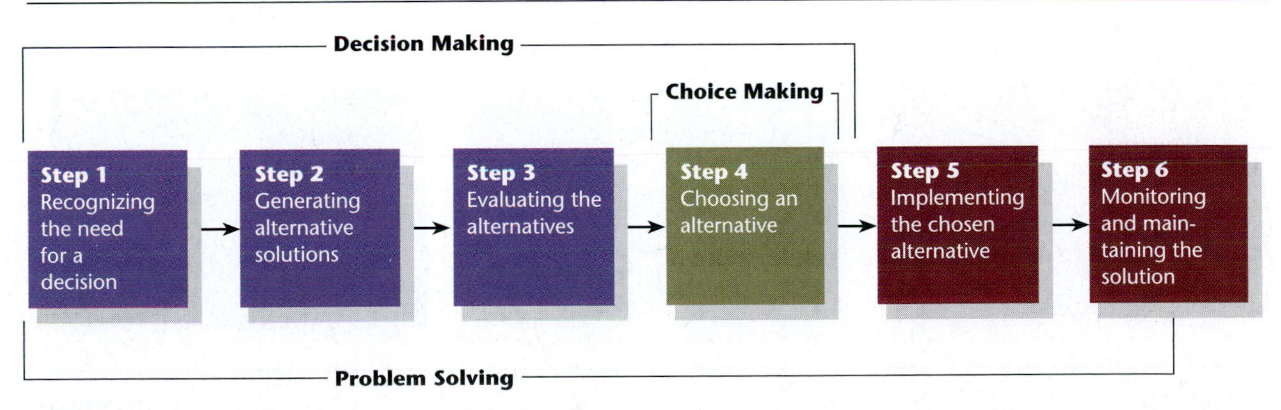

Source: Adapted from *Managerial decision making* by G. R. Huber. Copyright © 1980. Reprinted by permission of Pearson Education, Inc., Upper Saddle River, NJ 07458.

Many decision occasions require managers to make decisions quickly and under pressure. In all cases, decision making focuses on choosing an alternative that managers expect will lead their organization to a desired goal.

Decision Characteristics

As previously noted, organizational members are continuously called on to make decisions and act on behalf of the organization. Occasions that give rise to decision making, such as problems or opportunities, create a set of conditions that can be characterized by the degree of risk, uncertainty, conflict, structure, and politics that the decision maker must address.

Conditions of Certainty, Risk, and Uncertainty Risk and uncertainty characterize decisions and their contexts (see Figure 9-2). Some decisions entail little uncertainty and little risk. Others entail great risk and high levels of uncertainty.

When a decision maker is aware of all available alternatives and the factors (outcomes) and probabilities associated with each, a state of *certainty* exists. Few organizational decisions are made under conditions of true certainty, but some decision situations are relatively certain. Under these conditions, decision making requires the collection and use of accurate, measurable, and reliable information.

Managers who make decisions under conditions of *risk* also know all of the available alternatives. They do not know what will happen if they choose a particular alternative, but they do possess enough information to subjectively assign probabilities of success to each alternative. When decisions are made under risk, managers must collect information that helps them estimate as accurately as possible the probable outcome of each alternative.

http://www.boeing.com

Under conditions of *uncertainty,* decision makers are not aware of all possible courses of action, even though they may be aware of several. For those alternatives that can be identified, there is not enough information to permit certain identification of probable outcomes. For example, as Boeing works on the new supersonic airplane that will fly just above the earth's atmosphere and make the trip between San Francisco and Tokyo in just over two hours, the newness of the venture means that they will have to make many decisions under extremely high levels of uncertainty. Many aspects of the market's reac-

FIGURE 9-2 Degree of Certainty and Decision Making

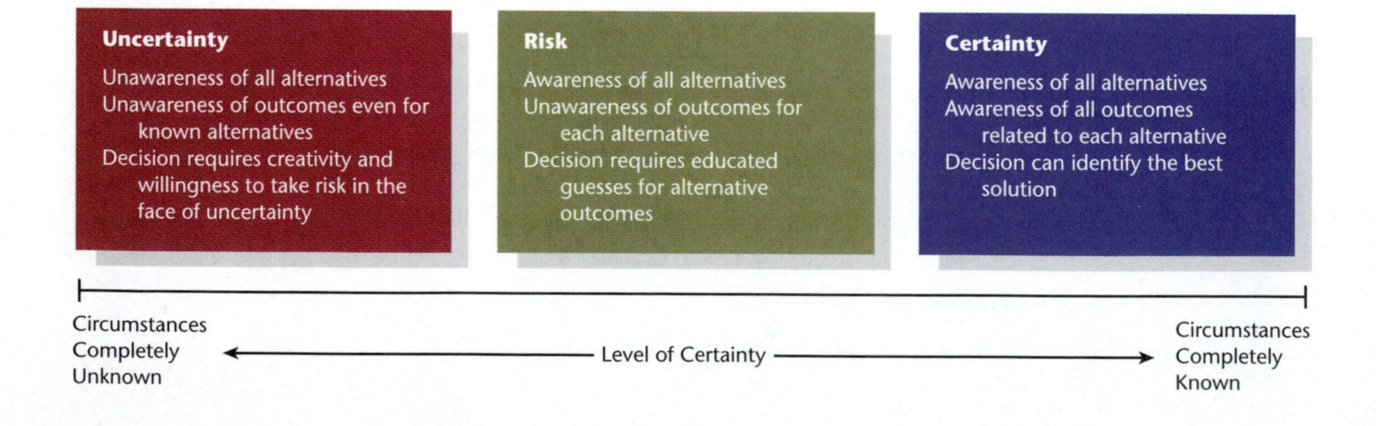

tion and the plane's environmental impact will not fully surface during the planning stages.

Decisions made under high levels of uncertainty can be difficult, and they can make managers very uncomfortable, particularly those managers with a low tolerance for ambiguity. On the positive side, however, decisions made under uncertainty can be very challenging, can provide opportunities for creativity, and can be especially rewarding when they lead to success.

Although many managers are perfectly comfortable making decisions under conditions of risk or uncertainty, they should always try to reduce the uncertainty surrounding their decisions. They can do so by conducting comprehensive and systematic research. The research can tell them more about their alternatives, give them a firmer basis for estimating possible outcomes, and help them look at best and worst alternatives.

Problem Structure The concept of problem structure is primarily concerned with the nature of the existing state, of the desired state, and of the means/methods that can resolve the problem confronting the organization. Problems range from completely structured to completely unstructured.

structured problem problem whose nature and context are well defined

unstructured problem problem characterized by a lack of problem and context definition

A **structured problem** is one where the existing problem and its context are well defined. The desired end state is clear and the course of action to get to the end state is clear.[6] At the other extreme, an **unstructured problem** is characterized by lack of problem and context definition. The desired end state is not clearly understood, and therefore the appropriate cause of action is unknown.

Structured problems entail role clarity, and unstructured problems entail role ambiguity. For the organizational member, role ambiguity is a major cause of on-the-job stress.[7]

Conflict Decision making rarely unfolds in a simple and straightforward manner. In addition to problems related to risk, uncertainty, and poorly defined structure, decision makers frequently have to deal with conflict.

On occasion the conflict can be psychological. As decision makers we are frequently trapped by our own history, preferences, training, and biases, finding ourselves having to do things that do not square with who we are. Human resource managers in many of Japan's largest firms, who for years were able to embrace "employment-for-life" policies, experienced an incredible amount of personal conflict when economic conditions during the 1990s forced their organizations to cut back personnel.

In addition to intra-individual conflict, interpersonal (individual-to-individual and group-to-group) conflict frequently accompanies decision making. Disagreement over the desirability of outcomes and/or disagreement over the means to achieve these outcomes are common. A recent decision at Minnesota Power to construct a new paper recycling facility produced several groups actively lobbying for competing uses of the resources that were to be used for this venture. One group lobbied to expand the paper-making capacity of Lake Superior Paper Industries, another group lobbied to increase investments in the company's Topeka Group, while a third group pushed hard for the development of Superior Recycled Fiber Industries. Few organizational decisions are likely to be unanimous or uncompromised, and conflict is commonplace.

http://www.mnpower.com/main.html

Politics Decision making, as revealed by Minnesota Power's decision to construct a paper recycling facility, frequently unfolds amidst organizational politics. Political activities are those that increase one's power base over other individuals and groups. Organizational politics recognize that individuals and groups in organizations often have preferences both for outcomes and for how things will be done. Thus, *politics* in decision making represents the use of power to achieve and/or protect one's self-interests in the presence of other interest groups.

Political decision making has a number of distinct characteristics. It often involves attempts to overcome an opponent by building coalitions, bargaining, trading support across issues at different points in time, working to achieve key positions, and controlling resources (like withholding information central to the decision at hand) in an effort to outmaneuver the opposition. The decisions that emerge when organizational politics are at work are commonly focused on what is desired by one or more intra-organizational interest groups, as opposed to what is good for the organization as a whole.

Types of Decisions

Managers make many different types of decisions every day. When should an organization construct a new building? How should a company react to a competitor's price cut? Is it time to develop and market a new product? How should a manager deal with absenteeism and low levels of performance? In this section we discuss some of the many types of decisions that confront managers.

means decision concerns procedures or actions undertaken to achieve particular goals; that is, it specifies how a goal is to be reached

ends decision focuses on the articulation of a desired goal (outcome)

strategic decision identifies the ends and means associated with positioning an organization in its external task environment

managerial (tactical) decision specifies how an organization intends to integrate its institutional level with its technical core, and how it will coordinate the diverse work systems within the technical core

operating decision deals with the day-to-day operation of an organization

Means vs. Ends Decisions Decisions may be about how to achieve goals (the means) or about the goals themselves (the ends). **Means decisions** concern procedures or actions undertaken to achieve particular goals—in other words, how a goal is to be reached. **Ends decisions** are those decisions that focus on the goals (outcomes) that are to be pursued. For example, during the 1990s, many American organizations were downsizing. They had set a goal (an ends decision) to reduce the size of the work force. (It could be argued that the ends decision to reduce the work force was itself a means decision, the end being reducing costs and increasing flexibility.) To achieve this goal, many companies engaged in massive layoffs, while others offered early retirement programs to encourage employees to leave the work force voluntarily. The means to reaching the ends goal of a reduced work force was to encourage early retirement. In practice, means and ends decisions are often linked. In fact, ends decisions are more likely to be successful when they are combined with means decisions.

Decision Levels Managers make decisions that affect various levels of the organization. At the broadest level, **strategic decisions** reflect management's strategies for positioning an organization in its external environment. Brad Rogers, manufacturer of peat-based briquettes, for example, made a strategic decision to begin marketing his company's products in a new state. At an intermediate level, **managerial** (or **tactical**) **decisions** specify how an organization intends to integrate its institutional level with its technical core and how it will coordinate work systems within the technical core. Because Brad has decided to market the briquettes in other states, for example, he must decide how to allocate resources for the expanded operations; this is a managerial decision. At a narrower level, **operating decisions** deal with the day-to-day operations of an organization. Brad will have to coordinate the daily activities, such as customer contacts, sales reports, and delivery problems, to handle the expanded operations. Because organizations are dynamic, integrated entities, decisions at one level are likely to be felt at many other levels. Operating decisions ultimately affect strategic decisions, just as strategic decisions affect decisions made at lower levels.

programmed decision routines employed to deal with frequently occurring situations

nonprogrammed decision the process of addressing unique or novel situations confronting the organization

functional decision relates to one of the organization's functions (production, marketing, accounting, finance, human resources)

job content decision relates to the inherent nature of the work performed by an individual or work group

job context decision relates to issues that surround the job, but are not a part of the job per se

Programmed vs. Nonprogrammed Decisions Some decisions cover routine circumstances and may become formal company policy. Other decisions cover special or novel circumstances. **Programmed decisions** are routines that deal with frequently occurring situations, such as requests for vacations by employees. In routine situations, where problems are structured, it is usually much more efficient for managers to use a programmed decision rather than make a new decision for each similar situation. In programmed decisions, managers make a decision only once, when the program is created. Subsequently, the program itself specifies procedures to follow when similar circumstances arise. The creation of these routines results in the formulation of rules, procedures, and policies. Programmed decisions are not necessarily confined to simple issues, such as vacation policies or the appropriate dress for the sales force; they also deal with complex issues, such as the types of tests that a doctor needs to conduct before performing major surgery on a patient with diabetes.

Nonprogrammed decisions generally are made in unique or novel situations. They tend to arise when decision makers deal with unstructured problems. Nonprogrammed decisions are necessary when no prior routine or practice exists to guide the decision-making process. For example, when the first Sears employee with Acquired Immune Deficiency Syndrome (AIDS) was identified, a decision had to be made about whether the employee could continue to work as long as he was able. The decision required special consideration and could not have been made at that time simply by referring to a policy manual.

Looking at control-oriented management and the mechanistic organization, we generally find the institutional level of the organization absorbing the majority of unstructured problems, and as a consequence a high incidence of unprogrammed decision making unfolds at this level. The contemporary move toward the high-involvement organization, organizational restructuring, and empowerment of organizational members reflects an increase in the frequency with which unstructured problems and nonprogrammed decision making occur in the organization's technical core.

Other Types of Decisions Three additional ways to think about the types of decisions common to organizations are functional, job content, and job context. **Functional decisions** are those that relate to one of the organization's functional areas (for example, operations, marketing, human resources). **Job content decisions** focus on the inherent nature of a job, such as decisions about the amount of autonomy and variety to be designed into the job. **Job context decisions** address issues that surround the job, but are not a part of the job per se. Decisions about the hours that employees work and the amount of flexibility they have in choosing those hours, along with pay, do not define the job, but are clearly related to the job.

THE DECISION-MAKING PROCESS AND MANAGERIAL PRACTICES

Ask several managers how they make decisions and solve problems and you will probably hear many say, "I don't know," "There are no rules; you just do it," and "I just do what feels right." In reality, good decision makers, acting either consciously or unconsciously, follow a fairly consistent pattern. This pattern can be identified and used to improve the quality of decisions. The following sections identify a number of distinct stages in the decision-making process.

A Systematic Approach to the Decision-Making Process

Earlier in this chapter, we distinguished among decision making, choice making, and problem solving. In this section we examine in greater detail four distinct steps involved in a systematic decision-making process (review Steps 1–4 in Figure 9-1). The remaining two steps in Figure 9-1, implementing the chosen alternative and monitoring and maintaining the solution, are part of the problem-solving process.

http://www.orglearner.com

Step 1: Recognizing the Need for a Decision: Problem Sensitivity, Definition, and Understanding The first step in the decision-making process consists of recognizing that a decision is needed. (Much of the following discussion of the decision-making process assumes the existence of a problem. It is important, however, to remember that a number of situations, including opportunities, also give rise to the need for decision making.) Problem recognition begins when a decision maker is alerted by a signal that a decision is needed—as discussed in Chapter 5, the sensation part of the perceptual process has been triggered. A habitually tardy employee, slipping sales, an unusual hum in a computer console, or an angry supervisor signal that a problem may exist. A manager may sense something is wrong but cannot describe the problem yet. Sometimes people identify problems automatically. For example, Tanya returns to her dorm after a difficult examination to listen to Mozart, only to discover that her old stereo has conked out. This is an obvious signal: She has a problem, and she needs to decide whether to fix the old system or buy the new (and expensive) system that she wants.

One way to look at this first step of the decision process is as *detecting symptoms.* After detecting a problem (opportunity), decision makers need to identify and define the problem in detail. They must understand why the situation is a problem, what its sources are, and what it affects. In essence, the manager must develop an understanding of the anatomy of the situation. Frequently decision makers fail to explore the context sufficiently and come to believe that the symptom *is* the problem. Subsequent efforts to get rid of the symptom are ineffective because the problem simply manifests itself in other ways. Managers at Miller Dwan Hospital came to believe that employee absenteeism was too high and that it was an organizational problem that needed correcting. The resulting policy docked employees a certain percent of their wages after three unexcused absences. What these managers failed to recognize was that the absenteeism was a symptom of a much deeper problem that they failed to resolve, and it resurfaced through a decline in productivity and increased turnover. In this case, job dissatisfaction was extremely high, and employees stayed away from work to avoid some very undesirable working conditions. Under the new policy, the employees came to work, but they found other ways to avoid the undesirable conditions—they simply avoided work while at work, and productivity declined further. Others found jobs with other health care providers.

To reach a detailed understanding, many decision makers employ *decomposition.* That is, they break a problem into a series of subproblems (decompose the problem), analyze the subproblems, and then recombine them into a better understood whole.

Decision makers employ several guidelines to assist them in understanding the decision situation. First, they differentiate between events and the language used to describe an event. Managers should make sure that they are looking at the event itself and not at an interpretation of it—and perhaps an incorrect one at that. For example, Eric Jon, a union leader, stated that "the labor-management conflict that has characterized this place for the past three years stems directly from management's continued exploitation of the work force." This characterization of labor-management problems is not an objective analysis of the problems or their causes. It is the speaker's perception of events, not necessarily the true cause and effect. Second, managers must identify whether the available information is fact or opinion, and they must evaluate the degree of certainty that surrounds the problem. For example, Madison Lee, a sales manager for Dunham Business Systems, commented to her boss, "Mark Johnson is lazy, and, as a result, he is by far our poorest salesperson." To diagnose the problem, Madison's boss must know whether he is dealing with opinion or with actual performance. Third, determine the underlying cause rather than placing blame or giving credit. In other words, understand rather than judge; that is, investigate the dynamics of the situation and determine its cause. If Mark's performance is low, is it because he is lazy—or because he was assigned a difficult territory? Successful problem diagnosis entails looking for causes and not placing blame or giving credit. Fourth, effective decision makers look for several causes. Problems and opportunities usually have more than one cause. When people identify only a single source of a problem, they are probably overlooking information that might help them formulate a better solution. Finally, decision makers are encouraged to be specific. That is, to explicitly formulate a diagnosis of the problem and state it so that others can understand as clearly as possible what the problem is and why it has arisen. In the previous example, it would have been helpful for Madison to specify that Mark's poor sales performance is due to a lack of motivation, to the unattractiveness of the rewards for good sales performance, and to distractions caused by his problems at home.[8]

http://www.decisionstrategies.com

Identifying and understanding a problem can be extremely difficult. Problems and crises frequently introduce uncertainty and discomfort. For these reasons, people sometimes avoid or take problem definition for granted. They gloss over the first step in the decision-making process and rush to step 2.

Management expert Tom Peters notes that managers and organizational members must learn to "thrive on chaos." Change must be relished with enthusiasm and energy. Rush and uncertainty are a part of today's organizational environment.[9] The high-achieving organizations will be those that develop the ability to scan their internal and external environments and identify and seize opportunities for change.

Step 2: Generating Alternative Solutions After a problem has been identified, diagnosed, and understood, a manager is ready to move into the second stage of the decision-making process—generating a set of alternative solutions. In developing these solutions, decision makers must first specify the goals they hope to achieve. Are they trying to reduce costs? Improve product quality? Increase sales? Once they determine their goals, they can search for alternative means of reaching them.

Alternative solutions generally fall into two categories: existing solutions and custom solutions. **Existing solutions** are alternatives that have been used (or at least considered) by other decision makers in similar situations. Thus, they can be seen as programmed solutions. For example, many organizations purchase programs—compensation systems, for instance—that have worked well in other organizations. Existing solutions are frequently adapted, with or without modification, to new situations. Existing solutions sometimes prove an easy way out—perhaps too easy. Managers frequently rely more on existing solutions and their own previous experiences than on fresh information for making their

existing solution
a solution to decision occasions (a problem) that has been previously developed

Reprinted with special permission of King Features Syndicate, Inc.

decisions.[10] In failing to consider fresh information, managers might fail to develop solutions that fit the organization and its current problem.

custom solution
a solution to decision occasions (problems) that is specifically developed for the situation at hand

Custom solutions are developed specifically for a current situation. Custom solutions are called for by unstructured problems. It is at this stage that creativity enters the decision-making process, whether through fresh adaptations of existing alternatives, a combination of alternatives, or the development of new alternatives.

Fostering creativity is not an easy task. People's creative powers tend to get stifled through formal educational processes, where people are taught rote memorization, precision, logic, and accuracy instead of freewheeling thought. However, creativity can be nurtured. Solomon H. Snyder, Director of the Department of Neuroscience at the Johns Hopkins School of Medicine, noted that "breakthroughs stem frequently from chance observations. A scientist notices something peculiar and has the curiosity to suspect that something significant has transpired. . . . I encourage my students to heed what they see, hear, or smell with their experimental animals, tissues, and test tubes."[11] This comment underlines the importance of honing our powers of observation. We need to work hard at seeing and listening to the world around us, then take these signals and study them. In addition to honing our powers of observation as a means to idea generation and creative problem solving, a variety of steps can be taken to generate ideas. Procter & Gamble, for example, instituted a toll-free number as one means of getting customer input. Their 800-line has become a major source of product improvement ideas. Other organizations make frequent use of brainstorming sessions (see Chapter 15)—a freewheeling group thinking and idea generation process—to help stimulate creative thought as a part of the decision-making process and the development of alternatives.

http://www.pg.com

An important component in this step is the generation of multiple alternatives. Lee Iacocca, while an executive with Chrysler, advocated this decision-making principle. He said that he doesn't like to settle for "either chocolate or vanilla." Instead, he always wanted "strawberry" as an option. According to management consultant William F. O'Dell, "The more alternatives that you get to choose from, the more leeway you have for creative discussion."[12]

http://www.chrysler.com

Step 3: Evaluating Alternatives Once managers develop a list of alternative solutions, their next task is to evaluate them. Research, experimentation, and drawing on experience are common tools for this step of the decision process. To begin, managers estimate how well each alternative meets the organization's goals and objectives. That is, how well would each alternative be expected to reduce costs, improve quality, or increase sales? The goal is to evaluate how satisfactory each alternative is.

As a part of this process, decision makers focus on the strengths and weaknesses, pros and cons, and latent and manifest consequences of each alternative. In addition, it is important to evaluate their feasibility. In doing so, managers should ask such questions as

- How much will each alternative cost, both in money and in human resources?
- Is the alternative acceptable to those who have to make it work?
- What risks are associated with the alternative?
- Are there legal, regulatory, social responsibility, or ethical barriers associated with the alternative?
- How will this alternative influence other aspects of the organization?

Step 3 of the decision-making process usually eliminates some alternatives. Some alternatives are eliminated because they are not satisfactory. Perhaps the evaluation suggests that they increase rather than decrease costs. Other alternatives are eliminated because they are too risky or uncertain. Increasing the size of the O-rings on the space shuttle's engine just before liftoff is, of course, too risky. Still other alternatives simply are not feasible. Evaluation might, for example, identify a law that prohibits an alternative or might suggest an adverse social consequence to a particular alternative.

Procter & Gamble and many other organizations commonly evaluate decisions in terms of what they add to the "bottom line." Given the difficulty of forecasting long-term profitability, they sometimes use short-term profits as a predictor of the longer term. This can be a risky strategy as P&G discovered with Duncan Hines cookies. The product got off to a fast start, the short term suggested a good long-term return, but it soon ran into stiff competition with same-niche entries from Nabisco, Frito-Lay, and Keebler. Ford Motor Company often evaluates an option's impact on profitability using a surrogate criteria. Employing consumer "intention to buy" survey information facilitates evaluation of alternatives.[13]

http://www.duncanhines.com

http://www.nabisco.com

http://fritolay.com

Step 4: Choosing an Alternative If, after all possible solutions have been evaluated, only one viable alternative remains, the decision is essentially made. Usually, however, several alternatives remain under consideration after the evaluation process; therefore, the final stage in the decision process involves making judgments and choices.

Quantitative and qualitative tools often help managers select the most favored alternative. Examples of two quantitative tools are *queuing models,* which identify the best number of waiting lines, and *break-even analysis,* which identifies the point at which sales revenue will equal the total cost of producing a product or service. The *delphi, synetics,* and *nominal group technique* (discussed in Chapter 15) represent three qualitative tools that aid decision makers with their choice.

The tools of the trade only *help* decision makers choose, however. Decision makers must ultimately decide what they want to accomplish. Three decision criteria are optimizing, maximizing, and satisficing. If decision makers hope to *optimize,* they want to find the best possible decision—a next to impossible task! To *maximize,* decision makers must determine whether an alternative meets the maximum number of objectives. To **satisfice,** decision makers try only to find the first satisfactory solution. This is the criterion, according to Nobel Prize winner Herbert Simon, that decision makers most commonly follow. As explained in later sections, different approaches to decision making favor one of these

satisfice the selection of a decision alternative that is just "satisfactory" in nature decision criteria. The nature of the decision process can change substantially, depending on which approach is chosen. It usually takes more time, for example, to maximize than to satisfice—and still more time to optimize (if this is even possible).

Many organizational decisions are made by compromising and achieving consensus.[14] Touching base with the boss and/or colleagues is commonplace. This is particularly true where there is a high level of task interdependence (that is, where a decision made in one area impacts other areas of the organization because of the way tasks are tied together). Consensus-based decisions are difficult to make. Frequently these decisions are governed by emotion and personal opinions instead of rational thought.[15]

Contingency Approaches to Decision Making

The variety of situations confronting managers calls for various approaches to decision making. Two popular situation-based (contingency) approaches come from James Thompson and Arthur Tudin, and Victor Vroom and his colleagues Philip Yetton and Arthur Jago.

The Thompson and Tudin Model The Thompson and Tudin model is presented in Figure 9-3. Two critical situational conditions guide the selection of a decision strategy: preferences about outcomes and belief about causation.[16] Thus, Thompson and Tudin advise that a decision maker ask two questions: (1) Is there agreement about the outcome that will result from the decision we are about to make? And, (2) Is there agreement about the processes we should use to achieve our goal? These two questions give rise to four very different decision situations that work groups face. Thompson and Tudin have identified a decision-making approach for three of these situations.

computational decision-making approach reliance on an expert to guide the decision-making process

The **computational decision-making approach** is a rational, mechanical process. The computational approach works when there is agreement on the desired outcomes and the existence of a well-developed body of knowledge that instructs an organization on how to proceed. Under these conditions, relevant

FIGURE 9-3 Decision Strategies

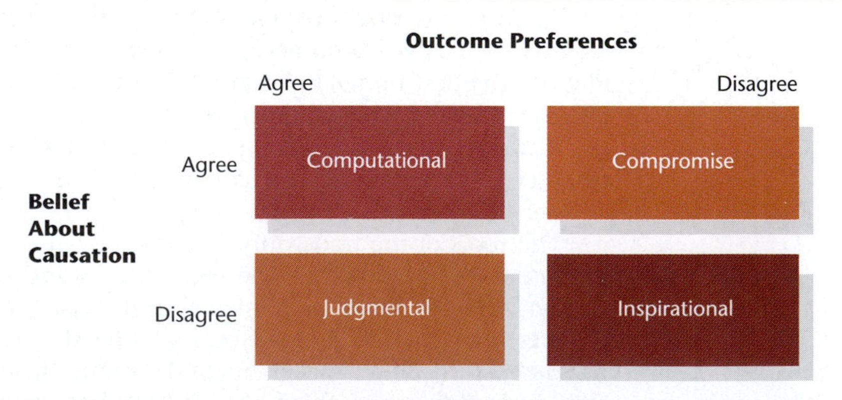

Source: Adapted from J. D. Thompson and A. Tudin. 1959. Strategies, structures, and processes of organizational decisions. In J. D. Thompson, P. B. Hammond, R. W. Hawkes, B. H. Junker and A. Tudin (Eds.), *Comparative studies in administration.* Pittsburgh: University of Pittsburgh Press, 195–216.

information, including facts regarding the problem and desired outcomes, is turned over to an expert, who may be a manager, staff manager, or subordinate. This expert interprets the existing body of knowledge, makes the decision, and directs others on how to respond. When Ford Motor Company detects a safety problem with one of its models, managers do not solve the problem. Instead, engineers are instructed to apply the technology they control to develop an engineering solution to the problem.

judgmental decision-making approach reliance on majority rule from the personal judgments rendered by a group of experts

The **judgmental decision-making approach** is used when managers agree on their goals but have no body of knowledge to guide them on how to achieve these goals. They therefore ask experts to share their knowledge, ideas, and opinions and to use their creativity to develop solutions in the face of uncertainty. Personal judgments that result from the group's interaction and personal reflections are combined to arrive at a decision. The decision rule that gets applied is majority rule, reflecting the fact that no one has a "corner on the opinion of correctness." For example, when Chrysler's managers noted a drop in station wagon sales in the late 1970s, they sought a wide range of input and generated many alternative solutions. The judgmental solution they settled on from among all the possibilities was the minivan (possibly the best decision made by Chrysler in the last three decades).

compromise decision-making approach reliance on a negotiated decision from representatives of competing interest groups

In the **compromise decision-making approach**, individuals or groups who disagree about preferred outcomes bargain. Differences in terms of preferences, values, or ideological differences call for bargaining and negotiation. This approach requires broad-based participation by members from each preference group, yet with a limit on the size of the actual negotiating group. In order to move effectively toward a resolution of their conflict over goals, each interest group selects a spokesperson to represent them in the group decision process. This strategy calls for participation through representation, with each interest group agreeing that its top priority must be resolving the conflict. It is important that each group have access to all relevant information and veto power over emerging decisions. The ultimate aim is to reach a compromise for which each group member feels ownership, such as when departments agree on a release date for a new product.

inspirational decision-making approach reliance on intuition (inspiration) to resolve decision occasions (a problem) under conditions of ends and means disagreements within a decision-making body

The **inspirational decision-making approach** is characterized by extremely high levels of uncertainty, because there is no agreement on either goals or methods. Thompson and Tudin were unable to identify a successful strategy for this situation. Such conditions frequently cause managers to procrastinate in the hope that the problem will go away.

When there is no agreement on either how to move forward or which goals are preferred, commitment to finding a resolution to the impasse, continued dialogue, and open and complete sharing of information are crucial, or the organization is likely to weaken. This is a time for creativity and intuition.[17] Finding ways to reduce the national deficit, for example, may well call for the inspirational approach. The synetics, delphi, and nominal group techniques are structured group processes that can aid inspirational decision making.

Thompson and Tudin's contingency model suggests that managers must be flexible in their approaches to decision making. Under some conditions, they will make the decisions and direct others. At other times, they will look to experts to make decisions and provide the needed direction. Still other conditions will call for any number of group decision processes.

Research suggests that several organizational factors should be considered as managers decide on an appropriate decision-making strategy. Decision making is typically done on a hierarchical basis, with managers directing the activities of their group when a decision is being made for a large department, when there is little task uncertainty, when an established set of procedures defines how an activity should be performed, and when there is little interdependence among those who will be affected by the decision. Group forms of decision making (to be discussed more fully in Chapter 15) are effective when there are high levels of interdependence among those affected by the decision, when group size is small, and when task uncertainty is high. Finally, individual employees are likely to exercise high levels of discretion in the performance of their jobs under conditions of low interdependence and high levels of task uncertainty.[18] Thus, two technology dimensions—task uncertainty and task interdependence—and social system size play a major role in influencing the use of hierarchical, group, and individual approaches to decision making.

The Decision Tree Decision making is commonly hindered by the fact that managers often select the wrong approach to decision making. In answer to this common pitfall, Victor Vroom of Yale University and his colleagues (Philip Yetton of the University of New South Wales in Australia, and Arthur Jago from the University of Missouri) developed the decision tree.[19] Their decision tree technique helps managers "decide how to decide." That is, it is a tool that helps managers decide the extent to which their group should be involved in making decisions.

http://www.mindtools.com/dectree.html

Most managers have their own way of involving (or not involving) their employees in planning and decision making. Some managers conduct these tasks in an autocratic and authoritarian manner. They develop plans and make decisions solo, without asking for input from others. Other managers work with their group and reach the decision by consensus. These two styles define the extremes of the continuum. In reality, neither of these two styles—nor the styles in between—is best for every planning and decision situation. Instead, managers (team leaders) should analyze each situation and then select an approach that best fits it.

The decision tree model helps managers select the appropriate amount of employee involvement in the decision-making process. They described five approaches:

1. *Autocratic I (AI):* A manager makes plans and decisions alone, without any input from employees.
2. *Autocratic II (AII):* A manager asks for information from employees, who may or may not be informed as to why they are being asked. The manager then makes the plans and decisions alone.
3. *Consultative I (CI):* A manager shares the situation with the group and asks each individual member for information and an evaluation of the problem. No group meetings are held. The manager makes the plans and decisions alone.
4. *Consultative II (CII):* A manager shares the situation with the group and asks them for information and an evaluation of the problem. The manager makes the plans and decisions alone.
5. *Group (G):* A manager shares the situation with the group and asks them for information and an evaluation of the problem. The manager accepts and implements the plan or decision agreed on by the group.

Decision trees help managers find the best style for a particular situation. After managers answer a specified set of questions, they follow the decision tree to one of its many branches (see Figure 9-4). To use the tree, begin on the left and answer each prescribed question (see below). Depending on your answer, a branch on the decision tree leads you to the next question, and the process is repeated until you arrive at the end of a branch. Next to the branch you will find a list of appropriate strategies for your situation. If more than one alternative appears at the end of a branch, use the one with the lowest costs or the one you prefer if cost is not an issue. It is often possible to combine the characteristics of two or more acceptable alternatives.

The appropriate degree of employee participation in the decision-making process revolves around the nature of the problem, the required level of decision quality, and the importance of having employees commit to the decision. The following are questions managers should focus on as they work their way through the decision tree: How important is the quality of this decision? How important is employee commitment to the decision? Do I have sufficient information to make a high-quality decision? Is the decision problem well structured? If I make the decision myself, is it reasonably certain that my employees will be committed to the decision? Do subordinates share the organizational goals to be attained in solving this problem? Is conflict over preferred solutions likely to occur among subordinates? Do employees have enough information to make a high-quality decision? As shown in Figure 9-4, these decisions are answered in terms of "high/low" or "yes/no."

Prescriptively, the model, for example, calls for "group decision making" when the importance of (a) the quality of the decision is low, (b) subordinate commitment to the decision is high, and (c) if you were to make the decision by yourself, it is reasonably certain that your subordinates would not be committed to the decision. Autocratic decision making, for example, would be called for when the importance of (a) the quality of the decision is low, and (b) group commitment to the decision is low. The decision tree has generated a great deal

FIGURE 9-4 Illustration of a Decision Tree Model

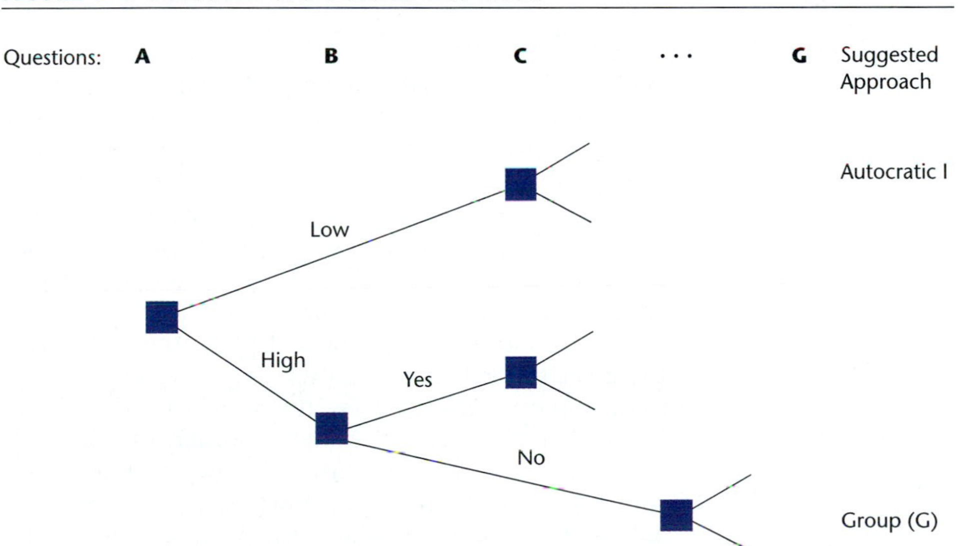

of interest and acceptance by a large number of managers. At Wisconsin Tissue Mills, for example, both management and employees have on numerous occasions expressed their enthusiasm about the way decisions are handled as a result of management's use of this decision-making tool. In addition, research evidence supports the model's prescriptions.[20]

Muddling Through

Many observers of organizational decision making conclude that managers do not seclude themselves and deliberately and systematically move from problem definition to alternative generation to alternative evaluation to the choice stages. Much of the decision making in organizations unfolds in a sea of uncertainty and turbulence, amidst several and competing streams of activity, as well as within the context of organizational politics.

According to Charles E. Lindblom, it is common to observe decision making that represents small adjustments to the status quo. Decision makers engage in a limited search for a small number of alternatives, undertake very little experimentation, and avoid risk taking and producing large effects. Tomorrow's actions are the result of small shifts from what is being done today.[21] This is the *incremental* approach to decision making.

http://www.kroger.com

Lindblom refers to this process as "muddling through."[22] The Kroger Company, after closing some 1200 supermarkets, essentially engaged in this decision-making strategy. Management decided to operate in markets where they might be able to achieve a 20 to 25 percent market share. This enabled them to minimize operating expenses, and to use one or a limited number of stores to experiment with and learn from the array of services that they offered. Kroger then added a cheese shop in one or two stores and observed its performance before deciding on further expansion. Adopting this incremental decision-making approach, they gradually, rather than abruptly, moved into providing the variety of services they now provide, such as cheese shops, beauty salons, flower shops, and health food centers.[23] Research suggests that incrementalism can be effective, especially in unstable environments.[24]

Typical Managerial Practices

While it is easy to advocate a systematic approach to decision making, muddling through, incrementalism, and as illustrated by Kroger's slow and careful transition from one stage to the next suggest that many managers don't follow the systematic four-step approach discussed earlier. Many behaviors are not conscious in nature; instead, they are driven by habit. Many people don't know when it pays to be systematic in decision making. Habitual or intuitive responses are not necessarily bad; managers who have internalized the goals of an organization and developed a good sense for the management process may be able to handle uncomplicated problems quite easily from instinct. Some of the great researchers and entrepreneurs seem to "just know" when the time is right—they are able to "seize the moment." This is the "art of management." It is not that they haven't thought through the issues at hand, it is just that the decision *appears* to arise "from out of the blue," often while they are doing something totally unrelated. However, the vast majority of managers need to be able to diagnose the situations that they face, to judge the importance of a decision, and to determine whether to decide systematically or allow instinct to carry the day.

Not all decisions managers face are of equal importance. A decision about a habitually tardy employee clearly differs from a decision about marketing a new product. Problems and opportunities vary in their size and the length of commitment required, the flexibility of the plans emerging from the decision, the impact a particular decision carries, and who is affected by the decision. The need for a more systematic approach to decision making increases as the size and length of commitment expands, as the flexibility of plans diminishes, as uncertainty grows, and as the human impact of the decision rises.

Sometimes managers have to make decisions under extremely high levels of uncertainty. The problems, alternatives, solutions, and goals are ill defined. Cause-and-effect relationships are not clearly identified. The decision context is turbulent, a great deal of confusion surrounds the decision, and a myriad of things are happening all at once. Under such circumstances, there are times when problem identification and solution may not even be related to each other. Some problems are never solved, even when solutions are available. Solutions may be adopted independently of a recognized problem or in the absence of an agreed-on set of goals. Some decisions are random—they don't unfold in a logical, organized, and systematic manner. Sounds like a crazy and mixed-up place—it is! And unfortunately, it is not all that uncommon. The organization and its management process sometimes resemble a "garbage can" into which problems, solutions, participants, and choices are haphazardly tossed. Occasionally, a problem, solution, participant, and choice happen to connect at one point; in that case, the problem may be solved.[25] Usually, though, the *garbage can approach to decision making*[26] just plain "stinks"!

Despite the fact that a systematic approach to decision making is widely known to be effective, studies show that managers seldom progress smoothly through the stages of decision making.[27] The process is marked by frequent interruptions, delays, and periods of acceleration. Failures due to undesired results and poor planning frequently force a return to earlier stages of the process. It never hurts to ponder what constitutes a great management decision. See *An Inside Look* on page 322 for one perspective.

PROBLEMS IN THE DECISION-MAKING PROCESS

Professor of Management Science Paul C. Nutt recently observed that "half the decisions in organizations fail" as a result of "managers who employ poor tactics."[28] Regardless of whether decisions are made individually or in groups, several problems confront those managing decision situations. Many observers of decision making suggest that bad decisions frequently originate in the "way the decision was made." Decision makers often fall into several traps that contribute to poor decisions: displaying a bias toward alternatives that maintain the status quo, making future choices that serve to justify past choices, and seeking evidence to confirm our instincts or preference and avoiding evidence that contradicts it.[29] Two of the most common pitfalls are the tendency to misunderstand a situation and to rush the decision process. A third problem frequently made by managers is using the wrong decision-making approach.

AN INSIDE LOOK

A Great Management Decision

What constitutes a great management decision? In 1998, *Management Review* polled experts in the field and compiled a list of the 75 Greatest Management Decisions Ever Made. The list spans the ages from the Bible to Napoleon to the era of Microsoft, and offers instructive insight into management decisions that influence us to this day.

The history of the world is full of significant management decisions. None of the great monuments of the world would exist if managers had not coordinated their financing, labor, and construction. Most great management decisions were based on human resources, marketing, budgeting, operations, and planning, and influenced world history as well as industries and companies' futures.

Following are two recent examples of great management decisions that have influenced the way that businesses operate:

The Tylenol Poisoning Episode: In 1982, Tylenol capsules were found to be tainted with poison. Parent company Johnson & Johnson immediately pulled Tylenol from store shelves and shared openly with the media about the catastrophe. Their honesty with the public worked to their advantage and led to even greater customer trust in the product and the company.

The Malden Mills Fire: In 1995, a fire destroyed nearly the entire operation of clothing manufacturer Malden Mills. The head of Malden Mills, Aaron Feuerstein, retained his entire work force of 2400 employees and paid them out of his own pocket. At first, many thought that this was a foolish and sentimental decision. However, employee loyalty and gratitude paid off in the form of exceptional productivity, and Malden Mills was back on its feet in three months and became more profitable than ever.

Both Tylenol and Malden Mills are examples of ideal management decisions. They combine luck, intuition, and hard work and involve significant risks. They also demonstrate ethical management behavior. No matter how much managers try to use tangible data to make decisions, all managers must also rely on foresight and a little bit of luck for success.

These 75 Greatest Management Decisions resulted in great success for their organizations. However, not every management decision will succeed, and managers frequently make poor decisions. The key for managers to remember is to keep trying and to learn from one's mistakes and failures. Even Napoleon was not a success all of the time!

Source: Adapted from S. Crainer. November 1998. The 75 greatest management decisions ever made. *Management Review* 87(10):16–23.

Misunderstanding a Situation

To understand a decision situation, a manager must coordinate and organize a great deal of relevant information. If this information is incomplete or organized poorly, the manager may easily misconstrue the situation. Consider the case of Bill Bass, a manager inspecting information about a problematic product return level. If Bill sees information on returns organized by day of shipment and by quality-control inspector, he might conclude that the problem is linked to two particular quality-control inspectors who seem to have a heavy workload on Mondays. If the information is organized by customer, Bill will see that most of the returns are from one large customer whose regular standing order is always filled from the Monday morning production run.

Although it can be relatively straightforward to organize *concrete* information about costs, schedules, and units produced, the sheer quantity of such information can make it next to impossible to make sense of it all. Giving meaning to *abstract* information is even more difficult. Because abstract information is more difficult to identify, it frequently goes unnoticed, and problems that appear through abstract signals—low job satisfaction, for example—often go unrecognized.

Perceptions that influence how we understand decision situations vary from individual to individual. In addition, some individuals have limited information processing capabilities, which means they only partially understand situations. We often see what we are trained to see, or what we want or need to see (see our discussion of "selective perception" in Chapter 5). As a consequence, our perceptions of and reactions to situations aren't always accurate.

http://www.miller-dwan.com

Managers may also misinterpret a decision situation if they mistake the symptoms of a problem for the problem itself. As we saw earlier, the human resource manager at Miller Dwan Hospital came to believe that high absenteeism was a major problem confronting his hospital, when in fact it was only a symptom of a larger underlying morale problem. Efforts to attack the symptom often leave the problem to fester and manifest itself in other ways. The hospital's definition of its problem as one of absenteeism was a mistake that hampered their decision-making process.

Rushing the Decision-Making Process

For many reasons, perhaps to save money or to avoid the uncertainty associated with problems, both individual and group decision makers often rush the decision-making process. The results are inadequately defined problems, limited searches for and development of possible solutions, and inadequately evaluated courses of action. It has been reported that "half the decisions in organizations fail," because decision makers "limit the search for alternatives, and use power to implement their plans."[30]

For example, a company may rush to evaluate a situation before it has been fully defined. Perhaps the company has found that its sales are lower than desired. In a rush to attack the problem, the company defines the situation as a problem of too few sales representatives. Note that the problem has been defined in terms of its solution. Inadequate problem definition, in all likelihood, will adversely constrain subsequent stages in the decision-making process (for example, the development of alternative solutions). Is the problem too few sales representatives? The managers should cast the problem in the following manner: "Our sales volume is $500,000, but we targeted it at $750,000." With the problem defined as $250,000 of unmet targeted sales, the managers can generate more possible solutions. They might hire more sales representatives, advertise more or use different advertising strategies, or market the product in different outlets. With more potential solutions, the managers are closer to solving their real problem.

Reports suggest that rushed decision making was a major cause of NASA's third failed Mars mission, which resulted in the $165 million crash of the *Mars Polar Lander*. NASA's operating credo has become "faster, better, cheaper." Senior managers push too hard, stretch the system, and in an effort to "launch, launch, launch, and get projects off the ground," they fail to watch over projects carefully. In the case of the *Polar Lander*, it appears that an easy-to-fix software glitch caused the Lander's engines to shut down too soon.[31]

Because many decision makers dislike uncertainty, they tend to overlook unusual alternatives in favor of readily available and previously used alternatives. In their haste, they may overgeneralize and assume that solutions from vaguely similar situations are appropriate for new situations. Decision makers also develop a similar familiarity with certain sources of information and alternatives. Although this approach is handy and fast, these comfortable alternatives limit the range of choices.

In their eagerness to make a final decision, many decision makers collapse the alternative generation and evaluation phases of the decision-making process into a single step. In the process, they inhibit idea "hitchhiking," wherein the first idea generated stimulates the development of a second idea, and so on. When ideas are allowed to surface completely, without being prematurely cut off by the evaluation process, they serve as catalysts for developing other—and possibly better—ideas. The second problem associated with collapsing the generation and evaluation phases is that, people's first ideas and thoughts are often only partly formed and fall short of their full potential. Early ideas should be permitted to surface and develop fully. When decision makers simultaneously generate and evaluate ideas, those ideas tend not to mature into fully formed possibilities for solutions.

IMPROVING DECISION MAKING

The decision-making process can be improved by changing the roles of the individuals involved and through the use of structured decision-making techniques. It can also be enhanced through organizational learning—capitalizing on developing and changing employees.

Improving the Roles of Individuals

Managers can take a number of steps to improve their decision-making process. They can use heterogeneous groups, for example, to expand the information base and encourage the thorough definition of problems, searches for alternatives, and evaluations of alternatives. They can use a devil's advocate—that is, someone whose role is to look at alternatives and tentative decisions and challenge them. A devil's advocate helps a group focus on the possibly undesirable consequences of some alternatives or the possibly desirable consequences of others.

Most organizations and control-oriented managers, perhaps quite unintentionally, have reward and penalty systems that discourage employees from identifying occasions to make decisions. In many organizations, people are rewarded only for doing exactly what they are told to do—performing their jobs as they have been defined—and are discouraged from experimenting. As a consequence, many existing problems and potential opportunities go unnoticed. Other organizations do encourage their employees to look for new opportunities and to explore potential opportunities. Almost any organization, as is common in involvement-oriented systems, can develop an internal environment that makes it safe for members to pursue new ideas. Giving employees the freedom to try new things, plus the permission to fail or to be wrong occasionally, stimulates http://www.3m.com

the search for solutions and for new ways of doing things. One organization that systematically encourages employees to search for new opportunities is 3M (Minnesota Mining and Manufacturing). 3M encourages many of its employees to devote a portion of their workday to searching for opportunities. One result of this policy was the development of "Post-it" notes, a phenomenally successful product that fills what was a previously unmet need.

Training organization members in systematic decision making, providing them with the tools for collecting the necessary information, and allowing adequate time for decision making go a long way toward improving decisions. Supporting these actions with reward systems that emphasize careful, effective decision making reinforces their importance.

Structured Group Decision-Making Processes

As managers move toward increasing levels of employee involvement, there often is a struggle over individual versus group decision making and questions as to the advantages and costs associated with group processes. Group decision making, after all, takes people away from their jobs, and meetings are frequently a waste of time!

While there are compelling arguments against group decision making, such as the time involved, compelling evidence suggests that groups *can* significantly enhance the quality of decisions.[32] The issue does not appear to be an argument against the use of groups, but instead appears to be one of learning how to use groups effectively.

As will be discussed in Part IV—Groups in Organizations—there are a number of group processes/dynamics (for example, social loafing, groupthink) that those who use groups and teams need to manage. In addition, several structured group processes, such as the delphi and nominal group techniques, capture the "assets of group decision making, while managing the liabilities associated with that process."[33] In Part IV, we discuss several important group dynamics and structured group decision processes that make group decision making more effective.

Organizational Learning

http://www.fortune.com/fortune/fortune500

During the 1980s, over half of the *Fortune 500* firms went through corporate restructuring in search of a "new kind of organization" that would accommodate changing environmental demands. Organizations were experiencing rapid change in both their internal and external environments. In addition, most organizations, saw their task environments becoming increasingly complex. The rapid change and increased complexity placed new pressures on the organization decision-making and problem-solving systems and created an urgent need for improved decision-making capabilities.

Managers increasingly found that their old control-oriented, top-down driven organizations, bureaucratic machines were not fast enough to respond to environmental changes, not keen enough to spot opportunities, not sharp enough to deliver higher levels of customer service, and not smart and sensitive enough to provide the type of work that would motivate their people.[34] Organizations realized that to handle the challenges of the new marketplace, they needed to expand the learning capacity of their organizations. Efforts to create a learning organization are taken seriously by many of today's major corporations. GE, http://www.kodak.com

http://www.analog.com

organizational learning the process by which organizations gain new knowledge and insights that lead to a modification in behavior and action

AT&T, and Kodak, for example, make continuous learning an integral part of their organization and their decision-making capacity.[35]

According to Ray Stata, Chairman of the Board and President of Analog Devices, **organizational learning** is the process by which organizations gain new knowledge and insights that lead to modifications in behavior and action. At Analog Devices, corporatewide product, market, and technology task forces that draw together 150 professionals from throughout the company meet routinely in an effort to better understand the opportunities that face their corporation. These cross-functional discussions encourage organizational learning.[36] Differing from individual learning, organizational learning occurs through *shared* insights, knowledge, and mental models.[37] According to Peter Senge, an author and consultant at MIT, organizational learning refers to expanded capacity to produce new and improved results.[38]

Organizational learning consists of identifying and using ideas from other organizations, developing ideas within the organization, and regularly monitoring organizational events. The following actions can help an organization develop and maintain a healthy capacity to learn:

- Explicitly committing to new ideas
- Promoting policies that emphasize curiosity, experimentation, and learning; permit failure; and reward discovery
- Allocating organizational resources to support learning
- Systematically collecting, storing, and processing information
- Opening internal boundaries so that information flows more freely, vertically, horizontally, and diagonally within the organization
- Instilling a participative philosophy and practices to support it so that organizational members become aware of what is learned and collaborate on decision making and problem solving[39]

Organizations approach organizational learning differently. IBM has done an excellent job of creating an environment that nurtures organizational learning. Corporate philosophy clearly states the importance of individual education as well as institutional learning. Managers create work assignments that encourage creativity in dealing with both new and existing problems and opportunities. The company devotes considerable time and money to education. For example, IBM provides at least 40 hours of management development training opportunities for all managers every year. The company has communication systems that share information learned by one division quickly and freely with other divisions. Employees are encouraged to interact with the external environment. As a result, the company is learning from the activities of other business organizations. Quad/Graphics, a Wisconsin-based printing company, creates their learning organization by valuing learning; expecting and encouraging continuous change; placing organizational members in the classroom one-half day a week for life; putting line employees in direct contact with the organization's suppliers and customers; and creating an in-house technology center that works continuously on technological changes to advance the printing industry.

Organizations that effectively handle the vast number of decision-making and problem-solving situations that confront them do so because of their ability to learn. When managers deliberately prepare their organizations to learn, they also prepare them to make decisions and solve problems effectively.

MODELS OF INDIVIDUAL DECISION MAKING

Four general models of the individual as a decision maker have been identified (see Table 9-1).[40] The first of these, the *irrational person model,* suggests that many decisions stem from a variety of fears, anxieties, and drives.[41] The second model, the *creative/self-actualizing model,* assumes that individuals pursue total development of their inner selves rather than look for an external goal, such as profit seeking.[42] Contemporary managers, however, deal mostly with the last two models: the *classical model* and the *behavioral model.*

A Classical (Rational/Economic) Decision-Making Model

Classical, or rational/economic, decision-making models were most popular during the early part of the 20th century. They portray decision makers as rational in behavior, as dealing with objective and verifiable facts, and as economically motivated. They depict decision makers as completely informed, as infinitely sensitive, and, therefore, as making decisions under conditions of **objective rationality**.[43] By knowing all possible alternatives and their probable consequences, decision makers rationally select the "one best" alternative by following the decision-making process portrayed in Figure 9-1. This classical decision-making model discounts as unnecessary the effects of the attitudes, emotions, or personal preferences of the decision maker.

objective rationality
the notion that decision makers are completely informed, infinitely sensitive, and therefore make decisions based on fact and rational thought

A Behavioral (Administrative) Decision-Making Model

The ideal is different from the reality, however. Where the classical model argues that decision makers are aware of all possible alternatives, the behavioral, or administrative, decision-making theory proposes that this is seldom the case, and that it is unrealistic to think otherwise. According to this model, decision makers cannot possibly be aware of all consequences for each alternative,

TABLE 9-1 Four Decision-Making Models

The Irrational Person	The Creative/Self-Actualizing Person
Has a variety of fears, anxieties, and drives.	Pursues total development of the inner self.
Decisions are driven by the unconscious motives underlying these fears and anxieties.	Decisions are driven by desire to develop the self even at the expense of external factors.
The Rational/Economic Person	**The Administrative Person**
Is rational and deals with objective facts.	Is aware of only certain alternatives.
Is economically motivated.	Is limited by restricted cognitive capacity.
Decisions are driven by objective rationality and a search for the best possible alternative.	Decisions are driven by a desire to identify and select the first acceptable alternative.

or of their probabilities of occurring. Whereas classical theory argues that decision makers should make decisions that meet the greatest number of criteria, behavioral theory suggests that most decision makers actually choose the first satisfactory solution that they identify. That is, they "satisfice."

bounded rationality
the tendency of decision makers to behave rationally within the limits of their information-processing capabilities and within the context of their attitudes and emotions

According to Herbert Simon's administrative model of decision making, people operate in the realm of **bounded rationality**.[44] They try to behave rationally within the limits of their information-processing capabilities and within the context of their attitudes and emotions. They engage in restricted searches for information; have limited information-processing capabilities; rely on familiar sources of information; and, as a result, construct simplified models of reality from which their decisions are made.[45] Optimal decisions, those that are the "best" decisions, therefore are seldom made, and when they are made, it is generally by chance. According to Simon, once decision makers identify a limited number of alternatives, they deviate from the demands of rationality and select the first alternative that is deemed "satisfactory"—that is, "good enough." Instead of identifying all possible alternatives, then rank ordering them according to some well-ordered and stable set of preferences, emotions and biases and previously determined aspirations are set into motion, and the decision maker seeks a satisfactory solution. This is what Simon calls *satisficing*. Examples of satisficing behavior, as opposed to the maximizing behavior offered by the rational model, might be "33 percent market share" versus the "total market," "fair price" versus "best price," and "adequate profit" versus "maximum profit."[46]

Individual Differences in Decision Making

People differ in their styles of making decisions. Some people make decisions quickly, others slowly. Some people consider a large amount of information before reaching a decision, others a small amount. Although it is not fully understood why people behave differently when making decisions, their cognitive and personality attributes appear to account for a number of these differences.

Cognitive Attributes An individual's cognitive attributes appear to affect the *judgmental* aspects of decision making. Relevant cognitive processes include intelligence, learning, remembering, and thinking. These cognitive attributes affect the ability to engage in inductive and deductive reasoning, to deal in the abstract, to handle information, and to generate ideas. They affect problem recognition, comprehension, and diagnosis; the storage, retrieval, and assimilation of information for the development of alternative solutions; and the capability of storing, retrieving, and processing information for the evaluation of alternatives. Differences in intelligence mean that people differ in their information-processing capacities. Some people process only relatively small amounts of information before becoming overloaded, and they base their decisions on relatively small amounts of specific information. Decision makers with greater capacity tend to become more abstract decision makers.

Personality Attributes Personality and motivational attributes affect decision-making *style*. Style differences, for example, are reflected in the speed with which decisions are made, the level of risk taking, and the level of confidence attached to the decision once it has been made.

Several personality and motivational factors have been related to decision-making style. Those with a high *propensity toward risk* tend to make rapid decisions because they process less information and spend less time evaluating information before making a decision. People with *dogmatic* personalities possess fixed, narrow perspectives on life and thus often consider only the small set of alternatives that fits their existing view of the world. They make their decisions quickly and with great confidence, and they are highly resistant to change because they are convinced that they know how things are and should be. Individuals who are *impatient and competitive* tend to process information quickly and aggressively and thereby make decisions quickly. They are often better at making short-term decisions. People with *calm, reflective* personalities tend to be very good at long-term planning and decision making.

Decision makers also differ in their ability to accept uncertainty, a personality characteristic called *tolerance for ambiguity.* Not surprisingly, people with low tolerance for ambiguity are more likely to select alternatives with fairly certain consequences. They are not risk takers, most likely scoring low on "inquisitiveness" from the "Big Five" personality type. In fact, people with very low tolerance for ambiguity tend to be *problem avoiders.* If something unexpected occurs, problem avoiders often ignore the first signs of a problem; they function poorly at the symptom-detection stage of decision making. Thus, they often progress far into a decision situation without understanding the circumstances surrounding it. The self-assessment below offers an opportunity for you to profile your own tolerance for ambiguity.

SELF-ASSESSMENT Tolerance for Ambiguity

Instructions: The following questions ask you about the importance of certain work conditions.

Use the following response categories as you answer the questions:

1 = Very Unimportant	4 = Slightly Important
2 = Moderately Unimportant	5 = Moderately Important
3 = Slightly Unimportant	6 = Very Important

1. How important is it to you to know, in detail, what you have to do on a job? 1 2 3 4 5 6
2. How important is it to you to know, in detail, how you are supposed to do a job? 1 2 3 4 5 6
3. How important is it to you to know, in detail, what the limits of your authority are on a job? 1 2 3 4 5 6
4. How important is it to you to know how well you are doing? 1 2 3 4 5 6

Scoring:

Sum your responses to questions 1–4 and divide by 4.

Interpretation: A score of 5 or greater indicates a low tolerance for ambiguity. A score of 2 or less indicates a high tolerance for ambiguity.

Source: Patterned after T. Lyons. 1971. Role clarity, need for clarity, satisfactions tensions and withdrawal. *Organizational Behavior and Human Performances* 6:99–110.

SELF-ASSESSMENT

At intermediate levels of tolerance for ambiguity are *problem solvers*. Rather than taking extensive steps to prevent problems, these individuals anticipate difficulties and deal with them as they arise. They are usually the first to recognize the need for a decision and are likely to respond quickly. People who have a high tolerance for ambiguity tend to be *problem seekers*. Because problem seekers are so comfortable with novelty and uncertainty, they actually seek challenges of this type and derive great satisfaction from conquering uncertainty. Problem seekers often behave as entrepreneurs in an organization. They go out of their way to find potential opportunities and then attempt to develop decisions that capitalize on them.

EMPLOYEE REACTIONS TO ORGANIZATIONAL DECISION MAKING

We have presented decision making as a process that unfolds in numerous ways in the context of organizational functioning. Managers, as we have seen, employ a variety of decision-making strategies, ranging from "telling" others what they want them to do (closed decision processes), to employing group decision processes, to allowing employees to make decisions on their own. At this point, we want to explore the impact that decision making has on organizational members.

participative decision making joint decision making

In this section we pay particular attention to participative decision making and the effects of different degrees of participation. We want to know, for example, if increasing degrees of participation impact employee motivation, satisfaction, and performance. Also as a part of our discussion, we explore the effects that perceptions of a "fair decision making process" have on the organizational member.

© STEVE CHENN/CORBIS

Participative decision making is one employee involvement strategy. To make this process more effective, managers need to train employees in group decision making, give them power to implement their decisions, and also give them a share of the profits realized from their efforts.

Participative Decision Making

The past several decades have been marked by an increasing number of organizations subscribing to the human resources model and implementing employee-involvement strategies. Many of these strategies (participative decision making, quality control circles, self-directed work teams) encompass employee participation in the decision-making process.

Participative decision making is *joint* decision making. Today, organizations are choosing to involve those individuals who will be impacted by a decision in the decision-making process. There is, however, no single role for them to play. Instead, participative decision making should be viewed in terms of degrees of participation.[47] At one extreme, upper-level managers play a dominant and proactive role in carrying out each stage of the decision-making process (that is, from problem identification to solution generation to alternative evaluation to choosing what is to be done). In this situation, those impacted by decisions are passive players in the decision-making process. Most likely they are not consulted, yet they are responsible for carrying out the decision made by those above them in the organizational hierarchy. With increasing degrees of participation, those impacted by the decision (those employees who will implement the decision) play an expanded role in the decision-making process. Thus, they may be asked to help identify the problem, to generate viable solutions, to provide input into the evaluation of those solutions, and to recommend and/or vote in the final selection of an alternative. The greater the number of steps in the decision process that those impacted are involved with, the greater the degree of participative decision making.

Participative decision making can also be viewed along a number of other dimensions. Some of these dimensions are job content versus job context, within versus across functional area, and within organizational level versus across level decisions. Thus, the nature and character of employee involvement in organizational decision making can vary considerably.

Accompanying the current movement toward high-involvement management and high-involvement organizations, the conventional wisdom is that participative decision making contributes positively to employee attitudes and work-related behavior. During the past couple of decades, organizational researchers have been studying the effects of participative decision making. Two major questions have been posed by the organizational scientist. First, why or how should participation favorably impact employee job satisfaction and performance? Second, what is the relationship between participation and employee responses?

Two models (see Figure 9-5) provide us with insight into the "how or why" question.[48] The *cognitive model* simply states that the involvement of others in the decision-making process increases the amount of information and ideas that are available, thereby contributing to better decisions and subsequent performance effects. The *affective model* reasons that participation and feelings of involvement are satisfying. Participation is seen as contributing to the fulfillment (satisfaction) of the individual's higher-order needs (the need for self-expression, independence, self-esteem). The fulfillment of higher-order needs

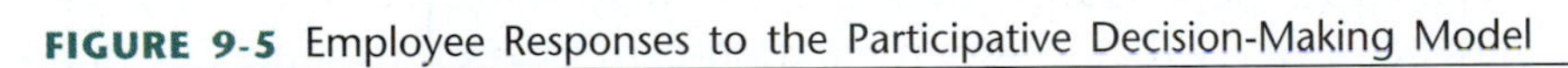
FIGURE 9-5 Employee Responses to the Participative Decision-Making Model

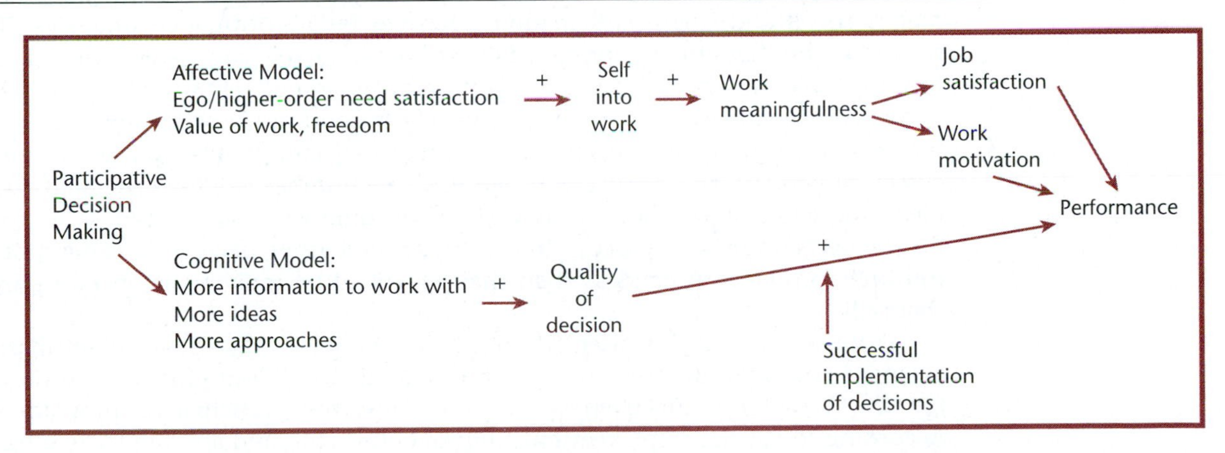

contributes to job satisfaction, increased motivation, and subsequent performance. A similar argument was offered by S. M. Sales in his discussion of the reinforcing value of work.[49] He argued that the value of work performed under democratic leadership should be higher than under autocratic leadership. As the value and experienced meaningfulness of work are enhanced, individuals invest more of their "self" in the job, job satisfaction rises, intrinsic motivation is strengthened, and performance increases.

While at the University of Michigan, Kurt Lewin provided us with some of the earliest insights into the effects of participation through his study of democratic, autocratic, and laissez-faire leadership. Lewin and his associates found that democratic styles of leadership can be efficient and that they lead to group mindedness, more friendliness, and higher levels of productivity should the leader be absent.[50] Since the writings of Lewin and his colleagues, researchers have examined the effects of participative decision making.

The evidence accumulated to date suggests that the effects of participation are neither simple, consistent, nor as strong as expected.[51] While many researchers report observations of a positive relationship between participation and employee satisfaction and performance, many studies indicate no relationship and at times a negative relationship.[52] While the research has generated inconsistent observations, by and large there does appear to be a positive relationship with job satisfaction. There is also evidence to suggest that psychological ownership is strengthened as a result of participative decision making.[53] This evidence supports the view that participation in the decision-making process provides the employee with increased control over job content and job context decisions. Over time, control over organizational activities promotes feelings of ownership for the organization and the targets of that control[54] (see our discussion of psychological ownership in Chapter 6).

As noted above, evidence of the relationship between participation and performance is inconclusive. Research results show both a positive relationship, and either no or at times a negative relationship. In general, there does appear to be a weak but generally positive relationship with productivity.[55] With regard to the participation-performance relationship, remember that while participation may enhance the quality of decisions made, these decisions still need to be successfully implemented before the performance effects associated with participation can be realized. Without a good implementation strategy, good decisions may fail to increase performance, and at times may actually cause a decline. Recent evidence reveals that the participation-performance relationship may materialize if and when participation improves task performance strategies. If, however, the participative process fails to generate the knowledge needed to improve task strategies, increases in performance are unlikely to occur.[56]

There is evidence that structured forms of group decision making, such as that generated by brainstorming and the nominal group technique (to be discussed in Part IV), are productive in terms of the number of ideas generated and idea uniqueness and creativity, as well as the number of alternative solutions for the decision-making process. In fact, structured group decision making quite routinely produces more ideas than that generated by individuals operating by themselves.

Professor Edward E. Lawler, III, in his discussion of high-involvement management and high-involvement organizations, identifies four critical conditions for the long-term effectiveness of any employee participative program.[57] According to Lawler, employees must have (1) the skills and abilities to be effective contributors, (2) the information needed to make a contribution, (3) the power to make something meaningful happen, and (4) the opportunity to participate in a gainsharing program that provides them with a reason to invest the time and energy to make meaningful contributions. Short of one or more of these conditions, employees' contributions will be limited in nature. Thus, managers choosing to use participative decision making should provide participation training, open up information sources important to the decisions at hand, give the decision participants the power to make things happen, and create mechanisms that enable them to share in the profits that are realized as a result of their efforts.

Distributive and Procedural Justice

Employees react to organizational decision making in two very important ways. Not only are they affected by the "outcomes" of the decisions that do and do not get made, they are also affected by the "way" decisions are made. Both significantly affect the work-related attitudes, motivation, and behavior of organizational members.

Distributive justice (see Chapter 7) refers to the fairness in outcomes that derive from organizational decisions. When an organizational member perceives a balance in what is received from the organization relative to what is given, distributive justice is realized. As noted in our discussion of employee motivation, distributive justice operates at a personal level and is based entirely on the employee's perceptions.

Those interested in the psychology of exchange relationships recognize that organizational members experience fairness (justice) not only in terms of the outcomes of exchange relationships, but also in terms of the process. The later is referred to as procedural justice. More specifically, **procedural justice** refers to whether the processes used to achieve an end are themselves experienced as fair.[58] Thus, the focus shifts from the outcomes to how they were determined. Distributive justice focuses on the fairness of the distribution of resources, while procedural justice focuses on the fairness of the procedures (that is, the decision-making processes) used to make those distribution decisions.

procedural justice perception that the processes employed to make a decision were fair

Employee reactions (for example, satisfaction, motivation, performance, goal acceptance, and commitment) to organizational decisions can be better understood in light of these principles of distributive and procedural justice. Understanding employee responses is complicated by the fact that employees can experience four different conditions:

- A poor perceived procedure (procedural injustice) produces a good outcome (distributive justice).
- A poor perceived procedure (procedural injustice) produces a bad outcome (distributive injustice).
- A good perceived procedure (procedural justice) produces a good outcome (distributive justice).
- A good perceived procedure (procedural justice) produces a bad outcome (distributive injustice).

These conditions impact attitudes, motivation, and behavior, as every organizational decision is experienced from both a procedural and distributive justice perspective.

FIGURE 9-6 Procedural and Distributive Justice Effects

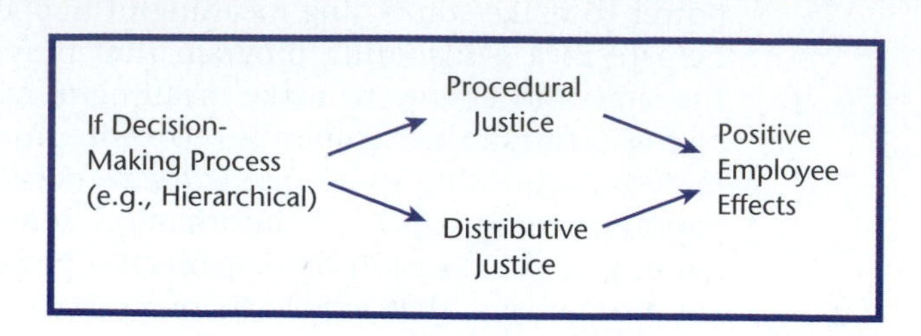

It is assumed that the highest levels of satisfaction will be experienced when organizational decisions result in both procedural and distributive justice (see Figure 9-6). In many cases, achieving procedural justice becomes a necessary though not sufficient condition for employees to experience satisfaction with either hierarchical or participative decision making. If the process is not experienced as fair, it is often difficult for the outcome to be judged as fair.

Research indicates that the *opportunity* to participate in a decision process promotes perceptions of fairness, and thus job satisfaction.[59] This occurs because participation provides employees with the opportunity to have input (voice) into the process and some control over the outcome. Both enhance employees' perceptions of procedural justice.[60] Researchers have observed a positive relationship between experiences of procedural justice and job satisfaction, commitment (attachment), and trust in the organization.[61] (See Figure 9-7.) These observations lead us to believe that under conditions where hierarchical decision processes are necessary, it is important that management ensure that employees perceive the process as fair. Thus, managers can reduce the likelihood that hierarchical decision making adversely impacts on employee satisfaction, commitment, and trust.

One set of procedural rules is believed to ensure perceptions of fairness in decision-making processes. Adherence to these rules appears to be of particular importance for managers engaged in hierarchical decision making, because it is under these conditions that employees have neither voice nor control. The emergence of procedural justice appears to be influenced by:[62]

- Consistency—procedures should be consistent across people and over time.
- Bias suppression—decision makers should not be influenced by self-interest.
- Accuracy—decisions should be based on good information and informed opinion.
- Correctability—opportunities should exist to modify or reverse bad decisions.

FIGURE 9-7 Participative Decision Making and Procedural Justice Effects

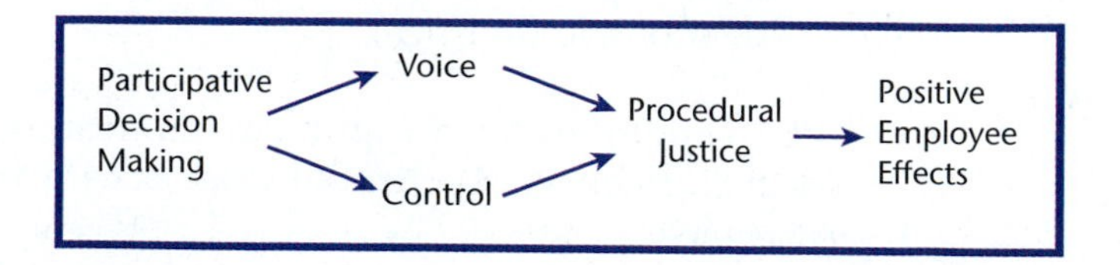

FIGURE 9-8 Determinants of Procedural Justice

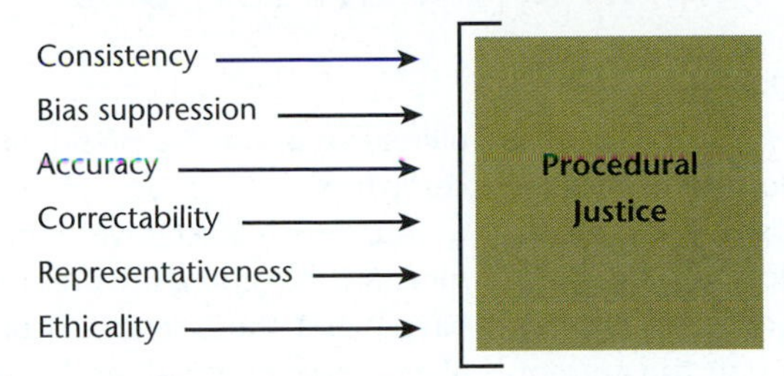

- Representativeness—processes should represent the concerns of all important subgroups and individuals affected by the decisions.
- Ethicality—process should be compatible with prevailing moral and ethical standards.

Figure 9-8 summarizes what are believed to be among the major determinants of procedural justice.

In summary, the effect of organizational decision making on employee attitudes, motivation, and subsequent behavior (like performance behavior) are affected by perceptions of fairness in both the outcomes and the processes used to make the decision. If the outcomes of hierarchical decision making are perceived as fair (and equitable), employee job satisfaction will be favorably affected. In addition, if hierarchical decision-making processes are experienced as procedurally just, there should be positive effects on employee satisfaction, organizational commitment, intent to stay, trust in supervision, and acts of good organizational citizenship. It is somewhat easier to create perceptions of procedural justice in participative decision making, since employees have both a voice and control. Thus, the same effects produced under procedurally just hierarchical conditions should be realized under participative conditions.

CONTROL- AND INVOLVEMENT-ORIENTED APPROACHES TO DECISION MAKING

Contrast decision making in mechanistic organizations with their control-oriented management practices, and organic organizations with their involvement-oriented management practices. (See *An Inside Look*.) In the mechanistic organization decisions are generally made near the top of the organizational hierarchy and then passed down the chain of command. In the organic organization and under involvement-oriented management practices, decisions are made close to where they will be carried out by involving the very people who will be executing them. The former represents centralized decision making; the latter has been variously referred to as delegated, decentralized, and/or participative decision making.

Control-oriented management attempts to minimize the risk and uncertainty confronting lower-level decision makers. Efforts are made to standardize operations, so that the majority of decisions made in the organization's technical

AN INSIDE LOOK

Decision Scenarios

A Control-Oriented Management Approach

A manufacturing decision in a control-oriented organization is about to be made by the general manager. He has thought through the current problem, has discussed it with the assistant general manager, and they have come to terms with some product design changes that can be made. Several additional individuals in manufacturing have consulted about the problem and the proposed course of action. The general manager has decided to move forward with his ideas. Before the ideas can be implemented, however, they must be approved upstairs.

The proposal gets passed upward, finally reaching the Vice President of Manufacturing who, upon review and consideration of the general manager's proposal, concludes that the decision and proposed course of action do not have any significant and negative ramifications for the other areas of manufacturing for which she is responsible.

Next the Vice President of Manufacturing has to take the proposal to next week's executive committee meeting. The proposed course of action is put on the agenda for the upcoming executive committee meeting. A brief summary of the project is prepared and circulated to the other members of the executive committee, consisting of the Vice Presidents of Finance, Marketing, Human Resources, Engineering, and Research and Development. They will have an opportunity to review the proposal, question its merits, make sure that the plan does not interfere with activities in their functional areas, and ultimately advise the president of the company.

After the executive committee meeting, the company president will have heard the discussions on manufacturing's proposal, and a decision to either move forward, stop the proposal, or return it to the general manager for further study and development will be made. The president chooses to accept the proposal, and instructions flow from the Vice President of Manufacturing back down to the general manager, instructing him to move forward with the proposed product design changes and the retooling that will be needed. The general manager, employing the hierarchy, instructs individuals below him to move forward with the implementation plans and to keep him informed of developments as he needs to periodically keep those upstairs informed of future events.

An Involvement-Oriented Management Approach

A team of men and women who perform the diverse set of activities needed to make greeting cards a reality are no longer housed in functionally pure departments; instead, writers, artists, accountants, and lithographic personnel work together as a self-managing work team creating birthday greeting cards. This birthday card team has a team leader, whose primary responsibility it is to work the team's boundary with other greeting card teams, with an advisory customer group, and with the organization's administrative and strategic management teams.

One of the production teams in this greeting card company has come up with an idea that would make a major change in the manufacture of its greeting cards. The idea gets developed to the proposal stage. As the production team creates its tentative proposal, the team leader carries the group's thoughts and ideas to other teams in the organization, keeping them abreast of the proposal and carrying back to the production team questions, concerns, and suggestions.

Once the production team has worked out the details of their proposal, they send out a communication through the company's electronic mail network informing others in the organization of their tentative proposal, and inviting people and other teams in the organization to meet with them and discuss the details of the proposal. In addition, several firms who serve as the company's external suppliers and customers have been invited to participate in this decision-making process from its inception.

At subsequent meetings, the production team meets with other team leaders representing functional areas from throughout the organization, reviewing the proposal with them, and getting feedback on the proposal before its implementation. Thus, representatives from other production areas, marketing, finance, middle, and strategic management all have input as the proposal unfolds.

Through this process the proposal is strengthened, and commitment and ownership are attached to the proposal from throughout the organization. A network not unlike a spider's web surrounds the proposal; this differs dramatically from the top-to-bottom single strand of the mechanistic organization's proposal.

core are structured and programmed decisions. Under involvement-oriented management, considerably less hierarchical decision making occurs, and in its place a greater reliance is placed on individual and group decision making. With higher levels of participative decision making, greater emphasis tends to be placed on developing systems for organizational learning and the use of structured decision-making processes at lower levels in the organization.

As we have seen, the uncertainty confronting an organization can originate in conditions in its external environment, as well as from its technology. Uncertainty coupled with task interdependence significantly influences the effectiveness of the different approaches to decision making. As depicted in Figure 9-9, decision making is likely to become more participative and less hierarchical as the amount of uncertainty experienced by the organization increases.

Finally, we would expect to witness somewhat higher levels of need fulfillment, greater experienced meaningfulness of work, stronger intrinsic motivation, more job satisfaction, and somewhat higher levels of individual performance among employees working under the participative conditions provided by involvement-oriented management practices than experienced under control-oriented conditions.

FIGURE 9-9 Control- and Involvement-Oriented Management and Organizational Decision Making

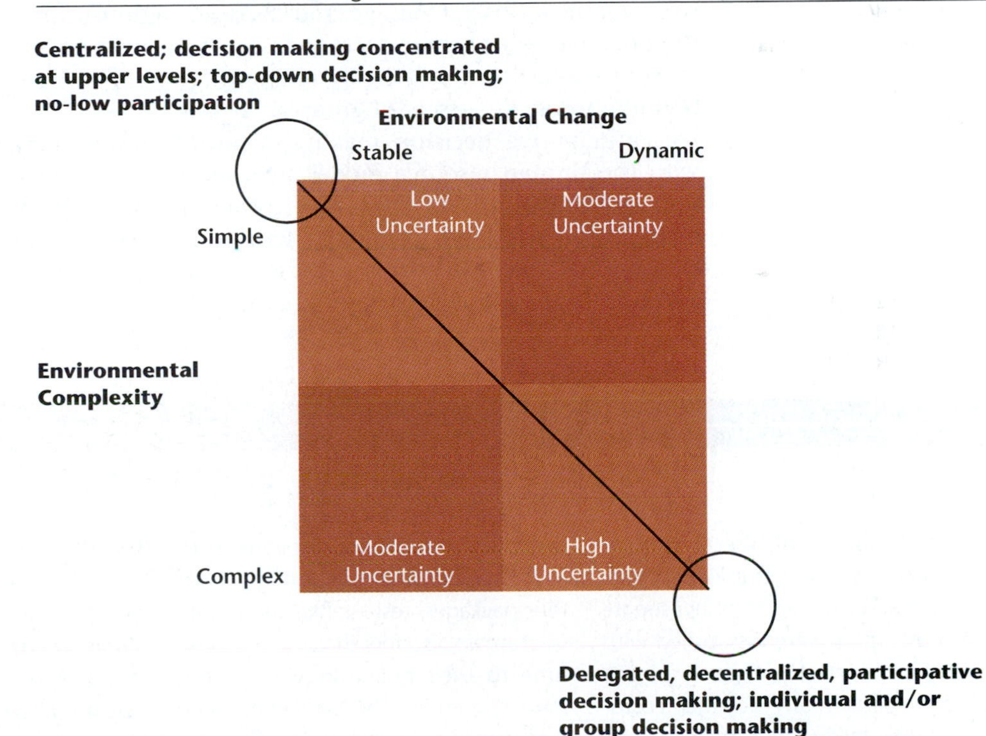

ORGANIZATIONAL DECISION MAKING IN REVIEW

Decision making, the process through which a course of action is chosen, is distinguished from choice making, which is simply the stage of decision making when a choice is made from previously defined alternatives. Decision making also differs from problem solving, which includes not only the entire decision-making process, but also the steps required to implement, monitor, and maintain the results of the decision.

In a four-step decision-making model, step 1 recognizes that a decision is needed and defines the nature of the decision situation. Step 2 generates a list of alternative solutions. Step 3 evaluates these alternatives. In step 4, an alternative is chosen. Problem solving involves these steps, plus a fifth and a sixth step that implement the chosen decision and monitor and maintain its effectiveness.

Unfortunately, the systematic decision models often are not followed, for a variety of reasons. Furthermore, people differ dramatically in how they make decisions. Knowledge of these differences helps managers select decision makers wisely and improve their effectiveness.

Common decision-making problems include misunderstanding a situation and rushing decisions. Managers can counteract these problems by providing access to needed information, by training individuals and groups in systematic decision making, by providing adequate time for the process, and by offering rewards that encourage effective decision making. In addition, the most effective organizations encourage and support organizational learning to improve the effectiveness of their decisions over time, and have implemented strategies to improve decision making by attempting to control group dysfunctions while building upon the assets of group processes.

Participative decision making is joint decision making and is consistent with the human resource model. As a managerial approach, participative decision making is part of the move toward high-involvement management and high-involvement organizations. Research indicates a generally positive relationship between participative decision making and employee job satisfaction, and to a lesser extent with performance.

A FINAL LOOK

Before the board of directors meeting, Deborah conducts in-depth qualitative market research to investigate why customers were dissatisfied with Voyagers' online travel services. She discovers that many Voyager customers enjoy talking with travel agents in the office or on the phone because it's much more personal and helps them plan their trips. Voyagers specializes in international travel, and the customers overwhelmingly feel the need to talk to someone with in-depth knowledge of foreign cities, tour packages, restaurants, and hotels. Customers also feel that the response time to their online inquiries is too long. Much of the personal touch was necessarily lost when Voyager went online, and customers were making themselves heard by going elsewhere.

Deborah reports to the board of directors that Voyagers has entered the field of online travel too impulsively. Customer service has suffered, and Voyagers needs a recovery plan. While many decisions benefit from inspiration, this particular decision has not succeeded. Deborah vows to make more informed decisions by learning more about actual client needs before acting. Together, Deborah and the board of directors generate alternatives to exclusively offering their services online.

KEY TERMS

bounded rationality, 328
compromise decision-making approach, 317
computational decision-making approach, 316
custom solution, 314
decision, 306
decision making, 306
ends decision, 310
existing solution, 313
functional decision, 311
inspirational decision-making approach, 317
job content decision, 311
job context decision, 311
judgmental decision-making approach, 317
managerial (tactical) decision, 310
means decision, 310
nonprogrammed decision, 311
objective rationality, 327
operating decision, 310
organizational learning, 326
participative decision making, 330
procedural justice, 333
programmed decision, 311
satisfice, 315
strategic decision, 310
structured problem, 309
unstructured problem, 309

ISSUES FOR REVIEW AND DISCUSSION

1. Briefly define decision making.
2. Identify four attributes that characterize the decisions that organizational members must attempt to deal with.
3. Identify and explain three types of decisions.
4. Discuss a systematic approach to the decision-making and problem-solving processes.
5. How do the decision process of incrementalism and the garbage can approach differ from one another?
6. Discuss the influence of personality and cognitive factors on individual decision making.
7. Discuss the contingency model to decision making. As a part of your discussion, identify the different conditions under which decisions are made and the appropriate decision-making strategy for each condition.
8. What is participative decision making and how does it affect employee job satisfaction and performance?
9. What is organizational learning and how does it fit into the decision-making process?
10. Compare and contrast decision making under control- and involvement-oriented approaches to management.

EXERCISES

CHOOSING A LEADERSHIP STYLE: APPLYING THE VROOM-YETTON MODEL

PROCEDURE

Step 1: 10 Minutes

Review Figure 9-4. Discuss any questions that you may have about it. Be sure that you understand the Vroom and Yetton model before proceeding to **step 2**.

Step 2: 25 Minutes

In groups of three to five, analyze each of the four cases given below. Using the model in Figure 9-4, decide on the appropriate decision style to be used in each case. Try to achieve consensus, but if you reach an impasse, go on to the next case and return to the disputed one later. Pick a spokesperson to report your group's solutions to the rest of the class.

CASE I

You are general foreman in charge of a large gang laying an oil pipeline. It is now necessary to estimate your expected rate of progress in order to schedule material deliveries to the next field site.

You know the nature of the terrain you will be traveling and have the historical data needed to compute the mean and variance in the rate of speed over that type of terrain. Given these two variables, it is a simple matter to calculate the earliest and latest times at which materials and support facilities will be needed at the next site. It is important that your estimate be reasonably accurate. Underestimates result in idle foremen and workers, and overestimates result in tying up materials for a period of time before they are to be used.

Progress has been good, and your five foremen and other members of the gang stand to receive substantial bonuses if the project is completed ahead of schedule.

CASE II

You are supervising the work of 12 engineers. Their formal training and work experience are very similar, permitting you to use them interchangeably on projects. Yesterday your manager informed you that a request had been received from an overseas affiliate for four engineers to go abroad on extended loan for a period of six to eight months. You and he agreed that this request should be met from your group.

All your engineers are capable of handling this assignment, and from the standpoint of present and future projects there is no particular reason why any one should be retained over any other. The problem is somewhat complicated by the fact that the overseas assignment is in what is generally regarded in the company as an undesirable location.

CASE III

You are the head of a staff unit reporting to the vice president of finance. He has asked you to provide a report on the firm's current portfolio, which will include recommendations for changes in the selection criteria currently employed. Doubts have been raised about the efficiency of the existing system in the current market conditions, and there is considerable dissatisfaction with prevailing rates of return.

You plan to write the report, but at the moment you are quite perplexed about what approach you should take. Your specialty is the bond market, and it is clear to you that a detailed knowledge of the equity market, which you lack, would greatly enhance the value of the report. Fortunately, four members of your staff are specialists in different segments of the equity market. Together, they possess a vast knowledge about the intricacies of investment. However, they seldom agree on the best way to achieve anything when it comes to the stock market. Although they are obviously conscientious as well as knowledgeable, they have major differences when it comes to investment philosophy and strategy.

The report is due in six weeks. You have already begun to familiarize yourself with the firm's current portfolio and management has provided you a specific set of constraints that your recommended portfolio must satisfy. Your immediate problem is to come up with some alternatives to the firm's present practices and select the most promising for detailed analysis in your report.

CASE IV

You are on the division manager's staff and work on a wide variety of problems both administrative and technical in nature. Your current assignment is to develop a universal method that will be used in each of the division's five plants for manually reading equipment registers, recording the readings, and transmitting the scorings to a centralized information system. All plants are located in a relatively small geographical region.

Until now the error rate in the reading and/or transmittal of data has been high. Some locations have considerably higher error rates than others, and the methods used to record and transmit the data vary between plants. It is probable, therefore, that part of the error variance is a function of specific local conditions rather than anything else, and this will complicate establishing a system common to all plants. You have the information on error rates but no information on the local practices that generate these errors or on the local conditions that necessitate the different practices.

Everyone would benefit from improved data, as they are used in a number of important decisions. Your contacts with the plants are through the quality control supervisors who are responsible for collecting the data. They are a conscientious group committed to doing their jobs well, but are highly sensitive to interference on the part of higher management in their own operations. Any solution that does not receive the active support of the various plant supervisors is unlikely to reduce the error rate significantly.

Step 3: 15 Minutes

Meet again as a total class group. First, each group reports on the decision style it believes is appropriate for each case. (If there are more than three or four groups, take a vote to see how many groups chose which style for each case.) Next, group leaders will present Vroom's analysis of each case and the styles that are appropriate according to his analysis. Finally, discuss Vroom's and the class's analyses and the discrepancies (if any) between them.

Discussion Questions

1. How much agreement is there within the class about the appropriate decision style for each case? Why?
2. How much agreement is there between the class's solutions and Vroom's analysis? Why? When in doubt between two styles, which one would you choose? Why?

Source: D. T. Hall, D. D. Bowen, R. J. Lewicki, and F. S. Hall. 1982. *Experiences in management and organizational behavior* (2nd ed.). New York: Wiley. Reprinted by permission of John Wiley & Sons, Inc.

INFOTRAC

INFOTRAC COLLEGE EDITION

The articles listed below are a sampling of those available through InfoTrac College Edition. You can search for them by title or by the author's name.

Articles

1. Decision-making traps we all fall into. Kare Anderson. *Journal of Property Management* Sept 2000 v65 i5 p12
2. Strategic decision making: the influence of CEO experience and use of tacit knowledge. (Chief Executive Officers) Erich N. Brockmann, Paul G. Simmonds. *Journal of Managerial Issues* Winter 1997 v9 n4 p454(14)
3. Participative decision-making: an integration of multiple dimensions. J. Stewart Black, Hal B. Gregersen. *Human Relations* July 1997 v50 n7 p859(20)
4. Business vs. Cultural Frames of Reference in Group Decision Making: Interactions Among Austrian, Finnish, and Swedish Business Students. Werner Auer-Rizzi, Michael Berry. *The Journal of Business Communication* July 2000 v37 i3 p264
5. Structuring Family Business Succession: An Analysis of the Future Leader's Decision Making. Dean A. Shepherd, Andrew Zacharakis. *Entrepreneurship: Theory and Practice* Summer 2000 v24 i4 p25

Questions

For Article 1:

The article "Decision-Making Traps We All Fall Into" elaborates on the decision-making problems introduced in this chapter. Consider these traps vis-à-vis a significant decision you have recently made in your life (changing employment, changing your major, buying a car). Which traps did you fall into—or avoid? What explanations can you offer for your behavior?

For Other Articles:

Form small groups and assign the other articles in this list to various members. After everyone has read these articles, discuss the practical advice you have gathered about the process and practice of decision making.

WEB EXERCISE

Identify and visit the web site of several online business journals. Read at least three articles in these journals that deal with organizational decision making. What are organizations doing to improve the process of decision making? What problems are they encountering?

Many organizations hire consultants and consulting firms to help their managers learn how to make better decisions. One firm that provides these services is Action Management Associates, Inc. Check out their web site at: **http://www.actionm.com/products.cfm**.

Do you think consultants can help improve managerial skills in decision making? Or do you think actual decision-making experiences are a better teacher?

CASE

The Sydney Olympics Torch Relay: A Myriad of Decisions for Di Henry

The Olympic Games in Sydney 2000 present an extraordinary management challenge, involving as they do thousands of participants, as well as worldwide media representation and massive audiences. Covering 130 days, and with an accredited media entourage of 4000, as well as 10,000 torch bearers in Australia and 20,000 individuals running thousands of kilometers from Greece to Oceania and Australia via hundreds of towns and roads, the torch relay that opens the games is really a smaller version of the full Games. Can this huge event be managed by just one person, making the myriad of decisions necessary to ensure its success?

Di Henry joined the Sydney Organizing Committee for the Olympic Games (SOCOG) in October 1995 as Special Events Manager. Her brief was to oversee launches, sponsor events, marketing events, the Olympic tour (comprising parades, picnics, and exhibitions throughout Australia), and the torch relay. Her goal for the torch relay was to take it to all states and territories and places of national interest in Australia, as well as Oceania, within the constraints of an immovable time frame and a small budget. Literally thousands of decisions were needed to make this happen.

Faced with this daunting task, Henry began to set the parameters that would allow decisions to be made. She picked the symbolic number of 100 days for the relay, which tied the event to the millennium. She then cast a budget relevant to the length of the event by breaking down the cost of items, such as reconnaissance, the advance team, the number of torch bearers, headquarters costs such as wages and equipment, and the service costs associated with uniforms, road crew, the torches themselves, food, and accommodation. She also added the costs of stretching the relay to Oceania. From her experience in special events management, she knew that the important task was to break this gargantuan event into blocks of items that could be managed.

The next step was to check the calculations of the cost and range of the event. Henry read all the relevant literature, went to Atlanta to observe a torch relay in action, and had discussions with anyone available who had been involved in such events previously. This allowed her to clarify and modify her initial calculations. In Sydney she began recruiting staff, as set out in her initial plan. The milestones of the first plan were met, and the ongoing job of selling the event to SOCOG itself continued. As in any organization, selling the undertaking internally was as important as selling it to the external world.

Di Henry then wrote the major scope paper. The first plan had largely been guesswork, but now that the original calculations had been checked, it needed to be formalized so that everyone knew exactly what they were working to. The plan covered the vision for the event and its objectives, the parameters, the issues, the policy and the goals, and contained a Gantt chart that provided an overview of how the various activities would be scheduled to meet required deadlines. From this point on, the decision making was increasingly delegated, with Henry giving people direction so that they could achieve the results needed. A communications plan was prepared which set the objectives for disseminating information to the outside world, and an operations plan outlined the fine detail. Each plan divided large undertakings into manageable and relevant tasks for different players.

The team operated in three main functional areas: Advance, Operations, and Media and Marketing. Interaction between these three divisions was essential, as the relay could work successfully only if it were a collaborative, integrated effort.

Initially, the spotlight was on the Advance Division, with route selection and community networking highlighted. The spotlight then shifted to the Media and Marketing Division, with launches held, and efforts made to attract sponsors to the event. Finally, the Operations Division carefully scrutinized such issues as the convoy, the design and manufacture of the torches, security, and torch bearer selection. Those responsible for the torch relay in Atlanta ran workshops for the team, based on their own experience. Further checks helped to reinforce and consolidate decisions made thus far, or to further modify others.

As a manager, Di Henry was aware of the vital need for good communication. Regular staff meetings were held, with fun time planned to keep up morale and enthusiasm over the long preparatory period. There were team lunches, parties, and bonding weekends, which allowed the team to feel at ease with each other—an important factor given that they would be living together when the relay was on. Interaction with other divisions in SOCOG was also maintained, so that the relay was seen as an essential aspect of the Games.

From the beginning there were no boundaries drawn around information. All members of the team had equal access to information, and all members shadowed each other and multi-tasked, so that everyone fully understood all aspects of the undertaking. Henry notes that there are two parts to the process of planning such a big event—the big plan that can be seen, and the surprise elements that are hard, but cannot be avoided. For example, the team decided early on that it would not reveal the route during planning. This was supported by a decision that the route would not be changed once announced, even though Henry knew that various communities would be disappointed if their preferences were not included.

Henry stresses that nothing works without preparation. Most decisions can be pressure time, and she tried either to get all the players involved before the decision was made, or if a decision had to be made rapidly without the luxury of consultation, she ensured that the reasons for the decision were communicated to everyone as soon as possible. She observes: "If you leave someone out of the loop it can become a problem. A very important part of being a manager is knowing who you need to talk to, and knowing that you can never get all the decisions right. Get the majority right and live with the ones you don't get right."

Questions

1. What methods of decision making are apparent in this case? What are their strengths and weaknesses? Could they have been improved? Though this is an example of a single-use plan, what "learnings" could Henry have brought in from observation of similar events? What modifications to these former plans did she make, and what contingencies did she plan for? Why?
2. Did Di Henry face conditions of certainty, risk, or uncertainty? What procedures did she undertake to deal with these conditions?

Source: P. Davidson and R. W. Griffin. 1999. Management Australia in a global context. *Brisbane: Wiley & Sons Australia, Ltd. [New York: John Wiley & Sons; Boston: Houghton Mifflin Company]. Reprinted with permission of John Wiley & Sons Australia.*

Outline

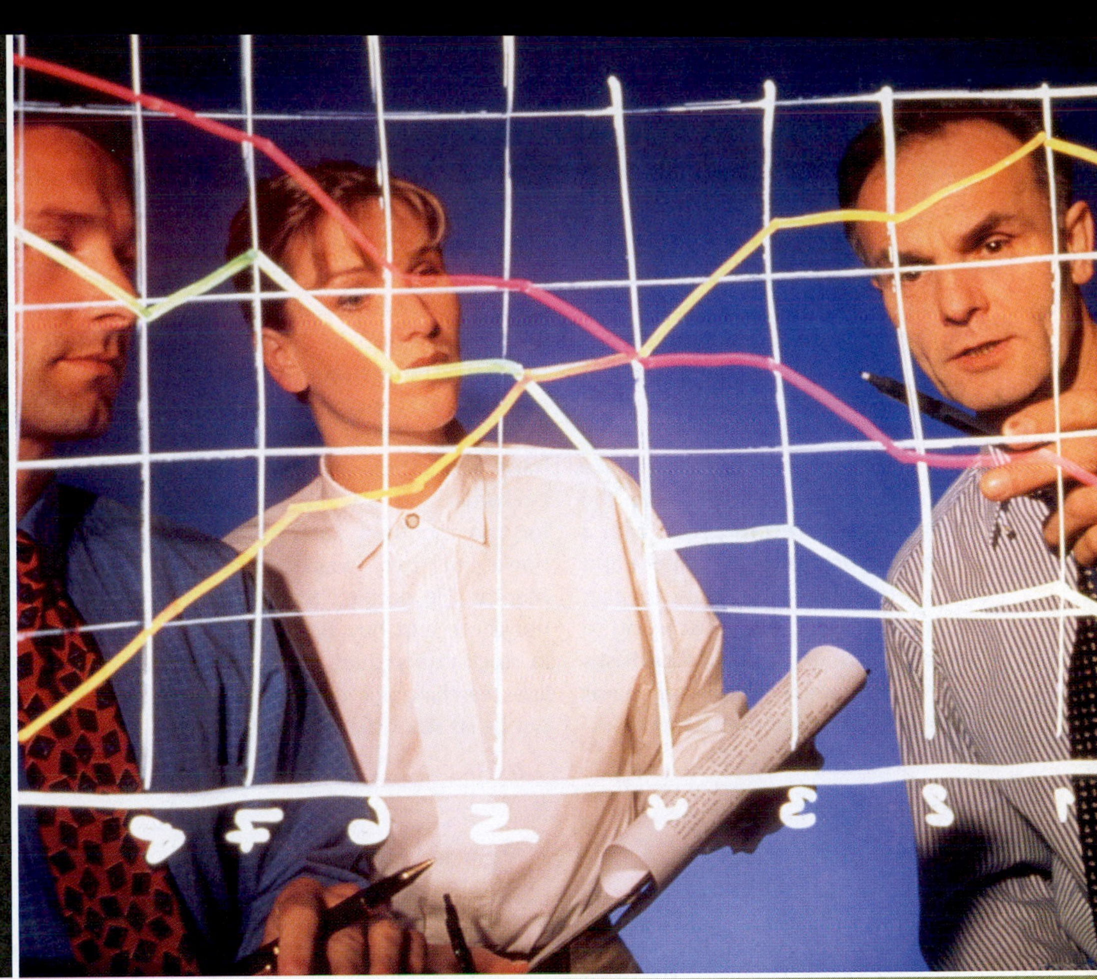

CHAPTER 10

Organizational Planning and Controlling

Learning Objectives

After reading this chapter, you should be able to

1. Outline the planning and controlling processes.
2. Identify different types of plans and control systems employed by organizations.
3. Discuss why organizations need to plan and control.
4. Explain the individual and organizational effects associated with goal setting and planning.
5. Discuss the impact that control has on organizational members.
6. Describe management by objectives as a philosophy, and as a management tool/technique; describe its effects.
7. Differentiate between the execution of the planning and controlling activities under control- and involvement-oriented management practices.

PHOTO: © PREMIUM STOCK/CORBIS

A FIRST LOOK

ChezPastis.com, the brainchild of Elisabeth Charbonnier, specializes in selling French and other gourmet foods online. Before starting ChezPastis.com, Elisabeth and her partners were professional chefs, and their goal for their company is to make gourmet products available to the world. ChezPastis.com began with a bang, and before long Elisabeth and her partners were too busy to plan for the future and were just trying to survive. After six months, ChezPastis.com experienced growing pains similar to other Internet start-ups.

One of the partners, Zack Fortuna, was online one day trying to order some books for his daughter's birthday. The message he got after attempting to place his order was frustrating: "Sorry! The items you have requested are currently on backorder and will not be available for two months." Zack needed the books in two weeks, not two months. He decided to drive to the bookstore and buy books that were in stock rather than waste time online searching for items that might not be in stock. Suddenly, Zack realizes that ChezPastis.com frequently runs out of items as well and this delays customer orders. Perhaps ChezPastis.com's growing pains have something to do with their supply problems.

Question: Is ChezPastis.com's inventory problem attributable to poor planning, poor control, or both? How can Elisabeth, Zack, and the other partners improve the situation?

If you are good enough, it isn't necessary to set aside time for formal planning. After all, 'planning time' takes away from 'doing time.'" Managers often make such statements, possibly as a way of rationalizing their lack of a formal planning program. These claims are simply not valid—planning *does* influence the effectiveness of the entire organization.

Some years ago, the Calico Candy Company developed and produced a highly successful salt water taffy Santa Claus. Buoyed by this success, the company planned and manufactured a salt water taffy Easter Bunny and produced the Santa at Christmas again. This time, however, Calico got stuck with its taffy through faulty planning. Market research clearly showed that consumer preferences had shifted from taffy to chocolate. Rather than plan its products to meet this new preference, the company stayed with what had worked in the past and lost a "ton of money." Yes, planning is important.

PLANNING AS AN ORGANIZATIONAL ACTIVITY

planning the process by which managers establish goals and specify how these goals are to be attained

outcome or **goal statements** end states—the targets and outcomes that managers hope to attain

> The essence of planning is to see opportunities and threats in the future and, respectively, exploit or combat them as the case may be. . . . Planning is a philosophy, not so much in the literal sense of that word but as an attitude, a way of life.[1]

Planning is the process by which managers establish goals and specify how these goals are to be attained. Plans have two basic components: outcome or goal statements and action statements. **Outcome** or **goal statements** represent the *end*

action statements the means by which an organization moves forward to attain its goals

http://www.nwa.com

state—the targets and outcomes managers hope to attain. **Action statements** reflect the *means* by which organizations move forward to attain their goals. Several years ago, United and Northwest Airlines set goals to strengthen their organizations internally and within the fiercely competitive airlines industry. As a part of their action statements, United considered putting pilots in its boardroom and Northwest implemented an employee ownership system.[2]

Planning is an intellectual activity.[3] It is difficult to see managers plan, because most of this activity unfolds in the mind of those doing the planning. While planning, managers have to think about What has to be done? Who is going to do it? How and when will they do it? Planners think both retrospectively (about past events) and prospectively (about future opportunities and impending threats). Planning involves thinking about organizational strengths and weaknesses, as well as making decisions about desired states and ways to achieve them.[4]

IS PLANNING IMPORTANT?

Planning for organizational events, whether in the internal or external environment, should be an ongoing process—part of a manager's daily, weekly, and monthly duties, and a routine task for all members of high-involvement organizations. Plans should be continually monitored. Managers and other organizational members should check to see if their plans need to be modified to accommodate changing conditions, new information, or new situations that will affect the organization's future. Plans need to be administered with flexibility, as organizations learn about new and changing conditions. Clearly, the Calico Candy Company failed to monitor its plans in this way. By thinking of planning as a continuous activity, methods can be formulated for handling emerging and unforeseen opportunities and threats. Planning is one process through which organizational activity can be given meaning and direction.

Why Should Managers Plan?

Managers have several reasons for formulating plans for themselves, their employees, and various organizational units: (1) to offset uncertainty and change; (2) to focus organizational activity on a set of objectives; (3) to provide a coordinated, systematic road map for future activities; (4) to increase economic efficiency; and (5) to facilitate control by establishing a standard for later activity.

Several forces contribute to the necessity for organizational planning. First, in the internal environment, as organizations become larger and more complex, the task of managing becomes increasingly complex. Planning maps out future activities in relation to other activities in the organization. Second, as the external environment becomes increasingly complex and turbulent, the amount of uncertainty faced by a manager increases. Planning enables organizations to approach their environment systematically.

A study commissioned by AT&T found that the absence of planning was one of the biggest reasons for the failure of small businesses. Those firms that followed a clearly defined plan in their day-to-day operations are more successful than those that do not. Of the declining firms in the AT&T survey, 38 percent indicated that they did not follow their plans closely.[5]

Do Managers Really Plan?

Managers should plan formally, but do they? Some observers contend that managers typically are too busy to engage in a regular form of systematic planning. McGill University management professor Henry Mintzberg notes:

> When managers plan, they do so implicitly in the context of daily actions, not in some abstract process reserved for two weeks in the organization's mountain retreat. The plans of the chief executives I have studied seemed to exist only in their heads—as flexible, but often specific, intentions. . . . The job of managing does not breed reflective planners; the manager is a real-time responder to stimuli.[6]

Others disagree. After reviewing a number of studies focused on the degree to which planning and other managerial activities are inherent parts of managing, management professors J. Carroll and J. Gillen state that "the classical management functions of Fayol, Urwick, and others are not "folklore as claimed by some contemporary management writers but represent valid abstractions of what managers actually do and what managers should do."[7] Barbara Allen, president of Sunbelt Research Associates, notes that she did a considerable amount of planning before launching her new business. Now that she is operating successfully, she reviews and updates her plans periodically.[8]

http://www.sunbeltresearch.com

Managers often are very busy people. Some act without a systematic plan of action; however, many managers do plan systematically.[9] For example, many managers develop systematic plans for how their organization will react to a crisis. United Airlines, for example, created a crisis planning group. The group developed United's crisis contingency plan book, which specifies what the airline's crisis management team should do in the event of a crisis. Several years ago, managers at the *Los Angeles Herald Examiner* developed contingency plans that enable the newspaper to go to press, through arrangements with other newspapers to use their presses, in the event of power outages.[10]

The question, Do managers really plan? and the observation that many times they are simply too busy to retreat to the mountaintop and reflect on where the organization should be going and how it should get there, misses the point: There are different types of planning.

THE PLANNING PROCESS

Planning is a process. Ideally it is future oriented, comprehensive, systematic, integrated, and negotiated.[11] It involves an extensive search for alternatives and analyzes relevant information, is systematic in nature, and is commonly participative.[12] The planning model described in this section breaks the managerial function of planning into several steps (see Figure 10-1). Following this step-by-step procedure helps ensure that organizational planning meets these requirements.

Step 1: Developing an Awareness of the Present State

According to management scholars Harold Koontz and Cyril O'Donnell, the first step in the planning process is *awareness*.[13] It is at this step that managers build the foundation on which they will develop their plans. This foundation specifies an organization's current status, pinpoints its commitments, recognizes its strengths and weaknesses, and sets forth a vision of the future. Because the

FIGURE 10-1 The Planning Process

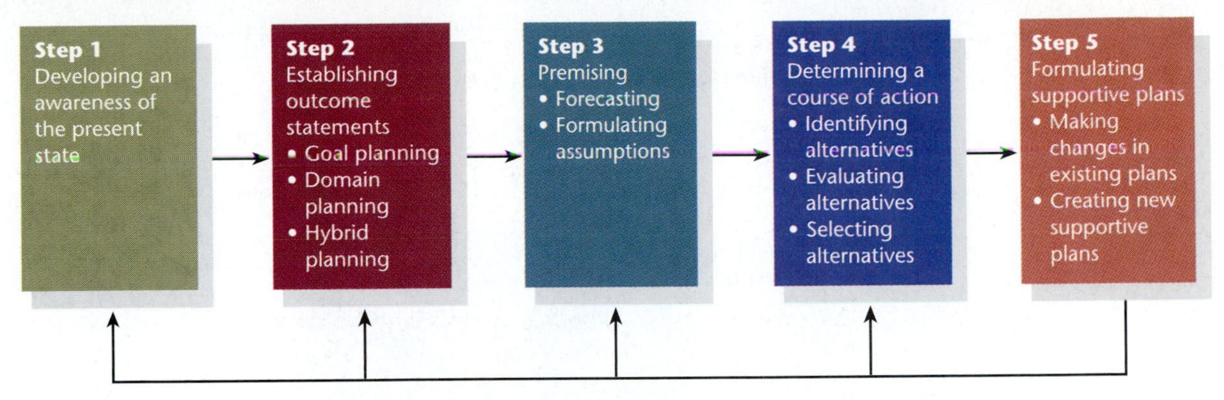

Source: Adapted from H. Koontz and C. O'Donnell. 1972. *Principles of management: An analysis of managerial functions.* New York: McGraw-Hill, 113. Reprinted with permission of The McGraw-Hill Companies.

past is instrumental in determining where an organization expects to go in the future, managers at this point must understand their organization and its history. It has been said—"The further you look back, the further you can see ahead."[14]

Step 2: Establishing Outcome Statements

The second step in the planning process consists of deciding "where the organization is headed, or is going to end up." Ideally, this involves establishing goals. Just as your goal in this course might be to get a certain grade, managers at various levels in the organization's hierarchy set goals. For example, plans established by a university's marketing department curriculum committee must fit with and support the plans of the department, which contribute to the goals of the School of Business, whose plans must, in turn, support the goals of the university. Managers therefore develop an elaborate *network of organizational plans*, such as that shown in Figure 10-2, to achieve the overall goals of their organization.

goal planning development of action statements to move toward the attainment of a specific goal

domain/directional planning the development of a course of action that moves an organization toward one domain or direction (and, therefore, away from other domains or directions)

Goal vs. Domain Planning Outcome statements can be constructed around specific goals or framed in terms of moving in a particular direction toward a viable set of outcomes. In **goal planning**, people set specific goals and then create action statements.[15] For example, freshman Kristin Rude decides that she wants a Bachelor of Science degree in biochemistry (the goal). She then constructs a four-year academic plan that will help her achieve this goal. Kristin is engaging in goal planning. She first identifies a goal and then develops a course of action to realize her goal.

Another approach to planning is **domain/directional planning**, in which managers develop a course of action that moves an organization toward one identified domain (and therefore away from other domains).[16] Within the chosen domain may lie a number of acceptable and specific goals. For example, high-school senior Manuel Marquart decides that he wants to major in a business-related discipline in college. During the next four years he will select a variety of courses from the School of Business curriculum, yet never select a major. After selecting courses based on availability and interest, he earns a sufficient number

FIGURE 10-2 Network of Organizational Plans

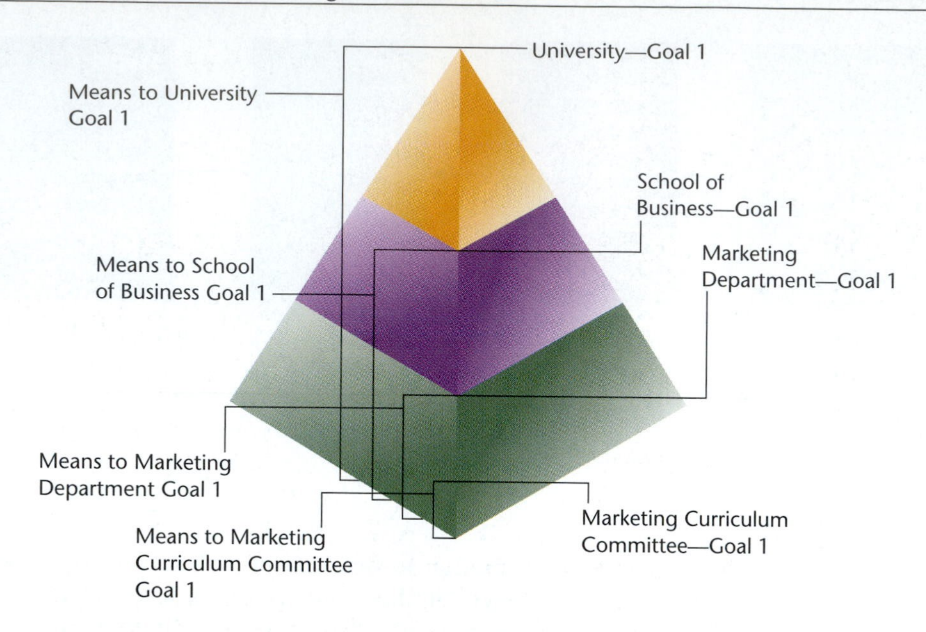

of credits within this chosen domain that enables him to graduate with a major in marketing. Manuel never engaged in goal planning, but in the end he will realize one of many acceptable goals within an accepted domain.

The development of the "Post-it®" product by the 3M Corporation demonstrates how domain planning works. In the research laboratories at 3M, efforts were being made to develop new forms and strengths of cohesive substances. One result was cohesive material with no known value because of its extremely low cohesive level. A 3M Division Specialist, Arthur L. Fry, frustrated by page markers falling from his hymn book in church, realized that this material, recently developed by Spencer F. Silver, would stick to paper for long periods and could be removed without destroying the paper. Fry experimented with the material as page markers and note pads—out of this came the highly popular and extremely profitable 3M product Scotch Post-it®.[17]

Situations in which managers are likely to engage in domain planning include (1) when there is a recognized need for flexibility; (2) when people cannot agree on goals; (3) when an organization's external environment is unstable and highly uncertain; and (4) when an organization is starting up or is in a transitional period. In addition, domain planning is likely to prevail at upper levels in an organization, where managers are responsible for dealing with the external environment and when task uncertainty is high. Goal planning (formulating goals compatible with the chosen domain) is likely to prevail in the technical core, where there is less uncertainty.

hybrid planning the coupling of domain and goal planning

Hybrid Planning Occasionally, coupling of domain and goal planning occurs, creating a third approach, called **hybrid planning**. In this approach, managers begin with the more general domain planning and commit to moving in a particular direction. As time passes, learning occurs, uncertainty is reduced, preferences sharpen, and managers are able to make the transition to goal planning as they identify increasingly specific targets in the selected domain. Movement from domain planning to goal planning occurs as knowledge accumulates, preferences for a particular goal emerge, and action statements are created.

Consequences of Goal, Domain, and Hybrid Planning Setting goals not only affects performance directly, but also encourages managers to plan more extensively. That is, once goals are set, people are more likely to think systematically about how they should proceed to realize the goals.[18] When people have vague goals, as in domain planning, they find it difficult to draw up detailed action plans and are therefore less likely to perform effectively. In Chapter 7, we examined goal theory. Research suggests that goal planning results in higher levels of performance than does domain planning alone.[19]

Step 3: Premising

In this step of the planning process, managers establish the premises, or assumptions, on which they will build their action statements. The quality and success of any plan depends on the quality of its underlying assumptions. Throughout the planning process, assumptions about future events must be brought to the surface, monitored, and updated.[20]

© SUSAN VAN ETTEN

Effective planning skills can be used throughout your life. The plan you develop to pay for and complete your education is an especially important one.

Managers collect information by scanning their organization's internal and external environments. They use this information to make assumptions about the likelihood of future events. As Kristin considers her four-year pursuit of her biochemistry major, she anticipates that in addition to her savings and funds supplied by her parents, she will need a full-time summer job for two summers in order to cover the cost of her undergraduate education. Thus, she includes finding full-time summer employment between her senior year of high school and her freshman year, and between her freshman and sophomore years of college as part of her plan. The other two summers she will devote to an internship and finding postgraduate employment—much to mom and dad's delight!

Step 4: Determining a Course of Action (Action Statements)

In this stage of the planning process, managers decide how to move from their current position toward their goal (or toward their domain). They develop an action statement that details what needs to be done, when, how, and by whom. The course of action determines how an organization will get from its current position to its desired future position. Choosing a course of action involves *determining alternatives* by drawing on research, experimentation, and experience; *evaluating alternatives* in light of how well each would help the organization reach its goals or approach its desired domain; and *selecting a course of action* after identifying and carefully considering the merits of each alternative.

Step 5: Formulating Supportive Plans

The planning process seldom stops with the adoption of a general plan. Managers often need to develop one or more supportive or derivative plans to bolster and explain their basic plan. Suppose an organization decides to switch from a 5-day, 40-hour workweek (5/40) to a 4-day, 40-hour workweek (4/40) in an attempt to reduce employee turnover. This major plan requires the creation of a number of supportive plans. Managers might need to develop personnel policies dealing with payment of daily overtime. New administrative plans will be needed for scheduling meetings, handling phone calls, and dealing with customers and suppliers.

Planning, Implementation, and Controlling

After managers have moved through the five steps of the planning process and have drawn up and implemented specific plans, they must monitor and maintain their plans. Through the controlling function (to be discussed in greater detail later in this chapter), managers observe ongoing human behavior and organizational activity, compare it to the outcome and action statements formulated during the planning process, and take corrective action if they observe unexpected and unwanted deviations. Thus, planning and controlling activities are closely interrelated (planning → controlling → planning . . .). Planning feeds controlling by establishing the standards against which behavior will be evaluated during the controlling process. Monitoring organizational behavior (the control activity) provides managers with input that helps them prepare for the upcoming planning period—it adds meaning to the awareness step of the planning process.

http://www.ibm.com

Influenced by Total Quality Management (TQM) and the importance of achieving continuous improvement in the processes used, as well as the goods and services produced, organizations like IBM-Rochester have linked their planning and controlling activities by adopting the Deming cycle (also known as the Shewart cycle).

Deming cycle a planning model directed toward attaining continuous improvement by integrating organizational learning into the planning process (plan, do, check, act)

It has been noted on numerous occasions that many organizations that do plan, fail to recognize the importance of continuous learning. Their plans are either placed on the shelf and collect dust, or they are created, implemented, and adhered to without a systematic review and modification process. Frequently plans are implemented without first measuring where the organization currently stands, so that future comparisons and evaluations of the plan's effectiveness cannot be determined. The **Deming cycle**, shown in Figure 10-3, helps managers assess the effects of planned action by integrating organizational learning into the planning process. The cycle consists of four key stages: (1) Plan—create the plan using the model discussed earlier. (2) Do—implement the plan. (3) Check—monitor the results of the planned course of action; organizational learning about the effectiveness of the plan occurs at this stage. (4) Act—on what was learned, modify the plan, and return to the first stage in the cycle, and the cycle begins again as the organization strives for continuous learning and improvement.

FIGURE 10-3 The Deming Cycle

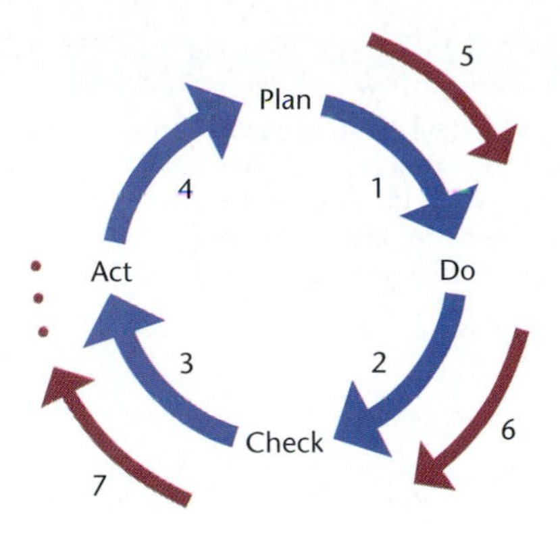

TYPES OF PLANS

From an activity perspective, organizations are relatively complex systems, as they are involved in numerous activities. Many of these activities require management's attention from both a planning and controlling perspective. Managers therefore create different types of plans to guide operations and to monitor and control organizational activities. In this section we introduce several commonly used plans. The major categories are hierarchical, frequency-of-use (repetitiveness), time-frame, organizational scope, and contingency. Table 10-1 provides a closer look at many types of plans that fall in each of these categories.

Hierarchical Plans

As you will recall from Chapter 1, the organization can be viewed as a three-layer cake, with its three levels of organizational needs. Each of the three levels—institutional, administrative, and technical core—is associated with a particular type of plan. As revealed in Table 10-1, the three types of hierarchical plans are strategic, administrative, and operating (technical core). The three hierarchical plans are interdependent, as they support the fulfillment of the three organizational needs.

In the organization's hierarchy, the technical core plans day-to-day operations.

Strategic Plans Strategic management is that part of the management process concerned with the overall integration of an organization's internal divisions, while simultaneously integrating the organization with its external environment. Strategic management formulates and implements tactics that try to match an organization as closely as possible to its task environment for the purpose of meeting its objectives.

TABLE 10-1 Organizational Plans

Hierarchical Plans

- Strategic plans (institutional)—define the organization's long-term vision; articulate the organization's mission and value statements; define what business the organization is in or hopes to be in; articulate how the organization will integrate itself into its general and task environments.
- Administrative plans—specify the allocation of organizational resources to internal units of the organization; address the integration of the institutional level of the organization (for example, vision formulation) with the technical core (vision implementation); address the integration of the diverse units of the organization.
- Operating plans (technical core)—cover the day-to-day operations of the organization.

Frequency-of-Use Plans

Standing Plans:

- Policies—general statements of understanding or intent; guide decision making, permitting the exercise of some discretion; guide behavior (for example, no employee shall accept favors and/or entertainment from an outside organization that are substantial enough in value to cause undue influence over one's decisions on behalf of the organization).
- Rules—guides to action that do not permit discretion in interpretation; specify what is permissible and what is not permissible.
- Procedures—like rules, they guide action; specify a series of steps that must be taken in the performance of a particular task.

Single-Use Plans:

- Programs—a complex set of policies, rules, and procedures necessary to carry out a course of action.
- Projects—specific action plans often created to complete various aspects of a program.
- Budgets—plans expressed in numerical terms.

Time-Frame Plans

- Short-, medium-, and long-range plans—differ in the distance into the future projected:
  - Short-range—several hours to a year
  - Medium-range—one to five years
  - Long-range—more than five years

Organizational Scope Plans

- Business/divisional-level plans—focus on one of the organization's businesses (or divisions) and its competitive position.
- Unit-/functional-level plans—focus on the day-to-day operations of lower-level organization units; marketing, human resources, accounting, and operations plans (production).
- Tactical plans—division-level or unit-level plans designed to help an organization accomplish its strategic plans.

Contingency Plans

- Plans created to deal with events that might come to confront the organization (e.g., natural disasters, terrorist threats); alternative courses of action that are to be implemented if events disrupt a planned course of action.

strategic plans
hierarchical plans that address an organization's institutional-level needs and attempt to position it advantageously within its task environment

Strategic plans address the organization's institutional-level needs (see Chapter 1). Strategic plans outline a long-term vision for the organization. They specify the organization's reason for being, its strategic objectives, and its operational strategies—the action statements that specify how the organization's strategic goals are to be achieved.

Part of strategic planning involves creating the organization's mission, a statement that specifies an organization's reason for being and answers the question "What business(es) should we undertake?" The mission and the strategic plan http://www.sps.org.uk

operating plans cover the day-to-day operations of the organization

administrative plans integrate institutional-level plans with operating plans as well as integrating all the operating plans

are major guiding documents for activities that the organization pursues. Strategic plans have several defining characteristics: They are long-term and position an organization within its task environment; they are pervasive and cover many organizational activities; they integrate, guide, and control activities for the immediate, and the long term; and they establish boundaries for managerial decision making. See *An Inside Look* for more insight into strategic planning.

Operating plans provide direction and action statements for activities in the organization's technical core. **Administrative plans** work to integrate institutional-level plans with the operating plans, and tie together all of the plans created for the organization's technical core.

AN INSIDE LOOK

Strategic Planning

Strategic planning, or the art of masterminding the future of an organization, became a high priority for organizations beginning in the 1960s. Big businesses hired strategic planners to think "outside the box" and guide their organizations to success by devising creative ways to compete. But in the 1980s, when many companies began to downsize and restructure due to the forces of global competition and new technologies, strategic planners were seen as an expendable luxury. Many companies downsized their strategic planners right out of a job.

As the maxim goes, "Those who fail to plan, plan to fail." Today's organizations are recognizing that they need the creative thinking of strategic planners now more than ever in an era of streamlining and cutbacks. Experts in the field of business have gone on record as stating that the most significant element of management in today's business world is strategy.

The early days of business strategy were characterized by the classical school of management. Top-level managers frequently generated strategic plans in isolation from the rest of the organization. Old-style strategic planning focused on financial and quantitative analysis, sometimes to the exclusion of forward-thinking ideas of competitive positioning and creating markets.

In the new era of strategic planning, all levels of the company can be involved. Everyone from line managers to staff managers to senior officers of an organization may be represented on the strategic planning team. Senior members of an organization who know the history and ropes inside out may be joined by junior members fresh out of school and ready to propose innovative ideas. Some organizations even include external stakeholders such as customers and suppliers on their strategy teams.

Strategic planners are called upon to think "big." Changing the rules and carving out future markets are expected results of a strategy team. Individuals from all levels of an organization, including internal and external environments, can help transform the future of an organization. Using high-involvement management on a strategy team not only ensures a more comprehensive and effective plan, but also helps to create a sense of ownership of the strategic goals throughout the organization.

Ideally, strategic planning should be part of every manager's day rather than a ritual annual activity that gets written up in a report and filed away. However, managers today frequently feel that they are too busy to take the time to think strategically. This phenomenon, which is known as "time famine," often results in disaster. In order to combat time famine, managers must deliberately make time and space for reflection. Getting away from the hectic environment of the office is often an effective strategy which can foster reflection, as is taking advantage of opportunities to learn new approaches and therefore think differently about problems. Leaders in today's fast-paced world should be role models for others in the organization and demonstrate the importance of thinking calmly and strategically. A leader must make time to think a priority in order to succeed.

Source: Adapted from J. A. Byrne. August 26, 1996. Strategic planning: After a decade of gritty downsizing, big thinkers are back in corporate vogue. *Business Week,* 46–52; and C. Comeau-Kirschner and L. Wah. Who has time to think? *Management Review* 89(1):16–23.

Frequency-of-Use Plans

standing plans rules, policies, and procedures about how to deal with issues that managers face repeatedly

Another category of plans is frequency-of-use plans. Some plans are used repeatedly; others are used for a single purpose. **Standing plans**, such as rules, policies, and procedures, are designed to cover issues that managers face repeatedly. For example, managers may be concerned about tardiness, a problem that may occur often in the entire work force. These managers might decide to develop a standing policy to be implemented automatically each time an employee is late for work. The procedure invoked under such a standing plan is called a standard operating procedure (SOP).

single-use plans plans developed for unique situations or problems and one-time use

Single-use plans are developed for unique situations or problems and are usually replaced after one use. Managers generally use three types of single-use plans: programs, projects, and budgets. See Table 10-1 for a brief description of standing and single-use plans.

Time-Frame Plans

http://www.mei.co.jp

http://www.panasonic.com

The organization's need to address the future is captured by its time-frame plans. This need to address the future through planning is reflected in short-, medium-, and long-range plans. Given the uniqueness of industries and the different time orientations of societies (recall Hofstede's differentiation of cultures around the world in terms of their orientation toward the future, as discussed in Chapter 5), the times captured by short, medium, and long range vary tremendously across organizations of the world. Konosuke Matsushita's 250-year plan, which he developed for the company that bears his name, is not exactly typical of the long-range plans of U.S. companies!

Short-, medium-, and long-range plans differ in more ways than the time they cover. Typically, the further a plan projects into the future, the more uncertainty planners encounter. As a consequence, long-range plans are usually less specific than shorter-range plans. Also, long-range plans are usually less formal, less detailed, and more flexible than short-range plans in order to accommodate such uncertainty. Long-range plans also tend to be more directional in nature.

Organizational Scope Plans

Plans vary in scope. Some plans focus on an entire organization. For example, the president of the University of Minnesota advanced a plan to make the university one of the top five educational institutions in the United States. This strategic plan focuses on the entire institution. Other plans are narrower in scope and concentrate on a subset of organizational activities or operating units such as the food services unit of the university. For further insight into organizational scope plans, see Table 10-1.

Contingency Plans

contingency plans plans that deal with alternative courses of action

Organizations often engage in contingency planning (also referred to as scenario or "what if" planning). You will recall that the planning process is based on certain premises about what is likely to happen in an organization's environment. **Contingency plans** are created to deal with what might happen if these assumptions turn out to be wrong. Contingency planning is thus the development of alternative courses of action to be implemented if events disrupt a planned course of action. A contingency plan allows management to act immediately if an unplanned occurrence, such as a strike, boycott, natural disaster, or major economic shift, render existing plans inoperable or inappropriate. For example, airlines develop contingency plans to deal with terrorism and air tragedies. Most contingency plans are never implemented, but when needed, they are of crucial importance.

GOALS OR OUTCOME STATEMENTS

official goals the aims of an organization that are expressed in highly abstract and general terms, generally employed for the organization's external constituents

operational goals the aims of an organization that reflect management's specific intentions

Creating goals is an inherent part of effective managerial planning. There are two types of organizational goals that are interrelated—official and operational goals.[21] **Official goals** are an organization's general aims as expressed in public statements, in its annual report, and in its charter. One official goal of a university, for example, might be to be "the school of first choice." Official goals are usually ambiguous and oriented toward achieving acceptance by an organization's constituencies. **Operational goals** reflect management's specific intentions. These are the concrete goals that organization members are to pursue.[22] For example, an operational goal for a hospital might be to increase the number of patients treated by 5 percent.

The importance of goals is apparent from the purposes they serve. Successful goals (1) guide and direct the efforts of individuals and groups; (2) motivate individuals and groups, thereby affecting their efficiency and effectiveness; (3) influence the nature and content of the planning process; and (4) provide a standard by which to judge and control organizational activity. In short, goals define organizational purpose, motivate accomplishment, and provide a yardstick against which progress can be measured.

Goal Formulation—Where Do Organizational Goals Come From?

There are two different views about how organizational goals are formulated. The first view focuses on an organization and its external environment. You will recall from Chapter 4 that there are many stakeholders (e.g., owners, employees, managers) who have a vested interest in the organization. Organizational goals emerge as managers try to maintain the delicate balance between their organization's needs and those of its external environment.[23] The second view concentrates on the set of dynamics in the organization's internal environment. Internally, an organization is made up of many individuals, coalitions, and groups who continually interact to meet their own interests and needs.[24] They bargain, trade, and negotiate and, through these political processes, organizational goals eventually emerge.

Neither approach to goal formulation can alone provide for long-term organizational success. Goals must fit an organization into its external environment, while satisfying the needs of external constituencies. In addition, goals must enable an organization's internal components to work in harmony. For example, the goals of its marketing department need to mesh with those of its production and finance departments. The challenge for managers is to balance these forces and preserve the organization.

Multiple Goals and the Goal Hierarchy

http://www.pfdf.org

Consistent with the two views of goal emergence, Peter Drucker offers the perspective that organizations must simultaneously pursue multiple goals. A well-known management scholar, consultant, and writer, Drucker believes that to achieve organizational success, managers must try to achieve multiple goals

TABLE 10-2 Hewlett-Packard's Corporate Goals

Profit. To achieve sufficient profit to finance our company growth and to provide the resources we need to achieve our other corporate objectives.

Customers. To provide products and services of the greatest possible value to our customers, thereby gaining and holding their respect and loyalty.

Field of Interest. To enter new fields only when the ideas we have, together with our technical, manufacturing and marketing skills, assure that we can make a needed and profitable contribution to the field.

Growth. To let our growth be limited only by our profits and our ability to develop and produce technical products that satisfy real customer needs.

People. To help our own people share in the company's success, which they make possible: to provide job security based on their performance, to recognize their individual achievements, and to help them gain a sense of satisfaction and accomplishment from their work.

Management. To foster initiative and creativity by allowing the individual great freedom of action in attaining well-defined objectives.

Citizenship. To honor our obligations to society by being an economic, intellectual and social asset to each nation and each community in which we operate.

Source: From Y. K. Shetty. 1979. New look at corporate goals. *California Management Review* 22(2): 71–79. Copyright © 1979 by the Regents of the University of California. Reprinted by permission of the Regents.

simultaneously—namely, market standing, innovation, productivity, profitability; physical and financial resources, manager performance and development, employee performance and attitude, and public responsibility.[25] Reflecting his concerns, the Hewlett-Packard Corporation has established the seven corporate goals listed in Table 10-2. Sometimes units within organizations may pursue goals that actually conflict with the goals of other internal units. The innovation goal of a research and development department, for example, might conflict with the production department's goal of efficiency.[26] Managers must strive to integrate the network of goals and resolve internal conflicts when they arise.

Broad organizational goals, such as productivity, innovation, and profitability, are likely to be broken into subgoals at various organizational levels. The complexities posed by many interrelated systems of goals and major plans can be illustrated by a **goal hierarchy**.[27] Thus, an organization sets organizational-level, divisional-level, departmental-level, and job-related goals. In the process, managers must make sure that lower-level goals combine to achieve higher-level goals.

goal hierarchy the interrelationship among an organization's job-, department-, divisional-, and organizational-level goals

FORMAL ORGANIZATIONAL PLANNING IN PRACTICE

Studies indicate that, in the 1950s, approximately 8.3 percent of all major U.S. firms (1 out of every 12) employed a full-time long-range planner. By the late 1960s, 83 percent of major U.S. firms used long-range planning. Today it is estimated that nearly all U.S. corporations with sales over $100 million prepare formal long-range plans.[28] Most formal plans extend five years into the future, and about 20 percent extend at least ten years.

Encouraging Planning

In spite of the advantages to be gained by planning, many managers resist it. Some feel that there is not enough time to plan, or that it is too complicated and costs too much. Others worry about the possible consequences of failing to reach the goals they set. Instead of *pre-planning,* sometimes referred to as blueprint planning (that is, formulating outcome and action statements before moving forward), many managers simply fail to plan, or at best engage in *in-process planning* (they read events, and think about the next step, just before acting). In-process planning works extremely well when individuals have a sense of what it is that they want to achieve and can improvise as they move forward in a sea of uncertainty and turbulence. This is much like skilled hockey players relying on their instincts, reading the defense, and improvising as they move up the ice and toward the opponent's net. This process often works better than attempting to implement a detailed pre-plan, as often characterizes plays in football.

In situations where we want to encourage pre-planning, certain techniques facilitate the process:

- Develop an organizational climate that encourages planning.
- Top managers support lower-level managers' planning activities—for example, by providing such resources as personnel, computers, and funds—and serve as role models through their own planning activities.
- Train people in planning.
- Create a reward system that encourages and supports planning activity and carefully avoids punishment for failure to achieve newly set goals.
- Use plans once they are created.

In order for managers to invest the time and energy needed to overcome resistance to planning, they must be convinced that planning does in fact pay off.

Does Planning Really Pay Off?

Managers of organizations in complex and unstable environments may find it difficult to develop meaningful plans, yet it is precisely conditions of environmental complexity and instability that produce the greatest need for a good set of organizational plans. Yet the question remains, does planning really pay off?

We know from our earlier discussion that setting goals is an important part of the planning process. Today, much is known about what characterizes effective individual goals. (We discuss this issue in greater detail later in this chapter.) Although group and organizational goals have been studied less, it is probably safe to assume that most of our knowledge about individual goals also applies to group and organizational goals. The research suggests that effective organizational goals should (1) be difficult but reachable with effort; (2) be specific and clearly identify what is desired; (3) be accepted by and have the commitment of those who will help achieve them; (4) be developed by employees if such participation will improve the quality of the goals and their acceptance; and (5) be monitored for progress regularly.

While the evidence is not abundant, studies suggest that firms that engage in planning are more financially successful than those that do not.[29] For example, one study reports that the median return on investment for a five-year period is 17.1 percent for organizations engaged in strategic planning, versus 5.9 percent for those that do not.[30] Similarly, of 70 large commercial banks, those that had strategic planning systems outperformed those that did not.[31]

Although planning clearly has observable benefits, it can be expensive. The financial commitment can be large for organizations with a formal planning staff. Even so, research suggests that planning is warranted.

The Location of the Planning Activity

Classical management thinking advocates a separation of "planning" and "doing." According to this school of thought, managers plan for technical core employees and formulate most of the plans for the upper levels of the organization, with little participation from lower-level managers and workers. In contrast, behavioral management theorists suggest involving organization members in drawing up plans that affect them. Implementation of a management-by-objectives program (to be discussed later in this chapter), for example, is one means by which this participative planning can be realized. Researchers at the Tavistock Institute in England promote the idea of self-managed work groups (to be discussed in Chapter 14) as a means of expanding the level of employee involvement. According to their socio-technical model, work groups assume a major role in planning (as well as in organizing, directing, and controlling) the work assigned to them. Many organizations—for example, Volvo and Motorola—have had successful experiences with employee involvement in planning and controlling activities.

http://www.tavinstitute.org

Planning Specialists

To keep pace with organizational complexity, technological sophistication, and environmental uncertainty, many organizations use planning specialists. Professional planners develop organizational plans and help managers plan. Boeing, General Electric, and Ford are among the many organizations with professional planning staffs. Planning specialists at United Airlines developed United's crisis management plan.

http://www.volvocars.com

Organizations have planning specialists and planning departments in place for a variety of reasons. These specialized roles have emerged because planning is time-consuming and complex and requires more attention than line managers can provide. In rapidly changing environments, planning becomes even more complex and often necessitates the development of contingency plans, once again demanding time for research and special planning skills. At times effective planning requires an objectivity that managers and employees with vested interests in a particular set of organizational activities cannot provide.

A planning staff's goals are varied. Their primary responsibility is to serve as planning advisors to top management, and to assist lower-level line managers in developing plans for achieving their many and varied organizational objectives. Frequently, they coordinate the complex array of plans created for the various levels within an organization. Finally, a planning staff provides encouragement, support, and skill for developing formal organizational plans.

EMPLOYEE RESPONSES TO PLANNING

Managers, of course, want their members to work hard. However, effort alone is not enough; it must be directed toward the appropriate target and executed in a proper manner. The question we explore here is, Do planning, goal setting,

For goals to be effective, they must be difficult, specific, and accepted by the employee, and they must be met with feedback from management. Manufacturers often use production goals to motivate employees.

and the development of action statements have a favorable impact on employee motivation, performance, and job satisfaction?

We turn to goal theory for our answer. Research provides us with a clear and unequivocal picture of the effects of setting goals for organizational members. *Goal theory* specifies that certain types of goals motivate employee behavior and thereby contribute to the level of employee performance. Goal theory, while somewhat narrow in scope, is the most completely supported theory of motivation.[32] We covered goal theory in detail in Chapter 7; here we review the implications of goal setting as a fundamental part of the planning process and as a standard for the exercise of control.

Characteristics of Goals That Motivate Performance

Goal theory (and the research related to it) highlights several important goal attributes—goal difficulty, goal specificity, goal acceptance and commitment, and goal feedback. As Figure 10-4 shows, workers who have a goal, even if it is quite general, usually perform better than those with no goals. Yet, certain types of goals are more effective than others. Two primary characteristics of goals that enhance their motivating potential are *goal specificity* and *goal difficulty*.[33] With regard to goal specificity, a goal that states "improve your performance" or "do your best" is generally not very effective because it is too general. Weyerhaeuser, for example, observed that their truck drivers hauling logs significantly increased their performance level when they were instructed to load their trucks to 94 percent of legal weight capacity, as opposed to simply "doing their best." The drivers found the specific goal to be motivating, and they often competed with one another to achieve the prescribed goal. In the first nine months following the introduction of the 94 percent target, Weyerhaeuser estimated its savings to be approximately $250,000.

FIGURE 10-4 The Effects of Goals on Performance

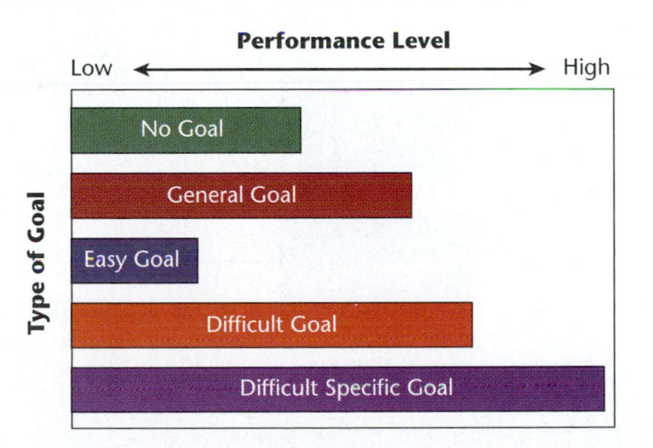

The second component of an effective goal is goal difficulty. People with difficult goals perform better than those with easy goals (note the third and fourth bars in Figure 10-4). If goals are perceived as "too difficult" or impossible, however, they lose their motivating effectiveness.[34] Ideally, goals will be both specific and difficult. Thus, setting specific and challenging goals contributes more to planning effectiveness and organizational performance than does working under "no-goal" or "do your best" goal conditions.[35]

Even a goal that is both difficult and specific, however, is not going to be effective unless it is accepted by the person who is expected to achieve it.[36] *Goal acceptance* is the degree to which people accept a goal as their own ("I agree that this report must be finished by 5 p.m.")[37] *Goal commitment* is more inclusive, referring to our level of attachment to or determination to reach a goal ("I *want* to get that report done on time").[38] Goals sometimes fail to motivate people when managers assign them without making sure that workers have accepted or committed to the goals. Figure 10-5 summarizes the conditions necessary to maximize goal-directed effort (motivation = direction + intensity), a major contributor to subsequent performance, while Figure 10-6 summarizes the three sets of factors that facilitate goal commitment.[39]

Goal feedback is the last important goal attribute. Goal feedback provides us with knowledge about the results of our efforts. This information can come from a variety of sources, such as our supervisor, peers, subordinates, customers, inanimate performance monitoring systems, and self-assessment. Regardless of the source, the right kind of feedback serves two important functions: "directional" and "effort." Directionally, good feedback tells employees whether they are on the right path and on target, or suggests the need for redirection. In addition, it should provide information that suggests the adequacy or inadequacy of the employee's level of effort. Thus, feedback is of critical importance!

The Negative Side of Goals

http://www.mit.edu/deming

There is, however, a negative side to goal setting. Total Quality Management (TQM) pioneer W. Edwards Deming fears that goals tend to narrow the performer's vision and invite people to slack off once the goal is achieved. TQM is also oriented more toward process (means) than toward success (goals, outcomes). Organizational learning and continuous improvement, a central component of

FIGURE 10-5 A Model of Goal Setting

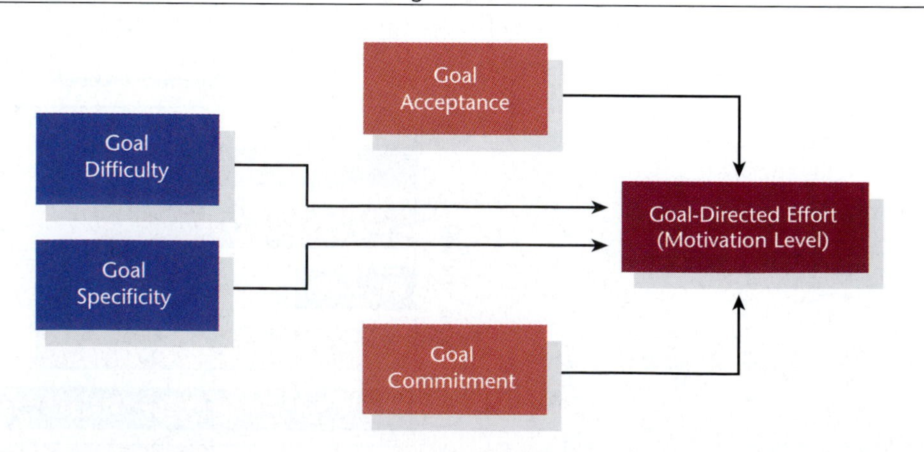

FIGURE 10-6 Determinants of Goal Commitment

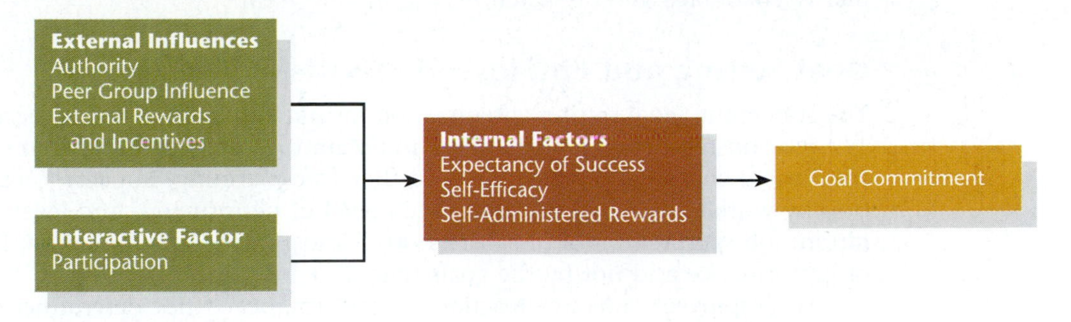

1. External influences: *authority*—being asked to do something by a person possessing legitimate authority increases goal commitment;

peer group influence—group dynamics, such as peers acting as role models and group norms, can produce commitment to goals;

rewards and incentives—commitment to goals is often the outgrowth of rewards and incentives that are associated with goal attainment

2. Interactive factor: *participation*—participation contributes to goal understanding and to a sense of goal ownership for those who want to be involved in the process

3. Internal factors: *expectancy of success*—perceptions of being able to achieve goals positively influence the commitment to those goals;

self-efficacy—people who have a strong belief in their ability to accomplish goals are more likely to have strong commitment to these goals;

self-administered rewards—self-generated feedback ("I did well") can lead to high goal commitment

Source: Adapted from E. A. Locke, G. P. Latham, and M. Erez. 1988. The determinants of goal commitment. *Academy of Management Review* 13:28. Copyright 1998 by Academy of Management. Reproduced with permission of Academy of Management in the format Textbook via Copyright Clearance Center; and from E. Erez and P. C. Earley. 1987. Comparative analysis of goal setting across cultures. *Journal of Applied Psychology* 72:658–665.

TQM, is oriented toward continually finding problems in the production process that when eliminated will result in performance increases.[40] Performance goals, on the other hand, generally focus the performer's attention on successfully achieving a specified level of accomplishment at some future point.

Recent evidence reveals a negative side to an employee's commitment to difficult goals. When organizational members are strongly committed to achieving difficult goals, their involvement in acts of good organizational citizenship (see Chapter 8) is likely to decline.[41] This negative relationship is unfortunate because organizations operating in highly turbulent, competitive, and uncertain environments are extremely fragile social systems. They need the commitment and the sense of ownership (see Chapter 6) that propel organizational members to spontaneously engage in behaviors that are not specified in their job descriptions, but that are important to the organization's success and well-being.

There are several other negative effects associated with goals: The methods and means created to accomplish organizational goals may themselves become the goal (means-ends inversion). Organizational goals may be in conflict with personal or societal goals. Goals that are too specific may inhibit creativity and innovation. Ambiguous goals may fail to provide adequate direction, and goals and reward systems are often incompatible. For example, universities commonly encourage faculty members to be better teachers, but their reward systems primarily encourage good research.[42]

Goal Setting and Employee Job Satisfaction

The statement "goal setting enhances job satisfaction" is not exactly accurate.[43] The relationship between goal setting and planning, and job satisfaction is somewhat more complex. Goal setting, and therefore planning, impacts job satisfaction by working through the employee's level of performance and level of aspiration. Job satisfaction (or dissatisfaction) is most likely determined by the level of performance and not by the goals that have been set.

An employee's affective reaction to performance is not determined by the performance level itself, but by the level of performance in relation to their aspiration level.[44] Job satisfaction, therefore, stems from the employee's evaluation of their actual performance in comparison to their aspiration level (or performance goal). In cases (see Figure 10-7) where performance reaches or passes the level aspired to, a positive emotion (job satisfaction) is likely to be produced. Performance that fails to reach aspirations causes a negative emotion (job dissatisfaction). In addition, if performance is valued by the employee because of the extrinsic rewards tied to it, high performance will create job satisfaction only if achieving the performance goal leads to the receipt of these valued extrinsic rewards.[45] Thus, goal setting is indirectly and contingently related to job satisfaction. If goal setting contributes to employees reaching their performance aspirations and/or the outcomes that are associated with that performance, job satisfaction is a likely by-product.

Managing Through Goal Setting

What can managers do to motivate employees through goal setting? First, it is important to encourage goal acceptance and commitment. This can be accomplished by working with organizational members to set difficult, specific, and

FIGURE 10-7 Performance, Aspiration Level, and Satisfaction

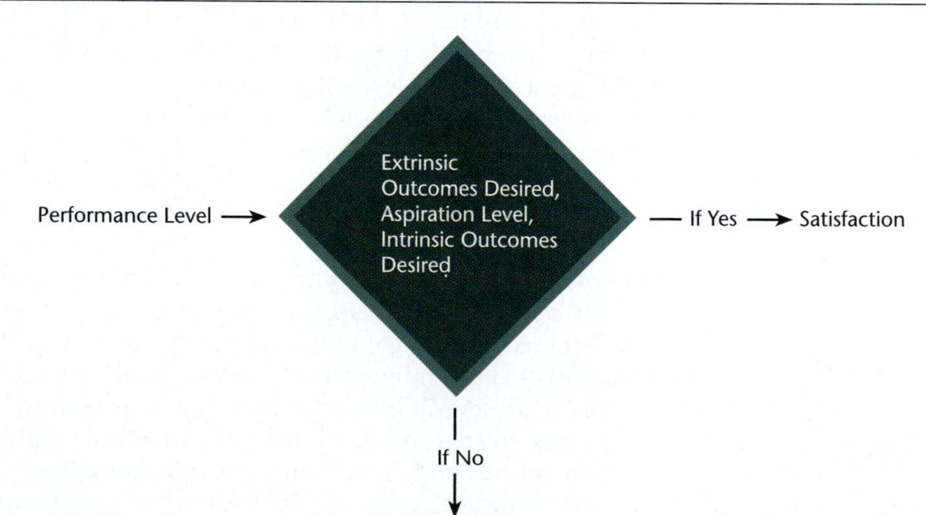

reasonable goals, and to make certain that members perceive them as reasonable. If necessary, provide training and other support needed to make the goals attainable. Offer feedback that lets people know when they are approaching the goal. Avoid using threats. Feedback that criticizes without providing insight into ways to contribute to performance improvements is both frustrating and unlikely to be effective (see our discussion of performance improvement plans in Chapter 8). One of Deming's concerns about goal setting is that it creates fear in employees—fear of the failure to reach the goal. He sees fear as a serious disease that contributes to poor organizational performance.[46] Instead, a positive, success-oriented approach is almost always more effective. If and when negative feedback is needed to correct errors, a manager's criticisms of an employee should be credible, constructive, and objective. In addition, it is important to recall that feedback that simply criticizes, without providing insight into how to make the needed corrections, will produce few if any positive results. Finally, keep in mind that, whereas goal acceptance occurs before people work on a task and can be encouraged through promises of reward, goal commitment can be nurtured throughout the performance period as workers receive rewards for progress.

Encourage the development of work group norms that contribute to goal commitment. Use legitimate authority to encourage the setting of specific and difficult goals. Stimulate workers to develop a sense of ownership in goals, thus producing goal acceptance and commitment. There are those who believe goal acceptance and commitment can be nurtured when workers come together as members of a family working toward the common goal of proving their worth.[47]

CONTROLLING AS AN ORGANIZATIONAL ACTIVITY

http://www.police.ci.duluth.mn.us

A few years ago, the Duluth Police Department found themselves struggling with employee morale. The summer had passed and the department discovered that it had allowed too much vacation time given the volume of summer activity facing the department. As they developed their staffing plans for the upcoming summer, they would have to grant fewer requests for summer vacations. Management soon learned that there would actually be more requests for summer vacation than they encountered the previous summer. A conflict between management and the police union appeared inevitable.

The department turned to creative problem solving. In the process they came up with the idea of moving from a 7-day week to an 8-day week. Under the old schedule a police officer worked a traditional 5 days a week, 8 hours a day, 40 hours a week arrangement with 2 days off each week. Under the new schedule, officers would work 12 hours a day and 48 hours a week. In addition, officers would work 4 days and then have 4 days off. This would in effect give officers half the upcoming summer off without taking a single day of vacation. The plan was endorsed by both the police union and the city council. Following the endorsement of the new staffing plan, the department developed a plan for monitoring the effectiveness of this new schedule, and collected base-line data so that subsequent assessment of the schedule could be compared to previous work schedules.[48]

In January, the new compressed work schedule was implemented. This was accompanied by a control system that would monitor the effectiveness of the new schedule. The department was particularly concerned about the impact of the schedule on stress levels, job satisfaction, and the overall effectiveness of their policing function. That is, would the 12-hour workday negatively affect performance? Periodically during the next couple of years, the department monitored the consequences of its new work schedule. There were several positive results. The level of stress appeared to decline along with the increases in hours worked and leisure time satisfaction, without any negative performance effects. Now, several years later, there is virtually no desire to return to the old, more traditional work schedule.

In effective organizations, the activities of planning and controlling are intricately interwoven. For each plan deemed important to the functioning of the organization, a system to monitor the plan's effectiveness must be designed and implemented. In the remainder of this chapter, we explore the nature of control, the control process, and its effects on the organization and its members.

CONTROLLING AND THE CONTROL PROCESS

controlling the process of monitoring and evaluating organizational effectiveness and the initiation of corrective actions needed to maintain or improve effectiveness

As you learned in Chapter 1, controlling is also a managing activity. **Controlling** is defined as the process of monitoring and evaluating organizational effectiveness and initiating the actions needed to maintain or improve effectiveness. Thus, managers who engage in the controlling activity watch, evaluate, and when needed, suggest corrective action.

Like the managerial functions of planning, organizing, and directing, controlling is a complex activity that is performed at many organizational levels. Upper-level managers, for example, monitor their organization's overall strategic plans, which can be implemented only if middle-level managers control the organization's divisional and departmental plans, which, in turn, rely on lower-level managers' control of groups and individual employees (see our earlier discussion of the goal hierarchy).

The Need for Control

Although there is a continual and universal need for control in organizations, the importance, amount, and type of control vary across organizational situations. Probably the most important influence on the nature of an organization's control systems is the amount of environmental change and complexity it faces.

Companies in low-wage, high-turnover industries may use organizational control mechanisms to ensure a quality outcome day after day, giving employees a solid structure and lessening the chance of any (unhappy) surprises for the customers, as shown in the Controlling: Sunshine Cleaning Systems video.

Organizations that operate with relatively stable external environments usually need to change very little, so managers eventually are able to control their organizations by using a set of routine procedures. With greater levels of environmental change and the accompanying uncertainty, however, controlling requires continual attention from managers. Routines and rigid control systems are simply not adequate for such conditions.

Environmental complexity also affects the nature of control systems. Simple environments contain a limited number of highly similar components that are relatively easy to control through common sets of rules and procedures. The same bureaucratic control system, for example, can be used at most branch offices of a large bank. As complexity increases through organizational growth, product diversification, and so on, managers' needs for up-to-date information and coordination among organizational activities intensify. The complexity that calls for increased control, however, also requires open, organic systems that can respond quickly and effectively to complex environments. In such complicated situations, organizations often specify the development of flexible sys-

FIGURE 10-8 Need for Control

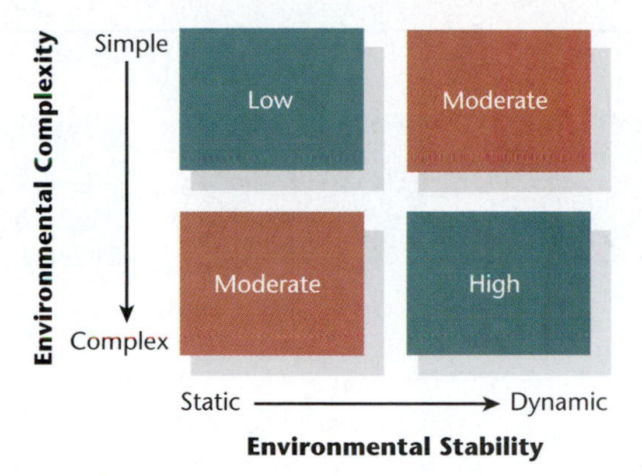

tems as a means goal: "To allow us to manage the complexities of our organization, we must remain flexible and open." Other control activities shift to ends goals, such as "We want to increase market share 10 percent in each of our divisions." Flexibility allows substantial choice as to how ends goals will be met: "Each division may decide how to achieve its 10 percent increase in market share." Figure 10-8 shows the level of control organizations need under different environmental conditions.

A Control Model

In essence, control affects every part of an organization. Among some of the major targets of the organization's control efforts are the resources it receives, the output it generates, its environmental relationships, organizational processes, and all managerial activities. Especially important targets of control include the functional areas of operations, accounting, marketing, finance, and human resources.

Traditional control models (see Figure 10-9) suggest that controlling is a four-step process:

1. *Establish standards.* Standards are the ends and means goals established during the planning process; thus, planning and controlling are intricately interwoven. Planning provides the basis for the control process by providing the standards of performance against which managers compare organizational activities. Subsequently the information generated as a part of the control process (see the subsequent steps in the control model) provides important input into the next planning cycle.
2. *Monitor ongoing organizational behavior and results.* After determining what should be measured, by whom, when, and how, an assessment of what has actually taken place is made.
3. *Compare actual behavior and results against standards.* Ongoing behavior is compared to standard. This assessment involves comparing actual organizational accomplishments relative to planned ends (what an organization is trying to accomplish) and means (how an organization intended for actions to unfold). The outcome of this comparison provides managers with the information they will evaluate in the final step.

FIGURE 10-9 The Traditional Control Model

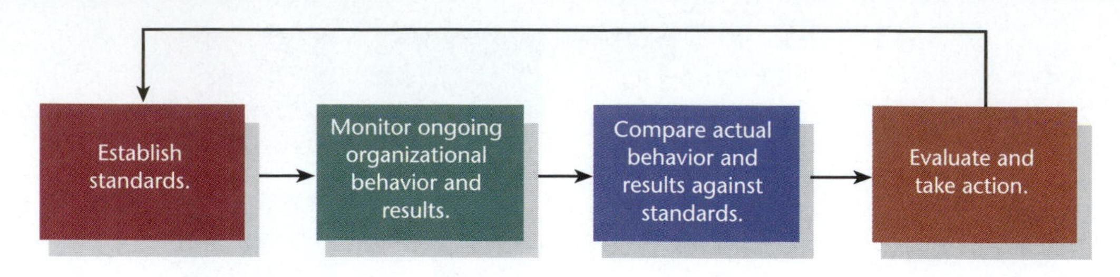

4. *Evaluate and take action.* Using their comparative information, managers form conclusions about the relationships found between expectations and reality, and then decide whether to maintain the status quo, change the standard, or take corrective action.

VARIATIONS IN CONTROL SYSTEMS

Although all good control systems follow the process described above, this doesn't mean that all control systems are identical. Control systems differ in terms of the degree to which they are self-managing, as opposed to externally managed, and by the point in the process at which control is exercised.

Cybernetic and Noncybernetic Systems

cybernetic control self-regulating control procedures

Control systems differ in the amount of outside attention required for them to operate effectively. Systems using **cybernetic control** are based on self-regulating procedures that automatically detect and correct deviations from planned activities and effectiveness levels. Few organizational control systems are totally cybernetic, but some come close. The control system for a coal-fired electrical generating station at Detroit Edison, for example, uses computers to monitor the flow of pulverized coal into the burning chamber. The computers speed up or reduce the flow as necessary to maintain adequate fuel supplies.

Cybernetic control systems automatically detect and correct deviations, but automating a control system does not mean it is cybernetic. This technician is adjusting the mixture in the vat, so this system is not self-regulating and thus is not cybernetic.

Merely automating a work system does not necessarily mean that the control system is cybernetic. The drone submarine sent to explore and photograph the sunken Titanic was fully automated, but humans on the surface monitored the effectiveness of the sub's operations and its adherence to the planned mission. To be classified as a cybernetic system, a work system must have built-in automatic control capabilities, although the built-in control need not be machine-based. A group of workers who control their own activities without outside assistance constitute a cybernetic system.

Control systems that are operated completely independently from the work system itself involve **noncybernetic control**. They rely on external monitoring systems in much the same way that a manufacturing company uses a separate quality assurance department to monitor and enforce quality standards rather than allowing production crews to perform this activity.

noncybernetic control control systems that operate independently from the work system that is being monitored; a monitoring system that is external to the target of control

Time Perspectives

Organizations can introduce the control activity at three stages in the work process: prior to, during, or after the performance of a work activity.[49] In practice, most managers use a **hybrid control system** that incorporates control at each of these intervals so that managers can prepare for a job, guide its progress, and assess its results.

hybrid control system control system that exercises control prior to, during, and after the performance of a work activity

Managers use **precontrols** (or preaction controls) to prevent deviation from a desired plan of action before work actually begins. For example, Butch Ledworowski, owner of Lil' America Building Contractors, inspects all construction materials to see that they meet industry standards. Managers can use two types of **concurrent controls** (steering and screening control) to prevent deviation from the planned course of action while work is in progress. *Steering controls* are reactive concurrent controls; they occur after work has begun but before it is completed. At Lil'America, for instance, Butch visits each construction site and watches his carpenters, offering advice and instruction as they work. *Screening controls* (also referred to as yes/no, go/no-go controls) are preventive concurrent controls. As activity at a critical stage is completed, managers use screening controls to assess work performed to that point and to judge whether progress is adequate. If it is, a yes decision is made to proceed to the next stage. At Lil' America, for example, Butch always inspects carpentry work after walls have been framed. Unless he approves the work, electricians cannot begin wiring the structure.

precontrols controls designed to prevent deviation from a desired plan of action before work actually begins

concurrent controls controls intended to prevent deviation from a planned course of action while work is in progress

Managers use **postaction controls** after the product or service is complete to examine the output. After each remodeling job, Butch assesses the work to determine whether it meets specifications, was completed on time, and came in at or under budget. Postaction controls play an important role in future planning, but their primary function is to provide feedback by describing the degree to which previous activities have succeeded.

postaction controls controls employed after a product or service is complete

CHARACTERISTICS OF EFFECTIVE CONTROL SYSTEMS

Successful control systems have certain common characteristics. First, a good control system follows the prescriptions in the control model (see Figure 10-9), and adequately addresses each organizational target. Next, to the extent possible, an effective control system takes a hybrid approach so that precontrol, concurrent, and postaction control systems can be used to monitor and correct activities at all points in an organization's operations. Other characteristics of a good control system include its treatment of information, its appropriateness, and its practicality.[50]

The control process itself and, certainly, all effective control systems are based on information. Without good information, managers cannot assess whether ends and means goals are met. They cannot determine the relationship between them or provide feedback to planners. To be effective, information must be accurate, objective, timely, and distributed to organization members who need it. High-involvement organizations work to make sure that virtually all organizational information is accessible by any employee who needs it order to make quality decisions. Oticon, a Danish manufacturer of hearing aids, for example, scans all company communications and places them in their information system that all employees can access.

http://www.oticon.com

Another characteristic of a good control system is its focus on issues of importance to the organization. Managers who develop control procedures for virtually all work activities and outcomes waste resources and, as will be discussed later in this chapter, risk creating a control system that produces negative feelings and reactions.

A final characteristic of a good control system is its practicality. Something that works well for another organization or looks wonderful in print still has to fit *your* organization to work well there. Some practical considerations to look for in a control system include feasibility, flexibility, the likelihood that organization members will accept it, and the ease with which the system can be integrated with planning activities.

THE IMPACT OF CONTROL ON ORGANIZATIONAL MEMBERS

Thus far, you have been learning about the importance of the controlling function. Consider now what the controlling function does for—or to—the organization's members. If designed well, control systems have many positive effects both for organizations and for the people who work in them (see Table 10-3).[51] Unfortunately, sometimes control systems can produce a number of negative effects.

Positive Effects

Organizational control systems can provide many positive effects for organization members in terms of motivation, performance, and satisfaction. This occurs by providing adequate structure, appropriate feedback, and effective goal-setting programs.

When workers want clarification of what they are expected to do, a leader can improve both their performance and satisfaction by providing structure. The guidance provided by both precontrol and concurrent control systems can likewise be received favorably. Another potential and related benefit for employees with an uncertainty avoidance (see Chapter 5) or low tolerance for ambiguity personality is that the structure of a good control system reduces the uncertainty of a work situation.

A good control system also provides constructive feedback. Most employees react quite favorably to the timely provision of accurate feedback about their effectiveness.[52] Feedback helps workers correct ineffective behaviors. Perhaps more importantly, feedback can be very rewarding. People who have a need to succeed (individuals with a high need for achievement) are gratified when feedback tells them that they are, in fact, succeeding. Feedback can improve job

TABLE 10-3 The Impact of Control on Organization Members

Potential Positive Effects of Control	
■ Clarifies expectations	■ Facilitates goal setting
■ Reduces ambiguity	■ Enhances satisfaction
■ Provides feedback	■ Enhances performance
Potential Negative Effects of Control	
■ Consumes resources	■ Fosters inappropriate behavior
■ Creates feelings of frustration and helplessness	■ Decreases satisfaction
■ Creates "red tape"	■ Increases absenteeism
■ Creates inappropriate goals	■ Increases turnover
	■ Creates stress

performance if workers use it to adjust their goals, approach, or effort levels appropriately. Both concurrent and postaction controls provide employees with feedback about the appropriateness of their behavior and the degree to which their work is producing successful results.

You have already seen that goal setting can be an important contributor to effective management. A good control system is very useful for identifying appropriate goals. Consider the control system used by the sales company where Maria Castro works. It specifies an expected sales approach (means goal) that helps her work toward a specific, difficult sales goal (ends goal). Precontrols help her understand how to achieve the desired sales level by providing such means goals as specific sales calls to make and promotional specials to offer. Concurrent controls and postcontrols provide feedback that helps Maria monitor her progress. The combined effects of goal setting and feedback about goal progress are particularly powerful.

Negative Effects

Unfortunately, control systems don't always function well. Excessive controls are a waste of money and energy. Donald Pemble, for example, needs a larger travel budget because he must personally inspect bridges under his new control system. His inspectors spend the time they could have used to inspect bridges in logging entries, painting numbers, and griping about the unfairness of the situation. Not only do excessive controls waste money because they fail to enhance effectiveness, but they can also create additional problems. For example, Shannon and her co-workers have changed from good corporate citizens who kept accurate records and conducted comprehensive inspections into harried workers who falsify log entries. Worse, unsuspecting motorists travel over what might be unsafe bridges.

The vast amount of paperwork and documentation called for by an excessive control system can also cause frustration and helplessness. The "red tape" created by many universities' control systems, for example, wastes students' time. Standing in lines for hours, they wait to pay dorm fees, purchase meal tickets, rent parking spaces, pay tuition, and register for classes. Their frustration and dissatisfaction are mirrored by many university employees who question the competence, the reasonableness, and perhaps even the intelligence of supervisors who insist on maintaining excessive control.

Another dysfunctional result of poor control systems can be seen in their effect on goal-setting programs. Whereas a good control system can help design and monitor valuable goal-setting programs, a poor control system can accomplish quite the opposite. A control system focused on unreasonable ends and means goals can motivate workers to establish inappropriate individual goals. For instance, the ends goal Donald Pemble established of having all bridges inspected within two years was unreachable, and his monthly inspection quotas (means goals) were unobtainable. Donald's insistence on maintaining these inappropriate goals was evident in his reactions when the inspectors failed to meet them. Consequently, Shannon and her co-workers focused on preserving their jobs as a primary goal, rather than on conducting quality inspections.

In addition to encouraging the formation of inappropriate goals, poor control systems emphasize and reward behaviors that, although not necessarily inappropriate, may hinder more productive behavior. Managers who concentrate on workers' attendance, for example, may not promote such desirable behaviors as creativity, cooperation, and team building.[53] Although there is nothing wrong with encouraging attendance, a control system that fosters attendance (by punishing tardiness) because it is easier to measure than creativity encourages rigid, uncreative behavior (on the part of employees who are almost always at work). An advertising agency that controls attendance but not creativity, for example, would soon be in serious trouble.

Even when control systems help identify appropriate goals and encourage appropriate behavior, rigid adherence to narrow goals can create problems. A large number of specific, concrete goals, for example, can inhibit creativity. The vast amount of time organization members must spend tending to concrete goals leaves them little time or energy to create. It is not only creativity that suffers, however. Every minute used taking attendance in a classroom is one less minute available for teaching. Every hour a police officer spends completing paperwork is one less hour available for public service. Managers should use only the goals they need, no more.

The Need for Personal Control

Organizations clearly have a need to control their members and operations, but individuals also have a need for *personal control*, a need to believe that they have the "ability to effect a change, in a desired direction, on the environment."[54] (See our discussion of cognitive evaluation theory in Chapter 7.) Sometimes organizations, through their structures and management processes, make people feel they have too little control. For example, managers can execute the control function by designing and demanding strict adherence to organizational rules and standard operating procedures. Colleges and universities, for example, tell students which classes they are allowed to take and when, what grades they have to maintain, how to behave outside the classroom, and so on. Companies tell employees when to come to work, how many hours to work, what to wear, when to take breaks, how to perform their jobs, and many other things. The challenge facing managers is to strike a balance between the amount of control their organization needs and the amount of personal control needed by its members. A recent study suggests that, when this balance is reached, both the satisfaction and performance of organization members can be enhanced.[55] In addition, evidence reveals that a number of other organizationally undesirable consequences can result from low or less than desired levels of personal control, such as withdrawal and health-related effects (stress, frustration, and depression).[56]

Finding the optimal balance between organizational and personal control is not an easy task, however, because most employees desire more personal control than their organizations allow. People will strive to gain greater control "in spite of (and frequently because of) the barriers and constraints the organization places on the attainment of personal control."[57] Repeated failures to gain personal control may cause workers to develop what has been called learned helplessness.[58] People who learn that they are helpless to influence their work environment are likely to be the source of low productivity, low quality, high absenteeism, dissatisfaction, and turnover. They tend to react with depression, anxiety, stress, frustration, hostility, anger, and alienation. Furthermore, once helplessness has been learned, people often continue to behave helplessly, even if the environment changes to permit them greater control. Managers must thus prevent employees from developing learned helplessness because reversing it is very difficult. They should allow workers to control the aspects of their work lives that they can adequately control and use only the necessary amount of organizational control.

In Search of Balance

At this point, it might seem that managers should just accede to workers' persistent demands for greater control. Research shows, however, that indiscriminately giving employees larger amounts of control actually causes performance to suffer if such control exceeds their capacity to use it.[59]

If a control system that is too excessive does not work, and if giving workers all of the personal control they desire is not effective, what do managers do to achieve the proper balance? First, people need to possess personal control; therefore, give them the amount of control they are able to handle. Second, make certain that workers given control believe they can use it effectively. Help them translate their effort into successful performance. Third, recognize that organizational control systems influence the personal control perceptions of organizational members. These, in turn, change behavior and attitudes.

By interviewing and/or surveying employees, managers can learn more about employees' needs for control. Through organizational scans, managers can determine the amount and location of control already existing in the organization, as well as the areas needing control. The objective then becomes one of achieving the best possible match between employees and their work environment.

MANAGEMENT BY OBJECTIVES—A PLANNING AND CONTROL TECHNIQUE

management by objectives (MBO)
a philosophy of management, a planning and controlling technique, and an employee involvement program

When people are personally committed to their organization's plans, those plans are more likely to be accomplished. This truism is the philosophy underlying management by objectives.

Management by objectives (MBO) is a philosophy of management, a planning and controlling technique, and an employee-involvement program.[60] As a management philosophy, MBO stems from the human resource model and Theory Y's assumption that employees are capable of self-direction and self-control (see Chapter 2). MBO also is anchored in Maslow's need theory (see

Chapter 7). The reasoning is that employee involvement in the planning and control processes provides opportunities for the employee to immerse the self in work-related activities, to experience work as more meaningful, to satisfy higher-order needs (like self-esteem), which leads to increased motivation and job performance (see Figure 10-10). It is hypothesized that, through involvement, employee commitment to a planned course of action will be enhanced and job satisfaction will be increased.

Although there are many variations in the practice of MBO, it is basically a process by which an organization's goals, plans, and control systems are defined through collaboration between managers and their employees. Together they identify common goals, define the results expected from each individual, and use these measurements to guide the operation of their unit and to assess individual contributions.[61] In this process, the knowledge and skills of many organizational members are used. Rather than managers' telling workers "These are your goals"—the approach of classical management philosophy—managers ask workers to join them in deciding what their goals should be.

After an acceptable set of goals has been established for each employee through a give-and-take, collaborative process, employees play a major role in developing an action plan for achieving these goals. In the final stage in the MBO process, employees develop control processes, monitor their own performance, and recommend corrections if unplanned deviations occur. At this stage, the entire process begins again. Figure 10-11 depicts the major stages of the MBO process.

The Theory of MBO

MBO has the potential to enhance organizational effectiveness. The following four major components of the MBO process are believed to contribute to its effectiveness: (1) setting specific goals; (2) setting realistic and acceptable goals; (3) joint participation in goal setting, planning, and controlling; and (4) feedback.[62] First, as we saw earlier in this chapter (and Chapter 7), employees working with goals outperform employees working without goals. Second, it is assumed that participation contributes to the setting of realistic goals for which there is likely to be goal acceptance and commitment. Setting realistic and acceptable goals is an important precondition for successful outcomes, especially if the goals are difficult and challenging in nature. Finally, feedback plays

FIGURE 10-10 MBO and Its Effects on Employees

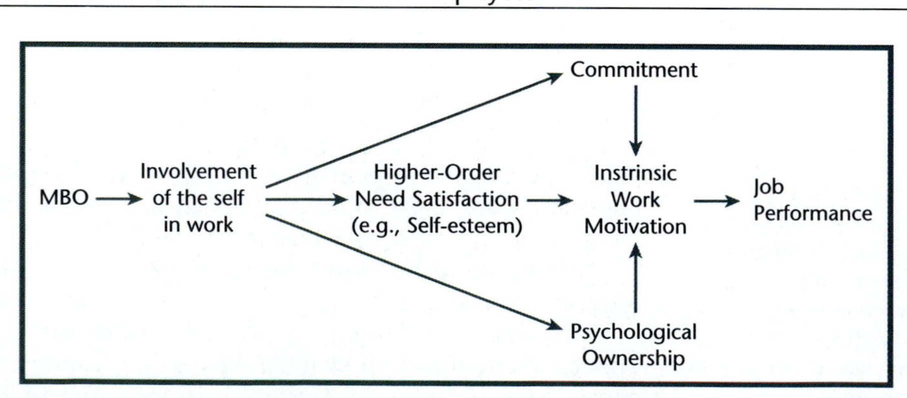

FIGURE 10-11 The Management by Objectives (MBO) Process

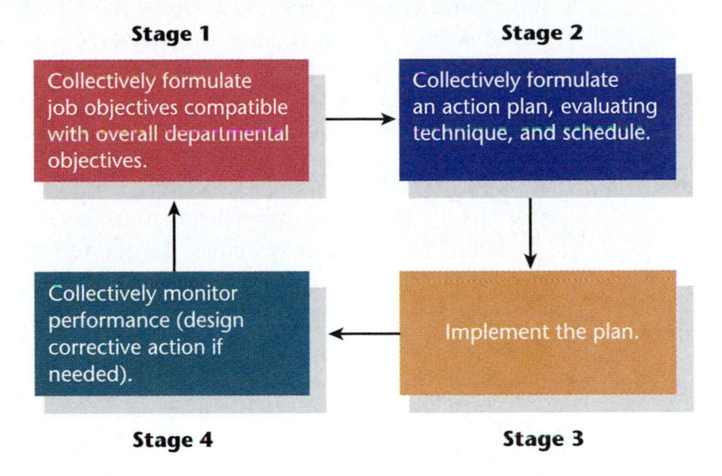

an important role. It is only through feedback that employees learn whether they should sustain or redirect their efforts in order to reach their goal, and it is only through feedback that they learn whether or not they are investing sufficient effort.

Thus, from a theoretical perspective, there are several reasons why MBO should produce a positive impact on employee performance, motivation, commitment, and job satisfaction. In the next section, we briefly look at what the research tells us about the effectiveness of MBO programs.

The Evidence

In both the public and private sectors, MBO is a widely employed management tool. A recent review of the research on MBO provides us with a clear and consistent view of the effects of these programs. In the 70 cases studied by Robert Rodgers and John Hunter, 68 showed increased productivity gains and only 2 showed losses.[63] In addition, the increases in performance were significant. Rodgers and Hunter report that the mean increase exceeded 40 percent.

While the results are generally positive in nature, differences in performance effects appear to be associated with the level of top management commitment. In those cases where top management is emotionally, intellectually (that is, top management espouses the value and importance of MBO), and behaviorally (top management actually uses MBO themselves) committed, the performance effects tend to be the strongest. The weakest MBO effects appear when top management does very little to "talk the value/importance of MBO" and they don't use the system themselves, even as they implement it for others.[64] This evidence tells us that "the processes" used to implement MBO may render a potentially effective program ineffective. Thus, managers should not only pay attention to the strategies used to facilitate planning and controlling (like MBO), they should also be concerned with how they go about implementing the plans. MBO requires top management commitment, and it should be initiated from the top down.[65]

Research shows that an MBO program can play a meaningful role in achieving commitment to a course of action and improving performance. In fact, research clearly documents instances where MBO programs have increased organizational effectiveness. Still, there have been failures. After reviewing 185 studies of MBO programs, one researcher concluded that they are effective under some circumstances, but not all.[66] For example, MBO tends to be more effective in the short term (less than two years), in the private sector, and in organizations removed from direct contact with customers. These factors also affect the success of an MBO program:

- The intensity of upper-level managers' commitment. Half-hearted commitment to an MBO system is associated with a higher failure rate.
- The time element: Is there enough time for employees to learn how to participate in an MBO process? That is, to learn how to set meaningful goals, develop good action statements, and develop effective monitoring systems? Is there enough time for employees to learn how to assume responsibility in a new context? Is there enough time for employees and managers to collaborate in a joint planning and controlling process?
- The legitimacy of the system: Is it integrated into an overall philosophy of management? Or does it seem like a gimmick to seduce employees into being more productive?
- The integration of employees' goals: Are goals for each employee integrated well enough into the goals of their larger work unit?

To be truly effective over the long haul, MBO programs probably need to be coupled with some type of gainsharing program (that is, programs whereby organizations share some of the financial gains accrued from the ideas, productivity improvements, and cost savings that stem from employee participation). Based on his extensive observation of involvement-oriented organizations, Professor Edward E. Lawler, III, notes that information, knowledge, power, and rewards are four key components of an effective and sustained high-involvement system (see our previous discussion of participation in Chapter 9).[67] Typically, MBO systems don't provide mechanisms through which employees share in the economic gains that may accrue to the organization as a result of their expanded role and responsibility. In light of the conditions that influence the effectiveness of MBO programs, management is challenged to provide an appropriate context for the design and maintenance of an effective MBO system.

THE CONTROL- AND INVOLVEMENT-ORIENTED APPROACHES TO PLANNING AND CONTROLLING

Planning and controlling are approached with distinctive differences under control-oriented and involvement-oriented approaches to management (see *An Inside Look*). In the mechanistic organization, both activities tend to be lodged with management in the organizational hierarchy, often above the point in the organization where the plans are being carried out. The hierarchy plays an active role in both the planning and controlling process, and the employee is often a passive player carrying out the planning directives and the target of the control activity.

The organic organization with its involvement-oriented management practices places the employee as an active player in both the planning and controlling activity. Management's role becomes one of a consultant, facilitator, enabler, philosopher, teacher, coach, and resource provider as employees take on active

AN INSIDE LOOK

Planning

Control-Oriented Management

A dominant coalition of upper-level managers, a centralized organizational brain center, and a top-down flow of organizational directives characterizes the approach to planning in the mechanistic organization. Planning in specialized and bureaucratic organizations is performed by top management and their planning staff. The results of these planning efforts are then passed down through the chain of command.

In many large and control-oriented organizations, top management is simply too busy to spend time crafting organizational plans. Many of these organizations have a planning department where planning specialists serve as an advisor to top management. Their job is to study the organization and its environment, and to create a number of different organizational plans. These plans are then submitted to top management for their review, revision, selection, and implementation. This centralization of the planning activity has been referred to as the "big brain" approach to planning. Implicitly it assumes that only top management and those trained in planning are capable of providing meaningful direction for the organization.

For years, GE was a corporate citadel characterized by the big brain and centralized planning. GE, with its multiple layers of bureaucracy, employed 350 planning specialists. They analyzed and reanalyzed GE, its products, its markets, its technology, and its competition. They produced volumes of plans and contingency plans, which were submitted to and reviewed by top-level line management.[a]

Upper-level management responsible for performance selected from the various planning options crafted by the planning specialists. Once a plan (or set of plans) was selected, the hierarchy implemented these plans. A large middle management monitored plans and reported information back up the chain of command that enabled upper-level management to stay informed on low-level organizational activity.

Involvement-Oriented Management

The organic organization is managed in accord with the "small brain theory." This approach to management and planning calls for integrating the observations, experiences, ideas, and information from multiple minds, both within and outside the organization instead of a few isolated individuals located at the top of the organizational pyramid.

GE, like many other organizations, is attempting to open itself up by removing boundaries that separate internal divisions and hierarchical levels, as well as the boundaries that separate the organization from those upon whom it is dependent for its key inputs as well as those to whom the organization delivers its products/services.

With Jack Welch at the helm of GE, there was a continuous attempt to cut out the bureaucratic jungle that was GE during the decades before his arrival. Welch slashed the company's entrenched bureaucracy. The 350 planning specialists are long gone. In their place, *everyone* plans. Each year the heads of GE's business units develop a plan that identifies opportunities and obstacles for their industry over the upcoming 24-month period.[b] In addition, frequent workout sessions provide organizational members with opportunities to raise questions, call out concerns, and offer suggestions for improving the current and future direction of the organization. As a part of Welch's attempt to mold GE into a borderless organization, he actively and continually sought input from the company's suppliers and customers.

[a] R. Henkoff. December 31, 1990. How to plan for 1995. *Fortune*, 70–79.

[b] Henkoff, 1990.

roles in planning and controlling and in assuming responsibility for the execution of both activities.

Upper-level managers assume responsibility for planning and controlling their units while employees assume the right and responsibility for planning and controlling at their job level. As upper-level managers carry out their planning and controlling activities, they do so by soliciting input from those below them in the organizational hierarchy.

Systems like MBO are much more likely to characterize the planning and controlling process in involvement-oriented organizations than in control-oriented organizations. Control in high-involvement organizations is diffused through many groups and is commonly focused on task accomplishment and overcoming obstacles, with a deemphasis on fixing blame with a particular individual for performance failures. In many control-oriented management systems, the reins of control are firmly held by the hierarchy and the activities of individuals are carefully controlled. Performance failures, therefore, tend to become focused on the individual who fails to perform.

Finally, mechanistic organizations are more likely to create large planning departments and to centralize the planning function with specialists. As organizations confront increasing environmental or technology-induced uncertainty, rapid environmental change, and turbulence, planning and controlling move closer to the point in the organization where the plans are implemented and carried out on a day-to-day basis. In place of hierarchy-based control, organizations rely more on professional employees and groups of employees to control their own actions as they execute organizational plans.

ORGANIZATIONAL PLANNING AND CONTROLLING IN REVIEW

Planning. Planning is the process through which managers establish goals and detail how these goals will be attained. There are five major stages in the planning process. First, an organization establishes its preplanning foundation, which reviews past events and describes the current situation. In the second step, the organization sets forth goals based on the preplanning foundation. In the third step, managers forecast what is likely to happen in the organization's internal and external environments in order to develop alternative courses of action. Then, managers identify possible courses of action for meeting their objectives, evaluate each alternative, and select a course of action. Finally, planners develop the supportive plans necessary to accomplish the organization's major plan of action. Once implemented, that plan is monitored and controlled so that it meets the goals established in the second step.

Managers create many types of plans based on hierarchical level, frequency of use, time frame, and organizational scope. Contingency plans to be used in case of unexpected events or wrong assumptions are critical for effective management in highly turbulent environments.

Goal development is an important part of the planning process. Goals developed for employees, for departments, and for entire organizations greatly enhance organizational effectiveness. Evidence reveals that performance is higher when organizations, as well as individuals, operate under difficult (but attainable), specific goals.

Plans reduce uncertainty and risk, focus attention on goals, and enhance understanding of the external environment. Although most major organizations engage in formal planning, many managers fail to plan appropriately. Lack of time, uncertainty about the future, and fear of failure are among the reasons given by managers for their failure to plan.

Controlling. The primary purposes of the controlling function are to monitor the extent to which an organization's plans are being followed and their effectiveness, and to identify when and where it is necessary to take corrective action. To accomplish these ambitious tasks, managers construct control systems that touch most aspects of an organization's functional areas, its relationship with the external and internal environments, and its relationships across different hierarchical levels.

The control process consists of four steps. In steps 1 and 2, managers create standards and monitor ongoing organizational behavior. In step 3, they examine the degree to which ongoing activity is consistent with their goals and means objectives, and the relationship between the two. In step 4, managers develop prescriptions to correct problems, to maintain strengths, and to provide feedback to an organization's planners.

Whereas all control systems have the same general purposes, they differ in their specifics. Some are self-managing cybernetic systems; noncybernetic systems require regular external supervision to be effective. Other variations in control systems include the point at which control activities are applied: before the work has begun (precontrols), while work is in progress (concurrent controls), and after work has been completed (postaction controls). A hybrid control system engages a variety of control activities at many points in time.

Although there are variations in control systems, all good systems have characteristics that enable them to work well in a given organization. Managers evaluating a control system might thus gauge its adequacy in providing accurate, timely, objective information to appropriate people in the organization. They also should examine whether the system focuses on the most critical aspects of their organization's conditions in a feasible, flexible manner that will be accepted by organizational members. Because of the importance of the information it provides, a good control system should also be integrated with planning activities.

Any control system can produce both positive and negative effects. If it is well designed, a control system provides needed structure and feedback and facilitates the development and execution of effective goal-setting programs. The result can be a satisfied, motivated, and productive work force. Inappropriate control systems, however, can cause frustration, dissatisfaction, and poor performance. Being aware of a control system's potential effects on organization members helps managers capitalize on its positive aspects, reduce the impact of negative effects, and promote workers' acceptance of the system.

The effort to maintain control is not restricted to managers. All employees have a need for personal control, a need that sometimes conflicts with their organization's need to maintain control. To achieve effectiveness, managers must balance the control needs of both the organization and its members.

Management by objectives (MBO), with its emphasis on goal setting, participation, and feedback, frequently contributes to increased employee goal commitment, motivation, and performance. If performance matches the employee's aspirations, job satisfaction is likely to be an important by-product of the organization's planning and controlling activities.

A FINAL LOOK

Zack comes to work the next day excited about his insight. The partners know that inventory has been an ongoing trouble spot but hadn't realized the effect it could be having on potential customers who get frustrated with delayed orders and go elsewhere. After collecting data on customer requests and backorders, the partners discover that they fill customer orders immediately only 50 percent of the time! Jolted by this thunderbolt, the partners decide to hold regular strategic planning meetings where they will view the big picture and plan for the future. The first things they decide to do are install better control systems over their inventory process and collect data on customer online experiences with ChezPastis.com.

Elisabeth proposes setting a goal of never having to tell a customer that their requested items are on backorder. Zack agrees that this is an admirable goal; however, he thinks they should set a daring but reachable goal of immediately filling customer orders 80 percent of the time. After all, they are a small business in an unpredictable environment, and they don't want to frustrate employees with a potentially impossible goal.

KEY TERMS

action statements, 345
concurrent controls, 367
contingency plans, 354
controlling, 364
cybernetic control, 366
Deming cycle, 350
domain/directional planning, 347
goal hierarchy, 356
goal planning, 347
hybrid control system, 367
hybrid planning, 348
management by objectives (MBO), 371
noncybernetic control, 367
official goals, 355
operational goals, 355
outcome or goal statements, 345
planning, 344
postaction controls, 367
precontrols, 367
single-use plans, 354
standing plans, 354
strategic plans, 352

ISSUES FOR REVIEW AND DISCUSSION

1. Define managerial planning and controlling.
2. Discuss the relationship between the two managerial functions of planning and controlling.
3. Identify and briefly describe each stage in the planning and controlling processes.
4. Compare and contrast three different types of planning.
5. What are multiple goals? What is a goal hierarchy? How are these concepts related?
6. Briefly describe the two views of the goal formulation process and explain how they differ.
7. Describe the MBO process, the philosophy behind it, and its relationship with performance.
8. Distinguish between cybernetic and noncybernetic control, and pre, concurrent, and postaction control systems.
9. Identify and discuss three positive and three negative effects often associated with control systems.
10. How does the desire for personal control affect managers, and how can they balance it with organizational control systems?

EXERCISES

PLANNING AND PRODUCTION TASK: REAL ESTATE PROBLEM

INTRODUCTION

Most textbooks describe the management process as one that involves four functions: planning, organizing, directing, and controlling. How each of these functions is performed will determine to a great extent whether a company is successful or not in meeting its objectives.

Like larger systems, small groups must also consider these functions if they are to be successful. Often, group task accomplishment involves interdependencies among members and requires a high degree of coordination.

In both cases, the tasks to be accomplished must be analyzed and objectives established in advance. Once the objectives are clear, the company or group can plan how it will organize its members and use resources to achieve these objectives. One key objective is always profitability. (In one sense, this is also true of nonprofit groups, because they seek to work within their budget and to expand their resources/donations.) Just as companies plan and organize for production, they also plan and organize to ensure that profit objectives are met.

In this exercise you will compete with other groups in constructing a building. The success of your group will be measured by the profit you make in your project. Profit is determined by subtracting costs from the total appraised value of the finished structure. As you will see, several factors determine appraised value. Therefore, it is essential that your group analyze this task carefully, set objectives, and plan the best possible organization that will allow you to meet them.

PROCEDURE

STEP 1. Each team should allow itself sufficient time to become familiar with the "Task Directions" given below. Discuss these until everyone understands them, then proceed to step 2.

Task Directions

Each team is to construct a building out of 5 × 8 index cards and to "sell" it at the end of the exercise. The sale price will be the total appraised value as determined by the real estate board valuation standards outlined below. The winning team will be the group with the greatest profit, regardless of the appraised value of the building.

Materials and Tools

Every team will use the same raw materials and tools. These are index cards, one ruler, one pair of scissors, one stapler, and one roll of tape. Extra staples and tape will be available, upon request, without extra charge.

Cost of Cards

Cards cost $70 each. At the beginning of the exercise, each team will receive a package of 100 cards and be charged $7,000, as the initial startup investment. Additional cards may be purchased from the supplier at the regular price. At the end of the exercise, you may redeem unused cards for $50 each. If you need to purchase or redeem cards, one person and only one person from your team will go to the supply depot to carry out the transaction. The team leader will designate the supply depot at the beginning of the exercise.

Construction and Delivery Time

At the beginning of the exercise, the group leader will announce the time you will be allotted to construct your building. No team is allowed to build until the group leader announces "Begin production." When the time is up, the group leader will announce "Stop production." No construction is allowed after this point. You will have 30 seconds in which to deliver your completed structure to the real estate board for appraisal. Buildings received after 30 seconds will not be appraised. No team members are allowed to remain with the building after it is delivered, except for the board members.

Real Estate Board

Each team should designate one member to serve on the board. The board is responsible for appraising each building and assuring that building codes are met. The board will convene during the construction period to decide on criteria for the "drop-shock" test and quality and aesthetic values. The board must appraise one building before going on to the next. The appraisals will stand; buildings cannot be reappraised.

Building Code

All buildings must be fully enclosed (floors and roofs). They must also have ceilings that are 3 inches from the floor, and be capable of withstanding a drop-shock test. The drop-shock test consists of dropping the building or dropping an object (for example a book) on the building. It will be the real estate board's responsibility to decide on the test.

Appraisal Values

Buildings are appraised on the basis of quality and aesthetics. The total of the quality and aesthetic values is then multiplied by the total square inches of floor space in the building to obtain the total appraised value.

Quality Valuation

Quality is determined by subjecting the building to the drop-shock test. Various qualities are assigned values as follows:

Minimal quality:	$12.00 per square inch of floor space
Good quality:	$14.00 per square inch of floor space
Better quality:	$16.00 per square inch of floor space
Top quality:	$18.00 per square inch of floor space

Aesthetic Valuation

The real estate board can set this anywhere from zero to $3.00 per square inch, depending on their appraisal of aesthetic value.

Other Instruction

Once construction begins (step 4), you are not allowed to ask the group leader to clarify game rules or resolve team difficulties. You are on your own. Five minutes before construction is to stop, the group leader will notify you of the time remaining. While the real estate board is appraising buildings, each team will be expected to clean up leftover raw materials and return them to the supply depot. All unused cards should be redeemed.

STEP 2. Your team should discuss the task and then establish the following:

1. What are your objectives in this project?
2. What plan will you use to achieve your objectives?
3. How will team members be organized and coordinated to accomplish the group's tasks?
4. How will you use resources?
5. Who will serve on the real estate board?
6. How will you deal with the uncertainties, that is, unknown time allocation and the drop-shock test?

One member of the team should be designated to report on your objectives, plan, and organization structure during the discussion at the end of the exercise.

STEP 3 (Beginning of Section). Each team should assemble at one work place (table or cluster of desks). The group leader will designate the following: (1) supply depot and supply person(s); (2) delivery station for real estate board; and (3) construction time. In addition, the group leader will distribute all materials and tools to team. Finally, the people designated to serve on the real estate board will be asked to convene. No one is to use any materials or tools at this point.

STEP 4. When the group leader announces "Begin production," you may build. When the group leader announces "Stop production," you must deliver your building to the real estate board.

STEP 5. The real estate board appraises the buildings. The groups clean up and return the raw materials. The group leader and supply person(s) compute total cost and enter figures on a board or easel. The real estate board enters the total value of buildings on a board or easel.

STEP 6. Compute the profit for each team. The total costs are subtracted from the total appraised value for each building. Determine the winning team.

STEP 7. The total group and the group leader should discuss the results in terms of the objectives, plan, and organization of each team to determine how these factors affected output and profits. Team members should respond to discussion questions for their own team.

Discussion Questions

1. What was the primary objective in this task?
2. Given this objective, what other objectives did your team set? Did you try to minimize/maximize floor space? Quality? Resources used? Aesthetic value? Costs?
3. Did your team's plan allow for the uncertainty associated with construction time? Did you establish any contingency plans or alternatives for long or short construction periods? Different shock tests?
4. Did your team members attempt to influence the real estate board either before or during the appraisal?
5. What factors in your team's efforts do you think account for its success or failure in this task?
6. How did your team's division of labor and coordination of efforts affect your performance?

Source: D. T. Hall, D. D. Bowen, R. J. Lewicki, and F. S. Hall. 1982. *Experiences in management and organizational behavior* (2nd ed.). New York: Wiley, 258–262. Reprinted by permission of John Wiley & Sons, Inc.

INFOTRAC INFOTRAC® COLLEGE EDITION

The articles listed below are a sampling of those available through InfoTrac College Edition. You can search for them either by title or by the author's name.

Articles

1. World class planning and decision-making. (Brief Article) David Paul. *Financial Executive* Nov 2000 v16 i6 p56
2. Strategic planning for real estate companies. Charles A. Hewlett. *Journal of Property Management* Jan-Feb 1999 v64 i1 p26(4)
3. Is your company measuring strategic planning effectiveness? (managerial accounting) Paul Phillips. *Management Accounting (British)* June 1998 v76 n6 p34(2)
4. A productive perspective on total data quality management. (Examining Data Quality special section) (Technology Information) (Cover Story) Richard Y. Wang. *Communications of the ACM* Feb 1998 v41 n2 p58(8)
5. Unconditional Wisdom—The secrets to successful e-business aren't secrets at all. They've been taught for years in the nation's top business schools. (Company Operations) Kayte Vanscoy. *Ziff Davis Smart Business for the New Economy* Oct 1, 2000 p78

Questions

For Article 1:

The article "World-Class Planning and Decision-Making" observes that planning is probably the "most-detested corporate process." From your reading of Chapter 10 and the articles on this list, explain why David Paul, the author, can make this statement. From your reading, also identify ways in which planning can be managed positively.

For Other Articles:

Other articles on this list discuss strategic planning in various industries and in e-business. Assign these articles to members of your group. In group discussion, identify the main points of each article. What common denominators do you find about the planning process?

WEB EXERCISE

Visit General Electric's web page (**http://www.ge.com**) and look at their most recent annual report. Describe the company's goals, objectives, and mission in terms of what you have learned in this chapter.

CASE

Product Development Planning at Display Electronics

The Display Electronics Corporation manufactures computer-driven electronic displays. These include such products as athletic scoreboards for college football stadiums; voting displays used by state legislatures; time-and-temperature signs used by banks; and larger displays sold as electronic billboards to coliseums, truck stops, and gambling casinos. In the early 1980s, opportunities for new products using this technology seemed endless.

Display Electronics grew as fast as company managers could develop marketing channels and raise funds to support the manufacture and sales of their new products. Despite this growth, company profits were irregular, and average return on sales was lower than company goals. Dr. Arthur Keene, the company president, became concerned that new product development was being driven more by technological than by economic considerations. Dr. Keene, who has a Ph.D. in electrical engineering, decided to put more emphasis on the profit potential of products at the earliest stage of development.

His first step was to create a marketing committee composed of himself,. the vice president for engineering, the vice president for sales and two members of his staff, and a representative of the company's advertising agency. The function of this committee was to review all new product development projects twice a month. The project managers, usually electrical engineers, who actually managed the development of new products, met with the committee as their projects were being reviewed. The procedures to be followed by the committee and project managers were outlined in the memorandum by Dr. Keene titled *Product Design Procedure*.

September 19, 1999

Product Design Procedure

1. All new product or product enhancement ideas are submitted to the marketing committee for consideration using Display Electronics Form No. 44.
2. Upon preliminary approval by the marketing committee, the idea is submitted to Engineering for design feasibility, estimated time and cost to complete the design, and estimated cost of the product. These data are presented to the marketing committee for final approval.
3. Upon final approval by the marketing committee, the development project is funded and scheduled for completion.
4. A project manager is assigned by the Engineering Vice President to manage each design project. It is his or her responsibility to successfully complete the project on schedule and within budget.

Dr. Keene further outlined the information to be required by the marketing committee for evaluating new product proposals. He did this by setting the requirements for product development requests in the memorandum, titled *Product Development Request*, which became Display Electronics Form No. 44.

September 19, 1999

Product Development Request

1. New Product ________________ Product Enhancement____________
2. Purpose: (check all appropriate items)
   - _____ Reduces manufacturing cost
   - _____ Takes advantage of new market
   - _____ Modifies another product in an existing product line
   - _____ Uses existing parts and subassemblies
   - _____ Uses existing distribution system
   - _____ Improves product reliability
   - _____ Other
3. Describe the new product idea. Carefully specify all key features.
4. Describe the market for the new product and the proposed method of distribution. Project total market size for the next five years.
5. Estimate the number of units that will be ordered and Display Electronics market share during the first year, the second year, and the third year. State product price at which these order quantities are feasible. State sensitivity of the market to product price. Carefully outline all assumptions made in arriving at your order projections.
6. List and describe all current and potential competitive products. Include company name, product description (brochures and manuals if available), market share, pricing, etc.
7. Describe the proposed marketing strategy for the new product (e.g. top of line, minimum first cost, complete system, etc.)
8. Describe the general manufacturing method and reference to currently used manufacturing methods.
9. Describe any unusual requirements and how these requirements are related to product success (e.g. critical product introduction date, special finish, size or weight, low power, etc.)
10. Additional comments as appropriate

Questions

1. What type of plans are being outlined in this case?
2. How does the planning process developed at the Display Electronics Corporation relate to the planning process stages outlined in this chapter?
3. Which organizational members are most likely to resist this process?
4. Do you see any other problems that might arise from the use of this planning process?

Source: This case was prepared by and is used with the permission of Phil Fisher of the University of Southern Indiana. It describes actual events, but the names of persons and the company have been disguised.

Outline

The nature of leadership

The trait approach to leadership

Behavioral approaches to leadership

Situational (contingency) approaches to leadership

Substitutes for and neutralizers of leadership

Transformational, visionary, and charismatic leadership

Leadership needs in the 21st century

Leading organizational members in review

CHAPTER 11

Leading Organizational Members

Learning Objectives

After reading this chapter, you should be able to

1. Discuss the nature of leadership and the leadership process.
2. Identify and discuss the processes associated with people coming to the position of leadership.
3. Describe how leaders influence and move their followers to action.
4. Compare and contrast the trait, behavioral, and situational perspectives on leadership.
5. Discuss the effect that leader behavior has on follower satisfaction and performance.
6. Explain transactional, transformational, and charismatic leadership.
7. Describe the concept "substitute for leadership." Identify and discuss two substitutes.
8. Comment on the impact that different approaches and styles of leadership have on the follower in terms of motivation, attitudes, and behavior.

PHOTO: © GEORGE SIMIAN/CORBIS

A FIRST LOOK

John Arroyo is thrilled with his new position as general manager of the Springfield Sea Lions, a minor league baseball team. A baseball fan all of his life, his hard work and degree in sports management are paying off. But, several months into his first season, he has to admit that all is not going as he had hoped.

The general manager whom John replaced, "T.J." Grevin, a much-loved old-timer, had been with the Sea Lions since their inception 14 years ago. John knew it would be difficult for whoever followed T.J., but he didn't realize how ostracized and powerless he would feel. He tried a pep talk: "I'm the general manager—the CEO of this ballclub! In time, the staff *will* respect me." However, after the first season ends, John is discouraged. Ticket and concession sales are down, and rumors have some long-time employees thinking about leaving. If John doesn't turn things around, he knows his tenure with the Sea Lions will be short.

Questions: Is John correct in assuming that the staff will learn to respect him in time? What can John do to earn the loyalty of his staff and improve the ball club's performance?

Sarah Elizabeth Roisland is the manager of a district claims office for a large insurance company. Fourteen people work for her. The results of a recent attitude survey indicate that her employees have extremely high job satisfaction and motivation. Conflict is rare in Sarah's office. Furthermore, productivity measures place her group among the most productive in the entire company. Her success has brought the company's vice president of human resources to her office in an attempt to discover the secret to her success. Sarah's peers, superiors, and workers all give the same answer: She is more than a good manager, she is an outstanding leader. She continually gets high performance from her employees and does so in such a way that they enjoy working for her.

There is no magic formula for becoming a good leader. There are, however, many identifiable reasons why some people are better and more effective leaders. You will come to see that leaders, especially effective leaders, are not created by simply attending a one-day leadership workshop, yet it is not totally in their genes either. You can become an effective leader if you are willing to invest the time and energy to develop all of the "right stuff."

A survey of American CEOs, conducted by *Fortune* magazine, indicates that in seeking management talent, *leadership* is an urgently needed quality.[1] Good leaders and good leadership are rare. Harvard management professor John P. Kotter notes that "there is a leadership crisis in the U.S. today,"[2] and Warren Bennis (former president of the University of Cincinnati, and management professor at the University of Southern California) states that many of our organizations are overmanaged and underled.[3]

http://www.harvard.edu

http://www.pfdf.org/leaderbooks/121/spring99/bennis.html

THE NATURE OF LEADERSHIP

There are many definitions of leadership, each with a different emphasis. Some definitions consider leadership an act or behavior, such as initiating structure so group members know how to complete a task. Others consider leadership as the center or nucleus of group activity, an instrument of goal achievement, a person endowed with a certain personality, a form of persuasion, the art of inducing compliance, and a power relationship.[4] Some see it in terms of the management of group processes—that is, developing a vision for the group, communicating that vision,[5] orchestrating the group's energy and activity toward goal attainment, "turning a group of individuals into a team," and "transforming good intentions into positive actions."[6]

leadership a social (interpersonal) influence relationship between two or more persons who depend on each other to attain certain mutual goals in a group situation

Leadership is frequently defined as a social (interpersonal) influence relationship between two or more persons who depend on each other to attain certain mutual goals in a group situation.[7] Effective leadership helps individuals and groups achieve their goals by focusing on the group's *maintenance needs* (the need for individuals to fit and work together by having, for example, shared norms) and *task needs* (the need for the group to make progress toward attaining the goal that brought them together).

Leader Versus Manager

The two dual concepts, leader and manager, leadership and management, are not interchangeable, nor are they redundant. The differences between the two can, however, be confusing. In many instances, to be a good manager one needs to be an effective leader. Many CEOs have been hired in the hope that their leadership skills, their ability to formulate a vision and get others to "buy into" that vision, will propel the organization forward. In addition, effective leadership often necessitates the ability to manage—to set goals; plan, devise and implement strategy; make decisions and solve problems; and organize and control. For our purposes, the two sets of concepts can be contrasted in several ways.

First, we define the two concepts differently. In Chapter 1, we defined management as a process consisting of planning, organizing, directing, and controlling. Here we define leadership as a social (interpersonal) influence relationship between two or more people who are dependent on each another for goal attainment.

Second, managers and leaders are commonly differentiated in terms of the processes through which they initially come to their position. Managers are generally appointed to their role. Even though many organizations appoint people to positions of leadership, leadership per se is a relationship that revolves around the followers' acceptance or rejection of the leader.[8] Thus, leaders often emerge out of events that unfold among members of a group.

Third, managers and leaders often differ in terms of the types and sources of the power they exercise. Managers commonly derive their power from the larger organization. Virtually all organizations legitimize the use of certain "carrots and sticks" (reward and coercive forms of power), as ways of securing the compliance of their employees. In other words, by virtue of the position that a manager occupies (president, vice president, department head, supervisor) certain "rights to act" (schedule production, contract to sell a product, hire and fire) accompany the position and its place within the hierarchy of authority. Leaders can also secure power and the ability to exercise influence from "carrots and sticks"; however, it is much more common for leaders to derive power from followers' perception of their knowledge (expertise), their personality and attractiveness, and the working relationship that has developed.

From the perspective of those who are under the leader and manager's influence, the motivation to comply often has a different base. The subordinate to a manager frequently complies because of the role authority of the manager, and because of the "carrots and/or sticks" that managers have at their disposal.

The follower of a leader complies because "they want to." Thus, leaders motivate primarily through intrinsic processes, while managers motivate primarily through extrinsic processes.

Finally, it is important to note that as managers attempt to direct their subordinates (or engage in what is frequently referred to as supervisory behavior), effective managers often succeed or fail because of their ability (or inability) to lead.[9] As noted above, effective leadership often calls for the ability to manage.

The Leadership Process

While an organization's success is influenced by its stakeholders (employees, investors, markets, and so on), it is the role of senior management—the CEO and his or her other executives—to lead the organization toward its strategic vision, as shown in the video Strategic Leadership: Vermont Teddy Bear Company.

Leadership is a process, a complex and dynamic exchange relationship, built over time, between leader and follower, and between leader and the group of followers who depend on each other to attain a mutually desired goal.[10] There are several key components (see Figure 11-1) to this "working relationship": the leader, the followers, the context (situation), the leadership process per se, and the consequences (outcomes).[11] Across time, each component interacts with and influences the other components, and whatever consequences (like leader-follower trust) are created influence future interactions. As any one of the components changes, so too will leadership.[12]

The Leader Leaders are people who take charge of, or guide, the activities of others. They are often seen as the focus or orchestrater of group activity, the people who set the "tone" of the group so that it can move forward to goal attainment. Leaders provide the group with what is required to fulfill its maintenance and task-related needs. We will return to the leader "as a person" as part of our discussion of the "trait approach" to leadership.

The Follower The follower is not a passive player in the leadership process. Edwin Hollander, after many years of studying leadership, suggested that the follower is the most critical factor in any leadership event.[13] It is, after all, the

FIGURE 11-1 The Leadership Process

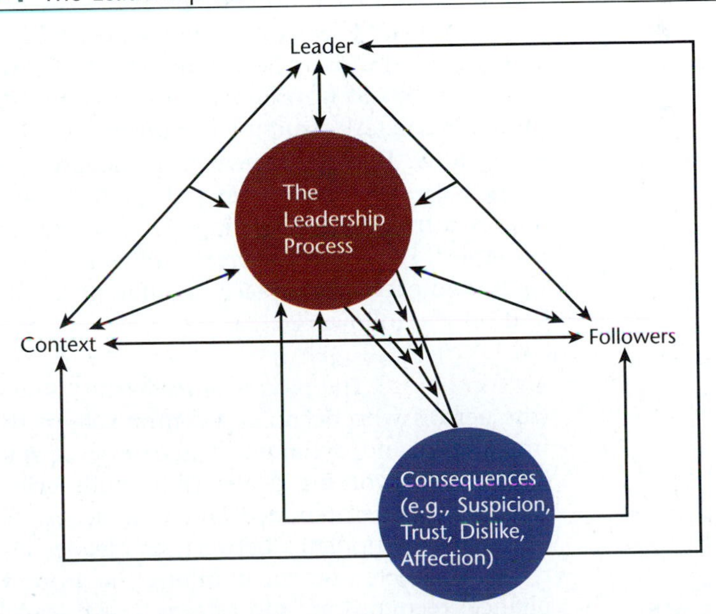

follower who perceives the situation and comes to define the needs that the leader must fulfill. In addition, it is the follower who either rejects leadership or accepts acts of leadership by surrendering his/her power to the leader to diminish task uncertainty, to define and manage the meaning of the situation to the follower, and to orchestrate the follower's action in pursuit of goal attainment.

The follower's personality and readiness to follow determine the style of leadership that will be most effective. For example, individuals with an internal locus of control are much more responsive to participative styles of leadership than individuals with an external locus of control.[14] Individuals with an authoritarian personality are highly receptive to the effectiveness of directive acts of leadership.[15] It is the followers' expectations, as well as their performance-based needs, that determine what a leader must do in order to be effective.

The strength of the follower's self-concept has also been linked to the leadership process. High self-esteem individuals tend to have a strong sense of self-efficacy, that is, a generalized belief they can be successful in difficult situations. They therefore tend to be strongly motivated to perform and persist in the face of adversity.[16] The high self-esteem follower tends to be responsive to participative styles of leadership. Low self-esteem individuals, with their doubts about their competence and worthiness, and about their ability to succeed in difficult situations, function better with supportive forms of leadership. This helps them deal with the stress, frustration, and anxiety that often emerge with difficult tasks. Followers without a "readiness to follow," limited by their inability to perform and lack of motivation and commitment, usually need more directive forms of leadership.[17]

Follower behavior plays a major role in determining what behaviors leaders engage in. For example, followers who perform at high levels tend to cause their leaders to be considerate in their treatment and to play a less directive role. Followers who are poor performers, on the other hand, tend to cause their leaders to be less warm toward them and to be more directive (controlling) in their leadership style.[18]

The Situation Situations make demands on a group and its members, and not all situations are the same. The situation is the context that surrounds the leader and the followers. Situations are multidimensional. We discuss the situation as it pertains to leadership in greater detail later in this chapter, but for now let's look at it in terms of the task and task environment that confront the group. Is the task structured or unstructured? Are the goals of the group clear or ambiguous? Is there agreement or disagreement about goals? Is there a body of knowledge that can guide task performance? Is the task boring, frustrating, and/or intrinsically satisfying? Is the environment complex or simple, stable or unstable? These factors create different contexts within which leadership unfolds, and each factor places a different set of needs and demands on the leader and on the followers.

The Process The *process* of leadership is separate and distinct from the leader (the person who occupies a central role in the group). The process is complex, interactive, and dynamic. It is a working relationship between leader and followers. This working relationship, built over time, is directed toward fulfilling the group's maintenance and task needs. Part of the process consists of an exchange relationship between the leader and follower. The leader provides a resource directed toward fulfilling the group's needs, and the group gives compliance, recognition, and esteem to the leader. To the extent that leadership is the exercise of influence, part of the leadership process is captured by the surrender of power by the followers and the exercise of influence over the followers by the leader.[19] Yet the influence process is not one way. Thus, the leader influences the followers and the followers influence the leader, the context influences the leader and the followers, and both leader and followers influence the context.

The Consequences A number of outcomes or consequences of the leadership process unfold between leader, follower, and situation. At the group level, two outcomes are important: Have the group's maintenance needs been fulfilled? (That is, do members of the group like and get along with one another, do they have a shared set of norms and values, and have they developed a good working relationship?); and Have the group's task needs been met? There are also important consequences of the leadership process for individuals: attendance, motivation, performance, satisfaction, citizenship, trust, and maintenance of their group membership.

The leader-member exchange (LMX) theory focuses our attention on consequences associated with the leadership process. The theory views leadership as consisting of a number of dyadic relationships linking the leader with a follower. A leader-follower relationship tends to develop quite quickly and remains relatively stable over time. The quality of the relationship is reflected by the degree of mutual trust, loyalty, support, respect, and obligation. High- and low-quality relationships produce in and out groups. Members of the in group come to be key players, and high-quality relationships tend to be associated with higher levels of performance, commitment, and satisfaction than are low-quality exchange relationships.[20] Attitudinal similarity and extroversion appear to be associated with a high-quality leader-member relationship.[21]

The nature of the leadership process varies substantially depending on the leader, the followers, and the situation. Thus, leadership is the function of an interaction between the leader, the follower, and the situation.

$$L = f\ [(\text{Person})(\text{Follower})(\text{Situation})].$$

The leadership context for the leader of a group of assembly line production workers is very different than for the leader of a self-managing production team, and is different than that confronted by the lead scientists in a research laboratory. The leadership tactics that work in the first context might fail miserably in the latter two.

Formal and Informal Leaders

Leaders hold a unique position in their groups, exercising influence and providing direction. Leonard Bernstein was part of the symphony, but his role as the New York Philharmonic conductor differed dramatically from that of the other symphony members. Besides conducting the orchestra, he created a vision for the symphony. In this capacity, leadership can be seen as a differentiated role and the nucleus of group activity.

formal leader that individual who is recognized by those outside the group as the official leader of the group

Organizations have two kinds of leaders: formal and informal. A **formal leader** is that individual who is recognized by those outside the group as the official leader of the group. Often, the formal leader is appointed by the organization to serve in a formal capacity as an agent of the organization. Jack Welch was the formal leader of General Electric, and Leonard Bernstein was the formal

© PHOTEX/CORBIS

Informal leaders are acknowledged by the group, and the group willingly responds to their leadership.

leader of the symphony. Practically all managers act as formal leaders as part of their assigned role. Organizations that use self-managed work teams allow members of the team to select the individual who will serve as their team leader. When this person's role is sanctioned by the formal organization, these team leaders become formal leaders. Increasingly, leaders in organizations will be those who "best sell" their ideas on how to complete a project—persuasiveness and inspiration are important ingredients in the leadership equation, especially in high-involvement organizations.[22]

Informal leaders, by contrast, are not assigned by the organization. The **informal leader** is that individual whom members of the group acknowledge as their leader. Athletic teams often have informal leaders, individuals who exert considerable influence on team members, even though they hold no official (formal) leadership position. In fact, most work groups contain at least one informal leader. Just as formal leaders, informal leaders can benefit or harm an organization, depending on whether their influence encourages group members to behave consistently with organizational goals.

informal leader that individual whom members of the group acknowledge as their leader

As we have noted, the terms *leader* and *manager* are not synonymous. Grace Hopper, retired U.S. Navy admiral, draws a distinction between leading and managing: "You don't manage people, you manage *things*. You lead *people*."[23] Informal leaders often have considerable leverage over their colleagues. Traditionally, the roles of informal leaders have not included the total set of management responsibilities because an informal leader does not always exercise the functions of planning, organizing, directing, and controlling. However, high-involvement organizations frequently encourage their formal and informal leaders to exercise the full set of management roles. Many consider such actions necessary for self-managing work teams to succeed.

Leader Emergence

People come to leadership positions through two dynamics. In many instances, people are put into positions of leadership by forces outside the group. University-based ROTC programs and military academies (like West Point) formally groom people to be leaders. We refer to this person as the **designated leader** (in this instance the designated and formal leader are the same person). **Emergent leaders**, on the other hand, arise from the dynamics and processes that unfold within and among a group of individuals as they endeavor to achieve a collective goal.

designated leader the person placed in the leadership position by forces outside the group

emergent leader the person who becomes a group's leader by virtue of processes and dynamics internal to the group

A variety of processes help us understand how leaders emerge. Gerald Salancik and Jeffrey Pfeffer observe that power to influence others flows to those individuals who possess the critical and scarce resources (often knowledge and expertise) that a group needs to overcome a major problem.[24] They note that the dominant coalition and leadership in American corporations during the 1950s was among engineers, because organizations were engaged in competition based on product design. The power base in many organizations shifted to marketing as competition became a game of "advertising" aimed at differentiating products in the consumer's mind. About 10–15 years ago, power and leadership once again shifted, this time to people with finance and legal backgrounds, as the critical contingencies facing many organizations were mergers, acquisitions, hostile takeovers, and creative financing. Thus, Salancik and Pfeffer reason that power and thus leadership flow to those individuals who have the ability to help an organization (group) overcome its critical contingencies. As the challenges facing a group change, so too may the flow of power and leadership.

Many leaders emerge out of the "needs of the situation." Different situations call for different configurations of knowledge, skills, and abilities. The group member who possesses the knowledge, skills, and abilities that the group requires to achieve its goal attainment needs is often turned to for leadership.[25] People surrender their power to define reality for themselves to individuals whom they believe will make meaningful contributions to those needs.[26] The individual to whom power is surrendered is often a member of the group who is in good standing. As a result of their contributions to the group's goals, they have accumulated *idiosyncrasy credits* (a form of competency-based status). These credits give the individual a status that allows him or her to influence the direction that the group takes as it works to achieve its goals.[27]

It is important to recognize that the traits possessed by certain individuals contribute significantly to their emergence as a leader. Research indicates that people are unlikely to follow individuals who, for example, do not display drive, self-confidence, knowledge of the situation, and honesty and integrity.

Leadership as an Exercise of Influence

As we have noted, leadership is the exercise of influence over those who are dependent on one another for the attainment of a mutual goal in a group setting. But *how* do leaders exercise this influence? This exercise is an essential ingredient of effective leadership. *Social (interpersonal) influence* is one's ability to effect a change in the motivation, attitudes, and/or behaviors of others. *Power*, then, essentially answers the "how" question: How do leaders move or influence their followers?

French and Raven provide us with a useful typology that identifies the source and types of power that may be at the disposal of leaders:

- *Reward power*—the power a person has because people believe that he or she can bestow rewards or outcomes, such as money or recognition that others desire.
- *Coercive power*—the power a person has because people believe that he or she can punish them by inflicting pain or by withholding or taking away something that they value.
- *Referent power*—the power a person has because others want to associate with or be accepted by him or her.
- *Expert power*—the power a person has because others believe that she or he has and is willing to share expert knowledge that they need. (The concept of *resource power* extends the idea of expert power to include the power that a person has because others believe that he or she possesses and is willing to share resources, such as information, time, or materials that are needed.)

- *Legitimate power*—the power that a person has because others believe that she or he possesses the "right" to influence them and they ought to obey. This right can originate in tradition; in the charisma or appeal of the person; and in laws, institutional roles within society, moralistic appeal, and rationality (that is, logical arguments, factual evidence, reason, and internally consistent positions).[28]

Not all forms of power are equally effective (see Figure 11-2), nor is one's total power base the simple sum of the powers at the leader's disposal. Different types of power elicit different forms of compliance: Leaders who rely on coercive power often have alienated followers who resist their influence attempts. Leaders who rely on reward power develop followers who are very "measured" in their responses; the use of rewards often leads people to think in terms of "how much am I getting," "how much should I give," or "am I breaking even." The use of referent power produces identification with the leader and their cause. The use of rationality, expert power, and/or moralistic appeal generally elicits commitment and the internalization of the leader's goals.[29]

Leaders who use referent and expert power commonly experience a favorable response in terms of follower satisfaction and performance. Reward and legitimate power (that is, relying on one's position to influence others) produce inconsistent results. Sometimes these powers lead to follower performance and satisfaction, yet they also sometimes fail. Coercive power can result in favorable performance, yet follower and resistance dissatisfaction are not uncommon. Research suggests that "rationality" is the most effective influence tactic in terms of its impact on follower commitment, motivation, performance, satisfaction, and group effectiveness.[30]

Good leaders, whether formal or informal, develop many sources of power. Leaders who rely on legitimate power (authority) alone seldom generate the influence necessary to help their organization and its members succeed. In the process of building their power base, effective leaders have discovered that the use of coercive power tends to "dilute" the effectiveness of other powers, and the development and use of referent power tends to "magnify" the effectiveness of other forms of power—a compliment or reward from a person we like generally has greater value than one from someone we dislike, and punishment from someone we love (such as "tough love" from a parent) is less offensive than the pain inflicted by someone we dislike.[31]

In sum, one key to effective leadership, especially as it pertains to the exercise of social and interpersonal influence, relates to the type of power employed by the leader. Overall leader effectiveness will be higher when people follow because of intrinsic processes and because they "want" to follow. This is much

FIGURE 11-2 The Leader-Follower Power Relationship

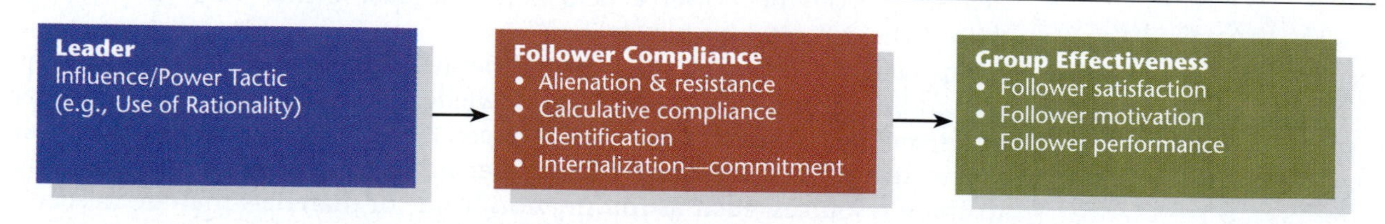

more likely to happen when the leader's influence flows out of rationality, expertise, moralistic appeal, and/or referent power.

Leadership is also about having a vision, and communicating that vision to others in such a way that it provides meaning for the follower.[32] Language, ritual, drama, myths, symbolic constructions, and stories are some of the tools leaders use to capture the attention of their "followers to be," to evoke emotion and to manage the meaning "of the task (challenges) facing the group."[33] (See *An Inside Look* at leaders as storytellers.) These tools help the leader influence the attitudes, motivation, and behavior of their followers.

AN INSIDE LOOK

Leaders as Storytellers

Everyone loves a good story. As many leaders these days are hoping, most people will remember and internalize a good story as well. Today's leaders are discovering the power of storytelling as a way of imparting the values and vision of an organization to employees.

Storytelling as a leadership technique has been used by leaders throughout history. Today, leaders are learning how to purposefully tell stories to help employees understand and become a part of the corporate culture. Generally, people view their lives similarly to a movie, where actions result in consequences. By hearing a story, employees can remember the consequences of an action and also retain the more subtle truths about the organization's culture.

The success of the restaurant chain Red Robin International has been driven by stories. The President and CEO of Red Robin, Michael Snyder, became inspired while watching his son's horse run free and unbridled through a field. As a result, he instituted the "Unbridled Philosophy" as a vision for the chain. The organization seeks stories of unbridled passion in its employees, publicizes them through advertisements and internal newsletters, and even uses them to recruit new employees. These examples of "unbridled passion" are inspiring stories about employees who go the extra mile for their customers. For example, one Red Robin manager volunteered to drive a group of teenagers to a dance after their chaperone's car died in the parking lot. Another assisted an out-of-breath customer by seating him and going to his car for his oxygen tank. Employees can see themselves in these stories and aspire to do similar kinds of acts for the good of the organization and its customers. The "Unbridled Philosophy" has infused Red Robin employees with enthusiasm and had led to a turnover rate that is well below the industry average.

Leaders should remember that effective stories do not have to be long or complicated. The best storytellers follow three steps to sharing experiences:

1. Describe the situation
2. Describe the action
3. Describe a memorable resolution

Besides helping employees to understand the corporate culture, leaders employ storytelling in other ways as well. Leaders can use stories to help employees remember examples of things that can go wrong. Rather than having to memorize a list of do's and don'ts, employees will be more likely to remember the outcome of a story illustrating things to do and things not to do. Storytelling can also be used to convince employees of the value of a new program by using memorable and illustrative examples. Another important use of stories is to demonstrate the real person behind the leader. When a leader share stories about his or her mistakes, the employees are likely to remember and learn from these failures. This can also help the leader build credibility by showing that he or she has a vulnerable side and is not immune to error.

Source: Adapted from N. L. Breuer. 1998. The power of storytelling. *Workforce* 77(12): 36–41; and M. Lovemore. 2000. Managing social capital. *Training & Development* 54(1):36–39.

Influence-based Leadership Styles

Many writers have explored how leaders can use power to address the needs of various situations. One view holds that in traditional organizations members expect to be told what to do and are willing to follow highly structured directions. Individuals attracted to high-involvement organizations, however, want to make their own decisions, expect their leader to allow them to do so, and are willing to accept and act on this responsibility. This suggests that power is employed in a variety of ways.

http://www.css.edu/users/dswenson/web/leadlink.htm

The Tannenbaum and Schmidt Continuum In the 1950s, Tannenbaum and Schmidt created a continuum (see Figure 11-3) in which leadership styles range from authoritarian to extremely high levels of worker operating freedom.[34] Subsequent to Tannenbaum and Schmidt's work, researchers adapted the continuum by categorizing leader power styles as autocratic (boss-centered), participative (workers are consulted and involved), or free-rein (members are assigned the work and decide on their own how to do it; the leader relinquishes the active assumption of the role of leadership).[35]

http://sol.brunel.ac.uk/~jarvis/bola/motivation/mcgregor.html

Theory X and Theory Y Leaders In Chapter 2, we introduced Douglas McGregor's Theory X and Theory Y, two different sets of attitudes about the individual as an organizational member.[36] Theory X and Y thinking gives rise to two different styles of leadership. The *Theory X leader* assumes that the average individual dislikes work and is incapable of exercising adequate self-direction and self-control. As a consequence, they exert a highly controlling leadership style. In contrast, *Theory Y leaders* believe that people have creative capacities, as well as both the ability and desire to exercise self-direction and self-control. They typically allow organizational members significant amounts of discretion in their jobs and encourage them to participate in departmental and organizational decision making. Theory Y leaders are much more likely to adopt involvement-oriented approaches to leadership and organically designed organizations for their leadership group.

FIGURE 11-3 Tannenbaum and Schmidt's Leadership Continuum

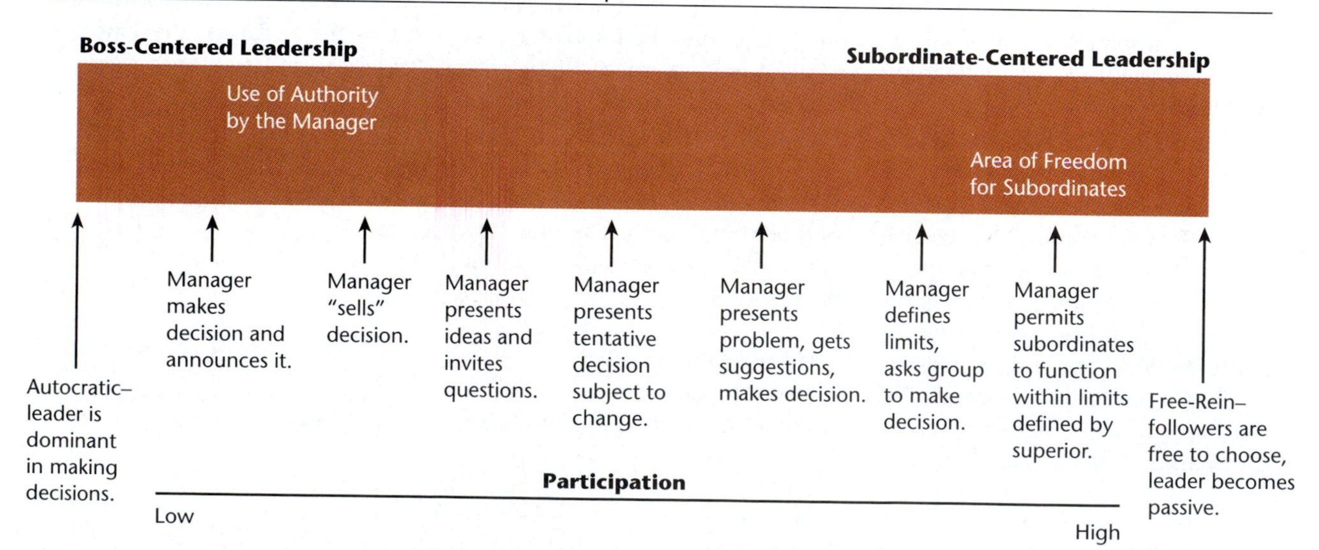

Source: Modified from R. Tannenbaum and W. H. Schmidt. May–June 1973. How to choose a leadership pattern. *Harvard Business Review,* 167.

Theory X and Theory Y thinking and leadership are not strictly an American phenomenon. Evidence suggests that managers from different parts of the global community commonly hold the same view. A study of 3600 managers from 14 countries reveals that most of them held assumptions about human nature that could best be classified as Theory X.[37] Even though managers might publicly endorse the merits of participatory management, most of them doubted their workers' capacities to exercise self-direction and self-control and to contribute creatively.[38]

Directive/Permissive Leadership Styles Contemplating the central role of problem solving in management and leadership, Jan P. Muczyk and Bernard C. Reimann of Cleveland State University offer an interesting perspective on four different leadership styles (see Figure 11-4) that revolve around decision-making and implementation processes.[39]

A *directive autocrat* retains power, makes unilateral decisions, and closely supervises workers' activities. This style of leadership is seen as appropriate when circumstances require quick decisions and organizational members are new, inexperienced, or underqualified. A doctor in charge of a hastily constructed shelter for victims of a tornado may use this style to command nonmedical volunteers. The captain of the *USS Cole* assumed this leadership style when a terrorist bomb ripped a whole in the side of his ship in Yemen during a refueling stop in October of 2000.

The *permissive autocrat* mixes their use of power, retaining decision-making power but permitting organizational members to exercise discretion when executing decisions. This leader behavior is recommended when decision time is limited, when tasks are routine, or when organizational members have sufficient expertise to determine appropriate role behaviors.

Also sharing power is the *directive democrat,* who encourages participative decision making but retains the power to direct team members in the execution of their roles. This style is appropriate when followers have valuable opinions and ideas, but one person needs to coordinate the execution of the ideas. A surgeon might allow the entire surgical team to participate in developing a plan for

FIGURE 11-4 Leadership Behavior and Uses of Power

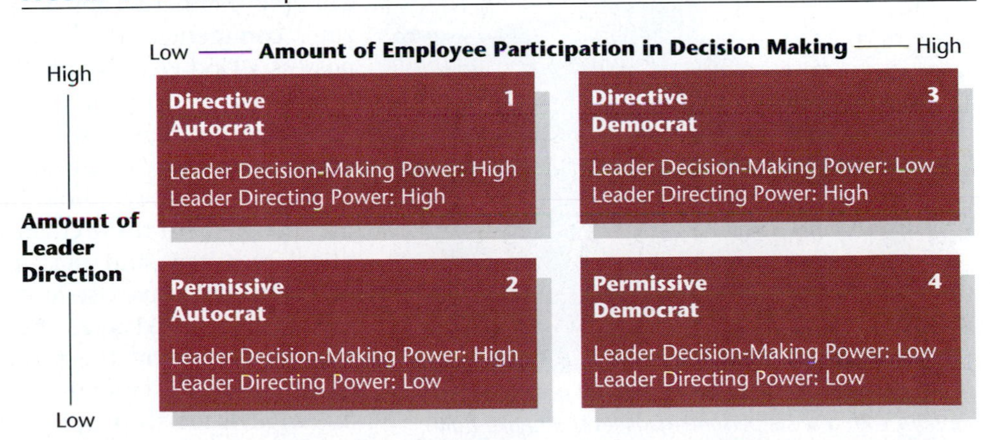

Source: Modified from J. P. Muczyk and B. C. Reimann. 1987. The case for directive leadership. *Academy of Management Executive* 1:304.

a surgical procedure. Once surgery begins, however, the surgeon is in complete charge.

Finally, the *permissive democrat* shares power with group members, soliciting involvement in both decision making and execution. This style is appropriate when participation has both informational and motivational value, when time permits group decision making, when group members are capable of improving decision quality, and when followers are capable of exercising self-management in their performance of work.

The permissive democratic approach to leadership is characteristic of leadership in high-involvement organizations. Here, leaders act as facilitators, process consultants, network builders, conflict managers, inspirationalists, coaches, teachers/mentors, and cheerleaders.[40] Such is the role of Ralph Stayer, founder, owner, and CEO of Johnsonville Foods. He defines himself as his company's philosopher. At Quad/Graphics, president Harry V. Quadracci is a permissive democrat because he encourages all Quad employees to play a major role in decision making and execution as they manage their teams as independent profit centers.

THE TRAIT APPROACH TO LEADERSHIP

great man theory of leadership the belief that some people are born to be leaders and others are not

Ancient Greek, Roman, Egyptian, and Chinese scholars were keenly interested in leaders and leadership. Their writings portray leaders as heroes. Homer, in his poem *The Odyssey*, portrays Odysseus during and after the Trojan War as a great leader who had vision and self-confidence. His son Telemachus, under the tutelage of Mentor, developed his father's courage and leadership skills.[41] Out of such stories there emerged the "great man" theory of leadership, and a starting point for the contemporary study of leadership.

© JEREMY HOMER/CORBIS

The great man theory of leadership holds that some people are born with a set of personal qualities that make truly great leaders. Mahatma Gandhi is often cited as a naturally great leader.

The **great man theory of leadership** states that some people are born with the necessary attributes to be great leaders. Alexander the Great, Julius Caesar, Joan of Arc, Catherine the Great, Napoleon, Mahatma Gandhi, and Mao Zedong are cited as naturally great leaders, born with a set of personal qualities that made them effective leaders. Even today, the belief that truly great leaders are born is common. For example, Kenneth Labich, writer for *Fortune* magazine, commented that "the best leaders seem to possess a God-given spark."[42]

During the early 1900s, scholars endeavored to understand leaders and leadership. They wanted to know, from an organizational perspective, what characteristics leaders hold in common in the hope that people with these characteristics could be identified, recruited, and placed in key organizational positions. This gave rise to early research efforts and to what is referred to as the *trait approach to leadership*. Prompted by the great man theory of leadership, and the emerging interest in understanding what leadership is, researchers focused on the leader—Who is a leader? What are the distinguishing characteristics of the great and effective leaders?

Leader Trait Research

Ralph Stogdill, while on the faculty at The Ohio State University, pioneered our modern (late 20th century) study of leadership.[43] Scholars taking the trait approach attempted to identify physiological (appearance, height, and weight), demographic (age, education, and socioeconomic background), personality (dominance, self-confidence, and aggressiveness), intellective (intelligence, decisiveness, judgment, and knowledge), task-related (achievement drive, initiative, and persistence), and social characteristics (sociability and cooperativeness) with leader emergence and leader effectiveness. After reviewing several hundred studies of leader traits, Stogdill in 1974 described the successful leader this way:

> The [successful] leader is characterized by a strong drive for responsibility and task completion, vigor and persistence in pursuit of goals, venturesomeness and originality in problem solving, drive to exercise initiative in social situations, self-confidence and sense of personal identity, willingness to accept consequences of decision and action, readiness to absorb interpersonal stress, willingness to tolerate frustration and delay, ability to influence other person's behavior, and capacity to structure social interaction systems to the purpose at hand.[44]

The last three decades of the 20th century witnessed continued exploration of the relationship between traits and both leader emergence and leader effectiveness. Edwin Locke from the University of Maryland and a number of his research associates, in their recent review of the trait research, observed that successful leaders possess a set of core characteristics that are different from those of other people.[45] Although these core traits do not solely determine whether a person will be a leader and a successful leader, they are seen as preconditions that endow people with leadership potential. Among the core traits identified are

- *Drive*—a high level of effort, including a strong desire for achievement as well as high levels of ambition, energy, tenacity, and initiative
- *Leadership motivation*—an intense desire to lead others
- *Honesty and integrity*—a commitment to the truth (nondeceit), where word and deed correspond
- *Self-confidence*—an assurance in one's self, one's ideas, and one's ability
- *Cognitive ability*—conceptually skilled, capable of exercising good judgment, having strong analytical abilities, possessing the capacity to think strategically and multidimensionally
- *Knowledge of the business*—a high degree of understanding of the company, industry, and technical matters
- *Other traits*—charisma, creativity/originality, and flexibility/adaptiveness[46]

While leaders may be "people with the right stuff," effective leadership requires more than simply possessing the correct set of motives and traits. Knowledge, skills, ability, vision, strategy, and effective vision implementation are all necessary for the person who has the "right stuff" to realize their leadership potential.[47] According to Locke, people endowed with these traits engage in behaviors that are associated with leadership. As followers, people are attracted to, and inclined to follow, individuals who display, for example, honesty and integrity, self-confidence, and the motivation to lead.

Personality psychologists remind us that behavior is a result of an interaction between the person and the situation—that is, Behavior = *f* [(Person) (Situation)]. To this, psychologist Walter Mischel adds the important observation that personality tends to get expressed through an individual's behavior in "weak" situations and to be suppressed in "strong" situations.[48] A strong situation is one with strong behavioral norms and rules, strong incentives, clear expectations, and rewards for a particular behavior. Our characterization of the mechanistic organization with its well-defined hierarchy of authority, jobs, and standard operating procedures exemplifies a strong situation. The organic social system exemplifies a weak situation. From a leadership perspective, a person's traits play a stronger role in their leader behavior and ultimately leader effectiveness when the situation permits the expression of their disposition. Thus, personality traits prominently shape leader behavior in weak situations.

Finally, about the validity of the "great person approach to leadership": Evidence accumulated to date does not provide a strong base of support for the notion that leaders are born. Yet, the study of twins at the University of Minnesota leaves open the possibility that part of the answer might be found in our genes. Many personality traits and vocational interests (which might be related to one's interest in assuming responsibility for others and the motivation to lead) have been found to be related to our "genetic dispositions" as well as to our life experiences.[49] Each core trait recently identified by Edwin A. Locke and his associates traces a significant part of its existence to life experiences. Thus, a person is not "born" with self-confidence. Self-confidence is developed, honesty and integrity are a matter of personal choice, motivation to lead comes from within the individual and is within his/her control, and knowledge of the business can be acquired. While cognitive ability does in part find its origin in the genes, it still needs to be developed. Finally drive, as a dispositional trait, may also have a genetic component, but it too can be self- and other-encouraged. It goes without saying that none of these ingredients are acquired overnight.

http://www.psych.umn.edu/psylabs/mtfs

Other Leader Traits

Sex and gender, disposition, and self-monitoring also play an important role in leader emergence and leader style.

Sex and Gender Role Much research has gone into understanding the role of sex and gender in leadership.[50] Two major avenues have been explored: sex and gender roles in relation to leader emergence, and whether style differences exist across the sexes.

Evidence supports the observation that men emerge as leaders more frequently than women.[51] Throughout history few women have been in positions where they could develop or exercise leadership behaviors. In contemporary society, being perceived as experts appears to play an important role in the emergence of women as leaders. Yet, gender role is more predictive than sex. Individuals with "masculine" (for example, assertive, aggressive, competitive, willing to take a stand), as opposed to "feminine" (cheerful, affectionate, sympathetic, gentle) characteristics are more likely to emerge in leadership roles.[52] In our society males are frequently socialized to possess the masculine characteristics, while females are more frequently socialized to possess the feminine characteristics.

Recent evidence, however, suggests that individuals who are androgynous (that is, who simultaneously possess both masculine and feminine characteristics) are as likely to emerge in leadership roles as individuals with only masculine characteristics. This suggests that possessing feminine qualities does not distract from the attractiveness of the individual as a leader.[53]

With regard to leadership style, researchers have looked to see if male-female differences exist in task and interpersonal styles, and whether or not differences exist in how autocratic or democratic men and women are. The answer is, when it comes to interpersonal versus task orientation, differences between men and women appear to be marginal. Women are somewhat more concerned with meeting the group's interpersonal needs, while men are somewhat more concerned with meeting the group's task needs. Big differences emerge in terms of democratic versus autocratic leadership styles. Men tend to be more autocratic or directive, while women are more likely to adopt a more democratic/participative leadership style.[54] In fact, it may be because men are more directive that they are seen as key to goal attainment and they are turned to more often as leaders.[55]

Dispositional Trait Psychologists often use the terms *disposition* and *mood* to describe and differentiate people. Individuals characterized by a positive affective state exhibit a mood that is active, strong, excited, enthusiastic, peppy, and elated. A leader with this mood state exudes an air of confidence and optimism and is seen as enjoying work-related activities.

Recent work conducted at the University of California–Berkeley demonstrates that leaders (managers) with positive affectivity (a positive mood state) tend to be more competent interpersonally, to contribute more to group activities, and to be able to function more effectively in their leadership role.[56] Their enthusiasm and high energy levels appear to be infectious, transferring from leader to followers. Thus, such leaders promote group cohesiveness and productivity. This mood state is also associated with low levels of group turnover, and is positively associated with followers who engage in acts of good group citizenship.[57]

Self-monitoring Self-monitoring as a personality trait refers to the strength of an individual's ability and willingness to read verbal and nonverbal cues and to alter one's behavior so as to manage the presentation of the self and the images that others form of the individual. "High self-monitors" are particularly astute at reading social cues and regulating their self-presentation to fit a particular situation. "Low self-monitors" are less sensitive to social cues; they may either lack motivation or lack the ability to manage how they come across to others.

Some evidence supports the position that high self-monitors emerge more often as leaders. In addition, they appear to exert more influence on group decisions and initiate more structure than low self-monitors. Perhaps high self-monitors emerge as leaders because in group interaction they are the individuals who attempt to organize the group and provide them with the structure needed to move the group toward goal attainment.[58]

BEHAVIORAL APPROACHES TO LEADERSHIP

The nearly four decades of research that focus on identifying the personal traits associated with the emergence of leaders and leader effectiveness resulted in two observations. First, leader traits are important—people who are endowed with the "right stuff" (drive, self-confidence, honesty, and integrity) are more likely to emerge as leaders and to be effective leaders than individuals who do not possess these characteristics. Second, traits are only a part of the story.

Traits only account for part of why someone becomes a leader and why they are (or are not) effective leaders.

Still under the influence of the great man theory of leadership, researchers continued to focus on the leader in an effort to understand leadership—who emerges and what constitutes effective leadership. Researchers then began to reason that maybe the rest of the story could be understood by looking at what it is that leaders *do*. Thus, we now turn our attention to leader behaviors, and the behavioral approaches to leadership.

It is now common to think of effective leadership in terms of what leaders do. CEOs and management consultants agree that effective leaders display trust in their employees, develop a vision, keep their cool, encourage risk, bring expertise into the work setting, invite dissent, and focus everyone's attention on that which is important.[59] Denny Perak, manager at a General Mills' cereal plant in Lodi, California, defines his leadership role in behavioral terms. He notes that he coaches his team on management techniques and serves as a boundary spanner linking the team and company headquarters.[60] Quad/Graphics' Harry V. Quadracci sees his primary organizational role as being the company's chief "disorganizer."[61] Apple founder Steve Jobs believes that the best leaders are coaches and team cheerleaders. Similar views have been frequently echoed by management consultant Tom Peters.

http://www.generalmills.com

During the late 1940s, two major research programs—The Ohio State University and the University of Michigan leadership studies—were launched to explore leadership from a behavioral perspective.

http://www.osu.edu

The Ohio State University Studies

A group of Ohio State University researchers, under the direction of Ralph Stogdill, began an extensive and systematic series of studies to identify leader behaviors associated with effective group performance. Their results identified two major sets of leader behaviors: consideration and initiating structure.

Consideration is the "relationship-oriented" behavior of a leader. It is instrumental in creating and maintaining good relationships (that is, addressing the group's maintenance needs) with organizational members. Consideration behaviors include being supportive and friendly, representing people's interests, communicating openly with group members, recognizing them, respecting their ideas, and sharing concern for their feelings.

consideration a "relationship-oriented" leader behavior that is supportive, friendly, and focused on personal needs and interpersonal relationships

Initiating structure involves "task-oriented" leader behaviors. It is instrumental in the efficient use of resources to attain organizational goals, thereby addressing the group's task needs. Initiating structure behaviors include scheduling work, deciding what is to be done (and how and when to do it), providing direction to organizational members, planning, coordinating, problem solving, maintaining standards of performance, and encouraging the use of uniform procedures.

initiating structure a "task-oriented" leader behavior that is focused on goal attainment, organizing and scheduling work, solving problems, and maintaining work processes

After consideration and initiating structure behaviors were first identified, many leaders believed that they had to behave one way or the other. If they initiated structure, they could not be considerate, and vice versa. It did not take long, however, to recognize that leaders simultaneously display any combination of both behaviors.

The Ohio State studies are important because they identified two critical categories of behavior that distinguish one leader from another. Both consideration and initiating structure behavior can significantly impact work attitudes and behaviors. Unfortunately, the effects of consideration and initiating structure are not consistent from situation to situation.[62] In some of the organizations studied, for example, high levels of initiating structure increased performance. In other organizations, the amount of initiating structure seemed to make little difference. Although most organizational members reported greater satisfaction when leaders acted considerately, consideration behavior appeared to have no clear effect on performance.

Initially, these mixed findings were disappointing to researchers and managers alike. It had been hoped that a profile of the most effective leader behaviors could be identified so that leaders could be trained in the best ways to behave. Research made clear, however, that there is no one best style of leader behavior for all situations.

The University of Michigan Studies

http://www.umich.edu

At about the same time that the Ohio State studies were under way, researchers at the University of Michigan also began to investigate leader behaviors. As at Ohio State, the Michigan researchers attempted to identify behavioral elements that differentiated effective from ineffective leaders.[63]

The two types of leader behavior that stand out in these studies are job-centered and organizational member-centered. *Job-centered behaviors* are devoted to supervisory functions, such as planning, scheduling, coordinating work activities, and providing the resources needed for task performance. *Employee member-centered* behaviors include consideration and support for organizational members. These dimensions of behavior, of course, correspond closely to the dimensions of initiating structure and consideration identified at Ohio State. The similarity of the findings from two independent groups of researchers added to their credibility. As the Ohio State researchers had done, the Michigan researchers also found that any combination of the two behaviors was possible.

The studies at Michigan are significant because they reinforce the importance of leader behavior. They also provide the basis for later theories that identify specific, effective matches of work situations and leader behaviors. Subsequent research at Michigan and elsewhere has found additional behaviors associated with effective leadership: support, work facilitation, goal emphasis, and interaction facilitation.[64]

These four behaviors are important to the successful functioning of the group in that support and interaction facilitation contribute to the group's maintenance needs, and goal emphasis and work facilitation contribute to the group's task needs. The Michigan researchers also found that these four behaviors do not need to be brought to the group by the leader. In essence, the leader's real job is to set the tone and create the climate that ensure these critical behaviors are present.[65]

The Leadership Grid®

http://www.nwlink.com/~donclark/leader/bm_model.html

Much of the credit for disseminating knowledge about important leader behaviors must go to Robert R. Blake and Jane S. Mouton, who developed a method for classifying styles of leadership compatible with many of the ideas from the Ohio State and Michigan studies.[66] In their classification scheme, *concern for results* (production) emphasizes output, cost effectiveness, and (in for-profit organizations) a concern for profits. *Concern for people* involves promoting working relationships and paying attention to issues of importance to group members. As shown in Figure 11-5, the Leadership Grid® demonstrates that any

FIGURE 11-5 Blake and Mouton's Leadership Grid®

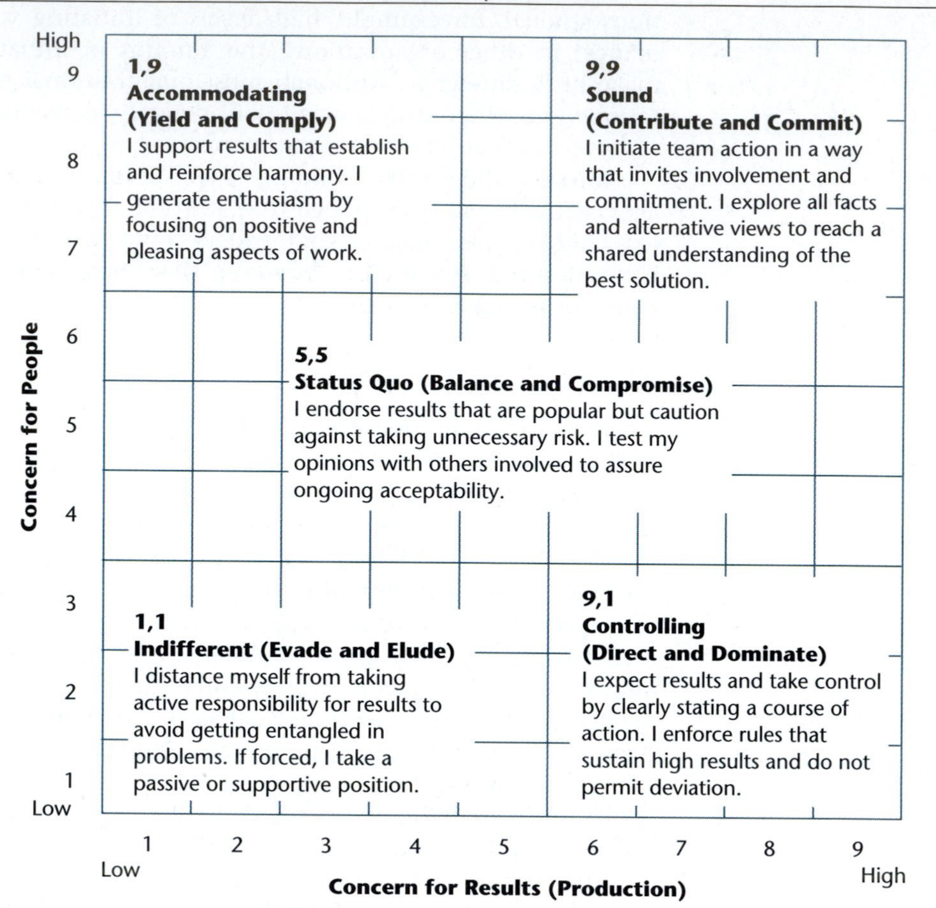

Source: This image is a black-and-white adaptation of The Leadership Grid® figure as it appears in *The Power to Change* by Rachel McKee and Bruce Carlson (Austin: Grid International, Inc.), p. 16. Copyright © 1999 by Grid International, Inc. Reproduced by permission of the owners.

combination of these two leader concerns is possible, and five styles of leadership are highlighted here.

Blake and Mouton contend that the sound (contribute and commit) leader (a high concern for results and people, or 9,9) style is universally the most effective.[67] While the Leadership Grid® is appealing and well structured, research to date suggests that there is no universally effective style of leadership (9,9 or otherwise).[68] There are, however, well-identified situations in which a 9,9 style is unlikely to be effective. Organizational members of high-involvement organizations who have mastered their job duties require little production-oriented leader behavior. Likewise, there is little time for people-oriented behavior during an emergency. Finally, evidence suggests that the "high-high" style may be effective when the situation calls for high levels of initiating structure. Under these conditions, the initiation of structure is more acceptable, favorably affecting follower satisfaction and performance, when the leader is also experienced as warm, supportive, and considerate.[69]

SITUATIONAL (CONTINGENCY) APPROACHES TO LEADERSHIP

As early as 1948, Ralph Stogdill stated that "the qualities, characteristics, and skills required in a leader are determined to a large extent by the demands of the situation in which he is to function as a leader."[70] In addition, it had been observed that two major leader behaviors, initiating structure and consideration, didn't always lead to equally positive outcomes. That is, there are times when initiating structure results in performance increases and follower satisfaction, and there are times when the results are just the opposite. Contradictory findings such as this lead researchers to ask, Under what conditions are the results positive in nature? and When and why are they negative at other times? Obviously, situational differences and key contingencies are at work.

Several theories have been advanced to address this issue. These are Fiedler's contingency theory of leadership, the path-goal theory of leader effectiveness, Hersey and Blanchard's life cycle theory, cognitive resource theory, the decision tree, and the decision process theory.[71] We explore two of the better-known situational theories of leadership, Fred Fiedler's contingency model and Robert J. House's path-goal theory, here. Victor Vroom, Phillip Yetton, and Arthur Jago's decision tree model was discussed in Chapter 9.

Fiedler's Contingency Model

One of the earliest, best-known, and most controversial situation-contingent leadership theories was set forth by Fred E. Fiedler from the University of Washington.[72] This theory is known as the **contingency theory of leadership.** According to Fiedler, organizations attempting to achieve group effectiveness through leadership must assess the leader according to an underlying trait, assess the situation faced by the leader, and construct a proper match between the two.

contingency theory of leadership a theory advanced by Dr. Fred E. Fiedler that suggests that different leadership styles are effective as a function of the favorableness of the leadership situation

least preferred co-worker (LPC) the person with whom the leader least likes to work

The Leader's Trait Leaders are asked about their **least preferred co-worker (LPC)**, the person with whom they *least* like to work. The most popular interpretation of the LPC score is that it reflects a leader's underlying disposition toward others—for example: pleasant/unpleasant, cold/warm, friendly/unfriendly, and untrustworthy/trustworthy. (You can examine your own LPC score by completing the LPC self-assessment on the following page.)

Fiedler states that leaders with high LPC scores are *relationship oriented*—they need to develop and maintain close interpersonal relationships. They tend to evaluate their least-preferred co-workers in fairly favorable terms. Task accomplishment is a secondary need to this type of leader and becomes important only after the need for relationships is reasonably well satisfied. In contrast, leaders with low LPC scores tend to evaluate the individuals with whom they least like to work fairly negatively. They are *task-oriented* people, and only after tasks have been accomplished are low LPC leaders likely to work on establishing good social and interpersonal relations.

The Situational Factor Some situations favor leaders more than others do. To Fiedler, *situational favorableness* is the degree to which leaders have control and influence and therefore feel that they can determine the outcomes of a

SELF-ASSESSMENT Fiedler's LPC Scale

Think of the person with whom you can work least well. This may be someone you work with now or someone you knew in the past. It does not have to be the person you like least well but should be the person with whom you had the most difficulty in getting a job done. Describe this person as he or she appears to you.

Pleasant	8	7	6	5	4	3	2	1	Unpleasant
Friendly	8	7	6	5	4	3	2	1	Unfriendly
Rejecting	1	2	3	4	5	6	7	8	Accepting
Helpful	8	7	6	5	4	3	2	1	Frustrating
Unenthusiastic	1	2	3	4	5	6	7	8	Enthusiastic
Tense	1	2	3	4	5	6	7	8	Relaxed
Distant	1	2	3	4	5	6	7	8	Close
Cold	1	2	3	4	5	6	7	8	Warm
Cooperative	8	7	6	5	4	3	2	1	Uncooperative
Supportive	8	7	6	5	4	3	2	1	Hostile
Boring	1	2	3	4	5	6	7	8	Interesting
Quarrelsome	1	2	3	4	5	6	7	8	Harmonious
Self-Assured	8	7	6	5	4	3	2	1	Hesitant
Efficient	8	7	6	5	4	3	2	1	Inefficient
Gloomy	1	2	3	4	5	6	7	8	Cheerful
Open	8	7	6	5	4	3	2	1	Guarded

Scoring:

LPC score is the sum of the answers to these 16 questions. High scores indicate a relationship orientation; low scores, a task orientation.

Source: Adapted from F. E. Fiedler and M. M. Chemers. 1974. *Leadership and effective management*. Glenview, IL: Scott, Foresman.

group interaction.[73] Several years later, Fiedler changed his situational factor from situational favorability to situational control—where situational control essentially refers to the degree to which a leader can influence the group process.[74] Three factors work together to determine how favorable a situation is to a leader. In order of importance, they are (1) *leader-member relations*—the degree of the group's acceptance of the leader, their ability to work well together, and members' level of loyalty to the leader; (2) *task structure*—the degree to which the task specifies a detailed, unambiguous goal, and how to achieve it; and (3) *position power*—a leader's direct ability to influence group members. The situation is most favorable for a leader when the relationship between the leader and group members is good, when the task is highly structured, and when the leader's position power is strong (cell 1 in Figure 11-6). The least favorable situation occurs under poor leader-member relations, an unstructured task, and weak position power (cell 8).

Leader-Situation Matches Some combinations of leaders and situations work well; others do not. In search of the best combinations, Fiedler examined a large number of leadership situations. He argued that most leaders have a relatively unchangeable or dominant style, so organizations need to design job situations to fit the leader.[75]

While the model has not been fully tested, and tests have often produced mixed or contradictory findings,[76] Fiedler's research indicates that relationship-oriented (high LPC) leaders are much more effective under conditions of intermediate favorability than under either highly favorable or highly unfavorable situations. Fiedler attributes the success of relationship-oriented leaders in situations with intermediate favorability to the leader's nondirective, permissive attitude; a more directive attitude could lead to anxiety in followers, conflict in the group, and a lack of cooperation.

For highly favorable and unfavorable situations, task-oriented leaders (those with a low LPC) are very effective. As tasks are accomplished, a task-oriented leader allows the group to perform its highly structured tasks without imposing more task-directed behavior. The job gets done without the need for the leader's direction. Under unfavorable conditions, task-oriented behaviors, such as setting

FIGURE 11-6 Fiedler's Contingency Model Leader-Situation Matches

Performance

Good

Poor

Favorable

Moderate

Unfavorable

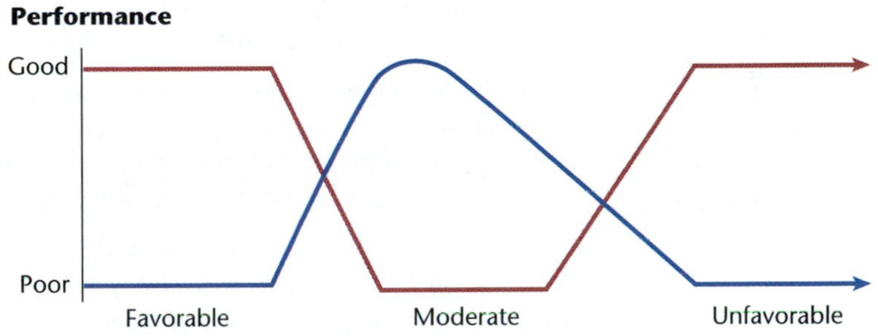

	1	2	3	4	5	6	7	8
Leader-Member Relations	Good	Good	Good	Good	Poor	Poor	Poor	Poor
Task Structure	High	High	Low	Low	High	High	Low	Low
Leader Position Power	Strong	Weak	Strong	Weak	Strong	Weak	Strong	Weak

Task Motivated

Relationship Motivated

Source: Adapted from F. E. Fiedler and M. M. Chemers. 1974. *Leadership and effective management.* Glenview, IL: Scott, Foresman.

goals, detailing work methods, and guiding and controlling work behaviors, move the group toward task accomplishment.

As might be expected, leaders with mid-range LPC scores can be more effective in a wider range of situations than high or low LPC leaders.[77] Under conditions of low favorability, for example, a middle LPC leader can be task-oriented to achieve performance, but show consideration for and allow organizational members to proceed on their own under conditions of high situational favorability.

Controversy over the Theory Although Fiedler's theory often identifies appropriate leader-situation matches and has received broad support, it is not without critics. Some note that it characterizes leaders through reference to their attitudes or personality traits (LPC), while it explains the leader's effectiveness through their behaviors—those with a particular trait will behave in a particular fashion. The theory fails to make the connection between the least preferred co-worker attitude and subsequent behaviors. In addition, some tests of the model have produced mixed or contradictory findings.[78] Finally, what is the true meaning of the LPC score—exactly what is being revealed by a person who sees their least preferred co-worker in positive or negative terms? Robert J. House and Ram N. Aditya recently noted that, in spite of the criticisms, there has been substantial support for Fiedler's theory.[79]

Path-Goal Theory

Robert J. House and Martin Evans, while on the faculty at the University of Toronto, developed a useful leadership theory. Like Fiedler's, it asserts that the type of leadership needed to enhance organizational effectiveness depends on the situation in which the leader is placed. Unlike Fiedler, however, House and Evans focus on the leader's observable behavior. Thus, managers can either match the situation to the leader or modify the leader's behavior to fit the situation.

path-goal theory of leadership posits that leadership is path- and goal-oriented, suggesting that different leadership styles are effective as a function of the task confronting the group

The model of leadership advanced by House and Evans is called the **path-goal theory of leadership** because it suggests that an effective leader provides organizational members with a *path* to a valued *goal*. According to House,

> the motivational function of the leader consists of increasing personal payoffs to organizational members for work-goal attainment, and making the path to these payoffs easier to travel by clarifying it, reducing road blocks and pitfalls, and increasing the opportunities for personal satisfaction en route.[80]

Effective leaders therefore provide rewards that are valued by organizational members. These rewards may be pay, recognition, promotions, or any other item that gives members an incentive to work hard to achieve goals. Effective leaders also give clear instructions so that ambiguities about work are reduced and followers understand how to do their jobs effectively. They provide coaching, guidance, and training so that followers can perform the task expected of them. They also remove barriers to task accomplishment, correcting shortages of materials, inoperative machinery, or interfering policies.

An Appropriate Match According to the path-goal theory, the challenge facing leaders is basically twofold. First, they must analyze situations and identify the most appropriate leadership style. For example, experienced employees who work on a highly structured assembly line don't need a leader to spend much time telling them how to do their jobs—they already know this. The leader of an archeological expedition, though, may need to spend a great deal of time telling inexperienced laborers how to excavate and care for the relics they uncover.

Second, leaders must be flexible enough to use different leadership styles as appropriate. To be effective, leaders must engage in a wide variety of behaviors. Without an extensive repertoire of behaviors at their disposal, a leader's effectiveness is limited.[81] All team members will not, for example, have the same need for autonomy. The leadership style that motivates organizational members with strong needs for autonomy (participative leadership) is different from that which motivates and satisfies members with weaker autonomy needs (directive leadership). The degree to which leadership behavior matches situational factors will determine members' motivation, satisfaction, and performance (see Figure 11-7).[82]

Behavior Dimensions According to path-goal theory, there are four important dimensions of leader behavior, each of which is suited to a particular set of situational demands.[83]

- *Supportive leadership*—At times, effective leaders demonstrate concern for the well-being and personal needs of organizational members. Supportive leaders are friendly, approachable, and considerate to individuals in the workplace. Supportive leadership is especially effective when an organizational member is performing a boring, stressful, frustrating, tedious, or unpleasant task. If a task is difficult and a group member has low self-esteem, supportive leadership can reduce some of the person's anxiety, increase his or her confidence, and increase satisfaction and determination as well.
- *Directive leadership*—At times, effective leaders set goals and performance expectations, let organizational members know what is expected, provide guidance, establish rules and procedures to guide work, and schedule and coordinate the activities of members. Directive leadership is called for when role ambiguity is high. Removing uncertainty and providing needed guidance can increase members' effort, job satisfaction, and job performance.
- *Participative leadership*—At times, effective leaders consult with group members about job-related activities and consider their opinions and suggestions when making decisions. Participative leadership is effective when tasks are unstructured. Participative leadership is used to great effect when leaders need help in identifying work procedures and where followers have the expertise to provide this help.

FIGURE 11-7 The Path-Goal Leadership Model

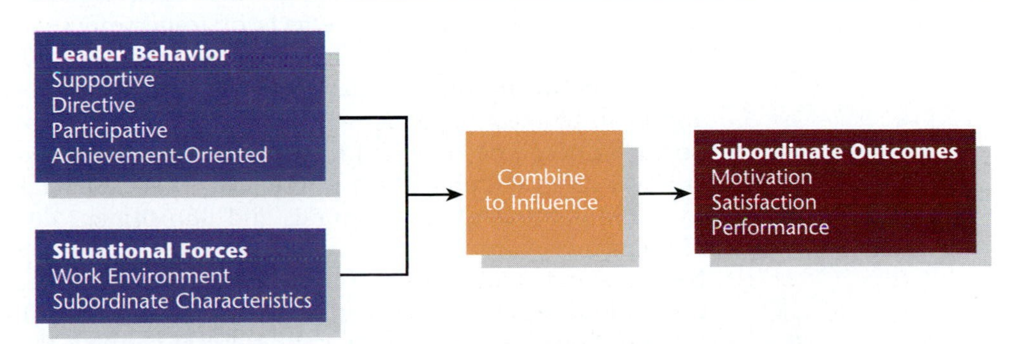

- *Achievement-oriented leadership*—At times, effective leaders set challenging goals, seek improvement in performance, emphasize excellence, and demonstrate confidence in organizational members' ability to attain high standards. Achievement-oriented leaders thus capitalize on members' needs for achievement and use goal-setting theory (described in Chapter 10) to great advantage.

Cross-Cultural Context

Frank Van Gogh, the Australian-born president of Rotoflow, a manufacturer of giant turbines used in the natural gas industry and located in Southern California, notes that there are 30 nationalities among his 200 employees.[84] *Multiculturalism* is a new reality as today's society and workforce become increasingly diverse (see Chapter 3). This naturally leads to the question, Is there a need for a new and different style of leadership?

The vast majority of the contemporary scholarship directed toward understanding leaders and the leadership process has been conducted in North America and Western Europe. Westerners have "developed a highly romanticized, heroic view of leadership."[85] Leaders occupy center stage in organizational life. We use leaders in our attempts to make sense of the performance of our groups, clubs, organizations, and nations. We see them as key to organizational success and profitability, we credit them with organizational competitiveness, and we blame them for organizational failures. At the national level, recall that President Reagan brought down Communism and the Berlin Wall, President Bush won the Gulf War, and President Clinton brought unprecedented economic prosperity to the United States during the 1990s.

This larger-than-life role ascribed to leaders and the Western romance with successful leaders raise the question, How representative is our understanding of leaders and leadership across cultures. That is, do the results that we have examined in this chapter generalize to other cultures?

As discussed in Chapter 5, Geert Hofstede points out that significant value differences (individualism-collectivism, power distance, uncertainty avoidance, masculinity-femininity, and time orientation) cut across societies. Thus, leaders of culturally diverse groups will encounter belief and value differences among their followers, as well as in their own leader-member exchanges.

There appears to be consensus that a universal approach to leadership and leader effectiveness does not exist. Cultural differences work to enhance and diminish the impact of leadership styles on group effectiveness. For example, when leaders empower their followers, the effect for job satisfaction in India has been found to be negative, while in the United States, Poland, and Mexico the effect is positive.[86] The existing evidence suggests similarities as well as differences in such areas as the effects of leadership styles, the acceptability of influence attempts, and the closeness and formality of relationships. The distinction between task and relationship-oriented leader behavior, however, does appear to be meaningful across cultures.[87] Leaders whose behaviors reflect support, kindness, and concern for their followers are valued and effective in Western and Asian cultures. Yet it is also clear that democratic, participative, directive, and contingent-based rewards and punishment do not produce the same results across cultures. The United States is very different from Brazil, Korea, New Zealand, and Nigeria. The effective practice of leadership necessitates a careful look at, and understanding of, the individual differences brought to the leader-follower relationship by cross-cultural contexts.[88]

SUBSTITUTES FOR AND NEUTRALIZERS OF LEADERSHIP

Several factors have been discovered that can substitute for or neutralize the effects of leader behavior (see Table 11-1).[89] *Substitutes* for leadership behavior can clarify role expectations, motivate organizational members, or satisfy members (making it unnecessary for the leader to attempt to do so). In some cases, these substitutes supplement the behavior of a leader. Sometimes it is a group member's characteristics that make leadership less necessary, as when a master craftsperson or highly skilled worker performs up to his or her own high standards without needing outside prompting. Sometimes the task's characteristics take over, as when the work itself—solving an interesting problem or working on a familiar job—is intrinsically satisfying. Sometimes the characteristics of the organization make leadership less necessary, as when work rules are so clear and specific that workers know exactly what they must do without help from the leader (see *An Inside Look* at flat management structure and the orchestra with no leader).

Neutralizers of leadership, on the other hand, are not helpful; they prevent leaders from acting as they wish. A computer-paced assembly line, for example, prevents a leader from using initiating structure behavior to pace the line. A union contract that specifies that workers be paid according to seniority prevents a leader from dispensing merit-based pay. Sometimes, of course, neutralizers can be beneficial. Union contracts, for example, clarify disciplinary proceedings, and

TABLE 11-1 Substitutes for and Neutralizers of Leader Behavior

	Leader Behavior Influenced	
Substitute or Neutralizer	**Supportive Leadership**	**Instrumental Leadership**
A. Subordinate Characteristics:		
1. Experience, ability, training		Substitute
2. "Professional" orientation	Substitute	Substitute
3. Indifference toward rewards offered by organization	Neutralizer	Neutralizer
B. Task Characteristics:		
1. Structured, routine, unambiguous task		Substitute
2. Feedback provided by task		Substitute
3. Intrinsically satisfying task	Substitute	
C. Organization Characteristics:		
1. Cohesive work group	Substitute	Substitute
2. Low position power (leader lacks control over organizational rewards)	Neutralizer	Neutralizer
3. Formalization (explicit plans, goals, areas of responsibility)		Substitute
4. Inflexibility (rigid, unyielding rules and procedures)		Neutralizer
5. Leader located apart from subordinates with only limited communication possible	Neutralizer	Neutralizer

Source: Leadership in organizations by G. A. Yukl. Copyright © 1981. Reprinted by permission of Pearson Education, Inc., Upper Saddle River, NJ 07458.

AN INSIDE LOOK

Flat Management Structure and the Orchestra with No Leader

A group of business students attend a seminar led by an orchestra with no conductor. What could these students possibly learn from leaderless musicians?

Orpheus is an orchestra made up of musicians who perform without the assistance of a conductor. In traditional orchestras, as in traditional hierarchical management, the conductor or leader guides the members of the group with his or her vision of how each piece should be played. The conductor/leader makes all creative decisions about interpreting the music, and the members of the orchestra follow this direction.

Under the direction of Orpheus, organizations and business schools worldwide are learning to operate with a less hierarchical structure. This leaderless orchestra show organizations how they can eliminate layers of management and remain successful and effective. Throughout the 1990s, organizations worked toward flatter management. This movement began as a way to cut costs. Now, however, companies recognize that flat organizations react more quickly to change—technological change in particular. And the more quickly an organization can react to change, the better its chances for survival in the turn-on-a-dime global economy.

Orpheus teaches organizations several important lessons. First, leaderless groups are more creative groups. Group members must create their own vision and therefore are stimulated to provide feedback and input themselves. With no recognized leader, members risk more; they dare to innovate.

Orpheus demonstrates that the input of all group members is needed and valuable. When members provide feedback to each other, the result is an organization with a balanced and equitable sense of direction.

Finally, Orpheus is about empowerment. When all members of the group feel they are essential to the success of the group and have influence over its direction, they take more pride in the group and invest more in its success. And empowerment translates into higher retention of group members. For modern organizations where employee turnover is a constant issue, retention is a significant benefit.

Orpheus has already won three Grammy awards, proving that leaders are not the only route to success. When all members of an organization are expected to lead, the results can be dynamic, exciting . . . and quite harmonious!

Source: Adapted from D. Leonhardt. November 10, 1999. A leaderless orchestra offers lessons for business. *New York Times*, 1, 14.

identify the responsibilities of both management and labor. Leaders must be aware of the presence of neutralizers and their effects so that they can eliminate troublesome neutralizers or take advantage of any potential benefits that accompany them (such as the clarity of responsibilities provided by a union contract). If a leader's effectiveness is being neutralized by a poor communication system, for example, the leader might try to remove the neutralizer by developing (or convincing the organization to develop) a more effective system.

Followers differ considerably in their *focus of attention* while at work, thereby affecting the effectiveness of the act of leadership. Focus of attention is an employee's cognitive orientation while at work. It reflects what and how strongly an individual thinks about various objects, events, or phenomenon, while physically present at work. Focus of attention reflects an individual difference in that not all individuals have the same cognitive orientation while at work—some think a great deal about their job, their co-workers, their leader, off-the-job factors, while others daydream.[90] An employee's focus of attention has both "trait" and "state" qualities. For example, there is a significant amount of minute-by-minute variation in an employee's focus of attention (the "state" component), and there is reasonable consistency in the categories of events that employees think about while they are at work (the "trait" component).

Research suggests that the more followers focus on off-job (nonleader) factors, the less they will react to the leader's behaviors. Thus, a strong focus on one's life "away from work" (for example, time with family and friends) tends to neutralize the motivational, attitudinal, and/or behavioral effects associated with any particular leader behavior. It has also been observed, however, that a strong focus on the leader, either positive or negative, enhances the impact that the leader's behaviors have on followers.[91]

TRANSFORMATIONAL, VISIONARY, AND CHARISMATIC LEADERSHIP

Many organizations struggling with the need to manage chaos, to undergo a culture change, to empower organizational members, and to restructure have looked for answers in "hiring the right leader." Many have come to believe that the transformational, visionary, and charismatic leader represents the style of leadership needed to move organizations through chaos.

The Transformational and Visionary Leader

Leaders who subscribe to the notion that "if it ain't broke, don't fix it" are often described as *transactional leaders*. They are extremely task oriented and instrumental in their approach, frequently looking for incentives that will induce their followers into a desired course of action.[92] These reciprocal exchanges take place in the context of a mutually interdependent relationship between the leader and the follower, frequently resulting in interpersonal bonding.[93] The transactional leader moves a group toward task accomplishment by initiating structure and by offering an incentive in exchange for desired behaviors. The **transformational leader**, on the other hand, moves and changes (fixes) things "in a big way"! Unlike transactional leaders, they don't cause change by offering inducements. Instead, they inspire others to action through their personal values, vision, passion, and belief in and commitment to the mission.[94] Through charisma (idealized influence), individualized consideration (a focus on the development of the follower), intellectual stimulation (questioning assumptions and challenging the status quo), and/or inspirational motivation (articulating an appealing vision), transformational leaders move others to follow.

transformational leader a leader who moves and changes things "in a big way" by inspiring others to perform the extraordinary

The transformational leader is also referred to as a visionary leader. The transformational leader is also referred to as a visionary leader. **Visionary leaders** are those who influence others through an emotional and/or intellectual attraction to the leader's dreams of what "can be." Vision links a present and future state, it energizes and generates commitment, provides meaning for action, and serves as a standard against which to assess performance.[95] Evidence indicates that vision is positively related to follower attitudes and performance.[96] As pointed out by Warren Bennis, a vision is effective only to the extent that the leader can communicate it in such a way that others come to internalize it as their own.[97]

visionary leader an individual who is capable of influencing others through an emotional and/or intellectual attraction to the leader's dream for that which "can be"

As people, transformational leaders are engaging, they are characterized by extroversion, agreeableness, and openness to experience (see Chapter 5 for a discussion of the Big Five personality variables).[98] They energize others. They increase followers' awareness of the importance of the designated outcome.[99] They motivate individuals to transcend their own self-interest for the benefit of the team, and inspire organizational members to self-manage (become self-leaders).[100] Transformational leaders move people to focus on higher-order needs (self-esteem and self-actualization). When organizations face a turbulent environment, intense competition, products that may die early, and the need to move fast, managers cannot rely solely on organizational structure to guide organizational activity. In these situations, transformational leadership can motivate followers to be fully engaged and inspired, to internalize the goals and values of the organization, and to move forward with dogged determination!

Transformational leadership is positively related to follower satisfaction, performance, and acts of citizenship. These effects result from the fact that transformational leader behaviors elicit trust and perceptions of procedural justice, which in turn favorably impact follower satisfaction and performance.[101] As R. Pillai, C. Schriesheim, and E. Williams note, "when followers perceive that they can influence the outcomes of decisions that are important to them and that they are participants in an equitable relationship with their leader, their perceptions of procedural justice [and trust] are likely to be enhanced."[102] Trust and experiences of organizational justice promote leader effectiveness, follower satisfaction, motivation, performance, and citizenship behaviors.

Charismatic Leadership

http://www.winstonchurchill.org

charisma a special personal magnetic charm or appeal that arouses loyalty and enthusiasm in a leader-follower relationship

http://www.reagan.webteamone.com

charismatic leader person who possesses legitimate power that arises from "exceptional sanctity, heroism, or exemplary character"

Ronald Reagan, Jesse Jackson, and Queen Elizabeth I have something in common with Martin Luther King, Jr., Indira Gandhi, and Winston Churchill. The effectiveness of these leaders originates, in part, in their **charisma,** a special magnetic charm and appeal that arouses loyalty and enthusiasm. Each exerted considerable personal influence to bring about major events.

It is difficult to differentiate the charismatic and transformational leader. True transformational leaders may achieve their results through the magneticism of their personality. In this case, the two types of leaders are essentially one and the same, yet it is important to note that not all transformational leaders have a personal "aura."

Sociologist Max Weber evidenced an interest in charismatic leadership in the 1920s, calling **charismatic leaders** people who possess legitimate power that arises from "exceptional sanctity, heroism, or exemplary character."[103] Charismatic leaders "single-handedly" effect changes even in very large organizations. Their personality is a powerful force, and the relationship that they forge with their followers is extremely strong.

The charismatic leadership phenomenon involves a complex interplay between the attributes of the leader and followers' needs, values, beliefs, and perceptions.[104] At its extreme, leader-follower relationships are characterized by followers' unquestioning acceptance; trust in the leader's beliefs; affection; willing obedience, emulation of, and identification with the leader; emotional involvement with his or her mission; and feelings of self-efficacy directed toward the leader's mission.[105] This can work to better the welfare of individuals, such as when Lee Iacocca saved thousands of jobs through his dramatic turnaround of a failing corporate giant, the Chrysler Corporation. It also can be disastrous, as when David Koresh led dozens and dozens of men, women, and children to their fiery death in Waco, Texas. Individuals working for charismatic leaders often have higher task performance, greater task satisfaction, and lower levels of role conflict than those working for leaders with considerate or structuring behaviors.[106] What are the characteristics of these people who can exert such a strong influ-

Reprinted with special permission of King Features Syndicate, Inc.

ence over their followers? Charismatic leaders have a strong need for power and the tendency to rely heavily on referent power as their primary power base.[107] Charismatic leaders also are extremely self-confident and convinced of the rightness of their own beliefs and ideals. This self-confidence and strength of conviction make people trust the charismatic leader's judgment, unconditionally following the leader's mission and directives for action.[108] The result is a strong bond between leader and followers, a bond built primarily around the leader's personality. Table 11-2 summarizes the characteristics of charismatic and noncharismatic leaders.

Although there have been many effective charismatic leaders, those who succeed the most have coupled their charismatic capabilities with behaviors consistent with the same leadership principles followed by other effective leaders. Those who do not add these other dimensions still attract followers but do not meet organizational goals as effectively as they could. They are (at least for a time) the pied pipers of the business world, with lots of followers but no constructive direction.

LEADERSHIP NEEDS IN THE 21ST CENTURY

Frequent headlines in popular business magazines like *Fortune* and *Business Week* call our attention to a major movement going on in the world of business. Organizations are being reengineered and restructured, and network, virtual, and modular corporations are emerging. People talk about the transnational organization, the boundary-less company, the post-hierarchical organization. By the end of the decade, the organizations that we will be living in, working with,

TABLE 11-2 Behavioral Characteristics of Charismatic and Noncharismatic Leaders

	Noncharismatic Leader	**Charismatic Leader**
Relation to Status Quo	Agrees with status quo and strives to maintain it	Opposed to status quo and strives to change it
Future Goal	Goal not too discrepant from status quo	Idealized vision that is highly discrepant from status quo
Likeableness	Shared perspective makes him or her likable	Shared perspective and idealized vision make him or her a likable and honorable hero worthy of identification and imitation
Trustworthiness	Disinterested advocacy in persuasion attempts	Disinterested advocacy by incurring great personal risk and cost
Expertise	Expert in using available means to achieve goals within the framework of the existing order	Expert in using unconventional means to transcend the existing order
Behavior	Conventional, conforming to existing norms	Unconventional or counternormative
Environmental Sensitivity	Low need for environmental sensitivity to maintain status quo	High need for environmental sensitivity for changing the status quo
Articulation	Weak articulation of goals and motivation to lead	Strong articulation of future vision and motivation to lead
Power Base	Position power and personal power (based on reward, expertise, and liking for a friend who is a similar other)	Personal power (based on expertise, respect, and admiration for a unique hero)
Leader-Follower Relationship	Egalitarian, consensus seeking, or directive Nudges or orders people to share his or her views	Elitist, entrepreneur, and exemplary Transforms people to share the radical changes advocated

Source: Modified from J. A. Conger and R. N. Kanungo. 1987. Toward a behavioral theory of charismatic leadership in organizational settings. *Academy of Management Review* 12:641.

and competeing against are likely to be vastly different from what we know today. (See *An Inside Look* at control- and involvement-oriented leadership.)

The transition will not be easy; uncertainty tends to breed resistance. We are driven by linear and rational thinking, which leads us to believe that "we can get there from here," by making some incremental changes in who we are and what we are currently doing. Existing paradigms frame our perceptions and guide our thinking. Throwing away paradigms that have served us well in the past does not come easily.

A look back tells most observers that the past decade has been characterized by rapid change, intense competition, an explosion of new technologies, chaos, turbulence, and high levels of uncertainty. A quick scan of today's business landscape suggests that this trend is not going away anytime soon. According to Professor Jay A. Conger from Canada's McGill University, "In times of great transition, leadership becomes critically important. Leaders, in essence, offer us a pathway of confidence and direction as we move through seeming chaos. The magnitude of today's changes will demand not only *more* leadership, but *newer forms* of leadership."[109]

AN INSIDE LOOK

Control- and Involvement-Oriented Leadership

Control-Oriented Leadership
Leadership in the mechanistic organization with its control-oriented management practices in one of position in the organizational hierarchy. Power is concentrated at the top. Plans and decisions get made by a dominant coalition of upper-level managers, and directives flow downward to those at lower levels.

Top, middle, and lower-level managers use their position in the hierarchy to exercise leadership over those below them. Rewards and punishment secure the compliance demanded. Directives are given in the form of written rules, policies, and procedures. Unanticipated events are handled by the manager/leader, who decides the direction to be taken and then communicates it to those below.

Involvement-Oriented Leadership
Leadership in the high-involvement organization is radically different from that in the control-oriented organization. As environments become increasingly turbulent, threatening, competitive, dynamic, and uncertain, a new type of leadership is called for. Today, many organizations need individuals who possess a new leadership skill—the ability to manage chaos.

A tough job lies ahead for the new leader/managers; they must operate the old organization, design a new organization, create the culture that will enable it to grow and prosper, and orchestrate the transition from the old to the new when the climate is ready to support and nurture it. While all of this is happening, the external environment is not sitting around, waiting for your transition; instead, it is "beating your brains out"!

Only leadership can succeed in turning top-down, highly controlled organizations into lean, flexible, open, involvement-oriented organizations. Chaos will be part of the process. Managing chaos will require the ability to simultaneously build trust, commitment, and a sense of community; to intellectually stimulate followers to adopt the challenge that lies ahead; and to design work systems that nurture psychological ownership for tasks at hand and for the organization.

According to Conger, two major forces are defining for us the genius of the next generation of leaders. The first force is the organization's external environment. Global competitiveness is creating some unique leadership demands. The second force is the growing diversity in organizations' internal environments. Diversity will significantly change the relationship between organizational member, work, and the organization, in challenging, difficult, and also very positive ways.

What will the leaders of tomorrow be like? Professor Conger suggests that the effective leaders of the 21st century will have to be many things.[110] They will have to be *strategic opportunists;* only organizational visionaries will find strategic opportunities before competitors. They will have to be *globally aware*; with 80 percent of today's organizations facing significant foreign competition, knowledge of foreign markets, global economics, and geopolitics is crucial. They will have to be *capable of managing a highly decentralized organization*; movement toward the high-involvement organization will accelerate as the environmental demands for organizational speed, flexibility, learning, and leanness increase. They will have be *sensitive to diversity*; during the first few years of the 21st century, fewer than 10 percent of those entering the workforce in North America will be white, Anglo-Saxon males; and the incoming women, minorities, and immigrants will bring with them a very different set of needs and concerns. They will have to be *interpersonally competent*; a highly diverse workforce will necessitate a leader who is extremely aware, and sensitive, to multicultural expectations and needs. They will have to be *builders of an organizational community*; work and organizations will serve as a major source of need fulfillment, and in the process leaders will be called on to help build this community in such a way that organizational members develop a sense of ownership for the organization and its mission.

Finally, it is important to note that leadership theory construction and empirical inquiry are an ongoing endeavor. While the study of traits, behavior, and contingency models of leadership provide us with a great deal of insight into leadership, the mosaic is far from complete. During the past 15 years, several new theories of leadership have emerged; among them are leader member exchange theory, implicit leadership theory, neocharismatic theory, value-based theory of leadership, and visionary leadership,[111] each of which over time will add to our bank of knowledge about leaders and the leadership process.

Leaders of the 21st century organization have a monumental challenge awaiting them and a wealth of self-enriching and fulfilling opportunities. The challenge and rewards awaiting effective leaders are awesome!

LEADING ORGANIZATIONAL MEMBERS IN REVIEW

Leadership is a primary vehicle for fulfilling the directing function of management. Because of its importance, theorists, researchers, and practitioners have devoted a tremendous amount of attention and energy to unlocking the secrets of effective leadership. They have kept at this search for perhaps a greater period of time than for any other single issue related to management.

Organizations typically have both formal and informal leaders. Their leadership is effective for virtually identical reasons. Leadership and management are not the same. Although effective leadership is a necessary part of effective management, the overall management role is much larger than leadership alone. Managers plan, organize, direct, and control. As leaders, they are engaged primarily in the directing function.

There are many diverse perspectives on leadership. Some managers treat leadership primarily as an exercise of power. Others believe that a particular belief and attitude structure makes for effective leaders. Still others believe it is possible to identify a collection of leader traits that produces a leader who should be universally effective in any leadership situation. Even today, many believe that a profile of behaviors can universally guarantee successful leadership. Unfortunately, such simple solutions fall short of the reality.

It is clear that effective leaders are endowed with the "right stuff," yet this "stuff" is only a precondition to effective leadership. Leaders need to connect with their followers, bring the right configuration of knowledge, skills, ability, vision, and strategy to the situational demands confronting the group.

We now know that there is no one best way to be an effective leader in all circumstances. Leaders need to recognize that how they choose to lead will affect the nature of their followers' compliance with their influence tactics, and ultimately impacts motivation, satisfaction, performance, and group effectiveness. In addition, the nature of the situation—contextual demands and characteristics of the follower—dictates the type of leadership that is likely to be effective. Fiedler focuses on leader traits and argues that the favorableness of the leadership situation dictates the type of leadership approach needed. He recommends selecting leaders to match the situation or changing the situation to match the leader. Path-goal theory focuses on leader behavior that can be adapted to the demands of a particular work environment and organizational members' characteristics. Path-goal theorists believe both that leaders can be matched with the situation and that the situation can be changed to match leaders. Together, these theories make clear that leadership is effective when the characteristics and behavior of the leader match the demands of the situation.

In recent years, there has been a renewed interest in key leader traits and behaviors. As organizations face increasing amounts of chaos in their external environments, searches for "the right leader" who can bring about major organizational transformations has intensified. This search once again focuses our attention on a set of "key" motives, knowledge, skills, and personality attributes. Emerging from this search has been the identification of the charismatic and transformational leader.

Characteristics of followers, tasks, and organizations can substitute for or neutralize many leader behaviors. Leaders must remain aware of these factors, no matter which perspective on leadership they adopt. Such awareness allows managers to use substitutes for, and neutralizers of, leadership to their benefit, rather than be stymied by their presence.

Leadership in the high-involvement organization differs dramatically from that in the traditional and control-oriented organization. Leaders external to the team have as one of their primary roles empowering group members and the teams themselves to self-lead and self-manage. Leaders internal to the team are peers; they work alongside and simultaneously facilitate planning, organizing, directing, controlling, and the execution of the team's work.

Although we know a great deal about the determinants of effective leadership, we have much to learn. Each theory presented in this chapter is put into practice by managers every day. None provides the complete answer to what makes leaders effective, but each has something important to offer.

Finally, our understanding of leadership has many shortcomings and limitations. The existing literature is largely based on observations from a Western industrialized context. The extent to which our theories of leadership are bound by our culture, limiting generalization to other cultures, is largely unknown. Cross-cultural leadership research will no doubt intensify as the global economy becomes an ever more dominant force in the world.

A FINAL LOOK

During the winter, John thinks long and hard about how he can earn the respect of the Sea Lions staff. Before the season opener, John announces his plan: "So I can better understand what your day is like, I'm going to spend one day in each of your shoes. I'm trading places with each of you. I will be a ticket taker, a roving hotdog vendor, and a janitor. And I will be a marketer, and an accountant—for a day. You in turn will have the day off so you can enjoy the game from the general manager's box." The staff laughs and whistles appreciatively. Then the Springfield mascot, Sparky the Sea Lion, speaks up: "Hey Mr. Arroyo, are you going to spend a day in my flippers?" "You bet!" says John, laughing. The entire staff cheers.

John continues. "At the close of the season, we will honor a staff member with the T.J. Grevin Award, for outstanding contributions to the Sea Lions organization. T.J. was such a great guy, it's only right that we honor him." The meeting ends, but John's staff linger to tell him how excited they are about his ideas. Amidst the handshakes, he hopes that this year may be the best year yet for the Sea Lions.

KEY TERMS

charisma, 412
charismatic leader, 412
consideration, 400
contingency theory of leadership, 403
designated leader, 390
emergent leader, 390
formal leader, 389
great man theory of leadership, 396
informal leader, 390
initiating structure, 400
leadership, 386
least preferred co-worker (LPC), 403
path-goal theory of leadership, 406
transformational leader, 411
visionary leader, 411

ISSUES FOR REVIEW AND DISCUSSION

1. Define leadership and distinguish between leadership and management.
2. Discuss the processes associated with people coming to positions of leadership.
3. Discuss the different forms of power available to leaders and the effects associated with each.
4. It has been observed that effective leaders have the "right stuff." What traits are commonly associated with leader emergence and effective leaders?
5. Both The Ohio State University and University of Michigan leadership studies identified central leader behaviors. What are these behaviors and how are they different from one another?
6. Blake and Mouton's work with the Leadership Grid® identified several leadership types. What are they and how does this leadership model look from the perspective of situation theories of leadership?
7. Identify and describe the three situational variables presented in Fiedler's contingency theory of leadership.
8. What are the four leadership behaviors in the path-goal theory of leadership?
9. Discuss the differences between the internal and external leadership roles surrounding self-managed work teams.
10. What are substitutes for leadership? What are neutralizers? Give an example of each.
11. What are the distinguishing features of the transformational and charismatic leader?

EXERCISES

LEADERSHIP: ITS ESSENCE

Exercise Schedule

	Unit Time	*Unit Time*
1. **Individual reflection**	**5 min**	**5 min**
2. **Small group discussion**	**10–15 min**	**15–20 min**
3. **Lists presented**	**5 min**	**20–25 min**
4. **Groups discuss leadership**	**5–10 min**	**25–35 min**
5. **Characteristics shared**	**5–15 min**	**30–35 min**

1. **Individual reflection** — **5 min** — **5 min**
Think of two leaders or bosses you have worked under. First think of a really awful boss, maybe the worst one you ever had and, in the following table, describe that person's behavior. Next, think of a really good boss, this time the best one, and describe that person's behavior. Be specific. Don't say merely, "motivating," but rather list what the person actually did that motivated you.

2. **Small group discussion** — **10–15 min** — **15–20 min**
In groups of 4–7, discuss what you see about leadership as a whole from these lists. Come up with a list of the behaviors you all agree with for both good and bad leadership. Post your lists for the whole class to see, or write them all on the blackboard.

3. **Lists presented** — **5 min** — **20–25 min**
Your instructor will quickly read the lists.

4. **Groups discuss leadership** — **5–10 min** — **25–35 min**
Resume discussion with your group. Using all the lists, determine the essence of what is being said about good and bad leadership. What are the main differences in these lists—what do all of the good things have in common? What do all the bad things have in common? Now try to state the essence of good leadership and bad leadership. Post these for the class to see.

5. **Characteristics shared** — **5–15 min** — **30–35 min**
Your instructor will now lead you in a whole-class discussion on the essence of leadership.

INDIVIDUAL WORKSHEET

Bad Leadership	Good Leadership

GROUP WORKSHEET 1

Bad Leadership	Good Leadership

THE ESSENCE OF LEADERSHIP WORKSHEET 2

List one characteristic in each space below.

Bad Leadership	Good Leadership

Source: Adapted by D. Marcic from M. McKnight, *Organizational behavior as a phenomenological free-will centered science,* presented at the Organizational Behavior Teaching Conference, June 1997. From *Organizational behavior: Experiences and cases* (6th ed.), by D. Marcic, J. Seltzer, and P. Vaill, copyright 2001. Reprinted with the permission of South-Western, a division of Thomson Learning. Fax 800-730-2215.

INFOTRAC

INFOTRAC® COLLEGE EDITION

The articles listed below are a sampling of those available through InfoTrac College Edition. You can search for them either by title or by the author's name.

Articles

1. How to influence leaders. (lessons in leadership) (Cover Story) Mary Lippitt. *Training & Development* March 1999 v53 i3 p18(5) Bus.Coll.: 115Q1259
2. Is it better to be loved or feared? (leadership) Michael A. Ledeen. *Across the Board* Sept 1999 v36 i8 p9(2)
3. Re-examining the components of transformational and transactional leadership using the Multifactor Leadership Questionnaire. Bruce J. Avolio, Bernard M. Bass, Dong I. Jung. *Journal of Occupational and Organizational Psychology* Dec 1999 v72 i4 p441
4. Another kind of leader. (George W. Bush) (Brief Article) Gloria Borger. *U.S. News and World Report* Jan 29, 2001 v130 i4 p21
5. A Leadership Credo for the New Millennium. (Brief Article) Jerome Tillman. *Black Issues in Higher Education* Jan 4, 2001 v17 i23 p136

Questions

For All Articles:

The articles in this list explore various leadership qualities. Have members of your group read them and report any new information on leadership skills that they discover. After all members read Chapter 11 and the assigned articles, ask each person to rank essential leadership skills in order of importance and then defend the ranking system to the other members of the group. Discuss the group's agreements and disagreements.

For All Articles:
Have members of your group brainstorm for a few minutes to name at least six people in leadership roles whom they admire or respect (it doesn't matter what area the leaders come from—business, government, sports, religion, or other areas). Then identify which leadership skills you think these people have and how they demonstrate these skills. Be as specific as possible.

WEB EXERCISE

Tour the website for the Center for Creative Leadership (http://www.ccl.org). What are the key issues being discussed at the Center today?

CASE
Which Style Is Best?

The ABC Company is a medium-sized corporation which manufactures automotive parts. Recently, the company president attended a leadership seminar and came away deeply impressed with the effect various leadership styles could have on the output and morale of the organization.

In mulling over how he might proceed, the president decided to use the services of Paul Patterson, a management consultant, who was currently reviewing the goals and objectives of the company. The president told Paul about the leadership seminar and how impressed he had been and that a leadership survey of the company was desired.

They determined that the division headed by Donald Drake should be the test case and that Paul would report to the president on completion of that survey. Some of the notes made by Paul in his interviews with the key managers in Drake's division follow.

Amy Allen

Amy is very proud of her section's output. She has always stressed the necessity for good control procedures and efficiency. She is very insistent that her subordinates fully understand project instructions and that follow-up communications be rapid, complete, and accurate. Amy serves as the clearinghouse for all incoming and outgoing work. She gives small problems to one individual to complete, but, if problems are large, she calls in several key people. Usually, her employees are briefed on what the policy is to be, what part of the report each subordinate is to complete, and the completion date. Amy considers this as the only way to get full coordination without lost motion or an overlap of work.

Amy considers it best for a boss to remain aloof from her subordinates and believes that being "buddy-buddy" tends to hamper discipline. She does her "chewing out" and praising in private. She believes that people in her section know where they stand.

According to Amy, the biggest problem in business today is that subordinates do not accept responsibility. She states that her people have lots of opportunities to show what they can do but not many try very hard.

Amy commented that she does not understand how her subordinates got along with the previous section head, who ran a very "loose ship." Amy stated that her boss is quite happy with the way things go in her section.

Bob Black

Bob believes that every employee has a right to be treated as an individual and espouses the theory that it is a boss's responsibility and duty to cater to employees' needs. He noted that he is constantly doing little things for his subordinates and gave, as an example, his presentation of two tickets to an art show to be held at the City Gallery next month. He stated that the tickets cost $15.00 each but that it will be both educational and enjoyable for the employee and her spouse. This was done to express his appreciation for a good job the person had done a few months back.

Bob says he always makes a point of walking through his section at least once each day, stopping to speak to at least 25 percent of the employees on each trip.

Bob does not like to "knock" anyone, but he noted that Amy Allen ran one of those "taut ships." He stated that Amy's employees are probably not too happy, but there is not much they can do but wait for her to move.

Bob said he had noticed a little bit of bypassing going on in the company but that most of it is due to the press of business. His idea is to run a friendly, low-key operation with a happy group of subordinates. Although he confesses that his section might not be as efficient in terms of speedy outputs as other units, he considers he has far greater subordinate loyalty and higher morale, and his subordinates work well as an expression of their appreciation of his (Bob's) enlightened leadership.

Charlie Carr

Charlie says his principal problem is the shifting of responsibilities between his section and others in the division. He considers his section the "fire drill" area that gets all of the rush, hot items, whether or not they belong in his section. He seems to think this is caused by his immediate superior's not being sure who should handle which jobs in the division.

Charlie admits he has not tried to stop this practice. He stated that it makes the other section heads jealous, but they are afraid to complain. They seem to think Charlie is a personal friend of the division manager, but Charlie says this is not true.

Charlie said he used to be embarrassed in meetings when it was obvious he was doing jobs out of his area but he has gotten used to it by now, and apparently the other section heads have also.

Charlie's approach to discipline is to keep everyone busy and "you won't have those kinds of problems." He stated that a good boss does not have time to hold anybody's hand, like Bob Black does, and tell them what a great job they are doing. Charlie believes that if you promise people you will keep an eye on their work for raises and promotion purposes, most of the problems will take care of themselves.

Charlie stated that he believes in giving a subordinate a job and then letting him or her do it without too much checking on the work. He believes most of his subordinates do their jobs reasonably well.

If Charlie has a problem, it is probably that the role and scope of his section have become a little blurred by current practices. Charlie stated that he thinks he should resist a recent tendency for "company people above my division manager's level" to call him up to their offices to hear his ideas on certain programs; however, Charlie is not sure that this can be stopped without creating a ruckus. He says he is studying the problem.

Don Drake

As division manager, Don thinks things are going pretty well, since he has not had any real complaints from his superiors in the company, beyond the "small problem" type of thing. He thinks his division is at about the same level of efficiency as the other divisions in the organization.

His management philosophy is to let the section managers find their own level, organizational niche, and form of operation and then check to see if the total output of the division is satisfactory. He stated that he has done this with his present section heads. This was the policy being used when Don was a section head, and it has worked fine for him.

Don considers his function to be that of a clearinghouse for division inputs and outputs. He sees his job basically as a coordinating one, coupled with the requirement for him to "front" for the division. He believes that subordinates should be allowed to expand their job activities as much as they are able to do so. Don noted that Charlie Carr had expanded greatly as a manager since Don had arrived. Don frequently takes Charlie with him to high-level meetings in the company, since Charlie knows more about the division's operations than anyone else.

Don noted that both Amy and Bob seem to do a credible job in their sections. He has very little contact with Amy's employees but occasionally has to see one of Bob Black's workers about something the employee has fouled up. This results from the fact that Bob considers such a face-to-face confrontation between a division manager and lower-level section employees a good lesson to impress on subordinates that they have let down their boss. Don Drake said he is not too keen on this procedure, but that Bob considers it a most valuable training device to teach employees to do a good job every time, so Don goes along with it.

Source: This case was prepared by W. D. Heier.

Questions

1. How would you characterize the leadership styles of each of the managers described in this case?
2. Where would you place each on the Leadership Grid®?
3. Which of the four would you prefer to have as a boss?
4. Which of the four appears to be the most effective? least effective?

Outline

The nature of organizing

Differentiation—organizational departmentalization

Differentiation—organizational superstructures

Integration—coordinating organizational activities and units

Employee responses to organizational design

Organizing and coordinating the work of the organization in review

PHOTO: © RAOUL MINSART/CORBIS

CHAPTER 12

Organizing and Coordinating the Work of the Organization

Learning Objectives

After reading this chapter, you should be able to

1. Discuss the meaning of organizing as a managerial activity and the different approaches to it.
2. Explain the difference between formal and informal organizations.
3. Identify and differentiate between the various approaches to departmentalization.
4. Identify the major approaches to organizational superstructure.
5. Outline the ways managers integrate the different levels in the organization's hierarchy and between activities at the same level in the hierarchy.
6. Describe the relationship between organizational differentiation and integration.
7. Discuss employee responses to several organizational design features.

A FIRST LOOK

At FourPaws, Inc., a mid-sized designer and manufacturer of pet supplies, business is booming. In light of the company's strong performance, the strategic planners are leaning on the marketing and operations teams to develop new and more innovative products. However, the operations team is swamped and under pressure to meet shipment deadlines.

The team leaders of the marketing and operations teams constantly lock horns about which products should get priority. Marketing leader Sam Truong has just met with Patricia Wetzel, the operations leader, and is fuming. Sam and the rest of the marketing team understand the strategy planner's big picture and have great ideas for new products. They just need operations to buy in. However, Patricia and her group always have reasons why they can't proceed with new products. For example, operations is already behind schedule on current products and doesn't believe they can add anything new. They argue that quality will be compromised if they continually begin assembly on new products. They have also requested a stable roll-out schedule, which the strategy and marketing teams have never provided.

Questions: Do you think that the tension at FourPaws is typical of similar companies? Are the strategy, marketing, and operations teams interdependent? What can be done to ease this tension and improve both marketing and productivity?

All organizations have work that must be done so they can achieve their mission, be it the delivery of health care, the creation and dissemination of knowledge, the manufacture of computers, the provision of psychiatric care, or extinguishing fires. Think, for a moment, about the activities employees perform at your university: scheduling courses, cleaning windows, ordering supplies, teaching classes, conducting research, maintaining student records, preparing food, photocopying, and so on. The management activity of organizing attempts to bring order and direction to the work of organizations so that plans are implemented effectively and goals are achieved. Without this activity, you might show up in a classroom only to have breakfast served, a lawn mower repaired, or a lecture given about a subject you are not studying. Without organizing, academic life would be chaotic for students, professors, and staff. This is true for all organizations, regardless of the societal need (see Chapter 1 for a discussion of societal needs and types of organizations) the organization serves. In this chapter and the next, we discuss organizing as a managing activity, organizational design that results from the organizing activity, and employee attitudinal, motivational, and behavioral responses to different organizational designs.

THE NATURE OF ORGANIZING

In Chapter 1, we introduced the concept of "organization." We suggested that some (for example, those managers who subscribe to the classical school of management thought) see organizations as tools, created and designed to fulfill a societal need. We also observed that for others, organizations are social systems. As previously noted, your authors view organizations as social-technical systems created to achieve a set of goals through people-to-people and people-to-work

http://www.frogleap.com
http://www.canucks.com

relationships. We suggested that the internal environments of Frog's Leap Winery, Steinlagger Brewery, the Vancouver Canucks, and the 3M Corporation will all look different, much as a saw looks different from a hammer, chisel, and pliers. The anatomy of the organization, those parts of its internal environment, is designed based on management's attitudes and assumptions about, for example, work, people, systems, the goals of the organization, as well as forces within the organization's task environment. A hospital, for example, has different organizational needs than a university, a museum, or a federal agency. As a consequence, these organizations will have very different designs.

Organizing Defined

organizing the activity of designing, structuring, arranging, and rearranging the components of an organization's internal environment

Organizing occurs when organizational members design, structure, arrange, and rearrange the components of their organization's internal environment (recall our discussion of internal environments in Chapter 2). It is this activity that creates the socio-technical system that managers believe will accomplish the organization's goals in an efficient and effective manner. In an effort to meet its goal of delivering high-quality health care, Merriner Hospital in Madison, Wisconsin, has placed both in- and outpatient facilities, emergency room, and trauma center on the first floor of the building to treat critical patients quickly.

Organizing creates the vehicle needed to reach a company's goals. When organizational goals are varied and complex, the organizing activity requires great sophistication. A hospital's housekeeping department may set a goal to clean all patient rooms by 3 p.m., which is, of course, very different from the surgical department's goal of losing no patients in open-heart surgery. The people-to-people and people-to-work relationships that function well for housekeeping will be very different from those that function well for the surgical unit. Each unit and network in the system is organized to help the hospital achieve its overall goal of high-quality health service.

An effective and efficient organizational design is critical to a hospital's mission.

Managers organize by defining and coordinating work at a number of different levels: Tasks are grouped to form jobs or teams, jobs and/or teams are combined into departments, and departments are organized into divisions. For example, answering phones and greeting visitors are part of the hospital receptionist's job. Secretaries open mail, process letters, and arrange meetings. Both jobs are found in the hospital's clerical services department. Processing applications, interviewing and hiring job applicants, and conducting performance appraisals are tasks performed in the hospital's human resources department. Together, the clerical services and human resources departments form the hospital's administrative services division. The hospital's linen and housekeeping departments are part of its environmental services division.

A variety of systems are created to support the organization and coordinate tasks, jobs, teams, departments, and divisions. Authority, communication, and coordination systems, for example, link and integrate jobs, teams, and departments. The coordination system of a data processing subsidiary enables its employees to present the following information at its parent company's annual meeting: number of new customers during the past year (from marketing), amount of revenue these contracts generated (from accounting), information on equipment downtime (from operations), and so forth. Managers must organize the systems needed to fulfill all of the organization's coordination needs.

Formal and Informal Organizations

formal organization the official structures and systems consciously designed by organizational members; the relatively enduring people-to-people and people-to-work interaction patterns created to accomplish organizational goals

informal organization joint activity between two or more individuals not formally designed that possibly contributes to joint results

In any organization, there are both formal and informal systems. The **formal organization** is that system that is consciously created through the organizing activity.[1] The formal organization consists of official structures and systems. These people-to-people and people-to-work systems are constructed to help people pool their time, energy, and talents to reach common objectives.

In contrast the **informal organization** exists when two or more people interact for a purpose or in a manner not specified by the formal organization. The informal organization refers to any *joint activity between two or more individuals without conscious joint purpose, even though possibly contributing to joint results*.[2] Informal groups reflect relationships that don't appear on the organizational chart. Such groups might include the water-cooler group, the morning-coffee regulars, and the Friday-evening bowlers.

Social psychologists have long researched why and how informal organizations emerge. Informal organizations evolve in a natural and unplanned manner. They are an outgrowth of the social and personal needs of organizational members. These needs, when coupled with physical proximity and opportunity, give rise to interactions that, when repeated, become an informal organization. As an informal organization the morning-coffee regulars are a group of people who interact on a regular basis, but they have no conscious common purpose (a work task to accomplish) toward which they are pooling their time and energies. Each member of the group brings their own needs/wants to their participation.

Over time, informal groups develop fairly stable memberships, their own communication networks, leaders, norms of acceptable and unacceptable behaviors, rewards and sanctions. Virtually all formal organizations have informal organizations, whose existence is neither "for" nor "against" the formal organization. Many of them have little or no impact on the successful operation of the formal organization. It is possible, however, for informal organizations to engage in activities that promote (or impede) the goals of the formal organization, such as was witnessed in the Hawthorne studies when employees exposed to management's lighting experiments decided to cooperate by becoming more productive.

Informal organizations may evolve into formal organizations, as when nurses in the geriatric ward of a hospital meet to discuss problems they have with doctors and patients and consciously form a "Work Problems Action Committee." Because members of the informal organization exchange information, satisfy individual needs, and influence one another, the informal organization can have direct and significant implications for the formal organization.

In the formal organization, managers prescribe expected behaviors through job descriptions, rules, policies, and operating procedures. In contrast, informal behaviors arise from the needs, norms, values, and standards of organizational members. The formal organization that assembles bathroom exhaust fans, for example, might specify the time to show up for work, the type of clothing permissible, the method to be used to assemble bathroom exhaust fans, and the minimum number of fans that must be produced per hour. The informal organization, however, may define a social norm that states that employees should not produce more than a certain number of fans per hour.

Managers need to recognize that both formal and informal organizations exist and that both influence the overall efficiency and effectiveness of their organization. Rather than fight informal organizations, managers should endeavor to benefit from them. Informal norms requiring ethical behavior, for example, can be useful, as can the "grapevine" that keeps people abreast of happenings at all levels of the formal organization.

Organizing—Timing and Tactics

When do managers engage in the organizing activity and what tactics do they use to guide the process?

Timing Organizing activities are performed at two distinct times in the organization's life cycle. First, the organizing activity accompanies the birth of the organization. Someone needs to create the organization for the very first time. Consider, for example, the emergence of the high-tech organizations (e.g., Gateway Computer, E-Bay, Cisco) that are now key players in the information revolution that is sweeping its way across the globe. Twenty-five years ago, there was no Amazon.com, Yahoo, or Oracle. Bill Gates and Paul Allen's vision in 1977 of a product and a radically different organization brought Microsoft, the formal organization, into being.

http://www.oracle.com

Second, the organizing activity is engaged in when organizations grow in size, take on new activities, downsize, or reshuffle internal arrangements to achieve better economies of operation. Microsoft has organized and reorganized as it endeavors to accommodate increased sales volume, product line, and changing market conditions. Mergers and acquisitions, such as the merger of America Online and Time Warner, necessitate organizing activities. Thus, these two organizations will need to find a way to integrate into a single organization, one that serves the purposes of the old needs and mission as well as the new organization that will evolve. Thus, organizing as a managing activity gets performed with the creation of organizations, and on a more-or-less continuing basis as the organization grows, downsizes, takes on new businesses, and reconfigures its internal activities.

http://www.timewarner.com

Tactics Managers approach the organizing activity in several ways: by working from the top of the organization down (the *top-down* approach), from the bottom up (the *bottom-up* approach), or from a *hybrid* perspective (a combination of the first two). Organizing also unfolds *incrementally*, with "a change here and a change there" as organizational needs dictate.

As a top-down activity, managers start with the mission of the organization and decide about what major divisions will accomplish this mission. Thus, the organization's super- or top structure is created. Each division is then divided into departments, as managers work from the top on down to the technical core to create their organization. Let's follow a hypothetical top-down General Motors decision. Suppose GM decides to manufacture two new brands of automobiles (family cars and mini-vans). GM also decides that the two brands should compete with each other. To make this plan a reality, GM creates a separate division for each brand. Virtually all of the activities needed to manufacture and market each automobile will be housed in their respective division. Following the creation of such departments as marketing, production, and human resources, activities are further subdivided, and finally each job in the manufacture and assembly process is structured.

Bottom-up organizing is, of course, just the reverse. All the tasks needed to manufacture and market the family cars and mini-vans are combined into jobs, which are grouped into departments, which are grouped into divisions. The organizing activity progresses from the bottom of the organization upward, building and ultimately integrating everything at the desk of the CEO. Thus, coordination, decision-making, and communication systems that link elements in the organization's technical core are put into place. Much like the strings attached to each moving part of a puppet, the lines run from the bottom of the puppet up and ultimately to the puppeteer—it is at this point that all the strings come together for their ultimate coordination and control.

The hybrid approach to organizing combines the top-down and bottom-up approaches. Management looks at the organization's institutional-level needs, its task environment, and the mission and strategies to be implemented. This guides their formation of the organization's superstructure (top-level or dominant structure). With an "eye focused on" the organization's institutional-level needs and superstructure, tasks, jobs, departments and divisions, communication, coordination, power, and decision-making structures are created, which results in the overall organization and its people-to-people and people-to-work interaction patterns.

Incremental organizing is ongoing. Incremental organizing is engaged in whenever an existing organization downsizes its operations (for example, some existing job is eliminated; a department, division, or product line is sold or outsourced) and/or when an existing organization takes on some new activity (a new job, department, division, product, service). Thus, managing in general and organizing in particular represent an ongoing activity where incremental changes are made to the design of jobs, the composition of work teams and departments, the location of decision-making authority, and communication and coordination systems that make the organization run more smoothly and efficiently.

DIFFERENTIATION—ORGANIZATIONAL DEPARTMENTALIZATION

Sources of Differentiation

organizational differentiation the differences in time and goal orientation, work performed, and organizational function and responsibility served by employees and work units

The concept differentiation means to become distinct or different in character. As applied to the organizational context, **organizational differentiation** focuses on the differences that exist among individuals, groups, departments, and organizational divisions. Differentiation occurs because of a number of forces, among them, differences in time orientation, goal orientation, work performed, and organizational function and responsibility served. Each force influences the cognitive and emotional orientation of the members of the organization, as well as differences between work units.[3]

The greater the degree of organizational differentiation (that is, the more differences there are among interdependent individuals and work units), the more complex and difficult the management process. For example, if research and development is working on projects for the organization's competitive position in the year 2030, and the production department is struggling to meet next week's production schedule, the two departments have a time differentiation such that R & D employees may be willing to take a couple of days out of their schedule for a mission meeting, while the production may be very resistant to participating. The greater the degree of organizational differentiation, the greater the organization's need for **integration** (organizational integration)—that is, finding ways to coordinate the work of these differentiated individuals and work units.

integration (organizational integration) the means used to coordinate and integrate the work of employees and work units

In the next section we discuss the different ways work activities are grouped into work units. This grouping process is one of the major forces that give rise to the differentiation experienced in organizations. Later in this chapter we discuss how organizations coordinate and integrate their needs.

Organizational Departmentalization

There are many activities (task and jobs) that need to be performed as organizations go about attempting to make their goals a reality. In addition, there are time, skill and ability, attention, and motivational limitations that constrain employees in terms of how much they can get done. Managers are no different; they also come to realize that there is an optimal level to the number of activities they can personally supervise. This limitation is referred to as the upper limit to one's *span of control*. This is why jobs are grouped into larger organizational units (such as work groups and departments) and work units into divisions. Without this organizing process, control of jobs, teams, and the coordination and integration of work would be impossible. The process of grouping jobs/teams into work units and those units into larger units, is called **departmentalization**.

departmentalization the process of grouping jobs/teams into organizational units and those units into larger units

http://www.zimbrick.com

Departmentalization answers the question, What activities do we want to "house together" and coordinate at the same place in the organizational hierarchy? For example, does Zimbrick, a large automobile dealer in the Midwest, want to locate (and therefore coordinate) all salespeople in one department, or does it want to coordinate new-car sales in one organizational unit and used-car sales in another? Should foreign and domestic car sales be combined? Should the purchasing department be coordinated with operations or with marketing? When a new job or group of jobs is created, where in the organizational hierarchy should these activities be managed? As shown in Figure 12-1, activities are grouped at all levels of the organization. Groupings at the very top of an organization create the organization's *superstructure,* which we discuss later in this chapter.

Through the years, various ways to group (departmentalize) organizational activities have been tried. Two basic approaches to departmentalizing dominate. The first approach groups activities that are within the same "family." "Family groupings" represent the most traditional approach to departmentalization. Among the traditional approaches to departmentalization are: function, product/service, territory, customer/client, process/equipment, and project. Traditional companies also take a hybrid approach. The second approach to departmentalization groups activities (jobs, departments, teams) by how interdependent they are. A third approach appears to be evolving with the advent of the high-involvement organization, in which groupings revolve around clusters of teams.

FIGURE 12-1 Departmentalization: The Grouping of Jobs at Different Levels

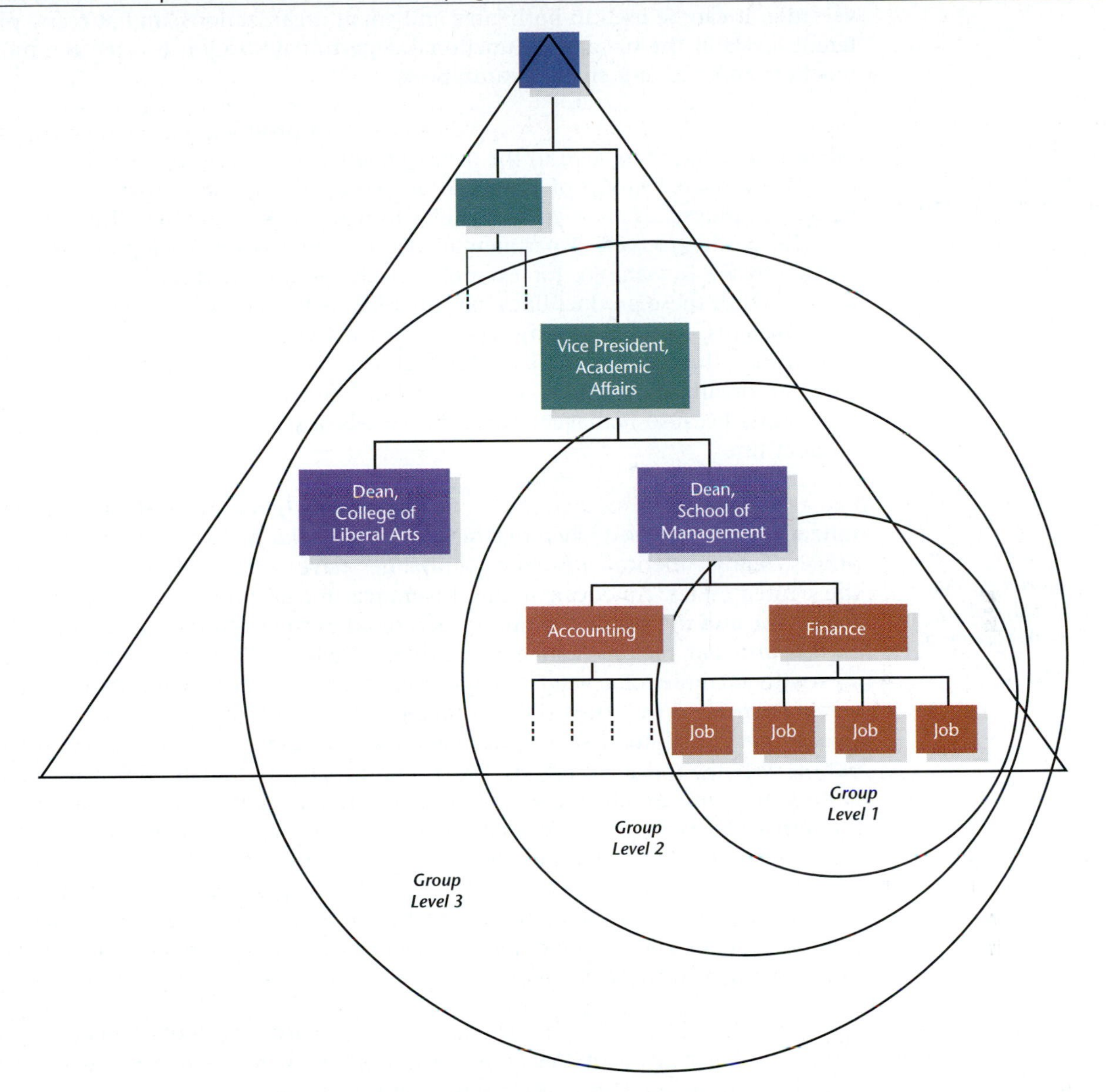

Departmentalization—Traditional Approaches

functional departmentalization the grouping of jobs by the organizational function served

Departmentalization by Function Managers create **functional departments** by grouping activities according to the nature of the work performed. Thus, similar activities are coordinated from a single place in the organizational hierarchy. Activities that support an organization's operations system, for example, are placed in an operations department. A marketing department controls only marketing activities. Each functional unit may be broken down further. Although the names given to functional departments vary from one organization to another, common terms in for-profit organizations are operations, marketing, finance, accounting, human resources, engineering, and research and development.

The functional approach to departmentalization is widely used because it is versatile. It can be used in both large and small organizations, and at many different levels in the hierarchy. Functional departmentalization is often the most practical approach for small organizations.

product/service departmentalization the grouping of jobs by products and/or services

Departmentalization by Product/Service In **product/service departmentalization,** activities related to the development and delivery of a single product (or closely related group of products) are grouped together. Progressive Video Images employs this approach with their movie, audio, and video departments.

The product/service departmentalization approach can be logical and efficient. Procter & Gamble, for example, produces and markets both soap and food. Each of these product lines has different technical and business properties and problems, so the company separates the activities that produce Ivory Soap from those that produce Crisco. Product/service departments are also useful when an organization wishes to treat product/service lines as independent business units, because managers can more readily assess the profitability of each product line.

territorial (geographical) departmentalization the grouping of organizational activities by different geographical areas

Departmentalization by Territory **Territorial (geographical) departmentalization** is often used when organizations have widely dispersed operations or offices. Many American insurance companies have regional offices throughout the United States. American Family Insurance, for example, has three separate territories, and the regional office in each handles the insurance issues that arise in its particular region. Similarly, Enbridge/Lakehead Pipeline Company operates with facilities in several Canadian Provinces (Alberta, Saskatchewan, and Quebec) and two U.S. states (North Dakota and Minnesota).

The territorial approach moves operations closer to raw materials, to distribution systems, and to customers. Sometimes geographic variations in laws, regulations, and customs change the nature of doing business enough that territorial arrangements work better. Regulations on the sale and servicing of insurance differ from state to state, and each American Family Insurance Company regional office is responsible for complying with the regulations within its territory. Territorial departmentalization makes it easier for American Family to develop systems and train employees to cope with the requirements of the various states served by each region.

customer/client departmentalization the grouping of organizational activities by different clients and client needs

Departmentalization by Customer/Client **Customer/client departmentalization** organizes activities around the type of customer or customer needs served by an organization. Wells Fargo Bank Company, like other banks, organizes its services around different types of customer groups. It is common, for example, for banks to have personal banking, small business, and commercial (big business) departments.

http://www.newsweek.com

This approach to departmentalization enables organizations to focus on and effectively serve the varying needs of identifiably different customer groups. Newsweek, Inc., for example, distributes the *Newsweek* magazine nationwide. It also prints *Newsweek Woman,* a version aimed at its female subscribers; *Newsweek Executive Plus,* for its professional and managerial subscribers; and a number of international versions, such as *The Bulletin with Newsweek,* the best selling magazine in Australia.

Departmentalization by Process There are two somewhat different approaches to departmentalization by process. The first focuses on the transformation process, commonly the equipment employed, in the production of the organization's product and services. The second refers to the activities that create something of value for the customer.

transformational process/equipment departmentalization the grouping of organizational activities by the equipment and/or processes used in the production process

Somewhat related to functional departmentalization is **transformational process/equipment departmentalization.** Consider an organization that manufactures a variety of paper products for home, office, and industrial use. A transformational process- or equipment-oriented department would house and run the equipment needed to make all rolled-paper products, while another department would run the equipment needed to make individual sheets of paper, and so forth. Thus, the activities (jobs) associated with particular equipment are housed in a work unit separate and distinct from those activities associated with other equipment.

http://www.hallmark.com

Experiencing excessively long delays in the development of new greeting cards, Hallmark decided to reorganize. After examining the *process* of developing new cards, they abandoned their old approach of organizing around tasks and instead organized around the process associated with greeting card development. Today, rather than having all artists in one department, writers in another, and so forth, teams of artists, writers, accountants, marketers, and lithographers are assigned a holiday and work together to develop cards for it. This form of **process departmentalization** groups activities around the processes that take one or more kinds of input and create output that is of value to someone downstream (a customer) from this stage in the transformation process.

process departmentalization the grouping of organizational activities around all of the processes needed to produce a product of value for an organizationally internal or external customer

project departmentalization the grouping of organizational activities by special and unique ventures, activities, or undertakings

Departmentalization by Project Grouping activities by projects gives rise to **project departments.** Project groups address specific organizational undertakings (ventures, assignments, activities, goals). They may, for example, have a design or developmental mission. A medical equipment manufacturer might form a project department to develop the processes needed to grow a heart valve. An engineering consulting firm might form a project department to determine the feasibility of constructing a high-speed electromagnetic rail system linking Vancouver, Chicago, Toronto, Montreal, and New York.

Project groups are interesting organizational arrangements. People are commonly brought into a project department because of their particular skills or expertise. They remain part of the department until they have made their contribution; thus, people may join and leave the project at various times during its existence, so the membership at the end of the project may be different from what it was at the beginning. The project director may be one of the few members who remains with the department until the project is finished. Once the project has been completed, the project department—having fulfilled its mission—ceases to exist.

Project departments typically have an involvement-oriented approach to management and an organic organizational design (see Chapter 2 for a discussion of these two concepts). Not only are members of a project department likely to come and go at different stages of the project, but authority and positions of leadership shift as members bring their particular expertise to various phases. In addition, the unit's communication, coordination, and control systems change frequently. The nature of the people-to-people and people-to-work relationships may change often to accommodate the uncertain nature of the project.

hybrid departmentalization the grouping of organizational activities by two or more forms of departmentalization

The Hybrid Approach to Departmentalization Rather than limiting the organization to just one departmentalization strategy, most organizations use a number of approaches. **Hybrid departmentalization** calls for the simultaneous

FIGURE 12-2 Hybrid Approach to Departmentalization: The Comfort-Living Corporation

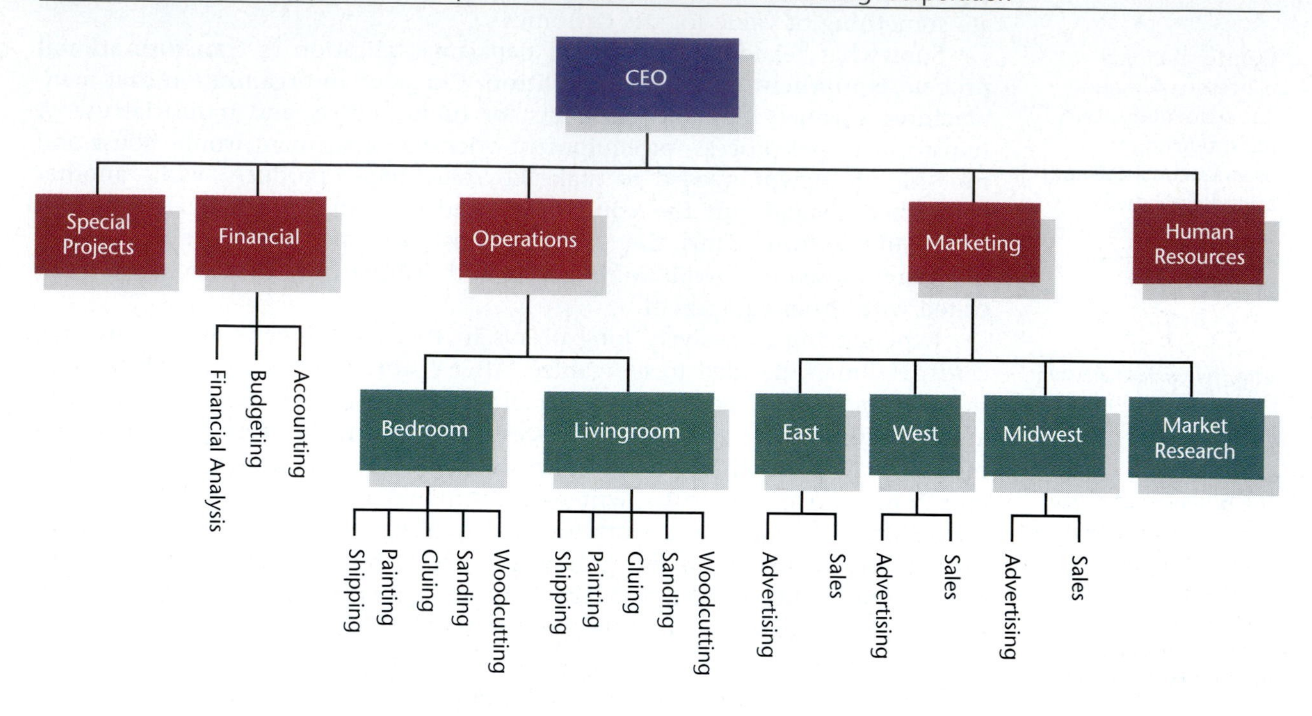

use of two or more departmentalization strategies. Figure 12-2 shows how managers at Comfort-Living Corporation, a home furnishings manufacturer and distributor, use the hybrid approach. Bjorn Eliason, owner of Comfort-Living, organizes top-level management according to organizational function and special projects. The operations department is subdivided by product into bedroom and livingroom departments, which are further broken down by process/equipment departmentalization. Gloria Troy, who supervises the marketing department's territories, is the head of a special project department on market research.

Thus far, we have discussed creating departments that group families of activities or mix family groups. There is a second approach to organizing departments—the interdependence approach.

Departmentalization—The Interdependence Approach

You may recall from Chapter 2 that the systems-theory perspective views each part of an organization as dependent on, and interrelated with, other organizational units. Operations managers, for example, need market information and financial resources from other departments to produce their organization's goods and services. As interdependence between jobs and organizational units increases, so do the costs and burdens of coordinating and controlling. As a consequence, many managers seek to minimize these problems by grouping together highly interdependent (tightly coupled) activities. This is called the **interdependence approach to departmentalization**. The idea is that costs and efficiencies will be minimized when such activities are coordinated from a common point (as opposed to being separated from one another) in the hierarchy.[4]

interdependence approach to departmentalization the grouping of activities based on the degree of coupling between them (jobs, teams, departments)

Four types of interdependence can exist between employees and work units (see Figure 12-3).[5] The lowest form of interdependence is *pooled interdependence*, in which employees, teams, or departments basically act independently, each doing their own work and depending only minimally on others. A group of sec-

FIGURE 12-3 Forms of Interdependence

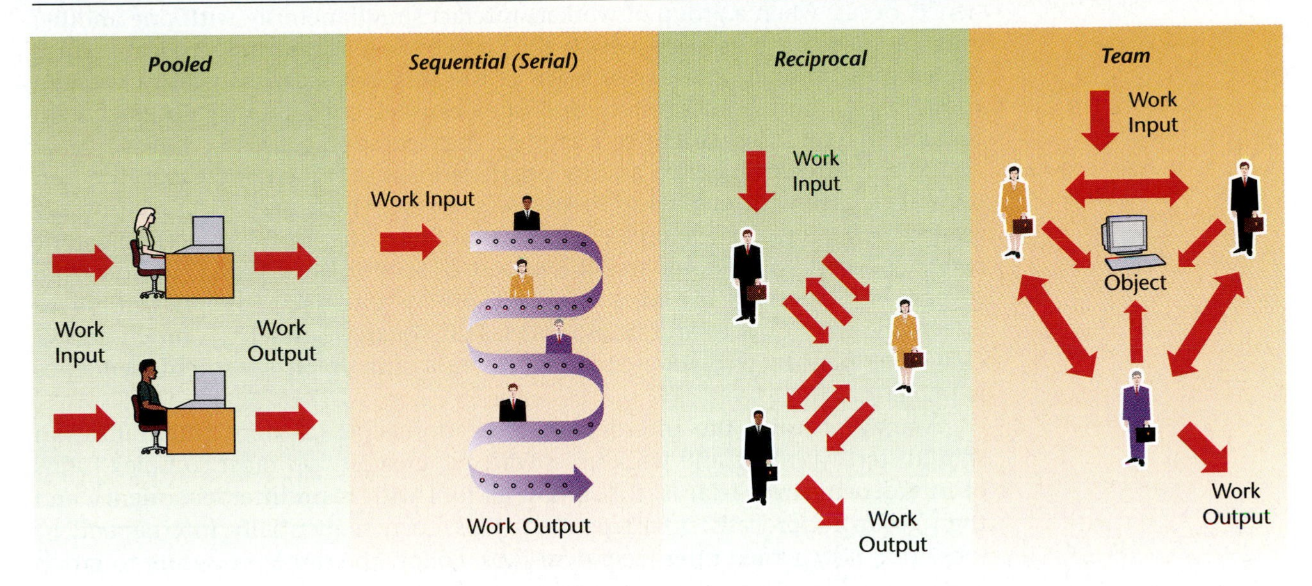

retaries, for example, is likely to have pooled interdependence. Each does their own piece of work from beginning to end. They are interdependent, however, in that the contribution from each secretary is necessary to the effectiveness of the entire organization, each has a job to perform, and the whole is affected if one does not do his or her work.

The next level of interdependence represents a more complex relationship. Under *sequential,* or *serial interdependence,* the object being worked on is passed from one worker or department to the next. The output of the first worker becomes the input for the second, whose output becomes the input for the third worker, and so on. This type of interdependence characterizes the assembly line. This workflow is characterized by both pooled and serial interdependence.

The third level is *reciprocal interdependence,* in which the object being worked on is passed back and forth among workers before the process is completed. When seeing a dentist, for example, a patient usually checks in with a receptionist. The receptionist guides the patient to a dental hygienist, who cleans the teeth before the dentist checks them. The dentist often transfers the checked patient back to the hygienist, who takes X rays and sends the patient back to the dentist for repair work. Finally, the patient revisits the receptionist to pay the bill and, perhaps, to schedule a future appointment before leaving the office. In reciprocal interdependence, production scheduling and coordinating are naturally more difficult than in pooled or sequential interdependence. Imagine what it would be like if your dental hygienist and your dentist, who have a reciprocal relationship with one another, were physically housed and coordinated out of different offices. You would then have to drive to the hygienist for X rays, cleaning, and preparation, then back to the dentist, then back to the hygienists for clean-up work—this is obviously ridiculous, time-consuming, costly, a burden, and a real pain. Hence the rationale for placing activities with reciprocal interdependence as close together as possible. The cost and burdens associated with coordination and control increase as the level of interdependence increases. Note that this workflow case is characterized by the simultaneous presence of pooled, serial, and reciprocal interdependencies.

Team interdependence, the highest and most complex form of interdependence, occurs when a group of workers interact simultaneously with one another and the object or person on which they're working. A hospital surgical team is the epitome of team interdependence as the surgeons, surgical assistants, anesthesiologist, nurses, and other support personnel continuously interact with one another and the patient to complete the operation.

As the interdependence among organizational members increases, the burdens associated with managing them also increase. Those managing reciprocally related activities, for example, must coordinate the flow of activities—the receipt of work to be done and the export of semifinished work—to and from several employees at the same time. A production delay by one employee affects the work flow to and from others. This situation presents a much greater challenge than the work flow along an assembly line in which interdependence is sequential.

Managers using the interdependence approaches to departmentalization should start with jobs and work units with the greatest and most complex forms of interdependence. That is, first group all jobs with team interdependence and then group reciprocally interdependent jobs, then sequentially interdependent jobs, and, last, pooled interdependent jobs. Follow the same procedure to group work units like teams in the hierarchy (see Figure 12-4). Those with reciprocal interdependence should have, if possible, a common point of coordination in the hierarchy and work units.

The interdependence approach is used by many hospitals. Groups with high levels of interdependence, such as surgical teams, are organized into a surgical department that covers of a wide range of jobs. A food service department might include dieticians, food preparation employees, and food delivery personnel, because these functions are interdependent; however, a maintenance department may consist only of those directly involved in the cleaning and repair of the physical facility.

FIGURE 12-4 Departmentalization of Interdependent Teams

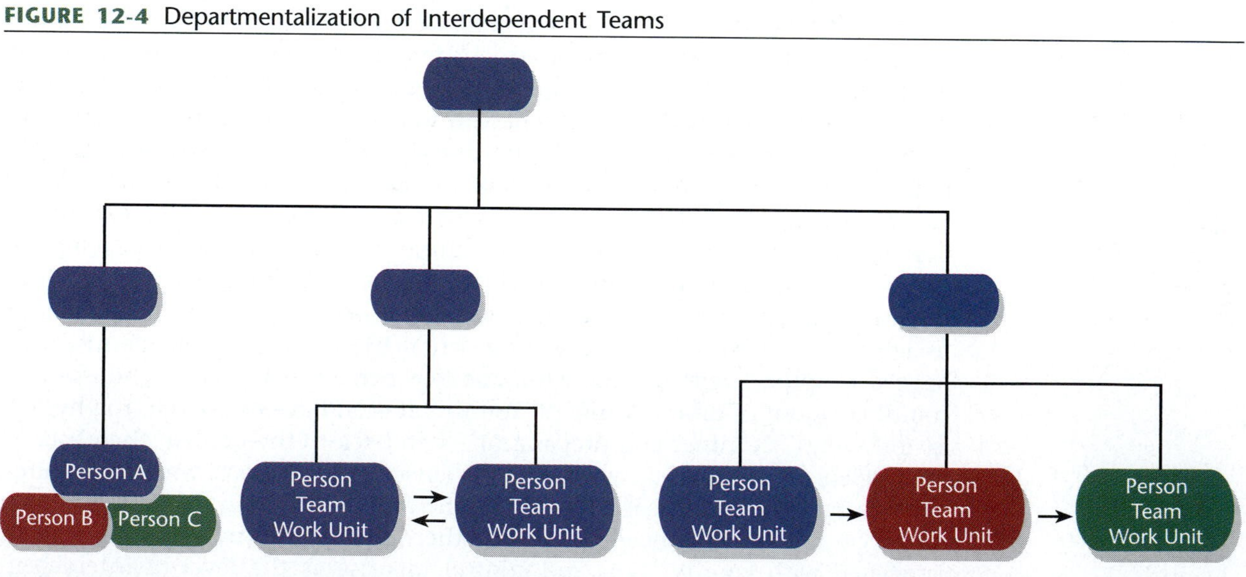

The obvious advantage to the interdependence approach to organizing is that it removes barriers to coordinating work. One person is in charge during surgery, or the process is drastically slowed. The primary problem with the interdependence approach is that it can be very difficult for one manager to direct such a wide range of individuals with diverse skills and needs. Often even the languages used by people from different technical areas are different, so communication can be difficult.

Departmentalization—The Team Cluster Approach

http://www.aal.org

In 1987, the employees at Aid Association for Lutherans (AAL), in Appleton, Wisconsin, a 90-year-old fraternal society that operates an insurance business, took their initial steps toward creating a high-involvement organization. Their goal, essentially, was to operate "entirely with self-directed teams in a highly participative work culture."[6]

team cluster approach to departmentalization the grouping of teams by shared interdependence, such as clients within a particular region of the country

The **team cluster approach** to departmentalization places several teams that have something in common (for example, the organization's clients from the Pacific Northwest of North America) in a single department/group. Team clusters commonly get defined in terms of shared interdependencies. For example, at GE's assembly plant in San Juan, Puerto Rico, one team cluster focuses on manufacturing, another on finished goods, and yet a third on supplies and raw materials.

In a team cluster approach to departmentalization, several teams that share a common bond are created within a department.

Prior to the creation of their team clusters, AAL organized its insurance activities along a traditional "assembly line model"; work flowed in a sequential pattern from individual to individual and department to department, which was coupled with control-oriented management. Insurance claims, coming in from the field, frequently took 20 days to process as they passed from clerk to clerk, and from department to department, with field agents often losing touch with their claim requests as they drifted around the organization.[7]

AAL's new structure consists of five groups (clusters), each of which serves agents from different regions around the country. Each group is made up of three to four teams of 20–30 employees who perform the nearly 170 tasks previously performed by the three departments. Under this new arrangement, field agents deal with one team who has been assigned to their business clients. Agents' cases can now be handled in 5 days and they have close relationships with members of the team.[8]

Simultaneous Departmental Arrangements

Many organizations simultaneously operate two structures in a side-by-side fashion. One structure may reflect control-oriented management and the mechanistic structure, while the second reflects involvement-oriented management with an organic design. The 3M Corporation exemplifies simultaneous structures at work. For years, 3M has encouraged its scientists to "steal" 15 http://www.enron.com

percent of their time from their daily schedule of preprogrammed activities and to experiment with the new and the different. The organization believes this arrangement fosters creativity. The remaining 85 percent of their time is devoted to completing scheduled work. Jeffrey K. Skilling, president of the energy company Enron Corporation, works to achieve a "loose and tight" structure. The "loose" structure's focus is creativity. MBAs and liberal arts graduates are hired, and according to Skilling "we stick them in the organization and tell them to figure something out." The "tight" side of the organization has to do with the controls management places on the employee-job relationship. This tight and loose grouping of organizational activities enables Enron to promote an entrepreneurial and innovative culture, while meeting the company's performance and productivity goals.[9]

DIFFERENTIATION—ORGANIZATIONAL SUPERSTRUCTURES

superstructure the division of activities at the top of the organizational hierarchy

When Cynthia plans a house, she first thinks about its overall design—a one-story ranch? a two-story colonial? a split-level? Only then does she focus on how to combine the pieces into rooms. Organizational members who are the architects of an organization's design commonly begin with an overall design. This gives their organization its **superstructure**—that is, the division of activities at the top of the hierarchy that gives the organization its primary structural form.[10]

The organization's superstructure reflects management's attempts to balance the efficient, effective operation of its internal environment and its strategic response to the external environment. The superstructure reflects the organization's dominant approach to grouping activities and specifies who has the power and legitimacy to guide its operations.

Note that the organization's superstructure is merely the approach to organizational departmentalization (the grouping of activities) that is used at the top of the organization and within the domain of the organization's institutional level. We have already identified a number of approaches that managers use to group organizational activities at various junctures in the hierarchy. Now let's see how these approaches work with the superstructure.

Several superstructure designs are widely used by organizations. We first consider some traditional designs based on functional, divisional, and hybrid arrangements, then the more complex approach known as the matrix superstructure. To close, we'll identify some emerging models.

Superstructures evolve over time (see Figure 12-5). As organizations grow in size and complexity, as goals become more elaborate, as technologies grow ever more sophisticated and complex, and as environments become more turbulent and uncertain, organizations' superstructures have also undergone significant transformations. The simple organization, with the owner-manager arrangement where one person assumed responsibility for performing the majority of the administrative and strategic activities, was the dominant organizational superstructure during the 1800s. Next came the multilevel functional structure, the divisional superstructure, and the hybrid and matrix superstructures, which were all evident by the early 1960s. Now, we increasingly see new experiments in organizational form with the network, modular, virtual, and high-involvement organizational superstructures as firms position themselves within the turbulent and competitive global economy.[11]

FIGURE 12-5 How the Corporation Has Evolved

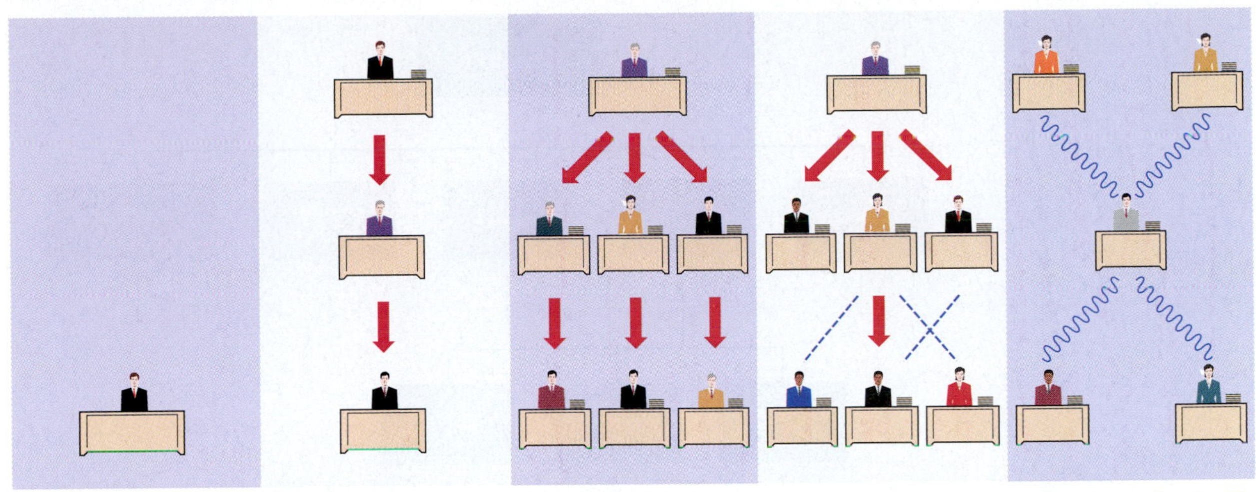

1800 Owner-managed Small companies, generally making one product for a regional market, are controlled by one person who performs many administrative tasks.

1850 Vertical – Companies grow larger and hire more managers, each to oversee a stage of the chain from raw material to finished product.

1900 Divisional – Large companies organize around a series of vertical chains of command to manage each product, or group of related products, that the company makes.

1950 Matrix – Large companies with vertical structures add a second, informal reporting chain that links managers with allied responsibilities or managers working together on temporary projects.

2000 Network – Small central organizations rely on other companies and suppliers to perform manufacturing, distribution, marketing, or other crucial business functions on a contract basis.

Source: Reprinted from March 3, 1986, issue of *Business Week* by special permission, copyright © 1986 by McGraw-Hill, Inc.

Traditional Superstructures

The three most common traditional superstructures are the functional, divisional, and hybrid. Each is appropriate for particular combinations of goal, technological, and environmental conditions.

functional superstructure the grouping of activities at the top of the organization by function

Functional Superstructure In a **functional superstructure,** upper-level activities and managers are organized around the basic functions—marketing, operations, finance, human resources, and so on—similar to the departmentalization-by-function approach adopted at lower levels. Functionally similar activities are grouped together and then connected with other homogeneous groups through a hierarchical network. The organization shown in Figure 12-6, for example, uses a functional superstructure. As shown here, all of the organization's marketing activities, such as market research, advertising, and sales, are coordinated from a single location in the hierarchy. The coordination of any of these activities with those of other functional areas is done at the very top of the organization and at a higher level than if the functions weren't separated by the structure. In addition, the organization's power base revolves around those who head these functions, as opposed, for example, to those who are responsible for the organization's products/services.

There are several advantages to this functional superstructure, which, historically, has been one of the most popular approaches to organizational design. It is versatile, and it is applicable regardless of the size of the organization. Employees in a given functional area are likely to have similar orientations in

FIGURE 12-6 A Functional Superstructure

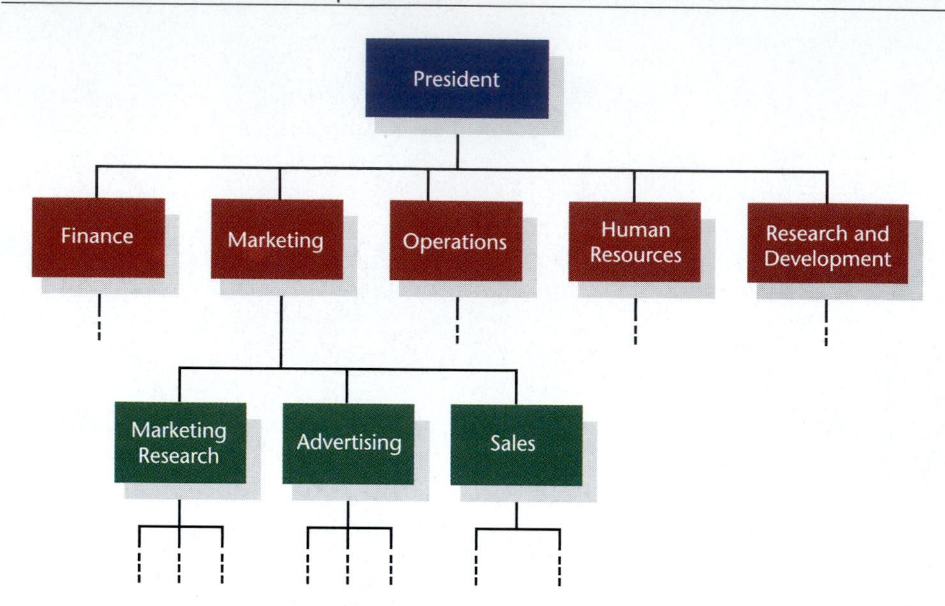

terms of their education and experiences, as well as time, interpersonal relationships, values, and goals. This similarity promotes collaboration, specialization, economies of scale, efficiency, and quality *within* the functional area. When all the advertising experts are in the same group, for example, they generate ideas more easily, negotiate better prices because of greater volume, and so on. Decision making and coordination are easier, because managers need to be familiar with only a relatively narrow set of activities.

There are, however, disadvantages associated with this design. Most common is the lack of communication, understanding, and coordination across units that can cause tension and conflict *between* work units. Strong functional groupings may prevent people from seeing the big organizational picture. Research personnel, for example, need to be creative, must focus on long-range time horizons, and require an open environment with no more than a moderate amount of tension. Personnel in the production department, on the other hand, have shorter time perspectives and goals centered on achieving immediately acceptable product quantity and quality. They need a structure that emphasizes order, predictability, and control. Coordinating work units in a functional superstructure can be complex and difficult, and is complicated by the fact that members of various functional units often operate with different time, value, and goal orientations. With these units not tied together until the top level, internal integration and conflict resolution often fall on the shoulders of CEOs, which can distract them from strategic issues.

divisional superstructure the grouping of activities at the top of the organization structure around nonfunctional activities, such as products and territories

Divisional Superstructure When an organization's superstructure is based on *non*functional factors, such as territories, products/services, customer base, process, or projects, a **divisional superstructure** results. The most common divisions are product and territory. Occasionally, divisional superstructures are also established on a customer/client basis. It is rare, however, for a superstructure to be based solely on a process or project approach. These arrangements are usually reserved for lower organizational levels. Figure 12-7 shows the superstructure of

FIGURE 12-7 A Territorial Divisional Superstructure

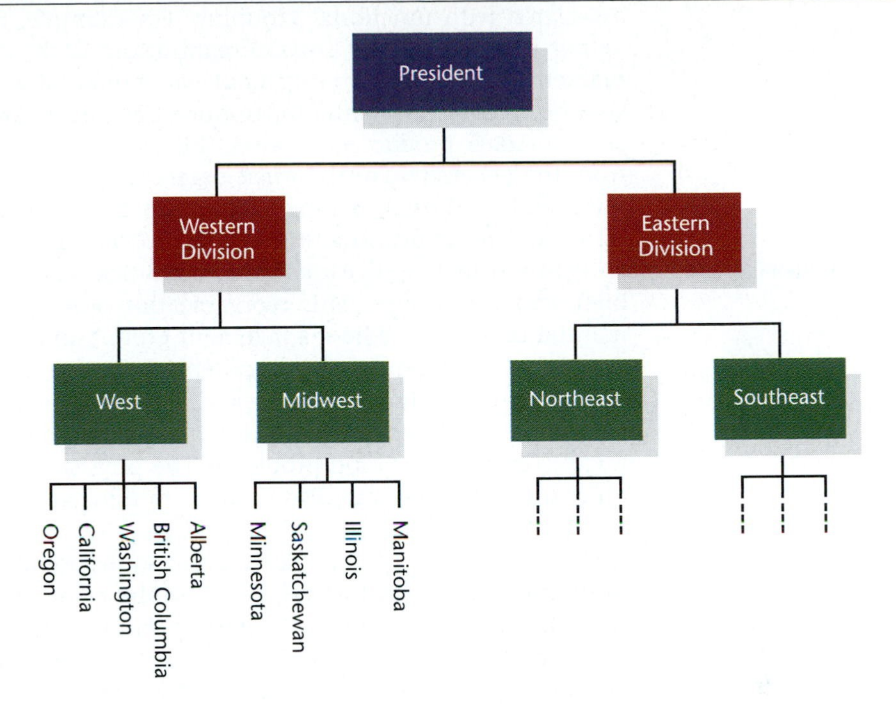

a retailing organization with operations in a number of different territories. A home care products company, on the other hand, may operate a product divisional structure with personal care, food, toothpaste, pharmaceutical, and soap product divisions.

One of the biggest advantages of a divisional superstructure design is that it can overcome both the inefficiencies caused by information overload and the bottlenecks that can affect upper-level managers in functional superstructures. For example, when CEOs have too much information to process, they tend to lose control over the internal operations of their organization and over strategic issues. With a divisional superstructure, however, upper-level managers divide the responsibility for internal and strategic control with divisional managers. For example, Michaelene Kelly, president of the bank, benefits from that firm's customer-based divisional superstructure, with a personal and business banking division. She uses input provided by the heads of the firm's personal, small business, and commercial divisions to focus on overall strategic issues. The three division heads are responsible for operating issues in their own divisions; thus, internal control improves because day-to-day operating responsibilities are delegated to the divisions. The resulting reduction in demands on Michaelene allows her more time to manage strategic activities.[12]

http://www.pg.com

A divisional superstructure lets managers exercise a high level of coordination within a division because division managers share similar goals and areas of expertise. It also promotes flexibility, adaptability, and specialization in meeting the needs of each territory or product. The division that produces Procter & Gamble's paper towels, paper diapers, sanitary napkins, and other paper products has very different needs from those of its foods division, which develops no-cholesterol cooking oils and sugar substitutes. The flexibility required in such cases generally is missing in the functional superstructure, which requires a high-level, consolidated point of coordination in the hierarchy.

Unfortunately, divisional superstructures can lose the economies of scale associated with functional grouping. For example, instead of having one marketing program for the entire organization, each division might have its own marketing unit. This arrangement can potentially create destructive competition between departments for resources as people are encouraged to be responsible for *their* product line. Also, this structure doesn't help people see issues from the perspective of the *whole* organization. Sharing resources, such as equipment and personnel, among divisions is generally more difficult than in functional arrangements. Reacting to this problem, several years ago General Motors reorganized its five divisions (Pontiac, Buick, Chevrolet, Cadillac, and Oldsmobile) into two groups. This reorganization was intended to lower the costs of maintaining five middle-management groups and to decrease the duplication of functional activities.[13] Another potential disadvantage is that, if product/service departments are duplicated in each territory, managers may not use standardized practices to run their departments. Although duplication may be necessary, it can create coordination problems. The physical separation of divisions in territorial superstructures can also create communication and coordination problems.

http://www.pontiac.com

Hybrid Superstructure Few organizations adopt a purely functional or divisional superstructure. Instead, most combine the characteristics of two or more structures to create a **hybrid superstructure.** The superstructure of Levi Strauss, for example, is hybrid. Near the top and reporting to the president, Levi Strauss has eight product divisions (each with its own marketing and manufacturing facilities) and four functional groups (research and development, corporate legal, market research, and traffic and transportation). The functional units serve each product division. For example, all research and development work for the eight divisions is done by the single R&D unit.

hybrid superstructure the grouping of activities at the top of the organizational structure around two or more activities

One advantage of a hybrid superstructure is that it lets organizations that operate in uncertain environments innovate, as well as monitor and respond to environmental changes. Managers at Levi Strauss, for example, must anticipate and shape fashion trends, while simultaneously dealing with the complexities of worldwide product distribution. A hybrid superstructure may also be adopted by organizations that don't want to support the costs of duplicating functional or other resources across divisional lines. Finally, a hybrid superstructure can give organizations high levels of efficiency by grouping particular units functionally and separating groups where necessary. It makes sense, for example, for Levi Strauss to have just one legal group. It also makes sense to place manufacturing and marketing in each product division so that those functions can capitalize on the advantages of product divisions. Overall, the hybrid superstructure makes it easier for the Levi organization to manage its wide range of products and markets.

http://www.levistrauss.com

The Matrix Superstructure

The matrix superstructure was developed during the early 1960s to help solve management problems that were emerging in the aerospace industry. The **matrix superstructure** is distinguished by its simultaneous use of two or more integrated structures. Thus, there is a gridlike intersection of multiple lines of authority and responsibility (see Figure 12-8). As is true at the departmental level, managers can create a matrix superstructure in numerous ways. They can, for example, blend function with territory, territory with product, or function

matrix superstructure the simultaneous and integrated use of two or more organizational structures

FIGURE 12-8 A Matrix Superstructure

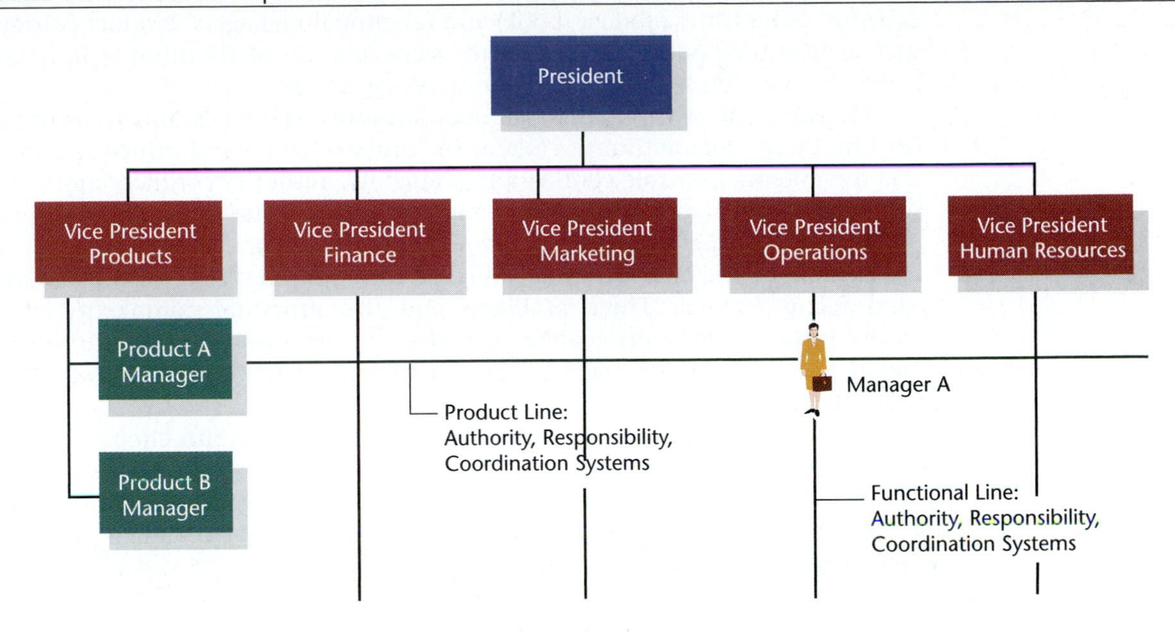

with territory with product. The company shown in Figure 12-8 superimposes a product division over a functional group to create its matrix superstructure. The functional finance, marketing, operations, and human resources units give the matrix a vertical structure, while the product division gives it a horizontal structure (thus, the simultaneous use of two superstructures).

As shown in Figure 12-8, the matrix superstructure allows coordination and sharing of knowledge among those working with a particular product due to its horizontal product component. At the same time, the vertical structure provides similar benefits in each functional area. The major advantage, however, is that the intersection of the horizontal and vertical structures makes both product and functional expertise available to all parts of the organization, thus providing greater control over operations. The matrix approach differs from the hybrid approach used by Levi Strauss, in which *part* of its superstructure is product-based and part is function-based. At Levi Strauss, the two parts can interact through hierarchical levels when needed. In the matrix approach shown in Figure 12-8, however, *all* of the superstructure is *both* product- and function-based; thus, hierarchical connections are much less critical.

A major advantage to matrix structures are their *dual authority systems* (two chains of command), which allow all units to benefit from dual authorities and some employees (usually upper-level managers) are accountable to two bosses. In Figure 12-8, for example, manager A is responsible to the vice president of operations, as well as to the manager for Product A. Consider the potential advantages of this arrangement for a publisher of college textbooks. The project team formed to produce a book might include a project (book) director, an acquisition editor, a developmental editor, a production manager, and a marketing manager. The acquisition, developmental, production, and marketing team members report to the project director as well as to their respective functional bosses. The developmental editor, for example, reports to the director of developmental editing, the marketing manager reports to the director of marketing, and so on. Because the matrix superstructure gives equal authority to all important organizational groups, each member of the team benefits from the expertise of both the product (book) and functional managers. Product concerns, such as how the book looks, receive the same amount of attention as functional issues, such as the kind of advertising strategy to use.

The strength of the matrix, its dual authority system is also its weakness. For one thing, dual authority violates the unity-of-command principle and creates the potential for role conflict and ambiguity, authority conflict, and responsibility gaps.[14] When the production manager reports that he or she needs more time to create a high-quality product and the marketing manager says that failure to produce the book on time will result in fewer sales, how do the two managers reconcile this? These problems and the structural complexity of the matrix have caused many managers to abandon it; however, the matrix design remains popular among many of the giant firms, such as Honeywell, IBM, and General Electric.

http://www.honeywell.com

Although a matrix design can be beneficial under certain circumstances, it creates unnecessary complexity, confusion, and overhead if used inappropriately. Research and the experiences of organizations that have used this superstructure reveal that managers should consider using a matrix design only when their organization must respond to such conditions as:

- *Multiple external demands.* Many organizations operate in an external environment that pressures them simultaneously for, say, technical quality, new products, and new markets. Environmental pressure for technical quality can often be addressed through a functional structure. Demands for new products are often satisfied through a product division, and a call for new markets can be dealt with well through a territorial design, but what happens when two (or all three) of these demands are made simultaneously and are of essentially equal importance? The matrix design, with its use of simultaneous structures, is a natural way to address these complex demands.
- *Extensive information needs.* When the external environment undergoes rapid, unpredictable change, managers must perform timely, often complex environmental scans, quickly collect and process large amounts of information, and then prepare the organization so that it can respond effectively to these new conditions. Sometimes the strong interdependence of several work units may increase information processing and integration needs. In these and other situations that call for upper-level managers to amass and analyze large amounts of information, a matrix design allows more rapid information processing, because the points of intersection become natural points of coordination.
- *Shared resources requirements.* When several work units need the same resources, but they are too expensive or not available in sufficient numbers to be supplied to each department, a matrix superstructure can be extremely useful. If the project manager of this book and the project manager of a psychology book both need art developed for their texts, a matrix can place an art specialist at a key intersection for all work units to share.[15]

In sum, a matrix design is complex, can be difficult to manage, and can create tension and role conflict. A dual-authority system requires the managers involved to form a consultative relationship, rather than the traditional superior and subordinate relationship. This relationship is a two-edged sword: It is beneficial, due to the professional atmosphere it can create, but problematic because of the absence of absolute authority. A matrix can produce high levels of conflict between managers. If this conflict is effectively managed, it works to the organization's advantage by capitalizing on the various skill and knowledge bases. Even so, it is time-consuming and often requires frequent meetings and conflict resolution sessions. These drawbacks are simply the price managers must pay if they are to benefit from the advantages of a matrix superstructure—a price well worth it for organizations requiring its special features, but a waste of money for organizations that can use a simpler superstructure effectively.[16]

The Network Organization Superstructure

network organization superstructure the partnership of several organizations who pool their core competencies

The **network organization superstructure** reflects several organizations coming together in a partnership and pooling their core competencies in order to take advantage of environmental opportunities. Two organizational superstructure arrangements, the virtual and modular corporation, represent the network organization superstructure. Visually, the network organization can be seen as an elaborate set of interconnected spiderwebs, with each web representing a different organization (see Figure 12-9).

http://www.iacocca-lehigh.org

Management experts at the Iacocca Institute talk about the virtual corporation as the company of the future and the ultimate in adaptability. The virtual corporation is an extension of project departmentation pushed to an interorganizational arrangement with a temporary organizational superstructure.

virtual corporation a temporary network of independent companies

The **virtual corporation** maintains a small central office. It is a temporary network of independent companies—suppliers, customers, partners, and sometimes rivals. It relies on other companies and suppliers to perform its manufacturing, marketing, distribution, and other crucial business functions that are typically done in-house. Linked by information technology, they share information, skills, costs, and access to one another's markets.[17] The virtual corporation is a fluid and flexible network of organizations that quickly come together, and collaborate in order to take advantage of a specific opportunity. Once the group has seized on the fast-changing opportunity, the network essentially dissolves.[18]

The virtual corporation does not have an elaborate organizational structure. It does not last long enough for a bureaucratic structure to emerge; as such, the organization is organic—fluid and flexible—in nature.

Three attributes are key components of this new corporate model. *Excellence,* each organization participating in the network brings a "core competence" to

FIGURE 12-9 The Network Organization Superstructure

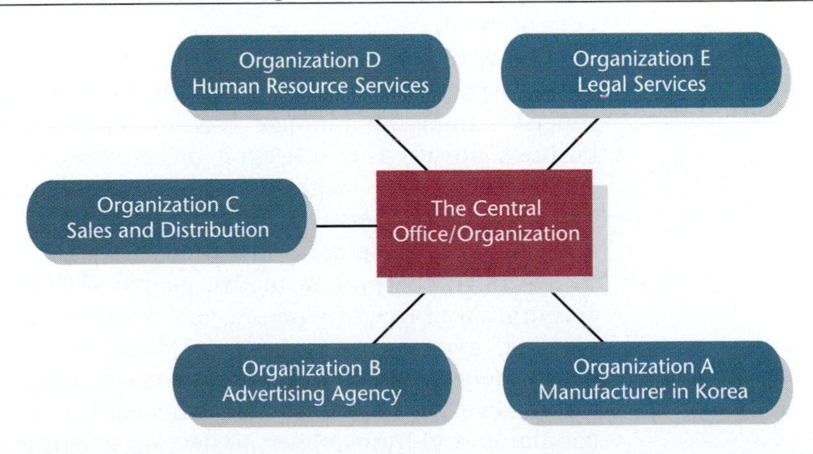

the partnership that the joint venture needs. *Opportunism*, the network revolves around the emergence of a fast-changing opportunity. The relationships remain informal and disband once the business opportunities have been realized. *Technology,* information networks enable organizations to form these networks around environmental opportunities.[19]

http://www.nike.com

This superstructure form is nothing new in the construction industry, where different companies frequently collaborate on specific projects, then dissolve when the building project is complete. Organizations like AT&T, IBM, Motorola, Nike, and Reebok have found that such structures work well for different phases of their operations. L.L.Bean, Nike, and Reebok do hundreds of millions of dollars in business without owning their own manufacturing facilities. TelePad Corporation of Reston, Virginia, used more than two dozen partners to bring its pen-based computer to market. MCI has adopted, as a part of its operating strategy, a number of networks to utilize the strengths (core competencies) of other organizations. They will produce telecommunication equipment by combining their competencies in network integration and software development.[20] Partnerships of this nature are one of the key attributes of the virtual corporation. (See *An Inside Look* into a network organization.)

modular corporation an organization that performs its core competency and outsources the performances of other vital business activities

Unlike the virtual corporation, the **modular corporation** identifies its own core competency and turns to outsourcing for performing other vital business activities, such as trucking, catering, data processing, and accounting. This organizing strategy enables a firm to direct its scarce resources toward its competitive advantage and away from support activities. In addition, this strategy enables the firm to hold down unit costs and the investments needed to produce new products.[21] Dell Computers epitomizes the modular corporation. They own no plants—they lease two small facilities where they assemble computers from parts that they purchase from others. Eliminating the middle person, Dell sells directly to the consumer through call-in orders, thereby bypassing the retailer mark-up and passing the savings on to consumers.

http://www.dell.com

High-Involvement Organization Superstructure

The superstructures of high-involvement organizations are essentially horizontal and process-oriented in nature. At its extreme, the high-involvement organization is one of groups and teams, flat in structure, operating with "unbridled" information.

At the top of the organization, we have the office of CEO and the organization's strategic team. This group assumes full responsibility for the organization in terms of its internal functioning and its strategic activity in the external environment.

Below the strategic team is the organization's core (central processes). Contrasted with the traditional approach, the focus is not on grouping tasks into a superstructure; the ultimate high-involvement model is process oriented. A business process is a collection of activities that takes one or more kinds of inputs and creates output that has value for those downstream from this process. Those downstream may be the ultimate consumer in the external environment, or an internal consumer.

http://www.butlermfg.com

Through the process model, people with different skills work together to accomplish a piece of work. At your local bank, the mortgage loan officer, title searcher, and credit checker work together. At Butler Manufacturing, people with different skills work together to assemble an entire grain dryer. As we saw earlier, several years ago Hallmark created teams of writers, artists, marketers, accountants, and lithographers to develop greetings cards faster. The result of their

AN INSIDE LOOK

Organizational Forms: Network Organizations

A new corporate look has emerged. Today, many organizations generate millions of dollars in annual product sales without a single employee involved in manufacturing. How can these companies perform that way? By using the newest corporate structure, the "network organization." A network organization maintains a very small central organizational structure. It then relies on other companies and suppliers to perform its manufacturing, marketing, distribution, or any other crucial business functions typically done in-house.

When Galoob Toys, Inc., selects a toy for its product line, it contracts with an outside firm—often in Hong Kong or China—to manufacture and package the product. The toys are then shipped to the United States, where they are distributed by commissioned manufacturers' representatives. Even accounts receivable are handled by an outside credit firm, so what do the president and executive vice president of the company spend their time doing? Making critical decisions and coordinating the various organizations on which they depend. You might say that Galoob is an idea and coordination business. The Galoobs make their money selling toys that never touch the hands of a Galoob employee.

Many network organizations in the United States arose out of their founders' desire to capitalize on lower labor costs found in other countries; however, many have extended this idea to capitalize on other potential advantages of the network structure. For example, network organizations need less capital and maintain lower overhead costs because they do not build their own facilities and employ a minimum number of employees per dollar of sales. They can move more quickly on a product or service idea or can adapt other advanced technologies more easily than can their traditional counterparts. Network organizations also tend to support an entrepreneurial spirit. The focus is on creativity, and profitable ideas that might not emerge in a traditionally structured organization are encouraged.

There are, however, some potential disadvantages to the network structure. A network organization usually has less control over production facilities than a traditional organization. If a supplier decides to sell its manufacturing capacity to a competitor, the network organization must look elsewhere. This decreased control can also affect a product's quality. If a supplier does not conform to the standards of the network organization, the network organization may not be able to remedy the situation quickly. Many people argue that networking causes a loss of the design and manufacturing expertise usually maintained by in-house production and that creativity and future product ideas are hampered.

No one knows for sure whether the network structure is here to stay. It is known, however, that with less bureaucracy, they are well suited to an era in which managers and workers are demanding a bigger say in their jobs. The network structure allows companies to zero in on what they do best and leave the rest to other experts.

work flows downstream to those responsible for producing the cards. These activities were previously housed in their own departments—writers, artists, lithographers—and greeting cards were passed from department to department. Now with the advent of e-mail cards, some of the traditional jobs (lithographers are no longer a part of the picture, and the person sending the card can customize their greeting). In San Juan, Puerto Rico, 172 of General Electric's Bayamon facility hourly workers, along with 15 salaried "advisors" and the plant manager, work as a 3-layered, 15-team facility, organized around the core processes used to manufacture surge protectors for power stations and transmission lines.[22]

Numerous advantages are associated with the high-involvement superstructure. Among them are increased responsiveness to changing environmental conditions, less and more direct communications between highly interdependent units, opportunities for multi-skilled training and worker flexibility, enhanced work meaningfulness and worker motivation, and the emergence of psychological ownership and responsibility.[23] On the negative side, people with a low tolerance for ambiguity and low self-esteem may not be highly motivated and contributing organizational members.

INTEGRATION—COORDINATING ORGANIZATIONAL ACTIVITIES AND UNITS

coordinating the linking of two or more organizational members and/or work units so that they function well together

When work is divided and various jobs and departments are created, someone must integrate and coordinate these organizational subsystems. Many management scholars consider the coordinating activity to be the essence of organizing. After all, the purpose of organizing is to achieve an integration among the diverse organizational units and activities. **Coordinating** links two or more organizational members and/or work units so that they function well together. Coordinating, for example, links the production of textbooks with the sale of textbooks; it connects student admissions to a university with the services they will need to acquire a high-quality education.

A look at an organization chart (see Chapter 1) reveals that organizational members and activities are separated both vertically—several hierarchical levels exist in virtually all organizations—and horizontally—most levels have several organizational members and activities. All of these people and organizational activities need to be coordinated and integrated if the organization is to accomplish its goals in an efficient and effective manner. Thus, organizations have two basic coordination needs: vertical and horizontal coordination.

Social scientists James March and Nobel prize winner Herbert Simon, from Carnegie Institute of Technology, note that organizations are coordinated by programming and feedback. *Coordination by programming* reflects a blueprint for action. For example, rules, policies, procedures, plans, and schedules guide and govern organizational activities.[24] This approach to coordination is impersonal in nature. For those of you who have played in a band or orchestra, reading and playing according to a sheet of music enables the brass and reed sections to play together and produce good music. The scores for the different instruments are written in such a fashion that they coordinate the activities (music) of the different musicians. Organizational sociologist James D. Thompson notes that *coordination by feedback* reflects the mutual adjustment between two or more organizational members.[25] As we shall see, this mode of coordination is personal in nature, requiring communication and interaction (team meetings, observations of each other, and so forth). Coordinating by feedback is easily envisioned with a sports example: Two wings and a center on the Bulldog's women hockey team are coming up the ice; reading the Saints' defense (feedback), the right wing cuts to the center of the ice as she approaches the Saints' blue line (adjustment); responding, the center cuts in behind her and moves toward the right side of the ice (mutual adjustment)—she shoots and she scores! Bulldogs 4—Saints 2—and the 2001 NCAA National Championship. For a well-developed hockey team, this movement up the ice is smooth and integrated, a result of players continually adjusting their actions to accommodate those of their teammates and the defensive strategies of the opponent. In our discussion of vertical and horizontal coordination, we introduce different coordination techniques, some of which are programmed (goal statements) and some of which are feedback (direct supervision).

In addition to coordination by programming and feedback, an organization's culture plays an important role in the coordination activity. The shared beliefs and values that comprise the culture also informs the thinking, decision making, and actions of organizational members and thereby brings about coordinated and integrated behavior.

Vertical Coordination

vertical coordination linking work units (individuals, teams, departments) separated by hierarchical level

To meet organizational goals, managers must coordinate the institutional level with the technical core. **Vertical coordination** links work units that are separated by hierarchical level. For example, if Bjorn Eliason, owner of the Comfort-Living Corporation, decides to boost sales through increased advertising, he will direct Emma Ericksson, his marketing manager, to come up with a new ad campaign. Emma, in turn, will ask territorial managers to contribute ideas and provide Bjorn with final recommendations. The marketing department will launch the chosen campaign.

The organization's vertical coordination needs can be achieved in a number of ways, including direct supervision, standardization, and goal statements.

Direct Supervision In small, uncomplicated organizations or within individual work units, managers, team leaders, and other unit members can meet face to face. This *direct supervision* facilitates communication, direction, and assistance, and integrates activities across organizational levels. Thus, the president of a paper company might communicate directly with the vice president of marketing who, in turn, talks to the director of sales, thereby tying together different levels.

Standardization Managers coordinate work across levels by standardizing activities. Large spans of control, high communication needs, desire for uniformity in operations, and physical dispersion all create pressure to standardize activities. Suppose that as manager at a collection agency, Julie Chi's span of control has gone from supervising five people to supervising twenty. This has made it increasingly difficult for her to deal face to face with each team member on all issues. If she standardizes activities, Julie can handle this increase. She simply develops *rules and procedures* to govern routine events for her group to follow. Of course, there will always be exceptions and unique events, for which rules and procedures have not been and, in fact, should not be created. At this point, the *exception principle* takes over, and managers then concentrate their efforts on matters that deviate from normal, such as a customer who threatens the physical safety of a collection agency employee.

Goal Statements When the nature of the work makes it difficult to designate specific behaviors, managers create a hierarchy of goals rather than specifying employee behaviors. A CEO of a publishing company, for example, might set a goal of increasing sales by 15 percent in the next year. The vice president of sales and marketing then assigns a sales goal to each regional manager in the division. They, in turn, assign sales goals to their sales force. These interrelated goals guide the actions of lower-level employees, and the accomplishment of the goals becomes the means through which the next higher level achieves its goals, and so on back up to the top of the hierarchy.

Horizontal Coordination

horizontal coordination linking work units (individuals, teams, departments) at the same hierarchical level

Horizontal coordination occurs at a single hierarchical level. At most levels in the hierarchy, jobs and work units have varying degrees of dependency and require varying amount of coordination. Horizontal coordination integrates the efforts of manufacturing and sales departments and allocates shared resources. Horizontal coordination thus makes it possible to coordinate organization members and units that don't have a hierarchical relationship.

Almost a century ago, manager and writer Henri Fayol talked about the need for creating horizontal coordination mechanisms. He noted that when conditions call for frequent and rapid exchange of information, strict adherence to a chain of command can create bottlenecks in the hierarchy, slowing down the communication process. To overcome such problems, he espoused the "gangplank principle."[26] Using the gangplank, the director of purchasing (see Figure 12-10) asks the director of finance for permission to deviate from the budget allotment. This eliminates the need to work through multiple layers of management for a budget change. The reduction in hierarchical levels, a growing phenomenon, is also intended to speed communication and coordination for horizontally separated units.

Horizontal coordination can be achieved in several ways.[27] In many instances, managers can use the same direct supervision, standardization, and goal statement techniques that bring about vertical coordination. Additional techniques include direct contact, liaisons, task forces/teams, integrators, managerial linking roles, and multiple command systems.

Direct Contact Achieving horizontal coordination for two managers who have a common problem can be as simple as talking to each other. This is the simplest application of Fayol's gangplank principle.

FIGURE 12-10 Fayol's Gangplank Principle

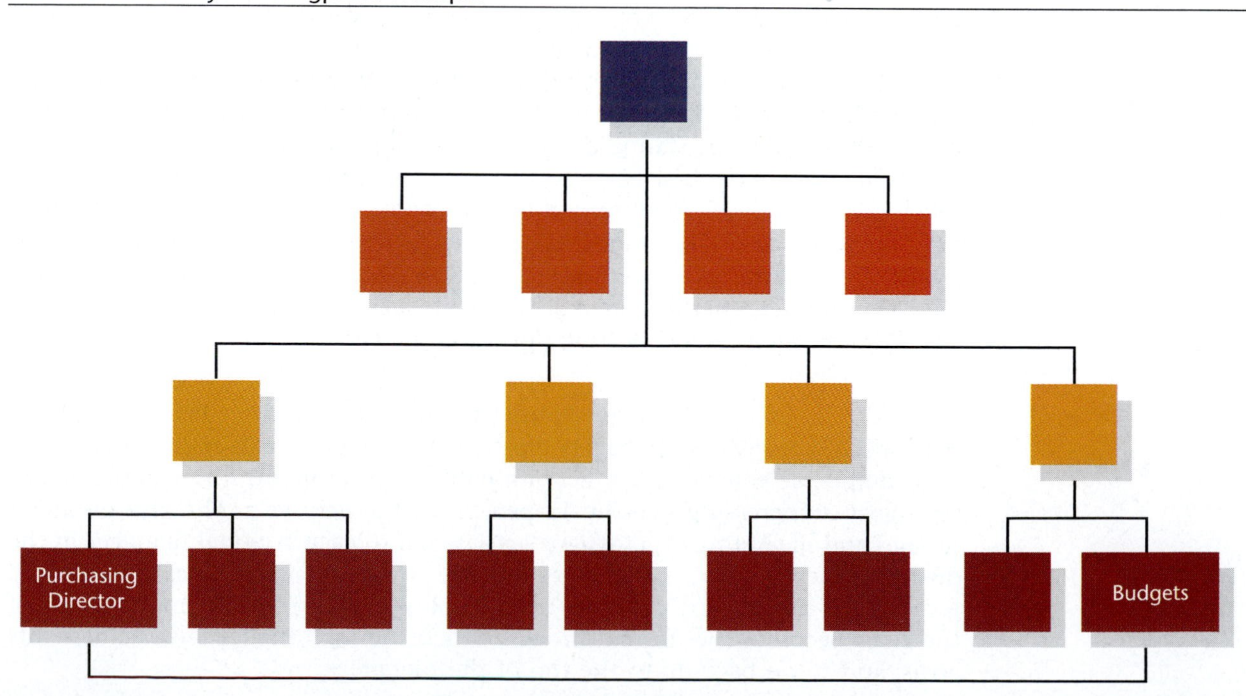

Liaison and Integrator Roles When the volume of contact between two work units becomes extremely heavy, management may assign a *liaison* to facilitate communication between the units. An organization designing a new jet airplane, for example, might assign a liaison to integrate the efforts of those designing the jet's engine with the those of the airframe team. This person constantly moves between the two groups to facilitate joint planning and problem solving.

Under other circumstances, an *integrator* might be appointed. The role of an integrator is more complex than that of a liaison. Liaisons primarily encourage and facilitate information exchange so that the units can coordinate their work. Integrators, on the other hand, provide leadership and actively influence the direction of the project through their expertise. Good political and conflict-resolution skills are important here.

Task Forces and Teams Integrators and liaisons work well in coordinating a limited number of work units, but when problems arise involving a larger number of units, managers may form a task force. The *task force* is a temporary group, composed of representatives from the units experiencing the difficulty, that tackles the problem and then dissolves when the problem is resolved. If the problem needs continual attention, and not a one-time solution, the task force becomes permanent and is referred to as a *task team*.

Managerial Linking Roles When conditions are highly uncertain, an integrator alone may not be able to coordinate highly heterogeneous, interdependent units. To deal with such situations, a linking manager must be given the formal authority to command action. The shift here is from a reliance on the influence that derives from expertise (integrator) to actual, formal authority (linking manager). The integrator may say, "Here is a way to solve the problem, and this is why I think you should choose this solution." A linking manager, however, has the authority to say, "We are going to solve it this way."

Companies with issues that cut across departmental lines will find that team or task force collaboration that engages a wide spectrum of views and experiences results in a better solution, as shown in the Valassis Communication video on teamwork.

Multiple Command Systems Coordination is sometimes achieved when two or more independent units each have command authority over an activity. Creating two such command centers violates Fayol's principle of unity of command, yet there are times when adopting this strategy brings about appropriate integration. Consider the case of Universe Products Limited, a manufacturer of electrical, chemical, mechanical, and aerospace products. Historically, the company coordinated all of its engineering and research activities out of its aerospace division; however, this functional grouping was ultimately unable to give special projects adequate attention. To resolve this problem, management created a second command system for its space projects. Members of the engineering and research department are now accountable to both their functional (aerospace) boss and to a Venus, Mars, or Space-Lab project manager. (Figure 12-11 illustrates the multiple-command system embedded in a matrix structure.)

Matching Coordination Techniques and Needs

Coordinating work units is seldom an easy task. In addition, we have observed that high levels of interdependence increase the difficulty of coordination. The degree of heterogeneity—the similarity or dissimilarity—of the units also may

FIGURE 12-11 Multiple Command Systems of Coordination

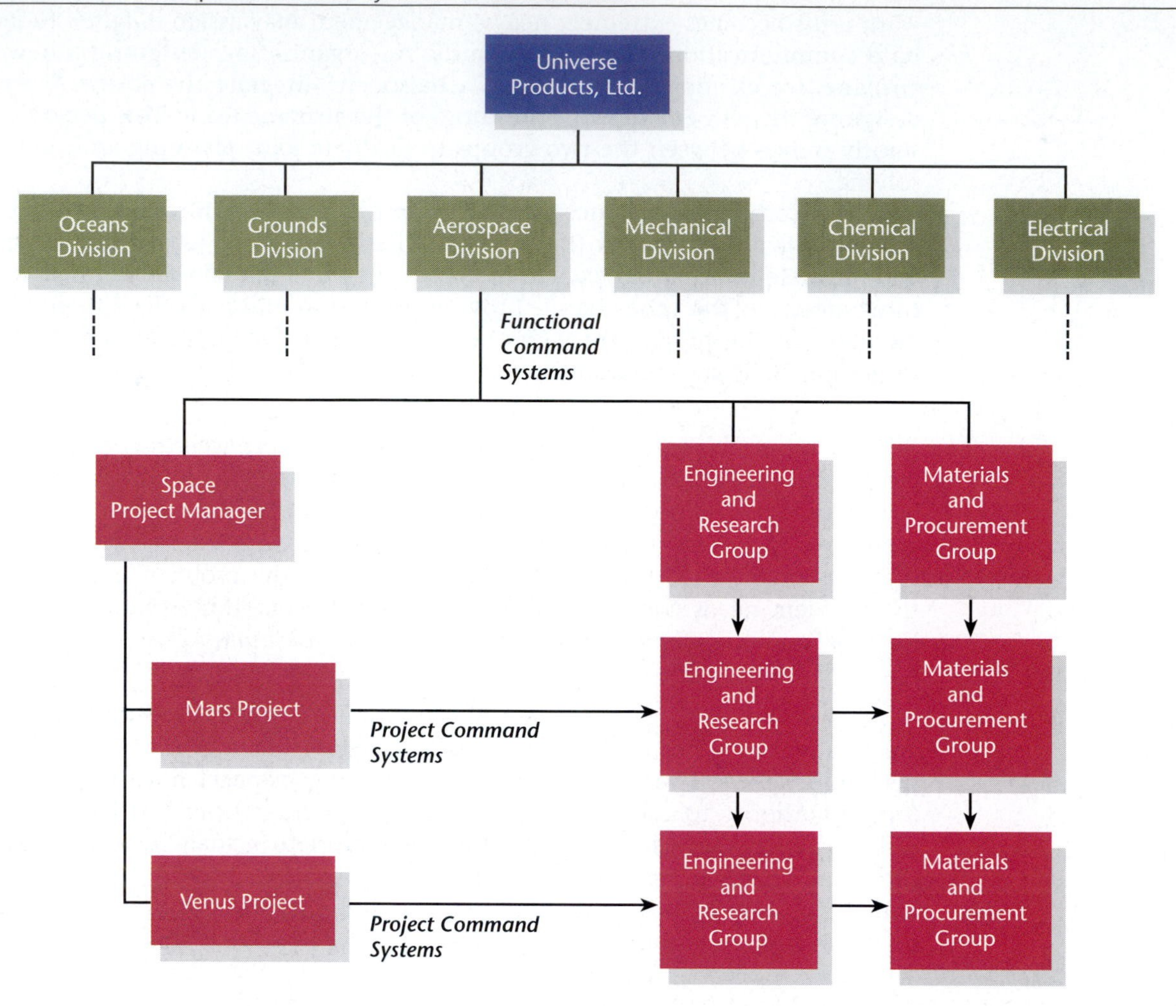

affect how easily they can be coordinated. The following four factors significantly affect management's ability to coordinate organizational units:

1. *Formality of structure.* Whether management systems are closed or open, mechanistic or organic, and flexible or rigid is an important factor.
2. *Interpersonal orientation.* The style characterizing human interactions affects coordination attempts. Task-oriented departments tend to concentrate on task-based issues in their interactions with colleagues; relationship-oriented departments focus more on developing, maintaining, and engaging in social interaction. Some of these differences are a function of the nature of the work performed. A production department that deals with the assembly of things, for example, may be more focused on task interactions than a marketing department, which deals with persuading people.
3. *Time orientation.* The time that elapses between the performance of a task and when workers learn about the consequences of their actions influences coordination. Sales and production departments, for example, generally deal with problems that give them rapid feedback, so employees' attention is usually focused on short-term matters. Research and development departments

deal with longer-term concerns, and feedback about the results of their work may be delayed for many years.

4. *Goal orientation.* Whether the goals of the units are compatible has an impact on coordination efforts. Production departments, for example, face high inventory costs for excess production, but sales departments face losses if inventory is too low to fill orders. The sales department wants a large inventory; the production department wants a smaller one.[28]

If each work unit had the same internal environment and the same interpersonal, time, and goal orientations, coordinating would be straightforward, but work unit differences in these factors can cause conflict and operating incompatibility. The challenge then is to find ways to integrate highly diverse work units. Fortunately, there are techniques available.

In selecting coordination techniques, first assess the needs of the situation and then identify the technique (or combination of techniques) that can satisfy those needs. The better the match, the better the results.[29] Table 12-1 lists typical coordination needs and indicates the ability of each technique to meet those needs.

In addition to a technique's ability to meet an organization's coordination needs, its cost—both in time and money—must also be considered. The simpler approaches, such as rules and procedures and direct supervision, are usually less expensive. When groups are involved, costs go up. When complex horizontal solutions are added to vertical solutions, costs rise still further. The more expensive techniques should be used only when less expensive alternatives will not suffice.

In general, the size of the organization and the nature of the task being performed determine the mode of coordination applied in organizations. With increasing size, managers often turn to programming and impersonal ways of integrating, relying less on the more personal modes of coordination (for example,

TABLE 12-1 Evaluation of Coordination Techniques

	Coordination Needs							
Coordination Strategy	**Size**	**Complexity**	**Span of Control**	**Interdependence**	**Uncertainty**	**Internal Differentiation**	**Communication**	**Horizontal Communication**
Direct supervision	L*	L	L	L-M	L-M	L	L	L
Rules and procedures	M-H	L-M	H	L	L	L	H	L
Goal statements	?	M	?	L-M	H	?	L	?
Direct manager contacts	L-M	M	?	M	M	L-M	L-M	M
Liaison roles	L-M	M	?	M	M	L-M	L-M	M
Task force/team	M	M-H	?	M-H	M-H	H	M	M-H

*Amounts of coordination: L = Low M = Medium H = High ? = Uncertain

Note: This table indicates the conditions under which each coordination strategy is expected to work well. Direct supervision, for example, usually works well with low size, low complexity, and low span of control. Further information relating to these issues may be found in M. Tushman and D. Nadler. 1978. Information processing as an integrating concept in organizational design. *Academy of Management Review* 3:613–624; J. G. March and H. A. Simon. 1958. *Organizations.* New York: Wiley; A. H. Van de Ven, A. L. Delbecq, and R. Koeing, Jr. 1976. Determinants of coordination modes within organizations. *American Sociological Review* 41:322–338; and P. R. Lawrence and J. W. Lorsch. 1967. *Organization and environment.* Homewood, IL: Irwin.

direct supervision and the use of team meetings). Under conditions of task uncertainty and high levels of interdependence, there tends to be less reliance on preprogramming of the system and more reliance on personal and group modes of coordination.[30]

EMPLOYEE RESPONSES TO ORGANIZATIONAL DESIGN

In this section, we summarize the impact organization design on employees.* We'll look at employee reactions to the employee's level in the hierarchy, occupying line and staff positions, project departmentalization, the matrix structure, and the coordination method the employee works under. We will also continue our discussion of employee responses to organizational design in the next chapter. The implicit assumption here is that the design of the organization impacts employee attitudes, motivation, and/or work-related behaviors through the processes described in Part II. As managers of organizational behavior, we must be both aware of, and able to predict, the likely outcome of our organizing activities.

No matter what the organizational design, effective managers must be able to predict the outcome of their organizing activities. In some circumstances, organizational design is critical.

Hierarchical Level

Our earlier discussion (see Chapter 1) called your attention to the fact that two social positions are operative in organizations (managers and nonmanagers), and that in the management social position there are generally multiple levels commonly referred to as top, middle, and first-level managers. We have encouraged you to envision the organization as a three-layer cake, based on the types of organizational responsibility that employees are assigned—institutional, administrative, and technical core. All of this means that organizational members work at multiple levels in the organizational hierarchy, with nonmanagers in the technical core, and managers carrying out managing activities associated with technical core, administrative, and institutional-level responsibilities.

The question that needs to be posed here has to do with whether meaningful differences in employee attitudes, motivation, and behavior are associated with their level in the hierarchy. For example, are managers generally more job satisfied than the rank-and-file? Are upper-level managers more satisfied than their lower-level counterparts? For years organizational scientists have been interested in whether significant differences exist across the organizational hierarchy. It was believed that differences in the physical, social, and psychological conditions across the hierarchy would result in higher levels of job sat-

* Our observations of employee responses to the design features discussed here and in the next chapter will be presented as though there are no interactive effects among the different design variables. In fact, many of the variables are highly interactive, which complicates our ability to interpret true relationships. Our comments do, however, provide a simple overview.

isfaction, motivation, and performance for managers than for nonmanagers, and that the same would also be true for upper- versus lower-level managers.

While it is important to recognize that there are a number of factors associated with jobs at different levels in the organization's hierarchy, the research conducted to date leads us to believe that most higher-level personnel are more satisfied with most aspects of their association with the organization than their lower-level counterparts, yet this relationship may not be a strong one.[31] Upper-level managers appear to be more satisfied with their esteem, autonomy, and self-actualization needs. A few studies suggest that these observations may be true in other cultural settings as well.[32] In addition to being somewhat more satisfied with most aspects of their jobs, higher-level personnel are somewhat more inner-directed, and perform better than do lower-level personnel. Their higher levels of job satisfaction may also contribute to reduced levels of voluntary absenteeism.

Line and Staff Positions

In Chapter 1, we introduced line and staff managers. Line personnel are those involved in the primary output of the organization, while staff personnel are indirectly involved and assist those in line positions. Line and staff positions each form their own hierarchy of authority. For example, in the legal department senior lawyers advise upper-level executives, while the junior legal staff generally advises middle-level managers.

Theorizing that because line managers are more self-directed, while staff managers are more other-directed due to their service role, line managers should be more job satisfied and have their needs for autonomy, esteem, and self-actualization met to a greater degree. The research evidence accumulated to date paints an incomplete picture. It does not appear that there is strong support for differences in satisfaction with line and staff positions.[33]

Project Groups

Jon L. Pierce, Tatiana Kostova, and Kurt Dirks in their discussion of psychological ownership note that this state is often the outgrowth of personal investments.[34] As people invest their time, ideas, and physical and emotional energies into things, these things become part of the self, and feelings of ownership for them emerge. Much like the artist who labors to create a painting, workers can come to experience ownership for the products of their creation. Philosopher John Locke in 1690 argued that we own ourselves, we own our labor, and therefore we are likely to feel that we own that which we create, shape, or produce.[35]

As we saw earlier, project departments are unusual in that project members are brought together to use their special skills and expertise to create something new and important to the organization. These settings therefore provide project members with vast opportunities to invest themselves in the project. Thus, we would hypothesize that high levels of psychological ownership will emerge for long-term members of project departments. Given the opportunity for high levels of self-investment, it is also predicted that high levels of intrinsic motivation, organization-based self-esteem, and job satisfaction will ensue. To date, these predictions have not been tested.

The very nature of the work assigned to project teams is, by and large, unusual and nonroutine in nature. This provides team members with opportunities for personal growth and development. The diversity in knowledge, skill, and ability produces conflict that often results in high levels of creativity and innovation. Such working conditions often promote high levels of commitment, teamwork, and cooperation.

Matrix Structures

As you may recall from Chapter 2, Henri Fayol feared that no employee could serve two or more bosses (managers) simultaneously and serve them well; he thus advocated the "unity of command" as one of his 14 principles of management. The matrix structure creates conditions where many organizational members (that is, the two-boss manager) find themselves trying to meet the demands and expectations of two managers at once.

While the matrix structure was developed to elevate and balance multiple organizational priorities (like product and function), to create conflict in the hope that such conflict stimulates creativity and improves performance, there is a price. Studies of the matrix organization have led researchers to hypothesize that employees exposed to this multiple-command structure are likely to experience role conflict, role ambiguity, and possibly role overload.[36] Researchers also theorize that work attitudes will be adversely impacted by the matrix structure. Specifically, satisfaction with work, supervision, co-workers, pay, and promotions will be adversely affected, and employee job involvement will decrease after lengthy exposure to the matrix arrangement.[37] The evidence quite consistently shows that prolonged exposure to role conflict, ambiguity, and overload is associated with physiological and psychological stress—both of which are costly to organizations.[38] Finally, the matrix organization provides the two-boss manager, and those within a level or two below them, more freedom and less structure, and opportunities for more personal responsibility, personal growth, and development.[39]

Coordination Modes

As previously noted, organizations are coordinated by programming and by feedback.[40] Coordination by preprogramming is an impersonal mode of coordination because blueprints—schedules, rules, policies, and procedures—guide actions. Coordination by feedback and mutual adjustment relies on the receipt and reaction to new information.[41] As such, it is achieved through personal and group interaction.[42] In the personal modes, individuals serve as the mechanism for mutual adjustment; they receive new information and then use it to orchestrate subsequent action. In the group mode, the mechanism for mutual adjustment is embedded in a group of role occupants, who, through meetings, process new information and adjust their subsequent actions.

While research has not looked extensively at employee reactions to impersonal, personal, and group coordination modes, the literature focuses on employee responses to formalization (discussed in the next chapter). It suggests that for many employees there is more job satisfaction and less alienation (that is, feelings of normlessness, powerlessness, and meaninglessness) when people have "human-to-human" conduct in their work relationships. The conventional wisdom among researchers is "the higher the formalization, the lower the job satisfaction."[43] Thus, it is expected that job dissatisfaction and alienation will be higher, and motivation lower under impersonal modes of coordination, and satisfaction and motivation higher under the personal and group modes of coordination.

ORGANIZING AND COORDINATING THE WORK OF THE ORGANIZATION IN REVIEW

Organizing is the management function focused on designing an organization and its internal systems. Throughout this text, we have talked about the major determinants of management practice and organizational design. We have suggested that managers engaged in the organizing activity should pay particular attention to the goals of their organization, to the level of environmental uncertainty, and to the nature of uncertainty embedded in the organization's task and then use this information to achieve a match between the organization's socio-technical systems and these different forces.

Organizing takes all of the tasks that need to be performed in order to effectively and efficiently accomplish the organization's goals and ties them together into a relatively enduring network of people-to-people and people-to-work interaction patterns. Tasks are organized into jobs or teams, jobs or teams into clusters of departments, departments into divisions, and divisions into the organization's overall superstructure. The primary purpose of the organizing activity is to integrate various work units so that the entire system is integrated into an efficient and effective goal-pursuing system.

Two major organizing activities were addressed in this chapter: departmentalization—separating and grouping activities, and coordination—the mechanisms that tie the different parts of the organization together. The grouping of activities is called departmentalizing. Departmentalization addresses two fundamental questions: What activities do we want to cluster or house together in the hierarchy? Where in the hierarchy do we want to place these activities? Several approaches to departmentalizing organizational activities were identified and discussed. The organization's dominant approach to departmentalization also gives rise to its superstructure, which identifies the organization's dominant coalition, major power structures, and insight into how it will attempt to deal strategically with its external task environment.

After discussing the different ways that managers organize internal activities and operations, we suggested that the more organizations become internally differentiated, the greater their need for integration. Two major coordination needs experienced by organizations were identified—vertical and horizontal. The major approaches to coordination were discussed, and we expanded on how managers fulfill horizontal and vertical integration needs.

Finally, we noted that organizational design—hierarchical levels, line and staff positions, matrix structure, project departmentalization, and coordination methods—impact organizational members. Since one of the things managers do is manage the behavior of their organization, managers must anticipate how their employees will respond from an attitudinal, motivational, and behavioral perspective to different organizational design features. We addressed how several of the design features can be expected to impact the attitudes, motivation, and behaviors of organizational members.

A FINAL LOOK

Both Sam and Patricia meet with their supervisor to discuss the tensions between the marketing and operations teams. As they make clear in the meeting, it isn't that they can't work together; it is just that their goals and driving forces are so different that they usually approach issues from completely opposite perspectives.

In an effort to solve this problem, a member of the strategy team, Hannah Shah, is made liaison between the two groups. Hannah has worked in both areas and is an ideal choice. She organizes a task force composed of members from both marketing and operations and meets regularly with them to work toward consensus on the issues. Conflicts arise and Hannah listens to both sides and brings the groups to decisions that they can live with.

Eventually, the task force decides that the issues are ongoing and that a task team is necessary. Both Sam and Patricia believe their concerns are being addressed and are confident that they can now move toward greater cooperation.

KEY TERMS

coordinating, 446
customer/client departmentalization, 430
departmentalization, 428
divisional superstructure, 438
formal organization, 425
functional departmentalization, 429
functional superstructure, 437
horizontal coordination, 448
hybrid departmentalization, 431
hybrid superstructure, 440
informal organization, 425
interdependence approach to departmentalization, 432
matrix superstructure, 440
modular corporation, 444
network organization superstructure, 443
organizational differentiation, 427
organizational integration, 428
organizing, 424
process departmentalization, 431
product/service departmentalization, 430
project departmentalization, 431
superstructure, 436
team cluster approach, 435
territorial (geographical) departmentalization, 430
transformational process/equipment departmentalization, 431
vertical coordination, 447
virtual corporation, 443

ISSUES FOR REVIEW AND DISCUSSION

1. Define organizing and discuss its purpose.
2. Specify the differences between formal and informal organizations.
3. Identify and briefly describe six forms of departmentalization.
4. What is the hybrid approach to departmentalization?
5. What is task interdependence, and how does it influence the grouping of organizational activities?
6. What does the concept organizational superstructure refer to, and what different approaches have been used by organizations?
7. Identify the two basic coordination needs of organizations, and discuss the three different mechanisms that managers use to meet them.
8. Identify and discuss the four factors that affect the integration of work units.
9. Discuss employee reactions to hierarchical level, line and staff positions, project departmentalization, matrix structure, and modes of coordination.

EXERCISES

WORDS-IN-SENTENCES COMPANY

INTRODUCTION

In this exercise you will form a "mini-organization" with several other people. You will be competing with other companies in your industry. The success of your company will depend on your (1) objectives, (2) planning, (3) organization structure, and (4) quality control. It may also depend on leadership style. It is important, therefore, that you spend some time thinking about the best design for your organization.

PROCEDURE

Step 1: 5 Minutes. Form companies and assign workplaces. The total group should be subdivided into small groups of comparable size. Since the success of any one group will not depend on size alone, do not be concerned if some groups are larger than others. *Each group should consider itself a company.*

Step 2: 10 Minutes. Read the directions below and ask the group leader about any points that need clarification. Everyone should be familiar with the task before beginning step 3.

DIRECTIONS

You are a small company that manufactures words and then packages them in meaningful (English language) sentences. Market research has established that sentences of at least three words but not more than six words each are in demand. Therefore, packaging, distribution, and sales should be set up for three- to six-word sentences.

The "words-in-sentences" (WIS) industry is highly competitive; several new firms have recently entered what appears to be an expanding market. Since raw materials, technology, and pricing are all standard for the industry, your ability to compete depends on two factors: (1) volume and (2) quality.

Group Task

Your group must design and run a WIS company. You should design your organization to be as efficient as possible during each 10-minute production run. After the first production run, you will have an opportunity to reorganize your company if you want to.

Raw Materials

For each production run, you will be given a "raw material word or phrase." The letters found in the word or phrase serve as the raw materials available to produce new words in sentences. For example, if the raw material word is "organization," you could produce the words and sentence: "Nat ran to a zoo."

Production Standards

Several rules are to be followed in producing "words-in-sentences." If these rules are not followed, your output will not meet production specifications and will not pass quality control inspection.

1. The same letter may appear only as often in a manufactured word as it appears in the raw material word or phrase; for example, "organization" has two *o*'s. Thus, "zoo" is legitimate, but "zoonosis" is not. It has too many *o*'s and *s*'s.
2. Raw material letters can be used again in different manufactured words.
3. A manufactured word may be used only once in a sentence and in only one sentence during a production run; if a word—for example, *a*—is used once in a sentence, it is out of stock.
4. A new word may not be made by adding *s* to form the plural of an already used manufactured word.
5. A word is defined by its spelling, not its meaning.
6. Nonsense words or nonsense sentences are unacceptable.
7. All words must be in the English language.
8. Names and places are acceptable.
9. Slang is not acceptable.

Measuring Performance

The output of your WIS company is measured by the total number of acceptable words that are packaged in sentences. The sentences must be legible, listed on no more than two sheets of paper, and handed to the Quality Control Review Board at the completion of each production run.

Delivery

Delivery must be made to the Quality Control Review Board 30 seconds after the end of each production run.

Quality Control

If any word in a sentence does not meet the standards set forth above, *all* the words in the sentence will be rejected. The Quality Control Review Board (composed of one member from each company) is the final arbiter of acceptability. In the event of a tie vote on the Review Board, a coin toss will determine the outcome.

Step 3: 15 Minutes. Design your organization using as many group members as you see fit to produce your "words-in-sentences." There are many potential ways of organizing. Since some are more efficient than others, you may want to consider the following:

1. What is your company's objective?
2. How will you achieve your objective? How should you plan your work, given the time allowed?
3. What division of labor, authority, and responsibility is most appropriate, given your objective, your task, and the technology?
4. Which group members are most qualified to perform certain tasks?

Assign one member of your group to serve on the Quality Review Board. This person may also participate in production runs.

Step 4: 10 Minutes—Production Run 1

1. The group leader will hand each WIS company a sheet with a raw material word or phrase.
2. When the instructor announces "Begin production," you are to manufacture as many words as possible and package them in sentences for delivery to the Quality Control Review Board. You will have 10 minutes.
3. When the group leader announces "Stop production," you will have 30 seconds to deliver your output to the Quality Control Review Board. Output received after 30 seconds does not meet the delivery schedule and will not be counted.

Step 5: 10 Minutes

1. The designated members from the companies of the Quality Control Review Board review output from each company. The total output should be recorded (after quality control approval) on the board or easel.
2. While the Board is completing its task, each WIS company should discuss what happened during production run 1.

Step 6: 10 Minutes. Each company should evaluate its performance and organization. Companies may reorganize for run 2.

Step 7: 10 Minutes—Production Run 2

1. The group leader will hand each WIS company a sheet with a raw material word or phrase.
2. Proceed as in step 4 (production run 1). You will have 10 minutes for production.

Step 8: 10 Minutes

1. The Quality Control Review Board will review each company's output and record it on the board or easel. The total for runs 1 and 2 should be tallied.
2. While the Board is completing its task, each WIS company should prepare an organization chart depicting its structure for both production runs.

Step 9: 10 Minutes. Discuss this exercise as a total group. The group leader will provide discussion questions. Each company should share the organization charts it prepared in step 8.

Source: D. T. Hall, D. D. Bowen, R. J. Lewicki, and F. S. Hall. 1982. *Experiences in management and organizational behavior* (2nd ed.). New York: Wiley, 238–241. Reprinted by permission of John Wiley & Sons, Inc.

INFOTRAC — INFOTRAC® COLLEGE EDITION

The articles listed below are a sampling of those available through InfoTrac College Edition. You can search for them either by title or by the author's name.

Articles

1. Selling Change: HR or PR's Job? Lloyd Corder, Jerry Thompson. *HR Focus* Feb 1999 v76 i2 p13(1)
2. Beyond the org chart. (organizational chart, social network mapping) Phyllis Gail Doloff. *Across the Board* Feb 1999 v36 i2 p43 (5)
3. Virtual corporation. (types and examples) (Industry Trend or Event) Joyce Chutchian-Ferranti. *Computerworld* Sept 13, 1999 p64(1)
4. Virtual department, power, and location in different organizational settings. Frank Symons. *Economic Geography* Oct 1997 v73 n4 p427(18)
5. Size and organizational differentiation in historical perspective. Jos C. N. Raadschelders. *Journal of Public Administration Research and Theory* July 1997 v7 n3 p419(23)

Questions

For Article 2:

The article "Beyond the Org Chart" proposes that there is an "invisible side of the organization." An organizational chart outlines authority, often referred to as the chain of command, but it may not tell you who is really important. Using organizations you have observed or participated in as a starting point (work, school, sports teams, etc.), discuss with your group various situations or decisions that did not follow the formal lines of authority. In what ways did the situation, decision, or organizational members deviate from the organizational chart? How far and how often did organizational members deviate from the organizational chart to make a decision? How did various organizational members respond to this deviation?

For All Articles:
Have members of your group read the other articles on this list that deal with various organizational structures. Discuss what problems surface in these different approaches.

WEB EXERCISE

Visit the website of a major corporation, like General Electric (http://www.ge.com); any major web search engine (like Yahoo) will find this for you. Look at its top-level management and identify the type of superstructure that this organization uses.

CASE
Arnco Products Company

The Arnco Products Company was founded in 1952 as a glass container supplier for the beer and soft drink segment of the beverage industry. Over the years, it branched into supplying other industries with glass containers. The first area was the dairy industry, which used returnable glass bottles for their delivery sales. Arnco then developed other forms of glass containers to allow it to expand into supplying food packers with jam and jelly glasses, which were reused by consumers. Eventually the Company became known as a specialist supplier of reusable glass containers. In all of the industries to which it sold, Arnco maintained high quality levels and sold at prices higher than their competitors.

When Paul Greenstone became president of Arnco, he replaced his uncle, Ronald Joyce. Mr. Joyce was an engineer and designer who concentrated his efforts on operations, particularly quality control. It was his belief that high-quality products would sell themselves. Mr. Greenstone, on the other hand, had left a major manufacturer of consumer goods, where he had been the national sales manager. His strong suit was in the development of accounts and channels of distribution. He believed that sales representatives (reps) should cultivate major accounts by providing the types of services that such accounts demanded.

At the time Mr. Greenstone became the president of Arnco, company sales had been flat for several years because of the increased use of cans, plastic containers, and nonreturnable bottles in the beverage industry. The one favorable factor was the increased use of returnable glass bottles in states requiring deposits on all beverage containers for environmental reasons. Mr. Greenstone believed that there was a new opportunity for Arnco if the company could take advantage of it. He came to believe that the company should investigate the characteristics and requirements of its customers, as well as the ability of Arnco's sales organization to meet their needs. To do this, he asked his staff to analyze Arnco's existing sales network and study customer buying patterns.

Arnco's sales force consisted of 20 sales reps organized on a geographical (territorial) basis. There were two regional managers supervising the sales reps. Each rep was expected to call on and service all accounts in his or her territory—an average of 100 accounts per rep. Two-thirds of the accounts were in the beverage industry, with an increasing number of food packers and a decreasing number of dairy accounts.

Because of the broad diversity of customer requirements, Arnco's product line was quite extensive. Each rep sold all items in the line. This required a great deal of knowledge on the part of the sales force, for beer and soft drink customers have different product requirements than food packers. Beverage accounts are concerned more with the serviceability of the container. Food packers tend to be more concerned with print requirements for container labels.

Once an order was placed, Arnco shipped directly to customers from either of two warehouses. One was located at company headquarters in Lancaster, Pennsylvania. It served all accounts east of the Mississippi River. The other warehouse was in Denver, Colorado, and handled the remainder of the country. Orders were faxed in each day by the sales reps, processed at the warehouse, and then filled and shipped by truck to the customer. The order-processing time varied from one to four days, depending on the volume of orders received on any one day. Truck delivery times varied from one to four days also; thus, total delivery time could vary from two to eight days once a customer placed an order.

Promotional efforts were totally concentrated in direct selling. No advertising had ever been used in the trade press, nor had direct mail or internet ever been used. When calling on an account, Arnco's representatives tended to stress their product quality and the company's reputation to get the order.

Arnco's customers purchased glass containers either through negotiating the purchase or through letting the purchase out for bids. Customers who used the bidding process typically wanted products made to their specifications and required more time on the part of Arnco's sales representatives. Arnco's survey showed that nearly 25 percent of their accounts used the bidding process exclusively and that about three-fourths used bids for 60 percent or more of their purchases. The survey also showed a strong relationship between the size of the customer and the use of competitive bidding, with the larger accounts using bidding more often than the smaller accounts.

The survey identified the importance of factors customers used to select their suppliers. The top five factors, in order of importance, were the following:

1. Quality
2. Speed of delivery
3. Service
4. Reputation
5. Price

The survey also showed that the larger customers who relied more on the bidding process placed more importance on speed of delivery than did smaller customers.

Another aspect of the survey examined competition from the customers themselves, who made some of their own containers. The survey showed that slightly fewer than 50 percent of their customers produced some of their own containers and that fewer than 10 percent made more than 40 percent of their required containers. None of their accounts produced more than 80 percent of their own containers.

After considering the results of the work done by his staff, Mr. Greenstone came to believe that the sales force would be more effective with a different organizational structure. He wondered what kind of structure was needed.

Questions

1. What do you think leads Mr. Greenstone to believe that the current structure needs improvement? What other changes might be made?
2. What are the most important aspects of the sales force's task environment?
3. What should be the basis for the sales force structure?
4. Prepare a new organizational chart for Arnco's sales force.

Source: This case was prepared by K. L. Jensen.

Outline

CHAPTER 13

Organizational Design

Learning Objectives

After reading this chapter, you should be able to

1. Identify the structural, process, and contextual dimensions of organizational design.
2. Discuss the concepts of influence, power, and authority and their relationships within organizations.
3. Describe how authority is transferred from one location in an organization to another.
4. Relate the importance of the classical (bureaucratic) mechanistic and organic models to organizational design.
5. Name and discuss two behavioral models of organizational design.
6. Identify the major features of the high-involvement organization.
7. Describe the relationship between the major contextual features and organizational design.
8. Discuss employee reactions to organizational design.

PHOTO: © JOSEPH SOHM: CHROMOSOHM, INC./CORBIS

A FIRST LOOK

Crystal Laser Printers has recently undergone an organizational change to self-managed work teams who share responsibility for meeting customer needs. Each member of the self-managed teams is now "on-call" for their particular group of clients. The teams' responsibilities go beyond fixed maintenance problems to designing proactive ways to prevent problems and monitor costs.

Stan Drummond is the team leader for a self-managed team that's struggling. Stan sees himself as a strong leader who isn't afraid to step in during a crisis. During meetings, he dominates the conversation and points out problems, then wonders why more people don't speak up. Team members collaborate infrequently and operate as individuals rather than as a group. Stan doubts the efficiency of his team and intervenes whenever problems arise.

Today, Stan personally takes a call from a team client with a recurring complaint. Instead of passing the complaint to the team per standard procedure, he handles it himself. Afterward, he senses hostility from his team. What has he done wrong?

Questions: Is Stan using a leadership style appropriate to the situation? Is the design of the team appropriate to the tasks they are assigned? Do you think that the team feels empowered to make decisions?

Picture two houses. In the first house, there are very few windows and doors, many corners, and small rooms; furniture is everywhere, and the hallways are crowded. The second house is open and spacious, with very few walls, and lots of doors and windows. The furniture is easy to move and does not restrict activity in the house. Organizations are not unlike houses. Just as architects design the features of houses, so do managers design the features of organizations. Architects create house designs to meet the needs of the families that will live in them. Managers design organizations to meet the needs of the organization and its members. In this chapter we discuss **organizational design**, the structures, systems, and processes that enable organizations to implement plans and to achieve goals.

organizational design the structures, systems, and processes that enable an organization to implement its plans and achieve it goals

In Chapter 1, we noted that if we looked at a picture of Steinlagger Brewery, Frog's Leap Winery, the Vancouver Canucks, and the 3M Corporation, each organization would look different because each has a somewhat different anatomy. In this chapter, we continue our discussion of organizational design, why design differs among organizations, and how different dimensions of organizational design impact the attitudes, motivation, and behavior of organizational members.

ORGANIZATIONAL DESIGN

The design that the architect creates for the house shapes the behavior that goes on in the home. Similarly, it is through the organization process that the organizational architect structures the people-to-people and people-to-work relationships, thereby enabling managers to shape and regulate the behavior that takes place within the organization as it moves toward goal attainment.

Much of this structure centers around the distribution and use of organizational power and authority. Deciding where to place power, deciding who shall decide, and deciding how to empower the work force are central to the exercise of organizational control. Deciding what type of authority system will work best is a major challenge.

Much like families neither want nor need the same design for their homes, managers do not need or want the same structure for their organizations. Consider the structure applied to the organization's authority system for three Midwestern utility companies. In one, the president of the organization accepts or rejects all appointments of new employees. In the second organization, the authority for making these decisions is given to employees in the human resources department, several levels below the president. In the third, a team of employees with whom the new hire will work makes the decision. These three companies differ in how their managers structure the organization's decision making. These and other distinctive characteristics of organizations are the major focus of this chapter.

DIMENSIONS OF ORGANIZATIONAL DESIGN

Much like the design of the house or the anatomy of the human body, organizations are multidimensional systems. Some dimensions concern the structure of the organization, some define its processes, and still others concern its contextual features. It is the contextual features that are the primary determinants of the organization's structure and the processes employed. As organizational members engage in organizing activity, they address issues pertaining to organizational design.

Organizational Structure

Like the structure of a house, organizational structure identifies and distinguishes the individual parts of an organization and ties them together to define an integrated whole.[1] Organizational structure differs from house structure, of course, because it encompasses more than inanimate walls, doors, and windows. **Organizational structure** includes the interaction patterns that link people to people and people to work, and these patterns are continually evolving.

organizational structure those attributes that characterize the interaction patterns that link people to people and people to work

The most important components of an organization's structure include the following:

- *Decentralization of authority*—the degree to which decision-making authority is spread throughout the organization or concentrated (centralized) at the top
- *Formalization*—the degree to which rules, policies, procedures, instructions, and communications are set forth in written records, documents, and procedure manuals
- *Standardization*—the extent to which work activities are described in detail and performed uniformly throughout the organization
- *Task specialization*—the degree to which organizational work is divided into narrow tasks, with extensive division of labor
- *Person specialization* (professionalism)—the level of formal education, training, and experience needed by the occupants of various organizational roles
- *Complexity*—the degree of formal structural differentiation within an organization, characterized by the number of specialized jobs, subunits (divisions and departments), levels of authority, and operating sites
- *Stratification*—the degree of status differences among individuals and groups in the organization

- *Configuration*—shape of the organization's structure, including the number of hierarchical levels; the spans of control—the number of people and/or activities under each manager's direction responsibility/supervision; and the ratios of managers to technical employees, support to operating personnel, and the like

Consider the structure of Progressive Video Images (PVI), a control-oriented organization. Because CEO Cindy Mertes makes most of the decisions, the company has a centralized structure. There is a high degree of formalization; PVI's employee handbook outlines in great detail the company's policies on hiring, firing, paying, retiring, and the like. All work tasks are standardized in a manual that specifies the procedures that PVI's staff should follow when converting movies to videotapes and custom editing videotapes. Tasks in the movie, video, and audio departments are highly specialized, with each film or videotape passing from person to person through a series of steps in which it is dubbed, spliced, and so forth. Some of PVI's employees have formal education in electronics or related fields, but most of them have gained their experience and expertise on the job. The organization is not very complex, as there are only three hierarchical levels and the number of specialized jobs are few. PVI is still a small concern, with little stratification and a simple configuration.

Because there is no one best structure for all situations, a wide variety of structures exist. Those designing organizations have many choices as they consider decentralization, formalization, standardization, and other structural components. Those performing the organizing function choose and combine these components as necessary to create structures that will serve their organization's needs. Units within the same organization commonly have different structures. For example, although the maintenance department at Eli Lilly Pharmaceutical is characterized by high levels of centralization, formalization, standardization, and task specialization, the company's R & D groups are decentralized and informal, with relatively little standardization and formalization.

Organizational Processes

Another dimension of an organization's design concerns the systems created to deal with such processes as decision making, coordinating, and communicating. Consider the decision-making process. Decision making is, of course, done in every organization; however, how it is done is a direct reflection of the organization's design. For example, will employees participate in the decision-making process, or will managers merely hand down edicts already "set in stone"? The coordinating process, as discussed in Chapter 12, is part of management's organizing function and integrates jobs, departments, divisions, and hierarchical levels. The systems that facilitate this can differ substantially. A coordination system can be personal (based on direct contact between managers and subordinates, task forces, and so on) or impersonal (relying on written rules, policies, and standard operating procedures). The communication process is an important part of the directing function, and the systems in place affect how information is prepared and exchanged. For example, one organizational design allows a worker to speak directly with the president of the company; in another design all requests and suggestions pass through the chain of command. To what extent does the organization's information technology lead to better informed members, increase the quality of decision making, or decrease the quality of working life of employees because of the impersonality of the communications?

There is no one best way to design coordination, decision making, communication, and other organizational processes to meet an organization's goals. Managers must examine the needs of their organization and design these systems so that they are consistent with, and support the structure of, the organization and the context in which it operates.

CENTRALIZATION AND DECENTRALIZATION OF AUTHORITY—A CLOSER LOOK

At the outset of this chapter, we indicated that a major objective of structure is to enable management to direct and control the activities of the organization in pursuit of its goals. Much of this control centers around authority—its placement and use. Deciding what type of authority system best fits the organization is a major challenge facing managers. In this section we take a close look at the centralization and decentralization of authority.

Influence and Power

As organizational members, we often assume that our organization's work *will* be successfully accomplished because formally defined jobs and departments specify how the work *should* be done. Things work this way for some people, in some jobs, at some times, but usually more is required to get the job done. In most situations, formal job definitions and coordinating strategies are not enough to get the work done. Organizations must also galvanize their workers into action, and, to do so, they must use influence. As we saw in Chapter 11 (Leading Organizational Members), **influence** is a person's ability to produce results and to bring about a change in the environment. **Interpersonal influence,** therefore, is the ability to produce a change in others—that is, to change their attitudes, motivation, and/or behavior. People derive influence from power and authority. **Power** simply answers the question, How do people effect change in their environment? In Chapter 11, we introduced several types and sources of interpersonal power—reward, coercive, referent, expert, resource, and legitimate power.[2] Each helps us understand "how" people (leaders, managers, and others) influence others. **Authority,** as we shall see, reflects the legitimate use of influence and organizationally sanctioned power.[3]

influence the ability to produce a change in one's environment

interpersonal influence the ability to produce a change in others—to change their attitudes, motivation, and/or behavior

power the means to achieve influence

authority legitimate power—the legitimate use of influence and organizationally sanctioned power

In practice, organizational members generally have—and need—more than one form of power in order to make things happen. When a manager makes a decision and directs others, employees usually follow this directive because of the legitimate power given to the manager by the organization, but this does not always happen. For example, what if the new manager is the company president's son, and employees resent "this young hotshot who only got the job because of his dad"? What if the new manager is a newly graduated M.B.A. from Cornell University, whose blue-collar employees don't think "the college kid" can possibly know how they should do their jobs?

In these and other cases, legitimate power (that is, the organizationally vested "right" to decide and act) alone is not enough. In reality, workers seldom give automatic and unconditional compliance to managers or team leaders. (After all, did you always do exactly as your parents told you? Do you always do exactly what your professor asks?) To reinforce their legitimate power, those who manage others must use other forms of power. If workers think that the president's son has the ability to fire them, their perceptions may give him coercive power. If the Cornell M.B.A. tells her group that she will pay a year-end bonus to employees whose use of new tools leads to an increase in production output, she is using reward power. Most public and private organizations have formal reward-and-punishment programs that enable managers to enhance their legitimate power.

Authority

Many equate authority with legitimate power. Max Weber, the influential German sociologist, saw authority as the legitimate "right" of a person to exercise influence.[4] According to Weber, this perception that someone has the legitimate right to exercise influence derives from such sources as legal systems, rationality, situational demands, relationships between people, tradition, and charismatic personalities. In the U.S. Army, for example, anyone wearing a lieutenant's uniform possesses the *right to command* privates, and privates have the *obligation to comply.* Contrast this with a project department, where influence is based on expertise each participant brings to a task and as a consequence influence shifts from person to person as their expertise becomes the critical path. In the next sections we look at the various types of authority found in organizations and their sources.

http://www.army.mil

A common view of authority arises from the classical school of management thought. According to **classical authority theory**, authority is the *institutional right* of organizational members to act, to decide, and to exercise influence. As authority flows from the institutional level down to the technical core, all managers eventually possess some formal authority to act, to decide, and to exercise influence on behalf of the organization. Thus, from this classical perspective, authority flows from the top down.

classical authority theory the belief that authority finds its origin and flow from the top of the organization down the hierarchy

A second perspective on authority is anchored in the nature of relationships between people in organizations, rather than in a formal hierarchy of relationships. In the **acceptance view of authority** proposed by Chester Barnard and other behavioral management advocates, authority flows upward from subordinates to superiors, based on the nature of the relationship between people and their perception of this relationship.[5] According to the acceptance view, the relationships between employees and their superiors become authoritative when the subordinates view those relationships as legitimate. If Ben Jeriode, sales manager, asks the salespeople in his department to prepare a report outlining their sales prospects for the upcoming year, the salespeople will accept the request as legitimate, will consider his request for action authoritative, and will comply if the nature of Ben's request falls within their zone of acceptance.[6]

acceptance view of authority the belief that authority finds its origin in subordinates' acceptance of directives and thus flows from the subordinates upward to the manager

A third perspective is the **situational view of authority** proposed by Mary Parker Follett. She argued that, rather than one person's giving orders to another, both should agree to take orders from the situation. Under these conditions, ultimate authority resides in the will and consent of the people who perform a particular task. Like Barnard, Follett treated acceptance as the key to establishing authority relationships. Unlike Barnard, however, Follett strongly emphasized the importance of considering each situation according to its particular demands (see also the discussion of power shifts of and leader emergence in Chapter 11). The knowledge and skills of people in relation to the task being executed should determine who will exercise authority, not their positions in the organizational hierarchy. Authority in a project department, for example, is

situational view of authority the belief that orders should flow from the situation, not from the person situationally based. Power may change hands more than once, depending on whether a project is in the development stage, the experimental stage, or the final report stage.

In all three views of authority, how employees perceive a manager's legitimacy is important. When people perceive attempts at influence as legitimate—whether because of hierarchical right, the nature of the people relationships, or the situation itself—they comply willingly. Although many managers treat authority as an institutional right that flows from the top down, effective use of formal authority depends on whether employees will accept directives. It is therefore imperative that managers make sure that their requests fall within their employees' zone of acceptance. Otherwise, their requests are likely to be met with resistance or at least something less than full support.

Types of Authority and Authority Relationships

As part of the organizing activity, managers must design an organization's authority system. This design creates authority relationships—the influence structures that define people-to-people and people-to-work relationships. There are three different types of authority found in these relationships: line, staff, and functional authority. The distinction between line and staff authority also gives rise to line and staff managers.

As you learned in Chapter 1, the roles and responsibilities of line and staff managers are different, and as a consequence they possess different types of authority. **Line authority** is a *command authority.* Line authority gives a person the right to make decisions and to commit the organization to action. **Staff authority,** on the other hand, is *advisory* authority.[7] It comes in the form of counsel, advice, and recommendation. Unlike line managers with formal command authority, people with staff authority—for example, staff managers—derive their power primarily from their expert knowledge and from the legitimacy they can establish for themselves in their relationships with line managers. A hospital's lawyer, for example, cannot dictate a contract that is negotiated between the industrial relations and its unionized employees. Instead, the lawyer, in a staff capacity, advises the hospital's contract negotiators about the advisability of the language contained in the contract. Similarly, the legal department at Sentury Insurance offers advice to the claims, underwriting, and human resource departments.

line authority command authority

staff authority advisory authority

Many variations on line and staff authority have come about because managers often have trouble getting their line managers to listen to and accept advice from staff personnel. Line managers often feel that staff people are isolated from the realities of their department and that their advice is therefore of limited value. In addition, because line managers are responsible for the action they take, many want to make their own decisions about what needs to be done, how, and why. To resolve this problem, many organizations have formally modified the role of staff personnel and the type of authority that they are permitted to exercise by increasing their directive powers (see Figure 13-1).

Functional authority is much less common than either line or staff authority. Functional authority is the right to direct or control specific activities that are under the span of control of other managers. Functional authority allows a manager (line or staff) to command specific processes, practices, and policies related to the activities undertaken by personnel in other departments. The human resources advisor, for example, may create policies guiding an organization's

functional authority the "right" to direct or control specific activities that are under the span of control of other managers

FIGURE 13-1 Variations in Staff Authority

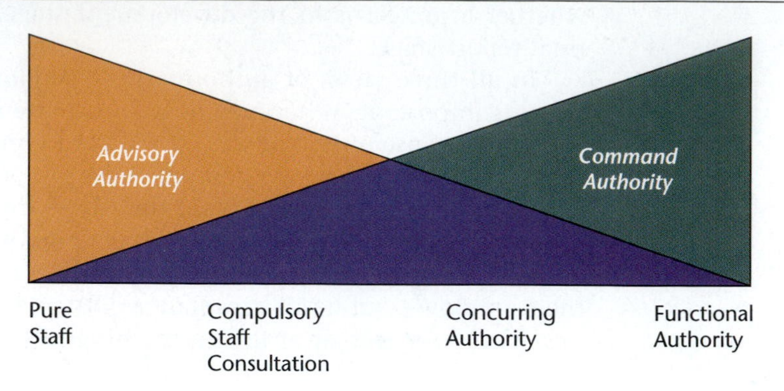

compliance with equal employment regulations. As work teams throughout the organization move to hire new team members, the organization's human resources advisor makes all final decisions to assure that there is compliance with the organization's equal employment opportunity policies (see Figure 13-2). Whereas line authority runs vertically in a traditional organization, functional authority cuts across the vertical chain of command and flows horizontally and diagonally across the hierarchy.

Delegating Authority

delegation transferring formal authority from one position to another in an organization

As organizations have rushed to restructure and moved toward employee involvement systems (for example, management by objectives, employee ownership, quality circles), the location of authority within the organization has been repositioned. The process through which this movement occurs is referred to as the delegation process. Specifically, **delegation** is the process managers use to transfer formal authority from one position to another and, thus, to put the

FIGURE 13-2 Functional Authority

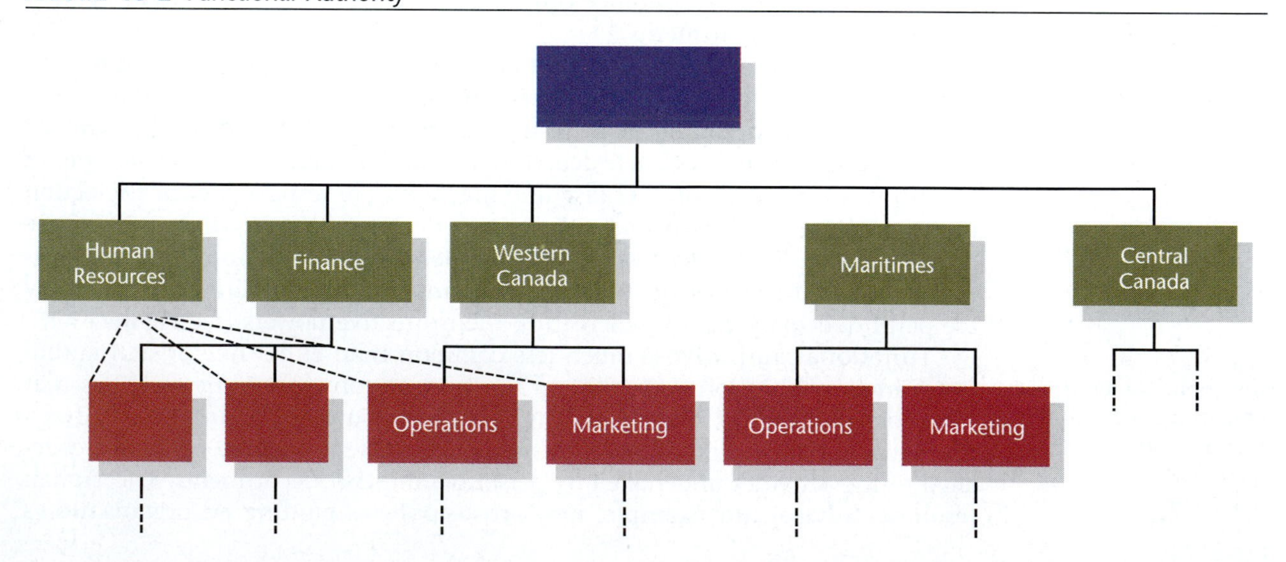

authority system they have designed into place. Architects delegate authority to draftspeople, senior law partners delegate authority to junior lawyers, high school principals delegate authority to assistant principals, and so on. While delegation generally is thought of as a transfer of authority from one person to another, it can also operate to and from organizational units, such as departments, committees, and self-managing work groups. For example, the self-managing work groups at Butler Manufacturing accepted the authority and responsibility for quality inspection, work scheduling, performance appraisals, and many other facets of the production process, in addition to the actual assembly of the company's grain dryers. While delegation commonly transfers authority downward, it is not confined to a downward process. Managers may delegate upward so that control can be exercised at a higher level.

The Delegation Process There are four distinct stages to the delegation process (see Figure 13-3), and each is critical to a complete and successful delegation.

In the first stage, the delegator assigns tasks that are to be performed by an employee or group of employees. In the second stage, the delegator transfers authority—the organizational right to command—to the delegatee. Up to this point, the delegator is the active participant, while the subordinate (delegatee) is more or less passive. Next comes the conditional third stage in the delegation process. Now, the delegatee either accepts or rejects the task assignment and the accompanying authority. If the assignment is refused, the delegation process is complete and will need to be restarted by assigning the activity to someone else. If the delegatee accepts the task assignment and authority, the delegation process continues. The fourth, and final, stage in the process is the creation of responsibility and an obligation on the part of the delegatee to perform the assigned tasks and to use the assigned authority properly. By accepting the assignment and its accompanying authority, the employee becomes accountable to the manager (delegator) and is responsible for completing the assigned work.

FIGURE 13-3 The Delegation Process

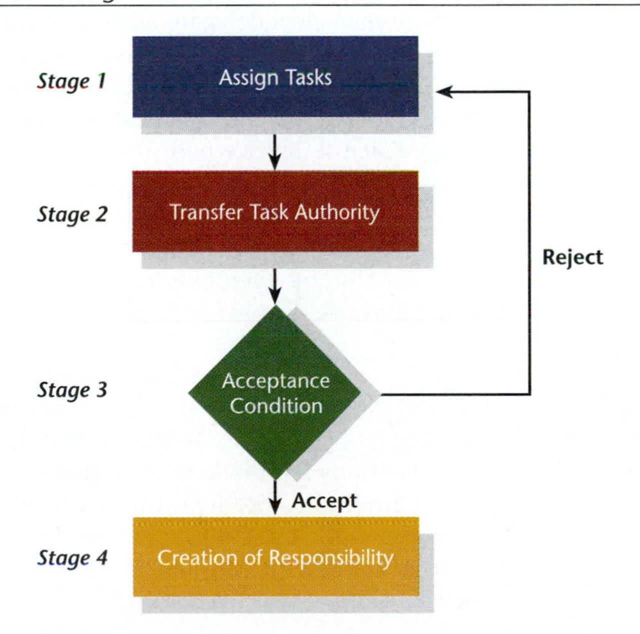

Unique Conditions It is important to note that to delegate means to grant or confer, not to give away or surrender. Thus, there is a unique aspect to the delegation process. A manager who delegates authority in no way abdicates the institutional right to act on behalf of the organization. The manager who delegates effectively retains authority, but does not exercise it unless the delegatee fails to act appropriately. It is the manager's responsibility to make sure that the assigned and accepted action is performed. For example, if Connie Johnson, purchasing manager for a national shoe distributor, authorizes Byron Hopkins, Midwest sales manager, to purchase a fleet of company cars: (1) Byron has the authority to make the purchase, even though Connie retains the authority to execute the purchase; and (2) Byron is responsible for performing the task and using the authority that has been delegated to him. Connie remains ultimately accountable for the purchase, however, and for the way in which the organization's money is spent. Connie exercises her authority and carries out her responsibility for the purchase of the fleet of cars through Byron.

If effectively executed, the act of delegation does not just create responsibility (accountability) on behalf of the delegatee. Ideally, the act of delegation inspires people to *want to* take responsibility. Through this process, psychological ownership (see Chapter 6) is likely to take root and a bond between the individual and the work unfolds.

Centralization and Decentralization

As we have noted several times, organizations enable management to control and direct activities in order to attain goals efficiently and effectively. The location and use of authority is a primary means through which the control of an organization is exercised. The location of the organization's decision-making authority is one dimension of organizational design because the placement of this authority influences how an organization is structured. A highly structured organization is comparable to a house whose walls, narrow hallways, and furniture arrangement controls our every movement. In this section, we explore this important part of the organization's structure.

Some managers delegate authority extensively, others hardly at all. The extent to which formal authority is concentrated at the top of the hierarchy determines its degree of **centralization**.[8] **Decentralization** exists when authority is diffused throughout an organization, and specific authority for decision making is lodged at the level where decisions get executed.[9] In the utility companies described earlier in this chapter, hiring authority is centralized at the company where the president approves the hiring of all new employees. In the other two companies, these decisions are made either by members of the human resources department or by members of the production work teams. These latter two companies have a more decentralized structure.

centralization formal authority is concentrated at the top of the organizational hierarchy

decentralization formal authority is diffused throughout an organization, and specific authority for decision making is lodged at the level where that decision gets executed

Nature and Importance At the extreme, absolute centralization exists when authority is concentrated at a single, central point in the organization. A highly centralized organization is typically designed so that all important organizational decisions are made at a high level in the organization. Upper-level managers or advisers to the institutional level make the decisions considered important and provide directives for lower-level employees to follow; thus, a decision to adopt a merit pay system is made at the top, with lower-level managers ordered to implement the plan.

With decentralization, authority is pushed down to the lowest possible hierarchical level. In a highly decentralized organization, authority is spread through the organization both horizontally and vertically. First-level managers and nonmanagers alike are expected to make important decisions that pertain to their work units. In high-involvement organizations, where authority is highly decentralized, the decision to implement a merit pay system could be made in a single unit or department.

People often confuse decentralization of authority with delegation of authority and participation. *Decentralization* is to the extent to which, by design, authority is spread through an organization and, thus, characterizes the organization's structure. It refers to the location in the organizational hierarchy at which decision-making authority is lodged. *Delegation* is the process through which authority is transferred, thus enabling an organization to become increasingly decentralized. Like decentralization, *participation* also involves a distribution of authority. Participation refers to joint decision making. Decisions that unfold collaboratively between managers and subordinates and/or among team members represent participation or participative decision making. Delegation without participation implies that superiors transfer authority to subordinates so that they can make decisions independently.[10]

Organizations vary in the degree to which their work units, departments, and divisions are decentralized.[11] In fact, work units need varying degrees of centralization and decentralization to accommodate differences in the work they perform, the environments with which they have to deal, and so on. Reporting of on-the-job accident rates to the Occupational Safety and Health Administration (OSHA) is centralized to facilitate effective, efficient reporting of inquiry statistics. Responsibility for preventing accidents, however, is often best decentralized to allow local control over hazardous situations.

http://www.osha.gov

Every organization needs an appropriate degree of decentralization to cope with the demands of its external environment, to coordinate activities within its formal structure, to do its particular kind of work, and to manage the attitudes and capabilities of its members. The appropriate degree of decentralization enables an organization to (1) become more flexible and capable of greater speed as it reacts to changes in the external environment; (2) deal with complex combinations of business activities; (3) cope with growth and change; (4) extract expertise from *more* organizational members by placing those most familiar with the work in positions to manage it; (5) relieve managers of information and decision overload; (6) motivate and improve human resources; and (7) increase a sense of ownership for work and for the organization.

Environmental uncertainty, turbulence, and growth bring with them an increasing need to collect and process information. A decentralized structure allows a greater number of workers to monitor and react to these environmental conditions—more individuals have the authority to interpret and make decisions on behalf of the organization. Decentralization is not a universally preferable way to design an organization's authority system, however. A great many reasons support centralization of authority as preferable in some cases. For example, in a stable environment, centralization lets managers exercise needed control over organizational activities. The concentration of authority in the hands of a few organizational members, as envisioned in Fayol's centralization, unity of command, and unity of direction principles, brings about consistency of operations, because only a limited number of people provide direction. Military organizations operate this way out of necessity.

Managers must find the best match between the degree of decentralization and their organization's external and internal environments. The challenge facing managers is to balance the advantages of decentralization without losing the coordination, integration, and control advantages provided by centralization.

Determinants of Appropriate Decentralization During the 1980s and 1990s, "downsizing," "rightsizing," "restructuring," and "organizational engineering" were common buzzwords characterizing the frantic scurry of activity in corporate America. Many managers once again looked for quick fixes to corporate woes, while others instituted a new philosophy of management, a new organizational culture, and a new management and organizational design to match.

With the external environment more competitive, turbulent, hostile, and uncertain, an increasing number of managers, like GE's Jack Welch, realized that a major drag on corporate productivity was corporate bureaucracy. In addition, it was becoming all too apparent that "If you're not faster than your competitors, you're in a tenuous position, . . . and if you're only half as fast, you're terminal."[12] Hence the need to remove the weight and cost associated with a bloated hierarchy and to make organizations more responsive to customer demands. Among the answers: more decentralization and involvement programs such as self-directed work teams. "Multi-multi-level organizations" simply cannot respond quickly enough.[13]

Another rationale for more delegation is that with the increasingly competitive and global environment, top-level management needs to spend more time thinking strategically. To gain this valuable time, they need to decentralize control and make better use of their human resources.[14]

Although today a myriad of forces in the organization's internal and external environments are calling for more delegation, decentralization, and participation, there is no one best way. There is no easy way to determine the ideal level of decentralization for any organization. There are, however, factors that managers should consider when designing their organization's authority system. Table 13-1 summarizes the conditions under which centralization and decentralization of authority are likely to be observed.

Decentralization is well suited to uncertain and rapidly changing *external environments*. The unpredictability of such environments demands that organizations acquire and process considerable amounts of information rapidly. Furthermore, they must respond quickly and appropriately to that information. Decentralization allows organizations to avoid delays and the information and decision overloads that occur if all information has to be collected, analyzed, and responded to at a central source of authority. For example, authority must be decentralized in a fire brigade battling a blaze. Each team of firefighters working a particular part of a fire must assess the needs of that location and have the authority to respond quickly. The fire chief would be overloaded if he or she retained all authority for all decisions, and the firefighters would be endangered if they could not react quickly when necessary.

Other factors influence decisions about decentralization. The *strategies pursued* by organizations influence the type of authority system that they create. A strategy of product diversification, for example, dictates a need for decentralization, because the complexity of doing business in many markets would overwhelm a single manager. Organization history and culture influence the level of decentralization as well. Organizations that grow from family ownership, such as the Ford Motor Company, are relatively centralized. So, too, are firms that have experienced slow growth under a strong leader. In contrast, organizations

http://www.ford.com

TABLE 13-1 The Decentralization Decision

Conditions	Appropriate Matches	
	Centralized	Decentralized
1. The External Environment		
Stability	Stable	Unstable
Uncertainty	Certain	Uncertain
2. The Organization		
Strategy	Narrow	Diverse
History/culture	Closed	Open
Growth rate	Slow	Rapid
Change rate	Slow	Rapid
Size	Small-med.	Large
Complexity	Simple	Complex
3. The Work		
Decision costs/risks	High	Low
Technology	Routine	Nonroutine
Task interdependence	Low	High
4. The People		
Upper managers—willing to "let go"	No	Yes
—confidence in lower managers	Low	High
Lower managers—managerial abilities	Low	High
—training needs	Low	High
—control desires	Low	High
—motivation needed	Low	High

formed through acquisition and consolidations, as well as those that have grown rapidly, tend to be more decentralized.

Size and *complexity* affect decentralization decisions. The larger an organization, the more it needs decentralization. Size eventually overwhelms an individual manager's span of control, and lower-level managers must take over many of the organizational decisions. Likewise, the more complex an organization, the more it needs decentralization. Regardless of its size, a complex organization needs decentralization to deal with its wide variety of work groups and types of decisions. Large and complex organizations, such as Procter & Gamble and IBM, need especially high levels of decentralization.

The *nature of the task* is also relevant to decentralization. Some tasks are simply better performed in centralized structures. Those that involve considerable interdependence, such as performing a heart transplant, are better suited to decentralization because monitoring of the work must be done at a "local" level. The same is true for tasks that involve considerable uncertainty and nonroutine technologies and thus require frequent consultation, advice, or direction. For these reasons, research and development are usually quite decentralized. In contrast, routine and nonambiguous tasks, such as converting taconite pellets to ingots or rolled steel, are well suited to centralization, in which decision making is handled higher in the organization.

The decision to decentralize is influenced as well by the characteristics of an organization's *managers*. Upper-level managers are fully in charge under centralization; lower-level managers take over under decentralization. Decentralization is unlikely to occur, therefore, unless upper-level managers release authority to, and have confidence in, the abilities of lower-level managers. Of course, decentralization is not appropriate if lower-level managers don't have the necessary abilities or motivation to make the required decisions. Decentralization, however, helps lower-level managers learn to make these decisions. In fact, unless an organization is prepared to recruit externally for upper-level managers, some degree of decentralization is necessary if the organization is to develop a supply of highly skilled managers for the future.

The potential psychological effects of decentralization on lower-level managers should not be overlooked. To the extent that these managers like to exercise control over their work, they find decentralization satisfying. When *employees'* needs for control are met, they are likely to complete their work quickly and come to work regularly. There is also ample evidence that decentralization often improves the quality of the decisions that people make because it improves their motivation.

Decentralization also has disadvantages for lower-level managers. It places major responsibilities and the worries and burdens associated with this work directly on their shoulders. The result can be longer hours and more intense work, often increasing stress.

Managers should take all of these considerations into account when making decisions to decentralize. Often these factors point to the same conclusion, making the manager's task easier, but when signals are mixed, the decentralizing becomes difficult. At that point, managers have to weigh the importance of each factor, as shown in Table 13-1, to arrive at a balanced decision.

Controls on Decentralization As we have seen, the internal operations of many organizations are inefficient because managers are reluctant to delegate and decentralize. In addition, many managers centralize their authority system all the more tightly in reaction to the very conditions—uncertainty and turbulence—that call for decentralization. To combat these problems, many organizations have found ways to decentralize and still maintain control over decision making through formalization and personal specialization.

As noted earlier, *formalization* is the degree to which the operating norms (that is, rules, policies, operating procedures) of an organization are explicitly stated.[15] Although the norms of an organization can be well developed yet remain unwritten, most organization scholars agree that a higher degree of formalization is achieved when rules, procedures, instructions, and major communications are contained in written documents, such as rule manuals and codes of conduct.[16] Many employees first encounter this formalization when they receive their organization's handbook, which endeavors to control their behavior by defining members' rights and obligations.

In many organizations, decentralization of authority and formalization go hand in hand. As managers delegate authority to people in lower organizational levels, they often create a set of rules, policies, and procedures (discussed in Chapter 10) to guide the decisions made by lower-level employees; thus, decentralization gives a supervisor of reservation agents at Northwest Airlines considerable authority to make decisions about special customer requests. The supervisor must follow a set of formal, written guidelines when making these decisions, however. Formalization thus becomes a way to control the decision making.

Formalization helps achieve consistency, coordination, economy, and standardization. By stating its expectations for employees, an organization reduces variability and helps ensure that decisions are made within an acceptable range.

© SUSAN VAN ETTEN

Organizations that rely on specialists to make decisions, such as schools, require less formalization to achieve control.

For example, zone managers at Ford Motor Company must decide when to honor customer requests for car repair work beyond that normally covered by the car's warranty. Although zone managers are encouraged to use personal judgment in their decisions, Ford provides guidelines so that decisions from zone to zone will not be dramatically different.

Personal specialization (also referred to as *professionalization*) refers to the level of education, training, and experience of employees. Specialists are both willing and able to make decisions based on their professional training and expertise. A skilled teacher, a master carpenter, a physician, and a diemaker are all specialists with strong work skills and norms of acceptable behavior acquired through educational and apprenticeship programs. Organizations that rely on personal specialization to guide the decision processes need less formalization in order to achieve control.[17]

Many organizations rely on personal specialization to control delegated authority. For example, law firms rely on professional training to guide lawyers' job performance and their exercise of the authority given to them by the firm. Managers can trust that selected employees will use organizational authority appropriately and delegate it successfully if they are technically competent, guided by professional norms, and intellectually capable of diagnosing and solving task-related problems. Under such conditions, organizations operate effectively and consistently, even with a decentralized authority system.

BASIC MODELS OF ORGANIZATIONAL DESIGN

In this section we look at the different approaches to organizational design. Each approach represents managerial attempts to manipulate the dimensions of organizational design to create their organization. As you read about the classical, behavioral, and organic approaches to organizational design, remember that an organization is a socio-technical system (Chapter 1) consisting of a relatively enduring network of people-to-people and people-to-work interaction patterns; two or more people with a conscious common purpose and a communication and command system that ties them together; and an input-throughput-output system. As such, an organization can be viewed as

> a formal collection of people that has been created for the purpose of accomplishing collective goals on a relatively continuous basis. The collection is characterized by a relatively identifiable boundary, norms of behavior, primary groups, channels of communication, task-related activities, [and] authority relationships . . . .[18]

This means that organizational members must design each formal arrangement—team, work unit, department, and division— as well as the total organization, while keeping in mind the context within which the unit functions. As suggested throughout this text, organizational purpose, technology, environment, and members are critical factors that play a meaningful role in defining the appropriate structure and processes for an organization.

As you may recall from Chapter 2, such people as Hugo Munsterberg, Walter Dill Scott, Mary Parker Follett, and Chester Barnard argued that the classical approach to management fails to consider the human side of organizations. Their work led to the development of *behavioral models,* which focused less on the rational and mechanical aspects of organizational design and more on its social and psychological sides. Behavioral models and the contemporary models that followed did not reject all of the classicists' design ideas. Instead, they shifted the emphasis to incorporating individuals and groups into the system as an integral part of managing. In this section we examine two behavioral models referred to as socio-technical systems theory and Rensis Likert's System 4 organization. Both models have contributed to the rise of the high-involvement organization.

Eric Trist and K. W. Bamforth's classic studies on alternative methods of coal mining suggested that managers should place substantial emphasis on the human side of their organization rather than focus strictly on its technical and mechanical side. Their research, and that of others conducted at England's Tavistock Institute, led to the development of the *socio-technical systems theory.*[19]

According to the socio-technical model, managers should design organizations from two premises. First, they should recognize that two systems operate inside every organization: a technical system that focuses on the tasks that produce the organization's product or service and a social system.[20] The technical systems involved in the manufacture of paper, for example, include machines and such activities as debarking, grinding, washing, bleaching, and cooking the wood. The social system that runs the machines and performs these activities includes individuals and groups whose motivation, interest, ideas, insights, creativity, and needs must also be maintained. The second premise focuses on the organization-task environment relationship. Because organizational survival and success depend on the task environment, managers must design their organization to be open and responsive to its needs and forces.

http://www.isr.umich.edu

When he was a social scientist at the University of Michigan's Institute for Social Research, Rensis Likert found a significant relationship between organizational design and effectiveness. Likert was most concerned with eight features of organizations: leadership, motivation, communication, interaction, decision making, goal setting, control, and performance goal setting. Through his research, Likert observed four design approaches that incorporate these features, which he referred to as Systems 1–4. Systems 2 and 3 have received little attention. The System 1 organization resembles the classical organization's bureaucratic model. Likert's most effective organization is classified as System 4.[21]

A *System 4 organization* emphasizes openness and has few boundary restrictions. People are not expected to adhere strictly to the chain of command in communicating information, coordinating work, or reporting accountability; thus, influence and information flow freely upward, downward, and laterally. Decentralization is the norm. The emphasis is on participatory decision making, and employees are expected to engage in self and group control. Authority flows from the nature of people's relationships and is based on achieving acceptance, rather than a hierarchical position.

Structurally, a System 4 organization has a traditional hierarchy laced with a hierarchy of groups (see Figure 13-4). Each manager is a member of several groups.

FIGURE 13-4 A Hierarchy of Groups

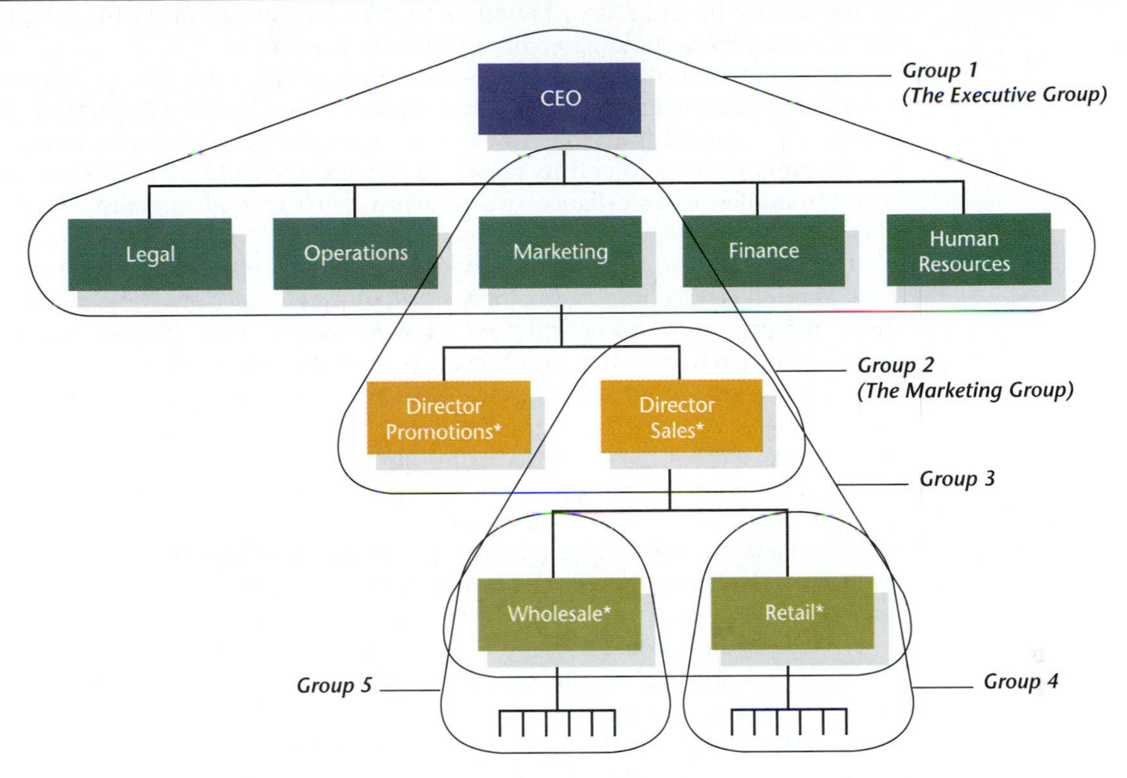

* Linking pin role

Mechanistic Model

bureaucratic organization a highly structured and formally designed organization

As you may recall from Chapter 2, classical management scholars, such as Henri Fayol, Frederick Taylor, and Max Weber, believed that a universal set of laws governs the efficient and effective functioning of organizations. They endeavored to identify these laws and to establish a set of guiding principles for the organizing process. Although members of the classical school did not agree on all issues, one major organizational design—the bureaucratic organization most often associated with the work of Max Weber—emerged from the classical period.[22] A **bureaucratic organization** is a highly structured and formally designed organization. Unfortunately, the term *bureaucracy* has become emotionally charged and synonymous with red tape and inefficiency.[23] This is too bad, because the bureaucratic model can create a high level of speed, order, predictability, and consistency of operations. Consider some of the characteristics that distinguish a bureaucratic design.

Characteristics of the Classical Bureaucratic Model Few organizations have a purely bureaucratic design, but virtually all possess at least some bureaucratic characteristics.[24] Chief among these is the emphasis on obeying one leader rather than many. This characteristic arises from Weber's well-defined hierarchy of authority, which specifies the lines of communication, command relationships, and the channels through which individual accountability should flow. A bureaucratic design thus centralizes its authority system and bases its legitimacy on inherent rationality. In a military setting, for example, it is rational for a field commander to possess the right to command troops. After all, there would hardly be time for a battalion to take a break during a firefight to see whether members could agree on a course of action!

A second characteristic of the bureaucratic design is its reliance on a set of rules that specify employee rights and duties and on standard operating procedures. This standardization and formalization delineate the relationship between the organization and its members. It tries to ensure that each task is uniformly handled in accordance with Weber's belief that an organization should clearly define each member's role and should position him or her relative to other members. The U.S. Marine Corps, for example, clearly defines each of its ranks and their accompanying rights and duties. The Corps also specifies in detail the procedures to be followed for work assignments, promotions, and so forth. In other words, the Corps manages "by the book" to ensure efficiency and uniform (pardon the pun) procedures. As an organization, McDonalds with its uniforms, emphasis on hierarchy, rules, and standardized food preparation procedures is also a bureaucratic organization.

http://www.hqmc.usmc.mil

http://www.mcdonalds.com

Other distinguishing features of the bureaucratic organization include:

- Members are selected because of their technical competence: So that it can select employees on objective standards of competence, the U.S. government bases selection decisions in part on the results of civil service exams that measure the qualifications of job applicants.
- Members advance in the organization as a result of tenure and technical competence: To avoid favoritism, the U.S. Post Office bases promotions on length of service and the development of job-related skills.
- Relationships are impersonal: Application of organizational rules, standards, and procedures is uniform and administered without consideration of individual needs or personal preferences.
- Labor is divided, individual specialization is encouraged, and tasks are routine: Each position is filled by an individual who will become an expert in the performance of a specific and limited number of activities.

As demonstrated by the U.S. Marine Corps and McDonalds, when a bureaucracy runs well, it is a model of order, stability, consistency, and predictability. Even when running well, however, the bureaucratic design has drawbacks.

Problems with Bureaucracy Although the rational approach espoused by the bureaucracy can work well for a mechanized organization, where people perform routine tasks under highly structured environmental conditions, it is less than ideal as environmental uncertainty increases and tasks become increasingly nonroutine.[25] At Hewlett-Packard, for example, the development and design of information systems requires a much more open and flexible working environment, which a highly programmed and controlled bureaucracy cannot provide.

Bureaucratic designs do not work well when an organization is highly dependent on the creativity of its members and their interdependencies.[26] The collaborative creativity needed to identify and develop movie ideas at Disney's Touchstone Studios would be inhibited by the rigid structure of a bureaucracy. Some other problems frequently associated with the bureaucratic organization include

http://www.disney.com

- People problems, such as alienation, frustration, low morale, and lack of motivation, stem from high levels of division of labor and imposed control. Workers with strong affiliation needs feel that bureaucracies thwart, rather than satisfy, their need for socialization and group interaction.

- The social and psychological sides of the organization, such as the informal organization, tend to be ignored. For example, the informal organization and strong culture that contribute substantially to Hewlett-Packard's innovativeness and effectiveness would undoubtedly be stifled by the rigidity of a bureaucratic design.
- Rules and procedures frequently become ends in and of themselves, replacing original goals. Some claim that the Occupational Safety and Health Administration (OSHA) provides a good example of this. OSHA inspections were designed to identify and correct industrial safety risks, but the detailed schedules and rules specified by its bureaucracy shift the emphasis from safety to conducting the appropriate number of inspections.
- Communication inside the organization must follow a rigid chain of command, resulting in tedious and time-consuming delays in information flow. Consider Earl, a distribution clerk who discovers a quality problem in the 20-inch bicycles he's shipping at a large bicycle plant. As trained, he reports the problem to his supervisor, who reports the problem to the director of transportation, who reports it to the director of quality control, who reports the problem to the manager of bicycle quality control, who reports it to Mary Ellen, who supervises inspection of 20-inch bikes. Mary confirms the problem and informs the production team, who corrects the error. Had there not been such a bureaucratic chain of command, Earl could have gone directly to Mary, who could have remedied the problem quickly and efficiently. (If you think this example was painful to read, consider how frustrating it would be in real life!)
- The organization becomes inflexible, incapable of responding quickly to environmental complexity and turbulence or to complex tasks and nonroutine technologies. For example, DuPont responded to research that showed the ozone-depleting effects of chlorofluorocarbons (CFCs) by announcing that it will no longer use CFCs in its products. When asked *when* the phasing-out process would be complete, the company's spokesperson indicated a time frame some two decades later.

Throughout the classical period, managers popularized the bureaucratic organization. During the past few decades, however, managers have experienced increasing inefficiencies associated with this design. As a result, alternative designs have emerged.

Organic Models

For highly uncertain environments and technologies, some people believe that even the behavioral models are too rigid a design. These people have drawn on the work of British researchers Tom Burns and George Stalker to create an organic design (see the discussion in Chapter 2 on organic and mechanistic management systems).[27] An **organic organization** is fluid and dynamic and is capable of evolution, redesign, and adaptation to both internal and external environments. This is in stark contrast to the classical bureaucratic design, which is mechanistic, rigid, and changes very little in response to these pressures (see Figure 13-5).[28]

organic organization
a fluid and dynamic organization capable of evolution, redesign, and adaptation

Consider the organizational design of W. L. Gore and Associates, the company that produces and markets Goretex® fabric. The company's plants each employ approximately 200 people, all of whom are encouraged to work with every other employee in a kind of corporate free-for-all. There are few chains of command, few hierarchies, few titles, and few formalized rule and policy

http://www.gore.com

FIGURE 13-5 Structures of Organic and Mechanistic Organizations

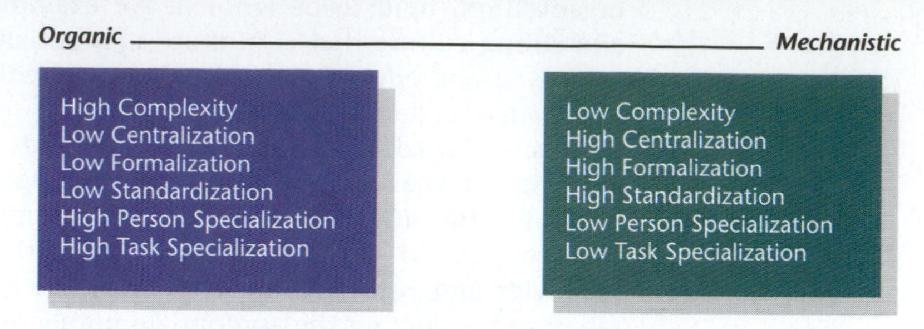

manuals. There is little fixed or assigned authority and responsibility. When people are hired, they are told to look around for something that they would like to do that will help the organization succeed. It sounds like anarchy, but Gore claims that its sales and earnings have been favorably affected as a result of his organizational design.

Although W. L. Gore and Associates is an extreme example, organic designs do allow goals, rather than highly formalized rules or standard operating procedures, to direct employees. Authority is vested in individuals and groups as a function of the task they are working on and the expertise they bring to the task. The loosely coupled, decentralized system changes as necessary to respond to environmental pressures, task needs, and participant expertise. Informal and spontaneous interactions facilitate the sharing of information and ideas. Participative decision making is common. Communication networks emerge and evolve to meet the needs of organizational members and the changing nature of the tasks. Control systems are personal and rely heavily on feedback about process and outcomes.

http://www.generaldynamics.com

Project teams and research labs often have organic designs. At the outset, the novelty of a project, such as developing a new laser-based communication system for General Dynamics, discourages highly formal job descriptions, rigid hierarchical arrangements, and centralized authority and communication systems. Instead, team members experiment with various relationships as they go along and let the evolving situations dictate the most effective arrangements. Structural arrangements change as the team proceeds from one set of activities with one set of demands to another set with different demands.

The virtual corporation, discussed in Chapter 12, possesses many organic attributes. An absence of an elaborate bureaucracy to regulate the joint organizational activity, coupled with a fluid and flexible structure, adjusts to take advantage of the core competencies of the participating organizations.

self-designing organization continuously experiments and tries new ways to respond to environmental demands; it continually appraises and revises itself in an effort to invent as well as to survive its future

The self-designing organization, with its organic design, has been receiving the attention of an increasing number of organization scholars.[29] Described as a "tinkering organization," a **self-designing organization** continuously experiments and tries new ways to respond to environmental demands.[30] It continually appraises and revises itself in an effort to invent as well as to survive its future.[31]

Self-designing organizations are a breed apart. They value impermanence rather than permanence. They generate conflict, invent rather than borrow solutions, pay little attention to tradition, and seek uncertainty. They permit work patterns to evolve to fit situations instead of designing patterns in anticipation of situational demands. Self-designing organizations are open, free, creative, alive (albeit often chaotic), and appeal to people who thrive in uncertainty. Others with a strong need for order, control, and predictability feel uncomfortable and

FIGURE 13-6 The Range of Organizational Designs

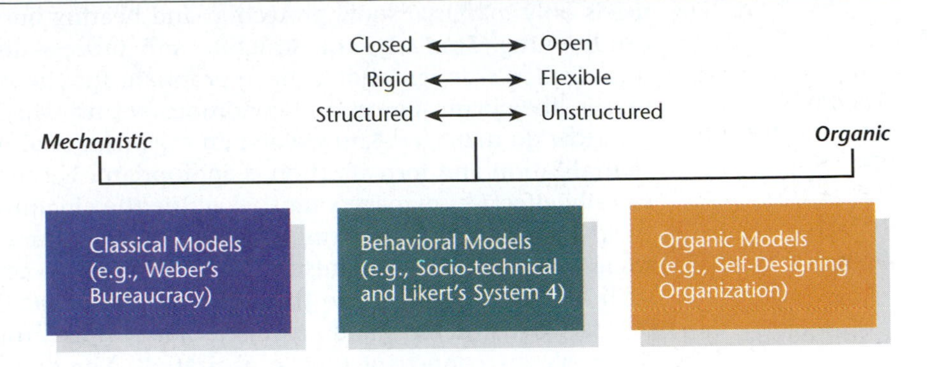

frightened by the concept of self-design. While it is too early to tell whether this organizational design will gain wide popularity in practice,[32] self-designing capability is a desired feature in high-involvement organizations.

The three basic approaches to the design of organizations and their internal units form a continuum (see Figure 13-6). At one extreme are organizations with rigid hierarchies, centralized authority systems, formalized rules, and standard operating procedures. These bureaucracies are mechanistic, with closed, rigid, and highly structured designs. At the other end of the continuum are organizations with flexible hierarchies, decentralized authority systems, and loosely structured designs. These organic organizations, as seen in self-designing organizations, can evolve quickly to meet changes in the environment, such as that brought on by increased foreign competition and technological innovation. Between the two extremes are behavioral models, such as the socio-technical system and System 4 organizations. System 4 organizations place a greater emphasis on open communication, lateral forms of influence and coordination, and participatory decision making than do mechanistic organizations, but they are not as open, fluid, and flexible as organic, self-designing organizations. Depending on its stage of evolution, high-involvement organizations align somewhere between the System 4, socio-technical organization and the true organic organization. Fluidity and flexibility in intra–work team design, openness between teams and their external environment, and an absence of a highly controlling hierarchy above the teams are key characteristics of organizations with organic properties.

In designing an organization, managers must consider internal and external factors—just as an architect designs a house to fit its inhabitants and the environment.

© SUSAN VAN ETTEN

ORGANIZATIONAL CONTEXT AND DESIGN INFLUENCES

When architect Cynthia Lockwood designs a house, she creates a structure and systems that take into account the characteristics of its inhabitants. The needs of a family with children, for example, differ from those of a retired couple, one of whom uses a wheelchair. Cynthia also considers the weather in the proposed location. A house to be built in Marquette, Michigan, needs a structure capable of supporting tons of standing snow on its roof and an excellent heating system. Contrast this with a house designed for southern Texas, which needs only marginal snow protection and heating but absolutely must have air conditioning. Similarly, the structure and process dimensions that define an organization's design should be appropriate for the **organizational context**—that is, the circumstances and conditions within which it operates.

organizational context the circumstances and conditions within which an organization operates

How do managers know when an organizational design with high levels of centralization and formalization is appropriate? Because no single design is universally effective, managers must examine the circumstances inside and outside their organization to determine the most appropriate and effective design. In some cases, highly mechanistic characteristics will be effective; in other cases, such a design could lead to the organization's immediate demise. As managers decide what structures and processes they will use, they must match these factors with the context of their organization. The design of an organization, its structure and processes, need to fit the context of the organization. In order to achieve organizational effectiveness, managers must consider several contextual factors that influence design decisions.[33] If they succeed, they will create an appropriate and effective design that significantly contributes to organizational success.

While several contextual factors influence design decisions, it is important to remember that the design of an organization is a function of strategic choices[34] (see Figure 13-7). Under ideal and rational conditions, strategic choices made by those who design organizations are guided by the following contextual factors.

Contingency theories of leadership are based on the observation that such contextual factors as technology and the external environment shape strategic choices and organizational structure. These contingency theories have led to a number of relatively simple and straightforward prescriptions: (1) Turbulent environments call for organic designs; (2) mass production and routine technologies call for mechanistic designs; and (3) a highly educated work force calls for less bureaucratization. In this section, we take a closer look at how context influences organizational design.

FIGURE 13-7 Strategic Choice and Organizational Design

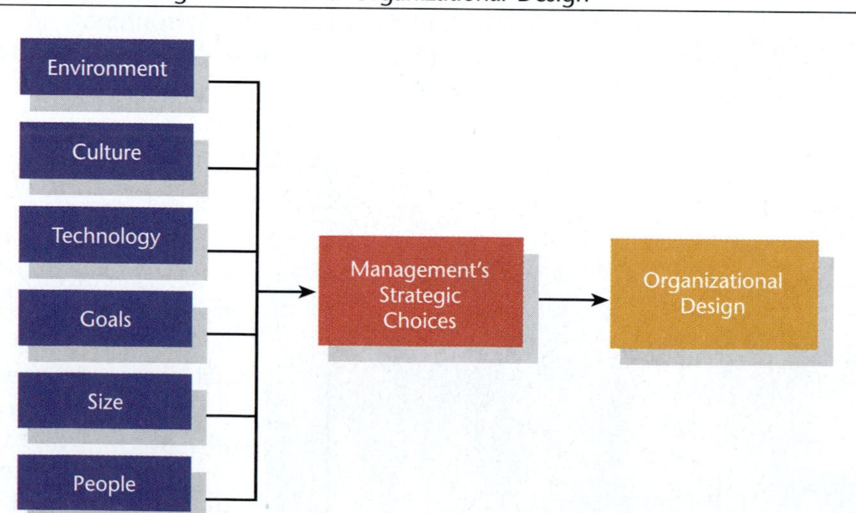

The External Environment

Particularly since the early 1960s, people who study organizations have stressed the importance of designing them so that they can respond better to their external environments. Organizations operating in the fiercely competitive airline industry must contend with threats of buyouts, price wars, changing schedules, and competition for lucrative routes. The uncertainty that accompanies such unstable and unpredictable environmental conditions requires a flexible organizational design, such as found in the organic models. In addition, as environmental demands change rapidly, organizations that can respond rapidly will have a competitive advantage. It took top management and the board of directors of GE only 36 hours to decide to spend approximately 50 billion dollars to purchase Honeywell. In stable environments, however, organizations have little need for speed and flexibility. Continuity and lack of environmental change thus enable managers to use standard operating procedures, centralized authority systems, and other efficient characteristics of mechanistically designed organizations, such as found in the bureaucratic model.

In addition to considering the external environment's influence on the organization as a whole, managers must judge the effects of the individual external environments that surround each organizational unit.[35] As you may recall from Chapter 4, Paul Lawrence and Jay Lorsch observed that firms operating in stable environments have work units with similar structures and comparable time, goal, and interpersonal orientations, but firms operating in unstable environments often have highly differentiated work units, with varying time, interpersonal, and goal orientations. It is important that managers match the design of each unit to the conditions of its external environment. For example, Colgate-Palmolive's production department, operating under relatively stable environmental conditions, might do well with a mechanistic structure, while its marketing group, operating in a more turbulent environment, might need an organic structure.

In sum, "successful firms competing in complex and dynamic industries have been found to have organic structures, . . . whereas successful firms competing in simple and static environments are characterized by mechanistic structures. . . ."[36] Why? The organic approach gives managers the flexibility and rapid response critical in dealing with environmental uncertainty and change; the bureaucratic model allows managers to streamline operations and compete in areas where efficiency, rather than innovation, determines success.

Societal Culture

The culture of the society that an organization operates in and the culture's attitudes toward authority also strongly influence organizational design. This effect is readily apparent if we compare organizations around the world. Researchers attribute many of the structural differences between British and American organizations to the fact that authority in British society often stems from tradition, whereas authority in the United States is based more on law and reason.[37] French organizational sociologist Michael Crozier attributes the strength of the bureaucracy in France to the value that society places on protecting individuals from those with power.[38] According to Crozier, the strong hierarchy, strict rules, and firmly established work procedures of the bureaucratic design keep authority figures from intruding into workers' daily lives. In contrast to their German counterparts, American organizations emphasize individualism and the need for achievement, which is reflected in the design of many U.S. organizations.[39] Finally, Japanese organizations and their group management systems may reflect the dominant role of society over that of individuals in Japanese culture.[40]

Technology

People often define technology as the machinery an organization uses, yet an organization's technology includes *any* process or technique that converts inputs to outputs, whether it is turning high school students into college graduates or transforming bolts of cloth into business suits.[41] An organization may use one overall technology, but each work unit also uses its own technology to accomplish its assigned task. For example, in a university, the routine technology used by the food service department to produce lunch in the cafeteria exists side by side with the nonroutine technology used in the biomedical research laboratory to pursue cancer research. The primary technology of the entire university is based on developing new knowledge and exchanging it through writing and direct, interpersonal interaction; thus, this technology focuses on the creation, transformation, and exchange of ideas.

Pioneering work on the relationship between technology and organizational design was done by British organization scholar Joan Woodward. In the early 1960s, she studied the relationship between technology and a number of organizational design features (span of control, hierarchy, decentralization of authority, and so on) in 100 British manufacturing firms.[42] Woodward classified firms according to three types of technology. In increasing order of technological complexity, they are *unit or small-batch technology*—products are custom-made to a customer's specification (for example, tailor-made suits, custom-built vacation homes) and usually are produced in very small quantities; *large-batch and mass-production technology*—a large number of products are manufactured assembly-line fashion (appliances and automobiles) before production changes over to another type of products; and *continuous process technology*—products are generated in a continuous stream such that the beginning of the second product is not distinguishable from the end of the first (refining of petroleum and other chemicals).

How does technology influence organizational design? Woodward noted that, as the technology becomes more complex, the number of hierarchical levels in an organization's structure increases. Span of control is influenced by type of technology. Top management's span increases as the technology becomes more complex. So does the size of the organization's staff. The span of control for lower-level supervisors is largest for organizations with large-batch or mass-production technologies. From these and other observations, Woodward noted that

> Successful firms inside the large-batch production range tended to have mechanistic management systems. On the other hand, successful firms outside the range tended to have organic systems.[43]

In structuring organizations, managers must consider what technology will be used. If it will be routine, a mechanistic (bureaucratic) design may be appropriate.[44] Organic designs, however, are better suited for organizations whose tasks and accompanying technology are nonroutine in nature.[45]

Goals

Alfred Chandler, while on the faculty at the Massachusetts Institute of Technology, observed a close relationship between the strategy pursued by an organization and its structure.[46] He analyzed the histories of such firms as General Motors, Standard Oil, Du Pont, and Sears and noted that each used simple and centralized structures when their product lines were limited; however, as the firms took on more complex goals, adopted new products, entered new markets, and increased output, each decentralized their structures.

Recent work shows that the strategies chosen by an organization's managers determine the tasks it undertakes, the technology it uses, and the environments in which it operates. Subsequently, these attributes—tasks, technology, and environment—have a strong impact on the design adopted by the organization.[47] General Motors, Standard Oil, Du Pont, and Sears all illustrate this finding.

http://www.sears.com

The design that an organization adopts, in turn, places constraints on its future goals. A mechanistic organization, for example, is likely to pursue goals that emphasize higher levels of productivity and operating efficiency. On the other hand, organizations that pursue innovation must be open and flexible, and must permit exchanges among individuals and groups that are highly heterogeneous in nature.[48]

Size

The size of an organization influences its design. As a department expands, a manager's span of control increases. As the span of control increases, coordination and control pressures mount. In response to these increased pressures, organizations frequently make structural changes. This reorganization often results in more work units, more hierarchical levels, and an ever more complex structure.

As organizations become larger, managers often increase both the number of specialized departments (especially staff departments) and job specialization. Individuals often become responsible for the performance of a narrow range of activities. In the early days at Progressive Video Images, for example, employee Liz Phinney was involved in virtually all of the company's business activities. On a given day, she would often work on 35-mm stills, 8-mm movies, VHS videos, Beta videos, transfers from film to video, and so on. As the company grew, however, it developed specialized departments. Now Liz works exclusively at transferring 8-mm movies to VHS videotape.

Often accompanying increased specialization is greater standardization and formalization, more delegation of authority, and increased decentralization of structure. Employees at lower levels make decisions to relieve upward pressure and bottlenecks in the hierarchy, but these decisions are guided by elaborate policies, rules, and standard operating procedures. Upper-level management then operates under the exception principle, handling only those issues that fall outside the formal guidelines and delegating specific assignments to lower-level employees.

Finally, size affects coordination and control activities. Managers tend to rely increasingly on impersonal modes of coordination and control as the organization grows. As a result, large organizations tend to be mechanistic in design.[49] As organizations move into the 21st century environment, efforts to achieve flexible, lean, and fast structures have been accompanied by a push to small size. Johnson & Johnson, a large company, has structured itself to enjoy the benefits of being small by creating 166 relatively autonomous units.[50]

People

The attitudes, values, beliefs, commitments, and behaviors of organizational members influence the design and, ultimately, the effectiveness of any organization. If employees are not good at self-direction and self-control, for example, the organization must rely on a mechanistic design.[51] If, on the other hand, employees are highly professional, committed, self-directed, and self-controlled, they work better in a less mechanistic design. Workers motivated by safety, security, and social needs tend to be comfortable and work well in a bureaucratic design. Employees with strong growth needs, however, find more challenge and greater satisfaction in an organically designed organization.[52]

Several scholars who study organizations argue that design is largely a function of the strategic preferences and choices of major organizational powerholders.[53] The values, beliefs, attitudes, and commitments of powerholders play a major role in shaping organizational design. Managers who subscribe to Theory X, for example, will design tightly controlled, bureaucratic organizations to keep a watchful eye over the actions of workers they feel must be told exactly what to do and how to do it. Theory Y managers, on the other hand, believe in an individual's capacity to exercise self-direction and self-control and, thus, will adopt organic designs.

Personality factors also influence managers' design preferences. Such factors as authoritarianism are, of course, particularly important. A manager with a highly authoritarian personality, for example, feels that power and status should be clearly defined and specified within organizations. This type of person will create a centralized and formalized structure with a distinct hierarchy of authority.

Clearly, there is no one best organizational design. Good managers review an organization's internal and external environments, technology, goals, size, and other contextual factors when they consider a structural design. They then compare the compatibility of design alternatives with existing and anticipated conditions. Through this systematic approach, managers can select and implement an overall design with supporting superstructures and processes that meet the requirements of their organization.

EMPLOYEE RESPONSES TO ORGANIZATIONAL DESIGN AND CONTEXT

In the preceding chapter we started to look at the impact that organizational design has on employees. We encourage you to review the employee effects of participation presented in Chapter 9 as well as the effects of power (reward, coercive, expert, referent, and legitimate power) discussed in Chapter 11. In this section we continue to explore the question, How does organizational design influence employee attitudes, motivation, and behavior? For an introduction to this issue, see *An Inside Look* at organization design and burnout in AIDS nurses.

Complexity

As noted earlier, the complexity of an organization's structure is reflected vertically and horizontally. Vertical complexity represents the number of hierarchical levels in the organization. The greater the number of levels, the more

AN INSIDE LOOK

Organization Design and Burnout in AIDS Nurses

The concept of burnout is one that nearly everyone knows and recognizes. Employees in human service professions such as nursing and counseling are particularly subject to burnout in the form of emotional fatigue, dissatisfaction, and lack of connection with clients or patients. High burnout also typically results in high employee turnover. One would expect that nurses working exclusively with AIDS patients would be particularly susceptible to burnout due to the level of stress and danger on the job. However, a 1997 study by Linda H. Aiken and Douglas M. Sloane found that AIDS nurses experienced less burnout and reported greater satisfaction with their work than other nurses. This satisfaction rate is due in large part to the organizational design of AIDS treatment facilities.

Aiken and Sloan propose that burnout in general is related most closely to the organizational environment in which the employee works rather than on personal characteristics. In a poorly designed work environment, employees feel victimized and unable to correct problems that arise. Aiken and Sloane discuss the ways in which AIDS nurses respond to two types of organizational design: hospitals that deal solely with AIDS patients vs. general "scattered-bed" hospitals; and hospitals that experience high nurse turnover vs. those who retain a satisfied nursing staff.

Nurses who work in hospitals that deal strictly with AIDS patients report a higher level of job satisfaction than those in the scattered-bed facilities. In specialized AIDS units, nurses' status is nearly equivalent to that of physicians. This is partially due to the fact that there is no known cure for AIDS, and the patients there require the care of nurses as much as or more so than they need doctors' care. Nurses in specialized AIDS hospitals are therefore given greater status, control over their patients, and decision-making autonomy. In addition, working with one type of patient allows AIDS nurses to gain and use specialized knowledge and feel fully competent in the area.

Hospitals that excel in retaining and attracting new nurses are known as magnet hospitals. Magnet hospitals share several organizational design features that result in their human resources' success. These features include a flat organization structure, decentralized decision making and authority for the nurses, support for the nurses' decisions at the management level, open communication between doctors and nurses, and representation of the nurse executive, or head nurse, in the organization responsible for making hospitalwide decisions.

Because hospitals rely heavily on qualified labor, effective human resource management is crucial to their success. The results of this study demonstrate that the design of a hospital's organizational environment can have dramatic effects on nurses and hospitals that result in better care for patients.

Source: Adapted from L. H. Aiken and D. M. Sloane. 1997. Effect of organizational innovations in AIDS care on burnout among urban hospital nurses. *Work and Occupations* 24(4): 453–477.

complex the organization's structure and the more difficulties for management as it attempts to integrate these different levels. Horizontal complexity represents the number of work units. The greater the number of differentiated units, relative to the size of the organization, the more complex the organization's structure, and the more difficult the integration of these units. Horizontal complexity signals greater role differentiation and specialization, thus a larger number of differentiated work units.

The question we address here is, How do organizational members respond to complexity in their organization's structure? The evidence that has emerged to date suggests that complexity, particularly vertical complexity, does affect member attitudes and behaviors. Those organizational members who work near the bottom of the organization appear to experience more need satisfaction in "flat" organizations—that is, in organizations with few hierarchical levels (low vertical complexity). Organizational members (managers) located near the top of the organization, however, tend to be more need satisfied in "tall" organizations—organizations with a greater number of hierarchical levels (high vertical complexity).[54]

Formalization

Formalization, like centralization, is another form of control used in bureaucratic organizations. As a structural dimension, formalization represents the degree to which a social system has standardized its operating norms and expressed them in written form. Organization scholars are consistent in their thinking about the effects of formalization—high levels of norm codification expressed in written rules, operating policies, and procedures that govern work behavior and other organizational relationships—on organizational members: "The higher the formalization, the lower the job satisfaction."[55] Empirical evidence, though limited in nature, tends to support this hypothesis.[56]

Centralization and Decentralization

Recall that centralization and decentralization indicate the location of decision-making authority in the organization's hierarchy. The farther the decision-making authority is removed from the employee charged with carrying out those decisions, the greater the negative effects. There appears to be somewhat less alienation from work, more satisfaction with supervision, and less job dissatisfaction when the organization's power structure is decentralized. In addition, some evidence suggests that there is more communication among co-workers and somewhat higher levels of performance under a decentralized structure.[57, 58, 59] There also appears to be support for the hypothesis that centralization has a negative relationship with performance and contributes to employee absenteeism.[60] Finally, with decentralization, organizational members have increased control over their work. Control is seen as a major route for developing feelings of ownership for different facets of the organization. As we have noted, acts of good organizational citizenship behavior increase with psychological ownership.[61]

Stratification

Stratification is seen as a status incongruence among organizational members. Scholars have consistently predicted that strong status systems (indoor vs. outdoor parking, separate entrances and dining rooms for managers and laborers, and so on) produce worker dissatisfaction—"the higher the stratification, the lower the job satisfaction."[62] Limited evidence appears to support this prediction.[63]

Size

Theory and research in organizational behavior provide us with two perspectives on the effects of the contextual variable size. First, researchers have looked into the impact of the size of the macro organization. Those taking this tack are interested in the attitudinal, motivational, and behavioral effects associated with being a member of a large organization like General Motors versus a small organization like the University Bar and Grill. Second, researchers have looked into the effects of work unit size and span of control. Those taking this perspective are interested in the employee effects associated with the size of the work unit (a department, for instance) in which one works on a day-to-day basis.

A review of the literature on the attitudinal and behavioral effects of size does not reveal a strong trend. In fact, the effects of size may be indirect and moderated by a number of other factors. For example, managers who cope with the burdens associated with managing large social systems via standardization and formalization tend to have different effects than those who choose to manage size by providing their employees with higher degrees of autonomy. In the former situation, size tends to be associated with higher levels of dissatisfaction, while in the latter situation, size tends to be associated with higher levels of job satisfaction. Thus, the effects are not due to size, but to the way in which size is managed.

If we look at effects from size alone, the evidence to date indicates that size appears to increase withdrawal behavior, with greater turnover and absenteeism associated with larger social systems.[64] The research conducted to date also suggests that job dissatisfaction is higher for people working in large social systems, and more labor disputes occur in large social systems.[65] Organization scholars reason that large social systems lead to low cohesiveness, poor communication, and division of labor; which in turn cause job dissatisfaction; and this contributes to absenteeism, turnover, and labor strife, each of which negatively impacts worker and firm productivity.[66]

Technology

Early studies of the effects of technology are quite consistent in their observations.[67] The abundance of evidence indicates that routine, long-linked, system-controlled, mass production technologies are associated with lower levels of job satisfaction, greater worker alienation, greater absenteeism, and lower levels of worker integration.

Jon L. Pierce and his colleagues[68] studied the effects of alternative sources of work environment structure (technology, job design, work unit, and leader behavior). They report a significant relationship between technology and satisfaction, supervisory ratings of effort, and performance. More favorable effects were associated with low levels of system-controlled technology. Other investigators report greater satisfaction, lower absenteeism, with no turnover effects among nurses working under minimal versus maximal technology in a nurse-managed special care unit.[69]

Technology-induced uncertainty has been shown to be associated with worker dissatisfaction, unless offset by increases in job complexity which frequently accompany technology-based uncertainty. As technology becomes increasingly under the control of people, and less programmed and system-controlled, challenge, intrinsic rewards, and satisfaction should increase. It is then—when the inability to preprogram the technology produces uncertainty, anxiety, and stress—that dissatisfaction, declining motivation, and performance decrements are likely to occur.[70] Thus, the lack of personal control associated with technology and the accompanying uncertainty may be the primary cause of negative effects.[71]

People—Management's Attitudes and Behaviors

For decades, managers and organization scholars have been keenly interested in organizational commitment. As we saw in Chapter 6, commitment is the nature and strength of an organizational member's attachment to the organization. Employees commit to—that is, want to maintain their affiliation with—an organization for a variety of reasons. This attachment reflects a need to belong (continuance commitment), a wanting to belong (affective commitment), and membership because it is perceived as the "right thing to do" (normative commitment). In addition to the employee's organizational commitment, there is the organization's commitment to the employee.

The norm of reciprocity, which is central to social exchange theory,[72] helps us understand the strength of the employee commitment. The norm of reciprocity suggests that organizational members feel obligated to respond positively to the favorable treatment they receive from their employer. If an organization demonstrates its loyalty and commitment to employees, employees will return loyalty and commitment. In fact, research reveals that organizational members commonly believe that their relationship with the organization is reciprocal.[73]

Current theory and research results indicate that the degree to which employees perceive that management is committed to them affects the strength of their affective commitment to the organization. This commitment from the organization also heightens employee job satisfaction, lowers absenteeism, decreases intentions to quit, lowers turnover, increases effort on behalf of the organization, raises performance, and causes employees to engage in more organizational citizenship behavior.[74] Employees come to experience management and organizational commitment to them by viewing the favorableness of those job conditions that management controls. Management's ability to affect certain job conditions is, of course, limited. Perceived support is more likely to stem from those acts where employees perceive management has discretion Thus, it is hypothesized (see Figure 13-8) that the organization's commitment to its employees is a significant determinant of the commitment returned by members.

empowerment the result of a process that enhances feelings of self-efficacy among organizational members, enabling them to feel as though they can perform their work effectively, and that they are responsible for doing so

Empowerment

One particularly significant emotional effect that often results from delegation is the empowerment of organizational members. **Empowerment** is the result of a process that enhances feelings of self-efficacy among organizational members, enabling them to feel as though they can perform their work effectively, and that they are responsible for doing so.[75] To empower, managers often transfer authority and responsibility, as both enable an individual to make things happen.[76]

FIGURE 13-8 The Commitment–Commitment Relationship

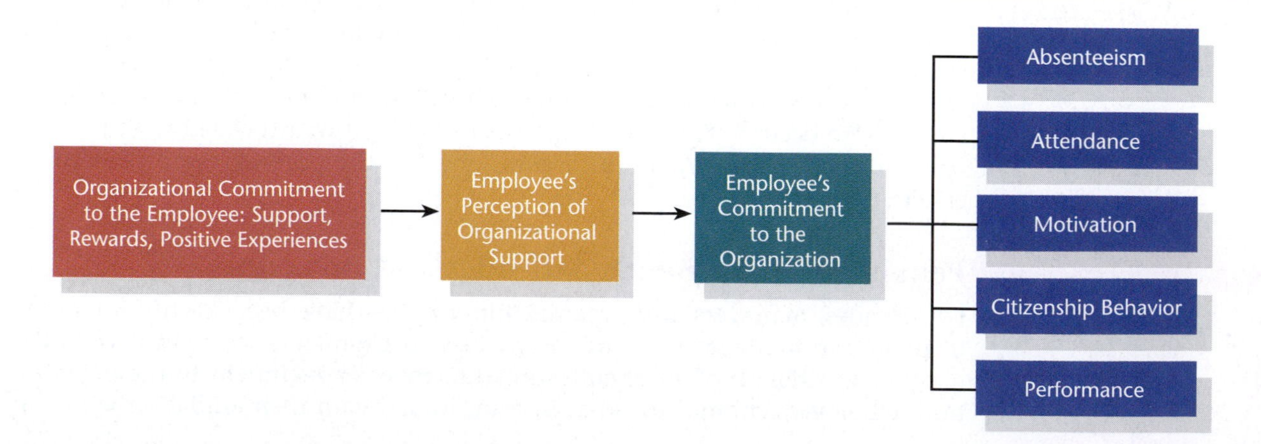

SELF-ASSESSMENT Psychological Empowerment

General Instructions: Think about your current job and answer each question using the following scale.

1 = Strongly Disagree
2 = Disagree
3 = Slightly Disagree
4 = Neither Agree nor Disagree
5 = Slightly Agree
6 = Agree
7 = Strongly Agree

1. The work that I do is meaningful to me.
2. I am confident about my ability to do my job.
3. I have significant autonomy in determining how I do my job.
4. I have significant influence over what happens in my department.

Scoring and Interpretation:

Sum your score for the four questions and divide by 4. This is your overall psychological empowerment.

A score of 6.0 and greater suggests a high level of empowerment, while a score of 2.0 or less suggests a low level of psychological empowerment. The four questions and your score on each reflect the meaning, competence, self-determination, and impact that you experience on your job.

Source: Sample items taken from G. M. Spreitzer's assessment of psychological empowerment. For the complete measure, see G. M. Spreitzer. 1995. Psychological empowerment in the workplace: Dimensions, measurement, and validation. *Academy of Management Journal* 38:1442–1465.

Empowerment is not a dimension of the personality (and thus an enduring state); instead it is a cognitive state that individuals experience while carrying out their organizational role. As such, psychological empowerment "reflects the ongoing ebb and flow of people's perceptions about themselves in relation to their work environment."[77] Empowerment is an intrinsic motivational state that manifests itself when the organizational member experiences the following cognitive states: (1) experiencing *meaning* in one's work; (2) having a belief in one's capacity to perform (feeling *competence* or experiencing self-efficacy); (3) experiencing a sense of choice (*self-determination* or autonomy) in initiating and regulating one's activities; and (4) feeling as though one has an *impact* upon what happens.[78] Empowered individuals take a proactive approach to their work. Such individuals prefer and feel as though they are capable of having a positive impact on their job and job context.

For those organizational members who feel powerless within the organizational context, there are many management strategies, such as training, keeping workers informed, job enrichment, and participative management, that can empower them. With delegation comes an expanded role, the creation of responsibility, the transfer of authority, and the opportunity to exercise more control. Management consultant William C. Byham suggests that the high-involvement organization is synonymous with the presence of authority and responsibility embedded at lower levels in the organizational hierarchy and thus empowered organizational members.[79]

http://www.assessmentcenters.org/pages/byhambio.html

AN INSIDE LOOK

Employee Empowerment as a Tool for Retention

One of the biggest challenges for organizations today is retaining a qualified and motivated work force. Retaining employees is a struggle because of the strong economy (increased demand for labor), and because employees do not feel the loyalty they once did. According to a recent survey, more than half the respondents stated that they would leave their current job for one offering a 20 percent raise in pay. As a result, organizations in the 21st century must be ever more creative as they strive to retain employees. One of best ways to do this is via employee ownership and employee empowerment.

As mentioned in Chapter 2, Starbucks offers all employees the opportunity to become "partners" in the company by investing in Bean Stock. This practice has helped Starbucks overcome the typical high turnover rate of the fast-food industry to post an amazingly low turnover rate of 16 percent for full-time employees.

Like Starbucks, Kinko's calls their employees "partners." They reward employees who remain with the organization one year or more by giving them $300 in company stock. In addition, they consolidated what had previously been a very decentralized organization and created a more controlled training program to provide employees with a common background and a vision of how they can make Kinko's their career. Since instituting these and other changes, Kinko's has reduced their employee turnover rate by nearly 30 percent.

Whole Foods Market, in Austin, Texas, also offers its employees stock options. But what is of interest to us here is how Whole Foods Market empowers its employees. New employees are hired provisionally and placed on an existing team. After one month, team members determine via vote whether they choose to work with this employee. This strategy encourages collaboration and cooperation among team members. Whole Foods also boasts an excellent retention record.

The retail giant Nordstrom has long empowered its employees. Nordstrom employees who are customer service and sales stars get their choice of prime working hours as well as financial bonuses. The company values respect and trust and treats its employees accordingly. And, not surprisingly, Nordstrom employees are loyal and Nordstrom's retention ratings are among the best in the industry.

One of the most tangible benefits of employee satisfaction and retention is improved organizational performance. Companies that utilize stock ownership plans tend to have increased profits, sales, and stock prices. A workforce that is highly motivated to succeed and therefore to help the organization succeed is the cornerstone to helping organizations compete in the 21st century.

Source: Adapted from C. Joinson. 1999. The cost of doing business? *HR Magazine* 44(13):86–92.

One major consequence associated with empowerment is that it produces energy. The more authority and responsibility held by an organizational member, the more energy they are likely to experience.[80] The most direct consequence of empowerment is that the energy produced results in a high level of intrinsic motivation, and as noted earlier, motivation is a prerequisite for effective human behavior. The stronger the motivation, assuming that people have the skills to perform and know how, the higher their level of performance (see Figure 13-9).

Summary: Employee Responses to Organizational Design and Context

Organizational members work in mechanistic or organically designed social systems, or some hybrid of the two. The mechanistic organization, as we have noted, can be characterized in terms of low complexity, high centralization, high

FIGURE 13-9 The Empowerment Model

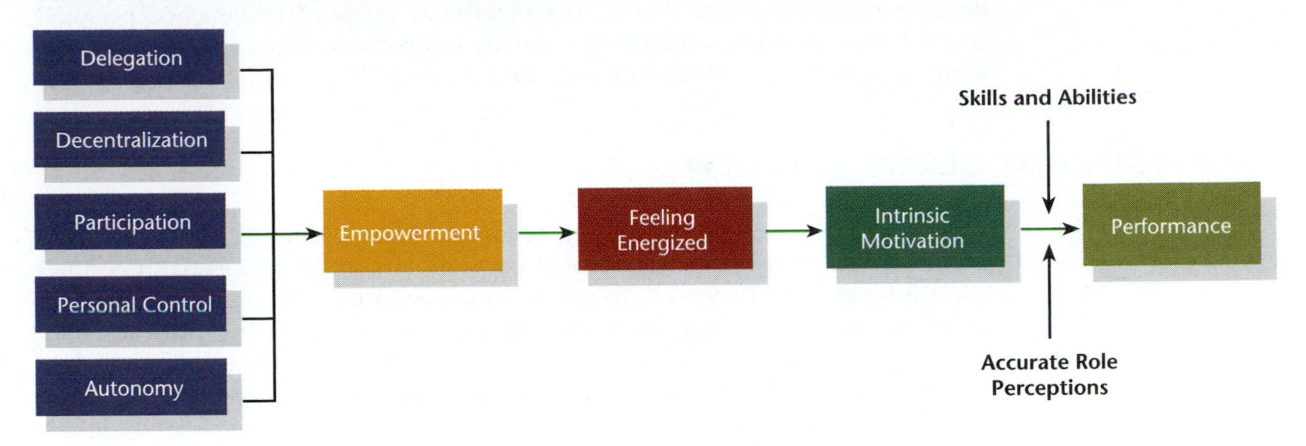

formalization, high stratification, and low specialization (task and person). The organic organization is structurally complex and decentralized, with low levels of formalization and stratification, accompanied by specialization.

Managers who need to emphasize productivity and efficiency commonly turn to the mechanistic organization design. This design also results in low levels of organizational flexibility, adaptiveness, and innovation. Emerging evidence suggests that organizational design affects employee perceptions of procedural justice (recall from Chapter 9 that procedural justice has to do with employee perceptions of fairness as it relates to the way decisions are made). Experiences of procedural injustice are likely to be higher in mechanistically designed organizations.[81] In addition, employees tend to have lower levels of job satisfaction, intrinsic motivation, and subsequently they display higher levels of withdrawal (absenteeism, tardiness, and turnover) and more resistance (union activity).

Managers who emphasize organizational adaptiveness and flexibility are more likely to adopt the organic structure because it is less bound by preprogrammed modes of coordination and control, and information flow bottlenecks, and concentrated authority. Organic organizations are more innovative, responsive, fast, flexible, and less resistant to change. As a consequence, the organic organization also has somewhat higher levels of inefficiency and lower levels of productivity. In addition, organizational members tend to be more intrinsically motivated, job satisfied, have higher levels of psychological ownership and stronger organizational identification, and experience procedural justice.[82] Simultaneously, experiences of role conflict, role ambiguity, and role overload are higher, and the pace of organizational life faster, all of which results in higher levels of stress.

The mechanistic and organic organizational designs allow organizational members to exercise very different levels of personal control. As organizations increase the amount of structure through centralization, formalization, and stratification, control shifts from the individual to the system. Thus, lower-level employees have less and less discretion in their work.

Evidence indicates that with increasing degrees of structure, lower-level organizational members experience and exercise less and less control, which in turn reduces the likelihood that they will develop feelings of ownership for either their work or the organization.[83] This comes at a cost to the organization, because research reveals that as organizational members experience personal control, they gain job satisfaction, intrinsic motivation, organizational commitment, and withdrawal behavior and stress decrease.[84]

ORGANIZATIONAL DESIGN IN REVIEW

As a part of the organizing activity, managers must decide how to design the overall organization. Managers should consider structural, process, and contextual dimensions as they work to achieve an appropriate organizational arrangement. In the last chapter, we addressed part of the organizing process as we considered how the work of organizations is organized and how departments and superstructure are created. In this chapter we examined to organizational design.

First, we looked at influence, power, and authority. Organizational members are able to influence others in the organization to the extent that they have the power and authority to do so. Authority provides individuals and groups the right to influence others. Merely having the authority is not enough, however, for managers to influence employees. The ability to exert authority requires managers to develop an adequate interpersonal power base that adds to the legitimate power base derived from their position in the organization's hierarchy. This is done by incorporating other sources of power, such as reward, coercion, and expertise.

Employees continually try to influence one another as they pursue organizational goals. Organizations try to control these influence patterns by creating formal authority systems. There are three views of the types and sources of authority. The classical view holds that people at the top of the hierarchy have the right to influence people at lower levels, resulting in a downward flow of authority. The acceptance view maintains that authority flows upward, because employees must accept managerial influence as legitimate before they will comply. The situational view proposes that authority is neither up nor down. Instead, the question of who has authority depends on the situation. The one belief shared by all three views is that employees must perceive managerial directives to be legitimate. If they do, then workers tend to comply, in part because they have learned to do so. The type of compliance—or lack of it—that managers can expect to receive can be predicted according to the types of influence the managers used.

The authority system defines an organization's authority relationships. Line authority is a command authority that follows an organization's vertical chain of command. Organizational members must comply with members above them in the hierarchy who have the right to issue directives. Staff authority is an advisory authority in which managers influence through their expertise and experience. Functional authority is a command authority over a set of functionally related activities. Unlike the vertical flow of line authority, however, functional authority can also flow horizontally and diagonally.

Managers receive some of their line, staff, or functional authority because members above them have transferred that authority to them through delegation. Although delegators may transfer authority and responsibility for certain tasks to others, the delegators remain ultimately responsible for the delegated activities. Delegating is a way to cope with large and complex work loads, but some managers and workers resist delegation. Organizations should encourage managers to delegate, by training employees, and by providing the necessary resources.

The amount of delegation that occurs in an organization determines its degree of decentralization. A highly decentralized authority system delegates authority to points in the hierarchy where decisions are implemented. Decentralization characterizes the authority structure of high-involvement organizations, and is appropriate for high levels of environmental and task-induced uncertainty that accompany nonroutine technologies. Organizations determine the level of decentralization appropriate for their needs by examining the external environment; the history, size, and complexity of the organization; the work performed in the organization; and the people who do the work.

Essentially, authority, delegation, and decentralization are the means by which managers try to control the powerful effects of influence in organizations. Whether this influence is exercised in the direction intended depends, in part, on how well the authority system matches the characteristics of an organization.

Several models of organizational design are operative and characterize today's organizational landscape. The bureaucratic (mechanistic) structure approach is advocated by classical management thinkers. It is relatively closed and rigid; it uses a high level of structured authority, communication, and coordination methods; and it uses many written standard operating procedures to control behavior.

To counter the classicists' concentration on the technical side of organizations, behavioral models emerged that stressed the human side of organizations. Socio-technical systems theory advocates argued that organizations designed strictly from a mechanical perspective are less effective than alternative designs. They called for the recognition of organizations as both technical and social systems that must be balanced. Similarly, Rensis Likert's System 4 design resulted in a network of interlocking groups, with managers' acting as linking pins to coordinate the flow of information and expertise. Both provide a structure that is more open and participatory than is the classical model.

The third model is the organic design. Created to permit an organization's structure to evolve quickly in response to changes in the internal and external environments, the organic approach has resulted in self-designing organizations. These are extremely fluid, flexible organizations that "go with the flow." This arrangement has advantages for organizations that must cope with foreign competition and technological innovation, but it may not be comfortable for workers who desire firm control and want procedures clearly outlined.

Managers contemplating various models and structures when designing organizations must take certain contextual factors into account. Environmental considerations, their organization's culture, the type and complexity of the technology to be used, their organization's goals, its size, and the attributes of organizational members give rise to variations in organizational design. These contextual factors make certain approaches more suitable than others.

Finally, the design of an organization shapes employee attitudes, motivation, and work-related behavior. We reviewed the relationship between several structural and contextual features and their impact on employees. We concluded by looking at the impact of mechanistic and organically designed social systems. It appears as though the majority of organizational members tend to prefer the structural features offered by organic organizations.

A FINAL LOOK

Over lunch, Stan confides to Sandra Montoya, another team leader, that his team isn't working effectively or cohesively. Sandra's team is known to be one of the most productive in the company, and Stan hopes she'll have some ideas.

After listening to Stan tell of intervening with a client earlier, Sandra suggests that he think of himself as less of a leader and as more of a coach. "Remember—these are self-managing teams," Sandra notes. "Maybe they aren't motivated to take responsibility for issues because you are constantly doing things for them. Try to facilitate more and direct less. I think you'll see some interesting results."

Stan is doubtful but decides to have a really open talk with his team. The group admits that they're team in name only. They are uncomfortable with Stan continually circumventing them to solve problems and agree that they want more decision-making authority. Stan resolves to stop running the meetings and start facilitating. The air is a lot clearer as the team heads back to work. Stan understands that this is just the first step, but it feels like a good first step.

KEY TERMS

acceptance view of authority, 466
authority, 465
bureaucratic organization, 477
centralization, 470
classical authority theory, 466
decentralization, 470
delegation, 468
empowerment, 490
functional authority, 467
influence, 465
interpersonal influence, 465
line authority, 467
organic organization, 479
organizational context, 482
organizational design, 462
organizational structure, 463
power, 465
self-designing organization, 480
situational view of authority, 466
staff authority, 467

ISSUES FOR REVIEW AND DISCUSSION

1. Explain the roles of structure, process, and context in organizational design.
2. Discuss the concepts of influence, power, and authority and their relationship.
3. Explain how authority is transferred from one location in an organization to another.
4. Compare and contrast the structures of mechanistic and organic organizations.
5. Under what conditions is an organic design appropriate?
6. Compare and contrast the bureaucratic and System 4 approaches to organizational design.
7. What are some attributes of high-involvement organizations?
8. Discuss the relationship between the different dimensions of an organization's context and its structure.
9. Discuss employee reactions to organizational design.

EXERCISES

ORGANIZATION DESIGN: ANALYZING A HOSPITAL DEPARTMENT CONSOLIDATION

The Four Frames Model*

BACKGROUND ON THE FOUR FRAMES MODEL

A book by Lee Bolman and Terrence Deal entitled *Reframing Organizations* introduces a novel approach to making sense of the chaotic environment we call organizational life. They suggest that effective leaders are able to view organizational problems from multiple perspectives or what they call "frames." The four frames of their model are structural, human resources, political, and symbolic.

Core Assumptions

The Structural Frame

1. Organizations exist primarily to accomplish established goals.
2. For any organization, there is a structure appropriate to the goals, the environment, the technology, and the participants.
3. Organizations work most effectively when environmental turbulence and the personal preferences of participants are contained by norms of rationality.
4. Specialization permits higher levels of individual expertise and performance.
5. Coordination and control are accomplished best through the exercise of authority and impersonal rules.
6. Structure can be systematically designed and implemented.
7. Organizational problems usually reflect an inappropriate structure and can be resolved through redesign and reorganization.

The Human Resource Frame

1. Organizations exist to serve human needs (and humans do not exist to serve organizational needs).
2. Organizations and people need each other. Organizations need the ideas, energy, and talent that people provide, while people need the careers, salaries, and work opportunities that organizations provide.
3. When the fit between the individual and the organization is poor, one or both will suffer: The individual will be exploited or will seek to exploit the organization, or both.
4. When the fit is good between the individual and the organization, both benefit: Humans can do meaningful and satisfying work while providing the resources the organization needs to accomplish its mission.

The Political Frame

The political frame views organizations as "alive and screaming" political arenas that house a complex variety of individuals and interest groups. Five propositions summarize the political perspective:

1. Most of the important decisions in organizations involve the allocation of scarce resources.
2. Organizations are coalitions composed of a number of individuals and interest groups (for example, hierarchical levels, departments, professional groups, ethnic groups).
3. Individuals and interest groups differ in their values, preferences, beliefs, information, and perceptions of reality. Such differences are usually enduring and change slowly if at all.
4. Organizational goals and decisions emerge from ongoing processes of bargaining, negotiation, and jockeying for position among individuals and groups.
5. Because of scarce resources and enduring differences, power and conflict are central features of organizational life.

The Symbolic Frame

1. What is most important about any event is not what happened but the meaning of what happened.
2. The meaning of an event is determined not simply by what happened but by the ways that humans interpret what happened.
3. Many of the most significant events and processes in organizations are substantially ambiguous or uncertain. It is often difficult or impossible to know what happened, why it happened, or what will happen next.
4. Ambiguity and uncertainty undermine rational approaches to analysis, problem solving, and decision making.
5. When faced with uncertainty and ambiguity, humans create symbols to reduce the ambiguity, resolve confusion, increase predictability, and provide direction. Events themselves may remain illogical, random, fluid, and meaningless, but human symbols make life meaningful. Improvements come through symbols, myth, and image.

Bolman and Deal offer the four frames as one way of organizing and making sense of large amounts of data. They want managers to be flexible in their diagnoses of events in organizational life so that they can recognize and cope with a variety of problems. Unfortunately,

---

* *Source:* L. Bolman and T. Deal. Copyright 1997. *Reframing Organizations* (2nd ed.). San Francisco: Jossey-Bass. This material is used by permission of Jossey-Bass, a subsidiary of John Wiley & Sons, Inc.

many managers limit their effectiveness by seeing most problems as stemming from a single source.

Exercise Schedule

	Unit Time	Total Time
1. **Groups from each frame**	**15 min**	**15 min**

Divide the class into four groups. Each group is assigned to one of the four frames. Discuss how the issues in the case study can be best understood from that particular frame of reference. (With a larger class, use multiple sets of four groups. Add 10 minutes to bring the groups that have the same frame together to form a single report.)

2. **Groups report**	**15 min**	**30 min**

Each group reports from the perspective of their own frame.

3. **Class discussion**	**10 min**	**40 min**

The instructor leads a discussion on how the Four Frames Model can be applied.

*Hospital Departmental Consolidation***

Janet Johns is the administrator of Suburban Memorial Hospital, a 125-bed hospital in an upper-class suburb located in a western state.

Ms. Johns recently asked the new assistant administrator, Sam Donalds, to investigate whether a consolidation of the EKG, Pulmonary Function, and Cardio-Pulmonary Rehabilitation departments would result in a significant savings to the hospital.

Background

The three departments do basically the same types of patient tests. As medicine has progressed, there has been a movement away from static (at-rest) testing to dynamic (in-motion) testing. Dynamic testing is used in the EKG department for tests on the heart, in the Pulmonary Function department for lung tests, and in the Cardio-Pulmonary Rehabilitation department for both heart and lung tests.

At present there is a duplication of services and equipment among the three departments at Suburban Memorial. In addition, three separate technicians are employed as well as three different part-time physicians who work on a percentage basis, according to the volume of work.

The EKG and Pulmonary Function departments make a significant contribution to Suburban's revenue. The contribution margin of Pulmonary Function has been 80 percent (for every $100 earned, the hospital spends only $20 to earn it) and that of EKG has been 60 percent. Revenues for each department have been:

Department	*Annual Revenue*	*Contribution Margin*
EKG	$460,000	60%
Pulmonary Function	$620,000	80%
Cardio-Pulmonary (new department, less than one year)	$180,000	unknown

The total annual revenue of Suburban Memorial is $21.4 million and the net income is $2.1 million. Mr. Donalds has calculated that a departmental consolidation could initially save the hospital $160,000 by selling duplicated equipment. In addition, the annual savings would amount to:

$ 74,000	personnel costs (fewer technicians needed, etc.)
25,000	ordering and supplies reduction (no duplication, less ordering)
175,000	reduced physician fees (only one physician would be needed)
26,000	plant and facilities (can lease out space not needed after consolidation)
$300,000	Total

Therefore, the annual savings, in essence additional revenue, would be $300,000 in addition to the initial $160,000 for the selling of equipment.

Physicians

Dr. Bartl, head of Pulmonary Function, is responsible for 80 percent of the pulmonary admissions to the hospital and about 4.7 percent of the total admissions. He is an extremely popular physician, attracting respiratory cases from well outside the normal service area of Suburban Memorial.

Dr. Neuman, head of EKG, controls 20 percent of the hospital's cardiac/internal medicine cases. She admits about 3 percent of the hospital's patients.

Finally, the head of the new Cardio-Pulmonary Rehabilitation department, Dr. Hermann, controls 100 percent of those cases, which at this point represent a negligible percentage of the hospital's patient revenue.

Ms. Johns is wondering what to do about the physicians if she decides to go through with the consolidation. One of the three physicians would have to be chosen (with a new reimbursement contract) to head this new department, or perhaps a new, salaried physician could be brought in. The combined workload would still be less than full-time.

** *Source:* © 1988 by Dorothy Marcic and Richard C. Housley. From *Organizational behavior: Experiences and cases* (6th ed.), by D. Marcic, J. Seltzer, and P. Vaill, copyright 2001. Reprinted by permission of South-Western, a division of Thomson Learning. Fax 800-730-2215.

However, Ms. Johns sees several problems with either of those two alternatives. One is that the physicians who would be "excluded" from the new department might become resentful and start admitting their out-of-service-area patients to other hospitals. Ms. Johns and Mr. Donalds have estimated a 25 percent probability that the three physicians would do so, which would mean a possible loss to the hospital of 15 percent of those physicians' admissions.

Ms. Johns has asked Mr. Donalds to prepare a report of the situation, including his recommendations, which will be discussed at the next management council meeting.

Discussion Questions

1. What are the main issues that should be considered in making the decision about consolidation?
2. If you were Mr. Donalds, what would you recommend?
3. Assuming that there is a consolidation, who should head the new department? Why?

INFOTRAC

INFOTRAC® COLLEGE EDITION

The articles listed below are a sampling of those available through InfoTrac College Edition. You can search for them either by title or by the author's name.

Articles

1. The Strands That Connect: An Empirical Assessment of How Organizational Design Links Employees to the Organization. Dr. Miles H. Overholt, Gerald E. Connally, Dr. Thomas C. Harrington, Dr. David Lopez. *Human Resource Planning* June 2000 v23 i2 p38
2. Is loyalty really dead? (includes related article on the US labor market) (employee loyalty) (Cover Story) John J Clancy. *Across the Board* June 1999 v36 i6 p14(6)
3. The Influence of Organizational Structure on the Effectiveness of TQM Programs. (Statistical Data Included) Jasmine Tata, Sameer Prasad, Rod Thorn. *Journal of Managerial Issues* Winter 1999 v11 i4 p440
4. The Pursuit of Managerial Entrepreneurship: Does Organization Matter? Myung Jae Moon. *Public Administration Review* Jan 1999 v59 i1 p31(1)
5. Developing employees for the 'new world.' (column) Ted Gautschi. *Design News* May 18, 1998 v53 n10 p154(1)

Questions

For Article 1:

The article by Overholt et al., "The Strands That Connect: An Empirical Assessment of How Organizational Design Links Employees to the Organization," describes a study that investigates how management uses organizational design to impact employee behavior within the framework of the People-Centered Organization. Two conclusions from this study are that "middle managers and supervisors are the key "to success and "bonding with the organization is a personal process." Explain the research that brings the authors to these conclusions.

For Other Articles:

Other articles on this list discuss organizational design and delegation of authority, and external forces that can impact organizational design. Assign these articles to various members of your group. Meet to discuss what new information they have learned from their readings.

WEB EXERCISE

Managers during the past decade have been downsizing, reengineering, reconfiguring, and restructuring in search of organizational forms that will better serve their organization's needs. Visit the website of an organization of your choice. Looking at the company's annual report or other documents, learn more about the type of structure of this organization.

CASE
Turning the Organization Chart Upside Down

In the book *Moments of Truth*, Jan Carlzon, president of Scandinavian Airlines (SAS), describes how he converted a $20 million loss one year into $54 million profit the following year by turning the organization chart upside down and putting power in the hands of the front-line employees who deal directly with customers. Carlzon argues that the traditional structure, in which top management tells people below what to do, is inefficient and out of place in today's customer-oriented market.

"Managing" [has] shifted from the executive suite to the operational level, where everyone is now a manager of his own situation. When problems arise, each employee has the authority to analyze the situation, determine the appropriate action, and see to it that action is carried out, either alone or with the help of others.

"It may seem like a mere word game to call everyone a 'manager,' but I use the term to remind my staff—and perhaps most of all those at the upper levels of the old pyramid—that their roles have undergone a fundamental change. If top executives who were once the managers must learn to be leaders, then those people out in the front lines must make the operational decisions. They are the ones who most directly influence the customer's impression of the company during those 'moments of truth.'

"Problems are solved on the spot as soon as they arise. No front-line employee has to wait for a supervisor's permission. No passenger boards the plane while still worried or dissatisified."

Carlzon provides some examples to illustrate how this upside-down organization operates. "Take, for example, the announcements made over a plane's public address system. In the old days, the SAS rule book included paragraphs that the crew read verbatim. When we gave the employees more flexibility, we encouraged them to toss out the script and improvise in a conversational manner that suited them, the passengers, and the current situation."

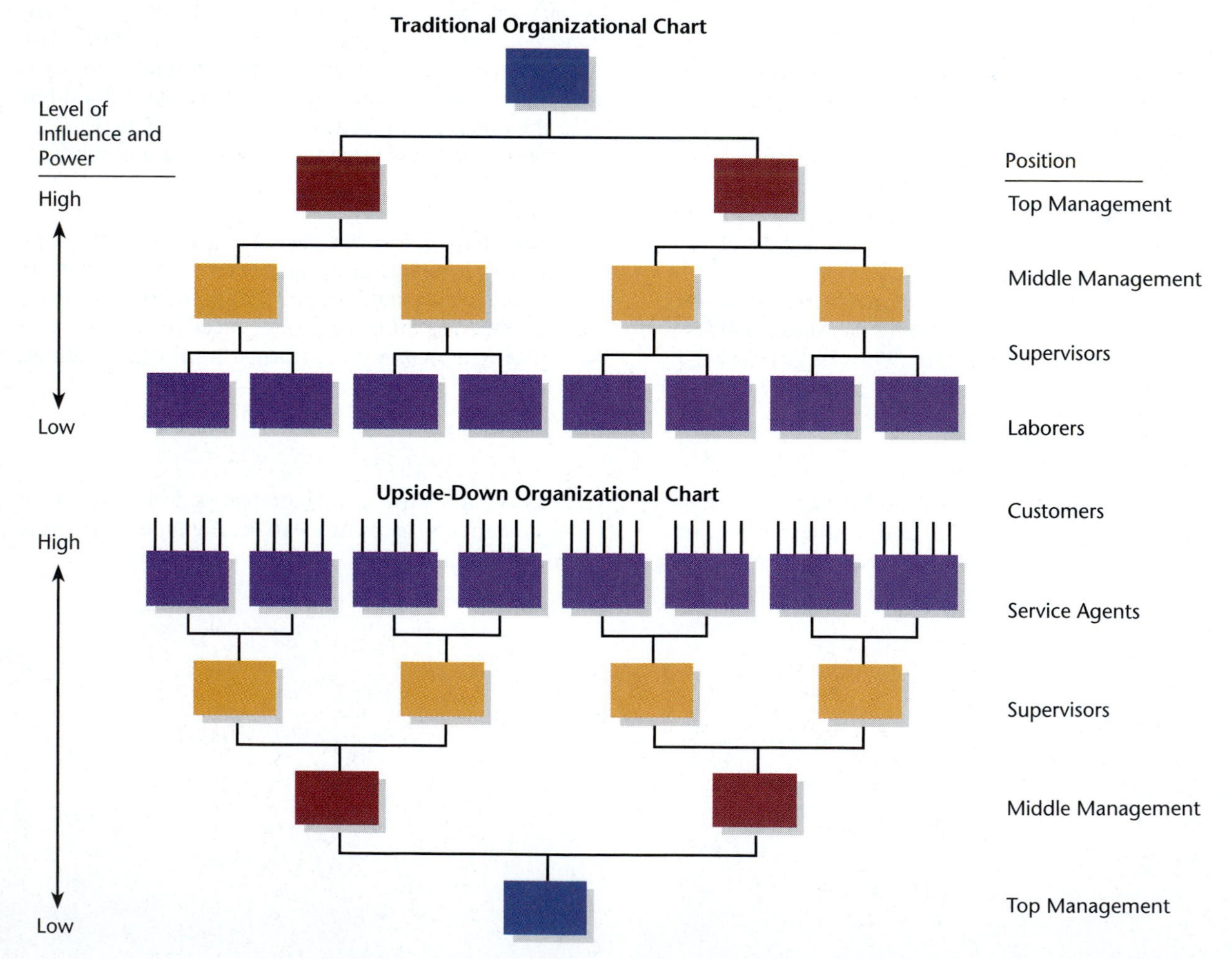

Occasionally, SAS confronted problems as they attempted to function with their organizational chart upside down.

"One day an SAS flight across Sweden has fallen far behind schedule because of snow. Taking responsibility for the situation, the purser decided on her own to compensate the customers for their inconvenience by offering them free coffee and biscuits. She knew from experience that because she was offering them at no charge, she would need about 40 additional servings. So she went to catering and ordered the extra coffee and biscuits.

"The SAS catering supervisor turned her down. It was against regulations to request more than the amount of food allotted to a particular flight, and the supervisor refused to budge. Not to be thwarted, the purser noticed a Finnair docked at the next gate. Finnair is an external customer of the SAS Catering Department and as such is not subject to SAS' internal regulations.

"Thinking quickly, the purser turned to her colleague in the Finnair plane and asked him to order 40 cups of coffee and 40 biscuits. He placed the order, which, according to regulations, the catering supervisor was obligated to fill. Then the SAS purser bought the snacks from Finnair with SAS petty cash and served the grateful passengers."

Questions

1. What does it mean to turn an organization's chart upside down? Is this change just "window dressing" in the form of customer service, or does it represent a significant change in decision making and responsibility?
2. How is an upside-down organization more appropriate to a customer-driven market?
3. How do the roles of front-line employees, upper management, and middle management change in an upside-down organization? What are the relationships between people, and who is responsible for what?

Source: D. J. Cherrington. Copyright © 1989. Organizational behavior: The management of individual and organizational performance. *Boston: Allyn & Bacon, 551–553. Reprinted by permission of Pearson Education, Inc., Upper Saddle River, NJ 07458.*

VIDEO COHESION CASE FOR PART III

Horizons: Strategies for Growth

As Horizons continues to gain experience and strengthen its client list, skills, and reputation, it hopes to grow in several ways.

Product/Market Strategies

Horizons has nine fully functioning divisions. All of the divisions have a full agenda and impressive levels of expertise. Collectively, the divisions provide Horizons a full complement of electronic media competencies. The company is currently focusing its efforts on serving three primary industry segments:

- Corporate business
- Educational publishers
- Entertainment

As part of its efforts to better penetrate these industry segments, Horizons is investigating potential joint venture opportunities, strategic alliances, and small-scale acquisitions. The company also views its clients as partners rather than customers. This mindset helps the company develop "win-win" partnerships with clients that facilitate repeat business.

To best serve the industry segments identified above, Horizons is currently pursuing opportunities in the following areas:

- Weekly television shows
- Feature films
- Children's videos and CDs for broadcast and retail distribution
- New educational products for the publishing industry

Progress is being made on several of these fronts. As mentioned earlier, the company is currently working with two other firms to produce the first educational CD-ROM to star Garfield. Another CD-ROM project will star Jim Henson's Muppets. A feature film is in the offing. Horizons CEO Don Lee and entertainment division head Mike Alu recently announced a venture to produce a feature film, "Crystal Messiah." The film portrays the story of a 12-year-old girl in a racially divided town when a mysterious drifter arrives whom she believes is the town's savior. In terms of website design and management, Horizons will soon launch a website called "restaurant.com." The site will feature a search engine that will help its patrons find the ideal restaurant to match their personal tastes and geographic location. The company has also recently added DVD-Video to its array of service offerings. Horizons hopes to take a leadership role in providing its clients with the highest quality DVD solutions available.

The Big House

To accommodate its projected growth, Horizons is once again preparing to move. The company is presently located in the remodeled Arlington Theater near downtown Columbus, which is not ideal. The company's employees are split in half, with some of them in the Arlington Theater and other in a facility across a busy street. The new facility, known as the DeSantis Estate, is a Tudor-style mansion with over five acres of grounds, horse stables, and a riding arena. The mansion and stables are being remodeled, and the company will put up a third building. The current stable area will be transformed into production studios. The main structure has large, open rooms that are conducive to teamwork and good communication. Because of its size and stature, Horizons employees affectionately call their future home the "Big House."

The move into the "Big House" will be a significant change for Horizons' Columbus employees. Not only will it increase the physical space they have available from 13,000 to 37,000 square feet, but will also create a campus type of atmosphere for the company's ongoing work. In addition, the company hopes to use the new facility to attract larger clients, instill a renewed sense of vitality into its operations, and attract freelancers who need a well-equipped place to practice their crafts.

Decision Making

Horizons has a unique mix of decision-making protocols and routines, primarily because most of the day-to-day decisions are made at the project team level. Strategic, financial, and facilities-related decisions are made by Don Lee and his management team. To keep things straight, the divisional managers meet with Lee once a week at a regularly scheduled staff meeting. Most decisions are made in house, with very little input from consultants or other outsiders. The company does not have an advisory board, although the formation of an advisory board is under consideration.

The Empowerment of Project Teams

Project teams have almost total autonomy to complete their assigned work. When the company gets a job, a project team is selected based on the nature of the work involved and the availability of personnel. Every project is a custom project—there is no cookie-cutter approach to getting things done. The teams typically start by conducting brainstorming sessions, and then they assign individuals specific tasks. Within the teams, the team leaders grant considerable autonomy to individual employees to complete their assigned tasks. The thinking is that autonomy breeds a sense of ownership and responsibility, which brings out the best in employees.

Fluid Nature of Decision Making and Teams

The fluid nature of the project teams gives Horizons somewhat of an amoeba structure. Teams are initiated and terminated, and people come together and separate, based on the ebb and flow of winning contracts and completing work. This can cause frustrations at times. For example, if an employee goes to a certain group of people to ask a question or get help solving a problem, that same group of people probably will not still be together the next time the employee needs help. The upside of the project team arrangement is that, over time, employees get the opportunity to work with a diverse set of people.

Related Website

Restaurant.com: **http://www.restaurant.com**

For Discussion:

1. Reflecting on the "early years" at Horizons, does it appear that Don Lee was engaged in goal or domain planning as it related to his business? What other observations do you infer about planning?
2. What is a mission statement and what purpose does it serve? What do you see as the key components of Horizon's mission statement?
3. In Chapter 3, you read about ethics and social responsibility. After examining Horizon's mission statement, how would you describe (characterize) this company's stance on issues pertaining to social responsibility?
4. Drawing on the task environment model presented in Chapter 4, how might you characterize the external task environment in which Horizons operates?
5. Describe "decision making" at Horizons. Does it fit with your interpretation of the degree of change and differentiation that characterizes its task environment?
6. Given Horizons' growth plans, do you have any concerns about the company's decision-making style? Explain your answer.
7. Describe Don Lee the leader—his traits, behavior/style, and philosophy (attitude).
8. Discuss Horizons' structure in terms of hierarchy, formalization, centralization, and so on. Do you think Horizons is best described as a mechanistic or organic organization? Why?

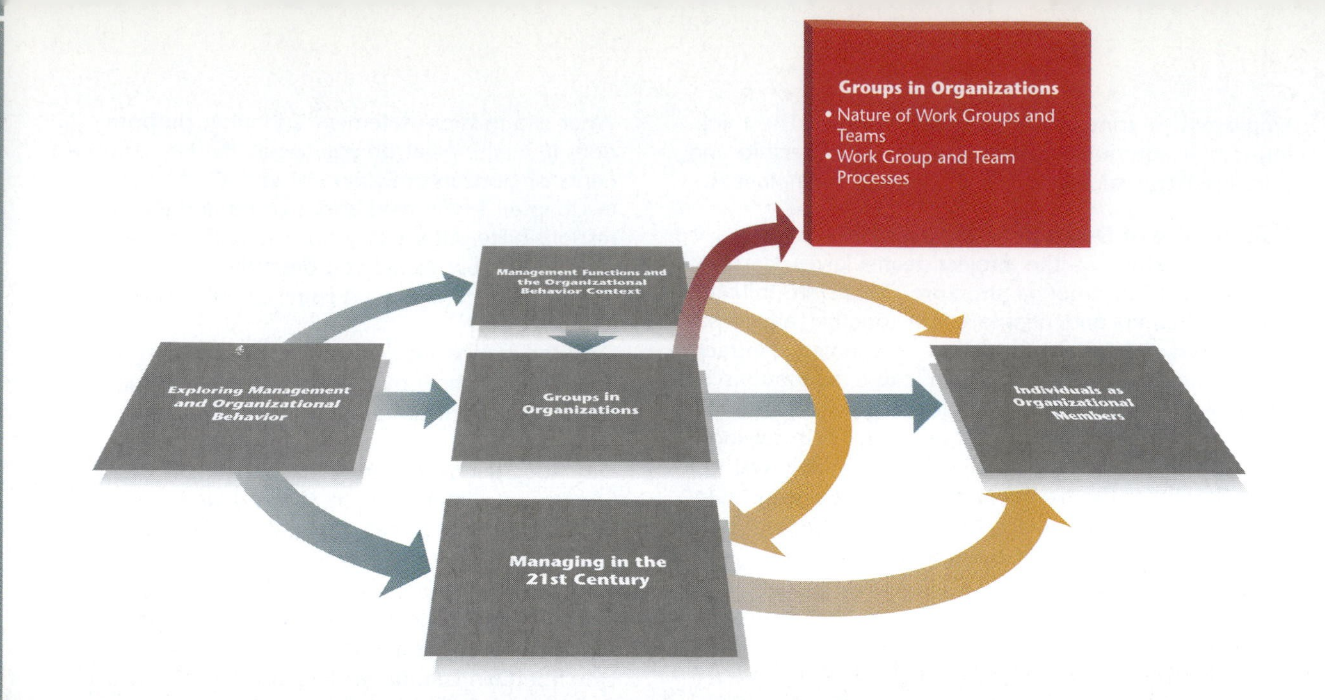

PART IV Groups in Organizations

As we saw in Part II, to understand how organizations function, we must understand how individuals function—through their perception and personality and through their attitudes, motivation, and behavior. Much of the work of organizations is done, not by individuals acting alone, but by individuals interacting as a work group or team. It is this aspect of organizational life, the nature of work groups and group processes, that we explore in Part IV.

In Chapter 1, we defined management as the activities of planning, organizing, directing, and controlling. The directing activity is about marshaling the organization's human resources in order to pursue organizational goals. So important is this activity that management is frequently defined as the process of getting things done through and with others. Given that teamwork is a key factor in today's successful organization, it will be your challenge, as a member of a 21st-century organization, to understand and manage teams effectively.

In Chapter 14, we explore the nature of work groups and teams within the organizational context. What stages do groups go through as they develop and what do they need to function well? What makes teams effective and what impedes their ability to get the job done? How do teams impact employee attitudes, motivation, and behavior? In Chapter 15, we explore work group processes. Key to the success of groups—and therefore of critical importance to managers—is the decision-making process itself. When should a manager encourage group decision making, and when are two heads *not* better than one? When group decision making is called for, how can a manager improve the quality of the decisions? We take an in-depth look at five of the most commonly used structured decision-making techniques used in today's high-involvement organizations: the stepladder technique, brainstorming, the Delphi technique, the nominal group technique, and synectics.

Other group processes that are of particular importance to managers include conflict within working relationships, communication between group members, and organizational politics. Conflict, though often negative, can also have a positive side *if* it is managed well. The same holds true for organizational politics and communication problems.

As illustrated in Figure IV-1, the nature of work groups (teams), and work group and team processes will affect: 1) team member attitudes, motivation, and behavior, 2) team performance and behavior, and 3) ultimately the organization's performance and behavior. Thus, managing work groups (teams) and their processes efficiently will be critical to an organization's success—and to your management career.

FIGURE IV-1 The Effects of Work Groups and Teams

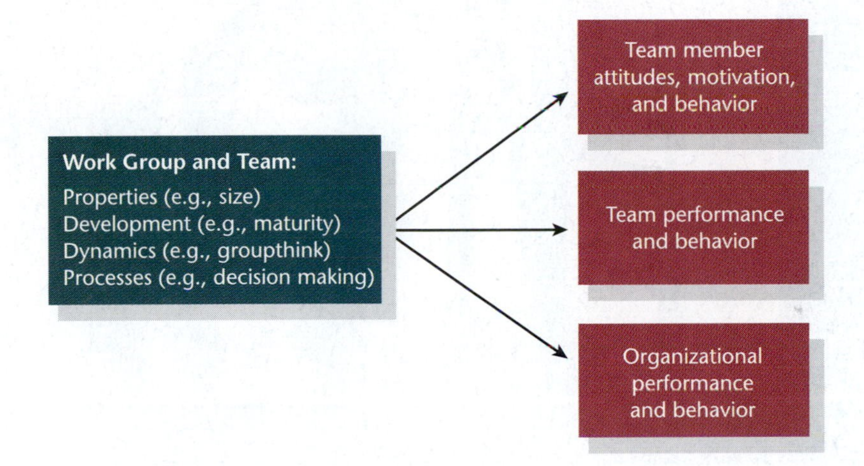

Outline

Groups and teams

Team properties

Team development

Individual differences and group fit

Team performance

Managing team effectiveness

Employee responses to work teams

The nature of groups and teams in organizations in review

CHAPTER 14

The Nature of Groups and Teams in Organizations

PHOTO: © STEVE CHENN/CORBIS

Learning Objectives

After reading this chapter, you should be able to

1. Discuss the concepts of groups and work teams.
2. Identify and differentiate between different types of teams.
3. Describe how self-managing teams differ from manager-led teams.
4. Identify the major properties of work teams.
5. Explain the stages in the evolution of a mature work team.
6. Discuss the determinants of team performance.
7. Identify and discuss the major impediments to team effectiveness.
8. Discuss how team involvement affects organizational members.

A FIRST LOOK

Day 15 of the Trent Database Project is ending on a sour note. Of the nine people assigned to the project, two left the office at 5:00 and the other seven reluctantly find themselves still working among empty Chinese takeout containers at 7:00 p.m.

"I can't believe Lee left. Doesn't he care about our deadline?"

"Celia hasn't exactly been putting in a lot of overtime, either."

"Why do we always end up doing all the work for this project?"

Susan interrupts. "Come on guys, you know that Lee's got to pick up his kids from day care, and Celia's dealing with some pretty heavy things, given her mother's stroke. I think they've been working extra hard to make up for leaving early. Aren't you being a bit hard on them?"

Several group members roll their eyes at this last comment. Their thoughts are almost audible: Susan's always trying to smooth things over. She doesn't seem to understand that we won't make our deadline unless *everyone* pulls their weight.

The conversation drifts from the touchy subject of Lee and Celia to another touchy subject—How are our users going to interface with this database? Four members prefer Grant's approach; the other two are adamant that it won't work. Grant, who is also the team leader, begins to think the upcoming deadline is a lost cause.

Questions: What stage of development is this group in? Can you identify the different roles the group members are playing? Do you agree with Susan that the group is being too hard on Lee and Celia? How can this group overcome its conflicts and improve its productivity?

During the past four decades, a new way of working has been quietly revolutionizing how people perform their work and how organizations are structured. Teams are everywhere—in the boardroom, on the production floor, and at every level in between. Project teams, quality control circles, joint labor-management teams, task teams, self-directed work teams, parallel teams, cross-functional teams, surgical teams, executive teams, action teams, negotiation teams, advise and involvement teams, and production and service teams—the list is endless.

http://www.fortune.com

Statistics reported during the 1990s reveal that 82 percent of organizations with 100 or more employees used teams. Of the *Fortune 1000* companies, 91 percent used employee participation groups in 1993, compared to 70 percent in 1987.[1] In another survey, 58.7 percent of employers reported using quality circles (teams that focus on quality improvement; see Chapter 17).[2] This is up from 29.3 percent in 1992. That same survey indicated that over 40 percent of organizations utilize self-managed teams. This is *not* a small change, it is a fundamental shift in paradigm. Perhaps the first question we should ask then, is, Why? Why the change to teamwork?

The answer, in retrospect, is simple: To survive! Faced with severe competition, rapidly changing market conditions, and an increasingly hostile and turbulent environment, managers urgently needed to make their organizations more flexible, responsive, and competitive. Reaching this goal has not been pleasant—to make management hierarchies smaller, many management and staff positions have been eliminated, and business ventures not central to core competencies have been dumped. The word *downsizing* still strikes terror in the heart of many a worker. But from "ashes" also comes innovation, innovation driven by the demands of the market. Phoenix rises, and incredibly successful concepts known only to a few just a decade ago—just-in-time inventory systems, quality management programs, self-managed teams, to name but a few—are now commonplace. With this innovation, productivity has risen to unprecedented levels.

The concept of work groups and teams arose from the belief that employee involvement, collaborative efforts, and the synergies created through group activity increase organizational efficiency and effectiveness. To this end, many industries (education, health care, transportation, insurance, manufacturing, and others) experimented with various configurations of work groups. The result? Work teams everywhere, from the shop floor to the upper echelons of management.

In this chapter we explore important questions about work groups and teams. What are groups and teams? What properties characterize them? What stages unfold as groups develop? What enhances team effectiveness? What impedes team effectiveness? How do teams impact employee attitudes, motivation, and behavior?

GROUPS AND TEAMS

As managers search for strategies that will help them compete, boost productivity, satisfy an increasingly educated work force, and negotiate an increasingly hostile environment, more and more organizations have come to believe that teams are the answer. What is it about groups and teams that enhances performance? Quite simply, managers believe that groups display synergy. **Synergy** occurs when group performance levels outpace levels achieved by employees working on their own. Expectations of increased productivity have prompted widespread experimentation with work groups and teams.

synergy a dynamic that causes group performance levels to be greater than that achieved by employees working on their own

What are groups? What is a team? Are there different types? These questions deserve careful answers.

Groups and Teams Defined

Social psychologists and those contributing to the small-group literature commonly define a **group** as two or more people who interact to achieve a common objective. According to Webster's dictionary, a group is "a number of individuals assembled together or having some unifying relationship." Thus, groups are seen as living, self-regulating systems that sense and interact with their environments. They develop structures and they affect, and are affected by, the members of the group. Groups develop in stages.[3]

group two or more people who interact with one another to achieve a common objective

Implicit in the definition of a group is the notion that groups are *real*. Many social scientists believe that a group is a living entity that transcends the individual. Proponents of this perspective thus argue that a group has a personality, can possess a sense of self-esteem and self-efficacy (see Chapter 5), and experiences intrinsic motivation. Not all social scientists agree with this perspective, however. The contrarians assert that "a group is simply the shared thoughts, feelings, and behavior patterns that exist among group members."[4] Thus, the level of motivation displayed by a group is simply that which is displayed by the members of the group.

Social scientists often talk about membership groups and reference groups. A **membership group** is one that an individual belongs to by virtue of birth or life circumstances. Association with a membership group is not voluntary in

membership group a group that an individual belongs to by virtue of birth or life circumstances nature, and is characterized by ethnic, racial, and sexual groupings. In contrast, a **reference group** is "any group to which we belong, or aspire to belong, and which we use as a basis for judging the adequacy of our behavior."[5] Political, friendship, work, professional, class, and relational (marriage, family) groupings are examples of reference groups.

reference group any group we belong to, or aspire to belong to, and that we use to judge the adequacy of our behavior

The term *team* has long been part of our sports vocabulary—the University of Florida football team (the Gators), the Johns Hopkins lacrosse team (the Blue Jays), the Chicago Bulls, Los Angeles Dodgers, and Green Bay Packers. In the workplace, however, team is a recent concept. Procter & Gamble (P&G) pioneered the contemporary use of teams in North America, although researchers at London's Tavistock Institute of Human Relations introduced the importance of organizations designed and managed as socio-technical systems shortly after World War II. The early research conducted in British coal mines and in an Indian textile mill focused on a social organization of work, based on cohesive and self-regulating groups of employees in production systems. In the 1960s, P&G envisioned teams as a way to achieve a significant competitive advantage, and for many years kept their idea secret. In fact, they went to great lengths to do this, at one point even asking their consultants and employees to sign nondisclosure statements. P&G had discovered that teamwork creates important performance synergies and a competitive edge over the competition.

http://www.cat.com
http://www.monsanto.com

Today, many organizations—Quad/Graphics, Gaines, Cummins Engine, Compaq, General Electric, Caterpillar, Monsanto, and AT&T, to name a few—use teams. These organizations all believe that work teams favorably affect the organization's responsiveness to its task environment, as well as the employee's motivation, commitment, satisfaction, and performance.

So, what do we mean by teams in the workplace? Once again, according to Webster's, a team is a group of two or more people joined in cooperative activity for work or play. "Cooperative" is the key term here. A "team" is something more than a "group." Team members not only interact with each other, they perceive themselves as a team, they have a common goal, and they endeavor, often strenuously, to attain that goal.[6] Attaining the goal results in a collective feeling of accomplishment, which further strengthens the team's emotional and intellectual bond. The primary distinguishing characteristics of teams, then, are the intensity with which team members work together, their emotional and interpersonal bonding, and the overriding pursuit of a collectively shared goal—their *esprit de corps,* in other words.

A pit crew is a good example of a team that works intensely to accomplish a common goal.

Those who distinguish between groups and teams commonly use the degree of "bondedness" as their primary criterion. A team is a group, yet not all groups are teams. Simply put, groups do not exhibit the cohesiveness, either emotionally or socially, that teams do. This bondedness is part of what makes the team work.

For students of organizational behavior, the reference group of interest is the work team—that small group of individuals who work collaboratively to their and their organization's mutual benefit. Teams in general, and reference groups in particular, not only influence the attitudes, motivation, and behavior of their members, but also engage in their own behaviors. That is, the whole (the team) is sometimes greater than the sum of its parts (its members). Therefore, organizations and managers have a keen interest in understanding how groups develop into teams.

For our final definition of teams, we borrow from the work of R. J. Hackman, professor of organizational behavior and social psychology at Harvard University. Dr. Hackman defines a **team** as "a collection of individuals who are interdependent in their tasks, who share responsibility for outcomes, who see themselves and who are seen by others as an intact social entity embedded in one or more larger social systems, and who manage their relationships across organizational boundaries."[7] A work team, therefore, is a work group, and hereafter we use the terms interchangeably.

team a collection of individuals who are interdependent in their tasks, who share responsibility for outcomes, who see themselves and are seen by others as an intact social entity embedded in one or more larger social systems, and who manage their relationships across organizational boundaries

Following are some distinguishing features of work groups.[8] Members and observers must be able to distinguish people who are part of the team from those who are not. Work groups have a distinct and recognizable task—a shared goal. Members work together and rely on each other's contributions to accomplish their common goal. Their goal, if attained, will affect other people. Members work together to complete a whole and identifiable piece of work. This allows them to see their accomplishments and experience meaningfulness from their work. Members have the authority to make a wide range of decisions on matters that affect them and their task performance, such as manage their work and internal processes. The membership of the team is both definable and relatively stable over time.

It is important here to distinguish between *teams* and *committees*. Frequently, efforts to create teams end up creating political bodies. When, in the formation of a group, much effort is expended on who will and will not be represented, a committee, not a team, is being formed. Committee members represent different constituencies. Their first and foremost obligation is to represent the interests of their constituency. This is a very different dynamic from a team, whose first and foremost obligation is to attain a goal.

Committees are usually less effective than teams in attaining goals. Committees often splinter. Members do not necessarily have a common goal, at least one that they all have committed to achieving. Their workings are conflictual in nature, as members maneuver to place their constituencies in positions of strength. What gets lost in this process is the organization as a cohesive whole. Teams, as opposed to committees, endeavor to keep as their focus the fact that the organization must function cohesively to move forward effectively and efficiently.

Types of Groups and Teams

Several types of teams are commonly seen in organizations today (see Table 14-1). They have been classified into typologies, and we examine a few of them here.

Just as organizations can be formal and informal (see Chapter 12), so too can groups and teams. **Formal groups** are consciously created to serve an organizational objective—for example, Boeing created a project team, a formal group, to design the 777 aircraft. Typically, managers identify one or more objectives for the group and specify who will be its members. In highly open and organic organizational settings, formal groups may also form as the result of employee initiative.

formal group (team) a group consciously created to serve an organizational objective

TABLE 14-1 Formal and Informal Groups

Formal Groups/Teams	Informal Groups/Teams
Vertical	Friendship groups
Horizontal	Interest groups
Cross-functional	
Quality control circles	
Employee involvement	
Standing committees	
Ad hoc committees	
Project teams	
Task forces	
Self-managing work teams	

informal group a group not intentionally created, arising spontaneously out of people's social needs, physical proximity, common interests, and mutual attraction

Unlike formal groups, **informal groups** arise spontaneously. They grow out of people's social needs, physical proximity, common interests, and mutual attraction. At Oscar Meyer in Madison, Wisconsin, the sausage department's 9:00 A.M. coffee group is one of many informal groups. Friendship groups are among the most common types of informal groups in organizations.

Many types of formal groups and teams operate in organizations. Their labels vary—task forces, project teams, top management teams, self-managed work teams, and so on.[9] High-involvement organizations commonly add employee involvement teams to the mix: Quality control circles, joint labor-management committees, and quality of work life groups are frequently formed to improve quality, innovation, productivity, and employee attachment to the organization, and to reduce costs.

manager-led team a team that places the responsibility for task performance with the group, while management functions (planning, organizing, directing, and controlling) remain the responsibility of management

Not all formal teams are alike. They differ not only in their original purpose, but also in terms of permanence (standing versus single use) and in their degree of autonomy. **Manager-led teams**, for example, place the responsibility for task performance with the group while retaining control of management functions (planning, organizing, directing, and controlling). This traditional team is very much in keeping with the classical school's control-oriented model of management. The team has very little authority, discretion, or ability to affect outcomes. This team exists to do the work—that is, to attain the goal—but they have little say in planning how to reach the goal.

self-managing work team a team that operates with goals set by management, but that is given the authority to plan for goal attainment

Self-managing work teams, on the other hand, operate with management-directed goals, but the members themselves plan how they will attain the goals. In addition, self-managed teams typically monitor their own performance and progress. These teams often design and redesign the work system to accommodate their changing needs. In order to accomplish this end of self-design, these teams place tremendous emphasis on organizational learning (see Chapter 9). Knowing when to modify the team's work structure to accommodate changes in the external environment and/or changing task demands requires a strong commitment to learning and feedback. Self-managing teams that successfully take on self-designing characteristics are well suited for complex, ill-defined, and ambiguous tasks embedded in a rapidly changing environment. During recent years, self-managing work teams have proliferated.

vertical team a team with members from several hierarchical levels

horizontal team a team with people from different departments at the same hierarchical level

cross-functional team a team with members from different functional areas of the organization

A popular classification scheme for teams refers to vertical, horizontal, and cross-functional teams. **Vertical teams** consist of members from several hierarchical levels. **Horizontal teams** are made up of individuals from different departments at the same hierarchical level. Both groups are **cross-functional teams** because they include members from different functional areas of the organization. A group whose members come from accounting, engineering, and marketing is a cross-functional team.

Influenced by the success of Japanese companies, many organizations in the 1970s and 1980s developed employee involvement systems using problem-solving teams.* Initially, the most popular form was the quality control circle, but eventually many other forms emerged. In many instances, the adoption of work teams involved a major change in the organization's technology. Organizations like Butler Manufacturing, Volvo, and Saab, for example, did away with assembly lines. Now, teams of workers assemble entire grain dryers and major components for automobiles. Once an organization institutes work teams, the next step toward the high-involvement system is self-management.

work team a group responsible for producing an organization's goods or services

Susan Cohen and Diane Bailey offer the following typology to capture the four types of teams used in today's organizations.[10] Work teams are the most common team and the type that first comes to mind when we think about teams in organizations. **Work teams** are groups of employees who produce an organization's goods or services.

parallel team a team that performs functions that the regular organization is not equipped to perform well

Parallel teams operate alongside the formal organization. **Parallel teams** perform functions that the regular organization is not equipped to perform well. For example, an organization may not have structures in place that facilitate problem solving or that generate suggestions for product or service improvements. Thus, a parallel team operates in tandem with that part of the organization the team is intended to serve. The U.S. Mint created quality circles to operate alongside its production facility, with an eye toward improving its production processes.

project team a team that is time-limited and formed to work on a single task; when the task is completed the team disbands

Project teams are time-limited teams. That is, they are formed to work on a single task and disband when that task is completed. At Boeing, a project team is designing a supersonic airplane that will fly just above the earth's atmosphere (a trip from the United States to Japan will take 2-3 hours). Once the plane's design is complete, the team will be disbanded. Project team's tasks are generally nonroutine in nature and require high levels of knowledge, judgment, and expertise. Members of project teams are frequently drawn from different disciplines and functional areas; hence, they are also cross-functional teams.

management team a team that manages (plans, organizes, directs, and controls) organizational subunits and activities under their control

Finally, **management teams** manage (plan, organize, direct, and control) organizational units and activities under their supervision. A management team at Robert Mondavi's Vineyards, for example, may assume control for red wines, while a second management team assumes responsibility for white wines. Each team coordinates activities associated with growing, harvesting, processing, storing, marketing, and research and development for its respective group. Management teams operate at many levels in the organization. At the top, a management team may be responsible for institutional-level activities, such as strategic planning. With the increasing environmental turbulence and complexity brought on by the global marketplace, use of top-management teams has expanded.[11]

* Japanese and Western management differ in their team practices. Japan, with its collectivist culture, creates low-level teams that work under a strong top-management influence. In the individualistic cultures of North America and Western Europe, empowered teams exercise greater discretion over work processes (see Stewart, Manz, & Sims, 1999; note 8).

http://www.citigroup.com

In their merger in the 1990s, Citibank and Travelers Insurance created the office of the president. John Reed and Sanford Weill, the respective CEOs of those two companies, formed a team to head the newly formed Citigroup. At Chemical Bank's headquarters in New York City, a three-president team deals with the organization's institutional-level responsibilities.

Self-Managing Work Teams

http://www.corning.com
http://www.kodak.com

Corning, Inc., Kodak, and GM's Saturn plant make extensive use of self-managing work teams. The Saturn plant represents a radical departure for the American automobile industry. At all levels, teams have replaced the old "hierarchy of bosses" system that has dominated the automobile industry since its inception. Representatives from management and the UAW work in a system of consultation to achieve smoother operations, greater efficiency and effectiveness, and enhanced cooperation. On the shop floor, teams of 6–15 workers give assignments, maintain equipment, order supplies, set vacation schedules, hire and discipline, and schedule their own work.[12]

Professor Hackman has written extensively about effective work groups. He suggests that effective self-managing work teams are best characterized by their stability, size, and intelligence.[13] Max Weber, the father of the bureaucratic organization, envisioned membership stability through the seniority system (see Chapter 2). Stability creates opportunities for members to develop trust, a crucial factor in virtually all effective organizations and in all aspects of organizational life. Small size is a second important feature for effective self-managing teams. Small teams facilitate both the development of interpersonal trust and rapid and flexible responses to the environment. Intelligence, the third feature, refers to the idea that effective self-managing teams have high levels of expertise and are learning and self-designing work units.[14]

Self-managing work teams generally control the task assignments of individual members.[15] They tend to perform a multiple-skill-based task and perform a whole and/or identifiable piece of work.[16] It is also common for these groups to be responsible for their own quality control, purchasing, bookkeeping, and basic human resource management tasks (such as hiring, performance appraisals, training, and discipline).[17] This high level of interdependence can lead to high commitment to the team by members. However, high interdependence is also conducive to conflict, which may detract from team commitment.[18]

Creating self-directed work teams can result in more motivated employees, with eyes on the bigger picture. A better appreciation of the work can result in changes to work processes and even to reinvention of jobs, as shown in the Next Door Food Store video on motivation and self-directed work teams.

Extensive research carried out at the Tavistock Institute suggests that there are several key components that managers should follow as they establish self-managing work teams:[19]

- collectively, the work team should be responsible for a whole and identifiable, though manageable, task;
- the work assigned to the team should be designed so that it causes social and cooperative interactions;
- members of the team should eventually learn all of the jobs that are a part of the team's total responsibility;
- the team should be self-contained—that is, it should have the power, information, skills and knowledge, materials, and equipment needed to perform the work assignment without having to turn to outside expertise;[20] and
- the team should have the information necessary to evaluate their own performance.

AN INSIDE LOOK

Self-Managing Work Teams as a Step to Success

In the field of production, many tangible measures of success distinguish a successful operation from an unsuccessful one. Safety records, productivity, and quality, for instance, separate forward-looking plants from those mired in older management concepts. In a recent survey of the best American plants, *Industry Week* recognized ten companies for succeeding in all of these measures. One element shared by most of them is their use of self-managing work teams.

Organizations committed to high-involvement management have adopted self-managing work teams as a key element in empowering employees. Employees involved in these teams work together to resolve issues regarding productivity, quality, and safety issues. Organizations transitioning from a traditional hierarchical structure to a flatter management approach utilize extensive training in team communications, group decision making, and problem solving to get the team-oriented structure off to a solid start. Communicating organizational and team goals effectively and making sure that they are accepted by all employees are also critical steps in using employee teams successfully. The survey showed that the most effective team size in these organizations is 7–15 people—small enough to promote contributions from all members, but large enough to distribute responsibilities equally.

Eaton Corporation, a manufacturer of hydraulic hoses in Arkansas, exemplifies the use of teams to improve plant effectiveness. Employees there are involved in two different types of teams: work teams and problem-solving teams. When this team-oriented structure was introduced in 1994, the production staff was less than impressed and felt that teams were a fad that would soon pass. Management thus spent a great deal of time assuring employees that they honestly sought and valued their involvement and opinions. One of the first employee teams focused on compensation issues and created an entirely new compensation plan based on employee input. A year after launching the teams program, managers were no longer present on the plant floor, and teams assumed responsibility for nearly all aspects of the production process. Safety, which was once a major problem at Eaton, improved dramatically after the safety team's recommendations were implemented.

Informal and friendly peer pressure contributes to employee bonding and morale, and is credited with maintaining smooth operations at Eaton. Formal employee peer reviews were discontinued several years ago because the teams felt that they could handle tardiness and absenteeism internally without the structured "finger-pointing" of a written review. New employees are hired on a temporary basis to evaluate how well they fit into the team-based structure; permanent employment requires the approval of the full team.

Since implementing self-managing work teams, Eaton has dramatically improved its productivity, customer service, and safety records. Empowered employees who make these teams work provide strength to the organization. Without the expertise and cooperation of all workers, the organization would not be able to reach and exceed its potential.

Source: Adapted from *Industry Week* and *industryweek.com,* February 21, 2000.

Experiences at Johnsonville Foods, Quad/Graphics, Butler Manufacturing, and General Mills suggest that self-managing work teams can be very successful. General Mills claims that production rose 40 percent at their Lodi, California, cereal plant following the introduction of work teams.[21] Similar increases in productivity have been reported at Chevron.[22]

http://www.chevron.com

TEAM PROPERTIES

All of us have been members of a number of groups, each with their own unique personality. There are several characteristics that serve to differentiate groups from one another. For example, teams differ in the level and scope of

TABLE 14-2 Team Properties

Level of Employee Involvement
- Authority/influence role
- Scope of work completed

Size
- Number of members

Norms
- Code of conduct; shared beliefs and values
- Collectively held expectations of member behavior

Roles
- Behaviors that characterize a person in a social setting

Social Facilitation and Impairment
- Increased and decreased performance due to the physiological and/or psychological arousal caused by the presence of others

Homogeneity/Heterogeneity
- Similarity/dissimilarity of values, demographics, time, goal, and interpersonal orientations

Cohesiveness
- How well group members "hang together"

the team's involvement, membership size, and the degree to which members are similar to one another (see Table 14.2). Team properties are important because they have an impact on the team's organizational behavior, including its level of performance.

Level of Employee Involvement

Work teams vary significantly in their level of involvement. Not all organizations are ready for self-managing teams, and not all teams are ready to manage themselves. At the lowest level of involvement, team members share information only, while management continues to make all of the operational decisions. Managers meet regularly with employees, inform them about what is going on and why, and respond to questions. But managers who think that true employee involvement can be achieved through such efforts are unlikely to achieve anything other than a "quick and short-lived fix" for their organizational woes.[23]

Moving along the involvement continuum, we find a selected group of team members—people with the expertise that management wants to tap into and who meet with management on a regular basis to work on predefined problems. These teams, often cross-functional in nature, explore problems and recommend a course of action. Finally, at the other extreme, we have self-managed work teams.[24] As suggested above, Quad/Graphics's venture into employee involvement was driven by owner/founder Harry Quadracci's strong belief in, and commitment to, the human resource model. Table 14-3 identifies eight levels of employee involvement, characteristics of each, and their primary outcome.

short team a team that handles a group of tasks originally performed by a traditional service or manufacturing department

Team involvement can also be characterized by the size of the team's "piece of the work." **Short teams** commonly handle a set of tasks that were traditionally

TABLE 14-3 Levels of Employee Involvement

Level	Action	Primary Outcome
1. Information sharing	Managers decide, then inform employees	Conformance
2. Dialogue	Managers get employee input, then decide	Acceptance
3. Special problem solving	Managers assign a one-time problem to selected employees	Contribution
4. Intra-group problem solving	Intact group meets weekly to solve local problems	Commitment
5. Inter-group problem solving	Cross-functional group meets to solve mutual problems	Cooperation
6. Focused problem solving	Intact group deepens daily involvement in a specific issue	Concentration
7. Limited self-direction	Teams at selected sites function full time with minimal supervision	Accountability
8. Total self-direction	Executives facilitate self-management in an all-team company	Ownership

Source: J. D. Orsburn, L. Moran, E. Musselwhite, and J. H. Zenger. 1990. *Self-directed work teams: The new American challenge.* Homewood, IL: Business One Irwin, 34.

http://www.nationalsteel.com

long team a team that performs a complete operation from its beginning to end

performed by service or manufacturing departments, such as electric motor assembly. On short teams, members commonly cross-train so that they can perform each assembly task.[25] At National Steel, for example, welders, pipe fitters, and millwrights cross-train, and team members rotate from one job to the next as needs dictate. A **long team** performs a complete operation from beginning to end. At Harley-Davidson, long teams build entire motorcycles.[26] At Volvo, short teams assemble complete drivetrains at the company's Kalmar, Sweden, plant. At its facility in Uddevalla, Sweden, long teams assembled entire automobiles in the 1990s.

Size

Teams should be small enough to form a social unit, but large enough to get the task done. The ideal size of a team is thought to be 5 to 7 members, but in practice teams commonly range from 3 to 15 members. Size affects such factors as team development and performance, as well as member attitude, motivation, and behavior.[27] As team size rises, it becomes increasingly difficult for members to build trust, to prevent subgroups from forming, to keep alienation from setting in, and to give all members opportunities for meaningful participation. Satisfaction also declines, as does members' ability to achieve consensus and to participate in group activities and decision making. Effective, efficient leadership emerges more slowly and with difficulty.

With increasing team size, members' opportunities to invest themselves in the team and its task diminishes, and psychological ownership weakens. This is a key ingredient of self-managing teams; without it, they cease to function.

Norms

team norms expectations with regard to the behavior of team members

The team forms expectations, called norms, with regard to the behavior of its members. Thus, **team norms** are collectively held expectations. They are the set of informal rules, shared beliefs, and values that guide member behavior.[28] Norms define the boundaries of acceptable and unacceptable behavior and are the standard against which member behavior is evaluated. As a code of conduct, norms define—sometimes explicitly and sometimes subtly—what members "dare" and "dare not" do either in the group or on the group's behalf.

Norms form around any subject that is important to the group. They both control behavior and provide consistency and predictability. Norms originate in diverse group dynamics, such as precedents set over time, values brought into the group from other situations, explicit statements from others, and critical events in the group's history.[29]

It is clear that citizenship behavior, work attendance, and quality of work are strongly influenced by group norms. At times norms will serve the interests of the organization; at other times they will work against its interests. Recall Western Electric's lighting and productivity experiments (the Hawthorne studies; see Chapter 2) conducted in the 1920s and 1930s. Those researchers concluded that cooperation with management, working hard, and coming to work on time became the work group values that guided member behavior. It does not always work that way, however.

Managers should be aware of group norms in their organization. They should also be aware of the level of conformity to these norms. Norms support or sabotage organizational activities. When a group's norms are consistent with an organization's goals, such as being courteous to customers, they are a source of organizational strength. Managers can work to develop groups, to shape group norms, and to satisfy group needs that make these groups organizational allies. Ford's slogan "Quality Is Job One" is a successful example of shaping group norms for the benefit of the organization, its employees, and its customers.

Roles

role a set of expected behaviors that characterize a person in a social setting

A **role** is a set of expected behaviors that characterize a person in a social setting.[30] Team members commonly take on different roles as the team works to achieve its purpose.

Groups must meet two basic needs if the group is to thrive—a task-oriented need and a social-emotional need (this relational need maintains the group).[31] To fulfill these needs, some group members play task-oriented roles, while others maintain the group through social roles. Members in task-oriented roles help the group achieve its production goals. That is, they plan, organize, direct, and control group activities, and work to achieve the task. Members who perform relational roles soothe conflicts, nurture relations, and provide social-emotional support that maintains a healthy social system. Table 14-4 summarizes the different activities associated with these two roles.

Group members also play other roles. Some members are self-oriented, often to the group's disadvantage; that is, they don't participate fully in the group. Nonparticipants contribute very little to either the group task or its maintenance needs. As a consequence, they occupy peripheral roles, and their commitment is at best tenuous. Self-oriented members may seek ego gratification by calling attention to personal feats. Other times they distance themselves from the group, yet not enough to lose the benefits that accrue to them from membership. Other group members take on peripheral roles and have low levels of

TABLE 14-4 The Task and Maintenance Roles of Groups

Maintenance Role: Activities that forward cohesiveness and morale

- Getting people acquainted, introducing one another, having informal gatherings.
- Meeting physical needs, temperature, rest breaks, food, comfort.
- Meeting emotional needs, letting people tell you their story, complimenting a person, showing sympathy.
- Gatekeeping, helping bring others into discussion, encouraging everyone to participate.
- Supporting, listening attentively, showing interest, encouraging more details.
- Compromising, willing to give up one's own ideas when group objectives require it.
- Harmonizing, helping people reach agreement or understanding, reducing areas of conflict.
- Reminding group of standards it has set, rights of individuals, etc.
- Reducing emotional tension by humor, suggesting a break, etc.

Task Role: Activities that facilitate task achievement for the group

- Stating the problem clearly, pointing out problems that need attention, getting others to state problems.
- Recognizing the need for information, facts, data and giving them and giving aid in securing them.
- Recognizing the need for opinions or feelings and getting them.
- Making suggestions, proposals for solving problems.
- Evaluating solutions and suggestions, testing for practicality.
- Summarizing group progress, decisions, or disagreements.
- Making procedural suggestions to help coordinate activities, subcommittees, buzz groups, role play, list suggestions on board, get group to assign priorities to agenda items, preventing "railroading."
- Calling attention to time limits, amount of time remaining to get the job done, agenda still to be covered.
- Serving as "group memory," recording suggestions, decision, being secretary.

commitment because of the lack of *management* support and commitment to the team concept. If managers expect teams to be a viable social system within the organization, their commitment must be real.

Group membership carries certain responsibilities. Members of groups and organizations all play more than one role. Each role comes with a set of expectations. Group members often experience contradictions (role conflict) and/or uncertainty (role ambiguity) about their roles.

Our perceptions strongly influence what group roles we play. First is our *expected role*—that is, our image of what our behavior should be. We hold this image, and so do others in the organization. We have an image of how we should perform our job, and so does our boss. A newspaper editor expects an investigative reporter to interview interesting people and write relevant, interesting articles. Expectations, however, don't always match the *transmitted role.* This is the written or verbal description of the role given to the person expected to fill it. The editor may or may not transmit the expected tasks to the reporter. The reporter, in turn, has a *perceived role,* that is, a definition of the job as he or she understands it. Finally, the *enacted role* is how the reporter actually fulfills it. Ideally, there should be no significant contradictions among these four roles.

In reality, there are often contradictions. It is the manager's job to see that contradictions are kept to a minimum.[32]

Social Facilitation and Impairment

We often feel and behave differently when other people are around than when we are alone. Sometimes this difference is a result of peer pressure. Sometimes it is simply due to the presence of others. Have you ever been in a play or given a talk to a large group? Did your heart race? Did your palms sweat? Did you feel extremely alert? These are all reactions to the presence of others.

social facilitation when performance is enhanced by the presence of others

social impairment when performance is diminished by the presence of others

Under some conditions, performance (for example, group decision making) is enhanced by the presence of others. This is called **social facilitation.** Under other conditions, performance is hindered. Social psychologists call this **social impairment.** The difference depends on the nature of the task, one's familiarity with the task, the level of arousal produced by the presence of others, and one's tolerance for high levels of arousal.

In general, increases in arousal facilitate individual performance. For example, we can often think of more problem solutions in the presence of others than when we work alone. There is, however, a critical point at which additional arousal overwhelms us and our performance suffers. This critical point differs from person to person and across tasks (see Figure 14-1). For easy tasks, when we deal with familiar things, our performance improves, even with very high levels of arousal. For difficult or new tasks, however, our performance begins to suffer at moderate or higher levels of arousal.[33]

homogeneous group a group whose members are similar in their demographics and values, goals, and time and interpersonal orientations

heterogeneous group a group whose members are highly diverse in their demographics and values, goals, and time and interpersonal orientations

This phenomenon is important in decision-making groups. If decision making involves simple, routine, or familiar situations, for example, working in the presence of others improves performance. If decision making deals with complex, difficult, and unfamiliar situations, tasks are better done privately, because the presence of others will impair effective decision making due to overarousal. It is important to recognize that overarousal in group settings inhibits the ability of some individuals to perform to their capacity. Steps can be taken to reduce the likelihood of overarousal and to take advantage of the social facilitation process. For example, directing individuals to write down their ideas in the presence of others rather than expressing them verbally is often effective (this is the nominal group technique, discussed in the next chapter).

Homogeneity/Heterogeneity

The composition of a team is key to its effectiveness. Group composition can be defined in terms of the **homogeneity/heterogeneity** of its members. Groups

FIGURE 14-1 How the Presence of Others Affects Performance

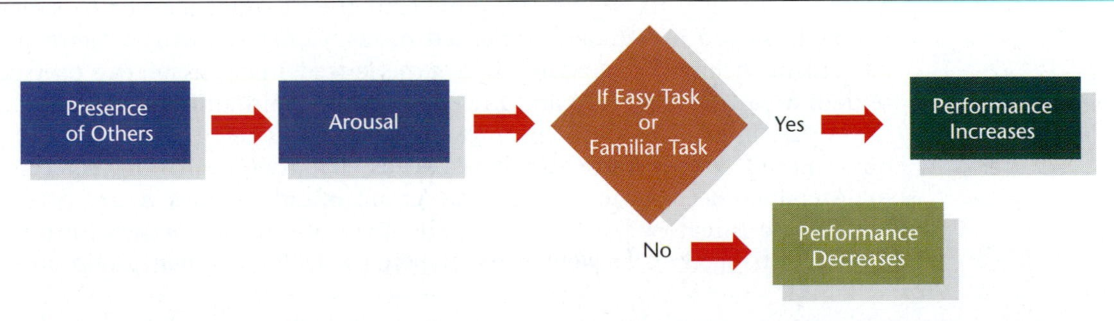

whose members are similar in demographics and values, goals, and time and interpersonal orientation are said to be homogeneous. Teams whose members are dissimilar along these dimensions are heterogeneous in their composition. As noted elsewhere in this text, numerous forces both in the workplace and in the larger societal context are making for growing diversity in the composition of teams and organizations.

The challenge facing team leaders and management is how to use this diversity to enhance the group's competitive advantage. The challenge is not a simple one.[34] Homogeneous groups encourage the building of good interpersonal relationships, and so communication in the group tends to be better, group coordination is easier, and reaching consensus is more likely than in a heterogeneous group. Under most circumstances, homogeneous groups are also easier for managers and team leaders to coordinate. Recent research reveals that good citizenship behaviors tend to be more prevalent in homogeneous groups. It has also been shown that group effectiveness is significantly related to the level of good citizenship behaviors displayed in these groups.[35]

http://www.dg.com

Heterogeneous groups also have advantages. Heterogeneous members bring a greater variety of information and ideas to the group. Research shows that decision quality increases as a result of such diversity.[36] Experiences at Data General, in Westborough, Massachusetts, demonstrate the organizational benefits that accrue with heterogeneous groups. The company set up several teams, constructed with diversity as a criterion, and had them compete in designing a new computer. According to Data General, "diversity gives a team a competitive advantage."[37] High-functioning heterogeneous groups are more creative than high-functioning homogeneous groups. Diverse groups generate a cross-fertilization of ideas that homogenous groups do not.[38] Building and sustaining trust, achieving open communication and shared norms, and establishing group cohesiveness in diverse groups *is* more difficult, but it is also worth the extra energy and effort.

Cohesiveness

Group cohesiveness has several meanings, including (1) attraction to the group and a resistance to leaving it; (2) morale, or the level of motivation displayed by members; and (3) coordination of efforts of members. For our purposes, we will define group **cohesiveness** as the interpersonal dynamic that reflects how well group members adhere to the group's norms. Cohesiveness is how well the group "hangs together."[39] The two forms of cohesiveness—task-oriented and social-emotional cohesion—parallel group needs.[40]

cohesiveness the degree to which group members accept the goals of the group, internalize its norms, and work to meet its task- and maintenance-oriented needs

Cohesiveness reflects the strength of a group's esprit de corps, whether members perceive themselves as "we" rather than as "I," and whether a "sense of belonging" exists. Members of highly cohesive teams accept the goals of the group, internalize its norms and adhere to them, and endeavor to satisfy the team's task- and maintenance-oriented needs. Cohesiveness is a factor in good citizenship behaviors[41] and is often experienced in terms of the pressures to remain a part of the group and to contribute to maintaining the group.

A variety of factors influence team cohesiveness (see Figure 14-2). As previously noted, groups have two basic needs. If either need (but especially the maintenance need) is threatened, the group often becomes more cohesive. In addition to threat (which may be in the form of outside competition), success, time spent together, attractiveness of being a team member, group size (large

FIGURE 14-2 Determinants and Consequences of Team Cohesiveness

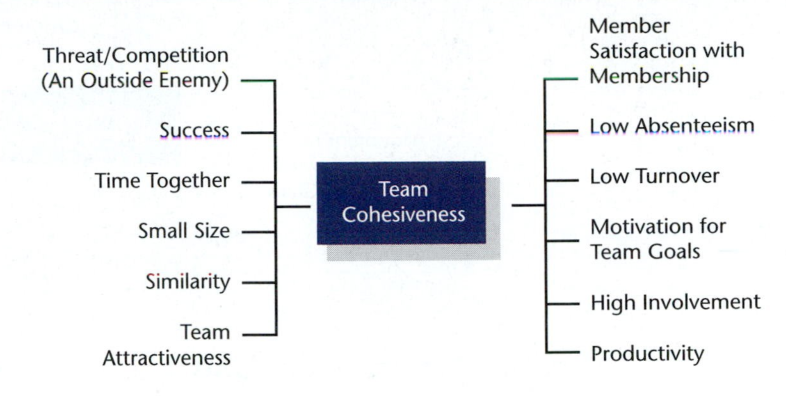

groups make cohesion less likely), and similarity play a significant role in developing group cohesiveness.

As we might expect, researchers and managers alike have observed a number of positive consequences associated with team cohesiveness. Team members enjoy working on cohesive teams; that is, cohesive teams are "attractive." After all, cohesion is in part a function of how well the group is meeting the needs of its members. This attractiveness results in low levels of voluntary turnover and absenteeism. The attractiveness of the team and desires for its success contribute to a high level of motivation directed toward one or both of the group's needs. Team members willingly accept the group's norms and goals and participate more fully. Cohesive groups frequently have higher productivity.[42]

Effective and efficient decision making is usually more difficult to achieve in groups that are not cohesive. Such groups struggle with communication, power relationships, and attempts to get to know and understand one another. The quality of decisions made in noncohesive groups, however, sometimes benefits from the conflict that ensues and from the lower conformity to group norms.

High levels of group cohesion and satisfaction don't always enhance performance. Cohesive groups tend to make decisions that meet group needs; if these needs are inconsistent with the organization's needs, their decisions can damage the organization. If the group's goals match those of the organization, all is well—group and organization are in synch. If group goals are inconsistent with organizational goals, organizational goals will not be met, even if the group's goals are. Highly cohesive groups can be very effective in counterproductive activities, such as work slowdowns and stoppages. Managers not only need to foster group cohesion, they must also direct it toward organizationally desirable goals (see Figure 14-3).

There are other potentially very negative consequences of team cohesion. Group members may follow the wishes of team leaders or other members even though the consequences for the group are negative. Social pressures to conform can be intense. In a dysfunctional group, a disproportionate amount of energy may be directed toward maintaining the group, with a simultaneous disregard for the group's task needs. This phenomenon is known as groupthink, discussed later in this chapter.

FIGURE 14-3 Effects of Group Cohesiveness on Performance

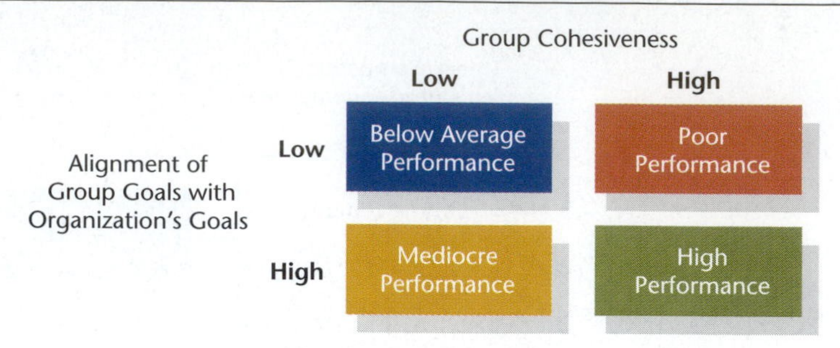

Spatial Arrangement and Team Structure

Where people are physically located—the spatial arrangements of their office, for example—strongly affects their behavior when they interact. This is an intriguing phenomenon that impacts such disparate behaviors as the transfer of information, conflict, and even the emergence of leaders.[43]

Researchers have examined this aspect of group behavior extensively. Their results have important consequences for performance. People sitting at a table, for example, talk to those next to them and to people directly across the table. People at the opposite corners of long, narrow tables will obviously have difficulty speaking to each other. This situation isn't subtle, but the results can be. Restrictions in information flow can create cliques, and cliques operate differently. Cliques by their very nature are dysfunctional; they cause conflict, with predictable results. Cliques are competitive, not cooperative. Achieving consensus, which is necessary to group decision making, can become impossible.

Team structure also affects team behavior, as well as the attitudes, motivation, and behavior of its members. We examine this component in our discussion of team performance. The role of social system structure was discussed in detail in Chapters 12 and 13.

TEAM DEVELOPMENT

In order to maximize team effectiveness, managers, team leaders, and team members must understand how and why teams form, what functions they serve, and the dynamics of team development.

Stages of Team Development

Like people, teams go through various stages as they mature, and their capacity for performance is not the same at each stage. Research in group dynamics has identified six stages in group development (see Figure 14-4).[44] Understanding these stages helps managers and team leaders develop effective teams. Organizations like Boeing, Caterpillar, Cummins Engine, LTV Steel, General Mills, Procter & Gamble, and Hewlett Packard, where employee involvement systems are a central part of internal work processes, have systematic programs in place to facilitate team development.[45] Their programs take advantage of each of the six stages.

http://www.cummins.com
http://www.ltvsteel.com

Stage 1: Orientation As teams first form, members don't know each other in the team context (even if they know each other outside this context). They are thus initially uncertain about the team's purpose, personal agendas, rules,

FIGURE 14-4 The Stages of Group (Team) Development

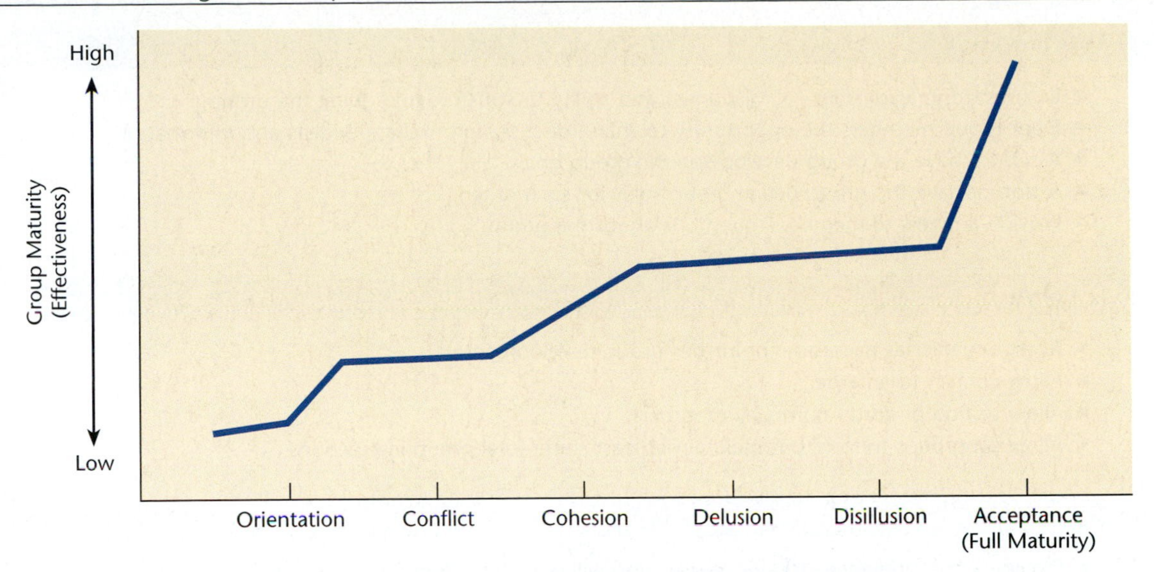

Source: Adapted from L. N. Jewell and H. J. Reitz. 1981. *Group effectiveness in organizations.* Glenview, IL: Scott, Foresman, 20.

procedures, leadership, and their own roles as team members. During this first stage, members exchange information, ask questions about other members, and attempt to define the nature of the team. Table 14-5 suggests ways leaders can meet the needs of a newly formed team and turn it into a functioning body.

Stage 2: Conflict Following orientation, teams enter a period of conflict as individual differences surface. Often, team members compete for leadership and role assignments. They may disagree over procedures and over the merits of the team itself. Tension and hard feelings may arise. The team may divide into subgroups that set off in different directions. Because the conflict stage is unpleasant and often ineffective, many teams try to deny its onset or deal with its issues superficially; however, bypassing the conflict stage greatly increases the chances of regression to this stage at a later date. It is far better to accept the stage as a necessary part of team development and to concentrate on effective ways to shorten its duration and minimize its impact (see Table 14-5).

Stage 3: Cohesion During this stage, team members work through personal differences, develop a set of norms, and agree on their roles. A group structure emerges, and operating procedures are established for guiding future activities. It is in this stage that a true sense of team identity emerges for the first time. Cooperation, low levels of emotionalism, and goal-directed activity are common characteristics of highly cohesive teams. Significant increases in team effectiveness are common during the cohesion stage (but remember that cohesive teams are sometimes dysfunctional). To harness the energy of a cohesive team, managers can follow the guidelines in Table 14-5. For teams that need to work together over long periods, it is important to move to the full maturity represented by stage 6—acceptance.

Stage 4: Delusion If a team develops beyond the cohesion stage, it will likely go through a stage of "delusion," in which members believe that significant problems no longer exist. (We could also call this stage complacency.) After all,

TABLE 14-5 Guidelines for Group Development

Stage 1: Orientation

- Ensure strong leadership—a willingness and ability to structure and guide the group.
- Offer group members the opportunity to share, discuss, and exchange ideas and information.
- Assign or have the group develop specific group goals.
- Assign or have the group define group roles for each other.
- Provide answers to members' questions about the group.

Stage 2: Conflict

- Accept conflict as necessary for further group development.
- Allow conflict to emerge.
- Allow testing of group norms by members.
- Allow subgroups to form but maintain at least some total group interactions.

Stage 3: Cohesion

- Provide a fair, nonpower-seeking leader who will work for the good of the group.
- Develop a system for addressing and resolving disagreements (conflict).
- Encourage a sense of group identity.
- Encourage written and/or public statements from the group as a whole.
- Develop and formalize a permanent operating structure to guide group actions.

Stage 4: Delusion

- Accept delusion as a normal stage necessary for further group development.
- Avoid the onset of groupthink by watching for symptoms and taking corrective steps as needed.
- Avoid prolonged continuation of delusion by challenging the unrealistic bases of the delusion.

Stage 5: Disillusion

- Accept disillusionment as necessary for further development.
- Allow disillusionment to occur openly.
- Force development of disillusionment by identifying and presenting group problems.
- Allow subgroups to form, but maintain at least some total group interactions.
- If the existing leader is unwilling or unable to manage conflicts, replace him/her with a directive leader who can do so.
- Emphasize how and why the group can mature effectively.

Stage 6: Acceptance

- Provide a leader with good interpersonal skills who will work for the good of the group, either by replacing the existing leader or by changing the behavior of the leader.
- Encourage open, honest discussion of issues.
- Discourage differences that focus on personalities.
- Dissolve subgroups through rewards for commitment to the total group.
- Identify to the group the unique qualities and contributions of each group member.
- Develop communication channels to exchange information accurately and realistically.
- Use issue-oriented decision-making strategies.

they have overcome the problems of conflict and gone on to significantly improve effectiveness. It is during this stage that teams sometimes succumb to groupthink and commit disastrous errors due to this false sense of perfection. The onset of the delusion stage is a natural consequence of the cohesion stage.

Stage 5: Disillusion For a team to achieve maturity, it must pass through the painful stage of disillusionment, in which the bubble of delusion bursts. Members are shocked into awareness of the problems that still confront the team and make few significant improvements in effectiveness. Cohesiveness decreases, and members may be tempted to leave the team. Absenteeism and tardiness are common. Subgroups emerge, and interpersonal conflict is frequent. Members blame each other for allowing the group to be deceived. Pessimism abounds.

Although unpleasant, mature teams, like organizations, have gone through this "team puberty." When teams bypass this stage, they are usually only postponing the inevitable. This stage—like the others—is necessary. It is better to live through it and to manage its impact rather than avoid it completely. The strategies noted in Table 14-5 help teams get through disillusion without being destroyed by it.

Stage 6: Acceptance With appropriate care and direction, a team moves through its disillusionment and into acceptance. This is the fully mature team. Fully mature teams discuss their differences rather than fight over them. They aggressively attack issues and deemphasize personal interests. Divisive subgroups tend to dissolve, and a strong sense of team identity emerges. The distinctive qualities of each team member are recognized and appreciated. Communication flows freely. Time and resources are used effectively and efficiently. Team effectiveness increases, as does members' satisfaction. Mature teams are great assets, but the route to maturity is neither short nor easy.

Alternative models of group development also exist. Bruce Tuckman and Mary Jensen's model acknowledges five developmental states: forming, storming, norming, performing, and adjourning.[46] Other models portray similar patterns of development, although they differ in their categorization schemes.

INDIVIDUAL DIFFERENCES AND GROUP FIT

The theory of work adjustment is one of many models that focus on the importance of the individual-organization fit. As in successful marriages, the employee and the organization are motivated to continue the relationship only as long as their needs are met. Both bring a set of needs to the relationship. The employee also brings a set of skills and abilities to the organization, while the organization offers a set of benefits and opportunities to the employee in return. Work adjustment—the fit between the individual and the organization—exists when (1) the needs of the individual are appropriately reinforced by the benefits and opportunities (inducements) offered by the organization, and (2) the needs of the organization are fulfilled by the skills and abilities (contributions) of the employee.[47]

The theory of work adjustment reminds us that a congruency has to exist between the individual and the work group if the group is to succeed—that is, if members will be motivated, satisfied, and productive enough to maintain their group membership. Research into personality and individual differences (see Chapter 5) provides us with some insight into which individuals find group membership to their liking. Effective team players are likely to be characterized by

- *extroversion*—extroverts "act on or engage their external environment" and as a consequence are outgoing and expressive, and tend to perform better at jobs that require a lot of interaction with people;
- *conscientiousness*—the extent of a person's dependability, level of organization, thoroughness, perseverance, and honesty;
- *agreeableness*—whether a person is trusting, accepting, and cooperative;
- *internal locus of control*—"internals" prefer to be active participants in decisions and processes that affect them, since they believe they control their own fate;
- *need for affiliation*—people with high needs for affiliation derive satisfaction from social and interpersonal relationships;
- *collectivism*—whether a person values "connection" with other people; collectivists feel good when they contribute to the success of the group.

In addition to the apparent conflict of the opposite of some of these personality factors (for example, introversion, individualism), a number of other personality factors make it difficult for certain people to be dedicated team members. Among them are a strong need for autonomy or independence, achievement, and Machiavellianism (see Chapters 5 and 7). Bear in mind, however, that these people can be highly effective in other situations.

To the extent that group membership can be managed, constructing groups with "team-friendly" versus "team-unfriendly" people is an effective strategy. Team-friendly people will be more likely to fit in with the group and to find their membership personally fulfilling. This in turn contributes to the likelihood of the group reaching the mature acceptance stage. Mature groups are most capable of self-management. Orpheus, a Boston-based chamber orchestra, exemplifies a high level of maturity, so much so that they no longer need a leader (conductor) to perform.[48] (See *An Inside Look* in Chapter 11.)

http://www.orpheusnyc.com

TEAM PERFORMANCE

As a part of their directing activity, managers are keenly interested in individual and team performance. The determinants of team performance appear to parallel those of individual performance. In Chapter 8, we noted that a behavior (say performance) results from the interaction of the person (their characteristics—ability, motivation) and the situation (resources, role perceptions) in which they perform their task. We can summarize this in the following manner:

$$\text{Individual Behavior} = f\,[(\text{Person})\ (\text{Situation})]$$

This same relationship operates in groups. That is, work group behavior (performance) results from the interaction of the group (its characteristics—norms, size) and the situation (resources, supervision) in which the group performs its task:

$$\text{Group Behavior} = f\,[(\text{Group})\ (\text{Situation})]$$

At the individual level, three personal factors shape performance. Recall from Chapter 8 that these determinants of performance consist of the individual's motivation to perform the task at hand, their skills and abilities to do so, and the accuracy of their role perceptions. That is, does the person know what is to be accomplished, and do they understand the processes they are to use to attain the goal? The final factor in individual performance is the environment, those forces outside the individual's control that impact them and/or their interaction with their work. For example, the speed of the assembly line significantly affects the amount of work an employee can accomplish.

At the group level, a near parallel set of factors affects the team's performance. As shown in Figure 14-5, team performance factors include team motivation, capacity, strategy, and the context.

By team capacity, we mean the attributes that affect the team's ability to perform—the combined knowledge, skills, abilities, and information that members bring to the team and its task. Team capacity also refers to a team's culture (shared beliefs, values and assumptions), norms, level of group development (cohesiveness), and structure and design (manager-led, self-managing, self-designing, and so on).

Research suggests that team structure plays a significant role in performance. Two important elements of team structure are interdependence, and autonomy or self-leadership.[49] By team interdependence (see Chapter 12), we mean how much members depend on each other as they perform their respective roles. Team autonomy or self-leadership addresses the level of external supervision. Autonomous teams have the freedom and authority to lead themselves, independent from external supervision, and high levels of interdependence suggest a strong set of interdependencies among team members—"what I do strongly affects you and your performance, and what you do strongly affects me and my performance."[50]

How team interpersonal processes, task-based processes (like idea generation and planning) and socio-emotional processes (like conflict resolution) unfold under different levels of interdependence and team autonomy affects team performance. While the evidence is inconclusive, researchers generally believe that strong team performance occurs in highly interdependent conditions. They also hypothesize that high levels of autonomy positively affect team performance.

FIGURE 14-5 The Determinants of Work Group/Team Performance

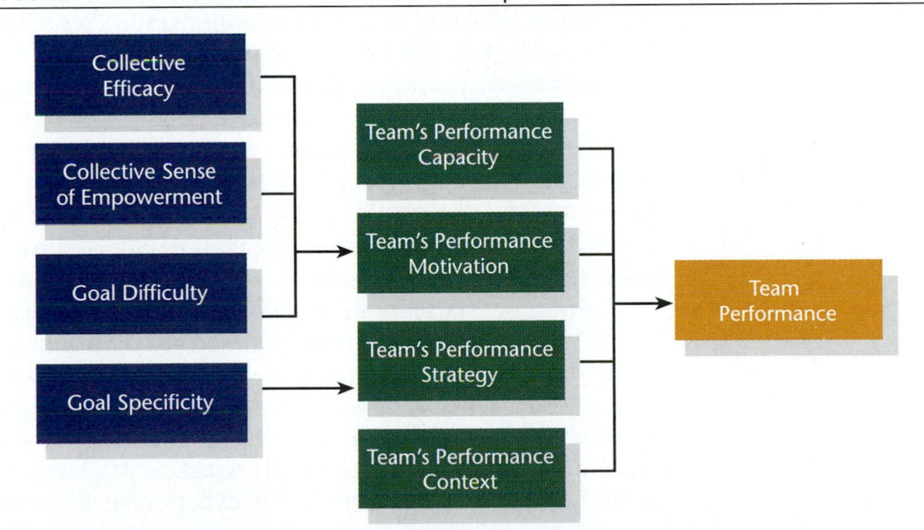

Sally Forth

Reprinted with special permission of King Features Syndicate, Inc.

High-capacity teams—that is, teams who possess the necessary skills, ability, knowledge, and information, who have a strong culture, norms that support performance, cohesiveness, and a self-managing design—meet one of the necessary conditions for high performance. Capacity, however, is not the sole determinant of team performance.

Team motivation is the second major determinant of performance. This should be readily apparent from previous discussions: Teams—like individuals—must not only have capacity, they must also be motivated to perform. Unlike individuals, the team's synergy, the sparks and impulses created as members feed off one another, is a significant factor in its motivation.

The incentives sparking motivation are both intrinsic and extrinsic in nature. *Extrinsic motivators* are incentives administered to the group by others. Examples include bonuses and other incentives that flow to the group for improving quality, reducing production costs, and increasing production. Intrinsic motivators are of two types. *Individual-based intrinsic motivators* are personal forces that operate on each member—their personal drive to achieve and grow, and so on. *Group-based intrinsic motivators* are forces that originate in the group and that operate on group members. For example, when the second-string football team sees the first string "pound" the opposing team, they want very badly to follow in the footsteps of their teammates. Individual- and group-based intrinsic forces work on team members as their aspirations grow and their ability to perform the task at hand expands.

collective efficacy the degree to which group members believe that the group has the capacity to achieve its performance objectives

The team must believe that it can be successful. Research on self-efficacy (the belief that one can achieve some result; see Chapter 7) at the individual level reveals that it is a powerful influence on motivation, on persistence in the face of adversity, and on performance. Emerging evidence suggests that a collective efficacy is crucial to group success. **Collective efficacy** has to do with whether group members believe that the group *can* achieve its objectives. The amount of effort the group will put into a task (that is, the team's performance motivation), whether the group will persist in the face of adversity, and the team's ultimate performance appear to be affected by the strength of the team's collective belief in its ability to perform.[51] It has been noted that the strength of a group lies partially in its sense of collective efficacy.[52]

While the social learning and social cognition theories of Albert Bandura from Stanford University provide insight into how self-efficacy emerges in individuals, it is less clear how collective efficacy emerges in groups. According to Bandura, five informational cues influence an individual's self-efficacy.[53] They are, in order of their influence: (1) enactive mastery—repeated accomplishments build skills, coping abilities, and experience; (2) vicarious experiences—other people model excellence for the individual; (3) verbal persuasion—other people tell the person they are capable; (4) emotional (physiological) arousal—the person is sufficiently stimulated to direct their full capacity toward performance; and (5) logical verification—the person derives new knowledge from things they already know. Collective efficacy appears to be shaped by a group's successes and failures, as well as by such forces as verbal persuasion and the level of emotional arousal. Others argue that a collective efficacy is more likely to develop among a group of individuals who have a collectivist set of values (group-oriented) as opposed to an individualistic set (see Chapter 5).[54]

empowered team
a team characterized by collective efficacy, meaningfulness, autonomy, and impact

Team empowerment has a lot to do with a team's motivation to perform. An **empowered team** is one in which the following four factors characterize the group: (1) collective efficacy—the team believes it can be effective; (2) meaningfulness—the team experiences its tasks as important, valuable, and worthwhile; (3) autonomy—team members experience substantial freedom, independence, and discretion in their workplace; and (4) impact—team members see that the work they're doing is significant and important to the organization. Research indicates that empowered work teams are more proactive and productive. In addition, their members experience more satisfaction in their jobs, and are more committed to the team and to the organization.[55]

Another determinant of team performance is the difficulty and specificity of its goals. As we saw in our discussion of goal setting (Chapters 7 and 10), setting specific and challenging goals has a positive impact on performance. Goal setting—especially when the goals are difficult—also contributes to team performance, because it both motivates and directs action. Setting specific goals clarifies performance expectations. We now turn our attention to this "directional" effect.

performance strategy
a clear outcome the team is working to achieve, coupled with an action plan that details how to proceed and how team members will interact

As you have no doubt surmised, having a direction affects performance. The team's direction is their **performance strategy.** When a team has a clear outcome members are working toward, when they have an action plan that details how they are to proceed and how individual members are to interact, they have a strategy. The notion of performance strategy parallels an individual's "accuracy of role performance." That is, the team understands the organization's expectations well enough to plan a strategy. Knowing what the organization wants positively impacts performance.

performance context
the environment that surrounds and impacts the team, yet remains out of its immediate and direct control

Finally, the team's **performance context** is its task environment. This environment surrounds the team and impacts it, yet remains out of its immediate and direct control. Given that teams are social entities embedded in one or more larger social systems (the organization),[56] the team's performance context includes that part of the organization that lies outside the team's formal boundaries. The resources given to a team to perform its task are a context factor that can significantly impact its ultimate performance.

MANAGING TEAM EFFECTIVENESS

http://www.visa.com

Professors Lee G. Bolman of Harvard University and Terrence E. Deal of Vanderbilt University asked several CEOs, What enables a group to push toward peak performance over an extended period?[57] Former Visa CEO Dee Hock responded, "In the field of group endeavor, you will see incredible events in which the group performs far beyond the sum of its individual talents. It happens in the symphony, in the ballet, in the theater, in sports, and equally in business. It is easy to recognize and impossible to define. It is a mystique. It cannot be achieved without immense effort, training, and cooperation. But effort, training, and cooperation alone rarely create it."[58] Bolman and Deal add that "the essence of teamwork is more than structure, political savvy, or talented people."[59] Based on their observations of teams like Data General's Eagle Team, they conclude that "soul" is the "real secret of a team's success."[60] Similarly, Peter Vaill, author of the popular book *Managing as a Performing Art,* suggests that members of high-performing teams like the Eagle group " 'felt the spirit,' and the feeling of spirit was essential to the meaning and value of the group's work, . . . , culture, soul, and spirit are the wellsprings of high performance."[61]

Team managers are, of course, continually concerned about team effectiveness.[62] (Table 14-6 highlights some of the dimensions of team effectiveness.) While the prescription that teams develop "soul," "spirit," and "culture" doesn't exactly give us concrete guidelines, researchers have identified a number of significant components of effective teams.

Group effectiveness unfolds over time; it does not happen overnight. Professor Hackman observes that group effectiveness is the direct result of group effort, the task knowledge and skills of members, and their choice of strategies. The group must also be given the resources it needs. So what, you may ask, *do* groups need? Many things, of course, but key among them is an organizational context that supports (for example, with education and information) and reinforces (with rewards) competent task performance. Groups also need a group design that promotes performance (see Chapter 12), and they need to create a group dynamic that promotes synergy.

Impediments to Team Effectiveness

Certain behaviors displayed by teams limit their effectiveness (see Figure 14-6).[63] Team managers and team members in both control-oriented and high-involvement organizations can, however, take steps to minimize the negative effects that result from these group behaviors.

social loafing when individual group members fail to put forth their best efforts because they believe that their contributions will essentially get lost in the group effort

Social Loafing **Social loafing** occurs when group members do not put forth their best efforts because they believe their contributions will essentially get lost (that is, will not be discernible) in the group effort.[64] Taking care to observe and evaluate individual effort is the most effective way to reduce social loafing. This can be accomplished by having team members work in close physical proximity, thereby permitting peer observation of individual contributions. In addition to providing member-to-member control, close proximity also reinforces the social needs of individuals and provides opportunities for feedback and helping behaviors.[65]

TABLE 14-6 Dimensions of Team Effectiveness

- Customer satisfaction
- Performance—quantity
- Performance—quality
- Member satisfaction
- Member commitment
- Cooperation
- Attendance
- Turnover
- Citizenship behavior

FIGURE 14-6 Impediments to Team Effectiveness

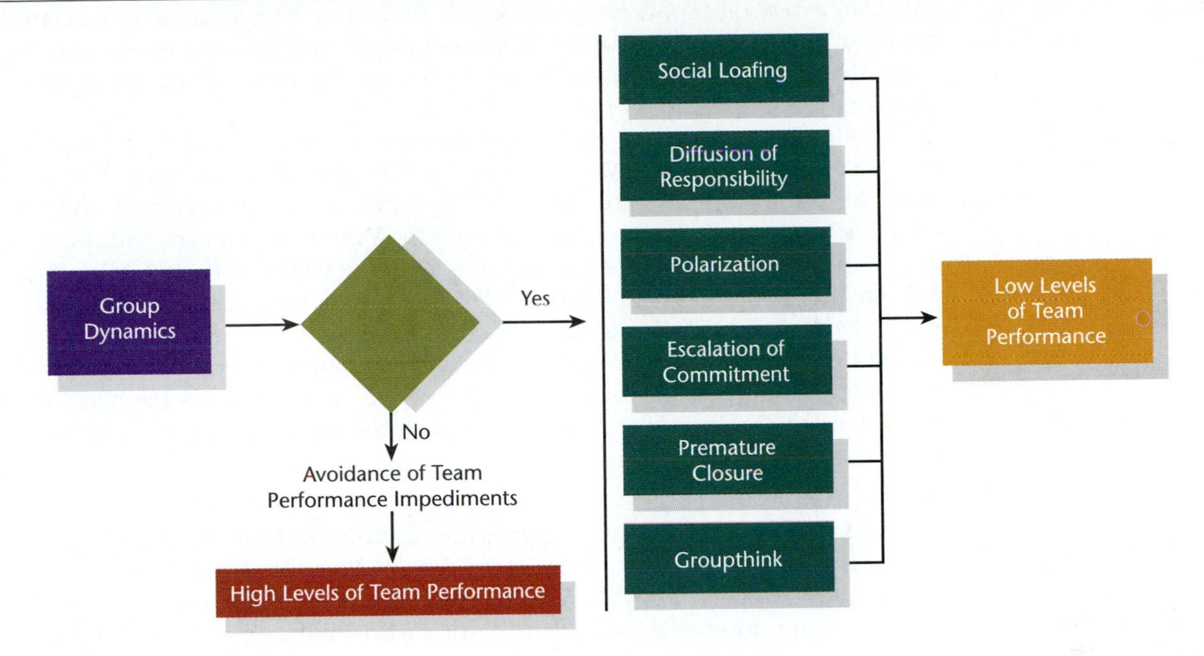

diffusion of responsibility a group dynamic in which individuals fail to act because they believe or expect that others will act, or because the presence of others reduces feelings of accountability

polarization when a group takes positions that are more extreme than members would take acting alone

Diffusion of Responsibility **Diffusion of responsibility** is a group dynamic where individuals fail to act because they believe that it is the job of others to act, or because the presence of others reduces their feelings of accountability.[66] (We have all done this at one time or another—"I thought *you* turned out the light.") Diffusion of responsibility is difficult to counteract because ascertaining whether an individual failed to take action is not always easy.[67]

Polarization Social psychologists note that group processes frequently result in groups taking positions that are "more extreme" than those taken by individuals acting alone.[68] This process is called **polarization.**[69] A *risky shift* occurs when groups make decisions that are more prone to risk; that is, members would not take this risk if they were operating alone (the *risky shift phenomenon*).[70] Groups can also become risk averse; this is another aspect of polarization.

While *cautious shifts* do occur, risky shifts are far more common. This happens for several reasons. First, through group discussion and the sharing of ideas and information, members become more familiar with a decision situation than they might if they were addressing it on their own. As they become less uncertain about goals and objectives and the probable outcomes of alternatives, they pursue alternatives that they previously considered too risky.

Second, the *diffusion of responsibility* phenomenon we discussed above factors in here. Because several people are acting, each individual feels less personally responsible for the group's decisions. The result? Decisions get riskier.[71] Remember the old adage, there is courage in numbers? Students in finance and investments at the University of Minnesota, for example, manage a portfolio worth over three million dollars. They admit that their investment decisions as a group are definitely riskier than their individual decisions. This shift appears to be rooted in the beliefs that "other group members will prevent a bad decision," and "if the decision doesn't work out, well, the group will be blamed—not me personally."

Third, most groups have at least one member who is willing to take greater risks. High risk takers also tend to be *risk persuaders*. The greatest risk takers in the group thus "push the outside of the envelope" and lead the group into decisions that are almost as risky as what they would make if the group wasn't "holding them back."

Finally, both risky and cautious shifts can be caused by *cultural values* (see the discussion of uncertainty avoidance in Chapter 5). Many group members strive for approval and status in the eyes of other members. To this end, they try to behave in a socially approved fashion. When the cultural values of the group (or organization) favor risk, individuals perceive this and take greater risks in the group. Conversely, when group values favor caution, these individuals take less risk in the group than they would alone. They hope to gain approval by being on the leading edge of the group's values. Social psychologists refer to this as the *group polarization effect*.[72] Because each member of the group tends to be influenced in a similar way, the group decision is often either quite risky or quite cautious.

escalation of commitment the process through which a group or individual continually extends a commitment even though signals suggest that a bad decision/investment has been made

Escalation of Commitment Sometimes a group and/or individual continually extends a commitment, even in the face of flagrant signals showing that a bad decision has been made.[73] This is called **escalation of commitment.** Remember the young options trader (Nick Leeson) who singlehandedly brought down the venerable Barings Bank in one afternoon in 1995 by compounding his bad investments? A variety of psychological (self-justification, ego-involvement), social (social-justification), and structural (political support, administrative inertia) forces cause people to continue to commit to a poor course of action.[74] The tendency to escalate can be reduced by frequent and timely feedback, numerous decision opportunities, and low visibility (that is, the person or group is not out on a "public limb," and therefore doesn't stand to lose as much face by withdrawing from the course of action).[75]

premature closure when a group rushes to identify the problem, to find an attractive or easily accessible solution, or to get on with things

Premature Closure Decision making and problem solving, as we saw in Chapter 9, are processes that can be managed. Group decision-making processes, unless appropriately managed, are often characterized by rush—a rush to identify the problem, a rush to find an attractive or easily accessible solution, and a rush to get on with things! This rush to resolution is called **premature closure.**[76]

The problem commonly manifests itself when one group member has a preferred solution. In order to avoid upsetting the person's feelings and to reduce uncertainty caused by the problem, the group doesn't explore the problem adequately. It doesn't identify enough alternatives, or it doesn't examine the costs and benefits of alternatives carefully enough.

This problem can be managed by adopting a systematic decision-making/problem-solving approach, one that ensures that appropriate attention is given to each stage in the process. In addition, several decision-making techniques, such as the nominal group technique (discussed in the next chapter), can help groups avoid premature closure.

groupthink when a group has illusions of invulnerability that lead it to accept excessive risks

Groupthink The late Irving Janis of Yale University documented the group phenomenon he dubbed groupthink.[77] **Groupthink** happens when a group's illusions of invulnerability lead it to take excessive risks. Thus, even with warning flags flying high, members rationalize their way out of believing that impending problems are real. Group members also believe that the group's purpose is so righteous that they don't question the morality of its assumptions or tactics. They use negative stereotyping to degrade outsiders who question the group and intensely pressure members to conform to group norms. If information from outside the group conflicts with the group's position, members protect their position by developing what Janis called "mind guards" to filter out the objectionable material. Highly cohesive groups are commonly victims of groupthink. Groupthink produces such a strong desire for consensus that it overwhelms individual thinking and the group's desire and ability to make realistic decisions. Potential consequences of groupthink include:

- Few alternatives are considered.
- Decisions, once made, are not reexamined.
- Rejected alternatives are not reexamined.
- Outside experts are seldom used.
- Facts that do not support the group are ignored.
- Risks are ignored or glossed over.

Groupthink can cause highly capable groups to make terrible decisions.[78] Janis noted that groups inflicted with this "disease" are driven to obtain consensus at almost any cost. This desire for unanimity can be so strong that dissent is almost eliminated.

In short, groupthink generally leads to bad—sometimes catastrophic—decisions. Numerous historic fiascoes—the doomed flight of the *Challenger,* the Bay of Pigs invasion, the escalation of the Vietnam conflict, and President Nixon's failed presidency—can all be laid at the feet of groupthink.[79] Fortunately, managers can take steps to reduce this insidious group dynamic.[80] Reducing it, however, is much more difficult than preventing it in the first place, because groups engaging in groupthink seldom realize that they are doing so. To avoid groupthink, managers can:

- Encourage each member to evaluate ideas openly and critically.
- Ask influential members to initially adopt a neutral stance on solutions.
- Enlist an independent outside body to evaluate the group's decision.
- Use expert advisers to challenge group views.
- Have outside experts attend group meetings to impartially evaluate the group's activities.
- Make one or more members devil's advocates so that ideas are frequently challenged.
- Expect members to explore alternative scenarios.
- Use subgroups to develop alternative solutions.
- Meet to reconsider decisions prior to implementation.

Although (as noted earlier) highly cohesive groups are prone to groupthink, fortunately, group cohesiveness doesn't always lead to groupthink. If a group's task-oriented cohesion is high and its social-emotional cohesion is low, groupthink is much less likely.[81] Knowing this, managers and team leaders can inhibit its onset by encouraging a task-oriented focus. Note that social-emotional cohesion can successfully coexist with task-oriented cohesion if the group's "reason for being" remains clear and the procedures designed to counteract groupthink are actively pursued.[82]

EMPLOYEE RESPONSES TO WORK TEAMS

As groups become a central part of organizational life, it is important to ask, What effects do work groups have on member attitudes, motivation, and behavior? We now turn our attention to this question.*

The Hawthorne Studies (see Chapter 2), conducted at Western Electric's Hawthorne Plant in Chicago during the 1920s and 1930s, demonstrated the powerful effects of groups in the workplace. Workers at the Hawthorne plant developed a strong group identity, and group norms affected employee attitudes, orientation toward the organization, and performance.[83] Another classic study of groups in the workplace took place during the 1940s and 1950s. Research conducted by the Tavistock Institute on the short- and longwall methods of coal mining corroborated yet again the powerful effects of groups. The shortwall method of coal mining involved a small group (eight or fewer) of miners working closely together to carry out virtually every phase of the mining process. The longwall method reconfigured work teams into groups of 40–50 men who often worked in separate parts of the mine and on different tasks. Soon after longwalling was introduced, productivity declined and worker alienation increased.[84] These two studies (and many others) remind us that the positive effects of groups should never be taken for granted.

Groups affect their members in four major ways: informational, affective, behavioral,[85] and motivational (see Figure 14-7). The informational effect has to do with the fact that groups influence the beliefs of their members. For example, if we respect the senior-level members of our team and they are loyal to the organization, it is highly likely that we will come to believe that management has a strong commitment to employees. As we saw in Chapter 6, an individual's affective state reflects feelings about attitude objects (in addition to the cognitive and behavioral intent components). Our job satisfaction is, of course, affected by the work we do; this is true whether we function as part of a group or as an individual contributor. As noted in earlier discussions, groups affect the behavior of their members through their size and cohesiveness, for example, which commonly affect member performance, attendance, and acts of citizen-

FIGURE 14-7 Immediate Group Effects

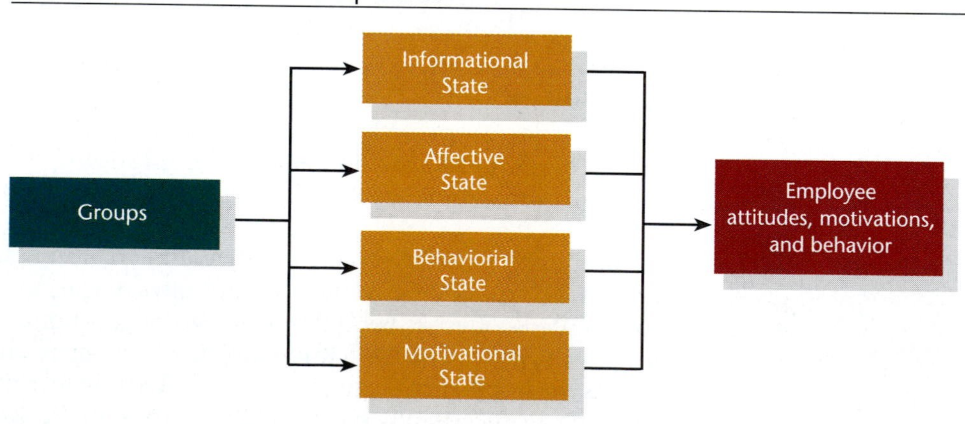

* We draw extensively on the work of J. R. Hackman (1992; note 85) for this discussion.

ship. Finally, groups impact member motivation. As organizational members, we bring a constellation of needs, wants, and expectations to our daily participation in the group. Group dynamics have the power to stir our enthusiasm, and also to drain it.

To understand group effects on employees (see Figure 14-8), we need to look at how participation (Chapter 9), planning and controlling (Chapter 10), leading (Chapter 11), organizing and organizational design (Chapters 12 and 13), and work design (Chapter 17) affect employees. Keep in mind that groups and teams also fit our definition of an organization: two or more people, with a common purpose, joined together with a communication and command system; a relatively enduring people-to-people and people-to-work interaction network. Of course, organizations nested within organizations, the group inside the department inside the division, and so on. Each group is an organization in miniature, with many of the organization's properties.

As we look at work teams as miniature organizations, it is obvious why they too have to be managed—groups make decisions, plan, direct, and control. Like organizations, groups can be structured and hence managed along the mechanistic-organic design continuum. As we have seen throughout this text, dramatic differences accrue from these two approaches.

FIGURE 14-8 Employee Responses to Groups

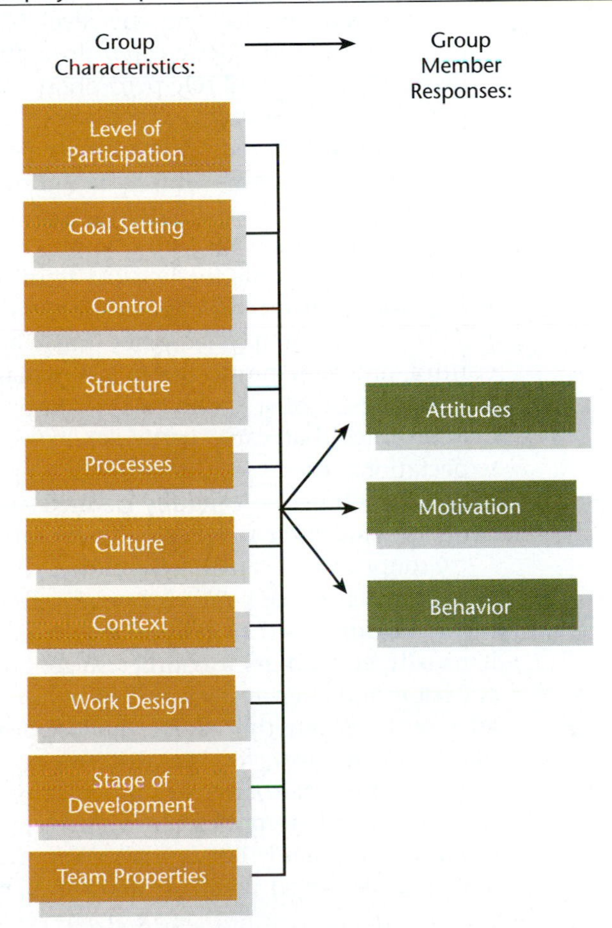

Finally, recent research indicates a consistently positive relationship between team membership and member satisfaction. However, the relationship between teams and performance is inconsistent. This is because work groups are better at some types of projects than others.

THE NATURE OF GROUPS AND TEAMS IN ORGANIZATIONS IN REVIEW

Buildings are made of bricks and mortar, but organizations are made of people. Just as engineers must be familiar with the nature and characteristics of their building materials, managers must understand the nature of people. They must know the effects of combining individuals into groups.

Groups can be formal or informal. They can bond firmly or stay barely intact. Many factors attract individuals to groups and contribute to the development of cohesion. Cohesion can benefit or injure an organization, depending, in part, on the group's norms and the level of consistency with the goals of the organization. Sometimes extremely high levels of cohesion lead to groupthink, a phenomenon in which the members of a group act disastrously in the face of conflicting information. Unfortunately, groupthink is not the only force that inhibits team performance. Groups can splinter as a result of their failure to overcome internal dynamics associated with group maturing processes. Several group dynamics—social loafing, diffusion of responsibility, polarization, escalation of commitment, and premature closure—can inhibit a team's effectiveness.

Team performance and the level of effectiveness attained are, in part, a function of the synergies created through the combination of members' energy, skills and abilities, and role perceptions. When given a supportive environment, a well-developed strategy, and a set of difficult and specific goals, work teams can be an effective tool in enhancing performance.

Work teams cannot simply be left on their own in the hope that they will make a significant contribution. Work teams can be seen as an employee involvement program. Like any employee involvement program, if work teams are going to be viable in the long term, it is crucial that knowledge and skills, information, power, and rewards be embedded into the team concept. Teams must be appropriately led, they must be empowered so that they experience control, and they must receive top management commitment.

Being part of a group has an impact on an individual. Group members assume roles that carry particular expectations. Although roles should clarify expectations, they often do just the opposite (thus creating ambiguity or conflict). Roles must be carefully defined and managed. Members of work groups generally find their work experiences satisfying.

Groups differ dramatically in their nature and effectiveness. The most effective groups become competent only after passing through a maturing process. In the beginning (the orientation stage), a group searches for its identity. Then it usually encounters a conflict stage. Successful further development leads to cohesion and then to a period of delusion, when members falsely believe that all is well. When this bubble bursts, disillusionment sets in. Through careful management, however, the disillusionment stage evolves into an acceptance stage. At this final point, full group maturity (and effectiveness) is realized.

Clearly, it is important for managers and team leaders to work to facilitate group development. But it is also important to recognize that there are several maladies like social loafing, groupthink, diffusion of responsibility, and premature closure that can become characteristic of groups. Those who rely on groups, especially managers in the high-involvement organizations, must be particularly attuned to these issues.

Managers cannot underestimate the importance of understanding groups of people. Guiding an organization without attending to its people is about as smart as driving a car without caring for its engine and transmission. The difference, of course, is that the "engines and transmissions" of organizations have psyches, group needs, and interpersonal dynamics.

A FINAL LOOK

Grant can see that the discord in his group is beginning to take its toll. Instead of focusing their energy on the project, members are ostracizing Lee and Celia, calling them "slackers." In addition, factions are forming over whose approach is more effective. Grant doesn't mind differing viewpoints; however, he knows that the group has to bond—and soon!

The next morning, Grant waits until all nine team members are settled. "As you know," he tells them, "our first deadline is only six days away. If we're going to succeed, we've got to get beyond our personal and professional differences. So, I think it's high time we aired our beefs. What is bothering *you*? Honesty is good—so name some problems. Come one, come all." Silence is the first "response," then Susan speaks up. "Some of us don't feel that everyone is pulling their weight. . . ."

The grievances come out, one by one, and the team establishes some guidelines to ensure that work will be distributed equitably. With the air in the office considerably clearer, the team decides a brainstorming session is in order. Members voice their opinions on the different user interface approaches without fear of being judged. Some members who previously agreed with Grant admit that the other side has some excellent points. Heaving a collective sigh of relief, the team is soon hard at work, and the deadline suddenly doesn't seem so impossible.

KEY TERMS

cohesiveness, 520
collective efficacy, 528
cross-functional team, 512
diffusion of responsibility, 531
empowered team, 529
escalation of commitment, 532
formal group (team), 510
group, 508
groupthink, 532
heterogeneous group, 519
homogeneous group, 519
horizontal team, 512
informal group, 511
long team, 516
management team, 512
manager-led team, 511
membership group, 508
parallel team, 512
performance context, 529
performance strategy, 529
polarization, 531
premature closure, 532
project team, 512
reference group, 509
role, 517
self-managing work team, 511
short team, 515
social facilitation, 519
social impairment, 519
social loafing, 530
synergy, 508
team norms, 517
team, 510
vertical team, 512
work team, 512

ISSUES FOR REVIEW AND DISCUSSION

1. Is there a difference between groups and teams?
2. How do formal and informal groups differ?
3. Discuss self-managing work teams. Why have they become so popular?
4. Identify and discuss the major properties of a team.
5. Discuss the different stages of group development.
6. What are the determinants of team performance?
7. Identify several dimensions of team effectiveness.
8. What are major impediments to team effectiveness?
9. How do teams impact members?
10. As a team member, what can you do to reduce the likelihood that groupthink will develop?

EXERCISES

FEEDBACK: INTERPERSONAL RELATIONSHIPS IN GROUPS

Purpose:
1. To learn effective methods of interpersonal feedback.
2. To develop a cohesive group.

Group Size:
Small ongoing (intact) groups of four to six (or up to eight) members.

Time Required:
50 minutes (longer for larger subgroups).

Room Arrangement Requirements:
Preferably a room large enough so that group members can give feedback in relative privacy.

Exercise Schedule

	Unit Time	*Total Time*
1. Introduction	**5 min**	**5 min**
2. Small groups give feedback	**35 min**	**40 min**
3. Class discussion	**10 min**	**50 min**

1. **Introduction** — 5 min / 5 min
The exercise and purpose are discussed by the whole class.

2. **Small groups give feedback** — 35 min / 40 min
The class is divided into groups of four to eight members. These should be groups that have worked together before. Each group member should think about how to fill out the Feedback Statements/Questions that follow. Be as specific as possible and use other group members' names when responding. Next, discuss your responses with all group members. Suggestion: One person at a time gives their answers to the statements, and other group members give additional feedback.

3. **Class discussion** — 10 min / 50 min
The instructor will lead a group discussion processing this exercise, discussing the importance of giving positive feedbaack and resolving issues and conflicts so that a group can function more efficiently.

FEEDBACK STATEMENTS/QUESTIONS

1. What I like most about this group is:

2. In this group, I have most difficulty discussing the following topics:

   a.

   b.

3. Group member behaviors that bother me the most are:

   a.

   b.

   c.

4. In this group, I would like to change:

5. I wish (____________________) would:
name(s)

6. If I could, I'd like to tell (____________________):
name(s)

7. a. In this group, the person with whom I have the strongest relationship is (____________________):
(name(s)

b. The strong relationship exists because:

8. I would like to ask (____________________) how he/she sees me.
name(s), or address to whole group

9. I would like to ask if (____________________) is angry or upset with me.
name(s)

10. I would like to ask (____________________) what my best contribution to the group is.
name(s)

11. I would like to ask (____________________) if I have seemed to change since entering the group.
name(s)

12. I would like to ask (____________________) what he/she is confused about me and . . .
name(s)

Source: Original idea adapted from Brian Holleran, Professor of Speech Communication, State University of New York, Oneonta.

INFOTRAC

INFOTRAC® COLLEGE EDITION

The articles listed below are a sampling of those available through InfoTrac College Edition. You can search for them either by title or by the author's name.

Articles

1. Giving teams a tune-up. (reviving tired work teams) Thomas J. Hackett. *HR Focus* Nov 1997 v74 n11 p11(2)
2. LEADERSHIP EMERGENCE IN AUTONOMOUS WORK TEAMS: ANTECEDENTS AND OUTCOMES. Simon Tagger, Rick Hackett, Sudhir Saha. *Personnel Psychology* Winter 1999 v52 i4 p899
3. Teams: it's all in the planning. (work groups) Lawerence Holpp. *Training and Development* April 1997 v51 n4 p44(4)
4. Building teams across borders. (Global Workforce) (includes related articles) (global work teams) (Cover Story) Charlene Marmer Solomon. *Workforce* Nov 1998 pNA
5. Measuring team effectiveness. (work teams) Jac Fitz-enz. *HR Focus* August 1997 v74 n8 p3(1)

Questions

For Article 4:

In the article "Building Teams across Borders," the author observes that "global teams can make major contributions to multinational organizations." While we often focus on the challenges in cross-cultural communication and working relationships, the cross-cultural work team can be a rich and dynamic asset in many organizations. After reading this article discuss with your group the benefits and advantages of a global work team, then list the advantages and benefits that you identified.

For All Articles:

Each of the articles on this list focuses on various steps in the team building process. After reading these articles, discuss the practical advice you gathered about the process and practice of team building.

WEB EXERCISE

Many organizations (for example, AT&T, Gaines, Caterpillar, Corning, Inc., Cummins Engine, Digital Equipment, General Electric, General Motors' Saturn Plant, Kodak, Lake Superior Paper Industries, Monsanto, Proctor & Gamble, Quad/Graphics, the U.S. Mint) have adopted the team approach to performance. Visit the website of one of these organizations and learn what kind of teams this organization uses and something about its experiences with work groups.

CASE
Team Building

You have been called in to implement a program of organizational change, the focus of which is to develop multidisciplinary teams in a mental health service that is part of a major hospital group. You are an external organizational consultant who has previously worked primarily with the private manufacturing sector, but you are keen, for both financial and personal development reasons, to apply your skills in a new arena. You want to do this piece of work well because there is a good possibility that you will be offered more consulting work in this organization.

More specifically, you are responsible for implementing one type of service delivery—the community mental health team (CMHT). The CMHT is one model of service delivery that brings together different mental health professionals to better meet the diverse needs of the clients. A widely held belief in the hospital is that such multidisciplinary teams provide a structure for bringing together different professional skills and that team-based organizational structures are an effective model of service delivery. The professions that typically input into current services are psychiatry, nursing, clinical psychology, occupational therapy, and social work.

At present, these professions work very much on their own, although they come together for "token" referral meetings. The function of these meetings is to allocate GP patient referrals for assessment and intervention. These meetings are usually dominated by the most powerful individual, the psychiatrist, or by the profession with the most members on the team (the nurses). Little effective information exchange about patient needs takes place, and there are long waiting lists.

You quickly notice during the course of your preliminary visits that the current service is piecemeal and fragmented. Different individuals with different professional roles and responsibilities work together on an ad hoc basis. Collaboration and skill mix are more often influenced by professional allegiance or by which individuals like each other (or dislike each other least) than by what is best for the client and/or the organization. The current situation is widely recognized as inefficient, and there is much overlap, replication, and frustration. Your initial contract is to focus on one team in the service that will act as a pilot. If this is successful, the model will be implemented across all the hospitals in the system.

The Team

The first team you meet has 12 people—a psychiatrist, a clinical psychologist, three senior nurses, two junior nurses, two support workers, an occupational therapist, and two administrative staff. The nurses, support workers, and secretaries are the only people employed full time on the team; everyone else belongs to other teams and/or occupies other job roles. The team is overwhelmed with referrals from GPs and other agencies.

There is no one overall administrative system to support the clinicians. Individuals pick up the work as they visit GP surgeries, day hospitals, and so on; there is no central point of access to the team. There is no joint discussion of patient needs, and everyone works in their own way. The team meets once a week to allocate work, and the ethos in the team is that no one says "no" to incoming work no matter how overloaded they are.

Everyone in the team holds their own individual waiting list and rushes around the city from dawn to dusk trying to carry out as many home visits as possible in order to keep the lid on their waiting list. The record-keeping systems are highly individualized. There is no team leader, although the psychiatrist (the person with the most formal power in the team) informally occupies this role.

It quickly becomes clear to you that the members appear to be either disinterested or resentful that the hospital is spending money on team development instead of buying additional resources to deal with the waiting list. The nurses are resistant to any changes in their role. They have worked in a particular way for a number of years now and have little motivation to change. Others (the clinical psychologist and the psychiatrist) are interested in the team development process and would do it themselves, but they are just too busy (in fact, almost too busy to attend many of the team meetings). There are significant power differences in the team. The psychiatrist is the most powerful, whereas the support workers are dependent on the nurses for clinical supervision and workload monitoring and thus are not keen to appear to dissent.

When you eventually get all the staff together (which takes some time as they are all too busy to meet), they sit round saying very little, staring at the floor.

Your contract with the staff is to run for a series of six team-building sessions that will explore multidisciplinary ways of working. Team building begins in earnest, but it remains a struggle to find times that everyone can meet.

Discussion Questions

1. Identify the feelings present at this point in the intervention and describe why they might be present. What is the pattern of relationships between you and the team and between individual team members? How might you respond?
2. What are the current operational problems (how the group gets things done) that require resolution?

Source: From C. Clegg, K. Legge, and S. Walsh. 1999. The experiencing of managing: A skills guide. *Hampshire, England: Macmillan Press Ltd., 281–283.*

Outline

Group decision making

Other work group and team processes

Work group and team processes in review

CHAPTER 15

Work Group and Team Processes

PHOTO: © R. W. JONES/CORBIS

Learning Objectives

After reading this chapter, you should be able to

1. Discuss the assets and liabilities associated with group decision making.
2. Comment on how group characteristics and dynamics affect group decision making.
3. Discuss when groups should and should not be employed in the decision-making process.
4. Describe how leaders can capture the advantages of group decision making while controlling for its liabilities.
5. Define the meaning of conflict and explain how and why it occurs in organizations.
6. Describe organizational politics and what you can do about them.
7. Explain the importance of organizational communication and the nature of communication in borderless organizations.

A FIRST LOOK

Janine Knight, general manager for KZNP, has been going over the numbers from the recent pledge drive with the station's management team. During this first year under her management, KZNP's fundraising efforts have fallen short. A public radio station, KZNP relies on pledges from organizations and individuals to obtain quality programming. Fewer organizations underwrote programs in the past year, which means the station has less financial support than ever. Janine feels that the station can weather this crisis; however, in the meantime, she sees major trouble brewing over which programs KZNP will keep and which they will have to let go.

Chip Gutierrez, the senior producer of one of KZNP's most revered shows, is scathing in his criticism for Lindsay Ferg, who oversaw the pledge drive. Lindsay is, not surprisingly, defensive and lashes out at Chip. She blames the community's lack of interest in the station's programming for the fundraising shortfall. Hank Estes worries that the new programs he has been producing will be cut before they have time to find an audience. While Janine knows that everyone on the team is threatened by the station's precarious financial position, prospects for resolving the ominous "musical chair" struggle look bleak.

Questions: How can Janine manage the conflict that the KZNP team is facing? What kinds of communication problems are the team experiencing?

Groups present many challenges to managers, team leaders, and team members. As we saw in Chapter 14, many issues relate to the nature and purpose of groups: group formation, development, and facilitation; group membership and fit; team properties; team performance; and the management of team effectiveness. In this chapter, we focus on group decision making. Organic organizations and involvement-oriented managers routinely employ groups in the decision-making process, and to the extent that control-oriented managers venture into the use of teams/groups, it is often as an aid to their decision-making processes.

Are groups more effective than individuals at making decisions? What are the perils associated with group decision making? When should groups be employed? How do you effectively manage the group decision-making process? These are some of the questions that we will explore.

While the primary focus of this chapter is on group decision-making processes, it is important to realize that several other work group and team processes (for example, conflict, communications, and organizational politics) impact decision making and other work group activities. If an organization is to function effectively using group decision-making processes, then managers, team leaders, and team members must learn how and when they should be used. Below, we discuss each of these processes and ways in which they can be managed effectively.

GROUP DECISION MAKING

As more and more organizations move away from mechanistic management and toward high-involvement systems, groups are used with increasing frequency as decision-making and problem-solving bodies. Consider the use of quality control circles at Design House. Employees there identified an inadequate production capacity related to plastic extruders. They studied the problem, obtained cost estimates, analyzed production increases, and looked at the potential payback numbers. Convinced they had a solution, the team recommended that management purchase two plastic extruders at a total cost of $400,000. Within four months, the company's expenses had been recouped and significant gains in productivity were realized.[1]

Not all team efforts are so successful, however. In fact, managers frequently comment that groups are slow, conflict is common, pressures to conform inhibit the development of good ideas, and subgroups frequently form—and work mostly "to get their own way." As a consequence, many managers hesitate to use groups as decision-making bodies or to give them true operating authority. Herein lies the central resistance to making the transition from control-oriented to involvement-oriented management, and from a mechanistically designed organization to an organic structure. As we discovered in our discussion of the high-involvement organization, the long-term viability of any employee involvement system is determined by its having true operating authority.

Despite the negative charges often directed at groups and teams, both the research and the experiences of organizations suggest that groups can be extremely productive. General Mills saw a 40 percent gain in productivity following the introduction of work teams at their Lodi, California, cereal plant. Stories like this abound.[2] So, what is the problem here? Is it one of groups and their inherent properties? Or do people not understand how to manage groups effectively? It is our contention that it is the latter situation. Organizations are still climbing the learning curve when it comes to using teams effectively. Managing groups and group processes represents a major shift in paradigm. Therefore, it behooves us to look at ways to help managers make this shift. Before we do this, however, let's review the assets and liabilities of group decision making.

http://www.generalmills.com

Group Decision Making—Assets and Liabilities

Spotted on an old Volkswagen minibus in New Orleans: a bumper sticker reading GROUPS DO IT BETTER!!! Organizations increasingly believe that groups make better decisions than individuals. The thinking goes, "two heads are better than one." That is, people involved in decision making feel a sense of ownership for the decision, and group decision making is safer because everyone shares in the risk. For these and other reasons, group decision making in organizations is everywhere—committees are formed, task forces are constructed, quality circles are installed, and self-managed work teams are created. However, despite all the enthusiasm, the fact remains that although groups often make excellent decisions, they make unwise and ill-fated ones as well. Why the mixed results?

Group decision making has both assets and liabilities.[3] A thorough understanding of the strengths and weaknesses of this process can help you, as a manager, determine when to encourage or discourage group decision making and how to improve the quality of group decisions.

What advantages do groups have over individuals in the decision-making process? Experts agree on these assets:

- *A greater wealth of knowledge and information.* Involving many people in the process brings more information and experience to the table.

- *More individual styles.* Because individuals search for information and analyze problems very differently, the problem can be attacked from many angles.
- *A greater number of alternatives.* Groups generate more possible solutions.
- *Increased acceptance of a decision.* Participating in decision making engages egos. The more people accept a decision and commit to it, the more likely the decision will be effectively implemented.
- *A better comprehension of a problem and decision.* More people understand the situation, and they understand it better. This is particularly important when group members will be implementing the decision.

These are strong arguments for using groups. Unfortunately, experts have also uncovered weaknesses in group use that have major implications for organizations. Here are some frequently mentioned liabilities:

- *Social pressure* can encourage group members to support emerging ideas blindly or discourage them from engaging in healthy disagreements. This desire to "not rock the boat" often causes groups to focus more on reaching agreement than on making a good decision.
- *Premature decisions* can result if groups choose solutions too early in the process. Groups often choose an alternative as soon as it is appears to have a positive outcome, and fail to consider other alternatives in appropriate depth.
- *An individual can dominate a group.* If one person's ideas and opinions overwhelm other group members, the benefits of group decision making are reduced. In addition, members resent being prevented from participating fully.
- *Conflicting secondary goals* can get in the way of the group's primary goal, which is to make a quality decision. Frequently, one faction just wants its side to "win." When too much energy is devoted to winning and too little to finding good solutions, the quality of decisions suffers.

Several group factors can be either assets or liabilities, depending on the situation:

- *Disagreement* between members can spark new ideas, but it can also cause hard feelings and threaten the group's existence.
- *Diverse and conflicting interests* of members expand the range of alternatives by providing a variety of perspectives. However, diversity also produces conflict that can threaten the group and hence the quality of its decisions.
- *Risk taking.* Groups are prone to making riskier decisions (the *risky shift* phenomenon noted in Chapter 14). This can be desirable (as many an entrepreneur will attest), but risk also comes with a greater chance for failure.
- *Groups often require more time* to decide. This, of course, uses more resources and slows the decision-making process. It can also be beneficial, however, if the group takes the time to understand the situation thoroughly and if they follow a good decision-making model.

Perhaps that bumper sticker should have read GROUPS DO IT BETTER—SOMETIMES!

The arguments for and against group decision making suggest that choosing this approach requires careful thought. Managers must evaluate whether, for a particular situation, the assets outweigh the liabilities. They need to ask if it is possible to manage the process to simultaneously take advantage of the assets and control the liabilities.

Effects of Group Properties and Dynamics on Decision Making

The previous chapter introduced several group properties and dynamics, including group size, physical arrangement, homogeneity/heterogeneity, social facilitation, and cohesiveness. Each of these properties can influence the group decision-making process. We also discussed several maladies that can afflict group activity (social loafing, diffusion of responsibility, polarization, escalation of commitment, premature closure, and groupthink). For managers to use groups effectively as decision-making bodies, they must manage each of these forces. This means, for example, that managers should consciously construct the size and homogeneity of the group and take steps to impede social loafing and premature closure. Managers, group leaders, and group members need to be prepared to confront these issues. The structured decision-making techniques discussed below are intended to assist with the achievement of that objective.

Group Conflict and Decision Making

Conflict is bad—isn't it? Agreement and consensus are much more desirable—aren't they? Contrary to these commonly held notions, ample evidence suggests that conflict sharpens decision making and enhances understanding.[4] Yet conflict can—and does—wreck team efforts, every day and through every level of the organizational world. The fact is, conflict can be contructive; it can also destroy. The determining factor is the *type* of conflict.

Cognitive conflict can contribute to group decision making if group members trust one another and are willing to express their opinions appropriately.

Cognitive conflict is task-oriented. It originates in differences in information held, in judgment, and in perspective. *Affective conflict,* on the other hand, is emotional. Affective conflict occurs because of personality clashes, incompatibilities, and disputes.[5]

© BILL VARIE/CORBIS

Cognitive conflict contributes to decision making because it facilitates the exchange of information, the analysis of information and ideas, and the development of personal and group judgment. Complex problems benefit from cognitive conflict because complex problems are best addressed by "a variety of skills, knowledge, abilities, and perspectives."[6] Affective conflict, on the other hand, leads to hard feelings, suspicion, and lack of trust among group members. It therefore inhibits effective decision making.[7]

Unfortunately, where cognitive conflict is present, affective conflict is frequently present, too. This occurs because the group has attributed cognitive conflict to sinister motives, and this creates affective conflict. Trust between group members minimizes this effect.[8] This finding has at least two implications. In newly formed groups, where trust has not yet developed, team leaders need to point out that cognitive conflict is a natural and healthy part of high-functioning groups and is not motivated by self-interest. Secondly, team leaders must make clear that aggressive behaviors like harsh language, yelling, and interrupting are unacceptable. Civility helps build trust and must be strongly encouraged. Trust among team members also appears to direct members' motivation into productive behaviors.[9] Both the judgmental decision strategy, which takes advantage of competing information and theories (Chapter 9), and the nominal group technique, discussed later in this chapter, are effective tools for managing cognitive-oriented conflict.

http://www.jnj.com
http://www.compaq.com

Some organizations have been able to make debate and the acceptance of healthy conflict a part of their culture. Apple, Ford, and Johnson & Johnson are prime examples. Compaq has created expectations that disagreement at all stages of new product development is natural. The focus of argument should not be to establish who is right and who is wrong, but to break positions down to reasons and facts and their underlying assumptions.[10] Forthright discussion, scrutiny, criticism, argument, and confrontation are an accepted part of GE's culture also. GE is no longer a formal, gentle, and stable work environment. Former CEO Jack Welch worked long and hard to make the company tough, aggressive, and iconoclastic.[11] The point is to generate good ideas, and then to build on them—this not only ensures survival, it puts a company at the top of the mountain.

The devil's advocate and dialectic processes build legitimate conflict into an organization's decision-making processes by making it okay to ask the hard and uncomfortable questions. The result is better answers, better solutions, and better decisions. A person or persons assigned to be *devil's advocates* ask the "what if" questions and critique the proposed course of action. Sometimes this role is handed around the group, allowing everyone a chance to develop their critiquing skills. The *dialectic method* is a structured debate, presented to the organization's key decision makers; one side presents the proposed plan and the other side presents a counterplan. Note, however, two major drawbacks to the dialectic method: The sophistication of the presentation can overwhelm its actual substance, and a "winning" debate can overshadow the identification of the strongest proposal.

Evidence suggests that organizations that promote open discussion and conflict tend to be more successful than those that do not. Consensus-driven decision making may work reasonably well in small, nondiversified, privately held organizations operating in relatively stable industries. But large organizations operating in uncertain environments appear to benefit from constructive dissent in their decision-making processes.[12]

When Should Groups Make Decisions?

Organizations are social systems, and much of what goes on in organizations takes place in groups. Because group decision making has drawbacks, managers must carefully consider when it is appropriate to use. These guidelines will help:

1. If a problem is of moderate difficulty, groups have a clear advantage over an individual. When a problem is extremely easy, a group is not necessary. When a problem is extremely difficult, a group may have trouble reaching a consensus, but it may also ultimately produce a better solution.

2. Problems that can be divided (decomposed) lend themselves to group problem solving. Information about various facets of a problem can be collected by subgroups and later assembled during the final stages of the decision-making process.
3. Groups with five to seven members are the most desirable, and a range of four to ten members is acceptable. Groups that are too small find it difficult to be highly productive. Groups that are too large tend to split into competing factions.
4. Groups whose members differ in experience, interest, and personal characteristics tend to be more productive than groups of similar individuals. This is a major reason why many organizations value diversity in their workforce, and train employees to value each other's diversity.
5. Partly structured interaction improves group functioning. Group leaders must encourage the free expression of ideas (from the majority as well as the minority) and prevent the premature evaluation of ideas.
6. Extreme status differences between group members—for example, president and secretary together—can inhibit group processes. Groups should be constructed without strong status differences, or various safeguards and inducements for low-status participants should be built into the process.
7. Groups that are too cohesive can get stuck in groupthink and become overly concerned with presenting a united front to outsiders. Moderately cohesive groups with a good communication system and an appropriate set of norms are thus more effective.[13]

These guidelines help managers obtain the best results from their groups. Always keep in mind, however, that groups are not a panacea; they bring both liabilities and assets to the process. The best managers recognize this and assess the characteristics of each situation before they assign decision-making responsibilities.

Managing Group Decision Making

Several structured group decision-making processes improve the efficiency and effectiveness of group decision making by controlling group liabilities and taking advantages of group assets. These include the stepladder technique, brainstorming, the Delphi technique, the nominal group technique, and synectics.

stepladder technique enhances decisions by structuring the addition of group members and their ideas into the process

Stepladder Technique The **stepladder technique** enhances group decisions by adding group members and their ideas into the process in a structured fashion.[14] Four basic tenets characterize the "stepladder." At the outset, individuals are identified as eventual participants in the decision-making process; two of these individuals are designated as the core group. First, each of the identified members is presented with the task and given time to think about the problem before they enter the core group. Second, as members join the core group, they present their preliminary solution. They make their presentation before they hear the core group's tentative solution. Third, the problem is again discussed each time a new member enters the core group. The idea is that each new discussion will "blend" the core group's tentative solution with that of the entering member. Fourth, a final group decision occurs only after all members have entered the core group, made their presentation, and the ensuing discussion has integrated the new ideas.[15]

Stepladder groups produce higher quality decisions than conventional groups, where all members work together from the outset. In addition, they tend to produce higher quality decisions than their best individual working alone.[16] In fact, it is not at all uncommon for stepladder groups to outperform their most proficient member.[17] This observation corroborates the idea that group processes create synergies and gains in proficiencies that individuals working alone cannot attain.

Preliminary observations of group performance with the stepladder technique indicate it works well for complex and novel problems. The technique appears to facilitate communication and the exchange of information, and inhibits social pressures to conform. Groups stay task-focused and draw on the contributions of all members.[18]

Brainstorming Brainstorming stimulates people to develop alternatives. Madison Avenue advertising executive Alex Osborn developed this technique in the 1950s after concluding that typical group decision-making processes inhibit rather than encourage creativity.[19] He observed that most groups discuss and evaluate an idea as soon as a group member generates it. Apparently, knowing that ideas will be evaluated immediately discourages people from developing and sharing ideas that are unusual and not well thought out. Creativity is inhibited.

brainstorming encourages the sharing of ideas in a setting free of the interruptions and risks that accompany immediate evaluation and discussion

Brainstorming encourages people to share ideas in a judgment-free setting. A set of basic ground rules governs a brainstorming session: No one may evaluate or criticize the ideas of others, and the more freewheeling the idea, the better. The more ideas produced, the better, and people are encouraged to "take off" on others' ideas (a technique called "hitchhiking").

In a brainstorming session, the problem is stated, and the group is asked to generate as many solutions as possible in a specified period. Participants are encouraged to suggest whatever comes to mind. Group facilitators emphasize that all ideas generated belong to the group, not to individuals. Criticism is forbidden.

The ideas generated in brainstorming sessions are recorded for later evaluation by either the group or the manager (depending on which strategy is used). Because the purpose is to generate a lot of ideas, it is expected that many of them will prove to be of little use. The hope is that, because so many ideas are generated, some will prove useful.

Advocates of brainstorming claim that it

1. reduces dependence on a single authority figure
2. encourages the open sharing of ideas
3. stimulates participation
4. provides individual safety in a competitive group
5. maximizes output for a short period
6. is enjoyable and stimulating[20]

How well does brainstorming work in practice? Compared to traditional group processes, brainstorming can work quite well.[21] The number and quality of ideas is better, and costs per idea generated tend to be more favorable. Brainstorming helps group members focus on the task at hand, and, as a result, conflict and pressures toward conformity decline. In addition, the ideas generated are more likely to be accepted by the group.

Unfortunately, what makes brainstorming successful also creates problems. Because ideas are not evaluated, at the end of a brainstorming session the only product is a list of ideas. There is no plan, there is no solution, and the initial problem still exists. This lack of closure can cause dissatisfaction among participants, especially when someone else (a manager or another group) evaluates the ideas generated.

Many organizations use brainstorming because it appears to have many advantages compared to traditional group decision making and only a few drawbacks. There is some evidence, however, that individuals brainstorming alone generate more and better-quality ideas than they do in the group.[22] Even in a relaxed atmosphere, the presence of others can still inhibit members.

Individual brainstorming works in some situations, group brainstorming in others. A group session encourages each member to devote the necessary time to idea generation, and, because group sessions are often more enjoyable than solitary work, they can create an *esprit de corps* and satisfy people's social needs. Group sessions remind each member that others have many good ideas, and they can improve group commitment to ideas and increase communication. When these factors are important, managers may use brainstorming groups rather than individual brainstorming.

Delphi Technique Sometimes solutions that come from groups in which participants interact face to face are of lower quality than solutions that come from individuals who work alone on the same problem. To address this issue, Norman C. Dalkey and his associates at the Rand Corporation developed the Delphi process.[23] The **Delphi technique** is a group process that brings information and the judgments of people together to facilitate planning and decision making. This process differs from others in that it gathers information and opinions without physically assembling the contributors. Instead, information is exchanged via mailed or e-mailed questionnaires. The Delphi technique is useful when a problem would benefit from group participation, but it is not feasible to assemble individuals for a meeting because of time constraints, geographical dispersion, or desires to remain anonymous.

http://www.rand.com

Delphi technique brings information and the judgments of people together without physically assembling the contributors

The Delphi technique, therefore, capitalizes on the combined creativity of a group of individuals, but avoids the problems that often arise in face-to-face groups. The procedure allows for anonymity among participants and encourages feedback, even among geographically dispersed participants. A group coordinator orchestrates the process through a series of formal communications (usually by mail, fax, or e-mail) to individual members (no two members communicate directly with one another). Although hundreds of individuals can participate in the Delphi technique, a maximum of 30 participants is usually desirable.[24]

The Delphi technique generally consists of several stages:

1. *Development of the Delphi question and the first inquiry:* The coordinator prepares a written statement of the problem and sends it to each group member. This statement is accompanied by a questionnaire requesting suggestions and potential solutions to the problem. The questionnaire asks them to present their ideas and emphasizes that, at this stage, ideas need not be fully developed or completely evaluated.
2. *The first response:* Participants, independently and anonymously, record their comments, suggestions, and potential solutions and return them directly to the coordinator.

3. *Analysis of the first response, feedback, and the second inquiry:* The coordinator prepares a written summary of all comments and sends this to each participant, along with another questionnaire. Depending on the first-round comments, this questionnaire might seek clarification of earlier comments, address apparent disagreements, or request more highly refined suggestions in particular areas.
4. *The second response:* Participants, again independently and anonymously, record their responses and send them to the coordinator.
5. *Continuation of the process:* The Delphi coordinator continues to follow this same procedure until a clear solution emerges, until a point of diminishing returns is reached, or until a vote is taken. Often, rather than take a formal vote, a statistical summary of the recommendations of group members is used. Research suggests that stability of opinion is generally reached after four rounds.[25]

Like other qualitative decision tools, the Delphi technique has both strengths and limitations. In its favor, the technique can involve large numbers of participants, and physical separation is not an issue. The technique produces a lot of information and many high-quality ideas. The negative aspects of face-to-face groups are greatly reduced. However, the technique is also slow. In fact, it has been estimated that a minimum of 45 days is required to complete a Delphi operation, although computer networks and electronic mail systems have greatly reduced this problem.[26] The delays and impersonality of the process do little to build group cohesiveness or commitment to the solution. In addition, group members need good written communication skills to participate effectively in a Delphi exercise. Participants also have to be motivated to produce timely and constructive responses. Finally, the success of the technique requires a coordinator who is adept at interpreting, translating, and summarizing input from members at each stage of the process.

nominal group technique (NGT) generates many creative potential solutions to a problem, evaluates them, and ranks them from best to worst

Nominal Group Technique The **nominal group technique (NGT)** generates a large number of creative potential solutions, evaluates these solutions, and ranks them from best to worst. First introduced in 1971, the NGT has become extremely popular.[27] It has proved particularly useful when individual group members have some expert knowledge, but no one has the knowledge required to solve the problem completely. Improving the quality of paper products produced by Wisconsin Tissue Mills, for example, requires the expertise of engineers, production managers, purchasing agents, quality control analysts, and others. In fact, in response to recommendations they generated using the Vroom-Yetton decision tree (see Chapter 9), managers at Wisconsin Tissue Mills formed 12 NGT groups to develop ideas for product quality and profitability improvements.

The NGT is a highly structured, interactive process that capitalizes on the strengths of group decision making and controls the inhibiting factors often associated with face-to-face groups. The NGT is a problem-solving and idea-generating approach designed for situations in which individual judgments must be identified and combined to reach a decision. It is not a technique for routine, noncomplex decision making.

The NGT process consists of at least four steps. It begins with a silent, individual generation of ideas. This is followed by a "round-robin" recording of these ideas. Next, ideas are discussed and evaluated sequentially by the group. Finally, there is a confidential vote on the relative importance of the ideas.

At the beginning of an NGT session, a "leader" presents the problem to be addressed by the group. Step 1—the silent generation of ideas—begins immediately. Each group member works independently for five to ten minutes, generating and recording their ideas. This phase of the process is identical to, and has all the advantages of, a short individual brainstorming session. Time is provided for people to ponder the problem. It avoids competition for the group's time and attention, it avoids pressures for conformity, it prevents the group from rushing toward a premature resolution, and it prevents the group from evaluating ideas as it generates them.

During step 2, ideas are combined in a master list. First, the leader asks one member of the group to state an idea and records it without discussing it. A second member of the group is then asked for one idea, and it is recorded. This process is continued round-robin, each member giving one idea at a time, until all ideas are listed. No discussion is permitted yet, but hitchhiking is encouraged. The round-robin approach separates ideas from their creators and focuses attention on sharing rather than on evaluating ideas. Finally, this process prevents anyone from talking too much or becoming argumentative. Lists of ideas generated by employee groups at Wisconsin Tissue Mills typically contained more than 30 suggestions for quality and cost improvements.

In step 3, the leader reads the first idea from the list and asks if any member would like to ask for or provide clarification of its meaning. Members can then briefly express their opinions about the strengths and weaknesses of the idea. Each item on the list is discussed sequentially in this manner. The leader discourages attempts to select any idea as a solution, thus preventing the group from spending too much time on a single issue. This approach also prevents a single individual from dominating the group.

Step 4 consists of a confidential vote on the merits of the various ideas. Members are asked to work alone and select a small number of ideas from the list (usually five to seven) that they feel are most important. Members then rank the ideas according to their personal evaluation and vote on them by assigning points based on their ranking. Individual votes are recorded anonymously on index cards and submitted to the leader, who tallies them. After the voting, the ideas are again ranked. The aggregation of individual votes determines the relative importance of ideas. The voting ensures that each member has equal influence on the outcome of the session. At Wisconsin Tissue Mills, the voting process typically identified 3 or 4 ideas that were rated highly, another 4 or 5 ideas considered moderately promising, and about 20 ideas that group members agreed were less promising.

Some NGT groups go to a fifth step, another serial discussion of ideas. People share additional information and discuss the voting pattern. Sometimes this discussion is focused only on those ideas that were ranked relatively high by the voters. Finally, in a sixth step, the group conducts a final vote.

The NGT can be extremely effective. It generates a large number of ideas, many of which are of high quality. It also produces a lot of low-quality ideas, but these "wash out" in the voting process. People have strong feelings of accomplishment and commitment to the solutions arrived at. They also feel committed to their group, enjoy the process, and feel a strong sense of having done a satisfying job because they can clearly see the results of their work.

The NGT process also has costs, however. It takes hours to implement, and it requires advanced planning. The high level of structure reduces feelings of involvement for some members. This structure also reduces the direct interaction among participants and, therefore, does not work well when situations require negotiation between two or more parties. Furthermore, the process can succeed only if all members agree to abide by the rules. As noted by its creators, Andre L. Delbecq and Andrew H. Van de Ven, the technique is best suited for complex situations that require the judgment of a number of experts and for which no single person has the only "right" solution.

synectic technique develops creative ideas and attempts to integrate diverse individuals into a problem-stating, problem-solving group

Synectics The Greek word *synectic* means "the joining together of different and apparently irrelevant elements."[28] The **synectic technique** integrates "diverse individuals into a problem-stating problem-solving group."[29] It gets people to focus on developing a single insightful solution and includes developing, evaluating, and critiquing ideas. Ideally, synectics produces a single, detailed potential solution. The strengths and weaknesses of the solution are identified during the process and attempts are made to resolve the weaknesses. As a result, a relatively complete plan often results with the synectic process.

Synectics is based on the assumption that we as individuals are divided into two parts. Our first part is concerned with safety and is analytical, suspicious, logical, and cautious—and thus inhibits experimentation and creativity. Our second part, though, strives to learn, is impulsive and sensation-seeking, and likes to have fun. Because the self-censoring part of our personality inhibits our impulsive, creative side, the synectic approach is structured to encourage our impulsive, creative aspects to override our self-censoring tendencies.[30] See *An Inside Look* for an interesting application of the synectics technique.[31]

Group Decision Strategies in Review

The qualitative decision techniques discussed above can help managers perform a number of managerial tasks. The Thompson and Tudin decision model and Vroom's decision tree (both are discussed in Chapter 9) help managers decide how to decide—whether to consult others or not. The decision tree is a system that can guide the making of decisions about planning, organizing, directing, and controlling organizational resources. The stepladder, brainstorming, Delphi, nominal group, and synectics techniques are structured processes that help team leaders gather others' ideas and information. These processes facilitate creativity and probe the judgment of experts. Many of these techniques structure group interaction in ways that reduce the liabilities associated with group decision making while simultaneously capitalizing on the assets of group processes.

Because each technique is designed for specific purposes, managers, team leaders, and members need to use them carefully and in the appropriate settings. Used well, systematic approaches are helpful. Used inappropriately, these models can erode the creativity, synergy, and trust of the group.

OTHER WORK GROUP AND TEAM PROCESSES

Other work group and team processes that affect group decision making and outcomes include interpersonal conflict, organizational politics, and organizational communications. The remainder of the chapter examines each of these in turn.

conflict a process that begins when one party perceives that another party has frustrated, or is about to frustrate, one or more of their concerns

Interpersonal Conflict

Conflict has been defined as a process that begins when one party perceives that the other has frustrated, or is about to frustrate, some concern. Conflict commonly exists when two or more people have incompatible goals, and they

AN INSIDE LOOK

Synectics: A Phone That Can't Be Beaten (or Stolen)

Get several of your friends together and spend half an hour brainstorming on the following issue: Identify ways to vandalize a pay telephone. Remember, feel free to come up with ideas that are as wild and unusual as possible. No matter how creative your solutions, they have probably all been used on phones owned by the New York Telephone Company. In fact, repairing and replacing damaged and stolen pay phones have become major expenses for the company during recent years.

New York Telephone decided to use the synectic approach to solve this vandalism problem. They enlisted the help of George Prince, developer of the synectic approach, and followed the five steps of the process.

At the *problem statement stage,* the scope of the problem was described, and it was agreed that an ideal solution to the problem would involve the total elimination of all pay phone vandalism and theft.

At the *goal-wishing stage,* a wide range of "wishes" was generated. One participant, for example, wished for an indestructible phone booth door that would open only after the insertion of money. Another participant wished that pay phones could be designed like punching bags, capable of withstanding repeated blows. Another wished the phones could be disguised as fire hydrants. This idea was hitchhiked on by someone who wished that the phone could be as indestructible as a fire hydrant. Continued discussion led to a wide range of creative ideas.

During the *excursion stage,* the leader suggested that the group follow up its ideas about indestructibility from the perspective of the Wild West. Discussion followed on the indestructibility of the bank safe, the indestructible relationship between a cowboy and his horse, and other equally "destruction-proof" ideas.

The *forced-fit stage* required participants to apply their Wild West ideas from the excursion stage to the problem of pay phone vandalism and theft in modern-day New York. When someone followed up on the idea of the impenetrable safe, for example, the suggestion was to build phones right into the wall of buildings. The idea of the indestructible pillars of rock found in western canyons gave rise to a suggestion for designing phones with no external appendages.

At the *itemized response stage,* a single solution to the problem of vandalism and theft of pay phones was specified. The group documented its advantages, its possible drawbacks, and ways to reduce these limitations.

The solution was to design a pay phone that resembles a bank's automated teller and to build it into the wall of a building so that it fits flush with the wall. The phone should have no appendages, not even buttons. Instead of a handset, it would have a speakerphone. Instead of a dial or buttons, the wall would have touch-sensitive areas. If a caller wanted privacy, he or she could attach a Walkman-type headset.

believe that the behavior of the other(s) will prevent their own goal attainment. The presence of incompatible goals alone is not sufficient to produce conflict. Conflict does not occur until the behavior of one of the parties interferes with, or is perceived as about to interfere with, the efforts of the other. Conditions that give rise to conflict include incompatibility of goals, scarcity of desired resources, and incompatible behavioral preferences.[32]

Clearly, conflict can, and often does, produce negative effects, such as decreased performance, lowered satisfaction, aggression, and anxiety. It wastes time, uses energy, and limits effectiveness. This is called *dysfunctional conflict.* In some situations, however, conflict can be beneficial. Conflict within a group can help members resolve underlying problems and move the group forward to a more effective stage of development. Conflict between groups can increase within-group cohesion and instigate needed organizational change. In some

© PHOTEX/CORBIS

It is important to manage conflict to reduce frustration, anger, and anxiety among team members.

cases, conflict can even produce creative and innovative results. Jerry Hirshberg, president of Nissan Design International, calls this "creative abrasion," which he colorfully describes as "the ability to transform pregnant moments of friction and collision into opportunities for breakthroughs."[33] When conflict produces positive results, it is called *functional conflict*.

Not all conflict needs to be avoided, but all conflict needs to be managed.

The Conflict Process Conflict does not suddenly appear in full bloom; it evolves from a series of occurrences. Figure 15-1 portrays the major stages of the conflict process, beginning with a person's experienced frustration and ending with conflict aftermath.[34]

People may first become aware of conflict when they experience frustration. This frustration can concern anything of importance—being denied a promotion, receiving only a small pay raise, or having difficulty accomplishing a work objective. The magnitude of conflict is usually proportional to the magnitude of the frustration experienced. Frustration, regardless of the cause, can lead to dissatisfaction, anxiety, anger, depression, and aggression. If a conflict is not fully resolved, some level of frustration will remain, along with the anxiety, anger, dissatisfaction, depression, stress, and aggression created by the conflict.

After experiencing frustration, people try to determine why the conflict is occurring and what it means. Some think, Why is that person doing this to me? Others are more analytical, wondering, Why do I feel this frustration? What has that person done to contribute to my frustration? What have *I* done to contribute to that person's frustration? How do I plan to behave during the remainder of this conflict? The more systematic a person is, the better they will conceptualize the nature and meaning of the conflict.

After people have conceptualized a conflict situation, they can take action to deal with it. The actions they engage in, of course, influence the reactions and behavior of others. Conflict behavior can take many forms, depending on the levels of cooperation and assertiveness of those involved. As shown in

FIGURE 15-1 The Conflict Process

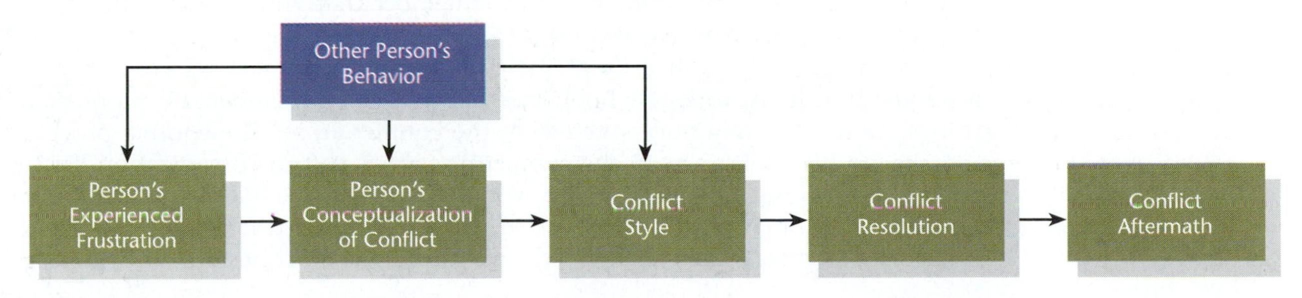

FIGURE 15-2 Conflict Behavior Styles

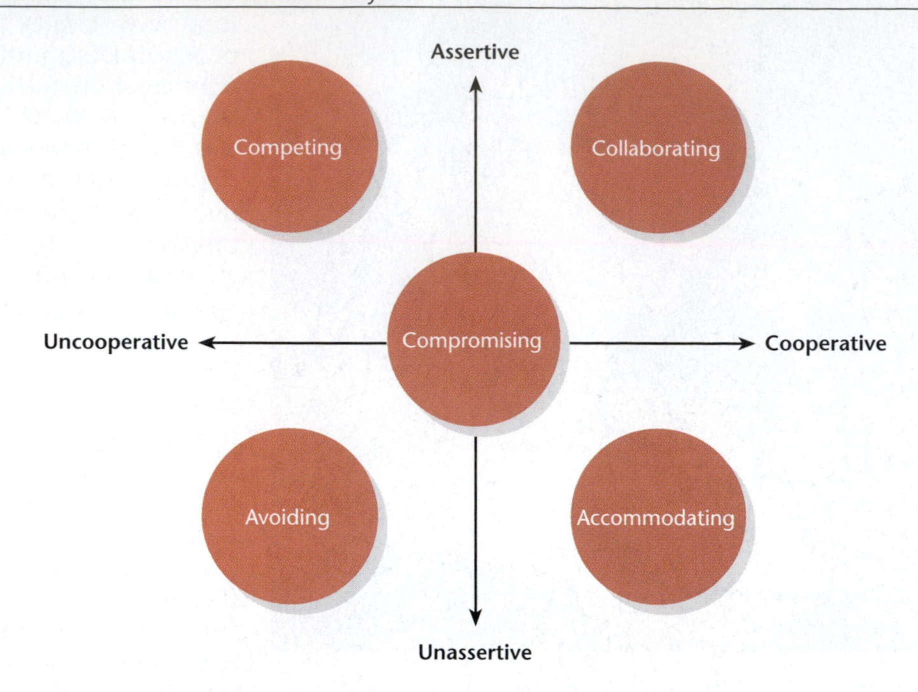

Figure 15-2, various combinations of cooperation and assertiveness create five distinct styles of conflict behavior: competition (an aggressive, often combative strategy in which one party tries to overpower the other), collaboration (an attempt to satisfy all parties' interests, often with a "win-win" solution), compromise (an agreement by both parties to give up something they value, often referred to as a "lose-lose" solution), avoidance (an uncooperative, unassertive style involving withdrawal from the conflict), and accommodation (a technique where one party tries to satisfy the interests of the other party at his or her own expense, producing a "win-lose" solution).

Most people have a dominant conflict-resolution style, though they usually incorporate aspects of the other styles as well. Furthermore, their dominant style may differ from one conflict to another, depending on how they conceptualize the situation.

The next stage of the conflict process deals with the other person's behavior. After all, there would be no conflict without the presence and behavior of another person. Your perceptions of the "other's" style substantially influence your own choice of conflict style. You are likely to behave differently, for example, if you perceive the other person as accommodating rather than competing. In conflict situations, it is important to remember that you and the other person simultaneously perceive and react to each other's behavior.

Finally, there is conflict aftermath. Think back to the last big conflict you were involved in at work or school. The fact that you remember it is proof that things are not the way they were before the conflict arose. The conflict process can exact a high toll on both the competing parties and the organization. Feelings of satisfaction, motivation, trust, and cohesiveness are likely to be affected. The aftermath of conflict can be positive as well. Conflict resolution often leads to needed organizational change, stronger feelings of cohesion, and greater

While most of us don't actively seek conflict, even healthy organizations encounter it—and stay healthy, even thrive by establishing processes to address and resolve it, as shown in the Jian conflict management video.

individual or group maturity. Whether conflict results in a gain or a loss for the people and organizations involved depends on how it is managed.

Managing Conflict Effectively People's instinctive choices in conflict situations are not necessarily good ones. For this reason, and because there is no one best conflict style, managers must carefully conceptualize each conflict situation and react appropriately. A new approach might be in order when quick, decisive action is vital and the other person in the conflict has a history of attacking noncompetitive opponents. An accommodating style might be more fitting when people discover they were wrong, when they know they will lose no matter what, or when future relations with the other person are more important than the outcome of the conflict at hand.

In sum, not all conflict must be avoided, but all organizational conflict must be managed. Good managers and team leaders possess the skills to minimize conflict and to emphasize the benefits of the conflict that does emerge.

Organizational Politics

politics the use of intrigue or strategy to obtain a position of power or control

organizational politics informal behaviors that protect or enhance the self-interests of an individual or group

One dictionary defines **politics** as the "use of intrigue or strategy in obtaining any position of power or control.[35] We normally think of politics in the context of government. However, politics exists in virtually all organizations, public and private. As group members act to satisfy their various individual and collective needs, they may act in political ways. Commonly, **organizational politics** are thought of as informal organizational behaviors designed to protect or enhance the self-interests of an individual or group of individuals.[36] These informal behaviors are not necessarily bad for the organization, but they are not formally approved or endorsed by the organization.[37]

While politics are active in every organization, the intensity of political activity increases in times of uncertainty, prior to resource allocation decisions, and when resource interdependence between individuals and groups is relatively high.[38] Organizational politics can be seen as "the management of influence to obtain ends not sanctioned by the organization or to obtain sanctioned ends through non-sanctioned influence means."[39]

Politics reflect an organizational reality. Coalitions form, labor and management bargain, and payments are made "on the side." In fact, it has been suggested by a noted organizational scholar that organizations are best defined as political coalitions in which decisions are made and goals are formed through the bargaining processes that unfold between individuals and groups.[40] Effective organizational members recognize the importance of organizational politics and act either to reduce their importance or to skillfully play the political game themselves.

What can you do about organizational politics? First, you cannot ignore them. Recognize that individuals and groups are interested in the acquisition of power and probably will use this power to serve their own interests. Be aware that decision making is often based not only on the merits of an issue, but also on the political consequences. Does the accounting department, for example, want to hire additional workers to help the organization function effectively or to build power for the accounting department? Be sensitive to the political concerns and interests of various individuals and groups as you evaluate the probable effects of alternative decisions. In short, learn about the political realities of your organization and anticipate their effects.

SELF-ASSESSMENT Perceptions of Politics Scale

Think of an organization that you have either worked for, belonged to, or are familiar with. Then, in the space provided, indicate how well the six statements below describe that organization. Use the following scale:

1	2	3	4	5
Strongly Disagree	**Mildly Disagree**	**Neither Agree nor Disagree**	**Mildly Agree**	**Strongly Agree**

_____ 1. Employees are discouraged from speaking out frankly when they are critical of well-established ideas.

_____ 2. You can usually get what you want around here if you know the right person to ask.

_____ 3. Overall, the rules and policies around here concerning promotion or pay are vague and ill-defined.

_____ 4. When you need help at work, you can never rely on a co-worker to lend a hand.

_____ 5. My co-workers help themselves, not others.

_____ 6. If a co-worker offers to lend some assistance, it is because they expect to get something out of it (it makes them look good, you owe them a favor now, and so on), not because they really care.

Scoring:

Add up the numbers for items 1–6. Enter that number here: ______

Interpretation

If your score is 1–13, your Perceptions of Politics score is LOW.

If your score is 14–19, your Perceptions of Politics score is AVERAGE.

If your score is 20–30, your Perceptions of Politics score is HIGH.

Questions

1. Do you agree with your score? Why or why not?
2. What types of other behaviors do you think characterize a highly political organization?
3. What could managers do to minimize the prevalence of behaviors like those described in the items above?

Source: Based on G. R. Ferris and K. M. Kacmar. 1992. Perceptions of organizational politics. *Journal of Management* 18:93–116.

Another tactic used by some is to take advantage of organizational politics. Supporting a politically powerful member can yield huge payoffs. If pay raises and promotions are influenced by people's political stance, so can learning the "party line" and behaving accordingly. Combining forces with other individuals or groups to build a political power base that dominates less powerful interests can also be effective.

Third, if you decide to play the political game, be aware of the possible ramifications. You cannot gain political advantage without expending energy that could be used for other purposes, such as increased performance. Furthermore, reliance on political support can be costly if the person you support has a fall from grace. If your favored status in an organization is heavily influenced by affiliation with a strong political leader, what happens to *you* when that leader is replaced by a political opponent? You undoubtedly will lose whatever political benefits you were enjoying. When you must stand on your own abilities rather than on your politics, you may also find that the energy you devoted to the political cause has been channeled away from activities that could have made you a more effective, competitive organizational member. Indeed, the use of political behaviors (ingratiation tactics) has been shown to result in lower levels of job satisfaction.[41]

Instead of playing the political game, you might wish to reduce the role of politics in your work life. Avoid using power solely as a show of force. Use power for organizational purposes when you need to, but do not flaunt it. Unfortunately, others may feel your behavior is politically motivated even when it is not. Take care to explain the reasons for your actions and be sensitive to the political concerns and awareness of others. Encourage open decision making and problem solving. Decisions made behind closed doors are often politically suspect. Participative leadership styles have been shown to reduce the negative effects of politics on employees.[42]

A final alternative is to try to reduce the role of politics in an organization as a whole and to diffuse responsibility throughout the organization rather than center it in the hands of a favored few. Over prolonged periods, political activity can have negative effects on performance and productivity. An atmosphere of shared responsibility makes the development of strong political coalitions less likely. Where political power does exist, try to channel it toward organizational rather than special-interest objectives.

As a member of an organization, you must decide whether to use or diffuse political power. Failure to recognize and deal with the political realities of organizational life will decrease your effectiveness, be it as employee or manager. It is also important to recognize that political behavior in organizations commonly produces negative effects, including uncertainty, suspiciousness, a weakening of interpersonal trust, heightened conflict, and increases in alienation.[43]

Organizational Communications

The importance of effective communication is not confined to managers. In today's high-involvement organization, teams—often self-managing teams—accomplish much of the work. It is not possible to coordinate the activities of a group without effective communication between its members. Although managers bear a heavy burden for coordinating communication across units, all members of an organization must acquire effective communication skills if they are to reach their full potential.

Communication should not be taken for granted or assumed to be effective. A survey by *Fortune* magazine several years ago revealed that while CEOs overwhelmingly said that morale among their middle managers was increasing, middle managers themselves reported the opposite.[44] Who is talking and listening to whom? W. Thomas Stephens, chairman of Manville Corporation, notes that in times of crises, "communication has to increase exponentially or you won't survive."[45] Other highly regarded CEOs like Frank Belatti of AFC Enterprises and John Horne of Navistar International consider organizational communication to be critically important to their companies.[46]

http://www.afc-online.com

http://www.navistar.com

communication the process of transferring information from one person or group to another

Communication is the process of transferring information from one person or group to another (see Figure 15.3). At Harley-Davidson, "It is a matter of top management getting out and talking with people, not at people. . . . "[47] *Effective* communication takes place when the information, or message, received matches the information the sender intended to transmit. Communication occurs, however, whenever a message is received—even if it is different from the message that was intended; thus, two major communication-related problems are *communication failure* (no meaningful information changes hands) and *miscommunication* (the message received is different from the one intended). Signs of communication failure include such telltale remarks as, "No, I never got that report," and "He didn't have anything new to say." Miscommunication is signaled by comments such as "I said you were expected to submit a ten-page paper, not a two-page paper," and "When I said I wanted this job done Wednesday, I meant *this* Wednesday, not next Wednesday."

Communications and Organizational Borders Barriers to effective communication abound in control-oriented organizations. Among them are the boundaries created among people and work units by status differentials, hierarchical levels, tight and narrowly defined job descriptions, and departments created along functional lines (divisions). These boundaries inhibit the flow of information, stymie the development of new ideas, reduce people's understanding of what is going on, prevent a sense of ownership from developing, and create morale problems.

Attempts to adopt involvement-oriented management practices and design an organic organization reflect, in part, an attempt to tear down some of these barriers. DANA Corporation's move from 15 hierarchical levels to 4 has put top-level management and the men and women on the production floor in closer contact. Hewlett-Packard's MBWA Program (management by walking around) and the brown-bag lunches held at Pacific Gas & Electric create opportunities for middle- and lower-level employees to have frequent face-to-face contact with management, creating greater opportunities for information exchange and simply getting a feel for "what is going on."

http://www.dana.com

http://www.pge.com

At General Electric, former CEO Jack Welch created "work-out" sessions. These three-day meetings enable managers to work on any issues they feel are pressing, from gripes to ideas for new products. Welch believes that the key to winning in the 21st century will be "to get every worker to have a new idea every day."[48] During one of these work-out sessions, a team from an aircraft engine plant lobbied for a plan that would cut the time to produce a jet engine part by 90 percent. Lake Superior Paper Industries, along with many other high-involvement organizations, has worked hard to eliminate status barriers that

FIGURE 15-3 The Communication Process

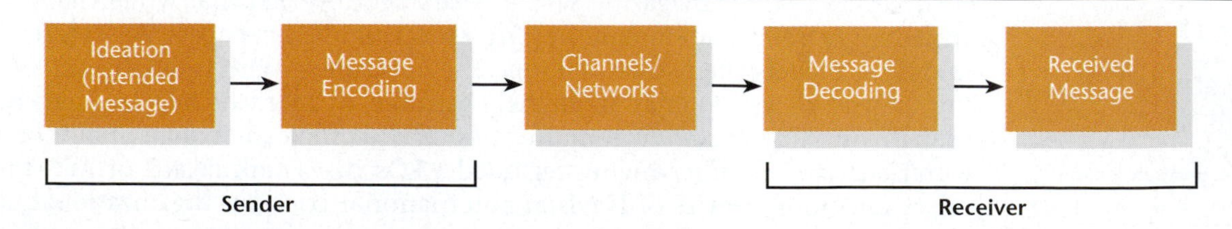

inhibit interpersonal communications. Top managers and workers park in the same lots (with no reserved spaces), enter the plant through the same doors, eat in the same lunch room, and dress casually.

Self-managing work teams have been instrumental in creating a system where people from different parts of the organization must communicate with one another. Minnesota Power employs cross-functional teams that link their power-generating work teams with members from other parts of the organization, cutting across all hierarchical levels. The men and women who run Quad/Graphics' printers deal directly with the company's customers—they are simultaneously the company's manufacturers and sales force. This strategy enhances the communication flow both into and out of the company's technical core. General Motors' Saturn plant designed new models with members of the automobile-consuming public sitting in on, and participating in, the design process. *An Inside Look* at Porter-Cable's strategies for eliminating communication problems describes some of these efforts in detail.

http://www.porter-cable.com

AN INSIDE LOOK

The Secret to Porter-Cable's Success

Home Depot has recognized Porter-Cable, a manufacturer of professional-quality power tools, multiple times as their Supplier of the Year. Less than ten years before earning this recognition, Porter-Cable faced flat sales and realized that something radical was needed. Managers in the operations division combined concepts from TQM, quality circles, and just-in-time (JIT) management to devise a new program to guide the company to success. The idea was to integrate the principles of safety, productivity, and teams. They dubbed their program AIMS—the American Integrated Manufacturing System.

One of the first orders of business under AIMS was to improve communications between management and employees on the plant floor. Component-focused teams now communicate directly with assembly teams, and quality issues are addressed quickly and effectively. Yellow lines painted on the factory floor delineate each team's areas of responsibility. Teams schedule their own work assignments and work toward production targets that they have helped to determine based on overall goals for the plant. Each month, teams are assessed by a management team and receive reports on their progress toward goals.

Rewards for accomplishing goals are a large reason that this system succeeds; it also contributes to the high level of employee motivation at Porter-Cable. Teams receive scores that count toward part of their annual achievement-sharing bonuses, which in 1998 averaged 8.7 percent of employees' gross paychecks. Most of this bonus is based on how well the plant achieves its overall goals. A percentage of any cost improvements in a team's area is also given back to each individual team.

The management team responsible for scoring each team's progress works with production teams to set goals and track performance. Teams take responsibility for failing to meet their goals, and excuses are not accepted. It is up to each individual team to rectify problems and to maintain their eligibility for the achievement bonuses. Because customer service is crucial to success in the manufacturing industry, teams communicate directly with customers to determine how to better serve their needs.

Porter-Cable attributes its transformation from an organization with lackluster sales to one regularly recognized as a high-performance organization to the AIMS program. Porter-Cable's willingness to change their processes and restructure the company to meet the demands of the marketplace is a key component of their success.

Source: Adapted from D. Drickhamer. October 18, 1999. People-powered change. *Industry Week,* 76–78.

Effective communication provides organizational members with necessary information and leads to increased motivation.

The Importance of Organizational Communication Communication within organizations is of critical importance for managers and leaders. The words of W. Thomas Stephens, chairman of Manville Corporation, are worth recalling: "We learned that, in times of stress, communication has to increase exponentially or you won't survive."[49] A survey of 54,000 business people by the Franklin Covey Company revealed that in building effective leadership, communication skills are second in importance only to integrity.[50]

It is through the communication process that organizational members become aware of, and are socialized into, the organization's culture. Organizations with strong cultures tend to be more successful than those lacking in cultural values. Consequently, the inculcation of the organization's values is of extreme importance. But the importance of the communication process does not stop there. It is through communication that organizational members come to see, understand, and share the vision that the organization is pursuing.

http://www.franklincovey.com

Effective organizations have members who understand how their jobs (roles) contribute to the larger organizational picture. This understanding frames their organizational role, reduces alienation, serves to satisfy their need to know and understand, and provides motivation, thereby contributing to individual and group performance.

Communication also represents one of the primary vehicles through which an employee involvement system can maintain itself as an effective and long-lasting management and organizational strategy. One of the keys to the long-term success of any employee involvement program is information. Organizational members need information to remain motivated and be equipped to make an effective contribution.[51] Communications is the means to the achievement of this end.

Goal theory, reinforcement theory, equity theory (discussed in Chapter 7), and the theories of job design (discussed in Chapter 16) all stress the importance of organizational members receiving feedback about their work and the results of their work. Communications between the members of an organization is one means to achieve these ends. It should also be noted that the strength of the psychological ownership that organizational members have for their work and for the organization contributes to their citizenship behaviors and overall levels of job performance. Evidence suggests that the sense of psychological ownership is in large part a function of the breadth and depth of "knowing." Communication is one important means through which intimate knowing of the organization gets created.[52]

WORK GROUP AND TEAM PROCESSES IN REVIEW

Many work group and team processes affect a manager's ability to direct the behavior of organizational members and the ability of each member to contribute to the effectiveness of the organization. Among these processes are group decision making, organizational politics, and organizational communications.

For many reasons (loss of control, time consumption, costs, lack of progress), managers often avoid using group decision-making and problem-solving processes. Yet, there remain many arguments in support of the use of groups, notably the "two heads are better than one" theory of idea generation. This prompts us to ask, is the problem really one of groups per se, or is it that too many managers simply don't know how to use groups in a way that simultaneously captures their assets and controls their liabilities? Several structured decision-making strategies (the nominal group technique, the devil's advocate) illustrate that this objective can be accomplished.

The qualitative decision-making techniques discussed here can help managers perform a number of tasks. The decision tree and the Thompson and Tudin model (Chapter 9) each present a systematic approach to the decision-making process and help managers decide how to decide—that is, whether to consult others or not. The stepladder, brainstorming, Delphi, nominal group, and synectics techniques are structured, systematic processes for helping team leaders gather others' ideas and information. These processes facilitate creativity and probe the judgment of experts. Many of these techniques structure group interaction in ways that reduce the liabilities associated with group decision making while simultaneously capitalizing on the assets that are associated with group processes.

Because each technique is designed for specific purposes, managers, team leaders, and team members need to use them carefully and in the appropriate settings. Used well, systematic approaches are helpful. Used badly, they may erode intuition, passion, and the art of management.

Conflict is a situation in which two or more people have incompatible goals, and one or both believe that the other is attempting to prevent their own goal attainment. A person going through the conflict process first experiences frustration, then tries to conceptualize or understand what is happening, reacts to their perceptions and the behavior of others, and lives with the aftermath. Most people have a dominant conflict management style.

Organizational behavior is very often influenced by political considerations, so an awareness of these issues is essential. Each person must decide how to respond to political pressures in organizations. Some available choices include learning to play the political game, avoiding politics as much as possible, and trying to diffuse the importance of politics in a specific organization.

While we did not discuss power within the work group context, it is important to remember that power and the use of power are an essential part of the functioning of effective work groups and teams. We discussed influence and power in Chapter 11, as a part of our discussion on "how leaders move others." Every member of an organization can accumulate legitimate, reward, coercive, expert, resource, and referent power. Some of these sources of power can be fed by formal organizational policies and practices, but others must be nurtured by individuals. Regardless of its source, power is "in the eyes of the beholder." You will not have reward power, for example, unless the person you wish to influence perceives that you have the ability and willingness to provide rewards. Development of an appropriate power base requires careful coordination of the various sources of power. Some combinations of sources can produce very strong power, such as fusing referent power with reward power. Other combinations are self-defeating, such as when a manager combines referent and coercive power.

Communication is an intricate but critical organizational process. The communication process includes formulation of an intended message, encoding of that message, transmission of the message through channels and networks, and decoding of the message by receivers. Distortion can occur at any step in the process. For messages to be received and interpreted as intended, organizational members must be very careful to match their communication choices to each situation.

A FINAL LOOK

Janine knows that there are no easy answers to KZNP's turmoil. Conflict is never easy, and her gut feeling is that whatever resolution they come to is not going to please everyone.

The management team argues for many hours over how to best distribute their funding. Lindsay suggests a supplemental pledge drive, and the team eventually agrees to mount one. Still, the current funds have to be distributed—there is no way around this. And sparks fly again. Chip and Hank clash over which programs need more support. Should the group support the established programs, which are more expensive to produce, or the newer programs, which Chip strongly feels are more expendable? A painful choice at best.

After much take and not a lot of give, people do begin to cooperate, and the team generates two potential solutions. They could tie pledges to programs that brought in the most donations, the reasoning being that listeners *are* voting with their money. Or, they could distribute funds equally among the programs, as the management team sees fit. While Janine is pleased that the team did eventually work together to resolve the problem, she knows the road ahead is going to be bumpy. When money and egos are involved, getting to resolution is never easy!

KEY TERMS

brainstorming, 549
communication, 560
conflict, 553
Delphi technique, 550
nominal group technique (NGT), 551
organizational politics, 557
politics, 557
stepladder technique, 548
synectic technique, 553

ISSUES FOR REVIEW AND DISCUSSION

1. Describe the advantages of group decision making.
2. What are the liabilities associated with using groups as decision-making and problem-solving bodies?
3. What types of conflict in group decision making are positive and what types are negative?
4. Describe when groups should be employed in decision making.
5. Identify and discuss five structured group decision-making processes.
6. Describe the stages in the evolution of conflict.
7. What are organizational politics and how might they influence group activity?
8. Why does politics emerge as an issue in organizations?
9. What is communication and why is it important to group functioning?

EXERCISES

WILDERNESS SURVIVAL

Purpose:
To understand group dynamics and group decision-making processes.

Group Size:
Any number of groups of 6–9 nine members.

Time Required:
50 minutes (more time for larger groups or if longer discussions are desired).

Related Topics: Leadership, Communications.

Background
Sometimes group decision making is more effective than individual decision making. Research shows that if the decision is simple, it is better to have one person responsible; however, if the problem is more complex, group decision making is more effective. In this exercise, you'll get a chance to compare the results of individual and group decision making.

The Situation
You have gone on a Boundary Waters canoe trip with five friends to upper Minnesota and southern Ontario in the Quetico Provincial Park. Your group has been traveling Saganagons Lake to Kawnipi Lake, following through Canyon Falls and Kennebas Falls and Kenny Lake.

The closest road is 15–18 miles away. Getting to it involves paddling through lakes and rivers and usually portaging (taking the land path) around numerous falls.

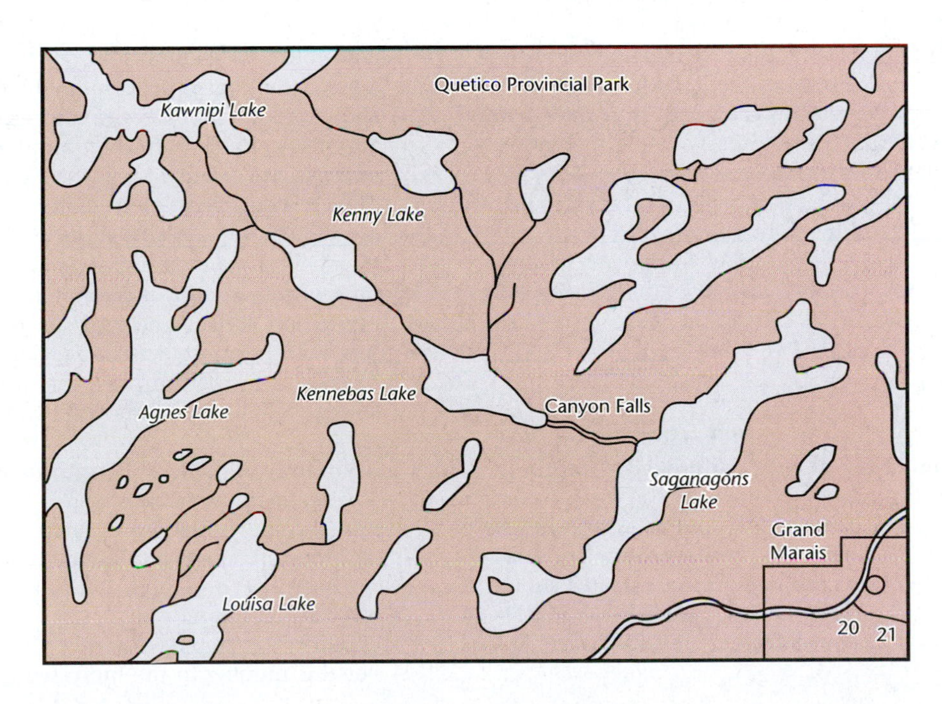

Saganagons Lake is impossible to cross in bad weather, generally because of heavy rain. The nearest town is Grand Marais, Minnesota, 60 miles away. That town has plenty of camping outfitters, but limited medical help, so residents rely on hospitals farther to the south.

The terrain is about 70 percent land and 30 percent water, with small patches of land here and there in between the lakes and rivers. Bears are not uncommon in this region. It is now mid-May, when the temperature (daytime) ranges from about 25° to 70°, often in the same day. Nighttime temperatures can be in the 20s.

Rain is frequent during the day (nights, too) and can be life-threatening if the temperature is cold. It is unusual for the weather to stay the same for more than a day or two. Generally, it will rain one day and be warm and clear the next, with a third day windy—and it is not easy to predict what type of weather will come next. In fact, it may be clear and warm, rainy and windy, all in the same day.

Your group of six was in two canoes going down the river and came to some rapids. Rather than taking the portage route on land, the group foolishly decided to shoot the rapids by canoe. Unfortunately, everyone fell out of the canoes and some were banged against the rocks. Luckily no one was killed, but one person suffered a broken leg and several others had cuts and bruises.

Both canoes were damaged severely. Both were bent completely in half, one with an open tear of 18″, while the other had two tears 12″ and 15″ long. Both had broken gunwales (upper edges on both sides). You lost the packs that held the tent, most clothing, nearly all the food, cooking equipment, fuel, first aid kit, and flashlight. Your combined possessions include one jack-knife, four canoe paddles, a pocketful of hard candies, five one-dollar bills, and 65 cents in change.

You had permits to take this trip, but no one knows for sure where you are, and the closest phone is in Grand Marais. You were scheduled back four days from now, so it is likely that a search party would be sent out in about five days (since you may have been delayed a day or so in getting back). Just now it has started to drizzle and it looks like more bad weather will follow.

Your task is to figure out how to survive in these unpredictable and possibly harsh conditions until you can get help.

Exercise Schedule

	Unit Time	*Total Time*
1. **Introduction and individual ranking**	**5 minutes**	**5 minutes**

Your instructor will brief you and then ask you to rank order the 14 items on the list in terms of survival value. The item considered most valuable should be ranked "1" and the least valuable should be ranked "14." Note your individual rankings in Table 1, column B.

	Unit Time	*Total Time*
2. **Group discussion**	**20 minutes**	**25 minutes**

Form groups of 6–9 members (with one or two optional observers) and come to a consensus on the ranking of the items. Use Table 1, column C. Members should not vote or "horse trade," but rather should try to have everyone more or less agree on the ranking. When someone disagrees, members should try to listen carefully. When someone feels strongly, that person should attempt to use persuasive techniques.

3. **Correct answers given**	**5 minutes**	**30 minutes**

Your instructor will post the correct answers and give the reasons for those rankings, according to the experts. Note these correct rankings in column D of Table 1.

4. **Computation of Table 1**	**5 minutes**	**35 minutes**

a. Compare your answer, listed under column B, with the correct answer, listed under column D. Subtract D from B in each row, taking the absolute value (do not count minus signs). That will be the individual error, which you should then note in column A. For example:

if you answered	and the correct answer was	the difference is:
2	11	9
10	5	5
12	1	11

b. Total the numbers in column A (none of which should be negative) to get your individual score.

c. Subtract column D from column C in each row, again using absolute values, to get the group error, and note it in column E.

d. Total the numbers in column E (none of which should be negative) to get your group score.

e. Subtract column C from column B in each row and put the results (absolute value) in column E. This is your persuasion score, which measures how much you are able to influence other group members to your thinking. Spend a few minutes during your group discussion talking about the persuasion score. Who had the lowest (this person was the most persuasive) and who had the highest (this person was the least persuasive) scores? Table 1 should now be complete.

5. **Computation of Table 2**	**5 minutes**	**40 minutes**

a. Average member score
Add the individual scores (step b, column A) of all group members and divide by the number of members in the group. Put this number in the indicated column.

b. Group score (step d, column E)
Put this number in the indicated column.

c. Synergy
If your group score is lower than your average member score, then put "yes" in the column for Synergy. If your group score is higher than your average member score, then put "no" in the column for Synergy.

d. Best member score
This is the number of the member who has the lowest individual score. Put this score in the indicated column.

TABLE 1

Rank the following in terms of survival assistance, assigning the most valuable a "1."

	A (B-D)	B	C	D	E (C-D)	F (B-C)
Items	**Individual Error**	**Your Ranking**	**Group Ranking**	**Expert Ranking**	**Group Error**	**Persuasion**
Fanny pack of food—cheese, salami, gorp						
Plastic-covered map of Boundary Waters						
Six PFDs (personal flotation devices)						
Two fishing poles, broken						
Set of clothes for three (wet)						
One yellow Frisbee						
Water purification tablets						
Duct tape, one 30-foot roll						
Whiskey, one pint, 180 proof						
Insect repellent, one bottle						
Matches, 30, dry						
Parachute cord, 35 feet						
Compass						
Six sleeping bags, synthetic, medium weight						

Individual Score (Total of A) ______ Group Score (Total of E) ______ Persuasion Score (Total of F) ______

6. **Group feedback (optional) 10+ minutes**
   Observers give feedback to your group, then your group talks about how it did in terms of decision making—who was most persuasive, and so on.
7. **Class discussion**
8. **Group discussion**
   As a class, discuss the following questions:
   a. To what extent did group discussion change the accuracy of the answers?
   b. Which behaviors helped/hindered the decision-making process?
   c. What happened if a person had a very accurate individual score, but was not very persuasive in the group; conversely, what happened if a person had a poor individual score and was very persuasive in the group?

TABLE 2 Groups

	1	2	3	4	5	6
Average Member Score						
Group Score						
Synergy						
Best Member Score						

Source: From *Organizational behavior: Experiences and cases* (6th ed.), by D. Marcic, J. Seltzer, and P. Vaill, copyright 2001. Reprinted with the permission of South-Western, a division of Thomson Learning. Fax 800-730-2215.

INFOTRAC

INFOTRAC® COLLEGE EDITION

The articles listed below are a sampling of those available through InfoTrac College Edition. You can search for them either by title or by the author's name.

Articles

1. Managing Conflict in the Workplace. (Industry Trend or Event) Peter Varhol. *Electronic Design* Oct 30, 2000 v48 i22 p155
2. Make Friends with the Wild Things. (managing employees and overcoming conflict) Tim Weitzel, Gary A. Had. *Training and Development* Nov 2000 v54 i11 p56
3. Can Your Job Make You Sick? Devon Madison. *Psychology Today* Nov 2000 v33 i6 p14
4. Toward a virtual politicking model. Celia T. Romm, Nava Pliskin. *Communications of the ACM* Nov 1997 v40 n11 p95(6)
5. True tales and tall tales: The power of organizational storytelling. (includes related articles on memorable organizational stories) Beverly Kaye, Betsy Jacobson. *Training & Development* March 1999 v53 i3 p44(7)

Questions

For Article 2:

The article "Make Friends with the Wild Things," delineates a strategy for managing conflict in organizations. As a group, identify the author's strategy and compare it to a strategy discussed here. How do these strategies for managing conflict differ and in what ways are they similar? Discuss which theory you believe would be more effective and explain why.

For Other Articles:

Chapter 15 and the articles on this list analyze organizational conflict and stress. "Managing Conflict in the Workplace," in particular, notes that workplace conflict "increases with cultural change." Have members of your group read the other articles. As a group, discuss how these writers suggest that managers help employees handle conflict and stress in a changing work environment.

WEB EXERCISE

The Center for the Study of Work Teams is the most well-known and well-respected organization devoted to the study of work teams in the world. The Center's overall goal is to help organizations improve the effectiveness of their work teams for the benefit of the organization and its members. Check out the Center's website at http://www.workteams.unt.edu/.

Do you think the Center would be helpful to most organizations? What do you find most interesting about the Center?

CASE
Changing Direction at Luminate

Bruce Fram was convinced that it was time to change the direction of the software firm he'd founded. Luminate (http://www.luminate.com) developed and installed software to help large corporations manage their enterprise resource planning (ERP) systems, the centralized computer systems that many firms had installed in the 1990s to automate management processes. Bristol-Myers Squibb, Dow Corning, and Tyson Foods were among the clients that relied on Luminate's software and services. In five years, the company had grown to 50 employees and Fram had high hopes that he'd be able to take Luminate public in the next few years.

However, Fram believed that Luminate's market was starting to change. New ERP installations were slowing down. Large corporations were now asking to have their software delivered over the Internet instead of being physically installed in their computers. Clients were also asking for additional consulting services that Luminate had never provided before. If Luminate could change its product mix, use the Internet for distribution, and develop broader services, Fram was confident that the company would become "not big, but huge."

Changing direction wouldn't be easy. It meant developing new products and altering the way the company had always operated. There was a chance that the change wouldn't be successful. Fram put together a team of six top company executives to work on the transition but asked that they keep their plans hidden from Luminate employees until they were finalized. "We were making a lot of tough decisions and wanted to make sure everything was right before we told employees," says Fram.

Fram hired Ron Gleason for the new position of vice president of e-services and put him in charge of spearheading the transition. Until the transition was complete, Gleason would telecommute from his home in Colorado and spend only part of each month in Luminate's Redwood City, California office.

Some of the executives chosen for the transition team were skeptical. Vice president of sales Jeff Johnson, for example, worried that the company would lose existing customers if it looked like Luminate no longer believed in its old products. Product-line manager Randy Keck, on the other hand, argued that Luminate had no choice but to proceed the way Fram wanted. The company had to keep up with the changing market, even if it meant losing long-term customers. Soon, the team divided into two factions: one that wanted the transition to happen quickly and another that wasn't sure the change was necessary.

During team meetings, tempers flared. The group argued about everything from staffing to which colors to use for Luminate's new website. Shouting matches frequently erupted. "You just don't understand!" Johnson yelled during one meeting when Keck refused to listen to his concerns. Gleason often didn't attend the meetings in person. Instead, he called in from his home in Colorado. On several occasions, when team members disagreed with his point of view, they simply hit the mute button on the conference room speakerphone and continued the discussion without him. "We were walking on eggshells," says one team member of the meetings, which often dragged on for hours.

Luminate employees, meanwhile, were growing anxious. They'd never been told why Gleason had been hired and suddenly he was making major changes. He split up entire departments, altered job responsibilities, and doubled the staff in preparation for the transition.

Rumors began to fly. Something big was going on, but most of the employees weren't sure what it was or what it would mean to their jobs. Some workers started talking about leaving the company. "Everyone was concerned," says Martin Van Ryswyk, vice president of engineering.

Finally, after careful testing showed the planned system would work, Fram announced Luminate's new direction to the staff. To calm employee fears, Fram and Gleason began holding monthly question and answer sessions, sending out daily e-mails about the transition, and meeting with staffers individually. Although employees now knew what was going on, dissatisfaction continued. When Luminate's new website debuted several months later, employees barraged the company's marketing department with over 500 angry e-mails about the site. "Logically, we understand what is going on now, but it takes emotions longer to settle," said one employee when the transition was completed.

For Discussion

1. What steps could Fram and Gleason have taken to reduce conflict among the transition team members? Between employees and management?
2. Do you agree or disagree with Fram's decision to keep the transition plan secret until it was finalized? Why or why not?
3. Discuss the role of communication in the Luminate transition. What, if anything, would you have done differently?

Sources: Adapted from C. Daniels. September 4, 2000. The trauma of rebirth. Fortune, *367; B. Weinstein. August 27, 2000. Transition from techie to senior manager a tough one.* Minneapolis Star Tribune, *J-1; and Zona Research, Inc., 2000. Luminate.* Internet Business Review.

VIDEO COHESION CASE FOR PART IV

Horizons: Leadership, Communications, and Motivation

Don Lee: A Multifaceted Leader

Don Lee, the founder and CEO of Horizons, is a multifaceted leader. On the one hand, he is a manager, and is respected by his employees for his command of technical issues and his ability to help them successfully complete projects. On the other hand, he is an inspirational leader, and has the type of personal qualities that employees find attractive and want to follow. He is also somewhat of an aberration. If he were put in a lineup of 10 people and 100 outsiders were asked to guess "who do you think is the leader of a $10 million company?" probably very few would select Lee. Yet, it is impossible to talk to a group of Horizons employees without sensing their genuine admiration and respect for Lee. It is also impossible to ignore Lee's success and the manner in which he has built Horizons from literally nothing to one of the Midwest's fastest-growing media production companies.

The CEO

According to the people who know him best, Lee has evolved as a CEO during his 17 years at the helm of Horizons. He started the company himself. The first person he hired was a cameraman, recognizing that he could stand behind only one camera at a time. He talks openly about his own spiritual awakening, and says that during the early years he decided to turn Horizons "over to God." He did this because he became aware that the company was bigger than he was. The early years of Horizons, and Lee as its CEO, parallel the story of how many companies grow and CEOs mature. Lee built the company step by step, with no real dramatic flair or spectacular event that catapulted Horizons or Lee himself into the limelight. Although his personal appearance (he has shoulder-length hair, a beard, and dresses casually) may strike one as a deterrent to business success, Lee seems to have developed a knack for getting people to look beyond that. One Horizons employee, reflecting on Lee and his accomplishments, said, "He has been able to take his free spirit and package it and market it in a way that is appealing even to very conservative clients and industries."

Like many successful CEOs, Lee clearly has position power, and he is respected in his office as the company's CEO. He has been able to take his creative flair for media and use it in areas such as finance and operations. His greatest strength as a manager seems to be finding the right mix of people and resources to do creative things. In terms of his day-to-day management style, he is informal and likes to "manage by walking around." It is not uncommon for Lee to sit down by an employee at their workstation and talk over the aspects of a particular task or job. So far, Lee's focus on people and his propensity to eschew structure have worked. He has Horizons moving in the right direction. The company is making money, is growing, is winning awards, and has a cadre of talented and committed employees.

The only unanswered question is Lee's capacity to manage and lead a larger organization effectively. His greatest strengths, which include caring about people, maintaining personal relationships with employees, and spending one-on-one time with new hires, will be difficult to maintain as the firm continues to grow. It is unfair to judge Lee prematurely and conclude that he will not be effective in more of a strategic, rather than an in-the-trenches, role. Yet, this is an issue that will affect the future success of Horizons, and Lee as its CEO.

The Leader and Friend

Lee also has charisma and other forms of personal power in his leadership role. Cherie Hatton, Lee's longtime protégé, has stated that her decision to come to work for Lee didn't have anything to do with "video, film, multimedia, or sound." She said that she came to work for Lee because he is a "godly man, who has integrity, who loves his wife and kids, and who I could be friends with—even if I wasn't working for him." Lee also seems to genuinely enjoy spending time with employees. For example, when Lee takes several employees on a business trip, he prefers to rent a suite, rather than a series of separate rooms, so that all of his employees and he can "laugh, have fun, and watch movies together." Lee's caring attitude and fun-loving nature have clearly made an impression on his employees. When listening to Horizons employees talk, the words *family, fun, respect,* and *people* are frequently mentioned in connection with the company's business operations.

Communications

Communications can be difficult in a project-oriented company. The fluid nature of people working in teams and/or working on location to shoot a film segment or commercial, makes finding an opportunity to talk to a specific person or getting the answer to a specific question a chore at times. E-mail has helped. Horizons is also rather cramped quarters presently, which has many disadvantages but does positively facilitate communication, simply because the employees are physically near one another. Whether the move to the "Big House" will help or hinder effect effective communication between company employees is unknown. Opening additional offices across the country will also further spread out the staff.

Motivation

Employee motivation at Horizons is facilitated by meeting each employee's basic needs and by providing employees with the opportunity to exercise their creativity. Along with a supportive work environment, employees are given the latest "cutting-edge" tools to perform their craft. Lee encourages employees to learn new software and ways of doing things. As evidence of this, Dave Fullen, a division manager, has said on several occasions Lee has told him that if his employees are not learning new software, then the company is falling behind. As mentioned earlier, the company also provides its employees with a fair amount of flexibility in terms of their work schedules, vacation time, and sick leave. This allows them to strike a fairly healthy balance between their work and personal life.

Employees are also given the opportunity to showcase their individual skills and leadership abilities. Mark Rigsby, a Horizons VP, described it like this: "I tell people what I want accomplished, I give them their schedule, I give them their budget, and then I tell them to go nuts and get it done. If you expect great things from people, You'll get great things." Rigsby is also a believer in granting employees considerable autonomy, in hopes of installing in them a sense of ownership for the quality of their work. The head of the company's Interactive Division, Dave Fullen, takes a similar approach. His approach is to provide employees autonomy, but also to provide them ample opportunity to ask for help. He characterizes his approach by comparing it to a tightrope act. He says that he gives people enough room to fall off their tightropes, but keeps the act close enough that the fall won't break anything.

In general, the company does a good job motivating its employees. The reward is an energized workplace and a high level of discretionary effort on the part of employees.

For Discussion:

1. What type of groups does Horizons use?
2. Lee seems to enjoy regarding his employees as friends. Is this a good attribute for a CEO? What are the pluses and minuses?
3. What stage of development is Horizons at and how did it get there? What other distinguishing characteristics describe the Horizons group?
4. Do you think the quality of communications between Horizons employees will improve or slip as the company continues to grow and moves into the "Big House?" Explain your answer.
5. As Horizons expands, will politics become an increasing part of organizational life?
6. What are project teams and how do they operate at Horizons?
7. Where do the "feelings of ownership" stem from within the team processes at Horizons?
8. What is teamwork and how/where is it evident at Horizons?

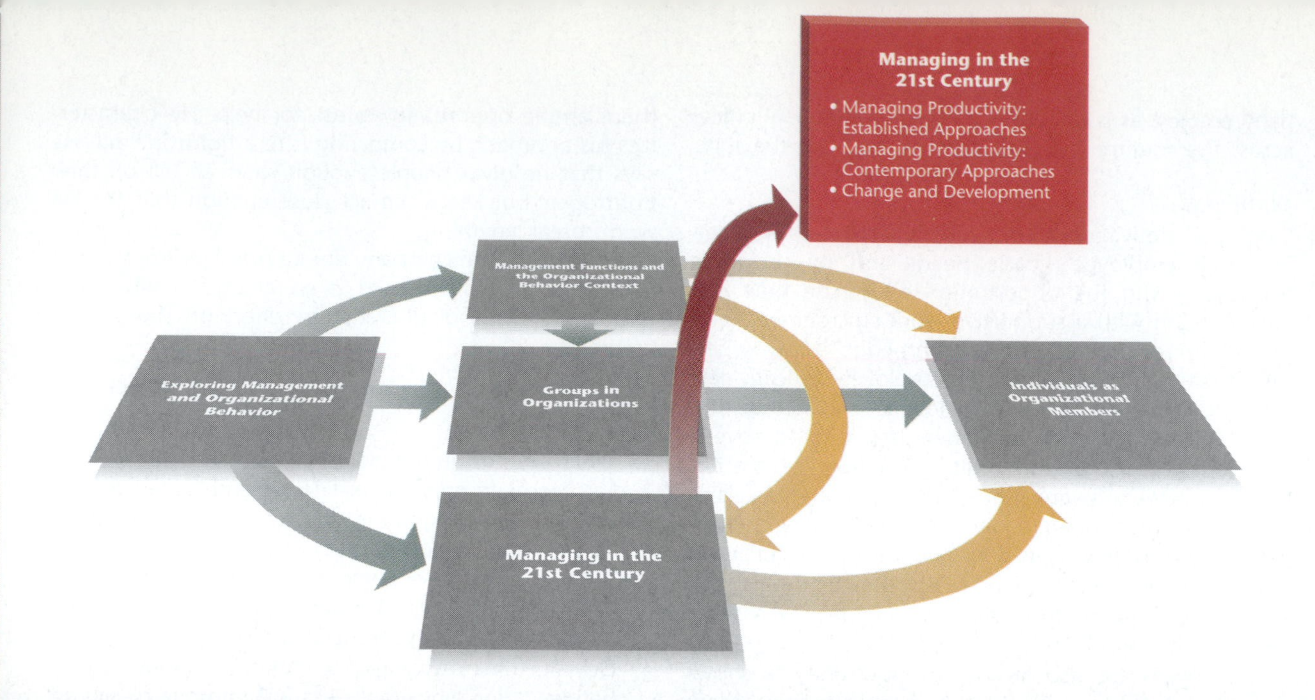

PART V Managing in the 21st Century

16. Managing Productivity: Established Approaches

17. Managing Productivity: Contemporary Approaches

18. Managing Organizational Change and Development

Throughout this text, we have highlighted the notion that many important issues and challenges confront today's managers. In this, the last part of your text, we address two important challenges awaiting those of you who will manage organizations in the 21st century—the management of productivity, and the management of organizational change and development. Your management philosophy and organizational culture will affect in profound and central ways which practices and policies you and your organization will use.

There is a long organizational history that revolves around the management of productivity. As far back as 1776, Adam Smith, in his *Wealth of Nations*, expressed the view that a division of labor would bring about dramatic increases in productivity. Throughout the 20th century, managers were preoccupied with identifying other ways to make organizations more productive and profitable. Standardization of work procedures, tool design, time and motion studies, lighting, length of rest periods, hot lunch programs, goal setting, human relations programs, participative decision making—these are all measures that have been developed and used to enhance productivity.

In Chapters 16 and 17 we examine the management of productivity in greater detail. In Chapter 16, we explore two established strategies used to manage productivity: organizational behavior modification and job design. Both have been found to have positive impacts.

In Chapter 17, we explore more recent productivity themes. We examine four contemporary programs implemented by a large number of organizations: alternative work schedules, employee ownership, quality control circles, and high-involvement management.

Many of these approaches to the management of productivity (such as job enlargement and enrichment, self-managing work teams, discretionary work schedules, employee ownership, quality control circles, and high involvement) are philosophically rooted in the human resource model. In addition, each approach reflects a model of the organizational member, which is consistent with McGregor's Theory Y, Argyris's conceptualization of the adult personality, and Maslow's growth-need motivated employee (see Figure V-1).

We conclude with a look at organizational change in Chapter 18. As we have noted throughout this text, organizations are experiencing rapid change in their external task environments. These changes are profound and are dramatically affecting organizations and those who manage organizations. Organizational change and development affects everyone in the workplace, and all organizational members need to understand it. In particular, managers of the 21st century will need to be masters of the processes of change and development. It is the intent of this chapter to start you on this journey.

FIGURE V-1 The Management of Productivity

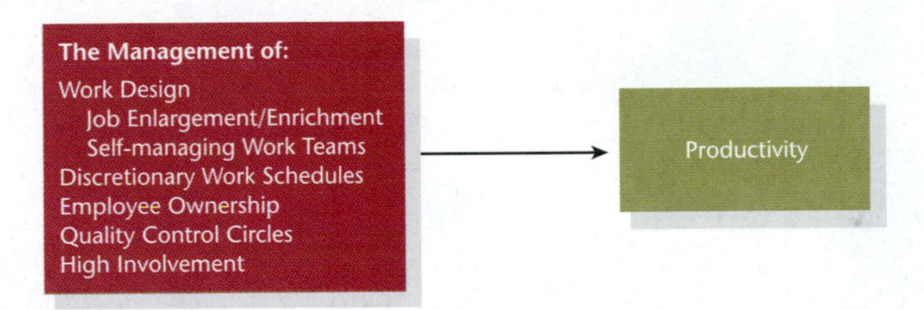

Outline

Organizational behavior modification

Job and work design

Managing productivity in review

PHOTO: © LAWRENCE MANNING/CORBIS

CHAPTER 16

Managing Productivity: Established Approaches

Learning Objectives

After reading this chapter, you should be able to

1. Summarize reinforcement theory.
2. Discuss organizational behavior modification.
3. Explain how to use behavior modification in the workplace.
4. Discuss your views on the ethics of organizational behavior modification.
5. Distinguish between the craft, classical, and job characteristics approaches to job design.
6. Compare and contrast job enlargement and job enrichment.
7. Describe the Job Characteristics Model, and summarize how job design affects employee attitudes, motivation, and behavior.
8. Discuss the self-management approach to job design.

A FIRST LOOK

The Admissions Staff at Ogden Community College (OCC) is composed of five well-educated, confident individuals. As the primary recruiters for OCC, they are responsible for attracting students to the institution. They are all gregarious and enjoy going out into the community to meet with prospective students and their families and generally like their responsibilities.

Lately, however, some of the veteran recruiters are feeling burned out. Jennifer Evans complains, "It's fun to introduce students to OCC on paper, but I never get to see them take the next step of enrolling and taking classes. I'd love to see how these guys do!"

Mary Hernandez, the president of OCC, overhears Jennifer's comment at a reception. "Hmm, maybe we ought to redesign the admissions staff positions. They could still recruit—they're so good at it—but their rapport with the students would also make them great academic advisors. We could reassign some of the academic advisors to pick up the slack in recruiting. Besides keeping staff enthused, this might also bring more students to OCC *and* help them persist in their studies."

Questions: What steps should Mary Hernandez follow as she considers redesigning these jobs? Do you think all of the admissions staff will be happy with this job redesign? If not, why? Would you be happy with the redesign? What other effects should this redesign contribute to?

Managers are forever looking for ways to increase productivity. As you may recall, the classical school of management thought grew out of concerns about inefficiency and ineffectiveness. This brought about what we call the science of work, and researchers ever since have endeavored to discover better management practices and organizational designs. The Hawthorne studies came along, and the search was somewhat the same—Are there additional ways to increase productivity beyond that found by scientific management and classical organization theorists? This time the focus was directed toward the environment in which work gets performed. Managers at the Hawthorne Plant had already focused their attention on work processes and tool and machine design as a way of achieving productivity gains, and now their attention turned to the work environment—lighting might make a difference. The human relations movement expanded the organization's view of the employee, and fulfilling social needs at work became yet another way to enhance performance.

Today, we are still keenly interested in productivity. Some things never seem to change: Productivity is a key component of competitiveness. In this and the next chapter, we will explore some recent strategies and programs to increase productivity. Each of these approaches to management impacts employee attitudes, motivation, and behavior, which ultimately reflect back on organizational productivity.

ORGANIZATIONAL BEHAVIOR MODIFICATION

People repeat some behaviors more often than others. One employee may be frequently late for work, whereas another is always suggesting improvements to production processes. Some employees perform just well enough to not get fired, while others strive to surpass performance standards. What encourages people to behave in a particular way? Simply put, people do what they are rewarded for doing.

Reinforcement theory (or operant conditioning) suggests that we repeat behaviors that result in desirable consequences and avoid behaviors that produce undesirable outcomes. We covered this topic extensively in Chapter 7. Here we focus on the implications of this theory for the workplace.

Reinforcement Theory Revisited

Managers need to ask themselves, What behaviors am I reinforcing? and then consciously reinforce ones they want to encourage. What behaviors will accrue if executives are compensated for quarterly profits? Rapid learning! Executives will discover that it doesn't personally pay to invest in R&D or in infrastructure. What behavior will your university get if it rewards faculty only for publishing?

Companies will use a variety of means to motivate employees, from the threat of firing to the opportunity to participate in the company's profits (even to becoming an owner through the acquisition of stock). As shown in the Valassis Communication video concerning motivating for performance, motivation can be established as a central tenet of the corporate culture.

To motivate employees to repeat a particular behavior, reinforcement theorists say that a desirable consequence must await the performance of the behavior. This can be anything that satisfies an active need, such as a promotion that fulfills a growth need, or that removes a barrier to need satisfaction, such as a flexible work schedule that allows parents to attend their children's school functions. When it is necessary to discourage behaviors, the consequence should be undesirable, something that frustrates need satisfaction or removes a currently satisfying circumstance—such as a reduction in pay or a demotion.

Reinforcement theory, when coupled with the content theories of motivation (again, see Chapter 7), provides management with a sound approach to employee motivation. The content theories identify the needs that motivate people. Managers can use these theories to identify what outcomes workers positively or negatively value. Reinforcement theory helps managers understand how to shape desired behavior by providing positively or negatively valued outcomes to encourage or discourage particular behaviors. For example, if Mary values personal esteem that stems from others' acknowledgment of her accomplishments, she should be rewarded by social recognition, such as a plaque presented at an awards banquet.

http://www.aptea.com

As you know, people learn to behave in certain ways because of the consequences from past behaviors.[1] Workers at A&P Grocers (Great Atlantic & Pacific Tea) began to make suggestions at meetings because their managers began to follow up on these suggestions. When the suggestions worked, the employees shared in the increased profits.

The learning process involves the coupling of a stimulus, a response, and a consequence. When Colleen receives praise from her boss for working hard, and if this praise is pleasurable, then she will probably continue to work hard. If, however, the supervisor ignores or criticizes Colleen's hard work, it is likely that she will stop working so hard. It is the experienced consequence (positive or negative) that influences whether a response will be repeated the next time the stimulus is presented.

reinforcement when a consequence makes a behavior more likely to be repeated

extinction when a consequence makes a response less likely to be repeated

When a consequence makes it *more likely* that a response will be repeated, **reinforcement** has occurred. Praise from Colleen's superior is a reinforcer. If a consequence makes the response *less likely,* **extinction** begins. Recall from Chapter 7 the three things that make a response more likely to recur: positive reinforcement (learning to respond to a stimulus in order to experience a desir-

Reprinted by special permission of NAS, Inc.

able outcome), negative reinforcement (learning to respond to a stimulus in order to terminate an undesired outcome), and avoidance learning (learning to respond to a stimulus in order to avoid an undesired outcome). Nonreinforcement and punishment make the response less likely to recur.

Organizational Behavior Modification (OBM)

organizational behavior modification (OBM) systematically applies operant conditioning theory to manage workplace behavior

Organizational behavior modification (OBM) takes operant conditioning theory and systematically applies it to manage workplace behavior. As you may recall, operant conditioning theory is rather quiet about what goes on in people's heads (their cognitions). Organizational behavior modification differs from basic operant theory in its heavy use of cognitive processes. That is, it looks at why behavior changes by trying to infer people's thoughts, and this can make OBM quite effective.

Operant theory requires that we *directly* experience stimulus → response → consequence (S → R → C) sequences before our behavior will change. OBM argues that behavior can change in *anticipation* of future S → R → C sequences. If you have been hired by a company that says it will pay you if you come to work, you go to work anticipating they will do so—even though you haven't yet received a paycheck. If a professor tells a class that cheaters will be flunked, many students will refrain from cheating. Thus anticipation of future consequences makes it possible to influence behavior.

OBM recognizes the importance of social learning—that is, learning from others' behaviors and those consequences. Social learning means we don't need to learn through personal trial-and-error experiences. Of course, we benefit from social learning every day of our lives, from not touching the hot stove because our brother got burned to imitating successful co-workers.

Organizational Behavior Modification Outcomes

To use OBM well, you need to understand how employees value certain outcomes. Outcomes are, of course, the consequences in the S → R → C sequence when they are intentionally made contingent on a desired response. If you fail to do this, your OBM plan may backfire. A reinforcer that is intended to be positive may actually act as punishment if the person sees it as a negative outcome. Need theory can help you select appropriately valued consequences. In doing so, you will improve the effectiveness of your organization's OBM programs.

Since OBM does pay attention to cognitive processes, both intrinsic and extrinsic outcomes are important. *Intrinsic consequences* are "self-administered" outcomes and can function in any aspect of behavior:

- *Positive reinforcement* ("Completing this task gives me a real feeling of accomplishment.")
- *Negative reinforcement* ("Finishing this task removes the nagging guilt feelings I have been experiencing.")
- *Punishment* ("I'm sorry I did a poor job on this assignment.")

Extrinsic consequences all come from outside the individual. Pay increases and promotions are extrinsic outcomes. Intrinsic and extrinsic consequences often exert joint influences on learning. When they are operating in a similar fashion, learning can occur rapidly. A worker who performs at a high level, for example, may feel a sense of accomplishment (intrinsic) and receive a cash bonus (extrinsic). When intrinsic and extrinsic factors oppose each other, conflict ensues and motivation is impaired ("Cheating on that last exam still feels awful, but I did get a high grade"). To use OBM optimally, consider both intrinsic and extrinsic consequences.

Intrinsic consequences are usually self-administered on a continuous reinforcement schedule ("I always feel like this when I behave this way."). This produces rapid learning during the early learning process. It can also result in quick extinction if the intrinsic experiences cease to occur. Edward Deci and others argue that, under certain circumstances, extrinsic reinforcement reduces the impact of intrinsic reinforcement.[2] In an intrinsically motivating job, for example, extrinsic reinforcements can shift your focus away from you and onto the external source of reinforcement. If true, this would reduce the reinforcing impact of intrinsic factors. Similarly, the parent of a child who is intrinsically motivated to mow the lawn may find that paying the child for the good deed has begun to snuff out his or her intrinsic motivation. The pay may be less for the child than the worker, but the reaction is the same as the perceptions of control shift from the self to the "other."

Behavioral Shaping in OBM

behavioral shaping learning a complex behavior through successive approximations of the desired behavior

OBM makes frequent use of **behavioral shaping** (learning a complex behavior through successive approximations of the desired behavior). Shaping is easier to accomplish if you can explain the desired behavior to the person learning it. You need to reinforce a behavior that is at least remotely similar to the ultimate behavior you desire. You then wait until a more similar behavior is shown by the learner, reinforce it, wait until an even more similar behavior is shown, and so on. Learning occurs much more rapidly when the ultimate desired behaviors and each desired step are explained to the learner.

Implementing an OBM Program

The most popular OBM program was developed by Fred Luthans (from the University of Nebraska, Lincoln) and Robert Kreitner (while at Western Illinois University).[3] They provide a five-step plan for installing OBM programs:

Step 1. Identify Performance Behaviors Think very carefully about what you expect employees to do on their jobs. Usually OBM focuses on only one set or type of behaviors (such as safe work practices). Identify exactly what behaviors constitute desired performance (say, always wearing steel-toed safety shoes). Identify conditions or behaviors that prevent the occurrence of the desired behaviors (safety shoes aren't always available, or co-workers make fun of people who wear them). A key OBM requirement is that the desired behavior be "countable." You must be able to count the initial displays of the behavior as well as the desired frequency.

Step 2. Determine the Base Rate of Performance Once a work behavior has been targeted, its initial rate (or base rate) must be determined. This means that you or your group counts how often the desired behavior occurs. So you might check the employee for safety boots twice a day for two weeks and record it. This is called sampling. The manager may find that the employee wears safety boots 50 percent of the time.

Step 3. Identify Existing Contingencies Now you must identify what stimuli (S) precede the behavior (R). Thus, the manager identifies conditions that precede both desired (wearing safety shoes) and undesired (not wearing them) behaviors. Then you identify the existing consequences (C). What happens after employees wear their safety shoes? When they don't wear them? Chances are that the desired behavior is rewarded less than the undesired behavior. Or maybe employees say the shoes are now uncomfortable (S), or it goes against the group norm and people who wear them are ridiculed (C).

Step 4. Select Intervention Strategy That is, how are you going to improve the base rate? This is your intervention. You will have to create new S → R → C sequences. Operant conditioning theory gives you four basic strategies. First, you can use positive reinforcements: Give $50 bonuses to employees who wear their safety shoes at all times for a month. Second, you can use negative reinforcement: Yell at employees every time they don't have the shoes on! Third, you can punish: Send employees home without pay every time they are caught without their safety shoes. Fourth, you can use extinction: Prohibit employees from making fun of co-workers for wearing safety shoes and thereby eliminate the existing punishment (derision). Most OBM programs use a combination of these strategies, as well as several reinforcers and punishments. OBM programs usually work with positive reinforcement because it is the most powerful cause of change in behaviors. It also is less likely to lead to abuse by managers (yelling at employees is *not* a good idea!), and poor employee morale.

Step 5. Evaluate After you implement the intervention, you must see whether it is working. That is, you determine the rate of performance of the desired behavior. In other words, you repeat step 2 and you compare this rate to the base rate. The key questions here are, is the after-intervention rate higher than the base rate, and if so, has it met my target? Let's say the safety-shoe-wearing rate has increased to 80 percent from the 50 percent base. This is an improvement, but your target is 100 percent. So you may decide to increase the bonus to $75, *or* you may look more closely at the comfort issue. Evaluating the OBM program is critical, or you will never know if it was worth the trouble and cost.

Effects of OBM Programs

Examples of OBM applications abound. When Marty asks you out on a date (S), you accept and go (R), and if you have a good time (a positive C), you are more likely to say yes if Marty asks you again. If you have a bad time (a negative C), you'll probably be busy next time Marty phones you. Furthermore, if you continue to have bad times, you stop dating altogether (generalized R).

Organizations use OBM every day. Pay is positive reinforcement. "Docking" pay is punishment. Improving your performance to get your boss "off your back" is negative reinforcement.

OBM techniques work for a wide range of purposes. During job training, OBM speeds learning. Continuous schedules of reinforcement initially speed learning. After this early learning period, intermittent schedules work to increase response rate and resistance to extinction. Explaining the total desired behavior and each successive training step helps shape complex behavior. Reinforcement practices "bring learners along" one step at a time as they master each element of the final desired behavior.[4]

Industrial safety programs commonly incorporate OBM principles. Warning lights, bells, and whistles (S) warn of unsafe conditions. Punch presses can be rigged to warn that a hand is in the way of a machine. Modern jetliners have ground proximity indicators that automatically start a spoken stimulus ("Pull up . . . pull up . . . pull up") when an aircraft approaches the ground from an unsafe altitude or rate. For obvious reasons, most safety applications of OBM don't have trainees actually experience consequences. Rather, a combination of social learning and simulation suffices.

http://www.emeryworld.com

OBM is used in turnover management, absenteeism control, performance motivation, and discipline. Perhaps the most widely publicized use of OBM occurred at Emery Worldwide.[5] Their OBM program was designed to increase the fill rate of shipping containers. Emery increased the percentage of full containers from 45 percent to 90 percent in one year. Supervisor praise was the primary reinforcement. Emery estimates that they saved $600,000 in the first year, and $2,000,000 in five years. Not bad for a cost free-reinforcer! See *An Inside Look* for another example.

AN INSIDE LOOK

OBM Improves Beaver Trapping

Two research teams (Latham/Dossett and Saari/Latham) studied how two types of OBM programs affected 12 rodent trappers.[6] The 12 trappers worked for a forest products company in the state of Washington. Their job was to capture beavers so they wouldn't damage newly planted seedlings. Trapping performance measured for a four-week period indicated an average of 0.52 trappings per hour per worker.

After the initial four-week period, half of the trappers were placed on a continuous reinforcement (CR) schedule. This schedule provided $1 above and beyond the regular hourly compensation for each beaver trapped. The remaining six trappers were placed on a variable ratio (VR) reinforcement schedule in which every fourth trapping was reinforced (at $4, so that both groups received an average of $1 per trapping). Every week, the groups alternated between the two schedules.

Figure 16-1 shows the results of the two OBM programs. Under the continuous reinforcement schedule, performance increased 50 percent (from an average of 0.52 to 0.78). Under the variable ratio schedule, performance was even higher (1.08, or a 108% increase). The study revealed that CR schedules were more effective for inexperienced employees (as would be expected during early learning periods).

Saari and Latham also explored why the VR schedule was more effective when both programs provided the same financial reinforcement. Interviews revealed that the trappers felt the VR schedule provided greater amounts of recognition and intrinsic reinforcement (a sense of task accomplishment and experienced meaningfulness of the work). After several years, the program was still operating with similar results.

FIGURE 16-1 Beaver Trapping and OBM

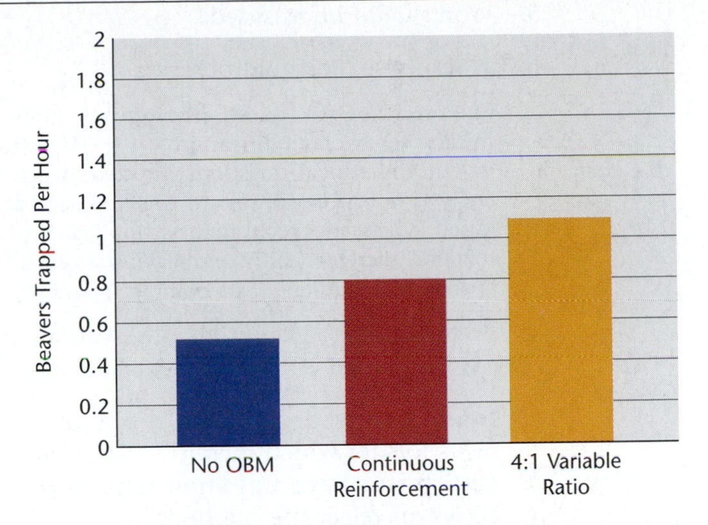

Source: L. M. Saari and G. P. Latham. 1982. Employee reactions to continuous and variable reinforcement schedules involving a monetary incentive. *Journal of Applied Psychology* 67:506–508.

Alexander Stajkovic (University of California at Irvine) and Fred Luthans (University of Nebraska, Lincoln) recently reviewed 20 years of research on the effects of OBM on task performance.[7] They found that OBM programs significantly and positively impact task performance. The results tend to be more positive in manufacturing organizations than in service organizations. In service organizations, it is often difficult to define and accurately assess performance and OBM outcomes. Therefore, designing interventions is also difficult. That said, OBM, when it can be used, also positively affects performance in service organizations.

The Ethics of OBM

Is organizational behavior modification ethical? A blanket answer is difficult, because different philosophies, both individual and organizational, come into play here. Some people feel that any attempt to influence behavior in any way is unethical. If you feel this way, OBM is clearly unethical for you. Others feel that OBM is ethical as long as behavior is not modified so as to compromise the focal person legally, morally, or emotionally. If you feel this way, whether or not OBM will be ethical for you depends on the behavior produced by its use. Still others believe that OBM is ethical so long as the person using it explains to the subject what behaviors are to be modified, why, and how. Even after taking all perspectives into consideration, you still may be left wondering, Who am I to decide whether what I am asking of this person is "illegal, immoral, or otherwise compromising"? There is no easy answer.

Howard Berthold of Lycoming College presented several frequently asked questions about OBM use:[8]

1. Isn't it unethical to modify another person's behavior?
2. Isn't behavior modification worse than some other methods because it is planned rather than unplanned—intentional rather than unintentional?
3. Aren't the techniques involved objectionable?

4. Wouldn't a successful program cause people to lose their individuality?
5. Won't OBM be misused?

In his response, Berthold observes

> The preceding five questions typify the kinds of concerns many people express toward behavior modification. . . . The bottom line to most of these concerns is that the ethical questions directed at behavior modification turn out upon analysis not to be unique to this approach at all, but are issues that should be raised when any technique is applied to the sphere of management. There remains, therefore, only one real question, and that is how one ensures that any approach, regardless of its name or methods, is ethical.[9]

Berthold then lays out six observations to consider when deciding whether OBM is being used ethically.[10] Behavioral modification is least controversial when

1. It uses positive techniques. It is also less controversial when it is applied to behaviors for which there is widespread agreement that changes are justified.
2. Participants have full knowledge of the methods and goals, and they can accept or reject the methods.
3. A need or reason for using it is clearly established.
4. All reasonable alternatives have been specified, and there is general agreement that a given alternative is best.
5. The people who practice it are well informed about the ethical issues involved, can discuss the issues intelligently with participants, and strive to follow established ethical guidelines.
6. It advances and supports personal and social ideals.

One other consideration may help you when contemplating the use of OBM: Is OBM being used to "force" organizational members to do things against their wishes, or is OBM helping these members to behave in a way they desire? The former is clearly manipulation; the latter is simple assistance. You may reject using OBM to manipulate. On the other hand, if your employees ask you to help them improve in some way, OBM should be one of your choices.

JOB AND WORK DESIGN

job (work) design
how tasks are combined to form a job; the formal and informal specification of task-related activities assigned to and carried out by a worker; the inherent nature and character of the work performed

Job (work) design has to do with how tasks are combined to form a job. It is the formal and informal specification of the task-related activities assigned to and carried out by organizational members. Job design focuses on the inherent nature and character of the work performed. "Central to the relationship between an individual and a work organization is the nature of the work that the individual is asked to do."[11] The nature and quality of our relationship with our employer is determined, to a large extent, by the nature of the work that we perform. As you now know, all kinds of employee responses—motivation, citizenship behavior, psychological ownership, performance, turnover, and organization-based self-esteem, to name a few—are strongly influenced by the nature of the work we do hour after hour, day after day. Thus, the way jobs are designed is of major importance to organizations and to organizational members.

The Craft Approach

Prior to the Industrial Revolution, the dominant approach to work design was the craft approach. In the *craft approach*, a single skilled worker designed and built products one at a time from beginning to end. The craftsperson raised and sheared sheep, washed and carded the wool, dyed it with berries or blossoms that he or she had gathered, dried and spun it into yarn, and wove it into clothing, which was eventually sold as the process continued.

For the craftsperson there were many tasks and a sea of activity that confronted them each day. To succeed, one needed a number of different skills and abilities, some more complex than others. The craftsperson was continually confronted with problems to solve and decisions to make—when to plant the crops, breed the sheep, shear the wool, and so on. The time needed to perform each task varied, and the entire process (from the breeding and raising of the sheep to the sale of wool scarves) spanned a long period. The Industrial Revolution forever changed the way we work. The small cottage industries and the craft approach rapidly disappeared with the advent of the machine and the division of labor.

The Classical Approach

http://www.adamsmith.org.uk

The *classical approach* divided the work into a small number of simple, repetitive, and standardized tasks and called them jobs. Economist Adam Smith, in his classic book *The Wealth of Nations* (published in 1776), first identified the economic advantages of the specialization, standardization, and simplification of work.[12] Smith cited pin manufacturing, where a craftsman pin maker made no more than 20 pins per day. Through division of labor and with new equipment, 10 workers could produce 48,000 pins a day.

Smith believed that each employee should perform only a limited number of activities that do not require elaborate skills. Smith gave five reasons for designing jobs this way:

1. *Skill and dexterity development.* A worker who repeatedly performs the same activity improves over time.
2. *Time savings and production gains.* Workers produce more if they do not lose time changing from one activity to another.
3. *Innovations.* People who specialize their efforts find ways to do their job better, faster, and more cheaply.
4. *Specialized equipment.* Narrowly defined tasks can often be done by machines developed for that specific purpose.
5. *Training time and costs.* Employees become productive almost immediately. It does not take long to train workers to perform a small number of simple tasks.

vertical specialization an approach to jobs that removes planning and controlling activites from production employees

horizontal specialization an approach to jobs that creates many low-skill-level, short-time cycle, repetitive positions

Succeeding generations of managers built on the division of labor,[13] and many jobs today are designed along specialization, standardization, and simplification.[14] Frederick W. Taylor and other advocates of scientific management refined this approach.[15] He advocated division of labor (1) that separated management from the rank and file, (2) within the ranks of management to achieve functional supervision, and (3) among the rank and file. His work resulted in **vertical specialization**, which removes planning and controlling activities from production employees, and **horizontal specialization**, which creates many low-skill-level, short-time cycle, repetitive jobs.

This classical approach to work design was seen as a way to enhance productivity, efficiency, control, and standardization. For decades, its supporters touted that it increased labor effectiveness, lowered production costs, and made system performance more predictable. Recall from Chapter 2 that Taylor's pig iron handlers went from 12½ to 52 tons per day, and Gilbreth's bricklayers went from 125 to 250 laid bricks per hour as a result of the development and application of scientific management. While it is not clear how much the favorable results were a function of division of labor or of other changes (such as wage incentive systems, new technologies, and the increased ability of management to administer large, complex production facilities),[16] there did emerge a belief in the efficacy of the classical approach to job design.

Critics of the classical approach argue that it leads to problems for organizations and for workers. They suggest that employees occupying simplified, low-skill-level, repetitive jobs eventually perceive them as monotonous and, thus, become bored and dissatisfied. Boredom and job dissatisfaction eventually translate into absenteeism, turnover, and various other forms of output restriction (see Figure 16-2).[17] Similarly, Chris Argyris (Harvard University) argues that vertical and horizontal specialization of work results in jobs designed for the "child" or "immature personality," versus for the adult. Thus, when adults are asked to perform these jobs, an inevitable conflict arises between the job's call for dependency and the person's need for independence; the job's call for few skills and abilities, and the person's need to develop and use many sophisticated skills and abilities; and the job's call for thinking in the here and now, and the person's need for a longer-term perspective.[18] According to Argyris, this person-organization conflict eventually results in physical and/or psychological resistance through such escape mechanisms as

- *Physical withdrawal.* Employees come late to work, are absent from work, and/or quit.
- *Psychological withdrawal.* Employees care little about their work or the product, feel apathetic and dissatisfied, and are not committed to their job and the organization.
- *Physical resistance.* Employees may join a union, engage in work slowdowns and stoppages, engage in "horse-play," or even commit sabotage.[19]

Although scientific management improved productivity, there were significant drawbacks. Whereas "[i]t is the aim of scientific management to induce men to act as nearly like machines as possible . . . ,"[20] people don't like to act like machines. Many workers in scientifically managed jobs experienced a sense of lost control. This reaction was anticipated by Karl Marx over 100 years ago:

> They [the capitalists] mutilate the laborer into a fragment of a man, degrade him into the level of an appendage to a machine, destroy every remnant of charm in his work, and turn it into a hated toil.[21]

Under scientific management, skill development was slowed because few skills were used on the job which, in turn, limited promotional opportunities. Employees perceived work as depersonalized, meaningless, and monotonous. The problem became worse over the years. Although pay levels rose with the advent of minimum wage laws and labor unions, workers became less content

FIGURE 16-2 The Curse of the Classical Job Design Model

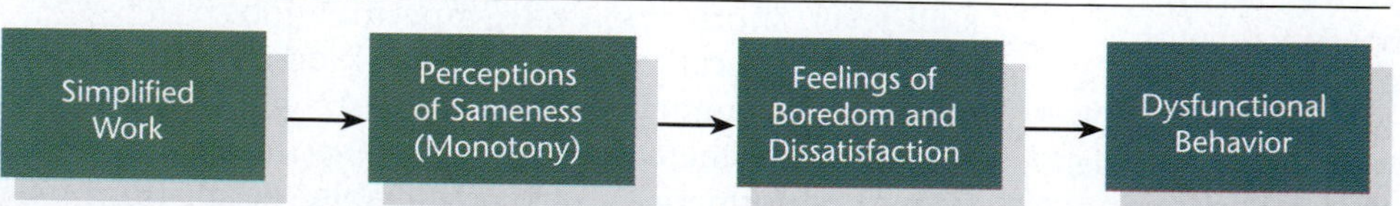

to do almost anything for a living wage. Further compounding the problem was the fact the workers were becoming better educated, and they wanted jobs that would use their knowledge as well as their hands! These experiences caused dissatisfaction, absenteeism, turnover, and general discontent to spread.[22] Scientific management may have been an appropriate approach to job design in its time, but it had became outdated for many workers in later years.

The Transition from Classical Job Design

The classical approach to job design tried to make organizations efficient and effective by making work *simple*. Adam Smith praised the division of labor and the redesign of jobs from skilled crafts to the simplified, repetitive jobs that accompanied the assembly line. Frederick Taylor, with stopwatch in hand, tested the maximum a man could produce. His protégé Henry Ford produced 14,000 cars in 1909. Five years later, with the assembly line firmly entrenched, the number skyrocketed to 230,000. "Ford's assembly line had its own speed, and the workers had to adapt to it."[23]

During the 1940s and 50s, members of the behavioral school of management began to suggest that higher productivity could be attained by making work *interesting*, as opposed to making it simple. Proponents rejected the idea of treating people as automatons, as "cogs in the industrial machinery." They wisely noted that although machines don't have emotions, people do. When people's needs are not met and their motives are frustrated, workers and their organizations suffer. The answer? An approach to job design that had a "human face."

Accompanying this emerging perspective, the bureaucratic organization and routine job designs were seen as incompatible with the personality of mature workers. Research evidence began to emerge suggesting that enlarged and enriched jobs are favorably associated with intrinsic motivation, job satisfaction, work attendance, and performance.

http://www.saab.com

Saab, Volvo, General Mills, Butler Manufacturing, Lake Superior Paper Industries, Hewlett-Packard, and 3M are among the myriad organizations that have rejected the classical approach to job design. They have responded with a move toward job enlargement, job enrichment, and self-managing work teams. As a Saab advertisement proclaimed:

BORED PEOPLE BUILD BAD CARS.
THAT'S WHY WE'RE DOING AWAY WITH THE ASSEMBLY LINE.

The Job Enlargement Approach

job enlargement
adding breadth to a job by increasing the number and variety of activities performed by an employee—horizontal loading

The first widespread attempts to counteract negative effects of simplified job design focused on job enlargement. **Job enlargement** adds breadth to a job by increasing the number and variety of tasks.[24] Intended to reverse the effects of horizontal specialization, these efforts are called *horizontal loading*.

Job enlargement efforts focused on increasing the number of activities engaged in by workers.* Instead of performing one simple task, workers were assigned multiple tasks. While these tasks were usually of similar difficulty, employees experienced more variety. Thus, insurance clerks, for example, who

* Although job enlargement theorists often proposed increasing discretion over work methods, most applications focused on providing a wider range of activities.

repeatedly complete one type of insurance application, get task variety by filling out other forms, filing duties, and communicating with clients and agents to maintain insurance histories.

Job enlargement was very popular from the late 1940s through the early 1960s. Among the many organizations to use job enlargement programs were IBM, AT&T, the U.S. Civil Service, the U.S. Social Security Administration, and Maytag. Research used to document the effectiveness of these programs was often inadequate, but cumulative evidence suggests that satisfaction and quality of performance increased. On the other hand, both training costs and job ability requirements increased, and the quantity produced was relatively unaffected.[25]

http://www.ssa.gov

Some organizations attacked employee boredom and job dissatisfaction through a *job rotation* strategy. In job rotation, employees rotate through different jobs to increase stimulation and task variety, and hopefully arrest monotony and boredom. While very few studies document the effects of job rotation, what evidence there is suggests that the results were disappointing.[26]

The Job Enrichment Approach

The most promising idea for job design, job enrichment, emerged in the 1960s. **Job enrichment** adds depth to a job by adding "managerial" activities (planning, organizing, directing, and controlling) to employees' responsibilities. These efforts to reverse the effects of vertical specialization are called *vertical loading*. Thus insurance clerks would make decisions about accepting new policy applications, rejecting claims, and so on. Job enlargement makes work less tedious, while job enrichment attempts to empower organizational members[27] by making work more "fun" and "rewarding."

job enrichment adding depth to a job by adding, for example, planning and controlling—vertical loading

A driving force behind job enrichment was Frederick Herzberg, developer of the motivation-hygiene theory (see Chapter 7).[28] Herzberg tells how in the 1950s he asked himself, "What can I do in organizations to keep the sane from going insane?"[29] He suspected from his research on mental health that highly routinized jobs had the potential to cause great mental harm. A self-avowed humanist,* Herzberg believed that work environments can be designed to satisfy the full range of needs of people. Pay and safe work conditions, the hygiene factors, only *prevent* dissatisfaction. They do not motivate or *create* satisfaction for the long-term. Only "motivator" factors can satisfy and motivate employees. To achieve this end, Herzberg sought to design and enrich jobs with a focus on:

1. Accountability—workers should be responsible for their performance.
2. Achievement—jobs should provide opportunities for workers to accomplish something worthwhile.
3. Control—workers should have control over how the work is done.
4. Feedback—workers should receive information about their effectiveness.
5. Personal growth and development—workers should be given opportunities to learn new skills.
6. Work pace—workers should have control over the work pace.[30]

Job enrichment has proven extremely popular. As was the case with job enlargement, however, studies on the effectiveness of early job enrichment pro-

* One who holds the view that man is capable of self-fulfillment, ethical conduct, and so on, without resorting to the supernatural.

grams had research design problems.* Thus, assessing the effectiveness and limitations of the approach was problematic. Critics also argued that this approach doesn't provide an adequate framework for identifying a job's strengths and weaknesses so that improvements can be made.[31] There were other criticisms of Herzberg's approach. He was criticized for being vague about how to enrich jobs, for assuming that all people have similar needs and will respond the same to enriched work, and for failing to develop ways to measure enrichment. Nevertheless, case studies of job enrichment indicated the approach had potential. Recent approaches to job design benefit and build from the job enrichment model, and much of the credit should be given to Herzberg.

The Job Characteristics Approach to Job Design

Early Development Arthur Turner and Paul Lawrence of Harvard University published results of the first large-scale job characteristics study in 1965. Although some have classified this approach as a radical departure from earlier job design perspectives, it is actually a logical progression. One major factor that distinguished the work of Turner and Lawrence was their technique for identifying and measuring job characteristics believed to influence worker attitudes and behaviors. They identified six requisite task attributes related to worker attitudes and, to a lesser extent, to worker attendance. These task attributes were variety, autonomy, required social interaction (with co-workers), opportunities for social interaction, knowledge and skill required, and responsibility. These six characteristics are fairly consistent with the factors used by the job enlargement and enrichment perspectives. Turner and Lawrence made it possible, however, to measure these characteristics. This would prove very useful later for managers and consultants as they planned their job redesign strategies.

The Importance of Worker Values Charles Hulin and Milton Blood, from the University of Illinois, discovered that not all workers respond equally strongly to high levels of the six characteristics. Workers from small towns appeared to respond quite positively to high levels, but workers from urban settings did not. Later, it was proposed that this finding might relate to the degree of alienation from the middle-class work norm. Workers who value achievement and responsibility and believe in the intrinsic value of hard work respond positively to jobs high on these task attributes. Those who do not hold these values do not respond positively.[32] This was one of the first attempts to determine which types of workers would react most favorably to enriched jobs.

The Hackman and Lawler Contributions Two major contributions were made by J. Richard Hackman and Edward E. Lawler, III, while they were at Yale University, in a study reported in 1971.[33] They modified the questionnaire developed by Turner and Lawrence to identify four "core job characteristics" (variety, autonomy, task identify, and feedback) and two less critical characteristics (dealing with others, and friendship opportunities). Their measure of "higher-order need strength" (a desire for higher-order outcomes like personal growth and accomplishment) attempted to identify why some workers respond more positively to job characteristics than others. Higher-order need strength is

* Herzberg still maintains that his research methods were not flawed.

closely related to some of the needs discussed in Chapter 7. Need for achievement, for esteem, and for self-actualization form a consistent group of human needs. The results of this study indicated that greater amounts of the job characteristics were associated with more positive worker reactions. Perhaps even more important was the finding that workers with strong higher-order needs responded most favorably to jobs where the design was more complex (with high levels of variety and autonomy) and less routine in nature.

Contemporary Job Characteristics Theory

The work of J. Richard Hackman of Harvard University and Greg Oldham of the University of Illinois has had the greatest impact in this area in recent years.[34] They spurred rigorous research on job design and its impact on workers. In the process, measures of job characteristics (the Job Diagnostic Survey) and individual characteristics (the Growth Need Strength Scale) have been developed. A more complete theoretical model, referred to as the Job Characteristics Model (JCM), has emerged for explaining how and why job enlargement and enrichment works.

Job Characteristics Model (JCM) a theory of job design and its individual effects

The **Job Characteristics Model (JCM)** is presented in Figure 16-3. In the discussion that follows, we look at several key components of the model. Hackman and Oldham also developed measures for assessing these components. You can use the self-assessment, which contains portions of their Job Diagnostic Survey (JDS), to assess your own job. While the JDS has been revised over the years,[35] the main body of the survey remains unchanged. It is by far the most used job diagnostic tool today.

FIGURE 16-3 The Job Characteristics Model

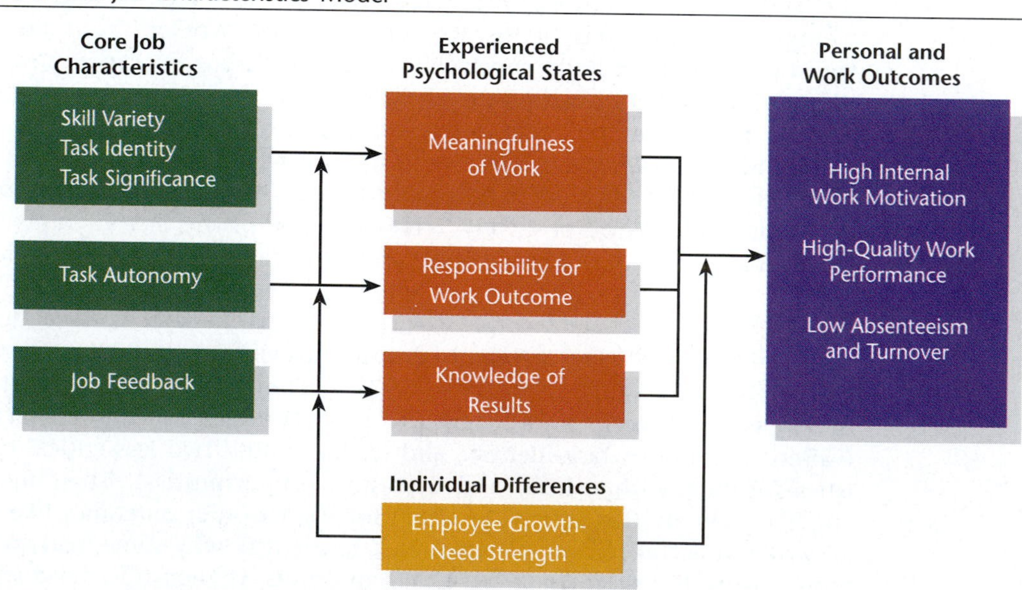

Source: J. R. Hackman and G. R. Oldham. 1976. Motivation through the design of work: Test of a theory. *Organizational Behavior and Human Performance* 16:250–279.

SELF-ASSESSMENT Sample Items—The Job Diagnostic Survey

SECTION ONE

This part of the questionnaire asks you to describe your job, as *objectively* as you can.

Please do *not* use this part of the questionnaire to show how much you like or dislike your job. Questions about that will come later. Instead, try to make your descriptions as accurate and as objective as you possibly can.

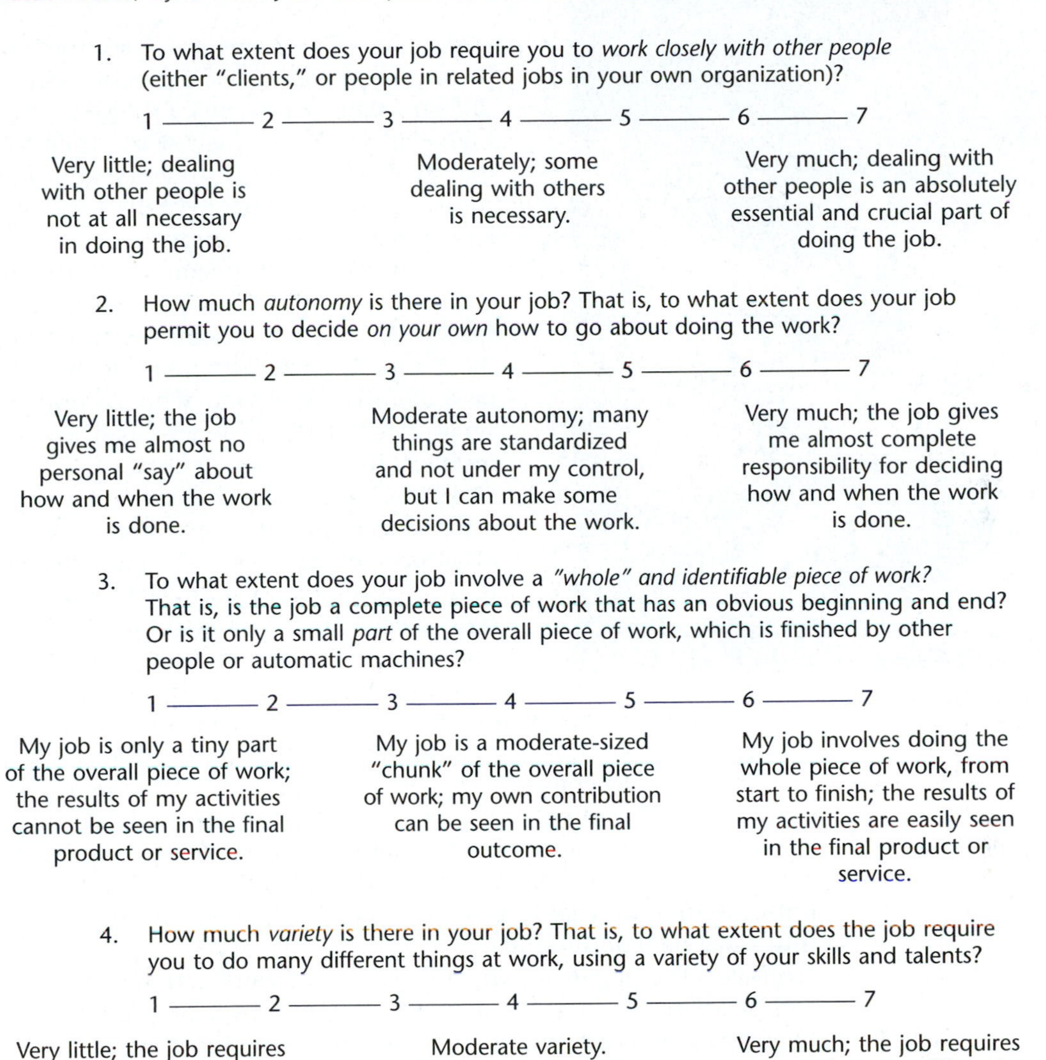

1. To what extent does your job require you to *work closely with other people* (either "clients," or people in related jobs in your own organization)?

1 ——— 2 ——— 3 ——— 4 ——— 5 ——— 6 ——— 7

1	4	7
Very little; dealing with other people is not at all necessary in doing the job.	Moderately; some dealing with others is necessary.	Very much; dealing with other people is an absolutely essential and crucial part of doing the job.

2. How much *autonomy* is there in your job? That is, to what extent does your job permit you to decide *on your own* how to go about doing the work?

1 ——— 2 ——— 3 ——— 4 ——— 5 ——— 6 ——— 7

1	4	7
Very little; the job gives me almost no personal "say" about how and when the work is done.	Moderate autonomy; many things are standardized and not under my control, but I can make some decisions about the work.	Very much; the job gives me almost complete responsibility for deciding how and when the work is done.

3. To what extent does your job involve a *"whole" and identifiable piece of work?* That is, is the job a complete piece of work that has an obvious beginning and end? Or is it only a small *part* of the overall piece of work, which is finished by other people or automatic machines?

1 ——— 2 ——— 3 ——— 4 ——— 5 ——— 6 ——— 7

1	4	7
My job is only a tiny part of the overall piece of work; the results of my activities cannot be seen in the final product or service.	My job is a moderate-sized "chunk" of the overall piece of work; my own contribution can be seen in the final outcome.	My job involves doing the whole piece of work, from start to finish; the results of my activities are easily seen in the final product or service.

4. How much *variety* is there in your job? That is, to what extent does the job require you to do many different things at work, using a variety of your skills and talents?

1 ——— 2 ——— 3 ——— 4 ——— 5 ——— 6 ——— 7

1	4	7
Very little; the job requires me to do the same routine things over and over again.	Moderate variety.	Very much; the job requires me to do many different things, using a number of different skills and talents.

5. In general, how *significant or important* is your job? That is, are the results of your work likely to significantly affect the lives or well-being of other people?

1 ——— 2 ——— 3 ——— 4 ——— 5 ——— 6 ——— 7

1	4	7
Not very significant; the outcomes of my work are *not* likely to have important effects on other people.	Moderately significant.	Highly significant; the outcomes of my work can affect other people in very important ways.

Note: These questions illustrate how the JDS assesses job design. This sample assesses five of the seven dimensions.

Source: J. R. Hackman and G. R. Oldham. 1975. Development of the Job Diagnostic Survey. *Journal of Applied Psychology* 60:159–170.

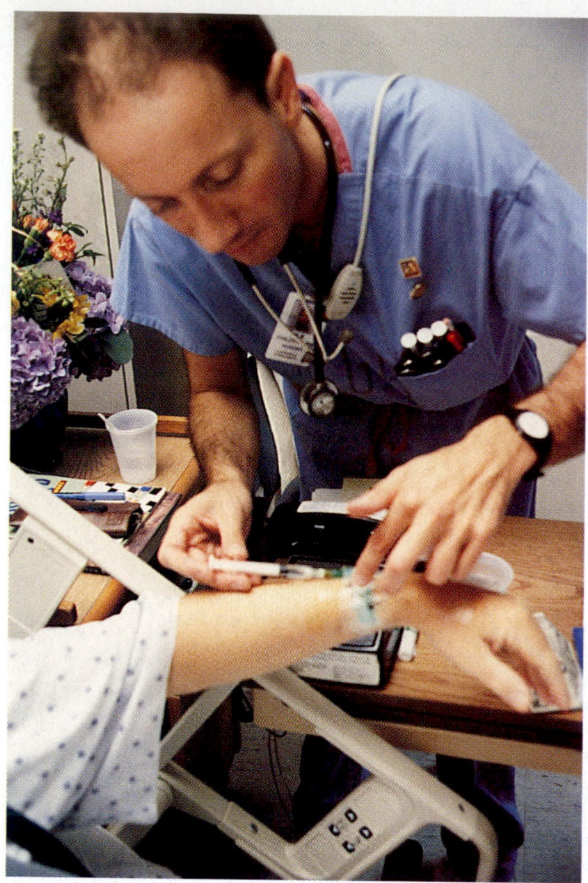

© SUSAN VAN ETTEN

Nurses' skill levels have a significant impact on the health and well-being of the patients in their care, so nursing is a high task-significance job.

Core Job Characteristics According to Hackman and Oldham's model (see Figure 16-3), five core job characteristics are of primary importance to a job's design. These core characteristics reveal how much a job has been enlarged and enriched and also its routineness or complexity:

1. *Skill variety*—The degree to which the job requires performing a variety of different activities using different skills and talents. College professors have high skill variety in their work; they teach, conduct research, counsel students, and many other things. Someone who tightens lug nuts on cars all day has low skill variety.
2. *Task identity*—The degree to which the job entails completing a "whole" and "identifiable" piece of work. Someone who assembles an entire product (be it a toaster, microchip, or telephone) has high task identity. Someone who completes only a small piece of the product (such as the lug nut installer) has low task identity.
3. *Task significance*—The degree to which the job has a substantial impact on the lives or well-being of other people, whether in the immediate organization or in the external environment. Again, professors have high task significance because they can affect the lives of hundreds of students a year. Nurses also have high task significance.
4. *Autonomy*—The degree to which the job provides substantial freedom, independence, and discretion to an individual, both in scheduling the work and in determining the procedures used to complete it. Higher-level managers in organizations have high autonomy. The higher you are in an organization, the fewer people supervise your activities. New Army recruits have little autonomy. Drill sergeants tell them what to do from the time they wake up until the time they go to bed. Self-employed people are their own boss and thus have high autonomy.
5. *Feedback*—The degree to which carrying out work activities results in direct and clear information about performance. Jobs that provide feedback by themselves, without relying on other people (like supervisors and co-workers) are high in this characteristic. Employees who do their own quality control have high feedback. A toaster assembler who ensures that her toasters function correctly after assembling them has high feedback. An office clerk who receives performance feedback once a year has low task feedback.

A job that incorporates high levels of skill variety, task identity, task significance, autonomy, and feedback is a complex job. It is also an enlarged and enriched job. Conversely, routine jobs have low levels of these characteristics. Hackman and Oldham theorized that jobs with high levels of the core job characteristics will have a strong *motivating potential*. Proponents of job enlargement and job enrichment encourage those who organize work to build high levels of these core components into jobs. They also recommend building in two socially oriented components—feedback from others, and interaction opportunities. Jobs with these seven characteristics, it is argued, avoid the problems inherent in the classical approach to job design and thus enhance organizational effectiveness.

Critical Psychological States As shown in Figure 16-3, from the core job characteristics emerge three critical psychological states—experienced meaningfulness of work, experienced responsibility for work outcomes, and knowledge of results. These states reflect on our cognitive orientation toward our job.

Skill variety, task identity, and task significance determine whether we will experience meaningfulness in our work. Task autonomy influences how responsible we feel for the work we do. Feedback determines how much we know about the results of our work activities.

Personal and Work Outcomes The three psychological states combine to influence personal and work outcomes. That is, the theory states that when we feel that our work is meaningful, that we are responsible for it and we know how well we're performing, we are likely to demonstrate high levels of intrinsic motivation, job satisfaction, high-quality work performance, and low levels of absenteeism, tardiness, and turnover behaviors.

Growth-Need Strength Growth-need strength reflects the intensity of an employee's motivation to satisfy their growth needs within the work context. Growth-need strength is similar to higher-order need strength, reflecting how much we want to satisfy our needs for achievement, esteem, and growth through work, as opposed to through off-work activities (hobbies, family, religion, and so on). Organizational members who are motivated by their growth needs want complexity and challenge in their jobs.

Employee growth-need strength plays two important roles in the Job Characteristics Model (see Figure 16-3). First, people with high growth-need strength are seen as more sensitive to the level of the core job characteristics. Thus, they experience high levels of the critical psychological states with high levels of the core job characteristics, and low levels of these states with low levels of the core job characteristics. The second impact of growth-need strength determines people's reactions when they experience the critical psychological states. People with high growth-need strength should react more favorably to high levels of the psychological states. They are, for example, more intrinsically motivated and job satisfied, and their work enables them to satisfy their needs on the job.

Employee Responses to Job/Work Design

So what does the research literature tell us about worker responses to job design? Does evidence support the Job Characteristics Model? The short answer is, yes. The job characteristics theory has generated a tremendous amount of research, which supports many of the hypothesized relationships in the model.[36]

The literature offers a number of observations. Research findings suggest that employees experience more job satisfaction when they work in complex jobs. Positive relationships are also found between job complexity and motivation and performance, although not as strong as the job design–job satisfaction relationship. In addition, tardiness, absenteeism, and turnover are generally less common in complex jobs. The findings for the behavioral responses (that is, performance, tardiness, absenteeism, and turnover) are neither as strong nor as consistent as the positive relationship between job design and employee satisfaction.[37]

Evidence also supports the central role of the three psychological states.[38] Thus, the core job characteristics help these states emerge. Employees who experience their work as meaningful, who have a sense of responsibility for their work outcomes, and who possess knowledge of the results of their work are likely to be intrinsically motivated, job satisfied, perform quality work, and avoid absenteeism. These observations imply that the five core attributes produce their effects by working through the three psychological states.[39]

As we have noted and as you no doubt know from personal experience, not all employees respond the same way to job design. Some people prefer complexity in their work. Others do not. So what explains the difference?

This issue has not been totally resolved. As noted above, there is some evidence to suggest that those individuals who are alienated from work values, those with a weaker work ethic, might be somewhat less responsive to complex jobs.[40] The most consistent evidence supports Hackman and Oldham's model and their prediction that people who are strongly motivated by their growth (high-order) needs are more responsive to enlarged and enriched jobs than people who are motivated by their lower-order needs. Thus, for employees with strong growth needs, the five core job characteristics will more likely produce the three psychological states, and organizations will gain in intrinsic work motivation, high-quality work, low absenteeism and turnover, and increased job satisfaction in their work force. Finally, the preponderance of the evidence suggests that most employees would respond favorably to more complexity in their jobs. Those employees strongly motivated by their growth needs simply respond more positively to enrichment than do their colleagues who are driven by lower-order needs.[41]

The theory of psychological ownership (see Chapter 6) provides additional insight into the process through which complex job design positively impacts employee motivation, attitudes, and behavior.[42] As shown in Figure 16-4, complex jobs provide us with the opportunity to exercise personal control, to invest ourselves in our work, and to develop an intimate association with our job. These are the three roots of psychological ownership. As we have noted before, feelings of ownership are associated with intrinsic motivation, commitment, job satisfaction, assumption of responsibility, and good citizenship behaviors.[43]

Current Job Design Issues

A number of "new" job design issues have emerged during recent years. Many have led to helpful changes in the model. Researchers have begun to explore (1) a

FIGURE 16-4 The Relationship Between Job Complexity and Psychological Ownership

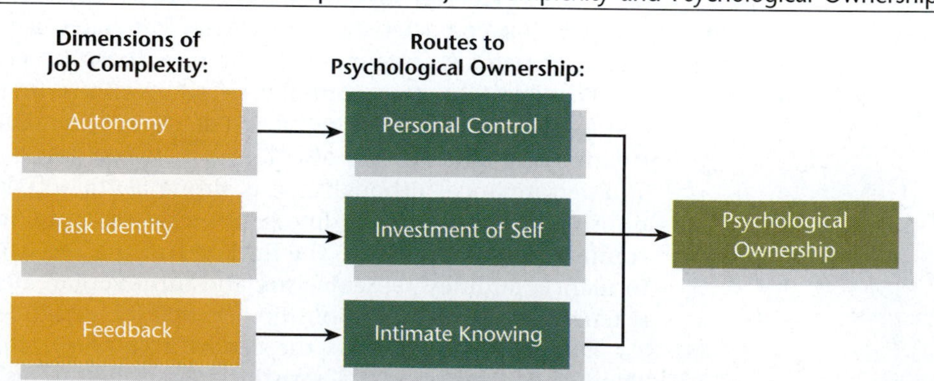

wider range of individual characteristics that influence worker reactions, (2) the impact of technology and work unit design, and (3) leader behaviors.

Individual Characteristics In addition to the strength of growth needs, a number of other personal characteristics may influence our reactions to job design. Since we often perceive the same sensory stimulus in very different ways (see Chapter 5), our perception of the objective characteristics of our job may be influenced by several factors. The perception of identical tasks varies significantly as a function of our age, education, job tenure, cognitive structure, dominance, and field independence.[44]

Moreover, when jobs are enriched, it is important to ensure that employees think about the job changes. Donald Gardner, Randall Dunham, Larry Cummings, and Jon Pierce found that employees who don't think much about their jobs (job versus nonjob focus of attention) don't react as positively to job enrichment as employees who are job focused do.[45] Given these findings, it is clear that organizations must manage not only job design but also the processes by which jobs are perceived.

Technology An organization's technology is defined by how it transforms materials and other inputs (information, ideas, and so on) into outputs (products, services). Technologies can be "long-linked" (assembly lines where tasks are performed in a predefined serial order), "mediating" (choosing one from a set of standardized processes, like banks and insurance companies), and "intensive or custom" (nonstandardized techniques with tasks performed in reaction to emerging demands).[46]

Several researchers have found an important relationship between an organization's technology and job design. While at Northwestern University, Denise Rousseau found that perceived job variety, identity, significance, and autonomy are all associated with the dominant technology of the organization.[47] This, and other research, suggests that routine jobs commonly accompany routine and system-controlled technologies.[48] These technologies are characterized by standard operating procedures, rigid workflow patterns, high levels of automation, serial interdependence, and standard variability in the nature of the raw material worked on, along with a well-developed body of knowledge to direct the transformation process. Nonroutine technologies, on the other hand, have just the opposite—more flexible workflow patterns, low levels of automaticity, and so on, and perhaps key to this situation, a still-developing body of knowledge. Thus, the men and women who operate these technologies need greater control. The result is that these employees are more likely to perceive their jobs as complex and not under the control of the system.

These and other findings lead to three conclusions: First, job design must match the nature of the technology. Second, when planning a major change in technology, managers should evaluate the effects of the change on job design and on worker reactions. Third, when planning a major change in job design, managers should take into account whether the existing technology will work with or against the changes.

Work Unit Design Through the years several organization scholars have proposed that an organization's design and its job designs should fit. Lyman Porter, J. Richard Hackman, and Edward E. Lawler III, for example, have proposed that employee motivation, job satisfaction, and performance are a function of how well employees are matched with their job and how well both match with the organization. Thus, they argued that a three-way interaction functions between work unit (organization) structure, job design, and individual differences.

Porter and his associates envision the organization's structure as mechanistic or organic (see Chapter 13), job design as simple/routine or complex, and the organizational member as having strong or weak needs for growth. They hypothesized that the high levels of motivation, job satisfaction, and performance will emerge under the congruent conditions of an employee with strong growth needs, on a complex job, in an organic organization. The lowest levels of motivation, job satisfaction, and performance exist when employees with strong growth needs are matched with a routine job in a mechanistically designed work unit.

Jon Pierce, Randall Dunham, and Richard Blackburn tested Porter's theory and found support for these two predictions. In addition, they found that virtually all employees respond more favorably to complex jobs, and also more favorably to organically designed work units. Employees with high growth-need strength respond more favorably to complex jobs and organically designed social systems than their low growth-need counterparts. Finally, these researchers observed a positive interaction between job design and social system design. This means that employees in complex jobs and organically designed work units tend to be more strongly motivated, satisfied with their jobs, and possibly higher performers. Thus, job designers need to simultaneously consider the design of jobs, the employee, and the design of the larger social system.[49]

Leader Behavior Ricky Griffin from Texas A&M University has developed and tested a conceptual framework which argues for considering job design and leader behavior simultaneously.[50] First, a leader should examine the degree to which a follower's needs are matched by the demands of the job. If there is a mismatch, the leader may need to take steps to supplement the lack of fit. Second, he observes that changes in job design may lead to changes in leader behavior. For example, if a follower is assigned decision-making responsibilities previously held by the leader, this change may have unintended consequences for the leader. Finally, Griffin notes that leader behavior can also influence job design. Leader attempts to provide a follower with some guidance by initiating structure may reduce some of the autonomy in the follower's job, thereby reducing experienced responsibility and producing several other effects.

An Interdisciplinary Job Design Model

Recent research reveals that workers not only look at their jobs in terms of complexity but also in terms of whether dealing with the general public is required, and how much physical effort is required. The Job Characteristics Model does not include these characteristics.[51]

In recent years, Michael Campion (Purdue University) has expanded thinking about job design, by looking at how to design work processes (industrial engineering) and how to design machines to "fit" people (ergonomics), in combination with known psychological aspects of job design.[52] Campion integrates job design by drawing from a number of different scientific fields.

Campion's interdisciplinary model looks at four approaches to job design. The first is *mechanistic*, which emphasizes efficiency. That is, it views workers as "machines," and seeks to minimize training costs and skill requirements. The second approach, *motivational*, parallels job enrichment and endorses complexity to prevent boredom. The goal here is to maximize job satisfaction and intrinsic

The perceptual/motor approach to job design seeks to minimize the amount of concentration a job requires. That makes it particularly effective for reducing concentration errors on high-stress jobs.

motivation. The third approach is *biological*, which endeavors to make jobs "comfortable" and less stressful. That is, good job design should result in less stress and strain, aches and pains, and health complaints. The fourth approach is *perceptual/motor*, which tries to minimize "mental load," the amount of concentration and mental effort required. Workers with too much mental load, like air traffic controllers, eventually make serious errors. Thus, jobs should give workers mental breaks; this should reduce errors and accidents, as well as stress, boredom, dissatisfaction, and fatigue. Table 16-1 summarizes Campion's views on job design.

These different approaches to job design have some common goals (maximize satisfaction, minimize errors), yet they result in very different job designs. As Campion writes,

> Although there are commonalities, the conflicts among the job design approaches . . . are more enlightening. Jobs can be simultaneously high on the mechanistic and perceptual/motor approaches because they both generally recommend design features that minimize mental demands, but the motivational approach gives nearly opposite advice by encouraging design features that enhance mental demands. As such, jobs high on the motivational approach may be more difficult to staff, require more training, have greater error-likelihood, and more mental overload and stress. Jobs high on the mechanistic and perceptual/motor approaches may have less satisfied and motivated employees and higher absenteeism. This suggests a basic trade-off between organizational benefits, such as efficiency and reliability, and individual benefits, such as satisfaction.[53]

The implications of Campion's work are many. Organizations need to carefully think about the types of workers they employ as well as the jobs they create. If an organization chooses to design jobs along mechanistic principles, it must be careful not to employ people who are overqualified for those jobs. If an organization tries to hire the best-qualified people with the greatest potential, then it must keep those employees challenged. Mismatches result in unnecessary stress, absenteeism, dissatisfaction, and poor productivity. Because of the education and aspirations of the U.S. work force, it is generally advisable to consider the motivational approach over the others.

The Self-Managing Team Approach

self-managing work teams groups of workers who collaborate in the management and performance of their work

The fourth and most recent approach to job design is the **self-managing work teams** that we have been emphasizing throughout the text. Instead of designing jobs for the individual employee, organizations design work around a team of individuals. The team is designed in such a way that members assume responsibility for completing a piece of work and play a major role in managing their own performance.

As noted in Chapter 14, Volvo is a strong proponent of such teams. Their production line for the manufacture of automobiles is essentially gone. In its place, a small group of workers build an entire automotive component (for instance, the drivetrain). Volvo has also used teams of workers to assemble entire

TABLE 16-1 Characterizing Jobs on Different Dimensions of Job Design

The mechanistic job design approach

1. *Job specialization:* Is the job highly specialized in terms of purpose and/or activity?
2. *Specialization of tools and procedures:* Are the tools, procedures, materials, etc., used on this job highly specialized in terms of purpose?
3. *Task simplification:* Are the tasks simple and uncomplicated?
4. *Single activities:* Does the job require the incumbent to do only one task at a time? Does it not require the incumbent to do multiple activities at one time or in very close succession?
5. *Job simplification:* Does the job require relatively little skill and training time?
6. *Repetition:* Does the job require performing the same activity or activities repeatedly?
7. *Spare time:* Is there very little spare time between activities on this job?
8. *Automation:* Are many of the activities of this job automated or assisted by automation?

The motivational job design approach

1. *Autonomy:* Does the job allow freedom, independence, or discretion in work scheduling, sequence, methods, procedures, quality control, and other types of decisions?
2. *Intrinsic job feedback:* Do the work activities themselves provide direct, clear information about the effectiveness (in terms of quality and quantity) of job performance?
3. *Extrinsic job feedback:* Do other people in the organization (such as managers and co-workers) provide information about the effectiveness (in terms of quality and quantity) of job performance?
4. *Social interaction:* Does the job provide for positive social interaction (such as teamwork or co-worker assistance)?
5. *Task/goal clarity:* Are the job duties, requirements, and goals clear and specific?
6. *Task variety:* Does the job have a variety of duties, tasks, and activities?
7. *Task identity:* Does the job require completion of a whole and identifiable piece of work? Does it give the incumbent a chance to do an entire piece of work from beginning to end?
8. *Ability/skill-level requirements:* Does the job require a high level of knowledge, skills, and abilities?
9. *Ability/skill variety:* Does the job require a variety of types of knowledge, skills, and abilities?
10. *Task significance:* Is the job significant and important compared with other jobs in the organization?
11. *Growth/learning:* Does the job allow opportunities for learning and growth in competence and proficiency?

---

http://www.volvo.com

automobiles. Workers have "confirmed Volvo's belief that responsibility, involvement, camaraderie and joy increase work satisfaction and raise product quality."[54]

Viewing the nature of work as critically important in defining the individual-organization relationship, high-involvement organizations generally adopt the job enlargement/job enrichment or self-managing team approach to job design. Butler Manufacturing in Sioux City, Iowa, employs self-managing teams to construct grain dryers.[55] Team members change job assignments frequently so that they learn the entire range of assembly activities. Quality inspection, employee

The biological job design approach

1. *Strength:* Does the job require fairly little muscular strength?
2. *Lifting:* Does the job require fairly little lifting, and/or is the lifting of very light weights?
3. *Endurance:* Does the job require fairly little muscular endurance?
4. *Seating:* Are the seating arrangements on the job adequate (with ample opportunities to sit, comfortable chairs, good postural support, etc.)?
5. *Size difference:* Does the workplace allow for all size differences between people in terms of clearance, reach, eye height, leg room, etc.?
6. *Wrist movement:* Does the job allow the wrists to remain straight, without excessive movement?
7. *Noise:* Is the workplace free from excessive noise?
8. *Climate:* Is the climate at the workplace comfortable in terms of temperature and humidity, and is it free of excessive dust and fumes?
9. *Work breaks:* Is there adequate time for work breaks given the demands of the job?
10. *Shift work:* Does the job not require shift work or excessive overtime?

The perceptual-motor job design approach

1. *Lighting:* Is the lighting in the workplace adequate and free from glare?
2. *Displays:* Are the displays, gauges, meters, and computerized equipment used on this job easy to read and understand?
3. *Programs:* Are the programs in the computerized equipment for this job easy to learn and use?
4. *Other equipment:* Is the other equipment (all types) used on this job easy to learn and use?
5. *Printed job materials:* Are the printed materials used on this job easy to read and interpret?
6. *Workplace layout:* Is the workplace laid out so that the employee can see and hear well enough to perform the job?
7. *Information-input requirements:* Is the amount of attention needed to perform this job fairly minimal?
8. *Information-output requirements:* Is the amount of information that the employee must output on this job, in terms of both action and communication, fairly minimal?
9. *Information-processing requirements:* Is the amount of information that must be processed, in terms of thinking and problem solving, fairly minimal?
10. *Memory requirements:* Is the amount of information that must be remembered on this job fairly minimal?
11. *Stress:* Is there relatively little stress on this job?
12. *Boredom:* Are the chances of boredom on this job fairly small?

Source: Reprinted by permission of publisher, from *Organizational Dynamics,* Winter 1987. New York: Elsevier.

training and development, work scheduling, assembly, and control activities are managed by the group. Team members also handle many group personnel issues, such as hiring, performance appraisals, promotions, and treating behavior problems. Teams at General Mills' cereal plant in Lodi, California, do just about everything that middle managers do, in addition to running the production process. General Mills claims that productivity is as much as 40 percent higher there, compared to its traditional factories.[56] (See *An Inside Look* for Professor J. Richard Hackman's perceptions on teams.)

AN INSIDE LOOK

Interview with J. Richard Hackman

J. Richard Hackman is Cahners-Rabb Professor of Social and Organizational Psychology at Harvard University. He conducts research on a variety of topics in social psychology and organizational behavior, including the performance of work teams, social influences on individual behavior, and the design and leadership of self-managing units in organizations.

1. What should a manager pay more attention to—the design of individual jobs or the design of groups?

I don't think that's really the question. The real question is how to design motivating work that is consistent with organizational objectives. Sometimes that involves designing autonomous work teams; and sometimes it involves designing an automated system for getting a piece of work done. The idea should be to design jobs that tap the resources of the people who are working in the organization, jobs that contribute to employee growth and development while also contributing to organizational objectives.

2. Are there conditions under which the design of individual jobs or the design of groups becomes particularly important?

In fact, sometimes there isn't any choice, or the choice is obvious. The only real error in such circumstances would be to go against the natural current. For example, for salespeople with a distinct geographical territory, a team design would be superfluous. On the other side, playing in a string quartet is a nice example of a team task; the interdependence at the core of the work can't be changed, so some situations clearly call for an individual design and others clearly call for a team design. It gets interesting in situations where you could go one way or the other. For example, in thinking about the work of an airplane cockpit crew, should you design a series of choreographed individual jobs or an intact team task? You see the kind of trade-offs that would have to be considered in making that decision. My advice is to actively think about that matter and not just "knee jerk" in one direction or the other.

Historically, there has been a "knee-jerk" reaction toward individual task design in traditional industrial practice, and in recent years there's been something of a "knee-jerk" reaction toward designing autonomous or self-managing work teams in new high-commitment-type organizations. I would encourage people on both sides of that fence to be a bit more thoughtful about the design choices they make because the choice will dictate, to a considerable extent, the organizational support structures and systems and the leadership style that will be needed. Also, the choice that's made will, over time, have an influence on the kind of organizational culture that emerges. Designers should be comfortable with the direction in which the design choices would move that culture—for example, toward a more individualistic or more collectivistic culture.

Finally, designers should keep in mind that a critical thing is to implement the choice well. In some organizations and with some technologies, it would be next to impossible to successfully implement either the individual option or the group option.

3. Your job characteristics theory has probably been generally more researched in the last ten years than any other theory. What's the good news or bad news about your research?

The good news is that I think we have pretty well tied down the fact that the characteristics of jobs really do make a difference—and it appears to be a very substantial difference—in the reactions people have to their work and to their behavior on the job. We've got that post in concrete, as it were, and can now move on from there to rather more interesting questions.

That leads me, of course, to the bad news, which is that we haven't moved on to more interesting questions nearly as vigorously as I would have hoped. We haven't, for example, really solved the individual differences question yet. It seems clear to observers of people at work that different people respond differently to motivating jobs, yet the growth-needs-strength measure Oldham and I developed doesn't seem to be quite right as the measure of whatever it is that accounts for those differences in responses. The dozen or so other measures that have been tried don't, in my view, quite capture it either, and so, we're still stuck with the question we were addressing a decade ago—namely, there are clearly individual differences in how people react to their work, but what are the key variables here, and how do they operate? We still don't know nearly as much as we ought to.

Proponents argue that self-managing teams provide all of the advantages of job enlargement and job enrichment and more. Work in a self-managing group is designed to offer variety, autonomy, significance, task identity, feedback, and opportunities for human interaction. Because teams manage themselves, members are more likely to accept, support, and actively pursue the team's procedures and goals. This approach moves organizational control from the hands of traditional managers to those of workers, and managers and workers must be able to accept this transformation, or the approach will fail. (See *An Inside Look* on work teams).

http://www.shenlife.com

While we don't know a great deal about effective leadership in high-involvement settings, we can distinguish between two: leadership internal to the team and leadership external to it. Self-managed teams don't operate totally independently from the rest of the organization. External leaders play several significant roles for teams.

AN INSIDE LOOK

Work Teams: Only People Can Give Wisdom to the Machines

Until recently, the majority of work performed in the United States was directed by the hands of people. Today, the bulk of work is guided by machines. When people were the instrument of production, managers were taught to control employees. Now that machines do the work, emphasis is shifting to teaching managers to loosen their control and encourage workers to use their creativity and initiative in controlling machines.

Modern plants in the United States rely heavily on robotics and other computer-driven systems for manufacturing. The Ex-Cell-O Corporation in Americus, Georgia, is typical. Ex-Cell-O manufactures a variety of plastic car parts, such as the shiny colored covers used for bumpers. In the past, each bumper cover was spray-painted by a worker. Now the job is done by robots—and quality and productivity are much higher. Employees at Ex-Cell-O's plant are responsible for operating and maintaining the robotics systems rather than for directly producing the goods.

The nature of work changes substantially when robotics take over production. Even though robotics and computerization have reduced the likelihood of a worker's making a simple production error, human errors in operating the technology can be magnified to dreadful levels: witness the nuclear accidents at Three Mile Island and Chernobyl. It is a fact of life in business today that many of our technologies are extremely complex, dangerous, and unforgiving. They cannot be operated without high levels of commitment and professional employees.

More and more organizations are turning to teamwork to nurture commitment to the organization and to manage the new technologies effectively. When Shenandoah Life Insurance Company placed employees into semiautonomous work teams of five to seven members, the time required to handle a policy conversion decreased from twenty-seven to two days. Overall, 50 percent more policies were handled with a smaller number of employees. Proctor & Gamble, a leader in the use of teams, claims that its team-based plants are significantly more productive than its traditional plants. Volvo's team-oriented plants in Sweden are reported to have production costs lower than the company's conventional plants.

Loosened controls, better use of employees' ideas, greater commitment, and stronger motivation go hand-in-hand in developing a more effective and more satisfied work force. Enlightened managers are discovering that one of the best decisions they can make is to allow workers to help make decisions. The solutions are not easy but the direction is clear: this is the decade of the worker!

The role of external leaders is that of coordinator, facilitator, consultant, and coach. They encourage teams to engage in self-management behaviors, self-observation, and self-evaluation.[57] Very few commands come from external leaders; they push team members to problem-solve—What do you think? How should this be done? What will happen if . . . ? An external leader at Lake Superior Paper Industries (LSPI) sums it up: "[F]irst teach and then allow them (the workers) to do."[58] External leaders help team members acquire the skills and knowledge they need to make meaningful contributions, and with this empowerment comes power, involvement, and responsibility.[59] Thus, external leaders expand and enrich the team's work assignment, and encourage them to enlarge and enrich each team member's role.

In the mechanistic organization, it is management that initiates structure—defines roles, launches new initiatives, makes decisions and solves problems, sets limits on freedom of expression, and orchestrates communications. In mature self-managed work teams, these activities get performed by the team leader and the members themselves.[60]

Observations of self-managed teams at a small parts manufacturing plant in the southern United States lead Professors Charles Manz (Arizona State University) and Henry Sims, Jr. (University of Maryland) to conclude that the external leaders exercise less control than leaders in control-oriented organizations. Instead, they devote their time to influencing and enabling the team and praising effort and success.[61] External leaders also encourage self-reinforcement, self-criticism, self–goal setting, self-observation, self-expectation, and rehearsal. Professors Manz and Sims note that "the dominant role of the external leader . . . is to lead others to lead themselves."[62]

At General Electric's facility in San Juan, Puerto Rico, external leaders occasionally attend team meetings where they facilitate and provide resources. Their role is to help the teams move forward—that is, to enable performance through coaching.

Internal leadership in teams varies depending on the team's stage in the maturing process. As Figure 16-5 shows, at stage 1 a leader (an expert, problem solver, mentor, and coordinator) directs the group's efforts. As the team develops (stage 2), this leader serves as helper, example setter, and teacher in a "side-by-side" capacity. During stage 3, the team nears maturity and the original leader moves "outside" to manage the team's boundaries as a resource provider, information provider, auditor, and advisor. Generally during this stage, the team selects an internal leader. Once the team fully matures (stage 4), the external leader counsels, facilitates, enables, and frequently represents the group (along with the internal leader) to other vertical and horizontally removed teams.[63]

The internal leader is selected by team members. Internal leaders train inexperienced workers, work alongside the other members, help the team organize, coordinate job assignments, and facilitate performance.

A Contingencies Perspective to Job/Work Design

A number of management scholars argue that no one approach to job design is universally appropriate. In the *contingency approach*, managers organize work and design jobs to fit worker characteristics, and to fit the organization's technology, environment, and other organizational design characteristics.[64]

Initially, proponents of this approach focused on the fit between individual characteristics and job design characteristics. They suggested that people have different needs and personality characteristics and, therefore, respond differ-

FIGURE 16-5 The Leader During a Team's Four Stages

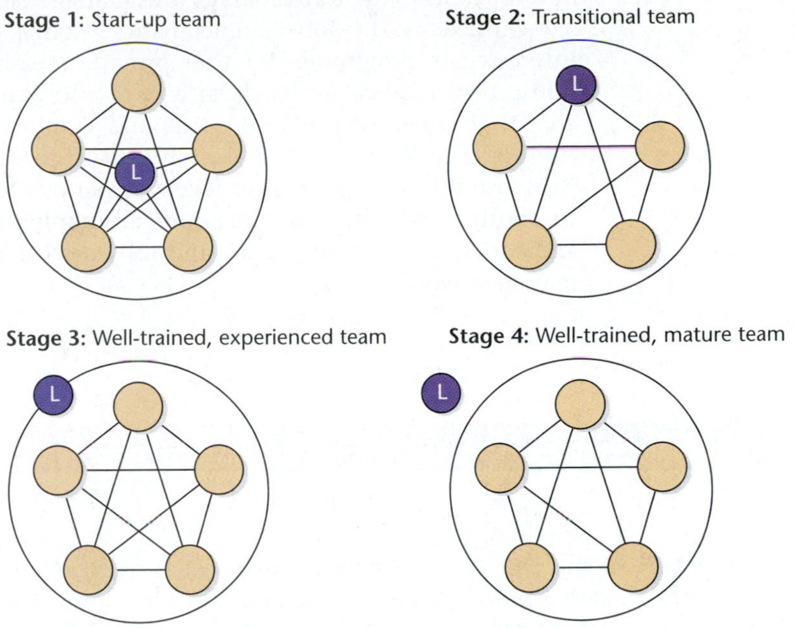

Stage 1: Start-up team

Stage 2: Transitional team

Stage 3: Well-trained, experienced team

Stage 4: Well-trained, mature team

Source: C. C. Manz and J. W. Newstrom. 1990. Self-managing team in a paper mill: The external leadership of self-managing work teams. *International Human Resources Management Review* 1:52.

ently to job designs.[65] Some employees, for example, prefer routine jobs, while others respond more favorably to complex jobs. If people don't enjoy social interaction, value social rewards, or seek complex and challenging work, it's unlikely that they will be happy in teams.[66] In addition to achieving a match between individual differences and work design, many contingency approach proponents assert that structural characteristics of an organization should be considered as well. It has been argued that routine jobs are compatible with mechanistic (bureaucratic) organizations, while complex jobs and self-managing work teams have design characteristics that match the structure of organic organizations.[67] Dynamic, organic organizations using rapidly changing technologies are unlikely to function well if jobs are overly specialized and routine.[68] Workers in such jobs won't be able to keep up with changing demands. Conversely, mechanistic organizations have little need for complex jobs and/or self-managing work teams. Because there is no one best way to design work, the contingency approach encourages managers to consider the fit between job design, the individual, technology, organization design, and the internal and external environments.

MANAGING PRODUCTIVITY: ESTABLISHED APPROACHES IN REVIEW

Endeavoring to increase productivity is not new. The classical school searched for principles of management and organizational design, and developed the science of work—all in the pursuit of performance. Organizations continue to search for ways to enhance performance.

In this chapter we discussed two contemporary and popular strategies for managing performance. Not surprisingly, people engage in behaviors that get rewarded. Building on this observation, Organizational Behavior Modification was developed as a way to encourage and manage desired behavior in the workplace.

Guided by the Job Characteristics Model, managers have become highly interested in designing jobs that provide meaningfulness, a sense of responsibility, performance feedback, and psychological ownership. They have discovered that when work is interesting and complex, when it helps employees fulfill higher-order needs, it is likely to be intrinsically motivating. Job satisfaction, work attendance, and higher levels of performance are consequences of intrinsic motivation. Many organizations are applying the principles of work design embedded in job enlargement and job enrichment as they design work for self-managed work teams.

A FINAL LOOK

Of the five members of the OCC's admissions staff, three like the president's proposed job redesign. Jennifer and two other recruiters think the change will make them more effective recruiters because they will have firsthand knowledge about students' actual experiences. They look forward to developing stronger relationships with students.

The other two recruiters are more hesitant. In fact, Joseph Candy dreads the idea. He has been recruiting at OCC for 15 years and enjoys the predictability of his position. He knows nothing about academic advising, is not interested in learning about it, and feels that the new responsibilities will simply add stress. He doesn't feel he has a choice, however, and this begins to show up in his attitude.

On meeting with the staff to discuss the changes, President Hernandez realizes she has made the redesign decision hastily and arbitrarily. She decides to allow the recruiters to redesign their task assignment. In three months, the team will make their recommendations.

KEY TERMS

behavioral shaping, 578
extinction, 576
horizontal specialization, 583
Job Characteristics Model (JCM), 588
job design, 582
job enlargement, 585
job enrichment, 586
organizational behavior modification (OBM), 577
reinforcement, 576
self-managing work teams, 595
vertical specialization, 583

ISSUES FOR REVIEW AND DISCUSSION

1. Explain operant learning theory.
2. Describe how a manager can influence employee behavior—that is, make it more likely to occur and less likely to occur.
3. What are the key steps in organizational behavior modification?
4. Explain the craft, classical, and behavioral approaches to job design.
5. Discuss job enlargement and job enrichment and contrast them with the classical approach.
6. Discuss the self-management team approach to work design.
7. Summarize employee reactions to job design.

EXERCISES

JOB ENRICHMENT ASSIGNMENT

Objective: To better understand the job characteristics model by applying it to a personal experience.

Rate a job that you currently have, have had in the past, or are familiar with, on the five core job characteristics from the job characteristics model. Use a 1–5 scale where 1 = very low and 5 = very high. For example, if the job is moderately low on autonomy, it might rate a 2. Rate the job for all five characteristics:

Skill variety:	_____
Task identity:	_____
Task significance:	_____
Autonomy:	_____
Feedback:	_____
Sum (Motivating Potential Score; MPS):	_____

Option 1 (Individual)

1. Briefly describe the job you are analyzing in a paragraph or two.
2. Identify **five** ways in which the job could be enriched. Focus on those characteristics with the lowest ratings. Remember, enrichment involves changing the job itself (what workers do), not things like pay or supervision (hygiene factors).
3. After you propose your changes, indicate which core job characteristics will affect each change.

Option 2 (Group)

1. Share your MPS with other group members. Determine who has the **lowest** MPS. That job has the greatest potential to be enriched and will be the focus of the remainder of the exercise.
2. The person who performed that job should briefly describe the job to the group.
3. As a group, identify **five** ways in which the job could be enriched. Again, focus on those characteristics with the lowest ratings.
4. After you propose your changes, indicate which core job characteristics affect each change.
5. Share your analysis and results with the class.

INFOTRAC

INFOTRAC® COLLEGE EDITION

The articles listed below are a sampling of those available through InfoTrac College Edition. You can search for them either by title or by the author's name.

Articles

1. Does employee involvement work? Yes, sometimes. (The Quality Function in Redesigned Organizations) John L. Cotton. *Journal of Nursing Care Quality* Dec 1997 v12 n2 p33(13)
2. A longitudinal study of the job perception-job satisfaction relationships: a test of the three alternative specifications. Chi-Sum Wong, Chun Hui, Kenneth S. Law. *Journal of Occupational and Organizational Psychology* June 1998 v71 n2 p127(20)
3. Practice your own successful habits. (tips for career success)(Editorial) Richard Koonce. *Training & Development* March 1998 v52 n3 p19(1)
4. On the contrary, job stress is in job design. Sheri Caudron. *Workforce* Sept 1998 v77 n9 p21(3)
5. Old friends, new faces: motivation research in the 1990's. (Yearly Review of Management) Maureen L. Ambrose, Carol T. Kulik. *Journal of Management* May-June 1999 v25 i3 p231(6)

Questions

For Article 1:

The article, "Does Employee Involvement Work? Yes, Sometimes," maintains that certain employee involvement programs are more successful than others. As a group, identify the seven types of employee participation listed in the article. Agree on a brief description of each and discuss their advantages and disadvantages for both employer and employee. Based on this article and the information in Chapter 16, which employee participation style do you believe would be most valuable to you and why?

For All Articles:

Read the other articles on this list and report to your group any new concepts you learned regarding job design or job characteristics. How will this information benefit you in your future career?

WEB EXERCISES

1. Visit the website for the National Center for Employee Ownership (**http://www.nceo.org**) and for Ownership Associates (**http://www.ownershipassociates.com**) and learn what is happening in the world of employee ownership, and what employee owners really think about ownership [see a piece written by Rodgers (1999) that addresses this issue].

2. For those of you interested in operant learning theory and organizational behavior modification, we suggest looking at B. F. Skinner's home page for some interesting and historical reading on the principles of reinforcement. See **http://www.bfskinner.org** and select "about B. F. Skinner," and then select and read "A brief survey of operant behavior." You might also find it interesting to read *A Glimpse of the Scientist,* written by Skinner's daughter, Julie. In this piece she talks about what is was like to have Skinner as a father. This piece was published in *Behaviorology,* Spring 1993, 1:55–60.

CASE

Medtronic: A "Human" Place to Work

Cindy Vang's job at Medtronic may seem tedious to some people. Wearing a zippered smock, a hair net, booties, and surgical gloves, she spends most of her workday in a blue vinyl chair at the end of an assembly line. She's one of 45 workers in a department that makes a small component that keeps battery-powered pacemakers—one of Medtronic's best-selling medical devices—working after they've been surgically implanted in the bodies of heart patients. Part of Vang's job is loading finished components into a storage block. Using tweezers to move the tiny components, it takes her about 15 minutes to fill each block with 275 components. Her department produces about 200,000 of the components each month. Vang makes around $500 a week, not enough to be able to participate in Medtronic's employee stock purchase plan.

Vang derives satisfaction from knowing that the components she makes save lives. Every year, the company invites people whose bodies function thanks to Medtronic medical devices to come to holiday parties and give testimonials about how their health and lives have been improved. "We have patients who come in who would be dead if it weren't for us," says one Medtronic production supervisor. "I mean, they sit right up there and tell us what their lives are like. You don't walk away from them not feeling anything." Vang proudly displays in her living room the Medtronic medallion she received when she joined the company. It was presented to her personally by retired Medtronic founder Earl Bakken and is inscribed with an excerpt from Medtronic's mission statement: "Alleviate pain, restore health, and extend life."

Vang also likes the opportunities Medtronic provides for learning. At her request, she's participated in company training programs that have enabled her to become certified in five of the fourteen skills listed in her department's cross-training grid. Because of this training, she can now perform a variety of tasks and finds her job more challenging. "I like it because of the flexibility of moving, sitting, standing, all the combinations together," she explains. It also doesn't hurt that while she works Vang is allowed to talk freely with her coworkers and listen to music and books-on-tape on her personal headphones.

Ask Vang why she likes her job at Medtronic, however, and the answer is more basic. She works from 5 A.M. until 1:30 four days a week and gets 80 hours of vacation time a year. That allows her to be home with her three school-aged children every afternoon and provides flexibility to care for them if they need to stay home from school because of illness. "Since my parents were there for me when I was young, that's what I feel for my kids now," says Vang. She says the real reason she stays at Medtronic is simple: It's close to home and family.

Meanwhile, at Medtronic's corporate headquarters, CEO Bill George understands the importance of keeping employees dedicated to meeting the company's objectives, but he acknowledges that a passion for the company's mission isn't always enough to spur individual employee productivity. He likes to call Medtronic a "human" place to work, where employees can find fulfillment in a variety of ways. "If it's not, we've failed totally," he says.

However, George knows that creating that atmosphere is difficult in a company that's been growing more than 20 percent each year for the past decade. Keeping up with that pace inevitably puts pressure on employees. "It's easy for them sometimes maybe not to keep the mission top-of-mind," he says.

Discussion Questions

1. Use Hackman and Oldham's Job Characteristics Model to evaluate Cindy Vang's job at Medtronic. Do you agree or disagree with Hackman and Oldham's theory that jobs designed with high levels of each core job characteristic have stronger motivating potential?

2. You are Vang's supervisor. Using the concepts discussed in this chapter, suggest how her job should be redesigned to improve her productivity. Give specific examples.
3. As Vang's supervisor, you've noticed that her production time has slowed. It now takes her 20 minutes instead of 15 to fill a storage block of components. Develop an Organizational Behavior Modification plan to improve Vang's productivity.

Sources: T. Fiedler. April 9, 2000. Medtronic CFO understands "big picture" for big success. Minneapolis Star Tribune, *1D; D. Jones. May 30, 2000. Product development can fill prescription for success.* USA Today, *7B; D. Whitford. January 8, 2001. A human place to work.* Fortune, *108.*

Outline

- Alternative work schedules
- Employee ownership
- Quality control circles
- The high-involvement organization and management
- Managing productivity: contemporary approaches in review

CHAPTER 17

Managing Productivity: Contemporary Approaches

Learning Objectives

After reading this chapter, you should be able to

1. Describe the different approaches to work scheduling: compressed workweek, discretionary-time systems, and shift-work scheduling.
2. Identify the conditions under which different work schedules are most effective.
3. Summarize employee reactions to the compressed workweek, discretionary-time systems, and shift-work scheduling.
4. Discuss the meaning of and approaches to employee ownership.
5. Explain how employee ownership produces its intended effects.
6. Discuss employee attitudinal, motivational, and behavioral reactions to employee ownership.
7. Describe the nature and purpose of the quality control (QC) circle.
8. Summarize the employee effects associated with Total Quality Management and QC circles.
9. Summarize the essence of the high-involvement organization and its overall effects.

PHOTO: © ED KASHI/CORBIS

A FIRST LOOK

Aunt Ruthie's Kitchen is a Darlington landmark. Loyal customers make their way here regularly from all over the city and beyond in search of Aunt Ruthie's fresh ingredients and home-made desserts. The restaurant is also a regular family favorite in local polls. Think Darlington, and people think "Made with love from Aunt Ruthie's." As Darlington has grown, so has Aunt Ruthie's. The owners point proudly to their five locations.

But now Aunt Ruthie's is no longer a local favorite. The restaurant was nowhere to be found on the latest poll of favorite city restaurants, and locals now regularly choose some of the new national chains that have sprouted up around the city (like weeds, sniff Aunt Ruthie's owners). And, piling insult on injury, the *Darlington Press*'s recent review of the restaurant criticizes both the food quality and the service, proclaiming that "the love" is gone from Aunt Ruthie's.

The owners are in a tizzy. (Wake-up calls can be brutal!) They had been so sure of their customers' loyalty. "OK, so sales *have* gone down, but that's just because we've got five restaurants and people find the new chains novel—but that'll wear off; they'll be back." Well, it hasn't worn off, and customers aren't back. Obviously, something has to change . . . but what?

Questions: Do you think the owners of Aunt Ruthie's could have foreseen these troubles coming? Why were they blind to the decrease in quality at their restaurants? What have the owners focused on instead of quality? Do the owners need a new vision, or should they turn to what originally made them successful?

As we have seen throughout this text, management continually searches for ways to make organizations more productive. Global competition, radical changes in technology, increasingly diverse work forces, and changing customer expectations characterize the external and internal environments of today's organizations. These forces serve as catalysts for new programs, new management practices, and new organizational systems that endeavor to increase productivity, yet maintain positive attitudes among organizational members.

In the preceding chapter we looked at two traditional techniques for managing productivity—organizational behavior modification and job design. Now we look at techniques that have been developed and refined over the past few decades—alternative work schedules, employee ownership, quality control (QC) circles, and high involvement. Each shows promise for enhancing productivity and morale.

ALTERNATIVE WORK SCHEDULES

As the general standard of living and leisure-time activities increased in the 19th and 20th centuries, organizations slowly moved toward a shorter workweek. This move was characterized by two trends. First, the days worked per week decreased, from 7 days to 5. Second, the workday shrank from 12 or 14 hours to 8. As a consequence, our standard workweek (for most nonprofessional and nonmanagerial workers) is defined in terms of an 8-hour day, 5 days a week—what we call the 5/40.

A number of forces have sparked renewed interest in work schedules, including more women in the work force, more single-parent and two-paycheck households, onerous commutes, and increasing demands for an improved quality of work life and quality of personal life. As a result, alternative work schedules are now the norm in many U.S. companies, and alternative work settings, particularly *telecommuting,* are also becoming increasingly popular.[1]

Scheduling Work

In this section we look at compressed workweeks and discretionary work schedules, and also at shift work. How working hours are scheduled has significant implications for employee morale and productivity.

Innovative work schedule arrangements, such as compressed workweeks and discretionary work scheduling, require careful planning by management.

compressed workweek a work scheduling arrangement that attempts to compress the traditional workweek into fewer days and/or fewer hours per week

discretionary-time system a work scheduling arrangement that provides the employee with an element of discretion in deciding when they will be at work

staggered start system a work scheduling arrangement that provides the employee with a set of management-defined options as to when the work day will commence

Compressed Workweeks Many configurations of the **compressed workweek** have been implemented. Compressed schedules typically follow one of three basic patterns: (1) fewer days worked per week, total hours remain constant (say from a 5/40 week to a 4/40 week); (2) fewer hours worked per week, total days remain constant (from a 5/40 week to a 5/35 week); and (3) fewer days and fewer hours worked per week (for example, from a 5/40 week to a 4/36 week).

The most popular compressed schedule is the 4-day, 40-hour workweek, the 4/40. This plan, if scheduled around four continuous 10-hour workdays (like Monday through Thursday, or Tuesday through Friday), gives employees long weekends throughout the year. In order to achieve more flexibility with compressed work schedules, some organizations now define a workweek as 8 days—Week 1: Monday through Monday; Week 2: Tuesday through Tuesday, and so on. In the 8-day 4/40 week, employees also work four 10-hour days, but unlike the 7-day 4/40 week, they get a 4-day break before they begin the next 4/40 cycle. This schedule enables organizations to employ two shifts of workers who alternate between being "on" or "off" the 4/40 cycle continuously throughout the year. Organizations get 7 days a week of work coverage, and employees get 4-day "weekends," though not always including Saturdays and Sundays.

Theoretically, the compressed workweek increases people's satisfaction with their jobs, hours worked, and leisure time. It can, however, result in increased fatigue because of the longer workday. Of course, the thinking is that for many the extended time away from work enables people to "recharge their batteries."[2]

Discretionary Work Schedules Another popular modification to the standard workweek uses **discretionary-time systems.** A number of different work schedules (staggered hours, flexible hours, variable hours) provide both flexibility and choice.

The **staggered start system** doesn't reduce the hours or days worked, but it does provide employees with flexibility and discretion in scheduling work and nonwork time. Under this system, employees as individuals, as a department, or organizationwide choose when to start their workday from a number of options (like 7, 8, or 9 A.M.; or every half hour from 7 to 9 A.M.). Some organizations permit occasional changes in the chosen starting time (once every year, once every three months, and so on).

flexible working hours a discretionary time, work scheduling arrangement that enables the employee to exercise a daily decision regarding the time of day that he or she will start and end their work day

Flexible working hours represent a variation of the discretionary-time system. During the 1960s, a German aerospace firm, Messerschmitt-Bolkow-Blohm (MBB), introduced a "gliding time" system to manage traffic congestion caused by its employees arriving at work at the same time on Munich's congested roads. In MBB's system, employees could start their 8-hour workday *any time* between 7 and 8 A.M. and leave any time between 4 and 5 P.M. The idea spread rapidly in Scandinavia and many western European countries, but initially found little enthusiasm in the United States. In 1972, Control Data Corporation became the first major U.S. employer to offer this scheduling option.[3]

Called flextime, gleitzeit, gliding time, or flexible hours, in its pure form employees decide *daily* what time they will come to work. In practice, many firms restrict this choice by permitting only weekly, bi-weekly, or monthly decisions.

The flexible working hour arrangement differs from the staggered start system. Under the staggered start system, the employee is given a limited number of starting time options, which are then adhered to for a fixed period. Organizations that use flexible working hours define the earliest possible starting time and the latest possible quitting time (for example, no one may start work before 7 A.M., and no one may work later than 5 P.M.). This is called the "band width." Within the band width, time is divided into "core hours" and "flex-hours." Everyone must be at work during the core hours, enabling interdependent activities to transpire in a predictable fashion. The flex-hours represent a component of time during which the employee can choose to be at work or not.

Figure 17-1 shows two different flexible working hour arrangements. In the top schedule, employees can start their 8-hour workday anytime between 7 and 9 A.M. (7:00, 7:01, 7:02 . . . 9:00), which makes the core hours fall between 9 A.M. and 3 P.M. If an employee chooses to arrive at work at 8:05 on Monday morning, their workday will end at 4:05 that afternoon. This system thus provides two discretionary hours in the morning and two in the afternoon. The system represented in the bottom schedule has three flex-hour and two core-hour periods. Thus, an employee can select when to start their workday between 7 and 9 A.M. and must be at work between 9 and 11 A.M. They can choose when to take their hour-long lunch break, but must be at work between 1 and 3 P.M. Depending on the choices made in the morning and midday, the end of their workday is determined. Thus, each employee gets five discretionary hours.[4]

FIGURE 17-1 Flexible Working Hour Arrangement

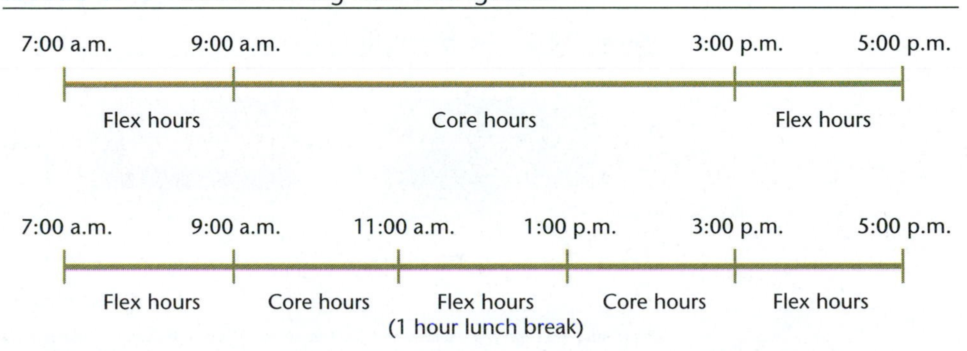

As you can imagine, many different flexible working hour arrangements are possible. Managers vary the schedule's flexibility and amount of employee discretion through:[5]

- the number of required *core minutes* at work
- formal or informal *change approval*—whether employees must seek formal approval before altering their schedule
- *schedule variability*—how often employees can change their schedule
- *time banking*—whether employees can debit and credit time (for example, work 10 hours one day and 6 hours another for a total of 16 hours over two days) and how long the debit or credit can be carried forward
- *schedule flexibility*—the size of the flexible-hour bands
- *band width*—the amount of time between the earliest possible starting time and the latest possible quitting time provided by the flexible working hour arrangement.

It is assumed that each of these dimensions affects the amount of flexibility experienced by the employee.

variable-hour arrangement a work scheduling arrangement that contracts with the employee for a specified amount of time to be worked on a daily, weekly, or monthly basis

The third discretionary-time system uses a **variable-hour arrangement.** In this system, employees "contract" with management for a specified amount of time to be worked on a daily, weekly, or monthly basis. The variable-hour arrangement removes all core hours, making the employee totally free to decide when they are going to work and not work.

The concept "alternative work schedules" should not be confused with "alternative work arrangements." The former refers to an organization's attempt to manage work-related time (such as the number of hours and days worked). Alternative work arrangements focus on other work-related factors. Some organizations, for example, have eliminated a "time requirement." Instead, they employ a *task contracting* arrangement, where the organization contracts with an employee for the performance of a task without regard to the total amount of time worked, hours worked per day, or days worked per week. The use of telecommuting often accompanies task contracting, and is another example of an alternative work arrangement.

Theoretically, discretionary-time schedules are seen as leading to increased job satisfaction and performance, reduced work-related stress, tardiness, absenteeism, and turnover, and less tension between work and nonwork demands.[6] Flexible hours are also seen as a way to attract people to the organization. The current thinking is, the more flexibility provided, the more positive the effects on employees (see Figure 17-2).[7]

FIGURE 17-2 The Effects of Flextime

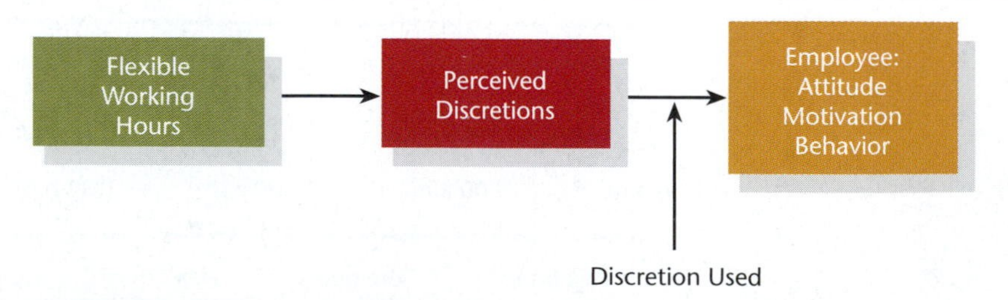

Source: Adapted from J. L. Pierce and J. W. Newstrom. 1983. The design of flexible work schedules and employee responses: Relationship and process. *Journal of Occupational Behaviour* 4:247–262.

Shift Work Schedules Many organizations use **shift work schedules**, where employees work different blocks of time on a regular basis. Under a three-shift arrangement, for example, one group of employees might work from 7 A.M. to 3 P.M., another group from 3 P.M. to 11 P.M., and a third group from 11 P.M. to 7 A.M. In some cases workers stay on one shift permanently, while in other instances employees rotate across scheduling blocks on a weekly or monthly basis.

A fire/police department is an example of an organization that must use shift work due to the need to be available to the public 24 hours a day.

Organizations adopt compressed workweeks and discretionary-time schedules under the assumption that these alternatives make the workplace more attractive to current and prospective employees. The driving forces behind shift work are quite different. Shift work enables manufacturers to obtain more hours of productivity per day from their physical resources. That is, machines and buildings are used 16 or 24 hours a day because the cost of idle plant time can be prohibitive. In some instances organizations employ a shift work schedule out of necessity. Hospitals, police and fire departments, as well as power plants and airports, for obvious reasons, need to remain open around the clock, day in and day out.

While employers (and the public in the case of hospitals and power plants) are perceived as reaping the greatest benefits from shift work, many employees actually prefer it. Shift workers often are able to live a "double life" because they learn to get by on less sleep, do their errands in the middle of the day instead of on the weekends when stores and banks are crowded, and receive premium wages for taking the "less desirable" shifts. Shift work also allows at least one parent to be home with young children while the family still benefits from two incomes.

shift work schedules a pattern of working-hour arrangements whereby the employee works organizationally defined and different blocks of time on a regular basis

Employee Responses to Alternative Work Schedules

Up to this point we have described several types of work schedules and looked at their theorized effects. But how do employees actually feel about all these new choices? Researchers have focused on how alternative work schedules affect employee attitudes, motivation, and work-related behaviors.[8] As previously suggested, management's interest in these alternatives has been driven by the belief that attractive work schedules will promote more effective organizational behavior and greater job satisfaction. The Theory of Work Adjustment[9] reasons that the greater the correspondence between employee needs and wants and a job's characteristics, the more compatible the relationship between employees and the organization. Thus, fitting the organization's work scheduling needs to employee needs will likely result in increased motivation, satisfaction, and other valued behaviors.[10]

Compressed Workweek Many employees report that they like the compressed workweek. Once they experience the 4/40, most do not want to return to the traditional 5/40 week. See *An Inside Look*—Impressing Employees with Compressed Schedules—for an in-depth perspective on this alternative.

AN INSIDE LOOK

Impressing Employees with Compressed Schedules

Have you ever noticed how difficult it can be to make it to a doctor's appointment or schedule a parent-teacher conference when you are working full time? Many of the realities of everyday life require that we take care of personal issues during the "normal" business hours of 8 A.M. to 5 P.M. If you are like the vast majority of us who work 8 to 5, then you know how hard it can be to take care of things as simple as a haircut or a car repair.

Today's employees put a high priority on not only earning a decent salary but also having adequate flexibility in their schedule to enjoy their personal life. Because productivity can be compromised when employees take an hour off here and there to run personal errands or when they worry about not spending enough time with their families, many organizations use compressed work schedules.

Compressed schedules take many forms. Some traditional office environments use a 4-day, 10-hour workweek, which gives employees 3 days off each week. Organizations that must be productive 24 hours a day, such as factories, hospitals, food services, and protective service organizations (police and fire departments), are even more innovative in scheduling work shifts. The large variety of shift-work configurations available ensures that organizations can find a schedule that will work for them.

As with other major changes that affect employees' lifestyle, organizations should always ask for employee input on the move to alternative work schedules. Educating employees about the options and then soliciting their opinions are a must. If employees are unhappy with the new schedules, it does not bode well for productivity or turnover rates. Some common concerns about compressed schedules include fatigue, which can impact safety. Exercise programs implemented in some organizations have helped to address these concerns. Supervising employees who are on a variety of schedules can be a headache for managers and can be another potential downside.

On a more positive note, organizations have discovered that there are usually more benefits than downsides to compressed workweeks. Compressed scheduling allows organizations to be more responsive to customers demanding efficient turnaround times or extended service hours. Many employees on compressed schedules report less stress and fatigue. Organizations report that employees are more productive because they are not distracted by personal or family issues, because they now have more time to focus on these issues away from work.

Organizations that have experience implementing compressed work schedules contend that if employees buy into the program, are given advanced notice of the scheduling change, and can subscribe to it voluntarily, the benefits to both employees and the organization can be enormous. Someday soon, the concept of a "normal" workweek may be a relic of the 20th century.

Sources: Adapted from N. Hatch Woodward. 2000. TGI Thursday. *HR Magazine* 45(7):73-76; and C. R. Maiwald, J. L. Pierce, and J. W. Newstrom, with B. Paik Sunoo. 1997. Workin' 8 P.M. to 8 A.M. and lovin' every minute of it! *Workforce* 76(7): 30–36.

Dislike of the schedule is usually associated with fatigue and an individual's leisure-time orientation. The longer workday does, in some instances, contribute to mental and/or physical fatigue. As the schedule becomes more tiring and stressful, dissatisfaction with the schedule builds.[11] Evidence suggests that differences in leisure-time orientation have an important effect on employees' attitudes toward compressed workweeks. Some individuals have an "hours-per-day" orientation, while others have a "days-per-week" orientation. For hours-per-day employees, the longer workday creates more role conflict, stress, and dissatisfaction. For people who have or can adjust to a days-per-week orientation, the compressed schedule is associated with greater job and leisure-time satisfaction.

As we all know firsthand, our work schedules often interfere with activities outside work—ones that involve family and friends, access to services, community events and entertainment, and personal business. The compressed schedule is experienced positively because it affords us larger blocks of time for our lives outside work, permitting a harmonization with family and community rhythms.[12]

While the compressed workweek is positively associated with employee satisfaction with hours worked and leisure time, its association with general job satisfaction is weaker, although rarely negative. This might be due to the simple fact that overall job satisfaction has many different facets (pay, supervision, coworkers, to name a few); the hours one works is only one of them.

Stress is an area of major concern when considering compressed schedules. Unfortunately, the evidence is inconclusive. Some studies indicate that stress and fatigue increase; others indicate no change, and still others show a decline. The latter observation appears to be related to the amount of time people have to "recharge their batteries." Evidence suggests that organizations that combine the 8-day week with the 4/40 or 4/48 schedule may be reducing employees' stress and fatigue. Apparently, four days between work schedules provides many people with the rest they need to mitigate the onset of stress and fatigue that stems from the longer workday.[13]

Finally, as with the studies on stress and fatigue, the evidence supporting a positive relationship between performance effectiveness and compressed schedules is mixed. That is, studies show performance increasing, decreasing, and not changing. Controlling for increased fatigue, there is no reason to believe that there should be a drop-off in performance. In addition, there is nothing inherent in the compressed schedule that should lead to significant increases in performance. The single exception might be on jobs where larger time blocks are more efficient for completing tasks, but such cases are probably few and far between.

Discretionary-Time Systems People typically show great interest in discretionary-time schedules, and once they've worked a flexible schedule generally don't want to return to a conventional one. Observations of people on flexible hours reveal some interesting patterns. First, the new schedules chosen by employees are frequently quite similar to their old ones. Second, most employees don't vary their daily starting and quitting times very often. While the flexibility is there, use of it tends to be quite limited.[14] However, this does not necessarily mean that having work scheduling discretion is unimportant.

It has also been noted that not all organizational members are positively inclined toward flexible working hours. Control-oriented supervisors generally don't like flexible hours, as they find it more difficult to track whom should be working and when. If an employee is sitting at his desk reading the newspaper during the 7 to 9 a.m. flex-band, how does the supervisor know if he is on his own time or company time? Another drawback for some is that everyone has to put in extra effort to get the common work (and especially meetings) done during the core hours.

Shift Work Research focusing on the effects of shift work does not paint a positive picture. Shift work can create havoc in people's lives.

The problems caused by shift work stem from a lack of harmony between the hours of work and family and community patterns. Another complication is that people who work shifts experience a constant battle between their hours of work and their body's circadian rhythms (our 24-hour cycle).

Adverse health effects from shift work—both physical and psychological—abound. Increased alcohol consumption, poorer appetites, low-quality sleep, and higher levels of fatigue have been widely documented. Higher levels of stress and interrupted gastrointestinal functioning, symptoms of psychological distress, lower levels of job satisfaction, and withdrawal behavior (absenteeism and turnover) have also been found to accompany shift work.[15] Some evidence suggests that more accidents and injuries occur on the night shift compared to either the morning or afternoon schedules. In addition, employees' social life is often impaired by shift work, which can reduce opportunities to participate in traditional social engagements and recreational activities. Shift workers typically spend more time in solitary activities.[16] Research also supports the claim that performance suffers. Employees who work fixed shifts tend to be more productive than rotating shift workers.

Several years ago the James River Paper Company in Ashland, Wisconsin, experimented with its shift schedules in an attempt to mitigate the adverse consequences of shift work.[17] James River implemented a *hybrid compressed week shift-work schedule* using a 12-hour, 8-day week. Management saw this as a way of eliminating many of the negative effects of shift work, while gaining the positive effects associated with the compressed workweek. The new schedule has two groups of workers who rotate between the day and night shifts. One group works a night shift that consists of four 12-hour days followed by four days off, at which point they rotate back to the day shift and a new workweek consisting of four 12-hour days and four days off. Then it's back to a new 8-day week and the night shift.

One study of the James River experiment reveals many positive effects. The hybrid shift workers were more satisfied with their hours of work and leisure time than were a comparable group of traditional shift workers. They also had a more positive perception of their work schedule's impact on their personal, social, and family lives. Fewer physiological and psychological symptoms of stress were noted among the hybrid shift workers. The researchers did uncover some individual differences, however. Employees with positive, upbeat, energetic, and optimistic dispositions had the most positive reactions to the hybrid schedule.[18]

Numerous attempts have been made to find a better fit between shift work and employees' personal needs. The following ideas appear to be especially promising:[19]

- To the extent possible, give employees their schedule preference. People who *choose* to work afternoons or nights experience fewer adverse effects than individuals who "have" to work these shifts.[20]
- Permanent shift assignment is better than rotating shifts for adjusting body rhythms.
- Rotate shifts forward, clockwise, from mornings to afternoons to nights.
- Shorten the night shift somewhat, and slightly lengthen the morning and afternoon shifts, to make the night shift more appealing.
- Make shift changes predictable so that people can better schedule their lives.
- Lengthen the intervals between shifts to permit employees more time to "recharge their batteries."[21]
- Keep shift rotations slow in order to give employees time to adjust.

EMPLOYEE OWNERSHIP

Before the 1970s, worker-owned companies were almost unheard of. By the end of that decade, however, headlines like "Miners Buy Mine to Save Their Jobs," "Employees Acquire Factory," and "Pilots Purchase Airline" were common. In fact, the last two and a half decades have been marked by an acceleration in the rate at which U.S. and Canadian firms have adopted some type of employee ownership arrangement. In 1976, approximately 300 U.S. companies were employee owned; by 1999, more than 11,000 organizations were operating under employee ownership arrangements. Today more than 10 million people are employee owners. In a few instances, employees own as much as 100 percent of the company, but only 3000 companies are majority employee owned.[22] Many well-known companies, including Anheuser-Busch, Lockheed, Procter & Gamble, and Polaroid, have implemented employee ownership plans. Avis Corporation is 100 percent employee owned. These firms frequently and proudly advertise their employee ownership arrangement—"For Rent by Owners."

http://www.anheuser-busch.com

http://www.avis.com

Employee-owned companies taking the form of worker cooperatives and characterized by "employee ownership" and "employee management" existed as long ago as 1791. The modern-day worker cooperative finds its roots in the plywood industry of the Pacific Northwest. In 1921, 125 lumber workers, carpenters, and mechanics pooled their money and built their own plywood mill in Olympia, Washington. In the ensuing years, Olympia Veneer's experiment prompted the formation of other worker-owned and worker-controlled mills. Electrical, agricultural, and food cooperatives emerged between 1920 and the late 1950s.

social ownership an arrangement whereby people in a society or community, including the employees, have an ownership stake in an organization

worker (producer) cooperatives an arrangement whereby employees are the exclusive owners of the organization

Employee ownership is driven by a variety of forces. It can occur as a result of a last-ditch effort to save a floundering organization, a negotiated settlement in a labor-management dispute, a strategy to avert a hostile takeover, a search for capital, a desire to enhance productivity, employee recruitment and retention issues, tax advantages, a philosophical ideal, or a respectful gesture and gift extended to a loyal and productive work force. Some of these reasons are clearly "business-oriented," while others are "employee-centered."

Employee Stock Ownership Plan (ESOP) an arrangement whereby employees may or may not be the exclusive owners of the organization; ownership is frequently the result of an employee-ownership trust having been established by the company on the employees' behalf

direct ownership an arrangement whereby employees purchase and hold stocks in the organization that employs them

Employee Ownership—What Is It?

There are four basic types of employee-owned organizations, with numerous variations of each:

- **social ownership**—people in a society or community, including employees, have an ownership stake in an organization
- **worker (producer) cooperatives**—employees are the exclusive owners
- **employee stock ownership plans (ESOPS)**—employees may or may not be the exclusive owners; ownership is frequently the result of an employee ownership trust established by the organization on employees' behalf
- **direct ownership**—employees purchase and hold stocks in the organization that employs them

Different ownership systems incorporate different degrees of employee ownership and control—some are built around employee ownership, some around employee control, and others around both.

AN INSIDE LOOK

Employees as Owners and Investors of Human Capital

"Our employees are our most important assets."

Phrases like this are common currency in annual reports, mission statements, and press releases these days, but in the 1980s and 1990s, frequent downsizing demonstrated that organizations viewed employees as just another cost to cut during economic downturns. As the economy improved, organizations turned once again to their employees to improve productivity. During the mid- to late 1990s, the business mantra for many organizations became "Employees Are Owners and Investors of Human Capital."

How do assets and capital differ? Assets are an organization's economic resources that are expected to be of benefit in the future. Some assets are physical—forklifts, buildings, computers, and so on. Some are intellectual—patents and production processes. But an organization's work force is also an asset, because without workers, companies cannot conduct business.

Capital differs from assets in that owners and investors control it. By human capital we mean employees' time, energy, abilities, attitudes, and behaviors. Because employees decide how much they are willing to invest in their jobs, they are therefore the owners and investors of capital—human capital.

Owners and investors of capital are keenly interested in getting the highest returns on their capital. Only by investing wisely can owners achieve strong returns. Training and education are wise investments of employee capital because they can lead to strong payoffs in productivity down the road. College degrees pay off in terms of higher salary, greater responsibilities, and overall higher job satisfaction, while training helps employees to be more effective; an investment that pays off both for the individual employee and the organization.

The overriding point is simple: Organizations and employees rely on each other for value. If organizations cannot attract and retain excellent employees by offering strong returns on their investment of time and energy, employees will take their talents elsewhere. Companies that provide challenging and satisfying work environments and opportunities for their people to continually invest their "human capital" will be rewarded with a productive work force.

Source: Adapted from T. O. Davenport. June 2000. Workers are not assets. *Across the Board,* 30–34.

The majority of employee ownership arrangements created during the closing years of the 20th century are ESOPs (employee stock ownership plans). A significant number of ESOPs define ownership simply as providing employee owners with an equity (shareholder) stake in the organization.

This equity-based approach has been criticized because it does not fully embody the essence of ownership as we generally experience it, like owning a car, for example.[23] Legally, ownership is commonly defined as a "bundle of rights" consisting of the right (1) to possess some share of the owned object's physical and/or financial value (equity); (2) to obtain information about the status of that which is owned; and (3) to exercise influence over the owned object. Many ESOPs do not come with informational and/or decision-making rights, but virtually all of them give employee owners an equity stake in the organization.

http://www.gwu.edu/~ccps/etzioni/

Ownership operates as both a legal and a psychologically experienced state. Sociologist Amitai Etzioni from George Washington University writes that "it is most productive to examine property [ownership] as a dual creation, part attitude, part object, part in the mind, part 'real.'"[24] People are likely to feel that they are owners when they legally own some share of the organization, have information about the organization's status, and exercise influence over the organization. We defined this state as *psychological ownership* (see Chapter 6)—that state where an individual feels as though the target of ownership (whether material or immaterial in nature) or a piece of it is "theirs."[25]

Popular Claims on the Efficacy of Employee Ownership

Ever since its inception, there have been myriad anecdotal claims and assertions about the efficacy of employee ownership. In 1912, Catherine Webb speculated that "by making [an employee] a shareholder in the business employing him . . . it stimulates his zeal and careful working." In the 1970s, an article in *U.S. News and World Report* suggested that "when a worker is given a piece of the action, he will be motivated to work harder, gripe less. Turnover, absenteeism, and grievances all might diminish."[26] P. Derrick and J. F. Phipps (1969) and E. Vanek (1975) expressed the view that worker alienation and effectiveness problems can be ameliorated through employee ownership systems. Among organizations that have recently converted to employee ownership, claims of improved morale and productivity are common. Brunswick Corporation's vice-president of finance claimed a 50 percent increase in sales following the implementation of their ESOP program.

http://www.brunswickcorp.com

Theory of Ownership

employee ownership an organizational arrangement in which a significant portion of the people who work in the firm hold rights to organizational equity, information, and influence

Theorists propose that **employee ownership** boosts motivation, contributes to job satisfaction, strengthens organizational commitment, reduces voluntary absenteeism and turnover, and enhances employee performance.[27] Ownership plans constructed around giving employees an equity stake in the organization, keeping them informed about organizational affairs, and permitting them to play an active role in influencing important organizational activities contribute to the emergence of psychological ownership.[28]

This theory also posits that employee ownership produces its positive effects through psychological ownership (see Figure 17-3). That is, only if formal ownership leads to psychological ownership does formal ownership favorably affect employee attitudes, motivation, and performance. Many employee ownership systems fail to achieve these results because they are designed exclusively around the equity component.

Employee Responses to Ownership

Organizational scientists have had many opportunities to study how employee ownership affects employees. Employee ownership (incorporating equity, information, and influence) tends to integrate the employee owner into the ownership experience.[29] A collective consciousness emerges, as do common interests, psychological partnership, identification with the organization, and organizational commitment. Employee owners appear to come together with a shared responsibility, enhanced cooperation, and teamwork, and also demonstrate increased job satisfaction.[30]

Giving employees an equity stake, sharing important organizational information, and involving them in organizational decision making send a powerful signal. The message flashed is, "you matter, you make a difference, and this difference is valued." As this message becomes internalized, employee owners come to believe that they are significant, worthy, and valuable to the organization. These beliefs are the essence of organization-based self-esteem (see Chapter 5).

FIGURE 17-3 How Employee Ownership Affects Psychological Ownership

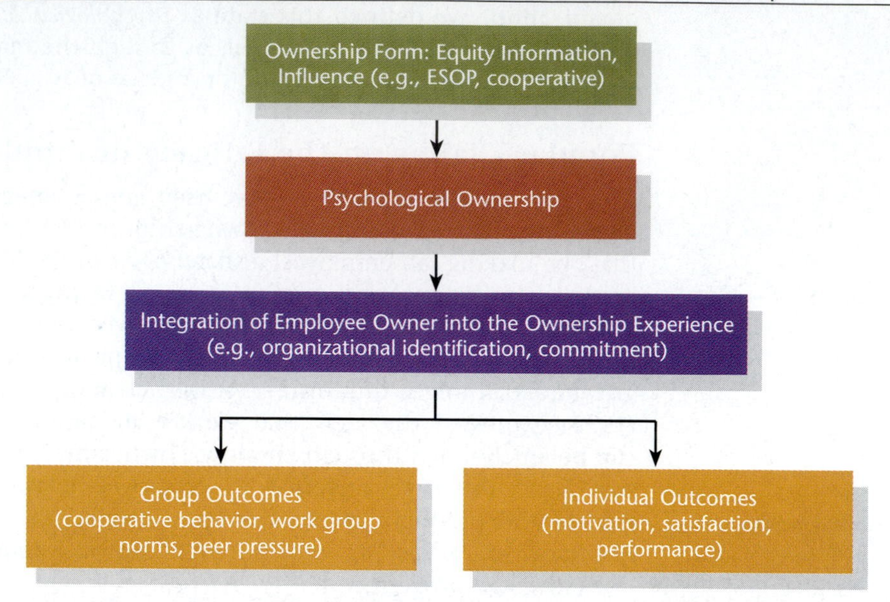

Source: Adapted from J. L. Pierce, S. A. Rubenfeld, and S. Morgan. 1991. Employee ownership: A conceptual model of process and effects. *Academy of Management Review* 16:123.

Because we are motivated to maintain and/or enhance our self-image, those of us with strong organization-based self-esteem put forth goal-directed efforts and sustain our motivation levels, and thus attain higher levels of performance. Thus, employee ownership is seen as a way to enhance employee performance.

The research findings are consistent: Virtually no performance effects are associated with equity-only ownership. The effects turn positive only when information sharing and decision participation are added to the mix.[31] Figure 17-4 illustrates how employee ownership operates to affect performance.

Finally, it is important to note that there are downsides to employee ownership. Employee owners often experience stress as they "worry" about the soundness of daily business decisions. It can be difficult to walk away from work at night without carrying home thoughts and concerns about "the business" and its troubles.

FIGURE 17-4 The Ownership–Performance Relationship

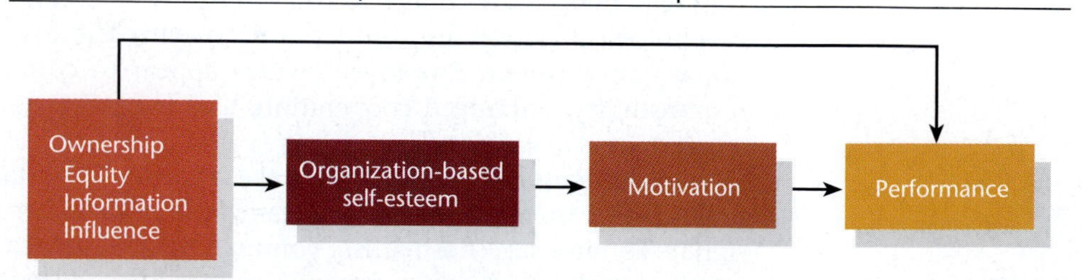

QUALITY CONTROL CIRCLES

It has been said that the Japanese changed the dominant business paradigm by launching the quality revolution. For years, U.S. companies focused solely on volume: produce large quantities, capitalize on economies of scale, and capture market share. Following World War II, Japan recognized that if they were to become a dominant player in the world economy, they would have to compete very differently—the "more is more" model would not work for them. Their response was to level the playing field by changing products and replacing the emphasis on quantity with a focus on quality.

http://www.caes.mit.edu/deming/

To achieve this end, the Japanese adopted American W. Edwards Deming as their business mentor. They listened to his ideas on quality management while the rest of the world turned a deaf ear. From this partnership there emerged Total Quality Management (commonly shortened to quality management) and the employee involvement practice known as the quality control circle.[32]

Total Quality Management (TQM) an approach to management that has as its primary focus the achievement of quality through continuous improvement of the processes employed to manufacture a product or deliver a service.

Total Quality Management (TQM) has come to mean many different things. However, the primary focus is on *continuous improvement* of the processes used to manufacture a product or deliver a service. TQM's four pillars are customer focus, measurement and evaluation, employee involvement, and continuous improvement.

The Quality Control Circle

quality control (QC) circle an employee involvement tool that generally consists of a small group of individuals who meet on a regular basis to discuss issues pertaining to quality and related problems

Quality control (QC) circles are one of many vehicles organizations use to achieve employee involvement and continuous improvement. QC circles generally consist of 5-15 employees who meet on a regular basis (usually once a week) to discuss issues pertaining to quality and related problems.[33] Participation in quality circles is often voluntary, and circles generally meet on company time. Typically, QC members are not financially rewarded for the ideas they generate, regardless of whether profits arise as a result. Many QC circle advocates assume that participation is rewarding per se, and a nice addition to the daily routine.

Most organizations don't delegate much authority to their QC circles, whose primary role is to explore problems and generate ways to cut costs, increase performance, and improve quality. As a rule, the ideas generated get passed along to others for review and a decision on whether action should be taken. TQM and QC circles are now an integral part of the management process in virtually every industry and every corner of the world.

Employee Responses to TQM and QC Circles

American organizations finally started to heed Deming's ideas in the 1980s. Today TQM is widespread, and QC circles are the most widely adopted TQM practice. Quality management is first and foremost a human process. Employees are key in the search for continuous improvement. Thus, cross-functional teams, self-directed work groups, and of course QC circles play important roles in TQM.

For TQM to bring results, organizational members must work smarter, harder, and more efficiently, and must take on more responsibility. Some of these changes are natural by-products of increased understanding of one's job and its place in the organizational framework. Others require better training and stronger commitment from the organization.

Deming and Karoru Ishikawa, another "father" of the quality movement, believed that their espoused TQM practices would positively impact employee motivation.[34] Quality management is very much in keeping with the human resource model (Chapter 2) and job enlargement and enrichment (Chapter 16). Expanded employee involvement, power, and responsibility contribute to increased intrinsic motivation and performance. In addition, it is assumed that employee job satisfaction is favorably impacted because employees experience their work as meaningful. Social motivation also appears to benefit from participation in QC circles because a synergy develops when people work together to achieve a desired outcome.

http://www.quality.nist.gov

On the down side, Professor Edward E. Lawler, III, argues that the design of most QC circles limits their ability to produce profound and sustained effects on motivation or performance. In his view, most QC circles are not designed as high-involvement systems.[35] He notes that to affect performance over the long term, employees must (1) have real power and understand that they can cause things to happen, (2) have the skills and abilities needed to improve performance, (3) receive relevant information, and (4) share in the gains that stem from their contributions.[36] (Deming argued strongly against the use of monetary rewards, but Lawler and many others believe that the sharing of monetary rewards is crucial.)

QC circles come up short in several of these areas. Missing from the design of the typical QC circle is the power to make things happen, training to equip participants with the necessary skills, and gain-sharing.[37] Organizational experiences with QC circles don't paint a very positive picture. While some beneficial effects have been reported, most circles are relatively short lived, and productivity and quality effects are inconsistent. In addition, QC circles don't appear to significantly affect worker motivation, commitment, or satisfaction.[38] This latter observation might be due to the fact that involvement in a QC circle consumes a very small portion of an employee's workday, often only one hour a week.

While QC circles may have great potential, it's easy to understand why they haven't produced the acclaimed results. Quality circles are easy to implement, so they are often installed as "quick fixes" without strong management commitment to employee involvement. Without fundamental changes in the organization's power, information, and reward structures, and with very little employee training in statistical control methods, few long lasting effects are likely to be realized.[39]

Other aspects of TQM appear to be more favorable. Evidence suggests that quality increases, new ideas, and processes are brought to market more rapidly, production costs decline, and profitability rises.[40] Vinod Singhal and Kevin Hendricks recently noted that TQM pays. They found that TQM award winners posted 37 percent higher sales growth and 44 percent fatter stock prices. These findings parallel those of the Malcolm Baldrige National Quality Award winners.[41] Wagner Lighting Products, for example, was generating 3700 defective products for every million produced. Today, following their adoption of TQM practices, they claim that fewer than a dozen defects are found annually.[42] TQM also helped Teradyne improve productivity (measured by sales per worker), which has soared from $120,000 to $219,000 annually in less than a decade.[43] Note, however, that TQM results are not entirely positive. For one thing, stress levels rise with expectations for continuous production improvements. Evidence also indicates that a significant number of quality management initiatives fail due to a lack of commitment on the part of both management and the work force.[44]

http://www.teradyne.com

THE HIGH-INVOLVEMENT ORGANIZATION AND MANAGEMENT

As noted in earlier chapters, a new type of organization—the high-involvement organization—is becoming increasingly visible. General Electric operates some of its manufacturing plants with no supervisors; self-managing work teams are the centerpiece of its approach to organization. Operators of paper machines at Lake Superior Paper Industries interview, hire, train, evaluate, discipline, promote, and fire those with whom they work. Printing press operators at Quad/Graphics, who are also part owners of the company, deal directly with vendors and customers in order to improve operating efficiency and responsiveness.

Each of these examples marks a radical departure from the traditional organizational structure, where top and middle management, along with their staff specialists, direct and control virtually all activities. While the high-involvement approach is not yet dominant in the United States, it is gaining popularity because of the experiences of a number of highly successful organizations.

High-involvement organizations strive to find people who are self-starters, who are motivated by intrinsic rewards, and who have feelings of competence and self-efficacy.

High-Involvement Systems[45]

As we have noted throughout the text, high involvement focuses on employee involvement as a way to increase organizational performance. It is a participative process designed to use workers' entire capacity and to encourage commitment to the organization's success.[46] In high-involvement organizations, people at all levels and in all positions—especially those who make the products or deliver the services—manage (plan, organize, direct, and control) all parts of the organization.

Management's job in the high-involvement organization is to try to achieve a fit between their people, their task/technology, and their information processes, rewards, and structure. High involvement is about each organizational member assuming responsibility for their work and for the mission of the organization because they psychologically experience ownership for their work and for the organization.

Involvement Strategies

Organizations adopt a number of strategies as they endeavor to utilize their human resources more fully. Work design is the heart of the high-involvement organization because the nature of the work establishes, defines, and maintains the individual's relationship with the organization. People are hired to perform a job, so jobs shape employee motivation, attitudes, and behavior in crucial ways.[47] Thus, job enrichment and work teams (discussed in earlier chapters) are central to making high involvement work.

Other strategies, also discussed throughout this book, include Management-by-Objectives, quality circles,[48] employee ownership, gainsharing,[49] and quality-of-work-life (QWL) programs. QWL programs are " 'cooperative labor-management programs' . . . designed to increase the involvement of employees" in order to improve conditions for both the organization and the worker.[50] Model programs were implemented at General Motors, Harman International Industries, and Ford. Employees at GM's Rochester plant routinely returned to school to learn more about the automotive industry, economics, competitiveness, problem solving, and a variety of other topics.[51] At Harman, shop floor committees were employed to give employees greater influence over plant decisions,[52] while Ford focused on collaborative problem solving at the shop floor level.[53] It would not be uncommon to see virtually all of these involvement strategies, in one form or another, as an integral part of the high-involvement organization.

http://www.harman.com

The Effects of High Involvement

Currently, very few companies are fully integrated high-involvement organizations. According to Professor Lawler, Motorola is one organization that has come close to implementing high-involvement organization-wide. He also notes that the approach is more popular in smaller organizations like W. L. Gore and Herman Miller.[54]

http://www.gore.com

http://www.hermanmiller.com

Evidence suggests that many high-involvement strategies have been associated with organizational improvements, indicating that they *can* make a difference. According to results offered by consultant Jack Orsburn and his associates, productivity at Procter & Gamble and General Mills increased significantly after they instituted self-directed work teams. Aid Association for Lutherans reduced their case processing time by 75 percent and boosted their productivity by 20 percent.[55] Marquette University's Professor John L. Cotton, after his review of employee involvement, summed up his findings this way: "I firmly believe that involvement is capable of generating world-class improvements in American industry."[56] "Our success in global competition demands brainpower—the ability to work smarter, not just harder. . . . We can win in the global competition, but it will require a new approach to management, one incorporating employee involvement."[57]

An organization that employs Management-by-Objectives, or quality circles, or employee ownership is not necessarily a high-involvement organization. High-involvement organizations are fully integrated systems marked by enriched jobs, teams extending from the shop floor to the executive suite, universal vigilance toward quality, and active participation by all employees in planning and controlling activities. They are built upon a philosophical commitment to employee involvement.

MANAGING PRODUCTIVITY: CONTEMPORARY APPROACHES IN REVIEW

Compressed workweeks, staggered starts, flexible working hours, and a variety of other schedules are now commonplace in North American organizations. Most of these innovations were implemented because of management's belief that a schedule that is more attractive to employees will promote retention, motivation, and job satisfaction. Many were also driven by a hope that performance would improve. For the most part, alternative work schedules have been favorably received. Rarely do employees who have switched from a traditional 5/40 schedule to staggered starts, flexible or variable hours, a compressed work week, or some hybrid variation want to return to the traditional schedule.

Many organizations have adopted an employee ownership arrangement as a way of positively influencing employee attitudes, motivation, and work-related behavior. Ownership arrangements designed to provide workers with the "bundle of rights" commonly associated with ownership in general have been found to promote psychological ownership, which positively affects group dynamics (teamwork, cooperation), and employee satisfaction, acts of good organizational citizenship, and performance.

Quality control circles are an integral part of Total Quality Management and a widely used employee involvement strategy. While a few short-term positive effects have been associated with QC circles, research by Professor Edward E. Lawler, III, predicts that long-term benefits are unlikely. Missing from most QC circles is the power to make changes and a gainsharing program that links rewards with quality and/or productivity improvements.

Finally, an increasing number of organizations are moving toward high-involvement management as a way of becoming high-performance organizations. The high-involvement organization builds employee participation and involvement into virtually all of its practices. These practices embrace the idea that an organization's human resources are key to its competitive advantage.

Practices such as organizational behavior modification, job enlargement and enrichment, self-directed work teams, alternative work schedules, employee ownership, Total Quality Management, QC circles, and high-involvement strategies have all been employed in an effort to manage productivity. Many of these strategies, if properly implemented and managed, can favorably affect the motivation, attitudes, and work-related behaviors of organizational members, as well as the overall efficiency and effectiveness of the organization.

A FINAL LOOK

The owners of Aunt Ruthie's Kitchen ask for ideas from employee volunteers. People from all aspects of the business, from cooks and busboys to menu designers and accountants, attend a brainstorming session. The first question thrown out is, What's wrong with us? People enlarge on this question to include What do our customers want from us? Why do they come to Aunt Ruthie's? Why are they not coming? How can we bring them back?

The quality circle makes three recommendations. First, Aunt Ruthie's needs to focus on what made it so popular for so long—homestyle cooking. Aunt Ruthie's has altered its menu to compete with chains that offer everything from spaghetti to stir-fry. It doesn't even make its own desserts anymore, and the quality circle feels that people miss that.

Second, the quality circle recommends several ways to improve service, including better training for new staff. They also suggest that the wait staff make taking orders by memory a standard, "signature" practice so that customers feel like regulars and to underscore the homestyle atmosphere.

Third, it was recommended that Aunt Ruthie implement a gainsharing program. Any time the QC circle offers a cost reduction, performance improvement, or quality program that results in increased profit, a share of those profits will be divided among the restaurant's employees.

The owners are pleased—their staff has a strong feel for the desires of their community. They decide to put these ideas into action immediately. Not all the QC circle's ideas will be used, but everyone is confident that they are going in the right direction and that Aunt Ruthie's will once again be the heart of the community.

KEY TERMS

compressed workweek, 608
direct ownership, 615
discretionary-time systems, 608
employee ownership, 617
Employee Stock Ownership Plan (ESOP), 615
flexible working hours, 609
quality control (QC) circles, 619
shift work schedules, 611
social ownership, 615
staggered start system, 608
Total Quality Management (TQM), 619
variable-hour arrangement, 610
worker (producer) cooperatives, 615

ISSUES FOR REVIEW AND DISCUSSION

1. Explain these approaches to scheduling work: compressed workweeks, discretionary-time systems, and shift work.
2. How do different work schedules impact employee attitudes, motivation, and behavior?
3. Discuss employee ownership. What forms does it take and what is the difference between legal and psychological ownership?
4. Explain how formal ownership impacts employee attitudes, motivation, and behavior.
5. Summarize the research findings on the relationship between ownership and employee attitudes, motivation, and behavior.
6. What are QC circles, why do they exist, and what purpose do they serve?
7. What effects on behavior has been observed as a result of QC circles?
8. What makes an organization a high-involvement organization?
9. How have high-involvement practices affected employees?

EXERCISES

QUALITY IMPROVEMENT QUESTIONNAIRE

For each item, circle the number that best describes your attitude or behavior on the job or at school.

	Disagree				Agree
1. I recognize the practical constraints of existing conditions when someone proposes an improvement.	5	4	3	2	1
2. I like to support change efforts, even when the idea may not work.	5	4	3	2	1
3. I believe that many small improvements are usually better than a few big improvements.	5	4	3	2	1
4. I encourage other people to express improvement ideas, even if they differ from mine.	5	4	3	2	1
5. There is truth to the statement, "If it isn't broke, don't fix it."	5	4	3	2	1
6. I work at the politics of change to build agreement for my improvement ideas.	5	4	3	2	1
7. I study suggestions carefully to avoid change just for the sake of change.	5	4	3	2	1
8. I like to have clear objectives that support improvement, even if changes upset my efficiency.	5	4	3	2	1
9. I constantly talk about ways to improve what I'm doing.	5	4	3	2	1
10. I am able to get higher-ups to support my ideas for improvement.	5	4	3	2	1

Total score ____________

Scoring and Interpretation:

Your score indicates the extent to which you are a positive force for quality improvement. The questions represent behaviors associated with the continuous improvement of quality.

40–50: Great. A dynamo for quality improvement.
30–40: Good. A positive force.
20–30: Adequate. You have an average attitude toward quality.
10–20: Poor. You may be dragging down quality efforts.

Go back over the questions on which you scored lowest and develop a plan to improve your approach toward quality. Discuss your ideas with other students.

Source: Excerpt from p. 647 of *Management* (3rd ed.) by Richard L. Daft, copyright © 1994 by The Dryden Press, reprinted by permission of the publisher.

INFOTRAC 

The articles listed below are a sampling of those available through InfoTrac College Edition. You can search for them either by title or by the author's name.

Articles

1. Ownership cultures create unity. Scott Hays. *Workforce* Feb 1999 v78 i2 p60(4) Bus.Coll.: 114X2338
2. Not knowingly undersold. (employee partnership in business) Paul Barker. *New Statesmen* (1996) Nov 15, 1999 v128 i4462 p29 Mag.Coll.: 101F2710
3. Good Career/Life Balance Makes for Better Workers. Ann Vincola, Caela Farren. *HR Focus* April 1999 v76 i4 p13(1)
4. Worker's ideas for improving alternative work situations. Shari Caudron. *Workforce* Dec 1998 v77 i12 p42(5)
5. Work-Family Concern Tops List. (results of survey by OfficeTeam) (Brief Article) (Statistical Data Included) Stephanie Overman. *HR Focus* July 1999 v76 i7 p4

Questions

For Article 1:

The article "Ownership cultures create unity" discusses the rising phenomenon of employee ownership and makes the troubling point that, in this country, "most people haven't been educated to be owners." After reading Chapter 17 and the above-mentioned article, ask your group to brainstorm a list of practical strategies to help employees assume corporate ownership. Be as specific as possible.

For Other Articles:

Several of the articles in the above list deal with the topic of alternative work schedules. Assign these articles to members of your group. Meet to discuss new information you have gathered about flexible work schedules.

WEB EXERCISE

The Center for Effective Organizations in the Marshall School of Business at the University of Southern California is a research center and has as a part of its mission the development of new knowledge focused on how organizations can be more effective and competitive.

Visit their website at **http://www.marshall.usc.edu/ceo/**. At this site select "publications" and then select "search publications—by topic." You will see several different topical areas that have been the focus of research activity at the Center. Each of these areas deals with ways of managing organizational behavior to make organizations more effective and competitive. Select one topical area (for example, employee involvement) that is of most interest to you. You should see several abstracts of articles on that topic that are available through the Center. Select one of these abstracts and prepare a summary.

CASE
Feeding Employee Satisfaction at la Madeleine

John Corcoran, CEO of the la Madeleine French Bakery & Café restaurant chain, believes his company has the recipe for success. All it will take is the right human resource ingredients.

The privately owned chain aims to bring "a little slice of France to America" by combining fast-food convenience with an upscale atmosphere. Customers order from a menu of French-style breads, sandwiches, soups, and pastries at the service counter. Meals can be taken out or enjoyed in the restaurant, where exposed beams and wood floors are designed to evoke the feel of a Parisian café.

Since the first la Madeleine restaurant was opened in Dallas in 1983, the chain has expanded to 63 units throughout Texas, Arizona, Georgia, Louisiana, Maryland, Virginia, and Washington, D.C. There are now 2,500 employees, called "associates," working for la Madeleine.

In the past three years, however, the company has had to deal with a number of challenges. Rapid expansion in the mid-1990s left the firm saddled with heavy debt. At the same time, competitors like Au Bon Pain and Panera Bread Company entered many of la Madeleine's markets, and its sales and profits declined.

When he assumed the CEO position in 1998, Corcoran found an astounding lack of consistency among la Madeleine restaurants. Service and product quality varied dramatically because there was little formal direction from headquarters about how each unit should operate. "The time had not been taken to put in place systems to evolve la Madeleine from a concept to a well-run company," says Corcoran. Employee turnover was also skyrocketing. Sixty percent of the chain's restaurant managers quit each year. Hourly employees were even less likely to stay, with turnover in some stores running as high as 300 percent each year.

Corcoran immediately began trying to improve employee retention and productivity. First, he hired an area training manager for each market. In addition to showing employees how to prepare la Madeleine's menu, the trainers stress the importance of preparing food in a way that gives customers an authentic French bakery experience. Corcoran also began sending each restaurant manager to France every year for a week of all-expenses-paid training, a powerful incentive for many to stay with the company.

In addition, the company also developed a clear, formal career ladder to show workers that they can advance through the system if they stay with the firm. Corcoran and other key executives regularly talk about opportunities for career advancement when they visit each market on a regular basis. During these visits, top management also discusses the company's mission and future plans.

With these programs in place, Corcoran says the company is making progress. Sales are rising and management turnover has dropped to 40 percent. Hourly worker turnover has also fallen, but remains high. Corcoran isn't satisfied yet. He'd like to bring management turnover rates down to at least 30 percent and keep hourly worker turnover to below three digits.

It won't be an easy task. The restaurant industry has traditionally faced a shortage of workers who are willing to put up with long hours, stressful conditions, and low pay. The National Restaurant Association surveyed restaurant workers to uncover the elements that would improve their job satisfaction. At the top of the list were competitive wages, incentive pay, and staffing schedules sufficient to handle the workload. Employees said they also want to feel they work for a well-managed company that treats employees fairly and cares about them and their family responsibilities.

Some restaurant chains are already successfully improving worker satisfaction, retention, and productivity. Starbucks Coffee, for instance, was the first chain restaurant to offer stock options to both salaried and hourly employees. Under this employee-ownership plan, every worker who stays with Starbucks for a minimum of six months and works at least 20 hours a week is eligible to purchase stock. Acapulco Restaurants, a California-based Mexican food chain, offers top-performing employees cash bonuses and days off. McDonald's Restaurants offer hourly workers a flexible scheduling policy to accommodate worker education and family responsibilities.

Corcoran says that, despite the increased competition, his strategy will remain the same: "We will emphasize with our associates to take care of our guests, to stay focused and do what we do well, which is deliver a high quality product to our loyal guests."

Discussion Questions

1. Evaluate the effectiveness of the programs Corcoran has already implemented and suggest how they could be improved.
2. If you were Corcoran, what additional approaches would you consider to improve employee productivity and satisfaction? Explain.
3. Could the QC-Circle concept be used at la Madeleine? Discuss the benefits and limitations of instituting QC-Circles at la Madeleine.

Sources: Adapted from C. Hutchcraft. February 1, 2001. The good fight. Restaurants & Institutions, *downloaded from* **http://www.rimag.com**; *J. Larson. February 16, 2000. Dough flies in Phoenix: la Madeleine feeds French bread need.* The Arizona Republic, *D2; J. Tahan. June 6, 2000. Bakery targets N. Texas for expansion.* The Arlington Morning News, *1C; Lisa Tanner. February 19, 2001. French bakery chain takes nouvelle approach.* Dallas Business Journal, *21.*

Outline

CHAPTER 18

Managing Organizational Change and Development

Learning Objectives

After reading this chapter, you should be able to

1. Identify the five primary reasons change does and should occur in organizations.
2. Understand the difference between proactive and reactive change.
3. Describe the major types of change that occur in organizations.
4. Describe the range of people's reactions to organizational change and the reasons underlying their reactions.
5. Understand the role that psychological ownership plays in both the promotion of, and resistance to, organizational change.
6. Identify and describe the relative strengths and weaknesses of the seven major techniques for developing support for organizational change.
7. Understand the special role of organizational development and how it can enhance effectiveness and benefit organizational members.
8. Describe a systematic approach to planning and managing organizational change.
9. Describe a learning organization and how it differs from traditional organizations.

A FIRST LOOK

Premier Plastics is a medium-sized, family-run company that operates in the same top-down, autocratic style favored by its founder, Sidney Carruthers. It has been profitable for many years, and given that it's a traditional assembly-line manufacturer, the Carruthers family saw no need to shake things up. Then last year, the company's sales dropped 20 percent.

Talk about a wake-up call! The entire family hunkers down in some bare-the-soul discussions about what's happening. Although retired, Mr. Carruthers dominates the discussion, and unfortunately no new ground is broken because the family members are hesitant to disagree with him. But it's obvious that they need an objective, clear-headed viewpoint, so the family finally agrees to bring in an outside consultant. Perhaps it's time to "think outside the box."

Question: What forces for change are evident at Premier Plastics? How do you think the family leaders, Sidney Carruthers in particular, will react to an outside consultant?

We have examined techniques that help managers effectively plan, organize, direct, and control, as well as create a culture that promotes healthy employee attitudes, motivation, and behavior. Managers use these techniques all the time when they create new organizations. Few of us, however, will have the opportunity to create a new organization from scratch. Instead, most of us will use this knowledge to effect change in an existing organization.

Change occurs for many reasons. Sometimes the change is simply advantageous—a new technology promises greater efficiency. Other times, there is no choice but to change, as when new governmental regulations dictate how business will be done. As a manager, you will soon find that it is not enough to have a good idea—you must make your idea work, and work well. In this chapter we explore common causes of organizational change, the types of changes you may face, and employee reactions to change. We also explore how you can develop support for change; techniques for structuring change; and a model for planning and managing the change process.

The topic of organizational change and development should be thought of in conjunction with the managing activity of control. As a part of the control process, managers observe actual organizational behavior and compare observed behavior with expectations. Through this comparison process, managers can determine how effective their organization has been and whether change is needed in order to maintain or enhance effectiveness.

WHY CHANGE OCCURS: FORCES FOR CHANGE

organizational change the movement of an organization from its current state to some future and preferred state

Organizational change is the movement of an organization from its current state to some future and hopefully more effective state. Organizational change does not occur spontaneously; it takes place when the forces encouraging change become more powerful than those resisting change. Most organizations face an incredible number of factors that "invite" them to change. The forces driving change can be internal or external. A strategic plan for product diversification can be a potent internal force for change. A new technological develop-

© R. W. JONES/CORBIS

New technology can create opportunity for change in organizations. For instance, video conferencing capabilities change how some organizations function because they facilitate communication between remote offices.

ment from outside an organization can provide a powerful external force for change—think about how digitalization has revolutionized communications, and how gene mapping has re-created the biotechnology industry.

Technological Forces

We live in the age of technological change. You might say we are bombarded with technology-induced change. Virtually all organizations employ a variety of technologies to produce their goods and services. Significant advancements in technologies continually compel organizations to change. Technological change can arise from internal sources, as when organizations develop their own new technologies. Medtronics' efforts to genetically engineer heart valves reflect a potential shift in their core technology that will have profound organizational effects. Technological change can also arise from external sources, as when St. Jude's acquired a sealant for arteries from research conducted at the University of Minnesota's research laboratories. Regardless of the source, changes in technology can sow the seeds for changes in management practice and organizational design.

http://www2.stjude.org

Employee Needs and Values

More than ever, managers are recognizing the importance of considering the needs and values of their members. Many of today's workers are leaning less toward financial rewards and more toward quality of life alternatives. Hence the advent of flexible working hours, the compressed work week, and on site childcare facilities. Changes in employees' needs and values can be an extremely strong force driving organizational change.

Social Forces

The general public is another strong force for change, sometimes simply by altering their interest for products. Changing public tastes means organizations must continually shift their marketing, sometimes their image, and always the way they do business. Society's increased concern for health and physical fitness, for example, has caused many food companies to market products containing less salt, fewer calories, lower cholesterol, and less saturated fat. At other times social pressures go beyond indicating what is desirable and define what is acceptable.

Business and Economic Forces

The inflation rate, gross domestic product, money supply, interest rates, and industry competition—all exert tremendous pressures on organizations. Extremely high interest rates plagued the United States in the early 1980s, for example, causing organizations to restrict expansion, reduce borrowing to finance new ventures, and minimize unsold inventories. The entire economy does not have

As shown in the Central Michigan Community Hospital video, a hospital can face a range of changes, from aging populations, reform in the industry, and changing regional economics—managing change means taking steps in anticipation of change, preempting the competition, and developing resources before they're needed.

to shift, however, for business and economic factors to drive change in an organization. Other change can be the simple outgrowth of competitive pressures. Potlatch Corporation worked long and hard to develop a genetically altered tree species in order to address its competitive pressures for rapidly growing trees to supply their paper manufacturing business faster and more cheaply.

Organizational Forces

Often the organization itself is the primary force behind change. For example, Boeing made a landmark strategic decision to move its corporate headquarters out of Seattle in order to better effect "global" thinking in the company.

These five forces seldom operate independently—rather, a combination of them drives change. Have organizations introduced robotics solely because technological advances have made it possible? Not likely. Economic constraints, employee desires for more challenging work, and societal demands for better-quality products have combined with the availability of new technologies in driving this change.

TYPES OF CHANGE

All changes occur either reactively or proactively. Reactive and proactive change can involve technological, structural/procedural (administrative), and/or human components.[1] Changes can also be distinguished based on the degree to which they are innovative.

Reactive Versus Proactive Change

reactive change when forces driving change pressure an organization to change

Reactive change occurs when the forces driving change provide so much pressure that an organization *must* change. The failure of existing equipment or systems, for example, is a powerful impetus for change. So too are government interventions. Microsoft may be facing profound change because of the federal government's anti-trust litigation against the corporation. As of this writing the courts have ordered Microsoft to split into at least two companies. No surprise—Microsoft is appealing the decision! However, should the decision be upheld, not only will an entire industry experience radical shifts but users worldwide will be affected.

proactive change when managers conclude that a change is desirable (as opposed to necessary)

http://www.aacsb.edu

Proactive change occurs when an organization concludes that a change is desirable (as opposed to necessary). Generally, proactive change is more orderly and more efficient because it is planned (although, as noted in previous chapters, not all planning is done well). The University of Minnesota Duluth's School of Business and Economics committed itself to attaining AACSB's* accreditation of its bachelor and masters of business administration degree programs. For six years the school worked to get the systems in place and received full accreditation early in the year 2000.

Change and Innovation

"All innovation is change, but not all change is innovation."[2] Despite the fact that many tend to equate the two concepts, it is important to differentiate between them. Change, as previously noted, involves any modification to an exist-

* Association to Advance Collegiate Schools of Business—International (formerly American Assembly for Collegiate Schools of Business and the International Association for Management Education).

innovation when an organization is one of the first users of an idea

ing organizational practice. **Innovation** occurs when an organization is one of the first users of an idea. The first airline to provide scheduled service in space will be innovative, as was the first hospital to perform a heart transplant and Henry Ford's use of the assembly line for the mass production of automobiles.

Because innovation provides more excitement, more challenge, and more uncertainty than most change, management of innovation requires special care. Thus, nurturing support for innovation and managing the change process systematically is crucial.[3]

http://www.thinksmart.com

Technological Changes

Some of the most visible and dramatic changes made in organizations during the last two decades introduced new technologies. Robotics in manufacturing processes, paperless offices, distance learning and the "virtual lecture"—the list is endless. For better or for worse, technology is pushing change at unprecedented rates (see Figure 18-1). The most common technological changes involve new equipment, new work procedures, new methods of processing information, and other automation.

Structural/Procedural Changes

While technological changes are about tools and processes, structural changes concentrate on organizational design and the methods to coordinate work. This can be as far-reaching as moving from a functional organization (one based on finance, operations, marketing, etc.) to a divisional organization (one centered on product lines, customer groups, or territories) or as minimal as changing the way authority is delegated and a manager's span of control. Restructuring has become a norm as organizations struggle to find effective ways to coordinate work, downsize, restructure, and enhance productivity.

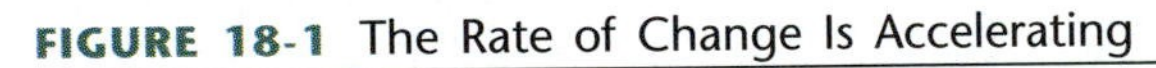

FIGURE 18-1 The Rate of Change Is Accelerating

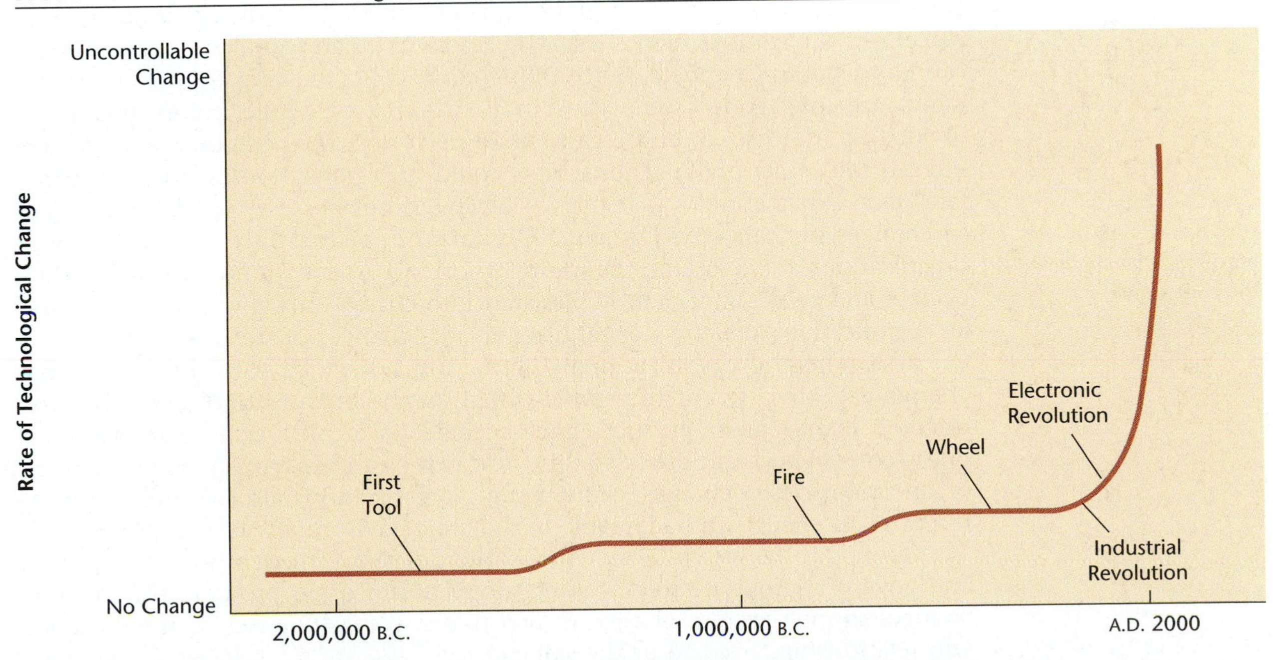

Source: R. B. Dunham. 1984. *Organizational behavior.* Homewood, IL: Irwin, 465.

People-Oriented Changes

Many organizations concentrate on people-oriented changes, such as improving employee skills, attitudes, motivation, and behaviors. These factors are so important that they constitute a major part of the work conducted by organizational development specialists. Sometimes this strategy involves replacing people—for example, when existing employees are unable to adapt to new technologies or new environments. At other times, organizations need "new blood" and fresh ideas. Replacing employees also sends a message to the external environment, as when a CEO is replaced. Some observers note that elevating G. Richard Wagoner, Jr., to CEO at General Motors signaled that GM intended to "move faster, act as one company globally, introduce more innovative vehicles, and set stretch targets."[4] However, most people-oriented change in organizations involves training, developing, and motivating the existing work force.

http://www.gm.com

Technostructural and Sociotechnical Changes

Distinguishing between technological, structural, and people-oriented changes is, in theory, easy. In reality, however, organizational change is rarely so neatly categorized. Accordingly, we define two hybrid approaches that "affect the work content and method and . . . the sets of relationships among workers."[5] **Technostructural changes** involve concurrent changes in organizational technology and structure. **Sociotechnical changes** are about changes in people and technology. As you may have guessed, these distinctions are seldom clear in practice. In fact, most changes using either of these hybrid titles involve changes in all technological, structural/procedural, and people-oriented change areas. Rather than debate the appropriate label to assign a given change, it is more important to use all three areas of potential change effectively.[6]

technostructural changes concurrent change in organizational technology and structure

sociotechnical changes concurrent change in people and technology

REACTIONS TO CHANGE

Look at the *Fortune 500* companies of 1979/1980 and of today. More than 50 percent of the familiar names that your mom and dad would recognize (American Motors, Allis-Chalmers, Getty Oil, Lipton, Schlitz Brewing, Searle, and Sperry Rand) are long gone—some gave in to bankruptcy, while others had to be divided up, downsized, and recast, while many lost their identity as they were merged into other organizations. How could such powerhouses come to such a fate? One explanation is that many simply did not possess the ability to adapt to changes in their environments. **Organizational inertia** is the tendency of organizations to maintain the status quo, and is a common cause of their decline and subsequent demise. Resistance to change can and often does lower an organization's effectiveness and reduces its chances of survival.

organizational inertia tendency to maintain the status quo

Researchers of organizational inertia and resistance to change note that change gets thwarted at three levels: first, at the organization level: Control-oriented management practices and mechanistic organizations emphasize stability, consistency, and predictability. Research clearly suggests that mechanistic organizations resist change, while organic organizations are significantly more receptive to change and adaptable to dynamic environmental conditions.

Second, at the group level: Groups often develop strong norms that specify and govern appropriate roles. Strong group norms often promote resistance to change, simply because change means that a whole new set of norms, roles, and relationships need to be developed.

Finally, at the individual level: As individuals, organizational members anticipate, notice, and react to change. Their reactions can range from quite positive and supportive, to quite negative and very resistant. In fact,

> [P]eople experience change in all manner of ways. For some, a particular change will bring satisfaction, joy, advantage, a sense of job well done; for others, that same change may bring disadvantage, pain, sadness, even humiliation. Still others may barely perceive the change at all, experiencing it indifferently at most.[7]

Habits, fear of uncertainty, fear of failure, insecurity—all can inhibit us from anticipating change in positive ways. Note that sometimes resistance to change finds it origin and motivation in a "healthy concern" for the welfare of the organization, as not all change increases organizational efficiency and effectiveness.[8]

Macro-level efforts to effect organizational change start with either structural or process changes at the organization or group level. Micro-level efforts to effect organizational change start at the individual level. A significant portion of the resistance to and promotion of organizational change can be dealt with at the micro level. As organizational members deal with change, their attitudes affect their work unit. In similar fashion, individual-level reaction to change can also be carried to the organization level via efforts to alter the organization's culture as well as its structural systems.

The Reasons Behind Our Reactions to Change

Why do reactions to change vary so widely? Why do some people actively support a change while others simply passively accept it, and still others actively resist it? People's reaction to change depends heavily on how they answer the following questions:

1. Will I gain or lose something of value?
2. Do I understand the nature of this change?
3. Do I trust the initiators of this change?
4. Do I agree with this change?
5. How do I feel about this change?[9]

In other words, most people react rationally and logically to change. In fact, most people resist change because past change has caused them problems or prevented them from satisfying important needs.[10] Knowing this should help you anticipate support or resistance and help you develop support for change.

Perceptions of Value. When we conclude that a proposed change will cause us to lose something of value, we have a vested interest in resisting it. The more we expect to gain from change, the more we support it.

Understanding the Change. We all fear the unknown, so we are less likely to support change if we don't understand it. If we are confused about the implications of change, we usually assume the worst and react accordingly.

Trust in the Initiators. If our trust in management is low, our first reaction is to ask, What is really going to happen and how is this going to harm me? When we don't trust the initiators of change, virtually any change tends to be received negatively. When trust is high, we are more likely to support change.

Agreement with the Change. It is amazing that organizations planning change often fail to assess who is likely to agree with the introduction of a change and who is apt to disagree. It is clearly logical to expect that those who think the change is a good idea will be more likely to support it than those who feel the change is a bad idea.

Personal Feelings. Our personal characteristics affect whether we will support or resist change. For example, if we lack confidence in our skills—skills required by the change—we will probably be resistant. Cynicism is another key element in our reactions to change.[11]

In addition to the influence of these and other personality attributes (such as dogmatic—closed-mindedness—and authoritarian personalities), attitudes toward change itself can also play an important role in shaping our reactions to any specific change. The items in the self-assessment below address the cognitive, affective, and behavioral tendency components of a person's attitude toward change,[12] and can thus help managers anticipate probable reactions to changes.

SELF-ASSESSMENT

SELF-ASSESSMENT What Is Your Attitude Toward Change?

Instructions: Thinking about "change in general," indicate whether you agree or disagree with the following statements. Mark your answers in the space provided.

1	2	3	4	5
Strongly Disagree	**Slightly Disagree**	**Neither Agree nor Disagree**	**Slightly Agree**	**Strongly Agree**

____ 1. I look forward to changes at work.
____ 2. I usually resist new ideas.
____ 3. I am inclined to try new ideas.
____ 4. Change usually benefits organizations.
____ 5. I usually support new ideas.
____ 6. Most of my co-workers benefit from change.
____ 7. I don't like change.
____ 8. Change frustrates me.
____ 9. Changes tend to stimulate me.
____ 10. Most changes at work are irritating.
____ 11. I often suggest new approaches to things.
____ 12. Change often helps me perform better.
____ 13. I intend to do whatever possible to support change.
____ 14. Other people think that I support change.
____ 15. I usually hesitate to try new ideas.
____ 16. Change usually helps improve unsatisfactory situations at work.
____ 17. I find most changes to be pleasing.
____ 18. I usually benefit from change.

Scoring:

Add your answers to questions 4, 6, 12, 14, 16, and 18, and then divide by 6. This is your "belief and opinion about change" score. Next, add your answers to questions 1, 7, 8, 9, 10, and 17, and divide by 6. This score reflects how "change makes you feel." Now, add your answers to questions 2, 3, 5, 11, 13, and 15, and divide by 6. This score reflects how "change makes you want to act (behave)." A score of 4 and greater reflects a positive attitude toward change. A score of 2 and less reflects an attitude that is negative and potentially resistant to change.

Source: R. B. Dunham, J. A. Grube, D. G. Gardner, J. L. Pierce, & L. L. Cummings. August 1989. *The development of an attitude towards change instrument.* Annual meeting of the Academy of Management, Washington, D.C.

Although the five categories of underlying causes just discussed seem to operate independently, this is usually not the case. Particular combinations of these factors can be especially powerful. What kind of reaction, for example, would emanate from a cynical person—who doesn't trust management, expects personal loss, and disagrees with a change? The person will probably actively resist the change or leave the organization. How about a highly dogmatic person who agrees with the change proposed by a trusted manager and believes that the change will benefit him or her personally?

PSYCHOLOGICAL OWNERSHIP AND ORGANIZATIONAL CHANGE

Additional insight into the conditions under which organizational members are likely to promote and resist organizational change can be had by looking at the dynamics of psychological ownership. As implied in our earlier discussion of psychological ownership (Chapter 5), from the time that we are small children, we have experiences of ownership for a variety of objects—"my blankie," "my ball," "my car," "my idea," and "my job." There are strong emotional, attitudinal, motivational, and behavioral effects that stem from this psychological state.

http://www.bus.sfu.ca/homes/kurt_d/kurt_d.pdf

Simon Fraser University management professor Kurt T. Dirks and his colleagues, Larry L. Cummings and Jon L. Pierce, have proposed a psychological theory of change. Their work provides insight into why we support or resist change and the conditions under which individuals both promote and resist organizational change.[13] Central to their theory is the strength of an individual's psychological ownership for the target of the change. The strength of an individual's psychological ownership for the target of change appears to influence their disposition toward change.

http://www.fed.org

In addition, psychological ownership will affect peoples' reactions to change, depending upon the type of change that is being initiated. Dirks and his colleagues categorize change three ways: (1) self-initiated versus imposed change, (2) evolutionary versus revolutionary change, and (3) additive versus subtractive change.

In the first categorization, change is self-initiated or imposed. There are times when we believe that some future state is more attractive than what currently exists, and as a result we personally initiate a move from the current condition toward that idealized state. Imposed change, on the other hand, is initiated by others and is something we must react to. In the second categorization, change is either evolutionary—gradual, incremental, and narrowly focused, *or* it is revolutionary—change that seeks to make quick and major alterations. Evolutionary change attempts to keep the core structure intact, while the target of change goes through slow development and growth. Quality management (Chapters 2 and 17), with its emphasis upon continuous improvement, exemplifies evolutionary change. Revolutionary change, on the other hand, is radical. It seeks to alter the basic structure of the target by tearing it down and rebuilding. The sudden mergers, takeovers, downsizings, and restructurings of the 1980s and 1990s exemplify revolutionary change. Finally, there is additive and subtractive change. Change may add to the organization or take some aspect of the organization's identity away. The introduction of flexible working hours to expand the number of options that an employee has for starting and ending their working day reflects an additive change, while the dropping of a course within your university is subtractive in nature. You can no doubt think of numerous other examples.

The different types of change have psychological implications for those exposed to the change. When change is directed toward some aspect of the organization (such as a program, work group, job assignment, office space) that we feel a strong sense of psychological ownership for, we will respond positively when the change is self-initiated, additive, and/or evolutionary in nature. Change under these conditions is likely to be accepted, actively supported, and satisfying.

Organizational efforts to bring about change to targets for which there is a strong sense of psychological ownership will be resisted when the change is imposed, subtractive, and/or revolutionary. This resistance to change will likely manifest itself through opposition, active resistance, a weakening of commitment, dissatisfaction, and withdrawal.

DEVELOPING SUPPORT FOR CHANGE

So, how can you as a manager develop support for an impending change?

Educate and Communicate It's simple—education and communication make a difference. People need to know—indeed they may have a right to know—*what* the change is, *when* it is to be introduced, *how* it will be introduced, *why* it is necessary, and *how* they will be affected.

Participate and Involve Education and communication *give* employees information. Participation and involvement, on the other hand, *ask* employees for information. There are two reasons for doing this: (1) to elicit information from members that might help improve the quality or effectiveness of a change, and (2) to increase the likelihood that employees will accept the change and become committed to its success.

© PICTURE PRESS/CORBIS

One way for management to develop support for change within an organization is to communicate with employees about the change. This requires that management inform employees about what the change is, when and how it will be introduced, and why it is necessary.

Task Support Organizations can help their members make a change more effective through tools, materials, and advice. An individual who lacks some of the skills required to operate a new computer system, for example, might be offered training. Providing support of this nature can enhance an employee's self-efficacy and thereby increase their work motivation and level of performance. The provision of appropriate support can make the difference between a failed and successful change effort.

Provide Emotional Support When change is major, emotional support is extremely important, and says "This organization cares about its members." It is natural for employees to be concerned about potential personal losses and to fear that they may be unable to work effectively under the change. Emotional support can come in the form of individual counseling or group discussions. In the majority of cases, however, emotional support comes primarily from one's immediate supervisor and co-workers.

Provide Incentives People often support or resist a change because they believe they will personally gain or lose something.[14] Management can emphasize the potential for personal gain by providing incentives when the change is implemented. People are more likely to support a change that benefits them personally and are more likely to resist a change that costs them something.

Manipulate and Co-opt Manipulation is the systematic control or distortion of information. Thus, the initiators of change provide information that makes a change appear positive, while information that might discourage support is withheld or distorted. Some managers believe that it is perfectly acceptable to provide only part of the information related to a change as long as the change information selectively provided is accurate. Co-optation is a special type of manipulation, which, on the surface, resembles participation. Instead of having a genuine interest in employee input, those initiating the change are merely trying to nurture support for their efforts. Thus, employees might be asked to get involved, creating the impression of participation, when in reality their ideas are neither wanted nor given serious consideration.

Coerce Often the most powerful and quickest technique for developing support, at least on a short-term basis, is coercion. The principle underlying the use of coercion is very simple: "Do this or else." For coercion to work, organizational members must believe that resistance to a change would result in punishment or the loss of something of value to them. Coercion can be effective, and sometimes it is necessary when change must be implemented quickly to avoid great loss.

Many of the techniques (the positive ones) are used extensively in organizational development efforts. Indeed, their use should be considered when implementing any organizational change. Table 18-1 summarizes each approach. In most situations, managers will want to choose an appropriate combination of these techniques to effectively manage their change efforts. Table 18-2 lists situations appropriate for each technique.[15]

THE SPECIAL ROLE OF ORGANIZATIONAL DEVELOPMENT

The techniques we've been discussing for managing change have been developed and refined by *organizational development specialists,* who apply these techniques to achieve planned and systematic organizational change.

organizational development (OD)
a process for diagnosing organizational problems by looking for incongruencies in environment, structures, processes, and people

What Is Organizational Development?

Michael Beer, from Harvard University, defines **organizational development (OD)** as "a process for diagnosing organizational problems by looking for incongruencies between environment, structures, processes, and people."[16] Although this definition sounds broad and loose, it can be argued that the openness of OD provides necessary breadth and flexibility.

TABLE 18-1 Advantages and Drawbacks of Change Techniques

Technique	Advantages	Drawbacks
Education and communication	After being convinced, members often assist with implementation.	Costs time and money.
Participation and involvement	Participants' input can be useful, and they are likely to be supportive when involved.	Heavy time costs; leads to poor change suggestions and disillusionment if ideas are not followed.
Facilitation	Enhances the successful implementation of change.	Costs time and money for support materials and training programs.
Emotional support	Relatively inexpensive, and a good way to help with personal adjustment problems.	Often done nonsystematically, resulting in time and cash outlays that may not remedy the problem.
Incentives	Can "head off" major resistance before it arises.	Can be expensive and can encourage resistance in hopes of gaining "compensation."
Manipulation and co-optation	Works fairly rapidly without substantial cost.	Is unethical and can destroy trust if workers find out they've been intentionally misled.
Coercion	Usually the fastest method, and suppresses resistance regardless of cause.	Decreases satisfaction, increases resentment, and makes other techniques less effective.

OD specialists have mined theories from psychology and organizational behavior to develop a series of actions that improve organizational effectiveness and/or the well-being of its members. OD practitioners refer to these actions as *interventions*. An OD specialist analyzes an organization's problems and needs, and plans an intervention, which can involve anything from individual or group counseling sessions to organizationwide structural changes.

Think of OD practitioners as "organizational doctors." What do good doctors do when they see patients? They talk—first to the patient to identify health

TABLE 18-2 Techniques for Developing Support/Reducing Resistance

Technique	Common Uses
Education and communication	When knowledge would alleviate fears due to inaccurate or sketchy information.
Participation and involvement	When change initiators need information from others to design change and when the probability of resistance is high.
Facilitation	When people lack the necessary skills or tools to be effective following change.
Emotional support	When people have personal concerns and anxiety about a change that supportive reassurance could alleviate.
Incentives	When key people will resist the change unless they benefit from it.
Manipulation and co-optation	When change is absolutely necessary and all other techniques would be ineffective or too costly.
Coercion	When change must occur quickly and the initiators have significantly more power than the resistors.

concerns. Then, employing the tools of the medical profession, they conduct a formal examination to assess the condition of the patient's body. Based on this information, they make their diagnosis and specify a treatment plan. Then they talk again, this time to explain to the patient what course of treatment should be undertaken. The patient's progress is assessed periodically and treatment is adjusted if necessary. If all goes as planned, the patient's health improves.

OD specialists—let's call them "Dr. O's"—do basically the same thing. Dr. O's talk to critical representatives of the organization to obtain details about organizational strengths and weaknesses. They then conduct a formal assessment, using such tools as surveys and interviews, to identify the affected components of the organization. Using this information, Dr. O's identify potential interventions that might remedy the problem or problems and discuss them with key organizational members. Appropriate interventions are then undertaken, and during this period, Dr. O's assess the organization's progress and fine-tune the interventions as necessary. As with medical doctors, Dr. O's sometimes succeed and sometimes fail, but the treatment of every organization, whether it leads to success or failure, enhances their ability to treat future "patients."

OD interventions can be as varied as the organizations in which they are implemented. Dr. D. D. Warrick of the University of Colorado at Colorado Springs has described some of the common features of OD interventions:[17]

1. The focus of change is on the system as a whole, and its interrelated parts. A whole system can be a whole organization, a department, or a work group, any of which can be targeted for OD as long as the changes will be supported by the larger organization or power structure.
2. The goal is to improve organizational health and effectiveness, with health being a means to effectiveness, and not an end in itself. Table 18-3 summarizes OD's view of healthy and unhealthy organizations.
3. OD is a long-range approach to change that emphasizes lasting rather than temporary change and seeks to change culture and norms by changing attitudes, knowledge, behavior, processes, and structures.
4. OD is a top-down strategy that recognizes that the commitment and involvement of top management, or lack thereof, significantly affect outcomes. Change begins at the top and is gradually applied downward through the organization.
5. OD is a collaborative strategy that involves those affected by the change and recognizes the importance of developing commitment to change.
6. OD is an approach that uses data to analyze and motivate change, and to solve problems, rather than making assumptions about what the real issues are. This is very important because forces driving change are often misperceived, unnoticed, and/or exaggerated. Validating these forces and the problems associated with them, with solid data, helps OD practitioners focus on what is real and not just imagined.
7. OD programs are guided by internal and/or external change agents. Change agents are specialists in managing organizational development and change. Their primary role is facilitator. The emphasis is on helping people plan and implement their own change.
8. OD is designed to develop a work climate where organizational members can accomplish meaningful objectives and healthy behavior is rewarded.
9. OD recognizes the need for planned follow-up to maintain and to evaluate the change effort. Monitoring plans ensures their implementation.

TABLE 18-3 Healthy and Unhealthy Organizations

Criteria	Healthy Characteristics	Unhealthy Characteristics
Organizational philosophies (explicit and implicit)	Strong employee-centered orientation that values, respects, and treats employees fairly regardless of position or status.	Employees not valued or treated with respect unless they hold special position or status.
	Strong customer-centered orientation that is shared throughout the organization.	Little interest shown in serving the customers.
	Long-term perspective that values both results and quality of work life.	Short-term perspective that pays little attention to quality of work life.
	Innovation and creativity encouraged and rewarded.	Innovation and creativity not encouraged nor rewarded.
Leadership	Top leader competent, respected, effective, people oriented; inspires people to action.	Top leader more interested in numbers than people; noninspirational or inspires unproductive behaviors.
	Top management functions as a team, has a big-picture perspective, and is skilled in teamwork and developing and accomplishing worthwhile goals and policies.	Top management does not function as a team, is ineffective, and multiplies its own problems throughout the organization.
Management	Managers get results in terms of both high performance and satisfaction.	Managers not results-oriented.
	High level of competence in management skills.	Lack of training and competence in management skills.
	Managers view management as a profession requiring continuous study and upgrading.	Managers do not view management as profession.
Human Resource management	Competent employees with positive attitudes recruited, trained, and retained.	Marginal employees with negative attitudes recruited and retained.
	Personnel policies and practices designed to help employees excel and develop quality of work life.	Human Resource policies antiquated, frustrate employee needs, result in underutilization of human resources.
	High performance, healthy behavior, growth, and collaboration encouraged and rewarded.	High performance, healthy behavior, growth, and collaboration not encouraged or rewarded.
Capital Resources	Strong financial planning and resources.	Marginal financial planning and inadequate financial resources.
	Excellent facilities and equipment.	Poor facilities and equipment.
	Technologically advanced.	Technologically behind.

http://www.dhutton.com/change

change agents individuals trained to facilitate organizational change

Who Practices OD?

Traditionally, organizational development was practiced primarily by consultants—referred to as **change agents.** These consultants tended to be trained in a behavioral science, such as psychology or sociology. (Today similar training is offered by many management programs in business schools.) More often than not, they were academics. Only a relatively small number of organizations had in-house OD specialists; however, some organizations have created OD depart-

Structure	Lean, flexible, nonbureaucratic, and results-oriented structure designed to achieve and reward high performance, healthy behavior, innovation, and entrepreneurship.	Strong bureaucracy or lack of structure results in low performance, unhealthy behavior, and lack of innovation.
	Clear and worthwhile goals, policies, and responsibilities.	Goals, policies, and responsibilities unclear and inspire little commitment.
	Minimal but effective controls for managing resources and performance.	Restrictive or ineffective controls.
	Excellent working conditions.	Poor facilities and equipment.
	Formal and informal structures reasonably congruent.	Formal and informal structures incongruent.
Processes	Communication open and straightforward.	Communication closed and guarded.
	Effective planning keeps organization vital.	Ineffective planning results in crisis management.
	Decision making is results-oriented, decentralized, and participative when appropriate.	Decision-making activities not results-oriented and tightly controlled by a few powerful members, or are delegated with little accountability.
	Problems and conflicts confronted openly and constructively.	Problems and conflicts approached through power, manipulation, or smoothing over.
	Meetings productive and evaluated for process as well as content issues.	Meetings unproductive with little regard given to process issues.
	Relationships between individuals and within and between groups supportive, productive, and developed by design.	Relationships characterized by lack of support and cooperation, conflict, and a self-serving attitude with development left to chance.
Growth and development	Continuous growth and development focused at an individual, group, intergroup, and whole-organization level.	Little interest or support demonstrated for growth and development.
	Managerial, technical, and personal development training encouraged and sponsored.	Minimal value placed on training and development.
Work climate	Work culture characterized by openness, trust, support, teamwork, fairness, results-orientation, and fun.	Work culture characterized by guarded behavior, lack of cooperation and teamwork, inconsistent treatment, and negative attitudes.
Performance	High productivity and work quality.	Low productivity and work quality.
	High employee satisfaction.	Low employee satisfaction.
	Success in terms of both goal attainment and quality of work life.	Minimal success in achieving goals and regression in quality of work life.

Source: D. D. Warrick. 1984. *Managing organization change and development.* Chicago: Science Research Associates. Reprinted with the permission of the author.

http://www.odnetwork.org

ments. For example, Minnesota Power created an OD department to move the organization to a more participative and open culture. Then, with the plan and commitment in place, each OD department member returned to their respective positions in the organization to assist with the implementation of the organizational change—a "within the ranks" (grass-roots) approach. *An Inside Look* gives another perspective on change agents.

AN INSIDE LOOK

Coaches as Agents of Change

In order to win, professional athletes must be in peak physical condition and must understand the rules of their game inside and out. However, most athletes could not reach their peak performance without someone motivating them to extend their capabilities and manage the stress that comes with competition. Enter the coach.

Some of the largest and best-known corporations—Kodak, AT&T, and IBM, to name a few—are taking cues from the sports world—they're hiring coaches to help their teams reach their full potential. Sometimes radical change is needed to shift direction and move toward a strategic plan for growth and innovation. Outside coaches jump-start the transformation process.

Because managers are often distracted by the everyday hustle and bustle of daily life and work crises, coaches help managers refocus and concentrate on the big picture. Many coaches work with individual managers to help them clarify organizational and personal goals and values and to serve as a sounding board. The result? Managers improve performance and make more objective and effective decisions. For many managers, intensive work with coaches prevents burnout and energizes them to motivate others in their organization to work for change.

Besides working with individual managers, coaches also work with groups. AT&T's Growth Markets sales organization brought in an outside coach to help transform their organization into a unit more responsive to expansion and outside forces. The coach inspired the team to increase their plan for revenue growth to an ambitious 16 percent, twice as much as their previous year's plan. After a few days of intensive training and some follow-up coaching, the organization ultimately reached their challenging goal. For AT&T, the cost was well worth it. The coach's leadership helped the group shift into a high-performance, flexible, and cooperative team that routinely exceeds past sales.

Coaches remind managers of the best ways to lead. Communication and listening skills are key, as are motivation techniques. In today's project team environment, coaches are especially useful as project coordinators. They teach team leaders better ways to communicate with each other and with their own teams and help leaders stay focused.

In today's fast-paced and ever-changing business world, coaches help people keep up and keep pace.

Source: Adapted from B. Morris. 2000. So you're a player, do you need a coach? *Fortune* 141(4): 144.

While OD specialists still conduct the majority of this work, the biggest growth since the 1980s has occurred among managers. Only recently have OD concepts, values, and methods been featured in the practitioner-oriented management literature. Now we commonly see managers driving OD activities that lead to innovative plant designs, participative management, collaborative union-management activities, and employee task forces.[18]

Common OD Activities

Because OD is a flexible, adaptive process, it is difficult to create a master list of tools. Medical doctors don't use every available tool on each patient. Neither do Dr. O's. But we can give you an overview of the process. First, let's look at some specific OD techniques (Table 18-4), which reflect the basic values and assumptions inherent in the OD process.[19]

For example, Dr. O's believe that people in organizations strive to satisfy high-level needs, such as personal growth and development. They believe that organizational members value work that is experienced as meaningful. They also believe that workers want to contribute to organizational effectiveness and

TABLE 18-4 Frequently Used OD Techniques

Technique	Examples
Organizational diagnoses	Interviews, surveys, group meetings
Team building	Improvement of existing groups; creation of teams for problem solving
Survey feedback	Provision of survey results to members; interpretation of results by members
Education	Classroom training for "sensitivity" skills and interpersonal skills
Intergroup activities	Communication development; conflict reduction
Third-party peace making	Negotiation, mediation by "outsider" for interperson and intergroup conflict
Technostructural/sociotechnical activities	Joint examination of technology, structure, and people systems
Process consultation	Observation of groups in action with immediate feedback on processes observed
Life/career planning	Future oriented—development of personal goals and acquisition of skills to help individuals fit into the organization and the organization match individual needs
Coaching	Nonevaluative feedback to individuals describing how others see them
Planning and goal setting	Training of individuals to improve Human Resource planning and goal-setting effectiveness; emphasis on individual's place in the overall organization

that they are capable of doing so. OD values stress that group relationships have a major impact on the satisfaction and productivity of individual organizational members and that groups are key to organizational success. Finally, they assume that organizational design, structure, policies, and practices influence the attitudes and behaviors of members and that management must therefore be prepared to change these factors to benefit both the organization and its members.

How Effective Is OD?

How well does organizational development actually work? It is hard to say. Most OD activities need to remain open to change while under way in order to adapt to organizational and individual complexities. The problem is that such flexibility makes it very difficult to judge the success of an intervention. Many OD practitioners choose not to collect evidence that could be used to assess their effectiveness. The literature contains many case studies and anecdotal reports on apparently successful OD interventions.[20]

A recent review of OD research in the 1990s took a different approach to the issue of OD effectiveness.[21] Rather than assemble a score card of "wins" and "losses," these authors focused on forces that caused organizations to seek change, on the OD interventions and processes used to implement them, and on the criteria by which OD efforts have been and should be evaluated. Two conclusions stand out. First, many, if not most, OD efforts that have any effect have multiple effects, and not always positive ones. Thus, improving customer service in one instance might also inadvertently reduce employee job satisfaction. Such mixed effects make it difficult to draw conclusions about the programs' overall effectiveness. Therefore, looking at the big-picture results is important. Second, OD results must be looked at over time. An OD intervention effective after one year might be ineffective in five years—members might even regard it as a "swindle."[22] Thus, to improve their craft, OD practitioners must not only focus on the process, but also the criteria used for evaluation, and the timing of their measurement.

Many OD interventions have produced moderate to substantial positive effects. Others have been conducted less well and have damaged organizations and their members. Finally, the OD interventions that prove most effective tend to follow a systematic approach, such as that presented in the next section, and are begun without prejudice about the nature of needed organizational change.

PLANNING AND MANAGING THE CHANGE PROCESS

To this point, the chapter has discussed the reasons for organizational change, the most common types of change, and the types of and reasons for the reactions to change. The chapter has also explored some techniques for reducing resistance to change and developing support. Now we provide an overview of a systematic procedure for the planning and management of organization change. We use the four-stage process shown in Figure 18-2.

http://www.change-management.net/index.html

The change process begins with the identification of a needed change. This is followed by planning for the implementation, and the implementation of the change. After implementation comes the assessment of the success of the change effort. It is at this stage that the need for alterations is identified. The key to effective management of change is the use of a systematic and orderly change process.

Stage 1: Identify

In the first stage of change, the organization, management, and/or employees recognize that they need to change, and figure out how they should change. Once a need for change has been identified, the nature of the necessary change(s) should be clarified. Sometimes the warning flags that alerted everyone only give a general idea of the needed change; other times they reveal the specific types of change needed.

During stage 1, it is important to specify—at least in a general sense—the objectives of a proposed change and the criteria that will be used to determine whether these objectives will be met. At times the change can be completely specified here. At other times, however, final planning carries over to stage 2. This might be the case, for example, when significant employee input is needed to aid in the design of the change.

Stage 2: Plan the Implementation

The second stage of the change process includes a diagnosis of the situation (context) in which the change is likely to occur, the selection of a general strategy for managing the change, and the choice of specific techniques to be used to develop support for and reduce resistance to the change. The situational

FIGURE 18-2 Managing Change

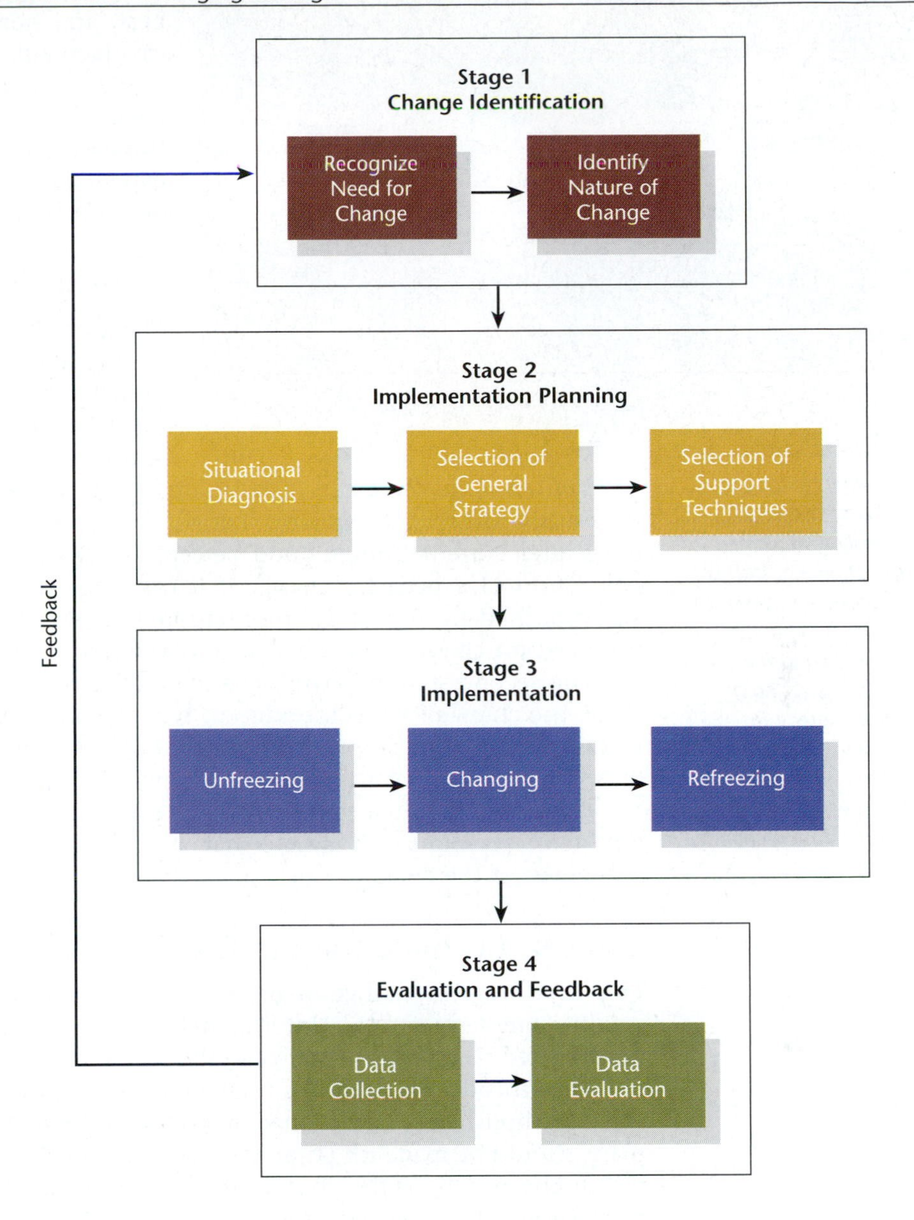

diagnosis involves the collection of a broad range of information. It is necessary, for example, to identify where the change will be implemented and which organization members will potentially be influenced by the change. It is also appropriate to identify who possesses the information needed to effectively design the change. At this point, the change agent may need to overcome **organizational silence**—that state where potentially important information is not passed along to those who need to know it and who have the authority to act on it.[23] Equally important is the identification of individuals whose support for the change is pivotal to its success. Finally, a risk and cost/benefit assessment should be conducted.

organizational silence when potentially important organizational information is not passed along to those who need to know it and who have the authority to act on it

Next, a change strategy is selected. Decisions must be made concerning how quickly the change will be implemented, when the planned change should

© LAYNE KENNEDY/CORBIS

One step in managing the change process effectively is implementation planning. In this step, managers design a blueprint for change that includes diagnosing the situation, selecting a general strategy for managing the change, and choosing specific techniques for overcoming resistance to the change.

be revealed to the organization's members, and how much participation and involvement there should be in the design and implementation of the change. Finally, a decision should be made about the amount of resources that should be expended to minimize resistance and develop support for the change effort.

Stage 3: Implement

The time has come for action. In psychologist Kurt Lewin's widely accepted model for implementing change,[24] he identifies three steps—unfreeze, change, and refreeze.

Unfreezing involves a systematic upsetting of the equilibrium between the forces driving and discouraging change. To unfreeze a system, the change agent must alter current thinking and perception. It may be necessary to *create* the perception of a need for change if it does not currently exist. This might be accomplished by providing information that will help employees understand the need for change and the change's potential for improvement.[25]

The second step in Lewin's change model is referred to as *changing*. At this stage, the change itself is introduced. The new machine is put in place, the new work procedures are adopted, and so forth. Unfreezing must occur first, or members won't be ready for the change and will be more likely to resist it.

Refreezing, the final step, involves stabilizing the situation and encouraging long-term acceptance. It is here that people must experience the positive consequences of the change.

Stage 4: Evaluate the Results and Seek Feedback

This final stage in change management is extremely important for the organization's long-term success. Unfortunately, it is also often overlooked. Data should be collected to assess whether objectives were achieved.

Next this data needs to be evaluated. Here, managers should compare what was accomplished by the change to what was desired. When discrepancies exist, plans should be made for potential alterations of the change or the processes by which the results of the change are managed. Based on this evaluation, feedback should be provided and, if necessary, the change process should begin again from stage 1. Careful adherence to systematic change management greatly increases your chances of being effective and succeeding in the global economy.

THE LEARNING ORGANIZATION

http://www.stanford.edu/group/SLOW/

Imagine an organization where members embrace change as a fact of life, where change is perceived as an opportunity, not as a threat. The prevailing attitude might be "if it isn't broken, break it!" Finally, employees share their knowledge and are willing to do whatever needs to be done. This is an organization with the capacity to continuously adapt and change as needed.

learning organization an organization that purposefully designs and constructs its structure, culture, and strategies with the capacity to learn so that it can continuously adapt and change as needed

http://www.solonline.org

We call this the **learning organization**; MIT management professor Peter Senge popularized this concept in his 1990 book *The Fifth Discipline.*[26] His ideas and prescriptions have become a major trend. Indeed, the Society for Organizational Learning was established worldwide for different organizations (and yes, even competitors) to collaborate, learn, and change by conducting joint research and sharing their best practices. Table 18-5 describes the purpose and principles that guide this influential group.

TABLE 18-5 The Society for Organizational Learning

Purposes and Principles

Purpose of SoL

SoL is a global learning community dedicated to building knowledge about fundamental institutional change. We aim to help build organizations worthy of people's fullest commitment, and are committed to any institution and individual that is committed to SoL's purpose and principles. To meet this goal, we discover, integrate, and implement theories and practices for the interdependent development of people and their institutions.

Guiding Principles of SoL

- *Drive to Learn*—All human beings are born with an innate, lifelong desire and ability to learn, which should be enhanced by all organizations.
- *Learning Is Social*—People learn best from and with one another, and participation in learning communities is vital to their effectiveness, well-being and happiness in any work setting.
- *Learning Communities*—The capacities and accomplishments of organizations are inseparable from, and dependent on, the capacities of the learning communities that they foster.
- *Aligning with Nature*—It is essential that organizations evolve to be in greater harmony with human nature and with the natural world.
- *Core Learning Capabilities*—Organizations must develop individual and collective capabilities to understand complex, interdependent issues; engage in reflective, generative conversation; and nurture personal and shared aspirations.
- *Cross-Organizational Collaboration*—Learning communities that connect multiple organizations can significantly enhance the capacity for profound individual and organizational change.

Ideals of the SoL Community

- *Subsidiarity*—Make no decision and perform no function at a higher or more central level than can be accomplished at a more local level.
- *Inclusiveness*—Conduct all deliberations and make all decisions by bodies and methods that reasonably represent all relevant and affected parties.
- *Shared Responsibility*—Advance the purpose in accordance with these principles in ways that enhance the capacity of the community as a whole, as well as that of each member.
- *Openness*—Transcend institutional and intellectual boundaries and roles that limit or diminish learning.
- *Adaptive Governance*—Continually conceive, implement, and practice governance concepts and processes that encourage adaptability, diversity, flexibility, and innovation.
- *Intellectual Output*—Use research generated by the community in ways that most benefit society.
- *Acknowledgment*—Openly and fairly acknowledge intellectual contributions to concepts, theories, and practices, both from within and from outside the community.
- *Participation & Quality*—Contribute to and/or participate in research, capacity building, and practice, striving for the highest standards of quality.

Much has been written on the learning organization in the past 10 years.[27] According to Senge, a learning organization has employees who (1) share a common vision; (2) discard their old ways of thinking and doing and embrace new ones; (3) have a systems view of the organization (think outside their work units); (4) openly communicate without fear of criticism or punishment; and (5) sublimate their self-interests and that of their work units to achieve the organization's vision. Another book, *The Learning Company,* elaborates on what learning organizations look like, and how they transform.[28]

A true learning organization embraces changes, is free from organizational politics, possesses completely open communications, is flexible and adaptive, and encourages learning and sharing of knowledge. This is, of course, the ideal, probably not attainable as there is no true and complete learning organization. Yet it is a worthy goal for all of those organizations operating in a turbulent, highly uncertain, and competitive task environment. Like other concepts we've examined in this book, becoming a learning organization serves as a useful and concrete objective for organization managers and their members to think about and strive for in their day-to-day activities. When organizational members strive for the very best every day, they and their organizations gradually but eventually end up where they wanted to be all along.

MANAGING ORGANIZATIONAL CHANGE AND DEVELOPMENT IN REVIEW

Stability and change are both present in organizations; the challenge facing those who manage organizational behavior is to maintain the delicate balance between these two states with appropriate organizational structures, processes, and systems.[29] Change is a fact of life, it will continue to occur, and it *must* occur to maintain organizational effectiveness. Change is driven by technology, employee needs and values, society, business and economic conditions, and by the organization itself.

Change is reactive when the forces driving it are so strong that it becomes *necessary* to change. Change is proactive when an organization assesses its status and concludes that change is *desirable.* Innovation is a special type of change that occurs when an organization is one of the first users of an idea.

A wide range of organizational change is possible. Some changes involve new technologies, others primarily structure and procedures. Still other changes are people oriented. The most effective changes—technostructural or sociotechnical—often combine these three types of change.

Reactions to change vary dramatically. Change can be actively resisted, actively supported, or anything in between. People base their reactions on whether they expect to personally gain or lose something of value because of the change. Their reactions are also shaped by their understanding of the change, whether they trust its initiators, and whether they agree with the change. People's personal characteristics and values shape their reactions. Finally, psychological ownership for the target of change, coupled with the type of change, influences support and resistance.

Developing support for a change and reducing resistance is very important. To that end, effective change agents educate and communicate, encourage participation and involvement, facilitate, and provide emotional support and incentives. Although sometimes necessary in emergencies, manipulating, coopting, and coercing should usually be avoided.

Organizational development is an evolving area of change management that shows much promise for the future. OD systematically plans and manages the change process. A typical OD intervention includes four stages: identification, planning for implementation, the actual implementation, and evaluation and fine-tuning.

A learning organization is one in which all members share a vision and will do what it takes to achieve that shared vision—hopefully in an ethical and socially acceptable way. A true learning organization embraces changes, is free from organizational politics, openly communicates, is flexible and adaptive, and encourages the learning and sharing of knowledge.

In many ways, this chapter is the most important one in this text. If your ideas are worth implementing, you must implement them well or they will not realize their potential. Good ideas only work well when they are managed effectively. One of the major factors that distinguishes strong managers from merely adequate ones is how well they manage change and its effects.

A FINAL LOOK

The Carruthers family and the OD consultant eventually decide that decreasing productivity is the major reason for Premier Plastics' plummeting profits. They need new perspectives on efficiency. What better source for ideas than our work force? An employee incentive program is instituted that gives $100 cash bonuses for productive ideas. Employees whose ideas are used receive $1,000. Quality circles are formed to find solutions to ongoing problems.

In the past, family leaders had not done much formal strategic planning. However, their Dr. O shows them why they need long-range planning and goal setting, and a strategy team is formed that includes both family leaders and team leaders from the plant's new action teams.

After the first year, results are nothing short of astounding—75 percent of the employees submit improvement ideas! New processes are instituted as a result of both employee ideas and the quality circles, and the entire plant is energized by the "bull market" in innovation. Premier Plastics is well on its way to enjoying the positive results of embracing change.

KEY TERMS

change agents, 640
innovation, 631
learning organization, 647
organizational change, 628
organizational development (OD), 637
organizational inertia, 632
organizational silence, 645
proactive change, 630
reactive change, 630
sociotechnical changes, 632
technostructural changes, 632

ISSUES FOR REVIEW AND DISCUSSION

1. Describe how the five forces drive organizational change.
2. Why should we differentiate between planned (proactive) and reactive change?
3. Your college changes to a grading system where all courses are graded pass/fail. Explain why you would expect a variety of student reactions using the underlying reasons discussed in this chapter.
4. What role do feelings of psychological ownership for the target of change play in both the promotion and resistance to change?
5. Briefly describe which techniques for developing support for change might be useful for organizations changing from traditional assembly-line production to automation.
6. Prepare a brief presentation explaining why OD should be required training for all managers.
7. Prepare a brief presentation explaining why OD should not be required training for all managers.
8. Summarize the process for planning and managing change systematically, and note why each stage is necessary.
9. Why would a traditional organization want to become a learning organization? Are there disadvantages to becoming a learning organization?

EXERCISES

DO YOU WORK FOR A LEARNING ORGANIZATION?

Directions: Indicate for each of the following statements whether it is mostly true or mostly false in relation to your current or most recent place of work. Indicate a question mark when the statement is either not applicable or you are not in a position to judge.

	Mostly true	?	Mostly false
1. Company employees often visit other locations or departments to share new information or skills they have learned.	____	____	____
2. Our company frequently repeats mistakes.	____	____	____
3. We get most of our market share by competing on price.	____	____	____
4. Loads of people in our organization are aware of and believe in our vision.	____	____	____
5. Top management assumes that the vast majority of employees are experts at what they do.	____	____	____
6. Almost all of our learning takes place individually rather than in groups or teams.	____	____	____
7. In our company, after you have mastered your job you do not have to bother with additional learning such as training programs or self-study.	____	____	____
8. Our firm shies away from inviting outsiders into our company to discuss our business because few outsiders could understand our uniqueness.	____	____	____
9. If it weren't for a few key individuals in our company, we would be in big trouble.	____	____	____
10. Our new product launches go smoothly and quickly.	____	____	____
11. Our company creates a lot of opportunities for employees to get together and share information, such as conferences and meetings.	____	____	____
12. We are effective at pricing the service we provide to customers.	____	____	____
13. Very few of our employees have any idea about company sales and profits.	____	____	____
14. I often hear employees asking questions about why the company has taken certain major actions.	____	____	____

15. The company maintains a current database about the knowledge and skills of almost all our employees. ____ ____ ____
16. Having specialized knowledge brings you some status in our company. ____ ____ ____
17. It would be stretching the truth to say that many of our employees are passionate about what our organization is attempting to accomplish. ____ ____ ____
18. Our performance appraisal system makes a big contribution to helping employees learn and improve. ____ ____ ____
19. Following established rules and procedures is important in our company, so creativity and imagination are not encouraged. ____ ____ ____
20. Most of our employees believe that if you do your own job well, you don't have to worry about what goes on in the rest of the organization. ____ ____ ____
21. We get loads of useful new ideas from our customers. ____ ____ ____
22. I have frequently heard our managers talk about how what goes on in the outside world has an impact on our company. ____ ____ ____
23. We treat customer suggestions with a good deal of skepticism. ____ ____ ____
24. During breaks, you sometimes hear employees discussing the meaning and implication of the work they are doing. ____ ____ ____
25. Employees at every level tend to rely on facts when making important decisions. ____ ____ ____
26. If a process or procedure works well in our company, we are hesitant to experiment with other approaches to a problem. ____ ____ ____
27. Our company treats mistakes as valuable learning experiences about what not to do in the future. ____ ____ ____
28. Our company rarely copies ideas from the successful practices of other companies. ____ ____ ____
29. Each time we face a significant problem, our company seems to start all over to find a solution. ____ ____ ____
30. It's a waste of time to be reading about a learning organization, when my real interest is in learning how to prevent problems. ____ ____ ____

Total score: ____

Scoring and Interpretation:

A. Record the number of Mostly true answers you gave to the following questions: 1, 4, 5, 10, 11, 12, 14, 15, 16, 18, 21, 22, 24, 25, 27.

B. Record the number of Mostly false answers you gave to the following questions: 2, 3, 6, 7, 8, 9, 13, 17, 19, 20, 23, 26, 28, 29, 30.

C. Add the numbers for A and B.

D. Add half of your ? responses to A, and half to B.

25 or higher: You are most likely a member of a learning organization. This tendency is so pronounced that it should contribute heavily to your company's success.

13–24: Your company has an average tendency toward being a learning organization, suggesting an average degree of success in profiting from mistakes and changing in response to a changing environment.

0–12: Your firm is definitely not a learning organization.

Source: A. J. DuBrin. 1999. *Looking around corners: The art of problem prevention.* Madison, WI: CWL Publishing Enterprises, 181–183. Used with permission of the publisher.

INFOTRAC

INFOTRAC COLLEGE EDITION

The articles listed below are a sampling of those available through InfoTrac College Edition. You can search for them either by title or by the author's name.

Articles

1. Making changes the right way. (Workforce Extra) (organizational changes) Randa A. Wilbur. *Workforce* March 1999 v78 i3 pE12(2) Bus.Coll.: 115Q2779.
2. Time for a change. (speeches on change management by Gordon Bethune and Mary Kay Ash) (Transcript) *Workforce* Sept 2000 v79 i9 p100
3. The roller coaster of downsizing. (managing a downsized company) Dean McMann. CMA *Management* Oct 1999 v73 i8 p42(3)
4. Navigating through organizational change. (Brief Article) Denis St-Amour. CMA *Management* June 2000 v74 i5 p16
5. The Emerging Dynamics of Change: Resistance, Readiness, and Momentum. Karen J. Jansen. *Human Resource Planning* June 2000 v23 i2 p53

Questions

For Article 5:

After reading "The Emerging Dynamics of Change: Resistance, Readiness, Momentum," think of changes in work situations you have experienced. In group discussion, identify reasons the employees had for resisting the changes. Explain how the organization dealt with this resistance. What were the outcomes?

For Other Articles:

Many articles on this list deal with the impact of organizational change on employees' lives. From the group's reading of these articles, discuss the strategies that organizations can use to help employees deal with the stresses brought about by change. Also discuss the strategies employees can use to deal with such stress.

WEB EXERCISE

In the past couple of decades, organizations have undergone major changes in an effort to increase their effectiveness and gain a competitive advantage. Locate the website of an organization that is making major organizational change. What type of change is being made, what obstacles and successes has the organization encountered?

CASE
Guarantee Corporation of America

Founded in Denver, Colorado, in 1958, the Guarantee Corporation of America (GCA) develops and markets a single product—mortgage insurance, which protects lenders in case of borrower default. Lenders' willingness to accept 5 percent down has greatly increased the number of mortgages issued, and their desire to reduce risk on such loans has made mortgage insurance extremely attractive. Today most lenders require mortgage insurance when down payments are less than 20 percent of the home's purchase price. The catch for borrowers? They pay for mortgage insurance. GCA has done quite well, competing effectively in the expanding market created by population growth and the desire of baby boomers to buy homes. In fact, GCA succeeded so well that a large financial corporation bought the company in 1975 and continued to operate it as GCA, a wholely owned subsidiary.

GCA maintains its home offices in Denver, but about half its 250 employees are spread across the country so they can better sell and service policies. Administrative (filing, reporting, clerical, and secretarial) services are performed by a centralized office administration department in Denver. The manager of this department, Mary-Jo Kovach, joined GCA in 1992 as an accountant and was promoted to management in 1995.

In a June 1996 employee attitude survey, the twenty members of the office administration department, as a group, scored as follows: satisfaction with physical work conditions, pay, promotional opportunities, and the work itself—a little above company averages; satisfaction with co-workers and supervision—far above company averages; and satisfaction with amount of work and company policies and practices—noticeably below company averages. Group cohesion was the highest of any department in the company.

Mary-Jo is proud of her department and her work. She feels her group is performing well, especially in light of the fact that conditions are considerably less than ideal. Her comments to a friend in January 1997 show her rising concern over the situation:

When I accepted this promotion, I didn't realize what I was getting myself into. My department is understaffed and constantly subjected to conflicting demands from marketing and policy services. My boss tells me to give equal treatment to both departments, but each acts as though the other doesn't exist. Worse, both act as if we do nothing but wait for them to drop work in our laps. Expectations for turnaround time on correspondence, major reports, and other information processing are totally unrealistic. I do everything I can to protect the members of my department from unreasonable demands, even though this sometimes makes us appear unresponsive to the needs of the people we are here to serve. Some days the stress gets to me so much that my stomach is just tied up in knots. Given the circumstances, we are doing an exemplary job, but nobody appreciates this.

After Carolyn Larson becomes GCA's executive vice president in April 1997, she holds a series of group meetings with each department to assess the "state of the company." She hears many favorable comments about the quality of the GCA product, the superb sales force, and the appropriateness of GCA's strategic and operational plans. She also hears the following from Bob Ley, Vice President of Marketing:

Our office administration department is a joke. I can't tell you how many potential sales we have lost because they failed to get our proposals out on time. Every time I send work over, I tell them it is a top priority but they seem to treat every piece of work as though it's just another meaningless task. What really irritates me is when they do the unimportant work and leave the important stuff undone. I don't get it—what's wrong with them?

Dave Womble, Vice President of Policy Services, adds:

I hate to be blunt but Mary-Jo has got to go. Her department doesn't have to sell policies, and they don't have to service them. All they have to do is keep track of them, and they can't even do that. What's needed for that department is a manager who is not afraid to manage employees. Mary-Jo spends too much time protecting her underlings and not enough time demanding work out of them.

Carolyn seeks Mary-Jo's input on Bob and Dave's comments:

I can understand how Bob and Dave would feel that way. To tell you the truth, I don't think we are meeting their needs well, but they do little to help. Telling me everything is a top priority doesn't help me plan. We are understaffed, underrespected, and I must admit, poorly organized. I would like to turn the department around, and I think I could if I could get some help and support to do so.

Based on this and other input, Carolyn decides Mary-Jo should get a chance to turn her department around. Specifically, she wants these results from Mary-Jo within two months:

1. A rank-ordered list of problems her department encounters in trying to meet the needs of the company
2. A rank-ordered list of internal problems
3. Criteria for evaluating the effectiveness of the department
4. A strategic plan for making the department effective
5. An implementation plan
6. An assessment procedure of the results

The next morning, Carolyn finds Mary-Jo's office empty of all personal effects and the following note:

Dear Ms. Larson:

I wish you the best of luck in managing the operations of the GCA. I have been managing the office administration department as effectively as humanly possible, given the unreasonable demands placed on us and the lack of adequate top managerial support. What you have asked me to do in two months—in addition to my current overwhelming responsibilities—is exactly what you should have done to help my department succeed. Asking me to do your work for you is of little help. It is with deepest regret that I resign my position with GCA, effective immediately.

Sincerely,

Mary-Jo Kovach

Mary-Jo Kovach

Questions:

1. What would you have done if you were Mary-Jo?
2. Did Carolyn do the right thing? What could she have done differently?
3. Using the model for planning and managing change and any other resources you think are necessary, describe how the six items presented to Mary-Jo by Carolyn could be addressed.
4. Who from GCA should be involved in addressing the six items?

Source: Provided by R. B. Dunham of the University of Wisconsin, Professor of Management and Organizational Behavior, 2001.

VIDEO COHESION CASE FOR PART V: EPILOGUE

Horizons: Standing at the Crossroads

Horizons is at an important crossroads in its corporate history. When the "Big House" is finally ready to move into, the company will be occupying a world-class facility for the first time. The company is also producing its first full-length motion picture, and it is on the leading edge of exciting new DVD technology. In addition, the quality of its projects seems to be moving up. Its partnership with Brighter Child Interactive to produce the first educational video featuring Garfield is a good example. If successful, these initiatives will lead to more opportunities and more high-quality strategic partnerships, and Horizons has the potential to literally take off.

But can the company pull it off? Does the company have the CEO, the management talent, the organizational structure, and enough depth at key positions to ride its positive momentum up the growth curve? And, more important, does it want to? It is a private company and does not have a board of directors and stockholders pushing management to increase its stock price through growth. In contrast, what it does have is a conscientious, even-tempered CEO who can basically do what he wants. And it also has a management team and a group of employees that seem to genuinely care about the company and the people who work there. As a result, there is a tension confronting Horizons that will not be easy to resolve. If it enters a period of rapid growth, it risks losing the family-oriented culture that its employees adore. If it chooses not to grow, it limits itself in terms of the opportunities that it provides its employees and the financial rewards that result. If it tries to have both a family-oriented culture and rapid growth, then the challenges will be compelling.

In evaluating the company's choices, one would be hard pressed to bet against Don Lee and his management team. They will probably get it right. Despite their lack of formality and structure, they seem to be a well-oiled machine. Yet the future is unknown, and the choices are difficult. What would you tell Don Lee if he asked you for your advice?

Glossary

ability: the knowledge, skills, and receptiveness to learning that an individual brings to a task or job

absenteeism: occurs when an employee does not report to work when scheduled

acceptance view of authority: the belief that authority finds its origin in subordinates' acceptance of directives and thus flows from the subordinates upward to the manager

action statements: the means by which an organization moves forward to attain its goals

administrative plans: integrate institutional-level plans with operating plans as well as integrating all the operating plans

administrative-level need: the organizational need to integrate the institutional level with the technical core and the diverse work systems within the technical core

affective commitment: an emotional attachment to the organization and its mission; an employee's emotional attachment to, identification with, and involvement in the organization

affective component: of an attitude consists of the feelings a person has toward an attitude object

association: occurs when a person transfers parts or all of an attitude about an old object to a new attitude object

attitude: an individual's predisposition to think, feel, perceive, and behave in certain ways toward a particular tangible or intangible phenomenon

attribution theory: explains how people assign responsibility and the cognitive processes by which they interpret the causes of their own behavior and the behavior of other people

authority: legitimate power—the "right" to decide and act on behalf of the organization

avoidable voluntary turnover: occurs when an employee elects to leave the organization and the employer could have prevented it by improving the employee's work conditions

avoidance learning: occurs when people learn to behave in a certain way to avoid encountering an undesired or unpleasant consequence

behavioral accounting: treats attitudinal measures as indicators of subsequent employee behavior, which in turn have economic implications for organizations that can be assessed using cost-accounting procedures

behavioral school: management thought and practice that views the organization from a social and psychological perspective

behavioral science movement: a movement that stressed the need to conduct systematic and controlled field and laboratory studies of workers and their motivation, attitudes, and behavior

behavioral shaping: learning a complex behavior through successive approximations of the desired behavior

behavioral tendency component: of an attitude is the way an individual is inclined to behave toward an attitude object

behaviorally anchored rating scales (BARS): use a scale for each relevant dimension of performance, but each scale has explicit behavioral anchors

"Big Five" personality theory: the view that all personality traits can be distilled into five big ones: extroversion, adjustment, agreeableness, conscientiousness, and inquisitiveness

boundary roles: those positions in organizations that link the organization with its external environment

boundary spanners: individuals whose job it is to span the organization's boundaries and integrate the organization with its external environment

boundary-spanning process: the means by which managers link the organization with its external environment.

bounded rationality: the tendency of decision makers to behave rationally within the limits of their information-processing capabilities and within the context of their attitudes and emotions

brainstorming: encourages the sharing of ideas in a setting free of the interruptions and risks that accompany immediate evaluation and discussion

bureaucratic organization: a highly structured and formally designed organization

centralization: when formal authority is concentrated at the top of the organizational hierarchy

change: the variety that causes a stimulus to be selected for perceptual processing

change agents: individuals trained to facilitate organizational change

charisma: a special personal magnetic charm or appeal that arouses loyalty and enthusiasm in a leader-follower relationship

charismatic leader: person who possesses legitimate power that arises from "exceptional sanctity, heroism, or exemplary character"

classical authority theory: the belief that authority finds its origin and flows from the top of the organization down the hierarchy

classical school: management thought and practice that emerged during the late 1800s and early 1900s and emphasized: control-oriented managers, the mechanistic organization, and a model of the employee as rational and economically motivated

closed system: an organization that is "shut-off" to its external environment and one in which managers look internally for ideas on productivity and efficiency improvements

closure: the tendency to organize perceptual stimuli so that, together, they form a complete message

code of ethics: an organizationally created code used to encourage ethical behavior by all organizational members

cognitive component: of an attitude is what we know, or think we know, about the attitude object

cognitive dissonance: an unpleasant psychological state that occurs when a person possesses conflicting thoughts about an attitude object

cohesiveness: the degree to which group members accept the goals of the group, internalize its norms, and work to meet its task- and maintenance-oriented needs

collective efficacy: the degree to which group members believe that the group has the capacity to achieve its performance objectives

communication: the process of transferring information from one person or group to another

comparative method: of performance appraisal requires supervisors to compare the performance of each worker to the performance of all co-workers

compressed workweek: a work scheduling arrangement that attempts to compress the traditional workweek into fewer days and/or fewer hours per week

compromise decision-making approach: reliance on a negotiated decision from representatives of competing interest groups

computational decision-making approach: reliance on an expert to guide the decision-making process

conceptual skills: the ability to examine, diagnose, understand, and evaluate complex concepts at an abstract level of analysis; to reason, store, and retrieve information

concurrent controls: controls intended to prevent deviation from a planned course of action while work is in progress

conflict: a process that begins when one party perceives that another party has frustrated, or is about to frustrate, one or more of their objectives

conscious information processing: involves consciously questioning the accuracy of what you perceive

consideration: a "relationship-oriented" leader behavior that is supportive, friendly, and focused on personal needs and interpersonal relationships

content motivation theories: focus on what motivates people

contingency perspective: the belief that the techniques appropriate for a manager to use depend on the specific situation

contingency plans: plans that deal with alternative courses of action

contingency theory of leadership: a theory advanced by Dr. Fred E. Fiedler that suggests that different leadership styles are effective as a function of the favorableness of the leadership situation least preferred

continuance commitment: attachment to an organization that is based on the costs an employee associates with leaving the organization

contrast: the difference between one stimulus and surrounding stimuli that makes that stimulus more likely to be selected for perceptual processing

controlling: monitoring the behavior of organizational members and the effectiveness of the organization itself to determine whether organizational goals are being achieved, and taking corrective action if necessary

coordinating: the linking of two or more organizational members and/or work units so that they function well together

covenantal relationships: exist between employees and employers when there is a state of mutual commitment and trust, and shared values

cross-functional team: a team with members from different functional areas of the organization

culture: the way in which a society as a whole perceives the world and how it should operate

custom solution: a solution to decision occasions (problems) that is specifically developed for the situation at hand

customer/client departmentalization: the grouping of organizational activities by different clients and client needs

cybernetic control: self-regulating control procedures

decentralization: formal authority is diffused throughout an organization, and specific authority for decision making is lodged at the level where that decision gets executed

decision: judgment that directly affects a course of action

decision making: the process of identifying a set of feasible alternatives and from these, choosing a course of action

decisional (strategy-making) role: the organizational role that involves serving as entrepreneur, disturbance handler, resource allocator, and negotiator for an organization

delegation: transferring formal authority from one position to another in an organization

Delphi technique: brings information and the judgments of people together without physically assembling the contributors

Deming cycle: a planning model directed toward attaining continuous improvement by integrating organizational learning into the planning process (plan, do, check, act)

departmentalization: the process of grouping jobs/teams into organizational units and those units into larger units

designated leader: the person placed in the leadership position by forces outside the group

deviant behavior: voluntary behavior that violates significant organizational norms and in doing so threatens the well-being of an organization, its members, or both

diffusion of responsibility: a group dynamic in which individuals fail to act because they believe or expect that others will act, or because the presence of others reduces feelings of accountability

direct ownership: an arrangement whereby employees purchase and hold stocks in the organization that employs them

directing: orchestrating interpersonal activities, leading, and motivating employees to work effectively and efficiently in the pursuit of organizational goals

direction: what a person is motivated to achieve

discretionary-time system: a work scheduling arrangement that provides the employee with an element of discretion in deciding when they will be at work

divisional superstructure: the grouping of activities at the top of the organization structure around nonfunctional activities, such as products and territories

domain/directional planning: the development of a course of action that moves an organization toward one domain or direction (and, therefore, away from other domains or directions)

economic domain: the rules and economic institutions that regulate business activity and govern the transfers of land, labor, capital, goods, and services that an organization needs to fulfill its goals

effort: the human energy directed toward achieving an organizational objective

effort-performance expectancy: E1, the perceived probability that effort will lead to performance (or $E \rightarrow P$)

emergent leader: the person who becomes a group's leader by virtue of processes and dynamics internal to the group

employee ownership: an organizational arrangement in which a significant portion of the people who work in the firm hold rights to organizational equity, information, and influence

Employee Stock Ownership Plan (ESOP): an arrangement whereby employees may or may not be the exclusive owners of the organization; ownership is frequently the result of an employee-ownership trust having been established by the company on the employees' behalf

empowered team: a team characterized by collective efficacy, meaningfulness, autonomy, and impact

empowerment: the result of a process that enhances feelings of self-efficacy among organizational members, enabling them to feel as though they can perform their work effectively, and that they are responsible for doing so

ends decision: focuses on the articulation of a desired goal (outcome)

environmental change: reflects the degree to which the organization's task environment is stable/shifting

environmental segmentation: reflects the degree of homogeneity (similarities) and heterogeneity (differences) among components of the organization's task environment

equity theory: states that human motivation is affected by the outcomes people receive for their inputs, compared to the outcomes and inputs of other people

ERG theory: compresses Maslow's five need categories into three: existence, relatedness, and growth

escalation of commitment: the process through which a group or individual continually extends a commitment even though signals suggest that a bad decision/investment has been made

essay method: of performance appraisal requires the rater to write a narrative about the employee's performance strengths and weaknesses, as well as ways the employee can improve job performance

ethics: the set of standards and code of conduct that defines what is right, wrong, and just in human actions

excused absences: are those in which employees notify their employer in advance that they will not be at work on a given day, and the employer approves of the absence

existing solution: a solution to decision occasions (a problem) that has been previously developed

expatriates: employees who are sent on assignments in foreign countries

expectancy effect: occurs when people perceive stimuli in ways that will confirm their expectations

expectancy theory: posits that people will exert high effort levels to perform at high levels so that they can obtain valued outcomes

external environment: a set of conditions, circumstances, and influences that surround and affect the functioning of an organization

external locus of control: people who believe that external factors such as luck, other people, or organizations are the primary determinants of their destiny

extinction: occurs when a consequence or lack of a consequence makes it less likely that a behavior will be repeated in the future

extrinsic motivation: occurs when a person performs a given behavior to acquire something that will satisfy a lower-order need

extrinsic outcomes: are awarded or given by other people (like a supervisor)

field dependence: a characteristic of people that reflects the degree to which they differ in their ability to differentiate figure from ground

figure-ground differentiation: the tendency to distinguish and focus on a stimulus that is classified as figure as opposed to background (ground)

first-level managers: those managers at the lowest level in the organization

flexible working hours: a discretionary time, work scheduling arrangement that enables the employee to exercise a daily decision regarding the time of day that he or she will start and end their work day

formal group (team): a group consciously created to serve an organizational objective

formal leader: that individual who is recognized by those outside the group as the official leader of the group

formal organization: the official structures and systems consciously designed by organizational members; the relatively enduring people-to-people and people-to-work interaction patterns created to accomplish organizational goals

functional authority: the "right" to direct or control specific activities that are under the span of control of other managers

functional decision: relates to one of the organization's functions (production, marketing, accounting, finance, human resources)

functional departmentalization: the grouping of jobs by the organizational function served

functional managers: those managers responsible for the organization's functions of production, marketing, finance, accounting, and human resources

functional superstructure: the grouping of activities at the top of the organization by function

fundamental attribution error: our tendency to overestimate the effects of internal causes and underestimate the effects of external causes when we judge other peoples' actions

general environment: that part of the external environment that represents the organization's sociocultural, economic, technological, legal/political, and international domains

goal commitment: the degree to which people dedicate themselves to achieving a goal

goal hierarchy: the interrelationship among an organization's job-, department-, divisional-, and organizational-level goals

goal planning: development of action statements to move toward the attainment of a specific goal

goal theory: states that people will perform better if they have difficult, specific, accepted performance goals or objectives

graphic rating scale: a method of performance appraisal that requires the rater to judge the performance of the ratee on dimensions (criteria) using scaled standards (poor, excellent, etc.)

great man theory of leadership: the belief that some people are born to be leaders and others are not

group: two or more people who interact with one another to achieve a common objective

groupthink: when a group has illusions of invulnerability that lead it to accept excessive risks

halo effect: the process of generalizing from an overall evaluation of an individual to specific characteristics of the person

Hawthorne studies: worker productivity studies carried out at Western Electric that led to the creation of the human relations school of thought

hedonism: assumes that people are motivated to satisfy mainly their own needs (seek pleasure, avoid pain)

heredity: the transmission from parents to offspring of certain defining characteristics; a genetic predisposition to behave or think in certain ways

heterogeneous group: a group whose members are highly diverse in their demographics and values, goals, and time and interpersonal orientations

high-involvement management and organization: a participative process that uses the entire capacity of workers, designed to encourage employee commitment to organizational success

homogeneous group: a group whose members are similar in their demographics and values, goals, and time and interpersonal orientations

horizontal coordination: linking work units (individuals, teams, departments) at the same hierarchical level

horizontal specialization: an approach to jobs that creates many low-skill-level, short-time cycle, repetitive positions

horizontal team: a team with people from different departments at the same hierarchical level

human (interpersonal) skills: the ability to work with and understand others, to lead, motivate, resolve conflict, and build group effort

human relations model: a management model that views the employee as socially motivated and operates from the assumption that a social need–satisfied worker is a productive worker

human resource accounting: the application of accounting principles and practices to the evaluation and management of human assets

human resource model: the belief that through employee involvement in organizational decision making performance would be enhanced, leading to employee satisfaction, commitment and motivation for further involvement

hybrid control system: control system that exercises control prior to, during, and after the performance of a work activity

hybrid departmentalization: the grouping of organizational activities by two or more forms of departmentalization

hybrid planning: the coupling of domain and goal planning

hybrid superstructure: the grouping of activities at the top of the organizational structure around two or more activities

hygienes: factors in the work environment that are based on the basic human need to "avoid pain"

implicit personality theory: the tendency to ascribe personality traits to people because they share certain characteristics with others

individualism-collectivism: the degree to which individuals in a society prefer to act as individuals, as opposed to a group

influence: the ability to produce a change in one's environment

informal group: a group not intentionally created, arising spontaneously out of people's social needs, physical proximity, common interests, and mutual attraction

informal leader: that individual whom members of the group acknowledge as their leader

informal organization: joint activity between two or more individuals not formally designed that possibly contributes to joint results

informational role: the organizational role that involves monitoring, disseminating, and serving as a spokesperson for an organization

initiating structure: a "task-oriented" leader behavior that is focused on goal attainment, organizing and scheduling work, solving problems, and maintaining work processes

innovation: when an organization is the first or one of the first users of an idea

inputs: any personal qualities that a person views as having value and that are relevant to the organization

inspirational decision-making approach: reliance on intuition (inspiration) to resolve decision occasions (a problem) under conditions of ends and means disagreements within a decision-making body

instincts: our natural, fundamental needs, basic to our survival

institutional-level need the organizational need to become integrated with the external environment

integration (organizational integration): the means used to coordinate and integrate the work of employees and work units

intensity: (1) the degree to which people try to achieve their targets; (2) the forcefulness that enhances the likelihood that a stimulus will be selected for perceptual processing

interdependence approach to departmentalization: the grouping of activities based on the degree of coupling between them (jobs, teams, departments)

internal environment: all that is the organization—such as its space, climate, machines/equipment, work and work processes, management and management practices, and organizational members

internal locus of control: people who believe that internal factors like their skills and ability are the primary determinants of their destiny

international domain: organizations and the economic, legal/political, technological, and sociocultural domains of other countries with which they have contact

interpersonal influence: the ability to produce a change in others—to change their attitudes, motivation, and/or behavior

interpersonal role: the organizational role that involves serving as figurehead, leader, and liaison for an organization

intrinsic motivation: arises out of performing a behavior in and of itself, because it is interesting or "fun" to do

intrinsic outcomes: are awarded or given by people to themselves (such as a sense of achievement)

involuntary absenteeism: occurs when an employee is absent because of illness or factors out of the employee's direct control

involuntary turnover: occurs when the organization, against an employee's preferences, discontinues their employment, or when an employee has to quit for personal reasons that are outside of their control.

Job Characteristics Model (JCM): a theory of job design and its individual effects

job content decision: relates to the inherent nature of the work performed by an individual or work group

job context decision: relates to factors that surround the job, but are not a part of the job per se

job description: a written document that identifies the job duties for a particular job in an organization

job (work) design: how tasks are combined to form a job; the formal and informal specification of task-related activities assigned to and carried out by a worker; the inherent nature and character of the work performed

job duties: the activities, tasks, and behaviors expected of anyone performing a particular job

job enlargement: adding breadth to a job by increasing the number and variety of activities performed by an employee—horizontal loading

job enrichment: adding depth to a job by adding, for example, planning and controlling—vertical loading

job involvement: an employee's psychological involvement with a particular job

job performance: how well (or poorly) employees perform their job duties compared to expectations for the job

job satisfaction: the attitude that results from the appraisal of one's job as attaining or enabling the attainment of one's important job values

Johari window: one way to conceptualize the possible combinations of what you know about yourself and what others know about you

judgmental decision-making approach: reliance on majority rule from the personal judgments rendered by a group of experts

latent needs: cannot be inferred from a person's behavior at a given time, yet the person may still possess those needs

leadership: a social (interpersonal) influence relationship between two or more persons who depend on each other to attain certain mutual goals in a group situation

learning organization: an organization that purposefully designs and constructs its structure, culture, and strategies with the capacity to learn so that it can continuously adapt and change as needed

least preferred co-worker (LPC): the person with whom the leader least likes to work

legal/political domain: those systems that allocate power among various groups in society and settle disputes as they arise, and that develop, administer, and enforce the law

line authority: command authority

line managers: those managers who have "direct" responsibility for producing the organization's products and/or services

locus of causality: occurs when people observe the behavior of others and attribute the behavior to internal causes (ability, effort) or external causes (luck, easy or difficult task)

locus of control: the degree to which people believe their actions determine what happens to them in life

long team: a team that performs a complete operation from its beginning to end

Machiavellian personalities: believe that it is appropriate to behave in any manner that will meet their needs

management: the process of planning, organizing, directing, and controlling organizational resources in the pursuit of organizational goals

management by objectives (MBO): a philosophy of management, a planning and controlling technique, and an employee involvement program

management team: a team that manages (plans, organizes, directs, and controls) organizational subunits and activities under their control

managerial (tactical) decision: specifies how an organization intends to integrate its institutional level with its technical core, and how it will coordinate the diverse work systems within the technical core

manager-led team: a team that places the responsibility for task performance with the group, while management functions (planning, organizing, directing, and controlling) remain the responsibility of management

managers: those members of the organization assigned the primary responsibility for carrying out the management process

manifest needs: are needs motivating a person at a given time

manifest needs theory: assumes that human behavior is driven by the desire to satisfy needs

masculinity-femininity the degree to which a society displays mostly traditionally male or traditionally female traits

matrix superstructure: the simultaneous and integrated use of two or more organizational structures

McKinsey 7-S framework: a perspective on management that calls for the harmonious management of strategy, structure, systems, staff, style, skills, and superordinate goals (shared goals)

means decision: concerns procedures or actions undertaken to achieve particular goals; that is, it specifies how a goal is to be reached

mechanistic organization: an organization whose structure is fixed and rigid (also referred to as a bureaucracy)

membership group: a group that an individual belongs to by virtue of birth or life circumstances

modular corporation: an organization that performs its core competency and outsources the performances of other vital business activities

moral audit: an internal assessment of a firm's moral and ethical conduct

motivation: an internal state that energizes, directs, and sustains behavior

motivators: relate to the jobs that people perform, and people's ability to feel a sense of achievement as a result of performing them

motive: a source of motivation; the need that a person is attempting to satisfy

nature advocates: assume that part of personality finds its origins in biology—our heredity

need: a human condition that becomes energized when people feel deficient in some respect

need for achievement (nAch): the need to excel at tasks, especially tasks that are difficult

need for affiliation (nAff): the need to establish and maintain warm and friendly relationships with other people

need for power (nPow): the need to control things, especially other people; reflects a motivation to influence and be responsible for other people

negative reinforcement: occurs when a behavior causes something undesirable to be removed, increasing the likelihood of the behavior reoccurring

network organization superstructure: the partnership of several organizations who pool their core competencies

nominal group technique (NGT): a structured group process that generates many potential solutions to a problem, evaluates them, and ranks them from best to worst

noncybernetic control: control systems that operate independently from the work system that is being monitored; a monitoring system that is external to the target of control

nonprogrammed decision: the process of addressing unique or novel situations confronting the organization

nonreinforcement: occurs when no consequence follows a worker's behavior

normative commitment: attachment to an organization that is based on the belief that it is the "right" thing to do

novelty: when the stimulus we are sensing differs from stimuli we have experienced in the past

nurture advocates: argue that personality and intelligence find their basis in life experiences, especially those experienced early in life

objective rationality: the notion that decision makers are completely informed, infinitely sensitive, and therefore make decisions based on fact and rational thought

objective reality: what exists in the physical world

official goals: the aims of an organization that are expressed in highly abstract and general terms, generally employed for the organization's external constituents

open system: an organization that attempts to integrate itself with its external environment and looks to the outside for ideas on productivity and efficiency improvements

operant conditioning: a learning process based on the results produced by a person "operating on" the environment

operant conditioning theory: posits that people learn to behave in a particular fashion as a result of the consequences that followed their past behaviors

operating decision: deals with the day-to-day operation of an organization

operating plans: cover the day-to-day operations of the organization

operational goals: the aims of an organization that reflect management's specific intentions

organic organization: a fluid and dynamic organization capable of evolution, redesign, and adaptation

organization: (1) the process of placing selected perceptual stimuli into a framework for "storage"; (2) a tool or technical system, as well as a social system and a relatively enduring people-to-people and people-to-work interaction system

organization-based self-esteem (OBSE): an evaluation of our personal adequacy (worthiness) as an organizational member

organizational behavior modification (OBM): systematically applies operant conditioning theory to manage workplace behavior

organizational change: the movement of an organization from its current state to some future state

organizational chart: a schematic drawing that depicts the hierarchical relationship among all positions within the organization

organizational citizenship behaviors (OCBs): behaviors that employees exhibit on and off their jobs that reflect sacrifices for, and commitment to, the prosperity of the organization

organizational climate: the prevailing organizational condition that reflects the overall organizational tone or character

organizational commitment: the relative strength of an individual's identification with and involvement in a particular organization

organizational context: the circumstances and conditions within which an organization operates

organizational culture: a pattern of basic assumptions invented, discovered, or developed by a given group as it learns to cope with problems of external adaptation and internal integration

organizational design: the structures, systems, and processes that enable an organization to implement its plans and achieve it goals

organizational development (OD): a process for diagnosing organizational problems by looking for incongruencies in environment, structures, processes, and people

organizational differentiation: the differences in time and goal orientation, work performed, and organizational function and responsibility served by employees and work units

organizational diversity: a hetereogeneous work group where no one group occupies a majority position

organizational functions: the work of organizations, which consists of production, marketing, finance, accounting, human resources, and management

organizational humanism: a system that promoted an interest in understanding the psychological forces that tie individuals to organizations, and promoted management practices that lead to employee satisfaction and well-being

organizational inertia: tendency to maintain the status quo

organizational learning: the process by which organizations gain new knowledge and insights that lead to a modification in behavior and action

organizational nesting: organizations embedded within organizations

organizational politics: informal behaviors that protect or enhance the self-interests of an individual or group

organizational silence: when potentially important organizational information is not passed along to those who need to know it and who have the authority to act on it

organizational structure: those attributes that characterize the interaction patterns that link people to people and people to work

organizing: the activity of designing, structuring, arranging, and rearranging the components of an organization's internal environment

outcome or goal statements: end states—the targets and outcomes that managers hope to attain

outcomes: anything a person perceives as getting back from an organization in exchange for the person's inputs

overall job satisfaction: a combination of facet satisfactions that describes a person's overall affective reaction to a set of work and work-related factors

overreward inequity: occurs when people perceive their outcome/input ratio to be greater than that of their referent other

parallel team: a team that performs functions that the regular organization is not equipped to perform well

participative decision making: joint decision making between managers and subordinates

path-goal theory of leadership: posits that leadership is path- and goal-oriented, suggesting that different leadership styles are effective as a function of the task confronting the group

perceived reality: what individuals experience through one or more of the human senses, and the meaning they ascribe to those experiences

perception: the process by which people organize and obtain meaning from the sensory stimuli they receive from the environment

perceptual defense: the way a person retains existing perceptions in the face of new information that conflicts with those perceptions

performance: the behaviors of organizational members that help meet organizational objectives

performance appraisal: the process of evaluating how effectively members are fulfilling their job responsibilities and contributing to organizational goals

performance context: the environment that surrounds and impacts the team, yet remains out of its immediate and direct control

performance environment: refers to those factors that impact employees' performance but are essentially out of their control

performance improvement plan: a formal agreement between a manager and an employee that covers (1) the employee's performance problem, (2) why performance is deficient, and (3) what the employee must do and by when to eliminate the performance problem

performance strategy: a clear outcome the team is working to achieve, coupled with an action plan that details how to proceed and how team members will interact

performance-outcome expectancy: E2, the perceived relationship between performance and outcomes (or $P \rightarrow O$)

personal aggression: deviant behavior that is serious and directed at a specific individual(s)

personal experience: in forming attitudes occurs by coming in direct contact with an attitude object

personality: the collection of psychological characteristics or traits that determines a person's preferences and individual style of behavior

physical withdrawal: the act of physically removing oneself from the work environment through such behaviors as tardiness, absence, and turnover

planning: the process by which managers establish goals and specify how these goals are to be attained

polarization: when a group takes positions that are more extreme than members would take acting alone

political deviance: deviant behavior that is minor and directed at a specific individual

politics: the use of intrigue or strategy to obtain a position of power or control

positive reinforcement: occurs when a desirable consequence that satisfies an active need, or that removes a barrier to need satisfaction, increases the likelihood of a behavior reoccurring

postaction controls: controls employed after a product or service is complete

power: the means to achieve influence through personal qualities or role conditions

power distance: the acceptance of large differences in power between the most and least powerful in a society

precontrols: controls designed to prevent deviation from a desired plan of action before work actually begins

premature closure: when a group rushes to identify the problem, to find an attractive or easily accessible solution, or to get on with things

primacy effect: the disproportionately high weight given to the first information obtained about a stimulus

primary needs: are instinctual in nature and include physiological needs for food, water, and sex (procreation)

principle of charity: suggests that those who have plenty should give to those who do not

principle of stewardship: suggests that organizations have an obligation to see that the public's interests are served by corporate action and the ways in which profits are spent

proactive change: when managers conclude that a change is desirable (as opposed to necessary)

procedural justice: perception that the processes employed to make a decision were fair

process departmentalization: the grouping of organizational activities around all of the processes needed to produce a product of value for an organizationally internal or external customer

process motivation theories: focus on the how and why of motivation

process perspective of management: an activity concerned with the orchestration of people, work, and systems in the pursuit of organizational goals

product/service departmentalization: the grouping of jobs by products and/or services

product, territory, and process managers: those who manage an organization's product, territorial, and process divisions

production deviance: deviant behavior that is minor and directed at the organization

profit-maximizing management: the belief that business's primary responsibility to society is to underwrite the country's economic growth and to oversee the accumulation of wealth

programmed decision: routines employed to deal with frequently occurring situations

project departmentalization: the grouping of organizational activities by special and unique ventures, activities, or undertakings

project team: a team that is time-limited and formed to work on a single task; when the task is completed the team disbands

projection: the process by which people attribute their own feelings and characteristics to other people

property deviance: deviant behavior that is serious and directed at an organization

proximity in space: occurs when the physical nearness of stimuli to one another affects their perceptual organization

proximity in time: occurs when one stimulus is observed at about the same point in time as another stimulus

psychological ownership: the state in which an individual feels as though the target of ownership (or a piece of that target) is theirs

psychological withdrawal: a mental state in which an employee is disengaged from the work environment

punishment: an aversive consequence that follows a behavior and makes it less likely to reoccur

quality control (QC) circle: an employee involvement tool that generally consists of a small group of individuals who meet on a regular basis to discuss issues pertaining to quality and related problems

quality management perspective: an approach to management that has as its goal the achievement of customer satisfaction by providing high-quality goods and services

quality-of-life management: the belief that managers have to do more than achieve narrow economic goals, but that they should manage the quality-of-life by helping develop solutions for society's ills

rater error: occurs when an employee's performance rating does not reflect their true or actual performance level

reactive change: when forces driving change pressure an organization to change

reality testing: occurs when you compare your perceptions about a stimulus object to some other measure of that object

recency effect: the disproportionately high weight given to the last information obtained about a stimulus

reference group: any group we belong to, or aspire to belong to, and that we use to judge the adequacy of our behavior

referent others: workers that a person uses to compare inputs and outcomes, and who perform jobs similar in difficulty and complexity to the employee making an equity determination

reinforcement: occurs when a consequence makes it more likely a behavior will be repeated in the future

rights theory: concentrates on respecting the rights to which people are entitled (e.g., the right to privacy)

role: a set of expected behaviors that characterize a person in a social setting

role perceptions: the set of behaviors employees think they are expected to perform as members of an organization

satisfice: the selection of a decision alternative that is just "satisfactory" in nature

schedules of reinforcement: the frequency at which effective employee behaviors are reinforced

scientific management: that kind of management which conducts a business or affairs by standards established by facts or truths gained through systematic observation, experiment, or reasoning

second-level managers: those managers who direct first-level managers

secondary needs: are learned throughout one's life span and are psychological in nature

selection: the process a person uses to eliminate some of the stimuli that have been sensed and to retain others for further processing

selective perception: occurs when people select for perception those things that are consistent with their views of themselves and the world, and reject or argue against those that are inconsistent

self-managers: individuals who manage themselves and the performance of their own work; thus, they plan, problem-solve, make decisions, and control their own work activities

self-designing organization: continuously experiments and tries new ways to respond to environmental demands; it continually appraises and revises itself in an effort to invent as well as to survive its future

self-determination theory (SDT): seeks to explain not only what causes motivation, but also the effects of extrinsic rewards on intrinsic motivation

self-efficacy: a belief about the probability that one can successfully execute some future action or task, or achieve some result

self-esteem: how we perceive ourselves in terms of our abilities, competencies, and effectiveness

self-fulfilling prophecy (Pygmalion) effect: occurs when people unconsciously adjust their behaviors to reflect their expectations in a situation

self-managing work team: a team that operates with goals set by management, but that is given the authority to plan for goal attainment

self-understanding: acknowledgment that you and people who interact with you are susceptible to perceptual errors

sensation: our ability to detect stimuli in our immediate environment

shift work schedules: a pattern of working-hour arrangements whereby the employee works organizationally defined and different blocks of time on a regular basis

short team: a team that handles a group of tasks originally performed by a traditional service or manufacturing department

similarity: the physical resemblance of some stimuli that causes them to be associated during perceptual organization

single-use plans: plans developed for unique situations or problems and one-time use

situational view of authority: the belief that orders should flow from the situation, not from the person

social audit: a detailed examination and evaluation of an organization's social performance

social facilitation: when performance is enhanced by the presence of others

social impairment: when performance is diminished by the presence of others

social learning: of attitudes occurs when people with whom a person works affect the attitudes one develops

social loafing: when individual group members fail to put forth their best efforts because they believe that their contributions will essentially get lost in the group effort

social ownership: an arrangement whereby people in a society or community, including the employees, have an ownership stake in an organization

social responsibility: an organization's obligation to engage in activities that protect and contribute to the welfare of society

socialization: the process through which people develop beliefs about what is right, wrong, and just

sociocultural domain: the values, customs, mores, and demographic characteristics of the people within a society

sociological perspective of management: the belief that management consists of a certain group of people in the organization

socio-technical changes: concurrent change in people and technology

socio-technical system: an organization viewed as both a social and a technical system

staff authority: advisory authority

staff managers: managers whose responsibility it is to "support" line managers

staggered start system: a work scheduling arrangement that provides the employee with a set of management-defined options as to when the work day will commence

standing plans: rules, policies, and procedures about how to deal with issues that managers face repeatedly

state of equity: occurs when people perceive their outcome/input ratio to be equal to that of their referent other

stepladder technique: enhances decisions by structuring the addition of group members and their ideas into the process

stereotyping: occurs when a person has certain beliefs about a class of stimulus objects, and then generalizes those beliefs to encounters with members of that class of objects

strategic decision: identifies the ends and means associated with positioning an organization in its external task environment

strategic plans: hierarchical plans that address an organization's institutional-level needs and attempt to position it advantageously within its task environment

structured problem: problem whose nature and context are well defined

subjective performance appraisal methods: include all of those performance appraisal methods that require one employee (usually a manager) to rate another employee

superstructure: the division of activities at the top of the organizational hierarchy

synectic technique: develops creative ideas and attempts to integrate diverse individuals into a problem-stating, problem-solving group

synergy: a dynamic that causes group performance levels to be greater than that achieved by employees working on their own

system factors: impediments to job performance over which the employee has no direct control

systems theory: a view of an organization as made up of a number of interrelated elements, each functioning to contribute to the purpose of the whole

task environment: that part of the external environment that consists of the organization's suppliers, customers/markets, regulatory and influence groups, competitors, and allies

task (project) managers: individuals who have been assigned responsibility for a particular organizational task or project

team: a collection of individuals who are interdependent in their tasks, who share responsibility for outcomes, who see themselves and are seen by others as an intact social entity embedded in one or more larger social systems, and who manage their relationships across organizational boundaries

team cluster approach to departmentalization: the grouping of teams by shared interdependence, such as clients within a particular region of the country

team managers: those who assume responsibility for the orchestration of group performance activities

team norms: expectations with regard to the behavior of team members

technical core need: the organizational need to accomplish the day-to-day activities associated with producing a product or delivering a service

technical skills: the ability to use and understand the use of tools, procedures, and techniques needed to perform a task

technological domain: the knowledge, processes, means, systems, hardware, and software available to an organization to convert its inputs (raw materials, unfinished goods, energy) into outputs (products or services)

technostructural changes: concurrent change in organizational technology and structure

termination: the unilateral canceling of an employment contract by an organization, whether the contract is written or not

territorial (geographical) departmentalization: the grouping of organizational activities by different geographical areas

theory of justice: emphasizes engaging in acts that are fair and impartial

Theory X: a management view of the worker as inherently disliking work, lacking work-related motivation, resistant to change, gullible and dull, and indifferent to the needs of the organization

Theory Y: a management view of the worker as liking work, motivated to achieve objectives, capable of self-direction and self-control, and for whom the expenditure of effort at work is as natural as play

Theory Z: a theory of management based upon an integration of the best Japanese and American practices

360° feedback: occurs when employees (especially managers) receive feedback from a number of sources

time orientation: the degree to which cultures possess a short or long perspective on time

Total Quality Management (TQM): an approach to management that has as its primary focus the achievement of quality through continuous improvement of the processes employed to manufacture a product or deliver a service

transformational leader: a leader who moves and changes things "in a big way" by inspiring others to perform the extraordinary

transformational process/equipment departmentalization: the grouping of organizational activities by the equipment and/or processes used in the production process

translation: the stage of the perceptual process at which stimuli are interpreted and given meaning

trusteeship management: the belief that corporate managers need to maintain an equitable balance among the competing interests of all groups with a stake in the organization

turnover: occurs when an employee or employer cancels the employment relationship

uncertainty avoidance: the degree to which cultures differ in the extent to which they tolerate uncertainty

underreward inequity: occurs when people perceive their outcome/input ratio to be less than that of their referent other

unexcused absences: occur when an employee, with no advance approval, simply fails to show up for work when scheduled

unstructured problem: problem characterized by a lack of problem and context definition

utilitarian theory: concentrates on social consequences; an action is considered morally right if its consequences for everyone affected by the action are greater than those which would be realized by a different action

valences: the degree to which a person perceives an outcome as being desirable, neutral, or undesirable

variable-hour arrangement: a work scheduling arrangement that contracts with the employee for a specified amount of time to be worked on a daily, weekly, or monthly basis

vertical coordination: linking work units (individuals, teams, departments) separated by hierarchical level

vertical specialization: an approach to jobs that removes planning and controlling activites from production employees

vertical team: a team with members from several hierarchical levels

virtual corporation: a temporary network of independent companies

visionary leader: an individual who is capable of influencing others through an emotional and/or intellectual attraction to the leader's dream for that which "can be"

voluntary absenteeism: occurs when an employee chooses not to go to work when they could have (they are not ill) and should have (they were expected)

voluntary turnover: occurs when the employee chooses to leave an organization

whistleblowing: a member's disclosure that someone within the organization has engaged in an illegal, immoral, unethical, or illegitimate act

withdrawal: the physical and/or psychological avoidance by employees of their workplace

work involvement: an employee's devotion to or alienation from work in general

work motivation: the amount of effort a person exerts to achieve a level of job performance

work team: a group responsible for producing an organization's goods or services

worker (producer) cooperatives: an arrangement whereby employees are the exclusive owners of the organization

Endnotes

PART I. Exploring Management and Organizational Behavior

Chapter 1. The Nature of Organizations and Management

1. T. Parsons. 1951. *The social system*. Glencoe, IL: Free Press; T. Parsons. 1954. *Essays in sociological theory*. Glencoe, IL: Free Press; T. Parsons. 1956. Suggestions for a sociological approach to the theory of organizations. *Administrative Science Quarterly*, 1:63–85, 225–239.

2. C. I. Barnard. 1938. *The functions of the executive*. Cambridge, MA: Harvard University Press.

3. A. K. Rice. 1958. *Productivity and social organization: The Ahmedabad experiment*. London: Tavistock.

4. J. E. Haas & T. E. Drabek. 1973. *Complex organizations: A sociological perspective*. New York: Macmillan.

5. H. Fayol. 1916/1949. *General and industrial management*, C. Storrs, trans. London: Sir Isaac Pitman and Sons, Ltd. (Original work published in 1916.)

6. For a discussion of a creative new approach to organizational charts, see: H. Mintzberg & L. Van der Heyden. 1999. Organigraphs: Drawing how companies really work. *Harvard Business Review* (Sept.–Oct.): 87–94.

7. M. P. Follett. 1949. *Freedom and coordination: Lecture in business organization*. London: Pitman.

8. Fayol, 1916/1949.

9. Ibid.

10. Barnard, 1938; R. C. Davis. 1951. *The fundamentals of top management*. New York: Harper & Row; J. B. Miner. 1973. *The management process: Theory, research, and practice*. New York: Macmillan.

11. T. Teal. 1996 (Nov.–Dec.). The human side of management. *Harvard Business Review* 74(6):35–44.

12. Teal, 1996.

13. M. W. McCall, Jr., A. M. Morrison, & R. L. Hannan. 1978. *Studies of managerial work: Results and methods*. (Technical Report 9.) Greensboro, NC: Center for Creative Leadership.

14. R. A. Mackenzie. 1969 (Nov.–Dec.). The management process in 3-D. *Harvard Business Review*, 87.

15. J. P. Kotter. 1999 (March–April). What effective general managers really do. *Harvard Business Review* 77(2):148.

16. H. Mintzberg. 1975 (July–Aug.). The manager's job: Folklore and fact. *Harvard Business Review*, 49–61.

17. P. F. Drucker. 1988 (Sept.–Oct.). Management and the world's work. *Harvard Business Review*, 65–76.

18. W. W. Torrow & P. R. Pinto. 1976. The development of a managerial job taxonomy: A system for describing, classifying, and evaluating executive positions. *Journal of Applied Psychology*, 61:410–418; W. Whitely. 1985. Managerial work behavior: An integration of results from two major approaches. *Academy of Management Journal* 28:358.

19. "Given the failures that plagued Greyhound, it is evident that they failed to do so and has contributed to loss of market share." [John W. Teets, chairman of the Board for Greyhound Corp., in an advertisement]. 1986 (Mar. 31). *Fortune*, 46.

20. T. A. Mahoney, T. H. Jerdee, & S. J. Carroll, Jr. 1963. *Development of managerial performance: A research approach*. Cincinnati: South-Western; T. A. Mahoney, T. H. Jerdee, & S. J. Carroll, Jr. 1965. The jobs of management. *Industrial Relations* 4: 97–110.

21. J. Horne & T. Lupton. 1965. The work activities of middle managers: An exploratory study. *Journal of Management Studies* 2:14–33.

22. D. Katz. 1974 (Sept.–Oct.). Skills of an effective administrator. *Harvard Business Review* 90–102.

23. G. Colvin. 2000 (Mar. 6). Managing in the info era. *Fortune* 141(5):F6.

24. L. J. Peter & R. Hull. 1969. *The Peter principle: Why things always go wrong*. New York: William Morrow.

25. L. B. Koran. 1989 (May 22). How the next CEO will be different. *Fortune*, 157–161.

26. P. F. Drucker. 1999. *Management challenges for the 21st century*. New York: McGraw-Hill.

Chapter 2. Philosophies and Approaches to Management Practice

1. G. D. Babcock. 1927. *The Taylor system in Franklin management*, 2nd ed., New York: Engineering Magazine Company, 31.

2. C. Babbage. 1832. *On the economy of machinery and manufactures*. London: Charles Knight, 132.

3. F. W. Taylor. 1947. *Scientific management*. New York: Harper.

4. F. W. Taylor. 1912. *The art and science of shoveling*. Testimony before a special committee of the U.S. House of Representatives.

5. Taylor, 1947.

6. H. Fayol. 1949. *General and industrial management*, C. Storrs, trans. London: Pitman, 19.

7. M. Weber. 1922. *The theory of social and economic organization*, A. M. Henderson & T. Parsons, ed. and trans. (1947), New York: Oxford University Press.

8. E. Mayo. 1933. *The human problems of industrial civilization*. New York: Macmillan; F. J. Rothlisberger & W. J. Dickson. 1947. *Management and the worker*. Cambridge, MA: Harvard University Press.

9. An interesting historical treatment of Hugo Munsterberg and his contributions to industrial psychology is presented by F. J. Landy. 1992. Hugo Munsterberg: Victim or Visionary? *Journal of Applied Psychology* 77:787–802.

10. H. Munsterberg. 1913. *Psychology and industrial efficiency*. New York: Arno Press.

11. M. P. Follett. 1918. *The new state*. Gloucester, MA: Smith.

12. L. D. Parker. 1984. Control in organizational life: The contribution of Mary Parker Follett. *Academy of Management*

Review 9:736–745; P. Graham. 1995. *M. P. Follett—Prophet of Management: A celebration of writings from 1920s*. Boston: Harvard Business School Press.

13. G. Powell. 1998. The abusive organization. *Academy of Management Executive* 12 (2):95–96.
14. A. H. Maslow. 1957. *Motivation and personality*. New York: Harper & Row.
15. D. M. McGregor. November 1957. The human side of enterprise. *Management Review*, 22–28, 88–92; D. M. McGregor. 1960. *The human side of enterprise*. New York: McGraw-Hill.
16. McGregor, 1957, 23.
17. D. M. McGregor. 1957 (Apr. 9). The human side of enterprise, *Proceedings of the 5th Anniversary Convocation of the School of Industrial Management*. Cambridge, MA: Massachusetts Institute of Technology, 15; D. M. McGregor. 1960. *The human side of enterprise*. New York: McGraw-Hill.
18. C. Argyris. 1957. *Personality and organization*. New York: Harper.
19. R. Likert. 1961. *New patterns of management*. New York: McGraw-Hill; R. Likert. 1967. *The human organization*. New York: McGraw-Hill.
20. A. Kornhauser & A. Sharp. 1932. Employee attitudes: Suggestions from a study in a factory. *Personnel Journal* 10: 393–404.
21. A. Brayfield & W. Crockett. 1955. Employee attitudes and employee performance. *Psychological Bulletin* 35:396–424.
22. R. Miles. 1964. Conflicting elements in managerial ideologies. *Industrial Relations* 4:77–91; R. Miles. 1975. *Theories of management: Implications for organizational behavior and development*. New York: McGraw-Hill, 42.
23. E. E. Lawler, III. 1986. *High involvement management*. San Francisco: Jossey-Bass; E. E. Lawler, III. 1992. *The ultimate advantage: Creating the high involvement organization*. San Francisco: Jossey-Bass.
24. J. L. Cotton. 1993. *Employee involvement: Methods for improving performance and work attitudes*. Newbury, CA: Sage, 3; E. E. Lawler, III, & S. A. Mohrman. 1989. With HR help, all managers can practice high-involvement management. *Personnel* 66(4):26–31.
25. T. L. Peters & R. H. Waterman, Jr. 1982. *In search of excellence: Lessons from America's best-run companies*. New York: Harper & Row.
26. W. Ouchi. 1981. *Theory Z: How American business can meet the Japanese challenge*. Reading, MA: Addison-Wesley.
27. W. A. Pasmore. 1988. *Designing effective organizations: The sociotechnical systems perspective*. New York: Wiley; E. L. Trist. 1981. The sociotechnical perspective: The evolution of sociotechnical systems as a conceptual framework and as an action research program. In A. H. Van de Ven & W. F. Joyce (eds). *Perspectives on organization design and behavior*. New York: Wiley, 19–75.
28. J. R. Hackman & R. Wageman, 1995. Total quality management: Empirical, conceptual, and practical issues. *Administrative Science Quarterly* 40:309–342.
29. W. E. Deming. 1986. *Out of crisis*. Cambridge, MA: MIT Press.
30. R. A. Johnson, F. E. Kast, & J. E. Rosenzweig. 1963. *The theory and management of systems*. New York: McGraw-Hill.
31. Johnson, Kast, & Rosenzweig, 1963.
32. R. T. Pascale & A. G. Athos. 1981. *The art of Japanese management: Applications for American executives*. New York: Simon & Schuster; Peters & Waterman, 1982.
33. Pascale & Athos, 1981, 81.
34. Ouchi, 1981.
35. T. A. Stewart, A. Taylor, P. Petre, & B. Schlender. 1999 (Nov. 22). Henry Ford, Alfred P. Sloan, Tom Watson, Jr., Bill Gates: The businessmen of the century. *Fortune* 140(10):108–128.

Chapter 3. Social Responsibility and Ethics

1. Bill gives big: Mr. Microsoft will send 20,000 minority students to college. 1999 (Sept. 27). *Time*, 48 (www.time.com).
2. "Lilly leading supporter of minority investment company." 1991 (Sept. 13). *Dateline* 6:35, 1.
3. Anti-sweatshop efforts continue. 2000 (Spring). *On Wisconsin* 101(1):14. University of Madison: University of Wisconsin Alumni Association.
4. B. Dumaine. 1990. Making education work. *Fortune*, 12–22.
5. K. Labich. 1999 (Sept. 6). No more crude at Texaco. *Fortune* 205–212.
6. T. K. Grose. 1999 (Oct. 4). Called to account. *Time*, 104–106.
7. KBJR News, Duluth, MN, Sept. 26, 1999.
8. T. Parsons. 1951. *The social system*. Glencoe, IL: Free Press; T. Parsons. 1954. *Essays in sociological theory*. Glencoe, IL: Free Press.
9. K. Davis & R. L. Blomstrom. 1971. *Business society and environment: Social power and social response*. New York: McGraw-Hill.
10. J. Goodwin & D. Goodwin. 1999. Ethical judgments across cultures: A comparison between business students from Malaysia and New Zealand. *Journal of Business Ethics* 18 (3): 267–281; K. Davis & W. C. Frederick. 1984. *Business and society: Management, public policy, and ethics*, 5th ed. New York: McGraw-Hill.
11. D. Votaw & S. P. Sethi. 1973. *The corporate dilemma: Traditional values versus contemporary problems*. Englewood Cliffs, NJ: Prentice-Hall; S. P. Sethi. 1975. Dimensions of corporate social performance: An analytical framework. *California Management Review* 17(3):58–64.
12. After all the smoke cleared: An in-the-trenches look at how the war against Big Tobacco got won. 1999 (Sept. 27). *Time*, 98 (www.time.com).
13. B. Cohen & J. Greenfield. 1997. *Ben & Jerry's double dip: Lead with your values and make money too*. New York: Simon & Schuster; S. Rign. 1990 (Feb.). Cloths are an adventure at Patagonia. *COMPASS* 22–30; W. Roessing. 1990 (Mar.). High marks for Hallmark. *COMPASS* 32–40.
14. W. C. Frederick, K. Davis, & J. E. Post. 1988. *Business and society: Corporate strategy, public policy, ethics*. New York: McGraw-Hill.
15. M. Heald. 1970. *The social responsibilities of business: Company and community: 1900–1960*. Cleveland: Case-Western Reserve University Press.
16. Frederick, Davis, & Post, 1988.
17. Ibid.
18. P. L. Berger. 1999 (Sept./Oct.). New attack on the legitimacy of business. *Harvard Business Review*, 82–89.
19. R. Hay & E. Gray. 1974. Social responsibilities of business managers. *Academy of Management Journal* 17:135–143.
20. Hay & Gray, 1974, 142.
21. Johnson & Johnson Annual Report. 1998. "Our Credo."
22. A discussion of the social audit can be found in R. A. Bauer & D. H. Fenn, Jr., 1972. *The corporate social audit*. New York: Sage.
23. Grand Metropolitan Annual Report—Partnership with the Community. 1990. Range of Community Activities, 2.
24. T. K. Grose. 1999 (Oct. 4). Called to account. *Time*, 104–106 (www.time.com).
25. Sethi, 1975, 63.
26. Ibid., 62.
27. D. A. Rondinelli & G. Vastag. 1996 (Fall). International environmental standards and corporate policies: An integrative framework. *California Management Review*, 106–122.
28. Frederick, Davis, & Post, 1988, 32.

29. W. C. Rappleye, Jr. 2000 (Mar.). From apprehension to comprehension to leadership: How the private sector has made environmental issues its own. *Across the Board,* 32–57.

30. D. Dalton & R. Cosier. 1982 (May–June). The four faces of social responsibility. *Business Horizons,* 19–27.

31. M. Orey. 1999. *Assuming the risk: The mavericks, the lawyers, and the whistle blowers who beat Big Tobacco.* Boston: Little Brown.

32. See M. E. Porter & C. Van der Linde. 1995 (Sept./Oct.). Green and competitive: Ending the stalemate. *Harvard Business Review,* 120–134.

33. TIAA/CREF Variable Account Report. 1999; P. A. Stanwick & S. D. Stanwick. 1998. The relationship between corporate social performance, and organizational size, financial performance, and environmental performance: An empirical examination. *Journal of Business Ethics* 17 (2):195–204; K. E. Aupperle, A. B. Carroll, & J. D. Hatfield. 1985. An empirical examination of the relationship between corporate social responsibility and profitability. *Academy of Management Journal* 28:446–63.

34. Stanwick & Stanwick, 1998.

35. Frederick, Davis, & Post, 1988, 36–39.

36. T. Parsons. 1960. *Structure and process in modern society.* Glencoe, IL: Free Press; P. M. Blau & W. R. Scott. 1962. *Formal organizations: A comparative approach.* San Francisco: Chandler.

37. Frederick, Davis, & Post, 1988. 39–43.

38. M. Friedman. 1970 (Sept.). The social responsibility of business is to increase profits. *The New York Times Magazine* 33: 122–26; M. Friedman. 1971 (Apr.). Does business have social responsibility? *Bank Administration,* 13–14.

39. K. Davis. 1973. The case for and against business assumption of social responsibility. *Academy of Management Journal* 16: 312–22.

40. J. Kahn. 1999 (Oct. 11). The world's most admired companies. *Fortune,* 267–82.

41. L. E. Preston. 1986. Social issues in management: An evolutionary perspective. In D. A. Wren & J. A. Pearce (eds.), *Papers dedicated to the development of modern management.* Chicago: Academy of Management, 52–57.

42. Preston, 1986, 56.

43. R. Ford & F. McLaughlin. 1984. Perceptions of socially responsible activities and attitudes: A comparison of business school deans and corporate chief executives. *Academy of Management Journal* 27:666–674.

44. H. Geneene. 1984. *Managing.* New York: Doubleday, 258.

45. P. F. Drucker. 1973. *Management: Tasks, responsibilities, practices.* New York: Harper & Row; H. Mintzberg. 1983. *Power in and around organizations.* Englewood Cliffs, NJ: Prentice-Hall.

46. D. J. Dunn. 1987 (Mar. 16). Directors aren't doing their jobs. *Fortune,* 17–19.

47. I. F. Kesner, B. Victor, & B. T. Lamont. 1986. Board composition and the commission of illegal acts: An investigation of Fortune 500 Companies. *Academy of Management Journal* 29: 789–99.

48. Korn/Ferry International. 1981. *Board of directors: Eighth annual study.* Los Angeles: Author.

49. Geneene, 1984.

50. Kesner, Victor, & Lamont, 1986; J. Milliman & A. Feyerherm. 1999. responding to community expectations on corporate environmental performance: How to develop effective citizen advisory panels. *Corporate Environmental Strategy* 6:164–174.

51. R. A. Buchholtz. 1989. *Fundamental concepts and problems in business ethics.* Englewood Cliffs, NJ: Prentice-Hall.

52. Parsons, 1960.

53. A. Colby & L. Kohlberg. 1987. Theoretical foundations and research validation. In A. Colby & L. Kohlberg, with A. Abraham (eds.): *The measurement of moral judgment.* Cambridge, England: Cambridge University Press, Chapter 1, Volume 1.

54. T. J. Peters & R. H. Waterman, Jr. 1982. *Lessons from America's best run corporations.* New York: Harper & Row, 26.

55. J. G. Longenecker. 1985. Management priorities and management ethics. *Journal of Business Ethics.* 4:65–70.

56. P. B. Jubb. 1999. Whistleblowing: A restrictive definition and interpretation. *Journal of Business Ethics* 21:77–94; M. P. Miceli & J. P. Near. 1984. The relationship among beliefs, organizational position, and whistle-blowing status: A discriminant analysis. *Academy of Management Journal* 27:687–705.

57. J. P. Near & M. P. Miceli. 1995. Effective whistle-blowing. *Academy of Management Review* 20:679–708.

58. A. L. Otten. 1986 (July 14). Ethics on the job: Companies alert employees to potential dilemmas. *The Wall Street Journal,* 17; M. Brody. 1986 (Nov. 24). Listen to your whistleblower. *Fortune,* 77.

59. Johnson & Johnson 1996 Annual Report, 40.

60. E. I. duPont de Nemours and Company, 1996 Annual Report, 28.

61. "We're building a premier company." 1999. PepsiCo, Inc., Annual Report, 10.

62. L. McAneny & L. Saad. 1997 (Dec.). Pharmacists strengthen their position as the most highly rated profession. *The Gallup Poll Monthly,* 21–24.

63. B. Z. Posner & W. H. Schmidt. 1984. Values and the American manager: An update. *California Management Review* 26(3):202.

64. T. K. Grose. 1999 (Oct. 4). Called to Account. *Time,* 104–106 (www.time.com).

65. Posner and Schmidt, 1984, 202–216; Brenner & Mollander, 1977; R. Baumhart. 1961 (July/Aug.). How ethical are businessmen? *Harvard Business Review,* 6–12, 16, 19, 156–76.

66. W. H. Hegarty & H. P. Sims, Jr. 1978. Some determinants of unethical decision behavior: An experiment. *Journal of Applied Psychology* 63:451–457; W. H. Hegarty & H. P. Sims, Jr. 1979. Organizational philosophy, policies, and objectives related to unethical decision behavior: A laboratory experiment. *Journal of Applied Psychology* 64:331–338.

67. L. Hosmer. 1987. *The ethics of management.* Homewood, IL: Irwin, 107–109.

68. D. J. Fritzsche & H. Becker. 1984. Linking management behavior to ethical philosophy: An empirical investigation. *Academy of Management Journal* 27, 166–175.

69. D. B. McFarlin & P. D. Sweeney. 1992. Distributive and procedural justice as predictors of satisfaction with personal and organizational outcomes. *Academy of Management Journal* 35: 626–637.

70. J. Wilke. 1987 (May 7). BioTechnica to get OK to test genetically altered bacteria. *Boston Globe,* 61.

71. F. N. Brady. 1985. A Janus-Headed model of ethical theory: Looking two ways at business/society issues. *Academy of Management Review* 10:568–576.

72. L. K. Trevino. 1986. Ethical decision making in organizations: A person-situation interactionist model. *Academy of Management Review* 11:601–617.

73. R. B. Dunham. 1984. *Organizational behavior: People and processes in management.* Homewood, IL: Irwin.

74. Dunham, 1984, 495.

75. M. L. Nichols & V. E. Day. 1982. A comparison of moral reasoning of groups and individuals on the "defining issues test." *Academy of Management Journal* 25:201–208.

76. G. J. Benson. 1989. Codes of ethics. *Journal of Business Ethics* 8:305–319.

77. W. H. Hegarty & H. P. Sims, Jr. 1979. Organizational philosophy, policies, and objectives related to unethical decision behavior: A laboratory experiment. *Journal of Applied Psychology* 6:331–338.

78. C. J. Cowton & P. Thompson. 2000. Do codes make a difference? The case of bank lending and the environment. *Journal of Business Ethics* 24:165–178.

79. C. Wiley. 1998. Reexamining perceived ethics issues and ethics roles among employment managers. *Journal of Business Ethics* 17:147–161.

80. G. R. Weaver, L. K. Trevino, & P. L. Cochran. 1999. Corporate ethics practices in the mid-1999's: An empirical study of the Fortune 1000. *Journal of Business Ethics* 18:283–294.

81. D. A. Morf, M. G. Schumacher, & S. J. Vitell. 1999. A survey of ethics officers in large organizations. *Journal of Business Ethics* 20:265–271.

82. G. R. Weaver, L. K. Trevion, & P. L. Cochran. 1999. Corporate ethics programs as control systems: Influences of executive commitment and environmental factors. *Academy of Management Journal* 42:41–57.

83. C. C. Verchoor. 1998. A study of the link between a corporation's financial performance and its commitment to ethics. *Journal of Business Ethics* 17:1509–1516.

84. J. R. W. Joplin & C. S. Daus. 1997. Challenges of leading a diverse workforce. *Academy of Management Executive* 11 (3):32–47.

85. See, for example, A. M. Morrison, M. N. Ruderman, & J. M. Hughes. 1993. *Making diversity happen.* Greensboro, NC: Center for Creative Leadership, and U.S. Bureau of Labor Statistics. 1992. *Occupational Outlook Handbook.* Washington, D.C.: U.S. Government Printing Office.

86. Society for Human Resource Management. 1999. *Workplace diversity: A product of the SHRM diversity initiative.* Alexandria, VA: The Society for Human Resource Management.

87. Foreign-born drawn to Miami. 1999 (Oct. 16). *The Denver Post,* 16A.

88. SHRM, *Workplace diversity,* ibid.

89. G. Colvin. 1999 (July 19). The 50 best companies for Asians, Blacks, and Hispanics. *Fortune,* 53–58.

90. J. A. Gilbert, B. A. Stead, & J. M. Ivancevich. 1999. Diversity management: A new organizational paradigm. *Journal of Business Ethics* 21:61–76.

91. Colvin, 1999.

92. Ibid, 54.

93. Prejudice a worry on millennial eve. 1999 (Oct. 5). *Denver Post,* A6.

94. C. Eichenwald. 1997 (Jan. 4). Texaco to let U.S. check bias-law compliance. *New York Times,* 36.

95. G. Robinson & K. Dechant. 1997. Building a business case for diversity. *Academy of Management Executive* 11(3):21–31; Society for Human Resource Management. 1999. *Workplace diversity: A product of the SHRM diversity initiative.* Alexandria, VA: The Society for Human Resource Management.

96. S. E. Jackson, K. E. May, & K. Whitney. 1995. Understanding the dynamics of diversity in decision-making teams. In R. Guzzo, E. Salas, & Associates (eds.), *Team effectiveness and decision making in organizations.* San Francisco: Jossey-Bass.

Chapter 4. The Organizational Environment

1. J. Child. 1981. Culture, contingency and capitalism in the cross-national study of organizations. In L. L. Cummings & Barry M. Staw (Eds.), *Research in organizational behavior,* Greenwich, CT: JAI Press, 303–356; M. Crozier. 1973. Cultural determinants of organizational behavior. In A. R. Negandhi (ed.), *Modern organizational theory,* Kent, OH: Kent State University Press, 219–228.

2. E. B. Taylor. 1871. *Primitive culture.* London: Murray, 71.

3. M. Crozier. 1972. The relationship between micro and macro sociology. *Human Relations* 25:239–251.

4. A. Ranney. 1971. *The governing of men.* New York: Holt, Rinehart & Winston.

5. R. N. Osborn, J. G. Hunt, & L. R. Lauch. 1980. *Organization theory: An integrated approach.* New York: J. Wiley, 150.

6. M. E. Porter. 1986 (Winter). Changing patterns of international competition. *California Management Review* 28:2, 11.

7. M. Crozier. 1964. Bureaucracy, integration, and alienation. *The Bureaucratic Phenomenon.* Chicago: University of Chicago Press.

8. G. Hofstede. 1980. *Culture's consequences.* Beverly Hills, CA: Sage; G. Hofstede, B. Neuijen, D. D. Ohayv, & G. Sandeers. 1990. Measuring organizational cultures: A qualitative and quantitative study across 20 cases. *Administrative Science Quarterly* 35:286–316.

9. G. Hofstede, 1980, 1993.

10. Personal communication, 1987.

11. W. R. Dill. 1958. Environment as an influence on managerial autonomy, *Administrative Science Quarterly* 2:409–443; J. D. Thompson. 1967. *Organizations in action.* New York: McGraw-Hill.

12. P. E. Connor. 1980. *Organizations: Theory and design.* Chicago: Science Research Associates.

13. Thompson, 1967.

14. Ibid., 23.

15. Ibid., 18–24.

16. Ibid., 26–36.

17. J. Pfeffer. 1976. Beyond management and the worker: The institutional function of management. *Academy of Management Review* 1:36–46.

18. Lobbying 101: Colleges discover the pork barrel. 1986 (Oct. 27). *Business Week,* 116, 118.

19. Thompson, 1967.

20. T. J. Peters. 1987. *Thriving on Chaos.* New York: Knopf.

21. T. Burns & G. M. Stalker. 1961. *The management of innovation.* London: Tavistock.

22. Dumaine, B. 1993 (Feb. 22). The new non-managers. *Fortune,* 80–84.

23. E. E. Lawler, III. 1992. *The ultimate advantage: Creating the high involvement organization.* San Francisco: Jossey-Bass.

24. P. R. Lawrence & J. W. Lorsch. 1969. *Organization and environment.* Homewood, IL: Irwin.

25. Connor, 1980, 15.

26. Mintzberg, 1973.

27. S. Kerr, K. D. Hill, & L. Broedling. 1986. The first-line supervisor: Phasing out or here to stay? *Academy of Management Review* 11:103–117.

28. H. Mintzberg. 1973. *The nature of managerial work.* Englewood Cliffs, NJ: Prentice-Hall.

29. J. L. Pierce, R. B. Dunham, and L. L. Cummings. 1984. Sources of environmental structuring and participant responses. *Organizational Behavior and Human Performance* 33:214–242.

30. E. H. Schein. 1985. *Organizational culture and leadership.* San Francisco: Jossey-Bass, 9.

31. P. Selznick. 1957. *Leadership in administration.* Evanston, IL: Row, Peterson.

32. What makes a company great? 1998 (Oct. 26). *Fortune,* 218.

33. D. R. Denison. 1984. Bringing corporate culture to the bottom line. *Organizational Dynamics* 13:5–22; H. Schwartz and S. M. Davis. 1989. Matching corporate culture and business strategy. *Organizational Dynamics* 10:34–48.

34. W. H. Glick. 1985. Conceptualization and measuring organizational and psychological climate: Pitfalls in multilevel research. *Academy of Management Review* 10:601–616.

PART II. Individuals as Organizational Members

Chapter 5. Individuals in Organizations: Perception, Personality, and Cultural Differences

1. Berlyne, D. E. 1960. *Conflict, arousal, and curiosity.* New York: McGraw-Hill.

2. D. G. Gardner & E. F. Stone. 1981 (Aug.). Effects of biasing factors on student ratings of teaching. Annual Meeting of the American Psychological Association, Los Angeles.

3. And in fact is on the rise again, as evidenced by the racially motivated violence that has occurred in California, Illinois, Indiana, and Texas over the last several years, and the increasing numbers of "hate groups" in the United States as a whole.

4. S. M. Andersen, R. L. Klatzky, & J. Murray. 1990. Traits and social stereotypes: Efficiency differences in social information processing. *Journal of Personality and Social Psychology* 59:192–201.

5. R. Rosenthal & L. Jacobsen. 1968. *Pygmalion in the classroom.* New York: Holt, Rinehart, & Winston.

6. J. Luft. 1970. *Group processes.* Palo Alto, CA: National Press Books.

7. A. R. Cohen, S. L. Fink, H. Gadon, & R. D. Willits. 1999. *Effective behavior in organizations* (7th ed.). Chicago, IL: Irwin McGraw-Hill.

8. D. Dunning, D. W. Griffin, J. D. Milojkovic, & L. Ross. 1990. The overconfidence effect in social prediction. *Journal of Personality and Social Psychology* 58:568–581.

9. M. B. Lupfer, L. F. Clark, & H. W. Hutcherson. 1990. Impact of context on spontaneous trait and situational attributions. *Journal of Personality and Social Psychology* 58:239–249.

10. E. H. Schein. 1985. *Organizational culture and leadership.* San Francisco: Jossey-Bass.

11. Ibid.

12. R. Suskind. 1990. Peterborough, N.H., "Site of 'Our Town' still resists change." *Wall Street Journal,* 123:1.

13. H. H. Kelly & J. L. Michela. 1980. Attribution theory and research. *Annual Review of Psychology* 31:457–501; and B. Weiner, I. Freize, A. Kukla, L. Reed, S. Rest, & R. M. Rosenbaum. 1971. Perceiving the causes of success and failure. In E. Jones, D. Kanouse, H. Kelly, R. Nesbitt, S. Valins, & B. Weiner (eds.). *Attribution: Perceiving the causes of behavior,* pp. 45–61. Morristown, NJ: General Learning Press.

14. For example, see A. G. Miller & T. Lawson. 1989. The effect of an informational option on the fundamental attribution error. *Personality and Social Psychology Bulletin* 20:194–204.

15. M. E. Heilman & R. A. Guzzo. 1978. The perceived cause of work success as a mediator of sex discrimination in organizations. *Organizational Behavior and Human Decision Processes* 21:346–357.

16. W. F. Cascio. 1989. *Managing human resources: Productivity, quality of life, profits.* New York: McGraw-Hill.

17. P. A. Casselden & S. E. Hampson. 1990. Forming impressions from incongruent traits. *Journal of Personality and Social Psychology* 59:353–362.

18. H. A. Murray. 1938. *Explorations in personality.* New York: Oxford University Press.

19. R. D. Arvey, T. J. Bouchard, Jr., N. L. Segal, & L. M. Abraham. 1989. Job satisfaction: Environmental and genetic components. *Journal of Applied Psychology* 74:187–192.

20. J. Brockner. 1988. *Self-esteem at work: Research, theory, and practice.* Lexington, MA: Heath.

21. D. G. Gardner & J. L. Pierce. 1998. Self-esteem and self-efficacy within the organizational context. *Group & Organization Management* 23(1):48–70; and S. Coopersmith. 1967. *The antecedents of self-esteem.* New York: Freeman; Rosenberg, M. 1965. *Society and the adolescent self-image.* Princeton, NJ: Princeton University Press.

22. M. Rosenberg. 1965. *Society and the adolescent self-image.* Princeton, NJ: Princeton University Press.

23. P. Tharenou. 1979. Employee self-esteem: A review of the literature. *Journal of Vocational Behavior* 15:1–29. A closely related concept is self-efficacy, which is the self-perceived ability to perform well in the future on a specific task (such as write a report). It is a more narrow concept than job-based self-esteem. Self-efficacy is discussed further in Chapter 7.

24. J. L. Pierce, D. G. Gardner, L. L. Cummings, & R. B. Dunham. 1989. Organization-based self-esteem: Construct definition, measurement, and validation. *Academy of Management Journal* 32:622–648.

25. A. K. Korman 1976. Hypothesis of work behavior revisited and an extension. *Academy of Management Review* 1:50–63.

26. Pierce, Dunham, Cummings, & Dunham, 1989.

27. J. B. Rotter. 1966. Generalized expectancies for internal versus external control of reinforcement. *Psychological Monographs* 80:1–28.

28. Interesting studies include C. Anderson, D. Hellriegel, & J. Slocum. 1977. Managerial response to environmentally induced stress. *Academy of Management Journal* 19:260–272; and T. Mitchell, C. Smyser, & S. Weed. 1975. Locus of control: Supervision and work satisfaction. *Academy of Management Journal* 17:623–631.

29. N. Machiavelli. 1513. *The prince.* (Written, but not published, in 1513.) English translations include: R. M. Adams. 1977. *The prince.* New York: Norton.

30. Research on Machiavellianism includes R. Christie & F. L. Geis (eds.). 1970. *Studies in Machiavellianism.* New York: Academic Press; F. L. Geis & T. H. Moon. 1981. Machiavellianism and deception. *Journal of Personality and Social Psychology* 41:766–775.

31. J. M. Digman. 1990. Personality structure: Emergence of the five-factor model. *Annual Review of Psychology* 41:417–440; M. K. Mount & M. R. Barrick. 1998. Five reasons why the "Big Five" article has been frequently cited. *Personnel Psychology* 51:849–857; M. K. Mount & M. R. Barrick. 1991. The "Big Five" personality dimensions and job performance: A meta-analysis. *Personnel Psychology* 44:1–26; and R. P. Tett, D. N. Jackson, & M. Rothstein. 1991. Personality measures as predictors of job performance: A meta-analytic review. *Personnel Psychology* 44:703–742.

32. Mount & Barrick, 1991, 1998.

33. D. G. Gardner. 1986. Activation theory and task design: A test of several new predictions. *Journal of Applied Psychology* 71:411–418.

34. For example, see M. A. Shaffer & D. A. Harrison. 1998. Expatriates' psychological withdrawal from international assignments: Work, nonwork, and family influences. *Personnel Psychology* 51:87–118.

35. J. S. Black. 1988. Work role transitions: A study of American expatriate managers in Japan. *Journal of International Business Studies* 19:277–294; and R. L. Tung. 1988. *The new expatriates.* Cambridge: Ballinger.

36. R. Shannonhouse. 1996 (Nov. 8). Overseas-assignments failures. *USA Today/International Edition,* 8A.

37. See, for example, N. J. Adler. 1991. *International dimensions of organizational behavior* (2nd ed.), Boston: PWS-Kent; and G. Hofstede. 1980. *Cultures' consequences: international differences in work-related values,* Beverly Hills, CA: Sage.

38. Hofstede, 1980.

Chapter 6. Attitudes in Organizations

1. F. N. Kerlinger. 1973. *Foundations of behavioral research,* 2nd ed. New York: Holt, Rinehart, & Winston.

2. R. D. Arvey, T. J. Bouchard, N. L. Segal, & L. N. Abraham. 1989. Job satisfaction: Environmental and genetic components. *Journal of Applied Psychology* 74:187–192; and N. G. Martin, L. J. Eaves, A. C. Heath, R. Jardine, L. M. Feingold, & H. J. Eysenck. 1986. Transmission of social attitudes. *Proceedings of the National Academy of Science* 83:4363–4368.

3. Arvey et al., 1989; Martin et al., 1986.

4. L. Festinger. 1957. *A theory of cognitive dissonance.* Evanston, IL: Row, Peterson.

5. For a related study, see D. G. Gardner, R. L. Dukes, & R. Discenza. 1993. Effects of computer use on computer attitudes and computer confidence: A causal modeling approach. *Computers in Human Behavior* 9:427–440.

6. K. Edwards. 1990. The interplay of affect and cognition in attitude formation and change. *Journal of Personality and Social Psychology* 59:202–216.

7. G. R. Salancik. 1977. Commitment and the control of organizational behavior and belief. In B. M. Staw & G. R. Salancik (eds.), *New directions in organizational behavior.* Chicago: St. Clair, 1–54.

8. M. Fishbein & I. Ajzen. 1975. *Belief, attitude, intention, and behavior.* Reading, MA: Addison-Wesley.

9. R. P. Steel & N. K. Ovalle. 1984. A review and meta-analysis of research on the relationship between behavioral intentions and employee turnover. *Journal of Applied Psychology* 69:673–686.

10. E. A. Locke. 1976. The nature and causes of job satisfaction. In M. Dunnette (ed.), *Handbook of industrial and organizational psychology.* Chicago: Rand McNally, 1297–1350.

11. Ibid., 1319.

12. B. M. Staw & J. Ross. 1985. Stability in the midst of change: A dispositional approach to job attitudes. *Journal of Applied Psychology* 70:469–480.

13. G. R. Salancik & J. Pfeffer. 1977. A social information processing approach to job attitudes and change. *Administrative Science Quarterly* 23:224–253.

14. R. D. Arvey, T. J. Bouchard, N. L. Segal, & L. M. Abraham. 1989. Job satisfaction: Environmental and genetic components. *Journal of Applied Psychology* 74:187–192.

15. I. Levin & J. P. Stokes. 1989. Dispositional approach to job satisfaction: Role of negative affectivity. *Journal of Applied Psychology* 74:752–758. Also see Staw & Ross, 1985.

16. See C. J. Cranny, P. C. Smith, & E. F. Stone. 1992. *Job satisfaction.* New York: Lexington Books; and E. F. Stone. 1978. *Research in organizational behavior.* New York: Goodyear.

17. The male faces were originally developed by T. Kunin, 1955, as reported in *Personnel Psychology* 8:65–78. The matching female faces were created by R. B. Dunham & J. B. Herman, 1975, and published in the *Journal of Applied Psychology* 60: 629–631.

18. D. J. Weiss, R. V. Dawis, G. W. England, & L. H. Lofquist. 1967. *Manual for the Minnesota Satisfaction Questionnaire* (Minnesota Studies in Vocational Rehabilitation: XXII). Minneapolis: Work Adjustment Project, Industrial Relations Center, University of Minnesota.

19. P. C. Smith, L. M. Kendall, & C. L. Hulin. 1969. *The measurement of satisfaction in work and retirement.* Chicago: Rand McNally.

20. For detailed comparisons of these four approaches and their relative strengths and weaknesses, see R. B. Dunham, F. J. Smith, & R. S. Blackburn. 1977. Validation of the index of organizational reactions with the JDI, the MSQ, and the faces scales. *Academy of Management Journal* 20:420–432.

21. ASPA-BNA Survey No. 37. 1979. Personnel policies: Research and evaluation. Washington, D.C.: Bureau of National Affairs.

22. D. W. Organ & M. Konovsky. 1989. Cognitive versus affective determinants of organizational citizenship behavior. *Journal of Applied Psychology* 74:157–164.

23. D. W. Organ. 1977. A reappraisal and reinterpretation of the satisfaction-causes-performance hypothesis. *Academy of Management Review* 2(1):46–53.

24. L. W. Porter, R. M. Steers, R. T. Mowday, & P. V. Boulian. 1974. Organizational commitment, job satisfaction, and turnover among psychiatric technicians. *Journal of Applied Psychology* 59:603–609; and R. T. Mowday, L. W. Porter, & R. M. Steers. 1982. *Employee-organizational linkages.* New York: Academic Press.

25. M. J. Allen & J. P. Meyer. 1990. The measurement and antecedents of affective, continuance and normative commitment to the organization. *Journal of Occupational Psychology* 63: 1–18.

26. J. P. Meyer, N. J. Allen, & I. R. Gellatly. 1990. Affective and continuance commitment to the organization: Evaluation of measures and analysis of concurrent and time-lagged relations. *Journal of Applied Psychology* 75:710–720.

27. J. L. Pierce & R. B. Dunham. 1987. Organizational commitment: Pre-employment propensity and initial work experiences. *Journal of Management* 13:163–178.

28. D. Omrani. 1992. Business process re-engineering: A business revolution? *Management Services* 36(10):12–16.

29. I. Sager. 1998 (Mar. 30). Stock options: Lou takes a cue from Silicon Valley. *Business Week,* 34.

30. S. Lease. 1998. Annual review, 1993–1997: Work attitudes and outcomes. *Journal of Vocational Behavior* 53:154–183.

31. S. Rabinowitz. 1981. Towards a developmental model of job involvement. *International Review of Applied Psychology* 30: 31–50; and S. D. Saleh & J. Hosek. 1976. Job involvement: Concepts and measurements. *Academy of Management Journal* 19: 213–224.

32. T. L. Brown. June 19, 1989. What will it take to win? *Industry Week,* 15.

33. J. L. Pierce, T. Kostova, & K. T. Dirks. 2001. Toward a theory of psychological ownership in organizations. *Academy of Management Review* 23:298–310.

34. T. Peters. 1991. 20 ideas on service. *Executive Excellence* 8(7):3–5.

35. J. L. Pierce & L. Van Dyne. 1993. *Psychological ownership within the organizational context.* A paper presented at the eighth annual conference of the Society for Industrial and Organizational Psychology, San Francisco; and L. Van Dyne & J. L. Pierce. 1993. *Employee ownership: Empirical support for mediated relationships.* A paper presented at the eighth annual conference of the Society for Industrial and Organizational Psychology, San Francisco.

36. I. Ajzen & M. Fishbein. 1977. Attitude-behavior relations: A theoretical analysis and review of empirical research. *Psychological Bulletin* 48:888–918.

37. W. H. Mobley, S. O. Horner, & A. T. Hollingsworth. 1978. An evaluation of precursors of hospital employee turnover. *Journal of Applied Psychology* 63:408–414.

38. Pierce & Van Dyne, 1993.

39. J. Welch. 1993 (Jan.). "Jack Welch's lessons for success," book excerpt. *Fortune,* 38.

40. J. L. Pierce, R. B. Dunham, & L. L. Cummings. 1984. Sources of environmental structuring and participant responses. *Organizational Behavior and Human Performance* 33:214–242; J. L. Pierce. 1979. Employee affective responses to work unit structure and job design: A test of an intervening variable. *Journal of Management* 5:193–211; G. R. Oldham & J. R. Hackman. 1981. Relationship between organizational structure and employee reactions: Comparing alternative frameworks. *Administrative Science Quarterly* 26:66–83; and J. L. Pierce, R. B. Dunham, & R. S. Blackburn. 1979. Social system structure, job design, and growth need strength: A test of a congruency model. *Academy of Management Journal* 22:223–249.

41. R. Brummet, E. Flamholtz, & W. Pyle. 1968. Human resource accounting—A challenge for accountants. *The Accounting Review,* 10:217–224.

42. R. Likert & D. G. Bowers. 1973. Improving the accuracy of P/L reports by estimating the change in dollar value of the human organization. *Michigan Business Review* 25:15–24.

43. P. H. Mirvis & E. E. Lawler, III. 1977. Measuring the financial impact of employee attitudes. *Journal of Applied Psychology* 62:1–8. Also see W. F. Cascio. 1991. *Costing human resources: The financial impact of behavior in organizations,* 3rd ed. Boston: PWS-Kent.

44. Readers who are interested in the financial impact of attitudes should see W. F. Cascio. 2000. *Costing human resources: The financial impact of behavior in organizations.* Cincinnati: South-Western College Publishing.

45. These are discussed more thoroughly, as is the entire attitude survey process, in R. B. Dunham & F. J. Smith. 1979. *Organizational surveys: An internal assessment of organizational health.* Glenview, IL: Scott, Foresman.

46. Guidance is available for the measurement of behaviors such as turnover and absenteeism. One source for such information is the Bureau of National Affairs *Policies and Practice Guide,* a publication updated biweekly to reflect current organizational practices. Also see R. W. Hollmann. 1999. *Absenteeism: Analyzing work absences.* SHRM White Paper, Alexandria, VA: Society for Human Resource Management; and C. Wiley. 1999. *Employee turnover: Analyzing employee movement out of the organization.* SHRM White Paper, Alexandria, VA: Society for Human Resource Management.

47. B. A. Macy & P. H. Mirvis. 1976. Measuring quality of work and organizational effectiveness in behavioral-economic terms. *Administrative Science Quarterly* 21:212–226.

48. Ibid.

49. Allen & Meyer, 1990.

Chapter 7. Work Motivation

1. J. E. Hunter & R. E. Hunter. 1984. Validity and utility of alternative predictors of job performance. *Psychological Bulletin* 96: 72–98.

2. Chapter 4 presents statistics on the prevalence of this choice.

3. H. A. Murray. 1938. *Explorations in personality.* New York: Oxford University Press.

4. Murray also hypothesized that people would differ in the degree to which they felt these needs. His list of secondary needs became a basis for his theory of personality.

5. Representative references include J. W. Atkinson & D. C. McClelland. 1948. The projective expression of needs. II. The effect of different intensities of the hunger drive on thematic apperception. *Journal of Experimental Psychology* 38:643–658; D. C. McClelland, J. W. Atkinson, R. A. Clark, & E. L. Lowell. 1953. *The achievement motive.* New York: Appleton-Century-Crofts; R. C. DeCharms. 1957. Affiliation motivation and productivity in small groups. *Journal of Abnormal Psychology* 55:222–276; D. C. McClelland. 1961. *The achieving society.* Princeton, NJ: Van Nostrand; and D. C. McClelland. 1975. *Power: The inner experience.* New York: Irvington.

6. In fact, McClelland argued that the success of entire societies is dependent on its achievement needs.

7. D. C. McClelland. 1970. The two faces of power. *Journal of International Affairs* 24:29–47.

8. A. H. Maslow. 1943. A theory of human motivation. *Psychological Bulletin* 50:370–396; A. H. Maslow. 1954. *Motivation and personality.* New York: Harper & Row; A. H. Maslow. 1965. *Eupsychian management.* Homewood, IL: Irwin.

9. D. McGregor. 1960. *The human side of enterprise.* New York: McGraw-Hill; D. McGregor. 1967. *The professional manager.* New York: McGraw-Hill.

10. Maslow, 1943, 382.

11. C. P. Alderfer. 1972. *Existence, relatedness, and growth: Human needs in organizational settings.* New York: Free Press.

12. D. T. Hall & K. E. Nougaim. 1968. An examination of Maslow's need hierarchy in an organizational setting. *Organizational Behavior and Human Performance* 3:12–35; E. E. Lawler, III & J. L. Suttle. 1972. A causal correlational test of the need hierarchy concept. *Organizational Behavior and Human Performance* 7:265–287; M. A. Wahba & L. G. Bridwell. 1973. Maslow reconsidered: A review of research on the need hierarchy theory. *Proceedings of the thirty-third annual meeting of the Academy of Management,* 514–520.

13. C. P. Alderfer. 1972. *Existence, relatedness, and growth: Human needs and organizational settings.* New York: Free Press.

14. Note that Herzberg's theory has often been labeled the "two-factor theory" because it focuses on two continua. This name, however, implies that only two factors are involved, which is not correct. Herzberg prefers not to use the term "two-factor theory" because his two *sets* of needs identify a much larger *number* of needs.

15. F. Herzberg, B. Mausner, & B. Snyderman. 1959. *The motivation to work.* New York: Wiley; F. Herzberg. 1966. *Work and the nature of man.* New York: Crowell; F. Herzberg. 1968. One more time: How do you motivate employees? *Harvard Business Review* 46:54–62.

16. R. B. Dunham, J. L. Pierce, & J. W. Newstrom. 1983. Job context and job content: A conceptual perspective. *Journal of Management* 9:187–202.

17. R. M. Ryan & E. L. Deci. 2000. Self-determination theory and the facilitation of intrinsic motivation, social development, and well-being. *American Psychologist* 55:68–78.

18. B. F. Skinner. 1953. *Science and human behavior.* New York: Free Press; B. F. Skinner. 1969. *Contingencies of reinforcement.* East Norwalk, CT: Appleton Century-Crofts; B. F. Skinner. 1971. *Beyond freedom and dignity.* New York: Bantam Books.

19. Ibid.

20. R. W. Kempen & R. V. Hall. 1977. Reduction of industrial absenteeism: Results of a behavioral approach. *Journal of Organizational Behavior Management* 20:1–21.

21. J. S. Adams. 1965. Inequity in social exchange. In L. Berkowitz (ed.), *Advances in experimental social psychology* (Vol. 2). New York: Academic Press; G. C. Homans. 1961. *Social behavior: Its elementary forms.* New York: Harcourt, Brace, & World.

22. Ibid.

23. J. Kane & E. E. Lawler, III. 1979. Performance appraisal effectiveness. In B. Staw (ed.), *Research in organizational behavior* (Vol. 1). Greenwood, CT: JAI Press.

24. E. E. Lawler, III. 1972. Secrecy and the need to know. In M. Dunnette, R. House, & H. Tosi (eds.), *Readings in managerial motivation and compensation.* East Lansing: Michigan State University Press.

25. I. R. Andrews. 1967. Wage inequity and job performance: An experimental study. *Journal of Applied Psychology* 51:39–45; J. S. Adams. 1963a. Towards an understanding of inequity. *Journal of Abnormal Social Psychology* 67:422–436; J. S. Adams. 1963b. Wage inequities, productivity and work quality. *Industrial Relations* 3:9–16.

26. R. C. Huseman., J. D. Hatfield, & E. W. Miles. 1987. A new perspective on equity theory: The equity sensitivity construct. *Academy of Management Review* 12:222–234; E. W. Miles, J. D. Hatfield, & R. C. Huseman. 1989. The equity sensitivity construct: Potential implications for worker performance. *Journal of Management* 15:581–588.

27. R. J. Bies. 1987. The predicament of justice: The management of moral outrage. In B. M. Staw & L. L. Cummings (eds.), *Research in organizational behavior* (Vol. 9). Greenwich, CT: JAI Press, 289–319; J. Greenberg. 1987. A taxonomy of organizational justice theories. *Academy of Management Review* 12:9–22.

28. E. L. Locke. 1978. The ubiquity of the technique of goal setting in theories of and approaches to employee motivation. *Academy of Management Review* 3:594–601; F. W. Taylor. 1911. *The principles of scientific management.* New York: Norton; K. Lewin. 1935. *A dynamic theory of personality.* New York: McGraw-Hill; K. Lewin. 1938. *The conceptual representation and the measurement of psychological forces.* Durham, NC: Duke University Press; K. Lewin, T. Dembo, L. Festinger, & P. S. Sears. 1944. Level of aspiration. In J. McVicker Hunt (ed.), *Personality and behavior disorders.* New York: Ronald Press, 333–378; P. Drucker. 1954. *The practice of management.* New York: Wiley; D. McGregor. 1957. An uneasy look at performance appraisal. *Harvard Business Review* 35:89–94; E. A. Locke. 1968. Toward a theory of task motivation and incentives. *Organizational Behavior and Human Performance* 3:157–189; E. A. Locke, K. N. Shaw, L. M. Saari, & G. P. Latham. 1981. Goal setting and task performance: 1969–1980. *Psychological Bulletin* 90:125–152; G. P. Latham & E. A. Locke. 1984. *Goal setting: A motivational technique that works!* Englewood Cliffs, NJ: Prentice Hall.

29. C. C. Pinder. 1984. *Work motivation: Theory, issues, and applications.* Glenview, IL: Scott, Foresman.

30. Locke, 1979.

31. T. R. Mitchell & W. S. Silver. 1990. Individual and group goals when workers are interdependent: Effects on task strategies and performance. *Journal of Applied Psychology* 75:185–193.

32. A. Bandura. 1977. Self-efficacy: Toward a unifying theory of behavioral change. *Psychological Review* 84:191–215; A. Bandura. 1986b. The explanatory and predictive scope of self-efficacy theory. *Journal of Social and Clinical Psychology* 4:359–373; A. Bandura. 1997. *Self-efficacy: The exercise of control*. New York: Freeman.

33. D. G. Gardner & J. L. Pierce. 1998. Self-esteem and self-efficacy within the organizational context: An empirical comparison. *Group and Organization Management* 23:48–70.

34. Locke, 1978.

35. M. L. Ambrose & C. T. Kulik. 1999. Old friends, new faces: Motivation research in the 1990s. *Journal of Management* 25: 231–292.

Chapter 8. Behavior in Organizations

1. R. L. Cardy & G. H. Dobbins. 1994. *Performance appraisal: Alternative perspectives*. Cincinnati: South-Western; G. Latham & K. Wexley. 1994. *Increasing productivity through performance appraisal*. Reading, MA: Addison-Wesley; and K. R. Murphy & J. N. Cleveland. 1995. *Understanding performance appraisal: Social, organizational, and goal-based perspectives*. Thousand Oaks, CA: Sage.

2. M. R. Edwards & A. J. Ewen. 1996. *360-degree feedback*. New York: American Management Association.

3. W. T. Gregor. 1990 (May/June). Alternative strategies for successful cost management. *Bankers Magazine* 173(3), 20–28.

4. D. L. Deadrick & D. G. Gardner. 2000. Performance distributions: Measuring employee performance using total quality management principles. *Journal of Quality Management* 4:225–241.

5. P. C. Smith & L. M. Kendall. 1963. Retranslation of expectations: An approach to the construction of unambiguous anchors for rating scales. *Journal of Applied Psychology* 47:249–255; and J. P. Campbell, M. D. Dunnette, R. D. Arvey, & L. V. Hellervik. 1973. The development and evaluation of behaviorally based rating scales. *Journal of Applied Psychology* 57:15–22.

6. For example, see Deadrick & Gardner, 2000; and Cardy & Dobbins, 1994.

7. Murphy & Cleveland, 1995.

8. F. T. Coleman. 2000. *Cardinal rules of termination*, SHRM White Paper. Alexandria, VA: Society for Human Resource Management.

9. A. H. Brayfield & W. H. Crockett. 1955. Employee attitudes and employee performance. *Psychological Bulletin* 52:396–424; M. T. Iaffaldano & P. M. Muchinsky. 1985. Job satisfaction and job performance: A meta-analysis. *Psychological Bulletin* 97: 251–273; and V. H. Vroom. 1964. *Work and motivation*. New York: Wiley.

10. Deadrick & Gardner, 2000.

11. Cardy & Dobbins, 1994; and Deadrick & Gardner, 2000.

12. T. A. Wright & B. M. Staw. 1999. Affect and favorable work outcomes: Two longitudinal tests of the happy-productive worker thesis. *Journal of Organizational Behavior* 20:1–23.

13. Ibid.

14. D. G. Gardner, R. B. Dunham, J. L. Pierce, & L. L. Cummings. 1989. Focus of attention at work: Construct definition and empirical validation. *Journal of Occupational Psychology* 62: 61–77.

15. R. W. Hollmann. 2000. *Absenteeism: Analyzing work absences*, SHRM White Paper. Alexandria,VA: Society for Human Resource Management.

16. D. A. Harrison & J. J. Martocchio. 1998. Time for absenteeism: A 20-year review of origins, offshoots, and outcomes. *Journal of Management* 24:305–346.

17. Bureau of National Affairs. 2000. *Bulletin to management: BNA's quarterly report on job absence*. Alexandria, VA: Society for Human Resource Management.

18. Harrison & Martocchio, 1998.

19. P. W. Hom & R. W. Griffeth. 1995. *Employee turnover*. Cincinnati: South-Western.

20. T. W. Lee, T. R. Mitchell, B. C. Holtom, L. S. McDaniel, & J. W. Hill. 1999. The unfolding model of voluntary turnover: A replication and extension. *Academy of Management Journal* 42: 450–464.

21. R. Deems. 1998. Employee turnover costs. *Ivey Business Journal* 62(4):19.

22. Bureau of National Affairs, 2000.

23. W. H. Turnley & D. C. Feldman. 1999. The impact of psychological contract violations on exit, voice, loyalty, and neglect. *Human Relations* 52:895–922.

24. B. Davison. 1997. Special report: Strategies for managing retention. *HR Focus* 74(10):3; C. D. Fyock. 2000. *Retention tactics that work*. SHRM White Paper, Alexandria, VA: Society for Human Resource Management; N. Stein. 2000. Winning the war to keep top talent. *Fortune* 141(11):132; R. J. Vandenberg, H. A. Richardson, & L. J. Eastman. 1999. The impact of high involvement work processes on organizational effectiveness: A second-order latent variable approach. *Group and Organization Management* 24:300–339; and T. B. Weiss. 1997. Show me more than the money. *HR Focus* 74(11):3.

25. Fyock, ibid.

26. Ibid.

27. J. L. Cotton. 1993. *Employee involvement*. Newbury Park, CA: Sage.

28. Vandenberg et al., 1999.

29. D. Katz & R. Kahn. 1966. *The social psychology of organizations*. New York: Wiley.

30. P. M. Podsakoff & S. B. MacKenzie. 1997. Impact of organizational citizenship on organizational performance: A review and suggestions for future research. *Human Performance* 10:133–152; L. VanDyne & J. A. LePine. 1998. Helping and voice extra-role behaviors: Evidence of construct and predictive validity. *Academy of Management Journal* 41:108–119.

31. M. C. Bolino. 1999. Citizenship and impression management: Good soldiers or good actors? *Academy of Management Review* 24:82–98; and D. W. Organ. 1988. *Organizational citizenship behavior: The good soldier syndrome*. Lexington, MA: Lexington Books.

32. L. VanDyne, J. W. Graham, & R. M. Dienesch. 1994. Organizational citizenship behavior: Construct redefinition, measurement, and validation. *Academy of Management Journal* 37: 765–802.

33. D. W. Organ & K. Ryan. 1995. A meta-analytic review of attitudinal and dispositional predictors of organizational citizenship behaviors. *Personnel Psychology* 48:775–801.

34. Also see J. A. Chatman & S. G. Barsade. 1995. Personality, organizational culture, and cooperation: Evidence from a business simulation. *Administrative Science Quarterly* 40:423–444.

35. Anonymous. 2000 (May 14). Bloody delusions? Insanity defense eyed as Xerox massacre trial starts Monday. Associated Press.

36. F. Tartakovsky. 1999 (Nov. 15). You're safer at work. *Time* 154(20):86.

37. Anonymous. 2000 (Apr.). Exclusive HR focus survey: Safe, not sorry, is the best approach. *HR Focus* 77(4):1,4; Anonymous. 2000 (Mar.). How to "fight" workplace violence. *HR Focus* 77(3):8–9; D. B. Fogelman. 2000. Minimizing the risk of violence in the workplace. *Employment Relations Today* 27(1):83–99; B. Leonard. 2000. Workplace violence is top security concern for execs. *HR Magazine* 45(5):20; S. Schroeder. 1999. The high cost of violence. *Risk Management* 46(11):54.

38. Schroeder, 1999.

39. Fogelman, 2000.
40. Leonard, 2000.
41. Schroeder, 1999.
42. A. M. O'Leary-Kelly, R. W. Griffin, & D. J. Glew. 1996. Organization-motivated aggression: A research framework. *Academy of Management Review* 21:225–254.
43. S. L. Robinson & R. J. Bennett. 1995. A typology of deviant behaviors: A multidimensional scaling study. *Academy of Management Journal* 38:555–572.
44. D. C. Gundersen & J. Nicolletti. 1999 (Mar.). *Workplace violence*. Presentation to Colorado Department of Transportation.
45. O'Leary-Kelly et al., 1996.
46. Gundersen & Nicoletti, 1999; J. J. Keller. 1999. *Safety managers handbook*. New York: American Management Association.
47. E. F. Ferraro. 1995. *What every employer should know about workplace violence*. Golden, CO: ASET.
48. J. Marks. 1996 (Apr. 22). The American uncivil wars. *U.S. News & World Report,* 66–72.
49. R. A. Baron & J. H. Neuman. 1996. Workplace violence and workplace aggression: Evidence on their relative frequency and potential causes. *Aggressive Behavior* 22:161–173; H. J. Ehrlich & B. E. K. Larcom. 1994. *Ethnoviolence in the workplace*. Baltimore: Center for the Applied Study of Ethnoviolence; J. H. Neuman & R. A. Baron. 1997. Aggression in the workplace. In R. A. Giacalone & J. Greenberg (eds.), *Antisocial behavior in organizations,* 37–67. Thousand Oaks, CA: Sage.
50. L. M. Andersson & C. M. Pearson. 1999. Tit for tat? The spiraling effect of incivility in the workplace. *Academy of Management Review* 24:452–471.
51. Anonymous. 1999. Dealing with drugs. *Occupational Safety and Health* 68(7):78–80; D. R. Comer. 2000. Employees' attitudes toward fitness-for-duty testing. *Journal of Managerial Issues* 12(1): 61–75; G. Flynn. 1999. How to prescribe drug testing. *Workforce* 78(1):107–110; J. Germignani. 1999. Substance abusers: Terminate or treat? *Business and Health* 17(6):32–38; T. D. Hartwell, P. D. Steele, & N. F. Rodman. 1998. Workplace alcohol testing programs: Prevalence and trends. *Monthly Labor Review* 121(6): 27–34; S. Overman. 1999. Splitting hairs. *HR Magazine* 44(8):42–48; R. G. Perry. 1998. Fitness-for-duty testing. *Occupational Safety and Health* 67(4):41–43; D. Rhode. 1998. Drugs in the workplace. *Occupational Safety and Health* 67(10):136–138.
52. Hartwell et al., 1998; Rhodes, 1998.
53. For example, see M. Cranford (1998). Drug testing and the right to privacy: Arguing about the ethics of workplace drug testing. *Journal of Business Ethics* 17:1805–1815.
54. Rhodes, 1998.
55. Germignani, 1999.
56. Hartwell et al., 1998.
57. Flynn, 1999.
58. E. F. Ferraro. 1995. *Workplace substance abuse*. Chino Hills, CA: Group Dynamics.
59. Anonymous. 1999. Dealing with drugs. *Occupational Safety and Health* 68(7):78–80.

PART III. Management Functions and the Organizational Behavior Context

Chapter 9. Organizational Decision Making

1. B. M. Bass. 1983. *Organizational decision making*. Homewood, IL: Irwin, 2; H. A. Simon. 1960. *The new science of management decision*. Englewood Cliffs, NJ: Prentice-Hall.
2. Bass, 1983, 3.
3. G. Huber. 1980. *Managerial decision making*. Glenview, IL: Scott, Foresman, 8–9.
4. W. F. O'Dell. 1991. *Effective business decision making*. Lincolnwood, IL: NTC Business Books; Simon, 1960.
5. P. L. Koopman, J. W. Broekhuysen, & M. Meijn. 1984. Complex decision making at the organizational level. In P. J. Drenth, H. Thierry, P. J. Wilems, & C. J. DeWolff (eds.), *Handbook of work and organizational psychology*. New York: Wiley, 831–854.
6. K. R. MacCrimmon & R. N. Taylor. 1976. Decision making and problem solving. In M. D. Dunnette (ed.), *Handbook of industrial and organizational psychology*. Chicago: Rand McNally.
7. S. M. Jex, 1998. *Stress and job performance: Theory, research, and implications for managerial practice*. Thousand Oaks, CA: Sage.
8. A. Elbing. 1978. *Behavioral decisions in organizations*. Glenview, IL: Scott, Foresman, 74–83.
9. T. Peters. 1987. *Thriving on chaos*. New York: Knopf.
10. D. Isenberg. 1986. Thinking and managing: A verbal protocol analysis of managerial problem solving. *Academy of Management Journal* 29:775–88.
11. S. Snyder. 1989 (Dec.). Getting to eureka. *Johns Hopkins Magazine,* 26.
12. W. F. O'Dell. 1991 (Sept.). Executive book summary of *Effective Business Decision Making*. 13:9, 4.
13. Ibid.
14. Ibid.
15. Ibid.
16. J. D. Thompson & A. Tudin. 1959. Strategies, structures, and processes of organizational decisions. In J. D. Thompson, P. B. Hammond, R. W. Hawkes, B. H. Junker, & A. Tudin (eds.). *Comparative studies in administration*. Pittsburgh: University of Pittsburgh Press, 195–216.
17. L. A. Burke & M. K. Miller. 1999. Taking the mystery out of intuitive decision making. *Academy of Management Executive* 13:4, 91–99.
18. A. H. Van de Ven. 1977. A panel study on the effects of task uncertainty, interdependence, and size on unit decision making. *Organization and Administrative Sciences* 8:237–53.
19. V. H. Vroom & P. H. Yetton. 1973. *Leadership and decision making*. Pittsburgh, PA: University of Pittsburgh Press; V. H. Vroom & A. G. Jago. 1988. *The new leadership: Managing participation in organizations*. Englewood Cliffs, NJ: Prentice-Hall.
20. A. G. Jago. 1982. Leadership: Perspectives in theory and research, *Management Science* 28:315–336; R. J. House & M. L. Baetz. 1979. Leadership: Some empirical generalizations and new research directions. In B. M. Staw (ed.), *Research in organizational behavior,* vol. 1, Greenwich, CT: JAI Press, 341–423.
21. C. E. Lindblom. 1959. The science of "muddling through." *Public Administration Review* 19:79–88.
22. Ibid.
23. E. A. Locke & G. P. Latham. 1984. *Goal setting for individuals, groups, and organizations*. Chicago: Science Research Associates, 26.
24. P. J. Brews & M. R. Hunt. 1999. Learning to plan and planning to learn: Resolving the planning school/learning school debate. *Strategic Management Journal* 20:889–913.
25. R. L. Daft. 1983. *Organization theory and design*. St. Paul, MN: West, 361.
26. M. D. Cohen, J. G. March, & J. P. Olsen. 1972. A garbage can model of organizational choice. *Administrative Science Quarterly* 17:1–25; J. G. March & Johan P. Olsen. 1986. Garbage can models of decision making in organizations. In J. G. March & R. Weissinger-Baylon (eds.), *Ambiguity and Command: Organizational Perspectives on Military Decision Making,* Marshfield, A: Pitman, 11–35.
27. H. Mintzberg, D. Raisinghani, & A. Theoret. 1976. The structure of "unstructured" decision processes. *Administrative Science Quarterly* 21:246–75.
28. P. C. Nutt. 1999. Surprising but true: Half the decisions in organizations fail. *Academy of Management Executive* 13:4, 75.
29. J. S. Hammond, R. L. Keeney, & H. Raiffa. 1998 (Sept.–Oct.). The hidden traps in decision making. *Harvard Business Review* 76(5):47–58.

30. Nutt, 1999.

31. A. Murr. 2000 (Apr. 10). Final answer: It crashed. *Newsweek,* 46.

32. D. C. Feldman. 1984. The development and enforcement of group norms. *Academy of Management Review* 9:47–53.

33. N. R. F. Maier. 1970. Assets and liabilities in group problem solving: The need for an integrative function. In N. R. F. Maier (ed.), *Problem solving and creativity: In individuals and groups.* Belmont, CA: Brooks/Cole, 431–444.

34. W. Kiechel, III. 1990 (Mar. 12). The organization that learns. *Fortune,* 133–135.

35. Ibid.

36. R. Stata. 1989. Organizational learning—The key to management innovation. *Sloan Management Review* 30(3):63–74.

37. Ibid.

38. P. Senge. 1990. *The fifth discipline: The art and practice of the learning organization.* New York: Doubleday.

39. J. W. Gardner. 1965 (Oct.). How to prevent organizational dry rot. *Harper's Magazine,* 20–26.

40. M. J. Driver. 1979. Individual decision making and creativity. In S. Kerr (ed.), *Organizational behavior.* Columbus, OH: Grid, 59–91.

41. S. Freud. 1920. *A general introduction to psychoanalysis.* New York: Pocket Books.

42. C. Argyris. 1957. *Personality and organization.* New York: Harper & Row; C. G. Jung. 1957. *The undiscovered self.* Boston: Little, Brown; A. H. Maslow. 1962. *Toward a psychology of being.* Princeton: Van Nostrand; D. McGregor. 1960. *The human side of enterprise.* New York: McGraw-Hill.

43. H. A. Simon. 1976. *Administrative behavior: A study of decision-making processes in administrative organizations,* 3rd ed. New York: Free Press; H. Simon. 1965 (March). Administrative decision making. *Public Administrative Review,* 31–37.

44. Simon, 1976.

45. Ibid.

46. A. G. Bedeian & R. F. Zammuto. 1991. *Organizations: Theory and design.* Chicago: Dryden Press, 525.

47. R. Tannenbaum. & W. H. Schmidt. 1958. How to choose a leadership pattern. *Harvard Business Review,* 95–101.

48. K. I. Miller & P. R. Monge. 1988. Participation, satisfaction, and productivity: A meta-analytic review. *Academy of Management Journal* 29:727–753.

49. S. M. Sales. 1966. Supervisory style and productivity. *Personnel Psychology* 19:275–286.

50. R. White & R. Lippitt. 1960. Leader behavior and member reaction in three social climates. In D. Cartwright and A. Zander (eds.), *Group dynamics,* 3rd ed. New York: Harper & Row, 318–335.

51. E. A. Locke, M. Alavi, & J. A. Wagner. 1997. Participation in decision making: An information exchange perspective. In G. Ferris (ed.), *Research in personnel and human resources management.* Greenwich, CT: JAI Press, 15:293–331.

52. E. A. Locke & D. M. Schweiger. 1979. Participation in decision-making: One more look. In B. M. Staw & L. L. Cummings (eds.), *Research in organizational behavior,* 1. Greenwich, CT: JAI Press; K. I. Miller & P. R. Monge. 1988. Participation, satisfaction, and productivity: A meta-analytic review. *Academy of Management Journal* 29:727–753; D. M. Schweiger & C. R. Leana. 1986. Participation in decision making. In E. A. Locke (ed.), *Generalizing from laboratory to field studies.* Lexington, MA: Heath, 147–166; J. A. Wagner, III. 1994. Participation's effects on performance and satisfaction: A reconsideration of research evidence. *Academy of Management Review* 19:312–330.

53. J. L. Pierce, M. P. O'Driscoll, & A. Coghlan. 2001. *Work environment structure and psychological ownership: The mediating effects of control.* Department of Psychology, University of Waikato Working Paper, Hamilton, New Zealand; Y. Bonadona. 2000. *Perception of control: A route to psychological ownership in organizations.* Master of Social Sciences Thesis, University of Waikato, Hamilton, New Zealand.

54. J. L. Pierce, T. Kostova, & K. Dirks. 2001. Toward a theory of psychological ownership in organizations. *Academy of Management Review* 26:298–310.

55. Miller & Monge, 1988.

56. J. A. Scully, S. A. Kirkpatrick, & E. A. Locke. 1995. Locus of knowledge as a determinant of the effects of participation on performance, affect, and perceptions. *Organizational Behavior and Human Decision Processes* 61:276–288.

57. E. E. Lawler, III. 1986. *High involvement management.* San Francisco: Jossey-Bass; E. E. Lawler, III. 1992. *The ultimate advantage.* San Francisco: Jossey-Bass.

58. J. Thibaut & L. Walker. 1975. *Procedural justice: A psychological analysis.* Hillsdale, NJ: Erlbaum; J. Thibaut & L. Walker. 1978. A theory of procedure. *California Law Review,* 66:541–566; D. M. Rousseau. 1995. *Psychological contracts in organizations: Understanding written and unwritten agreements.* Thousand Oaks, CA: Sage.

59. Q. M. Roberson, N. A. Moye, & E. A. Locke. 1999. Identifying a missing link between participation and satisfaction: The mediating role of procedural justice perceptions. *Journal of Applied Psychology* 84:585–593.

60. Ibid.

61. R. H. Lowe & S. J. Vodanovich. 1995. A field study of distributive and procedural justice as predictors of satisfaction and organizational commitment. *Journal of Business and Psychology* 10(1):99–113; M. A. Korsgaard, D. M. Schweiger, & H. J. Sapienza. 1995. Building commitment, attachment, and trust in strategic decision-making teams: The role of procedural justice. *Academy of Management Journal* 38:60–84; K. W. Mossholder, N. Bennett, & C. L. Martin. 1988. A multilevel analysis of procedural justice context. *Journal of Organizational Behavior* 19:131–141.

62. R. J. Bies & J. S. Moag. 1986. Interactional justice: Communication criteria of fairness. In M. H. Bazerman, R. Lewicki, & B. Sheppard (eds.), *Research on negotiations in organizations* 1: 43–55. Greenwich, CT: JAI Press; D. Levinthal. 1988. A survey of agency models of organizations. *Journal of Economic Behavior and Organization* 9:153–185.

Chapter 10. Organizational Planning and Controlling

1. G. A. Steiner. 1969. *Top management planning.* London: Macmillan, 6–7.

2. United once more. 1987 (June 22). *Time,* 46–47; Two largest unions reach tentative pact with Northwest Airlines, 1993, May 3. St. Paul, MN: UPI News.

3. H. Koontz & C. O'Donnell. 1972. *Principles of management: An analysis of managerial functions.* New York: McGraw-Hill, 113–114.

4. B. E. Goetz. 1949. *Management planning and control.* New York: McGraw-Hill.

5. L. A. Williams. 1993 (Aug. 15). Planning can save small business. *Duluth News-Tribute,* 5-B.

6. H. Mintzberg. 1975 (July–Aug.). The manager's job: Folklore and fact. *Harvard Business Review,* 51.

7. S. J. Carroll & D. J. Gillen. 1984. The classical management functions: Are they really outdated? *Academy of Management Proceedings* 44:132–136.

8. Williams, 1993.

9. T. A. Mahoney, T. H. Jerdee, & S. J. Carroll, Jr. 1963. *Development of managerial performance: A research approach.* Cincinnati: Southwestern; T. A. Mahoney, T. H. Jerdee, & S. J. Carroll, Jr. 1965. The jobs of management. *California Management Review* 4:97–110; J. A. Hass, A. M. Porat, & J. A. Vaughan. 1969. Actual vs. ideal time allocations reported by managers: A study of managerial behavior. *Personnel Psychology* 22:61–75; R. V. Penfield. 1975. Time allocation patterns and effectiveness of managers. *Personnel Psychology* 27:245–255.

10. S. Fink. 1986. *Crisis management: Planning for the inevitable*. New York: AMACOM, 56; 64–65.

11. P. Lorange & R. V. Vancil. 1977. *Strategic planning systems*. Englewood Cliffs, NJ: Prentice-Hall; Steiner, 1969.

12. K. G. Smith, E. A. Locke, & D. Barry. 1986. *Goal setting, planning effectiveness and organizational performance: An experimental simulation*. Unpublished manuscript, University of Maryland, College of Business and Management, College Park, Maryland.

13. Koontz & O'Donnell, 1972, 124–128.

14. J. F. Clemens & D. F. Mayer. 1987. *The classic touch: Lessons in leadership from Homer to Hemingway*. Homewood, IL.: Dow Jones-Irwin, 147.

15. Steiner, 1969, 7; M. B. McCaskey. 1974. A contingency approach to planning: Planning with goals and planning without goals. *Academy of Management Journal* 17:281–291.

16. McCaskey, 1974.

17. T. J. Peters & R. J. Waterman, Jr. 1982. *In search of excellence: Lessons from America's best-run companies*. New York: Harper & Row.

18. P. C. Earley, P. Wojnarock, & W. Prest. 1987. Task planning and energy expended: An exploration of how goals influence performance. *Journal of Applied Psychology* 47:107–104; P. C. Earley & B. Perry. 1987. Work plan availability and performance: An assessment of task strategy priming on subsequent task completion. *Organizational Behavior and Human Decision Processes*, 39:279–302.

19. Smith, Locke, & Barry, 1986.

20. R. H. Kilman. 1984. *Beyond the quick fix*. San Francisco: Jossey-Bass, 50–51.

21. C. Perrow. 1961. The analysis of goals in complex organizations. *American Sociological Review* 26:854.

22. P. E. Connor. 1980. *Organizations: Theory and design*. Palo Alto, CA: Science Research Associates, 92–96.

23. J. D. Thompson & W. J. McEwen. 1958. Organizational goals and environment. *American Sociological Review* 23:23–30.

24. R. M. Cyert & J. G. March. 1963. *A behavioral theory of the firm*. Englewood Cliffs, NJ: Prentice-Hall.

25. P. F. Drucker. 1954. *The practice of management*. New York: Harper.

26. J. Hage. 1965. An axiomatic theory of organizations. *Administrative Science Quarterly* 10:289–320.

27. M. R. Richards. 1978. *Organizational goal structures*. St. Paul, MN: West, 27.

28. J. J. Reitz & L. N. Jewell. 1985. *Managing*, Glenview, IL.: Scott, Foresman, 66.

29. P. J. Brews & M. R. Hunt. 1999. Learning to plan and planning to learn: Resolving the planning school/learning school debate. *Strategic Management Journal* 20:889–913; W. Lindsay & L. Rue. 1980. Impact of the organization environment on the long-range planning process: A contingency view. *Academy of Management Journal* 23:385–404; D. Herold. 1972. Long-range planning and organizational performance: A cross-validation study. *Academy of Management Journal* 15:91–102; C. Saunders & F. D. Tuggle. 1977. *Toward a contingency theory of planning*. Presented at the 37th Annual Meeting of the Academy of Management, Orlando, FL; S. S. Thune & R. J. House. 1970. Where long-range planning pays off. *Business Horizons* 13:81–87.

30. E. H. Bowman. 1976. Strategy and the weather. *Sloan Management Review* 17:53.

31. D. R. Wood & R. L. LaForge. 1979. The impact of comprehensive planning on financial performance. *Academy of Management Journal* 22:516–526.

32. E. A. Locke & G. P. Latham. 1990. *A theory of goal setting and task performance*. Englewood Cliffs, NJ: Prentice-Hall; E. A. Locke & G. P. Latham. 1984. *Goal setting: A motivational technique that works!* Englewood Cliffs, NJ: Prentice-Hall.

33. E. A. Locke. 1982. Relation of goal performance with a short work period and multiple goal levels. *Journal of Applied Psychology* 67:512–514; G. P. Latham & J. J. Baaldes. 1975. The practical significance of Locke's theory of goal setting. *Journal of Applied Psychology* 60:187–90; G. P. Latham & E. A. Locke. 1979. Goal setting—A motivational technique that works. *Organizational Dynamics*, 68–80.

34. Locke, 1982.

35. E. A. Locke, K. N. Shaw, L. M. Saari, & G. P. Latham. 1981. Goal setting and task performance: 1969–1980. *Psychological Bulletin* 90:125–152.

36. Locke, 1982; H. Garland. 1983. Influence of ability-assigned goals, and normative information of personal goals and performance: A challenge to the goal attainability assumption. *Journal of Applied Psychology* 68:20–30; J. R. Hollenbeck & H. J. Klein. 1987. Goal commitment and the goal setting process: Problems, prospects, and proposals for future research. *Journal of Applied Psychology* 72:212–20.

37. Locke, Shaw, Saari, & Latham, 1981.

38. E. A. Locke, G. P. Latham, & M. Erez. 1988. The determinants of goal commitment. *Academy of Management Review* 13: 23–39.

39. Ibid.

40. R. R. Hackman & R. Wageman. 1995. Total quality management: Empirical, conceptual, and practical issues. *Administrative Science Quarterly* 40:309–342; W. E. Deming. 1993. *The new economics for industry, government, education*. Cambridge, MA: MIT Center for Advanced Engineering Study; W. E. Deming. 1986. *Out of the crises*. Cambridge, MA: MIT Center for Advanced Engineering Study.

41. P. W. Wright, J. M. George, S. R. Farnsworth, & G. C. McMahan. 1993. Productivity and extra-role behavior: The effects of goals and incentives on spontaneous helping. *Journal of Applied Psychology* 78:374–381.

42. R. M. Steers. 1977. *Organizational effectiveness: A behavioral view*. Santa Monica, CA: Goodyear, 20–23.

43. Locke & Latham, 1990.

44. K. Lewin. 1958. Psychology of success and failure. In C. L. Stacey and M. F. Demartino, *Understanding human motivation*. Cleveland: Allen.

45. Locke & Latham, 1990.

46. Deming, 1986.

47. Jay A. Conger. 1991 (Feb.). Inspiring others: The language of leadership. *Academy of Management Executive* 5(1):31–45.

48. See the following article for the findings from this work schedule change: J. L. Pierce & R. B. Dunham. 1992. The 121-hour work day: A 48-hour, 8-day week. *Academy of Management Journal* 35:1086–1098.

49. W. H. Newman. 1975. *Constructive control*. Englewood Cliffs, N. J.: Prentice Hall, 6.

50. W. H. Newman. 1984. Managerial control. In J. E. Rosenzweig & F. E. Kast (eds.), *Modules in management series*. Chicago: Science Research Associates, 1-42; W. H. Newman, J. R. Logan, & W. H. Hegarty. 1985. *Strategy, policy, and central management*. Cincinnati: Southwestern; W. H. Sihler. 1979. Toward better management control systems. *California Management Review*, 14:33–39; E. P. Strong & R. D. Smith. 1968. *Management control models*. New York: Holt, Rinehart & Winston.

51. M. S. Taylor, C. D. Fisher, & D. R. Ilgen. 1984. Individuals' reactions to performance feedback in organizations: A control theory perspective. In K. M. Rowland & G. R. Ferris (eds.), *Research in Personnel and Human Resources Management*. Greenwich, CT: JAI Press, 81–124.

52. E. A. Locke & G. P. Latham. 1984. *Goal setting: A motivational technique that works*. Englewood Cliffs, NJ: Prentice-Hall.

53. Interview with Steven Kerr appearing in R. D. Dunham 1984. *Organizational behavior: People and processes in management*. Homewood, IL: Irwin, 147; S. Kerr. 1987. On the folly of rewarding A, while hoping for B. *Academy of Management Journal* 18: 769–783.

54. D. B. Greenberger, S. Strasser, L. L. Cummings, & R. B. Dunham. 1989. The impact of personal control on performance and satisfaction. *Organizational Behavior and Human Decision Processes* 43:31; D. B. Greenberger & S. Strasser. 1986. Development and application of a model of personal control in organizations. *Academy of Management Review* 11:164.

55. Greenberger, Strasser, Cummings, & Dunham, 1989.

56. S. M. Miller. 1977. Controllability and human stress: Method, evidence and behavior. *Research and Therapy,* 171, 287–304; M. E. P. Seligman. 1975. *Helplessness: On depression, development and death.* New York: Freeman.

57. Greenberger & Strasser, 1986, 174.

58. J. B. Ovmier & M. E. P. Seligman. 1967. Effects of inescapable shock upon subsequent escape and avoidance learning. *Journal of Comparative and Physiological Psychology* 63:28–33; M. J. Martinko & W. L. Gardner. 1982. Learned helplessness: An alternate explanation for performance deficits. *Academy of Management Journal* 7:195–204.

59. M. H. Bazerman. 1982. Impact of personal control on performance: Is added control always beneficial? *Journal of Applied Psychology* 67:472–479.

60. P. Drucker, 1954; A. P. Raia. 1974. *Managing by objectives.* Glenview, IL: Scott, Foresman; R. G. Greenwood. 1981. Management by objectives: As developed by Peter Drucker, assisted by Harold Smiddy. *Academy of Management Review* 6:225–230.

61. G. S. Odiorne. 1979. *M.B.O. II.* Belmont, CA: Fearon.

62. R. Rodgers & J. E. Hunter. 1991. Impact of management by objectives on organizational productivity. *Journal of Applied Psychology Monograph* 76:322–336.

63. Ibid.

64. R. W. Hollmann. 1976. Applying MBO research to practice. *Human Resource Management* 15(4):28–36; J. M. Ivancevich, J. H. Donnelly, & J. M. Gibson. 1976. Evaluating MBO: The challenge ahead. In J. M. Gibson, J. M. Ivancevich, & J. H. Donnelly (eds.), *Readings in organizations: Behavior, structure, process.* Dallas, TX: Business Publications, 401–414.

65. J. C. Aplin & P. P. Schoderbek. 1976. MBO: Requisites for success in the public sector. *Human Resource Management* 15(2): 30–36.

66. J. N. Kondrasuk. 1981. Studies in MBO effectiveness. *Academy of Management Review* 6:419–30.

67. E. E. Lawler, III. 1986. *High-involvement management.* San Francisco: Jossey-Bass; E. E. Lawler, III. 1992. *The ultimate advantage: Creating high involvement organizations.* San Francisco: Jossey-Bass.

68. R. Henkoff. 1990 (Dec. 31). How to plan for 1995. *Fortune,* 70–79.

69. Ibid.

Chapter 11. Leading Organizational Members

1. L. S. Richman. 1993 (July 12). CEO's: Help not wanted. *Fortune,* 43.

2. K. Labich. 1988 (Oct. 24). The seven keys to business leadership. *Fortune,* 58.

3. W. Bennis. 1989. *Why leaders can't lead.* San Francisco: Jossey-Bass.

4. B. M. Bass. 1990. *Bass & Stogdill's handbook of leadership: Theory, research, and managerial applications.* New York: The Free Press.

5. W. Bennis. 1989. *Why leaders can't lead.* San Francisco: Jossey-Bass; W. Bennis, & B. Nanus. 1985. *Leaders: The strategies for taking charge.* New York: Harper & Row.

6. T. B. Pickens, Jr. 1992 (Fall/Winter). Pickens on leadership. *Hyatt Magazine,* 21.

7. E. P. Hollander & J. W. Julian. 1969. Contemporary trends in the analysis of leadership process. *Psychological Bulletin* 7(5): 387–397.

8. E. P. Hollander. 1964. Emergent leadership and social influence. In E. P. Hollander (ed.), *Leaders, groups, & influence.* New York: Oxford University Press.

9. F. E. Fiedler. 1996. Research on leadership selection and training: One view of the future. *Administrative Science Quarterly* 41:241–250.

10. Hollander & Julian, 1969.

11. R. M. Stogdill. 1948. Personal factors associated with leadership: A survey of the literature. *Journal of Psychology* 28: 35–71.

12. A. J. Murphy. 1941. A study of the leadership process. *American Sociological Review* 6:674–687.

13. Hollander, 1964.

14. R. J. House & T. R. Mitchell. 1974 (Autumn). Path-goal theory of leadership. *Journal of Contemporary Business* 81–97.

15. G. Yukl. 1971. Toward a behavioral theory of leadership. *Organizational Behavior and Human Performance* 6:414–440.

16. D. G. Gardner & J. L. Pierce. 1998. Self-esteem and self-efficacy within the organizational context. *Group & Organization Management* 23(1):48–70.

17. P. Hersey & K. H. Blanchard. 1988. *Management of organizational behavior utilizing human resources.* Englewood Cliffs, NJ: Prentice-Hall.

18. C. N. Greene. 1975. The reciprocal nature of influence between leader and subordinate. *Journal of Applied Psychology* 60: 187–193.

19. Hollander & Julian, 1969.

20. B. B. Graen & M. Wakabayashi. 1994. Cross-cultural leadership-making: Bridging American and Japanese diversity for team advantage. In M. D. Dunnette (ed.), *Handbook of industrial and organizational psychology,* 4 (2nd ed.): 415–446. Palo Alto: Consulting Psychologists Press.

21. C. A. Schriesheim, S. L. Castro, & F. J. Yammarino. 2000. Investigating contingencies: An examination of the impact of span of supervision and upward controlling on leader-member exchange using traditional and multivariate within- and between-entities analysis. *Journal of Applied Psychology* 85:659–677; A. S. Phillips & A. G. Bedeian. 1994. Leader-follower exchange quality: The role of personality and interpersonal attributes. *Academy of Management Journal* 37:990–1001.

22. J. A. Conger. 1993. The brave new world of leadership training. *Organizational Dynamics* 21(3):46–59.

23. Pickens, 1992, 21.

24. G. R. Salancik & J. Pfeffer. 1977 (Winter). Who gets power and how they hold on to it: A strategic contingency model of power. *Organizational Dynamics,* 3–21.

25. A. J. Murphy. 1941. A study of the leadership process. *American Sociological Review* 6:674–687.

26. L. Smircich & G. Morgan. 1982. Leadership: The management of meaning. *Journal of Applied Behavioral Science* 18(3): 257–273; Stogdill, 1948.

27. Hollander, 1964.

28. J. R. P. French, Jr. & B. Raven. 1959. The bases of social power. In D. Cartwright (ed.), *Studies in social power.* Ann Arbor, MI: Institute for Social Research, University of Michigan, 150–167.

29. A. Etzioni. 1961. *A comparative analysis of complex organizations, on power, involvement, and their correlates.* New York: Free Press of Glenco; H. C. Kelman. 1958. Compliance, identification, and internalization: Three processes of attitude change. *Journal of Conflict Resolution,* 51–61.

30. G. Yukl & J. B. Tracey. 1992. Consequences of influence tactics used with subordinates, peers, and the boss. *Journal of Applied Psychology* 77:525–535; T. R. Hinkin & C A. Schriesheim. 1990. Relationships between subordinate perceptions of supervisor influence tactics and attributed bases of supervisory power. *Human Relations* 43:221–237; P. M. Podsakoff & C. A. Schriesheim. 1985. Field studies of French and Raven's bases of power:

Critique, reanalysis, and suggestions for future research. *Psychological Bulletin* 97:398–411.

31. T. R. Hinkin & C. A. Schriesheim. 1990. Relationships between subordinate perceptions of supervisor influence tactics and attributed based of supervisory power. *Human Relations* 43:221–237.

32. Bennis, 1989.

33. L. Smircich & G. Morgan. 1982. Leadership: The management of meaning. *Journal of Applied Behavioral Sciences* 18(3): 257–273.

34. R. Tannenbaum & W. H. Schmidt. 1958 (Mar.–Apr.). How to choose a leadership pattern. *Harvard Business Review,* 95–101; R. Tannenbaum & W. H. Schmidt. 1973 (May–June). How to choose a leadership pattern. *Harvard Business Review,* 162–175.

35. K. Davis & J. W. Newstrom. 1985. *Human behavior at work: Organization behavior.* New York: McGraw-Hill.

36. D. McGregor. 1957. The human side of enterprise, *Management Review* 46:22–28, 88–92; D. McGregor. 1960. *The human side of enterprise.* New York: McGraw-Hill.

37. M. Haire, E. E. Ghiselli, & L. W. Porter. 1966. *Managerial thinking: An international study.* New York: Wiley.

38. R. E. Miles. 1975. *Theories of management: Implications for organizational behavior and development.* New York: McGraw-Hill.

39. J. P. Muczyk & B. C. Reimann. 1987. The case for directive leadership. *The Academy of Management Executive* 1:301–311.

40. W. A. Pasmore. 1988. *Designing effective organizations: The sociotechnical systems perspective.* New York: Wiley; T. J. Peters & R. H. Waterman, Jr. 1982. *In search of excellence: Lessons from America's best-run companies.* New York: Harper & Row.

41. F. A. Kramer. 1992 (Summer). Perspectives on leadership from Homer's Odyssey. *Business and the Contemporary World* 168–173.

42. K. Labich. 1988 (Oct. 24). The seven keys to business leadership. *Fortune,* 58.

43. Stogdill, 1948; R. M. Stogdill. 1974. *Handbook of leadership: A survey of theory and research.* New York: Free Press.

44. Ibid., 81. See also Stogdill, 1948.

45. S. A. Kirkpatrick & E. A. Locke. 1991. Leadership: Do traits matter? *The Executive* 5(2):48–60. E. A. Locke, S. Kirkpatrick, J. K. Wheeler, J. Schneider, K. Niles, H. Goldstein, K. Welsh, & D.-O. Chad. 1991. *The essence of leadership: The four keys to leading successfully.* New York: Lexington.

46. Kirkpatrick & Locke. 1991. The best managers: What it takes. 2000 (Jan. 10). *Business Week,* 158.

47. Locke et al., 1991; T. A. Stewart. 1999 (Oct. 11). Have you got what it takes? *Fortune* 140(7):318–322.

48. W. Mischel. 1973. Toward a cognitive social learning reconceptualization of personality. *Psychological Review* 80:252–283.

49. R. J. House & R. N. Aditya. 1997. The social scientific study of leadership: Quo vadis? *Journal of Management* 23:409–473; T. J. Bouchard, Jr., D. T. Lykken, M. McGue, N. L. Segal, & A. Tellegen. 1990. Sources of human psychological differences: The Minnesota study of twins reared apart. *Science* 250:223–228.

50. S. Helgesen. 1990. *The female advantage.* New York: Doubleday/Currency; J. Fierman. 1990 (Dec. 17). Do women manage differently? *Fortune* 122:115–120; J. B. Rosener. 1990 (Nov.–Dec.). Ways women lead. *Harvard Business Review* 68(6): 119–125.

51. J. B. Chapman. 1975. Comparison of male and female leadership styles. *Academy of Management Journal* 18:645–650; E. A. Fagenson 1990. Perceived masculine and feminine attributes examined as a function of individual's sex and level in the organizational power hierarchy: A test of four theoretical perspectives. *Journal of Applied Psychology* 75:204–211.

52. R. L. Kent & S. E. Moss. 1994. Effects of sex and gender role on leader emergence. *Academy of Management Journal* 37: 1335–1346.

53. Ibid.

54. A. H. Early & B. T. Johnson. 1990. Gender and leadership style: A meta-analysis. *Psychological Bulletin* 108:233–256.

55. G. H. Dobbins, W. S. Long, E. Dedrick, & T. C. Clemons. 1990. The role of self-monitoring and gender on leader emergence: A laboratory and field study. *Journal of Management* 16:609–618.

56. B. M. Staw & S. G. Barsade. 1993. Affect and managerial performance: A test of the sadder-but-wiser vs happier-and-smarter hypothesis. *Administrative Science Quarterly* 38:304–331.

57. J. M. George & K. Bellenhausen. 1990. Understanding prosocial behavior, sales performance, and turnover: A group-level analysis in a service context. *Journal of Applied Psychology* 75:698–709.

58. Dobbins et al., 1990.

59. K. Labich, 1988, 58–66.

60. B. Dumaine. 1990 (May 7). Who needs a boss? *Fortune,* 52–60.

61. T. Peters. 1987. *Thriving on chaos.* Schaumburg, IL: Video Publishing House.

62. E. A. Fleishman. 1953. The description of supervisory behavior. *Personnel Psychology* 37:1–6; E. A. Fleishman & E. F. Harris. 1962. Patterns of leadership behavior related to employee grievances and turnover. *Personnel Psychology* 15:43–56; A. W. Halpin & B. J. Winer. 1957. A factorial study of the leader behavior descriptions. In R. M. Stogdill & A. C. Coons (eds.), *Leader behavior: Its description and measurement.* Columbus: Bureau of Business Research, Ohio State University; J. K. Hemphill & A. E. Coons. 1975. Development of the leader behavior description questionnaire. In R. M. Stogdill & A. E. Coons (eds.), *Leader behavior*; S. Kerr & C. Schriesheim. 1974. Consideration, initiating structure, and organizational criteria—an update of Korman's 1966 review. *Personnel Psychology* 27:555–568.

63. D. Katz & R. L. Kahn. 1952. Some recent findings in human relations research. In E. Swanson, T. Newcomb, & E. Hartley (eds.), *Readings in social psychology,* New York: Holt, Rinehart, & Winston; D. Katz, N. Macoby, & N. Morse. 1950. *Productivity, supervision, and morale in an office situation,* Ann Arbor, MI: Institute for Social Research; F. C. Mann & J. Dent. 1954. The supervisor: Member of two organizational families. *Harvard Business Review* 32:103–112.

64. D. G. Bowers & S. C. Seashore. 1966. Pretesting organizational effectiveness with a four-factor theory of leadership. *Administrative Science Quarterly* 11:238–262; Yukl, 1971; D. A. Nadler, G. D. Jenkins, Jr., C. Cammonn, and E. E. Lawler, III. 1975. *The Michigan organizational assessment package progress report.* Ann Arbor: Institute for Social Research, University of Michigan.

65. Bowers & Seashore, 1966.

66. R. R. Blake & J. S. Mouton. 1964. *The managerial grid.* Houston: Gulf; R. R. Blake & J. S. Mouton. 1981. *The versatile manager: A grid profile,* Homewood, IL: Dow Jones-Irwin; R. R. Blake & J. S. Mouton. 1984. *The new managerial grid III.* Houston: Gulf.

67. R. R. Blake & J. S. Mouton. 1981. Management by grid® principles or situationalism: Which? *Group and Organization Studies* 6:439–455.

68. L. L. Larson, J. G. Hunt, & R. N. Osborn. 1976. The great hi-hi leader behavior myth: A lesson from Occam's razor. *Academy of Management Journal* 19:628–641.

69. D. Tjosvold. 1984. Effects of warmth and directiveness on subordinate performance on a subsequent task. *Journal of Applied Psychology* 69:422–427; A. W. Halpin. 1957. The leader behavior and effectiveness of aircraft commanders. In R. M. Stogdill & A. E. Coons (eds.). *Leader Behavior: Its description and measurement.* Columbus, OH: The Ohio State University, Bureau of Business Research.; E. A. Fleishman & J. Simmons. 1970. Relationship between leadership patterns and effectiveness ratings among Israeli foremen. *Personnel Psychology* 23:169–172.

70. Stogdill, 1948, 63.

71. House & Aditya, 1997.

72. F. E. Fiedler & M. M. Chemers. 1974. *Leadership and effective management.* Glenview, IL: Scott, Foresman.

73. F. E. Fiedler. 1976. The leadership game: Matching the men to the situation. *Organizational Dynamics,* 4, 9.

74. Personal conversation between Robert J. House and Fred Fiedler in September 1996, as reported in House & Aditya, 1997.

75. F. E. Fiedler. Sept.–Oct. 1965. Engineering the job to fit the manager. *Harvard Business Review,* 115–122.

76. See, for example, the supporting results of M. M. Chemers & G. J. Skrzypek. 1972. Experimental test of the contingency model of leadership effectiveness. *Journal of Personality and Social Psychology* 24:172–177; and the contradictory results of R. P. Vecchio. 1977. An empirical examination of the validity of Fiedler's model of leadership effectiveness. *Organizational Behavior and Human Performance* 19:180–206.

77. R. B. Dunham. 1984. [Interview with Fred E. Fiedler.] *Organizational behavior: People and processes in management.* Homewood, IL: Irwin, 368; J. L. Kennedy, Jr. 1982. Middle LPC leaders and the contingency model of leadership effectiveness. *Organizational Behavior and Human Performance* 30:1–14.

78. Chemens & Skrzpek, 1972; Vecchio, 1977.

79. House & Aditya. 1997; L. H. Peters, D. D. Hartke, & J. T. Pohlman. 1985. Fiedler's contingency model of leadership: An application of the meta-analysis procedure of Schmidt and Hunter. *Psychological Bulletin* 97:274–285.

80. R. J. House. 1971. A path goal theory of leader effectiveness. *Administrative Science Quarterly* 16:324.

81. R. Hoojiberg. 1996. A multidimensional approach toward leadership: An extension of the concept of behavioral complexity. *Human Relations* 49(7):917–946.

82. R. J. House & T. R. Mitchell. 1974 (Autumn). Path-goal theory of leadership, *Journal of Contemporary Business,* 86; R. J. House & G. Dessler. 1974. The path-goal theory of leadership: Some post hoc and a priori tests. In J. Hunt & L. Larson (eds.). *Contingency approaches to leadership.* Carbondale, IL: Southern Illinois University Press.

83. House & Mitchell, 1974; House & Dessler, 1974; R. T. Keller. 1989. A test of the path-goal theory of leadership with need for clarity as a moderator in research and development organizations. *Journal of Applied Psychology* 74:208–212.

84. L. Uchitelle. 1994. The new faces of U.S. manufacturing. *The New York Times,* July 3, Section 3, 1, 6.

85. J. R. Meindl, S. B. Ehrlich, & J. M. Dukerich. 1985. The romance of leadership. *Administrative Science Quarterly* 30:78–102.

86. C. Robert, T. M. Probst, J. J. Martocchion, F. Drasgow, & J. J. Lawler. 2000. Empowerment and continuous improvement in the United States, Mexico, Poland, and India: Predicting fit on the basis of the dimensions of power distance and individualism. *Journal of Applied Psychology* 85:643–658.

87. P. W. Dorfman & S. Roonen. 1991. *The universality of leadership theories: Challenges and paradoxes.* Paper presented at the Academy of Management Meetings, Miami.

88. P. W. Dorfman, J. P. Howell, S. Hiblino, J. K. Lee, U. Tate, & A. Bautista. 1997. Leadership in Western and Asian countries: Commonalities and differences in effective leadership processes across cultures. *Leadership Quarterly* 8(3):233–274.

89. P. M. Podsakoff, B. P. Niehoff, S. B. MacKenzie, & M. L. Williams. 1993. Do substitutes for leadership really substitute for leadership: An empirical examination of Kerr and Jermier's situational leadership model. *Organizational Behavior and Human Decision Processes* 54:1–44; S. Kerr. 1977. Substitutes for leadership: Some implications for organizational design. *Organization and Administrative Sciences* 8:135–146; S. Kerr & J. M. Jermier. 1978. Substitutes for leadership: Their meaning and measurement. *Organizational Behavior and Human Performance* 22:375–403; J. P. Howell & P. W. Dorfman. 1981. Substitutes for leadership: Test of a construct. *Academy of Management Journal* 24:714–728; J. L. Pierce, R. B. Dunham, & L. L. Cummings. 1984. Sources of environmental structuring and participant responses. *Organizational Behavior and Human Performance* 33:214–242.

90. D. G. Gardner, R. B. Dunham, L. L. Cummings, & J. L. Pierce. 1989. Focus of attention at work: Construct definition and empirical validation. *Journal of Occupational Psychology* 62:61–77.

91. D. G. Gardner, R. B. Dunham, L. L. Cummings, & J. L. Pierce. 1987. Focus of attention at work and leader-follower relationships. *Journal of Occupational Behaviour* 8:277–294.

92. G. A. Yukl. 1981. *Leadership in organizations.* Englewood Cliffs, NJ: Prentice-Hall.

93. B. Kellerman. 1984. *Leadership: Multidisciplinary perspectives.* Englewood Cliffs, NJ: Prentice-Hall; F. L. Landy. 1985. *Psychology of work behavior.* Homewood, IL: Dorsey Press.

94. J. M. Burns. 1978. *Leadership.* New York: Harper & Row; B. M. Bass. 1985. *Leadership and performance beyond expectations.* New York: Free Press.

95. R. L. Daft. 1999. *Leadership: Theory and practice.* Fort Worth, TX: Dryden Press.

96. J. R. Baum, E. A. Locke, & S. A. Kirkpatrick. 1998. A longitudinal study of the relation of vision and vision communication to venture growth in entrepreneurial firms. *Journal of Applied Psychology* 83:43–54; J. M. Howell & P. J. Frost. 1989. A laboratory study of charismatic leadership. *Organizational Behavior and Human Decision Processes* 43:243–269.

97. Bennis, 1989.

98. T. A. Judge & J. E. Bono. 2000. Five-factor model of personality and transformational leadership. *Journal of Applied Psychology* 85:751–765.

99. R. Pillai, C. A. Schriesheim, & E. S. Williams. 1999. Fairness perceptions and trust as mediators for transformational and transactional leadership: A two-sample study. *Journal of Management* 25:897–933.

100. C. C. Manz & H. P. Sims, Jr. 1987. Leading workers to lead themselves: The external leadership of self-managed work teams. *Administrative Science Quarterly* 32:106–129.

101. Pillai, Schriesheim, & Williams, 1999.

102. Ibid., 901.

103. S. N. Eisenstadt. 1968. *Max Weber: On charisma and institution building.* Chicago: University of Chicago Press, 46.

104. J. A. Conger & R. N. Kanungo. 1987. Toward a behavioral theory of charismatic leadership in organizational settings. *Academy of Management Review* 12:637–647; Howell & Frost, 1989.

105. R. J. House & M. L. Baetz. 1979. Leadership: Some empirical generalizations and new research directions. *Research in Organizational Behavior* 1:341–423; Conger and Kanungo, 1987.

106. Howell & Frost, 1989.

107. R. J. House. 1977. A 1976 theory of charismatic leadership. In J. G. Hunt & L. L. Larson (eds.). *Leadership: The cutting edge.* Carbondale, IL: Southern Illinois University Press.

108. A. R. Willner. 1984. *The spellbinders: Charismatic political leadership.* New Haven, CT: Yale University Press.

109. Conger, 1993.

110. Ibid.

111. House & Aditya, 1997.

Chapter 12. Organizing and Coordinating the Work of the Organization

1. C. Barnard. 1938. *The functions of the executive.* Cambridge, MA: Harvard University Press.

2. Ibid.

3. J. W. Lorsch & J. J. Morse. 1974. *Organizations and their members: A contingency approach.* New York: Harper & Row, 7.

4. J. D. Thompson. 1967. *Organizations in action.* New York: McGraw-Hill.

5. Ibid.; A. H. Van de Ven, A. L. Delbecq, & R. Koenig, Jr. 1976. Determinants of coordination modes within organizations. *American Sociological Review* 41:322–338.

6. J. Hoerr. 1988 (Nov. 28). Work teams can rev up paper-pushers, too. *Business Week,* 64–68.

7. Hoerr, 1988.

8. Ibid.

9. A. Salpukas. 1999 (June 27). Firing up an idea machine. *New York Times,* 1–3, 13.

10. R. Robey. 1982. *Designing organizations: A macro perspective.* Homewood, IL: Irwin.

11. J. W. Wilson with T. D. Dobrzynski. 1986 (Mar. 3). And now, The post-industrial corporation. *Business Week,* 64–71; E. E. Lawler, III. 1992. *The ultimate advantage: Creating the high involvement organization,* San Francisco: Jossey-Bass; S. Tullman. 1993 (Feb. 8). The modular corporation. *Fortune,* 106–117; J. Byrne with R. Brandt. 1993 (Feb. 8). The virtual corporation: The company of the future will be the ultimate in adaptability. *Business Week,* 98–102.

12. R. E. Hoskisson. 1987. Multidivisional structure and performance: The contingency of diversification strategy. *Academy of Management Journal* 30:625–644.

13. W. J. Humpton. 1986 (Feb. 17). GM's shuffle: The calm before a slaughter. *Business Week,* 35.

14. W. F. Joyce. 1986. Matrix organization: A social experiment. *Academy of Management Journal* 29:536–561.

15. S. M. Davis & P. R. Lawrence. 1977. *Matrix.* Reading, MA: Addison-Wesley, 11–24; R. B. Duncan. 1979. What is the right organization structure? Decision tree analysis provides the answer. *Organizational Dynamics* 7(3):59–80.

16. E. W. Larson & D. H. Gobeli. 1987. Matrix management: Contradictions and insights. *California Management Review* 29(4):126–138.

17. W. H. Davidow & H. S. Malone. 1992. *The virtual corporation.* New York: Burlingame; Byrne & Brandt, 1993.

18. Byrne & Brandt, 1993.

19. Ibid.

20. Ibid.

21. Tullman, 1993.

22. T. A. Stewart. 1992 (May 18). The search for the organization of tomorrow. *Fortune,* 91–96.

23. E. E. Lawler, III. 1986. *High-involvement management.* San Francisco: Jossey-Bass.

24. J. G. March & H. A. Simon. 1958. *Organizations.* New York: Wiley.

25. Thompson, 1967.

26. H. Fayol. 1916. *General and industrial management.* London: Pitman.

27. J. R. Galbraith. 1974. Organization design: An information processing view, *Interfaces* 4:28–36.

28. P. R. Lawrence & J. W. Lorsch. 1967. *Organization and environment.* Homewood, IL: Irwin.

29. Ibid.

30. A. H. Van de Ven, A. L. Delbecq, & R. Koenig, Jr. 1976. Determinants of coordination modes within organizations. *Administrative Science Quarterly* 41:322–338.

31. C. J. Berger & L. L. Cummings. 1979. Organizational structure, attitudes and behaviors. In B. M. Staw (ed.), *Research in organizational behavior,* Vol. 1, 169–208; L. W. Porter & E. E. Lawler, III. 1965. Properties of organization structure in relation to job attitudes and job behavior. *Psychological Bulletin* 64: 23–51.

32. Ibid.

33. Berger & Cummings, 1979.

34. J. L. Pierce, T. Kostova, & K. Dirks. 2001. Toward a theory of psychological ownership in organizations. *Academy of Management Review* 26:298–310.

35. J. Locke. 1690. *Two treatises of government.* Oxford: Oxford University Press.

36. W. F. Joyce. 1986. Matrix organization: A social experiment. *Academy of Management Journal* 29:536–561.

37. Ibid.

38. C. Cooper, M. O'Driscoll, & P. Dewe. 2000. *Occupational stress.* Thousand Oaks, CA: Sage.

39. S. M. Davis & P. R. Lawrence. 1977. *Matrix.* Reading, MA: Addison-Wesley.

40. J. G. March & H. A. Simon. 1958. *Organizations.* New York: Wiley.

41. Thompson, 1967.

42. A. H. Van de Ven, A. L. Delbecq, & R. Koenig, Jr. 1976. Determinants of coordination modes within organizations. *American Sociological Review* 41:322–338.

43. J. Hage. 1965. An axiomatic theory of organizations. *Administrative Science Quarterly* 10:289–320.

Chapter 13. Organizational Design

1. R. H. Miles. 1980. *Macro organizational behavior.* Santa Monica, CA: Goodyear, 18; R. H. Hall. 1987. *Organizations: structures, processes, and outcomes.* Englewood Cliffs, NJ: Prentice-Hall.

2. W. G. Astley & P. S. Sachdeva. 1984. Structural sources of intraorganizational power: A theoretical synthesis, *Academy of Management Review* 9:104–113; J. R. P. French, Jr. & B. Raven. 1959. The bases of social power. In D. Cartwright (ed.), *Studies of social power.* Ann Arbor, MI: Institute for Social Research; D. J. Hickson, C. R. Hinings, C. A. Lee, R. E. Schneck, & J. M. Pennings. 1971. A strategic contingencies' theory of intraorganizational power. *Administrative Science Quarterly* 16:216–229; G. R. Salancik & J. Pfeffer. 1977. Who gets power and how they hold on to it: A strategic-contingency model of power. *Organizational Dynamics* 5:3–21.

3. The problems associated with defining power and the major approaches are discussed by A. T. Cobb. 1984. An episodic model of power: Toward an integration of theory and research. *Academy of Management Review* 9:482–493.

4. M. Weber. 1947. *The theory of social and economic organization.* Glencoe, IL: Free Press.

5. C. Barnard. 1938. *The functions of the executive.* Cambridge, MA: Harvard University Press.

6. Ibid.; H. A. Simon. 1976. *Administrative behavior* (3rd ed.). New York: Macmillan.

7. H. Stieglitz. 1974. On concepts of corporate structure. *The Conference Board Record,* 11:7–13.

8. R. H. Hall. 1982. *Organizations.* Englewood Cliffs, NJ: Prentice-Hall; J. Hage & M. Aiken. 1967. Program change and organizational properties: A comparative analysis. *American Journal of Sociology* 72:503–519.

9. C. R. Leana. 1987. Power relinquishment versus power sharing: Theoretical clarification and empirical comparison of delegation and participation. *Journal of Applied Psychology* 72: 228–233; D. M. Schweiger & C. R. Leana. 1986. Participation in decision making. In E. Locke (ed.), *Generalizing from laboratory to field settings: Research findings from industrial-organizational psychology, organization behavior, and human resource management.* Boston: Heath, 147–166; E. A. Locke & D. M. Schweiger. 1979. Participation in decision-making: One more look. In B. M. Staw (ed.). *Research in organizational behavior,* vol. 1. Greenwich, CT: JAI Press, 265–340.

10. Leana, 1987.

11. R. H. Hall. 1962. Intraorganizational structural variation: Applications of the bureaucratic model. *Administrative Science Quarterly* 7:295–308; E. Litwak. 1961. Models of organizations which permit conflict. *American Journal of Sociology* 76:177–184; P. R. Lawrence & J. W. Lorsch. 1967. *Organization and environment.* Homewood, IL: Irwin.

12. George Stalk of the Boston Consulting Group, quoted by J. D. Orsburn, L. Moran, E. Musselwhite, & J. H. Zenger. 1990.

Self-directed work teams: The new American challenge. Homewood, IL: Business One Irwin, 3–4.

13. Raymond Miles, University of California, Berkeley, cited by T. A. Stewart. 1989 (Nov. 6). New ways to exercise power. *Fortune* 121:54.

14. Stewart, 1989, 52–64.

15. Hall, 1982.

16. D. Pugh, D. J. Hickson, C. R. Hinings, & C. Turner. 1968. Dimensions of organizational structure. *Administrative Science Quarterly* 12:65–105.

17. P. M. Blau. 1970. Decentralization in bureaucracies. In M. N. Zald (ed.), *Power in organizations*. Nashville, TN: Vanderbilt University Press; J. Hage & M. Aiken. 1967. Relationship of centralization to other structural properties. *Administrative Science Quarterly* 12:72–91.

18. P. E. Connor. 1980. *Organizations: Theory and design*. Chicago: SRA.

19. E. Trist & K. W. Bamforth. 1951. Some social and psychological consequences of the long-wall method of coal getting. *Human Relations* 4:3–38.

20. W. A. Pasmore. 1988. *Designing effective organizations: The sociotechnical systems perspective*. New York: Wiley.

21. R. Likert. 1967. *The human organization*. New York: McGraw-Hill; R. Likert. 1961. *New patterns in management*. New York: McGraw-Hill.

22. M. Weber. 1922. *The theory of social and economic organization*. A. M. Henderson & T. Parsons (eds. and trans.). 1947. New York: Oxford University Press.

23. P. S. Adler. 1999. Building better bureaucracies. *Academy of Management Executive* 13(4):36–47; P. M. Blau & M. W. Meyer. 1987. *Bureaucracy in modern society*. New York: Random House.

24. Litwak, 1961; Hall, 1962.

25. Litwak, 1961; C. Perrow. 1967. A framework for the comparative analysis of organizations. *American Sociological Review* 32: 194–208; A. H. Van de Ven & A. L. Delbecq. 1974. A task contingent model of work unit structure. *Administrative Science Quarterly* 19:183–197; W. A. Randolph & G. G. Dess. 1984. The congruence perspective of organization design: A conceptual model and multivariate research approach. *Academy of Management Review* 9:114–127.

26. C. Argyris. 1973. Personality and organization theory revisited. *Administrative Science Quarterly* 18:141–167; C. Argyris. 1957. *Personality and organization*. New York: Harper & Row; W. Bennis. 1965. Beyond bureaucracy. *Transaction* 2:31–35; R. Blauner. 1964. *Alienation and freedom*. Chicago: University of Chicago Press.

27. T. Burns & G. M. Stalker. 1961. *The management of innovation*. London: Tavistock.

28. Litwak, 1961; Hall, 1962; G. Hage. 1965. An axiomatic theory of organizations. *Administrative Science Quarterly* 10:289–320.

29. B. L. T. Hedberg, P. C. Nystrom, & W. H. Starbuck. 1976. Camping on seesaws: Prescriptions for a self-designing organization. *Administrative Science Quarterly* 21:46–65; B. L. T. Hedberg, P. C. Nystrom, & W. H. Starbuck. 1977. Designing organizations to match tomorrow. North-Holland/TIMS *Studies in Management Sciences* 5:171–181; K. E. Weick. 1977. Organization design: Organization as self-designing systems. *Organizational Dynamics* 6(2): 30–46; A. Wildavsky. 1972. The self-evaluating organization. *Public Administration Review* 32(5):509–520.

30. A. G. Bedeian. 1984. *Organizations: Theory and analysis*. Chicago: Dryden Press, 499.

31. Hedberg, Nystrom, & Starbuck, 1977, 171.

32. Weick, 1977, 37.

33. D. S. Pugh, D. J. Hickson, C. R. Hinings, & C. Turner. 1969. The context of organization structures. *Administrative Science Quarterly* 14:91–114.

34. J. Child. 1972. Organization structure, environment, and performance: The role of strategic choice. *Sociology* 6:369–393.

35. Lawrence & Lorsch, 1967.

36. Randolph & Dess, 1984, 121.

37. S. Richardson. 1956. Organizational contrasts on British and American ships. *Administrative Science Quarterly* 1:189–207.

38. M. Crozier. 1964. *The bureaucratic phenomenon*. Chicago: University of Chicago Press.

39. A. Reudi & P. R. Lawrence. 1970. Organizations in two cultures. In J. W. Lorsch & P. R. Lawrence (eds.). *Studies in organization design*. Homewood, IL: Irwin.

40. W. G. Ouchi. 1981. *Theory Z: How American business can meet the Japanese challenge*. Reading, MA: Addison-Wesley.

41. Randolph & Dess, 1984.

42. J. Woodward. 1965. *Industrial organization: Theory and practice*. London: Oxford University Press.

43. Ibid., 71.

44. Perrow, 1967; Van de Ven & Delbecq, 1974.

45. J. W. Alexander & W. A. Randolph. 1985. The fit between technology and structure as a predictor of performance in nursing subunits. *Academy of Management Journal* 28:840–859; J. V. Singh. 1986. Technology, size, and organizational structure: A reexamination of the Okayama study data. *Academy of Management Journal* 29:800–812.

46. A. D. Chandler, Jr. 1962. *Strategy and structure: Chapters in the history of the American industrial enterprise*. Cambridge, MA: MIT Press.

47. H. Mintzberg. 1979. *The structuring of organizations*. Englewood Cliffs, NJ: Prentice-Hall.

48. J. L. Pierce & A. L. Delbecq. 1977. Organization structure, individual attitudes, and innovation. *Academy of Management Review* 2:27–37; M. Aiken & J. Hage. 1971. The organic organization and innovation. *Sociology* 5:63–82; Burns & Stalker, 1961.

49. Singh, 1986.

50. J. Weber. 1992 (May 4). A big company that works. *Business Week,* 124–132.

51. D. McGregor. 1960. *The human side of enterprise*. New York: McGraw-Hill.

52. L. W. Porter, E. E. Lawler, III, & J. R. Hackman. 1975. *Behavior in organizations*. New York: McGraw-Hill.

53. J. Child, 1972. J. R. Montanari. 1977 (Aug.). *Operationalizing strategic choice*. A paper presented at the 37th National Meeting of the Academy of Management, Orlando, FL; D. C. Hambrick & P. A. Mason. 1984. Upper echelons: The organization as a reflection of its top managers. *Academy of Management Review* 9:193–206.

54. C. J. Berger & L. L. Cummings. 1979. Organization structure, attitudes, and behaviors. In B. M. Staw (ed.), *Research in Organizational Behavior,* vol. 1, 169–208, Greenwich, CT: JAI Press.

55. J. Hage. 1965. An axiomatic theory of organizations. *Administrative Science Quarterly* 10:289–320.

56. J. L. Pierce. 1979. Employee affective responses to work unit structure and job design: A test of an intervening variable. *Journal of Management* 5(2):193–211.

57. L. L. Cummings & C. J. Berger. 1976 (Autumn). Organization structure: How does it influence attitudes and performance? *Organizational Dynamics,* 34–49.

58. Leana. 1986.

59. C. M. Bonjean & M. D. Grimes. 1970. Bureaucracy and alienation: A dimensional approach. *Social Forces* 48:365–373; M. Aiken & J. Hage. Aug. 1966. Organizational alienation: A comparative analysis. *American Sociological Review,* 497–507; J. Hage, M. Aiken, & C. Marrett. 1971. Organization structure and communications. *Administrative Science Quarterly* 36:860–871.

60. B. P. Indik. 1965. Organization size and member participation. *Human Relations* 18:339–350; G. H. Litwin. 1968. Climate and motivation: An experimental study. In R. Taginri and G. H. Litwin (eds.). *Organizational climate: Explorations of a concept*. Boston: Harvard University, Graduate School of Business, 169–190.

61. J. L. Pierce, T. Kostova, & K. T. Dirks. 2001. Towards a theory of psychological ownership in organizations. *Academy of Management Review* 21:298–310.

62. Hage, 1965; C. Barnard. 1964. Functions and pathology of status systems in formal organizations. In W. F. Whyte (ed.). *Industry and society.* New York: McGraw-Hill.

63. Bonjean & Grimes. 1970; J. Hage. 1974. *Communication and organizational control.* New York: Wiley.

64. Indik, 1965; G. Ingham. 1970. *Size of industrial organization and worker behavior.* Cambridge: Cambridge University Press; Porter & Lawler, 1965.

65. S. G. Green, S. E. Anderson, & S. L. Shivers. 1996. Demographic and organizational influences on leader-member exchange and related work attitudes. *Organizational Behavior and Human Decision Processes* 66:203–214; Porter & Lawler, 1965; Berger & Cummings, 1979; Pierce, 1979.

66. Porter & Lawler, 1965.

67. R. Blauner. 1964. *Alienation and freedom.* Chicago: University of Chicago Press; M. Fullan. 1970. Industrial technology and worker integration in the organization. *American Sociological Review* 35:1028–1039; J. Hage & M. Aiken. 1969. Routine technology, social structure, and organizational goals. *Administrative Science Quarterly* 16:216–229; R. B. Peterson. 1975. The interaction of technological process and perceived organizational climate in Norwegian firms. *Academy of Management Journal* 18: 288–299; A. K. Rice. 1958. *Productivity and social organization: The Ahmedabed experiment.* London: Tavistock; J. Shepard. 1969. Functional specialization and work attitudes. *Industrial Relations* 8:185–194; E. L. Trist & K. W. Bamforth. 1951. Some social and psychological consequences of the long-wall method of coal getting. *Human Relations* 4:3–38.

68. J. L. Pierce, R. B. Dunham, & L. L. Cummings. 1984. Sources of environmental structuring and participant responses. *Organizational Behavior and Human Performance* 33:214–242.

69. R. Song, B. J. Daly, E. B. Rudy, S. Douglas, & M. A. Dyner. 1997. Nurses' job satisfaction, absenteeism, and turnover after implementing a special care unit practice model. *Research in Nursing and Health* 20(5):443–452; D. M. Rousseau. 1977. Technological differences in job characteristics, employee satisfaction, and motivation: A synthesis of job design research and sociotechnical systems theory. *Organizational Behavior and Human Performance* 19:18–42; G. R. Jones. 1984. Task visibility, free riding, and shirking: Explaining the effect of structure and technology on employee behavior. *Academy of Management Review* 9:684–695.

70. B. M. Bass. 1985 *Leadership and performance beyond expectations.* New York: Free Press.

71. R. Karasek. 1979. Job demands, job decision latitude, and mental strain: Implications for job redesign. *Administrative Science Quarterly* 24:285–306.

72. P. M. Blau. 1964. *Exchange and power in social life.* New York: Wiley; A. G. Gouldner. 1960. The norm of reciprocity: A preliminary statement. *American Sociological Review* 25:161–178.

73. D. M. Rousseau. 1989. Psychological and implied contracts in organizations. *Employee Rights and Responsibilities Journal* 2:121–139; D. M. Rousseau. 1990. New hire perceptions of their own and their employer's obligations: A study of psychological contracts. *Journal of Organizational Behavior* 11:389–400.

74. R. Eisenberger, R. Huntington, S. Hutchinson, & D. Sowa. 1986. Perceived organizational support. *Journal of Applied Psychology* 71:500–507; R. Eisenberger, J. Cummings, S. Armeli, & P. Lynch. 1997. Perceived organizational support, discretionary treatment, and job satisfaction. *Journal of Applied Psychology* 82:812–820.

75. W. C. Byham. 1993 (May). Empowerment: *The generator of human energy.* Presented at the Symposium on psychological ownership: individual and organizational consequences, at the 8th annual conference of the Society for Industrial and Organizational Psychology, San Francisco; K. W. Thomas & B. A. Velthouse. 1990. Cognitive elements of empowerment: An "Interpretive" model of intrinsic task motivation. *Academy of Management Review* 15:666–681; J. A. Conger & R. N. Kanungo. The empowerment process: Integrating theory and practice. *Academy of Management Review* 13:471–482.

76. Byham, 1993; Thomas & Velthouse, 1990.

77. G. M. Spreitzer. 1995. Psychological empowerment in the workplace: Dimensions, measurement, and validation. *Academy of Management Journal* 38:1444.

78. Ibid.

79. Byham, 1993.

80. Ibid.

81. M. Schminke, M. L. Ambrose, & R. S. Cropanzano. 2000. The effect of organization structure on perceptions of procedural fairness. *Journal of Applied Psychology* 85:294–304.

82. Hage, 1965; P. F. Nemiroff & D. L. Ford, Jr. 1976. Task effectiveness and human fulfillment in organizations. *Academy of Management Review* 1(4):83–97; J. L. Pierce, R. B. Dunham, & R. S. Blackburn. 1979. Social systems structure, job design, and growth need strength: A test of a congruency model. *Academy of Management Journal* 22:223–240; L. W. Porter, E. E. Lawler, III, & J. R. Hackman. 1975. *Behavior in organizations.* New York: McGraw-Hill.

83. J. L. Pierce, M. P. O'Driscoll, & A. M. Coghlan. 2001. *Work environment structure and psychological ownership: The mediating effects of control.* Bureau of Business and Economics, School of Business and Economics working paper, University of Minnesota Duluth.

84. D. J. Dwyer & D. C. Ganster. 1991. The effects of job demands and control on employee attendance and satisfaction. *Journal of Organizational Behavior* 12:595–608; R. Karasek, R. Russell, & T. Theorell. 1982 (March). Physiology of stress and regeneration in job related cardiovascular illness. *Journal of Human Stress,* 29–42; M. P. O'Driscoll & T. A. Beehr. 2000. Moderating effects of perceived control and need for clarity on the relationship between role stressors and employee affective reaction. *Journal of Social Psychology* 140:151–159.

PART IV. Groups in Organizations

Chapter 14. The Nature of Groups and Teams in Organizations

1. S. G. Cohen & D. E. Bailey. 1997. What makes teams work?: Group effectiveness research from the shop floor to the executive suite. *Journal of Management* 23:239–290; E. E. Lawler, III, S. A. Mohrman, & G. E. Ledford, Jr. 1995. *Creating high performance organizations: Practices and results of employee involvement and total quality management in Fortune 1000 companies.* San Francisco: Jossey-Bass.

2. P. Osterman. 2000. Work reorganization in an era of restructuring: Trends in diffusion and effects on employee welfare. *Industrial and Labor Relations Review* 53:179–196.

3. J. Luft. 1984. *Group processes: An introduction to group dynamics.* Palo Alto, CA: Mayfield, 2.

4. S. A. Wheelan. 1994. *Group processes: A developmental perspective.* Boston: Allyn & Bacon, 2; F. H. Allport. 1924. *Social psychology.* Boston: Houghton Mifflin.

5. R. A. Jones, C. Hendrick, & U. M. Epstein. 1979. *Introduction to social psychology.* Sunderland, MA: Sinauer, 486.

6. M. E. Shaw. 1981. *Group dynamics: The psychology of small group behavior,* 3rd ed. New York: McGraw-Hill.

7. Cohen & Bailey, 1997, 241.

8. This definition is taken from G. L. Stewart, C. C. Manz, & H. P. Sims. 1999. *Team work and group dynamics.* New York: Wiley, 3. They were influenced by R. A. Guzzo & M. W. Dickson. 1996. Teams in organizations: Research on performance and effectiveness. *Annual Review of Psychology* 47:307–338.

9. J. A. Pearce, II, & E. C. Ravlin. 1987. The design and activation of self-regulating work groups. *Human Relations* 40:751–782.

10. Cohen & Bailey, 1997.

11. D. Mankin, S. G. Cohen, & T. K. Bikson. 1996. *Teams and technology: Fulfilling the promise of the new organization.* Boston: Harvard Business School Press.

12. J. Hoerr. Feb. 20, 1989. Is teamwork a management plot? Mostly not. *Business Week,* 70; J. Hoerr. Aug. 5, 1985. How power will be balanced on Saturn's shop floor. *Business Week,* 65–66.

13. J. R. Hackman. 1987. The design of work teams. In J. W. Lorsch (ed.), *Handbook of organizational behavior.* Englewood Cliffs, NJ: Prentice-Hall.

14. W. A. Pasmore. 1988. *Designing effective organizations: The sociotechnical systems perspective.* New York: Wiley.

15. T. G. Cummings & S. Srivastva. 1977. Management of work: A sociotechnical systems approach. Kent, OH: Kent State University Press; T. I. Chacko, T. H. Stone, & A. P. Brief. 1979. Participation in goal setting programs: An attributional analysis. *Academy of Management Review* 4:433–438.

16. J. E. Kelly. 1978. A reappraisal of socio-technical theory. *Human Relations* 31:1069–1099; W. Pasmore, C. Francis, J. Haldeman, & A. Shani. 1982. Sociotechnical systems: A North American reflection on empirical studies of the seventies. *Human Relations* 35:1179–1204.

17. Pearce & Ravlin, 1987.

18. J. W. Bishop & K. D. Scott. 2000. An examination of organizational and team commitment in a self-directed team environment. *Journal of Applied Psychology* 85:439–450.

19. Pearce & Ravlin, 1987.

20. E. E. Lawler, III. 1992. *The ultimate advantage: Creating the high involvement organization.* San Francisco: Jossey-Bass.

21. B. Dumane. 1990 (May 7). Who needs a boss? *Fortune,* 52–60.

22. M. Attaran & T. T. Nguyen. 1999. Succeeding with self-managed teams. *Industrial Management* 41:24–28.

23. R. H. Kilmann. 1984. *Beyond the quick fix: Managing five tracks to organizational success.* San Francisco: Jossey-Bass; R. H. Kilmann. 1984. Beyond the quick fix: Why managers must disregard the myth of simplicity as a direct route to organizational success. *Management Review* 73(11):24–28, 37.

24. J. D. Orsburn, L. Moran, E. Musselwhite, & J. H. Zenger. 1990. *Self-directed work teams: The new American challenge.* Homewood, IL: Business One Irwin.

25. Ibid., 66.

26. Ibid.

27. L. L. Cummings, G. P. Huber, & E. Arendt. 1974. Effects of size and spatial arrangements on group decision making. *Academy of Management Journal* 17:460–475.

28. J. R. Hackman. 1990. Group influences on individuals in organizations. In M. D. Dunnette (ed.), *Handbook of industrial/organizational psychology.* Palo Alto, CA: Consulting Psychologists Press.

29. D. C. Feldman. 1984. The development and enforcement of group norms. *Academy of Management Review* 9:47–53.

30. B. J. Biddle. 1979. *Role theory: Expectations, identities, and behavior.* New York: Academic Press.

31. K. D. Benne & P. Sheats. 1948. Functional roles of group members. *Journal of Social Issues* 4:41–49.

32. J. Schaubroeck, D. G. Ganster, W. E. Sime, & D. Ditman. 1993. A field experiment testing supervisory role clarification. *Personnel Psychology* 46:1–24.

33. J. E. MacGrath. 1976. Stress and behavior in organizations. In M. D. Dunnette (ed.). *Handbook of industrial and organizational psychology.* Chicago: Rand McNally; A. S. Luchins. 1942. Mechanisation in problem solving. *Psychological Monographs* 54: 1–95; R. M. Yerkes & J. D. Dodson. 1908. The relation of strength of stimulus to rapidity of habit formation. *Journal of Comparative Neurological Psychology* 18:459–483.

34. R. Hall. 1975. Interpersonal compatibility and workgroup performance. *Journal of Applied Behavioral Science* 2:210–219; Huber, 1980; P. R. Laughlin & L. G. Branch. 1972. Individual vs. tetradic performance on a complementary task as a function of initial ability level. *Organizational Behavior and Human Performance* 8:201–216.

35. L. Van Dyne. 1993. *In-role and extra-role behaviors: Cross level and longitudinal effects of individual similarity to other group members.* Unpublished doctoral dissertation. Minneapolis: University of Minnesota, Carlson School of Management.

36. J. P. Wanous & M. A. Youtz. 1986. Solutions diversity and the quality of group decisions. *Academy of Management Journal* 29:149–159.

37. L. G. Bolman & T. E. Deal. 1992. What makes a team work? *Organizational Dynamics* 21(2):34–44.

38. P. C. Earley & E. Mosakowski. 2000. Creating hybrid team cultures: An empirical test of transnational team functioning. *Academy of Management Journal* 43:26–49.

39. M. E. Shaw. 1981. *Group dynamics: The psychology of small group behavior,* 3rd ed. New York: McGraw-Hill.

40. P. R. Bernthal & C. A. Insko. 1993. Cohesiveness without groupthink. *Group and Organization Management* 18(1):66–87.

41. R. E. Kidwell, Jr., K. W. Mossholder, & N. Bennett. 1997. Cohesiveness and organizational citizenship behavior: A multilevel analysis using work groups and individuals. *Journal of Management* 23:775–793; L. N. Jewell & H. J. Reitz. 1981. *Group effectiveness in organizations.* Glenview, IL: Scott, Foresman, 5–6.

42. R. M. Stogdill. 1972. Group productivity, drive, and cohesiveness. *Organizational Behavior and Human Performance* 8:26–43; D. Cartwright. 1968. The nature of group cohesiveness. In D. Cartwright & A. Zander (eds.), *Group dynamics: Research and theory,* 3rd ed. New York: Harper & Row, 91–109; M. E. Shaw. 1981. *Group dynamics: The dynamics of small group behavior,* 3rd ed. New York: McGraw-Hill.

43. Cummings et al., 1974, 463.

44. L. N. Jewell & H. J. Reitz. 1981. *Group effectiveness in organizations.* Glenview, IL: Scott, Foresman.

45. Orsburn et al., 1990.

46. B. W. Tuckman & M. A. C. Jensen. 1977. Stages in small group development revisited. *Group and Organizational Studies* 2:49–427; B. W. Tuckman. 1965. Developmental sequences in small groups. *Psychological Bulletin* 63:384–399.

47. R. V. Dawis, G. W. England, & L. H. Lofquist. April 1968. A theory of work adjustment (revision). University of Minnesota, Minnesota Studies in Vocational Rehabilitation XXIII, Bulletin 47.

48. D. Leonhardt. 1999 (Nov. 10). Soothing savage structures. *New York Times,* C1, 14.

49. S. G. Cohen & D. E. Bailey. 1997. What makes teams work? Group effectiveness research from the shop floor to the executive suite. *Journal of Management* 23:239–290; M. A. Campion, G. J. Medsker, & A. C. Higgs. 1993. Relations between work group characteristics and effectiveness: Implications for designing effective work groups. *Personnel Psychology* 46:823–850.

50. G. L. Stewart & M. R. Barrick. 2000. Task structure and performance: Assessing the mediating role of intrateam process and the moderating role of task type. *Academy of Management Journal* 43:135–148.

51. M. Erez & P. C. Earley. 1993. *Culture, self-identity, and work.* New York: Oxford University Press; P. C. Earley. 1993. East meets west meets mideast: Further explorations of collectivistic and individualistic work group. *Academy of Management Journal* 36:319–348.

52. Erez & Earley, 1993.

53. A. Bandura. 1977. Self-efficacy: Toward a unifying theory of behavioral change. *Psychological Review* 84:191–215; A. Bandura. 1982. Self-efficacy mechanism in human agency. *American*

Psychologist 37:122–147; A. Bandura. 1989. Human agency in social cognitive theory. *American Psychologist* 44:1175–1184; A. Bandura. 1997. *Self-efficacy: The exercise of control.* New York: Freeman.

54. Erez & Earley, 1993.

55. B. L. Kirkman & B. Rosen. 1999. Beyond self-management: Antecedents and consequences of team empowerment. *Academy of Management Journal* 42:58–74.

56. Hackman, 1987.

57. Bolman & Deal, 1992.

58. Quoted in Bolman & Deal, 1992, as taken from L. Schlesinger, B. Ecles, & J. Gabarro. 1983. *Managerial behavior in organizations.* New York: McGraw-Hill.

59. Bolman & Deal, 1992, 34.

60. Ibid., 42.

61. Ibid., 43.

62. D. Nadler, J. R. Hackman, & E. E. Lawler, III. 1979. *Managing organizational behavior.* Boston: Little Brown.

63. D. Polley & L. Van Dyne. 1993. *The limits and liabilities of self managed work teams.* A paper presented at symposium on Self-Managed Work Teams. University of North Texas, Denton, TX.

64. B. Latane, K. Williams, & S. Harkins. 1979. Many hands make light the work: The causes and consequences of social loafing. *Journal of Personality and Social Psychology* 37:822–832; S. G. Harkins & K. Szymanski. 1987. Social loafing and social facilitation. In C. Hendrick (ed.), *Review of Personality and Social Psychology* 9:167–184.

65. Polley & Van Dyne, 1993.

66. J. M. Darley & B. Latane. 1968. Bystander intervention in emergencies: Diffusion of responsibility. *Journal of Personality and Social Psychology* 8(4):377–383.

67. Polley & Van Dyne, 1993.

68. Ibid.

69. D. I. Isenberg. 1986. Group processes: Advances in experimental social psychology. *Journal of Personality and Social Psychology* 50:1141–1151; H. Lamm & D. G. Meyer. 1978. Group-induced polarization of attitudes and behavior. In L. Berkowitz (ed.), *Advances in experimental social psychology,* New York: Academic Press, 11.

70. R. D. Clark, III, W. H. Crockett, & R. L. Archer. 1971. Risk-as-value hypothesis: The relationship between perception of self-others, and the risky shift. *Journal of Personality and Social Psychology* 20:425–29; J. H. Davis, P. R. Laughlin, & S. S. Komorita. 1976. The social psychology of small groups: Cooperative and mixed-motive interaction. In M. R. Rosenzweig & L. W. Porter (eds.), *Annual Review of Psychology* 27:501–541; L. B. Rosenfeld. 1973. *Human interaction in the small group setting.* Columbus, OH: Merrill.

71. R. S. Baron, G. Roper, & P. H. Baron. 1974. Group discussions and the risky shift. *Journal of Personality and Social Psychology* 30:538–545; Isenberg, 1986.

72. E. Burnstein & A. Vinokur. 1977. Persuasive argumentation and social comparison as determinants of attitude polarization. *Journal of Experimental Social Psychology* 13:315–332; J. M. Jellison & R. M. Arkin. 1977. Social comparison of abilities: A self-presentational approach to decision making in groups. In J. M. Suls & R. L. Miller (eds.), *Social comparison processes.* New York: Halsted Press, 235–257.

73. B. M. Staw. 1976. Knee deep in the big muddy: A study of escalating commitment to a chosen course of action. *Organizational Behavior and Human Performance* 16:27–44; J. Brockner & J. Z. Rubin. 1985. *Entrapment in escalating conflicts: A social psychological analysis.* New York: Springer-Verlag; B. M. Staw & J. Ross. 1987a. Behavior in escalation situations: Antecedents, prototypes, and solutions. In L. L. Cummings and B. M. Staw (eds.), *Research in Organizational Behavior* 9:39–78, Greenwich, CT: JAI Press; B. M. Staw & J. Ross. 1987b. (Mar.–Apr.). Knowing when to pull the plug. *Harvard Business Review* 68–74; M. Bazerman, T. Guiliano, & A. Appleman. 1984. Escalation of commitment in individual and group decision making. *Organizational Behavior and Human Performance* 33:141–152.

74. Staw & Ross, 1987a.

75. Polley & Van Dyne, 1993.

76. J. B. Harvey. 1974 (Summer). The Abilene paradox: The management of agreement. *Organizational Dynamics* 3:63–80.

77. I. L. Janis. 1971. Groupthink. *Psychology Today* 5:43ff; I. L. Janis. 1982. *Groupthink: Psychological studies of policy decisions,* 2nd ed. Boston: Houghton Mifflin.

78. Ibid.

79. R. J. Aldag & S. R. Fuller. 1993. Beyond fiasco: A reappraisal of the groupthink phenomenon and a new model of group decision processes. *Psychological Bulletin* 113(3):533–552.

80. P. R. Bernthal & C. A. Insko. 1993. Cohesiveness without groupthink. *Groups and Organization Management* 18(1):66–87.

81. Ibid.

82. Ibid.

83. G. C. Homans. 1950. *The human group.* New York: Harcourt, Brace & World.

84. E. L. Trist & K. W. Bamforth. 1951. Some social and psychological consequences of the longwall method of coal-getting. *Human Relations* 4:1–38.

85. J. R. Hackman. 1992. Group influences on individuals in organizations. In M. D. Dunnette & L. M. Hough (eds.), *Handbook of industrial and organizational psychology,* 2nd ed. Palo Alto, CA: Consulting Psychologists Press, 198–267.

Chapter 15. Work Group and Team Processes

1. J. L. Cotton. 1993. *Employee involvement: Methods for improving performance and work attitudes.* Newbury Park, CA: Sage, 62–63.

2. B. Dumaine. 1990 (May 7). Who needs a boss? *Fortune* 121(10):52–60.

3. N. R. F. Maier. 1970. Assets and liabilities in group problem solving: The need for an integrative function. In Norman R. F. Maier (ed.), *Problem solving and creativity: In individuals and groups.* Belmont, CA: Brooks/Cole, 431–44.

4. A. C. Amason, & D. M. Schweiger. 1994. Resolving the paradox of conflict: Strategic decision making and organizational performance. *International Journal of Conflict Management* 5:239–253; C. R. Schwenk. 1990. Conflict in organizational decision making: An exploratory study of its effects in for-profit and not-for-profit organizations. *Management Science* 36:436–448.

5. A. C. Amason & H. J. Sapienza. 1997. The effects of top management team size and interaction norms on cognitive and affective conflict. *Journal of Management* 23:495–516.

6. K. A. Bantel & S. E. Jackson. 1989. Top management innovations in banking: Does the composition of the top team make a difference? *Strategic Management Journal* 10:109.

7. Amason & Sapienza, 1997.

8. T. L. Simons & R. S. Peterson. 2000. Task conflict and relationship conflict in top management teams: The pivotal role of intragroup trust. *Journal of Applied Psychology* 85:102–111.

9. K. T. Dirks. 1999. The effects of interpersonal trust on work group performance. *Journal of Applied Psychology* 84:445–455.

10. R. A. Cosier & C. R. Schwenk. 1990. Agreement and thinking alike: Ingredients for poor decisions. *Academy of Management Executive* 4(1):69–74.

11. Cosier & Schwenk, 1990.

12. Ibid.

13. H. J. Reitz & L. N. Jewell. 1985. *Managing.* Glenview, IL: Scott, Foresman.

14. S. G. Rogelbert, J. L. Barnes-Farrell, & C. A. Lowe. 1992. The stepladder technique: An alternative group structure facilitating effective group decision making. *Journal of Applied Psychology* 77:730–737.

15. Ibid.

16. Ibid.

17. W. Watson, L. K. Michaelsen, & W. Sharp. 1991. Member competence, group interaction, and group decision making: A longitudinal study. *Journal of Applied Psychology* 76:803–809; L. K. Michaelsen, W. E. Watson, & R. H. Black. 1989. A realistic test of individual versus group consensus decision making. *Journal of Applied Psychology* 74:834–839.

18. Rogelberg et al., 1992.

19. A. F. Osborn. 1957. *Applied imagination.* New York: Scribner's.

20. R. W. Napier & M. K. Gershenfeld. 1985. *Groups: Theory and experience,* 3rd ed. Boston: Houghton Mifflin, 334.

21. D. W. Taylor, P. C. Berry, & C. H. Block. 1958. Does group participation when using brainstorming techniques facilitate or inhibit creative thinking? *Administrative Science Quarterly* 3:23–47; J. K. Murnighan. 1981. Group decision making: What strategies should you use? *Management Review* 70:55–62.

22. Taylor et al., 1958.

23. N. C. Dalkey & O. Helmer. 1963. An experimental application of the Delphi method to the use of experts. *Management Science* 9:458–467; A. L. Delbecq, A. H. Van de Ven, & D. H. Gustafson. 1975. *Group techniques for program planning: A guide to nominal group and delphi processes.* Glenview, IL: Scott, Foresman; C. M. Moore. 1987. *Group techniques for idea building.* Newbury Park, CA: Sage.

24. Delbecq et al., 1975.

25. R. C. Erffmeyer, E. S. Erffmeyer, & I. M. Lane. 1986. The Delphi technique: Empirical evaluation of the optimal number of rounds. *Group and Organizational Studies* 11:120–128.

26. Delbecq et al., 1975.

27. A. L. Delbecq & A. H. Van de Ven. 1971. A group process model for problem identification and program planning. *Journal of Applied Behavioral Science* 7:466–92; A. L. Delbecq & A. H. Van de Ven. 1971. Nominal versus interactive group processes for committee decision-making effectiveness. *Academy of Management Journal* 14:203–211.

28. W. J. Gordon. 1961. *Synectics: The development of creative capacity.* New York: Harper & Row, 3.

29. Ibid.

30. G. Prince. 1980. *Problem solving strategies: The synetic approach.* Del Mar, CA: CRM McGraw-Hill Films.

31. Ibid.

32. S. B. Sitkin & R. J. Bies. 1992. Social accounts in conflict situations: Using explanations to manage conflict. *Human Relations* 46(3):349–368.

33. In S. Caudron. 2000. Keeping team conflict alive. *Public Management* 82:5–10.

34. K. W. Thomas. 1976. Conflict and management. In M. D. Dunnette (ed.), *The handbook of industrial and organizational psychology,* 891. Chicago: Rand-McNally.

35. L. Urdang (ed.). 1968. *The Random House dictionary of the English language.* New York: Random House.

36. L. W. Porter, R. W. Allen, & H. L. Angle. 1983. The politics of upward influence in organizations. In R. W. Allen & L. W. Porter (eds.), *Organizational influence processes.* Glenview, IL: Scott, Foresman, 408–422.

37. L. A. Witt, M. C. Andrews, & K. M. Kacmar. 2000. The role of participation in decision-making in the organizational politics job satisfaction relationship. *Human Relations* 53:341–351.

38. D. Buchanan & R. Badham. 1999. Politics and organizational change: The lived experience. *Human Relations* 52:609–626; A. Drory. 1993. Perceived political climate and job attitudes. *Organization Studies* 14(1):59–71.

39. B. T. Mayes & R. W. Allen. 1977. Toward a definition of organizational politics. *Academy of Management Review* 2:672–678.

40. J. G. March 1962. The business firm as a political coalition. *Journal of Politics* 24:662–678.

41. G. Harrell-Cook, G. R. Ferris, & J. H. Dulebohn. 1999. Political behaviors as moderators of the perceptions of politics–work outcomes relationships. *Journal of Organizational Behavior* 20:1093–1105.

42. Witt, Andrews, & Kacmar, 2000.

43. P. Kumar & R. Ghadially. 1989. Organizational politics and its effects on members of organizations. *Human Relations* 42:305–314.

44. A. B. Fisher. 1991 (Nov. 18). CEOs think that morale is dandy. *Fortune,* 83–74.

45. Ibid., 83.

46. R. Nemec. 2000. Leaders, take us to your communicator. *Communication World* 17:29–33.

47. Fisher, 1991, 83.

48. J. Greenwald. 1992 (Jan. 27). Is Mr. Nice Guy back? *Business Week,* 43.

49. Fisher, 1991, 83.

50. Greenwald, 1992, 42.

51. E. E. Lawler, III. 1986. *The high involvement organization.* San Francisco: Jossey-Bass.

52. J. L. Pierce, T. Kostova, & K. T. Dirks. 2001. Towards a theory of psychological ownership in organizations. *Academy of Management Review* 26:298–310; L. Van Dyne & J. Pierce. 1993. *Employee ownership: Empirical support for mediated relationships.* Paper presented at the eighth annual conference of the Society for Industrial and Organizational Psychology, San Francisco.

PART V. Managing in the 21st Century

Chapter 16. Managing Productivity: Established Approaches

1. B. F. Skinner. 1953. *Science and human behavior.* New York: Free Press; B. F. Skinner. 1969. *Contingencies of reinforcement.* East Norwalk, CT: Appleton-Century-Crofts; B. F. Skinner. 1971. *Beyond freedom and dignity.* New York: Bantam.

2. E. L. Deci. 1972. Intrinsic motivation, extrinsic reinforcement, and inequity. *Journal of Personality and Social Psychology* 22:113–120.

3. F. Luthans & R. Kreitner. 1974. The management of behavioral contingencies. *Personnel* 51:7–16; F. Luthans & R. Kreitner. 1975. *Organizational behavior modification.* Glenview, IL: Scott, Foresman.

4. The interested reader might wish to explore these issues in P. K. Duncan & E. E. Lloyd. 1982. Training format in industrial behavior modification. In R. M. O'Brien, A. M. Dickinson, & M. P. Rosow (eds.). *Industrial behavior modification: A management handbook.* Maxwell House, NY: Pergamon Press, 387–404.

5. W. F. Dowling. 1973. At Emery Air Freight: Positive reinforcement boosts performance. *Organizational Dynamics* 2(1):41–50; W. C. Hamner & E. P. Hamner. 1976. Behavior modification on the bottom line. *Organizational Dynamics* 4(4):8–21.

6. G. P. Latham, & D. L. Dossett. 1978. Designing incentive plans for unionized employees: A comparison of continuous and variable ratio reinforcement schedules. *Personnel Psychology* 63: 47–61; L. M. Saari & G. P. Latham. 1982. Employee reactions to continuous and variable ratio reinforcement schedules involving a monetary incentive. *Journal of Applied Psychology* 62:506– 508.

7. A. D. Stajkovic & F. Luthans. 1997. A meta-analysis of the effects of organizational behavior modification on task performance, 1975–1995. *Academy of Management Journal* 40:1122–1149.

8. H. C. Berthold, Jr. 1982. Behavior modification in the industrial/organizational environment: Assumptions and ethics. In R. M. O'Brien, A. M. Dickinson, & M. P. Rosow (eds.), *Industrial behavior modification: A management handbook.* Maxwell House, NY: Pergamon Press, 405–427.

9. Ibid., 415.

10. Ibid., 415–424.

11. E. E. Lawler, III. 1992. *The ultimate advantage: Creating the high involvement organization.* San Francisco: Jossey-Bass, 77.

12. A. Smith. 1776. *The wealth of nations.* New York: Modern Library.

13. C. Babbage. 1832. *On the economy of machinery and manufacturers.* London: Knight.

14. J. L. Pierce & R. B. Dunham. 1976. Task design: A literature review, *Academy of Management Review* 1:83–97.

15. F. W. Taylor. 1947. *Scientific management.* New York: Harper; F. B. Gilbreth & L. M. Gilbreth. 1910. *Applied motion study.* New York: Sturgis & Walton; H. L. Gantt. 1910. *Work wages and profits.* New York: The Engineering Magazine Co.

16. J. L. Pierce. 1980. Job design in perspective. *The Personnel Administrator* 25:67–74.

17. M. R. Blood & C. L. Hulin. 1967. Alienation, environmental characteristics and worker responses. *Journal of Applied Psychology* 51:284–290; J. L. Pierce, 1980.

18. C. Argyris. 1957. *Personality and organization: The conflict between system and the individual.* New York: Harper Torchbooks.

19. C. Argyris. 1957. *Integrating the individual and the organization.* New York: Wiley.

20. Gilbreth, 1914, 50.

21. In D. Sirota & A. D. Wolfson. 1972 (May–June). Job enrichment: What are the obstacles? *Personnel,* 8–17.

22. R. T. Golembiewski. 1965. *Men, management, and morality: Toward a new organizational ethic.* New York: McGraw-Hill.

23. A. Harrington. 1999 (Nov. 22). The big ideas. *Fortune,* 152.

24. F. Herzberg, B. Mausner, & B. Snyderman. 1959. *The motivation to work.* New York: Wiley; F. Herzberg. 1968. One more time: How do you motivate employees? *Harvard Business Review* 46:54–62.

25. R. W. Griffin. 1982. *Task design: An integrative approach.* Glenview, IL: Scott, Foresman.

26. Ibid.

27. R. C. Liden, S. J. Wayne, & R. T. Sparrowe. 2000. An examination of the mediating role of psychological empowerment on the relations between the job, interpersonal relationships, and work outcomes. *Journal of Applied Psychology* 85:407–416.

28. F. Herzberg, B. Mausner, & B. Snyderman. 1959. *The motivation to work.* New York: Wiley; F. Herzberg. 1968. One more time: How do you motivate employees? *Harvard Business Review* 46:53–62.

29. E. L. Plumlee. 1991. A visit with Fred Herzberg. *Management Newsletter* 4(3):2–6.

30. F. Herzberg. 1974 (Sept.–Oct.). The wise old Turk. *Harvard Business Review,* 70–80.

31. R. L. Aldag & A. P. Brief. 1979. *Task design and employee motivation.* Glenview, IL: Scott, Foresman.

32. M. R. Blood & C. L. Hulin. 1967. Alienation, environmental characteristics, and worker responses. *Journal of Applied Psychology* 51:284–290; C. L. Hulin & M. R. Blood. 1968. Job enlargement, individual differences, and worker responses. *Psychological Bulletin* 69:41–55; C. L. Hulin. 1971. Individual differences and job enrichment—the case against general treatments. In J. Mahler (ed.), *New perspectives in job enrichment.* New York: Van Nostrand-Reinhold.

33. J. R. Hackman & E. E. Lawler, III. 1971. Employee reactions to job characteristics. *Journal of Applied Psychology Monograph* 55:259–286.

34. J. R. Hackman & G. R. Oldham. 1975. Development of the job diagnostic survey. *Journal of Applied Psychology* 60:159–170; J. R. Hackman & G. R. Oldham. 1976. Motivation through the design of work: Test of a theory. *Organizational Behavior and Human Performance* 16:250–279; J. R. Hackman & G. R. Oldham. 1980. *Work redesign.* Reading, MA: Addison-Wesley.

35. J. R. Idaszak & F. Drasgow. 1987. A revision of the Job Diagnostic Survey: Elimination of a measurement artifact. *Journal of Applied Psychology* 72:69–74.

36. Pierce & Dunham, 1976; Aldag & Brief, 1979; Griffin, 1982; K. H. Roberts & W. Glick. 1981. The job characteristics approach to task design: A critical review. *Journal of Applied Psychology* 66:193–217; Y. Fried & G. R. Ferris. 1987. The validity of the job characteristics model. *Personnel Psychology* 40:287–322.

37. Pierce & Dunham, 1976; B. T. Loher, R. A. Noe, N. L. Moeller, & M. P. Fitzgerald, 1985. A meta-analysis of the relation of job characteristics to job satisfaction. *Journal of Applied Psychology* 70(2):280–289; Fried & Ferris, 1987.

38. R. W. Renn & R. J. Vandenberg. 1995. The critical psychological states: An underrepresented component in Job Characteristics Model research. *Journal of Management* 21(2):279–303.

39. Ibid.

40. Turner & Lawrence, 1965; Blood & Hulin, 1967.

41. Pierce & Dunham, 1976; Loher et al., 1985.

42. J. L. Pierce, T. Kostova, & K. Dirks. 2001. Toward a theory of psychological ownership in organizations. *Academy of Management Review* 26:298–310. J. L. Pierce, M. P. O'Driscoll, & A. M. Coghlan, A. M. 2001. *Work environment structure and psychological ownership: The mediating effects of control.* University of Minnesota-Duluth, School of Business and Economics Working Paper.

43. Pierce, Kostova, & Dirks, 2001.

44. R. J. Aldag, & A. P. Brief. 1977. Moderators of relationships of job behaviors to perceptions of core task dimensions. *Proceedings of the 8th annual Midwest conference of the Midwest division of the American institute for decision sciences,* 327–329; E. F. Stone. 1979. Field independence and perceptions of task characteristics: A laboratory investigation. *Journal of Applied Psychology* 64:305–310.

45. D. G. Gardner, R. B. Dunham, L. L. Cummings, & J. L. Pierce. 1987. Employee focus of attention and reactions to organizational change. *Journal of Applied Behavioral Science* 23:351–370.

46. J. D. Thompson. 1967. *Organizations in action.* New York: McGraw-Hill; D. M. Rousseau. 1977. Technological differences in job characteristics, employee satisfaction, and motivation: A synthesis of job design research and sociotechnical systems theory. *Organizational Behavior and Human Performance* 19:18–42.

47. Rousseau, 1977.

48. D. J. Bass. 1985. Technology and the structuring of jobs: Employee satisfaction, performance, and influence. *Organizational Behavior and Human Decision Processes,* 35:216–240; C. L. Hulin & M. Roznowski. 1985. Organizational technologies: Effects on organizations' characteristics and individuals' responses. In L. L. Cummings & B. M. Staw (eds.), *Research in Organizational Behavior,* 39–87. Greenwich, CT: JAI Press; J. L. Pierce. 1984. Job design and technology: A sociotechnical systems perspective. *Journal of Occupational Behaviour* 5:147–154.

49. J. L. Pierce, R. B. Dunham, & R. S. Blackburn. 1979. Social system structure, job design, and growth need strength: A test of a congruency model. *Academy of Management Journal* 22:223–240; L. W. Porter, E. E. Lawler, III, & J. R. Hackman. 1975. *Behavior in organizations.* New York: McGraw-Hill.

50. R. W. Griffin. 1980. Relationships among individual, task design, and leader behavior variables. *Academy of Management Journal* 65:665–683; Griffin, 1982.

51. E. F. Stone & H. G. Gueutal. 1985. An empirical derivation of the dimensions along which characteristics of jobs are perceived. *Academy of Management Journal* 28:376–396.

52. M. A. Campion. 1988. Interdisciplinary approaches to job design: A constructive replication with extensions. *Journal of Applied Psychology* 73:467–481; M. A. Campion & P. W. Thayer. 1985. Development and field evaluation of an interdisciplinary measure of job design. *Journal of Applied Psychology* 70: 29–43.

53. Campion, 1988, 468.

54. Volvo. 1990 (Apr. 2). *Business Week,* 44–45.

55. Hackman & Oldham, 1980, 165–168.

56. B. Dumaine. 1990 (May 7). Who needs a boss? *Fortune* 121(10):52–60.

57. C. C. Manz & H. P. Sims, Jr. 1987. Leading workers to lead themselves: The external leadership of self-managing work teams. *Administrative Science Quarterly* 32:106–129.

58. C. C. Manz & J. W. Newstrom. 1990. Self-managing teams in a paper mill: Success factors, problems, and lessons learned. *International Human Resource Management Review* 1:52.

59. Ibid.; E. E. Lawler, III. 1986. *The high involvement organization.* San Francisco: Jossey-Bass.

60. C. A. Schriesheim, R. J. House, & S. Kerr. 1976. Leader initiating structure: A reconciliation of discrepant research results and some empirical tests. *Organizational Behavior and Human Performance* 15:297–321.

61. Manz & Sims, 1987.

62. Ibid., 119.

63. Manz & Newstrom, 1990, 48.

64. Lawler, 1992; Hackman & Oldham, 1975; Pierce & Dunham, 1976; C. I. Hulin & M. R. Blood. 1968. Job enlargement, individual differences and worker responses. *Psychological Bulletin* 69:41–55; Argyris, 1957; F. Herzberg. 1966. *Work and the nature of man.* Cleveland: World.

65. Griffin, 1982; Pierce & Dunham, 1976; Hulin & Blood, 1968.

66. Hackman & Oldham, 1980.

67. Pierce, Dunham, & Blackburn, 1979; Porter, Lawler, & Hackman, 1975.

68. Ibid.; Pierce, 1984; W. Slocum, Jr., & H. P. Sims, Jr. 1980. A typology for integrating technology, organizations, and job design. *Human Relations* 33:143–212.

Chapter 17. Managing Productivity: Contemporary Approaches

1. R. B. Dunham & J. L. Pierce. 1997. Flexible workplace—telecommuting. In L. H. Peters, C. R. Greer, & S. A. Youngblood (eds.). *The Blackwell Encyclopedic Dictionary of Human Resource Management.* Oxford, England: Blackwell.

2. J. L. Pierce & R. B. Dunham. 1992. The 12-hour workday: A 48-hour, 8-day week. *Academy of Management Journal* 35:1086– 1098; J. L. Pierce, J. W. Newstrom, R. B. Dunham, & A. E. Barber. 1989. *Alternative work schedules.* Boston: Allyn & Bacon.

3. Pierce et al., 1989.

4. J. L. Pierce & J. W. Newstrom. 1983. The design of flexible work schedules and employee responses: Relationships and process. *Journal of Occupational Behaviour* 4:247–262.

5. R. T. Golembiewski & C. W. Proehl, Jr. 1978. A survey of the empirical literature on flexible work hours: Character and consequences of a major innovation. *Academy of Management Review* 3:837–853; Pierce & Newstrom, 1983.

6. J. L. Pierce & J. W. Newstrom. 1980. Toward a conceptual clarification of employee responses to flexible working hours: A work adjustment approach. *Journal of Management* 6:117–134; Pierce et al., 1989.

7. J. L. Pierce & J. W. Newstrom. 1982. Employee responses to work schedules: An inter-system–inter-organization comparison. *Journal of Management* 8:9–25; Pierce & Newstrom, 1983.

8. Our discussion of the research findings on the effects of alternative work schedules on employees is drawn from Pierce et al., 1989; and from B. B. Baltes, T. E. Briggs, J. W. Huff, J. A. Wright, & G. A. Neuman. 1999. Flexible and compressed workweek schedules: A meta-analysis of their effects on work-related criteria. *Journal of Applied Psychology* 84:496-513.

9. R. V. Davis, G. W. England, & L. H. Lofquist. 1968. A theory of work adjustment (a revision). University of Minnesota. Minnesota Studies in Vocational Rehabilitation XXIII, Bulletin 47 (April).

10. Pierce & Newstrom, 1980.

11. Pierce et al., 1989.

12. R. B. Dunham, J. L. Pierce, & M. Castenada. 1987. Alternative work schedules: Two quasi-experiments. *Personnel Psychology* 40:215–242; R. B. Dunham & J. L. Pierce. 1986. Attitudes toward work schedules: Construct definition, instrument development, and construct validation. *Academy of Management Journal* 29:170–182.

13. Pierce & Dunham, 1992; C. R. Maiwald, J. L. Pierce, J. W. Newstrom, & B. P. Sunoo. 1997. Working 8 p.m. to 8 a.m. and lovin' every minute of it. *Workforce* 76(7):30–36.

14. Pierce et al., 1989.

15. Ibid.

16. Pierce et al., 1989.

17. Maiwald et al., 1997.

18. These findings from the James River Paper Company are consistent with and complement the findings reported by Pierce & Dunham, 1992. The Pierce and Dunham study reports on the conversion from an 8-hour 5-day schedule to a 12-hour day, 8-day schedule in the police department in Duluth, Minnesota.

19. Pierce et al., 1989.

20. J. Barton. 1994. Choosing to work at night: A moderating influence of individual tolerance to shift work. *Journal of Applied Psychology* 79:449–454.

21. P. Totterdell, E. Spleten, L. Smith, J. Barton, & S. Folkard. 1995. Recovery from work shifts: How long does it take? *Journal of Applied Psychology* 80:43–57.

22. J. R. Blasi, M. Conte, & L. Kruse. 1999. Employee ownership National Center for Employee Ownership Report; C. Rosen & M. Quarrey. 1987. How well is employee ownership working? *Harvard Business Review* 65(5):126–128, 132; J. Schwartz. April 1989. Giving workers a piece of the action. *Newsweek,* 17, 45.

23. J. L. Pierce & L. Rodgers. 2001. Employee ownership: Worker-owner productivity and related processes. University of Minnesota-Duluth, School of Business and Economics Working Paper; J. L. Pierce, S. Rubenfeld, & S. Morgan. 1991. Employee ownership: A conceptual model of process and effects. *Academy of Management Review* 16:121–144; A. Etzioni. 1991. The socio-economics of property. In F. W. Rudmin (ed.). *Journal of Social Behavior and Psychology,* Special Edition, 12:427–468.

24. A. Etzioni. 1991. The socio-economics of property. In F. W. Rudmin (ed.), *Journal of Social Behavior and Psychology* 6(6): 466.

25. J. L. Pierce, T. Kostova, & K. Dirks. 2001. Toward a theory of psychological ownership in organizations. *Academy of Management Review* 26:298–310.

26. Stocks for workers spreading but raising question too. *U.S. News and World Report* (August 1976), 68–70.

27. Pierce, Rubenfeld, & Morgan, 1991.

28. Pierce, Kostova, & Dirks, 2001.

29. D. VandeWalle, L. Van Dyne, & T. Kostova. 1995. Psychological ownership: An empirical examination of its consequences. *Group and Organization Management* 20(2):210–226; R. J. Long. 1978. The effects of employee ownership on organizational identification, employee job attitudes, and organizational performance: A tentative framework and empirical findings. *Human Relations* 31:29–48; Pierce et al., 1991.

30. Pierce, Rubenfeld, & Morgan, 1991.

31. Rosen & Quarrey. 1987; M. Quarrey & C. Rosen. 1986. *Taking stock: Employee ownership in America: The equity solution.* Lexington, MA: Lexington Books.

32. Our discussion of Total Quality Management draws heavily on J. R. Hackman & R. Wageman. 1995. Total quality management: Empirical, conceptual, and practical issues. *Administrative Science Quarterly* 40:309–342. In addition, we draw heavily on J. L. Cotton, 1993, *Employee involvement: Methods for improving performance and work attitudes,* Newbury, CA, Sage, for our discussion of the effects of quality control circles on employees.

33. Cotton, 1993.
34. Hackman & Wageman, 1995.
35. E. E. Lawler, III. 1992. *The ultimate advantage: Creating the high involvement organization.* San Francisco: Jossey-Bass; E. E. Lawler, III. 1989. *High involvement management.* San Francisco: Jossey-Bass; E. E. Lawler, III, & S. A. Mohrman. 1987. Quality circles: After the honeymoon. *Organizational Dynamics* 15(4):42–54; E. E. Lawler, III. 1988. Choosing an involvement strategy. *Academy of Management Executive* 2(3):197–204.
36. Lawler, 1992.
37. Cotton, 1993.
38. Ibid.
39. Lawler, 1986; Cotton, 1993.
40. Hackman & Wageman, 1995.
41. O. Port. 1999. Innovations. *Business Week* (September 7).
42. L. Chappell. 1998. Transplants ushered in quality revolution. *Automotive News* (April 27):N8.
43. G. Bylinsky. 1999. America's elite factories. *Fortune* 140 (August 16):4136–C.
44. M. Brown, D. Hitchcock, & M. Willard. 1994. *Why TQM fails and what to do about it.* Burr Ridge, IL: Irwin.
45. We would like to note that much of our understanding and thinking about high-involvement management and organizations has been influenced by the work of Edward E. Lawler, III. Dr. Lawler received his doctorate from the University of California-Berkeley. Currently he is professor of management and the director of the Center for Effective Organizations at the University of Southern California. Three books capture much of his thinking, observations, and experience with high-involvement management and organizations: *High involvement management,* 1986, San Francisco: Jossey-Bass; *Strategic Pay,* 1990, San Francisco: Jossey-Bass; and *The ultimate advantage: Creating the high involvement organization,* 1992, San Francisco: Jossey-Bass.
46. Cotton, 1993, p. 3; E. E. Lawler, III, & S. A. Mohrman. 1989. With HR help, all managers can practice high-involvement management. *Personnel* 66(4):26–31.
47. F. Herzberg, B. Mausner, & B. Synderman. 1959. *The motivation to work.* New York: Wiley; J. L. Pierce, R. B. Dunham, & L. L. Cummings. 1984. Sources of environmental structuring and participant responses. *Organizational Behavior and Human Performance* 33:214–242; R. W. Griffin. 1991. Effects of work redesign on employee perceptions, attitudes, and behaviors: A long-term investigation. *Academy of Management Journal* 34:425–435.
48. R. E. Cole. 1979. *Work, mobility, and participation: A comparative study of American and Japanese industry.* Berkeley: University of California Press; G. Munchus. 1983. Employer-employee based quality circles in Japan: Human resource policy implications for American firms. *Academy of Management Review* 8:255–261.
49. Lawler, 1986; Cotton, 1993.
50. Cotton, 1993, 33–34.
51. Ibid.
52. B. A. Macy. 1979. The Bolivar quality of work life program: A longitudinal behavioral and performance assessment. *Proceedings of the 32nd annual meeting of the Industrial Relations Research Association,* Madison, WI: Industrial Relations Research Association, 83–93.
53. R. H. Guest. 1982. The Sharonville story: Worker involvement at a Ford Motor Company plant. In R. Zager & M. R. Posow (eds.), *The innovative organization: Productivity programs in action.* New York: Pergamon, 88–106.
54. Lawler, 1992, 45.
55. J. D. Orsburn, L. Moran, E. Musselwhite, & J. H. Zenger. 1990. *Self-directed work teams: The new American challenge.* Homewood, IL: Irwin.
56. Cotton, 1993, 243.
57. Ibid., 243–44.

Chapter 18. Managing Organizational Change and Development

1. H. J. Leavitt. 1964. Applied organization change in industry: Structural, technical, and human approaches. In W. W. Cooper, H. J. Leavitt, & M. W. Shelly II (eds.). *New perspectives in organization research.* New York: Wiley, 55–71.
2. Based on a similar quote by J. L. Price. 1972. *Handbook of organizational measurement.* Lexington, MA: D. C. Heath, 118.
3. This definition is consistent with that provided by S. W. Becker & T. L. Whisler. 1967. The innovative organization: A selective view of current theory and research. *Journal of Business* 40: 462–469.
4. S. Zesiger. 2000 (Feb. 21). GM's big decision: Status quo. *Fortune,* 101.
5. F. Friedlander and L. D. Brown. Organizational development. *Annual Review of Psychology* 25:235.
6. Leavitt, 1964.
7. C. A. Carnall. 1986. Toward a theory for the evaluation of organizational change. *Human Relations* 39:745–766.
8. S. K. Piderit. 2000. Rethinking resistance and recognizing ambivalence: A multidimensional view of attitudes toward an organizational change. *Academy of Management Review* 25:783–794.
9. Many of the issues use ideas from J. P. Kotter & L. A. Schlesinger of Harvard University in March/April 1979. Choosing strategies for change. *Harvard Business Review,* 106–113 and from J. P. Kotter, L. A. Schlesinger, & V. Sathe. 1979. *Organization: Text, cases, and readings on the management of organizational design and change.* Homewood, IL: Irwin.
10. L. W. Mealiea. 1978. Learned behavior: The key to understanding and preventing employee resistance to change. *Group & Organization Studies* 3:211–223.
11. J. P. Wanous, S. T. Reichers, & J. T. Austin. 2000. Cynicism about organizational change: Measurement, antecedents, and correlates. *Group and Organization Management* 25:132–153.
12. S. K. Piderit. 2000. Rethinking resistance and recognizing ambivalence: A multidimensional view of attitudes toward an organizational change. *Academy of Management Review* 25:783–794.
13. K. T. Dirks, L. L. Cummings, & J. L. Pierce. 1996. Psychological ownership in organizations: Conditions under which individuals promote and resist change. In R. W. Woodman & W. A. Pasmore (eds.), *Research in Organizational Change and Development.* Greenwich, CT: JAI Press, 9, 1–23.
14. Mealiea, 1978.
15. Some of these are based on Kotter & Schlesinger, 1979.
16. M. Beer. 1980. *Organization change and development: A systems view.* Santa Monica, CA: Goodyear; M. Beer & A. E. Walton. 1987. Organization change and development. *Annual Review of Psychology* 38:339–340.
17. Much of this section is based on D. D. Warrick. 1984. *Managing organization change and development.* Chicago: Science Research Associates.
18. M. Beer & B. Spector. 1985. Corporate-wide transformations. In R. Walton & P. Lawrence (eds.), *HRM trends and challenges.* Boston: Harvard Business School Press.
19. W. L. French & C. H. Bell, Jr. 1978. *Organizational development: Behavioral science interventions for organization improvement,* 2nd ed. Englewood Cliffs, NJ: Prentice-Hall.
20. Z. E. Barnes. 1987 (Feb.). Visions, values, and strategies: Changing attitudes and culture. *The Academy of Management Executive,* 33–42; R. N. Beck. 1987 (Feb.). The theory practice gap: Myth or reality? *Academy of Management Executive,* 31–32; J. J. Renier. 1987 (Feb.). Turnaround of information systems at Honeywell. *Academy of Management Executive,* 47–50.

21. A. A. Armenakis & A. G. Bedeian. 1999. Organizational change: A review of theory and research in the 1990s. *Journal of Management* 25:293–310.

22. M. Beer & R. Eisenstat. 1996. Developing an organization capable of implementing strategy and learning. *Human Relations* 49:597–619.

23. E. W. Morrison & F. J. Milliken. 2000. Organizational silence: A barrier to change and development in a pluralistic world. *Academy of Management Review* 25:706–725.

24. K. Lewin. 1947. Frontiers in group dynamics. *Human Relations* 1:5–41; K. Lewin. 1951. *Field theory in social science*. New York: Harper & Row.

25. W. G. Bennis, D. E. Berlew, E. H. Schein, & F. I. Steele. 1973. *Interpersonal dynamics: Essays and readings on human interaction*. Homewood, IL: Dorsey Press; D. A. Nadler. 1981. Managing organizational change: An integrative perspective. *Journal of Applied Behavioral Science* 17:191–211.

26. P. M. Senge. 1990. *The fifth discipline: The art and practice of the learning organization*. New York: Doubleday Currency.

27. We encourage the interested reader to look at *Organizational Dynamics*, 1998, volume 27, number 2. This special issue of the journal—Teaching Smart Companies to Learn: Organizational Learning Revisited—was devoted entirely to organizational learning and provides a close and updated look at the subject.

28. M. Pedler, J. Burgoyne, & T. Boydell. 1997. *The learning company: A strategy for sustainable development* (2nd ed.). London: McGraw-Hill.

29. C. R. Leana & B. Barry. 2000. Stability and change as simultaneous experiences in organizational life. *Academy of Management Review* 25:753–759.

Index